GO! Premium Media Site

Improve your grade with hands-on tools and resources!

- Master *Key Terms* to expand your vocabulary.
- Assess your knowledge with fun *Crossword Puzzles* and *Flipboards*, which let you flip through the definitions of the key terms and match them with the correct term.
- Prepare for exams by taking practice quizzes in the *Online Chapter Review*.
- Download *Student Data Files* for the application projects in each chapter.
- Answer matching and multiple choice questions to test what you learned in each chapter.

And for even more tools, you can access the following Premium Resources using your Access Code. Register now to get the most out of *GO!*.

- *Student Training Videos* for each Objective have been created by the author - a real instructor teaching the same types of courses that you take.*
- *GO! to Work* videos are short interviews with workers showing how they use Office in their job.*
- *GO! for Job Success* videos related to the projects in the chapter cover such important topics as Dressing for Success, Time Management, and Making Ethical Choices.*

*Access code required for these premium resources

Your Access Code is:

GMOV1-STOUP-GOPAK-XYLAN-METIS-HIKES

Note: If there is no silver foil covering the access code, it may already have been redeemed, and therefore may no longer be valid. In that case, you can purchase online access using a major credit card or PayPal account. To do so, go to **www.pearsonhighered.com/go**, select your book cover, click on "Buy Access" and follow the on-screen instructions.

To Register:

- To start you will need a valid email address and this access code.
- Go to **www.pearsonhighered.com/go** and scroll to find your text book.
- Once you've selected your text, on the Home Page for the book, click the link to access the Student Premium Content.
- Click the Register button and follow the on-screen instructions.
- After you register, you can sign in any time via the log-in area on the same screen.

System Requirements

Windows 7 Ultimate Edition; IE 8
Windows Vista Ultimate Edition SP1; IE 8
Windows XP Professional SP3; IE 7
Windows XP Professional SP3; Firefox 3.6.4
Mac OS 10.5.7; Firefox 3.6.4
Mac OS 10.6; Safari 5

Technical Support

http://247pearsoned.custhelp.com

D1384695

Photo credits: Goodluz/wrangler/Elena Elisseeva/Shutterstock

PEARSON

ALWAYS LEARNING

GO! with Microsoft® Office 2013

CIS 105

Fifth Custom Edition for HACC Central Pennsylvania's Community College

Taken from:
GO! with Microsoft® Office 2013, Volume 1
by Shelley Gaskin, Alicia Vargas, and Carolyn McLellan

GO! with Microsoft® Windows™ 8: Getting Started
by Shelley Gaskin

GO! with Microsoft® Windows™ 7: Getting Started
by Shelley Gaskin and Robert L. Ferrett

GO! with Computer Concepts: Getting Started
by Shelley Gaskin and Jill Carney

Cover Art: Courtesy of Photodisc/Getty Images.

Taken from:

GO! with Microsoft® Office 2013, Volume 1
by Shelley Gaskin, Alicia Vargas, and Carolyn McLellan
Copyright © 2014 by Pearson Education, Inc.
Published by Prentice Hall
Upper Saddle River, New Jersey 07458

GO! with Microsoft® Windows™ 8: Getting Started
by Shelley Gaskin
Copyright © 2014 by Pearson Education, Inc.
Published by Prentice Hall

GO! with Microsoft® Windows™ 7: Getting Started
by Shelley Gaskin and Robert L. Ferrett
Copyright © 2011 by Pearson Education, Inc.
Published by Prentice Hall

GO! with Computer Concepts: Getting Started
by Shelley Gaskin and Jill Carney
Copyright © 2014 by Pearson Education, Inc.
Published by Prentice Hall

This special edition published in cooperation with Pearson Learning Solutions.

All trademarks, service marks, registered trademarks, and registered service marks are the property of their respective owners and are used herein for identification purposes only.

Pearson Learning Solutions, 501 Boylston Street, Suite 900, Boston, MA 02116
A Pearson Education Company
www.pearsoned.com

Printed in the United States of America

4 5 6 7 8 9 10 V064 17 16 15 14

000200010271792007

JA

ISBN 10: 1-269-40754-6
ISBN 13: 978-1-269-40754-0

The following content is taken from:

GO! with Computer Concepts: Getting Started
by Shelley Gaskin and Jill Carney

GO!

with

Computer Concepts
Getting Started

Shelley Gaskin and Jill Carney

Boston   Columbus   Indianapolis   New York   San Francisco   Upper Saddle River
Amsterdam   Cape Town   Dubai   London   Madrid   Milan   Munich   Paris   Montréal   Toronto
Delhi   Mexico City   São Paulo   Sydney   Hong Kong   Seoul   Singapore   Taipei   Tokyo

GO!

with

Computer Concepts

Getting Started

Shelley Gaskin and Jill Carney

PEARSON

Table of Contents

Basic Computer Concepts

OBJECTIVES

Mastering these objectives will enable you to:

1. Define Computer and Identify the Four Basic Computing Functions
2. Identify the Different Types of Computers
3. Describe Hardware Devices and Their Uses
4. Identify Types of Software and Their Uses
5. Identify Ethically Responsible and Safe Computing Practices
6. Describe Networks and Define Network Terms

Photo-K / Fotolia

In This Chapter

Computers are an integral part of our lives. They are found everywhere today, in both personal and business settings. Computers are part of cars and phones, and they enable you to access bank accounts from home, shop online, and quickly communicate with people around the world by means of email and the Internet. It is difficult to find a business or occupation that doesn't rely on computers, whether it's a truck driver who keeps an electronic travel log, a high-powered stockbroker who needs up-to-the-second market information, or a doctor who sends in your prescription and has it filled while you are at your appointment. Computers can make these tasks faster, easier, more efficient, and more accurate.

Computers are all around us, which makes it important to learn basic computing skills and gain the knowledge to be a responsible computer user. Knowing how to use and maintain a computer ethically and responsibly makes you **computer fluent**.

This chapter looks at different types of computers and their functions. It discusses computer hardware and software, and the benefits of networking, responsible behaviors of both physical and social networking, and the importance of safe computing practices. It shows the ways with which you can protect your computer from various threats and be proactive in its maintenance.

What are the benefits of becoming computer fluent? Becoming computer fluent can benefit you in several ways. One advantage of being computer fluent is that it makes employees more attractive to potential employers. Most employers expect employees to have basic computer skills when they are hired, whether you work indoors or outdoors. Computers have certainly changed the way people work. The traditional memo has given way to email messages. Business reports can be shared on a network, enabling a group of individuals to collaborate by adding their own notes and comments before a report is finalized. Presentation graphic software is widely used to share information with an audience in a conference room or through the organization's intranet. Spreadsheet software is a key tool in presenting financial information and developing sound business plans.

Also, if you are knowledgeable about computers and their uses, it makes you a better consumer. You feel more comfortable when it comes to purchasing the right computer hardware and software for your needs, adding a peripheral for a specific use, or detecting basic problems when a system does not work properly. If you have a basic understanding of today's technology, you can better understand and use new technologies.

What are the basic functions of a computer? A *computer* is a *programmable* electronic device that can input, process, output, and store data. The term *programmable* signifies that a device can be instructed to perform a task or a function when provided with a program or software. A computer takes data and converts it into information. **Data** represents text, numbers, graphics, sounds, and videos entered into the computer's memory during input operations.

Information is data that has been processed so that it can be presented in an organized and meaningful way. Think of data as the pieces of a jigsaw puzzle and information as the finished puzzle. Putting the pieces of the puzzle together gives you the overall picture. For example, CIS1100, the letter B, and the name Amy Stevens are pieces of data. Individually, these pieces of data seem meaningless. However, when processed, this data becomes the information on a grade report that indicates Amy Stevens received a grade of B in her CIS 1100 class.

These four basic computer functions work in a cycle known as the *information processing cycle*. See Figure 1.1.

FIGURE 1.1 These are the four computer functions in the information processing cycle. Memory is not considered a function, but it is the center of the flow of data and information within this cycle.

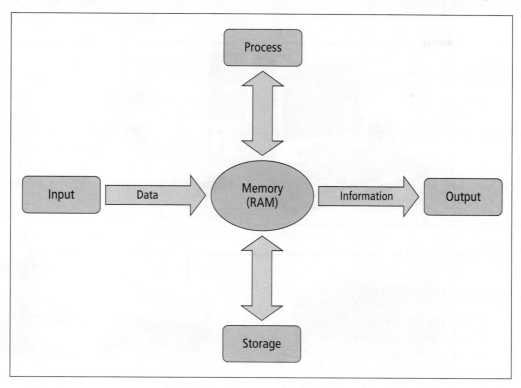

The functions of this cycle are:

- *Input*—The computer gathers data or enables a user to enter data.
- *Process*—Data is manipulated and converted into information.
- *Output*—Information is displayed or shown to the user in a way that is understandable.
- *Storage*—Data or information is stored for future use.

In the grade report, the instructor used a computer to enter, or input, the students' grades into the school's computerized grading system. A computer then processed this data along with data for other classes the student might have taken. In the example, the student Amy then received a written record of her grade or she accessed her grades online. The grade report was output by the computer. In addition, her grades remain stored in the system so they can be used to generate her transcript or to determine her future grade point average as she continues to take classes. See Figure 1.2.

FIGURE 1.2 The components of a typical computer system and the appropriate step in the information processing cycle.

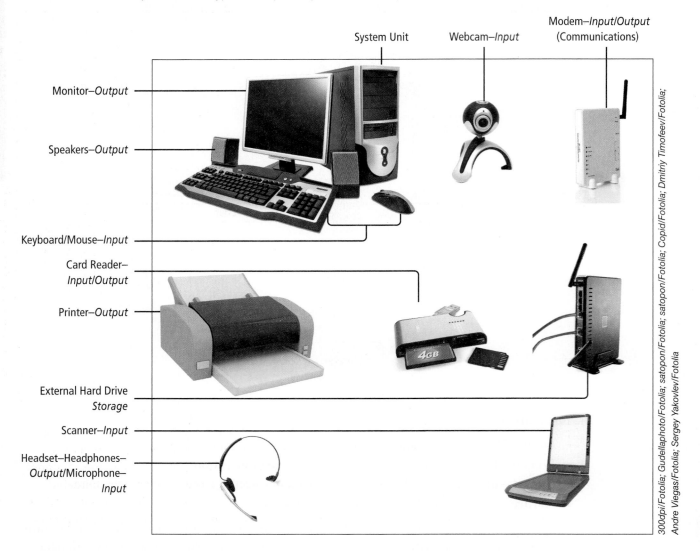

System Unit

Webcam–*Input*

Modem–*Input/Output*
(Communications)

Monitor–*Output*

Speakers–*Output*

Keyboard/Mouse–*Input*

Card Reader–
Input/Output

Printer–*Output*

External Hard Drive
Storage

Scanner–*Input*

Headset–Headphones–
Output/Microphone–
Input

4GB

300dpi/Fotolia; Gudellaphoto/Fotolia; satopon/Fotolia; Copid/Fotolia; Dmitriy Timofeev/Fotolia; Andre Viegas/Fotolia; Sergey Yakovlev/Fotolia

Objective 2 | Identify the Different Types of Computers

What are the different types of computers and what are their uses? Although computers come in a variety of sizes and shapes, the basic components required to complete the information processing cycle must be present in them. In addition to ***microcomputers*** (see Figure 1.3), which include the desktop, laptop, tablet computers, and mobile devices that many of you are familiar with, there are also specialty computers, including servers, mainframes, supercomputers, and embedded computers.

FIGURE 1.3 Types of microcomputers

Desktop PC

Tablet PC

Smartphone

Laptop

PDA

Microcomputers

What are microcomputers? The term ***microcomputer*** means that the main component of a computer is a ***microprocessor***, a tiny but powerful chip that is very small in size compared to a mainframe or a supercomputer. Microcomputers are classified as small, inexpensive, and designed for personal use or as part of a network of computers in a business environment. Computers in this category range in size from a desktop size system that is ideal when portability is not required, to ***handheld devices*** that fit in your pocket. Some of the most common types of microcomputers include the following:

- ***Desktop computers*** are computers that sit on the desk, floor, or table, and typically have a detachable keyboard, mouse, monitor, and possibly other peripheral devices, such as ***digital cameras***, scanners, and music players. ***Desktop computers*** are used in many homes and in business environments where portability is not needed. They can be configured in a multitude of arrangements depending on the specific needs and budget constraints. To ***configure*** means to put together by selecting a specific combination of components, features, and options.

  Desktop computers generally fall into two main categories: PCs or Macs. The PC, or personal computer, originally referred to as the IBM personal computer when it was released in the early 1980s, is now manufactured by a variety of companies including Lenovo, HP, and Dell. Today, the term PC applies to any personal computer based on an Intel microprocessor, or on an Intel-compatible microprocessor. The Apple Macintosh computer, now known as Mac, is manufactured exclusively by Apple Inc. with an Intel microprocessor and can perform the same functions as the PC.

  There are pros and cons to both types of computers, but in reality both are good systems and the choice usually comes down to personal preference. The primary differences between the PC and the Mac relate to the different operating system and user interface, the application software, and the cost and availability of parts and accessories.

The PC typically uses the Microsoft Windows operating environment, and the Mac uses the Mac operating system. Although the PC and the Mac each process information differently, both can perform the same types of tasks. The PC has a larger market share among general computer users and in business settings, whereas the Mac is popular with graphic design, advertising, and professional audio and film industries. Applications have become cross-platformable between the Mac and PC over the years, so regardless of your preference, these days you can share most files between operating systems.

- *Gaming computers* are mostly used by video game enthusiasts. They are usually configured with a fast *central processing unit (CPU)*, a large amount of memory, a special video card, a joystick or game pad, and a sound card with a surround sound speaker system.

- *Laptop computers* are ideal for people "on-the-go." Equipped with rechargeable batteries, they are designed to be portable, permitting them to be used in a variety of places. Averaging about 6 pounds, a laptop's size and weight can also limit its computing power. Laptops typically have a built-in display screen, a keyboard, and a pointing *device*; although it is possible to connect them to detachable devices for more comfortable desktop use. You can use a *docking station* to connect a laptop to a full-size keyboard, monitor, and other devices in any setting.

- *Tablet computers* are similar to laptops because they are portable; however, they have some special features that set them apart. Tablet computers have a convertible *touchscreen* that swivels, enabling the tablet to be used like a standard laptop computer in one position or like a clipboard in the second position. When used in the tablet configuration, the user can actually write directly on the screen by using a special pen known as a *stylus*, which is a pointed device used to input information and access various features right on the device's screen. Tablets use advanced handwriting-recognition technology to convert handwriting to digital text. Many also use *speech-recognition* technology, such as JAWS or ADA free, which enables the user to record discussions or lectures, or to control the computer functions by using voice commands.

- *Mobile devices* include items such as smartphones, portable music players, and e-readers. These devices vary in size and purpose, but they are all ultra-lightweight and portable. *Smartphones* add Internet capability to the wireless communication aspects of cell phones. Portable music players permit people to download, store, and enjoy music, podcasts, and sometimes videos, while e-readers make it possible to do the same thing with books, magazines, and other publications.

Servers

What are servers? When computers are connected together in a network environment, *servers* are specialized computers that manage network resources through the use of administrative software. See Figure 1.4.

FIGURE 1.4 Network server

Edelweiss/Fotolia

They provide other computers with access to the network and can handle a variety of functions or may be assigned to only one particular type of task. Thus, within the same organization, you might find an Intranet server that handles the organization's private, internal network, a web server that stores and delivers the organization's webpage, a file server that handles the storage and retrieval tasks for all of the organization's files, and a printer server that handles all print requests. Also, virtual servers (not real, but an abstraction) can manage other specialized servers without the added cost of additional hardware.

What are mainframe computers? *Mainframe computers* are large computers often found in large businesses, organizations, and government agencies where thousands of users must simultaneously use the data and resources of their institution (see Figure 1.5).

FIGURE 1.5 Mainframe computer

zentilla/Fotolia

Mainframe computers **multitask**; that is, they can perform more than one task at a time. Mainframes can store vast amounts of data by using a variety of storage. Mainframes are often used for high-security applications, bulk data processing such as data surveys, census, and statistics. Early mainframe computers were very large and required separate rooms to house them, while today's mainframes are significantly smaller, faster, and more powerful than their predecessors.

Supercomputers

What are supercomputers? *Supercomputers* are large, powerful, and ultrafast computers that perform specialized tasks. Some of these are used for research, processing intensive scientific calculations, and multi-scale simulations.

Supercomputers (see Figure 1.6 for an example of a supercomputer) are the fastest and most expensive computers. Unlike a mainframe computer that can handle a number of programs simultaneously, the supercomputer is designed to run fewer programs at one time, but to do so as quickly as possible. They perform sophisticated mathematical calculations, track weather patterns, monitor satellites, and perform other complex, dedicated tasks.

The Titan, a supercomputer at the Oak Ridge National Laboratory in Tennessee, was built by Cray (**www.cray.com**), and features the same types of CPUs used in current personal computers and *GPU*s (graphical processing units) used in gaming computers today. By example, this would be the equivalent of 1,000 people performing one calculation per second for 60,000 years to be able to complete what the Titan can complete in only one second. Titan's ultimate accomplishment, however, is its miniscule use of energy while performing these intense calculations at lightning speed (Lavelle, 2012). Its cost was approximately $100 million.

FIGURE 1.6 A supercomputer's common configuration. It would take 1,000 people performing one calculation per second for 60,000 years to be able to complete what the Titan supercomputer can complete in only one second.

apops/Fotolia

There are many high-level scientific uses touted for the astonishing Titan. Some of the most anxiously anticipated tasks currently scheduled are creating climate change models with extreme accuracy, designing more fuel-efficient sustainable automobile systems, improved output and safety of nuclear power reactors, and producing super-powered magnets to drive electric motors and generators, especially in automobiles.

Embedded Computers

What are embedded computers? *Embedded computers* are small specialized computers built into larger components such as automobiles. Functions such as emission control systems, antilock braking systems (ABS), airbags, and stability control systems are common in today's vehicles. These computers use a specially programmed microprocessor to perform a set of predefined tasks, and may require little or no input from the user. Other devices that use embedded computers include electronic devices, microwave ovens, digital cameras, programmable thermostats, medical devices, clocks, and diagnostic equipment.

Objective 3 | Describe Hardware Devices and Their Uses

What is computer hardware? *Hardware* is the computer and any equipment connected to it. Hardware devices are the physical components of the computer. Items such as the monitor, keyboard, mouse, and printer, or any hardware connected through your network, are known as *peripheral devices*, because they attach to the computer, are accessed from the computer, and are controlled by the computer.

The computer itself is known as the *system unit*, and it contains many of the critical hardware and electrical components. In a desktop PC, the system unit is sometimes referred to as the tower, box, computer, or console. When the system unit is combined with the appropriate peripheral devices, the system can perform the four basic computer functions: input, process, output, and storage. Peripheral devices are used to input and output data and information, and the system unit processes and stores the data.

System Unit

What is inside the system unit? If you remove the cover from the system unit, you will find several key components inside. One of the most essential components is the ***motherboard***, a large printed circuit board to which all the other components are connected (see Figure 1.7). The microprocessor chip is also known as the ***central processing unit (CPU)***. ***RAM***, also known as random access memory, is the computer's main memory (temporary working memory). ***ROM*** (read only memory) is nonvolatile, cannot be changed, and provides quick execution of commands due to the fact that it does not have to be processed each time. All of these components are connected to the motherboard (see the table in Figure 1.8). The motherboard also provides some of the ports used to connect peripheral devices to the system.

FIGURE 1.7 The motherboard and some of its components

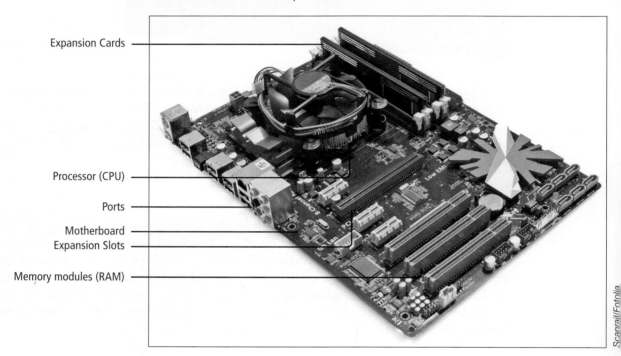

Expansion Cards

Processor (CPU)

Ports

Motherboard

Expansion Slots

Memory modules (RAM)

Scanrail/Fotolia

List 5 embedded computers you use daily
1
2
3
4
5

FIGURE 1.8 Motherboard features

MOTHERBOARD FEATURES	
COMPONENT	**DESCRIPTION**
Motherboard/System board	The main computer circuit board into which all components are plugged. It is installed safely inside the box or case called the system unit.
Central Processing Unit (CPU)	The central processing unit is responsible for getting data from memory, performing arithmetic and logical operations, and converting data to information.
Random Access Memory (RAM)	Temporary storage area where data is stored before processing, output, or storage. RAM is the center of the flow of data and information within the information processing cycle.
Read Only Memory (ROM)	Nonvolatile, permanent read-only memory, which contains the initial program that runs at startup of the computer, known as the boot process.
Expansion slots	Connectors on the motherboard that allow you to connect expansion cards.
Expansion cards	Removable circuit boards used to add new peripherals or increase the computer's capabilities. If the motherboard does not have a specific port to connect a peripheral device, the appropriate expansion card will allow you to do so.
Ports	Connecting points used as an interface between peripherals and the motherboard.

Input devices are used to enter data into temporary memory (RAM). The two most familiar input devices are the keyboard and the mouse, but they are not the only ones. See Figure 1.9.

FIGURE 1.9 Input devices

Wireless Laser Mouse

Multimedia Keyboard

Underside of Wireless Laser Mouse

Microphone

grounder/Fotolia; IMAphotos/Fotolia; V.R.Murralinath/Fotolia

Are there different types of keyboards? The **keyboard** is the primary input device for computers. There are actually several different kinds of keyboards. The QWERTY keyboard is the most common one. It is based on the original typewriter keyboard and is named for the arrangement of the letters on the upper left alphabetic row of keys. Another style is the Dvorak keyboard, which arranges the letters and numbers in a different pattern for increased typing speed.

Some ergonomic keyboards use a split keyboard arrangement, offsetting each half at an angle to reduce the incidence of repetitive stress injuries such as carpal tunnel syndrome.

Keyboard size and layout on laptop and tablet computers can differ slightly from a standard keyboard due to space constraints. Keyboards usually send information to the computer through a cable connected to a USB port; however, wireless keyboards are gaining in popularity. A *wireless* keyboard communicates with the computer by infrared or radio frequency technology. These wireless devices require batteries.

What are all these other keys used for? In addition to the standard alphanumeric keys originally found on typewriters, computer keyboards have a variety of keys that provide additional functionality.

Control keys, such as the Ctrl, Alt, and Windows keys, often provide shortcuts or increased functionality to the keyboard when used in combination with another key. If you press the Shift key and a letter, the result is an uppercase, rather than a lowercase, letter. In the same way, using one of the control keys enables the standard keys to be used for additional purposes. For example, pressing Ctrl and the letter P opens the Print dialog box. Another example of a control key is the Esc key, which can often be used to stop, or escape, from a currently running task. A unique control key that is found only on Windows-based keyboards is the Windows key.

The *numeric keypad*, located at the right of the keyboard, provides an alternate method of quickly entering numbers. This is useful for individuals who are accustomed to using an adding machine or calculator.

Function keys are located above the standard row of number keys. Numbered F1 through F12, these keys are generally associated with certain software-specific commands. Pressing the F1 key will usually open the Help menu for a program; however, pressing one of the other function keys can produce different results, depending on the software program running.

Arrow keys are the keys located at the lower portion of the keyboard between the standard keys and the numeric keypad. These keys enable the user to move the insertion point around the window one space at a time.

Toggle and other keys, which are located just above the arrow keys, are used for various purposes including navigation and editing. The *Insert*, *Num Lock*, and *Caps Lock* keys are all examples of toggle keys. A *toggle key* works like a light switch; press it once and the feature is turned on, press it again and it is turned off. If you've ever accidentally pressed the Caps Lock key and typed a long string of all capital letters, you've seen this feature in action. Pressing the Caps Lock key again allows you to return to normal keyboarding mode. Num lock allows you to switch the number pad from numeric entry (when on) to navigational uses (when off).

Multimedia and *Internet control keys* are typically found at the upper edge of the keyboard. The precise placement and function of these keys usually depend on the keyboard manufacturer. However, most modern keyboards have at least a few keys or buttons that can be used for such tasks as muting or adjusting speaker volume, opening a web browser, and sending an email message. Generally, each key has an icon that indicates its function and is programmable to use your default email and web applications, among others.

Is there an easier way to control the action on the computer screen? Yes, the *mouse* is an input device (also called a pointing device) that, together with the keyboard, enables the user to control the operations of the computer. The mouse became popular with the introduction of graphical user interfaces, such as Microsoft Windows. This point-and-click device is useful for positioning the *insertion point* by translating hand movements into corresponding actions on the screen. The mouse is represented on the screen by a symbol called the *mouse pointer*. The user can move the mouse and position this pointer anywhere on the screen, click and drag to move objects, or make selections from available program icons or menus.

Older mice may have a roller ball on the bottom that, as you move it, translates your movement into electrical impulses. Newer mice use laser technology (optical) to control the pointer movement. Because the bottom of an optical mouse is sealed, dirt and debris are less likely to get inside and interfere with the mouse's internal mechanisms. This laser beam can be harmful if pointed at your eyes; do not look at it directly or point it at anybody else's eyes. Like a keyboard, the mouse can be wired or wireless. Laptop and tablet computers can use a mouse, but most of them have a built-in touchpad, a trackball, or track point to move the insertion point and mouse pointer. Most mice today are equipped with two buttons and a scroll wheel in the center that provides easy zoom and scroll functions.

How can the mouse be used more efficiently? Although there are different kinds of mice, the traditional mouse has two buttons and a scroll wheel. The palm of your hand should rest comfortably over the mouse in such a way that your index finger rests on the left mouse button and the middle finger on the right mouse button. The following provides a brief description of some of the ways the mouse can be used:

- *Click*—By default, the left mouse button is considered the primary button. When instructed to click, it is understood that the mouse pointer is moved to a certain location on the screen and the left mouse button is pressed and released one time to reposition the insertion point.
- *Double-click*—When instructed to double-click, it is understood that the mouse pointer is moved to a certain location on the screen and the left mouse button is pressed and released two times in rapid succession. Double-clicking is used to open an item or launch an application. It is important that the mouse does not move while double-clicking or the command will not produce the expected results.
- *Drag*—This means to press the left mouse button and continue to hold it while dragging, or moving, the mouse then releasing it. This action can be used to select large blocks of text, to move objects, or to resize other objects.
- *Right-click*—Pressing and releasing the right mouse button one time will open a shortcut menu. *Shortcut menus* are usually context-sensitive, which means they will vary depending on what or where you have clicked and what program you are using. The right mouse button is also known as the secondary button and is not typically pressed more than one time; no double-clicking for the right button. After the shortcut menu has been opened, you select the appropriate choice by clicking it with the left mouse button.
- *Right-drag*—This is done by pressing the right mouse button and continuing to hold it while dragging, or moving, the mouse. This action is used when copying, moving, or linking files or folders within different storage devices.
- *Scroll wheel*—If your mouse is equipped with a scroll wheel, it can be used to quickly move a page up or down in a window, thus the name of the action *to scroll*. It is an easy way to navigate through lengthy documents or websites. Combined with the control key, the scroll wheel can easily zoom in or out of pages on the web and in most applications.

Are there other input devices? Although the keyboard and mouse are the two most common input devices, there are many other input devices. *Scanners* are similar to copy machines, but instead of producing a paper copy, they convert documents or photos to digital files that can then be saved on your computer. Microphones are used to digitally capture and record sounds. Game controls such as joysticks are used to control movement within video games. Digital cameras and *digital video recorders* enable you to capture digital images and movies and transfer them directly to your computer.

What does the CPU do? The *CPU* or *processor* (see Figure 1.10) is the brain of the computer and is responsible for executing program instructions and manipulating data to convert to information. It has two main parts—the *control unit* and the *arithmetic logic unit (ALU)*. The control unit is responsible for obtaining and executing instructions from the computer's memory. Example: The user wants to print a document and selects the "Print" command from an icon on the screen. The CPU gets the command from memory (RAM), interprets the command, and sends the document as output to a selected printer. In other words, the CPU coordinates the internal activities and the activities of all the other computer components. The arithmetic logic unit (ALU) performs the arithmetic and logic functions for the computer. The ALU handles addition, subtraction, multiplication, and division, and also makes logical and comparison decisions. This enables the CPU to perform tasks such as sorting data alphabetically or numerically and filtering data to locate specific criteria.

FIGURE 1.10 Two sides of a CPU

nexusseven/Fotolia

Different Types of CPUs

As important as the CPU is to your computer, you might expect it to take up a large amount of space in the console. However, the CPU is actually rather small, thus the term *microchip*. Over the years, manufacturers have successfully reduced the size of microprocessor chips while continuing to increase their computing power. In fact, Moore's law (formulated in 1965 by Gordon Moore, cofounder of Intel) addresses this increase in computing power, observing that current production methods enable CPU capacity to double about every 24 months or so! Where will we be next year? Exabyte may be typical.

Are there different brands of CPUs? Yes, the most well-known chip manufacturers include Intel and Advanced Micro Devices (AMD). Chip manufacturers often produce several different models of chips. Some of the chips that Intel makes include the Intel® Core™ i7 processor Extreme Edition, the Intel® Core™2 Quad Processor for desktops, and the Intel® Centrino® 2 Processor Technology for portable computers. AMD manufactures chips such as the AMD Phenom™ II X4 for desktops and the AMD Turion™ X2 Ultra Dual-Core Mobile Processor for portable computers. Intel and AMD chips are the mainstays for PCs. Using multiple processors (***dual-core*** or ***quad-core***) has several advantages over a single-processor CPU, including improved ***multitasking*** capabilities and system performance, lower power consumption, reduced usage of system resources, and lower heat emissions.

How is a CPU's processing power measured? One indicator of a CPU's processing power is its clock speed. ***Clock speed*** measures the speed at which a CPU processes data (number of instructions per second) and is measured in hertz (Hz); these days usually ***gigahertz (GHz)***. Early computers had CPUs that processed at speeds of less than 5 ***megahertz (MHz)***, whereas modern processors can operate at over 3 GHz (the equivalent of 3,000 MHz) and newer processors continue to surpass these numbers.

What types of memory does a computer have? Memory is another critical computer component of a computer system. The term ***memory*** signifies storage. There are two basic types of memory: temporary or volatile and permanent or nonvolatile.

Permanent memory includes read-only memory (ROM), which is prerecorded on a chip. The information on a ROM chip cannot be changed, removed, or rewritten, and is generally inaccessible to the computer user. ROM is *nonvolatile* memory because it retains its contents even if the computer is turned off. ROM contains critical information, such as the program used to start up or *boot* the computer.

Storage devices such as hard disks and flash drives and storage media such as CDs and *DVDs* are considered permanent or nonvolatile memory. These are presented later in this chapter.

Temporary memory, the computer's *volatile* memory, is Random Access Memory (RAM). (See Figure 1.11.)

FIGURE 1.11 Random Access Memory (RAM) / RAM chips on left and Read Only Memory (ROM) / ROM chip on right.

Vladimir Vydrin / Fotolia; Devyathkin / Fotolia

Random access memory (RAM) acts as the computer's short-term memory and stores data and program instructions waiting to be processed. RAM is considered volatile because it's always in flux, constantly changing, and its contents are erased when the computer is turned off.

Why is it important to have enough RAM? The more tasks your computer performs at the same time, or the more programs you have open, the more RAM it uses. Recall the description of RAM as the center of the flow of data and information in the information processing cycle (see Figure 1.1). That flow slows down when there is not enough RAM. Your computer's RAM is like the upper portion of your desk. The size of the desk that you need is determined by the work you do at a given moment. You may use a laptop computer, several books, a clipboard with notes, a holder for pens and pencils, and a telephone. If your desk is not big enough to fit these items, you cannot work with all of them at the same time. If you do not have a sufficient amount of RAM in your system, you might notice your computer slows down or even stops responding when you try to perform tasks.

Computer users often think this means they have too much information saved on their computers' hard drives. What it actually means is that they are running out of memory, not permanent storage space. To fix this problem, you can reduce the number of programs running at the same time, disable some features of the operating system, or add more RAM to your system. Installing additional memory is one of the most inexpensive and easiest upgrades for your computer and often results in noticeable performance improvements. It is, in fact, the combination of the processor's speed and amount of RAM that gives your computer its overall quickness of performance.

Memory is measured in units of bytes such as megabytes (MB), gigabytes (GB), and terabytes (TB). One megabyte is approximately one million bytes, one gigabyte is one billion bytes, and one terabyte is one trillion bytes. Additional information can be found in the table in Figure 1.12.

UNITS TO MEASURE MEMORY				
NAME	**ABBREVIATION**	**NUMBER OF BYTES**	**EQUIVALENT**	**RELATIVE SIZE**
Byte	B	1 byte	8 bits	Holds one character of data
Kilobyte	KB	1,024		Holds about a half page of double-spaced text
Megabyte	MB	1,048,576	1,024 KB	Holds about 768 pages of typed text
Gigabyte	GB	1,073,741,824	1,024 MB	Holds approximately 786,432 pages of text
Terabyte	TB	1,099,511,627,776	1,024 GB	Represents a stack of typewritten pages almost 51 miles high
Petabyte	PB	1,125,899,906,842,624	1,024 TB	Represents a stack of typewritten pages almost 52,000 miles high
Exabyte	EB	11,522,921,504,606,846,976	1,024 PB	All data transferred over the internet in a year equals several hundred EB.
Zettabyte	ZB	1,099,511,627,776 GB	1,024 EB	It is estimated that all information in the world equals a few ZB.
Yottabyte	YB	1,208,925,819,614,629,174,706,176	1,024 EB	A number so large that humans cannot comprehend it.

RAM size requirements vary depending on the operating system in use. Older computers that run Windows XP should have between 512 MB to 1 GB of RAM. For newer computers, a minimum of 2 GB or more is recommended. Computers today are commonly configured with anywhere from 2 GB to 1 TB of RAM.

Output Devices

Output devices display information after data has been processed in a useful format. This format can be text, graphics, audio, or video. Monitors and printers are the two most common output devices.

What are monitors? *Monitors* are display devices that show images of text, graphics, and video once data has been processed. The image on a monitor is called *soft copy*; you can view it, but you cannot touch it; it is intangible. See Figure 1.13.

FIGURE 1.13 Output devices—monitors

Touch screen display   LCD Wide monitor

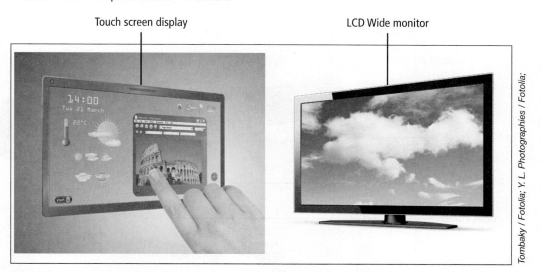

Tombaky / Fotolia; Y. L. Photographies / Fotolia;

What is an LCD monitor? Monitors come in a variety of sizes and styles, but the standard today is the *liquid crystal display (LCD)*. *Flat-panel* LCD monitors use a liquid crystal display and are thin and energy efficient.

What factors determine a monitor's display quality? A monitor's display is made up of millions of tiny dots known as *pixels* or picture elements. Each pixel represents a single point on a display screen or in a graphic image. The number of pixels on the screen determines a monitor's sharpness and clarity, also known as its *resolution*. A higher number of pixels results in a clearer and sharper monitor resolution and smaller image size. A standard screen resolution might be expressed as 1,024 × 768, which means there are 1,024 columns, each containing 768 pixels, for a total of more than 786,000 pixels on the screen. Monitor sizes are determined by measuring their screens diagonally.

Dot pitch is another display characteristic and refers to the diagonal distance between two pixels of the same color. Dot pitch is measured in millimeters with smaller measurements resulting in a crisper viewing image because there is less blank space between the pixels. For best viewing, monitors should have a dot pitch measurement of .28 mm or less. LCD monitors use an electric current to illuminate the pixels.

Refresh rate is the speed at which the pixels are reilluminated and it's measured in cycles per second, expressed as hertz (Hz). Refresh rates generally run 75 Hz or higher, which means the screen image is redrawn 75 or more times per second. Higher refresh rates result in less screen flicker and less eye strain.

What are touchscreen monitors? Touchscreen monitors are both input and output devices. They display images like regular monitors, but also enable users to touch their surfaces and make selections directly from the screen. These monitors are widely used in retail stores at checkout counters and in airports for passengers' fast check-ins. Android touchscreens include 7 and 10 inch tablets. Apple's iPad and iPhone also use touchscreens.

Which monitor is best? Choosing the right monitor is always a combination of what you like, want, and can afford. A higher resolution, small dot pitch, fast refresh rate, and large monitor size are desirable, but all come with a higher price tag.

Using a monitor is a good way to view the information on your computer, but sometimes a soft copy isn't sufficient for your needs. *Printers* generate *hard copies* or *printouts*, which are a permanent record of your work on paper. See Figure 1.14 for some examples of printers.

FIGURE 1.14 Output devices—printers

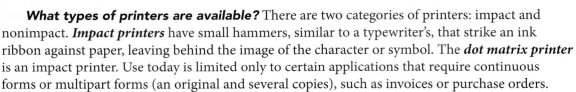

Ink-Jet Printer Cartridge

Dot Matrix Printer

Ink-Jet Printer

Laser Printer

Multifunction Printer

Laser Printer Cartridge

Aleksandar Jocic / Fotolia; Unclesam / Fotolia; Konstantin Shevtsov / Fotolia;

What types of printers are available? There are two categories of printers: impact and nonimpact. ***Impact printers*** have small hammers, similar to a typewriter's, that strike an ink ribbon against paper, leaving behind the image of the character or symbol. The ***dot matrix printer*** is an impact printer. Use today is limited only to certain applications that require continuous forms or multipart forms (an original and several copies), such as invoices or purchase orders.

How does a ***nonimpact printer*** work? Nonimpact printers do not actually touch the paper when printing. There are a variety of nonimpact printers, but the two most commonly used with home computers are the ink-jet printer and the laser printer. The ink-jet printer uses a special nozzle and ink cartridges to spray ink in small droplets onto the surface of the paper. ***Ink-jet printers*** easily print in color, in black, and in grayscale to produce good quality printouts. They are relatively inexpensive to buy and maintain. ***Laser printers*** use the same process as photocopiers to produce their output. They use a special cylinder known as a drum, dry ink or toner, and a laser. Static electricity attracts toner to the surface of the drum, and the laser distributes the toner in the correct pattern. The drum transfers the toner to the paper and heat is used to permanently fuse the toner to the paper. Laser printers are generally more expensive to purchase than ink-jet printers, although they often print more quickly and are more cost effective. Lower-end laser printers print only in black and white; however, more expensive printers can produce color copies.

How do you assess a printer's capabilities? When you select a printer, there are some key characteristics to consider.

Print speed is often expressed as ***pages per minute (ppm)***. Print speed can vary depending on the manufacturer and model, and is also affected by whether the page is text-only, if it includes graphics, and if the printout is in color, black, or grayscale.

Just as with monitors, resolution is also important to print quality. For printing purposes, resolution is expressed as ***dots per inch*** or ***dpi***. The higher the dpi, the better the print quality will be. Print qualities of 300 to 600 dpi are typical of most printers, although special photo printers can offer resolutions up to 1,200 dpi. Professional printers can reach 2,400 to 3,600 dpi for pages such as art plates in high quality reproduction books and textbooks.

Color output and its related cost is another important consideration. Ink-jet printers offer four- or six-color options. Many ink-jet printers use one cartridge for black ink and one or more cartridges for color. When available, printers that offer a separate cartridge for each color are a practical choice because you can replace only one color at a time as the cartridges run out. Laser printers use separate toner cartridges for each color.

What are all-in-one printers? All-in-one printers, or *multifunction devices (MFD)*, bundle multiple capabilities in one device. All-in-one devices usually include:

- A printer, either ink-jet or laser (output)
- A scanner to convert text or images into files that can be stored and further manipulated by the computer (input)
- A copier function to duplicate documents (output)
- Network capabilities to enable this multifunction device (MFD) to work as part of a wired or wireless network environment (communications)
- A facsimile (fax) function to send and receive documents through the telephone (communications)

Are there other output devices? *Speakers* and *multimedia projectors* are also examples of output devices. Many computers include small speakers to enable the user to listen to CDs or DVDs and hear any auditory signals the computer sends. However, if you're serious about multimedia, you will probably want to invest in a better set of speakers for improved performance. Multimedia projectors are used to conduct presentations and training sessions. These projectors enable information to be displayed on a big screen, so it can be easily viewed by a large group of attendees.

Under what category do digital cameras fall? A *digital camera* is a device that stores pictures digitally rather than by using conventional film. After images are captured, they are stored in the camera's internal memory. Some cameras use removable *flash memory cards* as storage media. These cards can be read by a computer, which can then edit them and save them as files. So, the camera itself is a form of handheld computer, which, if connected to a computer, serves as an *input/output device (I/O)*. The same thing can be said to describe camcorders.

Storage Devices

What are storage devices? *Storage devices* are used to store data, information, and programs for future use. This storage is often referred to as *permanent memory* because, unlike data that is in RAM, data saved to a storage device remains there until the user deletes or overwrites it. Data can be stored by using internal hardware devices located in the system unit or in removable units that enable portability. See Figure 1.15.

FIGURE 1.15 Storage devices

STORAGE MEDIUM	CAPABILITIES	STORAGE CAPACITY
 Hard Drive	Read and write	External: Up to 3 TB Internal: Up to 3 TB
 CD CD-RW	Read-only Read and write	700 MB
 DVD DVD+RW	Read-only Read and write	4.7 GB (for single-sided, single-layered DVDs) 9.4 GB (for single-sided, double-layered DVDs)
 Flash Memory Cards	Read and write	16 MB to 128 GB
 Flash Drive	Read and write	Up to 1 TB

Martin Garnham / Fotolia; popov48 / Fotolia; dimedrol68 / Fotolia; kittipak

How is a storage device different from storage media? A device is a piece of hardware such as a hard drive or a ***DVD drive***. Media is the removable part that actually contains the stored data. Media requires a device to ***read and write*** on it. Read is the action of retrieving or opening existing data and write is the action of saving or storing data. Following is a list of devices and their media:

- CD and DVD optical drives read and write on CDs and DVDs, which are the media.
- Card readers read and write on flash memory cards, which are the media.
- USB drives, also known as flash drives or thumb drives, are media that require a connection to a USB port for read/write operations.
- Tape backup drives read and write onto tape cartridges, which are the media.
- The exception to this is the hard drive, in which the hardware and the media are all contained in a sealed unit that cannot be taken apart.

How is data stored? Data is generally stored by using one of three forms of storage: magnetic, optical, or solid state storage:

Magnetic storage uses tape or film covered in a thin, magnetic coating that enables data to be saved as magnetic impulses. It works in much the same fashion as an audiocassette or videotape works. Hard drives and backup tape drives are both forms of magnetic storage. Before magnetic storage can occur, media has to be formatted. This is the process in which media is divided into ***tracks*** and ***sectors***. Tracks are magnetic concentric circles and sectors are segments within those circles. Data is stored magnetically within the spaces created by these tracks and sectors. Magnetic media has ***read/write*** capability, which means it is possible to use it over and over again, enabling you to delete or revise existing data and save new data.

Hard disk drive—A hard disk drive is the computer's main internal magnetic storage device. Also referred to as a hard drive, its storage space is usually measured in gigabytes (GB). In the 1990s, the 1 GB drive was developed. By 2013, computers' drives ranged in size from 500 GB up to 4 TB. Hard drives are permanent storage devices fixed inside the system unit.

Backup tape drives are storage devices that resemble audiocassette tape recorders and save data to magnetic tape media. Although they are rarely used for home computers anymore, many businesses and organizations still rely on tape backup systems to safeguard their data on a daily basis. See Figure 1.16.

FIGURE 1.16 Tape backup drive and media

The capacity of the components found in your system unit is measured in terms of storage size or speed. Computer systems continue to increase in storage capacity and computing speed, while decreasing in physical size. Generally, higher measurements indicate a system that is quicker and more powerful than a system with lower measurements. However, it is important to balance size and speed with financial considerations too. Although it is tempting to consider buying a computer with the most power possible, a lesser computer may be more reasonably priced and still be sufficient for the typical user's needs. Recall that CPU speed is measured in gigahertz (GHz). The amount of RAM and storage space in a computer are measured in gigabytes (GB).

- **Optical storage** uses flat plastic disks coated in a special reflective material. Data is saved by using a laser beam to **burn** tiny pits into the storage medium. A less intensive laser is used to read the saved data. The saved data is organized by using tracks and sectors, similar to those used in magnetic media. **Compact discs (CDs)** and **digital video discs (DVDs)** are examples of optical media. Unlike magnetic media, not all optical storage is read/write capable. **CD-ROMs**—CD media that was burned once and from that moment on can only be read—and **DVD-ROMs**—DVD media that is burned once and from that moment on can only be read—are considered read-only media (ROM). The information contained on them can be read, but not changed or deleted, and it is not possible to save new data to them. If you purchase new software, music, or a movie, it is most likely on a CD-ROM or DVD-ROM. A record-only disk (**CD-R**) enables you to record, or burn, information to the disk one time only; information saved this way cannot be deleted or rewritten. A rewritable disk (**CD-RW**) enables information to be recorded, revised, or deleted, and new data can also be written to the disk, similar to magnetic media. The same possibilities are available in DVDs. However, there are currently two competing formats DVD-R/RW, known as "DVD dash," and DVD+R/RW, known as "DVD plus." The R/RW suffix indicates the DVD can be used to record and can also be rewritten. Although most DVD players can play either format, if you want to record to a DVD, you must know which format the DVD recorder requires.

CD and DVD drives—Your computer may have one or two of these optical drives in the system unit. It's important to know whether these drives are simple CD-ROM drives, which can only read CDs, or if it is a CD-RW drive, also known as a ***CD burner***. A CD burner gives you the ability to save, or burn, files to a CD-R (compact disk recordable). You might also have a separate drive that can read and write DVDs.

Although CDs and DVDs look alike, DVDs are capable of holding much more information than CDs. A CD can hold up to 700 MB of data, but a DVD can store almost 10 GB! Because of their differences, a ***CD drive*** is unable to read DVDs, although a DVD drive can read CDs.

- ***LightScribe*** is a disk-labeling technology that burns text and graphics onto the surface of a specially coated LightScribe CD or DVD. This is an alternative to printing a conventional sticker label and attaching it to a regular CD or DVD, but it does require that you purchase LightScribe media. See Figure 1.17.

FIGURE 1.17 LightScribe direct disk labeling

LightScribe / Hewlett Packard

- ***Solid-State Storage*** uses solid-state technology. It is completely electronic and has no moving mechanical parts. Also called flash memory, it is a quick and easy form of rewritable storage and is often used in mobile devices such as smartphones, digital cameras, and MP3 players. Depending on the manufacturer, flash memory cards may be called Memory Stick, CompactFlash, Secure Digital, or MultiMediaCard. Typically, a device can use only one style of memory card; however, a computer equipped with the appropriate card reader can read any of them. Small, removable storage devices known as USB drives, flash drives, or thumb drives also use solid-state technology, require a USB port to connect to the system unit, and are very popular for transporting data.

Flash drives are removable storage devices that use flash memory and connect to the computer by a USB port. Flash drives are also known as thumb drives, universal serial bus (USB) drives, and jump drives. The flash drive is typically a device small enough to fit on a keychain or in a pocket and, because of its solid-state circuitry and lack of moving parts, it is extremely durable. Available in several common storage sizes ranging from 16 MB to 512 GB; the Victorinox company has released both a 512 GB secure SSD flash drive and a Swiss Army Knife 256 GB and 1 TB solid state storage (Victorinox, 2012). A flash drive is a quick and easy way to save and transport files. To use one of these devices, you plug it into a computer's USB port. The computer recognizes the new device and enables the user to save or retrieve files from the flash drive.

Is it possible to add a storage device to a system? If you are running out of hard disk space or your system doesn't have a particular storage device, it may be possible to add a storage device, provided your system has enough space for it. You would need an available drive bay, which is the physical location within the system unit, or you might consider removing an existing device and replacing it with another. For instance, if you only have a CD-ROM drive, you could remove that and replace it with a DVD±RW drive, thereby giving you the ability to play and burn both CDs and DVDs. It is also possible to purchase many of these units as external storage devices. An external storage device is a peripheral that attaches to the computer through a port and performs the same tasks as its corresponding internal device. One of the most popular of these today is the external hard drive, which can greatly increase a computer's storage capacity and make your data fully portable. In 2013, you could purchase a 5.1" × 1.6" × 6.6" external 3 TB, USB 3.0, removable hard drive for approximately $150. How far we have come in such a short time!

Ports

A *port* acts as an interface or connector between a system's peripheral devices and the computer, enabling data to be exchanged easily. The ports shown on the laptop in Figure 1.18 have different shapes and sizes. The same ports are typically found on a desktop too, although they might be arranged in a different order. Various input and output devices use different data exchange methods, requiring different types of ports and connectors (or plugs). If your computer does not have a particular port, you can buy an expansion card that connects to the motherboard and provides the needed connection.

FIGURE 1.18 Ports on a laptop.

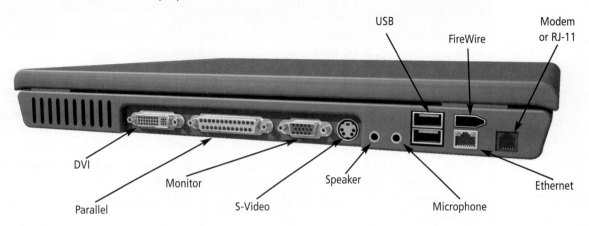

How do you determine which port a peripheral device needs? Manufacturers have attempted to make the process of connecting peripheral devices less complicated on newer computers. Rather than trying to match the size and shape of a connector to its port, many manufacturers use a color-coding system that coordinates the colors of the connectors with their corresponding ports. Additionally, most desktop computers include ports, such as USB and audio ports, on the front panel of the system unit to provide easier access to them. Locating these ports on the front panel makes it a simple process to connect and disconnect devices that are used only occasionally, such as digital cameras, external hard drives, or MP3 players. Peripherals that are rarely disconnected, such as a keyboard or printer, are generally plugged into the ports on the back of the computer.

What are the different ports used for? Serial and parallel ports are two of the oldest types of ports found on a computer. *Serial ports* are ports that can send data only one bit at a time, so the data exchange rate is slow compared to newer technology. The maximum rate at which a standard serial port can transfer data is 115 *kilobits (Kbps)* or one thousand bits per second. The mouse and modem are examples of devices that might use a serial port. A *parallel port* is a port that sends data in groups of bits, at transfer rates of up to 500 Kbps, so it is a considerably faster method of transferring data than the serial port. Older printers were often connected to a computer through a parallel port.

Are there faster ports? Over the years, newer ports have come into existence. One of these is the *universal serial bus (USB) port*. This type of port is able to interface with several different peripheral devices, which reduces the need for individual, dedicated ports. USB ports are also able to transfer data at extremely high rates of speed. Original USB ports, known as USB 1.1, are capable of speeds of 12 *megabits (Mbps)* or one million bits per second. The next version, USB 2.0, can attain a rate of 480 Mbps, 40 times faster than USB 1.1 technology and over 400 times faster than a serial port! USB 2.0 ports are backward compatible, which means that older USB devices work with them; however, data will transfer only at the slower USB 1.1 speed. The newer *USB 3.0* attains blazing transfer rates of 4.8 Gbps! The higher data transfer capabilities of USB ports, coupled with their capability to work with multiple devices, have made the older serial and parallel ports obsolete. Because of the USB port's speedy data transfer rate and its capability to be used with numerous devices, new computers often include six or more USB ports. Devices using USB ports include keyboards, mice, printers, scanners, digital cameras, MP3 players, and external hard drives. In general, it's a good idea to get a computer with as many USB ports as possible. See the table in Figure 1.19.

FIGURE 1.19 Port speeds and uses

PORTS AND THEIR USES		
PORT NAME	**DATA TRANSFER SPEED**	**TYPICAL USE**
Serial	115 Kbps	Mice/External modems
Parallel	500 Kbps	Printers
USB 1.1	12 Mbps	Mice/Keyboards/Printers/Scanners/Game controllers
USB 2.0	400 Mbps	Same as USB 1.1 but at faster transfer rates. Also, camcorders, digital cameras, and MP3 players. It maintains compatibility with USB 1.1.
USB 3.0	4.8 Gbps	Same devices as older USB devices, backward compatible
FireWire 400/ FireWire 800	400 Mbps/800 Mbps	Digital video camcorders/Digital cameras
Ethernet/Gigabit Ethernet	Up to 100 Mbps/Up to 1,000 Mbps	Network connections/Cable modems

The *FireWire port*, developed by Apple and also known as IEEE 1394, is another means of transferring data quickly. The FireWire 400 has a data transfer rate of 400 Mbps, while the newer FireWire 800 transfers data at a mighty 800 Mbps; two times as fast as USB 2.0. This port is typically used to connect devices that must transfer huge amounts of data to a computer quickly, such as digital cameras or digital video recorders, or external hard drives. FireWire ports are standard on many Apple products, but are usually found only on higher-end Windows PCs and peripheral devices. USB 3.0 was originally developed for use with fiber optic cables, with transfer capabilities of 5Gbps, theoretically 10 times faster than USB 2.0. It is considered overkill unless you are working with extremely large HDMI or video files constantly. Some peripheral devices offer users a choice of connecting by using a USB port or a FireWire port.

What kind of port is used to connect to another computer? *Connectivity ports*, such as Ethernet and modem ports, are used to connect a computer to a local network or to the Internet. An *Ethernet port*, also known as an *RJ-45 jack*, resembles a standard phone jack, but is slightly larger. The Ethernet port is used for network access and can also be used to connect a cable modem or router for Internet access. A *modem port* is the same size and shape as a phone jack and is used to connect the modem to a phone system, enabling *digital subscriber line (DSL)* or dial-up Internet access. DSL is a type of communications line in which signals travel through copper wires between a telephone switching station and a home or business. The maximum data transfer rate for a dial-up modem is 56 Kbps, whereas the most common Ethernet standard, Fast Ethernet, transfers data at the rate of 100 Mbps. However, Gigabit Ethernet, with a potential transfer rate of 1,000 Mbps, is becoming an option on higher-end systems and is standard on many Mac systems.

Even faster Ethernet technologies, such as 10 Gigabit Ethernet or 10 GbE exist, but they are currently used for network backbones and enterprise network infrastructures rather than home users. We currently have the technology to create Ethernet with speeds ranging from 400 Gbps to 1 Tbps; however, the cost may make their production prohibitive.

Are there special-purpose ports? Despite the prevalence of USB ports, which can be used for a variety of peripherals, there are still some devices that require special ports. These ports include Musical Instrument Digital Interface (MIDI), High-Definition Multimedia Interface (HDMI), IrDA, Bluetooth, video, and audio ports.

MIDI ports are used to connect electronic musical devices, such as keyboards and synthesizers, to a computer, enabling musicians to create digital music files.

HDMI ports are used to connect electronic devices, such as an iPad, to a digital television, computer, or projector. Due to the fact that HDMI is compatible with digital video interface (DVI), no conversion is necessary. HD movies can be played directly on TV from your digital device.

The *IrDA port* is used to enable devices such as keyboards, mice, and printers to transmit data wirelessly to another device by using infrared light waves. To transmit information, each of the devices must have an IrDA port, and a clear line of sight, with no other objects blocking the transmission.

Bluetooth is another type of wireless technology that relies on radio wave transmission and doesn't require a clear line of sight. Bluetooth-enabled devices such as smartphones or other mobile devices can communicate only with each other over short distances, typically less than 30 feet.

Video ports include standard monitor ports, DVI ports, and S-video ports. A *monitor port* is used to connect the monitor to the graphics processing unit, which is usually located on the motherboard or on a video card. However, to get the best results from an LCD monitor, the *Digital Video Interface (DVI) port* should be used instead. The DVI port transmits a pure digital signal, eliminating the need for digital to analog conversion and resulting in a higher quality transmission and a clearer picture on the monitor. The **S-video port** is typically used to connect other video sources, such as a television, projector, or digital recorder, to the computer.

Similar to video ports, **audio ports** connect audio devices, such as speakers, headphones, and microphones, to the computer's sound card. These jacks will be familiar to anyone who is used to using standard stereo components.

Evaluating Your System

The way a computer system is set up or the combination of components that make up the system is called its **configuration**. Different computers can be configured in different ways. This is important when buying a computer, expanding an existing system, or when connecting computers together in a network environment.

Now that you have learned most of the hardware components of a typical personal computer, you are ready to explore the computer's configuration, specifications, and features. If you didn't buy your computer brand new, you might not know all the details about your computer. If you did buy a new computer, the easiest way to find out is to check your paperwork; all the basic information should be there. However, if your computer isn't new or you didn't keep the paperwork, there are some ways to determine exactly what is in your system. Also if you start a new job or a new position and are given a computer system, you can do a number of things again to determine exactly what is in your system.

What kind of computer do you have? This is one of the easiest questions to answer. Like almost every other appliance you've used, you can probably find the manufacturer's name and a brand name or model number on the case of the computer. If not, check the back of the unit; there should be a metal tag that includes the manufacturer's name, model number, and serial number. This information might be necessary if you have to have service performed under warranty. To see your system properties in Windows 7 or 8, press ⊞ + Pause—the Properties window will open automatically using this keyboard shortcut. Alternatively, in Windows 8, from the Control Panel, click System and Security and then click System.

What operating system does the computer use? If you watch carefully as a computer boots up, you can often determine the operating system. You will usually see a **splash screen** showing the version of Windows that runs—for example, Windows XP, Windows 7, or Windows 8 which was released in December 2012.

How much memory is in the computer? What is the type and speed of the CPU? See Figure 1.20 that displays the System Properties window for several versions of Windows, with information on the computer's operating system, the type and speed of the CPU, and the amount of RAM that is installed.

FIGURE 1.20 Evaluating your system—General Properties

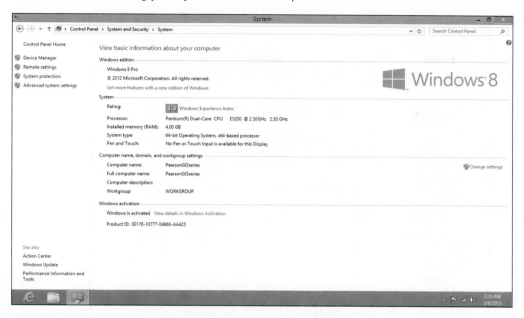

My Computer's Specifications	
Manufacturer	
Model/Type	
Operating System	
Amount of RAM	
C drive size	
Processor type	
Processor speed	

How do you determine what drives are on the system and how much storage space is available? It's important to know how much information you can store on your computer, what disk drives are available, and how much space you have left on each drive. Is there enough storage space or are the storage devices getting full? Use File Explorer in Windows 8 or Windows Explorer in previous versions of Windows to find the answers. You can open File Explorer (or Windows Explorer) by using the shortcut key 🪟 + E.

Figure 1.21 shows the the File Explorer window open to the Computer view in which the user can see all available local drives (devices within the system unit or peripherals connected to that unit) and network drives (devices available through a network). You can also right-click on any drive symbol and select Properties from the shortcut menu. A new dialog box displays the drive's information similar to the one shown in Figure 1.22. The pie chart displayed on the General Tab is a good visual tool that shows the size of your storage device and how much space is free.

FIGURE 1.21 Using File Explorer to view the drives available to your computer

FIGURE 1.22 The properties of one of the storage drives (the hard drive)

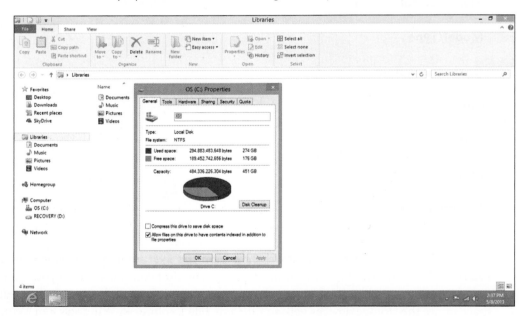

Objective 4 | Identify Types of Software and Their Uses

So far we have described computer hardware, the physical components of the system. However, without software, the computer would only be a collection of useless electronic and mechanical parts. Software provides the instructions or commands that tell the computer what to do. To perform various tasks, the computer requires a set of instructions called *programs* or *applications.* These programs enable individuals to use the computer without the need for special programming skills. There are two categories of computer software—system software and application software. Both types of software are required to work effectively with your computer.

System Software

System software provides the instructions that the computer needs to run. It contains the directions needed to start up the computer (known as the *boot process*), checks to ensure everything is in good working order, and enables you to interface or interact with the computer and its peripheral devices so that you can use them. System software consists of two main programs: the operating system and utility programs.

What is the operating system? The *operating system (OS)* is a special computer program that is present on every desktop computer, laptop, smartphone, server, or mainframe. The operating system controls the way the computer works from the time it is turned on until it is shut down. The operating system manages the various hardware components, including the CPU, memory, storage devices, peripheral devices, and network devices. It also coordinates with the various software applications presently running and provides the interaction with the user (*user interface*).

FIGURE 1.23 System Software Hierarchy, Model by Kari Pace Meck

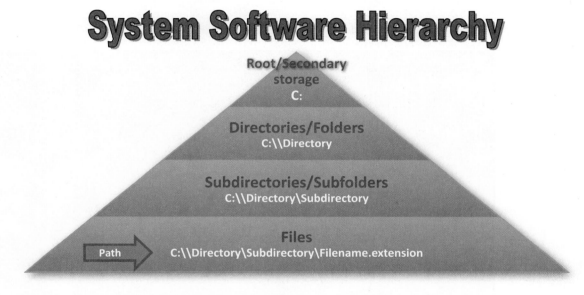

Figure 1.23 demonstrates the organizational hierarchy of system software. All software, system and application, is a collection of files working together to provide the user experience. All are stored within the system software hierarchy, which keeps track of where they are located. Deleting software files randomly disrupts this organization and can create problems. To properly add or remove software, installation and removal programs must be run to insure all related files are added or removed appropriately throughout the system hierarchy.

Is it possible to communicate with the operating system? Although the operating system communicates with the computer and its peripherals, it also includes a user interface that you can use to interact and communicate with the computer. Early operating systems used a text-based or keyboard-driven interface. The early *Disk Operating System (DOS)* required knowledge of special commands that had to be typed accurately to achieve the desired results. This type of system was not very user friendly. Most current operating systems use a point-and-click format known as a *graphical user interface (GUI)*. GUIs are more user friendly and intuitive than DOS systems. Rather than typing specific commands, you can use a mouse to select from on screen objects such as *icons* (a graphical depiction of an object such as a file or program), *menus* (lists of available commands), or *dialog boxes* (windows used to make choices or give the system specific instructions as to the action you want to take or task to perform). GUI operating systems display information on the monitor in the form of rectangular boxes called *windows*. Although you interact with system software every time you use the computer, in some ways you don't notice it.

Do all computers need an operating system? Yes, the operating system is a critical part of a computer system. Without an OS to provide specific instructions, the computer would be unable to fulfill its four main functions. The operating system provides a way for the user to interact with the computer, it manages the processor, memory and storage, and the system's hardware and peripherals. It provides a consistent means for software applications to work with the CPU. However, different computers require different types of operating systems. There are several popular operating systems available for home computers. They include Microsoft Windows, Mac OS, and Linux.

Microsoft Windows has the largest market share of the three main operating systems and is found on most of today's desktop and laptop computers. There have been many versions of Microsoft Windows, including Windows XP, Windows Vista, Windows 7, and Windows 8. Although a previous version of Windows might be found on an older computer, new computers are shipped with Windows 8 already installed. A sample of the new Windows 8 desktop is displayed in Figure 1.24.

FIGURE 1.24 A sample of the Windows 8 desktop

Why are there so many versions of Windows? Software developers are always updating and refining their software to adapt to new technology, respond to vulnerabilities, and improve their product. Because Microsoft also manufactures application software, some of its products have similar names and users can become confused. It's important to note that even though your computer might use Microsoft Windows for its operating system, it might not have Microsoft Office (an application software suite) installed. The newest operating system is Windows 8, which has been optimized for touchscreen performance. Microsoft's newest suite of office productivity software is Office 2013, which has *cloud* capabilities (see Objective 6, Describe Networks and Define Network Terms for cloud computing).

Mac OS is an operating system designed specifically for Apple's Macintosh computers. Figure 1.25 shows the Mac OS desktop that is similar to Windows because it also uses a GUI. In fact, Apple was the first company to introduce a commercially successful GUI operating system in 1984, named System, for the consumer market. The naming convention was OS1 through OSX. Versions 10.0 through 10.8, now use names of big cats. They are: Cheetah, Puma, Jaguar, Panther, Tiger, Leopard, Snow Leopard, Lion, and the current OS, Mountain Lion.

FIGURE 1.25 Mac OS desktop

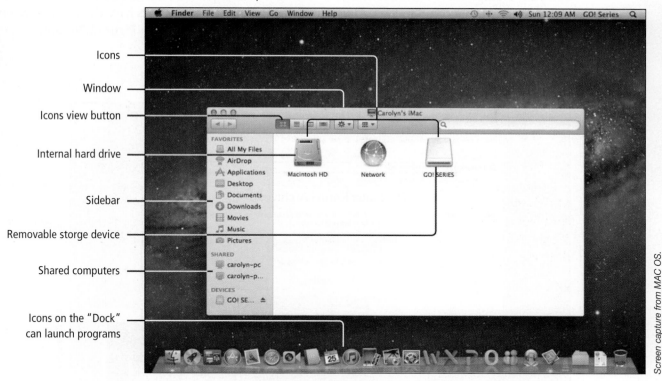

Icons

Window

Icons view button

Internal hard drive

Sidebar

Removable storge device

Shared computers

Icons on the "Dock" can launch programs

Screen capture from MAC OS.

Due to the popularity of the Windows-based PCs, Mac OS has a much smaller market share. If you are looking to purchase a PC or a peripheral for a PC, you have a variety of choices among different manufacturers. Apple manufactures products and peripherals solely for its computers and they tend to be a bit pricier.

Can Windows run on an Apple computer? Yes, there is software available to enable a Mac to run Windows applications. Microsoft's Virtual PC or Apple's Bootcamp allow you to perform tasks such as:

- Access all types of files, networks, and devices with your Mac from your PC
- Cut and paste between platforms; share applications, file types, folders, and other media between OS platforms
- Easily shut down virtual PC and re-launch right where it left off
- Use PC and Mac peripherals

Linux is an alternative operating system. Based on the UNIX operating system developed for mainframe computers, it also has a dedicated group of users. Linux is an open-source operating system, which means it is not owned by a single company and some versions are available at no cost.

How is open-source software different from other types of software? *Open-source software* makes its source code, essentially the program instructions, available to anyone who would like to see it. Programmers are encouraged to work with and change the code as they see fit, in the hope that having many "eyes" looking at the code will streamline and improve it. Proprietary software, such as Microsoft Windows, keeps this code secret and inaccessible to programmers who are not authorized by the software development company.

Why is Linux used? Linux is rarely used by novice desktop computer users although it is popular among developers and other technologically advanced individuals who prefer to use an alternative operating system for building a variety of computing systems. Some people appreciate the opportunity to work in this more "open" programming environment. Because no single company is responsible for the software, users might find help from various resources such as user groups and Internet communities. Alternatively, some software companies have chosen to develop and sell a version of Linux that includes a warranty and technical support. Figure 1.26 shows where the Linux kernel source code can be downloaded online.

FIGURE 1.26 Example of one of the versions of the Linux operating system

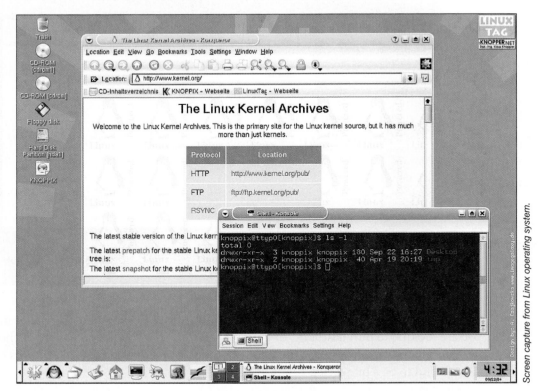

Screen capture from Linux operating system.

What are utility programs? Operating system software is the most critical software on the computer, because nothing can run without it. However, utility programs are another important component of system software. These small applications handle many important tasks involved with the management and maintenance of your system. *Utility programs* can be used to help back up important files, remove unwanted files or programs from your system, and schedule various tasks to keep your system running smoothly. Some of these utilities are included with the operating system, whereas others are stand-alone versions that you can purchase or download for free. The table in Figure 1.27 displays a variety of utility programs that ship with the Windows operating system, describing the function of each utility.

FIGURE 1.27 Windows utility programs

PROGRAM	FUNCTION
File Explorer (Windows Explorer in older versions)	Create folders, manage files, and compress/extract files. Read disk drive's properties including storage capacity and free disk space, check drive for errors
Windows Task Manager (Ctrl + Alt+ Delete)	Allows user to view the list of active applications, and switch or end any of them. Also, check the performance of the computer including CPU usage, RAM availability, and network utilization
Control Panel • System and Security • Network and Internet • Hardware and sound • Programs • User Accounts and Family Safety • Appearance and Personalization • Clock, Language, and Region • Ease of Access	Review your computer's status Back up your computer Find and fix problems View network status and tasks Choose home group and sharing options View devices and printers Add a device Connect to a projector Adjust commonly used mobility settings Install/uninstall programs Add desktop gadgets Add or remove user accounts Set up parental controls for any user Change the theme Change desktop background Adjust screen resolution Change keyboards or other input methods Change display language Let Windows suggest settings Optimize visual display
Administrative Tools	Schedule tasks
Security • Security Configuration Manager • Firewall and Advanced Security	Set account policies, local policies, network list manager policies, software restriction policies, and application control policies Set firewall and advanced security on local computer

Application Software

Application software or applications consists of programs that enable you to accomplish tasks and use the computer in a productive manner. Applications are programs created to perform a specific task, solve a specific problem, or address a specific need.

How do system software and application software work together? System software is like the breathing you must do to live; however, you don't usually think much about it unless something goes wrong. Application software might be compared to a musical instrument like a flute. When a musician combines each of these breaths and her flute, the result may be a beautiful melody (if she has practiced, of course!). Computer software works together similarly; the system software acts as the "breath," while the application software provides the "instrument," enabling you to create something.

There are many different kinds of application software, although they often fall into one of several general categories, each of which has a different purpose. You might be most familiar with productivity software, which includes the following applications:

- **Word processing software** is used to create, edit, format, print, and save documents and other text-based files. Word processing software enables you to create or edit letters, reports, memos, and many other types of written documents that you can print or attach to an email message. Revisions to existing documents can be made quickly and easily, without having to re-create the entire document. Documents created with this type of software can also include pictures, charts, hyperlinks, and other graphic elements. A **hyperlink** is a connection to another area of a document or a connection to an Internet location. Microsoft Word, Lotus Word Pro, and Corel WordPerfect are all examples of word processing programs. A document created by using Microsoft Word 2013 is shown in Figure 1.28.

FIGURE 1.28 Sample document created with Microsoft Word 2013

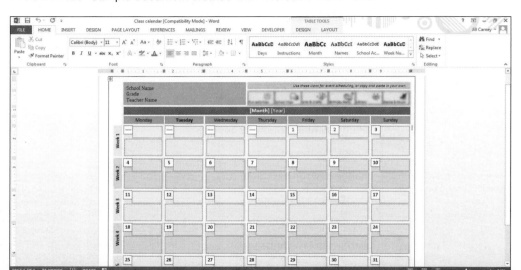

Notice that the document contains a graphic element in addition to text. Using word processing software replaces the use of conventional typewriters on which editing was virtually impossible once the document was finished.

Spreadsheet software enables the user to enter data in rows and columns format and:

- Perform calculations on numeric data with user-defined formulas.
- Convert part of the data into one or more charts, such as a column chart, pie chart, or line chart.

- Work with lists to organize data and sort it in alphabetic or numeric order.
- Create different scenarios and perform "what-if" analyses, the basis for sound decision making.

A key advantage of spreadsheet software is its capability to recalculate spreadsheets without user intervention. When data used in a calculation or a formula is changed, the spreadsheet software automatically updates the worksheet with the correct result. Microsoft Excel, Lotus 1-2-3, and Corel Quattro Pro are examples of spreadsheet programs. Figure 1.29 shows a worksheet and a chart created with Microsoft Excel 2013. The use of spreadsheet software replaces the old manual method of entering data in ledgers or journals and using a desktop calculator to do the math computations.

FIGURE 1.29 Example spreadsheet created with Microsoft Excel 2013

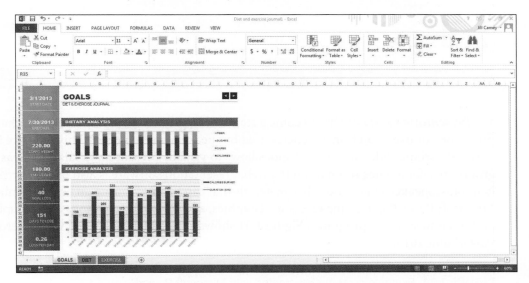

*A **database*** is a collection of data or unorganized facts. Database software is used to store, organize, update, and retrieve large amounts of data. ***Relational database management software (RDBMS)*** stores information in tables, which enable users quick access to the data by connecting tables with common fields. ***Data mining*** is a function in some databases that looks for hidden patterns in the data to anticipate future patterns. This is commonly used in scientific applications and as a marketing tool to predict future consumer trends. Typically, ***database software*** can be used to manage various types of information, such as that found in large mailing lists, inventories, students' records, order histories, and invoicing. Databases help you to enter, store, sort, filter, retrieve, and summarize the information they contain and then generate meaningful reports. Common database programs include Microsoft Access, Lotus Approach, and Corel Paradox. Figure 1.30 shows a database object created in Microsoft Access 2013. Database software replaces an old manual filing system where information is stored in filing cabinets in a single location.

FIGURE 1.30 Example of database software

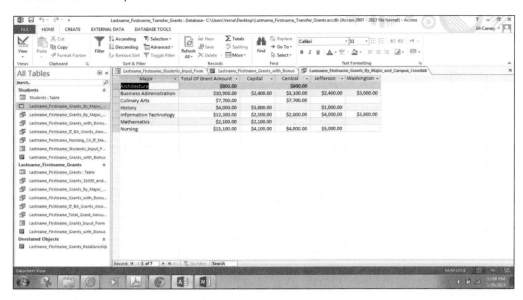

Presentation software has become a standard in presentations, replacing flip charts, slide projectors, or overhead transparencies used by speakers and lecturers. This software is used to create electronic slides and project slide shows to visually present materials and ideas to large groups in a conference room or on the web. Presentation software is also used to create audience handouts, speaker notes, and other materials that can be used during an oral presentation. Microsoft PowerPoint, Lotus Freelance Graphics, and Corel Presentations are examples of presentation software programs. Figure 1.31 shows a presentation created with Microsoft PowerPoint 2013.

FIGURE 1.31 Example presentation created with Microsoft PowerPoint 2013

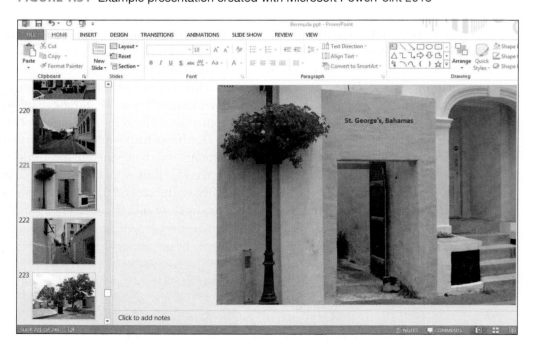

Business ***communication and organizational software*** can cover a broad range of tasks including ***video conferencing*** and telephony. However, applications in this productivity category are most often used to send and receive email messages. These applications typically include an address book (contacts list), a scheduler, a calendar, and task functions, which help users organize their personal and professional responsibilities. Microsoft Outlook, Lotus Notes, and Corel WordPerfect Mail are examples of communication and organizational software. Figure 1.32 shows an example of a calendar in Microsoft Outlook 2013.

FIGURE 1.32 Example of a calendar in Microsoft Outlook 2013

Social Communication and Personal Networking Software

Dictionary.com defines *social network* (for computers) as:

a) an online community of people with a common interest who use a website or other technologies to communicate with each other and share information, resources, and so on: a business-oriented social network.

b) a website or online service that facilitates this communication.

Social communication, by nature, includes any group of individuals who wants to interact with each other in a personal or business atmosphere. You can avoid the cost of phone calls, postage, and the time constraints of communicating with each other (locally or globally). Meetings that could take hours to get to, attend, and return from, now are at your disposal in moments. Only "a few clicks of a mouse," "swipes" of a finger, or "pinches" to reduce an image, and you are at your meeting!

All forms of social networking are located in the cloud (including using an intranet for secure purposes at businesses large or small). You can communicate in real time using ***IM***, Facetime, Skype, MagicJack, and VoIP; this type of communication is called ***synchronous***, where both parties must be connected at the same time. ***Asynchronous*** software includes email, Facebook, LinkedIn, and text messaging. All forms of these applications may include text, pictures, documents, video, voice, streaming video, or any combination of these.

Whether using social communication for business or personal reasons, you always must remember your netiquette and tone. Even with the rampant use of emoticons ☺, and knowing that typing in all caps is not only lazy, it's like yelling at someone; your physical expressions are not apparent and can easily be miscomprehended. Never respond asynchronously without careful consideration of how the content will be perceived. Likewise, remember that anything you post, whether text or image, IS PUBLIC FOREVER, perhaps long after you have forgotten about it.

Regarding the integrity of responsible, fluent computing, never post anything that could possibly be viewed in a negative light, especially if it does not belong to you, without permission of those involved.

What is a software suite? Although it is possible to buy any of the previous applications separately, most software manufacturers, including Microsoft, Corel, and Lotus, also group applications together into a package called a **software suite**. There is an alternative suite called OpenOffice and it's free. It is designed as open-source software, and users can report bugs, request new features, or change and improve the software.

Another advantage of using a suite is that because products from the same organization have many common elements, such as basic window design and layout, toolbars containing similar tools, dictionaries, and media galleries, many users find this familiarity with the similar interfaces makes it easier to switch between the programs in a suite. Examples of suites include Microsoft Office, Corel WordPerfect Office, Lotus SmartSuite, and Adobe Creative Suites.

What are some other common software applications? Recall that there are many different types of application software besides productivity software, each one with a specific function. Some of these include the following:

- You might use Microsoft Publisher, QuarkXPress, or Adobe InDesign to create newsletters, brochures, or advertising pieces.
- Bookkeepers rely on special accounting packages such as Peachtree Accounting or QuickBooks to balance the books and handle other accounting functions.
- Graphic designers turn to packages such as Adobe Photoshop or Adobe Illustrator to develop creative artwork.
- You might use Microsoft Expression Web or Adobe Dreamweaver to create your own website.

Web Browser Software

Web browsers are software used to locate and display websites and their pages and navigate through them. They also enable users to store their frequently used links for quick access to a particular location on the web. Current web browsers include Internet Explorer, Firefox, Safari, Mozilla, and Google Chrome.

If you have a specific question, chances are there is a **search engine**, to be accessed through any browser that will address those needs. Today, the best way to find software/hardware updates or find a plethora of information on a topic, both true and false, is to do a web search by using a search engine. Current free search engines include Google, Yahoo, Bing, Ask, and many others.

Objective 5   Identify Ethically Responsible and Safe Computing Practices

Being computer fluent implies you are a responsible computer user. This means more than just understanding the key components of a computer or the differences between hardware and software. Responsible computer users also know how to properly maintain their computers, back up necessary data, and protect themselves and others from security breaches and attacks.

Computer Maintenance

Backup! The first step to protect your computer and the valuable information it contains is to establish a regular maintenance routine. Backup utility programs, which may be part of your system software or purchased separately, enable you to back up your files. You can back up everything on your computer, only one or two important files, or anything in between. People often think that the computer is the most expensive item to replace if their hard drive fails. In reality, it is usually all the lost information that was contained on the hard drive that is the most costly to replace, if it is even possible to do so. Think about the types of files you might have on your own computer like financial records, your personal phone/address directory, resumes, scanned images of important documents, homework or school projects, your CD collection and purchased music files, and family photos and videos. Imagine how you would re-create these files if they were irretrievably damaged. Would you be able to find them again? If you back up files on a regular basis and store the backups in a secure location, you lessen the impact that a mechanical failure or security breach will have on your data. Remember: your backup needs to be in a different location (drive) than the original; use flash, email attachment, cloud, or any other universal media. Trust me, you don't usually do it until you lose something precious.

What other types of maintenance tasks should be performed? In addition to backing up files, regular file maintenance also helps to maintain order in your system. In Windows 7, several useful Windows utilities can be accessed from the System Tools folder. You can access the System Tools folder by clicking Start, clicking All Programs, and then clicking Accessories. In Windows 8, go to the Control Panel, click System and Security, and then click Administrative Tools. **Disk Defragmenter** scans the hard drive and attempts to relocate files so they use the available hard drive space more efficiently. Recall that data is stored on hard drives in sectors and tracks. As file sizes change, they can outgrow their original location. When that happens, the remaining portion of the file may be stored elsewhere. If a file size decreases, or a file is deleted, this can create a blank area on the hard drive. Defragmenting a hard drive enables scattered portions of files to be regrouped and open spaces to be rearranged. This results in faster and more efficient file access, which improves the response time of the hard drive.

Is there a way to automate maintenance tasks? Running these programs can be time consuming, especially when you want to use your computer for other tasks. It is also easy to forget to do these things on a regular basis. That is why newer versions of Windows include a **Task Scheduler.** This utility enables you to create a task and select the best time for each task to run, in addition to how often, which makes the whole process automatic. Figures 1.33 and 1.34 show the steps to follow to reach the Task Scheduler dialog box for Windows 7 and Windows 8 users, respectively.

FIGURE 1.33 Computer maintenance—steps to set a task in the Task Scheduler (Windows 7 users)

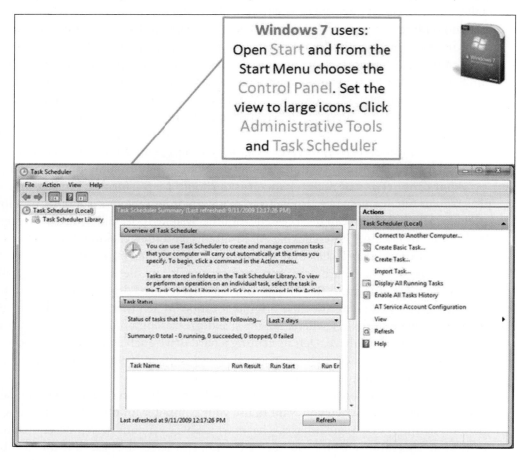

FIGURE 1.34 Computer maintenance—Task Scheduler (Windows 8 users)

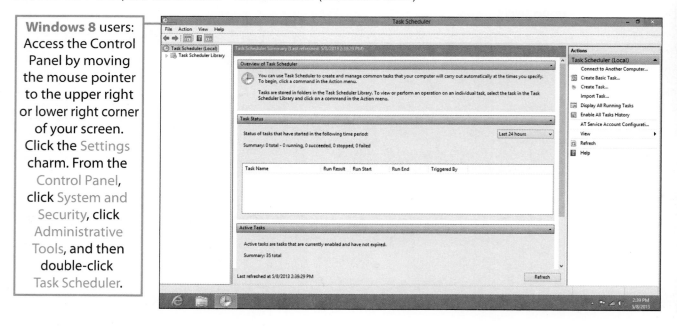

Can changes to my system be undone? Sometimes when new software is installed on a computer, the results are not what you anticipated. Instead of playing a new game, you find your system stops responding each time you start it. Or, you might find the new driver you installed for your printer is causing conflicts. Even though you've tried to uninstall the software, the system is still not right.

Fortunately, if you are running a newer version of Windows, the ***System Restore*** utility comes to the rescue. Periodically, Windows creates a ***restore point***, which records all the settings for your system. It's similar to taking a picture of how everything is currently set up. Figures 1.35 and 1.36 show steps to create a restore point for Windows 8 and 7 users, respectively.

FIGURE 1.35 Computer maintenance—steps to create a Restore Point (Windows 8 users)

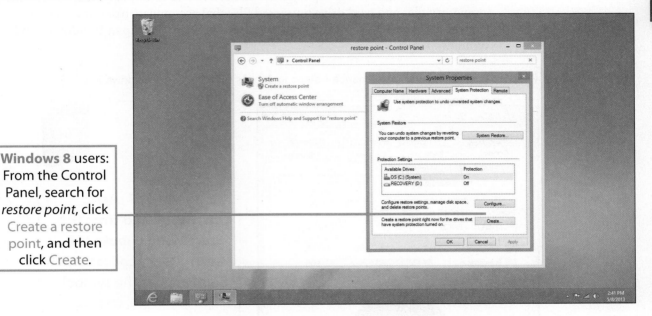

Windows 8 users:
From the Control Panel, search for *restore point*, click Create a restore point, and then click Create.

FIGURE 1.36 Computer maintenance—steps to create a Restore Point (Windows 7 users)

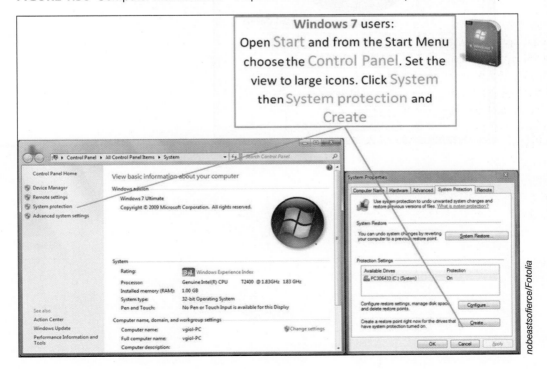

Windows 7 users:
Open Start and from the Start Menu choose the Control Panel. Set the view to large icons. Click System then System protection and Create

nobeastsofierce/Fotolia

It is also possible to set manual restore points, and it is highly recommended that you set one before installing new software or hardware, or when making any major changes to your system. If you experience a problem with your system after the new software is installed, you can roll your system back to an earlier restore point when the system was working correctly. Think of it as an Undo button for your operating system. The good news is, returning to an earlier restore point affects only your system settings. It does not delete any of the data files you may have created during the interval.

What other functions can you use to maintain a "healthy" computer? Following are some of the other things that keep computers healthy:

- **Disk Cleanup**—This is a group of tasks intended to free disk space occupied by Internet temporary files and hard drive unwanted files that accumulate from time to time. Figures 1.37 and 1.38 show the steps for accessing Disk Cleanup in Windows 8 and Windows 7.

FIGURE 1.37 Computer maintenance—steps to access Disk Cleanup (Windows 7 users)

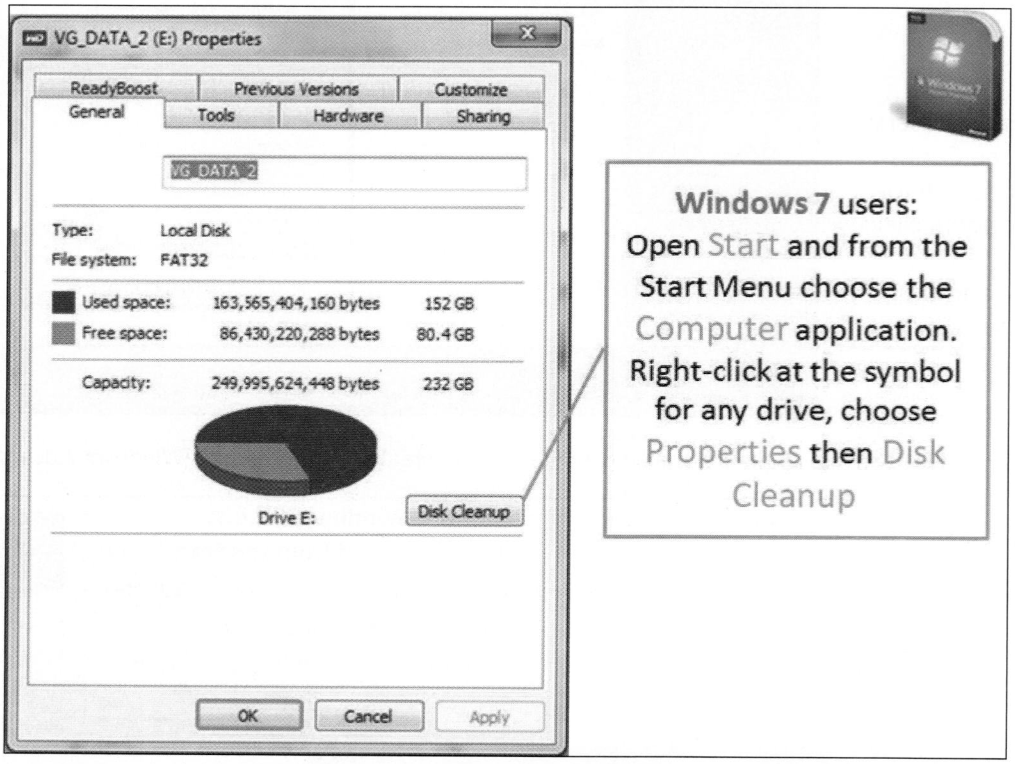

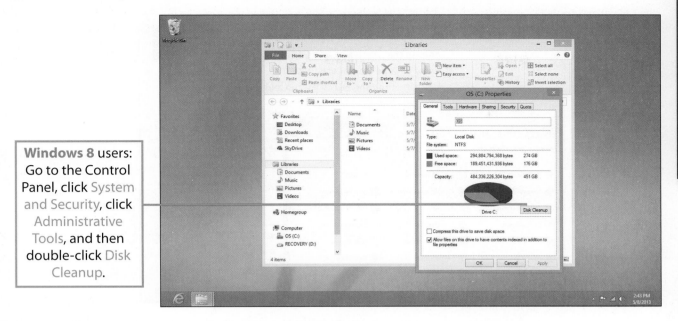

Windows 8 users: Go to the Control Panel, click System and Security, click Administrative Tools, and then double-click Disk Cleanup.

Part of this routine includes:

- Emptying the Recycle Bin.
- Activating and setting up the Internet Pop-up Blocker—This allows the user the select options to allow or to block advertising and other pop-up windows while surfing the Net (Figures 1.39 and 1.40).

FIGURE 1.39 Computer maintenance—steps to access the Pop-up Blocker (Windows 8 users)

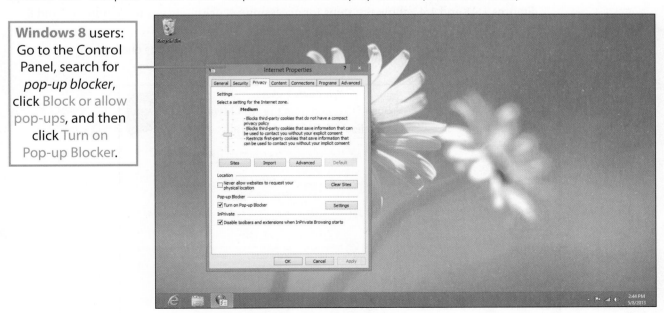

Windows 8 users: Go to the Control Panel, search for *pop-up blocker*, click Block or allow pop-ups, and then click Turn on Pop-up Blocker.

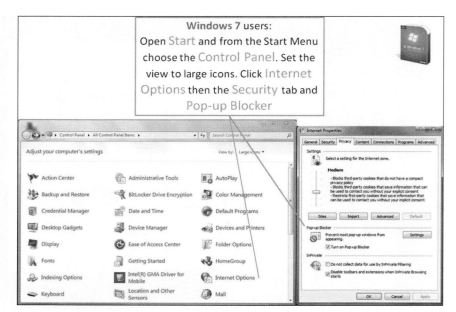

- Accessing and setting up Security settings—You can set security settings and even set them up with the Task Scheduler so you don't have to remember to do it manually, such as:

  - Check for security updates
  - Select the settings for the Windows Firewall
  - Check for Windows software updates
  - Scan for spyware and other potentially unwanted software
  - Change Internet security options

Figures 1.41 and 1.42 show the steps for accessing Security settings in Windows 7 and 8.

FIGURE 1.41 Computer maintenance—steps to access the Security settings and other functions (Windows 7 users)

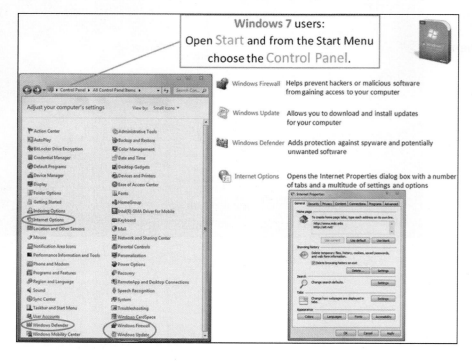

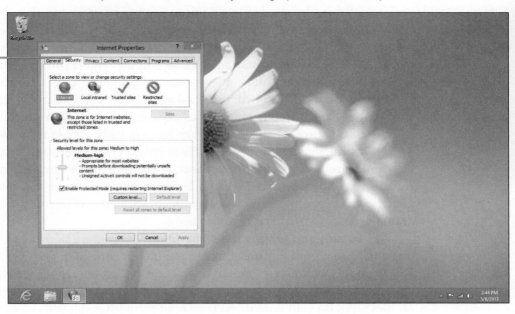

Windows 8 users:
From the Control
Panel, click
Network and
Internet, click
Internet Options,
and then
click the
Security tab.

FIGURE 1.43

Rafal Olechowski / Fotolia

Malware (Malicious Software)

Establishing the habit of performing regular maintenance on your computer is one way to protect your system, and yourself, from data loss. But there are many other dangers you must be aware of, too (see Figure 1.43). Viruses, spyware, and hackers are all out there waiting to pounce on the unwary computer user. *Malware* is any malicious software, usually acquired from spam or questionable web links. The term *hacker*, as used here, signifies an expert in computers and programming languages who uses his/her expertise to obtain unauthorized access to computer systems with the purpose of corrupting data or stealing information or only creating havoc with your system.

What are viruses and how do they get on the computer? Computer *viruses* are malicious code or software designed to invade your computer system and alter or destroy data without your knowledge and against your will. The severity of a virus can vary. Some viruses merely seem to be nuisances or might not even be obvious to the user; some cause files to be corrupted or erased; and others are capable of shutting down a computer and erasing the entire hard drive. Viruses infect a system and then attach themselves to a program or file to spread to other users.

Viruses can be distributed in several ways. In the early days of computers, viruses were spread by sharing infected floppy disks. Now, due to the ease in which files can be shared over the Internet, viruses are able to spread much more quickly. One of the most common ways to send a virus is through email attachments. Security experts recommend that you never open an email attachment unless you have first scanned it with antivirus software to determine that it is virus-free. Experts also recommend that unless you know the sender and have been expecting the email attachment, it is best to delete the attachment without ever opening it. File-sharing services are another source for these types of problems.

Are viruses and worms the same thing? *Worms* are similar to viruses because they are also malicious programs that spread from computer to computer; however, unlike viruses, worms are able to do this without any human interaction and are able to replicate themselves, so numerous copies can be sent. Worms can burrow into your email address book, or locate email addresses on files saved on your hard drive, then send themselves out without any help from you. When it reaches the email recipient, it does the same thing to the recipient's address book. Also, because worms can quickly replicate themselves, they can repeat this scenario over and over. The sheer amount of traffic they cause on a network can be enough to bring an entire organization to a grinding halt. Worms can also open a "back door" to your system, which provides hackers access to it and gives them the ability to control your computer remotely. Sasser, Blaster, NetSky, and MyDoom are all worms that have created a great deal of trouble in recent years.

Trojan horses are not truly viruses because they do not duplicate themselves or infect other files; however, they can be problematic because they may enable malware to be downloaded or allow hackers access to the computer. A *botnet* is a popular term for a group of software robots that run automatically in networks such as instant messenger, chat rooms, and discussion groups that have been made vulnerable by the presence of Trojan horses. Once inside a chat room, for instance, a botnet can generate *spam*, which is bulk unsolicited email messages sent to random lists of computer users. At first glance, a Trojan horse often appears to be a desirable software program, but in fact they facilitate unauthorized access to a computer system. Perhaps it is a free screensaver program or a set of animated mouse pointers. Unfortunately, these programs come with unwanted and hidden agendas. After the software is installed, the effects can be similar to those of viruses or worms. Before you install new software, it is important to scan the program files with antivirus software to ensure there are no Trojan horses lurking there. And, as with unknown email attachments, it is important to be skeptical about free software and shareware; it's seldom that you really get something for nothing!

Spyware

How is spyware different from viruses? *Spyware* is software designed to capture personal and confidential information that resides on your system and send it elsewhere. It has quickly become as large a problem as viruses. Spyware's primary threat is to your privacy and confidentiality. Although spyware is not usually intended to harm your system, it can sometimes have that effect on it. *Adware* is spyware that tracks your Internet browsing and can install malicious cookies on your computer. A *cookie* is a small text file that contains information that can identify you to a website. Cookies are not necessarily bad. They are useful when they are used to help personalize your web browsing experience, but cookies can threaten your privacy if they are used to reveal too much information.

How can you tell if spyware is on a computer? One symptom that indicates adware is on a computer is an increase in the number of pop-up ads the user receives, some of which might even address the user by name! Adware can generate pop-up ads even when you're not online. Some types of adware can also reset a web browser's home page to a page of its choosing and take control of the search engine, directing you to websites that have been predetermined by the adware.

Are there other privacy threats? *Key loggers* are another type of spyware. In this case, a software program records every keystroke made on the computer. Key loggers can capture all sorts of confidential information this way—passwords, credit card numbers, bank account numbers, and so on—and then relay this information elsewhere. Entire email messages and instant messaging conversations can be recorded this way too. Some key loggers are hardware, rather than software, although they perform the same devious function. Such hardware devices can be attached between the keyboard and the computer. The information stolen through the use of key loggers can easily make you a victim of identity theft. Trojan horses can be used to distribute key loggers and other types of spyware just as easily as they deliver viruses.

How can you avoid being a victim? To minimize the risk of having spyware installed on your computer, there are some practical precautions you can take. One of the most prevalent methods of spreading spyware is through file-sharing services, email attachments, and email or pop-up ad links. Not only can the file-sharing software include spyware, but often the files you think you are downloading for free are infected too. Although it's tempting to get the newest video for free from such a site, don't risk it!

This problem can be avoided if you use one of the legitimate, pay-as-you-go file-sharing services such as iTunes. Do not automatically trust files or software sent by friends or acquaintances and make it a habit to scan these items for viruses and spyware. Additionally, be cautious when you download and install freeware or shareware software. Be sure you deal with a reputable software publisher, scan the downloaded software for viruses and spyware, and read the licensing agreement. Some licensing agreements actually include information about additional software that will be automatically installed if you accept it. This could include anything from sharing all of your email contacts to authorizing unwanted spyware, which could possibly log every keystroke on your personal computer and return it to the hacker.

Another way to prevent spyware is to avoid pop-up and banner ads whenever possible. You should never click on them. Often the "No Thanks" button is only a ruse to get you to click it and enable the spyware installation. Close pop-up ads by clicking the Close button in the upper right corner. Installing pop-up blocking software can help to eliminate this risk almost entirely. If you have all pop-pup blockers turned on for security and want to over-ride it, hold the Ctrl key while clicking on the link.

If you are running the most recent version of Windows, you already have a pop-up blocker available to you. You can view the pop-up blocker settings for Windows 7 and 8 in Figures 1.39 and 1.40 and access this dialog box through Internet Explorer's Tools menu. Many popular search engines, such as Google and Yahoo! also include pop-up blocking features in their toolbars, which you can download at no charge. It is also wise to avoid questionable websites, because some of them can install spyware on your system simply by visiting the site.

Protecting Yourself and Your Computer

In addition to being cautious in your Internet travels, there are some proactive measures you can take to protect yourself and your computer from viruses and spyware. These include:

- **Software updates and patches**—Keeping your operating system and software up to date is critical. Software manufacturers are constantly on the lookout for security threats, and they issue updates and patches to help protect your system. Check for these and install them regularly. Software manufacturers have begun to implement automated procedures to check and install such updates. If your computer has this capability, it's a good idea to use this feature.

- **Antivirus and antispyware software**—Antivirus software is a utility program used to search your hard drive and files for viruses, and remove those that are found. Antispyware software works in a similar fashion, but searches for spyware rather than viruses. No computer should be without this protection. Many users erroneously think that because they aren't regularly online or use only a slow dial-up connection, they aren't a target. Nothing could be further from the truth! Recent studies show more than two-thirds of all computer users have some form of virus or spyware on their system. Smartphone users and Apple users are also vulnerable to malware and should use protective software too.

There are a variety of *antivirus* and *antispyware* products available. Unfortunately, there are also a lot of dishonest companies purporting to offer these products. Too often, these are really scams that will actually install spyware or viruses on your system! To avoid being scammed or downloading something malicious, you should never respond to offers that are received in a pop-up ad or unsolicited email message. To obtain legitimate products, it is best to purchase them from the manufacturer's website or from a local retailer, or from a trusted site (see Figure 1.44). Additionally, some Internet service providers are beginning to provide some of these products as part of their services.

FIGURE 1.44

Freeware with a proven record	
Product	**Website and Description**
AVG by Grisoft	http://free.avg.com/us-en/free-antivirus-download Detects viruses, threats, and malware; stops them
Ad-Aware Antivirus by Lavasoft	http://www.lavasoft.com/products/ad_aware_free.php Antivirus and spyware detector
Spybot Search and Destroy	http://www.safer-networking.org/private/ Removes spyware, malware, adware and other malicious software
SpywareBlaster	http://www.brightfort.com/sbdownload.html Does not clean, but does immunize well
Other popular sites	www.download.com
	www.tucows.com

Some well-known antivirus products include Norton AntiVirus (www.symantec.com), and McAfee VirusScan (www.mcafee.com), both of which are free from some *Internet Service Providers (ISP).* You should be sure to read the software reviews and evaluate their usefulness before downloading or installing them.

It is best to use only one antivirus product, because running more than one can cause conflicts between the programs. However, because there are so many different types of spyware, antispyware products may address these problems in different ways. Experts recommend running at least two different antispyware applications to catch as many spyware programs as possible. It's not enough to install antivirus and antispyware software on your system; you must update it frequently, at least once a week. Doing so will protect you against any new viruses or spyware created since the last time you checked. Software should be set to scan incoming data files, email messages, and so on, but regular full-system scans should also be conducted on a weekly basis.

Personal firewalls—*Firewalls* may be software programs or hardware devices, although their purpose is the same—to prevent unauthorized access to your computer. When a firewall is installed properly, it can make your computer invisible to hackers and other invaders. Not only can a good firewall help prevent infections and identity theft, it can also prevent hackers from accessing your computer and turning it into a zombie. A *zombie* computer is one that can be added to a botnet and controlled remotely and can be used to help spread viruses, spyware, or junk email messages known as spam. Zombie computers can also be used in *denial of service (DoS)* attacks. DoS attacks occur when a large number of computers try to access a website at the same time, effectively overloading it and causing it to shut down. If you are using Windows XP or any newer version of Windows, you already have a firewall available to you.

You can access the firewall settings in Windows 7 by clicking Start, clicking Settings, clicking Control Panel, clicking Security, and then clicking Windows Firewall. In Windows 8, from the Control Panel, click System and Security, and then click Windows Firewall.

What else should I look for? It might sound simple, but when online, do not give out personal information unless it is for legitimate purposes. It is important to avoid spam email messages, and *phishing* attacks—email messages that masquerade as authentic entities, such as banks and credit card companies, and ask for confidential information. Legitimate organizations will not ask for passwords, bank account numbers, or credit card details through email. It is also possible to check for hoaxes and scams at a variety of websites (Snopes.com is a very good one), including many of the antivirus and antispyware sites. When in doubt, do some research to see if the request you've received is legitimate. If necessary, make a telephone call to the agency in question. Viewing such requests with a critical eye can help you avoid online scams and hoaxes.

You should never perform transactions on a site that does not have *https:* in its address. The *s* stands for secure. You will also see a closed lock icon, usually in your browser's address bar, when you are on a secure site.

Objective 6 | Describe Networks and Define Network Terms

What are the components of a network? Connecting one computer to another creates a network. Recall that computers and the various peripherals that are connected to them are called hardware. *Networks* consist of two or more connected computers plus the various peripheral devices that are attached to them. Each object connected to a network, whether it is a computer or a peripheral device, is known as a *node*.

Why are computers connected to networks? Some of the benefits of computer networks include the capability to share data, software, and resources such as printers, scanners, Internet access, video conferencing, and VoIP. Computers can be connected to a network by using several types of media, the conductors of the network signals: existing telephone wires, power lines, coaxial cables, unshielded twisted pair (UTP) cables, and fiber optic.

Wireless networks use radio waves instead of wires or cables to connect. Most networks use a combination of wired and wireless communications (see Figure 1.45).

FIGURE 1.45 Types of network media, the conductor of network signals

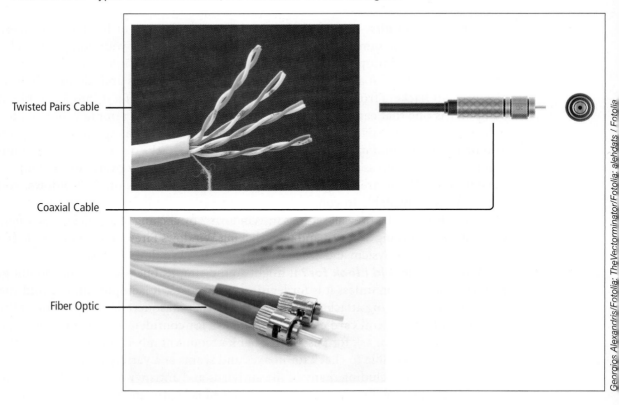

Twisted Pairs Cable

Coaxial Cable

Fiber Optic

Georgios Alexandris/Fotolia: TheVectorminator/Fotolia: alehdats / Fotolia

Today, by using computer networks, institutions are able to *video conference*, that is, simultaneously transmit audio and video between two or more individuals in different locations, optimizing communications, information sharing, and decision making.

Voice over Internet Protocol (*VoIP*) enables voice, facsimile, and voice-messaging communications over networks and the Internet.

Can networks be different sizes? A network that connects computers reasonably close together, say within a few city blocks in adjacent buildings, is called a *local area network (LAN)*. See Figure 1.46.

FIGURE 1.46 Example of a local area network, a college campus network that covers several buildings within a few city blocks

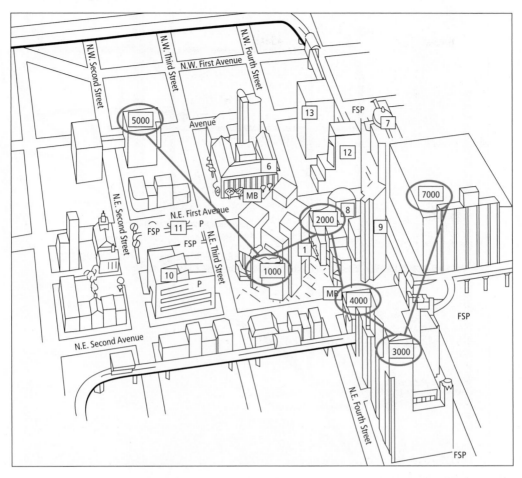

If the network grows to cover a larger geographic area or begins to include other networks, it becomes a *wide area network (WAN)*. An example is a state college campus that connects its computers with a LAN while all of its campuses connected together form a WAN. Because the different campuses are connected through WANs, students, faculty, staff, and administrators can easily and seamlessly use the resources of the entire network. Both LANs and WANs can be wired, wireless, or a combination of both. See Figure 1.47. The Internet is actually the largest WAN because it connects computer networks all around the world.

FIGURE 1.47 Example of a wide area network, which is a college network that links campus *LAN*s in several cities within a county

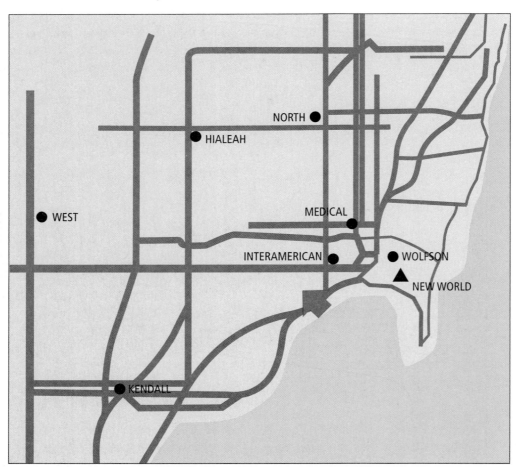

Are networks public or private? They can be either. If you want to post information and make it available to any user, you post it on a website with no restrictions. If you want to protect certain information, you create an ***intranet*** in which access is restricted to authorized users only. Within an intranet, network administrators can limit the specific rights and privileges of different users.

How are networks configured? Networks can be configured in several ways. There are two main categories: peer-to-peer and client-server. ***Peer-to-peer*** or ***P2P*** networks are most commonly found in homes and small businesses. In a peer-to-peer network, each node can communicate with every other node without a dedicated server or hierarchy among computers. Peer-to-peer networks are relatively easy to set up, but tend to be rather small. This makes them ideal for home use, although not as desirable in the workplace. If a network grows to more than, say, ten to fifteen nodes, it is generally best to use the client-server network. In a ***client-server network***, the server manages and controls all network resources. Therefore, it isn't difficult to find more than ten nodes in an office or business setting.

How is a client-server network different from a P2P network? Client-server networks typically have two different types of computers. The ***client***, also known as a node, is the computer used at your desk or workstation to write letters, send email messages, produce invoices, or perform any of the many tasks that can be accomplished with a computer. The client computer is the one most people directly interact with. In contrast, the server computer is typically kept in a secure location and is used by network technicians and administrators to manage network resources. If a server is assigned to handle only specific tasks, it is known as a ***dedicated server***. For instance, a web server is used to store and deliver web pages, a file server is used to store and archive files, and a print server manages the printing resources for the network. Each of these is a dedicated server.

As a client-server network grows in number of nodes and geographical distance covered, servers are assisted by distance-spanning devices such as switches and routers to optimize data traffic.

Network topology describes the different types of network architecture used for networks (see Figure 1.48). Just as there are different sizes and styles of buildings that are designed for different purposes, networks are designed to be physically configured and connected in different ways.

FIGURE 1.48 Common network topologies

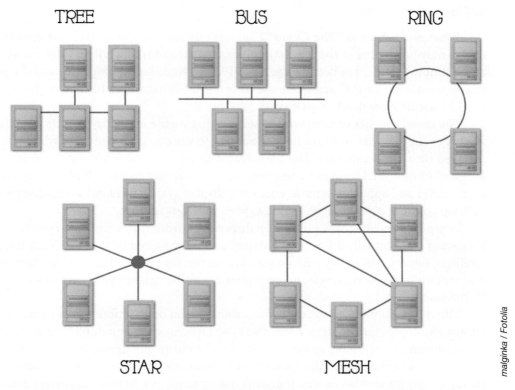

malginka / Fotolia

Which topologies are used most often? The most common layouts are explained in the following list:

- *Bus topology*—connects each node to a single, central high-speed line known as a bus. No server is used, and although it is possible for each node to communicate with all the others, they can only do so one at a time. If one computer or device is sending over the network, all the others must wait until the transmission is complete before they can begin. Because this is an inexpensive and easy way to connect, this topology is often found in peer-to-peer networks.

- *Ring topology*—sometimes known as token-ring topology, connects each node to the next, forming a loop or a circle. The data that's sent is passed from node to node, traveling around the circle in only one direction. A token travels around the ring until one of the nodes is ready to send a transmission. The node then holds the token until the transmission is finished, preventing any of the other devices from sending until the token is released to make its way around the circle again. This type of topology gives each device an equal chance of being able to send data and prevents one node from doing all the communicating. This topology is being phased out in favor of star topology.

- *Star topology*—is the most frequent networking style used for businesses and homes. It offers a high degree of flexibility. Each node is connected to a special device known as a switch, which is centrally located. Each node must go through the switch to communicate with the others. If something happens to one node, the others are still able to communicate through the switch.

- *Mesh topology*—is redundant (meaning the duplication of elements to allow constant backup or non-interruption of services), a more reliable network than the others we have discussed. It is used for situations when the nodes are spread around in no particular order. If one node goes down, the others can communicate through a working node or directly. In the past, it was cost prohibitive because of the large number of cables and connections required. In this day of wireless networking, it has become more popular.

- *Fully connected topology*—is based on mesh topology, with the distinction being that each and every node is connected to all the others. Therefore, if any connection goes down, no one loses access to the network. Any fault or clog in the network can find a better path, of least resistance.

The Cloud Topologies

What and where is "The Cloud"? Sounds ethereal, doesn't it? Well, we don't see it or touch it. You may have some of these questions since this cloud is intangible: Why are we only hearing about it now, when it has been in use since 1976 in some large companies and the government (those were intranets)? Can anyone use it? Is it safe? What would be the point of using it, and how would I use it? How much does it cost?

The cloud consists of a network of servers that we use every day. This is more familiarly known as the Internet. We now have the ability to use computer software while not having it installed on a local computer. The files created can then be stored in the cloud on a server and accessed or modified from any computer that has Internet access. All of your application software dictionaries and application preferences will display as they were last used, along with your desktop configuration being the same as your previous settings.

When we send an email message, it does not go from my computer to your computer directly. Packets of code actually follow network paths, whether wired or wireless. They bounce off satellites, towers, and so on, when it gets to a server, the packets reassemble, then are recompiled and sent on to the next server, and on it goes … until it reaches your personal device, perhaps all at different times.

The cloud allows us to store all of our information on a remote server so we can access it from almost *any* computerized device and also sync (synchronize—no duplications, no deletions, and so on, automatically). Now you can access any data from any device you have synced in to your other devices in the cloud. All of your file locations are linked to each other; some may be on one server, others on another server. It doesn't matter to us. We just hit the correct command.

Google Drive, for instance, includes free file upload, download, and storage (larger storage for monthly fees, personal or business class). Google is easily navigated by new users. The interface is very similar to Microsoft Office 2010.

Microsoft Office 2013 has the ability to use cloud-based computing through Microsoft's online storage product, SkyDrive. This permits many users to actually use application software from the server located anywhere in the cloud. If you choose to use Microsoft Office in this way, you would not purchase or install the actual application software on your own system; rather you would rent the services. A good example is the current offering from Apple. Sign up for a Creative Suite for 29.99/ month (Jan 2013), and you can use any application from any of their suites. You get every new update and upgrade, forever, for all apps in that suite, in addition to any newly developed apps in that suite for as long as you continue to pay the monthly fee. This keeps you up to date always.

This brings many new options and security issues. We are all wondering about some of the questions listed: Is it safe? It is supposedly safer than receiving constant updates to your computer, which can contain threats. All of that updating is done in the cloud, along with saving our files there.

What would be the point of using it, and how would I use it? You could use it for a backup for your non-protected documents or links. Do not save passwords, account information, or monetary statements there. Save working documents, ideas, and projects. You will be able to access your files from any location that has Internet access. If you also have cloud computing, which includes your application software, you will be able to edit anything anywhere!

END OF CHAPTER

SUMMARY

In this chapter, you examined the benefits of responsible computer fluency and identified the four basic functions of computing. You explored the various types of computers and their components, including CPUs, RAM, and storage devices. This chapter also discussed how to evaluate a computer system and understand the terminology used to measure storage capacity, memory, and microprocessor speed. Various hardware and peripheral devices were reviewed, including input and output devices, and different types of storage devices and media. You explored the basic types of computer software—system software and application software—and the different uses for each type. You identified various types of networks and the different ways networks can be configured. You also reviewed ways to maintain your computer and keep it safe from various threats, including malware.

KEY TERMS

CONTENT-BASED ASSESSMENTS

MATCHING

Match each term in the second column with its correct definition in the first column. Write the letter of the term on the blank line in front of the correct definition.

_____ 1. Computer programs.

_____ 2. Programs that enable you to accomplish a specific task or solve a specific need.

_____ 3. Two or more computers connected together to enable resource sharing.

_____ 4. Used to manage network resources, this type of computer can be dedicated to a specific task.

_____ 5. Optical disk drives use this type of storage media.

_____ 6. The layout or design/arrangement of computers connected to a network.

_____ 7. A peripheral device uses this to attach to the computer.

_____ 8. A programmable electronic device that can input, process, output, and store data.

_____ 9. The physical components of a computer system.

_____ 10. Hardware connected outside the computer's system unit.

_____ 11. The hardware unit that typically contains the CPU, RAM, a hard disk, and a power supply.

_____ 12. A large printed circuit board to which all the other components are connected.

_____ 13. The temporary storage that holds data and instructions waiting to be processed.

_____ 14. The processing unit.

_____ 15. This type of program threatens a user's privacy.

A Application software

B Computer

C Computer network

D Console/system unit

E CPU

F Hardware

G DVDs or CDs

H Memory (RAM)

I Motherboard/system board

J Peripherals

K Port

L Server

M Software

N Spyware

O Topology

MULTIPLE CHOICE

Circle the correct response.

1. Which of the following requires one byte of storage?
   a. Page   b. Paragraph   c. Sentence   d. Character

2. Which of the following units represents the fastest CPU clock speed?
   a. 733 MHz   b. 286 MHz   c. 2 GHz   d. 2 GB

3. Which of the following is not an input device?
   a. Keyboard   b. Speaker   c. Mouse   d. Stylus

4. Which of the following is an example of optical storage media?
   a. Disk drive   **b.** Flash card   **c.** RAM   **d.** Compact disc

5. Which of the following is not a type of computer?
   a. Mainframe   **b.** Multitask   **c.** Server   **d.** Supercomputer

6. Before a computer can process data, where must data be stored?
   a. In RAM   **b.** On a disk   **c.** In the control unit   **d.** On the monitor

7. What term, related to computers, means billions?
   a. Byte   **b.** Mega   **c.** Giga   **d.** Hertz

8. Which of the following is not a type of microcomputer?
   a. Desktop   **b.** Laptop   **c.** Smartphone   **d.** Microprocessor

9. Which of the following can prevent the easy and casual connection to your computer by a nonauthorized user?
   a. Disk defragmenter   **b.** Antivirus software   **c.** Firewall   **d.** Key logger

10. Which of the following is capable of opening a "back door" on a computer and is able to spread without human interaction?
    a. Trojan horse   **b.** Worm   **c.** Adware   **d.** Zombie

GLOSSARY

Adware Spyware that tracks your Internet browsing and can install malicious cookie on your computer.

Antispyware software A utility program used to search your hard drive for spyware, and remove those that are found.

Antivirus software A utility program used to search your hard drive for viruses, and remove those that are found.

Application A synonym for program.

Application software Programs that accomplish specific tasks, such as word processing, photo editing, or sending email messages, and using the computer in a productive manner.

Arithmetic logic unit (ALU) Handles addition, subtraction, multiplication, and division, and also makes logical and comparison decisions.

Arrow keys Keys located at the lower right of the keyboard between the standard keys and the numeric keypad that enable the user to move the insertion point around the active window.

Audio port Similar to video ports, these ports connect audio devices, such as speakers, headphones, and microphones to the computer's sound card.

Backup! The operation of creating copies of files on a media device other than the hard drive, so you have an extra copy if your original file gets corrupted.

Backup tape drive A storage device used to save data to media resembling a cassette tape.

Bluetooth A type of wireless technology that relies on radio wave transmission and doesn't require a clear line of sight. It is typically limited to less than 30 feet.

Boot The process of starting up the computer; the process occurs after the computer's power is turned on.

Botnet Computer network composed of zombie computers and used by hackers.

Browser See web browser.

Burn A process that saves data by using a laser beam that burns tiny pits into the storage media.

Bus topology In a computer network, it connects each node to a single central high-speed line known as a bus.

Caps Lock A key that will allow you to type in all caps without using the shift key.

CD Acronym for compact disk, a polycarbonate material with one or more metal layers capable of optically storing digital information.

CD burner Type of optical drive capable of reading and writing data from and to a CD (provided the media is recordable, like CD-Rs and CD-RWs).

CD drive Type of optical drive that can read CDs (compact disks).

CD-R Also known as CD Recordable, a type of computer disk that can be recorded by using a CD burner (drive).

CD-ROM CD media that was burned once and from that moment on can only be read.

CD-RW A rewritable disk that enables data to be recorded, revised, or deleted and new data written to the disk, similar to magnetic media.

Central processing unit (CPU) The part of the computer responsible for controlling all the commands and tasks the computer performs, acting as the brain of the computer.

Click A mouse function in which you point at an object, press and release the left (or primary) button once.

Client In a client-server network, the computer used to perform any of the many tasks that can be accomplished with a computer.

Client-Server network A network in which two different types of computers have different functions. See also client and server.

Clock speed A measure of the speed at which a CPU processes data (number of instructions per second).

Cloud Consists of a network of servers; more familiarly known as Internet servers.

Communication and organizational software A program such as Microsoft Outlook 2013 used to send or receive email messages, manage day-to-day tasks such as making appointments and creating contact lists.

Computer A programmable electronic device that can input, process, output, and store data.

Computer fluent Describes a person who understands the capabilities and limitations of computers and know how to use computer technology to accomplish tasks.

Configuration Arrangement of components, either within the computer or the network topology.

Configure To put together by selecting a combination of components, features, and options.

Connectivity port Ports such as Ethernet and modem that are used to connect a computer to a local network or to the Internet.

Control keys Keys such as Ctrl, Alt, and the Windows key that provide shortcuts or increased functionality to the keyboard when used in combination with other keys.

Control unit In the CPU, the component responsible for obtaining and executing instructions from the computer's memory.

Cookie A small text file that contains information that can identify you to a website.

CPU See Central Processing Unit.

Data Represents text, numbers, graphics, videos, and sounds entered into the computer's memory during input operations.

Database software Programs such as Microsoft Access used to store and organize large amounts of data and perform complex tasks such as sorting and query and to generate specialized reports.

Data mining A function in some database software that looks for hidden patterns in the data to anticipate future trends.

Dedicated server A server in a network that is assigned to handle only specific tasks.

Denial of service (DoS) Attacks that occur when a large number of computers try to access a website at the same time, effectively overloading it and causing it to shut down.

Desktop computer A class of microcomputer, such as PC or Mac, that typically occupies a working area around a desk.

Device A hardware component that attaches to a computer, includes disk drives, printers, mice, keyboards, and modems.

Dialog box A frame or window that shows the presets or defaults for a specific function and requires the user to make changes before moving ahead.

Digital camera A device that stores pictures digitally rather than using conventional film.

Digital Video Interface (DVI) port Ports that transmit a pure digital signal, eliminating the need for digital-to-analog conversion and resulting in a higher quality picture on an LCD monitor.

Digital video recorder Device that allow you to capture digital images and movies and transfer them directly to your computer.

Disk Cleanup System utility that scans the hard drive and removes unnecessary files.

Disk Defragmenter System utility that attempts to relocate files so they use the available hard drive space more efficiently.

Docking station Device that enables the user to connect a laptop to a full-size keyboard, monitor, and other devices in an office setting.

DOS The original OS for personal computers in the early 1980s. This was a text-based or keyboard-driven operating system.

Dot matrix Printers that have small hammers, similar to a typewriter's, that strike a ribbon against paper, leaving behind the image of a character or symbol.

Dot pitch A display characteristic in monitors that refers to the diagonal distance between two pixels of the same color. A smaller dot pitch will result in a crisper viewing image because there is less blank space between two pixels.

Dots per inch (dpi) How resolution is expressed. The higher the dpi, the better the print quality.

Double-click The action of clicking and releasing the left mouse button two times in rapid succession while keeping the mouse still.

Drag The action of moving something from one location on the screen to another; the action includes pointing and clicking (releasing the mouse button at the desired time or location).

DSL Acronym for digital subscriber line. Type of communications line in which signals travel through copper wires between a telephone switching station and a home of business.

Dual-boot A computer that can run more than one operating system.

Dual-core Processors that have several advantages over a single processor CPU, including improved multitasking capabilities, system performance, and lower power consumption.

DVD Acronym for digital video disk or diversified video disk; media that holds data written by an optical device.

DVD drive Digital video disk drive capable of reading and writing DVD media.

DVD-ROM Digital Video media that was burned once and from that moment on can only be read.

DVI port See Digital Video Interface.

Embedded computers Small, specialized computers built into larger components such as automobiles and appliances.

Ethernet port A port, slightly larger than a telephone jack, that can transmit data at a speed up to 1,000 megabits per second (Mbps) and is usually used to connect to a cable modem or network.

Exabyte One quadrillion bytes.

Firewall A combination of hardware and software used to prevent unauthorized access to your computer.

FireWire port A port used to send data at rates up to 800 megabits per second (Mbps), frequently used for digital cameras or digital video recorders.

Flash drive A small, portable, digital storage device that connects to a computer's USB port (Universal Serial Bus); also called a thumb drive, jump drive, or USB drive.

Flash memory Portable, nonvolatile memory that uses electronic, solid-state circuitry.

Flat-panel displays Flat-panel displays are monitors that use a liquid crystal display and are thin and energy efficient.

Function keys Keys that are located above the standard row of number keys and numbered F1 through F12. These keys are generally associated with certain software-specific commands and can be reassigned by the user.

Gaming computers Computers that are mostly used by video game enthusiasts. They are usually configured with a fast CPU, large amount of memory, a special video card, sound card, and surround sound speakers.

Gigabyte (GB) Approximately one billion bytes; a unit used to measure memory size and storage space.

Gigahertz (GHz) One billion hertz; a hertz is the unit used to measure processor speed. One hertz is one cycle (instructions read) per second.

Graphical Processing Units (GPU) Processor type used in gaming computers today.

Graphical user interface (GUI) Today's operating systems provide a user-friendly way to operate a computer with their graphical user interface. The user controls the action by using the keyboard, a mouse, or a touchscreen to make selections from on the screen objects such as icons, menus, or dialog boxes.

GUI See graphical user interface.

Hackers Derogatory term to describe individuals who gain unauthorized access to computer systems for the purpose of corrupting or stealing data.

Handheld devices Small portable computers that might include personal productivity software and enable the user to play music, take photos and videos, make phone calls, and access the Internet. Smartphones and personal music players fall into this category.

Hard copy The output of a printer, which is tangible (synonymous with printout).

Hard disk drive A combination of a device and media used as the main storage in most computers.

Hardware The physical or tangible components of the computer and any equipment connected to it.

HDMI (High-Definition Multimedia Interface) used for digital video or audio components.

Hyperlink A connection to another area of a document or a connection to an Internet URL.

Icon A graphic representation of an object on the screen. Icons can be selected with the mouse or by using your fingers on a touchscreen.

IM Acronym for Instant Messaging, software that enables users to communicate in real time like a phone conversation, but by using text only.

Impact A type of printer that resembles a typewriter; a key punches an inked ribbon to imprint a character on paper.

Information Data that has been organized in a useful manner.

Information processing cycle The cycle composed of the four basic computer functions: input, process, output, and storage.

Ink-jet A nonimpact printer that uses a special nozzle and ink cartridges to distribute liquid ink on the surface of paper.

Input During this step of the information processing cycle, the computer gathers data or allows a user to enter data into memory.

Input devices Computer hardware used to input data and instructions into a computer; examples include the keyboard, mouse, stylus, scanner, microphone, and digital camera.

Input/output device (I/O) A device which can input to a computer and also output them to other devices. Some include: CD-RW, USB drive, scanner, and all-in-one devices.

Insert key Can be set to turn on and off the overwrite feature in Microsoft Word and other applications.

Insertion point A blinking vertical line on the screen that shows where the next data entered will appear.

Internet control key Typically located at the upper or left on the keyboard. These keys enable the user to assign to each key a unique web browser function such as sending email messages, browsing a specific site, or accessing an online bank account.

Intranet A network or part of a network in which access is restricted to authorized users only. Usually present in large organizations.

IrDA port A port that is used to allow devices such as keyboards, mice, and printers to transmit data wirelessly to another device by using infrared light waves.

ISP Internet Service Provider; a company who collects a monthly fee to pay for your connection to the Internet through phone, DSL, cable, or fiber optic modem.

Joystick Game controller that is an input device used to control movement within video games.

Keyboard The primary input device for computers.

Key logger A type of spyware that records every keystroke made on the computer and can capture all sorts of confidential information such as passwords, credit card numbers, bank account info, and so on.

Kilobit One thousand bits. It takes eight bits to make one byte.

Kilobyte Approximately one thousand bytes.

Laptop computer Also known as a laptop, this microcomputer is smaller than a desktop and designed to be portable.

LAN Acronym for local area network. A network that connects computers that are reasonably close together.

Laser printer A type of nonimpact printer that uses a drum, static electricity, and a laser to distribute dry ink or toner on the surface of the paper.

LightScribe A disk-labeling technology that burns text and graphics onto the surface of a specially coated LightScribe CD or DVD.

Linux An alternative operating system. It is open-source software, which means it is not owned by a single company and is available at no cost. There is no technical support available except from the users of the OS.

Liquid crystal display (LCD) Technology used in flat-panel monitors, resulting in thinner, lighter monitors that consume less energy.

Local area network (LAN) A network that connects computers that are reasonably close together in a small geographical area.

Mac OS An operating system designed specially for Apple's Macintosh computers.

Magnetic A type of storage process using magnetized film to store data; used by devices such as hard disks, or media such as tape cartridges.

Mainframe computers Computers often found in large businesses, organizations, and government agencies where thousands of users must simultaneously use the data and resources for their everyday operations.

Malware Any malicious software, usually acquired from spam or questionable web links.

Megabit (Mb) Approximately one million bits. It takes eight bits to make a byte.

Megabyte (MB) Approximately one million bytes; a unit of storage to measure memory and storage space.

Megahertz (MHz) One million hertz; a hertz is one of the units used to measure processor speed. One hertz cycle (instruction read) per second.

Memory A generic term that signifies storage.

Menu A list of commands that perform specific tasks within a program.

Mesh topology If one node goes down, the others can communicate through a working node or directly

MFD Acronym for Multifunction Device.

Microchip The main component in the computer. CPU is a microchip, also referred to as the brain of the computer.

Microcomputer The type of computer that most people are familiar with and that ranges in size from large desktop systems to handheld devices. The name comes from its main component or brain called the microchip or microprocessor.

Microprocessor A microcomputer's main component; it is a tiny but powerful chip compared to a mainframe or a supercomputer.

Microsoft Windows The operating system that runs most PCs today and provides a graphical user interface to make the computer user friendly.

MIDI port Ports used to connect electronic equipment, such as keyboards and synthesizers, to a computer.

Mobile devices These devices fall into the category of handheld computers; they are small enough to fit in the palm of your hand, are usually wireless, and enable users to access personal productivity software, send and read email messages, and navigate the Internet.

Modem port Port used to connect a computer to a local network or to the Internet.

Monitor (or display screen) Display devices that show images of text, graphics, and video once data has been processed.

Monitor port A port that is used to connect the monitor to the graphics processing unit, which is usually located on the motherboard or on a video card.

Motherboard A large printed circuit board located in the system unit to which all other boards are connected; the motherboard contains the central processing unit (CPU), memory (RAM), expansion card slots, and ports.

Mouse An input device (pointing device) used to enter commands and user responses into a computer. This device controls a symbol on the screen (insertion point or mouse pointer) used to manipulate objects and select commands.

Mouse pointer The icon associated with the mouse. It changes to queue you into what operations can be performed within applications.

Multifunction device (MFD) Hardware device such as all-in-one printers that provide a number of functions in one unit.

Multimedia control key Modern keyboards have at least a few keys or buttons that can be used for such tasks as muting or adjusting speaker volume, opening a web browser, or sending email messages.

Multimedia projectors Output devices used to display information on a large screen for audiences.

Multitask To perform more than one task simultaneously.

Network A group of two or more computers (or nodes) connected together through cables or wirelessly to share information and resources.

Network topology The layout and structure of a computer network.

Node Any object connected to a network that is a computer or a peripheral device.

Nonimpact Printers that generate hard copies by means other than striking element on the ribbon and paper. They do not touch the paper when printing.

Nonvolatile Means permanent when referring to storage. It holds its contents even when the computer is shut down. ROM is a type of permanent storage, while your C drive (main hard disk in most computers) is your main storage device.

Numeric keypad A cluster of keys located on the right side of the keyboard. It

is an alternative method for entering numbers, similar to a calculator.

Num Lock key A toggle key that switches its ability between the number pad (when on) and by using the arrow keys on the number pad for uses like gaming (when off).

Open-source Software not owned by a company and can be changed by those with the appropriate programming knowledge. This includes the LINUX operating system.

Operating system (OS) The software that controls the way the computer works from the time it starts (boots up) until it is shut down.

Optical A type of storage process that uses a laser to read and write data; used to burn media such as CDs or DVDs.

OS See Operating system.

Output Data that has been processed and converted into information.

Output device Computer hardware components used to display information to the user, such as monitor, printer, or speakers.

P2P network (Peer-to-peer) A type of network in which each node can communicate directly with the other. No PC controls the others.

Parallel port A port that sends data in groups of bits as opposed to one bit at a time.

Peripheral A hardware device connected to a computer but not inside the system unit, such as a monitor, printer, scanner, or mouse.

Permanent memory Type of memory that retains data and information even if the computer's power is turned off.

Personal firewall Software or hardware that, when installed properly, can make your computer invisible to hackers and other invaders.

Phishing The process of attempting to acquire sensitive information such as usernames, passwords, and credit card details by pretending to be a reputable entity.

Pixel An abbreviated name for "picture element." Tiny dots that make up images on computer monitors.

Port An interface or a connecting point by which peripherals are connected to the computer's system unit.

Ppm (pages per minute) Acronym for "pages per minute." A measure of the speed of a printer.

Presentation software A program, such as PowerPoint 2013, used to create dynamic slideshows and generate speaker notes and audience handouts.

Printer An output device used to generate hard copy or printout.

Printout The output of a printer (synonymous with hard copy).

Process A CPU function in which data is converted into information.

Processor See CPU.

Program Also known as software, sets of instructions or commands that tell the computer what to do and are used by the computer to perform certain tasks.

Programmable A device that can be programmed or instructed to perform a specific task guided by commands or instructions.

Quad-core Processors that have several advantages over a single processor CPU, including improved multitasking capabilities, system performance, and lower power consumption. They perform similarly to dual core processors, having four processors instead of two.

RAM Acronym for Random Access Memory.

Random Access Memory (RAM) The computer's temporary storage space (short-term memory). It stores data on chips connected to the motherboard. This data is held only before processing by the CPU.

RDBMS Acronym for Relational Database Management System and is a database software that stores information in tables, which enable users quick access to the data by connecting tables with common fields.

Read-Only Memory (ROM) See ROM.

Read/write Read is the action of retrieving or opening existing data and write is the action of saving or storing data.

Refresh rate The speed at which the screen's (monitor) image is redrawn.

Resolution The measurement used to access the clarity and sharpness of an image on a monitor, determined by pixel density.

Restore point A file in which all your computer system settings are stored. It's similar to taking a picture of how everything is currently set up. If there is a system failure, Windows can come to the rescue.

Right-click The action of pressing and releasing the right mouse button.

Right-drag A mouse function done by pressing the right mouse button and continuing to hold it while dragging, or moving, the mouse pointer to another location.

Ring (or token-ring) topology A network layout that connects each node to the next, forming a loop or circle.

RJ-45 jack This jack resembles a standard phone jack, but is slightly larger. The Ethernet port that is used for network access and can also be used to connect a cable modem or router for Internet access.

ROM Acronym for Read-Only Memory. A type of prerecorded chip or other media that the computer can only "read," not write to or change its contents.

S-video port Short for Super-Video, a technology for transmitting video signals over a cable by dividing the video information into two separate signals, color and brightness.

Scanners Input device used to convert hard copy documents or images into digital files.

Scroll wheel A button on some mice, useful when scrolling within a document; rolling the wheel enables you to quickly move up or down in a window. Also, holding down the Ctrl (control) key while moving the wheel button lets you zoom in or out for varied distance of viewing.

Search engine Applications on www that are used to search for any type of information.

Sectors Wedge-shaped section of a hard disk drive or on any magnetic storage media, each measured from the center point to the outside edge.

Serial port Ports that can send data only one bit at a time.

Server In a client-server network, a server is the computer that manages shared network resources and provides access to the client computer.

Shortcut menu A menu displayed when the user right-clicks an object on the screen. These menus are "context-sensitive." That means the displayed commands and options specifically relate to the object being pointed at.

Smartphones Handheld devices that combine mobile phone capabilities with other features associated with pocket PCs and PDAs.

Social communication Includes any type of software to allow persons to interact with each other in a personal or business atmosphere that can often be viewed by other users of that social application, such as Facebook.

Soft copy The image generated on screen after data has been processed.

Software Suite A group of applications bundled together by software companies to allow for special pricing. A suite is always less expensive than purchasing each program separately.

Solid-State Storage It is completely electronic and has no moving mechanical parts.

Spam Unwanted or unsolicited bulk email messages.

Speech recognition Technology that enables the user to record discussions or lectures, or to control the computer functions by using voice commands.

Speakers Output devices that allow the user to hear auditory signals the computer sends, or even to play music.

Spreadsheet software A program such as Microsoft Excel used to organize data in rows and columns, perform calculations, create charts, and perform numerical analyses.

Spyware Software designed to capture personal and confidential information that resides on your system and send it elsewhere.

Star topology Each node in this type of network is connected to a special device known as a switch, which is centrally located. Each node must go through the switch to communicate with other nodes.

Storage To retain data or information for future use.

Storage devices Hardware components that retain data or information for future use.

Stylus A pen-like input device used to write on a tablet computer or touchscreen.

Supercomputer A large, very powerful computer typically devoted to one specialized task.

System Restore An operating system utility that comes to the rescue when you have loaded unwanted software. Periodically, Windows creates a restore point, which records all the settings for your system; you may also create your own manually.

System software The set of programs that enables a computer's hardware devices and program to work together; it includes the operating system and utilities.

System unit The tower, box, console that contains the critical hardware and electrical components of a computer. Typically, the motherboard, the CPU, RAM, and the hard drive are contained within the system unit.

Tablet computer A portable computer that features a screen that can be touched or written on by using advanced handwriting recognition.

Toggle key Keystroke combinations that activate a function or, if pressed again de-activate that function.

Temporary memory Short-term memory that stores data and program instructions that are waiting to be processed.

Terabyte One trillion bytes; a measure for memory and storage.

Token-Ring topology A network topology that connects each node with the next, forming a loop or circle.

Touchscreen A part of a tablet computer that displays information and can also be used to input data by touching or writing on its surface. These screens are considered input/output devices.

Touchscreen technology A type of display screen that has a touch-sensitive panel, which enables the user to touch and make selections from objects on the screen by the touch of a finger.

Tracks Concentric circles on a hard disk or any magnetic media that together with sectors provide the storage space for data and information.

Trojan horse A destructive program that presents itself as a genuine application.

Universal serial bus (USB) port A type of port able to interface with several different peripheral devices, which reduces the need for individual dedicated ports. The fastest to date is USB 3.0.

User interface The feature of a computer's operating system that enables you to interact with the computer. Also see GUI and DOS.

Utility program A component of system software, typically small programs used to perform routine maintenance and housekeeping tasks for the computer.

Video conferencing The use of networks to communicate audio and video between two or more individuals in different locations, optimizing communications, information sharing, and decision making.

Virus Malicious programs that are usually installed on your computer without your knowledge. They require human interaction to allow the file to run. Viruses can cause files to be corrupted or erased, are capable of shutting down a computer, or erasing the hard disk drive.

VoIP Acronym for Voice over Internet Protocol. Allows voice, fax, and voice messaging communications over a network and the Internet.

Volatile Nonpermanent, constantly changing; refers to a type of storage (RAM) that is lost when the computer is turned off before saving.

WAN Acronym for Wide Area Network.

Web browser Software used to locate and display web pages and navigate through them.

Wide area network (WAN) A network composed of local area networks connected over long distances.

Window A frame on the computer that holds programs or objects. It can be resized if desired.

Wireless Technology that transmits and receives data without a physical connection.

Wireless network A network that connects by using radio waves instead of wires or cables.

Word processing software A program that allows users to create, edit, print, and save documents. Microsoft Word is an example.

Worm Similar to viruses, malicious programs that spread from computer to computer; however, unlike viruses, worms are able to do this without any human interaction.

Zombie A computer that can be controlled remotely by a hacker and can be used to spread viruses, spyware, or spam.

Lavelle, Marianne. "National Geographic." 12 October 2012. *National Geographic News.* 25 3 2013 <http://news.nationalgeographic.com/news/energy/2012/10/121029-titan-fastest-supercomputer/>.

Victorinox Swiss Army. 9 January 2012. https://www.swissarmy.com/us/app/content/news_page/nc_new_electronicspressrelease_20120116. 25 January 2013.

Index

The following content is taken from:

GO! with Microsoft® Windows™ 7 : Getting Started
by Shelley Gaskin and Robert L. Ferrett

Students

How to Find the Student Data Files to Complete the Projects in This Book

Projects in this book begin either with a new blank file or from a student data file that has already been started for you.

The student data files can be accessed from the enclosed CD-ROM or from the GO! Website.

Files from the *CD-ROM*

As specifically directed in each project, navigate to the CD-ROM, and then save and rename the file according to the instructions in the project.

Files from www.pearsonhighered.com/go

1. Decide where you want to store your student data files.

- If you are storing on the hard drive of your computer or on a network drive, you may want to create a folder with an appropriate name on that drive.

- If you are storing on a removable storage device such as a USB flash drive, Zip disk, or floppy disk, insert the device now.

2. From your Web browser, go to **www.pearsonhighered.com/go**

3. From the list of books provided, point to the title of this book, click the active link and then follow the instructions as specified on the Website.

GO!

with Microsoft®

Windows 7
Getting Started

Shelley Gaskin and Robert L. Ferrett

Contents

Getting Started with Windows 7

OUTCOMES

At the end of this chapter, you will be able to:

PROJECT 1A
Familiarize Yourself
with Windows 7.

PROJECT 1B
Manage Files and Folders.

OBJECTIVES

Mastering these objectives will enable you to:

Dmitriy Shironosov/Shutterstock

In This Chapter

Windows 7 is the software that coordinates the activities of your computer's hardware. Windows 7 controls how your screen is displayed, how you open and close programs, and the start-up, shut-down, and navigation procedures for your computer. It is useful to become familiar with the basic features of the Microsoft Windows operating system, especially working with the Start button and the taskbar; opening, closing, moving, and resizing windows; and finding, saving, and managing files and folders.

Project 1A Familiarize Yourself with Windows 7

In Activities 1.01 through 1.09, you will explore the Windows 7 screen and practice navigating Windows 7. You will open, close, resize, and move windows, and you will open several windows at one time. The screens that you will be working with will look similar to those in Figure 1.1.

For Project 1A, you will need the following files:

No files are needed for this project

You will save your documents as

Lastname_Firstname_1A_Taskbar (not submitted)
Lastname_Firstname_1A_Windows (not submitted)
Lastname_Firstname_1A_WordPad

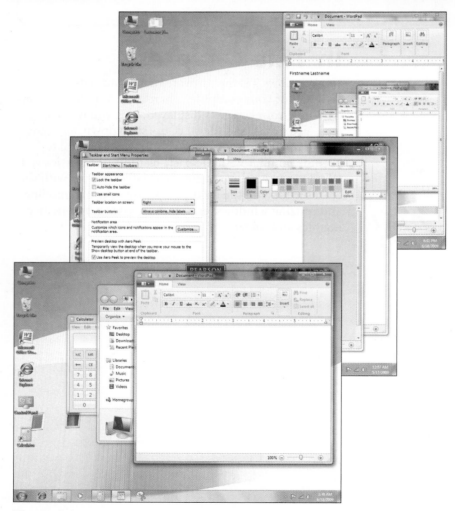

Figure 1.1

Objective 1 | Get Started with Windows 7

Windows 7 is an ***operating system***—software that controls the ***hardware*** attached to your computer, including its memory, disk drive space, attached devices such as printers and scanners, and the central processing unit. Windows 7 and earlier versions of Windows are similar; they use a ***graphical user interface (GUI)***. A GUI uses graphics or pictures to represent commands and actions and lets you see document formatting on the screen as it will look when printed on paper. ***Windows***, when spelled with a capital *W*, refers to the operating system that runs your computer.

Starting Windows is an automatic procedure; you turn on your computer, and after a few moments, the version of Windows installed on your computer displays. Some computers require that you log in, and some do not. Windows 7 is available in several versions: Starter, Home Premium, Professional, and Ultimate. For large institutions, there is also an Enterprise edition. For most tasks, the Home Premium, Professional, and Ultimate editions work the same. The Starter edition is typically used only on small notebook computers.

> **Alert! | Does your screen differ?**
>
> This chapter uses Windows 7 Ultimate edition, and there may be some differences in the look of this edition and the other editions. More importantly, the look of the screen will depend largely on the setting options that have been selected for your computer, the shape of your monitor, and on the type of hardware installed in your computer—especially the video card and memory.

Activity 1.01 | Exploring the Windows 7 Desktop

In this activity, you will examine the different components of the Windows 7 desktop.

1 Turn on your computer and wait for the Windows program to display, or follow the log-on instructions required for the computer you are using. For example, you might have to click a name on a Welcome screen, or enter a user ID or password. If this is your home computer and you are the only user, it is likely that you need do nothing except wait for a few moments.

The Windows ***desktop***, which is the working area of the Windows 7 screen, displays. The screen look will vary, depending on which version of Windows you are using and what you have on your own desktop.

2 Compare your Windows desktop with Figure 1.2 and then take a moment to study the Windows elements identified in the table in Figure 1.3. Your icons may vary.

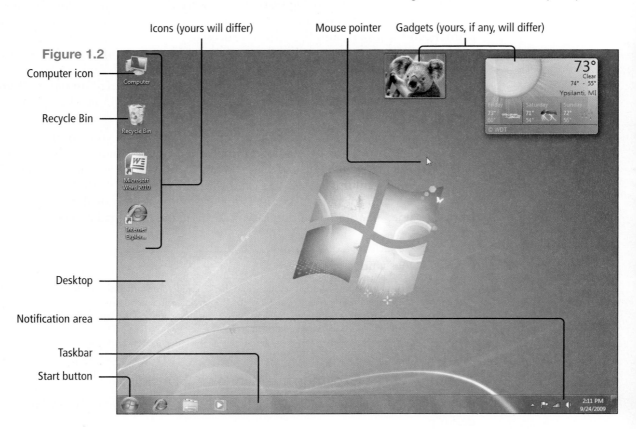

Figure 1.2

- Computer icon
- Recycle Bin
- Desktop
- Notification area
- Taskbar
- Start button
- Icons (yours will differ)
- Mouse pointer
- Gadgets (yours, if any, will differ)

Windows Screen Elements

Screen Element	Description
Command bar	A toolbar that offers easy access to settings or features.
Computer icon	An icon that represents the computer on which you are working, and that provides access to the drives, folders, and files on your computer.
Desktop	The working area of the Windows 7 screen, consisting of program icons, a taskbar, gadgets (optional), and a Start button.
Gadgets	Small dynamic programs that run on the desktop, such as a clock, a stock market ticker, or a weather forecast.
Icon	A graphic representation of an object that you can select and open, such as a drive, a disk, a folder, a document, or a program.
Mouse pointer	The arrow, I-beam, or other symbol that moves when you move the mouse or other pointing device, and that indicates a location or position on your screen—also called the **pointer**.
Notification area	The area on the right side of the taskbar, formerly called the **system tray** or **status area**, where the clock and system notifications display. These notifications keep you informed about active processes.
Recycle Bin	A temporary storage area for files that you have deleted from hard drives. Files can be either recovered or permanently removed from the Recycle Bin.
Start button	The button on the left side of the taskbar that is used to start programs, change system settings, find Windows help, search for programs or documents, or shut down the computer.
Taskbar	Displays the Start button and icons for any open programs. The taskbar also displays shortcut buttons for other programs.

Figure 1.3

3 On the left side of the taskbar, *click*—press the left mouse button one time—the **Windows Explorer** button 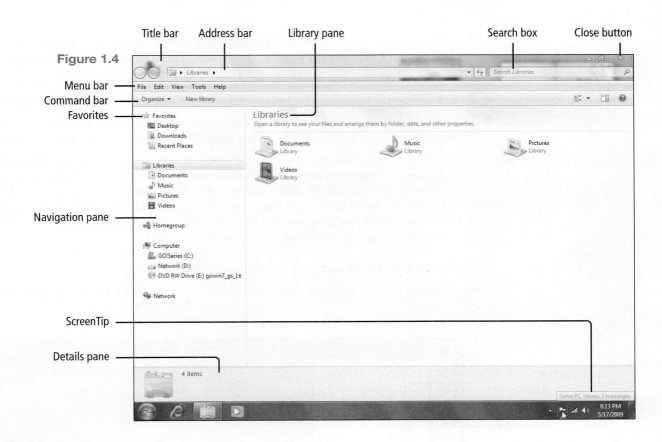. Compare your screen with Figure 1.4, and then take a moment to study the *Windows Explorer* window elements in the table in Figure 1.5. **Windows Explorer** is a program used to create and manage folders, and to copy, move, sort, and delete files. If the Windows Explorer button does not display on your taskbar, click the Start button, click All Programs, click Accessories, and then click Windows Explorer. If the Menu bar does not display, on the Toolbar, click the Organize button, point to Layout, and then click Menu bar.

The Windows Explorer window displays. When you click the Windows Explorer button, the window opens with *Libraries* selected in the Navigation pane and displayed in the file list. A *window*—spelled with a lowercase *w*—is a rectangular box that displays information or a program. When a window is open, the name of the window is sometimes displayed in the title bar.

Alert! | Does your screen differ?

Because the configuration of your Windows Explorer window depends on how it was last used, your window may not display all of the elements shown in Figure 1.4, in particular the Menu bar, Details pane, Navigation pane, and Search pane. A Preview pane may display on the right side of the window, and the window may cover the entire screen.

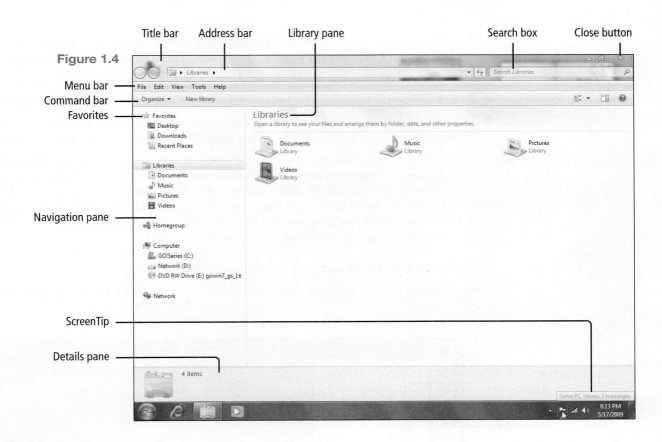

Figure 1.4

Parts of a Window

Screen Element	Description
Address bar	A toolbar that displays the organizational path to the active file, folder, or window.
Close button	A button in a title bar that closes a window or a Program
Details pane	Displays details about the drive, folder, or file selected in the file list.
Favorites	The upper part of the Navigation pane that displays favorite destinations associated with the current user.
File list	Displays the contents of the current folder or library.
Library pane	Displays above the file list when a Library is selected in the Navigation pane.
Menu bar	The bar near the top of a window that lists the names of menu categories.
Navigation pane	The pane on the left side of the Windows Explorer window that contains personal Favorites, Libraries, access to personal files and folders, and other items.
ScreenTip	A small box, activated by pointing to a button or other screen object, that displays the name of or further information about the screen element.
Search box	A box in which you type a search word or phrase.
Title bar	The area at the top of a window that includes the Minimize, Maximize, and Close buttons. The title bar also often contains the name of the program and the name of the open document.
Toolbar	A row of buttons that activates commands with a single click of the left mouse button.

Figure 1.5

4 In the upper right corner of the **Windows Explorer** window title bar, point to, but do not click, the **Close** button ![close button], and then notice that the ScreenTip *Close* displays.

A *ScreenTip* is a small note that provides information about or describes a screen element.

5 Click—press the left mouse button one time—the **Close** button ![close button] to close the window.

6 Point to the **Computer** icon in the upper left corner of the desktop and click the right mouse button—this action is known as a *right-click*. Compare your screen with Figure 1.6.

A shortcut menu displays. A *menu* is a list of commands within a category. *Shortcut menus* list *context-sensitive commands*—commands commonly used when working with the selected object. On this shortcut menu, the Open command is displayed in bold because it is the default action that occurs when you double-click this icon. To *double-click* an icon, point to the icon and then press the left mouse button quickly two times in succession, taking care not to move the mouse between clicks.

> **Alert!** | Does the Computer icon not display on your desktop?
>
> If the Computer icon does not display on the desktop, click the Start button ![start button]. On the right side of the Start menu, right-click Computer, and then from the shortcut menu, click *Show on Desktop*.

Figure 1.6

Command in bold is the default action

Shortcut menu

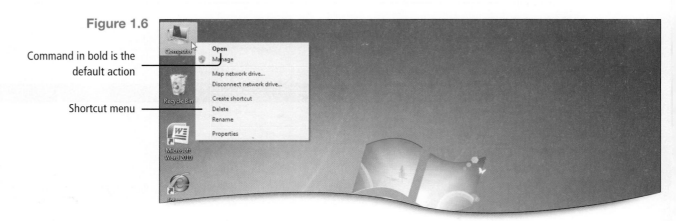

7 From the displayed shortcut menu, point to **Open** to select the command, and then click one time. Compare your screen with Figure 1.7.

> The Windows Explorer window displays, but this time the pane on the right is a file list, not a Libraries pane. The *file list* displays the contents of the item selected in the Navigation pane; in this case, the fixed and removable drives attached to the computer. A *drive* is an area of storage that is formatted with the Windows file system, and that has a drive letter such as C, D, E, and so on. The main drive inside your computer is referred to as the *hard drive*—there may be more than one hard drive in a computer. Also, network drives may display here.

Figure 1.7

Fixed local drives

Removable drives

File list

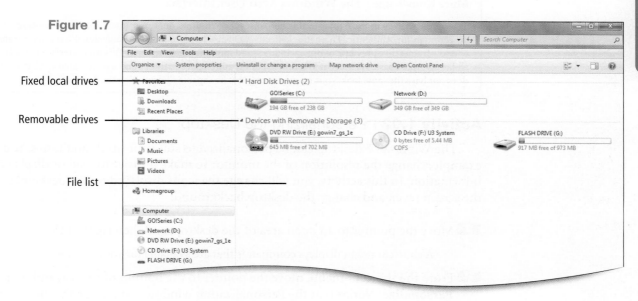

8 Near the top of the **file list**, point to and then click the disk drive labeled **(C:)**, and then notice the **Details** pane. Compare your screen with Figure 1.8.

Figure 1.8

Drive C: selected

Details of drive C: (your drive name may vary)

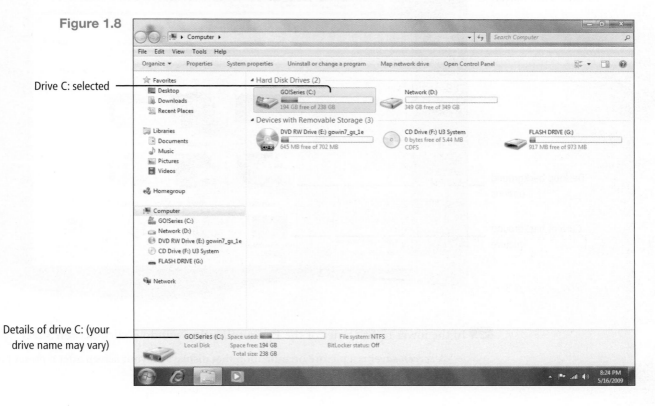

> **Alert!** | **Is your Details pane missing?**
>
> Recall that the configuration of your Windows Explorer window may vary, depending on how it was last configured. If your Details pane does not display, in the Command bar, click Organize, point to Layout, and then click *Details pane*.

9 In the **Windows Explorer** window title bar, click the **Close** button .

> **More Knowledge** | **The Windows Aero User Interface**
>
> The screen you see in the figures in this book uses the Windows Aero user interface. **Windows Aero**—which is an acronym for *A*uthentic, *E*nergetic, *R*eflective, *O*pen—features a three-dimensional look, with transparent window frames, live previews of open windows, and multiple color schemes. This user interface is available with all but the most basic versions of Windows 7, but requires extra memory and a good video card. If your screen does not have the same look, your computer may not be capable of displaying the Aero interface.

Activity 1.02 | Personalizing the Desktop

The Windows 7 desktop can be personalized to suit your needs and tastes. You can, for example, change the resolution of the monitor to make it easier to read or display more information. In this activity, you will change the icons displayed on the desktop, change the screen saver, and change the desktop background.

1 Move the pointer to an open area of the desktop, and then right-click.

A shortcut menu displays commands that are available for your desktop.

2 From the shortcut menu, move the pointer to the bottom of the list, and then click **Personalize**. Notice that the Personalization window displays, as shown in Figure 1.9.

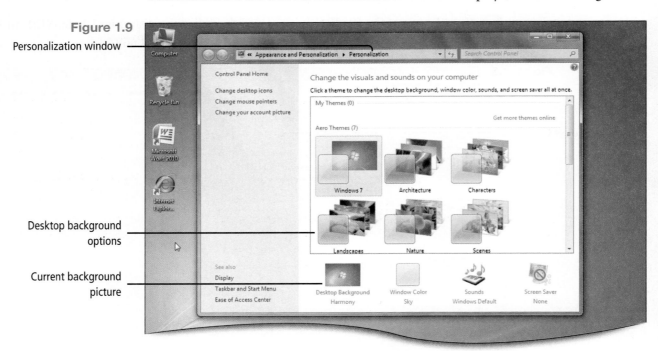

Figure 1.9
Personalization window ———

Desktop background
options ———

Current background
picture ———

3 In the lower right corner of the **Personalization** window, click **Screen Saver**.

A *screen saver* is a picture or animation that displays on your screen after a preset period of computer inactivity.

4 In the **Screen Saver Settings** dialog box, click the **Screen saver box arrow**. From the displayed list, click **Ribbons**, and then compare your screen with Figure 1.10.

A *dialog box* is a box that asks you to make a decision about an individual object or topic. The Ribbons screen saver is selected, and a preview displays near the top of the dialog box. The default length of inactivity to trigger the screen saver is 1 minute.

Figure 1.10

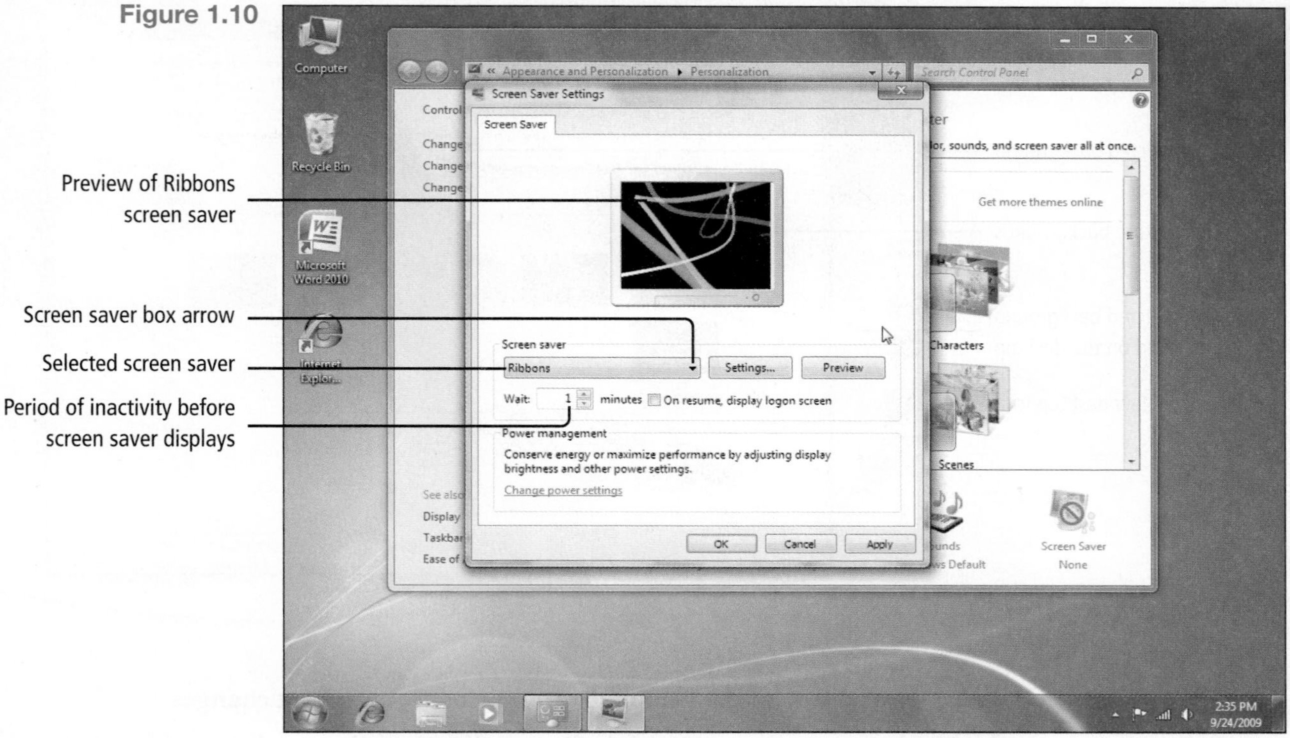

Preview of Ribbons screen saver

Screen saver box arrow

Selected screen saver

Period of inactivity before screen saver displays

5 In the **Screen Saver Settings** dialog box, click the **Preview** button to preview a full-screen version of the screen saver. When you are through, move the mouse to turn off the full-screen screen saver preview. If you want to turn on the screen saver, click **OK**; otherwise, click **Cancel**.

6 In the left panel of the **Personalization** window, click **Change desktop icons**.

7 At the top of the **Desktop Icon Settings** dialog box, select—click to add a check mark to—the **Control Panel** check box. Click **OK** to save your changes and close the Desktop Icon Settings dialog box. Notice that a Control Panel icon is added to the left side of the desktop.

8 At the bottom of the **Personalization** window, click **Desktop Background**. Click the **up arrow** ![up arrow] at the top of the scroll bar several times to move to the top of the backgrounds list. Under **Architecture**, click the third picture—the picture of the white building. The new background previews on the screen, as shown in Figure 1.11.

The *desktop background* is the picture, pattern, or color that displays on the desktop.

Figure 1.11

Selected background

Architecture backgrounds

Selected background previewed on the desktop

New desktop icon

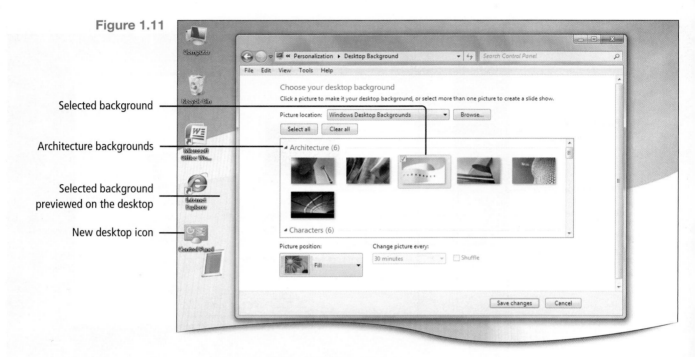

9 At the bottom of the **Personalization** window, click **Save changes**.

10 In the upper right corner of the **Personalization** window, click the **Close** button ![close button], and then compare your screen with Figure 1.12.

Figure 1.12

New background applied to desktop

Activity 1.03 | Adding and Removing Gadgets

Gadgets are used to display dynamic programs such as a currency converter, a calendar, a stock market ticker, or a clock. You can move the gadgets anywhere on the screen, and you can modify or resize most of them.

1 In an open area of the desktop, right-click to display a shortcut menu. On the shortcut menu, click **Gadgets**. Compare your screen with Figure 1.13.

Figure 1.13

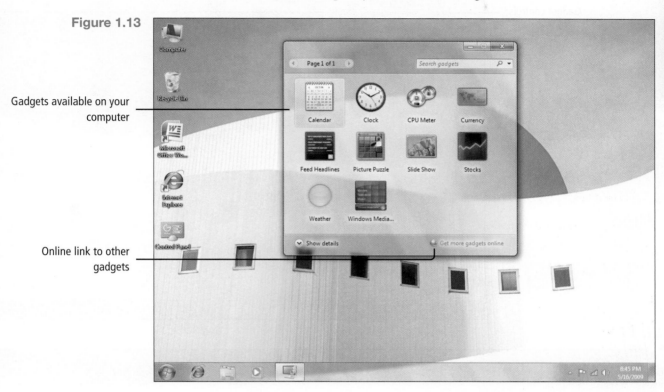

Gadgets available on your computer

Online link to other gadgets

2 In the **Gadgets** window, double-click the **Weather** gadget. In the upper right corner of the **Gadgets** dialog box, click the **Close** button.

Alert! | Are there already gadgets on your desktop?

Your desktop may contain one or more gadgets, including a Weather gadget. In fact, you can have more than one of the same gadgets on the desktop at a time. For example, if you are interested in the weather in two different locations, you can add two weather gadgets to the desktop and keep an eye on two locations at one time.

---

3 Point to the **Weather** gadget. Notice that a four-button tool set, called the *gadget controls*, displays on the right, as shown in Figure 1.14. Take a moment to study the functions of the buttons, as shown in the table in Figure 1.15.

Figure 1.14

Weather gadget

Gadget controls

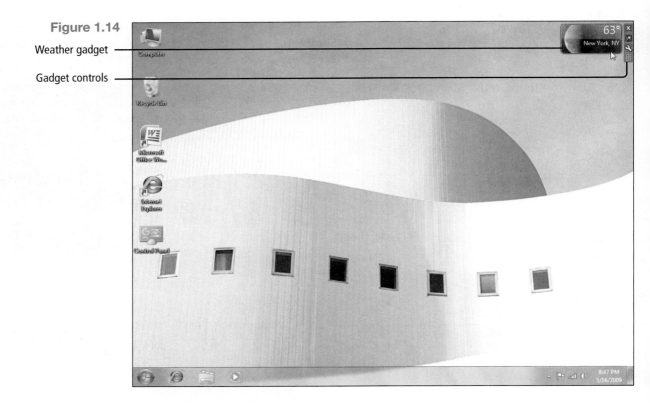

Gadget Controls		
Button Name	**Button**	**Description**
Close	☒	Closes the gadget.
Larger size	▣	Increases the size of the gadget; occupies the same position as the Smaller size button.
Smaller size	▣	Decreases the size of the gadget; occupies the same position as the Larger size button.
Options	◈	Displays different settings for each gadget.
Drag gadget	▦	Used to move the gadget anywhere on the desktop.

Figure 1.15

4 Point to the **Weather** gadget, click the **Larger size** button ⬚, and then click the **Options** button ⬚. In the **Select current location** box, type **Madison, Wisconsin** and then press Enter. Click **OK**, and then compare your screen with Figure 1.16.

Figure 1.16

Weather gadget enlarged —

Selected city —

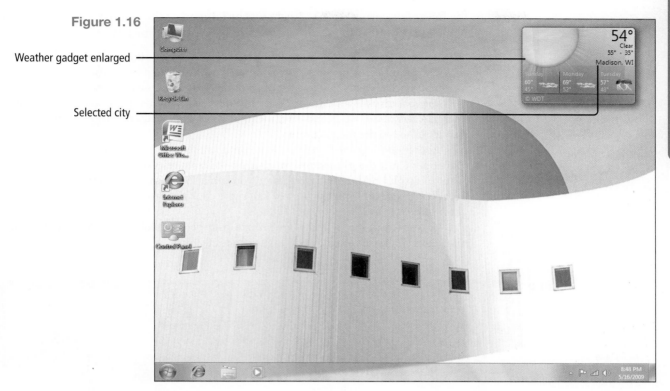

5 In an open area of the desktop, right-click to display a shortcut menu. On the short-cut menu, click **Gadgets**. In the **Gadgets** window, double-click the **Slide Show** gadget, and then double-click the **Slide Show** gadget again. In the upper right corner of the **Gadgets** dialog box, click the **Close** button ⬚.

Two additional gadgets are added to the desktop.

6 Point to either of the **Slide Show** gadgets, and then in the gadget controls, click the **Close** button ⬚ to remove the gadget from the desktop.

7 Point to the remaining **Slide Show** gadget, point to the **Drag gadget** button ⬚, and then drag the gadget near the upper edge of the desktop. Notice that as you move near the top of the desktop, the gadget snaps into position, slightly below the top of the desktop.

Objective 2 | Use the Start Menu and Manage Windows

Some programs and documents are available from the desktop. For most things, however, you will turn to the Start menu. The *Start menu* gives you access to all of the programs on your computer, and also enables you to change the way Windows operates, to access and configure your network, and to get help and support when it is needed. After you have opened several programs, you can rearrange and resize the program windows to fit your needs.

Activity 1.04 | Using the Start Menu

In this activity, you will use the Start menu to open a program, and also to open the Windows Explorer window.

Another Way

Press the Start button on your keyboard—a key with the Windows logo, often found to the left of the spacebar.

1 In the lower left corner of the screen, on the left end of the taskbar, point to and then click the **Start** button ⊙. Compare your screen with Figure 1.17.

The left side of the Start menu contains four areas. At the bottom is the Search box, which enables you to search for files or programs. Above the Search box is the **All Programs** command, which takes you to a list of all of the programs you can access on the computer. *All Programs* displays an arrow, which indicates that a submenu is available for a command. A **submenu** is a second-level menu; the arrow indicates that more items can be found related to the menu command.

Above *All Programs* is an area that contains the most recently opened programs. On the upper left is the **pinned programs area**—an area reserved for programs that you want to display permanently, although you can also remove programs from this area. To remove a program from the pinned list, right-click the program, and then click *Remove from this list*.

On the top of the right side are links to your personal folders, while the bottom sections give you access to computer management features.

Figure 1.17

Current user (yours will differ)

Pinned programs area (your items will vary)

Recently used programs (your items will vary)

Arrow indicates submenus are available

All Programs command

Search box

Start button

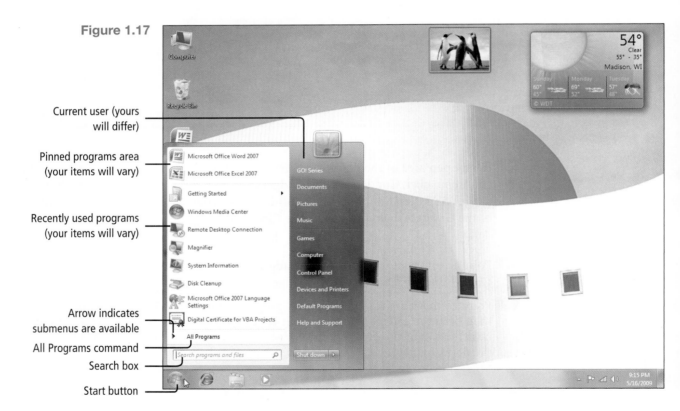

Alert! | Is your taskbar hidden?

Some computers are set up to hide the taskbar when it is not in use. This adds more workspace to the desktop, and is particularly useful on portable computers with small screens. When the taskbar is hidden, move the pointer to the bottom of the screen, and it will display. However, in this chapter, it is assumed that the taskbar is displayed at all times.

To keep the taskbar displayed on your screen, find an open area on the taskbar, right-click, and then from the shortcut menu, click Properties. In the Taskbar and Start Menu Properties dialog box, on the Taskbar tab, locate the *Auto-hide the taskbar* check box. If the taskbar is hidden, there will be a check mark in the check box. To remove the Auto-hide feature, click the check box one time to clear—remove—the check mark.

2 From the **Start** menu, point to, but do not click, the **All Programs** command. Compare your screen with Figure 1.18.

The All Programs submenu displays—displaying a portion of the contents found within All Programs—and the *All Programs* command changes to a *Back* command. Your menu will differ from the one shown in Figure 1.18 because your computer will have different programs installed. Folders in the menu contain more programs or more folders or some of each.

Figure 1.18

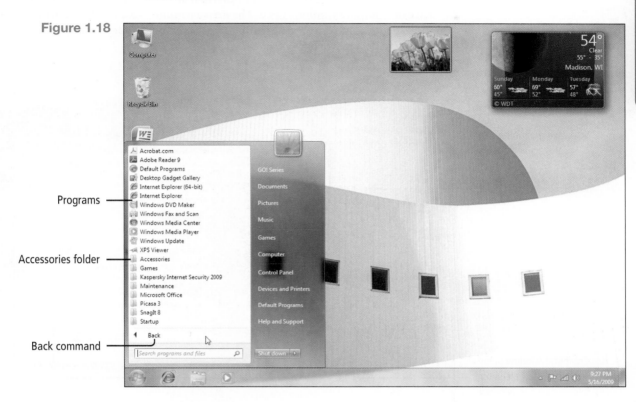

Programs

Accessories folder

Back command

3 Click the **Accessories** folder, and then from the displayed list, click **Calculator**. Notice that the *window name*—*Calculator*—displays in the title bar.

The Calculator window opens, and the Start menu closes. You can access the Accessories programs from the Start menu and use them while you are using other programs. For example, you might want to make a quick calculation while you are typing a document in Microsoft Word. You can open the calculator, make the calculation, and then place the result in your Word document without closing Word.

4 Click the **Start** button ⊕ again, and near the middle of the right side of the **Start menu**, click **Computer**. If the Windows Explorer window fills the entire screen, near the right side of the title bar, click the Restore Down button ⊡ . Compare your screen with Figure 1.19.

> The Windows Explorer window opens, but the Calculator window is either partially or completely hidden, as shown in Figure 1.19. The buttons in the taskbar, however, indicate that two programs are open. The buttons that are outlined indicate the programs that have one or more windows open. The *active window*—the window in which the pointer movements, commands, or text entry occur when two or more windows are open—displays a darker title bar.

Figure 1.19

Darker title bar indicates the active window

Window name in title bar

Computer window hides most of the Calculator window

Calculator window button

Computer window button

5 Click the **Start** button ⊕, and then click in the **Search programs and files** box. Type **wordpad** and press ⏎. If the WordPad window fills the entire screen, near the right side of the title bar, click the Restore Down button ⊡ .

> If you type a program name into the Start menu Search box, the program will open, which enables you to quickly open programs rather than try to find them. *WordPad* is a simple word processing program that comes with Windows 7.

Activity 1.05 | Adding Shortcuts to the Start Menu, Desktop, and Taskbar

There are programs that you will seldom use, and there are programs that you will use all the time. To make frequently used programs easily and quickly available, you can pin a shortcut to the program in the Start menu *pinned programs area*, or you can add a short-cut icon to the desktop or pin the program to the taskbar.

1 Click the **Start** button ⊕, point to **All Programs**, click **Accessories**, and then right-click **Calculator**.

2 From the displayed shortcut menu, click **Pin to Start Menu**. At the bottom of the **Start menu**, click the **Back** button, and notice that *Calculator* has been added to the pinned programs area, as shown in Figure 1.20.

Figure 1.20

Calculator program pinned to Start menu

3 Click the **Start** button , point to **All Programs**, if necessary click **Accessories**, right-click **Calculator**, and then point to—but do not click—**Send to**. Notice the available commands on the *Send to* list, as shown in Figure 1.21.

Figure 1.21

Shortcut menu

Send to command

Desktop (create shortcut) command

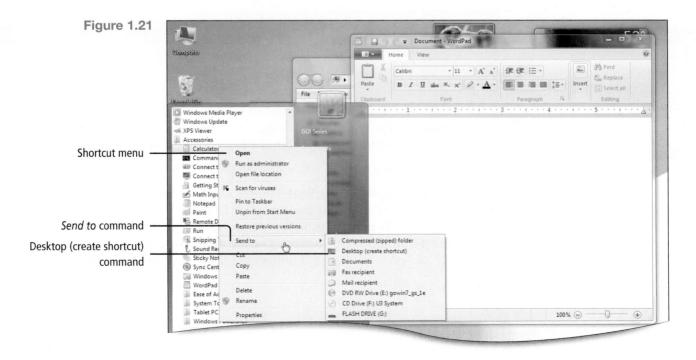

4 From the displayed shortcut menu, click **Desktop (create shortcut)**, and then click in any open area of the desktop.

> A Calculator icon is placed on the desktop. The shortcut icon has a small blue arrow in the lower left corner. Depending on the windows you have open, and the number of icons on your desktop, your Calculator shortcut icon may be hidden.

5 Click the **Start** button 🔘, point to **All Programs**, if necessary click **Accessories**, right-click **Snipping Tool**, and then click **Pin to Taskbar**. Click in an open area on the desktop, and then compare your screen with Figure 1.22.

> You can use *Snipping Tool* to capture a screen shot, or *snip*, of the entire screen or of any object on your screen, and then make notes on, save, or share the image. You will use this tool throughout this chapter.

Figure 1.22

Calculator shortcut icon added to the desktop

Snipping Tool added to taskbar

6 On the taskbar, click the **Snipping Tool** button ✂️.

> The Snipping Tool window displays, and the rest of the screen appears faded.

7 In the **Snipping Tool** window, click the arrow to the right of the **New** button to display a list of potential snips. From the list, click **Full-screen Snip**.

> The entire screen is captured, and displays in the Snipping Tool window.

8 Near the top of the **Snipping Tool** window, click the **Save Snip** button 💾. In the **Save As** dialog box, in the left column, click **Desktop** to save the snip to the desktop. In the **File name** box, using your own last and first names, type **Lastname_Firstname_1A_Taskbar** Use the underscore between words—hold down Shift and press the dash (-) button to the right of the numbers near the top of the keyboard. Click in the **Save as type** box, and then from the menu, click **JPEG file**. Compare your screen with Figure 1.23.

Figure 1.23

File will be saved on the desktop

File name

File saved in JPEG format

Save button

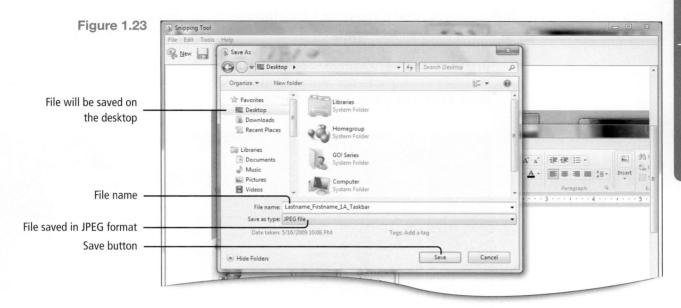

9 At the bottom of the **Save As** dialog box, click **Save** to save the snip on the desktop.

10 In the upper right corner of the **Snipping Tool** window, click the **Close** button. Notice that your file displays as an icon on the desktop.

Activity 1.06 | Minimizing, Maximizing, and Restoring a Window

You can **maximize** a window, which enlarges the window to occupy the entire screen, and you can **restore** a window, which reduces the window to the size it was before being maximized. You can also **minimize** a window, which reduces the window to a button on the taskbar, removing it from the screen entirely without actually closing it. When you need to view the window again, you can click the taskbar button to bring it back into view.

1 Click anywhere in the **WordPad** window to make it the active window, and then examine the three buttons in the upper right corner of the window. The left button is the **Minimize** button, the middle button is the **Maximize** button, and the right button is the **Close** button.

Another Way
Double-click in the bar at the top of the window.

2 In the **WordPad** window, click the **Maximize** button. Notice that the window expands to cover the entire screen, and the Maximize button changes to a Restore Down button, as shown in Figure 1.24.

Figure 1.24

Maximize button changes to Restore Down button

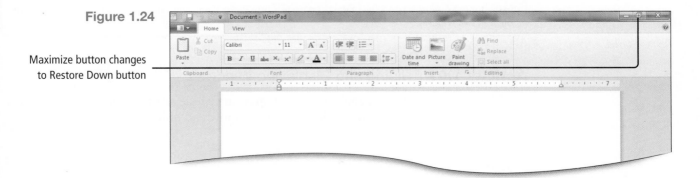

3 In the **WordPad** window, click the **Restore Down** button. Notice that the window resumes its former shape, size, and location.

4 In the **WordPad** window, click the **Minimize** button. In the taskbar, click the **Calculator** button to make it the active window, and then in the **Calculator** window, click the **Minimize** button to display the Windows Explorer window. Notice that the Windows Explorer window now displays as the active window. Notice also that the two programs that you minimized are not closed—their buttons are still outlined on the taskbar, as shown in Figure 1.25.

Figure 1.25

WordPad window minimized to taskbar

Calculator window minimized to taskbar

5 In the taskbar, click the **Calculator** button to restore the Calculator window. Then, click the **WordPad** button to restore the WordPad window.

More Knowledge | Keeping More Than One Program Window Open at a Time

The ability to keep more than one window open at a time will become more useful as you become more familiar with Microsoft Office. For example, if you want to take information from two word processing documents to create a third document, you can open all three documents and use the taskbar to move among them, copying and pasting text from one document to another. Or, you could copy a chart from Excel and paste it into Word or take a table of data and paste it into PowerPoint. You can even have the same document open in two windows.

Activity 1.07 | Hiding and Displaying Windows

There is a shortcut that enables you to temporarily hide all open windows and view the desktop, and also a way to display just one window and hide the rest.

1 Move the pointer to the lower-right corner of the desktop to point to the **Show desktop** button. Notice that all open windows become transparent to give you a *peek* at the desktop—all desktop items display, as shown in Figure 1.26.

This only works if the Aero interface is turned on.

Figure 1.26

Outlines of transparent windows

Show desktop button

2 Move the pointer away from the **Show desktop** button and notice that the windows display again.

3 Point to the **Show desktop** button, but this time click the button. Notice that all open windows are hidden, and no outlines display.

4 Click the **Show desktop** button again to display all open windows.

5 In the taskbar, locate and click the **Calculator** button to make the Calculator the active window. Notice that the background of the Calculator icon on the taskbar is brighter than the icons for the other open windows.

6 Point to the **Calculator** title bar, hold down the left mouse button, and then *shake*—move the window back and forth quickly—the window.

All windows except the shaken window are hidden.

7 Shake the **Calculator** window again to display all of the open windows.

Objective 3 | Resize, Move, and Scroll Windows

When a window opens on your screen, it generally opens in the same size and shape as it was when last used. If you are using more than one window at a time, you can increase or decrease the size of a window, or move a window so that you can see the information you need.

As you work within a program, the information you create will likely grow larger than the screen can display. When the information in a window extends beyond the right or lower edges of the window, scroll bars display at the bottom and right. Using the *horizontal scroll bar*, you can move left and right to view information that extends beyond the left or right edge of the screen. Using the *vertical scroll bar*, you can move up and down to view information that extends beyond the top or bottom of the screen.

Activity 1.08 | Customizing and Using the Taskbar

When you have a number of windows open, you can use the taskbar to quickly review the contents of each document to determine which one to use. You can also move the taskbar to the top, left, or right edges of the desktop.

1 On the taskbar, point to—but do not click—the **Windows Explorer** button, and then compare your screen with Figure 1.27.

> A thumbnail of the window displays. A *thumbnail* is a miniature representation of a window or a file. If two documents are open in the same program, two thumbnails will display. The Aero interface must be turned on for this feature to work.

Figure 1.27

Thumbnail of the
Computer window

2 On the taskbar, point to—but do not click—the **Calculator** button. Move the pointer and point to the **WordPad** button.

3 Click the **Start** button, point to **All Programs**, click **Accessories**, and then click **Paint**.

> If the Paint window is maximized, click the Restore Down button.

> *Paint* is a simple drawing program that comes with Windows 7. Four programs are now open, and there are icons on the taskbar for other unopened programs, such as Snipping Tool.

4 Hold down the [Alt] key, and then press the [Tab] key. Compare your screen with Figure 1.28.

> The screen displays thumbnails of the windows that are open, including the desktop; if the Aero interface is not turned on, only the program icons display.

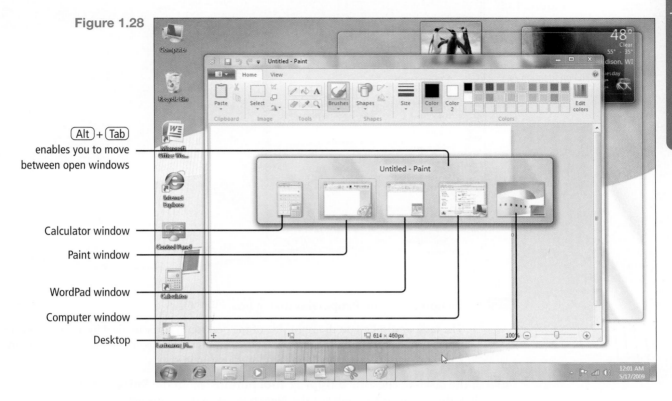

Figure 1.28

[Alt] + [Tab] enables you to move between open windows

Calculator window

Paint window

WordPad window

Computer window

Desktop

5 Continue to hold down [Alt], but press [Tab] several times. Notice that the selected window moves from left to right in the list of thumbnails.

> When you release the [Alt] key, the window in the active thumbnail becomes the active window on the desktop.

6 Move to the **Calculator** window, and then release the [Alt] button.

7 On the taskbar, point to the **Windows Explorer** window, and then right-click.

> A *jump list* displays frequent destinations you might want to jump to from the Windows Explorer window. If you display a jump list for a program such as a word processor or a spreadsheet, a list of recently edited files also displays, enabling you to quickly open any desired files.

8 Right-click an open area of the taskbar, and then from the shortcut menu, click **Properties**.

9 In the **Properties** dialog box, be sure the Taskbar tab is selected. Under **Taskbar appearance**, click the **Taskbar location on screen arrow**, and then click **Right**. Compare your screen with Figure 1.29.

Figure 1.29

Taskbar tab

Screen location of the taskbar

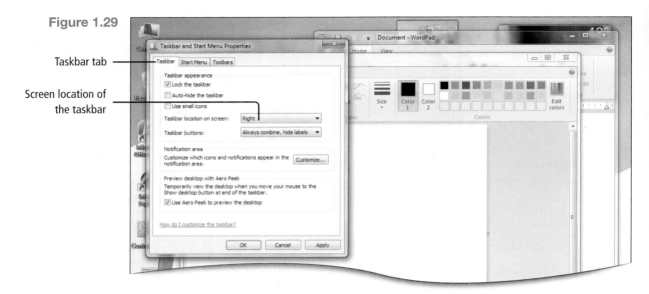

10 At the bottom of the **Properties** dialog box, click **OK**.

> The taskbar displays on the right side of the desktop. This is an ideal location if you are using a widescreen monitor or a portable computer with a wide monitor because it gives you more vertical space on the screen for your documents.

11 In the taskbar, click the **Snipping Tool** button ✂. In the **Snipping Tool** window, click the arrow to the right of the **New** button to display a list of potential snips. From the list, click **Full-screen Snip**.

12 Near the top of the **Snipping Tool** window, click the **Save Snip** button 💾. In the **Save As** dialog box, in left column, click **Desktop**. In the **File name** box, using your own last and first names, type **Lastname_Firstname_1A_Windows** Click in the **Save as type** box and be sure **JPEG file** is selected.

13 At the bottom of the **Save As** dialog box, click **Save** to save the snip on the desktop.

14 In the upper right corner of the **Snipping Tool** window, click the **Close** button [✕]. Notice that your file displays as an icon on the desktop.

15 Use the procedure you practiced in Steps 8 through 10 to return the taskbar to the bottom of the desktop.

Activity 1.09 | Resizing, Moving, Scrolling, and Closing Windows

In the following activity, you will resize and move the Windows Explorer window. You will also use the vertical scroll bar in the window to view information that does not fit in the window.

1 On the right end of the taskbar, click the **Show desktop** button to hide all of the windows.

2 On the taskbar, click the **Windows Explorer** button 🗀 to display the Windows Explorer window.

3 Move the pointer to the lower right corner of the window to display the diagonal resize pointer, and then compare your screen with Figure 1.30.

When the mouse pointer is in this shape, you can use it to change the size and shape of a window.

Figure 1.30

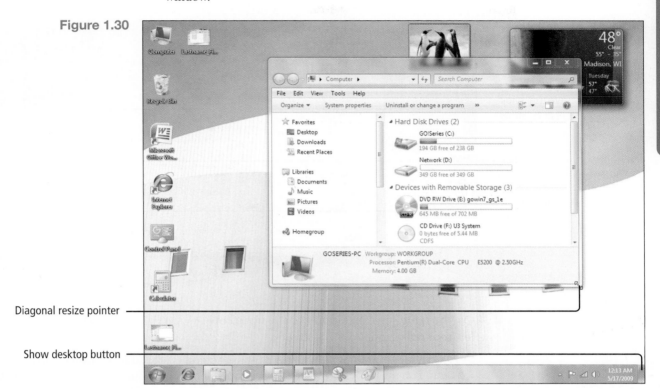

Diagonal resize pointer

Show desktop button

4 Hold down the left mouse button, *drag*—move the mouse while holding down the left mouse button and then release at the appropriate time—diagonally up and to the left until you see a scroll bar at the right side of the window, and then release the mouse button. Adjust as necessary so that the Windows Explorer window is the approximate size of the one shown in Figure 1.31.

Notice that a vertical scroll bar displays on the right side of the window, and another one displays on the right side of the Navigation pane. A scroll bar is added to the window whenever the window contains more than it can display.

Figure 1.31

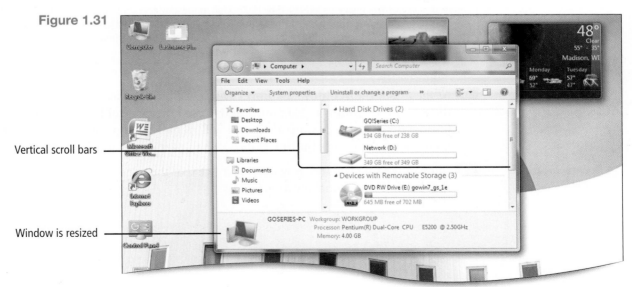

Vertical scroll bars

Window is resized

5 In the **Windows Explorer** window **file list**, at the bottom of the vertical scroll bar, point to the **down arrow** ▼ and click two times. Notice that information at the bottom of the window scrolls up so that you can see the information that was not visible before, as shown in Figure 1.32.

Figure 1.32

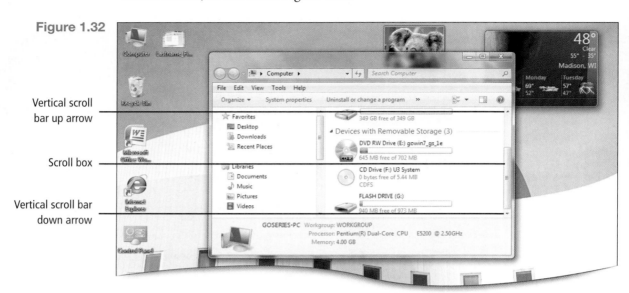

Vertical scroll bar up arrow

Scroll box

Vertical scroll bar down arrow

6 On the same scroll bar, point to the **up arrow** ▲, and then click and hold down the left mouse button.

The window scrolls to the top of the file list. You can click and hold down the left mouse button on the up or down scroll arrows to scroll rapidly through a long list of information.

7 Point to the scroll box, and then drag it downward.

The *scroll box* displays within the vertical and horizontal scroll bars and provides a visual indication of your location within the information displayed. It can also be used with the mouse to reposition the information on the screen. Moving the scroll box gives you more control as you scroll because you can see the information as it moves up or down in the window.

Note | Moving a Screen at a Time

You can move up or down a screen at a time by clicking in the gray area above or below the vertical scroll box. You can also move left or right a screen at a time by clicking in the area to the left or right of a horizontal scroll box. The size of the scroll box indicates the relative size of the display to the whole document. If the scroll box is small, it means that the display is a small portion of the entire document.

---

8 At the top of the **Windows Explorer** window, point to a blank area in the title bar to the left of the Minimize, Maximize, and Close buttons. Hold down the left mouse button, drag the window up as far as it will go past the top edge of the window, and then release the mouse button. Notice that the window is maximized.

9 Click in the title bar and drag down. Notice that the window is restored to its original size, but not its original location.

10 In the **Windows Explorer** window title bar, click the **Close** button ☒. In the taskbar, right-click the **Paint** button 🖌, and then click **Close window**. Use the same technique to close the **Calculator** window 🖩.

11 In the taskbar, click the **WordPad** button to display the WordPad window. Using the title bar, drag the WordPad window to the right edge of the desktop until it changes shape to occupy the right half of the desktop, and then release the mouse button.

> You can use this method to open two windows side by side if you drag a second window to the left border.

12 Click in the WordPad window, type your first and last names, and then press [Enter]. Locate the **Lastname_Firstname_1A_Taskbar** icon on the desktop—you may have to click the two snip files to find the correct file.

13 Drag the **Lastname_Firstname_1A_Taskbar** file to the line below your name in the WordPad document, and then release the mouse button. Compare your screen with Figure 1.33.

> The contents of the file you dragged are pasted into the WordPad document.

Figure 1.33

Your name

File dragged into WordPad document

File icon

14 Drag the **Lastname_Firstname_1A_Windows** file to the line below the figure you just inserted into the WordPad document. In the WordPad title bar, click the **Save** button 🖫.

15 In the **Save As** dialog box, in the **Navigation** pane, click **Desktop**. In the **File name** box, type **Lastname_Firstname_1A_WordPad** and then click **Save**.

16 If you are to print your document, hold down [Ctrl] and then press [P] to display the Print dialog box. Be sure the correct printer is selected, and then click **Print**. If you are to submit this document electronically, follow your instructor's directions.

17 **Close** ☒ the WordPad window.

End **You have completed Project 1A** ——————————

Project 1B Manage Files and Folders

Project Activities

In Activities 1.10 through 1.18 you will create folders, and then copy, move, rename, and delete files and folders. You will add tags to files and use the Windows 7 search features to search for files. Your screens will look similar to those in Figure 1.34.

Project Files

For Project 1B, you will need the following files:

36 sample files, and two folders containing 14 additional files

You will save your documents as:

Lastname_Firstname_1B_Renamed_Folder

Lastname_Firstname_1B_Compressed_Folder

Lastname_Firstname_1B_Search_Folder

Project Results

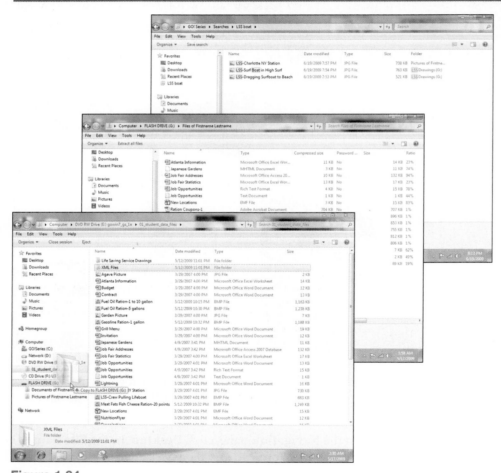

Figure 1.34

Objective 4 | Create, Move, and Rename Folders

Information that you create in a computer program is stored in the computer's memory, which is a temporary storage location. This data will be lost if the computer is turned off. To keep the information you create, you must save it as a file on one of the drives available to you. For example, a five-page term paper that you create in a word processing program such as Microsoft Word, when saved, is a *file*. Files can be stored directly on a drive, but more commonly are stored in a folder on the drive. A *folder* is a container for programs and files, represented on the screen by a picture of a common paper file folder.

Use folders to organize your files so that you can easily locate them for later use. Folders and files must be created and stored on one of the drives attached to your computer. Your available drives fall into three categories: 1) the nonremovable hard drive, also called the *local disk*, inside the computer; 2) removable drives that you insert into the computer, such as a flash drive, an external hard drive, or a writable CD or DVD; or 3) a shared network drive connected to your computer through a computer network, such as the network at your college.

Activity 1.10 | Opening and Navigating Windows Explorer

Windows Explorer is a program that enables you to create and manage folders, and copy, move, sort, and delete files. In the following activity, you will create a folder on one of the three types of drives available to you—the local disk (hard drive), a removable drive (USB flash drive, an external hard drive, or some other type of removable drive), or a network drive. If you are using a computer in a college lab, you may have space assigned to you on a shared network drive. You can create these folders on any drive that is available to you. For the rest of this chapter, a flash drive will be used.

1 On the taskbar, click the **Windows Explorer** button ⬚. If this button is not available, click the **Start** button ⬚, point to All Programs, click Accessories, and then click Windows Explorer.

> The Windows Explorer window opens, with the Navigation pane displayed on the left, and the Libraries pane displayed on the right. You may also see a Details pane just above the taskbar and a Preview pane on the right side of the window.

> **More Knowledge | Using Libraries**
>
> *Libraries* are folders used to sort files with similar content. By default, Windows 7 sets up four libraries: Documents, Music, Pictures, and Videos. Each of these libraries is assigned two folders—a user folder and a public folder. For example, the Documents library contains the My Documents subfolder for the current user, along with the Public Documents subfolder on the hard disk, which contains files that can be shared with all users. If you have other fixed drives on your computer, or permanent network drives, you can add other folders to a library so that all files of a similar type can be accessed quickly using the library.

Another Way

On the right side of the title bar, click the Maximize button ⬚.

2 If the window is not maximized, drag the title bar to the top of the screen.

3 On the Command bar, click the **Organize** button, and then point to **Layout**. If the Details pane does not display at the bottom of your window, click Details Pane. If the Navigation pane does not display on the left side of your window, repeat the procedure and click Navigation Pane. Compare your screen with Figure 1.35.

Figure 1.35

Organize button

Libraries pane

Navigation pane

Details pane

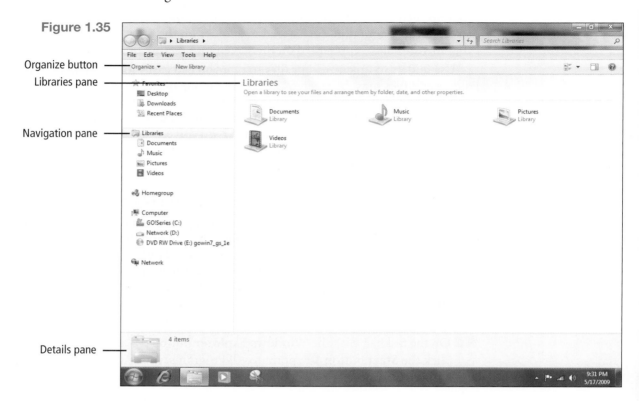

4 In the **Navigation** pane, if necessary scroll down, and then click **Computer**.

The file list displays a list of hard drives, removable storage devices, network drives, and other devices connected to the computer.

5 In the **Navigation** pane, if necessary, to the left of **Computer**, click the open arrow ▷ . Notice that the arrow changes to a filled arrow pointing downward at an angle ◢ .

The open arrow indicates that there are other folders and drives to be displayed. When you click the open arrow, the next level of folders and drives displays. The list of drives in the Navigation pane matches the list of drives in the file list.

6 Insert your USB flash drive or other removable drive. If an AutoPlay dialog box displays asking what you want Windows to do, click the Close button. In the **Navigation** pane, under **Computer**, click your removable drive—for this chapter, the removable drive name will be FLASH DRIVE (G:); yours will be different.

7 Compare your screen with Figure 1.36. Notice that the file list in the figure is empty; your storage device or drive may already contain files and folders.

Figure 1.36

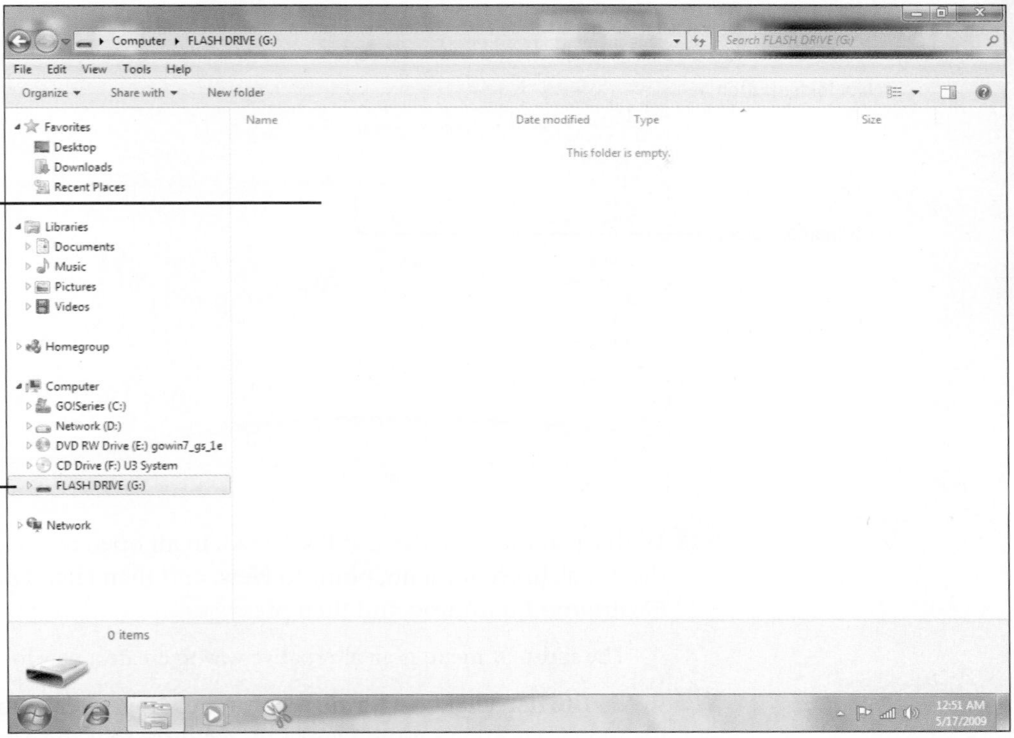

File list is empty; yours
may have files and folders

Flash drive (your drive
name and letter will vary)

More Knowledge | Computer Storage Devices

The hard drive (local disk) is usually identified on your computer by the notation C: (and sometimes D:, E:, and so on for additional drives). *Flash drives*—also known as *USB drives* or *thumb drives*—are small storage devices that plug into a computer's Universal Serial Bus (USB) port, which provides a connection between a computer and a peripheral device such as a printer, a mouse, a keyboard, or a USB drive.

You may also have access to files on another type of storage device, a *CD*—Compact Disc, or a *DVD*—Digital Video (or Versatile) Disc. CD and DVD drives are optical storage devices that come in two formats—read-only and read-write. If you are using files stored on a read-only CD or a DVD disc, you will need to open a file from the disc, and then save it to a writable drive, or copy a file to another disk and then open it.

Activity 1.11 | Creating a New Folder

It is always a good idea to create a new folder when you have a new category of files to store. You do not need to create a new folder for each type of file, however. You can store many different kinds of files in the same folder.

Another Way

If you accidentally press
Enter before you have a
chance to name the
folder, you can still
rename it. Right-click
the folder, click Rename
from the shortcut
menu, type a new
name, and then press
Enter.

1 With the flash drive selected, in the Command bar, click the **New folder** button.

A new folder—named *New folder*—is created with the name of the folder displayed in the *edit mode*. Edit mode enables you to change the name of a file or folder, and works the same in all Windows programs.

2 With *New Folder* selected, substitute your name where indicated, and type **Pictures of Firstname Lastname** and then press Enter. Click anywhere in the blank area of the file list to deselect the new folder and compare your screen with Figure 1.37.

Figure 1.37

New folder button

Renamed folder

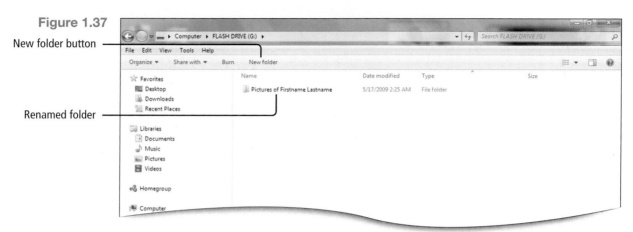

3 With the removable drive still selected, in an open area of the **file list**, right-click to display a shortcut menu, point to **New**, and then click **Folder**. Type **Documents of Firstname Lastname** and then press Enter.

The shortcut menu is an alternative way to create a new folder.

4 In the **file list**, click the **Name** column heading several times to sort the folders and file names from *a* to *z* and from *z* to *a*. Notice that the arrow in the Name column heading points up when the folders are displayed in *ascending order* (*a* to *z*), and points down when the folders are displayed in *descending order* (*z* to *a*). Stop when the folders are sorted in descending alphabetical order—from *z* to *a*.

5 In the **file list**, move the pointer to the line at the right of the **Name** column heading to display the resize pointer ✛, as shown in Figure 1.38. Drag the resize pointer ✛ to the right or left to make the column slightly wider than the longest folder name.

Figure 1.38

Name column heading with arrow indicating sort order

Folders in descending alphabetical order

Resize pointer

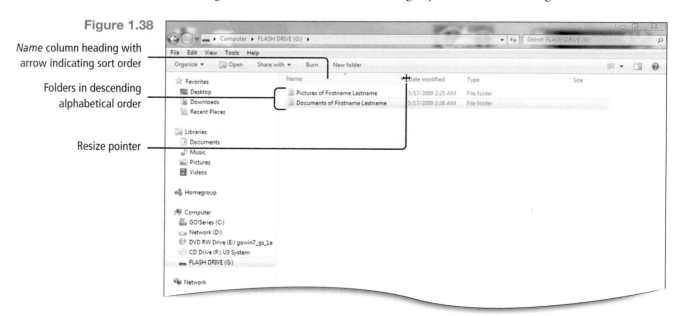

Activity 1.12 | Moving and Renaming Folders

Your student files and folders for this book are stored on a CD or another location chosen by your instructor. You can move the folders, including the files in the folders, from another location to your flash drive or other storage device.

1 Navigate to the location where your student files for this book are stored. They may be stored on a CD, in a course management system, on a hard drive, or on a shared network drive. In this chapter, the data CD is used.

2 In the **Navigation** pane, on the data CD, click the open arrow ▷ to display the folder on the disc. Click the **01_student_data_files** folder, and then compare your screen with Figure 1.39. If your files and folders do not display the way they display in the figure, on the Command bar, to the right of the *Change your view* button, click the *More options* arrow, and then click Details.

There are two folders and a number of files in this folder. The total number of files and folders is displayed in the Details pane at the bottom of the screen. There are more files in the two folders, but they are not included in the totals in the Details pane—only the files and the folders currently displayed in the file list are counted.

Figure 1.39

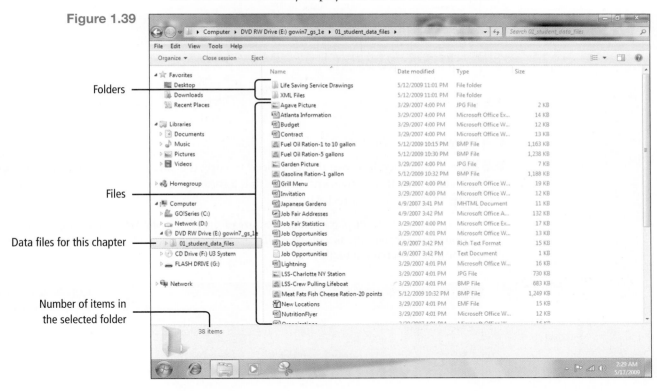

3 In the **file list**, move the pointer to the right border of the **Name** column heading to display the ✛ pointer. Double-click to resize the border to the widest folder or file name. Repeat this procedure to display the full **Date modified** and **Type** column contents.

> **Note** | Changing the Columns that Display in the File List
>
> If one or more of the columns displayed in Figure 1.39 do not display, right-click anywhere in the file list column titles, and then click the desired column.

4 In the **Navigation** pane, if necessary, click the open arrow ▷ to the left of your flash drive. Be sure your student files and folders from the data CD still display in the file list.

5 Near the top of the **file list**, locate the **XML Files** folder. Click on the folder, hold the mouse button down, and drag the folder to the **Navigation** pane directly on top of your storage drive, as shown in Figure 1.40. Notice that a folder displays attached to the pointer, and a ScreenTip says *Copy to FLASH DRIVE (G:)*—your folder or drive name will vary.

Figure 1.40

ScreenTip indicates copy location

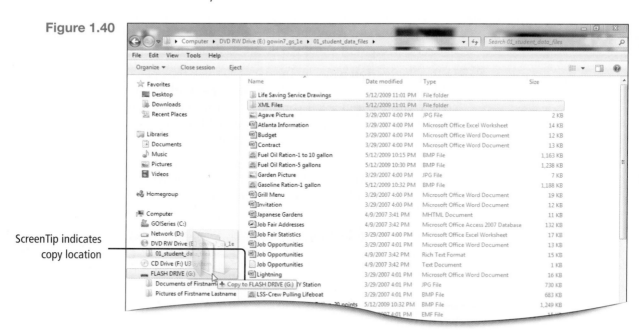

6 Release the mouse button.

7 Repeat the procedure you just practiced to copy the **Life Saving Service Drawings** folder to your flash drive, and notice that a message box indicates the progress of the copy, as shown in Figure 1.41.

The message box displays because the size of the *Life Saving Service Drawings* folder is much larger than the size of the *XML Files* folder and takes a few seconds to copy. The original files remain on the CD.

Figure 1.41

Message box indicates progress of the copy

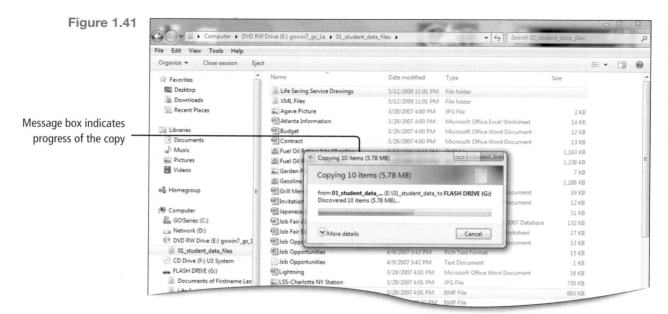

8 In the **Navigation** pane, click the flash drive or other device where you are storing your files and folders. In the **file list**, right-click the **Life Saving Service Drawings** folder, and then from the displayed shortcut menu, click **Rename**.

9 With the folder name in edit mode, type **LSS Drawings** and then press Enter.

The folder name is changed. When text is selected, typing replaces all of the selected text.

10 Use the skills you practiced earlier to create a **Full-screen Snip**. Click the **Save Snip** 🖫 button. In the **Save As** dialog box, in the left pane, scroll down to display the **Computer** drives. Click your flash drive, and then in the Command bar, click the **New folder** button. Name the new folder **Windows Chapter 1** Press Enter, and then press Enter again to open the new folder. In the **File name** box, type **Lastname_Firstname_1B_Renamed_Folder** Click **Save**, and then **Close** the Snipping Tool window.

Objective 5 | Copy, Move, Rename, and Delete Files

Copying files from one folder to another is a frequent data management task. For example, you might want to make a backup copy of important information, copy a file from a CD to a local disk, or copy information from your local disk drive to a removable drive. Copying files works the same regardless of the type of drive.

Performing other operations on files, such as deleting them or moving them, also works the same regardless of the type of drive. As you accumulate files, you will likely need to delete some to reduce clutter on your hard drive. You might also want to move documents into other folders on another drive to *archive* them—place them somewhere for long-term storage. Finally, you may want to change the names of file to make the names more descriptive. All of these tasks are functions of your Windows 7 operating system.

Activity 1.13 | Copying Files

1 In the **Navigation** pane, under **Computer**, scroll to the location where your student data files for this book are stored. Locate and click the folder named **01_student_data_files** to display the files and folders in the folder.

2 In the **Navigation** pane, scroll as necessary to display your flash drive or other storage device. Be sure your student data files and folders still display in the file list.

3 Near the middle of the **file list**, locate the **Garden Picture** file, and then drag it to your storage device. Recall that dragging also includes releasing the mouse button at the destination location.

When you drag a file or folder from one device to another, it is copied, which means that the original file remains on the original drive and a copy of the file is placed on the new drive. If you drag a file or folder to another place (such as a folder) on the same drive—for example, from one folder to another—the file or folder is moved and no longer resides in the original location.

4 Locate the **Grill Menu** file, right-click the file, and then click **Copy**.

This creates a copy of the Grill Menu file and places it in a temporary storage area called the *Clipboard*. Files in the Clipboard can be placed in other folders using the Paste command.

5 In the **Navigation** pane, click your storage device. In the **file list**, right-click in an open area, and then from the shortcut menu, click **Paste**. Notice that the file is copied to the open folder.

6 Click the **Name** column heading as necessary to sort the folders in ascending order—the arrow in the column heading should be pointing up. Compare your screen with Figure 1.42.

> The file list should display five folders—the three that you created and the two that you copied. In addition, the two files that you copied should display below the folders. When you sort a folder in ascending order, the folders always display first.

Figure 1.42

Folders display first

Folders and files sorted in alphabetical order by Name

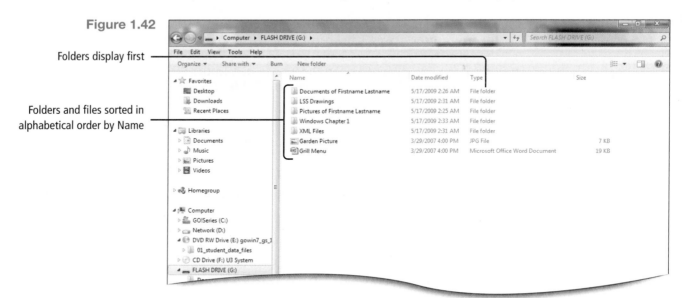

7 Display the files and folders in the **01_student_data_files** folder again. Click the **Atlanta Information** file, hold down Shift, and then click the **Fuel Oil Ration-1 to 10 gallon** file.

> By holding down the Shift key, you select the two files you click and all of the files in between.

8 In the **Navigation** pane, scroll as necessary to display your storage area. Drag the selected files to your storage area.

9 Click the **Agave Picture** file, hold down Ctrl, and then click the **Fuel Oil Ration-5 gallons** file, and then the **Gasoline Ration-1 gallon** file. Notice that by using the Control key, you can select several files that are not next to each other, as shown in Figure 1.43.

Figure 1.43

Selected files

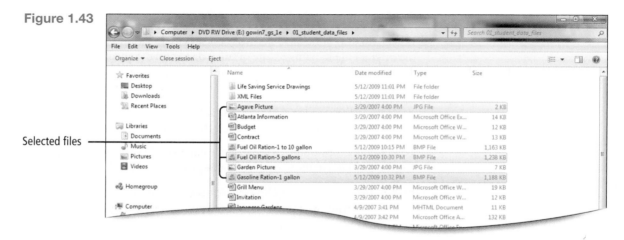

10 Drag the selected files to your storage area.

11 In the **file list**, click the **Invitation** file, and then use the vertical scroll bar to scroll to the bottom of the file list. Hold down Shift, and then click the **Volunteers** file. In the Detail area, notice that the number of files displays, as shown in Figure 1.44. If the total size of the files does not display, in the Details pane, click Show more details.

Figure 1.44

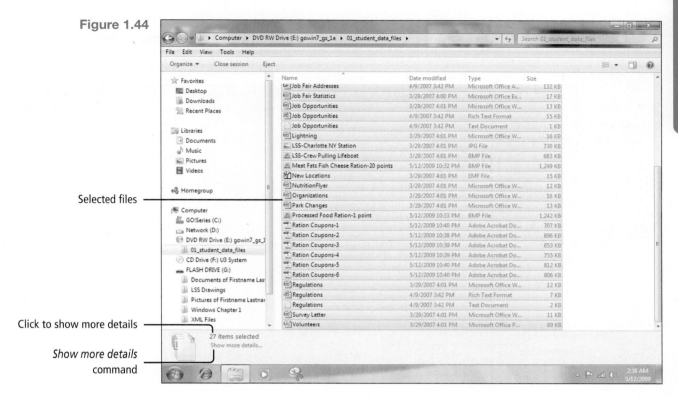

Selected files

Click to show more details

Show more details command

12 Drag the selected files to your storage area.

More Knowledge | File Extensions

The files you see may display three or four letters following the file name, such as *.docx*. These are *file extensions*, and most files have these extensions—although they may or may not display on your system. Files created by Microsoft Office programs have a standard set of extensions that identify the type of program used to create the file. For example, Microsoft Word documents end in *.doc* or *.docx*, Excel worksheets end in *.xls* or *.xlsx*, PowerPoint presentations end with *.ppt* or *pptx*, and so on. The default setting in Windows 7 is to hide the file extensions.

Activity 1.14 | Moving, Renaming, and Deleting Files

In the following activity, you will move files from one location on your removable drive to another location on the same drive. You will also rename and delete files.

1 In the **Navigation** pane, scroll as necessary and then click on your flash drive or other storage device.

> Your storage device should display five folders at the top, and a total of 36 files in the drive—41 objects, as displayed in the Details pane.

2 In the **file list**, click the **Type** column header to sort the files by file type. Move the pointer to the right border of the **Type** column heading to display the ➕ pointer. Double-click to resize the border to the widest file type.

3 In the **file list**, use the wheel in the middle of your mouse, or the vertical scroll bar, to scroll down until you can see all of the **Microsoft Office Word Document** files.

4 Click the **Budget** file, hold down ⟨Shift⟩, and then click the **Survey Letter** file to select all of the Word documents. Drag the selected files to the **Documents of Firstname Lastname** folder.

> The files are moved to the new folder, and no longer display in their original location.

5 In the **Navigation** pane, click the **Documents of Firstname Lastname** folder, and then compare your screen with Figure 1.45.

Figure 1.45

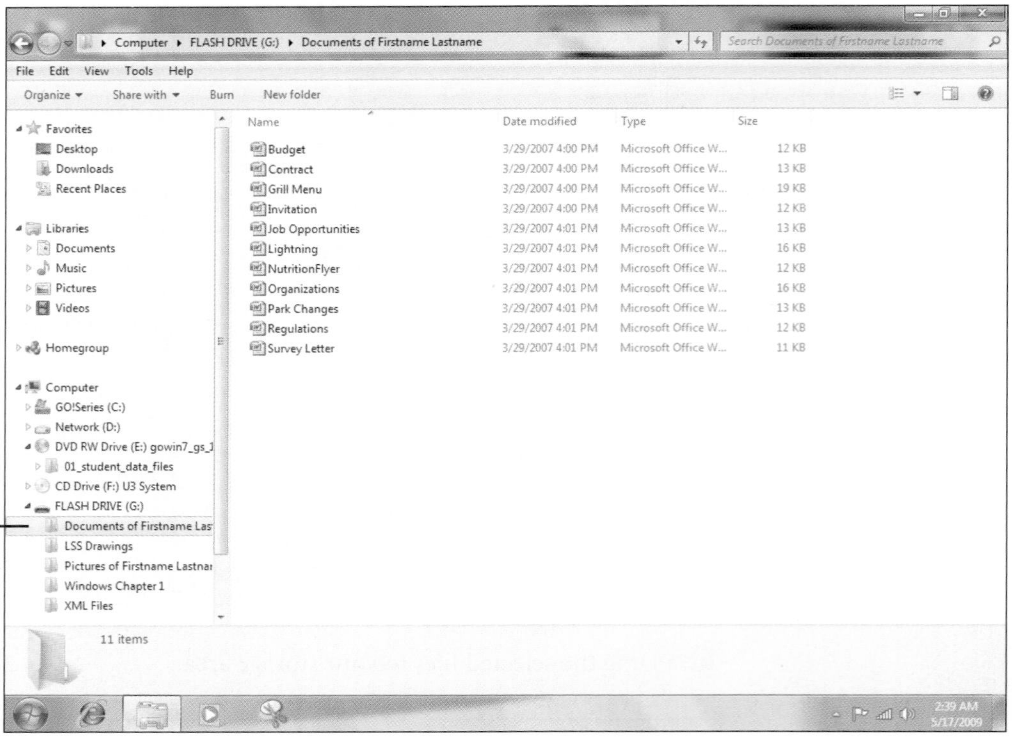

Word files moved to different folder

6 In the **Navigation** pane, click on your flash drive or other storage device. Using the technique you just practiced, select the three **JPG Images**, and then drag them to the **Pictures of Firstname Lastname** folder.

> **Alert! | What if your file types differ?**
>
> Files can be associated with several different programs, and will display a different file type in the Type column. For example, the three files labeled JPG in Figure 1.46 could be called JPEG files on your computer.

7 Select the six **BMP Files** and drag them to the **Pictures of Firstname Lastname** folder. If you do not see files labeled *BMP File*, select the six files beginning with *Fuel Oil Ration-1 to 10 gallon* and ending with *Processed Food Ration-1 point*.

8 In the **Navigation** pane, click the **Pictures of Firstname Lastname** folder, and then compare your screen with Figure 1.46.

Figure 1.46

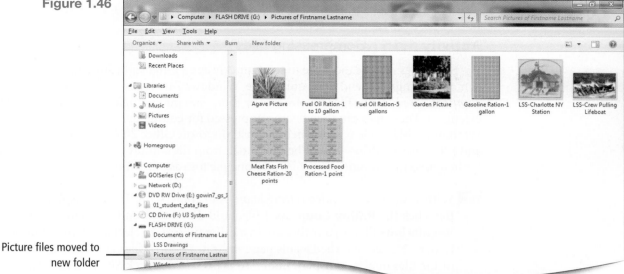

Picture files moved to new folder

9 If thumbnails do not display for the files, on the Command bar, to the right of the **Change your view** button, click the **More options arrow**, and then click **Large Icons**.

10 In the **file list**, right-click the **Agave Picture** file, and then click **Rename**. Type **Agave Cactus** and then press Enter.

11 In the **file list**, right-click the **Garden Picture** file, and then click **Delete**. The **Delete File** message box displays, as shown in Figure 1.47.

Figure 1.47

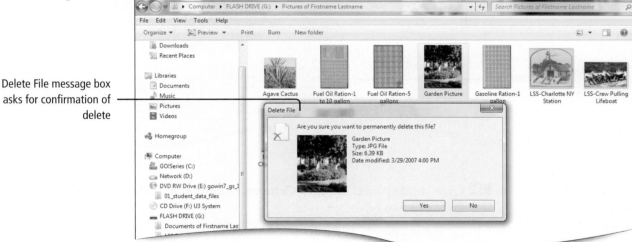

Delete File message box asks for confirmation of delete

Another Way

In the Navigation pane, click your flash drive or other storage location name.

12 In the **Delete File** message box, click **Yes** to send the file to the Recycle Bin.

13 In the upper left corner of the window, click the **Back** button to move back to your main storage area.

14 In the **file list**, right-click the **XML Files** folder, and then click **Delete**. In the displayed **Delete Folder** message box, click **Yes**.

> When you delete a folder, all files in the folder are also deleted.

Activity 1.15 | Compressing Files

Some files may be too large to send quickly as an e-mail attachment. For example, files containing graphics tend to be quite large. Windows 7 includes a feature with which you can *compress*—reduce the file size of—one or more files into a single file that uses a *.zip* file extension. These files can then be uncompressed for editing on any other computer running Windows 7. Many file types—such as most Microsoft Office 2007 files, Adobe Acrobat files, and JPEG picture files—do not benefit much from file compression. However, compression is often used to combine many files into one file for easy distribution.

1 With your storage device selected, and four folders and 16 files displayed in the **file list**, click the **Ration Coupons-1** file, hold down [Shift], and then click the second **Regulations** file. If your files are in a different order, select all 16 files, but not the folders. Notice that the Details pane indicates that 16 files are selected. If the total size of the files does not display, under *16 items selected*, click *Show more details*. Notice that the 16 files have a total size of 5.00 MB.

2 In the **file list**, right-click any of the selected files, and then from the displayed shortcut menu, point to **Send to**. Compare your screen with Figure 1.48.

Figure 1.48

Compressed (zipped) folder command ——

Selected files ——

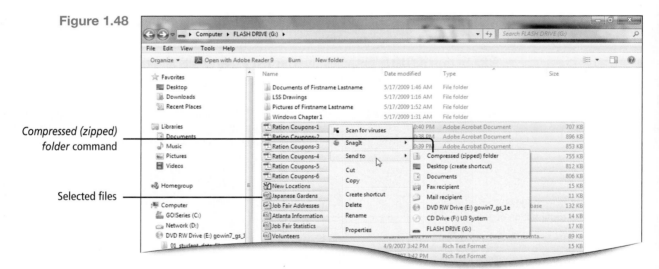

3 From the displayed list, click **Compressed (zipped)** folder, and then wait a moment for the files to be compressed.

> The compressed folder displays the name of the file you right-clicked, but displays in edit mode so you can change the file name.

Note | To Work with Third-Party Zip Programs

If you are using a third-party zip program, such as WinZip™ or PKZIP™, you will need to use that program to complete this task—the procedure listed below will not work.

---

4 With the compressed folder name still in edit mode, type **Files of Firstname Lastname** and then press Enter. Notice that the compressed folder size is approximately 4.9 MB, which is not a great space savings. Compare your screen with Figure 1.49.

Figure 1.49

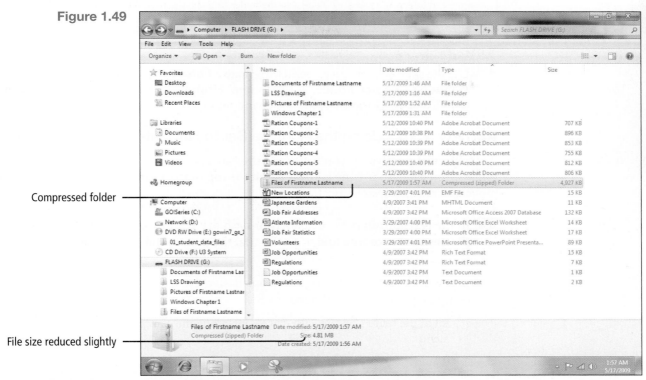

Compressed folder

File size reduced slightly

5 In the **file list**, double-click the **Files of Firstname Lastname** compressed folder. Compare your screen with Figure 1.50.

The files in the compressed folder are listed, along with their original sizes and their compressed sizes. The percent of space saved is indicated for each file. Some of the files show very little space savings, while in others the space saved is considerable. To extract the files from the compressed folder, you would click the *Extract all files* button on the Command bar. You can also open the files directly from the compressed folder.

Figure 1.50

Original file size

Extract all files button

Compressed file size

Files in compressed folder

Percent of space saved

Compressed folder

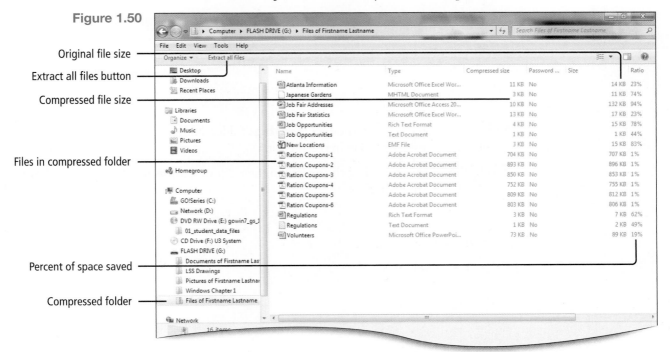

> **More Knowledge** | Adding More Items to a Compressed Folder
>
> You can add more files to an existing compressed folder by dragging files and dropping them on the compressed folder. You can drag the files to the folder from anywhere, and you can also drag folders into a compressed folder.

6 Use the skills you practiced earlier to create a **Full-screen Snip. Save Snip** 💾 to your **Windows Chapter 1** folder as **Lastname_Firstname_1B_Compressed_Folder** and then **Close** ❎ the Snipping Tool window.

Activity 1.16 | Using the Address Bar to Navigate Drives and Folders

In previous activities, you have used the Navigation pane to move between drives and folders. You can also use the address bar at the top of the Windows Explorer window to move quickly to a desired location.

1 In the **Navigation** pane, display your flash drive, and then click the **Pictures of Firstname Lastname** folder. Notice that the path to the current folder displays in the address bar.

2 In the Address bar, to the right of your flash drive name, click the **arrow**, and then compare your screen with Figure 1.51.

All of the folders on the flash drive—including the compressed folder—display in a menu.

Figure 1.51

Flash drive arrow

Folders in flash drive, including compressed folder

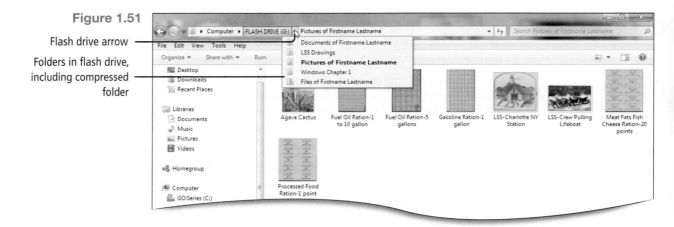

3 From the menu, click the **LSS Drawings** folder. Notice that the contents of the *LSS Drawings* folder display in the file list.

4 In the address bar, click the **arrow** to the right of **Computer**. Notice that all of the available drives display.

5 To the left of **Computer**, click the **arrow**, and then compare your screen with Figure 1.52.

> The top-level items in the Navigation pane display in a menu, along with commands for the Control Panel and the Recycle Bin.

Figure 1.52

Top-level items in Navigation pane

Opens the Control Panel

Opens the Recycle Bin

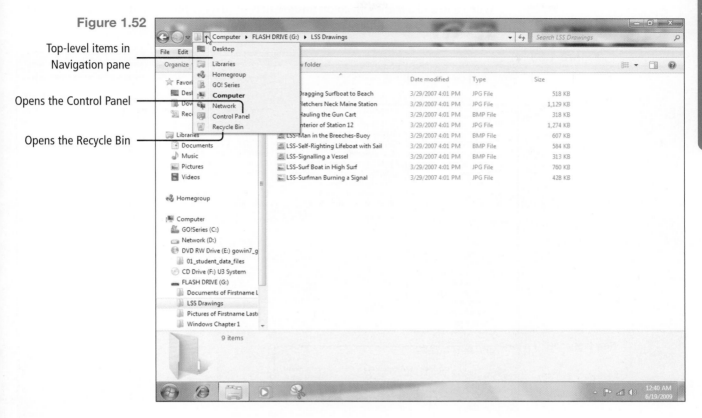

6 Click anywhere in the **file list** to close the menu.

Objective 6 | Find Files and Folders

As you use a computer, you will likely accumulate a large number of files and folders. It's easy to forget where you stored a file, or what you named it. Windows 7 provides several search functions with which you can find files and folders. You can also add tags to files. *Tags* are custom file properties that help you find and organize your files. Tags are part of a file's *metadata*—items that record and display information about a file, such as a title, a rating, the file name, and the file size.

Activity 1.17 | Adding Descriptions and Tags to Files

1 Be sure your storage device is selected, with the contents of the **LSS Drawings** folder displayed in the file list. Also be sure the **Details** pane is open at the bottom of the window.

2 Click the first file in the **file list**—**LSS-Dragging Surfboat to Beach**. Move the pointer to the line at the top of the **Details** pane to display the ⬍ pointer, and then drag the top of the Details pane to display three lines of details.

3 In the **Details** pane, click in the **Tags** box—to the right of the word *Tags*. Type **LSS** and then press →. Type **LSS Boat** and then press →. Type **Surfboat** and then compare your screen with Figure 1.53. Notice on the left side of the Details pane that the file type for this file is JPG—one of a number of image file types.

> When you add a tag, a semicolon immediately displays to the right of the insertion point. Semicolons separate multiple tags.

Figure 1.53

Selected file

New tags added

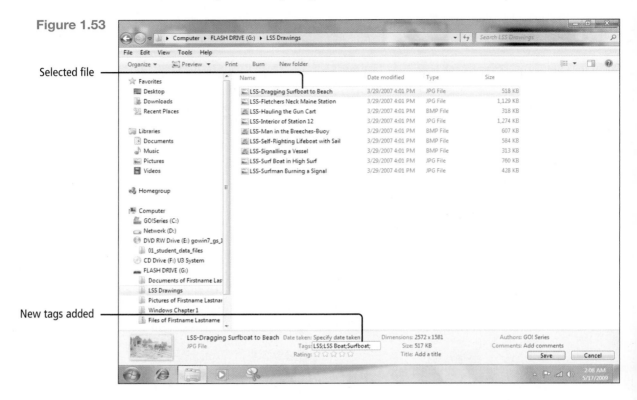

4 Press Enter to confirm the tags. Using the procedure you just practiced, add the same three tags to the **LSS-Surf Boat in High Surf** file. Notice on the left side of the Details pane that the file type for this file is JPG or JPEG.

5 Click the **LSS-Self-Righting Lifeboat with Sail** file. Notice that there is no place to add a tag.

> This image is a bitmap image, which does not support tags. Most Microsoft Office 2007 and 2010 default file formats support tags, as do many other file formats.

6 In the **Navigation** pane, click the **Pictures of Firstname Lastname** folder, and then click the file **LSS-Charlotte NY Station**. Add the following tags: **LSS** and **LSS Boat** and **LSS Boat Ramp** and then press Enter.

7 In the **Details** pane, click the **Title** box, type **Life Saving Station at Charlotte, NY** and then press Enter.

8 In the **file list**, right-click the **LSS-Charlotte NY Station** file, and then from the shortcut menu, click **Properties**. In the **Properties** dialog box, click the **Details tab**.

> The items you entered in the Details pane display, and there are several other categories of tags that you can add, including a rating of the picture or document.

9 In the **Properties** dialog box, under **Description**, click the fourth **Rating** star from the left. Under **Origin**, click the **Copyright** box, type **Public Domain** and then compare your screen with Figure 1.54.

Figure 1.54

Selected file

Rating tag

Copyright box

Title added

New tags added

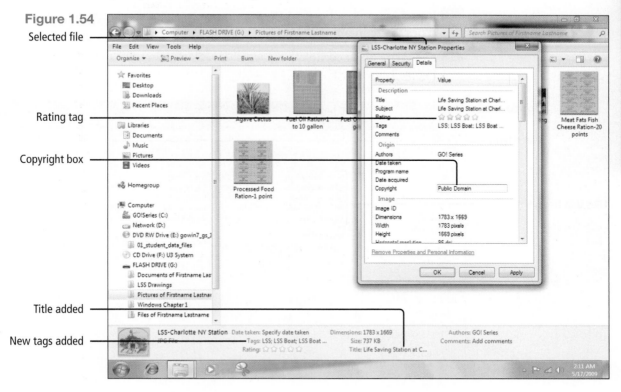

10 At the bottom of the **Properties** dialog box, click **OK**.

Activity 1.18 | Finding Files and Folders and Creating a Search Folder

1 In the **Navigation** pane, click your storage location name. Be sure your storage device is selected, and four folders, one compressed folder, and 16 files display in the file list.

2 Near the upper right corner of the window, click in the **Search** box, type **J** and then in the **file list**, examine the results of your search, as shown in Figure 1.55. If your search results do not display in the list format, to the right of the *Change your view* button [icon], click the *More options* arrow, and then click Details.

The program found all files and folders with words that begin with the letter *J*, along with all file types (file extensions) with words that begin with the letter *J*—in this case, all JPEG image files. Your files may display in a different order.

Figure 1.55

Letter to search for

File types beginning with the letter *J*

Files beginning with the letter *J*

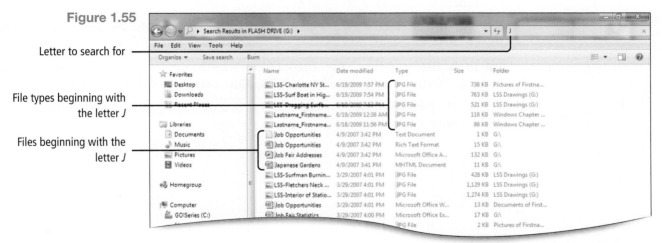

3 With the letter *J* already in the **Search** box, type the letter **P** and examine the search results. Notice that the only files, folders, or file types in your storage device that begin with the letters *JP* are the JPEG image files.

4 Press (Bksp), and notice that the search results again display all files, folders, and file types that contain the letter *J*.

5 Now type **ob** to complete the word *Job*. Notice that five files display, as shown in Figure 1.56.

Figure 1.56

Search term ————

Files that begin with *Job* ————

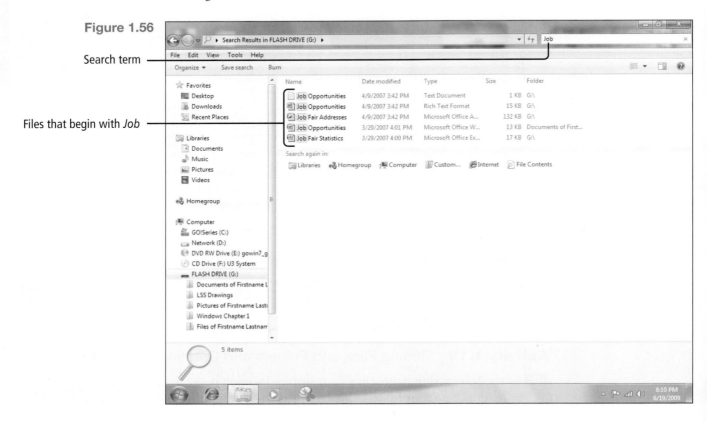

6 Press (Bksp) three times, type **LSS** and then notice that files and folders from various locations display in the file list.

7 Press (Spacebar), type **boat** and then notice that only one file or folder meets this search condition, even though you added *LSS Boat* as a tag to several files. Also notice that the file that was found had both search words, but they do not have to be next to each other.

> When you enter a word or phrase in the Search pane, only the file names, folder names, and file types are searched.

8 In the **file list**, below the displayed file, notice the search alternatives that are available. Under **Search again in**, click **File Contents**. Notice that three files display.

> The *File Contents* search extends the search to include tags, text that is a portion of a file name, or text inside the file.

9 On the Command bar, click the **Save search** button. In the displayed **Save As** dialog box, click **Save**. Compare your screen with Figure 1.57.

> A *search folder* is saved on your computer under **Favorites**—not on your removable storage device. A search folder retains all of the search conditions you specified during your search, and recreates the search every time you click the search folder. As you add more pictures with the *LSS Boat* tag to your removable storage device, the search folder will find them. It is important to remember that the search folder will only search the location you specified—it will not search the rest of the computer.

Figure 1.57

New search folder ———

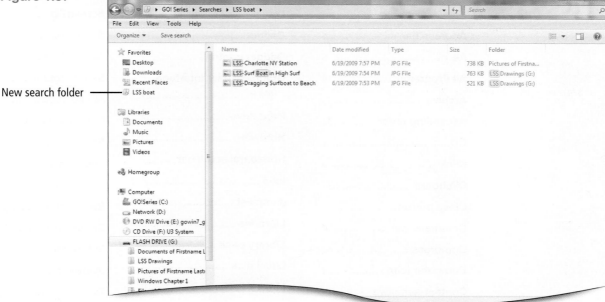

10 Use the skills you practiced earlier to create a **Full-screen Snip**. Save the snip to your **Windows Chapter 1** folder as **Lastname_Firstname_1B_Search_Folder** and submit all three file snips from Project 1B as directed. If you are directed to print the files, use the skills practiced in Activity 1.9 to create a WordPad document, add your name, drag the three snip files from this project, and then print the document. It is not necessary to save the WordPad file once you have printed it.

11 In the title bar, click the **Close** button to close the Windows Explorer window. Select and **Delete** the files and shortcuts you saved on the desktop, and then **Close** the gadgets that you added to the desktop.

More Knowledge | Using Wildcards in Searches

When you are searching for a particular type of file, you can specify the extension by using a wildcard, followed by the extension. A *wildcard* takes the place of one or more characters in a search. For example, if you wanted to search for all of your Excel 2007 files in the My Documents folder, select the folder, and then type *.xlsx* in the Search box. All files with the *.xlsx* extension will display. If you want to display all of your Excel files, including older versions (with the *.xls* extension), type *.xls*. This search will locate all *.xls* and *.xlsx* files. Similarly, you can search for all files beginning with *Fun* by typing *Fun**, which will return all files with those first three letters, including *Fundamentals of Business* and *Fun with Trombones*.

End **You have completed Project 1B** ————————————————————————

Content-Based Assessments

Summary

Windows 7 is a robust operating system that enables you to easily locate information and programs. It enables you to create, rename, move, copy, and delete files and folders. You can add key words and other information to the files to make searching easier and more accurate.

Key Terms

Screen ID

Identify each element of the screen by matching callout numbers shown in Figure 1.58 to a corresponding description.

Figure 1.58

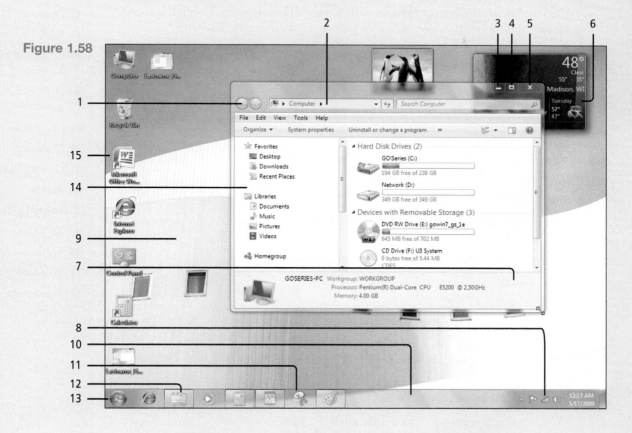

____ A. Address bar

____ B. Back button

____ C. Close button

____ D. Desktop

____ E. Details pane

____ F. Gadget

____ G. Icon

____ H. Maximize button

____ I. Minimize button

____ J. Navigation pane

____ K. Notification area

____ L. Snipping Tool button

____ M. Start button

____ N. Taskbar

____ O. Windows Explorer button

Matching

Match each term in the second column with its correct definition in the first column. Write the letter of the term on the blank line in front of the correct definition.

_____ 1. The Windows 7 user interface that features a three-dimensional look, with transparent window frames, live previews of open windows, and multiple color schemes.

_____ 2. A program that captures a screen or part of a screen.

_____ 3. Displays information about the drive, folder, or file selected in the file list.

_____ 4. A set of instructions that coordinates the activities of your computer.

_____ 5. A computer interface that shows documents as they will look in their final form and uses icons to represent programs.

_____ 6. A simple drawing program included with Windows 7.

_____ 7. Displays the Start button and the name of any open documents; it may also display shortcut buttons for other programs.

_____ 8. Command at the bottom of the Start menu that takes you to all available programs on your computer.

_____ 9. To remove the window from the screen without closing it.

_____ 10. To increase the size of a window to fill the screen.

_____ 11. The bar at the right side of a window that enables you to move up and down to view information that extends beyond the top and bottom of the screen.

_____ 12. The bar at the bottom of a window that enables you to move left and right to view information that extends beyond the left and right edges of the screen.

_____ 13. Move the mouse pointer while holding down the left mouse button, and then release at the appropriate time.

_____ 14. Work that you save and store on a drive, such as a Word document or a PowerPoint presentation.

_____ 15. A program that enables you to create and manage folders, and copy, move, sort, and delete files.

A All Programs

B Details pane

C Drag

D File

E Graphical user interface

F Horizontal scroll bar

G Maximize

H Minimize

I Operating system

J Paint

K Snipping Tool

L Taskbar

M Vertical scroll bar

N Windows Aero

O Windows Explorer

Content-Based Assessments

Multiple Choice

Circle the correct answer.

1. In the Windows Explorer window, this pane displays Favorites, Libraries, Computer, and Network information.
   - **a.** Preview
   - **b.** Navigation
   - **c.** Details

2. The working area of the Windows 7 screen—consisting of program icons, a taskbar, a Start button, and gadgets—is the:
   - **a.** desktop
   - **b.** window
   - **c.** Notification area

3. The arrow, I-beam, or other symbol that shows the location or position of the mouse on your screen is the mouse:
   - **a.** button
   - **b.** cursor
   - **c.** pointer

4. The area on the right side of the taskbar that keeps you informed about processes that are occurring in the background, such as antivirus software, network connections, and other utility programs, is the:
   - **a.** Quick Launch toolbar
   - **b.** Notification area
   - **c.** program icon

5. Custom file properties such as names, places, and descriptions that are added to files are called:
   - **a.** jump lists
   - **b.** details
   - **c.** metadata

6. You can activate this by pointing to an object and clicking the right mouse button.
   - **a.** active window
   - **b.** shortcut menu
   - **c.** gadget

7. When you create a new folder, the folder name displays:
   - **a.** in edit mode
   - **b.** in the Details pane
   - **c.** on the desktop

8. When you create a search folder, it displays in the Navigation pane under this category:
   - **a.** Favorites
   - **b.** Computer
   - **c.** Libraries

9. A dynamic program—such as a clock, a stock market ticker, or a weather window—that displays on the desktop is a:
   - **a.** gadget
   - **b.** tag
   - **c.** snip

10. The three or four characters to the right of the period in a file name is called:
    - **a.** metadata
    - **b.** a wildcard
    - **c.** a file extension

Content-Based Assessments

Skills Review | Project 1C Using Windows 7

Apply a combination of the 1A and 1B skills.

In the following Skills Review, you will copy files from your student data disk to a flash drive, create and rename folders, and move files. You will also add tags to files and search for files using the Search box. Your completed documents will look similar to the ones shown in Figure 1.59.

Project Files

For Project 1C, you will need the following files:

36 sample files, and two folders containing 14 additional files

You will save your documents as:

Lastname_Firstname_1C_Screen_Saver
Lastname_Firstname_1C_Desktop
Lastname_Firstname_1C_Folders
Lastname_Firstname_1C_Tags

Project Results

Figure 1.59

(Project 1C Using Windows 7 continues on the next page)

Content-Based Assessments

Skills Review | Project **1C** Using Windows 7 (continued)

1 Turn on your computer and if necessary follow the log-on instructions required for the computer you are using.

2 Move the pointer to an open area of the desktop, and then right-click. From the shortcut menu, move the pointer to the bottom of the list, and then click **Personalize**. At the bottom of the **Personalization** window, click the **Screen Saver** button. Click the **Screen saver box arrow**, and then from the displayed list, click **Bubbles**.

3 If the **Snipping Tool** does not display on your taskbar, click the **Start** button, point to **All Programs**, click **Accessories**, right-click **Snipping Tool**, and then click **Pin to Taskbar**. On the taskbar, click the **Snipping Tool** button. In the **Snipping Tool** window, click the arrow to the right of the **New** button, and then click **Full-screen Snip**.

4 In the **Snipping Tool** window, click the **Save Snip** button. In the **Save As** dialog box, in the left pane, scroll down to display the **Computer** drives. Click your flash drive, and then in the Command bar, click the **New folder** button. Name the new folder **Windows Project C** Press [Enter], and then press [Enter] again to open the new folder. In the **File name** box, type **Lastname_Firstname_1C_ Screen_Saver** Be sure the **Save as type** box displays *JPEG file*. Click **Save**, and then **Close** the Snipping Tool window.

5 If you want to use the Bubbles screen saver, at the bottom of the Screen Saver Settings dialog box, click OK; otherwise, click Cancel.

6 At the bottom of the **Personalization** window, click **Desktop Background**. Use the vertical scroll bar to display the **United States** desktop backgrounds, and then click the picture of the **stone arch**. Click **Save changes** to apply the new background, and then **Close** the Personalization window.

7 Click the **Start** button, point to **All Programs**, and then click **Accessories**. Right-click **WordPad**, point to **Send to**, click **Desktop (create shortcut)**, and then click in any open area of the desktop.

8 In an open area of the desktop, right-click to display a shortcut menu, and then click **Gadgets**. Double-click the **Clock** gadget, double-click the **Stocks** gadget, and then double-click the **CPU Meter** gadget. **Close** the Gadgets window. Point to the **CPU Usage** gadget, and then click the **Larger size** button. Drag the **CPU Usage** gadget to the top of the desktop.

9 Use the skills you practiced to create a **Full-screen Snip** of the desktop, **Save** it in the **Windows Project C** folder as **Lastname_Firstname_1C_Desktop** and then **Close** the Snipping Tool window.

10 On the taskbar, click the **Windows Explorer** button. If this button is not available, click the Start button, point to All Programs, click Accessories, and then click Windows Explorer. Insert your student data CD. In the **Windows Explorer** window, in the **Navigation** pane, click the drive that contains your student data files. To the left of the drive name, click the open arrow to display the **01_student_data_files** folder, and then click that folder to display the folders and files in the file list.

11 In the **Navigation** pane, in the drive that contains your student files, be sure the folders display. In the **file list**, drag the **XML Files** folder to the **Windows Project C** folder on your flash drive.

12 At the top of the **file list**, click the **Type** column heading. Widen the **Type** column so you can see all of the file types. Click the first **Adobe Acrobat** document—*Ration Coupons-1*—, hold down [Shift], and then click the last **Adobe Acrobat** document—*Ration Coupons-6*. Drag the selected files to the **Windows Project C** folder on your flash drive. Then, select all of the files with a **Type** that begins *Microsoft Office*. Drag these 15 files to the **Windows Project C** folder on your flash drive.

13 In the **Navigation** pane, locate your flash drive, and then click the **Windows Project C** folder. On the Command bar click the **New Folder** button, and then name the folder **Adobe Acrobat Files** Select the six **Adobe Acrobat Files** and drag them to the folder you just created. In the **Navigation** pane, expand the **Windows Project C** folder, and then click the **Windows Project C** folder to display the folder contents.

14 In the **file list**, right-click the file **Volunteers**, and then click **Rename**. Rename the file **Job Fair Volunteers** In the same list of files, right-click the **Lightning** file, and then from the shortcut menu, click **Delete**. In the message box, click **Yes**.

15 At the top of the **file list**, click the **Name** column heading as necessary to display the folders and files in ascending (*a* to *z*) order. Use the skills you practiced to create a **Full-screen Snip** of the Windows Explorer window, **Save** it in the **Windows Project C** folder as

(Project 1C Using Windows 7 continues on the next page)

Skills Review | Project **1C** Using Windows 7 (continued)

Lastname_Firstname_1C_Folders and then **Close** the Snipping Tool window.

16 In the **file list**, click the **Job Fair Statistics** file. In the **Details** pane, click to the right of **Tags**. In the **Tags** box, type **Atlanta** press →, and then type **Job Fair** Add the same tags to the **Atlanta Information** file.

17 In the **Search** box, type **Atlanta** and then press Enter. In the **file list**, click **File Contents** to include files with the word *Atlanta* in the files or in the file tags. If necessary, change the display to Details. Use the skills you practiced to create a **Full-screen Snip** of the Windows Explorer window, **Save** it in the **Windows Project C**

folder as **Lastname_Firstname_1C_Tags** and then **Close** the Snipping Tool window.

18 Submit all four snips as directed. If you are directed to print the files, use the skills practiced in Activity 1.9 to create a WordPad document, add your name, drag the four snip files from this project, and then print the document. It is not necessary to save the WordPad file once you have printed it.

19 Remove all desktop and taskbar shortcuts that you created in this project, and then **Close** all three gadgets that you added.

 You have completed Project 1C —————————

Glossary

Active window The window in which the mouse pointer's movements commands, or text entry occur when two or more windows are open.

Address bar A toolbar that displays the organizational path to the active file, folder, or window.

Aero See Windows Aero.

All Programs Command at the bottom of the Start menu that takes you to all available programs on your computer.

Archive To back up files and store them somewhere other than the main hard drive.

Ascending order Files or folders listed from *a* to *z* when sorted.

Background See Desktop background.

CD A compact disc—an optical storage device used to store data and which can be read-only or read-write.

Click To press the left mouse button one time.

Clipboard A temporary storage area in Windows that stores the most recently copied item.

Close button A shortcut button in a title bar that closes a window or a program.

Command bar The area at the top of a window that displays commands relevant to the open window.

Compress Reduce the size of a file or combine several files into one.

Computer icon An icon that represents the computer on which you are working, and that provides access to the drives, folders, and files on your computer.

Content pane Displays files and folders stored in the selected disk drive or folder in the Navigation pane.

Context-sensitive command A command associated with activities in which you are engaged; often activated by right-clicking a screen item.

Descending order Files or folders listed from *z* to *a* when sorted.

Desktop The working area of the Windows 7 screen, consisting of program icons, a taskbar, a sidebar, and a Start button.

Desktop background The picture, pattern, or color that displays on the desktop.

Details pane Displays details about the drive, folder, or file selected in the Content pane.

Dialog box A box that asks you to make a decision about an individual object or topic. Dialog boxes do not have Minimize buttons.

Double-click Press the left mouse button two times in rapid succession, using caution not to move the mouse.

Drag Move the mouse pointer while holding down the left mouse button, and then release at the appropriate time.

Drive An area of storage that is formatted with the Windows file system and that has a drive letter such as C.

DVD A digital video (or versatile) disc—an optical storage device used to store data, and which can be read-only or read-write.

Edit mode A Windows mode that enables you to change the name of a file or folder, and works the same in all Windows applications.

Favorites The top part of the Navigation pane that displays favorite destinations associated with the current user.

File Work that you save and store on a drive, such as a Word document or a PowerPoint presentation.

File extension The three or four characters to the right of the period in a file name. Extensions tell the computer the program to use to open the file. File extensions can be displayed or hidden.

File list Displays the contents of the current folder or library.

Flash drive A small storage device that plugs into a computer USB port; also called a thumb drive or a USB drive.

Folder Storage area, represented on the screen by a picture of a paper file folder, used to store files or other folders.

Gadget A dynamic program—such as a clock, a stock market ticker, or a weather window—that displays on the desktop, usually in the Windows Sidebar.

Gadget controls A set of tools that includes a Drag gadget button in the shape of 12 small dots, an Options button in the shape of a wrench, a Larger/Smaller size button, and a Close button.

Graphical user interface (GUI) A computer interface that shows documents as they will look in their final form and uses icons to represent programs.

Hard drive A large disk drive inside your computer, also referred to as a Local Disk.

Hardware The computer memory, disk drive space, attached devices such as printers and scanners, and the central processing unit (CPU).

Horizontal scroll bar The bar at the bottom of a window that enables you to move left and right to view information that extends beyond the left and right edges of the screen.

Icon A graphic representation; often a small image on a button that enables you to run a program or program function.

Jump list A shortcut menu from an icon on the taskbar that displays frequent destinations you might want to visit from that program.

Libraries Folders used to sort files by file type.

Library pane Displays above the file list when a library is selected in the Navigation pane.

Local disk A large disk drive inside your computer, also referred to as a hard disk.

Maximize To increase the size of a window to fill the screen.

Menu A list of commands within a category.

Menu bar The bar near the top of a window that lists the names of menu categories.

Metadata Information about a file, such as tags, a title, a rating, the file name, and the file size.

Minimize To remove the window from the screen without closing it. Minimized windows can be reopened by clicking the associated button in the taskbar.

Mouse pointer The arrow, I-beam, or other symbol that shows the location or position of the mouse on your screen. Also called the pointer.

Navigation pane The pane on the left side of the Computer or Windows Explorer window that contains Favorites, Libraries, access to personal files and folders, and other items.

Notification area Area on the right side of the taskbar that keeps you informed about processes that are occurring in the background, such as antivirus software, network connections, and other utility programs. It also displays the time.

Operating system A set of instructions that coordinates the activities of your computer. Microsoft Windows 7 is an operating system.

Paint A program included with Windows in which graphics are created or edited.

Peek Use the *Show desktop* button to make the open windows transparent so you can see the desktop.

Pinned programs area An area at the top of the Start menu that is reserved for programs that you want to display permanently, although you can also delete programs from this area.

Pointer See mouse pointer.

Recycle Bin A storage area for files that have been deleted. Files can be recovered from the Recycle bin or permanently removed.

Restore Return a window to the size it was before it was maximized, using the Restore Down button.

Right-click Click the right mouse button to activate a shortcut menu.

Screen saver A picture or animation that displays on your screen after a set period of computer inactivity.

ScreenTip A small box, activated by holding the pointer over a button or other screen object, that displays the name of a screen element.

Scroll box The box in the vertical and horizontal scroll bars that can be dragged to reposition the document on the screen. The size of the scroll box also indicates the relative size of the document.

Search box A box in which you type a search word or phrase.

Search folder Retains all of the search conditions you specified during your search, and recreates the search every time you click the search folder.

Shake Use the title bar to move a window back and forth quickly to hide all other open windows.

Shortcut menu A menu activated by placing the pointer over an object and clicking the right mouse button.

Snip A screen or part of a screen captured using the Snipping Tool.

Snipping tool A program used to capture a screen or part of a screen.

Start button The button on the left side of the taskbar that is used to start programs, change system settings, find Windows help, or shut down the computer.

Start menu A menu that enables you to access the programs on your computer, and also enables you to change the way Windows operates, to access and configure your network, and to get help and support when it is needed.

Status area Another name for the notification area on the right side of the taskbar.

Submenu A second-level menu activated by selecting a menu option.

System tray Another name for the notification area on the right side of the taskbar.

Tags Custom file properties such as names, places, and descriptions that are added to files to enable you to categorize and find files more quickly.

Taskbar Displays the Start button and the name of any open documents. The taskbar also displays shortcut buttons for other programs.

Thumb drive A small storage device that plugs into a computer USB port; also called a USB drive or a flash drive.

Thumbnail A miniature representation of the contents of a window or file.

Title bar Displays the program icon, the name of the document, and the name of the program. The Minimize, Maximize/Restore Down, and Close buttons are grouped on the right side of the title bar.

USB drive A small storage device that plugs into a computer USB port; also called a thumb drive or a flash drive.

Vertical scroll bar The bar at the right side of a window that enables you to move up and down to view information that extends beyond the top and bottom of the screen.

Wildcard A character, such as an asterisk, that can be used to match any number of characters in a file search.

Window A box that displays information or a program, such as a letter, Excel, or a calculator. Windows usually consist of title bars, toolbars, menu bars, and status bars. A window will always have a Minimize button.

Window name The name that displays in a window's title bar.

Windows An operating system that coordinates the activities of a computer.

Windows Aero The Windows user interface that features a three-dimensional look, with transparent window frames, live previews of open windows, and multiple color schemes. Aero is an acronym for **A**uthentic, **E**nergetic, **R**eflective, **O**pen.

Windows Explorer A program that enables you to create and manage folders, and manage copy, move, sort, and delete files.

WordPad A simple word processing program that comes with Windows 7.

Index

The following content is taken from:

GO! with Microsoft® Windows™ 8: Getting Started
by Shelley Gaskin

GO!

with Microsoft®

Windows 8

Getting Started

Shelley Gaskin

PEARSON

Boston   Columbus   Indianapolis   New York   San Francisco   Upper Saddle River
Amsterdam   Cape Town   Dubai   London   Madrid   Milan   Munich   Paris   Montréal   Toronto
Delhi   Mexico City   São Paulo   Sydney   Hong Kong   Seoul   Singapore   Taipei   Tokyo

Table of Contents

Getting Started with Windows 8

violetkaipa/Fotolia

In This Chapter

In this chapter, you will use Microsoft Windows 8, which is software that manages your computer's hardware, software, and data files. Windows 8 also helps you create a personal dashboard to connect you to the things that matter to you. You will use the taskbar and desktop features to get your work done with ease and use Windows Store apps to get your latest personal information and to find information and entertainment. You will sign in to your computer, explore the features of Windows 8, create folders and save files, use Windows Store apps, manage multiple windows, sign out of your computer, and examine user accounts.

The projects in this chapter relate to the **Bell Orchid Hotels**, headquartered in Boston, and which own and operate resorts and business-oriented hotels. Resort properties are located in popular destinations, including Honolulu, Orlando, San Diego, and Santa Barbara. The resorts offer deluxe accommodations and a wide array of dining options. Other Bell Orchid hotels are located in major business centers and offer the latest technology in their meeting facilities. Bell Orchid offers extensive educational opportunities for employees. The company plans to open new properties and update existing properties over the next decade.

Getting to Know Windows 8

PROJECT ACTIVITIES

In Activities 1.01 through 1.10, you will participate in training along with Steven Ramos and Barbara Hewitt, both of whom work for the Information Technology Department at the Boston headquarters office of the Bell Orchid Hotels. After completing this part of the training, you will be able to sign in and sign out of your computer, create folders and save files on a removable storage device, use Windows Store apps, and manage your user account. You will capture two screens that will look similar to Figure 1.1.

PROJECT FILES

For Project 1A, you will need the following files:

A new Snip file and a new Windows 8 screen capture that you will initiate when prompted to do so

You will save your files as:

Lastname_Firstname_1A_Zoom_Snip
Lastname_Firstname_1A_Graph_Snip

PROJECT RESULTS

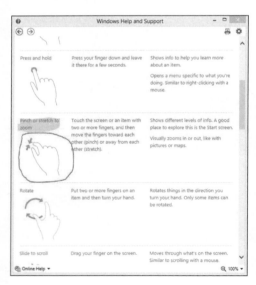

FIGURE 1.1 Project 1A Getting to Know Windows 8

1

WINDOWS 8

A *program* is a set of instructions that a computer uses to accomplish a task. A program is also referred to as an *application* or simply as an *app*—the shortened version of the word *application*. Apps help you perform tasks for a specific purpose; for example, to create a document using word processing software, to play a game, to view the latest weather report, or to manage information.

Windows 8 is an *operating system* developed by Microsoft Corporation that works with mobile computing devices of all types and also with traditional PCs. An operating system is a specific type of computer program that manages the other programs on a computer, and that includes computer devices such as desktop computers, laptop computers, smartphones, tablet computers, and game consoles. You need an operating system to:

- use apps
- coordinate the use of your computer hardware such as a keyboard, mouse, touchpad, touchscreen, game controller, or printer
- organize data that you store on your computer or access data that you store in other locations

The term *desktop app* commonly refers to a computer program that is installed on the hard drive of your computer and requires a computer operating system like Microsoft Windows or Apple OS to run. The programs in Microsoft Office such as Word and Excel are popular desktop apps. Adobe's Photoshop is a popular desktop app. Desktop apps typically have hundreds of features that take time to learn and use efficiently.

Apps installed on your computer's hard drive are referred to as *desktop apps* and apps that run from the device software or the browser software on PCs, tablet computers, game consoles, or smartphones are referred to simply as *apps*.

An app is usually a smaller application designed for a single purpose. You might already be familiar with apps that run on an Apple iPhone or an Android phone or a Windows phone; for example, games like Angry Birds and Words with Friends; information apps like The Weather Channel and ESPN ScoreCenter; apps provided by your bank to enable you to conduct transactions on your smartphone; and services like Skype or Google Search.

Similarly, *Windows Store apps* are built for specific purposes; for example, to view your photos, read sports information, play games, organize your list of contacts, or read updates to your social networks like Facebook and Twitter.

> **ALERT!** **Variations in Screen Organization, Colors, and Functionality Are Common in Windows 8**
>
> Individuals and organizations can determine how Windows 8 displays; therefore, the colors and the organization of various elements on the screen can vary. Your college or organization may customize Windows 8 to display a college picture or logo, or restrict access to certain features. The basic functions and structure of Windows 8 are not changed by such variations. You can be confident that the skills you will practice in this textbook apply to Windows 8 regardless of available functionality or differences between the figures in the book and your screen.

Activity 1.01 | Understanding User Accounts in Windows 8

> **NOTE** **Comparing Your Screen with the Figures in This Textbook**
>
> Your screen will more closely match the figures shown in this textbook if you set your screen resolution to 1280 × 768. At other resolutions, your screen will closely resemble, but not match, the figures shown. To view your screen's resolution, on the desktop, right-click in a blank area, click *Screen resolution*, and then click the Resolution arrow. To adjust the resolution, move the slider to the desired setting, and then click OK.

On a single computer, Windows 8 can have multiple user accounts. You can share a computer with other people in your family or organization and each person can have his or her own information and settings—none of which others can see. Each user on a single computer is referred to as a *local account*.

But what if you have or use more than one computer? Perhaps you have a computer at home and also a laptop computer that you use at school or when traveling. Maybe you have, or are thinking about getting, a tablet computer. The frustration of working on multiple computers is that they do not look the same. Settings and favorite websites that you have on one PC do not automatically appear on other PCs that you use. Additionally, if you get a new PC, you must try to set it up all over again to look like your old PC.

With Windows 8, you can create a *Microsoft account*, and then use that account to sign in to *any* Windows 8 system. Signing in with a Microsoft account is recommended because you can:

- download apps from the Windows Store.
- get your online content—email, social network updates, updated news—automatically displayed in an app when you sign in.
- sync settings online to make every Windows 8 computer you use look and feel the same.

To use a Windows 8 computer, you must establish and then sign in with either a local account or a Microsoft account. Regardless of which one you select, you should provide an email address to associate with the user account name.

If you create and then sign in with a local account, you can still connect to the Internet, but you will not have the advantage of having your personal arrangement of apps displayed to you every time you sign in to a Windows 8 PC. As shown in Figure 1.2, a new user added to a Windows 8 PC can provide an email address to associate with the account. You can use any email address to create a local account—similar to other online services where an email address is your user ID.

FIGURE 1.2

To create a Microsoft account, supply a *hotmail.com*, a *live.com*, or an *outlook.com* email address—or create one from the link at the bottom of the screen to display the form for a new Microsoft account. After you create a Microsoft account, you *do not* have to use it for your email or for any purpose other than to use the Windows 8 interface and to *roam* all of your computing devices. To roam means that you can set up one computer, for example your desktop computer, and then synchronize—roam—all the same settings to your laptop, to your tablet PC, to your Windows phone—to any other device you have that uses Windows 8.

By signing in with a Microsoft account, your computer becomes your connected device where you—not your files—are the center of activity.

To check how well you understand user accounts in Windows 8, take a moment to answer the following questions:

1 ▶ On a single Windows 8 computer, multiple people can have a user account with their own information and _____.

2 ▶ On a Windows 8 computer, it is recommended that you create a Microsoft account—if you do not have one—and then use that account to sign in because you can sync settings online to make every Windows 8 computer you sign in to _____ and feel the same.

3 ▶ To use a Windows 8 computer, you must establish and then sign in with either a _____ account or a Microsoft account.

4 ▶ After you create a Microsoft account, you do not have to use it for your _____ or for any other purpose.

5 ▶ To _____ means that you can set up one computer and then sync (synchronize) all the same settings to any other device you have that uses Windows 8.

Activity 1.02 | Turning On Your Computer, Signing In to a Windows 8 User Account, and Exploring the Windows 8 Environment

Before you begin any computer activity, you must, if necessary, turn on your computer. This process is commonly referred to as **booting the computer**. Because Windows 8 does not require you to completely shut down your computer except to install or repair a hardware device, in most instances moving the mouse or pressing a key will wake your computer in a few seconds. So most of the time you will skip the lengthier boot process.

In this activity, you will turn on your computer and sign in to Windows 8. Within an organization, the sign-in process may differ from that of your own computer.

ALERT! **You Must Have a User Account—Preferably a Microsoft Account—on the Computer at Which You Are Working**

On a Windows 8 PC, you must have a user account in order to sign in. On your own computer, you created your user account when you installed Windows 8 or when you set up your new computer that came with Windows 8. In a classroom or lab, check with your instructor to see how you will sign in to Windows 8. Recall that signing in with a Microsoft account, as described in the previous activity, will enable you to use apps with updated data.

---

1 ▶ If necessary, turn on your computer, and then compare your screen with Figure 1.3.

The Windows 8 **Lock screen** displays a picture—this might be a default picture, or a picture that you selected if you have personalized your system already. The Lock screen displays the time, day, and date, and one or more icons—sometimes referred to as **badges**—representing the status of your Internet connection, your battery if you are using a tablet or laptop, and any **Lock screen apps** you might have selected.

Your organization might have a custom sign-in screen with a logo or sign-in instructions, which will differ from the one shown.

FIGURE 1.3

Lock screen picture (yours may differ)

Time/Day/Date (yours will differ)

Icons can display under date indicating Internet and battery status (none shown here)

2 Determine whether you are working with a mouse and keyboard system or with a touchscreen system. If you are working with a touchscreen, determine whether you will use a stylus pen or the touch of your fingers.

Windows 8 is optimized for touchscreen computers and also works with a mouse and keyboard in the way you are probably most accustomed. If your device has a touchscreen, you can use the following gestures with your fingers in place of mouse and keyboard commands:

- Tap an item to click it.
- Press and hold an item for a few seconds and then release to right-click it.
- Touch the screen or an item with two or more fingers and then pinch together to zoom in or stretch your fingers apart to zoom out.
- Slide your finger on the screen to scroll—slide left to scroll right and slide right to scroll left.
- Slide to rearrange—similar to dragging with a mouse.
- Swipe from edge—from right to expose charms; from left to expose open apps, snap apps, or close apps; from top or bottom to show commands or close an app.
- Swipe—slide an item a short distance with a quick movement—to select an item and bring up app commands, if any.

> **NOTE** | **This Book Assumes You Are Using a Mouse and Keyboard but You Can Also Use Touch**
>
> The instruction in this textbook uses terminology that assumes you are using a mouse and keyboard, but you need only substitute the gestures listed above to move through the instruction easily using touch. If a touch gesture needs more clarification, a *By Touch* box will assist you in using the correct gesture. Because more precision is needed, for desktop operations touching with a stylus pen may be preferable to touch using your fingers. When working with Windows Store apps, finger gestures are precise.

3 Press Enter to display the Windows 8 sign-in screen.

> **⟳ BY TOUCH** | On the Lock screen, swipe upward to display the sign-in screen. Tap your user image if necessary to display the Password box.

4 If you are the displayed user, type your password (if you have established one) and press Enter. If you are not the displayed user, click your user image if it displays or click the *Switch user* arrow and then click your user image. Type your password, and then compare your screen with Figure 1.4.

The Windows 8 *Start screen* displays with square and rectangular boxes—referred to as *tiles*—from which you can access apps, websites, programs, and tools for using your computer by simply clicking or tapping them.

Think of the Start screen as your connected *dashboard*—a one-screen view of links to information and programs that matter to *you*—through which you can connect with the people, activities, places, and apps that you care about. Some tiles are referred to as *live tiles*, meaning they are constantly updated with fresh information relevant to you—the number of new email messages you have, new sports scores that you are interested in, or new updates to social networks such as Facebook or Twitter. Live tiles are at the center of your Windows 8 experience.

As you progress in your study of Windows 8, you will learn to customize the Start screen and add, delete, and organize tiles into meaningful groups. Your Start screen will not look like anyone else's; you will customize it to suit your own information needs.

FIGURE 1.4

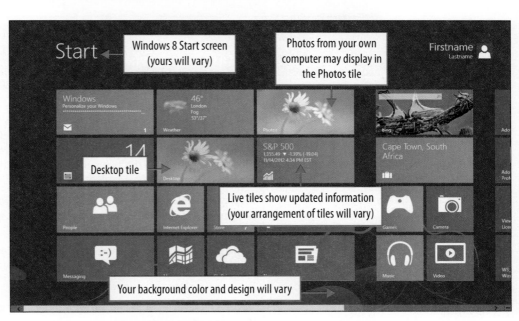

NOTE   **Differing Sign-In Procedures and Passwords**

Depending on whether you are working on your own computer, in a college lab, or in an organization, your sign-in process may differ. If you have a different sign-in screen, sign in as directed and move to Step 5 of this activity. If you are working in a classroom or lab, ask your instructor or lab assistant about the user account name and password to use. On your own computer, use your own user account name and password if you established a password.

---

5 On your **Start screen**, locate and then move the mouse pointer over—*point to*—the **Desktop tile**, and then *click*—press the left button on your mouse pointing device—to display the **Windows desktop**.

The *mouse pointer* is any symbol that displays on your screen in response to moving your mouse.

6 ▷ Compare your screen with Figure 1.5, and then take a moment to study the parts of the Windows desktop as shown in the table in Figure 1.6.

FIGURE 1.5

Recycle Bin

Desktop (your background may vary)

Program buttons for Internet Explorer and File Explorer (your group may differ)

Taskbar

Expand notification area button

Notification area

Network notification icon

Action Center icon

Speakers icon

FIGURE 1.6

PARTS OF THE WINDOWS 8 DESKTOP	
Action Center icon in the notification area	Displays the **Action Center**—a central place to view alerts and take actions related to things that need your attention.
Desktop	Serves as a surface for your work, like the top of an actual desk. Here you can arrange **icons**—small pictures that represent a file, folder, program, or other object—on the desktop such as shortcuts to programs, files, folders, and various types of documents in the same manner you would arrange physical objects on top of a desk.
Desktop background	Displays the colors and graphics of your desktop; you can change the **desktop background** to look the way you want it, such as using a picture or a solid color. Also referred to as **wallpaper**.
Expand notification area button	Displays additional icons related to your notifications.
Network notification icon	Displays the status of your network.
Notification area	Displays notification icons and the system clock and calendar; sometimes referred to as the **system tray**.
Program buttons	Launch **Internet Explorer**, the web browser program developed by Microsoft that is included with Windows 8, and **File Explorer**, the program that displays the contents of libraries, folders, and files on your computer, and also enables you to perform tasks related to your files and folders such as copying, moving, and renaming.
Recycle Bin	Contains files and folders that you delete. When you delete a file or folder, it is not actually deleted; it stays in the Recycle Bin if you want it back, until you take an action to empty the Recycle Bin.
Speakers icon	Displays the status of your computer's speakers (if any).
Taskbar	Contains program buttons to launch programs and buttons for all open programs; by default, it is located at the bottom of the desktop, but you can move it. You can customize the number and arrangement of buttons.

Activity 1.03 | Pinning a Program to the Taskbar

Snipping Tool is a program within Windows 8 that captures an image of all or part of your computer's screen within desktop apps. A *snip*, as the captured image is called, can be annotated, saved, copied, or shared via email. This is also referred to as a *screen capture* or a *screenshot*.

1 Point to the lower left corner of your screen to display the **Start screen** icon ▦ and then click one time to display the **Start screen**. Although you will not immediately see your typing, begin to type **snipping** and then compare your screen with Figure 1.7.

> The easiest and fastest way to search for an app is to use the *Start search* feature—from the Start screen, just start to type. By default, Windows 8 searches for apps, but you can easily change to search for settings or files.
>
> The Start search feature searches for all apps—both desktop apps and Windows Store apps.

⟳ BY TOUCH   On a touchscreen, swipe in from right edge of the screen, and then tap Search. Tap in the Search box to display the on-screen keyboard, and then begin to type *snipping*.

FIGURE 1.7

2 On the left, with **Snipping Tool** bordered in white—referred to as the *focus* of the search—press ⏎ one time.

> The desktop redisplays, the Snipping Tool dialog box displays on the desktop, and on the taskbar, the Snipping Tool program button displays framed in a lighter shade to indicate that the program is open.
>
> A *dialog box* is a small window that displays options for completing a task.

⟳ BY TOUCH   Tap the Snipping Tool app.

3 On the taskbar, point to the **Snipping Tool program button** 📷 and then *right-click*—click the right mouse button one time. On the displayed **Jump List**, click **Pin this program to taskbar**.

> A *Jump List* displays destinations and tasks from a program's taskbar button.

⟳ BY TOUCH   On the taskbar, use the *Swipe to select* technique—swipe upward with a short quick movement—to display the Jump List. On the list, tap *Pin this program to taskbar*.

4 Point to the upper right corner of the **Snipping Tool** dialog box, and then click **Close** ▣.

> Because you will use Snipping Tool frequently while completing the projects in this textbook, it is recommended that you leave Snipping Tool pinned to your taskbar.

A *file* is a collection of information stored on a computer under a single name. Examples of a file include a Word document, an Excel workbook, a picture, a song, or a program. A *folder* is a container in which you can store files. Windows 8 organizes and keeps track of your electronic files by letting you create and label electronic folders into which you can place your files.

In this activity, you will create a new folder on a *removable storage device*. Removable storage devices, such as a USB flash drive, are commonly used to transfer information from one computer to another. Such devices are also useful when you want to work with your files on different computers. For example, you probably have files that you work with at your college, at home, and possibly at your workplace.

A *drive* is an area of storage that is formatted with a file system compatible with your operating system and is identified by a drive letter. For example, your computer's *hard disk drive*—the primary storage device located inside your computer where some of your files and programs are typically stored—is usually designated as drive C. Removable storage devices that you insert into your computer will be designated with a drive letter—the letter designation varies from one computer to another.

As you progress in your study of Windows 8, you will also learn to use *cloud storage*—storage space on an Internet site that can also display as a drive on your computer. When you create a Microsoft account, free cloud storage called *SkyDrive* is provided to you.

ALERT! You will need a USB flash drive to complete this activity.

---

1 Be sure your Windows desktop is still displayed. Insert a USB flash drive into your computer.

If this is the first time you have used this device in the computer, in the upper right portion of your screen, a message might indicate *Tap to choose what happens with removable drives*.

You might also hear a sound and see a message in the taskbar that the device software is being installed.

2 If necessary, click the message in the upper right corner, and then click *Take no action*. If a window opens displaying the contents of your USB device, in the upper right corner click **Close ⊠**.

3 On the taskbar, click **File Explorer** 📄. Compare your screen with Figure 1.8.

The *folder window* for *Libraries* displays. A folder window displays the contents of the current location—folder, library, or drive—and contains helpful parts so that you can *navigate*—explore within the file organizing structure of Windows.

A *library* is a collection of items, such as files and folders, assembled from various locations. A *location* is any disk drive, folder, or other place in which you can store files and folders.

FIGURE 1.8

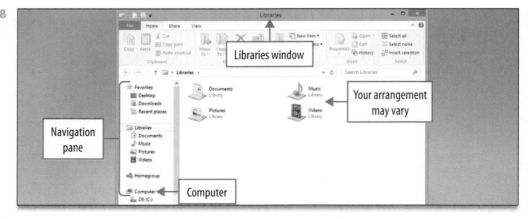

4 ▸ On the left, in the **navigation pane**, click **Computer**, and then compare your screen to Figure 1.9.

The *navigation pane* is the area on the left side of a folder or library window; it displays favorites, libraries, and an expandable list of drives and folders. If you are connected to a network, the name of the network, such as *Homegroup*, displays.

In the Computer window, you have access to all the storage areas inside and connected to your computer such as your hard disk drive, DVD or CD drives, removable storage devices, and network drive locations if you are connected to a network and have storage space there.

FIGURE 1.9

5 ▸ Under **Hard Disk Drives**, locate **OS (C:)**, point to the device name to display the ▨ pointer, and then right-click to display a shortcut menu. Compare your screen with Figure 1.10.

A *shortcut menu* is a context-sensitive menu that displays commands and options relevant to the active object.

Your hard disk drive may be referred to by another name such as Local Disk (C:).

⟲ **BY TOUCH**　　　Press and hold briefly to display a shaded square and then release.

FIGURE 1.10

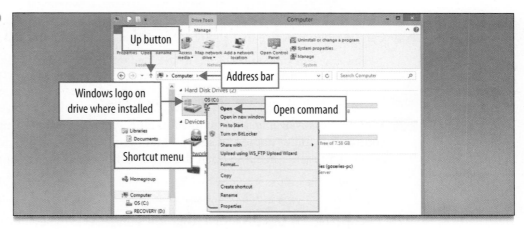

6 ▸ On the shortcut menu, click **Open** to display the *file list* for this drive.

A file list displays the contents of the current folder or library. Here, in the C: drive, Windows 8 stores various files related to your operating system. The Windows logo on the C: drive indicates this is where the Windows 8 operating system is stored.

⟲ **ANOTHER WAY**　　　Point to the device name and double-click to display the file list for the device.

7 To the left of the **address bar**, click the **Up** button $\boxed{\uparrow}$ to move up one level in the drive hierarchy and close the file list.

The ***address bar*** displays your current location in the folder structure as a series of links separated by arrows.

8 Under **Devices with Removable Storage**, click your **USB flash drive** to select it, and notice that the drive is highlighted in blue, indicating it is selected. At the top of the window, on the ribbon, click the **Computer tab**, and then in the **Location group**, click **Open**. Compare your screen with Figure 1.11.

N O T E	**Does Your Ribbon Show Only the Tab Names?**

By default, the ribbon is minimized and appears as a menu bar, displaying only the ribbon tabs. If only the tabs of your ribbon are displayed, click the Expand the Ribbon arrow $\boxed{\vee}$ on the right side to display the full ribbon.

The file list for your USB flash drive displays. If this is a new USB flash drive, there may be no files or only a few files related to the USB device itself.

The ***ribbon*** is a user interface in Windows 8 that groups the commands for performing related tasks on tabs across the upper portion of a window.

FIGURE 1.11

9 On the ribbon, notice that a tab for **Drive Tools** displays above the **Manage tab**.

This is a ***contextual tab***, which is a tab added to the ribbon automatically when a specific object is selected and that contains commands relevant to the selected object.

10 On the ribbon, in the **New group**, click **New folder**.

11 With the text *New folder* highlighted in blue, type **Windows 8 Chapter 1** and press Enter to confirm the folder name and select—highlight in blue—the new folder. With the folder selected, press Enter again to open the folder window. Compare your screen with Figure 1.12.

To ***select*** means to specify, by highlighting, a block of data or text on the screen with the intent of performing some action on the selection.

A new folder is created on your removable storage device. The address bar indicates the ***path*** from Computer to your device to your folder. A path is a sequence of folders that leads to a specific file or folder.

 BY TOUCH   You may have to tap the keyboard icon in the lower right corner of the taskbar to display the on-screen keyboard.

FIGURE 1.12

Address bar indicates current location

Folder window name

New folder on your device

Activity 1.05 | Creating and Saving a File

1 In the upper right corner of the folder window, click **Help** ⊘, and then under the **Search** box, click **Help home**. Click **Get started**, and then click **Touch: swipe, tap, and beyond**. Compare your screen with Figure 1.13.

> A vertical *scroll bar* displays on the right side of this window. A scroll bar displays when the contents of a window are not completely visible. A scroll bar can be vertical as shown or horizontal and displayed at the bottom of a window.

> Within the scroll bar, you can move the *scroll box* to bring the contents of the window into view. The position of the scroll box within the scroll bar indicates your relative position within the window's contents. You can click the *scroll arrow* at either end of the scroll bar to move within the window in small increments.

> Each computer manufacturer has some control over the Windows Help and Support opening screen. At the top of this screen, the manufacturer may place links to its own support and information about your computer's hardware.

FIGURE 1.13

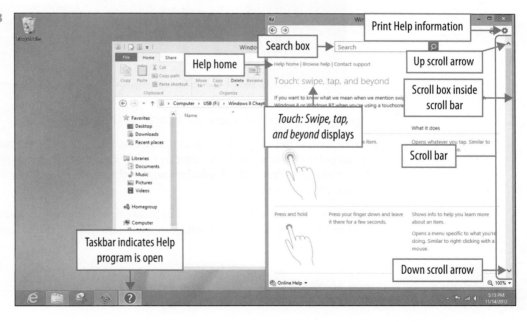

Search box

Print Help information

Help home

Up scroll arrow

Touch: Swipe, tap, and beyond displays

Scroll box inside scroll bar

Scroll bar

Taskbar indicates Help program is open

Down scroll arrow

2 Click the **down scroll arrow** as necessary—or drag the scroll box down—until the information and diagram for **Pinch or stretch to zoom** displays in the center of the window, as shown in Figure 1.14.

FIGURE 1.14

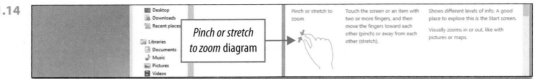

3 On the taskbar, click **Snipping Tool** to display the small **Snipping Tool** window.

4 On the **menu bar** of the **Snipping Tool**, click the **arrow** to the right of *New*—referred to as the **New arrow**—and then compare your screen with Figure 1.15.

> An arrow attached to a button will display a menu when clicked. Such a button is referred to as a *split button*—clicking the main part of the button performs a command and clicking the arrow opens a menu with choices. A *menu* is a list of commands within a category, and a group of menus at the top of a program window is referred to as a *menu bar*.

FIGURE 1.15

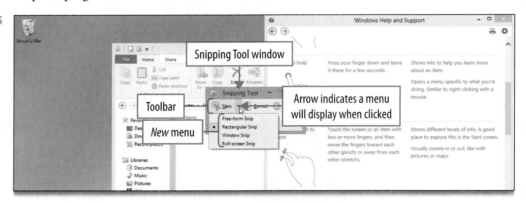

5 On the menu, notice that there are four types of snips.

> A *free-form snip* lets you draw an irregular line, such as a circle, around an area of the screen. A *rectangular snip* lets you draw a precise box by dragging the mouse pointer around an area of the screen to form a rectangle. A *window snip* captures the entire displayed window. A *full-screen snip* captures the entire screen.

> To *drag* is to move something from one location on the screen to another while holding down the left mouse button; the action of dragging includes releasing the mouse button at the desired time or location.

BY TOUCH   Slide your finger to drag and then lift your finger to release.

6 On the menu, click **Window Snip**. Then, move your mouse pointer over the open **Windows Help and Support** window, and notice that a red rectangle surrounds the window; the remainder of your screen dims.

7 With the pointer positioned anywhere over the surrounded window, click the left mouse button one time. Use the scroll bar to position the snip near the top of the window, and then compare your screen with Figure 1.16.

> Your snip is copied to the Snipping Tool mark-up window. Here you can annotate—mark or make notes on—save, copy, or share the snip.

FIGURE 1.16

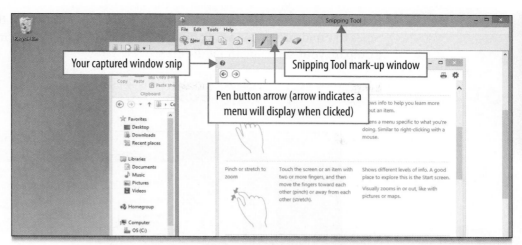

8 On the toolbar of the **Snipping Tool** mark-up window, click the **Pen button arrow** , and then click **Red Pen**. Notice that your mouse pointer displays as a red dot.

9 In the illustration for *Pinch or stretch to zoom*, point to the end of one of the blue arrows, and then while holding down the left mouse button, draw a red free-form circle around the illustration. If you are not satisfied with your circle, on the toolbar, click **Eraser** , point anywhere on the red circle, click to erase, and then begin again with Step 8.

10 On the toolbar of the **Snipping Tool** mark-up window, click **Highlighter** . Notice that your mouse pointer displays as a small yellow rectangle.

11 Point to the text *Pinch or stretch to zoom*, hold down the left mouse button, and then drag over the text to highlight it in yellow. If you are not satisfied with your yellow highlight, on the toolbar, click **Eraser** , point anywhere on the yellow highlight, click to erase, and then begin again with Step 10. Compare your screen with Figure 1.17.

 BY TOUCH   Use your finger to draw the circle and to highlight text.

FIGURE 1.17

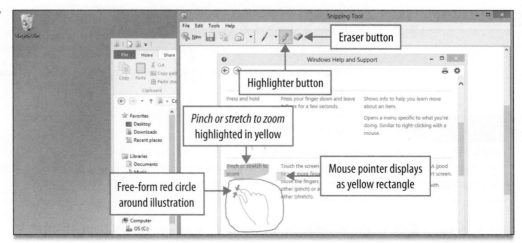

12 On the **Snipping Tool** mark-up window's toolbar, click **Save Snip** to display the **Save As** dialog box.

13 In the **Save As** dialog box, in the **navigation pane** on the left, drag the scroll bar down as necessary to view **Computer**. If necessary, to the left of **Computer**, click ▷ to expand the list, and then click the name of your **USB flash drive**.

14 In the **file list**, scroll as necessary, locate and ***double-click***—press the left mouse button two times in rapid succession while holding the mouse still—your **Windows 8 Chapter 1** folder. Compare your screen with Figure 1.18.

⟳ **ANOTHER WAY** Right-click the folder name and click Open.

FIGURE 1.18

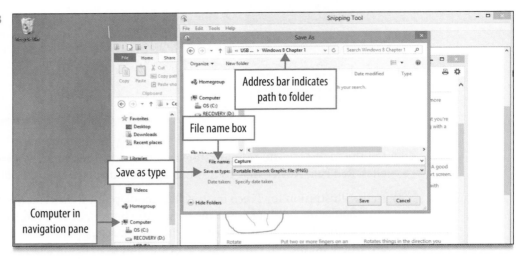

| NOTE | Successful Double-Clicking Requires a Steady Hand |

Double-clicking needs a steady hand. The speed of the two clicks is not as important as holding the mouse still between the two clicks. If you are not satisfied with your result, try again.

15 At the bottom of the **Save As** dialog box, locate **Save as type**, click anywhere in the box to display a list, and then on the displayed list click, **JPEG file**.

JPEG, which is commonly pronounced *JAY-peg* and stands for Joint Photographic Experts Group, is a common file type used by digital cameras and computers to store digital pictures. JPEG is popular because it can store a high-quality picture in a relatively small file.

16 At the bottom of the **Save As** dialog box, click in the **File name** box to select the text *Capture*, and then using your own name, type **Lastname_Firstname_1A_Zoom_Snip**

Within any Windows-based program, text highlighted in blue—selected—in this manner will be replaced by your typing.

| NOTE | File Naming in This Textbook |

Windows 8 recognizes file names with spaces. You can use spaces in file names, however, some programs, especially when transferring files over the Internet, may insert the extra characters *%20* in place of a space. In this textbook you will be instructed to save files using an underscore instead of a space. The underscore key is the shift of the ⎯ key—on most keyboards located two or three keys to the left of ⌫Backspace.

17 In the lower right corner of the window, click the **Save** button.

18 **Close** ☒ the **Snipping Tool** mark-up window, the **Windows Help and Support** window, and your **USB folder** window. Hold this file until you finish Project 1A, and then submit as directed by your instructor.

You have successfully created a folder on a removable storage device and saved a file within that folder.

Traditionally, the three major tasks of an operating system are to:

- Manage your computer's hardware—the printers, scanners, disk drives, monitors, and other hardware attached to it.

- Manage the application software installed on your computer—programs like those in Microsoft Office and other programs you might install to manage your money, edit photos, play games, and so on.

- Manage the *data* generated from your application software. Data refers to the documents, worksheets, pictures, songs, and so on that you create and store during the day-to-day use of your computer.

The Windows 8 operating system continues to perform these three tasks, and additionally is optimized for touchscreens; for example, tablets of all sizes and convertible laptop computers. Windows 8 works equally well with any input device, including a mouse, keyboard, touchscreen, and pen—a pen-shaped stylus that you tap on a computer screen.

The apps you use from the Start screen are referred to as *immersive*—they have no borders, no menus, and they behave differently from the traditional Windows desktop programs you just practiced. Because there is no taskbar, these apps cannot be minimized, nor can they be dragged around the screen as smaller windows. This look and behavior of apps is called *Microsoft Design Language*, which refers to the design principles in Windows 8 that include tiles with white text on deeply colored backgrounds, consistent fonts, simpler navigation, and the use of the entire screen. The idea is that you are immersed in the app with no screen distractions.

In most instances, when you purchase a computer, the operating system software is already installed. The operating system consists of many smaller programs, stored as system files, which transfer data to and from the disk and transfer data in and out of your computer's memory. Other functions performed by the operating system include hardware-specific tasks such as checking to see if a key has been pressed on the keyboard and, if it has, displaying the appropriate letter or character on the screen.

When using a Windows 8 computer, you can write and create using traditional desktop apps, and you can also read and socialize and communicate by using the Windows Store apps. With Windows 8, as compared to earlier versions of Windows, your PC behaves like a smartphone or tablet—it is connected, it is mobile, and it is centered on people and activities. If, as Microsoft predicts, the laptop and tablet will ultimately merge into one device—like the Microsoft Surface shown in Figure 1.19—then you will be well prepared by learning to use Windows 8 and the Windows Store apps.

FIGURE 1.19

Surface with Windows RT   Surface with Windows 8 Pro

Windows 8, in the same manner as other operating systems and earlier versions of the Windows operating system, has a desktop that uses a ***graphical user interface***—abbreviated as ***GUI*** and pronounced *GOO-ee*. A GUI uses graphics such as an image of a file folder or wastebasket that you click to activate the item represented. A GUI commonly incorporates the following:

- A ***pointer***—any symbol that displays on your screen in response to moving your mouse and with which you can select objects and commands.
- A ***pointing device***, such as a mouse or touchpad, to control the pointer.
- ***Icons***—small images that represent commands, files, applications, or other windows. By selecting an icon and pressing a mouse button, you can start a program or move objects to different locations on your screen.
- A ***desktop***—a simulation of a real desk that represents your work area; here you can arrange icons such as shortcuts to programs, files, folders, and various types of documents in the same manner you would arrange physical objects on top of a desk.

In Windows 8, you now also have the Start screen, organized by tiles, that serves as a connected dashboard to all of your important sites and services. On the Start screen, your view is tailored to your information and activities; for example, pictures display as ***thumbnails***—reduced images of graphics—email messages say who they are from, and videos include their length.

The physical parts of your computer such as the central processing unit (CPU), memory, and any attached devices such as a printer, are collectively known as ***resources***. The operating system keeps track of the status of each resource and decides when a resource needs attention and for how long.

There will be times when you want and need to interact with the functions of the operating system; for example, when you want to install a new hardware device like a color printer. Windows 8 provides tools with which you can inform the operating system of new hardware that you attach to your computer.

Software application programs are the programs that enable you to do work on, and be entertained by, your computer—programs such as Word and Excel found in the Microsoft Office suite of products, Adobe Photoshop, and computer games. An application program, however, cannot run on its own—it must run under the direction of the operating system.

For the everyday use of your computer, the most important and most often used function of the operating system is managing your files and folders—referred to as ***data management***. In the same manner that you strive to keep your paper documents and file folders organized so that you can find information when you need it, your goal when organizing your computer files and folders is to group your files so that you can find information easily. Managing your data files so that you can find your information when you need it is an important computing skill.

To check how well you can identify operating system functions, take a moment to answer the following questions:

1 Of the three major functions of the operating system, the first is to manage your computer's _____ such as disk drives, monitors, and printers.

2 The second major function of the operating system is to manage the application _____ such as Microsoft Word, Microsoft Excel, and video games.

3 The third major function of the operating system is to manage the _____ generated from your applications—the files such as Word documents, Excel workbooks, pictures, and songs.

4 The Start screen, which displays live tiles with your updated information, is your connected _____ to all of your important sites and services.

5 One of the most important computing skills you can learn is how to manage your _____ _____ so that you can find your information quickly.

According to Microsoft, a billion people in the world use Windows and 93% of PCs in the world run some version of Windows. Increasingly people want to use Windows in a format that runs easily on mobile computing devices such as laptops, tablets, and convertibles; research shows this is where people now spend more time.

With only desktop apps to choose from, Windows is centered around files—typing and creating things—and that will continue to be an important part of what you do on your computer. Additionally, you are doing different kinds of things on your PC, and you probably expect your PC to be more like a smartphone—connected all the time, mobile, to have long battery life, and be centered on the people and activities that are important to you. It is for those activities that the Windows Store apps will become important to you.

Think of Windows 8 as a way to do work on your desktop or laptop computer, and then to read and be entertained on your laptop, tablet, or Xbox game console. Microsoft promotes Windows 8 as both serious for work and fun for entertainment and social networking.

Activity 1.07 | Using Windows Store Apps

An array of Windows Store apps displays on the Start screen immediately after you sign in to a Windows 8 computer. On a new computer, the apps might be preselected by your computer manufacturer and by Microsoft. You can use these right away, and later you can add, delete, and rearrange the apps so that your Start screen becomes your own personal dashboard. Recall that some apps are represented by live tiles that will update with your personal information, such as Mail, after you set them to do so.

1 With your **desktop** still displayed, point to the lower left corner of your screen to display and then click one time to display the **Start screen**.

You can use this technique to return to the Start screen from any other screen—including the desktop.

2 On your **Start screen**, locate and point to the **Sports** app tile that comes with Windows 8. If necessary, drag the scroll bar at the bottom of the screen to the right to locate the app. If you cannot locate the Sports app, select some other news app. Compare your screen with Figure 1.20.

BY TOUCH   To display the Start screen, always swipe in from the right and tap Start. To scroll, slide your finger to the left to scroll to the right.

FIGURE 1.20

3 Click the **Sports** app tile, if necessary wait a moment if this is the first time you have used this app, point anywhere on the screen, and then right-click to display the app bar. Compare your screen with Figure 1.21.

Here you can navigate directly to categories such as the NBA (National Basketball Association) or MLB (Major League Baseball). This feature is the *app bar*—an area at the top or bottom of a Windows Store app containing various controls pertaining to the app.

BY TOUCH   On a touchscreen, from the bottom or top of the screen, swipe slightly upward or downward to display the app bar.

ANOTHER WAY   Press ⊞ + Z to display the app bar in an app.

FIGURE 1.21

4 At the top of the screen, click the **Favorite Teams** tile, and then click ⊕ to add another Favorite Team. With the **insertion point** blinking in the **Enter team name** box, type **Los** and then compare your screen with Figure 1.22.

The *insertion point* is a blinking vertical line that indicates where text will be inserted when you type.

FIGURE 1.22

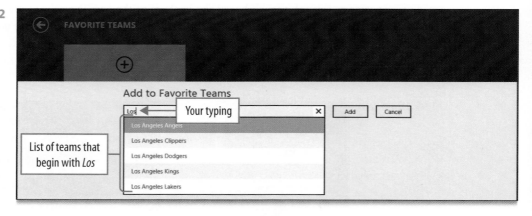

5 On the list, click **Los Angeles Dodgers**, and then compare your screen with Figure 1.23.

Depending on the time of year and the team's standing, the information will vary.

FIGURE 1.23

FAVORITE TEAMS

Los Angeles Dodgers
2nd in NL West
86-76,W1

Team information (yours will vary)

6　On your keyboard, in the lower left corner, locate and then press the ⊞ to display the **Start screen**.

This is the keyboard technique to display the Start screen.

7　On the **Start screen**, click the **Sports** app tile again.

The Favorite Teams screen with your selected team information displays because this was the last screen displayed before you returned to the Start screen.

8　On the **Favorite Teams** screen, click the **Los Angeles Dodgers** tile to see the latest *Top Story* regarding this team. Move your mouse slightly to display the gray scroll bar at the bottom of the screen, and then drag the scroll box to the right to see additional news stories related to the Los Angeles Dodgers.

BY TOUCH　　Slide your finger to the left to scroll to the right to view more articles.

9　Point to the top of the screen to display the ✋ pointer, hold down the left mouse button, and then drag the pointer to the bottom of the screen to close the app and redisplay the **Start screen**.

Use this technique to close an app. Leaving an app, for example by redisplaying the Start screen, does not close it.

BY TOUCH　　Swipe from the top of the screen to the bottom of the screen to close the app.

10　Locate and click the **Maps** app tile; click Allow if prompted to use your location. Then press ⊞ to return to the **Start screen**.

11　Locate and then click the **Finance** app tile. Right-click anywhere on the screen, and then at the top, click the **Watchlist** tile. Click ⊕, and then in the **Company name/Symbol** box, type **Microsoft** Click **Add** to add the NASDAQ stock listing for Microsoft. If Microsoft is already on your **Watchlist**, click **Cancel**.

A Watchlist tile for Microsoft Corporation, displaying their stock symbol MSFT, displays the latest information about Microsoft's stock price. Other companies might also display on your Watchlist.

12　Click the **MSFT tile** to see a graph of the day's stock price. At the bottom, click **1 Year** to see a graph representing one year.

13 With your Microsoft graph displayed, hold down ⊞ and press [PrintScrn] and then release the two keys. Notice that your screen dims momentarily; you will view the screenshot at the end of this activity.

> A *keyboard shortcut* is a combination of two or more keyboard keys used to perform a task that would otherwise require a mouse.

> On the Start screen or in a Windows Store app, use this technique to create a screenshot. Snipping Tool is not available for the Start screen or Windows Store apps. The screenshot file is automatically stored in your Pictures library.

🔁 **BY TOUCH**   Use or attach a keyboard; or, enable the on-screen keyboard, tap ⊞ to display it in white, and then tap the key labeled *PrtScn*. The keyboard will display in the picture.

---

14 Move the mouse slightly to display the gray scroll bar at the bottom of the screen, and then drag the scroll box to the right to read the latest news stories about Microsoft.

15 Press ⊞ to redisplay the **Start screen**.

> From any screen, recall that you can redisplay the Start screen by pointing to the lower left corner and clicking 🔲 or by pressing ⊞.

16 Locate and then click the **Travel** app tile. Move your mouse slightly to display the gray scroll bar at the bottom of the screen, and then drag the scroll box to the right to display pictures of featured travel sites.

17 Use one of the techniques you have practiced to redisplay the **Start screen**, and then point to the upper left corner of your screen. Notice a thumbnail of the last app you used—the Travel app. Compare your screen with Figure 1.24.

> This corner is referred to as the *Back tip*—it displays a thumbnail image of the last screen you were on, and you can use it to *go back* to your previous screen.

FIGURE 1.24

18 With the Back tip thumbnail displayed, notice faint vertical lines directly below and along the left edge of the screen. Without holding down any mouse buttons, move your mouse down slightly along the left edge of your screen. Compare your screen with Figure 1.25.

> This is the *app switcher*—the thumbnail view of open apps that displays when you move your mouse down from the Back tip in the upper left corner. To switch to an app that is still open, you can click any of the thumbnails. This feature is also referred to as simply *switcher*.

FIGURE 1.25

BY TOUCH   Swipe in slightly from the left edge of the screen and when the thumbnail of the previous app thumbnail appears, swipe slightly back to the left. Also, switcher stays docked on the side of the screen until you select something else. To close an app from switcher, drag it out of switcher and to the bottom of the screen.

19 ▶ Move your mouse out of the app switcher to close its view, and then point to the lower left corner of the screen; notice that a thumbnail of the last open app also displays here.

Because you already have the Start screen displayed, pointing to the lower left corner will display the last screen you were on that is still open. This corner is referred to as the *Start tip*.

20 ▶ Move the mouse slightly upward to display app switcher—thumbnails of all open apps.

To display app switcher, you must first point to either the upper left corner or the lower left corner, and then move the mouse upward or downward along the left edge of the screen.

21 ▶ In the app switcher, point to the **Finance** app, right-click, and then click **Close**.

Use this technique to close an app without redisplaying it.

22 ▶ Use the same technique to close the **Maps** app and the **Travel** app.

More Knowledge | **Use [⊞] + [Tab] to Display Switcher**

Hold down [⊞] and press [Tab] to display switcher. Continue to hold down [⊞] to keep the display open. Click any displayed app in the switcher to move to it.

Activity 1.08 | **Moving Between the Start Screen and Desktop and Saving a Windows Store App Screenshot as a File**

In the day-to-day use of your computer, depending on what you need to do, you will move between desktop apps and Windows Store apps, and it is easy to do so.

1 ▶ On your **Start screen**, locate the **Desktop** tile and click it one time.

If you move frequently from the Start screen to the desktop, you will want to keep your desktop tile easily visible.

ANOTHER WAY   From any Windows Store app or the Start screen, point to the lower left corner of the screen, right-click, and then on the shortcut menu, click Desktop.

---

2 ▶ From the taskbar, open **File Explorer** to display the **Libraries** window. In the **file list**, double-click **Pictures**, and then double-click **Screenshots**—this navigation is typically indicated as **Libraries ▶ Pictures ▶ Screenshots**. Compare your screen with Figure 1.26.

Your view might be the Large Icons view.

FIGURE 1.26

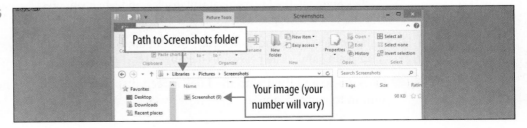

3 In the **file list**, click one time to select the **Screenshot (1)** file; if more than one Screenshot file displays, click to select the file that has the highest number.

> A screenshot captured in this manner from a Windows Store app is saved as a **.png** file, which is commonly pronounced **PING**, and stands for Portable Network Graphic. This is an image file type that can be transferred over the Internet.

4 On the ribbon, on the **Home tab**, in the **Organize group**, click **Rename**, and then using your own name, type **Lastname_Firstname_1A_Graph_Snip** Press Enter.

5 With the renamed file selected, on the ribbon, in the **Organize group**, click **Move to**, and then click **Choose location**. In the **Move Items** dialog box, scroll down, click **Computer** to expand it, click your **USB** drive, and then click your **Windows 8 Chapter 1** folder. In the lower right corner, click **Move**.

> Save this file until you complete Project 1A.

6 **Close** ☒ the **Screenshots** window.

Objective 4 Sign Out of Windows 8 and Turn Off Your Computer

On your own computer, when you are done working, sign out from Windows 8, and then set your computer properly so that your data is saved, you save energy, and your computer remains secure.

When you turn off your computer by using the *Sleep* command, Windows 8 automatically saves your work, the screen goes dark, the computer's fan stops, and your computer goes to sleep. You need not close your programs or files because your work is saved. When you wake your computer by pressing a key, moving the mouse, or using whatever method is appropriate for your device, you need only to dismiss the Lock screen and then enter your password; your screen will display exactly like it did when you turned off your computer.

When you *shut down* your computer, all open programs and files close, network connections close, and the hard disk stops. No power is used. According to Microsoft, about half of all Windows users like to shut down so that they get a "fresh start" each time they turn on the computer. The other half use sleep.

Activity 1.09 │ Locking, Signing Out of, and Shutting Down Your Computer

In an organization, there might be a specific process for signing out from Windows 8 and turning off the computer.

1 Use any of the techniques you have practiced to display the **Start screen**. In the upper right corner, click your user name.

> Here you can sign out or lock your computer, in addition to changing your account picture. If you click Sign out, the Lock screen will display, and when you press Enter, all the user accounts on this computer will display and are able to sign in.
>
> If you click Lock, the Lock screen will display, and when you press Enter, only you will be able to sign in again—unless no passwords have been set.

2 Click **Lock**, and then with the Lock screen displayed, click one time or press Enter, and then sign in to your computer again if necessary.

3 On the **Start screen**, point to the upper right corner of the screen to display the **charms** in a transparent view, and then move the mouse downward slightly into the displayed symbols along the right edge of the screen to display the **charms** in an opaque overlay. Compare your screen with Figure 1.27.

> *Charms* are a specific and consistent set of buttons that you can use in every app, whether a Windows Store app or a desktop app, and they enable you to search, share, access devices, or adjust your PC settings. Specifically you can:

- Use the Search charm to search for an app or search for content located in the active app or in another app.
- Use the Share charm to share content from the active app with people or services.
- Use the Start charm to go directly to the Start screen.
- Use the Devices charm to connect to devices and send content, stream media, and print.
- Use the Settings charm to configure the active app to your preferences and access help.

FIGURE 1.27

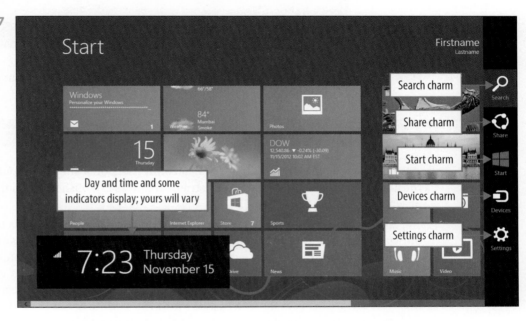

ANOTHER WAY   You can also display the charms from the *lower* right corner, but because this corner is also used to peek at the desktop when a desktop app is open or to zoom in on the Start screen, use the upper right corner to assure a consistent result.

4 Click the **Settings charm**, and then compare your screen with Figure 1.28.

FIGURE 1.28

5 At the bottom of the **Settings pane**, click **Power**, and then click **Shut down**.

Objective 5 | Manage User Accounts

Windows 8 supports multiple local account users on a single computer, and at least one user is the administrator—the initial administrator that was established when the system was purchased or when Windows 8 was installed.

As the administrator of your own computer, you can restrict access to your computer so that only people you authorize can use your computer or view its files. This access is managed through a local *user account*, which is a collection of information that tells Windows 8 what files and folders the account holder can access, what changes the account holder can make to the computer system, and what the account holder's personal preferences are. Each person accesses his or her user account with a user name and password, and each user has his or her own desktop, files, and folders. Users with a local account should also establish a Microsoft account so that their Start screen arrangement—personal dashboard of tiles—roams with them when they sign on to other Windows 8 computers.

An *administrator account* allows complete access to the computer. Administrators can make changes that affect other users, change security settings, install software and hardware, access all files on the computer, and make changes to other user accounts.

Activity 1.10 | Using PC Settings and Managing Your User Account

1 If necessary, turn on or wake your computer, and then sign in. Display the **Start screen**.

2 Point to the upper right corner to display the **charms**, move your mouse pointer down, and then click the **Settings charm**.

3 At the bottom of the **Settings pane**, click **Change PC settings**. On the left, be sure that **Personalize** is selected, and then compare your screen with Figure 1.29.

ANOTHER WAY   In the upper right corner, click your name, and then click *Change account picture* to display PC settings.

Here, in *PC settings*, you can control almost everything about how Windows looks and works. You can change colors and backgrounds, the picture on your Lock screen, and your account picture. Here you can also add other users, connect devices like printers, or set up a network.

FIGURE 1.29

4 In the upper right corner, click **Account picture**. Click **Browse**, and then if the Photos app does not display, to the right of **Files**, click ☑ to display all the file locations on your computer. At the bottom, scroll down if necessary, and then click **Photos** to open the **Photos app**. Compare your screen with Figure 1.30.

Assuming that you have signed in with a Microsoft account and that you have connected some of your services, you can get a photo from your Facebook account, your Flickr account, or any pictures you have stored on your SkyDrive—in addition to those in your Pictures library on your computer.

FIGURE 1.30

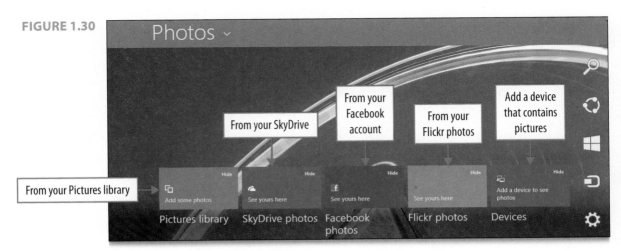

5 Click one of your locations, for example your Pictures library, select any picture, and then click **Choose image**. Compare your screen with Figure 1.31.

Your new image displays, and your previous image remains in case you want to choose it again. Here you can also create an account picture instantly from a camera on your computer if one is available.

FIGURE 1.31

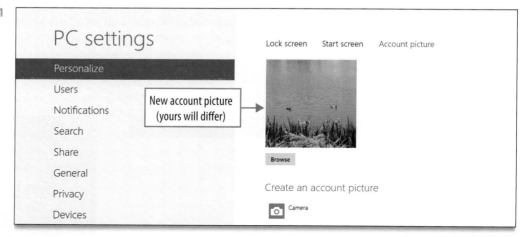

6 Point to the upper right corner of your screen to display the **charms**, click the **Settings charm**, click **Power**, and then click **Shut down** to close all apps and turn off your computer.

7 If you want to do so, turn your computer on, and then using the techniques you just practiced, change your account picture back to its previous picture.

END | You have completed Project 1A

PROJECT ACTIVITIES

In Activities 1.11 through 1.21, you will assist Barbara Hewitt and Steven Ramos, who work for the Information Technology Department at the Boston headquarters office of the Bell Orchid Hotels. Barbara and Steven have been asked to organize some of the files and folders that comprise the corporation's computer data. You will capture screens that will look similar to Figure 1.32.

PROJECT FILES

For Project 1B, you will need the following files:

The student data files that accompany this textbook stored on a USB flash drive

You will save your files as:

Lastname_Firstname_1B_WordPad_Snip
Lastname_Firstname_1B_Europe_Folders_Snip
Lastname_Firstname_1B_HR_Snip

PROJECT RESULTS

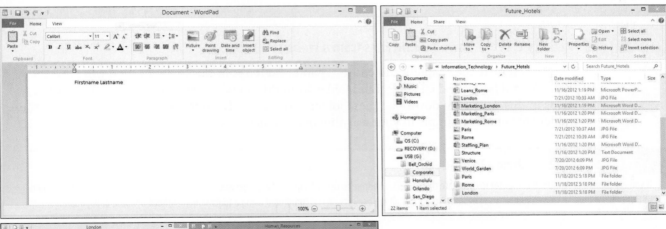

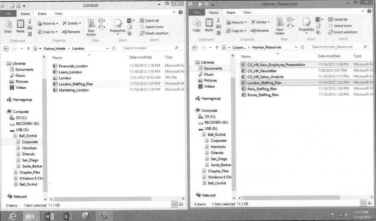

FIGURE 1.32 Project 1B Managing Files and Folders

A file is the fundamental unit of storage that enables Windows 8 to distinguish one set of information from another. A folder is the basic organizing tool for files. In a folder, you can store files that are related to one another. You can also put a folder inside of another folder, which is referred to as a subfolder.

Windows 8 arranges folders in a structure that resembles a *hierarchy*—an arrangement where items are ranked and where each level is lower in rank than the item above it. The hierarchy of folders is referred to as the *folder structure*. A sequence of folders in the folder structure that leads to a specific file or folder is a path.

A library is a collection of items, such as files and folders, assembled from various locations; the locations might be on your computer, on an external hard drive connected to your computer, or on another computer in your network. A library does not actually store your items; rather, a library provides a single access point from which you can open folders and files from different locations.

ALERT!

For the remainder of this textbook, you will need two of the folders that accompany this textbook. You will download these files in the following activity. Alternatively, your instructor might provide these files, or you can download the files from the Pearson website associated with this textbook. You will also need Microsoft Office 2013 (only Word, Excel, and PowerPoint) installed on the computer you are using. A trial version of Microsoft Office 2013 is sufficient for these projects.

Activity 1.11 | Downloading Files from a Website

To complete the chapters and end-of-chapter exercises in this textbook, you will need the Bell_Orchid folder and Chapter_Files folder from this book's companion website. Follow the steps in this activity to download these folders. Alternatively, your instructor might provide these folders to you, for example in your learning management system.

NOTE | **Using a Touchscreen**

If you are using a touchscreen computer to complete this project, continue to use the tap and swipe gestures that you practiced in Project 1A. The remainder of this textbook will assume a mouse and keyboard setup, but all the projects can be completed using a touchscreen without a mouse or keyboard.

---

1 Sign in to your computer, and then from the **Start screen**, display the **desktop**.

There are several ways to display the desktop from the Start screen when using a mouse and keyboard. You can click the desktop tile on the Start screen, press ⊞ + D, or point to the lower left corner, right-click, and then at the bottom of the menu click desktop.

2 If necessary, insert your **USB flash drive**.

3 On the taskbar, click **Internet Explorer** 🅮, click in the **address bar**, type **www.pearsonhighered.com/go** and then press Enter.

Recall that Internet Explorer is Microsoft's *web browser*—software with which you display webpages and navigate the Internet.

4 Scroll down the list, locate and click the name of this textbook, and then click the STUDENT DATA FILES tab.

5 Click the link for **Bell_Orchid Files**. In the **Windows Internet Explorer** dialog box, click **Save As**.

Recall that a dialog box is a small window that displays options for completing a task.

6 In the **Save As** dialog box, in the **navigation pane** on the left, scroll down, and if necessary, to the left of **Computer**, click ▷ to expand the list. Then click the name of your **USB flash drive**. Compare your screen with Figure 1.33.

FIGURE 1.33

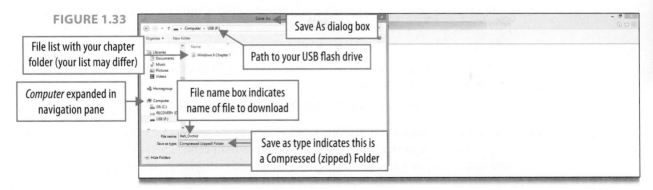

File list with your chapter folder (your list may differ)

Computer expanded in navigation pane

Save As dialog box

Path to your USB flash drive

File name box indicates name of file to download

Save as type indicates this is a Compressed (zipped) Folder

7 In the lower right corner, click **Save**.

At the bottom of your screen, the *Notification bar* displays information about pending downloads, security issues, and add-ons, and other issues related to the operation of your computer.

A *compressed file* is a file that has been reduced in size. Compressed files take up less storage space and can be transferred to other computers faster than uncompressed files. You can also combine a group of files into one compressed folder, which makes it easier to share a group of files.

8 In the **Notification bar**, when the download is complete, click **Open folder**, and then compare your screen with Figure 1.34.

FIGURE 1.34

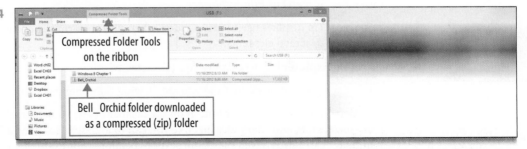

Compressed Folder Tools on the ribbon

Bell_Orchid folder downloaded as a compressed (zip) folder

9 With the compressed folder selected, on the ribbon, click the **Extract tab** to display the **Compressed Folder Tools**, and then click **Extract all**. Compare your screen with Figure 1.35.

Here you *extract*—decompress, or pull out—files from a compressed form. When you extract a file, an uncompressed copy is placed in the folder that you specify here.

You can navigate to some other location by clicking the Browse button and navigating within your storage locations.

FIGURE 1.35

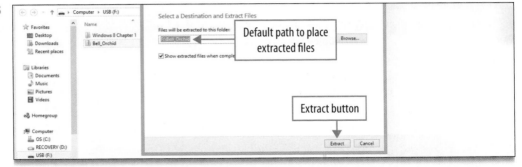

Default path to place extracted files

Extract button

10 Click the **Browse** button. In the **Select a destination** dialog box, click **Computer**, click the name of your **USB flash drive**, and then click **OK**.

11 In the lower right corner, click **Extract**, and notice that a progress bar indicates the progress of the extract process, and that when the extract is complete, the **Bell_Orchid** folder displays on the file list of your **USB flash drive**. If you want to do so, you can delete the compressed (zipped) folder from your flash drive because now you have an extracted *copy* of the folder.

> In a dialog box or taskbar button, a ***progress bar*** indicates visually the progress of a task such as a download or file transfer.

12 In the upper right corner of the **USB device** window, click **Close** ☒.

13 Using the techniques you just practiced, return to the website if necessary, and then download and extract the **Chapter_Files** folder to your **USB flash drive**. Then delete the compressed folder if you want to do so. **Close** ☒ all open windows and redisplay your desktop.

Activity 1.12 | Using File Explorer to Display Libraries, Folders, and Files

Recall that File Explorer is the program that displays the contents of libraries, folders, and files on your computer, and also enables you to perform tasks related to your files and folders such as copying, moving, and renaming. When you open a folder or library, a folder window displays to show its contents. The design of the folder window helps you navigate—explore within the folder structure for the purpose of finding files and folders—so that you can save and locate your files and folders efficiently.

In this activity, you will open a folder window and examine its parts.

1 With your desktop displayed, on the taskbar, *point to* but do not click **File Explorer** 🗔, and notice the ScreenTip *File Explorer*.

> A ***ScreenTip*** displays useful information when you perform various mouse actions, such as pointing to screen elements.

2 Click **File Explorer** 🗔 to display the **Libraries** window.

> File Explorer is at work anytime you are viewing the contents of a library, a folder, or a file.

> By default, the File Explorer button on the taskbar opens your Libraries. Within a library, you can organize, view, and share files just like you can in a folder. However, a library differs from a folder in that it can gather saved files from several locations. For example, from the Documents library, you can access documents in both your My Documents and Public Documents folders.

> In addition to the four default libraries—Documents, Music, Pictures, and Videos—you can create new libraries for other file collections you might have.

3 In the **file list**, click **Documents** one time to select it, and then on the ribbon, in the **Open group**, click **Open** 🗔.

> The window for the Documents library displays. You may or may not have files and folders already stored here.

🔄 **ANOTHER WAY**   Point to Documents, right-click to display a shortcut menu, and then click Open; or, point to Documents and double-click.

4 ▸ Compare your screen with Figure 1.36, and then take a moment to study the parts of the window as described in the table in Figure 1.37.

FIGURE 1.36

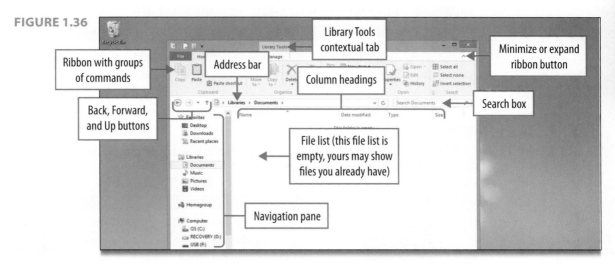

FIGURE 1.37

PARTS OF THE DOCUMENTS LIBRARY WINDOW	
WINDOW PART	**FUNCTION**
Address bar	Displays your current location in the file structure as a series of links separated by arrows. Tap or click a part of the path to go to that level or tap or click at the end to select the path for copying.
Back, Forward, Recent locations, and Up buttons	Provides the ability to navigate to other folders you have already opened without closing the current folder window. These buttons work with the address bar; that is, after you use the address bar to change folders, you can use the Back button to return to the original folder. Use the Up button to open the location where the folder you are viewing is saved—also referred to as the *parent folder*.
Column headings	Identify the columns. By clicking the column heading name, you can change how the files in the file list are organized; by clicking the arrow on the right, you can select various sort arrangements in the file list. Right-click a column heading to select other columns to add to the file list.
File list	Displays the contents of the current folder or library. If you type text into the Search box, only the folders and files that match your search will display here—including files in subfolders.
Library Tools contextual tab	Displays additional tools in context with the selected item.
Minimize or expand ribbon button	Changes the display of the ribbon. When minimized, the ribbon shows only the tab names and not the full ribbon.
Navigation pane	Displays locations to which you can navigate in an area on the left side of a folder window; for example, Favorites, Libraries, a Homegroup if you have one, and an expandable list of drives and folders. Use Favorites to open your most commonly used folders and searches; use Libraries to access your libraries. If you have a folder that you use frequently, you can drag it to the Favorites area so that it is always available.
Ribbon	Groups common tasks such as copying and moving, creating new folders, emailing and zipping items, and changing views on related tabs.
Search box	Enables you to type a word or phrase and then searches for a file or subfolder stored in the current folder that contains matching text. The search begins as soon as you begin typing; for example, if you type *G*, all the files that start with the letter *G* display in the file list.

5 ▶ Move your ⌖ pointer anywhere into the **navigation pane**, and notice that a **black arrow** (◢) displays to the left of *Favorites*, *Libraries*, and *Computer*, to indicate that these items are expanded, and a **white arrow** (▷) displays to the left of items that are collapsed (hidden).

You can click these arrows to collapse and expand areas in the navigation pane.

6 ▶ In the **navigation pane**, under **Computer**, click your **USB flash drive** one time to display its contents in the **file list**. Compare your screen with Figure 1.38.

In the navigation pane, *Computer* displays all of the drive letter locations attached to your computer, including the internal hard drives, CD or DVD drives, and any connected devices such as a USB flash drive.

The ribbon adds a Drive Tools contextual tab to provide commands you might need when working with various drives on your computer.

FIGURE 1.38

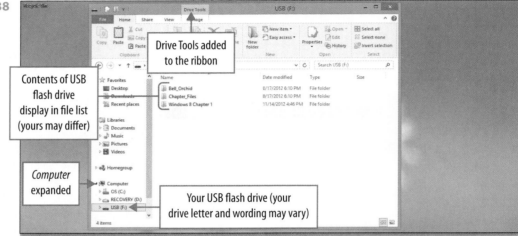

7 ▶ In the **file list**, double-click the **Bell_Orchid** folder—not the compressed folder—to display the subfolders.

Recall that the corporate office of the Bell Orchid Hotels is in Boston. The corporate office maintains subfolders labeled for each of its large hotels in Honolulu, Orlando, San Diego, and Santa Barbara.

🔁 **ANOTHER WAY**   Right-click the folder, and then click Open; or, select the folder and then on the ribbon click Open.

8 ▶ In the **file list**, double-click **Orlando** to display the subfolders, and then look at the **address bar** to view the path. Compare your screen with Figure 1.39.

Within each city's subfolder, there is a structure of subfolders for the Accounting, Engineering, Food and Beverage, Human Resources, Operations, and Sales and Marketing departments.

Because folders can be placed inside of other folders, such an arrangement is common when organizing files on a computer.

In the address bar, the path from the flash drive to the Bell_Orchid folder to the Orlando folder displays as a series of links.

FIGURE 1.39

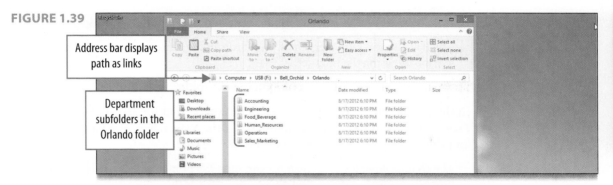

Address bar displays path as links

Department subfolders in the Orlando folder

9 In the **address bar**, to the right of **Bell_Orchid**, click the ▶ arrow to display a list of the subfolders in the **Bell_Orchid** folder. On the list that displays, notice that **Orlando** displays in bold, indicating it is open in the file list. Then, on the list, click **Honolulu**.

The subfolders within the Honolulu folder display.

10 In the **address bar**, to the right of **Bell_Orchid**, click the ▶ arrow again to display the subfolders in the **Bell_Orchid** folder. Then, on the **address bar** (not on the list), point to **Honolulu** and notice that the list of subfolders in the **Honolulu** folder displays.

After you display one set of subfolders in the address bar, all of the links are active and you need only point to them to display the list of subfolders.

Clicking an arrow to the right of a folder name in the address bar displays a list of the subfolders in that folder. You can click a subfolder name to display its contents. In this manner, the address bar is not only a path, but it is also an active control with which you can step from the current folder directly to any other folder above it in the folder structure just by clicking on a folder name.

11 On the list of subfolders for **Honolulu**, click **Sales_Marketing** to display its contents in the file list. Compare your screen with Figure 1.40.

ANOTHER WAY   In the file list, double-click the Sales_Marketing folder.

The files in the Sales_Marketing folder for Honolulu display. To the left of each file name, an icon indicates the program that created each file. Here, there is one PowerPoint file, one Excel file, one Word file, and four JPEG images.

FIGURE 1.40

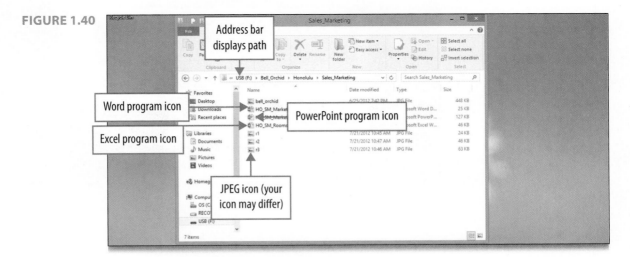

Address bar displays path

Word program icon

Excel program icon

PowerPoint program icon

JPEG icon (your icon may differ)

12 In the upper left corner of the folder window, click the **Back** button ⊙.

The Back button retraces each of your clicks in the same manner as clicking the Back button when you are browsing the Internet.

13 In the **file list**, point to the **Human_Resources** folder, and double-click to open the folder.

14 In the **file list**, click one time to select the PowerPoint file **HO_HR_New_Employee_ Presentation**, and then on the ribbon, click the **View tab**. In the **Panes group**, click **Details pane**, and then compare your screen with Figure 1.41.

The ***Details pane*** displays the most common ***file properties*** associated with the selected file. File properties refer to information about a file, such as the author, the date the file was last changed, and any descriptive ***tags***—properties that you create to help you find and organize your files.

Additionally, a thumbnail of the first slide in the presentation displays.

FIGURE 1.41

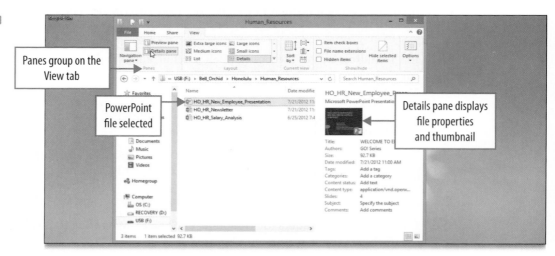

15 On the ribbon, in the **Panes group**, click **Preview pane** to replace the **Details pane** with the **Preview pane**. Compare your screen with Figure 1.42.

In the Preview pane that displays on the right, you can use the scroll bar to scroll through the slides in the presentation; or, you can click the up or down scroll arrow to view the slides.

FIGURE 1.42

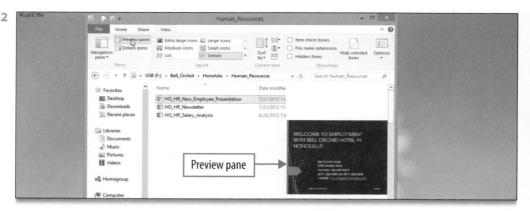

16 On the ribbon, click **Preview pane** to close the right pane completely.

Use the Details pane to see a file's properties and the Preview pane when you want to look at a file quickly without actually opening it.

17 **Close** ☒ the window.

Activity 1.13 | Using the Navigation Pane to Display the Folder Structure

When it is useful to do so, you can use the navigation pane on the left side of a folder window to navigate files and folders and to display the folder structure.

1 If necessary, **Close** ☒ any open windows, and then on the taskbar, click **File Explorer** 📁 to open the **Libraries** window.

2 On the left side of the window, in the lower portion of the **navigation pane**, if necessary click ▷ to expand **Computer**. Then point to your **USB flash drive** containing the Bell_Orchid files and click the white expand arrow ▷ to display the subfolders immediately below the name of your USB drive.

3 To the left of **Bell_Orchid**, click the expand arrow ▷ to display the subfolders. Scroll down if necessary, and then to the left of **San_Diego**, click the expand arrow ▷ to display the subfolders. Compare your screen with Figure 1.43.

In the navigation pane, the folder structure is shown in a visual hierarchy.

FIGURE 1.43

4 In the **navigation pane**, under **San_Diego**, click **Accounting** to display the files in the **Accounting** subfolder in the **file list**.

When you no longer see any ▷ arrows to expand further, clicking the folder will display the file list for that folder.

Optionally you can hide the display of the navigation pane, but it is recommended that you leave the navigation pane displayed because of its usefulness in displaying the drives on your computer and the folder structure when you want to see the structure in a hierarchical view.

5 In the upper right corner, click **Close** ☒.

When you are using the software programs installed on your computer, you create and save data files—the documents, workbooks, databases, songs, pictures, and so on that you need for your job or personal use. Therefore, most of your work with Windows 8 desktop apps is concerned with locating and starting your programs and locating and opening your files.

You can start programs from the Start screen or from the desktop by pinning a program to the taskbar. You can open your data files from within the program in which they were created, or you can open a data file from a folder window in File Explorer, which will simultaneously start the program and open your file.

Activity 1.14 | **Starting Programs and Opening Data Files**

1 With your desktop displayed, use any technique that you have practiced to display the **Start screen**, and then type **paint**

Recall that from the Start screen, you can begin typing and the Start search feature will immediately begin searching for apps.

Paint is a desktop app that comes with Windows 8 with which you can create and edit drawings and display and edit stored photos.

2 With the **Paint** app in focus—bordered in white—as the result of your search, press Enter to open the **desktop** app.

3 On the ribbon, with the **Home tab** active, in the **Tools group**, click the **Pencil** icon. Move your mouse pointer into the white drawing area, hold down the left mouse button, and then try writing your first name in the white area of the window.

BY TOUCH   Use your finger to draw on the screen.

4 In the upper left corner, to the left of the **Home tab**, click the **File tab** to display a menu of commands of things you can do with your picture.

5 On the menu, click **Exit**. In the displayed message, click **Don't Save**.

Messages like this display in most programs to prevent you from forgetting to save your work. A file saved in the Paint program creates a graphic file in the JPEG format.

6 Return to the **Start screen**, type **wordpad** and then open the **WordPad desktop** app. Notice that this program window has characteristics similar to the Paint program window; for example, it has a ribbon of commands.

7 With the insertion point blinking in the document window, type your first and last name.

8 From the taskbar, start **Snipping Tool**, and then create a **Window Snip**. Click anywhere in the WordPad window to display the **Snipping Tool** mark-up window. **Save** 🖫 the snip as a **JPEG** in your **Windows 8 Chapter 1** folder as **Lastname_Firstname_1B_WordPad_Snip** Hold this file until you finish Project 1B, and then submit this file as directed by your instructor.

9 **Close** ⊠ the **Snipping Tool** window. **Close** ⊠ WordPad, and then click **Don't Save**.

10 Display the **Start screen**, type **word 2013** and then open **Microsoft Word**. Compare your screen with Figure 1.44.

NOTE	**You Need Microsoft Word 2013**

For this project you need Microsoft Word 2013; you can use a trial version if necessary.

The Word program window has features that are common to other programs you have opened; for example, commands are arranged on tabs. When you create and save data in Word, you create a Word document file.

FIGURE 1.44

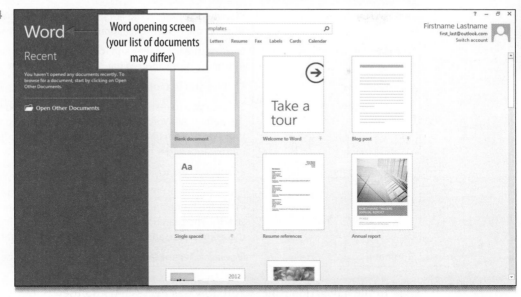

> **11** On the left, click **Open Other Documents**. Under **Open**, click **Computer**, and then click **Browse** to display the **Open** dialog box. Compare your screen with Figure 1.45, and then take a moment to study the table in Figure 1.46.

Recall that a dialog box is a window containing options for completing a task; its layout is similar to that of a folder window. When you are working in a desktop app, use the Open dialog box to locate and open existing files that were created in the desktop app.

By default, the Open dialog box displays the path to the *Documents* library of the user signed in. On your own computer, you can create a folder structure within the Documents library to store your documents. Alternatively, you can use the skills you have practiced to navigate to other locations on your computer, such as your removable USB flash drive.

FIGURE 1.45

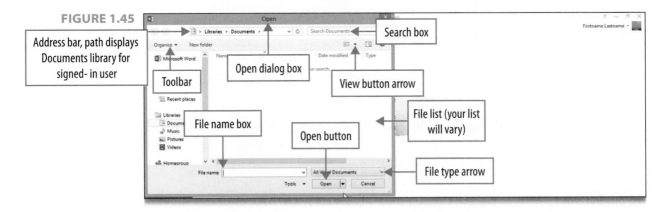

FIGURE 1.46

THE OPEN DIALOG BOX	
DIALOG BOX ELEMENT	**FUNCTION**
Address bar	Displays the path in the library or folder structure; by default, the path displays the Documents library for the signed-in user.
File list	Displays the list of files and folders that are available in the library or folder indicated in the address bar.
File name box	Enables you to type the name of a specific file to locate it.
File type arrow	Enables you to restrict the type of files displayed in the file list; for example, the default All Word Documents restricts the type of files displayed to only Word documents. You can click the arrow and adjust the restrictions to a narrower or wider group of files.
Navigation pane	Enables access to Favorites, Libraries, and Computer.
Search box	Filters the file list based on text that you type; the search is based on text in the file name and in the file itself, and on other properties that you can specify. The search takes place in the current folder or library, as displayed in the address bar, and in any subfolders within that folder.
Toolbar	Displays relevant tasks; for example, creating a new folder.

12 In the **navigation pane**, scroll down as necessary, and then under **Computer**, click your **USB flash drive**. In the **file list**, double-click the **Bell_Orchid** folder to open it and display its contents. In the upper right portion of the **Open** dialog box, click the **More Options arrow** ▦ ▾ , and then set the view to **Large icons**. Compare your screen with Figure 1.47.

Notice that the Live Icons feature indicates that each folder contains additional subfolders.

FIGURE 1.47

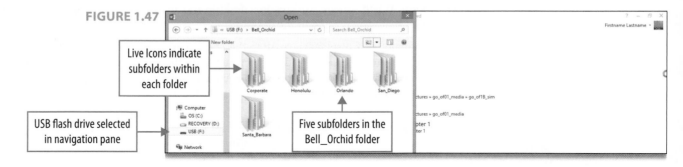

Live Icons indicate subfolders within each folder

USB flash drive selected in navigation pane

Five subfolders in the Bell_Orchid folder

13 In the **file list**, double-click the **Corporate** folder, and then double-click the **Accounting** folder.

The view returns to the Details view.

14 In the **file list**, notice that only one document—a Word document—displays. In the lower right corner, locate the **File type** button, and notice that *All Word Documents* displays as the file type. Click the **File type arrow**, and then on the displayed list, click **All Files**. Compare your screen with Figure 1.48.

When you change the file type to *All Files*, you can see that the Word file is not the only file in this folder. By default, the Open dialog box displays only the files created in the *active program*; however, you can display variations of file types in this manner.

Microsoft Office file types are identified by small icons, which is a convenient way to differentiate one type of file from another. Although you can view all the files in the folder, you can open only the files that were created in the active program, which in this instance is Microsoft Word.

FIGURE 1.48

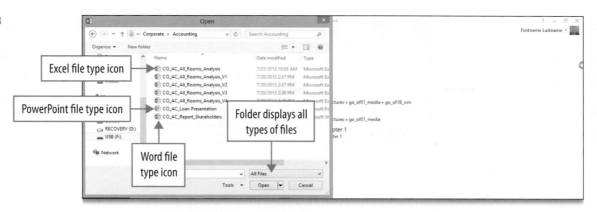

15 Change the file type back to **All Word Documents**. Then in the **file list**, double-click the **CO_AC_Report_Shareholders** Word file to open the document. Take a moment to scroll through the document. If necessary, **Maximize** ☐ the window.

16 **Close** ☒ the Word window. On the taskbar, click **File Explorer** ▦. In the **navigation pane**, under **Computer**, click your **USB flash drive** to display its contents in the **file list**.

17 In the **file list**, use any technique you have practiced to open folders to navigate to **Bell_Orchid ▶ Corporate ▶ Accounting**.

🔄 **ANOTHER WAY**   Expand each folder level in the navigation pane.

18 In the **file list**, double-click the **CO_AC_Loan_Presentation** file. When the **PowerPoint** window displays (a message regarding comments may display), if necessary **Maximize** ☐ the program window. Compare your screen with Figure 1.49.

FIGURE 1.49

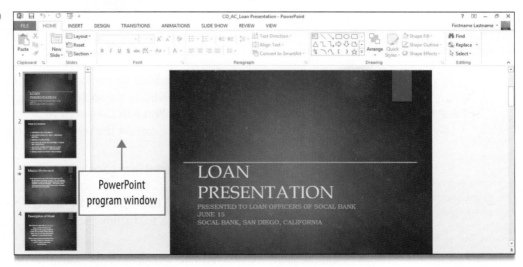

19 **Close** ☒ the PowerPoint window.

20 In the **address bar**, to the right of **Bell_Orchid**, click ▶ and then compare your screen with Figure 1.50.

Recall that the address bar is not just a path; rather, it contains active links from which you can click a folder name in the path, and then navigate directly to any displayed subfolders.

FIGURE 1.50

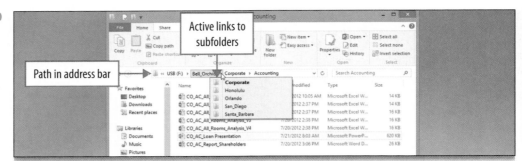

21 On the displayed list, click **Honolulu** to display the contents of the **Honolulu** folder in the **file list**. Open the **Food_Beverage** folder, and then open the **HO_FB_Banquet_Contract** file. Take a moment to view this document in the open Word program. **Close** [**x**] Word, and then **Close** [X] the folder window.

More Knowledge   **Storing Files and Creating Desktop Shortcuts for a Program on Your Desktop**

On your desktop, you can add or remove **desktop shortcuts**, which are desktop icons that can link to items accessible on your computer such as a program, file, folder, disk drive, printer, or another computer. In previous versions of Windows, many computer users commonly did this.

Now the Start screen is your personal dashboard for all your programs and online activities, and increasingly you will access programs and your own files in the cloud. So do not clutter your desktop with shortcuts—doing so is more confusing than useful. Placing desktop shortcuts for frequently used programs or folders directly on your desktop may seem convenient, but as you add more icons, your desktop becomes cluttered and the shortcuts are not easy to find. A better organizing method is to use the taskbar for shortcuts to programs. For folders and files, the best organizing structure is to create a logical structure of folders within your Documents library.

You can also drag frequently used folders to the Favorites area in the navigation pane so that they are available any time you open File Explorer. As you progress in your use of Windows 8, you will discover techniques for using the taskbar and the Favorites area of the navigation pane to streamline your work, instead of cluttering your desktop.

Objective 8   Personalize Your Windows 8 Start Screen

Because you will use some tiles on your Start screen more than others, you will want to reposition the tiles to suit your personal needs. To do so, simply drag the tiles with your mouse or your finger if you are using a touch device. You will also want to personalize the live tiles to display the information you want. For example, you can set the weather tile for your location.

Activity 1.15   Personalizing Your Windows 8 Start Screen

1 Display the **Start screen**, and then type **file explorer** On the left, point to the **File Explorer** app bordered in white, and then right-click to display the **app bar**. Compare your screen with Figure 1.51.

Here you can pin the app to the Start screen or to the taskbar on the desktop—or unpin from either of these locations.

FIGURE 1.51

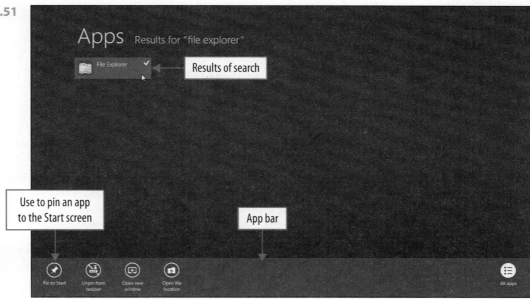

On the **app bar**, click **Pin to Start**, and then redisplay the **Start screen**. Point to the bottom of the screen to display the scroll bar, and then drag the scroll box to the right until the **File Explorer** tile comes into view as shown in Figure 1.52.

FIGURE 1.52

🔄 **BY TOUCH**   Drag your finger to the left to scroll to the right.

3 ▶ Drag the **File Explorer** tile to the top of the first column of tiles on your **Start screen**, and then drag the **Desktop** tile under it.

With this tile, you can easily go directly to File Explorer from your Start screen.

4 ▶ Click the **Weather** tile, if necessary, follow the prompts to set the app to your location, and then redisplay the **Start screen**.

5 ▶ On the **Start screen**, type **store** and press Enter to go the Windows Store. Type **twitter** and press Enter. If you want to do so, install a **Twitter** app—MetroTwit is one to try—so that you can view your Twitter feed on your **Start screen** as a live tile.

6 ▶ Redisplay your **Start screen**, point to an empty area, and then right-click. In the **app bar** at the bottom, click **All apps**.

Here you can view a small tile for every app—both desktop and Windows Store—in alphabetical order by category.

7 ▶ Press [⊞] to redisplay the **Start screen**. In the extreme lower right corner of your screen, click **Minimize** [–] to shrink the display of tiles.

This view enables you to see all of your tiles on one screen.

8 ▶ Click any empty area of the screen to return to the normal view.

ALERT!   **Allow Time to Complete This Lab in One Session**

If you are working on a computer that is not your own, for example in a college lab, plan your time to complete the remainder of this project in one working session.

Because you will need to store and then delete files on the hard disk drive of the computer at which you are working, it is recommended that you complete this project in one working session—*unless you are working on your own computer or you know that the files will be retained*. In your college lab, it is possible that files you store on the computer's hard drive will not be retained after you log off. Allow approximately 25–40 minutes for the remainder of this project.

Objective 9 ▌ Create, Rename, and Copy Files and Folders

File management includes organizing, copying, naming, renaming, moving, and deleting the files and folders you have stored in various locations—both locally and in the cloud.

Activity 1.16 ▏ Copying Files from a Removable Storage Device to the Documents Library on the Hard Disk Drive

Barbara and Steven have the assignment to transfer and then organize some of the corporation's files to a computer that will be connected to the corporate network. Data on such a computer can be accessed by employees at any of the hotel locations through the use of sharing technologies. For example, *SharePoint* is a Microsoft technology that enables employees in an organization to access information across organizational and geographic boundaries.

1 ▶ On the Windows 8 **Start screen**, click the **Desktop tile** to display your Windows 8 desktop. If necessary, insert the USB flash drive that contains the student data files that accompany this chapter that you downloaded from the Pearson website. Open **File Explorer** and display the folder window for your USB flash drive.

Recall that in the navigation pane, under Computer, you have access to all the storage areas inside your computer, such as your hard disk drives, and to any devices with removable storage, such as CDs, DVDs, or USB flash drives.

2 ▶ In the **file list**, click **Bell_Orchid** to select the folder. Compare your screen with Figure 1.53.

FIGURE 1.53

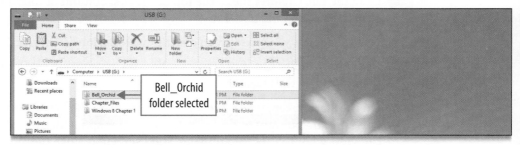

3 ▶ Point to the selected **Bell_Orchid** folder, hold down the left mouse button, and then drag the folder down to the taskbar until the ScreenTip *Pin to File Explorer* displays, and then release the left mouse button. Notice that the **Jump List** for File Explorer displays and that the **Bell_Orchid** folder is pinned to it.

By pinning the folder to the Jump List, you will be able to access it quickly.

4 Click anywhere on the desktop to close the Jump List. On the ribbon, on the **Home tab**, in the **Organize group**, click **Copy to**, and then on the displayed list, click **Documents**.

A progress bar displays in a dialog box, and also displays on the File Explorer taskbar button with green shading. A progress bar indicates visually the progress of a task such as a copy process, a download, or a file transfer.

The Documents library is one of several libraries within your *personal folder* stored on the hard disk drive. For each user account—even if there is only one user on the computer—Windows 8 creates a personal folder labeled with the account holder's name.

🔁 **ANOTHER WAY**   In the file list, point to the folder name and right-click. On the displayed shortcut menu, point to *Send to*, and then click Documents.

5 When the copy is complete, **Close** ☒ the window.

Activity 1.17 | Creating and Renaming Folders

Barbara and Steven can see that various managers have been placing files related to the new European hotels in the *Future_Hotels* folder. They can also see that the files have not been organized into a logical structure. For example, files that are related to each other are not in separate folders; instead they are mixed in with other files that are not related to the topic.

In this activity, you will create, name, and rename folders to begin a logical structure of folders in which to organize the files related to the European hotels project.

1 On the taskbar, right-click the **File Explorer** button 🗂 to display the **Jump List**, and then under **Pinned**, click **Bell_Orchid**.

🔁 **ANOTHER WAY**   If you were not able to pin the folder to the Jump List, click the File Explorer button, and then in the Documents library, navigate to the Bell_Orchid folder.

2 In the **address bar**, to the right of **Bell_Orchid**, click ▶, and then on the list click **Corporate**. To the right of **Corporate**, click ▶, and then click **Information_Technology**. To the right of **Information_Technology**, click ▶, and then click **Future_Hotels**.

Some computer users prefer to navigate a folder structure using the address bar in this manner. Use whichever method you prefer—double-clicking in the file list, or clicking in the address bar.

🔁 **ANOTHER WAY**   In the file list, double-click the Corporate folder, double-click the Information_Technology folder, and then double-click the Future_Hotels folder to display its contents in the file list. Or, in the navigation pane, click Documents, and expand each folder in the navigation pane.

3 Be sure the items are in alphabetical order by **Name**. If the items are not in alphabetical order, recall that by clicking on the column heading name, you can change how the files in the file list are ordered. On the ribbon, click the **View tab**, and then in the **Layout group**, be sure **Details** is selected. If necessary, set the view to **Details**.

The *Details view* displays a list of files or folders and their most common properties.

🔁 **ANOTHER WAY**   Right-click in a blank area of the file list, point to View, and then click Details.

4 On the ribbon, click the **Home tab**, and then in the **New group**, click **New folder**. With the text *New folder* selected, type **Paris** and press Enter. Click **New folder** again, and then type **Venice** and press Enter.

5 Create a new folder named **Essex** and press Enter. Click the **Venice** folder, and then on the ribbon, in the **Organize group**, click **Rename**. Notice that the text *Venice* is selected. Type **Rome** and press Enter.

🔄 **ANOTHER WAY**   Point to a folder or file name, right-click, and then on the shortcut menu, click Rename.

6 Click the **Essex** folder one time to select it. Point to the selected **Essex** folder, and then click one time again. With the text selected, type **London** and press Enter to change the folder name.

You can use either of these techniques to change the name of a folder.

7 From the taskbar, start **Snipping Tool**; if necessary drag the *title bar*—the bar across the top of a window that displays the program name—of Snipping Tool into a blank area of the desktop. Click the **New arrow**, and then click **Window Snip**. Point anywhere in the folder window and click one time. In the **Snipping Tool** mark-up window, click **Save Snip** 🖫.

8 In the **Save As** dialog box, in the **navigation pane**, scroll down as necessary, and then click your **USB flash drive** so that it displays in the **address bar**.

9 In the **file list**, double-click your **Windows 8 Chapter 1** folder to open it. Click in the **File name** box, and then replace the selected text by typing **Lastname_Firstname_1B_Europe_Folders_Snip**

10 Be sure the file type is **JPEG**. Click **Save** or press Enter. **Close** ⊠ the **Snipping Tool** window. Hold this file until you finish Project 1B. Leave the folder window open.

Activity 1.18 | Renaming Files

1 In the **address bar**, click **Information_Technology** to move up one level in the folder structure—or click the **Up button** ↑.

2 On the ribbon, click the **View tab**, and then in the **Current view group**, click **Size all columns to fit** ▦ to make it easier to see all the information about the files and folders.

3 Using any of the techniques you practiced to rename a folder, rename the **Dogs** file as **Dogs_1** and then rename the **MoreDogs** file to **Dogs_2** Compare your screen with Figure 1.54.

FIGURE 1.54

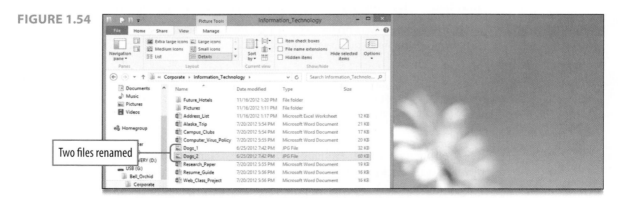

Two files renamed

4 **Close** ⊠ the folder window.

Activity 1.19 | Copying Files

Copying, moving, renaming, and deleting files and folders comprise the most heavily used features within File Explorer. Probably half or more of the tasks you complete in File Explorer relate to these tasks, so mastering these techniques will increase your efficiency.

When you *copy* a file or a folder, you make a duplicate of the original item and then store the duplicate in another location. In this activity, you will assist Barbara and Steven in making copies of the Staffing_Plan file, and then placing the copies in each of the three folders you created—London, Paris, and Rome.

1 ▶ In the taskbar, point to the **File Explorer** button 📁, hold down the left mouse button, and then drag upward slightly into the desktop to display the **Jump List**. Then, on the **Jump List**, under **Pinned**, click **Bell_Orchid**.

You will increase your efficiency if you make it a habit to work mostly from the taskbar and to display Jump Lists using this technique. After the Jump List displays, you need only move your mouse pointer upward a little more to select the action that you want.

🔄 **BY TOUCH**   Swipe upward with a quick short gesture to display the Jump List.

2 ▶ With the **Bell_Orchid** folder window displayed, by double-clicking in the **file list** or following the links in the **address bar**, navigate to **Corporate ▶ Information_Technology ▶ Future_Hotels**.

3 ▶ Maximize 🔲 the folder window. On the **View tab**, if necessary set the **Layout** to **Details**, and then in the **Current view group**, click **Size all columns to fit**.

4 ▶ In the **file list**, click the file **Staffing_Plan**, and then on the **Home tab**, in the **Clipboard group**, click **Copy**.

The Copy command places a copy of your selected file or folder on the *Clipboard* where it will be stored until you use the Paste command to insert the copy somewhere else. The Clipboard is a temporary storage area for information that you have copied or moved from one place and plan to use somewhere else.

In Windows 8, the Clipboard can hold only one piece of information at a time. Whenever something is copied to the Clipboard, it replaces whatever was there before. In Windows 8, you cannot view the contents of the Clipboard nor place multiple items there in the manner that you can in Microsoft Word.

5 ▶ At the top of the **file list**, double-click the **London folder** to open it, and then in the **Clipboard group**, click **Paste**. Notice that the copy of the **Staffing_Plan** file displays. Compare your screen with Figure 1.55.

FIGURE 1.55

File pasted to London folder

🔄 **ANOTHER WAY**   Right-click the file you want to copy, and on the menu click Copy. Then right-click the folder into which you want to place the copy, and on the menu click Paste. Or, select the file you want to copy, press Ctrl + C to activate the Copy command, open the folder into which you want to paste the file, and then press Ctrl + V to activate the Paste command.

6 ▶ With the **London** folder open, by using any of the techniques you have practiced, rename this copy of the **Staffing_Plan** file to **London_Staffing_Plan**

7 ▶ In the **address bar**, click **Future_Hotels** to redisplay this folder window and move up one level in the folder structure.

8 ▶ Click the **Staffing_Plan** file one time to select it, hold down Ctrl, and then drag the file upward over the **Paris** folder until the ScreenTip + *Copy to Paris* displays as shown in Figure 1.56, and then release the mouse button and release Ctrl.

> When dragging a file into a folder, holding down Ctrl engages the Copy command and places a *copy* of the file at the location where you release the mouse button. This is another way to copy a file or copy a folder.

FIGURE 1.56

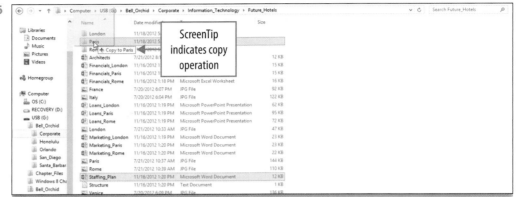

9 ▶ Open the **Paris** folder window, and then rename the **Staffing_Plan** file **Paris_Staffing_Plan** Then, move up one level in the folder structure to display the **Future_Hotels** folder window.

10 ▶ Double-click the **Rome** folder to open it. With your mouse pointer anywhere in the **file list**, right-click, and then from the shortcut menu click **Paste**.

> A copy of the Staffing_Plan file is copied to the folder. Because a copy of the Staffing_Plan file is still on the Clipboard, you can continue to paste the item until you copy another item on the Clipboard to replace it.

11 ▶ Rename the file **Rome_Staffing_Plan**

12 ▶ On the **address bar**, click **Future_Hotels** to move up one level and open the **Future_Hotels** folder window. Leave this folder open for the next activity.

Objective 10   Move and Delete Files and Folders

When you *move* a file or folder, you remove it from the original location and store it in a new location. To keep your computer organized, delete files you no longer need.

Activity 1.20 | Moving Files

In this activity, you will move items from the Future_Hotels folder into their appropriate folders.

1 ▶ With the **Future_Hotels** folder open, in the **file list**, click the Excel file **Financials_London** one time to select it. On the **Home tab**, in the **Clipboard group**, click **Cut**.

> The file's Excel icon dims. This action places the item on the Clipboard.

 **ANOTHER WAY**   Right-click the file or folder, and on the shortcut menu, click Cut; or, select the file or folder, and then press Ctrl + X.

2 ▶ Double-click the **London** folder to open it, and then on the **Home tab**, in the **Clipboard group**, click **Paste**.

ANOTHER WAY Right-click the folder, and on the shortcut menu, click Paste; or, select the folder, and then press Ctrl + V.

3 On the **address bar**, click **Future_Hotels** to move up a level. In the **file list**, point to **Financials_Paris**, hold down the left mouse button, and then drag the file upward over the **Paris** folder until the ScreenTip ➡*Move to Paris* displays, and then release the mouse button.

4 Open the **Paris** folder, and notice that the file was moved to this folder. On the **address bar**, click **Future_Hotels** to return to that folder.

5 Using either of the techniques you just practiced, move the **Financials_Rome** file into the **Rome** folder.

6 Hold down Ctrl, and then in the file list, click **Loans_London**, **London**, and **Marketing_London** to select the three files. Release the Ctrl key. Compare your screen with Figure 1.57.

> Use this technique to select a group of noncontiguous items in a list.

FIGURE 1.57

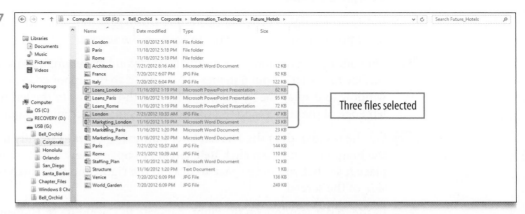

7 Point to any of the selected files, hold down the left mouse button, and then drag upward over the **London** folder until the ScreenTip ➡*Move to London* displays and *3* displays over the files being moved, and then release the mouse button.

ANOTHER WAY Right-click over any of the selected files, click Cut, right-click over the London folder, and then click Paste.

8 Using either the select and drag method, or the select and then Cut and Paste method, select the files **France**, **Loans_Paris**, **Marketing_Paris**, and **Paris**, and move these four files into the **Paris** folder.

9 Select the four files **Italy**, **Loans_Rome**, **Marketing_Rome**, and **Rome**, and move them into the **Rome** folder.

> You can see that by keeping related files together, for example, all the files that relate to the Rome hotel, in folders that have an appropriately descriptive name, it will be easier to locate information later.

ANOTHER WAY If a group of files to be selected are contiguous, or next to each other in the file list, click the first file to be selected and then press Shift and click the left mouse button on the last file to select all of the files between the top and bottom file selections.

10 Move the **Architects** file into the **London** folder.

11 In an empty area of the file list, right-click, and then click **Undo Move**. Leave the window open for the next activity.

> Any action that you make in a file list can be undone in this manner.

Activity 1.21 | Copying and Moving Files by Snapping Two Windows

Sometimes you will want to open, in a second window, another instance of a program that you are using; that is, two copies of the program will be running simultaneously. This capability is especially useful in the File Explorer program, because you are frequently moving or copying files from one location to another.

In this activity, you will open two instances of File Explorer, and then use the *Snap* feature to display both instances on your screen.

To copy or move files or folders into a different level of a folder structure, or to a different drive location, the most efficient method is to display two windows side by side and then use drag and drop or copy (or cut) and paste commands.

In this activity, you will assist Barbara and Steven in making copies of the Staffing_Plan files for the corporate office.

1 In the upper right corner, click **Restore Down** 🗗 to restore the **Future_Hotels** folder window to its previous size and not maximized on the screen.

2 On your desk, position your mouse so that you have enough space to drag it on your desk surface to the left about 6 inches. Then, point to the upper edge of the **Future_Hotels** folder window to display the 🔖 pointer and drag the window to the left until the pointer reaches the left edge of the screen and the window snaps into place and occupies the left half of the screen.

3 On the taskbar, drag the **File Explorer** button 📁 upward slightly into the desktop to display the **Jump List**, and then click **Bell_Orchid** to open a new folder window. Lift your mouse and place it so that you have space to drag to the right, and then snap this window to the right side of the screen.

4 In the folder window on the right, navigate to **Corporate ▶ Human_Resources**. Compare your screen with Figure 1.58.

FIGURE 1.58

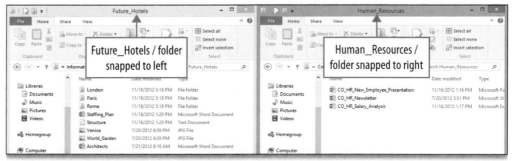

5 In the left window, open the **Rome** folder, and then select the file **Rome_Staffing_Plan**.

6 Hold down Ctrl, and then drag the file into the right window, into an empty area of the **Human_Resources file list**, until the ScreenTip + *Copy to Human_Resources* displays, and then release the mouse button and the Ctrl key.

7 In the left window, on the **address bar**, click **Future_Hotels** to redisplay that folder window. Open the **Paris** folder, point to **Paris_Staffing_Plan** and right-click, and then click **Copy**.

8 In the right window, point anywhere in the **file list**, right-click, and then click **Paste**.

9 Use either technique to copy the **London_Staffing_Plan** file on the left to the folder window on the right.

Copies of the three files regarding staffing plans for the three European locations display.

10 Start **Snipping Tool**, click the **New arrow**, and then click **Full-screen Snip**. In the **Snipping Tool** mark-up window, click **Save Snip** 🖫.

11 In the displayed **Save As** dialog box, notice the path in the **address bar**. If necessary, in the **navigation pane**, under **Computer**, click your **USB flash drive**, and then display the folder window for your **Windows 8 Chapter 1** folder.

12 Be sure the file type is **JPEG**. Using your own name, name the file **Lastname_Firstname_1B_HR_Snip** and press Enter.

13 **Close** 🗙 all open windows. Submit your three snip files from this Project to your instructor as directed.

More **Knowledge** | **Using the Recycle Bin Icon, Permanently Deleting an Item, and Restoring by Dragging**

It is good practice to delete files and folders that you no longer need from your hard disk drive and removable storage devices. Doing so frees up storage space on your devices and makes it easier to keep your data organized.

When you delete a file or folder from any area of your computer's hard disk drive, the file or folder is not immediately deleted. Instead, the deleted item is stored in the **Recycle Bin** and remains there until the Recycle Bin is emptied. Thus, you can recover an item deleted from your computer's hard disk drive so long as the Recycle Bin has not been emptied. Items deleted from removable storage devices like a USB flash drive and from some network drives are immediately deleted and cannot be recovered from the Recycle Bin.

To permanently delete a file without first moving it to the Recycle Bin, click the item, hold down Shift, and then press Delete. A message will display indicating *Are you sure you want to permanently delete this file?* Use caution when using Shift + Delete to permanently delete a file because this action is **not** reversible.

You can restore items by dragging them from the file list of the Recycle Bin window to the file list of the folder window in which you want to restore or you can restore them to the location they were deleted from by right-clicking the items in the file list of the Recycle Bin window and selecting Restore.

END | You have completed Project 1B

END OF CHAPTER

SUMMARY

Windows 8 is optimized for touchscreens and also works with a mouse and keyboard. You will probably use touch when you are reading or communicating on the web and a keyboard when creating files.

The Windows 8 Start screen is your connected dashboard—this is your one-screen view of information that updates continuously with new information and personal communications that are important to you.

The Windows Store apps you use from the Start screen are immersive—they have no borders or screen distractions. Windows Store apps typically have a single purpose; for example, to view Facebook updates.

File Explorer is at work anytime you are viewing the contents of a library, a folder, or a file. Use File Explorer to navigate your Windows 8 structure that stores and organizes the files you create.

GO! LEARN IT ONLINE

Review the concepts and key terms in this chapter by completing these online challenges, which you can find at **www.pearsonhighered.com/go**.

Matching and Multiple Choice:
Answer matching and multiple choice questions to test what you learned in this chapter. MyITLab®

Crossword Puzzle:
Spell out the words that match the numbered clues, and put them in the puzzle squares.

Flipboard:
Flip through the definitions of the key terms in this chapter and match them with the correct term.

GO! FOR JOB SUCCESS

Video: Email Etiquette

Your instructor may assign this video to your class, and then ask you to think about, or discuss with your classmates, these questions:

FotolEdhar / Fotolia

Why do you think it is important to follow specific etiquette when composing email?

Why is it important to include a greeting and sign every email you send?

What are the differences between sending a business email and a personal email, and what are three specific things you should never do in a business email?

END OF CHAPTER

REVIEW AND ASSESSMENT GUIDE FOR WINDOWS 8 CHAPTER 1

Your instructor may assign one or more of these projects to help you review the chapter and assess your mastery and understanding of the chapter.

	Review and Assessment Guide for Windows 8 Chapter 1		
Project	**Apply Skills from These Chapter Objectives**	**Project Type**	**Project Location**
1C	Objectives 1–5 from Project 1A	**1C Skills Review** A guided review of the skills from Project 1A.	On the following pages
1D	Objectives 6–10 from Project 1B	**1D Skills Review** A guided review of the skills from Project 1B.	On the following pages
1E	Objectives 1–5 from Project 1A	**1E Mastery** A demonstration of your mastery of the skills in Project 1A with decision making.	On the following pages
1F	Objectives 6–10 from Project 1B	**1F Mastery** A demonstration of your mastery of the skills in Project 1B with decision making.	On the following pages
1G	Combination of Objectives from Projects 1A and 1B	**1G Mastery** A demonstration of your understanding of the chapter concepts applied in a manner that you would outside of college. An analytic rubric helps you and your instructor grade the quality of your work by comparing it to the work an expert in the discipline would create.	On the following pages
1H	Combination of Objectives from Projects 1A and 1B	**1H GO! Think** A demonstration of your understanding of the chapter concepts applied in a manner that you would outside of college. An analytic rubric helps you and your instructor grade the quality of your work by comparing it to the work an expert in the discipline would create.	On the following pages
1I	Combination of Objectives from Projects 1A and 1B	**1I GO! Think** A demonstration of your understanding of the chapter concepts applied in a manner that you would outside of college. An analytic rubric helps you and your instructor grade the quality of your work by comparing it to the work an expert in the discipline would create.	On the following pages

GLOSSARY

.jpg An image file format, commonly pronounced *JPEG*, that stands for Joint Photographic Experts Group; this is a common file type used by digital cameras and computers to store digital pictures; JPEG is popular because it can store a high-quality picture in a relatively small file.

.png An image file format, commonly pronounced *PING*, that stands for Portable Network Graphic; this is an image file type that can be transferred over the Internet.

Action Center Located in the notification area, a central place to view alerts and take actions related to things that need your attention.

Address bar Displays your current location in the folder structure as a series of links separated by arrows.

Administrator account A user account that lets you make changes that will affect other users of the computer; the most powerful of the three types of accounts, because it permits the most control over the computer.

App The shortened version of the word *application*.

App bar An area at the bottom of every Windows Store app containing various controls pertaining to the app.

App switcher The thumbnail view of open apps that displays when you move your mouse down from the Back tip in the upper left corner; to switch to an app that is still open, you can click any of the thumbnails.

Application A set of instructions that a computer uses to accomplish a task; also called a program.

Back tip The upper left corner of the Start screen that when pointed to displays a thumbnail image of the last screen you were on; you can use it to *go back* to your previous screen.

Badge An icon that displays on the Lock screen, below the time, day, and date, that represents the status of your Internet connection, your battery if you are using a tablet or laptop, or any other Lock screen apps you might have selected.

Booting the computer The process of turning on a computer when the computer has been completely shut down.

Charms A set of buttons that display when you point or swipe in from the right side of the screen that you can use in every app—whether a Windows Store app or a desktop app—and that enable you to search, share, access devices, or adjust your PC settings.

Click The action of pressing the left mouse button.

Clipboard A temporary storage area for information that you have copied or moved from one place and plan to use somewhere else.

Cloud storage Storage space on an Internet site that can also display as a drive on your computer.

Compressed file A file that has been reduced in size and that takes up less storage space and can be transferred to other computers faster than uncompressed files.

Contextual tab Context-sensitive commands and options on the ribbon that are relevant to the active object.

Dashboard A descriptive term for the Windows 8 Start screen because it provides a one-screen view of links to information and programs that matter most to the signed-in user.

Data All the files—documents, workbooks, pictures, songs, and so on—that you create and store during the day-to-day use of your computer.

Data management The process of managing your files and folders in an organized manner so that you can find information when you need it.

Desktop The area in Windows 8 where you use desktop apps and that serves as a surface for your work, like the top of an actual desk.

Desktop app A computer program installed on the hard drive of a computer and that requires a computer operating system like Microsoft Windows or Apple OS to run.

Desktop background Displays the colors and graphics of your desktop; you can change the desktop background to look the way you want it.

Desktop shortcuts Desktop icons that link to any item accessible on your computer or on a network, such as a program, file, folder, disk drive, printer, or another computer.

Details pane Displays the most common properties associated with the selected file.

Details view The file list view in File Explorer that displays a list of files or folders and their most common properties.

Dialog box A small window that displays options for completing a task.

Double-click The action of pressing the left mouse button twice in rapid succession while holding the mouse still.

Drag The action of moving something from one location on the screen to another while holding down the left mouse button; the action of dragging includes releasing the mouse button at the desired time or location.

Drive An area of storage that is formatted with a file system compatible with your operating system and is identified by a drive letter.

Extract The action of decompressing—pulling out—files from a compressed form.

File A collection of information that is stored on a computer under a single name, for example a text document, a picture, or a program.

File Explorer The program within Windows 8 that displays the contents of libraries, folders, and files on your computer, and which also enables you to perform tasks related to your files and folders such as copying, moving, and renaming. File Explorer is at work anytime you are viewing the contents of a library, a folder, or a file.

File list Displays the contents of the current folder or library; if you type text into the Search box, only the folders and files that match your search will display here—including files in subfolders.

File properties Information about a file such as its author, the date the file was last changed, and any descriptive tags.

Folder A container in which you store files.

Folder structure The hierarchy of folders in Windows 8.

Folder window Displays the contents of the current folder, library, or device, and contains helpful parts so that you can navigate—explore within the organizing structure of Windows.

Free-form snip When using Snipping Tool, the type of snip that lets you draw an irregular line, such as a circle, around an area of the screen.

Full-screen snip When using Snipping Tool, the type of snip that captures the entire screen.

Graphical user interface The system by which you interact with your computer and which uses graphics such as an image of a file folder or wastebasket that you click to activate the item represented.

GUI The acronym for a graphical user interface, pronounced *GOO-ee*.

Hard disk drive The primary storage device located inside your computer and where most of your files and programs are typically stored; usually labeled as drive C.

Hierarchy An arrangement where items are ranked and where each level is lower in rank than the item above it.

Icons Small images that represent commands, files, applications, or other windows.

Immersive The term that describes the Windows 8 style screens, meaning they have no borders, no menus, and they behave differently from traditional Windows desktop programs because there is no taskbar, an app cannot be minimized like a desktop program, nor can an app be dragged around as a smaller window; the idea is that you are immersed in the app with no screen distractions.

Insertion point A blinking vertical line that indicates where text or graphics will be inserted.

Internet Explorer The web browser program developed by Microsoft that is included with Windows 8.

JPEG An acronym for Joint Photographic Experts Group, and which is a common file type used by digital cameras and computers to store digital pictures; JPEG is popular because it can store a high-quality picture in a relatively small file. A JPEG file has a .jpg file extension.

Jump List A list that displays when you right-click a button on the taskbar, and which displays locations (in the upper portion) and tasks (in the lower portion) from a program's taskbar button.

Keyboard shortcut A combination of two or more keyboard keys, used to perform a task that would otherwise require a mouse.

Library A collection of items, such as files and folders, assembled from various locations.

Live tiles Tiles on the Windows 8 Start screen that are constantly updated with fresh information relevant to the signed-in user; for example, the number of new email messages, new sports scores of interest, or new updates to social networks such as Facebook or Twitter.

Local account A user account in which the information associated with each user is local to a single Windows 8 computer.

Location Any disk drive, folder, or other place in which you can store files and folders.

Lock screen The first screen that displays after turning on a Windows 8 device, which displays the time, day, and date, and one or more icons representing the status of the device's Internet connection, battery status on a tablet or laptop, and any Lock screen apps that are installed such as email notifications.

Lock screen apps Apps that display on a Windows 8 Lock screen and that show quick status and notifications, even if the screen is locked, and include Calendar, Mail, Messaging, and Weather.

Menu A list of commands within a category.

Menu bar A group of menus.

Microsoft account A user account that allows you to set up one Windows 8 computer and then synchronize all the same settings from that computer to any other device you have that uses Windows 8.

Microsoft Design Language The design principles in Windows 8 that include tiles with white text on deeply colored backgrounds, consistent fonts, simpler navigation, and the use of the entire screen; the idea is that you are immersed in the app with no screen distractions.

Mouse pointer Any symbol that displays on your screen in response to moving your mouse.

Navigate (File Explorer) Explore within the file organizing structure of Windows 8.

Navigation pane The area on the left side of a folder window; it displays favorites, libraries, and an expandable list of drives and folders.

Notification area Displays notification icons and the system clock; sometimes referred to as the *system tray*.

Notification bar In Internet Explorer 10, a bar at the bottom of your screen that displays information about pending downloads, security issues, add-ons, and other issues related to the operation of your computer.

Operating system A specific type of computer program that manages the other programs on a computer—including computer devices such as desktop computers, laptop computers, smartphones, tablet computers, and game consoles.

Paint A program that comes with Windows 8 with which you can create and edit drawings and display and edit stored photos.

Parent folder In the file organizing structure of File Explorer, the location where the folder you are viewing is saved—one level up in the hierarchy.

Path A sequence of folders (directories) that leads to a specific file or folder.

PC settings The area from which you can control almost everything about how Windows 8 looks and works; you can change colors and backgrounds, the picture on your Lock screen, or your account picture, manage other users (if you are the administrator), connect devices like printers, or set up a network.

Personal folder A folder created for each user account on a Windows 8 computer, labeled with the account holder's name, and which contains the subfolders *Documents*, *Pictures*, *Music*, and *Videos*.

PING An acronym for Portable Network Graphic, and which is a common file type that can be transferred over the Internet. A PING file has a .png file extension.

Point to The action of moving the mouse pointer over a specific area.

Pointer Any symbol that displays on your screen in response to moving your mouse and with which you can select objects and commands.

Pointing device A mouse, touchpad, or other device that controls the pointer position on the screen.

Program A set of instructions that a computer uses to accomplish a task; also called an application.

Progress bar In a dialog box or taskbar button, a bar that indicates visually the progress of a task such as a download or file transfer.

Rectangular snip When using Snipping Tool, the type of snip that lets you draw a precise box by dragging the mouse pointer around an area of the screen to form a rectangle.

Recycle Bin A folder that stores anything that you delete from your computer, and from which anything stored can be retrieved until the contents are permanently deleted by activating the Empty Recycle Bin command.

Removable storage device A portable device on which you can store files, such as a USB flash drive, a flash memory card, or an external hard drive,

commonly used to transfer information from one computer to another.

Resources A term used to refer collectively to the parts of your computer such as the central processing unit (CPU), memory, and any attached devices such as a printer.

Ribbon The area at the top of a folder window in File Explorer that groups common tasks such as copying and moving, creating new folders, emailing and zipping items, and changing views on related tabs.

Right-click The action of clicking the right mouse button.

Roam The ability to set up one computer, for example a desktop computer, and then synchronize—roam—all the same settings to a laptop, to a tablet PC, to a Windows phone, or to any other device to which one signs in with the same Microsoft account.

Screen capture An image file that contains the contents of a computer screen.

Screenshot Another name for a screen capture.

ScreenTip Useful information that displays in a small box on the screen when you perform various mouse actions, such as pointing to screen elements.

Scroll arrow An arrow at the top and bottom, or left and right, of a scroll bar that when clicked, moves the window in small increments.

Scroll bar A bar that displays on the bottom or right side of a window when the contents of a window are not completely visible; used to move the window up, down, left, or right to bring the contents into view.

Scroll box The box in a vertical or horizontal scroll bar that you drag to reposition the document on the screen.

Select To specify, by highlighting, a block of data or text on the screen with the intent of performing some action on the selection.

SharePoint A Microsoft technology that enables employees in an organization to

access information across organizational and geographic boundaries.

Shortcut menu A context-sensitive menu that displays commands and options relevant to the active object.

Shut down Turning off your computer in a manner that closes all open programs and files, closes your network connections, stops the hard disk, and discontinues the use of electrical power.

SkyDrive A free file storage and file sharing service provided by Microsoft when you sign up for a Microsoft account.

Sleep Turning off your computer in a manner that automatically saves your work, stops the fan, and uses a small amount of electrical power to maintain your work in memory.

Snap (desktop apps) A Windows 8 desktop feature that automatically resizes windows when you move—*snap*—them to the edge of the screen.

Snip The image captured using Snipping Tool.

Snipping Tool A program included with Windows 8 with which you can capture an image of all or part of a computer screen, and then annotate, save, copy, or share the image via email.

Speakers icon Displays the status of the computer's speakers (if any).

Split button A button that has two parts—a button and an arrow; clicking the main part of the button performs a command and clicking the arrow opens a menu with choices.

Start screen The first screen that displays after signing in to a Windows 8 device, which displays square and rectangular boxes—referred to as tiles—from which one can access apps, websites, programs, and tools for using the computer by clicking or tapping them.

Start search The search feature in Windows 8 in which, from the Start screen, you can begin to type and by default, Windows 8 searches for apps; you can adjust the search to search for files or settings.

Start tip The thumbnail that displays when you point to the lower left corner of your screen.

Switcher Another name for *app switcher*.

System tray Another name for the notification area on the taskbar.

Tags Properties that you create and add to a file to help you find and organize your files.

Taskbar The area of the desktop that contains program buttons, and buttons for all open programs; by default, it is located at the bottom of the desktop, but you can move it.

Thumbnail A reduced image of a graphic.

Tiles Square and rectangular boxes on the Windows 8 Start screen from which one can access apps, websites, programs, and tools for using the computer by simply clicking or tapping them.

Title bar The bar across the top of the window that displays the program name.

User account A collection of information that tells Windows 8 what files and folders the account holder can access, what changes the account holder can make to the computer system, and what the account holder's personal preferences are.

Wallpaper Another term for the desktop background.

Web browser Software with which you display webpages and navigate the Internet.

Window snip When using Snipping Tool, the type of snip that captures the entire displayed window.

Windows 8 An operating system developed by Microsoft Corporation designed to work with mobile computing devices of all types and also with traditional PCs.

Windows Store apps Apps built for specific purposes; for example, to view photos, read sports information, organize a list of contacts, or read updates to social networks like Facebook and Twitter.

CHAPTER REVIEW

Apply 1A skills from these Objectives:

1 Use File Explorer and Desktop Apps to Create a New Folder and Save a File on a Removable Storage Device

2 Identify the Functions of the Windows 8 Operating System and Windows Store Apps

3 Use Windows Store Apps

4 Sign Out of Windows 8 and Turn Off Your Computer

5 Manage User Accounts

PROJECT FILES

For Project 1C, you will need the following files:

Your USB flash drive containing the student data files
win01_1C_Answer_Sheet (Word document)

You will save your file as:

Lastname_Firstname_1C_Answer_Sheet

1 Display the **Start screen**; point to the upper left corner and drag down slightly to display the app switcher, and then if necessary, close any open apps. Display the **desktop**. **Close** ☒ any open desktop windows. On the taskbar, click **File Explorer**. In the **navigation pane**, click your **USB drive** that contains the student files for this chapter, and then navigate to **Chapter_Files** ▶ **Chapter_01**. Double-click the Word file **win01_1C_Answer_Sheet** to open Word and display the document. If necessary, at the top click Enable editing; be sure the window is maximized. In the upper left corner, click **FILE**, click **Save As**, click **Computer**, and then click **Browse** to display the **Save As** dialog box. In the **navigation pane**, click your **USB drive** and then double-click to open your **Windows 8 Chapter 1** folder. Using your own name, save the document as **Lastname_Firstname_1C_Answer_Sheet** Click Save.

On the taskbar, click the **Word** button to minimize the window and leave your Word document accessible from the taskbar. **Close** the **Chapter_01** folder window. As you complete each step in this project, write the letter of your answer on a piece of paper; you will fill in your Answer Sheet after you complete all the steps in this project.

Display the **Start screen** and type **paint** Which of the following is true?

A. Applications that begin with the text *paint* display in the search results.

B. The Paint program opens on the desktop.

C. From this screen, you can remove the Paint program from your computer.

2 If necessary, press an arrow key on your computer to surround the name of the *Paint* program with a white border, and then press Enter. What is your result?

A. The Paint program tile displays on the Start screen.

B. The Paint program opens on the desktop.

C. File Explorer displays files created in the Paint program.

3 On the taskbar, point to the **Paint** button, right-click, and click **Pin this program to taskbar**. Then **Close** ☒ the **Paint** window. Which of the following is true?

A. Both B. and C. are true.

B. The Paint program closes.

C. The Paint program button displays on the taskbar because it is pinned there.

4 On the taskbar, click **File Explorer**. What is your result?

A. The window for your USB flash drive displays.

B. The Libraries window displays.

C. The Documents window displays.

(Project 1C Getting to Know Windows 8 continues on the next page)

CHAPTER REVIEW

5 In the **file list**, double-click **Documents**. What is your result?

A. The first document in the library opens in its application.

B. The contents of the Documents library display in the file list.

C. The contents of the Documents library display in the address bar.

6 In the **navigation pane**, click **Computer**. What is your result?

A. The storage devices attached to your computer display in the file list.

B. All of the files on the hard drive display in the file list.

C. Your computer restarts.

7 Close ☒ the **Computer** window. On the taskbar, point to the **Paint** button, right-click, and then click **Unpin this program from taskbar**. Display the **Start screen**. Type **store** and press Enter. What is your result?

A. All the storage devices attached to your computer display on the Start screen.

B. The Store app displays.

C. A list of games that you can download displays.

8 Display the **Start screen**, type **maps** and press Enter; if necessary, enable your current location. Display the **Start screen** again, type **weather** and then press Enter. Display the **Start screen** again, point to the upper left corner of the screen, and then move the mouse pointer down along the left edge of the screen to display all open apps. This display of all open apps is called what?

A. app navigator

B. app map

C. app switcher

9 Which of the following best describes the group of apps that display as open?

A. Weather, Desktop

B. Maps, Store, Weather

C. Weather, Maps, Store, Desktop

10 On the left side of the screen, point to each open app, right-click, and then click **Close** so that all apps are closed. What is your result?

A. The desktop redisplays.

B. The search results for *store* redisplay.

C. The Start screen displays.

To complete this project: Display the **desktop**, on the taskbar click the **Word** button, and type your answers into the correct boxes. Save and close your Word document, and submit as directed by your instructor. **Close** ☒ all open windows.

END | You have completed Project 1C

CHAPTER REVIEW

Apply 1B skills from these Objectives:

6 Use File Explorer to Display Libraries, Folders, and Files

7 Start Programs and Open Data Files

8 Personalize Your Windows 8 Start Screen

9 Create, Rename, and Copy Files and Folders

10 Move and Delete Files and Folders

Skills Review | Project 1D Managing Files and Folders

PROJECT FILES

For Project 1D, you will need the following files:

Your USB flash drive containing the student data files
win01_1D_Answer_Sheet (Word document)

You will save your file as:

Lastname_Firstname_1D_Answer_Sheet

1 ▸ Display the **Start screen**; point to the upper left corner and drag down slightly to display the app switcher, and then if necessary, close any open apps. Display the **desktop**. **Close** ☒ any open desktop windows. On the taskbar, click **File Explorer**. In the **navigation pane**, click your **USB drive** that contains the student files for this chapter, and then navigate to **Chapter_Files** ▶ **Chapter_01**. Double-click the Word file **win01_1D_Answer_Sheet** to open Word and display the document. If necessary, at the top click Enable editing; be sure the window is maximized. In the upper left corner, click **FILE**, click **Save As**, click **Computer**, and then click **Browse** to display the **Save As** dialog box. In the **navigation pane**, click your **USB drive** and then double-click to open your **Windows 8 Chapter 1** folder. Using your own name, save the document as **Lastname_Firstname_1D_Answer_Sheet** Click **Save**.

On the taskbar, click the **Word** button to minimize the window and leave your Word document accessible from the taskbar. **Close** the **Chapter_01** folder window. As you complete each step in this project, write the letter of your answer on a piece of paper; you will fill in your Answer Sheet after you complete all the steps in this project.

Open **File Explorer**, navigate to your **USB flash drive**, and then click to select the **Bell_Orchid** folder. On the ribbon, on the **Home tab**, in the **Organize group**, click **Copy to**, and then on the displayed list, click **Documents**. *You will need a new copy of the files for this Project.* If a message indicates **Replace or Skip Files**, click **Replace the files in the destination** so that you have a new copy of the original files from your USB drive.

From the **navigation pane**, double-click your **Documents** folder to open its folder window, and then double-click the **Bell_Orchid** folder. In the **file list**, how many *folders* display?

A. Four

B. Five

C. Six

2 ▸ Navigate to **Bell_Orchid** ▶ **Corporate** ▶ **Food_Beverage**. How many *folders* are in the **Food_Beverage** folder?

A. Three

B. Two

C. One

3 ▸ Open the **Restaurants** folder, and then click one time to select the file **Breakfast_Continental**. On the ribbon, click the **Home tab**. In which group of commands can you change the name of this file?

A. New

B. Select

C. Organize

(Project 1D Managing Files and Folders continues on the next page)

CHAPTER REVIEW

4 With the **Breakfast_Continental** file still selected, point to the file name and right-click. Which of the following is *not* true?

A. From this menu, you can rename the file.

B. From this menu, you can print the file.

C. From this menu, you can move the file to another folder within Bell_Orchid.

5 Click on the desktop to close the shortcut menu, and then click the **Up** button to move up one level in the hierarchy and display the file list for the **Food_Beverage** folder. On the ribbon, click the **View tab**. In the **Layout group**, click **Large icons**. What is your result?

A. The folder window fills the entire screen.

B. Files that are pictures are visible as pictures.

C. Only picture files display in the file list.

6 On the **View tab**, return the **Layout** to **Details view**. In the **file list**, click one time to select the file **CO_FB_Menu_Presentation**. In the **Panes group**, click the **Details pane** button. (*Hint*: you can point to a button to see its ScreenTip). By looking at the displayed details about this file on the right, which of the following is an information item you can determine about this file?

A. The number of words on each slide.

B. The number of slides in the presentation.

C. The number of people who edited this presentation.

7 In the **Panes group**, click the **Preview pane**. In the **Preview pane**, *slowly* drag the scroll box to the bottom of the scroll bar. Which of the following is *not* true?

A. The slide name displays as you drag the scroll box.

B. The PowerPoint program opens as you drag the scroll box.

C. The slide number displays as you drag the scroll box.

8 In the **Panes group**, click the **Preview pane** button again to close the pane. **Close** ☒ the folder window. Display the **Start screen**, type **paint** and then press Enter to display the **Paint** program on your desktop. On the taskbar, point to the **Paint** button and right-click. Which of the following is *not* true?

A. From the displayed menu, you can pin this program to the taskbar.

B. From the displayed menu, you can pin this program to the Start screen.

C. From the displayed menu, you can close the Paint program.

9 Click **Close window**, and then display the **Start screen**. Type **paint** and then in the Apps screen, right-click **Paint** to display the **app bar** at the bottom of the screen. Click **Pin to Start** and then redisplay the **Start screen**. Which of the following is true?

A. Windows 8 creates a tile for the Paint program on the Start screen.

B. The Paint program opens on your desktop.

C. A tile for the Paint program flashes on the Start screen.

(Project 1D Managing Files and Folders continues on the next page)

CHAPTER REVIEW

10 On the **Start screen**, locate and point to the **Paint** tile, and then right-click. Click **Unpin from Start**. Click the **Desktop** tile. Open **File Explorer**, display your **Documents** folder, and then click the **Bell_Orchid** folder one time to select it. On the **Home tab**, in the **Organize group**, locate **Delete**, and then click the **Delete button arrow**. What is your result?

A. The folder window for the Recycle Bin displays.

B. The folder is deleted and the Documents window closes.

C. A list of Delete options displays.

On the list, click **Permanently delete** (or Recycle if you prefer). Recall that you still have the original Bell_Orchid file on your USB flash drive. In the **Delete Folder** dialog box, click **Yes**. In the upper right corner of the folder window, click **Close** ⬛.

To complete this project: On the taskbar, click the **Word** button, and then type your answers into the correct boxes. Save and close your Word document, and submit as directed by your instructor. **Close** ⬛ all open windows.

END | You have completed Project 1D

CONTENT-BASED ASSESSMENTS

Mastering Windows 8   Project 1E Windows Help and Support

In the following Mastering Windows 8 project, you will capture and save a snip that will look similar to Figure 1.59.

Apply 1A skills from these Objectives:

1 Use File Explorer and Desktop Apps to Create a New Folder and Save a File on a Removable Storage Device

2 Identify the Functions of the Windows 8 Operating System and Windows Store Apps

3 Use Windows Store Apps

4 Sign Out of Windows 8 and Turn Off Your Computer

5 Manage User Accounts

PROJECT FILES

For Project 1E, you will need the following file:

Your USB flash drive containing the student data files
New Snip file

You will save your file as:

Lastname_Firstname_1E_Close_App_Snip

PROJECT RESULTS

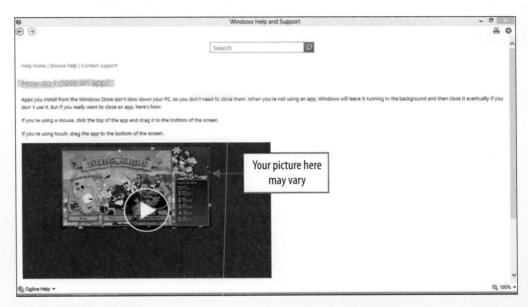

FIGURE 1.59

(Project 1E Windows Help and Support continues on the next page)

CONTENT-BASED ASSESSMENTS

1 On the **Start screen**, type **help and support** and press Enter to display the **Windows Help and Support** window. Search for **close an app** Click **How do I close an app?** Maximize ▫ the window.

2 On the taskbar, click **Snipping Tool**, click the **New button arrow**, and then click **Window Snip**. Click anywhere in the **Windows Help and Support** window to capture it.

3 On the toolbar of the **Snipping Tool** mark-up window, click the **Highlighter** and then highlight the text *How do I close an app?* Click the **Save Snip** button.

4 In the displayed **Save As** dialog box, in the **navigation pane**, scroll down, and then under

Computer, click your **USB flash drive**. In the **file list**, open your **Windows 8 Chapter 1** folder so that its name displays in the **address bar**, and then as the **File name**, and using your own name, save the snip as **Lastname_Firstname_1E_Close_App_Snip**

5 **Close** ☒ the **Snipping Tool** window. Take a moment to click the circled play button ▷ to watch the short video about how to close an app.

6 **Close** ☒ the **Windows Help and Support** window. Submit your snip file as directed by your instructor.

END | You have completed Project 1E

CONTENT-BASED ASSESSMENTS

Apply 1B skills from these Objectives:

6 Use File Explorer to Display Libraries, Folders, and Files

7 Start Programs and Open Data Files

8 Personalize Your Windows 8 Start Screen

9 Create, Rename, and Copy Files and Folders

10 Move and Delete Files and Folders

Mastering Windows 8 | Project 1F Managing Files and Folders

In the following Mastering Windows 8 project, you will capture and save a snip that will look similar to Figure 1.60.

PROJECT FILES

For Project 1F, you will need the following files:

Your USB flash drive containing the student data files
New Snip file

You will save your file as:

Lastname_Firstname_1F_San_Diego_Snip

PROJECT RESULTS

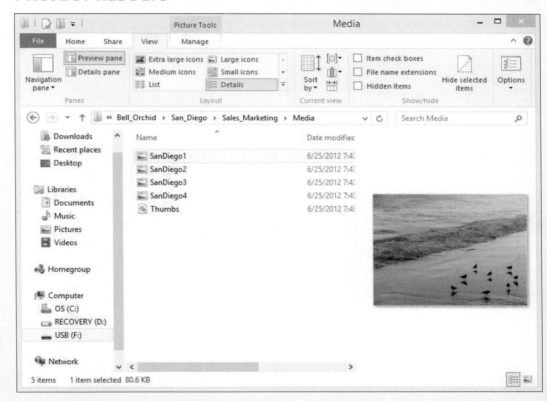

FIGURE 1.60

(Project 1F Managing Files and Folders continues on the next page)

CONTENT-BASED ASSESSMENTS

1 Display the **desktop**, and then on the taskbar, click **File Explorer**. Display the folder window for your **USB flash drive**, and then navigate to **Bell_Orchid ▶ San_Diego ▶ Sales_Marketing ▶ Media**.

2 On the **file list**, click one time to select the file **SanDiego1**.

3 Display the **Preview pane** for this file.

4 Start **Snipping Tool**, create a **Window Snip**, click anywhere in the **Media** folder window to capture it, and then click the **Save Snip** button.

5 In the displayed **Save As** dialog box, in the **navigation pane**, scroll down, and then under **Computer**, click your **USB flash drive**. In the **file list**, open your **Windows 8 Chapter 1** folder so that its name displays in the **address bar**, and then as the **File name**, and using your own name, save the snip as **Lastname_Firstname_1F_San_Diego_Snip**

6 **Close** ☒ the **Snipping Tool** window. Turn off the display of the **Preview pane**. **Close** ☒ the folder window. Submit your snip file as directed by your instructor.

END | You have completed Project 1F

OUTCOMES-BASED ASSESSMENTS

RUBRIC

The following outcomes-based assessments are *open-ended assessments*. That is, there is no specific correct result; your result will depend on your approach to the information provided. Make *Professional Quality* your goal. Use the following scoring rubric to guide you in *how* to approach the problem, and then to evaluate *how well* your approach solves the problem.

The *criteria*—Software Mastery, Content, Format and Layout, and Process—represent the knowledge and skills you have gained that you can apply to solving the problem. The *levels of performance*—Professional Quality, Approaching Professional Quality, or Needs Quality Improvements—help you and your instructor evaluate your result.

	Your completed project is of Professional Quality if you:	Your completed project is Approaching Professional Quality if you:	Your completed project Needs Quality Improvements if you:
1-Software Mastery	Choose and apply the most appropriate skills, tools, and features and identify efficient methods to solve the problem.	Choose and apply some appropriate skills, tools, and features, but not in the most efficient manner.	Choose inappropriate skills, tools, or features, or are inefficient in solving the problem.
2-Content	Construct a solution that is clear and well organized, contains content that is accurate, appropriate to the audience and purpose, and is complete. Provide a solution that contains no errors in spelling, grammar, or style.	Construct a solution in which some components are unclear, poorly organized, inconsistent, or incomplete. Misjudge the needs of the audience. Have some errors in spelling, grammar, or style, but the errors do not detract from comprehension.	Construct a solution that is unclear, incomplete, or poorly organized; contains some inaccurate or inappropriate content; and contains many errors in spelling, grammar, or style. Do not solve the problem.
3-Format & Layout	Format and arrange all elements to communicate information and ideas, clarify function, illustrate relationships, and indicate relative importance.	Apply appropriate format and layout features to some elements, but not others. Overuse features, causing minor distraction.	Apply format and layout that does not communicate information or ideas clearly. Do not use format and layout features to clarify function, illustrate relationships, or indicate relative importance. Use available features excessively, causing distraction.
4-Process	Use an organized approach that integrates planning, development, self-assessment, revision, and reflection.	Demonstrate an organized approach in some areas, but not others; or, use an insufficient process of organization throughout.	Do not use an organized approach to solve the problem.

OUTCOMES-BASED ASSESSMENTS

In this project, you will construct a solution by applying any combination of the skills you practiced from the Objectives in Projects 1A and 1B.

PROJECT FILES

For Project 1G, you will need the following file:

win01_1G_Help_Desk

You will save your document as:

Lastname_Firstname_1G_Help_Desk

From the student files that accompany this chapter, open the **Chapter_Files** folder, and then in the **Chapter_01** folder, locate and open the Word document **win01_1G_Help_Desk**. Save the document in your **Windows 8 Chapter 1** folder as **Lastname_Firstname_1G_Help_Desk**

The following email question arrived at the Help Desk from an employee at the Bell Orchid Hotel's corporate office. In the Word document, construct a response based on your knowledge of Windows 8. Although an email response is not as formal as a letter, you should still use good grammar, good sentence structure, professional language, and a polite tone. Save your document and submit the response as directed by your instructor.

To: Help Desk

We have a new employee in our department, and as her user picture, she wants to use a picture of her dog. I know that Corporate Policy says it is ok to use an acceptable personal picture on a user account. Can she change the picture herself within her standard user account, or does she need an administrator account to do that?

END | You have completed Project 1G

OUTCOMES-BASED ASSESSMENTS

GO! Think | Project 1H Help Desk

In this project, you will construct a solution by applying any combination of the skills you practiced from the Objectives in Projects 1A and 1B.

PROJECT FILES

For Project 1H, you will need the following file:

win01_1H_Help_Desk

You will save your document as:

Lastname_Firstname_1H_Help_Desk

From the student files that accompany this chapter, open the **Chapter_Files** folder, and then in the **Chapter_01** folder, locate and open **win01_1H_Help_Desk**. Save the document in your **Windows 8 Chapter 1** folder as **Lastname_Firstname_1H_Help_Desk**

The following email question arrived at the Help Desk from an employee at the Bell Orchid Hotel's corporate office. In the Word document, construct a response based on your knowledge of Windows 8. Although an email response is not as formal as a letter, you should still use good grammar, good sentence structure, professional language, and a polite tone. Save your document and submit the response as directed by your instructor.

To: Help Desk

When I'm done using my computer at the end of the day, should I use the Sleep option or the Shut down option, and what's the difference between the two?

END | You have completed Project 1H

OUTCOMES-BASED ASSESSMENTS

In this project, you will construct a solution by applying any combination of the skills you practiced from the Objectives in Projects 1A and 1B.

For Project 1I, you will need the following file:

win01_1I_Help_Desk

You will save your document as:

Lastname_Firstname_1I_Help_Desk

From the student files that accompany this chapter, open the **Chapter_Files** folder, and then in the **Chapter_01** folder, locate and open **win01_1I_Help_Desk**. Save the document in your **Windows 8 Chapter 1** folder as **Lastname_Firstname_1I_Help_Desk**

The following email question has arrived at the Help Desk from an employee at the Bell Orchid Hotel's corporate office. In the Word document, construct a response based on your knowledge of Windows 8. Although an email response is not as formal as a letter, you should still use good grammar, good sentence structure, professional language, and a polite tone. Save your document and submit the response as directed by your instructor.

To: Help Desk

I am not sure about the differences between copying and moving files and folders. When is it best to copy a file or a folder and when is it best to move a file or folder? Can you also describe some techniques that I can use for copying or moving files and folders? Which do you think is the easiest way to copy or move files and folders?

END | You have completed Project 1I

Index

The following content is taken from:

GO! with Microsoft® Office 2013, Volume 1
by Shelley Gaskin, Alicia Vargas,
and Carolyn McLellan

GO!

with Microsoft®

Office 2013

Volume 1

Shelley Gaskin, Alicia Vargas, and Carolyn McLellan

PEARSON

Boston   Columbus   Indianapolis   New York   San Francisco   Upper Saddle River
Amsterdam   Cape Town   Dubai   London   Madrid   Milan   Munich   Paris   Montréal   Toronto
Delhi   Mexico City   São Paulo   Sydney   Hong Kong   Seoul   Singapore   Taipei   Tokyo

Table of Contents

Chapter 3 Creating Research Papers, Newsletters, and Merged Mailing Labels 237

Introduction to Microsoft Office 2013 Features

1 OFFICE 2013

PROJECT **1A**

OUTCOMES
Create, save, and print a Microsoft Office 2013 document.

OBJECTIVES

1. Use File Explorer to Download, Extract, and Locate Files and Folders
2. Use Start Search to Locate and Start a Microsoft Office 2013 Desktop App
3. Enter, Edit, and Check the Spelling of Text in an Office 2013 Program
4. Perform Commands from a Dialog Box
5. Create a Folder and Name and Save a File
6. Insert a Footer, Add Document Properties, Print a File, and Close a Desktop App

PROJECT **1B**

OUTCOMES
Use the ribbon and dialog boxes to perform commands in Microsoft Office 2013.

OBJECTIVES

7. Open an Existing File and Save It with a New Name
8. Sign In to Office and Explore Options for a Microsoft Office Desktop App
9. Perform Commands from the Ribbon and Quick Access Toolbar
10. Apply Formatting in Office Programs
11. Compress Files and Use the Microsoft Office 2013 Help System
12. Install Apps for Office and Create a Microsoft Account

etse1112/Fotolia

In This Chapter

In this chapter, you will use File Explorer to navigate the Windows folder structure, create a folder, and save files in Microsoft Office 2013 programs. You will also practice using features in Microsoft Office 2013 that work similarly across Word, Excel, Access, and PowerPoint. These features include managing files, performing commands, adding document properties, signing in to Office, applying formatting, and using Help. You will also practice compressing files and installing Apps for Office from the Office Store. In this chapter, you will also learn how to set up a free Microsoft account so that you can use SkyDrive.

The projects in this chapter relate to **Skyline Metro Grill**, which is a chain of 25 casual, full-service restaurants based in Boston. The Skyline Metro Grill owners are planning an aggressive expansion program. To expand by 15 additional restaurants in Chicago, San Francisco, and Los Angeles by 2018, the company must attract new investors, develop new menus, develop new marketing strategies, and recruit new employees, all while adhering to the company's quality guidelines and maintaining its reputation for excellent service. To succeed, the company plans to build on its past success and maintain its quality elements.

Note Form

MyITLab®
Project 1A Training

PROJECT ACTIVITIES

In Activities 1.01 through 1.09, you will create a note form using Microsoft Word, save it in a folder that you create by using File Explorer, and then print the note form or submit it electronically as directed by your instructor. Your completed note form will look similar to Figure 1.1.

PROJECT FILES

For Project 1A, you will need the following file:

New blank Word document

You will save your file as:

Lastname_Firstname_1A_Note_Form

PROJECT RESULTS

Build from
Scratch

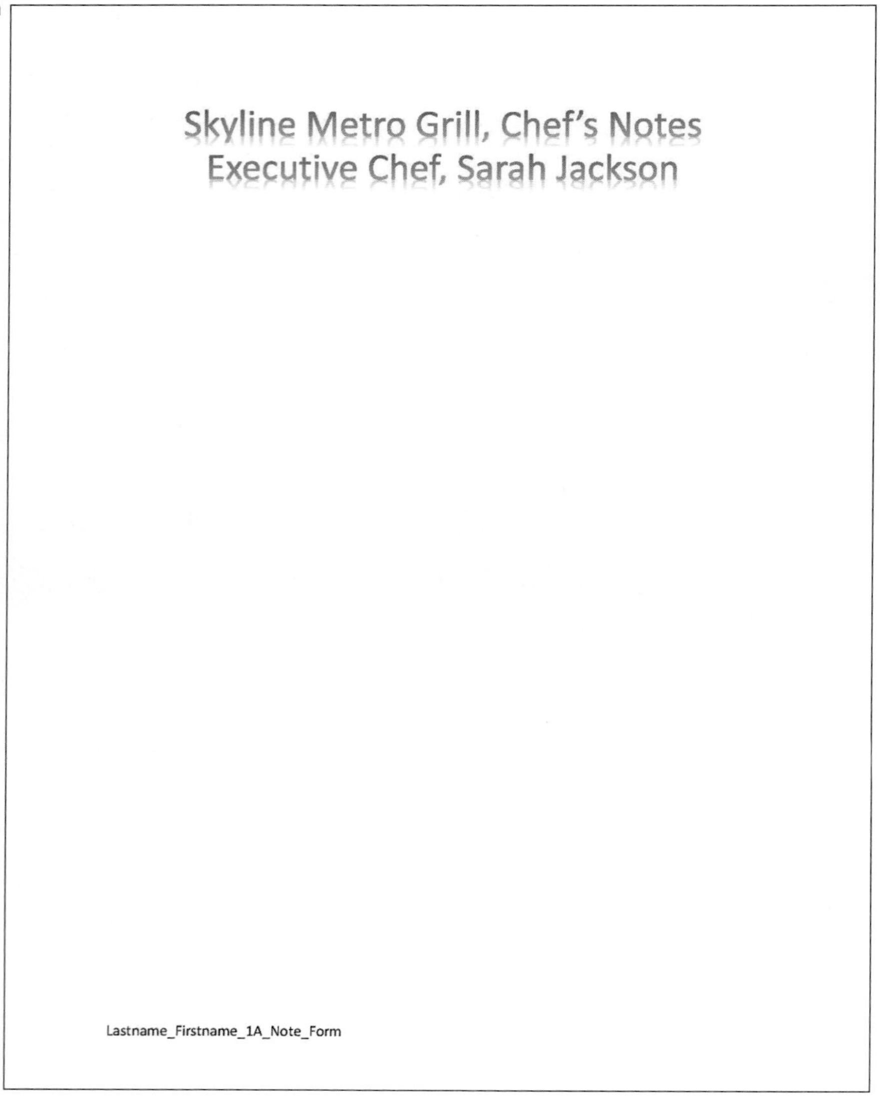

Skyline Metro Grill, Chef's Notes
Executive Chef, Sarah Jackson

Lastname_Firstname_1A_Note_Form

FIGURE 1.1 Project 1A Note Form

Objective 1 | Use File Explorer to Download, Extract, and Locate Files and Folders

Video OF1-1

A **file** is a collection of information stored on a computer under a single name, for example, a Word document or a PowerPoint presentation. A file is stored in a **folder**—a container in which you store files—or a **subfolder**, which is a folder within a folder. The Windows operating system stores and organizes your files and folders, which is a primary task of an operating system.

You **navigate**—explore within the organizing structure of Windows—to create, save, and find your files and folders by using the **File Explorer** program. File Explorer displays the files and folders on your computer and is at work anytime you are viewing the contents of files and folders in a **window**. A window is a rectangular area on a computer screen in which programs and content appear; a window can be moved, resized, minimized, or closed.

Activity 1.01 | Using File Explorer to Download, Extract, and Locate Files and Folders

| ALERT! | You Will Need a USB Flash Drive |

You will need a USB flash drive for this activity to download the Student Data Files for this chapter. If your instructor is providing the files to you, for example by placing the files at your learning management system, be sure you have downloaded them to a location where you can access the files and then skip to Activity 1.02.

| NOTE | Creating a Microsoft Account |

Use a free Microsoft account to sign in to Windows 8 and Office 2013 so that you can work on different PCs and use your SkyDrive. You need not use the Microsoft account as your primary email address unless you want to do so. To create a Microsoft account, go to **www.outlook.com**.

1 Sign in to Windows 8 with your Microsoft account—or the account provided by your instructor—to display the Windows 8 **Start screen**, and then click the **Desktop** tile. Insert a **USB flash drive** in your computer; **Close** ❌ any messages or windows that display.

The **desktop** is the screen in Windows that simulates your work area. A **USB flash drive** is a small data storage device that plugs into a computer USB port.

2 On the taskbar, click **Internet Explorer** 🌐. Click in the **address bar** to select the existing text, type **www.pearsonhighered.com/go** and press Enter. Locate and click the name of this textbook, and then click the **STUDENT DATA FILES tab**.

The **taskbar** is the area along the lower edge of the desktop that displays buttons representing programs—also referred to as desktop apps. In the desktop version of Internet Explorer 10, the **address bar** is the area at the top of the Internet Explorer window that displays, and where you can type, a **URL—Uniform Resource Locator**—which is an address that uniquely identifies a location on the Internet.

3 On the list of files, move your mouse pointer over—*point* to—**Office Features Chapter 1** and then *click*—press the left button on your mouse pointing device one time.

4 In the **Windows Internet Explorer** dialog box, click **Save As**.

A *dialog box* is a small window that contains options for completing a task.

5 In the **Save As** dialog box, on the left, locate the **navigation pane**, and point to the vertical **scroll bar**.

The Save As dialog box is an example of a *common dialog box*; that is, this dialog box looks the same in Excel and in PowerPoint and in most other Windows-based desktop applications—also referred to as programs.

Use the *navigation pane* on the left side of the Save As dialog box to navigate to, open, and display favorites, libraries, folders, saved searches, and an expandable list of drives. A *pane* is a separate area of a window.

A *scroll bar* displays when a window, or a pane within a window, has information that is not in view. You can click the up or down scroll arrows—or the left and right scroll arrows in a horizontal scroll bar—to scroll the contents up and down or left and right in small increments.

You can also drag the *scroll box*—the box within the scroll bar—to scroll the window or pane in either direction.

This is a *compressed folder*—also called a *zipped folder*—which is a folder containing one or more files that have been reduced in size. A compressed folder takes up less storage space and can be transferred to other computers faster.

NOTE   **Comparing Your Screen with the Figures in This Textbook**

Your screen will match the figures shown in this textbook if you set your screen resolution to 1280 × 768. At other resolutions, your screen will closely resemble, but not match, the figures shown. To view your screen's resolution, on the desktop, right-click in a blank area, and then click Screen resolution.

---

6 In the **navigation pane**, if necessary, on the scroll bar click ⌄ to scroll down. If necessary, to the left of **Computer**, click ▷ to expand the list. Then click the name of your **USB flash drive**.

7 With *Office_Features* displayed in the **File name** box, in the lower right corner click **Save**.

At the bottom of your screen, the *Notification bar* displays information about pending downloads, security issues, add-ons, and other issues related to the operation of your computer.

8 In the **Notification bar**, when the download is complete, click **Open folder** to display the folder window for your **USB flash drive**.

A *folder window* displays the contents of the current location—folder, library, or drive—and contains helpful parts so that you can navigate within the file organizing structure of Windows.

9 With the compressed **Office_Features** folder selected, on the ribbon, click the **Extract tab** to display the **Compressed Folder Tools**, and then click **Extract all**.

The *ribbon* is a user interface in both Office 2013 and Windows 8 that groups the commands for performing related tasks on tabs across the upper portion of a window.

In the dialog box, you can *extract*—decompress or pull out—files from a compressed folder.

You can navigate to some other location by clicking the Browse button and navigating within your storage locations.

10 In the **Extract Compressed (Zipped) Folders** dialog box, click to the right of the selected text, and then press Backspace until only the drive letter of your USB and the colon following it display—for example G:—and then click **Extract**. Notice that a progress bar indicates the progress of the extract process, and that when the extract is complete, the **Office_Features** folder displays on the file list of your **USB flash drive**.

> In a dialog box or taskbar button, a ***progress bar*** indicates visually the progress of a task such as a download or file transfer.
>
> The ***address bar*** in File Explorer displays your current location in the folder structure as a series of links separated by arrows, which is referred to as the ***path***—a sequence of folders that leads to a specific file or folder.
>
> By pressing Backspace in the Extract dialog box, you avoid creating an unneeded folder level.

11 Because you no longer need the compressed (zipped) version of the folder, be sure it is selected, click the **Home tab**, and then click **Delete**. In the upper right corner of the **USB drive** folder window, click **Close** ☒. **Close** ☒ the **Internet Explorer** window and in the Internet Explorer message, click **Close all tabs**.

> Your desktop redisplays.

Objective 2 — Use Start Search to Locate and Start a Microsoft Office 2013 Desktop App

Video OF1-2

The term ***desktop app*** commonly refers to a computer program that is installed on your computer and requires a computer operating system such as Microsoft Windows or Apple OS to run. The programs in Microsoft Office 2013 are considered to be desktop apps. Apps that run from the *device software* on a smartphone or a tablet computer—for example, iOS, Android, or Windows Phone—or apps that run from *browser software* such as Internet Explorer, Safari, Firefox, or Chrome on a desktop PC or laptop PC are referred to simply as ***apps***.

Activity 1.02 | Using Start Search to Locate and Start a Microsoft Office 2013 Desktop App

The easiest and fastest way to search for an app is to use the ***Start search*** feature—simply display the Windows 8 Start screen and start typing. By default, Windows 8 searches for apps; you can change it to search for files or settings.

1 With your desktop displayed, press [⊞] to display the Windows 8 **Start screen**, and then type **word 2013** With *word 2013* bordered in white in the search results, press Enter to return to the desktop and open Word. If you want to do so, in the upper right corner, sign in with your Microsoft account, and then compare your screen with Figure 1.2.

> Documents that you have recently opened, if any, display on the left. On the right, you can select either a blank document or a ***template***—a preformatted document that you can use as a starting point and then change to suit your needs.

 BY TOUCH

Swipe from the right edge of the screen to display the charms, and then tap Search. Tap in the Apps box, and then use the onscreen keyboard that displays to type *word 2013*. Tap the selected Word 2013 app name to open Word.

FIGURE 1.2

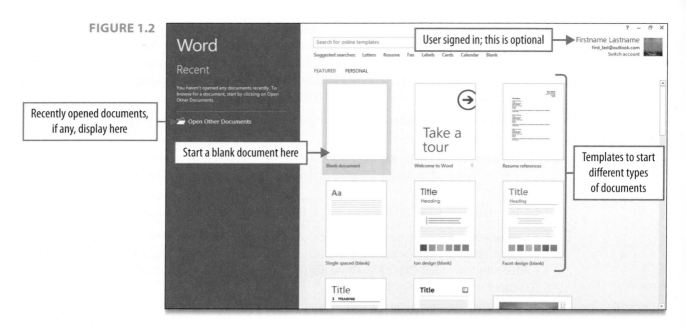

2 Click **Blank document**. Compare your screen with Figure 1.3, and then take a moment to study the description of these screen elements in the table in Figure 1.4.

NOTE	Displaying the Full Ribbon

If your full ribbon does not display, click any tab, and then at the right end of the ribbon, click 📌 to pin the ribbon to keep it open while you work.

FIGURE 1.3

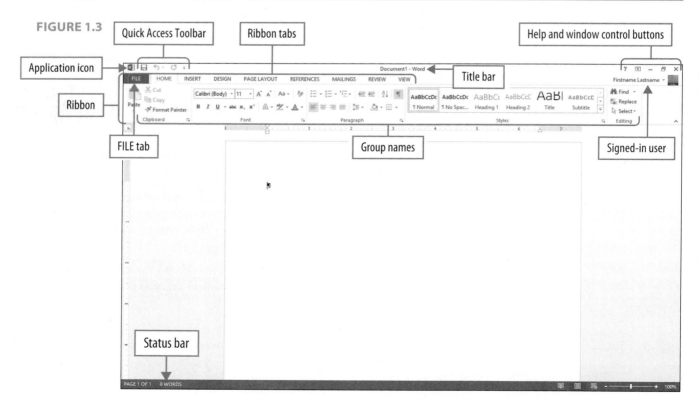

FIGURE 1.4

MICROSOFT OFFICE SCREEN ELEMENTS	
SCREEN ELEMENT	**DESCRIPTION**
FILE tab	Displays Microsoft Office Backstage view, which is a centralized space for all of your file management tasks such as opening, saving, printing, publishing, or sharing a file—all the things you can do *with* a file.
Group names	Indicate the names of the groups of related commands on the displayed tab.
Help and window control buttons	Display Word Help and Full Screen Mode and enable you to Minimize, Restore Down, or Close the window.
Application icon	When clicked, displays a menu of window control commands including Restore, Minimize, and Close.
Quick Access Toolbar	Displays buttons to perform frequently used commands and use resources with a single click. The default commands include Save, Undo, and Redo. You can add and delete buttons to customize the Quick Access Toolbar for your convenience.
Ribbon	Displays a group of task-oriented tabs that contain the commands, styles, and resources you need to work in an Office 2013 desktop app. The look of your ribbon depends on your screen resolution. A high resolution will display more individual items and button names on the ribbon.
Ribbon tabs	Display the names of the task-oriented tabs relevant to the open program.
Status bar	Displays file information on the left; on the right displays buttons for Read Mode, Print Layout, and Web Layout views; on the far right displays Zoom controls.
Title bar	Displays the name of the file and the name of the program. The Help and window control buttons are grouped on the right side of the title bar.
Signed-in user	Name of the Windows 8 signed-in user.

Objective 3 | Enter, Edit, and Check the Spelling of Text in an Office 2013 Program

Video OF1-3

All of the programs in Office 2013 require some typed text. Your keyboard is still the primary method of entering information into your computer. Techniques to enter text and to *edit*—make changes to—text are similar among all of the Office 2013 programs.

Activity 1.03 | Entering and Editing Text in an Office 2013 Program

1 On the ribbon, on the HOME tab, in the Paragraph group, if necessary, click Show/Hide ¶ so that it is active—shaded. If necessary, on the VIEW tab, in the Show group, select the Ruler check box so that rulers display below the ribbon and on the left side of your window.

The *insertion point*—a blinking vertical line that indicates where text or graphics will be inserted—displays. In Office 2013 programs, the mouse *pointer*—any symbol that displays on your screen in response to moving your mouse device—displays in different shapes depending on the task you are performing and the area of the screen to which you are pointing.

When you press Enter, Spacebar, or Tab on your keyboard, characters display to represent these keystrokes. These screen characters do not print and are referred to as *formatting marks* or *nonprinting characters*.

2 ▶ Type **Skyline Grille Info** and notice how the insertion point moves to the right as you type. Point slightly to the right of the letter *e* in *Grille* and click to place the insertion point there. Compare your screen with Figure 1.5.

A *paragraph symbol* (¶) indicates the end of a paragraph and displays each time you press Enter. This is a type of formatting mark and does not print.

FIGURE 1.5

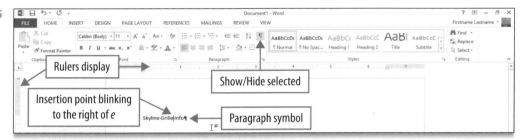

3 ▶ On your keyboard, locate and then press the Backspace key to delete the letter *e*.

Pressing Backspace removes a character to the left of the insertion point.

4 ▶ Press → one time to place the insertion point to the left of the *I* in *Info*. Type **Chef's** and then press Spacebar one time.

By *default*, when you type text in an Office program, existing text moves to the right to make space for new typing. Default refers to the current selection or setting that is automatically used by a program unless you specify otherwise.

5 ▶ Press Del four times to delete *Info* and then type **Notes**

Pressing Del removes a character to the right of the insertion point.

6 ▶ With your insertion point blinking after the word *Notes*, on your keyboard, hold down the Ctrl key. While holding down Ctrl, press ← three times to move the insertion point to the beginning of the word *Grill*.

This is a *keyboard shortcut*—a key or combination of keys that performs a task that would otherwise require a mouse. This keyboard shortcut moves the insertion point to the beginning of the previous word.

A keyboard shortcut is commonly indicated as Ctrl + ← (or some other combination of keys) to indicate that you hold down the first key while pressing the second key. A keyboard shortcut can also include three keys, in which case you hold down the first two and then press the third. For example, Ctrl + Shift + ← selects one word to the left.

7 ▶ With the insertion point blinking at the beginning of the word *Grill*, type **Metro** and press Spacebar.

8 ▶ Press Ctrl + End to place the insertion point after the letter *s* in *Notes*, and then press Enter one time. With the insertion point blinking, type the following and include the spelling error: **Exective Chef, Madison Dunham**

9 With your mouse, point slightly to the left of the *M* in *Madison*, hold down the left mouse button, and then ***drag***—hold down the left mouse button while moving your mouse—to the right to select the text *Madison Dunham* but not the paragraph mark following it, and then release the mouse button. Compare your screen with Figure 1.6.

The ***mini toolbar*** displays commands that are commonly used with the selected object, which places common commands close to your pointer. When you move the pointer away from the mini toolbar, it fades from view.

Selecting refers to highlighting, by dragging or clicking with your mouse, areas of text or data or graphics so that the selection can be edited, formatted, copied, or moved. The action of dragging includes releasing the left mouse button at the end of the area you want to select.

The Office programs recognize a selected area as one unit to which you can make changes. Selecting text may require some practice. If you are not satisfied with your result, click anywhere outside of the selection, and then begin again.

 BY TOUCH   Tap once on *Madison* to display the gripper—small circle that acts as a handle—directly below the word. This establishes the start gripper. If necessary, with your finger, drag the gripper to the beginning of the word. Then drag the gripper to the end of Dunham to select the text and display the end gripper.

FIGURE 1.6

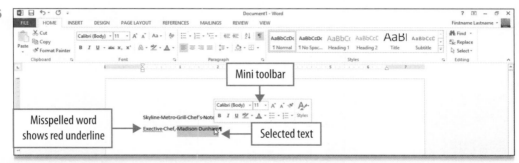

10 With the text *Madison Dunham* selected, type **Sarah Jackson**

In any Windows-based program, such as the Microsoft Office 2013 programs, selected text is deleted and then replaced when you begin to type new text. You will save time by developing good techniques for selecting and then editing or replacing selected text, which is easier than pressing the Del key numerous times to delete text.

Activity 1.04 | Checking Spelling

Office 2013 has a dictionary of words against which all entered text is checked. In Word and PowerPoint, words that are not in the dictionary display a wavy red line, indicating a possible misspelled word or a proper name or an unusual word—none of which are in the Office 2013 dictionary.

In Excel and Access, you can initiate a check of the spelling, but red underlines do not display.

1 Notice that the misspelled word *Exective* displays with a wavy red underline.

2 Point to *Exective* and then ***right-click***—click your right mouse button one time.

A ***shortcut menu*** displays, which displays commands and options relevant to the selected text or object. These are ***context-sensitive commands*** because they relate to the item you right-clicked. These types of menus are also referred to as ***context menus***. Here, the shortcut menu displays commands related to the misspelled word.

 BY TOUCH   Tap and hold a moment to select the misspelled word, then release your finger to display the shortcut menu.

3 Press [Esc] to cancel the shortcut menu, and then in the lower left corner of your screen, on the **status bar**, click the **Proofing** icon , which displays an *X* because some errors are detected. Compare your screen with Figure 1.7.

> The Spelling pane displays on the right. Here you have many more options for checking spelling than you have on the shortcut menu. The suggested correct word, *Executive*, is highlighted.
>
> You can click the speaker icon to hear the pronunciation of the selected word. You can also see some synonyms for *Executive*. Finally, if you have not already installed a dictionary, you can click *Get a Dictionary*—if you are signed in to Office with a Microsoft account—to find and install one from the online Office store; or if you have a dictionary app installed, it will display here and you can search it for more information.
>
> In the Spelling pane, you can ignore the word one time or in all occurrences, change the word to the suggested word, select a different suggestion, or add a word to the dictionary against which Word checks.

FIGURE 1.7

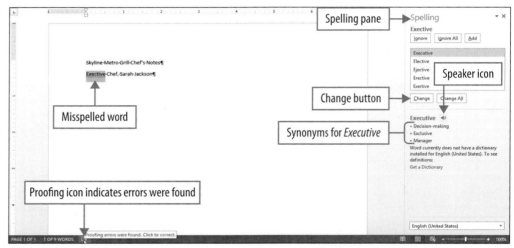

 ANOTHER WAY   Press [F7] to display the Spelling pane; or, on the Review tab, in the Proofing group, click Spelling & Grammar.

4 In the **Spelling** pane, click **Change** to change the spelling to *Executive*. In the message box that displays, click **OK**.

Objective 4   Perform Commands from a Dialog Box

In a dialog box, you make decisions about an individual object or topic. In some dialog boxes, you can make multiple decisions in one place.

Video OF1-4

Activity 1.05 │ Performing Commands from a Dialog Box

1 On the ribbon, click the **DESIGN tab**, and then in the **Page Background group**, click **Page Color**.

2 At the bottom of the menu, notice the command **Fill Effects** followed by an **ellipsis** (...). Compare your screen with Figure 1.8.

> An *ellipsis* is a set of three dots indicating incompleteness. An ellipsis following a command name indicates that a dialog box will display when you click the command.

FIGURE 1.8

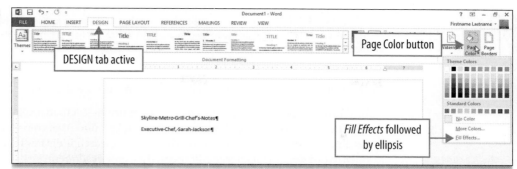

FIGURE 1.9

3 ▸ Click **Fill Effects** to display the **Fill Effects** dialog box. Compare your screen with Figure 1.9.

Fill is the inside color of a page or object. The Gradient tab is active. In a *gradient fill*, one color fades into another. Here, the dialog box displays a set of tabs across the top from which you can display different sets of options. Some dialog boxes display the option group names on the left.

4 ▸ Under **Colors**, click the **One color** option button.

The dialog box displays settings related to the One color option. An *option button* is a round button that enables you to make one choice among two or more options.

5 ▸ Click the **Color 1 arrow**—the arrow under the text *Color 1*—and then in the third column, point to the second color to display the ScreenTip *Gray-25%, Background 2, Darker 10%*.

A *ScreenTip* displays useful information about mouse actions, such as pointing to screen elements or dragging.

6 ▸ Click **Gray-25%, Background 2, Darker 10%**, and then notice that the fill color displays in the **Color 1** box. In the **Dark Light** bar, click the **Light arrow** as many times as necessary until the scroll box is all the way to right. Under **Shading styles**, click the **Diagonal down** option button. Under **Variants**, click the upper right variant. Compare your screen with Figure 1.10.

FIGURE 1.10

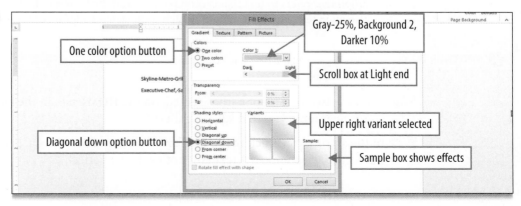

7 At the bottom of the dialog box, click **OK**, and notice the subtle page color.

In Word, the gray shading page color will not print—even on a color printer—unless you set specific options to do so. However a subtle background page color is effective if people will be reading the document on a screen. Microsoft's research indicates that two-thirds of people who open Word documents never edit them; they only read them.

Activity 1.06 | Using Undo

1 Point to the *S* in *Skyline*, and then drag down and to the right to select both paragraphs of text and include the paragraph marks. On the mini toolbar, click **Styles,** and then *point to* but do not click **Title**. Compare your screen with Figure 1.11.

A **style** is a group of **formatting** commands, such as font, font size, font color, paragraph alignment, and line spacing that can be applied to a paragraph with one command. Formatting is the process of establishing the overall appearance of text, graphics, and pages in an Office file—for example, in a Word document.

Live Preview is a technology that shows the result of applying an editing or formatting change as you point to possible results—before you actually apply it.

FIGURE 1.11

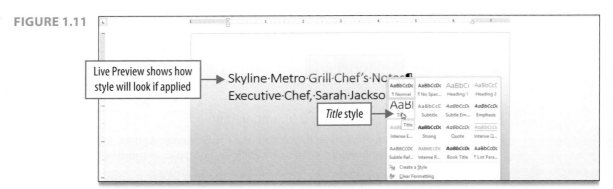

2 In the **Styles** gallery, click **Title**.

A **gallery** is an Office feature that displays a list of potential results.

3 On the ribbon, on the **HOME tab**, in the **Paragraph group**, click **Center** ⊟ to center the two paragraphs.

Alignment refers to the placement of paragraph text relative to the left and right margins. **Center alignment** refers to text that is centered horizontally between the left and right margins. You can also align text at the left margin, which is the default alignment for text in Word, or at the right.

ANOTHER WAY   Press Ctrl + E to use the Center command.

4 With the two paragraphs still selected, on the **HOME tab**, in the **Font Group**, click **Text Effects and Typography** Ⓐ ▾ to display a gallery.

5 In the second row, click the first effect—**Gradient Fill – Gray**. Click anywhere to *deselect*—cancel the selection—the text and notice the text effect.

6 Because this effect might be difficult to read, in the upper left corner of your screen, on the **Quick Access Toolbar**, click **Undo** ⟲.

The **Undo** command reverses your last action.

🔁 **ANOTHER WAY**   Press ⌨Ctrl + ⌨Z as the keyboard shortcut for the Undo command.

7 Display the **Text Effects and Typography** gallery again, and then in the second row, click the second effect—**Gradient Fill – Blue, Accent 1, Reflection**. Click anywhere to deselect the text and notice the text effect. Compare your screen with Figure 1.12.

As you progress in your study of Microsoft Office, you will practice using many dialog boxes and applying interesting effects such as this to your Word documents, Excel worksheets, Access database objects, and PowerPoint slides.

FIGURE 1.12

Text formatted with blue reflective text effect →

Gray page fill effects →

Skyline·Metro·Grill·Chef's·Notes¶
Executive·Chef,·Sarah·Jackson¶

Objective 5   Create a Folder and Name and Save a File

Video OF1-5

A *location* is any disk drive, folder, or other place in which you can store files and folders. Where you store your files depends on how and where you use your data. For example, for your college classes, you might decide to store on a removable USB flash drive so that you can carry your files to different locations and access your files on different computers.

If you do most of your work on a single computer, for example your home desktop system or your laptop computer that you take with you to school or work, then you can store your files in one of the Libraries—Documents, Music, Pictures, or Videos—that the Windows 8 operating system creates on your hard drive.

The best place to store files if you want them to be available anytime, anywhere, from almost any device is on your *SkyDrive*, which is Microsoft's free *cloud storage* for anyone with a free Microsoft account. Cloud storage refers to online storage of data so that you can access your data from different places and devices. *Cloud computing* refers to applications and services that are accessed over the Internet, rather than to applications that are installed on your local computer.

Because many people now have multiple computing devices—desktop, laptop, tablet, smartphone—it is common to store data *in the cloud* so that it is always available. *Synchronization*, also called *syncing*—pronounced SINK-ing—is the process of updating computer files that are in two or more locations according to specific rules. So if you create and save a Word document on your SkyDrive using your laptop, you can open and edit that document on your tablet. And then when you close the document again, the file is properly updated to reflect your changes.

You need not be connected to the Internet to access documents stored on SkyDrive because an up-to-date version of your content is synched to your local system and available on SkyDrive. You must, however, be connected to the Internet for the syncing to occur. Saving to SkyDrive will keep the local copy on your computer and the copy in the cloud synchronized for as long as you need it. If you open and edit on a different computer, log into the SkyDrive website, and then edit using Office 2013, Office 2010, or the ***Office Web Apps***, you can save any changes back to SkyDrive. Office Web Apps are the free online companions to Microsoft Word, Excel, PowerPoint, Access, and OneNote. These changes will be synchronized back to any of your computers that run the SkyDrive for Windows application, which you get for free simply by logging in with your Microsoft account at skydrive.com.

The Windows operating system helps you to create and maintain a logical folder structure, so always take the time to name your files and folders consistently.

Activity 1.07 | Creating a Folder and Naming and Saving a File

A Word document is an example of a file. In this activity, you will create a folder on your USB flash drive in which to store your files. If you prefer to store on your SkyDrive or in the Documents library on your hard drive, you can use similar steps.

1 If necessary, insert your **USB flash drive** into your computer.

As the first step in saving a file, determine where you want to save the file, and if necessary, insert a storage device.

2 At the top of your screen, in the title bar, notice that *Document1 – Word* displays.

The Blank option on the opening screen of an Office 2013 program displays a new unsaved file with a default name—*Document1, Presentation1*, and so on. As you create your file, your work is temporarily stored in the computer's memory until you initiate a Save command, at which time you must choose a file name and a location in which to save your file.

3 In the upper left corner of your screen, click the **FILE tab** to display **Backstage** view. Compare your screen with Figure 1.13.

Backstage view is a centralized space that groups commands related to *file* management; that is why the tab is labeled *FILE*. File management commands include opening, saving, printing, publishing, or sharing a file. The ***Backstage tabs***—*Info, New, Open, Save, Save As, Print, Share, Export,* and *Close*—display along the left side. The tabs group file-related tasks together.

Here, the ***Info tab*** displays information—*info*—about the current file, and file management commands display under Info. For example, if you click the Protect Document button, a list of options that you can set for this file that relate to who can open or edit the document displays.

On the right, you can also examine the ***document properties***. Document properties, also known as ***metadata***, are details about a file that describe or identify it, such as the title, author name, subject, and keywords that identify the document's topic or contents. To close Backstage view and return to the document, you can click ⬅ in the upper left corner or press (Esc).

FIGURE 1.13

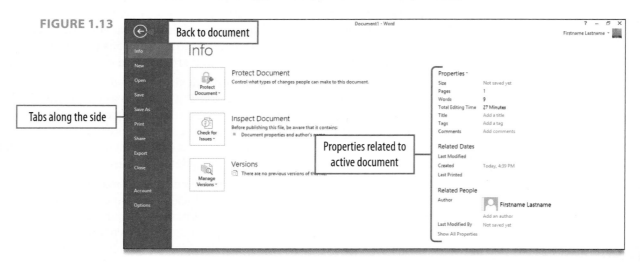

4 ▷ On the left, click **Save As**, and notice that the default location for storing Office files is your **SkyDrive**—if you are signed in. Compare your screen with Figure 1.14.

When you are saving something for the first time, for example a new Word document, the Save and Save As commands are identical. That is, the Save As commands will display if you click Save or if you click Save As.

FIGURE 1.14

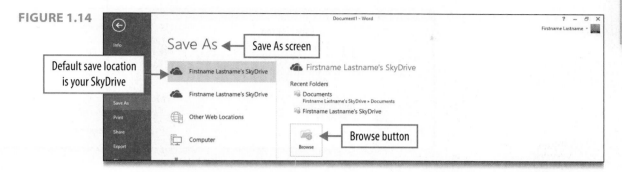

NOTE   **Saving after Your File Is Named**

After you name and save a file, the Save command on the Quick Access Toolbar saves any changes you make to the file without displaying Backstage view. The Save As command enables you to name and save a *new* file based on the current one—in a location that you choose. After you name and save the new document, the original document closes, and the new document—based on the original one—displays.

5 ▷ To store your Word file on your **USB flash drive**—instead of your SkyDrive—click the **Browse** button to display the **Save As** dialog box. On the left, in the navigation pane, scroll down, and then under **Computer**, click the name of your **USB flash drive**. Compare your screen with Figure 1.15.

In the Save As dialog box, you must indicate the name you want for the file and the location where you want to save the file. When working with your own data, it is good practice to pause at this point and determine the logical name and location for your file.

In the Save As dialog box, a *toolbar* displays. This is a row, column, or block of buttons or icons, that usually displays across the top of a window and that contains commands for tasks you perform with a single click.

FIGURE 1.15

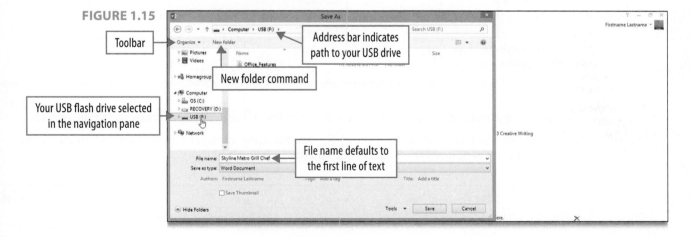

6 On the toolbar, click **New folder**.

In the file list, Word creates a new folder, and the text *New folder* is selected.

7 Type **Office Features Chapter 1** and press [Enter]. Compare your screen with Figure 1.16.

In Windows-based programs, the [Enter] key confirms an action.

FIGURE 1.16

8 In the **file list**, double-click the name of your new folder to open it and display its name in the **address bar**.

9 In the lower portion of the dialog box, click in the **File name** box to select the existing text. Notice that Office inserts the text at the beginning of the document as a suggested file name.

10 On your keyboard, locate the hyphen ⎯ key. Notice that the [Shift] of this key produces the underscore character. With the text still selected and using your own name, type **Lastname_Firstname_1A_Note_Form** and then compare your screen with Figure 1.17.

You can use spaces in file names, however, some people prefer not to use spaces. Some programs, especially when transferring files over the Internet, may insert the extra characters *%20* in place of a space. This can happen in **SharePoint**, so using underscores instead of spaces can be a good habit to adopt. SharePoint is Microsoft's collaboration software with which people in an organization can set up team sites to share information, manage documents, and publish reports for others to see. In general, however, unless you encounter a problem, it is OK to use spaces. In this textbook, underscores are used instead of spaces in file names.

FIGURE 1.17

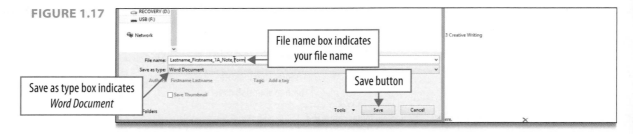

11 In the lower right corner, click **Save** or press [Enter]. Compare your screen with Figure 1.18.

The Word window redisplays and your new file name displays in the title bar, indicating that the file has been saved to a location that you have specified.

FIGURE 1.18

12 In the first paragraph, click to place the insertion point after the word *Grill* and type **,** (a comma). In the upper left corner of your screen, on the **Quick Access Toolbar**, click **Save** 🖫.

> After a document is named and saved in a location, you can save any changes you have made since the last Save operation by using the Save command on the Quick Access Toolbar. When working on a document, it is good practice to save your changes from time to time.

Video OF1-6

Objective 6 | Insert a Footer, Add Document Properties, Print a File, and Close a Desktop App

For most of your files, especially in a workplace setting, it is useful to add identifying information to help in finding files later. You might also want to print your file on paper or create an electronic printout. The process of printing a file is similar in all of the Office applications.

Activity 1.08 | Inserting a Footer, Inserting Document Info, and Adding Document Properties

N O T E	Are You Printing or Submitting Your Files Electronically?
In this activity, you can either produce a paper printout or create an electronic file to submit to your instructor if required.	

1 On the ribbon, click the **INSERT tab**, and then in the **Header & Footer group**, click **Footer**.

2 At the bottom of the list, click **Edit Footer**. On the ribbon, notice that the **HEADER & FOOTER TOOLS** display.

> The *Header & Footer Tools Design* tab displays on the ribbon. The ribbon adapts to your work and will display additional tabs like this one—referred to as *contextual tabs*—when you need them.

> A *footer* is a reserved area for text or graphics that displays at the bottom of each page in a document. Likewise, a *header* is a reserved area for text or graphics that displays at the top of each page in a document. When the footer (or header) area is active, the document area is dimmed, indicating it is unavailable.

3 On the ribbon, under **HEADER & FOOTER TOOLS**, on the **DESIGN tab**, in the **Insert group**, click **Document Info**, and then click **File Name** to insert the name of your file in the footer, which is a common business practice. Compare your screen with Figure 1.19.

> Ribbon commands that display ▼ will, when clicked, display a list of options for the command.

FIGURE 1.19

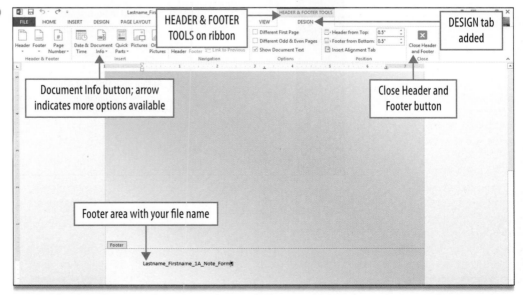

Document Info button; arrow indicates more options available

HEADER & FOOTER TOOLS on ribbon

DESIGN tab added

Close Header and Footer button

Footer area with your file name

Lastname_Firstname_1A_Note_Form

4 At the right end of the ribbon, click **Close Header and Footer**.

🔁 **ANOTHER WAY**   Double-click anywhere in the dimmed document to close the footer.

5 Click the **FILE tab** to display **Backstage** view. On the right, at the bottom of the **Properties** list, click **Show All Properties**.

🔁 **ANOTHER WAY**   Click the arrow to the right of Properties, and then click Show Document Panel to show and edit properties at the top of your document window.

6 On the list of **Properties**, click to the right of **Tags** to display an empty box, and then type **chef, notes, form**

> *Tags*, also referred to as *keywords*, are custom file properties in the form of words that you associate with a document to give an indication of the document's content. Adding tags to your documents makes it easier to search for and locate files in File Explorer and in systems such as Microsoft SharePoint document libraries.

🔁 **BY TOUCH**   Tap to the right of Tags to display the Tags box and the onscreen keyboard.

7 Click to the right of **Subject** to display an empty box, and then type your course name and section #; for example *CIS 10, #5543*.

8 Under **Related People**, be sure that your name displays as the author. If necessary, right-click the author name, click Edit Property, type your name, click outside of the Edit person dialog box, and then click OK. Compare your screen with Figure 1.20.

FIGURE 1.20

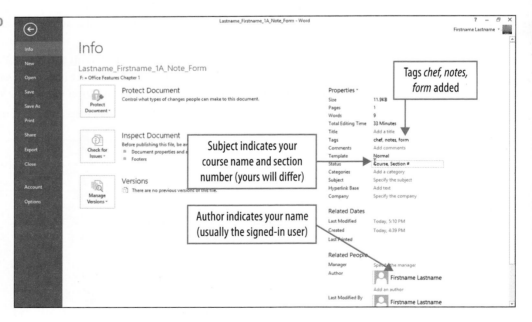

Activity 1.09 | Printing a File and Closing a Desktop App

1 On the left, click **Print**, and then compare your screen with Figure 1.21.

Here you can select any printer connected to your system and adjust the settings related to how you want to print. On the right, the **Print Preview** displays, which is a view of a document as it will appear on paper when you print it.

At the bottom of the Print Preview area, in the center, the number of pages and page navigation arrows with which you can move among the pages in Print Preview display. On the right, the Zoom slider enables you to shrink or enlarge the Print Preview. **Zoom** is the action of increasing or decreasing the viewing area of the screen.

ANOTHER WAY From the document screen, press Ctrl + P or Ctrl + F2 to display Print in Backstage view.

FIGURE 1.21

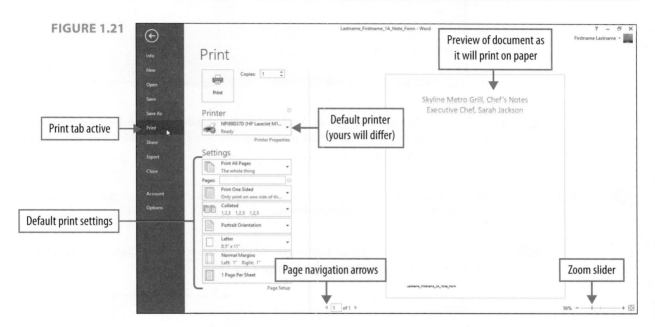

2 To submit your file electronically, skip this step and continue to Step 3. To print your document on paper using the default printer on your system, in the upper left portion of the screen, click the **Print** button.

The document will print on your default printer; if you do not have a color printer, the blue text will print in shades of gray. The gray page color you applied to the document does not display in Print Preview nor does it print unless you specifically adjust some of Word's options. Backstage view closes and your file redisplays in the Word window.

3 To create an electronic file, on the left click **Export**. On the right, click the **Create PDF/XPS** button to display the **Publish as PDF or XPS** dialog box.

PDF stands for **Portable Document Format**, which is a technology that creates an image that preserves the look of your file. This is a popular format for sending documents electronically, because the document will display on most computers.

XPS stands for **XML Paper Specification**—a Microsoft file format that also creates an image of your document and that opens in the XPS viewer.

4 On the left in the **navigation pane**, if necessary expand ▷ Computer, and then navigate to your **Office Features Chapter 1** folder on your **USB flash drive**. Compare your screen with Figure 1.22.

FIGURE 1.22

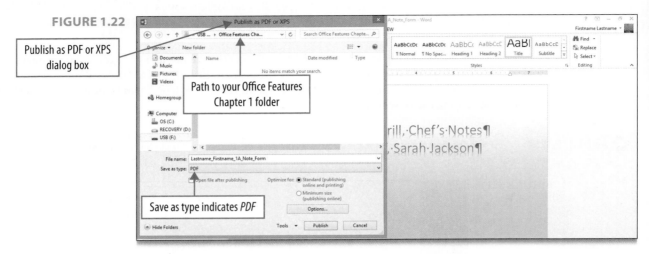

Publish as PDF or XPS dialog box

Path to your Office Features Chapter 1 folder

Save as type indicates *PDF*

5 In the lower right corner of the dialog box, click **Publish**; if your Adobe Acrobat or Adobe Reader program displays your PDF, in the upper right corner, click Close ☒. Notice that your document redisplays in Word.

ANOTHER WAY   In Backstage view, click Save As, navigate to the location of your Chapter folder, click the Save as type arrow, on the list click PDF, and then click Save.

6 Click the **FILE tab** to redisplay **Backstage** view. On the left, click **Close**, if necessary click Save, and then compare your screen with Figure 1.23.

FIGURE 1.23

Word window with all documents closed

Close button

7 In the upper right corner of the Word window, click **Close** ☒. If directed by your instructor to do so, submit your paper or electronic file.

END | You have completed Project 1A

Memo

PROJECT ACTIVITIES

In Activities 1.10 through 1.21, you will open, edit, and then compress a Word file. You will also use the Office Help system and install an app for Office. Your completed document will look similar to Figure 1.24.

PROJECT FILES

For Project 1B, you will need the following file:

of01B_Rehearsal_Dinner

You will save your file as:

Lastname_Firstname_1B_Rehearsal_Dinner

PROJECT RESULTS

Skyline Metro Grill

TO: Sarah Jackson, Executive Chef

FROM: Laura Mabry Hernandez, General Manager

DATE: February 17, 2016

SUBJECT: Wedding Rehearsal Dinners

In the spring and summer months, wedding rehearsal dinners provide a new marketing opportunity for Skyline Metro Grill at all of our locations. A rehearsal dinner is an informal meal following a wedding rehearsal at which the bride and groom typically thank those who have helped them make their wedding a special event.

Our smaller private dining rooms with sweeping city views are an ideal location for a rehearsal dinner. At each of our locations, I have directed the Sales and Marketing Coordinator to partner with local wedding planners to promote Skyline Metro Grill as a relaxed yet sophisticated venue for rehearsal dinners. The typical rehearsal dinner includes the wedding party, the immediate family of the bride and groom, and out-of-town guests.

Please develop six menus—in varying price ranges—to present to local wedding planners so that they can easily promote Skyline Metro Grill to couples who are planning a rehearsal dinner. In addition to a traditional dinner, we should also include options for a buffet-style dinner and a family-style dinner.

This marketing effort will require extensive communication with our Sales and Marketing Coordinators and with local wedding planners. Let's meet to discuss the details and the marketing challenges, and to create a promotional piece that begins something like this:

Skyline Metro Grill for Your Rehearsal Dinner

Lastname_Firstname_1B_Rehearsal_Dinner

FIGURE 1.24 Project 1B Memo

Video OF1-7

In any Office program, you can display the ***Open dialog box***, from which you can navigate to and then open an existing file that was created in that same program.

The Open dialog box, along with the Save and Save As dialog boxes, is a common dialog box. These dialog boxes, which are provided by the Windows programming interface, display in all Office programs in the same manner. So the Open, Save, and Save As dialog boxes will all look and perform the same regardless of the Office program in which you are working.

Activity 1.10 | Opening an Existing File and Saving It with a New Name

In this activity, you will display the Open dialog box, open an existing Word document, and then save it in your storage location with a new name.

1 Sign in to your computer, and then on the Windows 8 Start screen, type **word 2013** Press Enter to open Word on your desktop. If you want to do so, on the taskbar, right-click the **Word icon**, and then click **Pin this program to taskbar** to keep the Word program available from your desktop.

2 On Word's opening screen, on the left, click **Open Other Documents**. Under **Open**, click **Computer**, and then on the right click **Browse**.

3 In the **Open** dialog box, on the left in the **navigation pane**, scroll down, if necessary expand ▷ Computer, and then click the name of your **USB flash drive**. In the **file list**, double-click the **Office_Features** folder that you downloaded.

4 Double-click **of01B_Rehearsal_Dinner**. If **PROTECTED VIEW** displays at the top of your screen, in the center click **Enable Editing**.

In Office 2013, a file will open in ***Protected View*** if the file appears to be from a potentially risky location, such as the Internet. Protected View is a security feature in Office 2013 that protects your computer from malicious files by opening them in a restricted environment until you enable them. ***Trusted Documents*** is another security feature that remembers which files you have already enabled.

You might encounter these security features if you open a file from an email or download files from the Internet; for example, from your college's learning management system or from the Pearson website. So long as you trust the source of the file, click Enable Editing or Enable Content—depending on the type of file you receive—and then go ahead and work with the file.

5 With the document displayed in the Word window, be sure that **Show/Hide** is active; if necessary, on the HOME tab, in the Paragraph group, click Show/Hide to activate it. Compare your screen with Figure 1.25.

FIGURE 1.25

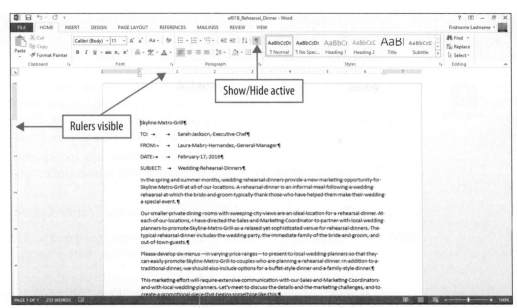

6 Click the **FILE tab** to display **Backstage** view, and then on the left, click **Save As**. On the right, click the folder under **Current Folder** to open the **Save As** dialog box. Notice that the current folder is the **Office_Features** folder you downloaded.

ANOTHER WAY   Press F12 to display the Save As dialog box.

7 In the upper left corner of the **Save As** dialog box, click the **Up** button ↑ to move up one level in the File Explorer hierarchy. In the **file list**, double-click your **Office Features Chapter 1** folder to open it.

8 Click in the **File name** box to select the existing text, and then, using your own name, type **Lastname_Firstname_1B_Rehearsal_Dinner** Compare your screen with Figure 1.26.

FIGURE 1.26

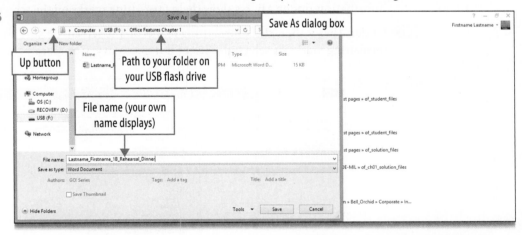

9 Click **Save** or press Enter; notice that your new file name displays in the title bar.

The original document closes, and your new document, based on the original, displays with the name in the title bar.

More Knowledge   **Read-Only**

Some files might display **Read-Only** in the title bar, which is a property assigned to a file that prevents the file from being modified or deleted; it indicates that you cannot save any changes to the displayed document unless you first save it with a new name.

Video OF1-8

If you sign in to Windows 8 with a Microsoft account, you may notice that you are also signed in to Office. This enables you to save files to and retrieve files from your SkyDrive and to *collaborate* with others on Office files when you want to do so. To collaborate means to work with others as a team in an intellectual endeavor to complete a shared task or to achieve a shared goal.

Within each Office application, an *Options dialog box* enables you to select program settings and other options and preferences. For example, you can set preferences for viewing and editing files.

Activity 1.11 | Signing In to Office and Viewing Application Options

1 In the upper right corner of your screen, if you are signed in with a Microsoft account, click the arrow to the right of your name, and then compare your screen with Figure 1.27.

Here you can change your photo, go to About me to edit your profile, examine your Account settings, or switch accounts to sign in with a different Microsoft account.

FIGURE 1.27

2 Click the **FILE tab** to display **Backstage** view. On the left, click the last tab—**Options**.

3 In the **Word Options** dialog box, on the left, click **Display**, and then on the right, locate the information under **Always show these formatting marks on the screen**.

4 Under **Always show these formatting marks on the screen**, be sure the last check box, **Show all formatting marks**, is selected—select it if necessary. Compare your screen with Figure 1.28.

FIGURE 1.28

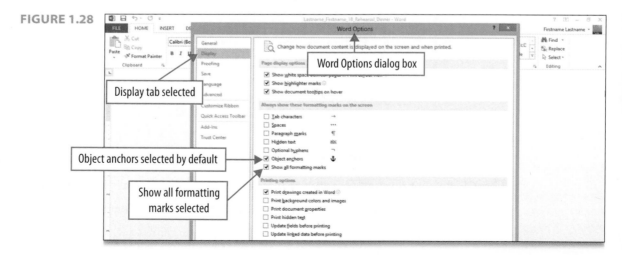

5 In the lower right corner of the dialog box, click **OK**.

Video OF1-9

The ribbon that displays across the top of the program window groups commands in a manner that you would most logically use them. The ribbon in each Office program is slightly different, but all contain the same three elements: *tabs*, *groups*, and *commands*.

Tabs display across the top of the ribbon, and each tab relates to a type of activity; for example, laying out a page. Groups are sets of related commands for specific tasks. Commands— instructions to computer programs—are arranged in groups and might display as a button, a menu, or a box in which you type information.

You can also minimize the ribbon so only the tab names display, which is useful when working on a smaller screen such as a tablet computer where you want to maximize your screen viewing area.

Activity 1.12 | Performing Commands from and Customizing the Ribbon and the Quick Access Toolbar

1 ▶ Take a moment to examine the document on your screen. If necessary, on the ribbon, click the VIEW tab, and then in the Show group, click to place a check mark in the Ruler check box. Compare your screen with Figure 1.29.

This document is a memo from the General Manager to the Executive Chef regarding a new restaurant promotion for wedding rehearsal dinners.

When working in Word, display the rulers so that you can see how margin settings affect your document and how text and objects align. Additionally, if you set a tab stop or an indent, its location is visible on the ruler.

FIGURE 1.29

2 ▶ In the upper left corner of your screen, above the ribbon, locate the **Quick Access Toolbar**.

Recall that the Quick Access Toolbar contains commands that you use frequently. By default, only the commands Save, Undo, and Redo display, but you can add and delete commands to suit your needs. Possibly the computer at which you are working already has additional commands added to the Quick Access Toolbar.

3 ▶ At the end of the **Quick Access Toolbar**, click the **Customize Quick Access Toolbar** button [▾], and then compare your screen with Figure 1.30.

A list of commands that Office users commonly add to their Quick Access Toolbar displays, including New, Open, Email, Quick Print, and Print Preview and Print. Commands already on the Quick Access Toolbar display a check mark. Commands that you add to the Quick Access Toolbar are always just one click away.

Here you can also display the More Commands dialog box, from which you can select any command from any tab on the ribbon to add to the Quick Access Toolbar.

 BY TOUCH   Tap once on Quick Access Toolbar commands.

FIGURE 1.30

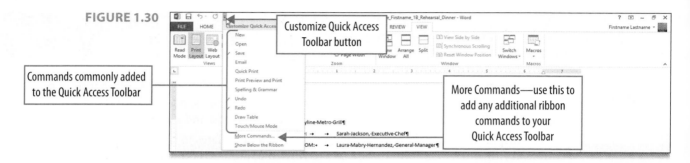

Commands commonly added to the Quick Access Toolbar

Customize Quick Access Toolbar button

More Commands—use this to add any additional ribbon commands to your Quick Access Toolbar

4 On the list, click **Print Preview and Print**, and then notice that the icon is added to the **Quick Access Toolbar**. Compare your screen with Figure 1.31.

> The icon that represents the Print Preview command displays on the Quick Access Toolbar. Because this is a command that you will use frequently while building Office documents, you might decide to have this command remain on your Quick Access Toolbar.

 ANOTHER WAY   Right-click any command on the ribbon, and then on the shortcut menu, click Add to Quick Access Toolbar.

FIGURE 1.31

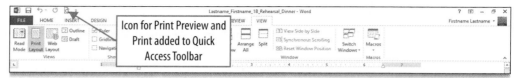

Icon for Print Preview and Print added to Quick Access Toolbar

5 In the first line of the document, if necessary, click to the left of the *S* in *Skyline* to position the insertion point there, and then press [Enter] one time to insert a blank paragraph. Press [↑] one time to position the insertion point in the new blank paragraph. Compare your screen with Figure 1.32.

FIGURE 1.32

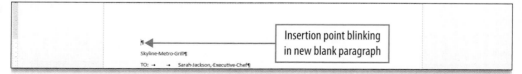

Insertion point blinking in new blank paragraph

6 On the ribbon, click the **INSERT tab**. In the **Illustrations group**, *point* to the **Online Pictures** button to display its ScreenTip.

> Many buttons on the ribbon have this type of *enhanced ScreenTip*, which displays useful descriptive information about the command.

7 Click **Online Pictures**, and then compare your screen with Figure 1.33.

> In the Insert Pictures dialog box you can search for online pictures using Microsoft's Clip Art collection. *Clip art* refers to royalty-free photos and illustrations you can download from Microsoft's Office.com site.

> Here you can also search for images using the Bing search engine, and if you are signed in with your Microsoft account, you can also find images on your SkyDrive or on your computer by clicking Browse. At the bottom, you can click the Flickr logo and download pictures from your Flickr account if you have one.

FIGURE 1.33

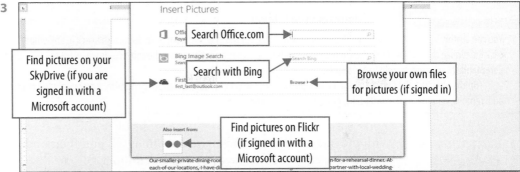

8 Click **Office.com Clip Art** and in the box that displays to the right, type **salad in a bowl** and press Enter. As shown in Figure 1.34, point to the illustration of the salad bowl to display its keywords.

You can use various keywords to find clip art that is appropriate for your documents.

FIGURE 1.34

9 Click the illustration of the salad to select it, and then in the lower right corner, click **Insert**. In the upper right corner of the picture, point to the **Layout Options** button 📷 to display its ScreenTip, and then compare your screen with Figure 1.35. If you cannot find the image, select a similar image, and then drag one of the corner sizing handles to match the approximate size shown in the figure.

Inserted pictures anchor—attach to—the paragraph at the insertion point location—as indicated by the anchor symbol. *Layout Options* enable you to choose how the *object*—in this instance an inserted picture—interacts with the surrounding text. An object is a picture or other graphic such as a chart or table that you can select and then move and resize.

When a picture is selected, the PICTURE TOOLS become available on the ribbon. Additionally, *sizing handles*—small squares that indicate an object is selected—surround the selected picture.

FIGURE 1.35

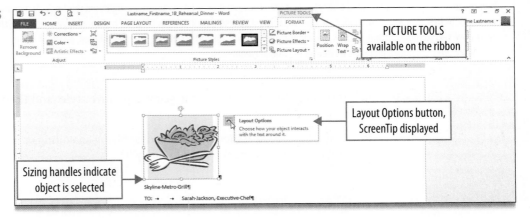

10 With the image selected, click **Layout Options** ⬛, and then under **With Text Wrapping**, in the second row, click the first layout—**Top and Bottom**.

11 Point to the image to display the 🔲 pointer, hold down the left mouse button to display a green line at the left margin, and then drag the image to the right and slightly upward until a green line displays in the center of the image and at the top of the image, as shown in Figure 1.36, and then release the left mouse button. If you are not satisfied with your result, on the Quick Access Toolbar, click Undo ↺ and begin again.

> *Alignment Guides* are green lines that display to help you align objects with margins or at the center of a page.

FIGURE 1.36

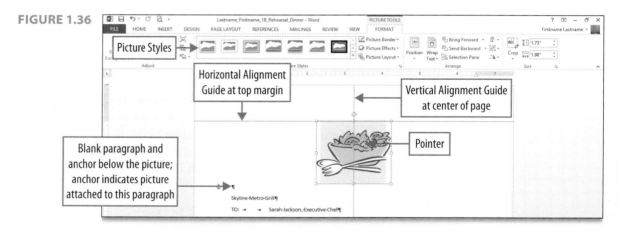

12 On the ribbon, in the **Picture Styles group**, point to the first style to display the ScreenTip *Simple Frame, White*, and notice that the image displays with a white frame.

13 Watch the image as you point to the second picture style, and then to the third, and then to the fourth.

> Recall that Live Preview shows the result of applying an editing or formatting change as you point to possible results—*before* you actually apply it.

14 In the **Picture Styles group**, click the second style—**Beveled Matte, White**—and then click anywhere outside of the image to deselect it. Notice that the *PICTURE TOOLS* no longer display on the ribbon. Compare your screen with Figure 1.37.

Contextual tabs on the ribbon display only when you need them.

FIGURE 1.37

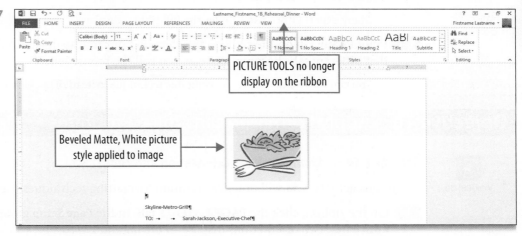

15 On the **Quick Access Toolbar**, click **Save** to save the changes you have made.

Activity 1.13 | Minimizing and Using the Keyboard to Control the Ribbon

Instead of a mouse, some individuals prefer to navigate the ribbon by using keys on the keyboard.

1 On your keyboard, press Alt, and then on the ribbon, notice that small labels display. Press N to activate the commands on the **INSERT tab**, and then compare your screen with Figure 1.38.

Each label represents a *KeyTip*—an indication of the key that you can press to activate the command. For example, on the INSERT tab, you can press F to open the Online Pictures dialog box.

FIGURE 1.38

2 Press Esc to redisplay the KeyTips for the tabs. Then, press Alt or Esc again to turn off keyboard control of the ribbon.

3 Point to any tab on the ribbon and right-click to display a shortcut menu.

Here you can choose to display the Quick Access Toolbar below the ribbon or collapse the ribbon to maximize screen space. You can also customize the ribbon by adding, removing, renaming, or reordering tabs, groups, and commands, although this is not recommended until you become an expert Office user.

4 Click **Collapse the Ribbon**. Notice that only the ribbon tabs display. Click the **HOME tab** to display the commands. Click anywhere in the document, and notice that the ribbon goes back to the collapsed display.

5 Right-click any ribbon tab, and then click **Collapse the Ribbon** again to remove the check mark from this command.

Many expert Office users prefer the full ribbon display.

6 Point to any tab on the ribbon, and then on your mouse device, roll the mouse wheel. Notice that different tabs become active as you roll the mouse wheel.

You can make a tab active by using this technique instead of clicking the tab.

Objective 10 | Apply Formatting in Office Programs

Video OF1-10

Activity 1.14 | Changing Page Orientation and Zoom Level

In this activity, you will practice common formatting techniques used in Office applications.

1 On the ribbon, click the **PAGE LAYOUT tab**. In the **Page Setup group**, click **Orientation**, and notice that two orientations display—*Portrait* and *Landscape*. Click **Landscape**.

In ***portrait orientation***, the paper is taller than it is wide. In ***landscape orientation***, the paper is wider than it is tall.

2 In the lower right corner of the screen, locate the **Zoom slider**.

Recall that to zoom means to increase or decrease the viewing area. You can zoom in to look closely at a section of a document, and then zoom out to see an entire page on the screen. You can also zoom to view multiple pages on the screen.

3 Drag the **Zoom slider** to the left until you have zoomed to approximately *60%*. Compare your screen with Figure 1.39.

FIGURE 1.39

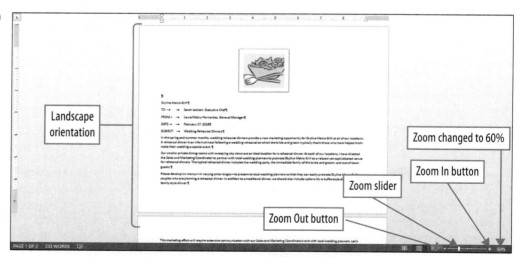

🔁 **BY TOUCH**   Drag the Zoom slider with your finger.

4 Use the technique you just practiced to change the **Orientation** back to **Portrait**.

The default orientation in Word is Portrait, which is commonly used for business documents such as letters and memos.

5 In the lower right corner, click the **Zoom In** button **+** as many times as necessary to return to the **100%** zoom setting.

Use the zoom feature to adjust the view of your document for editing and for your viewing comfort.

↻ ANOTHER WAY   You can also control Zoom from the ribbon. On the VIEW tab, in the Zoom group, you can control the Zoom level and also zoom to view multiple pages.

6 On the **Quick Access Toolbar**, click **Save** 🖫.

More **Knowledge**   **Zooming to Page Width**

Some Office users prefer Page Width, which zooms the document so that the width of the page matches the width of the window. Find this command on the VIEW tab, in the Zoom group.

Activity 1.15 | Formatting Text by Using Fonts, Alignment, Font Colors, and Font Styles

1 If necessary, on the right side of your screen, drag the vertical scroll box to the top of the scroll bar. To the left of *Skyline Metro Grill*, point in the margin area to display the 𝒜 pointer and click one time to select the entire paragraph. Compare your screen with Figure 1.40.

Use this technique to select complete paragraphs from the margin area—drag downward to select multiple-line paragraphs—which is faster and more efficient than dragging through text.

FIGURE 1.40

2 On the ribbon, click the **HOME tab**, and then in the **Paragraph group**, click **Center** ≡ to center the paragraph.

3 On the **HOME tab**, in the **Font group**, click the **Font button arrow** `Calibri (Body) ▾`. On the alphabetical list of font names, scroll down and then locate and *point to* **Cambria**.

A *font* is a set of characters with the same design and shape. The default font in a Word document is Calibri, which is a *sans serif* font—a font design with no lines or extensions on the ends of characters.

The Cambria font is a *serif font*—a font design that includes small line extensions on the ends of the letters to guide the eye in reading from left to right.

The list of fonts displays as a gallery showing potential results. For example, in the Font gallery, you can point to see the actual design and format of each font as it would look if applied to text.

4 Point to several other fonts and observe the effect on the selected text. Then, scroll back to the top of the **Font** gallery. Under **Theme Fonts**, click **Calibri Light**.

A *theme* is a predesigned combination of colors, fonts, line, and fill effects that look good together and is applied to an entire document by a single selection. A theme combines two sets of fonts—one for text and one for headings. In the default Office theme, Calibri Light is the suggested font for headings.

5 With the paragraph *Skyline Metro Grill* still selected, on the **HOME tab**, in the **Font group**, click the **Font Size button arrow** [11 ▾], point to **36**, and then notice how Live Preview displays the text in the font size to which you are pointing. Compare your screen with Figure 1.41.

FIGURE 1.41

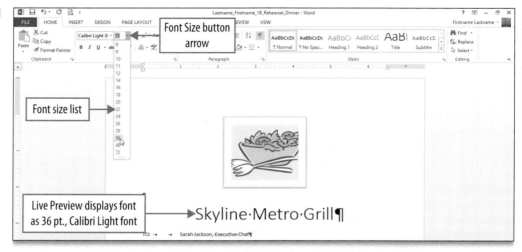

Font Size button arrow

Font size list

Live Preview displays font as 36 pt., Calibri Light font

→Skyline·Metro·Grill¶

6 On the list of font sizes, click **20**.

Fonts are measured in ***points***, with one point equal to 1/72 of an inch. A higher point size indicates a larger font size. Headings and titles are often formatted by using a larger font size. The word *point* is abbreviated as ***pt***.

7 With *Skyline Metro Grill* still selected, on the **HOME tab**, in the **Font group**, click the **Font Color button arrow** [A ▾]. Under **Theme Colors**, in the last column, click the last color—**Green, Accent 6, Darker 50%**. Click anywhere to deselect the text.

8 To the left of *TO:*, point in the left margin area to display the [pointer icon] pointer, hold down the left mouse button, and then drag down to select the four memo headings. Compare your screen with Figure 1.42.

Use this technique to select complete paragraphs from the margin area—drag downward to select multiple paragraphs—which is faster and more efficient than dragging through text.

 BY TOUCH   Tap once on TO: to display the gripper, then with your finger, drag to the right and down to select the four paragraphs.

FIGURE 1.42

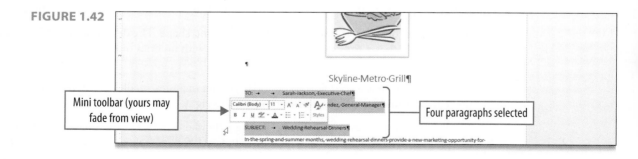

Mini toolbar (yours may fade from view)

Four paragraphs selected

9 With the four paragraphs selected, on the mini toolbar, click the **Font Color** button ▣ ▾, and notice that the text color of the four paragraphs changes.

The font color button retains its most recently used color—Green, Accent 6, Darker 50%. As you progress in your study of Microsoft Office, you will use other buttons that behave in this manner; that is, they retain their most recently used format. This is commonly referred to as *MRU*—most recently used.

Recall that the mini toolbar places commands that are commonly used for the selected text or object close by so that you reduce the distance that you must move your mouse to access a command. If you are using a touchscreen device, most commands that you need are close and easy to touch.

10 On the right, drag the vertical scroll box down slightly to position more of the text on the screen. Click anywhere in the paragraph that begins *In the spring*, and then **triple-click**—click the left mouse button three times—to select the entire paragraph. If the entire paragraph is not selected, click in the paragraph and begin again.

11 With the entire paragraph selected, on the mini toolbar, click the **Font Color button arrow** ▣ ▾, and then under **Theme Colors**, in the sixth column, click the last color— **Orange, Accent 2, Darker 50%**.

12 In the memo headings, select the guide word *TO:* and then on the mini toolbar, click **Bold** ▣ and **Italic** ▣.

Font styles include bold, italic, and underline. Font styles emphasize text and are a visual cue to draw the reader's eye to important text.

13 On the mini toolbar, click **Italic** ▣ again to turn off the Italic formatting.

A *toggle button* is a button that can be turned on by clicking it once, and then turned off by clicking it again.

Activity 1.16 | Using Format Painter

Use the Format Painter to copy the formatting of specific text or of a paragraph and then apply it in other locations in your document.

1 With *TO:* still selected, on the mini toolbar, click **Format Painter** ▣. Then, move your mouse under the word *Sarah*, and notice the ▣ mouse pointer. Compare your screen with Figure 1.43.

The pointer takes the shape of a paintbrush, and contains the formatting information from the paragraph where the insertion point is positioned. Information about the Format Painter and how to turn it off displays in the status bar.

FIGURE 1.43

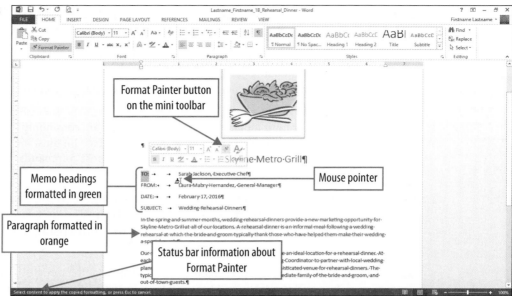

2 ▶ With the ⬚I pointer, drag to select the guide word *FROM:* and notice that Bold formatting is applied. Then, point to the selected text *FROM:* and on the mini toolbar, *double-click* **Format Painter** ⬚.

3 ▶ Select the guide word *DATE:* to copy the Bold formatting, and notice that the pointer retains the ⬚I shape.

> When you *double-click* the Format Painter button, the Format Painter feature remains active until you either click the Format Painter button again, or press (Esc) to cancel it—as indicated on the status bar.

4 ▶ With Format Painter still active, select the guide word *SUBJECT:*, and then on the ribbon, on the **HOME tab**, in the **Clipboard group**, notice that **Format Painter** ⬚ is selected, indicating that it is active. Compare your screen with Figure 1.44.

FIGURE 1.44

5 ▶ On the ribbon, click **Format Painter** ⬚ to turn the command off.

🔄 ANOTHER WAY   Press (Esc) to turn off Format Painter.

6 In the paragraph that begins *In the spring*, triple-click again to select the entire paragraph. On the mini toolbar, click **Bold** [B] and **Italic** [I]. Click anywhere to deselect.

7 On the **Quick Access Toolbar**, click **Save** [icon] to save the changes you have made to your document.

Activity 1.17 | Using Keyboard Shortcuts and Using the Clipboard to Copy, Cut, and Paste

The *Clipboard* is a temporary storage area that holds text or graphics that you select and then cut or copy. When you *copy* text or graphics, a copy is placed on the Clipboard and the original text or graphic remains in place. When you *cut* text or graphics, a copy is placed on the Clipboard, and the original text or graphic is removed—cut—from the document.

After copying or cutting, the contents of the Clipboard are available for you to *paste*—insert—in a new location in the current document, or into another Office file.

1 Hold down [Ctrl] and press [Home] to move to the beginning of your document, and then take a moment to study the table in Figure 1.45, which describes similar keyboard shortcuts with which you can navigate quickly in a document.

FIGURE 1.45

KEYBOARD SHORTCUTS TO NAVIGATE IN A DOCUMENT	
TO MOVE	**PRESS**
To the beginning of a document	[Ctrl] + [Home]
To the end of a document	[Ctrl] + [End]
To the beginning of a line	[Home]
To the end of a line	[End]
To the beginning of the previous word	[Ctrl] + [←]
To the beginning of the next word	[Ctrl] + [→]
To the beginning of the current word (if insertion point is in the middle of a word)	[Ctrl] + [←]
To the beginning of the previous paragraph	[Ctrl] + [↑]
To the beginning of the next paragraph	[Ctrl] + [↓]
To the beginning of the current paragraph (if insertion point is in the middle of a paragraph)	[Ctrl] + [↑]
Up one screen	[PgUp]
Down one screen	[PgDn]

2 To the left of *Skyline Metro Grill*, point in the left margin area to display the [icon] pointer, and then click one time to select the entire paragraph. On the **HOME tab**, in the **Clipboard group**, click **Copy** [icon].

Because anything that you select and then copy—or cut—is placed on the Clipboard, the Copy command and the Cut command display in the Clipboard group of commands on the ribbon. There is no visible indication that your copied selection has been placed on the Clipboard.

ANOTHER WAY   Right-click the selection, and then click Copy on the shortcut menu; or, use the keyboard shortcut [Ctrl] + [C].

3 On the **HOME tab**, in the **Clipboard group**, to the right of the group name *Clipboard*, click the **Dialog Box Launcher** button, and then compare your screen with Figure 1.46.

The Clipboard pane displays with your copied text. In any ribbon group, the ***Dialog Box Launcher*** displays either a dialog box or a pane related to the group of commands. It is not necessary to display the Clipboard in this manner, although sometimes it is useful to do so.

FIGURE 1.46

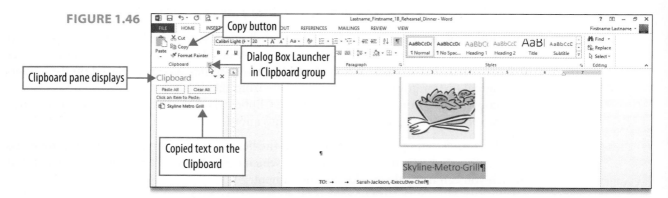

4 In the upper right corner of the **Clipboard** pane, click **Close** ☒.

5 Press Ctrl + End to move to the end of your document. Press Enter one time to create a new blank paragraph. On the **HOME tab**, in the **Clipboard group**, point to **Paste**, and then click the *upper* portion of this split button.

The Paste command pastes the most recently copied item on the Clipboard at the insertion point location. If you click the lower portion of the Paste button, a gallery of Paste Options displays. A ***split button*** is divided into two parts; clicking the main part of the button performs a command, and clicking the arrow displays a list or gallery with choices.

ANOTHER WAY   Right-click, on the shortcut menu under Paste Options, click the desired option button; or, press Ctrl + V.

6 Below the pasted text, click **Paste Options** as shown in Figure 1.47.

Here you can view and apply various formatting options for pasting your copied or cut text. Typically you will click Paste on the ribbon and paste the item in its original format. If you want some other format for the pasted item, you can choose another format from the ***Paste Options gallery***.

The Paste Options gallery provides a Live Preview of the various options for changing the format of the pasted item with a single click. The Paste Options gallery is available in three places: on the ribbon by clicking the lower portion of the Paste button—the Paste button arrow; from the Paste Options button that displays below the pasted item following the paste operation; or on the shortcut menu if you right-click the pasted item.

FIGURE 1.47

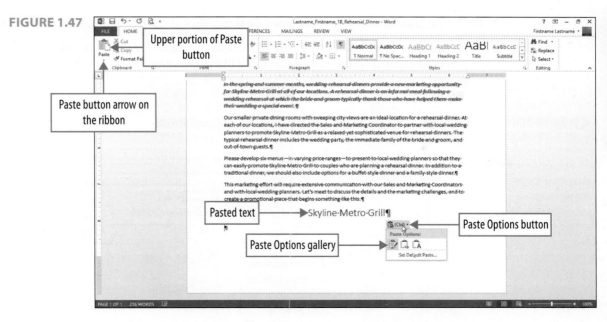

Upper portion of Paste button

Paste button arrow on the ribbon

Pasted text → Skyline·Metro·Grill¶

Paste Options button

Paste Options gallery

7 In the **Paste Options** gallery, *point* to each option to see the Live Preview of the format that would be applied if you clicked the button.

> The contents of the Paste Options gallery are contextual; that is, they change based on what you copied and where you are pasting.

8 Press Esc to close the gallery; the button will remain displayed until you take some other screen action.

9 Press Ctrl + Home to move to the top of the document, and then click the **salad image** one time to select it. While pointing to the selected image, right-click, and then on the shortcut menu, click **Cut**.

> Recall that the Cut command cuts—removes—the selection from the document and places it on the Clipboard.

 ANOTHER WAY   On the HOME tab, in the Clipboard group, click the Cut button; or, use the keyboard shortcut Ctrl + X.

10 Press Del one time to remove the blank paragraph from the top of the document, and then press Ctrl + End to move to the end of the document.

11 With the insertion point blinking in the blank paragraph at the end of the document, right-click, and notice that the **Paste Options** gallery displays on the shortcut menu. Compare your screen with Figure 1.48.

FIGURE 1.48

Paste Options on the shortcut menu

12 On the shortcut menu, under **Paste Options**, click the first button—**Keep Source Formatting**.

13 Point to the picture to display the pointer, and then drag to the right until the center green **Alignment Guide** displays and the blank paragraph is above the picture, as shown in Figure 1.49. Release the left mouse button.

FIGURE 1.49

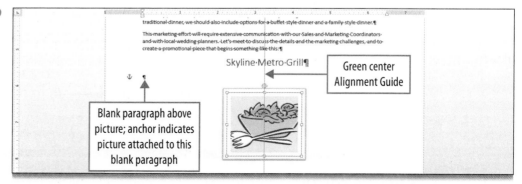

14 Above the picture, click to position the insertion point at the end of the word *Grill*, press Spacebar one time, type **for Your Rehearsal Dinner** and then **Save** 🖫 your document. Compare your screen with Figure 1.50.

FIGURE 1.50

15 On the **INSERT tab**, in the **Header & Footer group**, click **Footer**. At the bottom of the list, click **Edit Footer**, and then with the **HEADER & FOOTER Design tab** active, in the **Insert group**, click **Document Info**. Click **File Name** to add the file name to the footer.

16 On the right end of the ribbon, click **Close Header and Footer**.

17 On the **Quick Access Toolbar**, point to the **Print Preview and Print icon** 🔍 you placed there, right-click, and then click **Remove from Quick Access Toolbar**.

> If you are working on your own computer and you want to do so, you can leave the icon on the toolbar; in a lab setting, you should return the software to its original settings.

18 Click **Save** 🖫 and then click the **FILE tab** to display **Backstage** view. With the **Info tab** active, in the lower right corner click **Show All Properties**. As **Tags**, type **weddings, rehearsal dinners, marketing**

19 As the **Subject**, type your course name and number—for example *CIS 10, #5543*. Under **Related People**, be sure your name displays as the author (edit it if necessary), and then on the left, click **Print** to display the Print Preview. Compare your screen with Figure 1.51.

FIGURE 1.51

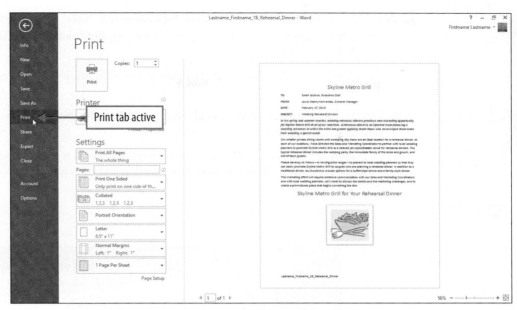

20 On the left side of **Backstage** view, click **Save**. As directed by your instructor, print or submit your file electronically as described in Project 1A, and then in the upper right corner of the Word window, click **Close** [**x**].

21 If a message indicates *Would you like to keep the last item you copied?* click **No**.

> This message displays if you have copied some type of image to the Clipboard. If you click Yes, the items on the Clipboard will remain for you to use in another program or document.

Objective 11 Compress Files and Use the Microsoft Office 2013 Help System

Video OF1-11

A **compressed file** is a file that has been reduced in size. Compressed files take up less storage space and can be transferred to other computers faster than uncompressed files. You can also combine a group of files into one compressed folder, which makes it easier to share a group of files.

Within each Office program, the Help feature provides information about all of the program's features and displays step-by-step instructions for performing many tasks.

Activity 1.18 | Compressing Files

In this activity, you will combine the two files you created in this chapter into one compressed file.

1 On the Windows taskbar, click **File Explorer** [icon]. On the left, in the **navigation pane**, navigate to your **USB flash drive**, and then open your **Office Features Chapter 1** folder. Compare your screen with Figure 1.52.

FIGURE 1.52

2 In the **file list**, click your **Lastname_Firstname_1A_Note_Form** Word file one time to select it. Then, hold down Ctrl, and click your **Lastname_Firstname_1B_Rehearsal_Dinner** file to select the files in the list.

> In any Windows-based program, holding down Ctrl while selecting enables you to select multiple items.

3 On the **File Explorer** ribbon, click **Share**, and then in the **Send group**, click **Zip**. Compare your screen with Figure 1.53.

> Windows creates a compressed folder containing a *copy* of each of the selected files. The folder name is selected—highlighted in blue—so that you can rename it.

BY TOUCH Tap the ribbon commands.

FIGURE 1.53

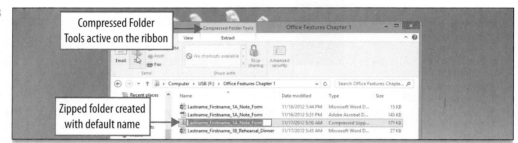

ANOTHER WAY Point to the selected files in the File List, right-click, point to Send to, and then click Compressed (zipped) folder.

4 Using your own name, type **Lastname_Firstname_Office_Features_Chapter_1** and press Enter.

> The compressed folder is ready to attach to an email or share in some other format.

5 In the upper right corner of the folder window, click **Close** ☒.

Activity 1.19 | Using the Microsoft Office 2013 Help System in Excel

In this activity, you will use the Microsoft Help feature to find information about formatting numbers in Excel.

1 Press ⊞ to display the Windows 8 **Start screen**, and then type **excel 2013** Press Enter to open the Excel desktop app.

2 On Excel's opening screen, click **Blank workbook**, and then in the upper right corner, click **Microsoft Excel Help** ❓.

ANOTHER WAY Press F1 to display Help in any Office program.

3 In the **Excel Help** window, click in the **Search online help** box, type **formatting numbers** and then press Enter.

4 On the list of results, click **Format numbers as currency**. Compare your screen with Figure 1.54.

FIGURE 1.54

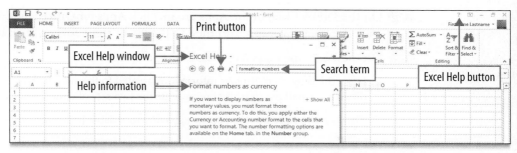

5 If you want to do so, at the top of the **Excel Help** window, click Print to print a copy of this information for your reference.

6 In the upper right corner of the Help window, click **Close**.

7 Leave Excel open for the next activity.

Objective 12   Install Apps for Office and Create a Microsoft Account

ALERT!   **Working with Web-Based Applications and Services**

Computer programs and services on the web receive continuous updates and improvements. Thus, the steps to complete the following web-based activities may differ from the ones shown. You can often look at the screens and the information presented to determine how to complete the activity.

Video OF1-12

Apps for Office 2013 and SharePoint 2013 are a collection of downloadable apps that enable you to create and view information within your familiar Office programs. Some of these apps are developed by Microsoft, but many more are developed by specialists in different fields. As new apps are developed, they will be available from the online Office Store.

An *app for Office* is a webpage that works within one of the Office applications, such as Excel, that you download from the Office Store. Office apps combine cloud services and web technologies within the user interface of Office and SharePoint. For example, in Excel, you can use an app to look up and gather search results for a new apartment by placing the information in an Excel worksheet, and then use maps to determine the distance of each apartment to work and to family members.

Activity 1.20 | **Installing Apps for Office**

ALERT!   **You Must Be Signed In to Office with a Microsoft Account to Complete This Activity**

To download an Office app, you must be signed in to Office with a free Microsoft account. If you do not have a Microsoft account, refer to the next activity to create one by using Microsoft's outlook.com email service, which includes free SkyDrive cloud storage.

1 On the Excel ribbon, click the **INSERT tab**. In the **Apps group**, click the **Apps for Office** arrow, and then click **See All**.

2 Click **FEATURED APPS**, and then on the right, click in the **Search for apps on the Office Store** box, type **Bing Maps** and press Enter.

3 Click the **Bing logo**, and then click the **Add** button, and then if necessary, click Continue.

4 **Close** Internet Explorer, and then **Close** the **Apps for Office** box.

5 On the **INSERT tab**, in the **Apps group**, click **Apps for Office**, click **See All**, click **MY APPS**, click the **Bing Maps** app, and then in the lower right corner, click **Insert**.

6 On the Welcome message, click **Insert Sample Data**.

Here, the Bing map displays information related to the sample data. Each state in the sample data displays a small pie chart that represents the two sets of data. Compare your screen with Figure 1.55.

This is just one example of many apps downloadable from the Office store.

FIGURE 1.55

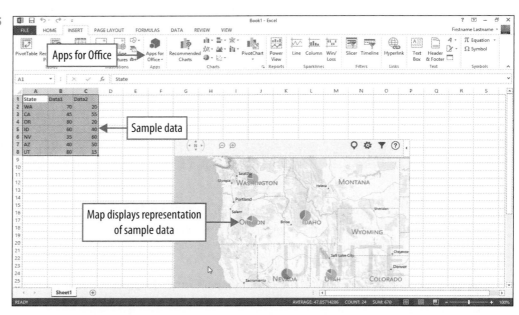

7 **Close** ☒ Excel without saving.

Activity 1.21 | Creating a Microsoft Account

In Windows 8, you can create a Microsoft account, and then use that account to sign in to *any* Windows 8 PC. Signing in with a Microsoft account is recommended because you can:

- Download Windows 8 apps from the Windows Store.
- Get your online content—email, social network updates, updated news—automatically displayed in an app on the Windows 8 Start screen when you sign in.
- Synch settings online to make every Windows 8 computer you use look and feel the same.
- Sign in to Office so that you can store documents on your SkyDrive and download Office apps.

1 Open Internet Explorer 🅔, and then go to **www.outlook.com**

2 Locate and click **Sign up now** to display a screen similar to Figure 1.56. Complete the form to create your account.

FIGURE 1.56

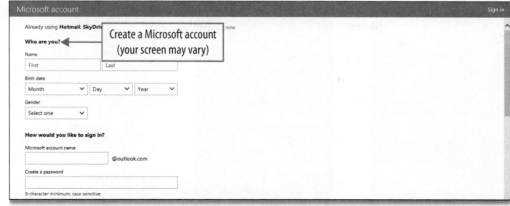

3 Close ☒ Internet Explorer.

END | You have completed Project 1B

END OF CHAPTER

SUMMARY

Many Office features and commands, such as the Open and Save As dialog boxes, performing commands from the ribbon and from dialog boxes, and using the Clipboard are the same in all Office desktop apps.

A desktop app is installed on your computer and requires a computer operating system such as Microsoft Windows or Apple OS to run. The programs in Microsoft Office 2013 are considered to be desktop apps.

Apps that run on a smartphone or tablet computer— for example, iOS, Android, or Windows Phone—or apps that run from browser software such as Internet Explorer or Chrome on a PC, are referred to as apps.

Within each Office app, you can install additional Apps for Office from the Office Store. You must have a Microsoft account, which includes free SkyDrive storage, to download Windows 8 or Office apps.

GO! LEARN IT ONLINE

Review the concepts and key terms in this chapter by completing these online challenges, which you can find at **www.pearsonhighered.com/go**.

Matching and Multiple Choice: Answer matching and multiple choice questions to test what you learned in this chapter. MyITLab®

Crossword Puzzle: Spell out the words that match the numbered clues, and put them in the puzzle squares.

Flipboard: Flip through the definition of the key terms in this chapter and match them with the correct term.

GLOSSARY

GLOSSARY OF CHAPTER KEY TERMS

Address bar (Internet Explorer) The area at the top of the Internet Explorer window that displays, and where you can type, a URL—Uniform Resource Locator—which is an address that uniquely identifies a location on the Internet.

Address bar (Windows) The bar at the top of a folder window with which you can navigate to a different folder or library, or go back to a previous one.

Alignment The placement of text or objects relative to the left and right margins.

Alignment guides Green lines that display when you move an object to assist in alignment.

App The term that commonly refers to computer programs that run from the device software on a smartphone or a tablet computer—for example, iOS, Android, or Windows Phone—or computer programs that run from the browser software on a desktop PC or laptop PC—for example Internet Explorer, Safari, Firefox, or Chrome.

App for Office A webpage that works within one of the Office applications, such as Excel, and that you download from the Office Store.

Apps for Office 2013 and SharePoint 2013 A collection of downloadable apps that enable you to create and view information within your familiar Office programs.

Backstage tabs The area along the left side of Backstage view with tabs to display screens with related groups of commands.

Backstage view A centralized space for file management tasks; for example, opening, saving, printing, publishing, or sharing a file. A navigation pane displays along the left side with tabs that group file-related tasks together.

Center alignment The alignment of text or objects that is centered horizontally between the left and right margins.

Click The action of pressing and releasing the left button on a mouse pointing device one time.

Clip art Downloadable predefined graphics available online from Office.com and other sites.

Clipboard A temporary storage area that holds text or graphics that you select and then cut or copy.

Cloud computing Refers to applications and services that are accessed over the Internet, rather than to applications that are installed on your local computer.

Cloud storage Online storage of data so that you can access your data from different places and devices.

Collaborate To work with others as a team in an intellectual endeavor to complete a shared task or to achieve a shared goal.

Commands An instruction to a computer program that causes an action to be carried out.

Common dialog boxes The set of dialog boxes that includes Open, Save, and Save As, which are provided by the Windows programming interface, and which display and operate in all of the Office programs in the same manner.

Compressed file A file that has been reduced in size and thus takes up less storage space and can be transferred to other computers quickly.

Compressed folder A folder that has been reduced in size and thus takes up less storage space and can be transferred to other computers quickly; also called a *zipped* folder.

Context menus Menus that display commands and options relevant to the selected text or object; also called *shortcut menus*.

Context-sensitive commands Commands that display on a shortcut menu that relate to the object or text that you right-clicked.

Contextual tabs Tabs that are added to the ribbon automatically when a specific object, such as a picture, is selected, and that contain commands relevant to the selected object.

Copy A command that duplicates a selection and places it on the Clipboard.

Cut A command that removes a selection and places it on the Clipboard.

Default The term that refers to the current selection or setting that is automatically used by a computer program unless you specify otherwise.

Deselect The action of canceling the selection of an object or block of text by clicking outside of the selection.

Desktop In Windows, the screen that simulates your work area.

Desktop app The term that commonly refers to a computer program that is installed on your computer and requires a computer operating system like Microsoft Windows or Apple OS to run.

Dialog box A small window that contains options for completing a task.

Dialog Box Launcher A small icon that displays to the right of some group names on the ribbon, and which opens a related dialog box or pane providing additional options and commands related to that group.

Document properties Details about a file that describe or identify it, including the title, author name, subject, and keywords that identify the document's topic or contents; also known as *metadata*.

Drag The action of holding down the left mouse button while moving your mouse.

Edit The process of making changes to text or graphics in an Office file.

Ellipsis A set of three dots indicating incompleteness; an ellipsis following a command name indicates that a dialog box will display if you click the command.

Enhanced ScreenTip A ScreenTip that displays more descriptive text than a normal ScreenTip.

Extract To decompress, or pull out, files from a compressed form.

File A collection of information stored on a computer under a single name, for example, a Word document or a PowerPoint presentation.

File Explorer The program that displays the files and folders on your computer, and which is at work anytime you are viewing the contents of files and folders in a window.

Fill The inside color of an object.

Folder A container in which you store files.

Folder window In Windows, a window that displays the contents of the current folder, library, or device, and contains helpful parts so that you can navigate the Windows file structure.

Font A set of characters with the same design and shape.

Font styles Formatting emphasis such as bold, italic, and underline.

Footer A reserved area for text or graphics that displays at the bottom of each page in a document.

Formatting The process of establishing the overall appearance of text, graphics, and pages in an Office file—for example, in a Word document.

Formatting marks Characters that display on the screen, but do not print, indicating where the Enter key, the Spacebar, and the Tab key were pressed; also called *nonprinting characters*.

Gallery An Office feature that displays a list of potential results instead of just the command name.

Gradient fill A fill effect in which one color fades into another.

Groups On the Office ribbon, the sets of related commands that you might need for a specific type of task.

Header A reserved area for text or graphics that displays at the top of each page in a document.

Info tab The tab in Backstage view that displays information about the current file.

Insertion point A blinking vertical line that indicates where text or graphics will be inserted.

Keyboard shortcut A combination of two or more keyboard keys, used to perform a task that would otherwise require a mouse.

KeyTip The letter that displays on a command in the ribbon and that indicates the key you can press to activate the command when keyboard control of the ribbon is activated.

Keywords Custom file properties in the form of words that you associate with a document to give an indication of the document's content; used to help find and organize files. Also called *tags*.

Landscape orientation A page orientation in which the paper is wider than it is tall.

Layout Options A button that displays when an object is selected and that has commands to choose how the object interacts with surrounding text.

Live Preview A technology that shows the result of applying an editing or formatting change as you point to possible results—*before* you actually apply it.

Location Any disk drive, folder, or other place in which you can store files and folders.

Metadata Details about a file that describe or identify it, including the title, author name, subject, and keywords that identify the document's topic or contents; also known as *document properties*.

Mini toolbar A small toolbar containing frequently used formatting commands that displays as a result of selecting text or objects.

MRU Acronym for *most recently used*, which refers to the state of some commands that retain the characteristic most recently applied; for example, the Font Color button retains the most recently used color until a new color is chosen.

Navigate The process of exploring within the organizing structure of Windows.

Navigation pane In a folder window, the area on the left in which you can navigate to, open, and display favorites, libraries, folders, saved searches, and an expandable list of drives.

Nonprinting characters Characters that display on the screen, but do not print, indicating where the Enter key, the Spacebar, and the Tab key were pressed; also called *formatting marks*.

Notification bar An area at the bottom of an Internet Explorer window that displays information about pending downloads, security issues, add-ons, and other issues related to the operation of your computer.

Object A text box, picture, table, or shape that you can select and then move and resize.

Office Web Apps The free online companions to Microsoft Word, Excel, PowerPoint, Access, and OneNote.

Open dialog box A dialog box from which you can navigate to, and then open on your screen, an existing file that was created in that same program.

Option button In a dialog box, a round button that enables you to make one choice among two or more options.

Options dialog box A dialog box within each Office application where you can select program settings and other options and preferences.

Pane A separate area of a window.

Paragraph symbol The symbol ¶ that represents the end of a paragraph.

Paste The action of placing text or objects that have been copied or cut from one location to another location.

Paste Options gallery A gallery of buttons that provides a Live Preview of all the Paste options available in the current context.

Path A sequence of folders that leads to a specific file or folder.

PDF The acronym for Portable Document Format, which is a file format that creates an image that preserves the look of your file; this is a popular format for sending documents electronically because the document will display on most computers.

Point The action of moving your mouse pointer over something on your screen.

Pointer Any symbol that displays on your screen in response to moving your mouse.

Points A measurement of the size of a font; there are 72 points in an inch.

Portable Document Format A file format that creates an image that preserves the look of your file, but that cannot be easily changed; a popular format for sending documents electronically, because the document will display on most computers.

Portrait orientation A page orientation in which the paper is taller than it is wide.

Print Preview A view of a document as it will appear when you print it.

Progress bar In a dialog box or taskbar button, a bar that indicates visually the progress of a task such as a download or file transfer.

Protected View A security feature in Office 2013 that protects your computer from malicious files by opening them in a restricted environment until you enable them; you might encounter this feature if you open a file from an email or download files from the Internet.

pt The abbreviation for *point*; for example, when referring to a font size.

Quick Access Toolbar In an Office program window, the small row of buttons in the upper left corner of the screen from which you can perform frequently used commands.

Read-Only A property assigned to a file that prevents the file from being modified or deleted; it indicates that you cannot save any changes to the displayed document unless you first save it with a new name.

Ribbon A user interface in both Office 2013 and File Explorer that groups the commands for performing related tasks on tabs across the upper portion of the program window.

Right-click The action of clicking the right mouse button one time.

Sans serif font A font design with no lines or extensions on the ends of characters.

ScreenTip A small box that that displays useful information when you perform various mouse actions such as pointing to screen elements or dragging.

Scroll bar A vertical or horizontal bar in a window or a pane to assist in bringing an area into view, and which contains a scroll box and scroll arrows.

Scroll box The box in the vertical and horizontal scroll bars that can be dragged to reposition the contents of a window or pane on the screen.

Selecting Highlighting, by dragging with your mouse, areas of text or data or graphics, so that the selection can be edited, formatted, copied, or moved.

Serif font A font design that includes small line extensions on the ends of the letters to guide the eye in reading from left to right.

SharePoint Collaboration software with which people in an organization can set up team sites to share information, manage documents, and publish reports for others to see.

Shortcut menu A menu that displays commands and options relevant to the selected text or object; also called a *context menu*.

Sizing handles Small squares that indicate a picture or object is selected.

SkyDrive Microsoft's free cloud storage for anyone with a free Microsoft account.

Split button A button divided into two parts and in which clicking the main part of the button performs a command and clicking the arrow opens a menu with choices.

Start search The search feature in Windows 8 in which, from the Start screen, you can begin to type and by default, Windows 8 searches for apps; you can adjust the search to search for files or settings.

Status bar The area along the lower edge of an Office program window that displays file information on the left and buttons to control how the window looks on the right.

Style A group of formatting commands, such as font, font size, font color, paragraph alignment, and line spacing that can be applied to a paragraph with one command.

Subfolder A folder within a folder.

Synchronization The process of updating computer files that are in two or more locations according to specific rules—also called *syncing*.

Syncing The process of updating computer files that are in two or more locations according to specific rules—also called *synchronization*.

Tabs (ribbon) On the Office ribbon, the name of each activity area.

Tags Custom file properties in the form of words that you associate with a document to give an indication of the document's content; used to help find and organize files. Also called *keywords*.

Taskbar The area along the lower edge of the desktop that displays buttons representing programs.

Template A preformatted document that you can use as a starting point and then change to suit your needs.

Theme A predesigned combination of colors, fonts, and effects that look good together and is applied to an entire document by a single selection.

Title bar The bar at the top edge of the program window that indicates the name of the current file and the program name.

Toggle button A button that can be turned on by clicking it once, and then turned off by clicking it again.

Toolbar In a folder window, a row of buttons with which you can perform common tasks, such as changing the view of your files and folders or burning files to a CD.

Triple-click The action of clicking the left mouse button three times in rapid succession.

Trusted Documents A security feature in Office that remembers which files you have already enabled; you might encounter this feature if you open a file from an email or download files from the Internet.

Uniform Resource Locator An address that uniquely identifies a location on the Internet.

URL The acronym for Uniform Resource Locator, which is an address that uniquely identifies a location on the Internet.

USB flash drive A small data storage device that plugs into a computer USB port.

Window A rectangular area on a computer screen in which programs and content appear, and which can be moved, resized, minimized, or closed.

XML Paper Specification A Microsoft file format that creates an image of your document and that opens in the XPS viewer.

XPS The acronym for XML Paper Specification—a Microsoft file format that creates an image of your document and that opens in the XPS viewer.

Zipped folder A folder that has been reduced in size and thus takes up less storage space and can be transferred to other computers quickly; also called a *compressed* folder.

Zoom The action of increasing or decreasing the size of the viewing area on the screen.

Introduction to Microsoft Word 2013

Fotowerk / Fotolia

Word 2013: Introduction

Video WA

Content! Defined by Merriam-Webster's online dictionary as "the topic or matter treated in a written work" and also as "the principal substance (as written matter, illustrations, or music) offered by a World Wide Web site," content is what you consume when you read on paper or online, when you watch video, or when you listen to any kind of music—live or recorded.

Content is what you *create* when your own words or performances are recorded in some form. For creating content in the form of words, Microsoft Office 2013 is a great choice. Rather than just a tool for word processing, Word is now a tool for you to communicate and collaborate with others. When you want to communicate with pictures or images in your Word document, Office 2013 has many new features to help you do so. Microsoft Word 2013 works best on a Windows 8 PC—desktop, laptop, or tablet—because if your PC is touch-enabled, you will be able to use your fingers to work with Word. For example, the ribbon expands to make it easy to tap commands and you can resize images by moving your fingers on the screen.

Best of all, Microsoft Word 2013 is integrated into the cloud. If you save your documents to your SkyDrive that comes with any free Microsoft account, such as one you can create at outlook.com, you can retrieve them from any device and continue to work with and share your documents. Enjoy learning Word 2013!

Creating Documents with Microsoft Word 2013

GO! to Work
Video W1

PROJECT 1A

OUTCOMES
Create a flyer with a picture.

PROJECT 1B

OUTCOMES
Format text, paragraphs, and documents.

OBJECTIVES

1. Create a New Document and Insert Text
2. Insert and Format Graphics
3. Insert and Modify Text Boxes and Shapes
4. Preview and Print a Document

OBJECTIVES

5. Change Document and Paragraph Layout
6. Create and Modify Lists
7. Set and Modify Tab Stops
8. Insert a SmartArt Graphic and an Online Video

A_ya / Fotolia

In This Chapter

In this chapter, you will begin your study of Microsoft Word, which is one of the most popular computer programs and one that almost everyone has a reason to use. You will use many of the new tools in Word 2013 such as applying attractive styles to your documents. You can use Microsoft Word to perform basic word processing tasks such as writing a memo, a report, or a letter. You can also use Word to complete complex tasks, such as creating sophisticated tables, embedding graphics, writing blogs, and creating publications. Word is a program that you can learn gradually, and then add more advanced skills, one at a time.

The projects in this chapter relate to **Sturgeon Point Productions**, which is an independent film company based in Miami and with offices in Detroit and Milwaukee. The film professionals produce effective broadcast and branded content for many industries, and provide a wide array of film and video production services. Sturgeon Point Productions has won awards for broadcast advertising, business media, music videos, and social media. The mission of the company is to help clients tell their stories—whether the story is about a social issue, a new product, a geographical location, a new company, or a person.

PROJECT ACTIVITIES

In Activities 1.01 through 1.16, you will create a flyer announcing two internships for a short documentary by Sturgeon Point Productions. Your completed document will look similar to Figure 1.1.

PROJECT FILES

For Project 1A, you will need the following files:

New blank Word document
w01A_Text
w01A_Bird

You will save your document as:

Lastname_Firstname_1A_Flyer

Build from
Scratch

PROJECT RESULTS

FIGURE 1.1 Project 1A Flyer

Objective 1   Create a New Document and Insert Text

Video W1-1

When you start Word, documents you have recently opened, if any, display on the left. On the right, you can select either a blank document or a ***template***—a preformatted document that you can use as a starting point and then change to suit your needs. When you create a new document, you can type all of the text or you can type some of the text and then insert additional text from another source.

Activity 1.01   Starting a New Word Document

1 **Start** Word, and then click **Blank document**. On the **HOME tab**, in the **Paragraph group**, if necessary, click **Show/Hide** ¶ so that it is active and the formatting marks display. If the rulers do not display, click the **VIEW tab**, and then in the **Show group**, select the **Ruler** check box.

2 Type **Internships Available** and then press Enter two times. As you type the following text, press the Spacebar only one time at the end of a sentence: **This summer, Sturgeon Point Productions will be filming a short documentary in Costa Rica about its native birds and has positions available for two interns. We are looking for a First Assistant Director and an Assistant Script Supervisor.**

As you type, the insertion point moves to the right, and when it approaches the right margin, Word determines whether the next word in the line will fit within the established right margin. If the word does not fit, Word moves the entire word down to the next line. This is ***wordwrap*** and means that you press Enter *only* when you reach the end of a paragraph—it is not necessary to press Enter at the end of each line of text.

> **N O T E**   **Spacing between Sentences**
>
> Although you might have learned to add two spaces following end-of-sentence punctuation, the common practice now is to space only one time at the end of a sentence.

3 Press Enter. Take a moment to study the table in Figure 1.2 to become familiar with the default document settings in Microsoft Word, and then compare your screen with Figure 1.3.

When you press Enter, Spacebar, or Tab on your keyboard, characters display in your document to represent these keystrokes. These characters do not print and are referred to as ***formatting marks*** or ***nonprinting characters***. These marks will display throughout this instruction.

FIGURE 1.2

DEFAULT DOCUMENT SETTINGS IN A NEW WORD DOCUMENT	
SETTING	DEFAULT FORMAT
Font and font size	The default font is Calibri and the default font size is 11 points.
Margins	The default left, right, top, and bottom page margins are 1 inch.
Line spacing	The default line spacing is 1.08, which provides slightly more space between lines than single spacing does.
Paragraph spacing	The default spacing after a paragraph is 8 points, which is slightly less than the height of one blank line of text.
View	The default view is Print Layout view, which displays the page borders and displays the document as it will appear when printed.

FIGURE 1.3

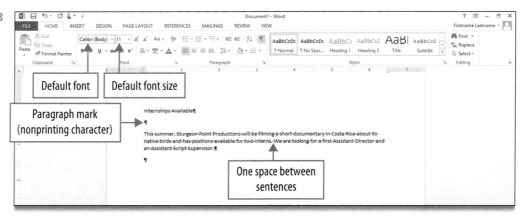

More Knowledge   **Word's Default Settings Are Easier to Read Online**

Until just a few years ago, word processing programs used single spacing, an extra blank paragraph to separate paragraphs, and 12 pt Times New Roman as the default formats. Now, studies show that individuals find the Word default formats described in Figure 1.2 to be easier to read online, where many documents are now viewed and read.

Activity 1.02 | **Inserting Text from Another Document**

1 ▷ On the ribbon, click the **INSERT tab**. In the **Text group**, click the **Object button arrow**, and then click **Text from File**.

ALERT!   **Does the Object Dialog Box Display?**

If the Object dialog box displays, you probably clicked the Object *button* instead of the Object *button arrow*. Close the Object dialog box, and then in the Text group, click the Object button arrow, as shown in Figure 1.4. Click *Text from File*, and then continue with Step 2.

2 ▷ In the **Insert File** dialog box, navigate to the student files that accompany this textbook, locate and select **w01A_Text**, and then click **Insert**. Compare your screen with Figure 1.4.

A *copy* of the text from the w01A_Text file displays at the insertion point location; the text is not removed from the original file.

FIGURE 1.4

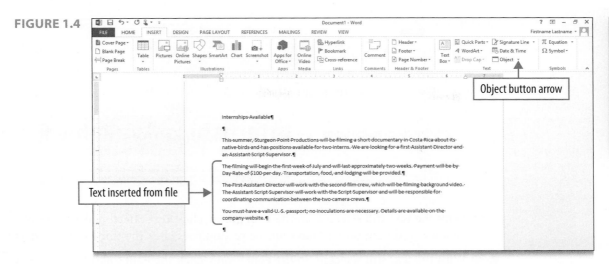

Object button arrow

Text inserted from file

🔄 **ANOTHER WAY**   Open the file, copy the required text, close the file, and then paste the text into the current document.

3 On the **Quick Access Toolbar**, click **Save** 🖫. Under **Save As**, click **Computer**, and then click **Browse**. Navigate to the location where you are saving your files for this chapter, and then create and open a new folder named **Word Chapter 1**. In the **File name** box, using your own name, replace the existing text with **Lastname_Firstname_1A_Flyer** and then click **Save**.

Objective 2 | Insert and Format Graphics

Video W1-2

To add visual interest to a document, insert *graphics*. Graphics include pictures, online pictures, charts, and *drawing objects*—shapes, diagrams, lines, and so on. For additional visual interest, you can apply an attractive graphic format to text; add, resize, move, and format pictures; and add a page border.

Activity 1.03 | Formatting Text by Using Text Effects

Text effects are decorative formats, such as shadowed or mirrored text, text glow, 3-D effects, and colors that make text stand out.

1 Including the paragraph mark, select the first paragraph of text—*Internships Available*. On the **HOME tab**, in the **Font group**, click **Text Effects and Typography** 🄰 ⋅.

2 In the **Text Effects** gallery, in the third row, point to the first effect to display the ScreenTip *Fill – Black, Text 1, Outline – Background 1, Hard Shadow – Background 1*, and then click this effect.

3 With the text still selected, in the **Font group**, click in the **Font Size** box [11 ⋅] to select the existing font size. Type **52** and then press [Enter].

When you want to change the font size of selected text to a size that does not display in the Font Size list, type the number in the Font Size box and press [Enter] to confirm the new font size.

4 With the text still selected, in the **Paragraph group**, click **Center** 🗐 to center the text. Compare your screen with Figure 1.5.

FIGURE 1.5

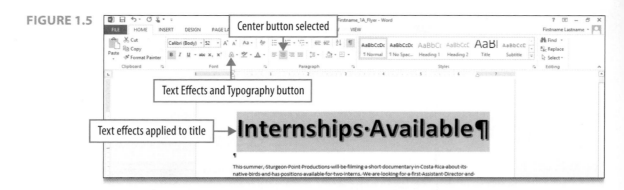

Center button selected

Text Effects and Typography button

Text effects applied to title → **Internships·Available¶**

This summer, Sturgeon Point Productions will be filming a short documentary in Costa Rica about its native birds and has positions available for two interns. We are looking for a first Assistant Director and

> **5** With the text still selected, in the **Font group**, click **Text Effects and Typography** [A ▾]. Point to **Shadow**, and then under **Outer**, in the second row, click the third style—**Offset Left**.

> **6** With the text still selected, in the **Font group**, click the **Font Color button arrow** [A ▾]. Under **Theme Colors**, in the sixth column, click the first color—**Orange, Accent 2**.

> **7** Click anywhere in the document to deselect the text, click **Save** [🖫], and then compare your screen with Figure 1.6.

FIGURE 1.6

Title color changed, shadow added → **Internships·Available¶**

More Knowledge | **Clear Existing Formatting**

If you do not like your text effect, you can remove all formatting from any selected text. To do so, on the HOME tab, in the Font group, click Clear All Formatting [✦].

Activity 1.04 | Inserting Pictures

> **1** In the paragraph that begins *This summer*, click to position the insertion point at the beginning of the paragraph.

> **2** On the **INSERT tab**, in the **Illustrations group**, click **Pictures**. In the **Insert Picture** dialog box, navigate to your student data files, locate and click **w01A_Bird**, and then click **Insert**.

> Word inserts the picture as an ***inline object***; that is, the picture is positioned directly in the text at the insertion point, just like a character in a sentence. The Layout Options button displays to the right of the picture. You can change the ***Layout Options*** to control the manner in which text wraps around a picture or other object. Sizing handles surround the picture indicating it is selected.

> **3** Notice the square sizing handles around the border of the selected picture, as shown in Figure 1.7.

> The corner sizing handles resize the graphic proportionally. The center sizing handles resize a graphic vertically or horizontally only; however, sizing with these will distort the graphic. A ***rotation handle***, with which you can rotate the graphic to any angle, displays above the top center sizing handle.

FIGURE 1.7

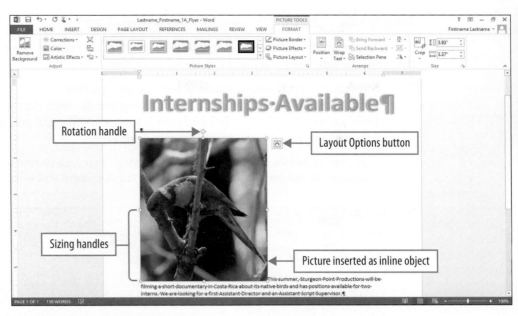

FIGURE 1.7

Activity 1.05 | Wrapping Text around a Picture Using Layout Options

Recall that Layout Options enable you to control *text wrapping*—the manner in which text displays around an object.

1 Be sure the picture is selected—you know it is selected if the sizing handles display.

2 To the right of the picture, click **Layout Options** 🖻 to display a gallery of text wrapping arrangements. Point to each layout option icon to view its ScreenTip.

Each icon visually depicts how text will wrap around an object.

🔄 **ANOTHER WAY** — On the FORMAT tab, in the Arrange group, click Wrap Text.

3 From the gallery, under **With Text Wrapping**, click the first layout—**Square**. Compare your screen with Figure 1.8.

Select Square text wrapping when you want to wrap the text to the left or right of an image. To the left of the picture, an *object anchor* displays indicating that the selected object is anchored to the text at this location in the document.

FIGURE 1.8

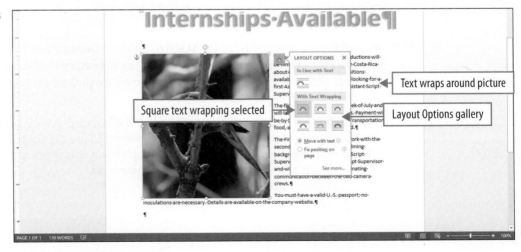

4 **Close** ✖ the **Layout Options**, and then **Save** 🖬 your document.

Activity 1.06 | Resizing Pictures and Using Live Layout

When you move or size a picture, *Live Layout* reflows text as you move or size an object so that you can view the placement of surrounding text.

1 If necessary, scroll your document so the entire picture displays on the screen. At the lower right corner of the picture, point to the sizing handle until the ⬛ pointer displays. Drag slightly upward and to the left and notice that as you drag, a green alignment guide displays at the left margin. Compare your screen with Figure 1.9.

Alignment guides display when you are moving or sizing a picture to help you with object placement, and Live Layout shows you how the document text will flow and display on the page.

FIGURE 1.9

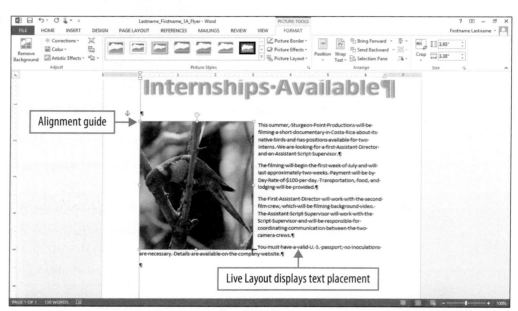

2 Continue to drag up and to the left until the bottom of the graphic is aligned at approximately **4 inches on the vertical ruler** and notice that the graphic is proportionally resized.

3 On the **Quick Access Toolbar**, click **Undo** ⟲ to restore the picture to its original size.

ANOTHER WAY On the FORMAT tab, in the Adjust group, click Reset Picture.

4 On the ribbon, under **PICTURE TOOLS**, on the **FORMAT tab**, in the **Size group**, click the **Shape Height spin box arrows**  as necessary to change the height of the picture to **3.8"**. If necessary, scroll down to view the entire picture on your screen, and then compare your screen with Figure 1.10.

A *spin box* is a small box with an upward- and downward-pointing arrow that lets you move rapidly through a set of values by clicking. When you use the Shape Height and Shape Width spin boxes to change the size of a graphic, the graphic will always resize proportionally; that is, the width adjusts as you change the height and vice versa.

FIGURE 1.10

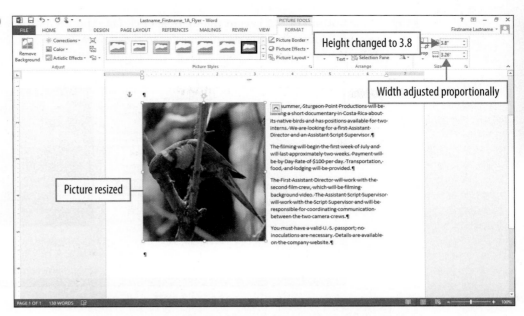

Height changed to 3.8

Width adjusted proportionally

Picture resized

5 Save 🖫 your document.

Activity 1.07 | Moving a Picture

There are two ways to move a picture in a document. You can point to the picture and then drag it to a new position. You can also change the picture settings in a dialog box, which gives you more precise control over the picture location.

1 Be sure the picture is selected. On the ribbon, click the **FORMAT tab**. In the **Arrange group**, click **Position**, and then click **More Layout Options**.

2 In the **Layout** dialog box, be sure the **Position tab** is selected. Under **Horizontal**, click the **Alignment** option button. To the right of **Alignment**, click the **arrow**, and then click **Right**. To the right of **relative to**, click the **arrow**, and then click **Margin**.

3 Under **Vertical**, click the **Alignment** option button. Change the **Alignment** options to **Top relative to Line**. Compare your screen with Figure 1.11.

With these alignment settings, the picture will move to the right margin of the page and the top edge will align with the top of the first line of the paragraph to which it is anchored.

FIGURE 1.11

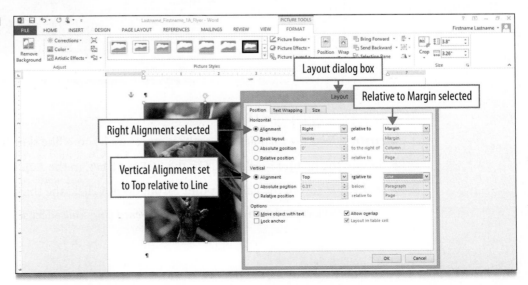

Layout dialog box

Relative to Margin selected

Right Alignment selected

Vertical Alignment set to Top relative to Line

4 At the bottom of the **Layout** dialog box, click **OK**, and then on the **Quick Access Toolbar**, click **Save** ⊟. Notice that the picture moves to the right margin, and the text wraps on the left side of the picture. Compare your screen with Figure 1.12.

FIGURE 1.12

Activity 1.08 | Applying Picture Effects

Picture styles include shapes, shadows, frames, borders, and other special effects with which you can stylize an image. *Picture Effects* enhance a picture with effects such as shadow, glow, reflection, or 3-D rotation.

1 Be sure the picture is selected. On the **FORMAT tab**, in the **Picture Styles group**, click **Picture Effects**.

2 Point to **Soft Edges**, and then click **5 Point**.

The Soft Edges feature fades the edges of the picture. The number of points you choose determines how far the fade goes inward from the edges of the picture.

3 Compare your screen with Figure 1.13, and then **Save** ⊟ your document.

FIGURE 1.13

Activity 1.09 | Applying Artistic Effects

Artistic effects are formats that make pictures look more like sketches or paintings.

1 Be sure the picture is selected. On the **FORMAT tab**, in the **Adjust group**, click **Artistic Effects**.

2 In the first row of the gallery, point to, but do not click, the third effect—**Pencil Grayscale**.

Live Preview displays the picture with the *Pencil Grayscale* effect added.

3 In the second row of the gallery, click the third effect—**Paint Brush**. **Save** 🖫 your document, and then notice that the picture looks more like a painting than a photograph. Compare your screen with Figure 1.14.

FIGURE 1.14

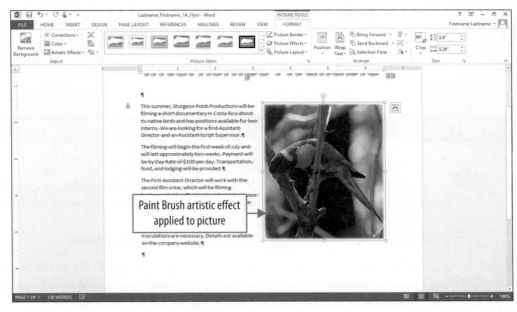

Paint Brush artistic effect applied to picture

Activity 1.10 | Adding a Page Border

Page borders frame a page and help to focus the information on the page.

1 Click anywhere outside the picture to deselect it. On the **DESIGN tab**, in the **Page Background group**, click **Page Borders**.

2 In the **Borders and Shading** dialog box, on the **Page Border tab**, under **Setting**, click **Box**. Under **Style**, scroll the list and click the seventh style—double lines.

3 Click the **Color arrow**, and then in the sixth column, click the first color—**Orange, Accent 2**.

4 Under **Apply to**, be sure **Whole document** is selected, and then compare your screen with Figure 1.15.

FIGURE 1.15

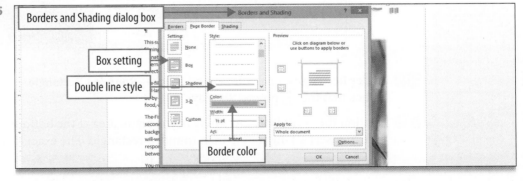

Borders and Shading dialog box

Box setting

Double line style

Border color

5 At the bottom of the **Borders and Shading** dialog box, click **OK**.

6 Press Ctrl + Home to move to the top of the document, click **Save** 🖫, and then compare your screen with Figure 1.16.

FIGURE 1.16

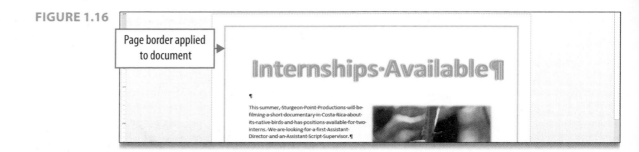

Page border applied to document

Internships·Available¶

¶

This·summer,·Sturgeon·Point·Productions·will·be·
filming·a·short·documentary·in·Costa·Rica·about·
its·native·birds·and·has·positions·available·for·two·
interns.·We·are·looking·for·a·first·Assistant·
Director·and·an·Assistant·Script·Supervisor.¶

Objective 3 | Insert and Modify Text Boxes and Shapes

Video W1-3

Word has predefined *shapes* and *text boxes* that you can add to your documents. A shape is an object such as a line, arrow, box, callout, or banner. A text box is a movable, resizable container for text or graphics. Use these objects to add visual interest to your document.

Activity 1.11 | Inserting, Sizing, and Positioning a Shape

1 Press ↓ one time to move to the blank paragraph below the title. Press Enter four times to create additional space for a text box, and notice that the picture anchored to the paragraph moves with the text.

2 Press Ctrl + End to move to the bottom of the document, and notice that your insertion point is positioned in the empty paragraph at the end of the document. Press Delete to remove the blank paragraph.

3 Click the **INSERT tab**, and then in the **Illustrations group**, click **Shapes** to display the gallery. Compare your screen with Figure 1.17.

FIGURE 1.17

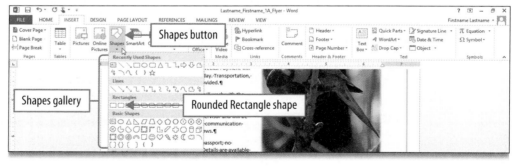

Shapes button

Shapes gallery

Rounded Rectangle shape

4 Under **Rectangles**, click the second shape—**Rounded Rectangle**, and then move your pointer. Notice that the ⊞ pointer displays.

5 Position the ⊞ pointer anywhere in the blank area at the bottom of the document. Click one time to insert a 1-inch by 1-inch rounded rectangle. The exact location is not important.

A blue rectangle with rounded edges displays.

6 To the right of the rectangle object, click **Layout Options** ⬚, and then at the bottom of the gallery, click **See more** to display the **Layout** dialog box.

ANOTHER WAY   On the FORMAT tab, in the Arrange group, click Position.

7 In the **Layout** dialog box, under **Horizontal**, click **Alignment**. To the right of **Alignment**, click the **arrow**, and then click **Centered**. To the right of **relative to**, click the **arrow**, and then click **Page**. Under **Vertical**, click in the **Absolute position** box to select the existing number, and then type **1** To the right of **below**, be sure that **Paragraph** displays. Click **OK**.

This action centers the rectangle on the page and positions the rectangle one inch below the last paragraph.

8 On the **FORMAT tab**, click in the **Shape Height** box ‡☐ Height: 0.19" ‡ to select the existing text. Type **1.5** and then click in the **Shape Width** box ⬚ Width: 6.49" ‡. Type **4.5** and then press Enter.

9 Compare your screen with Figure 1.18, and then **Save** 🖫 your document.

FIGURE 1.18

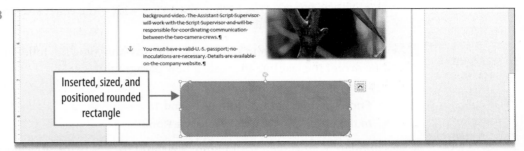

> Inserted, sized, and positioned rounded rectangle

Activity 1.12 | Typing Text in a Shape and Formatting a Shape

1 If necessary, select the rectangle shape. Type **To set up an interview, apply online at:** and then press Enter. Type **www.SturgeonPointProductions.com**

2 Press Ctrl + A to select the text you just typed. Right-click over the selected text to display the mini toolbar, and then click **Bold** B . With the text still selected, click **Increase Font Size** A˅ three times to increase the font size to **16 pt**.

The keyboard shortcut Ctrl + A is convenient to select all of the text in a text box.

3 With the text still selected, on the mini toolbar, click the **Font Color button arrow**. Under **Theme Colors**, click **Black, Text 1**.

4 Click outside the shape to deselect the text. Click the border of the shape to select the shape but not the text. On the **FORMAT tab**, in the **Shape Styles group**, click **Shape Fill**. In the sixth column, click the fourth color—**Orange, Accent 2, Lighter 40%**.

5 With the shape still selected, in the **Shape Styles group**, click **Shape Outline**. In the sixth column, click the first color—**Orange, Accent 2**. Compare your screen with Figure 1.19, and then **Save** 🖫 your document.

FIGURE 1.19

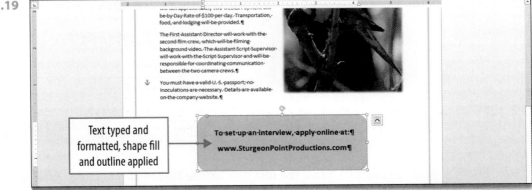

> Text typed and formatted, shape fill and outline applied

Activity 1.13 | Inserting a Text Box

A text box is useful to differentiate portions of text from other text on the page. Because it is a *floating object*—a graphic that can be moved independently of the surrounding text characters—you can place a text box anywhere on the page.

1 Press [Ctrl] + [Home] to move to the top of the document.

2 On the **INSERT tab**, in the **Text group**, click **Text Box**. At the bottom of the gallery, click **Draw Text Box**.

3 Position the ⊞ pointer over the first blank paragraph—aligned with the left margin and at approximately **1 inch on the vertical ruler**. Drag down and to the right to create a text box approximately **1.5 inches** high and **4 inches** wide—the exact size and location need not be precise.

4 With the insertion point blinking in the text box, type the following, pressing [Enter] after each line *except* the last line to create a new paragraph:

> **Interviews will be held:**
>
> **Friday and Saturday, January 14 and 15**
>
> **In the Career Services Conference Room**

5 Compare your screen with Figure 1.20, and then **Save** 🖫 your document

FIGURE 1.20

Activity 1.14 | Sizing and Positioning a Text Box and Formatting a Text Box Using Shape Styles

1 Point to the text box border to display the 🖑 pointer. In the space below the *Internships Available* title, by dragging, move the text box until a horizontal green alignment guide displays above the first blank paragraph mark and a vertical green alignment guide displays in the center of the page as shown in Figure 1.21.

FIGURE 1.21

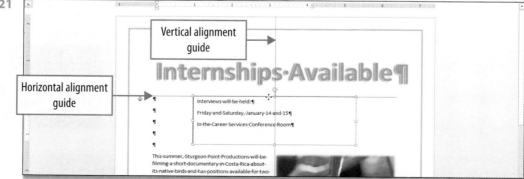

2 To precisely place the text box, on the **FORMAT tab**, in the **Arrange group**, click **Position**, and then click **More Layout Options**.

3 In the **Layout** dialog box, under **Horizontal**, click **Alignment**. To the right of **Alignment**, click the **arrow**, and then click **Centered**. To the right of **relative to**, click the **arrow**, and then click **Page**.

4 Under **Vertical**, click in the **Absolute position** box, select the existing number, and then type **1.25** To the right of **below**, click the **arrow**, and then click **Margin**.

5 In the **Layout** dialog box, click the **Size tab**. Under **Height**, select the number in the **Absolute** box. Type **1.25** and then under **Width**, select the number in the **Absolute** box. Type **4** and then click **OK**.

> The text box is sized correctly, centered horizontally, and the top edge is positioned 1.25 inches below the top margin of the document.

6 Click in the text box, and then press Ctrl + A to select all of the text. Right-click over the selected text to display the mini toolbar, change the **Font Size** to **16** and apply **Bold** B. Press Ctrl + E to center the text.

> Ctrl + E is the keyboard shortcut to center text in a document or object.

7 On the ribbon, under **DRAWING TOOLS**, click the **FORMAT tab**. In the **Shape Styles group**, click **More**, and then in the first row, click the third style—**Colored Outline – Orange, Accent 2**.

8 On the **FORMAT tab**, in the **Shape Styles group**, click **Shape Effects**. Point to **Shadow**, and then under **Outer**, in the first row, click the first effect—**Offset Diagonal Bottom Right**.

9 Click anywhere in the document to deselect the text box. Compare your screen with Figure 1.22, and then **Save** your document.

FIGURE 1.22

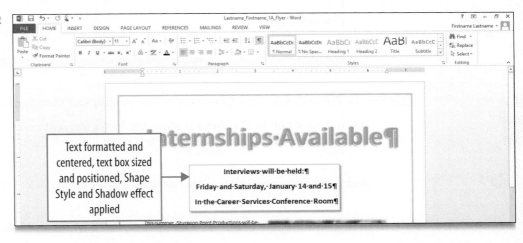

> Text formatted and centered, text box sized and positioned, Shape Style and Shadow effect applied

---

Objective 4 Preview and Print a Document

Video W1-4

While you are creating your document, it is useful to preview your document periodically to be sure that you are getting the result you want. Then, before printing, make a final preview to be sure the document layout is what you intend.

Activity 1.15 Adding a File Name to the Footer by Inserting a Field

Information in headers and footers helps to identify a document when it is printed or displayed electronically. Recall that a header is information that prints at the top of every page; a footer is information that prints at the bottom of every page. In this textbook, you will insert the file name in the footer of every Word document.

1 Click the **INSERT tab**, and then in the **Header & Footer group**, click **Footer**.

2 At the bottom of the gallery, click **Edit Footer**.

The footer area displays with the insertion point blinking at the left edge, and on the ribbon, the Header & Footer Tools display.

ANOTHER WAY   At the bottom edge of the page, right-click, and then on the shortcut menu, click Edit Footer.

3 On the ribbon, under the **HEADER & FOOTER TOOLS**, on the **DESIGN tab**, in the **Insert group**, click **Document Info**, and then click **File Name**. Compare your screen with Figure 1.23.

FIGURE 1.23

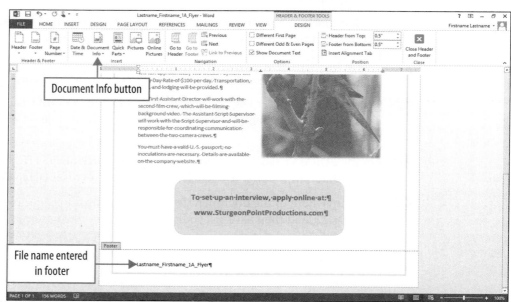

Document Info button

File name entered in footer

4 On the **DESIGN tab**, click **Close Header and Footer**, and then **Save** 🖫 your document.

When the body of the document is active, the footer text is dimmed—displays in gray. Conversely, when the footer area is active, the footer text is not dimmed; instead, the document text is dimmed.

ANOTHER WAY   Double-click in the document outside of the footer area to close the footer and return to the document.

Activity 1.16 | Adding Document Properties and Previewing and Printing a Document

1 Press (Ctrl) + (Home) to move the insertion point to the top of the document. In the upper left corner of your screen, click the **FILE tab** to display **Backstage** view. On the right, at the bottom of the **Properties** list, click **Show All Properties**.

2 On the list of **Properties**, click to the right of **Tags** to display an empty box, and then type **internship, documentary**

3 Click to the right of **Subject** to display an empty box, and then type your course name and section number. Under **Related People**, be sure that your name displays as the author. If necessary, right-click the author name, click **Edit Property**, type your name, press (Enter) and click **OK**.

4 On the left, click **Print** to display the **Print Preview**. Compare your screen with Figure 1.24.

Here you can select any printer connected to your system and adjust the settings related to how you want to print. On the right, Print Preview displays your document exactly as it will print; the formatting marks do not display. At the bottom of the Print Preview area, in the center, the number of pages and arrows with which you can move among the pages in Print Preview display. On the right, Zoom settings enable you to shrink or enlarge the Print Preview.

FIGURE 1.24

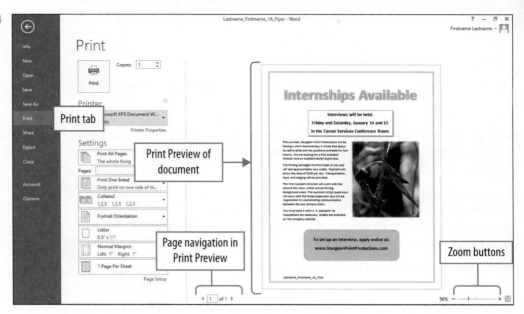

5 In the lower right corner of the window, click **Zoom In** ⊕ several times to view the document at a larger size, and notice that a larger preview is easier to read. Click **Zoom to Page** 🔲 to view the entire page.

6 To submit your file electronically, skip this step and move to Step 7. To print your document on paper using the default printer on your system, in the upper left portion of the screen, click **Print**.

The document will print on your default printer; if you do not have a color printer, colors will print in shades of gray. Backstage view closes and your file redisplays in the Word window.

7 To create an electronic printout, on the left, click **Export**. On the right, click **Create PDF/XPS**. In the **Publish as PDF or XPS** dialog box, navigate to your **Word Chapter 1** folder, and then click **Publish**. If your Adobe Acrobat or Adobe Reader program displays your PDF, in the upper right corner, click **Close** ⊠.

8 **Save** 🖫 your document. In the upper right corner of the Word window, click **Close** ✕ . If directed by your instructor to do so, submit your paper or electronic printout or your Word file.

END | You have completed Project 1A

Objective Create a Flyer in Word Web App

Build from Scratch

ALERT! **Working with Web-Based Applications and Services**

Computer programs and services on the web receive continuous updates and improvements, so the steps to complete this web-based activity may differ from the ones shown. You can often look at the screens and the information presented to determine how to complete the activity.

Activity | Creating a Flyer in the Word Web App

In this activity, you will use the Word Web App to create a flyer similar to the one you created in Project 1A.

1 From the desktop, start Internet Explorer. Navigate to **http://skydrive.com**, and then sign in to your Microsoft account. Open your **GO! Web Projects** folder—or create and then open this folder if necessary.

2 On the SkyDrive menu bar, click **Create**, and then click **Word document**. Using your own name, as the file name, type **Lastname_Firstname_WD_1A_Web** and then click **Create** to start a new file in the Word Web app.

3 Type **Sturgeon Point Productions** and then press Enter.

4 Type the following four lines of text, pressing Enter after each line *except* for the last line:

Internships Available for a Costa Rica
Native Birds Documentary
Interviews on Friday, January 14
Filming Begins the First Week of July

5 By using your I pointer, drag to select the first line in the document. On the **HOME tab**, in the **Font group**, click the **Font Size button arrow**, and then click **36**. Click the **Font Color button arrow**, and then in the fourth column, click the first color—**Blue Gray, Text 2**. In the **Paragraph group**, click **Center**.

In the Word Web App, you must drag to select text—triple-clicking a line will not select the line, nor will moving the pointer into the left margin and clicking. You can, however, double-click to select a single word.

6 Select the remaining text in the document, and then on the **HOME tab** in the **Font group**, click **Bold**. Click the **Font Size button arrow**, and then click **24**. In the **Paragraph group**, click **Center**. Compare your screen with Figure A.

FIGURE A

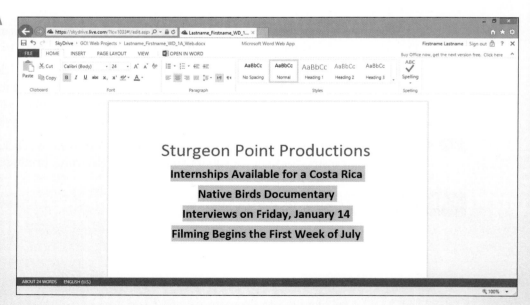

(GO! with Office Web Apps continues on the next page)

7 Click at the end of the line *Interviews on Friday, January 14*, and then press Enter to insert a blank line.

8 On the **INSERT tab**, in the **Pictures group**, click **Picture**. Navigate to the location where your student data files are stored, and then click **w01A_Bird**. Click **Open**. Notice that the picture is dimmed, indicating that it is selected.

9 Under **PICTURE TOOLS**, click the **FORMAT tab**, and then in the **Image Size group**, click **Shrink** several times until the **Scale** box displays **40.48%**. If the box does not display this exact number, click the **Shrink** or **Grow** buttons until the **Scale** is approximately this number.

10 With the picture still selected, on the **FORMAT tab**, in the **Picture Styles group**, click the sixth style—**Soft Edge Rectangle**.

11 Click anywhere in a blank area of the document so that the picture is not selected, and then compare your screen with Figure B.

12 In the upper left corner, above the **FILE tab**, click **Save** 🔲, and then submit as directed by your instructor. If you are instructed to submit an electronic printout of your file, create a PDF as indicated in the Note box that follows. Then, on the ribbon, click the **FILE tab** and click **Exit**. Sign out of your Microsoft account.

N O T E   **Creating a PDF from the Word Web App**

Click the FILE tab, click Print, and then click Print to PDF. In the Microsoft Word Web App message box, click Click here to view the PDF of your document. In the message bar at the bottom of your screen, click the Save arrow, and then click Save as. In the Save As dialog box, navigate to your Word Chapter 1 folder, and then save the file.

FIGURE B

Information Handout

PROJECT ACTIVITIES

In Activities 1.17 through 1.29, you will format an information handout from Sturgeon Point Productions that describes internships available to students. Your completed document will look similar to Figure 1.25.

PROJECT FILES

For Project 1B, you will need the following files:

w01B_Programs
w01B_Web

You will save your document as:

Lastname_Firstname_1B_Programs

PROJECT RESULTS

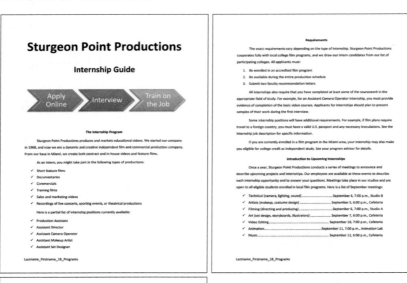

FIGURE 1.25 Project 1B Information Handout

Video W1-5

Document layout includes *margins*—the space between the text and the top, bottom, left, and right edges of the paper. Paragraph layout includes line spacing, indents, and tabs. In Word, the information about paragraph formats is stored in the paragraph mark at the end of a paragraph. When you press Enter, the new paragraph mark contains the formatting of the previous paragraph, unless you take steps to change it.

Activity 1.17 | Setting Margins

1 Start Word, and then click **Open Other Documents**. Navigate to the student files that accompany this textbook, and then open the document **w01B_Programs**. On the **HOME tab**, in the **Paragraph group**, be sure **Show/Hide** ¶ is active so that you can view the formatting marks.

2 Click the **FILE tab**, and then click **Save As**. Navigate to your **Word Chapter 1** folder, and then using your own name, **Save** the document as **Lastname_Firstname_1B_Programs**

3 Click the **PAGE LAYOUT tab**. In the **Page Setup group**, click **Margins**, and then take a moment to study the settings in the Margins gallery.

> If you have recently used custom margins settings, they will display at the top of this gallery. Other commonly used settings also display.

4 At the bottom of the **Margins** gallery, click the command followed by an ellipsis—**Custom Margins** to display the **Page Setup** dialog box.

5 In the **Page Setup** dialog box, under **Margins**, press Tab as necessary to select the value in the **Left** box, and then, with *1.25"* selected, type **1**

> This action will change the left margin to 1 inch on all pages of the document. You do not need to type the inch (") mark.

6 Press Tab to select the margin in the **Right** box, and then type **1** At the bottom of the dialog box, notice that the new margins will apply to the **Whole document**. Compare your screen with Figure 1.26.

FIGURE 1.26

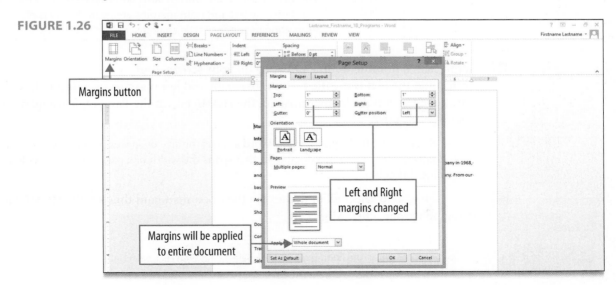

7 Click **OK** to apply the new margins and close the dialog box. If the ruler below the ribbon is not displayed, on the **VIEW** tab, in the **Show group**, select the **Ruler** check box.

8 Scroll to position the bottom of **Page 1** and the top of **Page 2** on your screen. Notice that the page edges display, and the page number and total number of pages display on the left side of the status bar.

9 Near the bottom edge of **Page 1**, point anywhere in the bottom margin area, right-click, and then click **Edit Footer** to display the footer area.

10 On the ribbon, under the **HEADER & FOOTER TOOLS**, on the **DESIGN tab**, in the **Insert group**, click **Document Info**, and then click **File Name**.

11 Double-click anywhere in the document to close the footer area, and then **Save** 🖫 your document.

Activity 1.18 | Aligning Text

Alignment refers to the placement of paragraph text relative to the left and right margins. Most paragraph text uses *left alignment*—aligned at the left margin, leaving the right margin uneven. Three other types of paragraph alignment are: *center alignment*—centered between the left and right margins; *right alignment*—aligned at the right margin with an uneven left margin; and *justified alignment*—text aligned evenly at both the left and right margins. The table in Figure 1.27 shows examples of these alignment types.

FIGURE 1.27

TYPES OF PARAGRAPH ALIGNMENT		
ALIGNMENT	**BUTTON**	**DESCRIPTION AND EXAMPLE**
Align Left	☰	Align Left is the default paragraph alignment in Word. Text in the paragraph aligns at the left margin, and the right margin is uneven.
Center	☰	Center alignment aligns text in the paragraph so that it is centered between the left and right margins.
Align Right	☰	Align Right aligns text at the right margin. Using Align Right, the left margin, which is normally even, is uneven.
Justify	☰	The Justify alignment option adds additional space between words so that both the left and right margins are even. Justify is often used when formatting newspaper-style columns.

1 Scroll to position the middle of **Page 2** on your screen, look at the left and right margins, and notice that the text is justified—both the right and left margins of multiple-line paragraphs are aligned evenly at the margins. On the **HOME tab**, in the **Paragraph group**, notice that **Justify** ☰ is active.

> To achieve a justified right margin, Word adjusts the size of spaces between words, which can result in unattractive spacing in a document that spans the width of a page. Many individuals find such spacing difficult to read.

2 Press [Ctrl] + [A] to select all of the text in the document, and then on the **HOME tab**, in the **Paragraph group**, click **Align Left** ☰.

🔄 **ANOTHER WAY**   On the HOME tab, in the Editing group, click Select, and then click Select All.

3 Press Ctrl + Home to move to the beginning of the document. In the left margin area, point to the left of the first paragraph—*Sturgeon Point Productions*—until the pointer displays, and then click one time to select the paragraph.

Use this technique to select entire lines of text.

4 On the mini toolbar, in the **Font Size** box, select the existing number, type **40** and then press Enter.

Use this technique to change the font size to a size that is not available on the Font Size list.

5 Select the second paragraph—*Internship Guide*—and then on the mini toolbar, change the **Font Size** to **26 pt**. Point to the left of the first paragraph—*Sturgeon Point Productions*—to display the pointer again, and then drag down to select the first two paragraphs, which form the title and subtitle of the document.

6 On the **HOME tab**, in the **Paragraph group**, click **Center** to center the title and subtitle between the left and right margins, and then compare your screen with Figure 1.28.

FIGURE 1.28

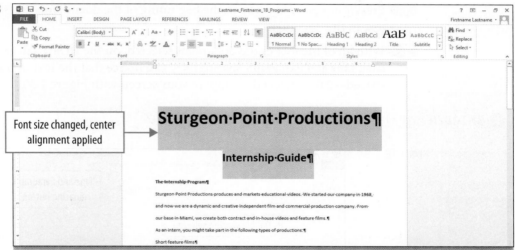

7 Near the top of **Page 1**, locate the first bold subheading—*The Internship Program*. Point to the left of the paragraph to display the pointer, and then click one time to select this text.

8 With *The Internship Program* selected, use your mouse wheel or the vertical scroll bar to bring the bottom portion of **Page 1** into view. Locate the subheading *Requirements*. Move the pointer to the left of the paragraph to display the pointer, hold down Ctrl, and then click one time. Scroll to the middle of **Page 2**, and then use the same technique to select the third subheading—*Introduction to Upcoming Internships*.

Three subheadings are selected; in Windows-based programs, you can hold down Ctrl to select multiple items.

9 Click **Center** to center all three subheadings, and then click **Save**.

Activity 1.19 | Changing Line Spacing

Line spacing is the distance between lines of text in a paragraph. Three of the most commonly used line spacing options are shown in the table in Figure 1.29.

FIGURE 1.29

ALIGNMENT	DESCRIPTION, EXAMPLE, AND INFORMATION
LINE SPACING OPTIONS	
Single spacing	**This text in this example uses single spacing**. Single spacing was once the most commonly used spacing in business documents. Now, because so many documents are read on a computer screen rather than on paper, single spacing is becoming less popular.
Multiple 1.08 spacing	**This text in this example uses multiple 1.08 spacing**. The default line spacing in Microsoft Word 2013 is 1.08, which is slightly more than single spacing to make the text easier to read on a computer screen. Many individuals now prefer this spacing, even on paper, because the lines of text appear less crowded.
Double spacing	**This text in this example uses double spacing**. College research papers and draft documents that need space for notes are commonly double-spaced; there is space for a full line of text between each document line.

1 ▶ Press Ctrl + Home to move to the beginning of the document. Press Ctrl + A to select all of the text in the document.

2 ▶ With all of the text in the document selected, on the **HOME tab**, in the **Paragraph group**, click **Line and Paragraph Spacing** ⬛▾, and notice that the text in the document is double spaced—**2.0** is checked. Compare your screen with Figure 1.30.

⟳ BY TOUCH   Tap the ribbon commands.

FIGURE 1.30

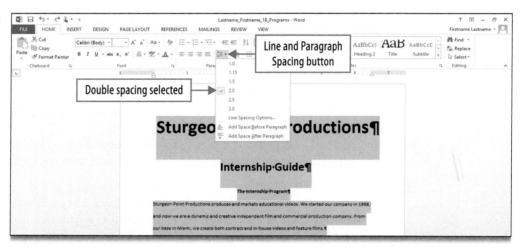

3 ▶ On the **Line Spacing** menu, click the *third* setting—**1.5**—and then click anywhere in the document to deselect the text. Compare your screen with Figure 1.31, and then **Save** ⬛ your document.

FIGURE 1.31

Activity 1.20 | Indenting Text

Indenting the first line of each paragraph is a common technique to distinguish paragraphs.

1 Below the title and subtitle of the document, click anywhere in the paragraph that begins *Sturgeon Point Productions produces.*

2 On the **HOME tab**, in the **Paragraph group**, click the **Dialog Box Launcher** .

3 In the **Paragraph** dialog box, on the **Indents and Spacing tab**, under **Indentation**, click the **Special arrow**, and then click **First line** to indent the first line by 0.5", which is the default indent setting. Compare your screen with Figure 1.32.

FIGURE 1.32

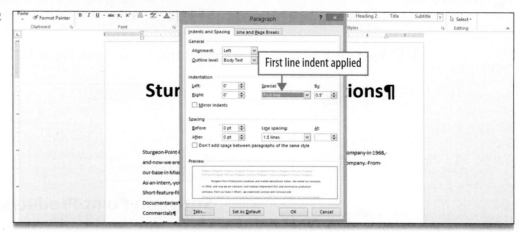

4 Click **OK**, and then click anywhere in the next paragraph, which begins *As an intern.* On the ruler under the ribbon, drag the **First Line Indent** marker to **0.5 inches on the horizontal ruler**, and then compare your screen with Figure 1.33.

FIGURE 1.33

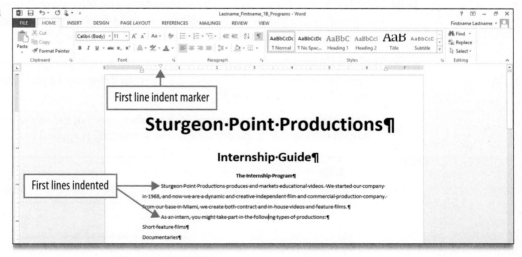

5 By using either of the techniques you just practiced, or by using the **Format Painter**, apply a first line indent of **0.5"** in the paragraph that begins *Here is a partial* to match the indent of the remaining paragraphs in the document.

6 **Save** your document.

Activity 1.21 | Adding Space Before and After Paragraphs

Adding space after each paragraph is another technique to differentiate paragraphs.

1 Press Ctrl + A to select all of the text in the document. Click the **PAGE LAYOUT tab**, and then in the **Paragraph group**, under **Spacing**, click the **After spin box up arrow** one time to change the value to **6 pt**.

> To change the value in the box, you can also select the existing number, type a new number, and then press Enter. This document will use 6 pt spacing after paragraphs to add space.

ANOTHER WAY   On either the HOME tab or the PAGE LAYOUT tab, display the Paragraph dialog box from the Paragraph group, and then under Spacing, click the spin box arrows as necessary.

2 Press Ctrl + Home, and then compare your screen with Figure 1.34.

FIGURE 1.34

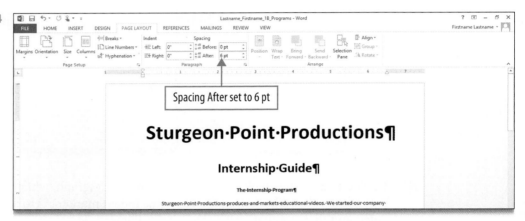

3 Near the top of **Page 1**, select the subheading *The Internship Program*, including the paragraph mark following it, scroll down, hold down Ctrl, and then select the subheadings *Requirements* and *Introduction to Upcoming Internships*.

4 With all three subheadings selected, in the **Paragraph group**, under **Spacing**, click the **Before up spin box arrow** two times to set the **Spacing Before** to **12 pt**. Compare your screen with Figure 1.35, and then **Save** your document.

> This action increases the amount of space above each of the subheadings, which will make them easy to distinguish in the document. The formatting is applied only to the selected paragraphs.

FIGURE 1.35

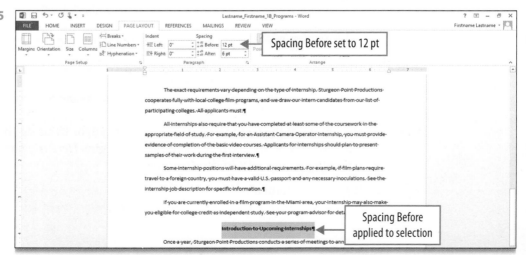

Video W1-6

To display a list of information, you can choose a **bulleted list**, which uses **bullets**—text symbols such as small circles or check marks—to introduce each item in a list. You can also choose a **numbered list**, which uses consecutive numbers or letters to introduce each item in a list.

Use a bulleted list if the items in the list can be introduced in any order; use a numbered list for items that have definite steps, a sequence of actions, or are in chronological order.

Activity 1.22 | Creating a Bulleted List

1 In the upper portion of **Page 1**, locate the paragraph *Short feature films*, and then point to this paragraph from the left margin area to display the pointer. Drag down to select this paragraph and the next five paragraphs.

2 On the **HOME tab**, in the **Paragraph group**, click **Bullets** to change the selected text to a bulleted list.

> The spacing between each of the bulleted points changes to the spacing between lines in a paragraph—in this instance, 1.5 line spacing. The 6 pt. spacing after each paragraph is eliminated with the exception of the last item in the list. Each bulleted item is automatically indented.

3 On the ruler, point to **First Line Indent** and read the ScreenTip, and then point to **Hanging Indent**. Compare your screen with Figure 1.36.

> By default, Word formats bulleted items with a first line indent of 0.25" and adds a Hanging Indent at 0.5". The hanging indent maintains the alignment of text when a bulleted item is more than one line.

> You can modify the list indentation by using Decrease Indent or Increase Indent. **Decrease Indent** moves your paragraph closer to the margin. **Increase Indent** moves your paragraph farther away from the margin.

FIGURE 1.36

4 Scroll down slightly, and then by using the pointer from the left margin area, select the five internship positions, beginning with *Production Assistant* and ending with *Assistant Set Designer*. In the **Paragraph group**, click **Bullets**.

5 Scroll down to view **Page 2**. Apply bullets to all of the paragraphs that indicate the September meetings and meeting dates, beginning with *Technical* and ending with *Music*. **Save** your document.

Activity 1.23 | Creating a Numbered List

1 Under the subheading *Requirements*, in the paragraph that begins *The exact requirements*, click to position the insertion point at the *end* of the paragraph, following the colon. Press Enter to create a blank paragraph. Notice that the paragraph is indented, because the First Line Indent from the previous paragraph carried over to the new paragraph.

2 To change the indent formatting for this paragraph, on the ruler, drag the **First Line Indent** marker ▽ to the left so that it is positioned directly above the lower button.

3 Being sure to include the period, type **1.** and press Spacebar. Compare your screen with Figure 1.37.

> Word determines that this paragraph is the first item in a numbered list and formats the new paragraph accordingly, indenting the list in the same manner as the bulleted list. The space after the number changes to a tab, and the AutoCorrect Options button displays to the left of the list item. The tab is indicated by a right arrow formatting mark.

FIGURE 1.37

A L E R T ! **Activating Automatic Numbered Lists**

If a numbered list does not begin automatically, click the FILE tab, and then click the Options tab. On the left side of the Word Options dialog box, click Proofing. Under AutoCorrect options, click the AutoCorrect Options button. In the AutoCorrect dialog box, click the AutoFormat As You Type tab. Under *Apply as you type*, select the *Automatic numbered lists* check box, and then click OK two times to close both dialog boxes.

---

4 Click **AutoCorrect Options** 📴, and then compare your screen with Figure 1.38.

> From the displayed list, you can remove the automatic formatting here, or stop using the automatic numbered lists option in this document. You also have the option to open the AutoCorrect dialog box to *Control AutoFormat Options*.

FIGURE 1.38

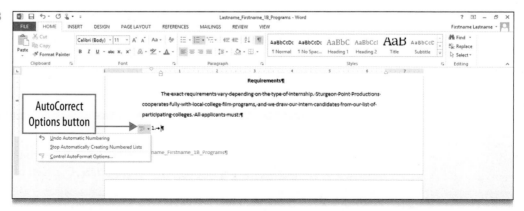

5 Click **AutoCorrect Options** 📴 again to close the menu without selecting any of the commands. Type **Be enrolled in an accredited film program** and press Enter. Notice that the second number and a tab are added to the next line.

6 Type **Be available during the entire production schedule** and press Enter. Type **Submit two faculty recommendation letters** Compare your screen with Figure 1.39, and then **Save** 💾 your document.

FIGURE 1.39

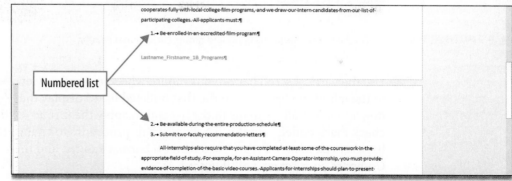

To End a List

To turn a list off, you can press Backspace, click the Numbering or Bullets button, or press Enter two times. Both list buttons—Numbering and Bullets—act as *toggle buttons*; that is, clicking the button one time turns the feature on, and clicking the button again turns the feature off.

Activity 1.24 | Customizing Bullets

You can use any symbol from any font for your bullet characters.

1 Press Ctrl + End to move to the end of the document, and then scroll up as necessary to display the bulleted list containing the list of meetings.

2 Point to the left of the first list item to display the 🖋 pointer, and then drag down to select all six meetings in the list—the bullet symbols are not highlighted.

3 On the mini toolbar, click the **Bullets button arrow** ≣▾ to display the **Bullet Library**, and then compare your screen with Figure 1.40.

FIGURE 1.40

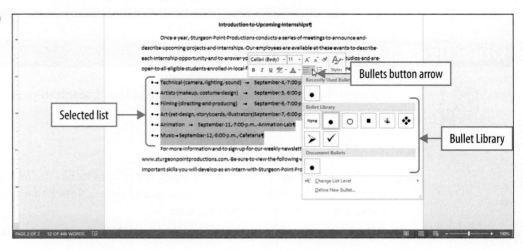

---

4 Under **Bullet Library**, click the **check mark** symbol. If the check mark is not available, choose another bullet symbol.

5 With the bulleted list still selected, right-click over the list, and then on the mini toolbar, double-click **Format Painter** .

🔄 **ANOTHER WAY**   On the HOME tab, in the Clipboard group, click Format Painter.

6 Use the vertical scroll bar or your mouse wheel to scroll to view **Page 1**. Move the pointer to the left of the first item in the first bulleted list to display the pointer, and then drag down to select all six items in the list and to apply the format of the third bulleted list—the check mark bullets—to this list. Repeat this procedure to change the bullets in the second list to check marks. Press Esc to turn off **Format Painter**, and then **Save** your document. Compare your screen with Figure 1.41.

FIGURE 1.41

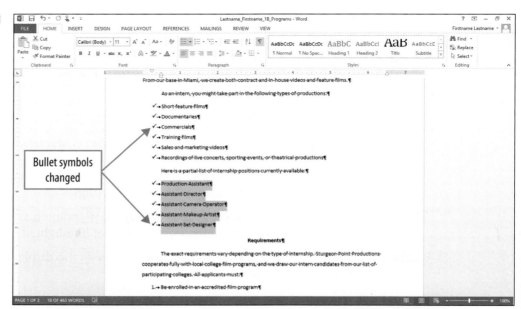

Objective 7   Set and Modify Tab Stops

Video W1-7

Tab stops mark specific locations on a line of text. Use tab stops to indent and align text, and use the Tab key to move to tab stops.

Activity 1.25 │ Setting Tab Stops

1 Scroll to view **Page 2**, and then by using the pointer at the left of the first item, select all of the items in the bulleted list of meetings and dates. Notice that there is a tab mark between the name of the meeting and the date.

The arrow that indicates a tab is a nonprinting formatting mark.

2 To the left of the horizontal ruler, point to **Tab Alignment** to display the *Left Tab* ScreenTip, and then compare your screen with Figure 1.42.

FIGURE 1.42

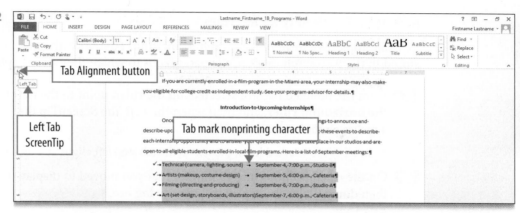

Tab Alignment button

Left Tab ScreenTip

Tab mark nonprinting character

3 Click **Tab Alignment** ⬜ several times to view the tab alignment options shown in the table in Figure 1.43.

FIGURE 1.43

TAB ALIGNMENT OPTIONS		
TYPE	**TAB ALIGNMENT BUTTON DISPLAYS THIS MARKER**	**RESULT OF TAB ALIGNMENT**
Left	⬜	Text is left aligned at the tab stop and extends to the right.
Center	⬜	Text is centered around the tab stop.
Right	⬜	Text is right aligned at the tab stop and extends to the left.
Decimal	⬜	The decimal point aligns at the tab stop.
Bar	⬜	A vertical bar displays at the tab stop.
First Line Indent	▽	Text in the first line of a paragraph indents.
Hanging Indent	⬠	Text in all lines except the first line in the paragraph indents.

4 Display **Left Tab** ⬜. Along the lower edge of the horizontal ruler, point to and then click at **3.5 inches on the horizontal ruler**. Notice that all of the dates left align at the new tab stop location, and the right edge of the column is uneven.

5 Compare your screen with Figure 1.44, and then **Save** 💾 your document.

FIGURE 1.44

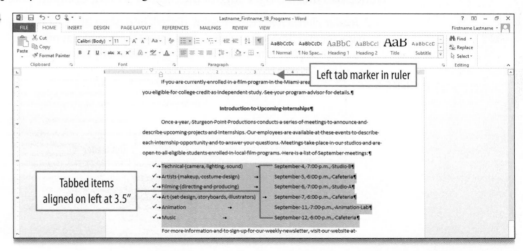

Left tab marker in ruler

Tabbed items aligned on left at 3.5"

Activity 1.26 | Modifying Tab Stops

Tab stops are a form of paragraph formatting. Therefore, the information about tab stops is stored in the paragraph mark in the paragraphs to which they were applied.

1 With the bulleted list still selected, on the ruler, point to the new tab marker at **3.5 inches on the horizontal ruler**, and then when the *Left Tab* ScreenTip displays, drag the tab marker to **4 inches on the horizontal ruler**.

In all of the selected lines, the text at the tab stop left aligns at 4 inches.

2 On the ruler, point to the tab marker that you moved to display the *Left Tab* ScreenTip, and then double-click to display the **Tabs** dialog box.

ANOTHER WAY   On the HOME tab, in the Paragraph group, click the Dialog Box Launcher. At the bottom of the Paragraph dialog box, click the Tabs button.

3 In the **Tabs** dialog box, under **Tab stop position**, if necessary, select *4"* and then type **6**

4 Under **Alignment**, click the **Right** option button. Under **Leader**, click the **2** option button. Near the bottom of the **Tabs** dialog box, click **Set**.

Because the Right tab will be used to align the items in the list, the tab stop at 4" is no longer necessary.

5 In the **Tabs** dialog box, in the **Tab stop position** box, click **4"** to select this tab stop, and then in the lower portion of the **Tabs** dialog box, click the **Clear** button to delete this tab stop, which is no longer necessary. Compare your screen with Figure 1.45.

FIGURE 1.45
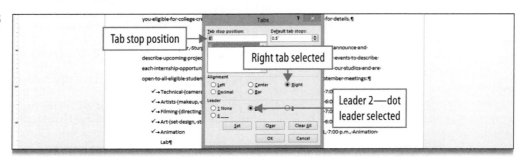

6 Click **OK**. On the ruler, notice that the left tab marker at *4"* no longer displays, a right tab marker displays at *6"*, and a series of dots—a ***dot leader***—displays between the columns of the list. Notice also that the right edge of the column is even. Compare your screen with Figure 1.46.

A ***leader character*** creates a solid, dotted, or dashed line that fills the space to the left of a tab character and draws the reader's eyes across the page from one item to the next. When the character used for the leader is a dot, it is commonly referred to as a dot leader.

FIGURE 1.46
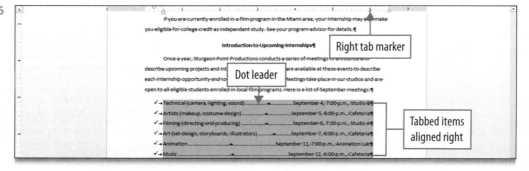

7 In the bulleted list that uses dot leaders, locate the *Art* meeting, and then click to position the insertion point at the end of that line, after the word *Cafeteria*. Press Enter to create a new blank bullet item.

8 Type **Video Editing** and press Tab. Notice that a dot leader fills the space to the tab marker location.

9 Type **September 10, 7:00 p.m., Cafeteria** and notice that the text moves to the left to maintain the right alignment of the tab stop.

10 Save 🖫 your document.

Objective 8 | Insert a SmartArt Graphic and an Online Video

Video W1-8

SmartArt graphics are designer-quality visual representations of information, and Word provides many different layouts from which you can choose. You can also insert a link to an online video from a variety of online sources, thus enabling the reader to view the video when connected to the Internet. SmartArt graphics and videos can communicate your messages or ideas more effectively than plain text and these objects add visual interest to a document or webpage.

Activity 1.27 | Inserting a SmartArt Graphic

1 Press Ctrl + Home to move to the top of the document, and then click to the right of the subtitle *Internship Guide*.

2 Click the **INSERT tab**, and then in the **Illustrations group**, point to **SmartArt** to display its ScreenTip. Read the ScreenTip, and then click **SmartArt**.

3 In the center portion of the **Choose a SmartArt Graphic** dialog box, scroll down and examine the numerous types of SmartArt graphics available.

4 On the left, click **Process**, and then by using the ScreenTips, locate and click **Basic Chevron Process**. Compare your screen with Figure 1.47.

At the right of the dialog box, a preview and description of the SmartArt displays.

FIGURE 1.47

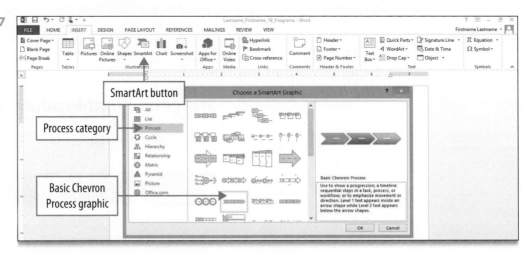

SmartArt button

Process category

Basic Chevron Process graphic

5 Click **OK** to insert the SmartArt graphic.

To the left of the inserted SmartArt graphic the text pane may display. The text pane provides one method for entering text into your SmartArt graphic. If you choose not to use the text pane to enter text, you can close it.

6 ▶ On the ribbon under **SMARTART TOOLS**, on the **DESIGN tab**, in the **Create Graphic group**, notice the **Text Pane** button. If the Text Pane button is selected, click **Text Pane** to close the pane.

7 ▶ In the SmartArt graphic, in the first blue arrow, click *[Text]*, and notice that *[Text]* is replaced by a blinking insertion point.

> The word *[Text]* is called ***placeholder text***, which is non-printing text that indicates where you can type.

8 ▶ Type **Apply Online**

9 ▶ Click the placeholder text in the middle arrow. Type **Interview** and then click the placeholder text in the third arrow. Type **Train on the Job** and then compare your screen with Figure 1.48.

FIGURE 1.48

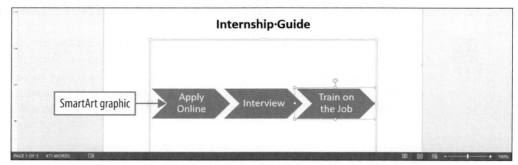

10 ▶ Save 🖫 your document.

Activity 1.28 | Sizing and Formatting a SmartArt Graphic

1 ▶ Click the SmartArt graphic border to select it. Be sure that none of the arrows have sizing handles around their border, which would indicate the arrow was selected, not the entire graphic.

2 ▶ Click the **FORMAT tab**, and then in the **Size group**, if necessary, click **Size** to display the **Shape Height** and **Shape Width** boxes.

3 ▶ Set the **Height** to **1.75"** and the **Width** to **6.5"**, and then compare your screen with Figure 1.49.

FIGURE 1.49

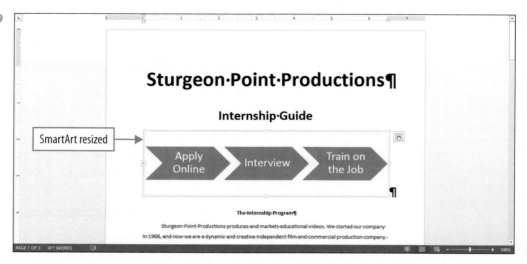

4 With the SmartArt graphic still selected, click the **SMARTART TOOLS DESIGN tab**, and then in the **SmartArt Styles group**, click **Change Colors**. Under **Colorful**, click the fourth style—**Colorful Range–Accent Colors 4 to 5**.

5 On the **SMARTART TOOLS DESIGN tab**, in the **SmartArt Styles group**, click **More** ⏷. Under **3-D**, click the second style—**Inset**. Click **Save** 🖫, and then compare your screen with Figure 1.50.

FIGURE 1.50

Activity 1.29 │ Inserting an Online Video

Microsoft's research indicates that two-thirds of people who open Word documents never edit them; they only read them. So with more and more documents being read online—and not on paper—it makes sense that you may want to include videos in your Word documents.

1 Press Ctrl + End to move to the end of the document.

2 On the **INSERT tab**, in the **Media group**, click **Online Video**. If the YouTube search box does not display, in the lower left corner of the Insert Video window, under Also insert from: click YouTube.

> Here you can search the web for an online video, search YouTube, or enter an **embed code** to insert a link to a video from a website. An embed code is a code that creates a link to a video, picture, or other type of **rich media** content. Rich media, also called **interactive media**, refers to computer interaction that responds to your actions; for example by presenting text, graphics, animation, video, audio, or games.

3 In the **Search YouTube** box, being sure to include the quotation marks, type **"Go 2013 1B Video"** and then press Enter.

4 Point to the displayed thumbnail and notice the ScreenTip. Click the **1B video**, and then click **Insert**. Compare your screen with Figure 1.51.

FIGURE 1.51

5 In the center of the video, point to the **Play** button ▶ to display the 👆 pointer, and then click. If a black screen displays, double-click one or more times until you see text on the screen, then point to the lower edge of the screen and click the Play button.

> A new window opens that contains the video and a play button. You can click the play button to view the video. When you insert an online video, the embed code is stored with the document and a link is created to the online content. In this manner, you can easily share video content that is relevant to the document without increasing the file size of the document.

6 View a few seconds of the video—more if you want—and then press (Esc) to return to your document.

7 Click **Save** 🖫, and then press (Ctrl) + (Home) to move to the top of your document.

8 Click the **FILE tab**, and then in the lower right portion of the screen, click **Show All Properties**. In the **Tags** box, type **internship** and in the **Subject** box, type your course name and section number. In the **Author** box, be sure your name displays; edit if necessary.

9 On the left, click **Print** to display **Print Preview**. At the bottom of the preview, click the **Previous Page** ◀ and **Next Page** ▶ buttons to move between pages. If necessary, return to the document and make any necessary changes.

10 As directed by your instructor, print your document or submit it electronically. **Save** 🖫 your document and **Close** ✕ Word.

END | You have completed Project 1B

GO! with Office Web Apps

Objective | Create a Handout in the Word Web App

You can use the Word Web App to edit your document if you are not at a computer on which Word 2013 is installed. You can change fonts and font sizes, modify paragraph alignment, and apply bullets and numbering.

> **ALERT!** **Working with Web-Based Applications and Services**
>
> Computer programs and services on the web receive continuous updates and improvements, so the steps to complete this web-based activity may differ from the ones shown. You can often look at the screens and the information presented to determine how to complete the activity.

Activity | Creating a Handout in the Word Web App

In this activity, you will use the Word Web App to edit a flyer similar to the one you edited in Project 1B.

1 Start Word, and then below the **Recent** list, click **Open Other Documents**. Navigate to your student data files, and then open **w01_1B_Web**. If necessary, in the upper right corner, log into Office with your Microsoft account. On the **FILE tab**, click **Save As**, and then on the right, click the name of your SkyDrive.

2 In the **Save As** dialog box, click your **GO! Web Projects** folder, and then click **Open**. In the **File name** box, type **Lastname_Firstname_WD_1B_Web** and then click **Save**.

3 Close Word, launch **Internet Explorer**, go to http://skydrive.com, sign in, and then open the file you just saved there. In the upper left, click **EDIT DOCUMENT**, and the click **Edit in Word Web App**.

4 Double-click the file that you just renamed, and then click **EDIT DOCUMENT**. On the list, click **Edit in Word Web App**.

5 Press Ctrl + A to select all the text in the document. On the **HOME tab**, in the **Paragraph group**, click **Align Text Left** .

6 Drag to select the first three lines in the document. On the **HOME tab**, in the **Paragraph group**, click **Center**. Compare your screen with Figure A.

7 Click at the beginning of the paragraph that begins *Sturgeon Point Productions produces*, and then press Tab. Click at the beginning of the paragraph that begins *As an intern*, and then press Tab.

8 Scroll the document and click at the beginning of the paragraph that begins *Here is a partial*, and then press Tab.

FIGURE A

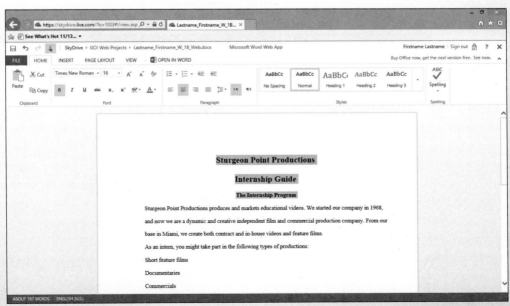

(GO! with Office Web Apps continues on the next page)

9 Click anywhere in the subheading *Introduction to Upcoming Internships*, and then on the **HOME tab**, in the **Paragraph group**, click **Center** . Click at the beginning of the paragraph that begins *Once a year*, and then press `Tab`.

10 Select the six paragraphs that begin with *Short feature films* and that end with *Recordings of live concerts*. On the **HOME tab**, in the **Paragraph group**, click **Bullets** to apply round, filled bullets to the selection.

11 Select the list that begins with *Production Assistant* and ends with *Assistant Set Designer*, and then click **Bullets** to apply bullets to the selection.

12 Select the first list to which you applied bullets. On the **HOME tab**, in the **Paragraph group**, click the **Bullets button arrow**, and then click **Square Bullet**. Notice that the same bullet style is applied to the second list.

13 Scroll the document and then select the list that begins with *Artists* and ends with *Music*. On the **HOME tab**, in the **Paragraph group**, click **Numbering** to apply numbers to the list.

14 Press `Ctrl` + `A` to select the entire document. On the **HOME tab**, in the **Paragraph group**, click **Line Spacing**, and then click **1.5** to change the line spacing for the entire document. Press `Ctrl` + `Home` to move to the top of the document and then compare your screen with Figure B.

15 **Save** your file and submit as directed by your instructor. Then, on the ribbon, click the **FILE tab** and click **Exit**.

FIGURE B

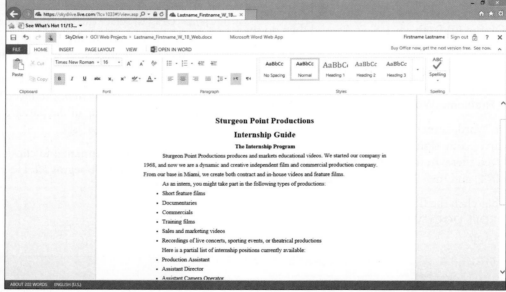

In every job, you must work and communicate with other people. A group of workers tasked with working together to solve a problem, make a decision, or create a work product is referred to as a *team*. For a team to succeed, the team members must be able to communicate with one another easily.

If all the team members work at the same location and work the same hours, communication is easy. You schedule face-to-face meetings and exchange documents and information among yourselves. But that is a rare arrangement in today's organizations. Rather, it is more likely that the members of your team work in different locations—even different countries— and work different hours or travel extensively away from the headquarters location. Also, for specific projects, teams are frequently organized across different departments of an organization or even across different organizations entirely. Then when the project is complete, the team disbands.

Collaboration is when you work together with others as a team in an intellectual endeavor to complete a shared task or achieve a shared goal; for example, when you and one or more of your classmates work together on a class project. Collaboration involves giving feedback to and receiving feedback from others on the team, and then revising the strategies to achieve the goal or produce the work product based on the feedback.

Microsoft Office 365 is a set of secure online services that enable people in an organization to communicate and collaborate by using any Internet-connected device—a computer, a tablet, or a mobile phone. Because Office 365 offers access from anywhere to email, Web conferencing, documents, and calendars, everyone on a team can work together easily. Office 365 is intended for use by multiple users in an organization.

Activity | Using the Exchange Online Outlook Meeting Tool to Collaborate

This group project relates to the **Bell Orchid Hotels**. If your instructor assigns this project to your class, you can expect to use the **Outlook Meeting tool** in **Office 365 Exchange Online** to collaborate on the following tasks for this chapter:

- If you are in the **Accounting Group**, you and your teammates will meet virtually to compose, format, proofread, and prepare a letter to send to shareholders.

- If you are in the **Engineering Group**, you and your teammates will meet virtually to compose, format, proofread, and prepare a letter to the three insurance companies that cover the hotel properties.

- If you are in the **Food and Beverage Group**, you and your teammates will meet virtually to compose, format, proofread, and finalize a letter to a customer planning a banquet.

- If you are in the **Human Resources Group**, you and your teammates will meet virtually to compose, format, proofread, and finalize a memo for employees regarding the new employee newsletter.

- If you are in the **Operations Group**, you and your teammates will meet virtually to compose, format, proofread, and finalize letters to three job applicants.

- If you are in the **Sales and Marketing Group**, you and your teammates will meet virtually to compose, edit, and finalize a letter to 20 groups of professional associations.

FIGURE A

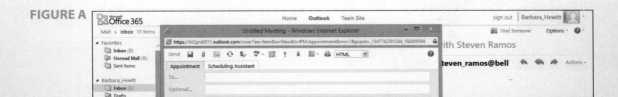

END OF CHAPTER

SUMMARY

In a document, you can type all of the text, or you can type some of the text and then insert additional text from another source such as another Word document. As you type, word wrap determines the line endings.

Graphics include pictures, shapes, and text boxes. Use graphics, text effects, and pictures to add visual appeal. When you insert pictures, Word provides many ways to position and format the pictures on the page.

SmartArt graphics visually represent your ideas and there are many SmartArt graphics from which to choose. You can also use online videos in your documents to provide visual information to the reader.

Word documents can be formatted to display your information attractively. You can add a page border, add bulleted and numbered lists, change margins and tabs, and modify paragraph and line spacing.

GO! LEARN IT ONLINE

Review the concepts and key terms in this chapter by completing these online challenges, which you can find at **www.pearsonhighered.com/go.**

Matching and Multiple Choice:
Answer matching and multiple choice questions to test what you learned in this chapter. MyITLab®

Crossword Puzzle:
Spell out the words that match the numbered clues, and put them in the puzzle squares.

Flipboard:
Flip through the definitions of the key terms in this chapter and match them with the correct term.

GO! FOR JOB SUCCESS

Video: Personal Branding

Your instructor may assign this video to your class, and then ask you to think about, or discuss with your classmates, these questions:

FotolEdhar / Fotolia

How do you suggest job seekers communicate their unique value—their *personal brand*—to potential employers online?

What are the best ways to network online and offline?

What are some of the biggest pitfalls in using social media to communicate a personal brand?

END OF CHAPTER
REVIEW AND ASSESSMENT GUIDE FOR WORD CHAPTER 1

Your instructor may assign one or more of these projects to help you review the chapter and assess your mastery and understanding of the chapter.

Project	Apply Skills from These Chapter Objectives	Project Type	Project Location
Review and Assessment Guide for Word Chapter 1			
1C	Objectives 1-4 from Project 1A	**1C Skills Review** A guided review of the skills from Project 1A.	On the following pages
1D	Objectives 5-8 from Project 1B	**1D Skills Review** A guided review of the skills from Project 1B.	On the following pages
1E	Objectives 1-4 from Project 1A	**1E Mastery (Grader Project)** A demonstration of your mastery of the skills in Project 1A with extensive decision making.	In MyITLab and on the following pages
1F	Objectives 5-8 from Project 1B	**1F Mastery (Grader Project)** A demonstration of your mastery of the skills in Project 1B with extensive decision making.	In MyITLab and on the following pages
1G	Objectives 1-8 from Projects 1A and 1B	**1G Mastery (Grader Project)** A demonstration of your mastery of the skills in Projects 1A and 1B with extensive decision making.	In MyITLab and on the following pages
1H	Combination of Objectives from Projects 1A and 1B	**1H GO! Fix It** A demonstration of your mastery of the skills in Projects 1A and 1B by creating a correct result from a document that contains errors you must find.	Online
1I	Combination of Objectives from Projects 1A and 1B	**1I GO! Make It** A demonstration of your mastery of the skills in Projects 1A and 1B by creating a result from a supplied picture.	Online
1J	Combination of Objectives from Projects 1A and 1B	**1J GO! Solve It** A demonstration of your mastery of the skills in Projects 1A and 1B, your decision-making skills, and your critical thinking skills. A task-specific rubric helps you self-assess your result.	Online
1K	Combination of Objectives from Projects 1A and 1B	**1K GO! Solve It** A demonstration of your mastery of the skills in Projects 1A and 1B, your decision-making skills, and your critical thinking skills. A task-specific rubric helps you self-assess your result.	On the following pages
1L	Combination of Objectives from Projects 1A and 1B	**1L GO! Think** A demonstration of your understanding of the chapter concepts applied in a manner that you would outside of college. An analytic rubric helps you and your instructor grade the quality of your work by comparing it to the work an expert in the discipline would create.	On the following pages
1M	Combination of Objectives from Projects 1A and 1B	**1M GO! Think** A demonstration of your understanding of the chapter concepts applied in a manner that you would outside of college. An analytic rubric helps you and your instructor grade the quality of your work by comparing it to the work an expert in the discipline would create.	Online
1N	Combination of Objectives from Projects 1A and 1B	**1N You and GO!** A demonstration of your understanding of the chapter concepts applied in a manner that you would in a personal situation. An analytic rubric helps you and your instructor grade the quality of your work.	Online
1O	Combination of Objectives from Projects 1A and 1B	**1O Cumulative Group Project for Word Chapter 1** A demonstration of your understanding of concepts and your ability to work collaboratively in a group role-playing assessment, requiring both collaboration and self-management.	Online

GLOSSARY

GLOSSARY OF CHAPTER KEY TERMS

Alignment The placement of paragraph text relative to the left and right margins.

Alignment guide Green vertical or horizontal lines that display when you are moving or sizing an object to assist you with object placement.

Artistic effects Formats applied to images that make pictures resemble sketches or paintings.

Bulleted list A list of items with each item introduced by a symbol such as a small circle or check mark, and which is useful when the items in the list can be displayed in any order.

Bullets Text symbols such as small circles or check marks that precede each item in a bulleted list.

Center alignment The alignment of text or objects that is centered horizontally between the left and right margin.

Collaboration The action of working together with others as a team in an intellectual endeavor to complete a shared task or achieve a shared goal.

Decrease Indent A command that moves your paragraph closer to the margin.

Dot leader A series of dots preceding a tab that guides the eye across the line.

Drawing objects Graphic objects, such as shapes, diagrams, lines, or circles.

Embed code A code that creates a link to a video, picture, or other type of rich media content.

Floating object A graphic that can be moved independently of the surrounding text characters.

Formatting marks Characters that display on the screen, but do not print, indicating where the Enter key, the Spacebar, and the Tab key were pressed; also called nonprinting characters.

Graphics Pictures, charts, or drawing objects.

Increase Indent A command moves your paragraph farther away from the margin.

Inline Object An object or graphic inserted in a document that acts like a character in a sentence.

Interactive media Computer interaction that responds to your actions; for example by presenting text, graphics, animation, video, audio, or games. Also referred to as rich media.

Justified alignment An arrangement of text in which the text aligns evenly on both the left and right margins.

Layout Options Picture formatting options that control the manner in which text wraps around a picture or other object.

Leader character Characters that form a solid, dotted, or dashed line that fills the space preceding a tab stop.

Left alignment An arrangement of text in which the text aligns at the left margin, leaving the right margin uneven.

Line spacing The distance between lines of text in a paragraph.

Live Layout A feature that reflows text as you move or size an object so that you can view the placement of surrounding text.

Margins The space between the text and the top, bottom, left, and right edges of the paper.

Microsoft Office 365 A set of secure online services that enable people in an organization to communicate and collaborate by using any Internet-connected device—a computer, a tablet, or a mobile phone.

Nonprinting characters Characters that display on the screen, but do not print; also called formatting marks.

Numbered list A list that uses consecutive numbers or letters to introduce each item in a list.

Object anchor The symbol that indicates to which paragraph an object is attached.

Picture Effects Formatting that enhances a picture with effects such as shadow, glow, reflection, or 3-D rotation.

Picture styles Frames, shapes, shadows, borders, and other special effects that can be added to an image to create an overall visual style for the image.

Placeholder text Non-printing text that holds a place in a document where you can type.

Rich media Computer interaction that responds to your actions; for example by presenting text, graphics, animation, video, audio, or games. Also referred to as interactive media.

Right alignment An arrangement of text in which the text aligns at the right margin, leaving the left margin uneven.

Rotation handle A symbol with which you can rotate a graphic to any angle; displays above the top center sizing handle.

Shapes Lines, arrows, stars, banners, ovals, rectangles, and other basic shapes with which you can illustrate an idea, a process, or a workflow.

SmartArt A designer-quality visual representation of your information that you can create by choosing from among many different layouts to effectively communicate your message or ideas.

Spin box A small box with an upward- and downward-pointing arrow that lets you move rapidly through a set of values by clicking.

Tab stop A specific location on a line of text, marked on the Word ruler, to which you can move the insertion point by pressing the Tab key, and which is used to align and indent text.

Team A group of workers tasked with working together to solve a problem, make a decision, or create a work product.

Template A preformatted document that you can use as a starting point and then change to suit your needs.

Text box A movable resizable container for text or graphics.

Text effects Decorative formats, such as shadowed or mirrored text, text glow, 3-D effects, and colors that make text stand out.

Text wrapping The manner in which text displays around an object.

Toggle button A button that can be turned on by clicking it once, and then turned off by clicking it again.

Wordwrap The feature that moves text from the right edge of a paragraph to the beginning of the next line as necessary to fit within the margins.

CHAPTER REVIEW

Apply 1A skills from these Objectives:

1 Create a New Document and Insert Text

2 Insert and Format Graphics

3 Insert and Modify Text Boxes and Shapes

4 Preview and Print a Document

Build from Scratch

Skills Review Project 1C Photography

In the following Skills Review, you will create a flyer announcing a photography internship with Sturgeon Point Productions. Your completed document will look similar to Figure 1.52.

PROJECT FILES

For Project 1C, you will need the following files:

New blank Word document
w01C_Building
w01C_Photographer

You will save your document as:

Lastname_Firstname_1C_Photography

PROJECT RESULTS

FIGURE 1.52

(Project 1C Photography continues on the next page)

CHAPTER REVIEW

1 ▶ Start Word and then click **Blank document**. On the **HOME tab**, in the **Paragraph group**, if necessary, click **Show/Hide** to display the formatting marks. If the rulers do not display, click the **VIEW tab**, and then in the **Show group**, select the **Ruler** check box.

  a. Type **Internship Available for Still Photographer** and then press Enter two times. Type the following text: **This fall, Sturgeon Point Productions will film a documentary on the historic architecture in and around Milwaukee, Wisconsin.** Press Enter.

  b. On the ribbon, click the **INSERT tab**. In the **Text group**, click the **Object button arrow**, and then click **Text from File**. In the **Insert File** dialog box, navigate to the student files that accompany this textbook, locate and select **w01C_Photographer**, and then click **Insert**. Delete the blank paragraph at the end of the document.

  c. Including the paragraph mark, select the first paragraph of text—*Internship Available for Still Photographer*. On the **HOME tab**, in the **Font group**, click **Text Effects and Typography**. In the **Text Effects** gallery, in the first row, click the fourth effect—**Fill – White, Outline – Accent 1, Shadow**.

  d. With the text still selected, in the **Font group**, click in the **Font Size** box to select the existing font size. Type **44** and then press Enter. In the **Font group**, click the **Font Color button arrow**. Under **Theme Colors**, in the fourth column, click the first color—**Blue-Gray, Text 2**.

  e. With the text still selected, in the **Font group**, click **Text Effects and Typography**. Point to **Shadow**, and then under **Outer**, in the second row, click the third style—**Offset Left**. In the **Paragraph group**, click **Center**.

  f. On the **Quick Access Toolbar**, click **Save**. Under **Places**, click **Computer**, and then click **Browse**. Navigate to your **Word Chapter 1** folder. In the **File name** box, replace the existing text with **Lastname_Firstname_1C_Photography** and then click **Save**.

2 ▶ In the paragraph that begins *The filming*, click to position the insertion point at the beginning of the paragraph. On the **INSERT tab**, in the **Illustrations group**, click **Pictures**. In the **Insert Picture** dialog box, navigate to your student data files, locate and click **w01C_Building**, and then click **Insert**.

  a. To the right of the selected picture, click the **Layout Options** button, and then under **With Text Wrapping**, click the first option—**Square**. **Close** the **Layout Options**.

  b. On the **FORMAT tab**, in the **Size group**, click the **Shape Height spin box down arrow** as necessary to change the height of the picture to **2.7"**.

  c. With the picture selected, on the **FORMAT tab**, in the **Arrange group**, click **Position**, and then click **More Layout Options**. In the **Layout** dialog box, on the **Position tab**, in the middle of the dialog box, under **Vertical**, click the **Alignment** option button. To the right of **Alignment**, click the arrow, and then click **Top**. To the right of **relative to**, click the arrow, and then click **Line**. Click **OK**.

  d. On the **FORMAT tab**, in the **Picture Styles group**, click **Picture Effects**. Point to **Soft Edges**, and then click **5 Point**. On the **FORMAT tab**, in the **Adjust group**, click **Artistic Effects**. In the fourth row, click the third effect—**Crisscross Etching**.

  e. Click anywhere outside the picture to deselect it. On the **DESIGN tab**, in the **Page Background group**, click **Page Borders**. In the **Borders and Shading** dialog box, on the **Page Border tab**, under **Setting**, click **Box**. Under **Style**, scroll the list and then click the third style from the bottom—a black line that fades to gray.

  f. Click the **Color arrow**, and then in the next to last column, click the first color—**Blue, Accent 5**. Under **Apply to**, be sure **Whole document** is selected, and then click **OK**. Click **Save**.

3 ▶ Click the **INSERT tab**, and then in the **Illustrations group**, click **Shapes** to display the gallery. Under **Basic Shapes**, in the second row, click the fifth shape—**Frame**.

  a. Position the ⊞ pointer anywhere in the blank area at the bottom of the document. Click one time to insert a 1" by 1" frame. The exact location need not be precise. To the right of the shape, click the **Layout Options** button, and at the bottom click **See more**.

  b. In the **Layout** dialog box, under **Horizontal**, click the **Alignment** option button. To the right of **Alignment**, click the arrow, and then click **Centered**. To the right of **relative to**, click the arrow, and then click **Page**. Under **Vertical**, click the **Absolute position**

(Project 1C Photography continues on the next page)

option button. In the **Absolute position** box, select the existing number, and then type **1** To the right of **below**, click the arrow, and then click **Paragraph**. Click **OK**.

c. On the **FORMAT tab**, click in the **Shape Height** box. Type **1.5** and then click in the **Shape Width** box. Type **5.5** and then press [Enter].

d. If necessary, select the frame shape. On the **FORMAT tab**, in the **Shape Styles group**, click **More** [▾]. In the **Shape Styles** gallery, in the first row, click the sixth style—**Colored Outline - Blue, Accent 5**. Type **Submit Your Application by June 30!** Select the text you just typed, and then on the mini toolbar, change the **Font Size** to **22**.

4 ▶ Click outside of the frame to deselect, and then press [Ctrl] + [Home] to move to the top of the document. Press [↓] two times to move to the blank paragraph below the title. Press [Enter] four times to make space for a text box.

a. On the **INSERT tab**, in the **Text group**, click **Text Box**. At the bottom of the gallery, click **Draw Text Box**. Position the [⊞] pointer over the first blank paragraph at the left margin. Drag down and to the right to create a text box approximately 1.5 inches high and 4 inches wide—the exact size and location need not be precise.

b. With the insertion point blinking in the text box, type the following, pressing [Enter] after the first two lines to create a new paragraph; do *not* press [Enter] after the last line:

This position requires skill in the use of:

Professional full-frame DSLR cameras

Tilt-shift lenses for tall buildings

c. To precisely place the text box, on the **FORMAT tab**, in the **Arrange group**, click **Position**, and then click **More Layout Options**. In the **Layout** dialog box, under **Horizontal**, click the **Alignment** button. To the right of **Alignment**, click the arrow, and then click **Centered**. To the right of *relative to*, click the arrow, and then click **Page**.

d. Under **Vertical**, click the **Absolute position** button. In the **Absolute position** box, select the existing number. Type **2** To the right of **below**, click the **arrow**, and then click **Margin**.

e. In the **Layout** dialog box, click the **Size tab**. Under **Height**, select the number in the **Absolute** box. Type **1** and then under **Width**, select the number in the **Absolute** box. Type **3.75** and then click **OK**.

f. In the text box, select all of the text. If necessary, right-click over the selected text to display the mini toolbar. Change the **Font Size** to **12**, apply **Bold**, and then press [Ctrl] + [E] to **Center** the text.

g. On the **FORMAT tab**, in the **Shape Styles group**, click **Shape Effects**. Point to **Shadow**, and then under **Outer**, in the first row, click the first style—**Offset Diagonal Bottom Right**.

h. In the **Shape Styles group**, click **Shape Outline**. In the fifth column, click the first color—**Blue, Accent 1** to change the color of the text box border. Click **Shape Fill**, and then in the fifth column, click the second color—**Blue, Accent 1, Lighter 80%**. Click **Save**.

5 ▶ Click the **INSERT tab**, and then in the **Header & Footer group**, click **Footer**. At the bottom of the menu, click **Edit Footer**. On the **HEADER & FOOTER TOOLS DESIGN tab**, in the **Insert group**, click **Document Info**, and then click **File Name**. Double-click in the document outside of the footer area to close the footer and return to the document.

a. Press [Ctrl] + [Home] to move the insertion point to the top of the document. In the upper left corner of your screen, click the **FILE** tab to display **Backstage** view. On the right, at the bottom of the **Properties list**, click **Show All Properties**.

b. On the list of Properties, click to the right of **Tags** to display an empty box, and then type **internship, photographer** Click to the right of **Subject** to display an empty box, and then type your course name and section #. Under **Related People**, be sure that your name displays as the author. If necessary, edit the author name.

c. **Save** your file and submit as directed by your instructor. **Close** Word.

END | You have completed Project 1C

CHAPTER REVIEW

Apply 1B skills from these Objectives:

5 Change Document and Paragraph Layout

6 Create and Modify Lists

7 Set and Modify Tab Stops

8 Insert a SmartArt Graphic and an Online Video

In the following Skills Review, you will edit an information handout regarding production and development internships with Sturgeon Point Productions. Your completed document will look similar to Figure 1.53.

PROJECT FILES

For Project 1D, you will need the following file:

w01D_Internship

You will save your document as:

Lastname_Firstname_1D_Internship

PROJECT RESULTS

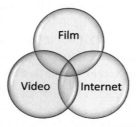

FIGURE 1.53

(Project 1D Internships continues on the next page)

CHAPTER REVIEW

1 Start Word, and then click **Open Other Documents**. Click **Computer**, and then click **Browse**. Navigate to your student files, and then open **w01D_Internship**. On the **HOME tab**, in the **Paragraph group**, be sure **Show/Hide** is active. Click the **FILE tab**, and then click **Save As**. Navigate to your **Word Chapter 1** folder, and then **Save** the document as **Lastname_Firstname_1D_Internship**

a. Click the **PAGE LAYOUT tab**. In the **Page Setup group**, click **Margins**, and then click **Custom Margins**. In the **Page Setup** dialog box, press Tab as necessary to select the value in the **Left** box. Type **1** and then press Tab to select the value in the **Right** box. Type **1** and then click **OK**.

b. Scroll down to view the bottom of **Page 1**, point anywhere in the bottom margin area, right-click, and then click **Edit Footer** to display the footer area. On the **HEADER & FOOTER TOOLS DESIGN tab**, in the **Insert group**, click **Document Info**, and then click **File Name**. Double-click anywhere in the document to close the footer area.

c. Press Ctrl + A to select all of the text in the document, and then on the **HOME tab**, in the **Paragraph group**, click **Align Left**.

d. Press Ctrl + Home. Select the document title, and then on the **HOME tab**, in the **Paragraph group**, click **Center**.

e. Locate the first bold subheading—*In-House Office Internships*. Point to the left of the paragraph to display the ⟰ pointer, and then click one time to select the text. With *In-House Office Internships* selected, locate the subheading *Additional Information*. Move the pointer to the left of the paragraph to display the ⟰ pointer, hold down Ctrl, and then click one time to select both paragraphs. In the **Paragraph group**, click **Center**.

f. Press Ctrl + A to select all of the text in the document. On the **HOME tab**, in the **Paragraph group**, click **Line and Paragraph Spacing**, and then click **1.5**.

2 Below the title of the document, click anywhere in the paragraph that begins *Sturgeon Point Productions is a full service*. On the **HOME tab**, in the **Paragraph group**, click the **Dialog Box Launcher** ▣.

a. In the **Paragraph** dialog box, on the **Indents and Spacing tab**, under **Indentation**, click the **Special**

arrow, and then click **First line** to indent the first line by 0.5". Click **OK**, and then click anywhere in the paragraph that begins *Sturgeon Point Productions is looking for*. On the ruler under the ribbon, drag the **First Line Indent** marker to **0.5 inches on the horizontal ruler**.

b. Press Ctrl + A to select all of the text in the document. Click the **PAGE LAYOUT tab**, and then in the **Paragraph group**, under **Spacing**, click the **After spin box up arrow** one time to change the value to **6 pt**.

c. Select the subheading *In-House Office Internships*, including the paragraph mark following it. Scroll down, hold down Ctrl, and then select the subheading *Additional Information*. With both subheadings selected, in the **Paragraph group**, under **Spacing**, click the **Before up spin box arrow** two times to set the **Spacing Before** to **12 pt**. **Save** your document.

3 Locate the first paragraph that begins *Development Department*, and then point to this paragraph from the left margin area to display the ⟰ pointer. Drag down to select this paragraph and the next five paragraphs so that six paragraphs are selected. On the **HOME tab**, in the **Paragraph group**, click **Bullets** to change the selected text to a bulleted list.

a. Under the subheading *In-House Office Internships*, in the paragraph that begins *Sturgeon Point Productions*, click to position the insertion point at the *end* of the paragraph, following the colon. Press Enter to create a blank paragraph. On the ruler, drag the **First Line Indent** marker to the left so that it is positioned directly above the lower button. Being sure to include the period, type **1.** and then press Spacebar to create the first item in a numbered list.

b. Type **Be enrolled as a film major at a participating local college or university** and then press Enter. Type **Maintain a 3.0 GPA** and then press Enter. Type **Receive satisfactory monthly progress reports from their direct supervisor**

c. Scroll down to view the bulleted list of departments, and then select all six bulleted items in the list. On the mini toolbar, click the **Bullets button arrow**, and then under **Bullet Library**, click the **check mark** symbol. If the check mark is not available, choose another bullet symbol.

(Project 1D Internships continues on the next page)

CHAPTER REVIEW

4 With the list selected, move the pointer to the horizontal ruler, and then point to and click at **3.5 inches on the horizontal ruler** to insert a tab and align the job titles at the tab mark.

   a. With the bulleted list still selected, on the ruler, point to the new tab marker at **3.5 inches on the horizontal ruler**, and then when the *Left Tab* ScreenTip displays, drag the tab marker to **4 inches on the horizontal ruler**.

   b. On the ruler, point to the tab marker that you moved to display the *Left Tab* ScreenTip, and then double-click to display the **Tabs** dialog box.

   c. In the **Tabs** dialog box, under **Tab stop position**, if necessary select *4"*, and then type **6** Under **Alignment**, click the **Right** option button. Under **Leader**, click the **2** option button. Near the bottom of the **Tabs** dialog box, click **Set**.

   d. Under **Tab stop position**, select **4"**, and then click **Clear** to delete the tab stop. Click **OK**. **Save** your document.

5 Press Ctrl + Home to move to the top of the document, and then in the title, click to the right of the *S* in *PRODUCTIONS*.

   a. Click the **INSERT tab**, and then in the **Illustrations group**, click **SmartArt**. On the left, click **Relationship**, and then scroll the list to the bottom. Locate and then click **Basic Venn**. Click **OK** to insert the SmartArt graphic. If necessary, close the Text Pane.

   b. In the SmartArt graphic, click on *[Text]* in the top circle shape. Type **Film** and then click on the placeholder *[Text]* in the lower left shape. Type **Video** In the third circle, type **Internet**

   c. Click the SmartArt graphic border to select it. Click the **FORMAT tab**, and then in the **Size group**, if necessary click **Size** to display the **Shape Height** and **Shape Width** boxes. Set the **Height** to **3"** and the **Width** to **6.5"**.

   d. With the SmartArt graphic still selected, on the ribbon, under **SMARTART TOOLS**, click the **DESIGN tab**, and then in the **SmartArt Styles group**, click **Change Colors**. Under **Colorful**, click the third style—**Colorful Range–Accent Colors 3 to 4**. On the **DESIGN tab**, in the **SmartArt Styles group**, click **More**. Under **3-D**, in the first row, click the third style—**Cartoon**. Click **Save**.

6 Hold down Ctrl and then press End to move to the end of the document. On the **INSERT tab**, in the **Media group**, click **Online Video**. If necessary, in the lower left corner of the Insert Video window, click YouTube. Click in the **Search YouTube** box. Including the quotation marks, type **"Go 2013 1B video"** and then press Enter. In the first row, click the first video, and then click **Insert**.

   a. Click the **FILE tab**, and then on the right, click **Show All Properties**. In the **Tags** box, type **internship** and in the **Subject** box, type your course name and section number. Be sure that your name displays as the author. Click **Save**.

   b. Click the **FILE tab** to display **Backstage** view. Click **Print** to display **Print Preview**. At the bottom of the preview, click the **Next Page** and **Previous Page** buttons to move between pages. If necessary, return to the document and make any necessary changes.

   c. As directed by your instructor, print your document or submit it electronically. **Close** Word.

END | You have completed Project 1D

CONTENT-BASED ASSESSMENTS

Mastering Word | Project 1E Documentary

MyITLab®
grader

In the following Mastery project, you will create a flyer announcing a special event being hosted by Sturgeon Point Productions. Your printed results will look similar to those in Figure 1.54.

Apply 1A skills from these Objectives:

1 Create a New Document and Insert Text

2 Insert and Format Graphics

3 Insert and Modify Text Boxes and Shapes

4 Preview and Print a Document

PROJECT FILES

For Project 1E, you will need the following files:

New blank Word document

w01E_Antarctica

w01E_Filmmaker

You will save your document as:

Lastname_Firstname_1E_Documentary

Build from
Scratch

PROJECT RESULTS

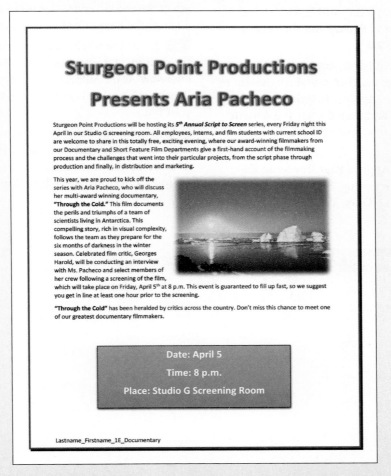

FIGURE 1.54

(Project 1E Documentary continues on the next page)

CONTENT-BASED ASSESSMENTS

1 **Start** Word and display a **Blank document** with the ruler and formatting marks displayed. Type **Sturgeon Point Productions Presents Aria Pacheco** and then press Enter. From your student data files, insert the text file **w01E_Filmmaker**. Using your own name, **Save** the document in your **Word Chapter 1** folder as **Lastname_Firstname_1E_Documentary**

2 To the document title, apply the **Fill – White, Outline – Accent 1, Glow – Accent 1** text effect, and then change the **Font Size** to 36. Change the **Font Color** to **Blue-Gray, Text 2**—in the fourth column, the first color. Apply an **Outer Shadow** using **Offset Left**—in the second row, the third style. **Center** the title.

3 Position the insertion point at the beginning of the paragraph that begins with *This year*, and then from your student data files, insert the picture **w01E_Antarctica**. Change the **Layout Options** to **Square** and then change the **Height** of the picture to **2.5**

4 Using the **Position** command, display the **Layout** dialog box, and then change the **Horizontal Alignment** to **Right relative to** the **Margin**. Apply a **10 Point Soft Edges** picture effect to the image, and then display the **Artistic Effects** gallery. In the third row, apply the fourth effect—**Mosaic Bubbles**.

5 Deselect the picture. Apply a **Page Border** to the document using the **Shadow** setting. Select the first style, and change the **Color** to **Blue-Gray, Text 2**. Change the **Width** to **3 pt**.

6 Below the last paragraph, draw a **Text Box** that is approximately 1.5 inches high and 4 inches wide—the exact size and location need not be precise. In the text box, type the following text:

> **Date: April 5**
>
> **Time: 8 p.m.**
>
> **Place: Studio G Screening Room**

7 Change the **Height** of the text box to **1.5** and the **Width** to **4.5** and then change the font size to **18**. Apply **Bold** and **Center**. To precisely place the text box, display the **Layout** dialog box. Change the **Horizontal Alignment** to **Centered**, **relative to** the **Page**, and then change the **Vertical Absolute position** to **0.5** below the **Paragraph**.

8 Apply a **Shape Style** to the text box—in the last row, select the second style—**Intense Effect – Blue, Accent 1**. Change the **Shape Outline** to **Black, Text 1**.

9 Insert the **File Name** in the footer, and then display the document properties. As the **Tags**, type **documentary, interview** As the **Subject**, type your course and section #. Be sure your name is indicated as the **Author**. **Save** your file.

10 Display the **Print Preview** and if necessary, return to the document and make any necessary changes. As directed by your instructor, print your document or submit it electronically. **Close** Word.

END | You have completed Project 1E

CONTENT-BASED ASSESSMENTS

Mastering Word Project 1F Pitch Festival

In the following Mastery project, you will edit a document with information regarding an event that Sturgeon Point Productions is holding for college students. Your printed results will look similar to those in Figure 1.55.

Apply 1B skills from these Objectives:

5 Change Document and Paragraph Layout

6 Create and Modify Lists

7 Set and Modify Tab Stops

8 Insert a SmartArt Graphic and an Online Video

PROJECT FILES

For Project 1F, you will need the following file:

w01F_Pitch_Festival

You will save your document as:

Lastname_Firstname_1F_Pitch_Festival

PROJECT RESULTS

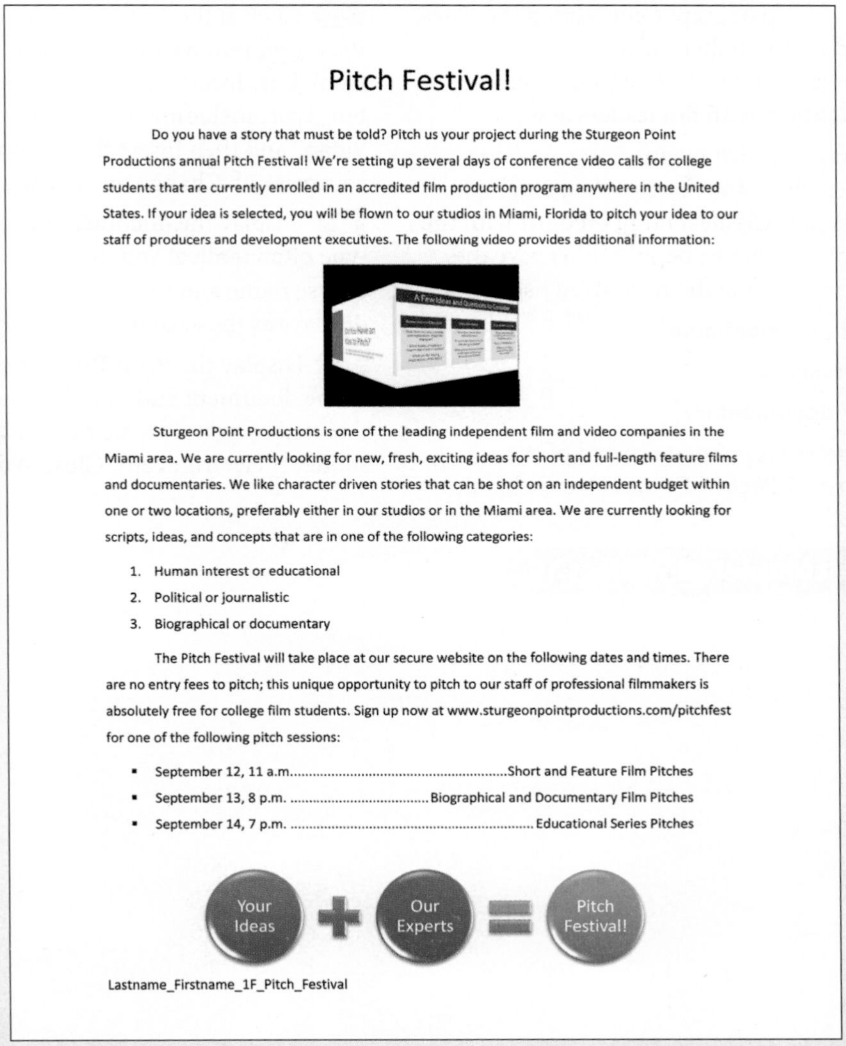

Pitch Festival!

Do you have a story that must be told? Pitch us your project during the Sturgeon Point Productions annual Pitch Festival! We're setting up several days of conference video calls for college students that are currently enrolled in an accredited film production program anywhere in the United States. If your idea is selected, you will be flown to our studios in Miami, Florida to pitch your idea to our staff of producers and development executives. The following video provides additional information:

Sturgeon Point Productions is one of the leading independent film and video companies in the Miami area. We are currently looking for new, fresh, exciting ideas for short and full-length feature films and documentaries. We like character driven stories that can be shot on an independent budget within one or two locations, preferably either in our studios or in the Miami area. We are currently looking for scripts, ideas, and concepts that are in one of the following categories:

1. Human interest or educational
2. Political or journalistic
3. Biographical or documentary

The Pitch Festival will take place at our secure website on the following dates and times. There are no entry fees to pitch; this unique opportunity to pitch to our staff of professional filmmakers is absolutely free for college film students. Sign up now at www.sturgeonpointproductions.com/pitchfest for one of the following pitch sessions:

- September 12, 11 a.m...Short and Feature Film Pitches
- September 13, 8 p.m. ....Biographical and Documentary Film Pitches
- September 14, 7 p.m. .... Educational Series Pitches

Lastname_Firstname_1F_Pitch_Festival

FIGURE 1.55

(Project 1F Pitch Festival continues on the next page)

CONTENT-BASED ASSESSMENTS

1 Start Word, and then from your student files, open **w01F_Pitch_Festival**. Display formatting marks, and then **Save** the file in your **Word Chapter 1** folder as **Lastname_Firstname_1F_Pitch_Festival**

2 Insert the **File Name** in the footer. Select all the document text, and then change the **Line Spacing** for the entire document to **1.5**. **Center** the document title, and then change the title font size to **24**. Change the **Top** and **Bottom** margins to **0.5**

3 Select the three paragraphs below the title, and then apply a **First line** indent of 0.5". Select the entire document, and then change the **Spacing Before** to **6 pt** and the **Spacing After** to **6 pt**.

4 Select the last three paragraphs containing the dates, and then apply filled square bullets. If the bullets are not available, choose another bullet style. With the bulleted list selected, set a **Right** tab with **dot leaders** at **6"**.

5 Locate the paragraph that begins *Sturgeon Point Productions*, and then click at the end of the paragraph, after the colon. Press [Enter]. Create a numbered list with the following three numbered items; be sure to remove the first line indent before creating the numbered list:

Human interest or educational

Political or journalistic

Biographical or documentary

6 Position the insertion point at the end of the document after the word *Pitches*. Do *not* insert a blank line. Insert a **SmartArt** graphic from the **Process** category. Toward the bottom of the gallery, select the **Equation** SmartArt. Select the outside border of the SmartArt, and then change the **Height** of the SmartArt to **1** and the **Width** to **6.5**

7 With the SmartArt selected, change the layout to **Square**, and change the **Horizontal Alignment** to **Centered relative to** the **Page**. Change the **Vertical Alignment** to **Bottom relative to** the **Margin**.

8 In the first circle type **Your Ideas** and in the second circle type **Our Experts** In the third circle type **Pitch Festival!** Change the SmartArt color to **Colorful Range – Accent Colors 4 to 5**. Apply the **3-D Polished** style.

9 Click at the end of the paragraph below the title. Press [Enter], remove the first line indent, and then center the blank line. Insert an **Online Video**. In the **Search YouTube** box, type, including the quotations marks, **"Go 2013 1F Video"** and then insert the video with the cube on a black background. Change the height of the video to **1.5**.

10 Display the document properties. In the **Tags** box, type **pitch festival** and in the **Subject** box, type your course name and section number. Be sure your name displays as the author.

11 Display the **Print Preview** and if necessary, return to the document and make any necessary changes. As directed by your instructor, print your document or submit it electronically. **Close** Word.

END | You have completed Project 1F

CONTENT-BASED ASSESSMENTS

Mastering Word Project 1G Educational Website

In the following Mastery project, you will create a flyer that details a new educational website that Sturgeon Point Productions has developed for instructors. Your printed results will look similar to those in Figure 1.56.

Apply 1A and 1B skills from these Objectives:

1 Create a New Document and Insert Text
2 Insert and Format Graphics
3 Insert and Modify Text Boxes and Shapes
4 Preview and Print a Document
5 Change Document and Paragraph Layout
6 Create and Modify Lists
7 Set and Modify Tab Stops
8 Insert a SmartArt Graphic and an Online Video

PROJECT FILES

For Project 1G, you will need the following files:

New blank Word document
w01G_Education
w01G_Media

You will save your document as:

Lastname_Firstname_1G_Educational_Website

PROJECT RESULTS

Build from Scratch

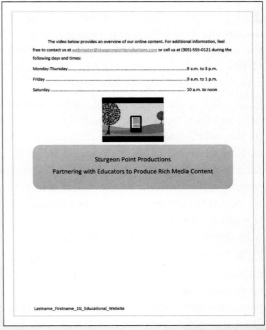

FIGURE 1.56

(Project 1G Educational Website continues on the next page)

CONTENT-BASED ASSESSMENTS

1 Start Word and display a blank document. Display formatting marks and the ruler. Type **Educational Websites** and then press Enter. Type **Sturgeon Point Productions is offering website tie-ins with every educational video title in our catalog, at no additional cost.** Press Spacebar, and then **Save** the document in your **Word Chapter 1** folder as **Lastname_Firstname_1G_Educational_Website**

2 With the insertion point positioned at the end of the sentence that you typed, insert the text from your student data file **w01G_Education**. Change the **Line Spacing** for the entire document to **1.5** and the spacing **After** to **6 pt**. To each of the four paragraphs that begin *Sturgeon Point Productions*, *As educators*, *When submitting*, and *The video*, apply a **First Line** indent of **0.5"**.

3 Change the font size of the title to **50** and then display the **Text Effects and Typography** gallery. Apply the second effect to the title—**Fill – Blue, Accent 1, Shadow**, and then **Center** the title. With only the title selected, change the **Line Spacing** to **1.0**.

4 Click at the beginning of the paragraph below the title, and then from your student data files, insert the picture **w01G_Media**. Change the picture **Height** to **2** and the **Layout Options** to **Square**. Format the picture with **Soft Edges** in **10 Point**, and then use the **Position** command to display the **Layout** dialog box. Change the picture position so that the **Horizontal Alignment** is **Right relative to** the **Margin**. Change the **Vertical Alignment** to **Top relative to** the **Line**.

5 Select the five paragraphs beginning with *Historic interactive timelines* and ending with *Quizzes and essay exams*, and then apply checkmark bullets. In the paragraph below the bulleted list, click after the colon. Press Enter and remove the first line indent. Type a numbered list with the following three numbered items:

> **The title in which you are interested**
>
> **The name of the class and subject**
>
> **Online tools you would like to see created**

6 With the insertion point located at the end of the numbered list, insert a **SmartArt** graphic. In the **Process** category, locate and select the **Basic Chevron Process**. In the first shape type **View** In the second shape type **Interact** and in the third shape type **Assess**

7 Change the SmartArt color to **Colorful Range – Accent Colors 4 to 5**, and then apply the **3-D Flat Scene** style. Change the **Height** of the SmartArt to **1** and the **Width** to **6.5** Change the **Layout Options** to **Square**, the **Horizontal Alignment** to **Centered relative to** the **Page**, and the **Vertical Alignment** to **Bottom relative to** the **Margin**.

8 Select the days and times at the end of the document, and then set a **Right** tab with **dot leaders** at 6". Click in the blank line below the tabbed list, and **Center** the line. Insert an **Online Video**. In the **Search YouTube** box, type **Pearson Higher Education Learning**, and then insert the first video that displays. Change the video **Height** to **1.5**

9 In the space below the video, insert a **Rounded Rectangle** shape. The exact location need not be precise. Change the **Shape Height** to **1.5** and the **Shape Width** to **6.5** Display the **Shape Styles** gallery, and then in the fourth row, apply the second style—**Subtle Effect - Blue, Accent 1**. Use the **Position** command to display the **Layout** dialog box, and then change the position so that both the **Horizontal** and **Vertical Alignment** are **Centered relative to** the **Margin**.

10 In the rectangle, type **Sturgeon Point Productions** and then press Enter. Type **Partnering with Educators to Produce Rich Media Content** and then change the font size to **16**.

11 Move to the top of the document and insert a **Text Box** above the title. The exact location need not be precise. Change the **Height** of the text box to **0.5** and the width to **3.7** Type **Sturgeon Point Productions** and then change the font size to **22 Center** the text.

12 Use the **Position** command to display the **Layout** dialog box, and then position the text box so that the **Horizontal Alignment** is **Centered relative to** the **Page** and the **Vertical Absolute position** is **0.5 below** the **Page**.

13 With the text box selected, display the **Shape Fill** gallery, and then in the next to last column, select the second color—**Blue, Accent 5, Lighter 80%**. Change the **Shape Outline** to the same color—**Blue, Accent 5, Lighter 80%**.

14 Deselect the text box. Apply a **Page Border** to the document. Use the **Box** setting, and choose the first style. Change the **Color** to **Blue, Accent 5**. Change the **Top** margin to **1.25** and insert the **File Name** in the footer.

15 Display the document properties. As the **Tags** type **website** and as the **Subject** type your course and section #. Be sure your name displays in the **Author** box, and then **Save** your file. Submit your document as directed.

END | You have completed Project 1G

CONTENT-BASED ASSESSMENTS

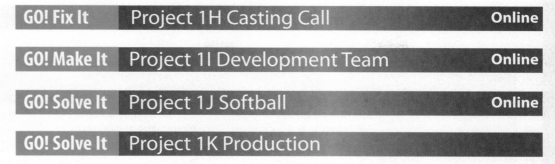

Build from Scratch

GO! Fix It	Project 1H Casting Call	Online
GO! Make It	Project 1I Development Team	Online
GO! Solve It	Project 1J Softball	Online
GO! Solve It	Project 1K Production	

PROJECT FILES

For Project 1K, you will need the following files:

w01K_Production
w01K_Studio

You will save your document as:

Lastname_Firstname_1K_Production

The Marketing Director for Sturgeon Point Productions is developing marketing materials aimed at filmmakers. Use the following information to format a flyer that uses text effects, an appropriately placed picture with an artistic effect and text wrapping applied, and an appropriately formatted SmartArt graphic.

From the student files that accompany this textbook, locate and open the file w01K_Production. Format the document using techniques you learned in this chapter. From your student data files, insert the picture w01K_Studio, and then format the picture with an artistic effect. Insert a **SmartArt** graphic that illustrates two or three important points about the company. Be sure the flyer is easy to read and understand and has an attractive design. Save the file in your **Word Chapter 1** folder as **Lastname_Firstname_1K_Production** and submit it as directed.

(Project 1K Production continues on the next page)

CONTENT-BASED ASSESSMENTS

Performance Level

Performance Criteria		Exemplary	Proficient	Developing
	Use text effects	Text effects applied to text in an attractive and appropriate manner.	Text effects applied but do not appropriately display text.	Text effects not used.
	Insert and format a picture	The picture is inserted and positioned correctly; text wrapping and an artistic effect are applied.	The picture is inserted but not formatted properly.	No picture is inserted in the document.
	Insert and format SmartArt	The SmartArt is inserted and appropriately formatted.	The SmartArt is inserted but no formatting is applied.	No SmartArt is inserted in the document.

END | You have completed Project 1K

OUTCOMES-BASED ASSESSMENTS

RUBRIC

The following outcomes-based assessments are *open-ended assessments*. That is, there is no specific correct result; your result will depend on your approach to the information provided. Make *Professional Quality* your goal. Use the following scoring rubric to guide you in *how* to approach the problem and then to evaluate *how well* your approach solves the problem.

The *criteria*—Software Mastery, Content, Format and Layout, and Process—represent the knowledge and skills you have gained that you can apply to solving the problem. The *levels of performance*—Professional Quality, Approaching Professional Quality, or Needs Quality Improvements—help you and your instructor evaluate your result.

	Your completed project is of Professional Quality if you:	Your completed project is Approaching Professional Quality if you:	Your completed project Needs Quality Improvements if you:
1-Software Mastery	Choose and apply the most appropriate skills, tools, and features and identify efficient methods to solve the problem.	Choose and apply some appropriate skills, tools, and features, but not in the most efficient manner.	Choose inappropriate skills, tools, or features, or are inefficient in solving the problem.
2-Content	Construct a solution that is clear and well organized, contains content that is accurate, appropriate to the audience and purpose, and is complete. Provide a solution that contains no errors in spelling, grammar, or style.	Construct a solution in which some components are unclear, poorly organized, inconsistent, or incomplete. Misjudge the needs of the audience. Have some errors in spelling, grammar, or style, but the errors do not detract from comprehension.	Construct a solution that is unclear, incomplete, or poorly organized; contains some inaccurate or inappropriate content; and contains many errors in spelling, grammar, or style. Do not solve the problem.
3-Format & Layout	Format and arrange all elements to communicate information and ideas, clarify function, illustrate relationships, and indicate relative importance.	Apply appropriate format and layout features to some elements, but not others. Overuse features, causing minor distraction.	Apply format and layout that does not communicate information or ideas clearly. Do not use format and layout features to clarify function, illustrate relationships, or indicate relative importance. Use available features excessively, causing distraction.
4-Process	Use an organized approach that integrates planning, development, self-assessment, revision, and reflection.	Demonstrate an organized approach in some areas, but not others; or, use an insufficient process of organization throughout.	Do not use an organized approach to solve the problem.

OUTCOMES-BASED ASSESSMENTS

Build from Scratch

GO! Think   Project 1L Classes

PROJECT FILES

For Project 1L, you will need the following file:

New blank Word document

You will save your document as:

Lastname_Firstname_1L_Classes

The Human Resources Director at Sturgeon Point Productions needs to create a flyer to inform full-time employees of educational opportunities beginning in September. The courses are taught each year by industry professionals and are designed to improve skills in motion picture and television development and production. Employees who have been with Sturgeon Point Productions for at least two years are eligible to take the courses free of cost. The classes provide employees with opportunities to advance their careers, gain valuable skills, and achieve technical certification. All courses take place in Studio G and interested employees should contact Elana Springs in Human Resources to sign up. Information meetings are being held at 5:30 p.m. according to the following schedule: television development on June 15; motion picture production on June 17; and recording services on June 21.

Create a flyer with basic information about the courses and information meetings. Be sure the flyer is easy to read and understand and has an attractive design. Save the document as **Lastname_Firstname_1L_Classes** and submit it as directed.

END | You have completed Project 1L

Build from Scratch

GO! Think   Project 1M Store   **Online**

Build from Scratch

You and GO!   Project 1N Family Flyer   **Online**

Build from Scratch

GO! Cumulative Group Project   Project 1O Bell Orchid Hotels   **Online**

Using Tables and Templates to Create Resumes and Cover Letters

GO! to Work
Video W2

2

PROJECT 2A

OUTCOMES
Write a resume by using a Word table.

PROJECT 2B

OUTCOMES
Write a cover letter and use a template to create a cover sheet.

OBJECTIVES
1. Create a Table
2. Format a Table
3. Present a Word Document Online

OBJECTIVES
4. Create a Custom Word Template
5. Correct and Reorganize Text
6. Use the Proofing Options and Print an Envelope
7. Create a Document Using a Predesigned Microsoft Template

onewordphoto / Fotolia

In This Chapter

Tables are useful for organizing and presenting data. Because a table is so easy to use, many individuals prefer to arrange tabular information in a Word table rather than setting a series of tabs. For example, you can use a table when you want to present rows and columns of information or to create a format for a document such as a resume.

When using Word to write business or personal letters, use a commonly approved letter format, and always use a clear writing style. You will make a good impression on prospective employers if you use a standard business letter style when you are writing a cover letter for a resume.

The projects in this chapter relate to the **College Career Center at Florida Port Community College** in St. Petersburg, Florida, a coastal port city near the Florida High Tech Corridor. With 60 percent of Florida's high tech companies and a third of the state's manufacturing companies located in the St. Petersburg and Tampa Bay areas, the college partners with businesses to play a vital role in providing a skilled workforce. The College Career Center assists students in exploring careers, finding internships, and applying for jobs. The Center offers workshops for resume and cover letter writing and for practice interviews.

Resume

PROJECT ACTIVITIES

In Activities 2.01 through 2.11, you will create a table to use as the format for a resume. The director of the Career Center, Mary Walker-Huelsman, will use this model when assisting students with building their resumes. Your completed document will look similar to Figure 2.1.

PROJECT FILES

For Project 2A, you will need the following files:

New blank Word document
w02A_Experience

You will save your document as:

Lastname_Firstname_2A_Resume

PROJECT RESULTS

Build from
Scratch

Josh Hayes
1541 Dearborn Lane, St. Petersburg, FL 33713

(727) 555-0313
jhayes@alcona.net

OBJECTIVE   Technology writing and editing position in the robotics industry, using research and advanced editing skills to communicate with customers.

SUMMARY OF QUALIFICATIONS
- Two years' experience in robotics lab for Aerospace Instruction Team
- Excellent interpersonal and communication skills
- Proficiency using Microsoft Office
- Proficiency using page layout and design software
- Fluency in spoken and written Spanish

EXPERIENCE

Instructional Lab Assistant, Florida Port Community College, St. Petersburg, FL July 2013 to present
- Assist robotics professors with sophisticated experiments
- Set up robotics practice sessions for Aerospace Instruction Team

Assistant Executive Editor, Tech Today Newsletter, St. Petersburg, FL September 2012 to June 2013
- Wrote and edited articles for popular college technology newsletter
- Responsible for photo editing, cropping, and resizing photos for newsletter
- Received Top College Technology Publication Award

Teacher's Assistant, Florida Port Community College, Aerospace Department, St. Petersburg, FL July 2011 to June 2012
- Helped students with homework, explained assignments, organized materials for professor
- Set up robotics lab assignments for students

EDUCATION

University of South Florida, Tampa, FL
Bachelor of Science, Mechanical Engineering, June 2015

Florida Port Community College, St. Petersburg, FL
Associate of Arts, Journalism, June 2013

HONORS AND ACTIVITIES
- Elected to Pi Tau Sigma, honor society for mechanical engineers
- Qualified for Dean's List six semesters
- Student Mentor, help other students in engineering program

Lastname_Firstname_2A_Resume

FIGURE 2.1 Project 2A Resume

Video W2-1

A *table* is an arrangement of information organized into rows and columns. The intersection of a row and a column in a table creates a box called a *cell* into which you can type. Tables are useful to present information in a logical and orderly format.

Activity 2.01 | Creating a Table by Defining Table Dimensions

1 **Start** Word and then click **Blank document**. On the **HOME tab**, in the **Paragraph group**, if necessary click **Show/Hide** to display the formatting marks. If the rulers do not display, click the **VIEW tab**, and then in the **Show group**, select the **Ruler check box**.

2 Click the **FILE tab**, and then in **Backstage** view, click **Save As**. In the **Save As** dialog box, navigate to the location where you are storing your projects for this chapter. Create a new folder named **Word Chapter 2**

3 **Save** the file in the **Word Chapter 2** folder as **Lastname_Firstname_2A_Resume**

4 On the **INSERT tab**, in the **Header & Footer group**, click **Footer**, and then at the bottom of the list, click **Edit Footer**. On the ribbon, in the **Insert group**, click **Document Info**, click **File Name**, and then at the right end of the ribbon, click **Close Header and Footer**.

5 On the **INSERT tab**, in the **Tables group**, click **Table**. In the **Insert Table** grid, in the fourth row, point to the second square, and notice that the cells are bordered in orange and *2x4 Table* displays at the top of the grid. Compare your screen with Figure 2.2.

FIGURE 2.2

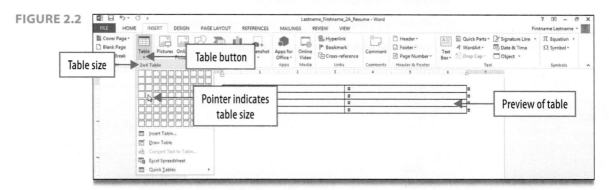

6 Click one time to create the table. Notice that formatting marks in each cell indicate the end of the contents of each cell; the mark to the right of each *row* indicates the row end. **Save** 🔲 your document, and then compare your screen with Figure 2.3.

> A table with four rows and two columns displays at the insertion point location, and the insertion point displays in the upper left cell. The table fills the width of the page, from the left margin to the right margin. On the ribbon, TABLE TOOLS and two additional tabs—*DESIGN* and *LAYOUT*—display. Borders display around each cell in the table.

FIGURE 2.3

Activity 2.02 | Typing Text in a Table

In a Word table, each cell behaves similarly to a document. For example, as you type in a cell, when you reach the right border of the cell, wordwrap moves the text to the next line. When you press Enter, the insertion point moves down to a new paragraph in the same cell. You can also insert text from another document into a table cell.

There are numerous acceptable formats for resumes, many of which can be found in Business Communications textbooks. The layout used in this project is suitable for a recent college graduate and places topics in the left column and details in the right column.

1 With the insertion point blinking in the first cell in the first row, type **OBJECTIVE** and then press Tab.

Pressing Tab moves the insertion point to the next cell in the row, or, if the insertion point is already in the last cell in the row, pressing Tab moves the insertion point to the first cell in the next row.

2 Type **Technology writing and editing position in the robotics industry, using research and advanced editing skills to communicate with customers.** Notice that the text wraps in the cell and the height of the row adjusts to fit the text.

3 Press Tab to move to the first cell in the second row. Type **SUMMARY OF QUALIFICATIONS** and then press Tab. Type the following, pressing Enter at the end of each line *except* the last line:

Two years' experience in robotics lab for Aerospace Instruction Team

Excellent interpersonal and communication skills

Proficiency using Microsoft Office

Proficiency using page layout and design software

Fluency in spoken and written Spanish

The default font and font size in a table are the same as for a document—Calibri 11 pt. The default line spacing in a table is single spacing with no space before or after paragraphs, which differs from the defaults for a document.

4 Save your document, and then compare your screen with Figure 2.4.

FIGURE 2.4

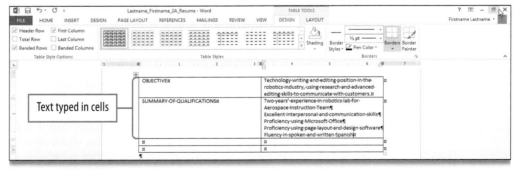

Activity 2.03 | Inserting Text from a File and Removing Blank Paragraphs

1 Press Tab to move to the first cell in the third row. Type **EXPERIENCE** and then press Tab.

2 Type the following, pressing Enter after each item, including the last item:

Instructional Lab Assistant, Florida Port Community College, St. Petersburg, FL July 2013 to present

Assist robotics professors with sophisticated experiments

Set up robotics practice sessions for Aerospace Instruction Team

3 Be sure your insertion point is positioned in the second column to the left of the cell marker below *Instruction Team*. Compare your screen with Figure 2.5.

FIGURE 2.5

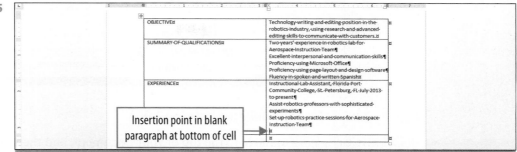

Insertion point in blank paragraph at bottom of cell

4 On the **INSERT tab**, in the **Text group**, click the **Object button arrow**, and then click **Text from File**. Navigate to your student files, select **w02A_Experience**, and then click **Insert**.

All of the text from the w02A_Experience document is added to the document at the insertion point.

ANOTHER WAY   Open the second document and select the text you want. Copy the text, and then paste at the desired location.

5 Press Backspace one time to remove the blank paragraph at the end of the inserted text, and then compare your screen with Figure 2.6.

FIGURE 2.6

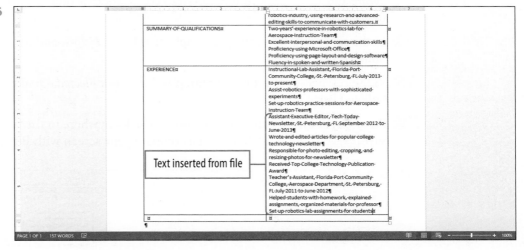

Text inserted from file

6 Press Tab to move to the first cell in the fourth row. Type **HONORS AND ACTIVITIES** and then press Tab.

7 Type the following, pressing Enter at the end of each item *except* the last one:

    Elected to Pi Tau Sigma, honor society for mechanical engineers

    Qualified for Dean's List, six semesters

    Student Mentor, help other students in engineering programs

8 **Save** 🖫 your document, and then compare your screen with Figure 2.7.

FIGURE 2.7

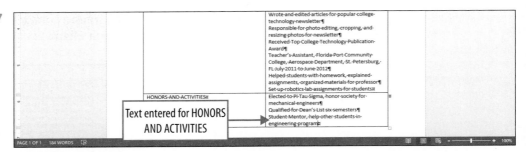

Text entered for HONORS AND ACTIVITIES

Activity 2.04 | Creating Bulleted Lists in a Table

1 Press Ctrl + Home to move to the top of your document, and then in the cell to the right of *SUMMARY OF QUALIFICATIONS*, select all of the text.

2 On the **HOME tab**, in the **Paragraph group**, click **Bullets** .

The selected text displays as a bulleted list to make each qualification more distinctive.

3 In the **Paragraph group**, click **Decrease Indent** one time to align the bullets at the left edge of the cell.

4 Scroll as necessary so that you can view the entire *EXPERIENCE* and *HONORS AND ACTIVITIES* sections on your screen. With the bulleted text still selected, in the **Clipboard group**, double-click **Format Painter**.

5 In the cell to the right of EXPERIENCE, select the second and third paragraphs—beginning *Assist* and *Set up*—to create the same style of bulleted list as you did in the previous step.

6 In the same cell, under *Assistant Executive Editor*, select the three paragraphs that begin *Wrote* and *Responsible* and *Received* to create another bulleted list aligned at the left edge of the cell.

7 In the same cell, select the paragraphs that begin *Helped* and *Set up* to create the same type of bulleted list.

8 In the cell below, select the paragraphs that begin *Elected*, *Qualified*, and *Student* to create a bulleted list.

9 Press Esc to turn off the **Format Painter**. Click anywhere in the table to deselect the text, **Save** your document, and then compare your screen with Figure 2.8.

FIGURE 2.8

Bullets added to text

Objective 2 | Format a Table

Video W2-2

Use Word's formatting tools to make your tables attractive and easy to read. Types of formatting you can add to a table include changing the row height and the column width, removing or adding borders, increasing or decreasing the paragraph or line spacing, and enhancing the text.

Activity 2.05 | Changing the Width of Table Columns and Using AutoFit

When you create a table, all of the columns are of equal width. In this activity, you will change the width of the columns.

1 ▶ Press Ctrl + Home. Click anywhere in the first column, and then on the ribbon, under **TABLE TOOLS**, click the **LAYOUT tab**. In the **Cell Size group**, notice the **Width** box, which displays the width of the active column.

2 ▶ Look at the horizontal ruler and locate the **1.5-inch mark**. Then, in the table, in any row, point to the vertical border between the two columns to display the ✛ pointer.

3 ▶ Hold down the left mouse button and drag the column border to the left until the white arrow on the ruler is at approximately **1.5 inches on the horizontal ruler** and then release the left mouse button.

4 ▶ In the **Cell Size group**, click the **Width box down spin arrow** as necessary to set the column width to **1.4"** and notice that the right border of the table moves to the right.

Adjusting column width by dragging a column border adjusts only the width of the column; adjusting column width with the Width box simultaneously adjusts the right border of the table.

5 ▶ In the **Cell Size group**, click **AutoFit**, and then click **AutoFit Window** to stretch the table across the page within the margins so that the right border of the table is at the right margin. **Save** 🖫 and then compare your screen with Figure 2.9.

🔄 **ANOTHER WAY**   You can adjust column widths by dragging the Move Table Column markers on the ruler. To maintain the right border of the table at the right margin, hold down Shift while dragging. To display measurements on the ruler, hold down Alt while dragging the marker.

FIGURE 2.9

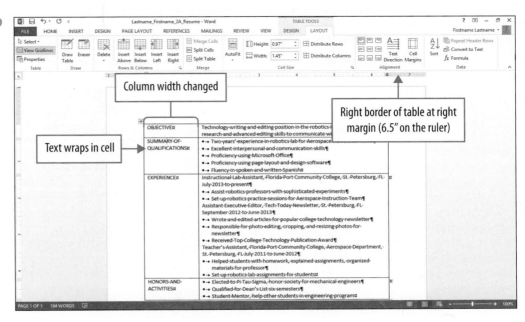

Activity 2.06 | **Using One-Click Row/Column Insertion to Modify Table Dimensions**

One of the most common actions you will take in a table is adding another row or another column. By using *One-click Row/Column Insertion* you can do so in context by pointing to the left or top edge where you want the row or column to appear and then clicking the ⊕ button to add it.

1 ▶ Scroll to view the lower portion of the table. On the left border of the table, *point* to the upper left corner of the cell containing the text *HONORS AND ACTIVITIES* to display the **One-click Row/Column Insertion** button ⊕. Compare your screen with Figure 2.10.

FIGURE 2.10

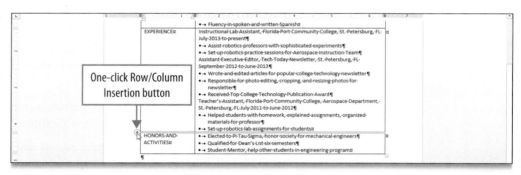

2 ▶ Click ⊕ one time to insert a new row above the HONORS AND ACTIVITIES row.

3 ▶ Click in the left cell of the new row, type **EDUCATION** and then press Tab.

4 ▶ Type the following, pressing Enter at the end of each item *except* the last one:

University of South Florida, Tampa, FL

Bachelor of Science, Mechanical Engineering, June 2015

Florida Port Community College, St. Petersburg, FL

Associate of Arts, Journalism, June 2013

5 ▶ Save 🖫 your document, and then compare your screen with Figure 2.11.

FIGURE 2.11

 **ANOTHER WAY**

When the insertion point is in the last cell in the bottom row of a table, you can add a row by pressing the Tab key; the insertion point will display in the first cell of the new row.

Activity 2.07 | Merging Table Cells

The title of a table typically spans all of the columns. In this activity, you will merge cells so that you can position the personal information across both columns.

1 Press Ctrl + Home to move to the top of your document, and then click anywhere in the top row of the table.

2 On the **LAYOUT tab**, in the **Rows & Columns group**, click **Insert Above**.

A new row displays above the row that contained the insertion point, and the new row is selected. This is another method to insert rows and columns in a table; use this method to insert a new row at the top of a table.

ANOTHER WAY Right-click in the top row, point to Insert, and then click Insert Rows Above.

3 Be sure the two cells in the top row are selected; if necessary, drag across both cells to select them.

4 On the **LAYOUT tab**, in the **Merge group**, click **Merge Cells**.

The cell border between the two cells no longer displays.

ANOTHER WAY Right-click the selected row and click Merge Cells on the shortcut menu.

Activity 2.08 | Setting Tabs in a Table

1 With the merged cell still selected, on the **HOME tab**, in the **Paragraph group**, click the **Dialog Box Launcher** to display the **Paragraph** dialog box.

2 On the **Indents and Spacing tab**, in the lower left corner, click **Tabs** to display the **Tabs** dialog box.

3 Under **Tab stop position**, type **6.5** and then under **Alignment**, click the **Right** option button. Click **Set**, and then click **OK** to close the dialog box.

4 Type **Josh Hayes** Hold down Ctrl and then press Tab. Notice that the insertion point moves to the right-aligned tab stop at 6.5".

In a Word table, you must use Ctrl + Tab to move to a tab stop, because pressing Tab is reserved for moving the insertion point from cell to cell.

5 Type **(727) 555-0313** and then press Enter.

6 Type **1541 Dearborn Lane, St. Petersburg, FL 33713** Hold down Ctrl and then press Tab.

7 Type **jhayes@alcona.net** Save your document, and then compare your screen with Figure 2.12.

FIGURE 2.12

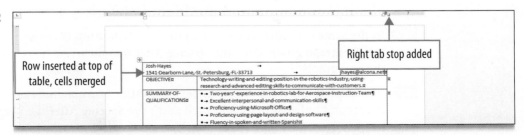

1 ▷ In the first row of the table, select the name *Josh Hayes*, and then on the mini toolbar, apply **Bold** ⎡B⎤ and change the **Font Size** to **16**.

2 ▷ Under *Josh Hayes*, click anywhere in the second line of text, which contains the address and email address.

3 ▷ On the **PAGE LAYOUT tab**, in the **Paragraph group**, click the **Spacing After up spin arrow** three times to add **18 pt** spacing between the first row of the table and the second row. Compare your screen with Figure 2.13.

> This action separates the personal information from the body of the resume and adds focus to the name.

FIGURE 2.13

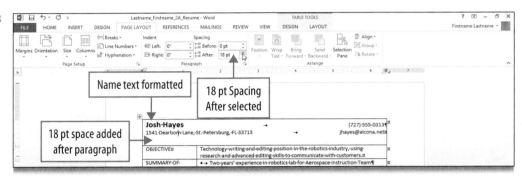

4 ▷ Using the technique you just practiced, in the second column, click in the last paragraph of *every cell* and add **18 pt Spacing After** including the last row; a border will be added to the bottom of the table, and spacing will be needed between the last row and the border.

5 ▷ In the second row, point to the word *OBJECTIVE*, hold down the left mouse button, and then drag downward in the first column to select all the headings in uppercase letters. On the mini toolbar, click **Bold** ⎡B⎤.

N O T E   **Selecting Only One Column**

When you drag downward to select the first column, a fast mouse might also begin to select the second column when you reach the bottom. If this happens, drag upward slightly to deselect the second column and select only the first column.

---

6 ▷ In the cell to the right of *EXPERIENCE*, without selecting the following comma, select *Instructional Lab Assistant* and then on the mini toolbar, click **Bold** ⎡B⎤.

7 ▷ In the same cell, apply **Bold** ⎡B⎤ to the other job titles—*Assistant Executive Editor* and *Teacher's Assistant*.

8 ▷ In the cell to the right of *EDUCATION*, apply **Bold** ⎡B⎤ to *University of South Florida, Tampa, FL* and *Florida Port Community College, St. Petersburg, FL*.

9 ▷ In the same cell, click anywhere in the line beginning *Bachelor*. On the **PAGE LAYOUT tab**, in the **Paragraph group**, click the **Spacing After up spin arrow** two times to add **12 pt** spacing after the paragraph.

10 ▷ In the cell to the right of *EXPERIENCE*, under *Instructional Lab Assistant*, click anywhere in the second bulleted item, and then add **12 pt Spacing After** the item.

11 ▷ In the same cell, repeat this process for the last bulleted item under *Assistant Executive Editor*.

12 Scroll to view the top of your document, **Save** 🔲 your document, and then compare your screen with Figure 2.14.

FIGURE 2.14

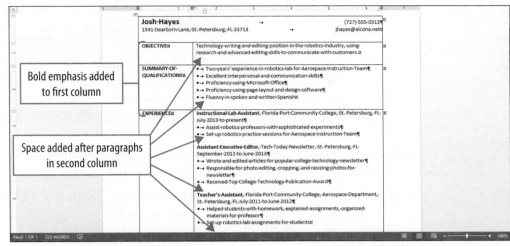

Activity 2.10 | Modifying Table Borders and Using Spacing Before

When you create a table, all of the cells have black 1/2-point, single-line, solid-line borders that print unless you remove them. Most resumes do not display any cell borders. A border at the top and bottom of the resume, however, is attractive and adds a professional look to the document.

1 Scroll as necessary to view the top margin area above the table, and then point slightly outside of the upper left corner of the table to display the **table move handle** ⊞.

2 With the ⟨⟩ pointer, click one time to select the entire table, and notice that the row markers at the end of each row are also selected.

> Shaded row markers indicate that the entire row is selected. Use this technique to select the entire table.

3 On the ribbon, under **TABLE TOOLS**, click the **DESIGN tab**. In the **Borders group**, click the **Borders button arrow**, and then click **No Border**.

> The black borders no longer display.

4 Press Ctrl + P, which is the keyboard shortcut to view the Print Preview, and notice that no borders display in the preview. Then, press **Back** ⬅ to return to your document.

5 With the table still selected, on the **DESIGN tab**, in the **Borders group**, click the **Borders button arrow**, and then at the bottom of the **Borders** gallery, click **Borders and Shading**.

6 In the **Borders and Shading** dialog box, on the **Borders tab**, under **Setting**, click **Custom**. Under **Style**, scroll down about one-third of the way, and then click the style with a **thick upper line and a thin lower line**.

7 In the **Preview** box at the right, point to the *top* border of the small preview and click one time.

🔄 **ANOTHER WAY**   Click the top border button, which is one of the buttons that surround the Preview.

8 Under **Style**, scroll down if necessary, click the opposite style—with the **thin upper line and the thick lower line**, and then in the **Preview** box, click the *bottom* border of the preview. Compare your screen with Figure 2.15.

FIGURE 2.15

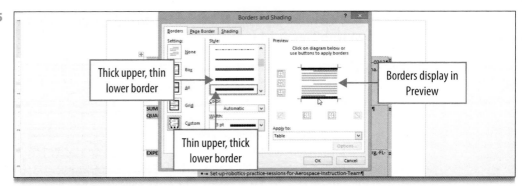

> Thick upper, thin lower border

> Borders display in Preview

> Thin upper, thick lower border

9 ▸ Click **OK**, click anywhere to cancel the selection, and then notice that there is only a small amount of space between the upper border and the first line of text.

10 ▸ Click anywhere in the text *Josh Hayes*, and then on the **PAGE LAYOUT tab**, in the **Paragraph group**, click the **Spacing Before up spin arrow** as necessary to add **18 pt** spacing before the first paragraph.

11 ▸ Press Ctrl + P to display **Print Preview**. Compare your screen with Figure 2.16.

FIGURE 2.16

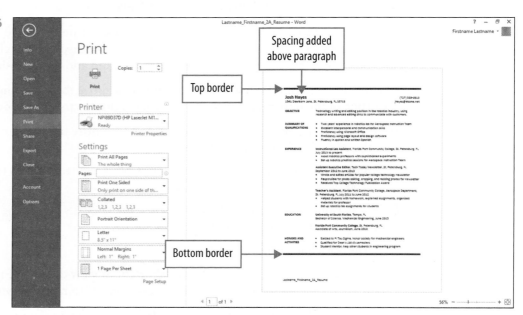

> Spacing added above paragraph

> Top border

> Bottom border

12 ▸ Press **Back** to return to your document, and then on the Quick Access Toolbar, click **Save**.

More **Knowledge** | **View Gridlines in a Table**

After you remove borders from a table, you can still view nonprinting gridlines, which show the cell boundaries of a table whenever the table does not have borders applied. Some people find this a useful visual aid. If you cannot see the gridlines, on the ribbon, under TABLE TOOLS, on the DESIGN tab, in the Borders group, click the Borders button arrow, and then click View Gridlines.

More **Knowledge** | **Convert Text to a Table**

To convert paragraphs or lists to a table, insert separator characters such as commas or tabs to show where to divide the text into columns. Then insert paragraph marks (press ENTER) to show where to begin the rows. Select the text, and then on the INSERT tab, in the Table group, click Convert Text to Table. In the Convert Text to Table dialog box, choose the options you want, and then click OK.

Video W2-3

Office Presentation Service enables you to present your Word document to others who can watch in a web browser. No preliminary setup is necessary; Word creates a link to your document that you can share with others via email or instant message. Anyone to whom you send the link can see your document while you are presenting online.

Individuals watching your presentation can navigate within the document independently of you or others in the presentation, so they can use a mouse, keyboard, or touch input to move around in the document while you are presenting it. If an individual is viewing a different portion of the document than the presenter, an alert displays on his or her screen. To return to the portion of the document that the presenter is showing, a Follow Presenter button displays.

While you are presenting, you can make minor edits to the document. If you want to share a copy of the document to the presentation attendees, you can select *Enable remote viewers to download the document* when you start the presentation. You can also share any meeting notes that you or others created in OneNote.

Activity 2.11 | Presenting a Word Document Online

If you are creating your own resume, it will be valuable to get feedback from your friends, instructors, or Career Center advisors before you submit your resume for a job application. In this Activity, you will present the resume document online for others to look at.

N O T E | **You May Be Asked to Sign in with Your Microsoft Account**

You may be asked to sign in with your Microsoft account, even if you are already signed in, to present your document online.

---

1 With your resume document displayed, click **Save** 🖫 .

2 Click the **FILE tab**, on the left click **Share**, and then under **Share**, click **Present Online**.

3 On the right, under **Present Online**, be sure **Office Presentation Service** displays; if necessary, click the arrow on the right to select it. Click the **Present Online** button. Wait a moment for the service to connect, and then compare your screen with Figure 2.17.

There are several methods to send your meeting invitation to others. You can click Copy Link to copy and paste the hyperlink; for example, you could copy the link into a *Skype* window. Skype is a Microsoft product with which you can make voice calls, make video calls, transfer files, or send messages—including instant messages and text messages—over the Internet.

You can also select Send in Email, which will open your Outlook email window if you use Outlook as your mail client.

N O T E | **Other Presentation Services May Display**

Under Present Online, you might have other services displayed. For example, if you are using Office 365, Microsoft Lync may display as the default presentation service.

FIGURE 2.17

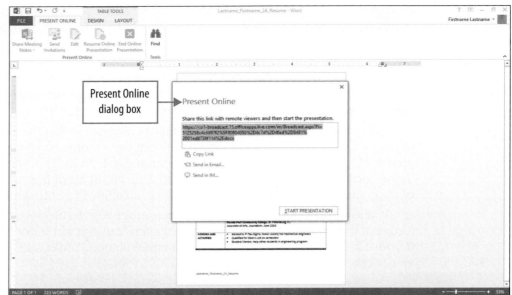

Present Online dialog box

4 ▶ If you want to do so, identify a classmate or friend who is at a computer and available to view your presentation, select one of the methods to share, click **START PRESENTATION**, and when you are finished, on the ribbon, click **End Online Presentation**. Otherwise, **Close** ✖ the **Present Online** dialog box.

> If you present online, you will need to initiate voice communication using Skype or by simply phoning the other person.

5 ▶ Be sure you have closed the **Present Online** dialog box. On the ribbon, on the **PRESENT ONLINE tab**, click **End Online Presentation**, and then in the message, click **End Online Presentation**.

6 ▶ Press Ctrl + Home to move to the top of your document. In the lower right corner, click **Zoom In** ➕ as necessary to set the Zoom level to **100%**. On the **HOME tab**, redisplay the formatting marks by clicking **Show/Hide**.

7 ▶ Click the **FILE tab**, and then in the lower right portion of the screen, click **Show All Properties**. In the **Tags** box, type **resume, Word table** and in the **Subject** box, type your course name and section number. In the **Author** box, be sure your name is indicated and edit if necessary.

8 ▶ On the left, click **Print** to display **Print Preview**. If necessary, return to the document and make any necessary changes.

9 ▶ As directed by your instructor, print your document or submit it electronically. **Save** 🖫 your document and **Close** ✖ Word.

More Knowledge   **Convert a Table to Text**

To convert a table to text, select the rows or table you want to convert to paragraphs, and then on the LAYOUT tab, in the Data group, click Convert to Text. In the Convert to Text dialog box, under Separate text at, click the separator character to use in place of the column boundaries, and then click OK.

END | You have completed Project 2A

GO! with Office Web Apps

Objective | Edit a Resume in Word Web App

You can create and edit tables in the Word Web App if you are not at a computer on which Word 2013 is installed.

A L E R T !   **Working with Web-Based Applications and Services**

Computer programs and services on the web receive continuous updates and improvements, so the steps to complete this web-based activity may differ from the ones shown. You can often look at the screens and the information presented to determine how to complete the activity.

Activity | Editing a Resume in Word Web App

In this activity, you will use the Word Web App to edit a Word table containing a resume similar to the resume you created in Project 1A.

1 From the desktop, start Internet Explorer. Navigate to **http://skydrive.com** and then sign in to your Microsoft account. Click your **GO! Web Projects** folder to open it—or create and then open this folder if necessary.

2 On the SkyDrive menu bar, click **Upload**. In the **Choose File to Upload** dialog box, navigate to your student data files, click **w02_2A_Web**, and then click **Open**.

3 Point to the uploaded file **w02_2A_Web**, and then right-click. On the shortcut menu, scroll down as necessary and then click **Rename**. Using your own last name and first name, type **Lastname_Firstname_WD_2A_Web** and then press [Enter] to rename the file.

4 Click the file that you just renamed, and then in the upper left, click **EDIT DOCUMENT**. On the list, click **Edit in Word Web App**.

5 If necessary, click to place the insertion point in the cell *OBJECTIVE*. On the ribbon, under **TABLE TOOLS**,

click the **LAYOUT tab**, and then in the **Insert group**, click **Insert Above**.

6 In the first cell of the new row, type **Daniela Frank** press [Enter], select the text you just typed, and then on the **HOME tab**, in the **Styles group**, click the **More Styles arrow**, and then click **Title**. With the text selected, change the **Font** to **Calibri (Body)**.

7 Click in the second cell of the new row, and then type **1343 Siena Lane, Deerfield, WI 53531** and press [Enter]. Type **(608) 555-0588** and press [Enter]. Type **dfrank@alcona.net** and press [Enter]. Right-click the email address, and then click **Remove Link**. Select all the text in the second cell that you just typed, and then on the **HOME tab**, in the **Paragraph group**, click **Align Text Right** ☰. Click anywhere to deselect, and then compare your screen with Figure A.

FIGURE A

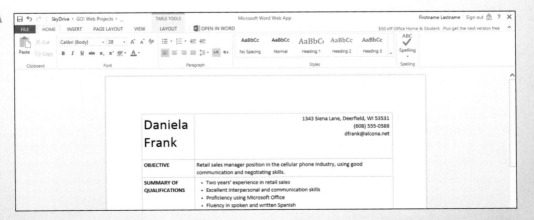

(GO! with Office Web Apps continues on the next page)

8 Scroll down and click anywhere in the *EXPERIENCE* cell. On the ribbon, under **TABLE TOOLS**, click the **LAYOUT tab**, and then in the **Insert group**, click **Insert Below**. In the first cell of the new row, press `Backspace` one time to move the insertion point to the left edge of the cell. Type **EDUCATION** Select the text you just typed, and then from the **HOME tab**, apply **Bold** `B`.

9 Press `Tab` to move to the second cell in the new row, press `Backspace` one time to move to the left edge of the cell, and then type **Madison Area Technical College, Madison, WI** and press `Enter`.

10 Type **Associate of Arts in Information Systems, June 2014** and press `Enter`. Select the upper line of text with the college information, and then press `Ctrl` + `B` to apply **Bold**. Click anywhere to deselect, and then compare your screen with Figure B.

11 On the ribbon, above the **FILE tab**, click Save `H`. Click the **FILE tab** and then click **Exit**. Submit the file as directed by your instructor. In the upper right, click your user name, and then click **Sign out**. **Close** `X` Internet Explorer.

FIGURE B

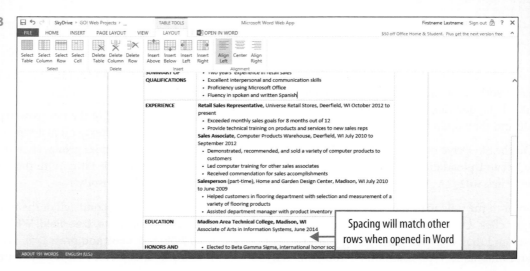

Spacing will match other rows when opened in Word

Cover Letter, Reference List, and Envelope

PROJECT ACTIVITIES

In Activities 2.12 through 2.24, you will create a letterhead, save the letterhead as a custom Word template, and then use the letterhead to create a cover letter to accompany a resume. You will also create a list of references from a Microsoft predesigned template and, if you have an envelope and printer available, format and print an envelope. Your completed documents will look similar to Figure 2.18.

PROJECT FILES

For Project 2B, you will need the following files:

New blank Word document
w02B_Cover_Letter_Text

You will save your documents as:

Lastname_Firstname_2B_Cover_Letter
Lastname_Firstname_2B_Reference_List

PROJECT RESULTS

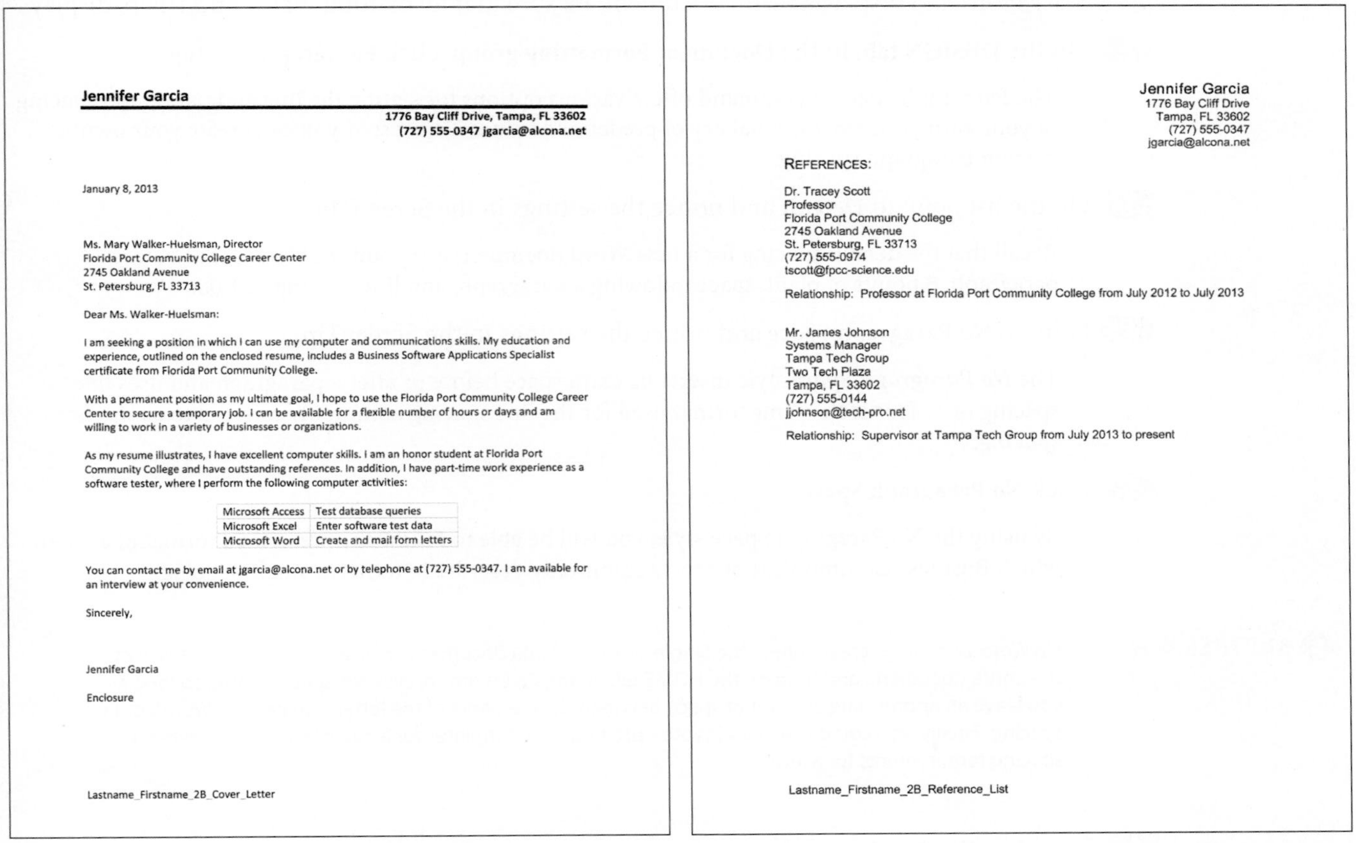

Jennifer Garcia

1776 Bay Cliff Drive, Tampa, FL 33602
(727) 555-0347 jgarcia@alcona.net

January 8, 2013

Ms. Mary Walker-Huelsman, Director
Florida Port Community College Career Center
2745 Oakland Avenue
St. Petersburg, FL 33713

Dear Ms. Walker-Huelsman:

I am seeking a position in which I can use my computer and communications skills. My education and experience, outlined on the enclosed resume, includes a Business Software Applications Specialist certificate from Florida Port Community College.

With a permanent position as my ultimate goal, I hope to use the Florida Port Community College Career Center to secure a temporary job. I can be available for a flexible number of hours or days and am willing to work in a variety of businesses or organizations.

As my resume illustrates, I have excellent computer skills. I am an honor student at Florida Port Community College and have outstanding references. In addition, I have part-time work experience as a software tester, where I perform the following computer activities:

Microsoft Access	Test database queries
Microsoft Excel	Enter software test data
Microsoft Word	Create and mail form letters

You can contact me by email at jgarcia@alcona.net or by telephone at (727) 555-0347. I am available for an interview at your convenience.

Sincerely,

Jennifer Garcia

Enclosure

Lastname_Firstname_2B_Cover_Letter

Jennifer Garcia
1776 Bay Cliff Drive
Tampa, FL 33602
(727) 555-0347
jgarcia@alcona.net

REFERENCES:

Dr. Tracey Scott
Professor
Florida Port Community College
2745 Oakland Avenue
St. Petersburg, FL 33713
(727) 555-0974
tscott@fpcc-science.edu

Relationship: Professor at Florida Port Community College from July 2012 to July 2013

Mr. James Johnson
Systems Manager
Tampa Tech Group
Two Tech Plaza
Tampa, FL 33602
(727) 555-0144
jjohnson@tech-pro.net

Relationship: Supervisor at Tampa Tech Group from July 2013 to present

Lastname_Firstname_2B_Reference_List

FIGURE 2.18 Project 2B Cover Letter and Reference List

Video W2-4

A ***template*** is a file you use as a starting point for a *new* document. A template has a predefined document structure and defined settings, such as font, margins, and available styles. On Word's opening screen, you can select from among many different templates—or you can create your own custom template.

When you open a template as the starting point for a new document, the template file opens a copy of itself, unnamed, and then you use the structure—and possibly some content, such as headings—as the starting point for a new document.

All documents are based on a template. When you create a new blank document, it is based on Word's ***Normal template***, which serves as the starting point for all blank Word documents.

Activity 2.12 | Changing the Document Style Set for Paragraph Spacing and Applying a Bottom Border to a Paragraph

A ***letterhead*** is the personal or company information that displays at the top of a letter, and which commonly includes a name, address, and contact information. The term also refers to a piece of paper imprinted with such information at the top. In this activity, you will create a custom template for a personal letterhead.

1 Start Word and display a blank document; be sure that formatting marks and rulers display.

2 On the **DESIGN tab**, in the **Document Formatting group**, click **Paragraph Spacing**.

The Paragraph Spacing command offers various options for setting the line and paragraph spacing of your entire document. A gallery of predefined values displays; or you can create your own custom paragraph spacing.

3 On the list *point* to **Default** and notice the settings in the ScreenTip.

Recall that the default spacing for a new Word document is 0 points of blank space before a paragraph, 8 points of blank space following a paragraph, and line spacing of 1.08.

4 Point to **No Paragraph Space** and notice the settings in the ScreenTip.

The ***No Paragraph Space*** style inserts *no* extra space before or after a paragraph and uses line spacing of 1. This is the same format used for the line spacing commonly referred to as ***single spacing***.

5 Click **No Paragraph Space**.

By using the No Paragraph Space style, you will be able to follow the prescribed format of a letter, which Business Communications texts commonly describe in terms of single spacing.

 **ANOTHER WAY** On Word's opening screen, select the Single spaced (blank) document; or, in a blank document, select the entire document, and then on the HOME tab, in the Styles group, click No Spacing. Also, so long as you leave an appropriate amount of space between the elements of the letter, you can use Word's default spacing. Finally, you could use one of Word's predesigned templates for a cover letter and observe all spacing requirements for a letter.

6 Type **Jennifer Garcia** and then press Enter.

7 Type **1776 Bay Cliff Drive, Tampa, FL 33602** and then press Enter.

8 Type **(727) 555-0347 jgarcia@alcona.net** and then press Enter. If the web address changes to blue text, right-click the web address, and then, click **Remove Hyperlink**.

9 Select the first paragraph—*Jennifer Garcia*—and then on the mini toolbar, apply **Bold** B and change the **Font Size** to **16**.

10 Select the second and third paragraphs. On the mini toolbar, apply **Bold** B and change the **Font Size** to **12**.

11 With the two paragraphs still selected, on the **HOME tab**, in the **Paragraph group**, click **Align Right** ▤.

↻ ANOTHER WAY   Press Ctrl + R to align text to the right.

12 Click anywhere in the first paragraph—*Jennifer Garcia*. In the **Paragraph group**, click the **Borders button arrow** ▦ ▾, and then at the bottom, click **Borders and Shading**.

13 In the **Borders and Shading** dialog box, on the **Borders tab**, under **Style**, be sure the first style—a single solid line—is selected.

14 Click the **Width arrow**, and then click **3 pt**. To the right, under **Preview**, click the bottom border of the diagram. Under **Apply to**, be sure *Paragraph* displays. Compare your screen with Figure 2.19.

FIGURE 2.19

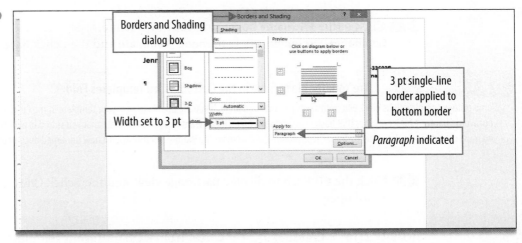

Borders and Shading dialog box

3 pt single-line border applied to bottom border

Width set to 3 pt

Paragraph indicated

↻ ANOTHER WAY   Alternatively, under Preview, click the bottom border button ▦ ▾.

15 Click **OK** to display a 3 pt line below *Jennifer Garcia*, which extends from the left margin to the right margin.

The border is a paragraph command and uses the same margins of the paragraph to which it is applied.

Activity 2.13 | Saving a Document as a Custom Word Template

After you create a document format that you like and will use again, for example, a letterhead for personal letters during a job search, you can save it as a template and then use it as the starting point for any letter.

1 Press F12 to display the **Save As** dialog box. In the lower portion of the dialog box, in the **Save as type** box, at the right edge, click the arrow, and then click **Word Template**.

ALERT!   Are You Using a Laptop Computer?

On some laptop computers, you might have to hold down the key labeled FN while pressing the F12 key in order to display the Save As dialog box.

2 At the top of the **Save As** dialog box, notice the path, and then compare your screen with Figure 2.20.

> By default, Word stores template files on your hard drive in your user folder, in a folder named Custom Word Templates. By doing so, the template is available to you from the Word opening screen.

FIGURE 2.20

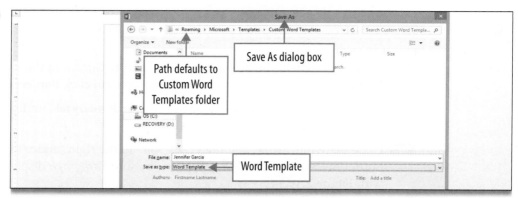

3 Click in the **File name** box, using your own name, type **Lastname_Firstname_2B_Letterhead_Template** and then click **Save**.

ALERT! **Are You Unable to Save in the Custom Word Templates Folder?**

Some college computer labs block you from saving on the hard drive. If you are unable to save your template in the Custom Word Templates folder, navigate to your Word Chapter 2 folder on your USB flash drive and save there. If you want to open a template that you stored in a location other than Word's default path, you must open the template directly from File Explorer—not from within Word—for it to open a new unnamed document based on the template.

---

4 Click the **FILE tab** to display **Backstage** view, and then click **Close** to close the file but leave Word open.

Activity 2.14 | Creating a Cover Letter from a Custom Word Template

A **cover letter** is a document that you send with your resume to provide additional information about your skills and experience. An effective cover letter includes specific information about why you are qualified for the job for which you are applying. Use the cover letter to explain your interest in the position and the organization.

ALERT! **Were You Unable to Save in the Custom Word Templates Folder?**

If you saved your template file on your USB flash drive because you were blocked from saving in the default folder on the hard drive, open your saved document, press [F12] to display the Save As dialog box, and then in your storage location, save the document—using your own name—as Lastname_Firstname_2B_Cover_Letter. Then move to Activity 2.15.

---

1 With Word open but no documents displayed, click the **FILE tab** to display **Backstage** view, and then click **New** to display the new document options. Compare your screen with Figure 2.21.

> Here you can create a new document from a blank document or from one of Word's many built-in or online templates.

FIGURE 2.21

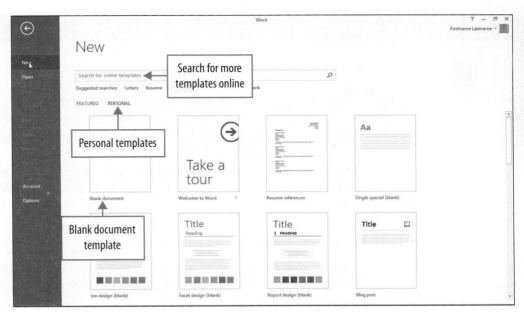

2 Under **Suggested searches**, click **PERSONAL**, *point* to the name of your letterhead template, and then compare your screen with Figure 2.22.

Custom templates that you create and that are stored in the Custom Word Templates folder on your hard drive are accessible to you here whenever you want to create a new document from your stored template.

FIGURE 2.22

3 Click your letterhead template.

Word opens a copy of your 2B_Letterhead_Template in the form of a new Word document—the title bar indicates *Document* followed by a number. You are not opening the original template file, and changes that you make to this new document will not affect the contents of your 2B_Letterhead_Template file.

4 Press [F12] to display the **Save As** dialog box, and then navigate to your **Word Chapter 2** folder. **Save** the file as **Lastname_Firstname_2B_Cover_Letter**

5 On the **INSERT tab**, in the **Header & Footer** group, click **Footer**, click **Edit Footer**, and then in the **Insert group**, click **Document Info**. Click **File Name**, and then click **Close Header and Footer**.

6 Save 🖫 your document.

Video W2-5

Business letters follow a standard format and contain the following parts: the current date, referred to as the *dateline*; the name and address of the person receiving the letter, referred to as the *inside address*; a greeting, referred to as the *salutation*; the text of the letter, usually referred to as the *body* of the letter; a closing line, referred to as the *complimentary closing*; and the *writer's identification*, which includes the name or job title (or both) of the writer and which is also referred to as the *writer's signature block*.

Some letters also include the initials of the person who prepared the letter, an optional *subject line* that describes the purpose of the letter, or a list of *enclosures*—documents included with the letter.

Activity 2.15 | Adding AutoCorrect Entries

Word's *AutoCorrect* feature corrects commonly misspelled words automatically; for example *teh* instead of *the*. If you have words that you frequently misspell, you can add them to the list for automatic correction.

1 Click the **FILE tab** to display **Backstage** view. On the left, click **Options** to display the **Word Options** dialog box.

2 On the left side of the **Word Options** dialog box, click **Proofing**, and then under **AutoCorrect options**, click the **AutoCorrect Options** button.

3 In the **AutoCorrect** dialog box, click the **AutoCorrect tab**. Under **Replace**, type **resumee** and under **With**, type **resume**

If another student has already added this AutoCorrect entry, a Replace button will display.

4 Click **Add**. If the entry already exists, click **Replace** instead, and then click **Yes**.

5 In the **AutoCorrect** dialog box, under **Replace**, type **computr** and under **With**, type **computer** Compare your screen with Figure 2.23.

FIGURE 2.23

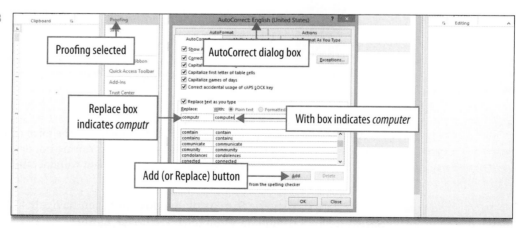

6 Click **Add** (or **Replace**) and then click **OK** two times to close the dialog boxes.

Activity 2.16 | Inserting the Current Date and Creating a Cover Letter

By using the *Date & Time* command, you can select from a variety of formats to insert the current date and time in document.

For cover letters, there are a variety of accepted letter formats that you will see in reference manuals and Business Communications texts. The one used in this chapter is a block style cover letter following the style in Courtland Bovee and John Thill, *Business Communication Today*, Eleventh Edition, Pearson Prentice Hall, 2012, p. A-2.

1 Press Ctrl + End to move the insertion point to the blank line below the letterhead, and then press Enter three times.

2 On the **INSERT tab**, in the **Text group**, click **Date & Time**, and then click the third date format. Click **OK** to create the dateline.

> Most Business Communication texts recommend that the dateline be positioned at least 0.5 inch (3 blank lines) below the letterhead; or, position the dateline approximately 2 inches from the top edge of the paper.

3 Press Enter four times, which leaves three blank lines. Type the following inside address on four lines, but do *not* press Enter following the last line:

Ms. Mary Walker-Huelsman, Director

Florida Port Community College Career Center

2745 Oakland Avenue

St. Petersburg, FL 33713

The recommended space between the dateline and inside address varies slightly among experts in Business Communication texts and office reference manuals. However, all indicate that the space can be from 1 to 10 blank lines depending on the length of your letter.

4 Press Enter two times to leave one blank line, and then compare your screen with Figure 2.24.

FIGURE 2.24

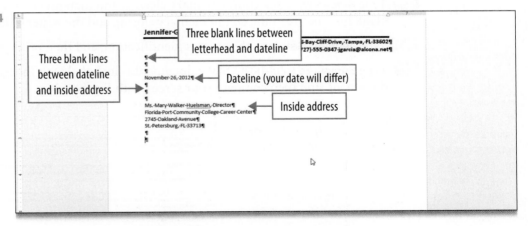

5 Type the salutation **Dear Ms. Walker-Huelsman:** and then press Enter two times.

> Always leave one blank line above and below the salutation.

6 Type, exactly as shown, the following opening paragraph that includes an intentional word usage error: **I am seeking a position in witch I can use my** and press Spacebar. Type, exactly as shown, **computr** and then watch *computr* as you press Spacebar.

> The AutoCorrect feature recognizes the misspelled word, and then changes *computr* to *computer* when you press Spacebar, Enter, or a punctuation mark.

7 ▶ Type the following, including the misspelled last word: **and communication skills. My education and experience, outlined on the enclosed resumee** and then type **,** (a comma). Notice that when you type the comma, AutoCorrect replaces *resumee* with *resume*.

8 ▶ Press Spacebar, and then complete the paragraph by typing **includes a Business Software Applications Specialist certificate from FPCC.** Compare your screen with Figure 2.25.

FIGURE 2.25

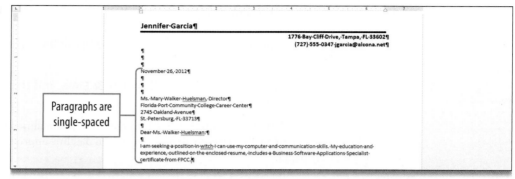

9 ▶ Press Enter two times. On the **INSERT tab**, in the **Text group**, click the **Object button arrow**, and then click **Text from File**. From your student files, locate and **Insert** the file **w02B_Cover_Letter_Text**.

Some of the words in the cover letter text display red or blue wavy underlines. These indicate potential spelling, grammar, or word usage errors, and will be addressed before the end of this project.

10 ▶ Scroll as necessary to display the lower half of the letter on your screen, and be sure your insertion point is positioned in the blank paragraph at the end of the document.

11 ▶ Press Enter one time to leave one blank line between the last paragraph of the letter and the complimentary closing.

12 ▶ Type **Sincerely,** as the complimentary closing, and then press Enter four times to leave three blank lines between the complimentary closing and the writer's identification.

13 ▶ Type **Jennifer Garcia** as the writer's identification, and then press Enter two times.

14 ▶ Type **Enclosure** to indicate that a document is included with the letter. **Save** 🖫 your document, and then compare your screen with Figure 2.26.

FIGURE 2.26

Activity 2.17 | Finding and Replacing Text

Use the Find command to locate text in a document quickly. Use the Find and Replace command to make the same change, or to make more than one change at a time, in a document.

1 ▸ Press [Ctrl] + [Home] to position the insertion point at the beginning of the document.

> Because a find operation—or a find and replace operation—begins from the location of the insertion point and proceeds to the end of the document, it is good practice to position the insertion point at the beginning of the document before initiating the command.

2 ▸ On the **HOME tab**, in the **Editing group**, click **Find**.

> The navigation pane displays on the left side of the screen with a search box at the top of the pane.

↻ ANOTHER WAY   Hold down [Ctrl] and press [F].

3 ▸ In the **navigation** pane, in the search box, type **ac** If necessary, scroll down slightly in your document to view the entire body text of the letter, and then compare your screen with Figure 2.27.

> In the document, the search letters *ac* are selected and highlighted in yellow for both words that begin with the letters *ac* and also for the word *contact* which contains this letter combination. In the navigation pane, the three instances are shown in context—*ac* displays in bold.

FIGURE 2.27

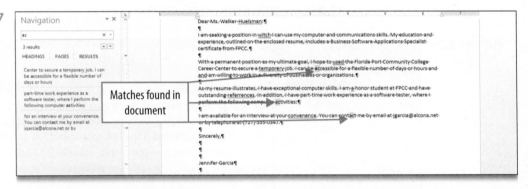

4 ▸ Click in the search box again, and type as necessary to display the word *accessible* in the search box.

> One match for the search term displays in context in the navigation pane and is highlighted in the document.

5 ▸ In the document, double-click the yellow highlighted word *accessible*, and then type **available** to replace the word.

6 ▸ **Close** [**✕**] the **navigation** pane, and then on the **HOME tab**, in the **Editing group**, click **Replace**.

7 ▸ In the **Find and Replace** dialog box, in the **Find what** box, replace the existing text by typing **FPCC** and in the **Replace with** box, type **Florida Port Community College** and then compare your screen with Figure 2.28.

FIGURE 2.28

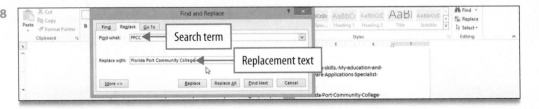

8 In the lower left corner of the dialog box, click **More** to expand the dialog box, and then under **Search Options**, select the **Match case** check box.

The acronym *FPCC* appears in the document two times. In a formal letter, the reader may not know what the acronym means, so you should include the full text instead of an acronym. In this instance, you must select the *Match case* check box so that the replaced text will match the case you typed in the Replace with box, and *not* display in all uppercase letters in the manner of *FPCC*.

9 In the **Find and Replace** dialog box, click **Replace All** to replace both instances of *FPCC*. Click **OK** to close the message box.

10 In the **Find and Replace** dialog box, clear the **Match case** check box, click **Less**, and then **Close** the dialog box. **Save** 🔲 your document.

The Find and Replace dialog box opens with the settings used the last time it was open. Therefore, it is good practice to reset this dialog box to its default settings each time you use it.

Activity 2.18 | Selecting and Moving Text to a New Location

By using Word's ***drag-and-drop*** feature, you can use the mouse to drag selected text from one location to another. This method is most useful when the text you are moving is on the same screen as the destination location.

1 Take a moment to study the table in Figure 2.29 to become familiar with the techniques you can use to select text in a document quickly.

FIGURE 2.29

SELECTING TEXT IN A DOCUMENT	
TO SELECT THIS:	**DO THIS:**
A portion of text	Click to position the insertion point at the beginning of the text you want to select, hold down Shift, and then click at the end of the text you want to select. Alternatively, hold down the left mouse button and drag from the beginning to the end of the text you want to select.
A word	Double-click the word.
A sentence	Hold down Ctrl and click anywhere in the sentence.
A paragraph	Triple-click anywhere in the paragraph; or, move the pointer to the left of the line, into the margin area. When the ⌐ pointer displays, double-click.
A line	Point to the left of the line. When the ⌐ pointer displays, click one time.
One character at a time	Position the insertion point to the left of the first character, hold down Shift, and press ← or → as many times as desired.
A string of words	Position the insertion point to the left of the first word, hold down Shift and Ctrl, and then press ← or → as many times as desired.
Consecutive lines	Position the insertion point to the left of the first word, hold down Shift and press ↑ or ↓.
Consecutive paragraphs	Position the insertion point to the left of the first word, hold down Shift and Ctrl and press ↑ or ↓.
The entire document	Hold down Ctrl and press A. Alternatively, move the pointer to the left of any line in the document. When the ⌐ pointer displays, triple-click.

2 Be sure you can view the entire body of the letter on your screen. In the paragraph that begins *With a permanent position*, in the second line, locate and double-click *days*.

3 Point to the selected word to display the ▨ pointer.

4 Drag to the right until the dotted vertical line that floats next to the pointer is positioned to the right of the word *hours* in the same line, as shown in Figure 2.30.

FIGURE 2.30

> I·am·seeking·a·position·in·witch·I·can·use·my·computer·and·communication·skills.·My·education·and· experience,·outlined·on·the·enclosed·resume,·includes·a·Business·Software·Applications·Specialist· certificate·from·Florida·Port·Community·College.¶
> ¶
> With·a·permanent·position·as·my·ultimate·goal,·I·hope·to·used·the·Florida·Port·Community·College· Career·Center·to·secure·a·temporery·job.·I·can·be·available·for·a·flexible·number·of·days·or·hours·and· and·am·willing·to·work·in·a·diversity·of·businesses·or·organizations.¶
> ¶
> As·my·resume·illustrates,·I·have·exceptional·computer·skills.·I·am·a·honor·student·at·Florida·Port· Community·College·and·have·outstanding·referrences.·In·addition,·I·have·part-time·work·experience·as·a· software·tester,·where·I·perform·the·following·computer·activities:¶

Word will be dragged to new location

5 Release the mouse button to move the text. Select *hours* and drag it to the left of the word *or*—the previous location of the word *days*. Click anywhere to deselect the text.

6 Examine the text that you moved, and add or remove spaces as necessary.

7 Hold down Ctrl, and then in the paragraph that begins *I am available*, click anywhere in the first sentence to select the entire sentence.

8 Drag the selected sentence to the end of the paragraph by positioning the small vertical line that floats with the pointer to the left of the paragraph mark. **Save** 🖫 your document, and then compare your screen with Figure 2.31.

FIGURE 2.31

Sentence moved to end of paragraph →

> ¶
> You·can·contact·me·by·email·at·jgarcia@alcona.net·or·by·telephone·at·(727)·555-0347.·I·am·available·for· an·interview·at·your·convenence.¶
> ¶ 🖺 (Ctrl) ▾
> Sincerely,¶
> ¶
> ¶
> Jennifer·Garcia¶
> ¶
> Enclosure¶

PAGE 1 OF 1   9 OF 188 WORDS   □⋉   100%

Activity 2.19 | Inserting a Table into a Document and Applying a Table Style

1 Locate the paragraph that begins *You can contact me*, and then click to position the insertion point in the blank line above that paragraph. Press Enter one time.

2 On the **INSERT tab**, in the **Tables group**, click **Table**. In the **Table** grid, in the third row, click the second square to insert a 2 × 3 table.

3 In the first cell of the table, type **Microsoft Access** and then press Tab. Type **Test database queries** and then press Tab. Complete the table using the following information:

Microsoft Excel	Enter software test data
Microsoft Word	Create and mail form letters

4 Point slightly outside of the upper left corner of the table to display the **table move handle** button ⊞. With the ⊹ pointer, click one time to select the entire table.

5 On the **LAYOUT tab**, in the **Cell Size group**, click **AutoFit**, and then click **AutoFit Contents** to have Word choose the best column widths for the two columns based on the text you entered.

6 With the table still selected, on the **DESIGN tab**, in the **Table Styles group**, click **More** ⊡. Under **Plain Tables**, click the second style—**Table Grid Light**.

> Use Table Styles to change the visual style of a table.

7 With the table still selected, on the **HOME tab**, in the **Paragraph group**, click **Center** ☰ to center the table between the left and right margins. Click anywhere to deselect the table.

8 **Save** 🖫 and then compare your screen with Figure 2.32.

FIGURE 2.32

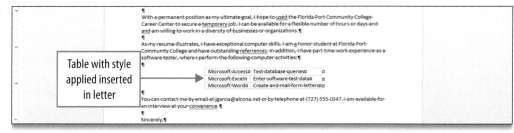

Table with style applied inserted in letter

Objective 6   Use the Proofing Options and Print an Envelope

Video W2-6

Word compares your typing to words in the Office dictionary and compares your phrases and punctuation to a list of grammar rules. This automatic proofing is set by default. Words that are not in the dictionary and words, phrases, and punctuation that differ from the grammar rules are marked with wavy underlines; for example, the misuse of *their*, *there*, and *they're*.

Word will not flag the word *sign* as misspelled even though you intended to type *sing a song* rather than *sign a song*, because both are words contained within Word's dictionary. Your own knowledge and proofreading skills are still required, even when using a sophisticated word processing program like Word.

Activity 2.20 | Checking for Spelling and Grammar Errors

There are two ways to respond to spelling and grammar errors flagged by Word. You can right-click a flagged word or phrase, and then from the shortcut menu choose a correction or action. Or, you can initiate the Spelling & Grammar command to display the Spelling and Grammar pane, which provides more options than the shortcut menus.

---

1 Position the body of the letter on your screen, and then examine the text to locate wavy underlines.

A list of grammar rules applied by a computer program like Word can never be exact, and a computer dictionary cannot contain all known words and proper names. Therefore, you will need to check any words flagged by Word with wavy underlines, and you will also need to proofread for content errors.

2 In the lower left corner of your screen, in the status bar, locate and point to the [icon] icon to display the ScreenTip *Proofing errors were found. Click to correct.* Compare your screen with Figure 2.33.

If this button displays, you know there are potential errors identified in the document.

FIGURE 2.33

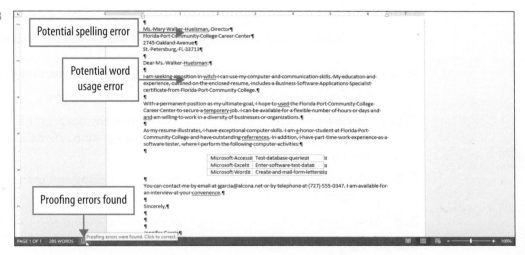

3 In the paragraph that begins *With a permanent*, in the second line, locate the word *temporery* with the wavy red underline. Point to the word and right-click, and then click **temporary** to correct the spelling error.

4 In the next line, locate the word *and* that displays with a wavy red underline, point to the word and right-click, and then on the shortcut menu, click **Delete Repeated Word** to delete the duplicate word.

5 Press Ctrl + Home to move the insertion point to the beginning of the document. Click the **REVIEW tab**, and then in the **Proofing group**, click **Spelling & Grammar** to check the spelling and grammar of the text in the document.

The Spelling pane displays on the right, and the proper name *Huelsman* is flagged. Word's dictionary contains only very common proper names—unusual names like this one will typically be flagged as a potential spelling error. If this is a name that you frequently type, consider adding it to the dictionary.

ANOTHER WAY   Press F7 to start the Spelling & Grammar command.

6 In the **Spelling** pane, click **Ignore All**. Compare your screen with Figure 2.34.

The word *witch* is highlighted as a grammar error, and in the Grammar pane, *which* is suggested.

FIGURE 2.34

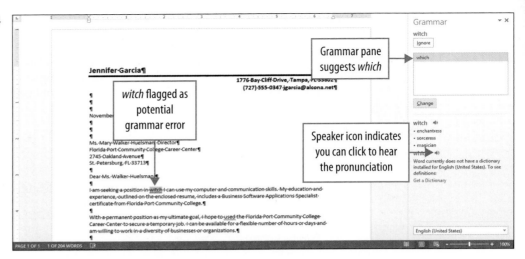

7 ▶ In the **Grammar** pane, click **Change** to change to the correct usage *which*.

The next marked word—a possible grammar error—displays.

8 ▶ Click **Change** to change *used* to *use*. Notice that the next error is a potential spelling error. In the **Spelling** pane, change *referrences* to the suggestion *references*. Notice that the next error is a possible grammar error.

9 ▶ Click **Change** to change *a* to *an*. Continue the spelling and grammar check and correct the spelling of *convenence*.

10 ▶ When Word displays the message *Spelling and grammar check complete*, click **OK**.

11 ▶ Save ⊞ your document.

Activity 2.21 | Using the Thesaurus

A ***thesaurus*** is a research tool that lists ***synonyms***—words that have the same or similar meaning to the word you selected.

1 ▶ Scroll so that you can view the body of the letter. In the paragraph that begins *With a permanent*, at the end of the second line, double-click to select the word *diversity*, and then in the **Proofing** group, click **Thesaurus**.

The Thesaurus pane displays on the right a list of synonyms; the list will vary in length depending on the selected word.

⟳ ANOTHER WAY   Right-click the word, on the shortcut menu, point to Synonyms, and then click Thesaurus.

2 ▶ In the **Thesaurus** pane, point to the word *variety*, and then click the arrow that displays. Click **Insert** to change *diversity* to *variety*.

3 ▶ In the paragraph that begins *As my resume*, double-click the word *exceptional*, and then on the ribbon, click **Thesaurus** again.

4 ▶ In the **Thesaurus** pane, point to *excellent*, click the **arrow**, and then click **Insert**. Compare your screen with Figure 2.35.

FIGURE 2.35

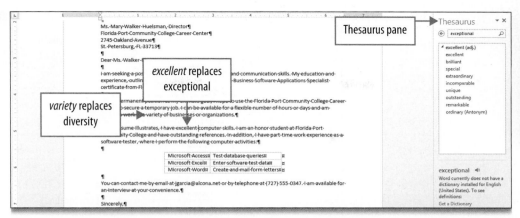

excellent replaces **exceptional**

variety replaces **diversity**

Thesaurus pane

Thesaurus

exceptional

excellent (adj.)
  excellent
  brilliant
  special
  extraordinary
  incomparable
  unique
  outstanding
  remarkable
  ordinary (Antonym)

exceptional
Word currently does not have a dictionary installed for English (United States). To see definitions:
Get a Dictionary

5 Close ☒ the **Thesaurus** pane.

6 Click the **FILE tab** to display **Backstage** view, and then on the **Info tab**, in the lower right portion of the screen, click **Show All Properties**. If you used your template, notice that it is indicated to the right of *Template*.

7 In the **Tags** box, type **cover letter** and in the **Subject** box, type your course name and section number. In the **Author** box, be sure your name is indicated and edit if necessary.

8 On the left, click **Print** to display **Print Preview**. If necessary, return to the document and make any necessary changes.

9 As directed by your instructor, print your document or submit it electronically. **Save** 🔲 your document and **Close** ☒ Word.

Activity 2.22 | Addressing and Printing an Envelope

Use Word's Envelopes command on the Mailings label to format and print an envelope.

> ### N O T E   This Is an Optional Activity
>
> This activity is optional. If you do not have an envelope and printer, or do not want to complete the activity at this time, move to Activity 2.23.

1 Display your **2B_Cover_Letter**, and then select the four lines that comprise the inside address.

2 On the **MAILINGS tab**, in the **Create group**, click **Envelopes**. Notice that the **Delivery address** contains the selected inside address.

3 Click in the **Return address** box, and then type **Jennifer Garcia** and press Enter. Type **1776 Bay Cliff Drive** and then press Enter. Type **Tampa, FL 33602**

4 In the lower portion of the **Envelopes and Labels** dialog box, click **Options**, and then compare your screen with Figure 2.36.

The default envelope size is a standard business envelope referred to as a Size 10.

FIGURE 2.36

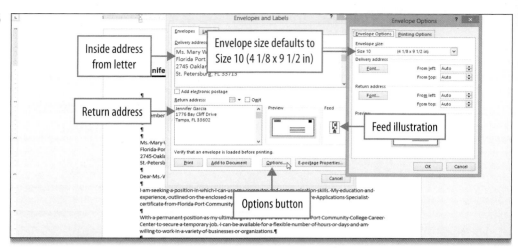

5 Click **OK** to close the **Envelope Options** dialog box. As shown under **Feed**, insert an envelope in your printer and then click **Print**.

Depending on the type and brand of printer you are using, your feed area may vary.

6 Close your **2B_Cover_Letter**, and then **Close** Word.

Objective 7 | Create a Document Using a Predesigned Microsoft Template

Video W2-7

Microsoft provides predesigned templates for letters, calendars, invoices, and other types of documents. Recall that when you open a template, it opens unnamed so that you can reuse it as often as you need to do so.

Activity 2.23 | Locating and Opening a Template

In this activity, you will use a predesigned template to create a list of references to accompany a resume. References are not included on a resume, because you want to use the resume space for personal information. Most employers do not check references until after the first interview and when they have decided to consider you for a position. Be sure that you have already notified these individuals, asked their permission to use their name as a reference, and then contact them to tell them that a specific employer may be contacting them.

1 **Start** Word, and then on the opening screen, in the **Search for online templates** box, type **resume references** and press Enter.

2 Locate the reference list that contains three left-aligned reference items as shown in Figure 2.37.

FIGURE 2.37

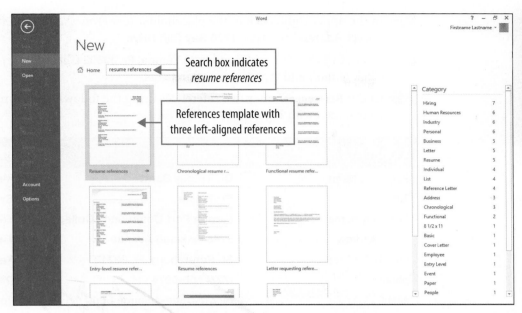

3 Click the three-item reference template, and then click **Create**. Compare your screen with Figure 2.38.

> The template opens a copy of itself in the form of a new Word document—the title bar indicates *Document* followed by a number. Recall that you are not opening the template itself, and that changes you make to this new document will not affect the contents of the template file.

FIGURE 2.38

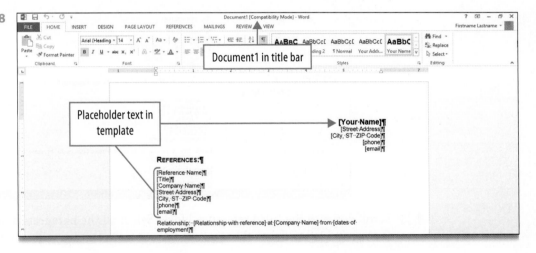

4 Press F12 to display the **Save As** dialog box. **Save** the document in your **Word Chapter 2** folder as **Lastname_Firstname_2B_Reference_List** and click **Save**. If a message indicates that you will be upgraded to the newest file format, click **OK**.

5 Add the file name to the footer, and then **Save** 🖫 your document.

Activity 2.24 | Replacing Template Placeholder Text and Removing Controls

After you save the template file as a Word document, you can begin to substitute your own information in the indicated locations. ***Placeholder text*** is text that indicates the type of information to be entered. Text surrounded by brackets is called a ***content control***. There are several different types of content controls, including date, picture, and ***text controls***. All of the controls in this template are text controls.

1 In the upper right, click in the placeholder text *[Your Name]* and type **Jennifer Garcia** Click *[Street Address]* and type **1776 Bay Cliff Drive**

2 Click *[City, ST ZIP Code]* and type **Tampa, FL 33602** Click *[phone]* and type **(727) 555-0347** Click *[email]* and type **jgarcia@alcona.net**

3 Under **References**, enter two references using the following information, and then compare your screen with Figure 2.39.

TEMPLATE FIELD	REFERENCE 1	REFERENCE 2
Reference Name	**Dr. Tracey Scott**	**Mr. James Johnson**
Title	**Professor**	**Systems Manager**
Company Name	**Florida Port Community College**	**Tampa Tech Group**
Street Address	**2745 Oakland Avenue**	**Two Tech Plaza**
City, ST ZIP Code	**St. Petersburg, FL 33713**	**Tampa, FL 33602**
phone	**(727) 555-0974**	**(727) 555-0144**
email	**tscott@fpcc-science.edu**	**jjohnson@tech-pro.net**
Relationship with reference	**Professor**	**Supervisor**
Company Name	**Florida Port Community College**	**Tampa Tech Group**
dates of employment	**July 2012 to July 2013**	**July 2013 to present**

FIGURE 2.39

4 Scroll down to the third reference block. Select all the paragraphs of placeholder text, and then press [Del] to delete these unneeded controls; this list will contain only two references.

ANOTHER WAY   Point to a content control, right-click, and then on the shortcut menu, click Remove Content Control.

5 Click **Save** [icon]. Click the **FILE tab**, and then in the lower right portion of the screen, click **Show All Properties**. In the **Tags** box, type **reference list** and in the **Subject** box, type your course name and section number. In the **Author** box, be sure your name is indicated and edit if necessary.

6 On the left, click **Print** to display **Print Preview**. If necessary, return to the document and make any necessary changes.

7 As directed by your instructor, print your document or submit it electronically. **Save** [icon] your document and **Close** [X] Word.

END | You have completed Project 2B

Objective | Create a Table in Word Web App

You can create and edit tables in the Word Web App if you are not at a computer on which Word 2013 is installed.

ALERT! **Working with Web-Based Applications and Services**

Computer programs and services on the web receive continuous updates and improvements, so the steps to complete this web-based activity may differ from the ones shown. You can often look at the screens and the information presented to determine how to complete the activity.

Activity | Creating a Table in Word Web App

In this activity, you will use the Word Web App to create a Word table within a document similar to Project 2B.

1 From the desktop, start Internet Explorer. Navigate to **http://skydrive.com** and then sign in to your Microsoft account. Open your **GO! Web Projects** folder—or create and then open this folder if necessary.

2 On the SkyDrive menu bar, click **Upload**. In the **Choose File to Upload** dialog box, navigate to your student data files, click **w02_2B_Web**, and then click **Open**.

3 Point to the uploaded file **w02_2B_Web**, and then right-click. On the shortcut menu, scroll down as necessary and then click **Rename**. Using your own last name and first name, type **Lastname_Firstname_WD_2B_Web** and then press Enter to rename the file.

4 Click the file that you just renamed, and then in the upper left, click **EDIT DOCUMENT**. On the list, click **Edit in Word Web App**.

5 Press Ctrl + End to move to the end of the document, and then press Enter.

6 On the **INSERT tab**, in the **Tables group**, click **Table**, and then insert a **3 × 4 Table**.

7 Type **Position** and press Tab. Type **Type** and press Tab. Type **Location** and press Tab.

8 In the second row type **Paralegal** and press Tab. Type **Part-time** and press Tab. Type **Tampa** and press Tab. Compare your screen with Figure A.

FIGURE A

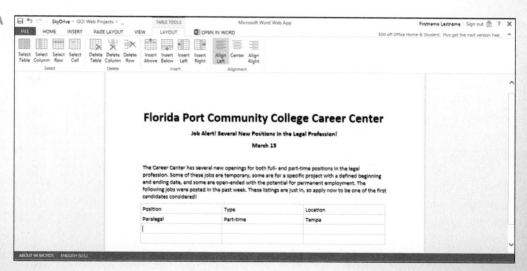

(GO! with Office Web Apps continues on the next page)

9 Type **Legal Records Clerk** and press Tab. Type **Full-time, 2 months** and press Tab. Type **North Tampa** and press Tab.

10 On the ribbon, under **TABLE TOOLS**, click the **LAYOUT tab**, and then in the **Delete group**, click **Delete Row**.

11 Drag to select all the cells in the first row, and then on the **HOME tab**, in the **Styles group**, click **Heading 1**.

With the three column titles still selected, in the **Paragraph group**, click **Center**. In the **Font group**, change the **Font Color** to **Black, Text 1**. Compare your screen with Figure B.

12 Above the **FILE tab**, click **Save**. Click the **FILE tab**, and then click **Exit**. Submit the file as directed by your instructor. In the upper right, click your user name, and then click **Sign out**. **Close** Internet Explorer.

FIGURE B

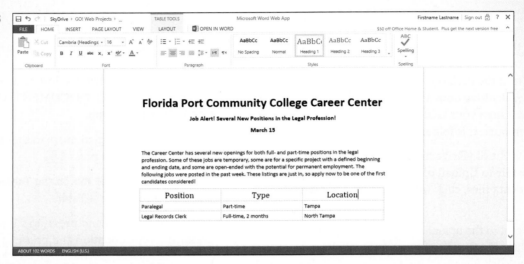

Office 365 combines tools for collaboration and productivity and delivers them to multiple users in an organization by using *cloud computing*—applications and services that are accessed over the Internet with multiple devices. For example, one cloud service with which you might be familiar is *SkyDrive*, a free web-based application with which you can save, store, organize, and share files online. This cloud service is available for anyone that has a free Microsoft account.

Another cloud service from Microsoft is *Office Web Apps*. These are the online companions to the desktop versions of Microsoft Office Word, Excel, PowerPoint, and OneNote that enable you to create, access, share, and perform light editing on Microsoft Office documents from any device that connects to the Internet and uses a supported *web browser*. A web browser is software, such as Internet Explorer, Firefox, Safari, or Chrome, that displays web pages.

For an organization, cloud computing enables the addition of services without investing in additional hardware and software. For you as a team member, you can simply use your web browser to access, edit, store, and share files. You do not need to have a full version of Office installed on your computer to do this. You have all the tools and security that large organizations have!

When you use using Office 365, your email and storage servers are hosted by Microsoft. Your organization gets business-class security from Microsoft—a large, well-established company. Sophisticated security and data management features are built into Office 365 so that you can control *permissions*—access rights that define the ability of an individual or group to view or make changes to documents—and provide secure email and communications.

Activity | Using Lync to Collaborate by Using a Video Call

This group project relates to the **Bell Orchid Hotels**. If your instructor assigns this project to your class, you can expect to use **Lync** in **Office 365** to collaborate on the following tasks for this chapter:

- If you are in the **Accounting Group**, you and your teammates will conduct a video call to discuss and agree on the letter that will be sent to shareholders.

- If you are in the **Engineering Group**, you and your teammates will conduct a video call to discuss and agree on the letter that will be sent to the three insurance companies that cover the hotel properties.

- If you are in the **Food and Beverage Group**, you and your teammates will conduct a video call to discuss and agree on the letter that will be sent to a customer planning a banquet.

- If you are in the **Human Resources Group**, you and your teammates will conduct a video call to discuss and agree on the memo for employees regarding the new employee newsletter.

- If you are in the **Operations Group**, you and your teammates will conduct a video call to discuss and agree on the letter that will be sent to three job applicants.

- If you are in the **Sales and Marking Group**, you and your teammates will conduct a video call to discuss and agree on the letter that will be sent to 20 groups of professional associations.

FIGURE A

END OF CHAPTER

SUMMARY

Word tables enable you to present information in a logical and orderly format. Each cell in a Word table behaves like a document; as you type in a cell, wordwrap moves text to the next line.

A good source of information for resume formats is a business communications textbook. A simple two-column table created in Word is suitable to create an appropriate resume for a recent college graduate.

Use Word's Office Presentation Service to present a Word document to others who can watch in a web browser. Word automatically creates a link to your document that you can share with others via email.

A template is useful because it has a predefined document structure and defined settings such as font, margins, and available styles. On Word's opening screen, you can select from thousands of templates.

GO! LEARN IT ONLINE

Review the concepts and key terms in this chapter by completing these online challenges, which you can find at **www.pearsonhighered.com/go**.

Matching and Multiple Choice: Answer matching and multiple choice questions to test what you learned in this chapter. MyITLab®

Crossword Puzzle: Spell out the words that match the numbered clues, and put them in the puzzle squares.

Flipboard: Flip through the definitions of the key terms in this chapter and match them with the correct term.

GO! FOR JOB SUCCESS

Video: Cover Letter and Resume Tips

Your instructor may assign this video to your class, and then ask you to think about, or discuss with your classmates, these questions:

FotolEdhar / Fotolia

A cover letter should contain different but complimentary information than the facts on your resume and be tailored to the specific job you are applying for. Name two different things that you could mention in a cover letter.

What type of information belongs in the Career Objective portion of your resume?

When is it best to use a chronological resume layout, and when is it appropriate to use a functional resume layout?

END OF CHAPTER

REVIEW AND ASSESSMENT GUIDE FOR WORD CHAPTER 2

Your instructor may assign one or more of these projects to help you review the chapter and assess your mastery and understanding of the chapter.

		Review and Assessment Guide for Word Chapter 2		
Project	**Apply Skills from These Chapter Objectives**	**Project Type**		**Project Location**
2C	Objectives 1-3 from Project 2A	**2C Skills Review** A guided review of the skills from Project 2A.		On the following pages
2D	Objectives 4-7 from Project 2B	**2D Skills Review** A guided review of the skills from Project 2B.		On the following pages
2E	Objectives 1-3 from Project 2A	**2E Mastery (Grader Project)** A demonstration of your mastery of the skills in Project 2A with extensive decision making.		In MyITLab and on the following pages
2F	Objectives 4-7 from Project 2B	**2F Mastery (Grader Project)** A demonstration of your mastery of the skills in Project 2B with extensive decision making.		In MyITLab and on the following pages
2G	Objectives 1-7 from Projects 2A and 2B	**2G Mastery (Grader Project)** A demonstration of your mastery of the skills in Projects 2A and 2B with extensive decision making.		In MyITLab and on the following pages
2H	Combination of Objectives from Projects 2A and 2B	**2H GO! Fix It** A demonstration of your mastery of the skills in Projects 2A and 2B by creating a correct result from a document that contains errors you must find.		Online
2I	Combination of Objectives from Projects 2A and 2B	**2I GO! Make It** A demonstration of your mastery of the skills in Projects 2A and 2B by creating a result from a supplied picture.		Online
2J	Combination of Objectives from Projects 2A and 2B	**2J GO! Solve It** A demonstration of your mastery of the skills in Projects 2A and 2B, your decision-making skills, and your critical thinking skills. A task-specific rubric helps you self-assess your result.		Online
2K	Combination of Objectives from Projects 2A and 2B	**2K GO! Solve It** A demonstration of your mastery of the skills in Projects 2A and 2B, your decision-making skills, and your critical thinking skills. A task-specific rubric helps you self-assess your result.		On the following pages
2L	Combination of Objectives from Projects 2A and 2B	**2L GO! Think** A demonstration of your understanding of the chapter concepts applied in a manner that you would outside of college. An analytic rubric helps you and your instructor grade the quality of your work by comparing it to the work an expert in the discipline would create.		On the following pages
2M	Combination of Objectives from Projects 2A and 2B	**2M GO! Think** A demonstration of your understanding of the chapter concepts applied in a manner that you would outside of college. An analytic rubric helps you and your instructor grade the quality of your work by comparing it to the work an expert in the discipline would create.		Online
2N	Combination of Objectives from Projects 2A and 2B	**2N You and GO!** A demonstration of your understanding of the chapter concepts applied in a manner that you would in a personal situation. An analytic rubric helps you and your instructor grade the quality of your work.		Online
2O	Combination of Objectives from Projects 2A and 2B	**2O Cumulative Group Project for Word Chapter 2** A demonstration of your understanding of concepts and your ability to work collaboratively in a group role-playing assessment, requiring both collaboration and self-management.		Online

GLOSSARY

GLOSSARY OF CHAPTER KEY TERMS

AutoCorrect A feature that corrects common typing and spelling errors as you type, for example changing *teh* to *the*.

Body The text of a letter.

Cell The box at the intersection of a row and column in a Word table.

Cloud computing Applications and services that are accessed over the Internet with multiple devices.

Complimentary closing A parting farewell in a business letter.

Content control In a template, an area indicated by placeholder text that can be used to add text, pictures, dates, or lists.

Cover letter A document that you send with your resume to provide additional information about your skills and experience.

Date & Time A command with which you can automatically insert the current date and time into a document in a variety of formats.

Dateline The first line in a business letter that contains the current date and which is positioned just below the letterhead if a letterhead is used.

Drag-and-drop A technique by which you can move, by dragging, selected text from one location in a document to another.

Enclosures Additional documents included with a business letter.

Inside address The name and address of the person receiving the letter and positioned below the date line.

Letterhead The personal or company information that displays at the top of a letter.

No Paragraph Style The built-in paragraph style—available from the Paragraph Spacing command—that inserts *no* extra space before or after a paragraph and uses line spacing of 1.

Normal template The template that serves as a basis for all Word documents.

Office Presentation Service A Word feature to present your Word document to others who can watch in a web browser.

One-click Row/Column Insertion A Word table feature with which you can insert a new row or column by pointing to the desired location and then clicking.

Placeholder text The text in a content control that indicates the type of information to be entered in a specific location.

Salutation The greeting line of a business letter.

Single spacing The common name for line spacing in which there is *no* extra space before or after a paragraph and that uses line spacing of 1.

Skype A Microsoft product with which you can make voice calls, make video calls, transfer files, or send messages—including instant message and text messages—over the Internet.

Subject line The optional line following the inside address in a business letter that states the purpose of the letter.

Synonyms Words with the same or similar meaning.

Table An arrangement of information organized into rows and columns.

Template An existing document that you use as a starting point for a new document; it opens a copy of itself, unnamed, and then you use the structure—and possibly some content, such as headings—as the starting point for a new document.

Text control A content control that accepts only a text entry.

Thesaurus A research tool that provides a list of synonyms.

Writer's identification The name and title of the author of a letter, placed near the bottom of the letter under the complimentary closing—also referred to as the *writer's signature block*.

Writer's signature block The name and title of the author of a letter, placed near the bottom of the letter, under the complimentary closing—also referred to as the *writer's identification*.

CHAPTER REVIEW

Skills Review Project 2C Student Resume

Apply **2A** skills from these
Objectives:

1 Create a Table

2 Format a Table

3 Present a Word Document
  Online

In the following Skills Review, you will use a table to create a resume for Ashley Kent. Your completed resume will look similar to the one shown in Figure 2.40.

PROJECT FILES

Build from Scratch

For Project 2C, you will need the following files:

New blank Word document

w02C_Skills

w02C_Experience

You will save your document as:

Lastname_Firstname_2C_Student_Resume

PROJECT RESULTS

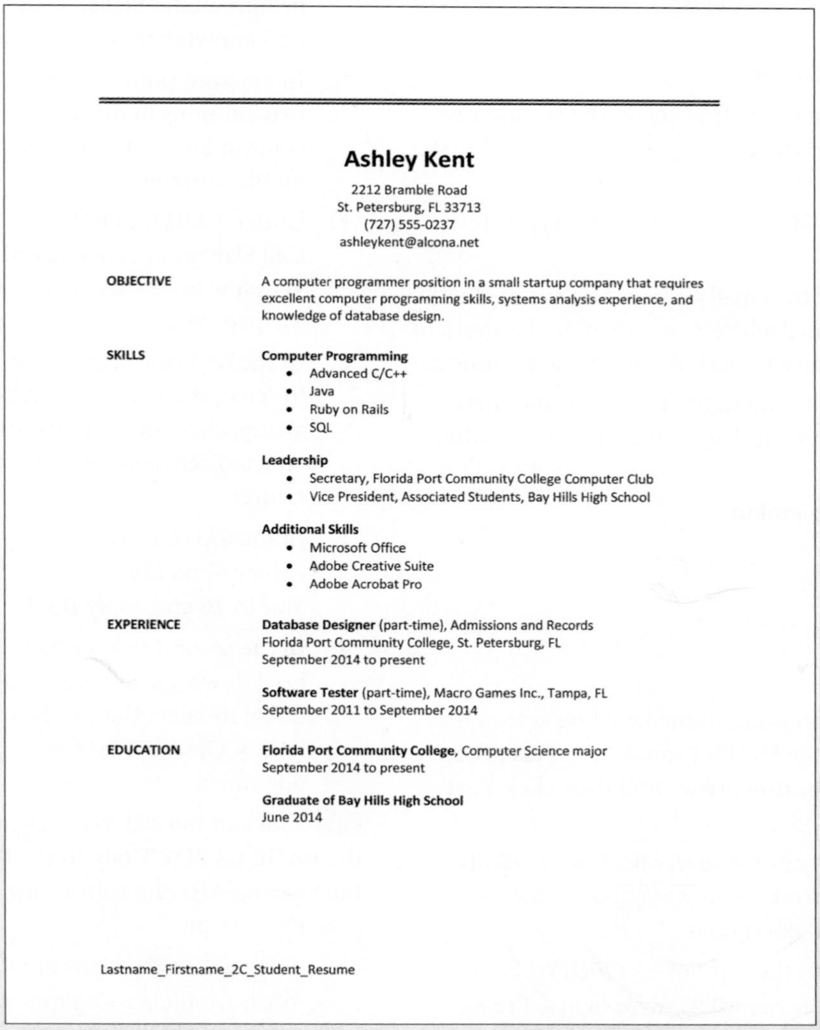

Ashley Kent

2212 Bramble Road
St. Petersburg, FL 33713
(727) 555-0237
ashleykent@alcona.net

OBJECTIVE	A computer programmer position in a small startup company that requires excellent computer programming skills, systems analysis experience, and knowledge of database design.
SKILLS	**Computer Programming** • Advanced C/C++ • Java • Ruby on Rails • SQL **Leadership** • Secretary, Florida Port Community College Computer Club • Vice President, Associated Students, Bay Hills High School **Additional Skills** • Microsoft Office • Adobe Creative Suite • Adobe Acrobat Pro
EXPERIENCE	**Database Designer** (part-time), Admissions and Records Florida Port Community College, St. Petersburg, FL September 2014 to present **Software Tester** (part-time), Macro Games Inc., Tampa, FL September 2011 to September 2014
EDUCATION	**Florida Port Community College,** Computer Science major September 2014 to present **Graduate of Bay Hills High School** June 2014

Lastname_Firstname_2C_Student_Resume

FIGURE 2.40

(Project 2C Student Resume continues on the next page)

CHAPTER REVIEW

1 **Start** Word and display a blank document. Be sure that formatting marks and rulers display. **Save** the document in your **Word Chapter 2** folder as **Lastname_Firstname_2C_Student_Resume**

a. Add the file name to the footer, and then close the footer area. Click the **INSERT tab**, and then in the **Tables group**, click **Table**. In the **Table** grid, in the fourth row, click the second square to insert a **2 × 4** table.

b. In the first cell of the table, type **Ashley Kent** and then press Enter. Type the following text, pressing Enter after each line *except* the last line:

   2212 Bramble Road

   St. Petersburg, FL 33713

   (727) 555-0237

   ashleykent@alcona.net

c. Press ↓ to move to the first cell in the second row. Type **SKILLS** and then press ↓ to move to the first cell in the third row.

d. Type **EXPERIENCE** and then press ↓. Type **EDUCATION**

e. In the first cell, if the email address displays in blue, right-click the email address, and then on the shortcut menu, click **Remove Hyperlink**. **Save** your document.

2 Click in the cell to the right of *SKILLS*, and then type the following, pressing Enter after each line including the last line:

   Computer Programming

   Advanced C/C++

   Java

   Ruby on Rails

   SQL

a. With the insertion point in the new line at the end of the cell, click the **INSERT tab**. In the **Text group**, click the **Object button arrow**, and then click **Text from File**.

b. Navigate to your student files, select **w02C_Skills**, and then click **Insert**. Press Backspace one time to remove the blank paragraph.

c. Click in the cell to the right of *EXPERIENCE*, and then insert the file **w02C_Experience**. Press Backspace one time to remove the blank line.

d. Click in the cell to the right of *EDUCATION*, and then type the following, pressing Enter after all lines *except* the last line:

   Florida Port Community College, Computer Science major

   September 2014 to present

   Graduate of Bay Hills High School

   June 2014

3 Point to the upper left corner of the *SKILLS* cell, and then click the **Row Insertion** button. In the first cell of the new row, type **OBJECTIVE** and then press Tab.

a. Type **A computer programmer position in a small startup company that requires excellent computer programming skills, systems analysis experience, and knowledge of database design.**

b. In any row, point to the vertical border between the two columns to display the ✛ pointer. Drag the column border to the left to approximately **1.5 inches on the horizontal ruler**.

c. Under **TABLE TOOLS**, on the **LAYOUT tab**, in the **Cell Size group**, click **AutoFit**, and then click **AutoFit Window** to be sure that your table stretches across the page within the margins.

d. In the first row of the table, drag across both cells to select them. On the **LAYOUT tab**, in the **Merge group**, click **Merge Cells**. Right-click over the selected cell, and then on the mini toolbar, click **Center**.

e. In the top row, select the first paragraph of text— *Ashley Kent*. On the mini toolbar, increase the **Font Size** to **20** and apply **Bold**.

f. In the second row, point to the word *OBJECTIVE*, hold down the left mouse button, and then drag down to select the row headings in uppercase letters. On the mini toolbar, click **Bold**. **Save** your document.

4 Click in the cell to the right of *OBJECTIVE*. On the **PAGE LAYOUT tab**, in the **Paragraph group**, click the **Spacing After up spin arrow** three times to change the spacing to **18 pt**.

a. In the cell to the right of *SKILLS*, apply **Bold** to the words *Computer Programming*, *Leadership*, and *Additional Skills*. Then, under each bold heading in

(Project 2C Student Resume continues on the next page)

CHAPTER REVIEW

the cell, select the lines of text, and create a bulleted list.

b. In the first two bulleted lists, click in the last bullet item, and then on the **PAGE LAYOUT tab**, in the **Paragraph group**, set the **Spacing After** to **12 pt**.

c. In the last bulleted list, click in the last bullet item, and then set the **Spacing After** to **18 pt**.

d. In the cell to the right of *EXPERIENCE*, apply **Bold** to *Database Designer* and *Software Tester*. Click in the line *September 2014 to present* and apply **Spacing After** of **12 pt**. Click in the line *September 2011 to September 2014* and apply **Spacing After** of **18 pt**.

e. In the cell to the right of *EDUCATION*, apply **Bold** to *Florida Port Community College* and *Graduate of Bay Hills High School*.

f. In the same cell, click in the line *September 2014 to present* and apply **Spacing After** of **12 pt**.

g. In the first row, click in the last line—*ashleykent@ alcona.net*—and then change the **Spacing After** to **18 pt**. Click in the first line—*Ashley Kent*—and set the **Spacing Before** to **30 pt** and the **Spacing After** to **6 pt**.

5 ▶ Point to the upper left corner of the table, and then click the **table move handle** ⊞ to select the entire table. Under **TABLE TOOLS**, on the **DESIGN tab**, in the **Table Styles group**, click the **Borders button arrow**, and then click **No Border**.

a. In the **Table Styles group**, click the **Borders button arrow** again, and then at the bottom of the gallery, click **Borders and Shading**. In the **Borders and Shading** dialog box, under **Setting**, click **Custom**. Under **Style**, scroll down slightly, and then click the style with two equal lines.

b. Click the **Width arrow**, and then click **1 1/2 pt**. Under **Preview**, click the top border of the preview box, and then click **OK**.

c. Click the **FILE tab** to display **Backstage** view, and then in the lower right portion of the screen, click **Show All Properties**. In the **Tags** box, type **resume, table** and in the **Subject** box, type your course name and section number. In the **Author** box, be sure your name is indicated and edit if necessary.

d. On the left, click **Print** to display **Print Preview**. If necessary, return to the document and make any necessary changes.

e. **Save** 🖫 your document, and then if you want to do so, present your document online to a fellow classmate. Then as directed by your instructor, print your document or submit it electronically. **Close** Word.

END | You have completed Project 2C

CHAPTER REVIEW

Apply 2B skills from these Objectives:

4 Create a Custom Word Template

5 Correct and Reorganize Text

6 Use the Proofing Options and Print an Envelope

7 Create a Document Using a Predesigned Microsoft Template

Skills Review Project 2D Cover Letter and Reference List

In the following Skills Review, you will create a letterhead, save the letterhead as a custom Word template, and then use the letterhead to create a cover letter to accompany a resume. You will also create a list of references from a Microsoft predesigned template and, if you have an envelope and printer available, format and print an envelope. Your completed documents will look similar to Figure 2.41.

PROJECT FILES

For Project 2D, you will need the following files:

Build from Scratch

New blank Word document
w02D_Cover_Letter_Text

You will save your documents as:

Lastname_Firstname_2D_Cover_Letter
Lastname_Firstname_2D_Reference_List

PROJECT RESULTS

Sarah Villmosky
7279 Rambling Brook Way, St. Petersburg, FL 33713
(727) 555-0117 svillmosky@alcona.net

October 20, 2016

Ms. Mary Walker-Huelsman, Director
Florida Port Community College Career Center
2745 Oakland Avenue
St. Petersburg, FL 33713

Dear Ms. Walker-Huelsman:

I am seeking the assistance of the Career Center in my job search.

Having recently graduated from Florida Port Community College with an Associate of Arts in Media Studies, I am interested in working for a newspaper, a magazine, or a publishing company.

I have previous work experience in the publishing industry as a writer and section editor for the local activities section of the St. Petersburg News and Times. I have the following skills that I developed while working at the St. Petersburg News and Times. I believe these skills would be a good fit with a local or national newspaper or publication:

Editorial experience:	Writing, editing, interviewing
Computer proficiency:	CS In Design, QuarkXPress, Microsoft Publisher
Education focus:	Media Studies and Journalism

I am willing to consider temporary positions that might lead to a permanent position. Please contact me at sarahvillmosky@alcona.net or by phone at (727) 555-0117. I am available immediately for an interview or for further training at the Career Center that you think would be beneficial in my job search.

Sincerely,

Sarah Villmosky

Enclosure

Lastname_Firstname_2D_Cover_Letter

Sarah Villmosky
7279 Rambling Brook Way
St. Petersburg, FL 33713
(727) 555-0177
svillmosky@alcona.net

REFERENCES:

Dr. Thomas Robins
Professor
Florida Port Community College
2745 Oakland Avenue
St. Petersburg, FL 33713
(727) 555-0902
trobins@fpcc-english.edu

Relationship: Professor at Florida Port Community College from July 2012 to July 2013

Ms. Janice Nguyen
Editor
St. Petersburg News and Times
One Gateway Center
St. Petersburg, FL 33713
(727) 555-0932
jnguyen@spnt-editorial.net

Relationship: Editor at St. Petersburg News and Times from July 2013 to present

Lastname_Firstname_2D_Reference_List

FIGURE 2.41

(Project 2D Cover Letter and Reference List continues on the next page)

CHAPTER REVIEW

1 **Start** Word and display a blank document; be sure that formatting marks and rulers display. On the **DESIGN tab**, in the **Document Formatting group**, click **Paragraph Spacing**, and then click **No Paragraph Space**.

a. Type **Sarah Villmosky** and then press Enter. Type **7279 Rambling Brook Way, St. Petersburg, FL 33713** and then press Enter.

b. Type **(727) 555-0117 svillmosky@alcona.net** and then press Enter. If the web address changes to blue text, right-click the web address, and then click **Remove Hyperlink.**

c. Select the first paragraph—*Sarah Villmosky*—and then on the mini toolbar, apply **Bold**, and change the **Font Size** to **16**.

d. Select the second and third paragraphs, and then on the mini toolbar, apply **Bold**, and change the **Font Size** to **12**.

e. Click anywhere in the first paragraph—*Sarah Villmosky*. On the **HOME tab**, in the **Paragraph group**, click the **Borders button arrow**, and then click **Borders and Shading**. Under **Style**, click the first style—a single solid line. Click the **Width arrow**, and then click **3 pt**. In the **Preview** area, click the bottom border, and then click **OK**.

f. Press F12 to display the **Save As** dialog box. In the lower portion of the dialog box, in the **Save as type** box, click the arrow, and then click **Word Template**. In the **File name** box, type **Lastname_Firstname_2D_Letterhead_Template** and then click **Save** to save the custom Word template in the default path, which is the Templates folder on the hard drive of your computer.

g. Click the **FILE tab** to display **Backstage** view, and then click **Close** to close the file but leave Word open.

h. With Word open but no documents displayed, click the **FILE tab**, and then click **New**. Under **Suggested searches**, click **PERSONAL**, and then locate and click the letterhead template that you just created.

i. Press F12 to display the **Save As** dialog box, navigate to your **Word Chapter 2** folder, and then **Save** the file as **Lastname_Firstname_2D_Cover_Letter**

j. On the **INSERT tab**, in the **Header & Footer group**, click **Footer**, click **Edit Footer**, and then in the **Insert**

group, click **Document Info**. Click **File Name**, and then click **Close Header and Footer**. Click **Save**.

2 Click the **FILE tab**. On the left, click **Options**. On the left side of the **Word Options** dialog box, click **Proofing**, and then under **AutoCorrect options**, click the **AutoCorrect Options** button.

a. In the **AutoCorrect** dialog box, click the **AutoCorrect tab**. Under **Replace**, type the misspelled word **assistence** and under **With**, type **assistance** Click **Add**. If the entry already exists, click **Replace instead**, and then click **Yes**. Click **OK** two times to close the dialog boxes.

b. Press Ctrl + End, and then press Enter three times. On the **INSERT tab**, in the **Text group**, click **Date & Time**, and then click the third date format. Click **OK**.

c. Press Enter four times. Type the following inside address using four lines, but do *not* press Enter after the last line:

Ms. Mary Walker-Huelsman, Director

Florida Port Community College Career Center

2745 Oakland Avenue

St. Petersburg, FL 33713

d. Press Enter two times, type **Dear Ms. Walker-Huelsman:** and then press Enter two times. Type, exactly as shown with the intentional misspelling, and then watch *assistence* as you press Spacebar: **I am seeking the assistence**

e. Type **of the Career Center in my job search.** Press Enter two times.

f. On the **INSERT tab**, in the **Text Group**, click the **Object button arrow**, and then click **Text from File**. From your student files, locate and insert the file **w02D_Cover_Letter_Text**.

g. Scroll to view the lower portion of the page, and be sure your insertion point is in the empty paragraph mark at the end. Press Enter, type **Sincerely,** and then press Enter four times. Type **Sarah Villmosky** and press Enter two times. Type **Enclosure** and then **Save** your document.

h. Press Ctrl + Home. On the **HOME tab**, in the **Editing group**, click **Find**. In the **navigation** pane, click in the search box, and then type **journalism** In the letter,

(Project 2D Cover Letter and Reference List continues on the next page)

CHAPTER REVIEW

Skills Review   Project 2D Cover Letter and Reference List (continued)

double-click the yellow highlighted word *Journalism* and type **Media Studies**

i. **Close** the **navigation** pane, and then on the **HOME tab**, in the **Editing group**, click **Replace**. In the **Find and Replace** dialog box, in the **Find what** box, replace the existing text by typing **SPNT** In the **Replace with** box, type **St. Petersburg News and Times** Click **More** to expand the dialog box, select the **Match case** check box, click **Replace All**, and then click **OK**. **Close** the **Find and Replace** dialog box.

j. In the paragraph that begins *I am available*, hold down Ctrl, and then click anywhere in the first sentence. Drag the selected sentence to the end of the paragraph by positioning the small vertical line that floats with the point to the left of the paragraph mark.

3 Below the paragraph that begins *I have previous*, click to position the insertion point in the blank paragraph, and then press Enter one time. On the **INSERT tab**, in the **Tables group**, click **Table**. In the **Table grid**, in the third row, click the second square to insert a 2 × 3 table. Type the following information in the table:

Editorial experience:	Writing, editing, interviewing
Computer proficiency:	CS In Design, QuarkXPress, Microsoft Publisher
Education focus:	Media Studies and Journalism

a. Point outside of the upper left corner of the table and click the **table move handle** button to select the entire table. On the **LAYOUT tab**, in the **Cell Size group**, click **AutoFit**, and then click **AutoFit Contents**.

b. With the table selected, on the **DESIGN tab**, in the **Table Styles group**, click **More** ⬇. Under **Plain Tables**, click the second style—**Table Grid Light**.

c. With the table still selected, on the **HOME tab**, in the **Paragraphs group**, click **Center**. **Save** your document.

4 Press Ctrl + Home. On the **REVIEW tab**, in the **Proofing group**, click **Spelling & Grammar**. For the spelling of *Villmosky*, in the **Spelling** pane, click **Ignore All**. For the spelling of *Huelsman*, click **Ignore All**.

a. For the grammar error *a*, click **Change**. Click **Change** to correct the misspelling of *intrested*. Click **Delete** to delete the duplicated word *for*. Change *activitys* to *activities*. Change *benificial* to *beneficial*. Click **OK** when the Spelling & Grammar check is complete.

b. In the paragraph that begins *I am willing*, in the third line, double-click the word *preparation*. In the **Proofing group**, click **Thesaurus**.

c. In the **Thesaurus** pane, point to *training*, click the arrow, and then click **Insert**. **Close** the **Thesaurus** pane.

d. Click **FILE tab**, and then in the lower right portion of the screen, click **Show All Properties**. In the **Tags** box, type **cover letter** and in the **Subject** box, type your course name and section number.

e. In the **Author** box, be sure your name is indicated and edit if necessary. On the left, click **Print**. If necessary, return to the document and make any necessary changes. **Save** your document, and then **Close** Word.

5 **Start** Word, and then on the opening screen, in the **Search online templates** box, type **resume references** and press Enter. Click the reference list that contains three left-aligned reference items, and then click **Create**.

a. Press F12 to display the **Save As** dialog box. **Save** the document in your **Word Chapter 2** folder as **Lastname_Firstname_2D_Reference_List** A message may indicate that the file will be upgraded to the newest file format.

b. Add the file name to the footer.

c. In the upper right, click in the placeholder text *[Your Name]* and type **Sarah Villmosky** Click *[Street Address]* and type **7279 Rambling Brook Way**

d. Click *[City, ST ZIP Code]* and type **St. Petersburg, FL 33713** Click *[phone]* and type **(727) 555-0177** Click *[email]* and type **svillmosky@alcona.net**

(Project 2D Cover Letter and Reference List continues on the next page)

CHAPTER REVIEW

6 Under **References**, enter two references using the information in Table 1:

a. Delete the remaining template controls.

b. Click the **FILE tab**, click **Show All Properties**, and then in the **Tags** box, type **reference list** and in the **Subject** box type your course name and section number. In the **Author** box, be sure your name is indicated and edit if necessary.

c. On the left, click **Print**. If necessary, return to the document and make any changes. Click **Save**. As directed by your instructor, print or submit electronically the two documents that are the results of this project. **Close** Word.

TABLE 1

Template Field	Reference 1	Reference 2
Reference Name	**Dr. Thomas Robins**	**Ms. Janice Nguyen**
Title	**Professor**	**Editor**
Company Name	**Florida Port Community College**	**St. Petersburg News and Times**
Street Address	**2745 Oakland Avenue**	**One Gateway Center**
City, ST ZIP Code	**St. Petersburg, FL 33713**	**St. Petersburg, FL 33713**
phone	**(727) 555-0902**	**(727) 555-0932**
email	**trobins@fpcc-english.edu**	**jnguyen@spnt-editorial.net**
Relationship with reference	**Professor**	**Editor**
Company Name	**Florida Port Community College**	**St. Petersburg News and Times**
dates of employment	**July 2012 to July 2013**	**July 2013 to present**

END | You have completed Project 2D

----▶ (Return to Step 6a)

CONTENT-BASED ASSESSMENTS

MyITLab® grader

Mastering Word | Project 2E Table of Job Listings

Apply 2A skills from these Objectives:

1. Create a Table
2. Format a Table
3. Present a Word Document Online

In the following Mastering Word project, you will create an announcement for new job postings at the Career Center. Your completed document will look similar to Figure 2.42.

PROJECT FILES

For Project 2E, you will need the following files:

New blank Word document
w02E_New_Jobs

Build from Scratch

You will save your document as:

Lastname_Firstname_2E_Job_Listings

PROJECT RESULTS

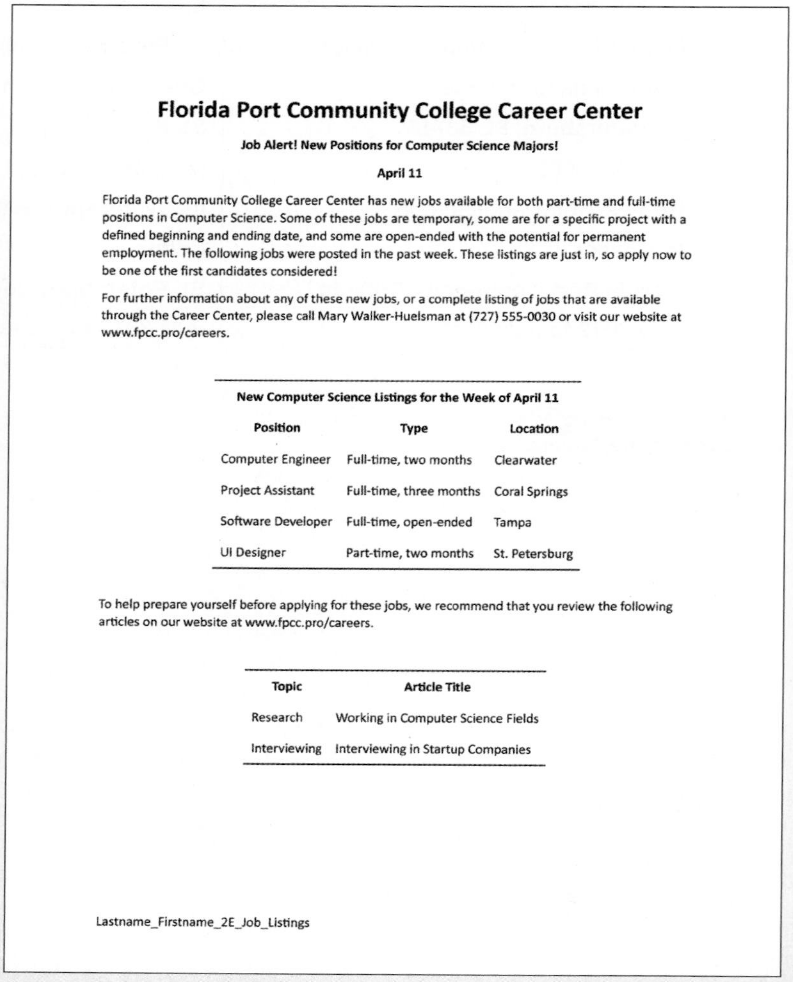

Florida Port Community College Career Center

Job Alert! New Positions for Computer Science Majors!

April 11

Florida Port Community College Career Center has new jobs available for both part-time and full-time positions in Computer Science. Some of these jobs are temporary, some are for a specific project with a defined beginning and ending date, and some are open-ended with the potential for permanent employment. The following jobs were posted in the past week. These listings are just in, so apply now to be one of the first candidates considered!

For further information about any of these new jobs, or a complete listing of jobs that are available through the Career Center, please call Mary Walker-Huelsman at (727) 555-0030 or visit our website at www.fpcc.pro/careers.

New Computer Science Listings for the Week of April 11

Position	Type	Location
Computer Engineer	Full-time, two months	Clearwater
Project Assistant	Full-time, three months	Coral Springs
Software Developer	Full-time, open-ended	Tampa
UI Designer	Part-time, two months	St. Petersburg

To help prepare yourself before applying for these jobs, we recommend that you review the following articles on our website at www.fpcc.pro/careers.

Topic	Article Title
Research	Working in Computer Science Fields
Interviewing	Interviewing in Startup Companies

Lastname_Firstname_2E_Job_Listings

FIGURE 2.42

(Project 2E Table of Job Listings continues on the next page)

CONTENT-BASED ASSESSMENTS

1 **Start** Word and display a blank document; display formatting marks and rulers. **Save** the document in your **Word Chapter 2** folder as **Lastname_Firstname_2E_Job_Listings** and then add the file name to the footer.

2 Type **Florida Port Community College Career Center** and press Enter. Type **Job Alert! New Positions for Computer Science Majors!** and press Enter. Type **April 11** and press Enter. **Insert** the file **w02E_New_Jobs**.

3 At the top of the document, select and **Center** the three title lines. Select the title *Florida Port Community College Career Center*, change the **Font Size** to **20 pt** and apply **Bold**. Apply **Bold** to the second and third title lines. Locate the paragraph that begins *For further*, and then below that paragraph, position the insertion point in the second blank paragraph. **Insert** a **3 × 4** table. Enter the following in the table:

Position	Type	Location
Computer Engineer	Full-time, two months	Clearwater
Software Developer	Full-time, open-ended	Tampa
UI Designer	Part-time, two months	St. Petersburg

4 In the table, point to upper left corner of the cell *Software Developer* to display the **Row Insertion** button, and then click to insert a new row. In the new row, type the following information so that the job titles remain in alphabetic order:

Project Assistant	Full-time, three months	Coral Springs

5 Select the entire table. On the **LAYOUT tab**, in the **Cell Size group**, click **AutoFit**, and then click **AutoFit Contents**. With the table still selected, on the **HOME tab**, **Center** the table. With the table still selected, on the **PAGE LAYOUT tab**, add **6 pt Spacing Before** and **6 pt Spacing After**.

6 With the table still selected, remove all table borders, and then add a **Custom 1 pt** solid line top border and bottom border. Select all three cells in the first row, apply **Bold**, and then **Center** the text. Click anywhere in the first row, and then on the **LAYOUT tab**, in the **Rows & Columns group**, insert a row above. Merge the three cells in the new top row, and then type **New Computer Science Listings for the Week of April 11** Notice that the new row keeps the formatting of the row from which it was created.

7 At the bottom of the document, **Insert** a **2 × 3** table. Enter the following:

Topic	Article Title
Research	Working in Computer Science Fields
Interviewing	Interviewing in Startup Companies

8 Select the entire table. On the **LAYOUT tab**, in the **Cell Size group**, use the **AutoFit** button to **AutoFit Contents**. On the **HOME tab**, **Center** the table. On the **PAGE LAYOUT tab**, add **6 pt Spacing Before** and **6 pt Spacing After**. With the table still selected, remove all table borders, and then add a **Custom 1 pt** solid line top border and bottom border. Select the cells in the first row, apply **Bold**, and then **Center** the text.

9 Click the **FILE tab** to display **Backstage** view, and then in the lower right portion of the screen, click **Show All Properties**. In the **Tags** box, type **new listings, computer science** and in the **Subject** box, type your course name and section number. In the **Author** box, be sure your name is indicated and edit if necessary.

10 On the left, click **Print** to display **Print Preview**. If necessary, return to the document and make any necessary changes. **Save** your document, and then if you want to do so, present your document online to a fellow classmate. Then as directed by your instructor, print your document or submit it electronically. **Close** Word.

END | You have completed Project 2E

CONTENT-BASED ASSESSMENTS

Apply 2B skills from these Objectives:

4 Create a Custom Word Template

5 Correct and Reorganize Text

6 Use the Proofing Options and Print an Envelope

7 Create a Document Using a Predesigned Microsoft Template

In the following Mastering Word project, you will create a memo and fax cover sheet that includes job tips for students and graduates using the services of the Florida Port Community College Career Center. Your completed documents will look similar to Figure 2.43.

PROJECT FILES

For Project 2F, you will need the following files:

w02F_Memo_Template
w02F_Memo_Text
Equity Fax template from Microsoft's installed templates

You will save your documents as:

Lastname_Firstname_2F_Career_Tips
Lastname_Firstname_2F_Fax

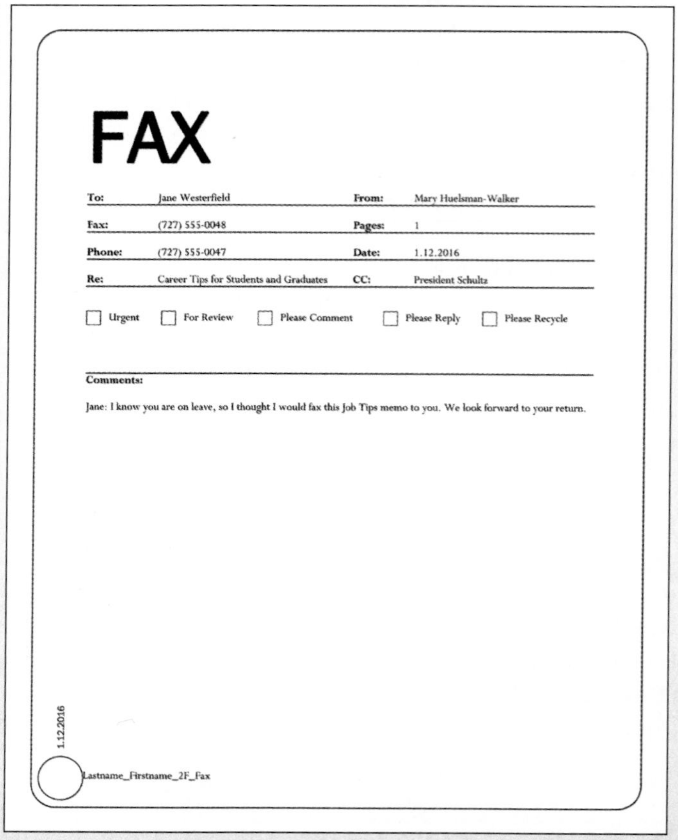

PROJECT RESULTS

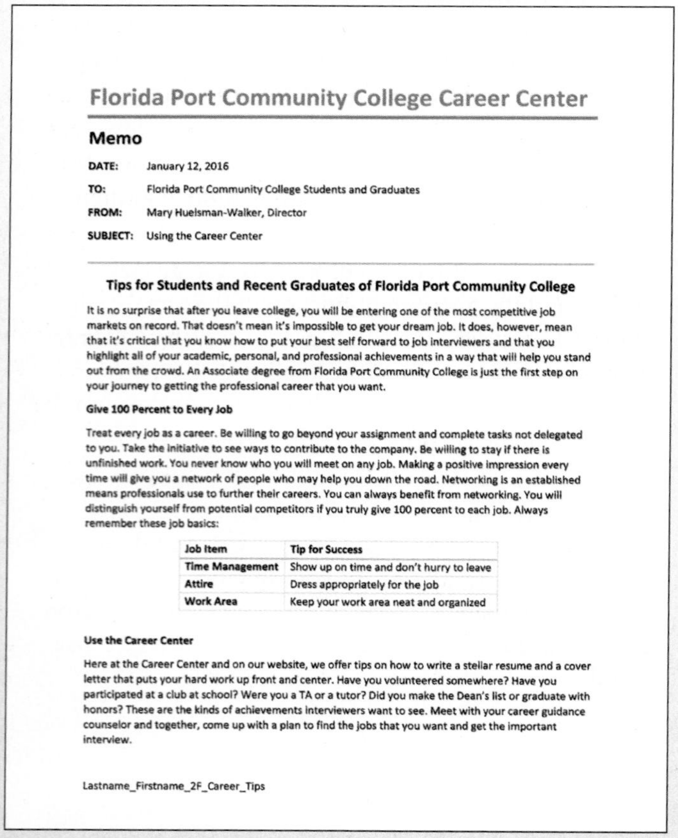

FIGURE 2.43

(Project 2F Career Tips Memo and Fax Cover Sheet continues on the next page)

CONTENT-BASED ASSESSMENTS

1 Be sure that Word is *closed*. On the taskbar, click **File Explorer**. Navigate to your student files and open **w02F_Memo_Template**. Notice that *Document1* displays in the title bar. (Recall that custom templates stored in a location other than the Templates folder on your hard drive must be opened directly from File Explorer in order for you to create and open a new document based on the template.)

2 Press F12. Navigate to your **Word Chapter 2** folder, and then in the **File name** box, using your own name, type **Lastname_Firstname_2F_Career_Tips**

3 Add the file name to the footer. At the top of your document, in the *DATE* paragraph, click to the right of the tab formatting mark, and then type **January 12, 2016** Use a similar technique to add the following information:

TO:	Florida Port Community College Students and Graduates
FROM:	Mary Huelsman-Walker, Director
SUBJECT:	Using the CC

4 Position the insertion point in the blank paragraph below the memo heading. **Insert** the file **w02F_Memo_Text**, and then press Backspace one time to remove the blank line at the end of the inserted text.

5 Select and **Center** the title *Tips for Students and Recent Graduates of Florida Port Community College*. By using either the **Spelling & Grammar** command on the **REVIEW** tab or by right-clicking words that display blue or red wavy underlines, correct or ignore words flagged as spelling, grammar, or word usage errors. Note: If you are checking an entire document, it is usually preferable to move to the top of the document, and then use the **Spelling & Grammar** command so that you do not overlook any flagged words.

6 In the paragraph that begins *Treat every job*, in the second line of the paragraph, locate and double-click *donate*. On the **REVIEW tab**, in the **Proofing group**, click **Thesaurus**, and then from the **Thesaurus** pane, change the word to *contribute*. In the last line of the same paragraph, point to *fundamentals*, right-click, point to **Synonyms**, and then click *basics*.

7 Using Match Case, replace all instances of *CC* with *Career Center*, and then in the paragraph that begins *An Associate degree*, move the first sentence to the end of the paragraph.

8 At the end of the paragraph that begins *Treat every job*, create a blank paragraph. **Insert** a 2 × 4 table, and then type the following information:

Job Item	Tip for Success
Time Management	Show up on time and don't hurry to leave
Attire	Dress appropriately for the job
Work Area	Keep your work area neat and organized

9 Select the entire table. **AutoFit Contents**, and then apply the **Grid Table 1 Light – Accent 1** table style—under **Grid Tables**, in the first row, the second style. **Center** the table.

10 Click the **FILE tab**, and then click **Show All Properties**. As the **Tags**, type **memo, job tips** and as the **Subject**, type your course name and section number. Be sure your name is indicated as the **Author**, and edit if necessary. **Save** and **Close** the document but leave Word open. Hold this file until you complete this project.

11 With Word open but no documents displayed, click the **FILE tab**, and then click **New**. In the **Search for online templates** box, type **fax (equity)** and press Enter, and then click the first **Fax (Equity theme)** template. Click **Create**. Press F12. Save the document in your **Word Chapter 2** folder, using your own name, as **Lastname_Firstname_2F_Fax** and then insert the file name in the footer. You may see a message indicating that the file will be upgraded to the newest format.

12 Use the following information to type in each control:

To:	Jane Westerfield
From:	Mary Huelsman-Walker
Fax:	(727) 555-0048
Pages:	1
Phone:	(727) 555-0047
Date:	1/12/2016
Re:	Career Tips for Students and Graduates
CC:	President Schultz
COMMENTS:	Jane: I know you are on leave, so I thought I would fax this Job Tips memo to you. We look forward to your return.

(Project 2F Career Tips Memo and Fax Cover Sheet continues on the next page)

CONTENT-BASED ASSESSMENTS

13 Click the **FILE tab**, and then click **Show All Properties**. As the **Tags**, type **memo, job tips** and as the **Subject**, type your course name and section number. The author will indicate *Mary Huelsman-Walker*. **Save** and **Close** the document. As directed by your instructor, print or submit electronically the two files that are the results of this project. **Close** Word.

END | You have completed Project 2F

CONTENT-BASED ASSESSMENTS

Mastering Word Project 2G Application Letter, Resume, and Fax Cover Sheet

In the following Mastering Word project, you will create a letter from a custom template, a resume, and a fax cover sheet from a Microsoft predesigned template. Your completed documents will look similar to Figure 2.44.

Apply 2A and 2B skills from these Objectives:

1 Create a Table
2 Format a Table
3 Present a Word Document Online
4 Create a Custom Word Template
5 Correct and Reorganize Text
6 Use the Proofing Options and Print an Envelope
7 Create a Document Using a Predesigned Microsoft Template

PROJECT FILES

For Project 2G, you will need the following files:

w02G_Letter_Text
w02G_Letterhead_Template
w02G_Resume
Equity Fax template from Microsoft's installed templates

You will save your documents as:

Lastname_Firstname_2G_Letter
Lastname_Firstname_2G_Resume
Lastname_Firstname_2G_Fax

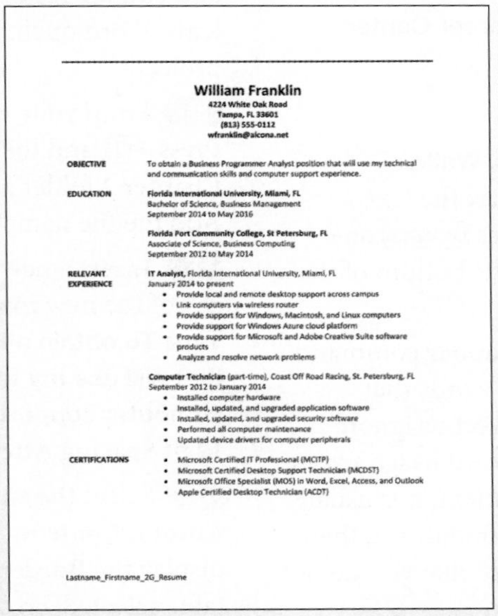

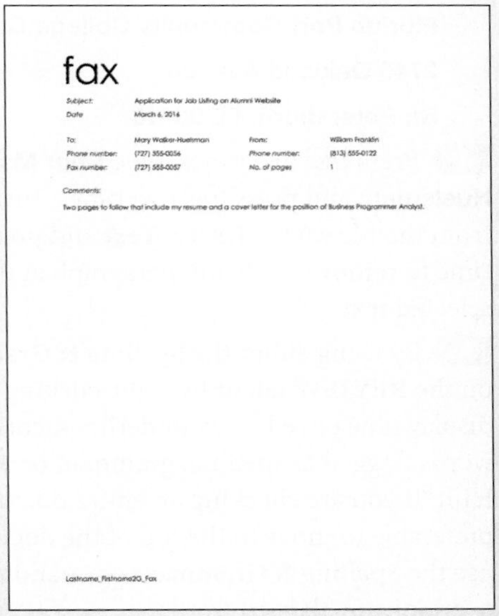

PROJECT RESULTS

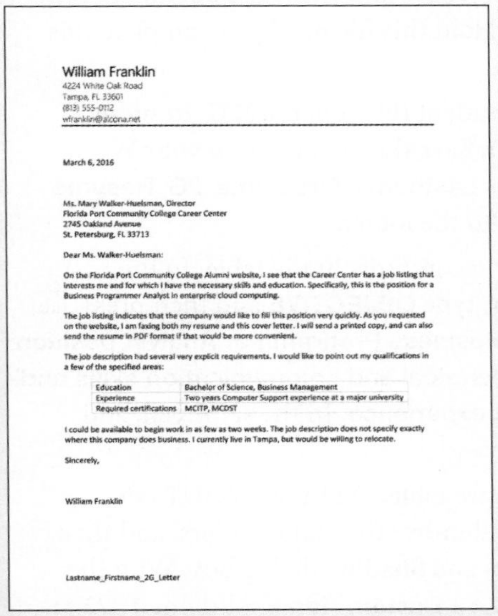

FIGURE 2.44

(Project 2G Application Letter, Resume, and Fax Cover Sheet continues on the next page)

CONTENT-BASED ASSESSMENTS

1 Be sure that Word is *closed*. On the taskbar, click **File Explorer**. Navigate to your student files and open **w02G_Letterhead_Template**. Notice that *Document1* displays in the title bar. (Recall that custom templates stored in a location other than the Templates folder on your hard drive must be opened directly from File Explorer in order for you to create and open a new document based on the template.)

2 Press [F12]. Navigate to your **Word Chapter 2** folder, and then in the **File name** box, using your own name, type **Lastname_Firstname_2G_Letter**

3 Add the file name to the footer. Be sure that rulers and formatting marks display. Move to the end of the document, and then press [Enter] three times. Use the **Date & Time** command to insert the current date using the third format, and then press [Enter] four times. Type the following:

> **Ms. Mary Walker-Huelsman, Director**
>
> **Florida Port Community College Career Center**
>
> **2745 Oakland Avenue**
>
> **St. Petersburg, FL 33713**

4 Press [Enter] two times, type **Dear Ms. Walker-Huelsman:** and press [Enter] two times. **Insert** the text from the file **w02G_Letter_Text** and press [Backspace] one time to remove the blank paragraph at the bottom of the selected text.

5 By using either the **Spelling & Grammar** command on the **REVIEW tab** or by right-clicking words that display blue or red wavy underlines, correct or ignore words flagged as spelling, grammar, or word usage errors. Hint: If you are checking an entire document, it is usually preferable to move to the top of the document, and then use the **Spelling & Grammar** command so that you do not overlook any flagged words.

6 Replace all instances of **posting** with **listing**. In the paragraph that begins *The job description*, use the **Thesaurus** pane or the **Synonyms** command on the shortcut menu to change *specific* to *explicit* and *credentials* to *qualifications*.

7 In the paragraph that begins *I currently live in Tampa*, select the first sentence of the paragraph and drag it to the end of the same paragraph. Click in the blank paragraph below the paragraph that begins *The job*

description, and then press [Enter] one time. **Insert a 2 × 3** table, and then type the text shown in Table 1.

TABLE 1

Education	Bachelor of Science, Business Management
Experience	Two years Computer Support experience at a major university
Required Certifications	MCITP, MCDST

8 Select the entire table. **AutoFit Contents**, and then apply the **Table Grid Light** table style—under **Plain Tables**, in the first row, the first style. **Center** the table.

9 Click the **FILE tab**, and then click **Show All Properties**. As the **Tags**, type **letter, alumni website** and as the **Subject**, type your course name and section number. Be sure your name is indicated as the **Author**, and edit if necessary. **Save** and **Close** the document but leave Word open. Hold this file until you complete this project.

10 From your student files, open **w02G_Resume**. Press [F12], and then **Save** the document in your **Word Chapter 2** folder as **Lastname_Firstname_2G_Resume** Add the file name to the footer.

11 Insert a new second row in the table. In the first cell of the new row, type **OBJECTIVE** and then press [Tab]. Type **To obtain a Business Programmer Analyst position that will use my technical and communication skills and computer support experience.** In the same cell, add **12 pt Spacing After**.

12 Select the entire table. On the **LAYOUT tab**, **AutoFit Contents**. Remove the table borders, and then display the **Borders and Shading** dialog box. With the table selected, create a **Custom** single solid line **1 1/2 pt** top border.

13 In the first row of the table, select both cells and then **Merge Cells**. **Center** the five lines and apply **Bold**. In the first row, select *William Franklin* and change the **Font Size** to **20 pt** and add **24 pt Spacing Before**. In the email address at the bottom of the first row, add **24 pt Spacing After**.

14 In the first column, apply **Bold** to the four headings. In the cell to the right of *EDUCATION*, apply **Bold** to the

(Project 2G Application Letter, Resume, and Fax Cover Sheet continues on the next page)

CONTENT-BASED ASSESSMENTS

name and address of the two colleges. Add **12 pt Spacing After** to the two lines that begin *September*. In the cell to the right of *RELEVANT EXPERIENCE*, apply **Bold** to the names of the two jobs—*IT Analyst* and *Computer Technician*. In the same cell, below the line that begins *January 2014*, apply bullets to the six lines that comprise the job duties. Create a similar bulleted list for the duties as a Computer Technician. Add **12 pt Spacing After** to the last line of each of the bulleted lists.

15 In the cell to the right of *CERTIFICATIONS*, select all four lines and create a bulleted list. Click the **FILE tab**, and then click **Show All Properties**. As the **Tags**, type **resume, business programmer analyst** and as the **Subject**, type your course name and section number. Be sure your name is indicated as the **Author**, and edit if necessary. **Save** and **Close** the document but leave Word open. Hold this file until you complete this project.

16 In Word's templates, search for **personal fax** and then select the second (shorter) template named **Fax cover sheet (informal)**. Click **Create**. **Save** the document in your **Word Chapter 2** folder as **Lastname_Firstname_2G_Fax** and then add the file name to the footer.

17 Type the text shown in Table 2 for the content controls.

TABLE 2

Subject:	**Application for Job Listing on Alumni Website**
Date:	**March 6, 2016**
To:	**Mary Walker-Huelsman**
From:	**William Franklin**
Phone number:	**(727) 555-0056**
Phone number:	**(813) 555-0122**
Fax number:	**(727) 555-0057**
No. of Pages	1
Comments:	**Two pages to follow that include my resume and a cover letter for the position of Business Programmer Analyst.**

18 Click the **FILE tab**, and then click **Show All Properties**. As the **Tags**, type **fax cover page** and as the **Subject**, type your course name and section number. Be sure your name is indicated as the **Author**, and edit if necessary. Click **Save**. As directed by your instructor, print or submit electronically the three files that are the results of this project. **Close** Word.

END | You have completed Project 2G

CONTENT-BASED ASSESSMENTS

Apply a combination of the 2A and 2B skills.

Build from Scratch

Build from Scratch

Build from Scratch

GO! Fix It   Project 2H New Jobs   **Online**

GO! Make It   Project 2I Training   **Online**

GO! Solve It   Project 2J Job Postings   **Online**

GO! Solve It   Project 2K Agenda

PROJECT FILES

For Project 2K, you will need the following file:

Agenda template from Word's Online templates

You will save your document as:

Lastname_Firstname_2K_Agenda

On Word's opening screen, search for an online template using the search term **formal meeting agenda**. Create the agenda and then save it in your Word Chapter 2 folder as **Lastname_Firstname_2K_Agenda** Use the following information to prepare an agenda for an FPCC Career Center meeting.

The meeting will be chaired by Mary Walker-Huelsman. It will be the monthly meeting of the Career Center's staff—Kevin Rau, Marilyn Kelly, André Randolph, Susan Nguyen, and Charles James. The meeting will be held on March 15, 2016, at 3:00 p.m. The old business agenda items (open issues) include (1) seeking more job listings related to the printing and food service industries, (2) expanding the alumni website, and (3) the addition of a part-time trainer. The new business agenda items will include (1) writing a grant so the center can serve more students and alumni, (2) expanding the training area with 20 additional workstations, (3) purchase of new computers for the training room, and (4) renewal of printing service contract.

Add the file name to the footer, add your name, your course name, the section number, and then add the keywords **agenda, monthly staff meeting** to the Properties area. Submit as directed.

Performance Level

Performance Criteria	Exemplary: You consistently applied the relevant skills	Proficient: You sometimes, but not always, applied the relevant skills	Developing: You rarely or never applied the relevant skills
Select an agenda template	Agenda template is appropriate for the information provided for the meeting.	Agenda template is used, but does not fit the information provided.	No template is used for the agenda.
Add appropriate information to the template	All information is inserted in the appropriate places.	All information is included, but not in the appropriate places.	Information is missing.
Format template information	All text in the template is properly aligned and formatted.	All text is included, but alignment or formatting is inconsistent.	No additional formatting has been added.

END | You have completed Project 2K

OUTCOMES-BASED ASSESSMENTS

RUBRIC

The following outcomes-based assessments are *open-ended assessments*. That is, there is no specific correct result; your result will depend on your approach to the information provided. Make *Professional Quality* your goal. Use the following scoring rubric to guide you in *how* to approach the problem and then to evaluate *how well* your approach solves the problem.

The *criteria*—Software Mastery, Content, Format and Layout, and Process—represent the knowledge and skills you have gained that you can apply to solving the problem. The *levels of performance*—Professional Quality, Approaching Professional Quality, or Needs Quality Improvements—help you and your instructor evaluate your result.

	Your completed project is of Professional Quality if you:	Your completed project is Approaching Professional Quality if you:	Your completed project Needs Quality Improvements if you:
1-Software Mastery	Choose and apply the most appropriate skills, tools, and features and identify efficient methods to solve the problem.	Choose and apply some appropriate skills, tools, and features, but not in the most efficient manner.	Choose inappropriate skills, tools, or features, or are inefficient in solving the problem.
2-Content	Construct a solution that is clear and well organized, contains content that is accurate, appropriate to the audience and purpose, and is complete. Provide a solution that contains no errors in spelling, grammar, or style.	Construct a solution in which some components are unclear, poorly organized, inconsistent, or incomplete. Misjudge the needs of the audience. Have some errors in spelling, grammar, or style, but the errors do not detract from comprehension.	Construct a solution that is unclear, incomplete, or poorly organized; contains some inaccurate or inappropriate content; and contains many errors in spelling, grammar, or style. Do not solve the problem.
3-Format & Layout	Format and arrange all elements to communicate information and ideas, clarify function, illustrate relationships, and indicate relative importance.	Apply appropriate format and layout features to some elements, but not others. Overuse features, causing minor distraction.	Apply format and layout that does not communicate information or ideas clearly. Do not use format and layout features to clarify function, illustrate relationships, or indicate relative importance. Use available features excessively, causing distraction.
4-Process	Use an organized approach that integrates planning, development, self-assessment, revision, and reflection.	Demonstrate an organized approach in some areas, but not others; or, use an insufficient process of organization throughout.	Do not use an organized approach to solve the problem.

OUTCOMES-BASED ASSESSMENTS

Build from
Scratch

GO! Think Project 2L Workshops

PROJECT FILES

For Project 2L, you will need the following files:

New blank Word document
w02L_Workshop_Information

You will save your document as:

Lastname_Firstname_2L_Workshops

The Florida Port Community College Career Center offers a series of workshops for both students and alumni. Any eligible student or graduate can attend the workshops, and there is no fee. Currently, the Career Center offers a three-session workshop covering Excel and Word, a two-session workshop covering Business Communication, and a one-session workshop covering Creating a Resume.

Print the w02L_Workshop_Information file and use the information to complete this project. Create an announcement with a title, an introductory paragraph, and a table listing the workshops and the topics covered in each workshop. Use the file w02L_Workshop_Information for help with the topics covered in each workshop. Format the table cells appropriately. Add an appropriate footer and document properties. Save the document as **Lastname_Firstname_2L_Workshops** and submit it as directed.

END | You have completed Project 2L

Build from
Scratch

GO! Think! Project 2M Planner **Online**

Build from
Scratch

You and GO! Project 2N Personal Resume **Online**

Build from
Scratch

GO! Cumulative Group Project Project 2O Bell Orchid Hotels **Online**

Creating Research Papers, Newsletters, and Merged Mailing Labels

GO! to Work
Video W3

3

WORD 2013

PROJECT 3A

OUTCOMES
Create a research paper that includes citations and a bibliography.

OBJECTIVES
1. Create a Research Paper
2. Insert Footnotes in a Research Paper
3. Create Citations and a Bibliography in a Research Paper
4. Use Read Mode and PDF Reflow

PROJECT 3B

OUTCOMES
Create a multiple-column newsletter and merged mailing labels.

OBJECTIVES
5. Format a Multiple-Column Newsletter
6. Use Special Character and Paragraph Formatting
7. Create Mailing Labels Using Mail Merge

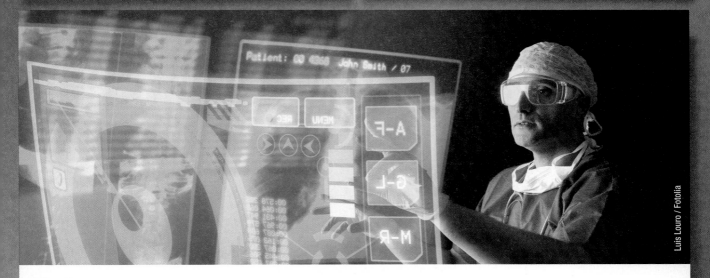

Luis Louro / Fotolia

In This Chapter

Microsoft Word provides many tools for creating complex documents. For example, Word has tools that enable you to create a research paper that includes citations, footnotes, and a bibliography. You can also create multiple-column newsletters, format the nameplate at the top of the newsletter, use special character formatting to create distinctive title text, and add borders and shading to paragraphs to highlight important information.

In this chapter, you will edit and format a research paper, create a two-column newsletter, and then create a set of mailing labels to mail the newsletter to multiple recipients.

The projects in this chapter relate to **University Medical Center**, which is a patient-care and research institution serving the metropolitan area of Memphis, Tennessee. Because of its outstanding reputation in the medical community and around the world, University Medical Center is able to attract top physicians, scientists, and researchers in all fields of medicine and achieve a level of funding that allows it to build and operate state-of-the-art facilities. A program in biomedical research was recently added. Individuals throughout the eastern United States travel to University Medical Center for diagnosis and care.

PROJECT ACTIVITIES

In Activities 3.01 through 3.14, you will edit and format a research paper that contains an overview of a new area of study. This paper was created by Gerard Foster, a medical intern at University Medical Center, for distribution to his classmates studying various physiologic monitoring devices. Your completed document will look similar to Figure 3.1.

PROJECT FILES

For Project 3A, you will need the following file:

w03A_Quantitative_Technology

You will save your document as:

Lastname_Firstname_3A_Quantitative_Technology

PROJECT RESULTS

FIGURE 3.1 Project 3A Research Paper

Objective 1 Create a Research Paper

Video W3-1

When you write a research paper or a report for college or business, follow a format prescribed by one of the standard *style guides*—a manual that contains standards for the design and writing of documents. The two most commonly used styles for research papers are those created by the *Modern Language Association (MLA)* and the *American Psychological Association (APA)*; there are several others.

NOTE | **If You Are Using a Touchscreen**

- Tap an item to click it.
- Press and hold for a few seconds to right-click; release when the information or commands displays.
- Touch the screen with two or more fingers and then pinch together to zoom in or stretch your fingers apart to zoom out.
- Slide your finger on the screen to scroll—slide left to scroll right and slide right to scroll left.
- Slide to rearrange—similar to dragging with a mouse.
- Swipe from edge: from right to display charms; from left to expose open apps, snap apps, or close apps; from top or bottom to show commands or close an app.
- Swipe to select—slide an item a short distance with a quick movement—to select an item and bring up commands, if any.

Activity 3.01 | Formatting the Spacing and First-Page Information for a Research Paper

When formatting the text for your research paper, refer to the standards for the style guide that you have chosen. In this activity, you will create a research paper using the MLA style. The MLA style uses 1-inch margins, a 0.5" first line indent, and double spacing throughout the body of the document with no extra space above or below paragraphs.

1 Start Word. From your student files, locate and **Open** the document **w03A_Quantitative_Technology**. If necessary, display the formatting marks and rulers. In the location where you are storing your projects for this chapter, create a new folder named **Word Chapter 3** and then **Save** the file in the folder as **Lastname_Firstname_3A_Quantitative_Technology**

2 Press Ctrl + A to select the entire document. On the **HOME tab**, in the **Paragraph group**, click **Line and Paragraph Spacing**, and then change the line spacing to **2.0**. On the **PAGE LAYOUT tab**, in the **Paragraph group**, change the **Spacing After** to **0 pt**.

3 Press Ctrl + Home to deselect and move to the top of the document. Press Enter one time to create a blank line at the top of the document, and then click to position the insertion point in the blank line. Type **Gerard Foster** and press Enter.

4 Type **Dr. Hillary Kim** and press Enter. Type **Biomedical Research 617** and press Enter. Type **February 15, 2016** and press Enter.

5 Type **Quantified Self Movement Gains Momentum** and then press Ctrl + E, which is the keyboard shortcut to center a paragraph of text. Click **Save**, and then compare your screen with Figure 3.2.

More Knowledge | **Creating a Document Heading for a Research Paper**

On the first page of an MLA-style research paper, on the first line, type the report author. On the second line, type the person for whom the report is prepared—for example, your professor or supervisor. On the third line, type the name of the class or business. On the fourth line, type the date. On the fifth line, type the report title and center it.

FIGURE 3.2

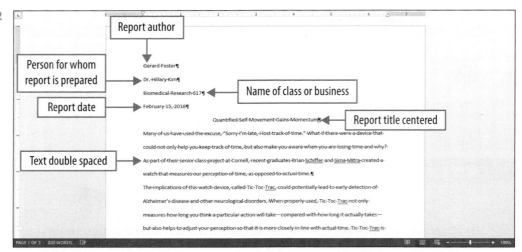

More Knowledge **Creating a Bookmark**

In a document, you can mark a place you want to find again easily. Select the content to which you want to assign the bookmark. On the INSERT tab, in the Links group, click Bookmark, and assign a name. To go to the bookmark, press CTRL + G, select Bookmark, and then click the bookmark name.

Activity 3.02 | **Formatting the Page Numbering and Paragraph Indents for a Research Paper**

1 On the **INSERT tab**, in the **Header & Footer group**, click **Header**, and then at the bottom of the list, click **Edit Header**.

2 Type **Foster** and then press Spacebar.

Recall that the text you insert into a header or footer displays on every page of a document. Within a header or footer, you can insert many different types of information; for example, automatic page numbers, the date, the time, the file name, or pictures.

3 Under **HEADER & FOOTER TOOLS**, on the **DESIGN tab**, in the **Header & Footer group**, click **Page Number**, and then point to **Current Position**. In the gallery, under **Simple**, click **Plain Number**. Compare your screen with Figure 3.3.

Word will automatically number the pages using this number format.

FIGURE 3.3

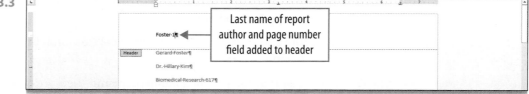

4 On the **HOME tab**, in the **Paragraph group**, click **Align Right** ≡. Double-click anywhere in the document to close the Header area.

5 Near the top of **Page 1**, locate the paragraph beginning *Many of us*, and then click to position the insertion point at the beginning of the paragraph. By moving the vertical scroll bar, scroll to the end of the document, hold down Shift, and then click to right of the last paragraph mark to select all of the text from the insertion point to the end of the document. Release Shift.

6 With the text selected, in the **Paragraph group**, click the **Dialog Box Launcher** button to display the **Paragraph** dialog box.

7 On the **INDENTS and SPACING tab**, under **Indentation**, click the **Special arrow**, and then click **First line**. In the **By** box, be sure **0.5"** displays. Click **OK**. Compare your screen with Figure 3.4.

The MLA style uses 0.5-inch indents at the beginning of the first line of every paragraph. *Indenting*—moving the beginning of the first line of a paragraph to the right or left of the rest of the paragraph—provides visual cues to the reader to help divide the document text and make it easier to read.

FIGURE 3.4

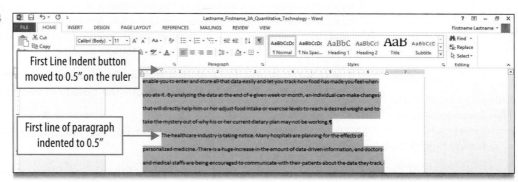

First Line Indent button moved to 0.5" on the ruler

First line of paragraph indented to 0.5"

ANOTHER WAY On the ruler, point to the First Line Indent button, and then drag the button to 0.5" on the horizontal ruler.

8 Press Ctrl + Home to deselect and move to the top of the document. On the **INSERT tab**, in the Header & Footer group, click **Footer**, and then at the bottom of the list click **Edit Footer**.

9 In the **Insert group**, click **Document Info**, and then click **File Name**. On the ribbon, click **Close Header and Footer**.

The file name in the footer is *not* part of the research report format, but it is included in projects in this textbook so that you and your instructor can identify your work.

10 Save your document.

More **Knowledge** | **Suppressing the Page Number on the First Page of a Document**

Some style guidelines require that the page number and other header and footer information on the first page be hidden from view—*suppressed*. To hide the information contained in the header and footer areas on Page 1 of a document, double-click in the header or footer area. Then, under HEADER & FOOTER TOOLS, on the DESIGN tab, in the Options group, select the Different First Page check box.

Objective 2 | Insert Footnotes in a Research Paper

Video W3-2

Reports and research papers typically include information that you find in other sources, and these must be credited. Within report text, numbers mark the location of *notes*—information that expands on the topic being discussed but that does not fit well in the document text. The numbers refer to *footnotes*—notes placed at the bottom of the page containing the note, or to *endnotes*—notes placed at the end of a document or chapter.

Activity 3.03 | Inserting Footnotes

You can add footnotes as you type your document or after your document is complete. Word renumbers the footnotes automatically, so footnotes need not be entered in order, and if one footnote is removed, the remaining footnotes automatically renumber.

1 ▶ Scroll to view the upper portion of **Page 2**, and then locate the paragraph that begins *Accurate records*. In the third line of the paragraph, click to position the insertion point to the right of the period after *infancy*.

2 ▶ On the **REFERENCES tab**, in the **Footnotes group**, click **Insert Footnote**.

Word creates space for a footnote in the footnote area at the bottom of the page and adds a footnote number to the text at the insertion point location. Footnote *1* displays in the footnote area, and the insertion point moves to the right of the number. A short black line is added just above the footnote area. You do not need to type the footnote number.

3 ▶ Type **The U.S. Department of Health & Human Services indicates that the widespread use of Health Information Technology will improve the quality of health care and prevent medical errors.**

This is an explanatory footnote; the footnote provides additional information that does not fit well in the body of the report.

4 ▶ Click the **HOME tab**, and then examine the font size and line spacing settings. Notice that the new footnote displays in 10 pt font size and is single-spaced, even though the font size of the document text is 11 pt and the text is double-spaced, as shown in Figure 3.5.

FIGURE 3.5

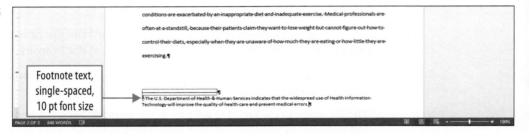

5 ▶ Scroll to view the top of **Page 1**, and then locate the paragraph that begins *Many of us*. At the end of the paragraph, click to position the insertion point to the right of the period following *time*.

6 ▶ On the **REFERENCES tab**, in the **Footnotes group**, click **Insert Footnote**. Type **Organizations such as airlines and the military could benefit because many employees are involved in time-sensitive operations, where errors can have catastrophic consequences.** Notice that the footnote you just added becomes the new footnote *1*. Click **Save** 🖫, and then compare your screen with Figure 3.6.

The first footnote that you typed, which is on Page 2 and begins *The U.S. Department of Health*, is renumbered as footnote *2*.

FIGURE 3.6

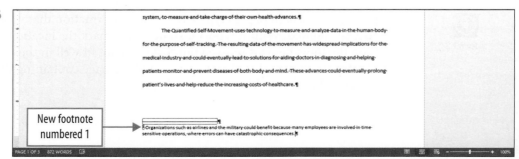

Activity 3.04 | Modifying a Footnote Style

Microsoft Word contains built-in paragraph formats called ***styles***—groups of formatting commands, such as font, font size, font color, paragraph alignment, and line spacing—that can be applied to a paragraph with one command.

The default style for footnote text is a single-spaced paragraph that uses a 10-point Calibri font and no paragraph indents. MLA style specifies double-spaced text in all areas of a research paper—including footnotes. According to the MLA style, first lines of footnotes must also be indented 0.5 inch and use the same font size as the report text.

1 ▶ At the bottom of **Page 1**, point anywhere in the footnote text you just typed, right-click, and then on the shortcut menu, click **Style**. Compare your screen with Figure 3.7.

> The Style dialog box displays, listing the styles currently in use in the document, in addition to some of the word processing elements that come with special built-in styles. Because you right-clicked on the footnote text, the selected style is the Footnote Text style.

FIGURE 3.7

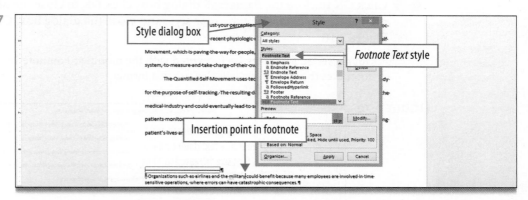

2 ▶ In the **Style** dialog box, click **Modify**, and then in the **Modify Style** dialog box, locate the small **Formatting** toolbar in the center of the dialog box. Click the **Font Size button arrow**, click **11**, and then compare your screen with Figure 3.8.

FIGURE 3.8

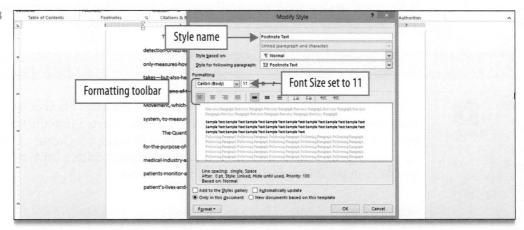

> **3** In the lower left corner of the dialog box, click **Format**, and then click **Paragraph**. In the **Paragraph** dialog box, on the **Indents and Spacing tab**, under **Indentation**, click the **Special arrow**, and then click **First line**.

> **4** Under **Spacing**, click the **Line spacing arrow**, and then click **Double**. Compare your dialog box with Figure 3.9.

FIGURE 3.9

> **5** Click **OK** to close the **Paragraph** dialog box, click **OK** to close the **Modify Style** dialog box, and then click **Apply** to apply the new style and **close** the dialog box. Compare your screen with Figure 3.10.

> Your inserted footnotes are formatted with the modified Footnote Text paragraph style; any new footnotes that you insert will also use this format.

FIGURE 3.10

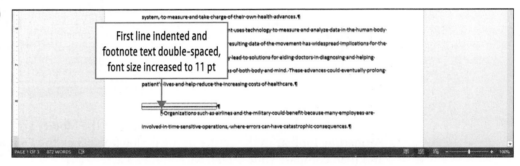

> **6** Scroll to view the bottom of **Page 2** to confirm that the new format was also applied to the second footnote, and then **Save** 🖫 your document.

Objective 3   Create Citations and a Bibliography in a Research Paper

Video W3-3

When you use quotations from or detailed summaries of other people's work, you must specify the source of the information. A ***citation*** is a note inserted into the text of a report or research paper that refers the reader to a source in the bibliography. Create a ***bibliography*** at the end of a research paper to list the sources you have referenced. Such a list is typically titled ***Works Cited*** (in MLA style), *Bibliography*, *Sources*, or *References*.

Activity 3.05 | Adding Citations for a Book

When writing a long research paper, you will likely reference numerous books, articles, and websites. Some of your research sources may be referenced many times, others only one time.

References to sources within the text of your research paper are indicated in an *abbreviated* manner. However, as you enter a citation for the first time, you can also enter the *complete* information about the source. Then, when you have finished your paper, you will be able to automatically generate the list of sources that must be included at the end of your research paper.

1 Scroll to view the middle of **Page 2**. In the paragraph that begins *Accurate records*, at the end of the paragraph, click to position the insertion point to the right of the quotation mark.

> The citation in the document points to the full source information in the bibliography, which typically includes the name of the author, the full title of the work, the year of publication, and other publication information.

2 On the **REFERENCES tab**, in the **Citations & Bibliography group**, click the **Style button arrow**, and then click **MLA** to insert a reference using MLA bibliography style.

3 Click **Insert Citation**, and then click **Add New Source**. Click the **Type of Source arrow**, and then click **Book**. Add the following information, and then compare your screen with Figure 3.11:

Author:	**Sopol, Eric J.**
Title:	**The Creative Destruction of Medicine**
Year:	**2012**
City:	**New York**
Publisher:	**Basic Books**
Medium	**Print**

FIGURE 3.11

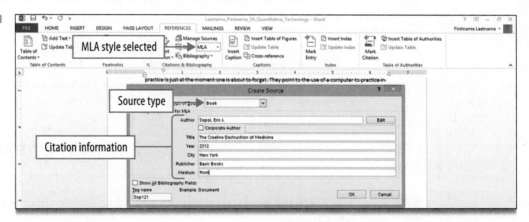

NOTE	Citing Corporate Authors and Indicating the Medium

If the author of a document is only identified as the name of an organization, select the Corporate Author check box and type the name of the organization in the Corporate Author box.

In the Seventh edition of the *MLA Handbook for Writers of Research Papers*, the category Medium was added and must be included for any item on the Works Cited page. Entries for this category can include Print, Web, Performance, and Photograph, among many others.

---

4 Click **OK** to insert the citation. Point to *(Sopol)* and click one time to select the citation.

> In the MLA style, citations that refer to items on the *Works Cited* page are placed in parentheses and are referred to as ***parenthetical references***—references that include the last name of the author or authors and the page number in the referenced source, which you add to the reference. No year is indicated, and there is no comma between the name and the page number.

5 Save 🖫 the document.

1 In the lower right corner of the box that surrounds the reference, point to the small arrow to display the ScreenTip *Citation Options*. Click this **Citation Options arrow**, and then on the list of options, click **Edit Citation**.

2 In the **Edit Citation** dialog box, under **Add**, in the **Pages** box, type **5** to indicate that you are citing from Page 5 of this source. Compare your screen with Figure 3.12.

FIGURE 3.12

3 Click **OK** to display the page number of the citation. Click outside of the citation box to deselect it. Then type a period to the right of the citation, and delete the period to the left of the quotation mark.

In the MLA style, if the reference occurs at the end of a sentence, the parenthetical reference always displays to the left of the punctuation mark that ends the sentence.

4 Press Ctrl + End to move to the end of the document, and then click to position the insertion point after the letter *e* in *disease* and to the left of the period.

5 In the **Citations & Bibliography group**, click **Insert Citation**, and then click **Add New Source**. Click the **Type of Source arrow**, if necessary scroll to the top of the list, click **Book**, and then add the following information:

Author:	Glaser, John P. and Claudia Salzberg
Title:	The Strategic Application of Information Technology in Health Care Organizations
Year:	2011
City:	San Francisco
Publisher:	Jossey-Bass
Medium:	Print

6 Click **OK**. Click the inserted citation to select it, click the **Citation Options arrow**, and then click **Edit Citation**.

7 In the **Edit Citation** dialog box, under **Add**, in the **Pages** box, type **28** to indicate that you are citing from page 28 of this source. Click **OK**.

8 On the **REFERENCES tab**, in the **Citations & Bibliography group**, click **Manage Sources**, and then compare your screen with Figure 3.13.

The Source Manager dialog box displays. Other citations on your computer display in the Master List box. The citations for the current document display in the Current List box. Word maintains the Master List so that if you use the same sources regularly, you can copy sources from your Master List to the current document. A preview of the bibliography entry also displays at the bottom of the dialog box.

FIGURE 3.13

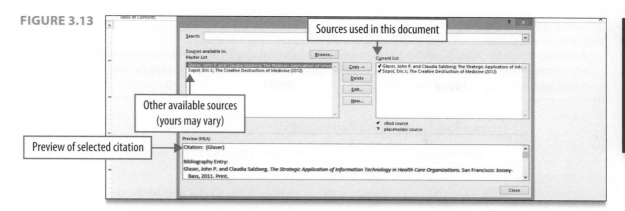

Sources used in this document

Other available sources (yours may vary)

Preview of selected citation

> **9** At the bottom of the **Source Manager** dialog box, click **Close**. Click anywhere in the document to deselect the parenthetical reference, and then **Save** your document.

Activity 3.07 | Adding Citations for a Website

> **1** In the lower portion of **Page 2**, in the paragraph that begins *Doctors have long*, in the third line, click to position the insertion point after the s in *States* and to the left of the period.

> **2** In the **Citations & Bibliography group**, click **Insert Citation**, and then click **Add New Source**. Click the **Type of Source arrow**, scroll down as necessary, and then click **Web site**. Type the following information:

Author:	Ogden, Cynthia L., Margaret D. Carroll, Brian K. Kit, and Katherine M. Flegal
Name of Web Page:	NCHS Data Brief Number 82
Year:	2012
Month:	January
Day:	15
Year Accessed:	2016
Month Accessed:	January
Day Accessed:	17
Medium	Web

> **3** Click **OK**. **Save** , and then compare your screen with Figure 3.14.

> A parenthetical reference is added. Because the cited web page has no page numbers, only the author name is used in the parenthetical reference.

FIGURE 3.14

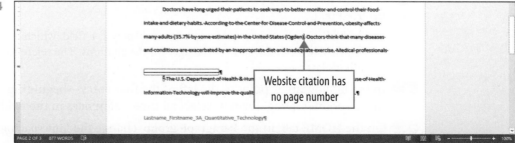

Website citation has no page number

Activity 3.08 | Inserting Page Breaks

Your bibliography must begin on a new page, so at the bottom of the last page of your report, you must insert a manual page break.

1 ▸ Press [Ctrl] + [End] to move the insertion point to the end of the document.

> If there is a footnote on the last page, the insertion point will display at the end of the final paragraph, but above the footnote—a footnote is always associated with the page that contains the citation.

2 ▸ Press [Ctrl] + [Enter] to insert a manual page break.

> A *manual page break* forces a page to end at the insertion point location, and then places any subsequent text at the top of the next page. Recall that the new paragraph retains the formatting of the previous paragraph, so in this instance the first line is indented.

> A *page break indicator*, which shows where a manual page break was inserted, displays at the bottom of Page 3.

3 ▸ On the **HOME tab**, in the **Paragraph group**, click the **Dialog Box Launcher** button to display the **Paragraph** dialog box.

4 ▸ On the **Indents and Spacing tab**, under **Indentation**, click the **Special arrow**, and then click **(none)**. Click **OK**, and then **Save** your document.

🔁 **ANOTHER WAY**   On the ruler, point to the First Line Indent button, and then drag the button to 0" on the horizontal ruler.

Activity 3.09 | Creating a Reference Page

At the end of a report or research paper, include a list of each source referenced. *Works Cited* is the reference page heading used in the MLA style guidelines. Other styles may refer to this page as a *Bibliography* (Business Style) or *References* (APA Style). Always display this information on a separate page.

1 ▸ With the insertion point blinking in the first line of **Page 4**, type **Works Cited** and then press [Enter]. On the **REFERENCES tab**, in the **Citations & Bibliography group**, in the **Style** box, be sure *MLA* displays.

2 ▸ In the **Citations & Bibliography group**, click **Bibliography**, and then near the bottom of the list, click **Insert Bibliography**.

3 ▸ Scroll as necessary to view the entire list of three references, and then click anywhere in the inserted text.

> The bibliography entries that you created display as a field, which is indicated by the gray shading. This field links to the Source Manager for the citations. The references display alphabetically by the author's last name.

4 ▸ In the bibliography, point to the left of the first entry—beginning *Glaser, John P.*—to display the pointer. Drag down to select all three references in the field.

5 ▸ On the **HOME tab**, in the **Paragraph group**, change the **Line spacing** to **2.0**, and then on the **PAGE LAYOUT tab**, in the **Paragraph group**, change the **Spacing After** to **0 pt**.

> The entries display according to MLA guidelines; the text is double-spaced, the extra space between paragraphs has been removed, and each entry uses a *hanging indent*—the first line of each entry extends 0.5 inch to the left of the remaining lines of the entry.

ANOTHER WAY   Display the Paragraph dialog box. Under Spacing, click the Line spacing arrow, and then click Double. Under Spacing, in the After box, type 0.

6 At the top of **Page 4**, click anywhere in the title text *Works Cited*, and then press Ctrl + E to center the title. Compare your screen with Figure 3.15, and then **Save** 💾 your document.

In MLA style, the *Works Cited* title is centered.

FIGURE 3.15

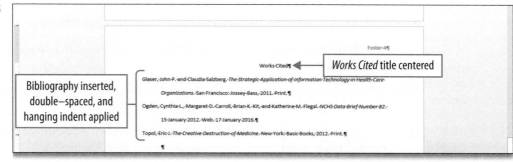

Activity 3.10 | Managing and Modifying Sources for a Document

Use the Source Manager to organize the sources cited in your document. For example, in the Source Manager dialog box, you can copy sources from the master list to the current list, delete a source, edit a source, or search for a source. You can also display a preview of how your citations will appear in your document.

1 On the **REFERENCES tab**, in the **Citations & Bibliography group**, click **Manage Sources**.

2 On the left, in the **Master List**, click the entry for *Sopol, Eric J.* and then between the **Master List** and the **Current List**, click **Edit**.

The name of this source should be *Topol* instead of *Sopol*.

3 In the **Edit Source** dialog box, in the **Author** box, delete *S* and type **T**

4 Click **OK**. When the message box indicates *This source exists in your master list and current document. Do you want to update both lists with these changes?* click **Yes**. Compare your screen with Figure 3.16.

In the lower portion of the Source Manager dialog box, a preview of the corrected entry displays.

FIGURE 3.16

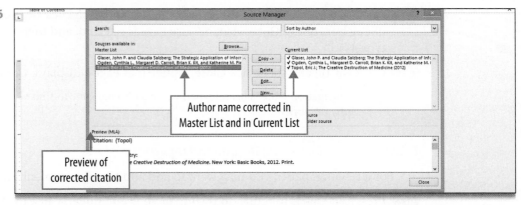

5 In the lower right corner, click **Close**. On your **Works Cited page**, notice that the author name is *not* corrected. Scroll to view the lower portion of **Page 2**, and notice that the author name *is* corrected and the citation is selected.

6 ▶ On the selected citation (*Topol 5*), click the **Citation Options arrow**, and then click **Update Citations and Bibliography**. Press Ctrl + End, and notice that this action updates the **Works Cited page** with the corrected name.

> Editing a source in Source Manager updates only the sources in the document; to update the Works Cited page, use the Update Citations and Bibliography command on the citation.

7 ▶ Drag to select all the lines for the three references. On the **HOME tab**, in the **Paragraph group**, click **Line and Paragraph Spacing** ⟰▾, and then click **2.0**. Click **Save** 🖫.

Activity 3.11 | Using the Navigation Pane to Go to a Specific Page

In a multipage document, use the navigation pane to move to a specific page or to find specific objects in the document.

1 ▶ Press Ctrl + Home to move to the top of the document. Click the **VIEW tab**, and then in the **Show group**, select the **navigation pane** check box.

2 ▶ In the **navigation pane**, on the right end of the **Search document** box, click the **Search for more things arrow**, and then compare your screen with Figure 3.17.

FIGURE 3.17

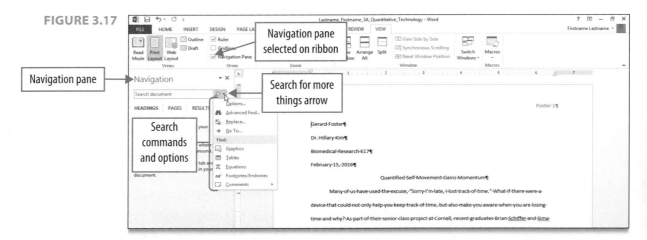

3 ▶ Under **Find**, click **Footnotes/Endnotes**. Notice that the first numbered footnote is selected.

4 ▶ In the **navigation pane**, to the right of *Result 1 of 2*, click the down arrow to move to the next numbered footnote.

5 ▶ Click the **Search for more things arrow** again, and then click **Go To**. In the **Find and Replace** dialog box, under **Go to what**, be sure **Page** is selected, and then in the **Enter page number** box, type **4**

6 ▶ Click **Go To**, and then click **Close**. Notice that **Page 4** displays. **Close** ✖ the **navigation pane**.

> The navigation pane is useful when you need to navigate to find various elements, especially in a lengthy document.

Activity 3.12 | Managing Document Properties

For a research paper, you may want to add additional document properties.

1 ▶ Press Ctrl + Home to return to the top of your document. Click the **FILE tab** to display **Backstage** view, and then in the lower right corner of the screen, click **Show All Properties**.

2 ▶ As the document **Title**, type **Quantified Self Movement Gains Momentum** and then as the **Tags**, type **quantified self, physiologic monitoring, research paper**

3 Click in the **Comments** box and type **Draft copy of a research report that will be distributed to class members** and then in the **Categories** box, type **Biomedical Research**

4 In the **Subject** box, type your course name and section number. In the **Company** box, select and delete any existing text, and then type **University Medical Center**

5 Click in the **Manager** box and type **Dr. Hillary Kim** Be sure your name displays as the **Author** and edit if necessary.

6 At the top of the **Properties** list, click the text *Properties*, and then click **Advanced Properties**. In the dialog box, click the **Summary tab**, and then compare your screen with Figure 3.18.

In the Advanced Properties dialog box, you can view and modify additional document properties.

FIGURE 3.18

7 Click the **Statistics tab**.

The document statistics show the number of revisions made to the document, the last time the document was edited, and the number of paragraphs, lines, words, and characters in the document. Additional information categories are available by clicking the Custom tab.

8 **Close** ☒ the dialog box, and then on the left, click **Save** to save and return to your document.

Objective 4   Use Read Mode and PDF Reflow

Video W3-4

Read Mode optimizes the view of the Word screen for the times when you are *reading* Word documents on the screen and not creating or editing them. Microsoft's research indicates that two-thirds of user sessions in Word contain no editing—meaning that people are simply reading the Word document on the screen. The Column Layout feature of Read Mode reflows the document to fit the size of the device you are reading so that the text is as easy to read on a tablet device as on a 24-inch screen. The Object Zoom feature of Read Mode resizes graphics to fit the screen you are using, but you can click or tap to zoom in on the graphic.

PDF Reflow provides the ability to import PDF files into Word so that you can transform a PDF back into a fully editable Word document. This is useful if you have lost the original Word file or if someone sends you a PDF that you would like to modify. PDF Reflow is not intended to act as a viewer for PDF files—for that you will still want to use the desktop app known as Adobe Reader or the ***Windows Reader app***, with which you can open a PDF or XPS file, zoom, find words or phrases, take notes, save changes, and then print or share the file.

Activity 3.13 | Using Read Mode

1 If necessary, press Ctrl + Home to move to the top of your document. On the **VIEW tab**, in the **Views group**, click **Read Mode**, and notice that **Read Mode** keeps footnotes displayed on the page associated with the footnote.

🔄 **ANOTHER WAY**   On the right side of the status bar, click the Read Mode button 📖.

2 ▸ In the upper left corner, click **TOOLS**.

You can use these tools to find something within the document or jump out to Bing to conduct an Internet search.

3 ▸ Click **Find**, and then in the **Search** box, type **Topol** Notice that Word displays the first page where the search term displays and highlights the term in yellow. Compare your screen with Figure 3.19.

FIGURE 3.19

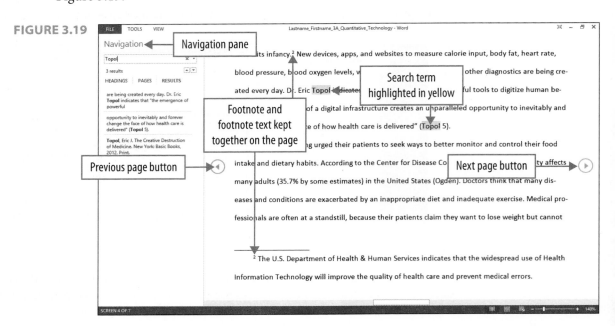

4 ▸ In the upper left corner, click **VIEW**, and then take a moment to study the table in Figure 3.20.

FIGURE 3.20

VIEW COMMANDS IN READ MODE	
VIEW COMMAND	**ACTION**
Edit Document	Return to Print Layout view to continue editing the document.
Navigation Pane	Search for specific text or click a heading or page to move to that location.
Show Comments	See comments, if any, within the document.
Column Width	Change the display of the document to fit more or less text on each line.
Page Color	Change the colors used to show the document to make it easier to read. Some readers prefer a sepia (brownish-gray) shading as the background or a black background with white text.
Layout	Read in different layouts. Select Column Layout, which is the default, or Paper Layout, which mimics the 8.5 × 11 format but without the ribbon.

5 ▸ On the **VIEW** menu, click **Edit Document** to return to **Print Layout** view. **Close** ✖ the **navigation pane**.

🔄 **ANOTHER WAY**   On the status bar on the right, click the Print Layout button 📄.

Activity 3.14 | Using PDF Reflow

1 Save 🖫 your document. Click the **FILE tab**, and then on the left, click **Close** to close your document but leave Word open.

2 Press Ctrl + F12 to display the **Open** dialog box, navigate to your student data files, and then click **w03A_PDF**. In the lower right corner, click **Open**. If a message indicates that *Word will now convert the PDF to an editable Word document…*, click **OK**.

3 If necessary, on the right side of the status bar, click **Print Layout** 🗐.

4 In the newsletter heading, change the **Volume** number to **3** Insert a footer, and then, using your own name, type **Lastname_Firstname_3A_PDF_Reflow** as shown in Figure 3.21.

FIGURE 3.21

Footer

Your first and last name in footer

Lastname_Firstname_3A_PDF_Reflow

5 Close the footer area. Press F12 to display the **Save As** dialog box, and then navigate to your **Word Chapter 3** folder. In the lower portion of the dialog box, click the **Save as type arrow**, and then click **PDF**.

6 In the **File name** box, type **Lastname_Firstname_3A_PDF_Reflow** and then in the lower right corner, click **Save** or press Enter.

This action re-saves the document as a PDF file.

⟳ ANOTHER WAY   Click the FILE tab, on the left click Export, click Create PDF/XPS, navigate to the desired folder, and then click Publish.

7 **Close** the **w03A_PDF** document without saving. **Close** ❌ Word. Print or submit electronically the two files that are the result of this project.

More **Knowledge**   **Inserting Watermarks**

You can add ghost text such as *Draft* or *Confidential* behind the content of a page. To do so, on the DESIGN tab, in the Page Background group, click Watermark, and select or create the watermark you want to use.

END | You have completed Project 3A

Objective | Insert a Link and Highlight Text in a Word Web App Document

You can use the Word Web App to insert a link to a website.

Activity | Inserting a Link and Highlighting a Text Selection

The Word Web App does not include the commands on the REFERENCES tab, so if you open a report that contains footnotes or citations created in the Word desktop app, you cannot edit them in the Word Web App. However, you can still make common text edits as you have practiced in other Web App projects. You can also insert a link to a website. In this activity, you will use the Word Web App to insert a link in a report, which you might want to do before sharing the report electronically for review by others.

1 From the desktop, start Internet Explorer. Navigate to **http://skydrive.com**, and then sign in to your Microsoft account. Open your **GO! Web Projects** folder; or create this folder if you have not done so.

2 In the SkyDrive menu bar, click **Upload**. Navigate to your student data files, click **w03_3A_Web**, and then click **Open**.

3 Point to the uploaded file **w03_3A_Web**, and then right-click. On the shortcut menu, scroll as necessary, and then click **Rename**. Using your own last name and first name, type **Lastname_Firstname_WD_3A_Web** and then press Enter to rename the file.

4 Click the file that you just renamed, and then click **EDIT DOCUMENT**. On the list, click **Edit in Word Web App**.

5 In the paragraph that begins *The implications*, drag to select *Tic-Toc-Trac*, and then on the **HOME tab**, in the **Font group**, click **Text Highlight Color**. Click the **Yellow** block to highlight this text in yellow.

6 Press Ctrl + End to move to the end of the document, and then press Enter.

7 On the **INSERT tab**, in the **Links group**, click **Link**. In the **Display text** box, type **See how Tic-Toc-Trac works!**

8 In the **Address** box, type **www.tictoctrac.com** and then click **Insert**. Compare your screen with Figure A.

9 To test the link, point to it, hold down Ctrl and then click one time. The site opens on a new tab.

10 In your browser, close the **TicTocTrac** tab.

11 Above the **FILE tab**, click **Save**. Click the **FILE tab**, and then click **Exit**. Submit as directed by your instructor. Sign out of your SkyDrive.

FIGURE A

Newsletter with Mailing Labels

PROJECT ACTIVITIES

In Activities 3.15 through 3.29, you will edit a newsletter that University Medical Center is sending to the board of directors and create the necessary mailing labels. Your completed documents will look similar to Figure 3.22.

PROJECT FILES

For Project 3B, you will need the following files:

New blank Word document
w03B_Environment_Newsletter
w03B_Addresses

You will save your documents as:

Lastname_Firstname_3B_Mailing_Labels
Lastname_Firstname_3B_Addresses
Lastname_Firstname_3B_Environment_Newsletter

PROJECT RESULTS

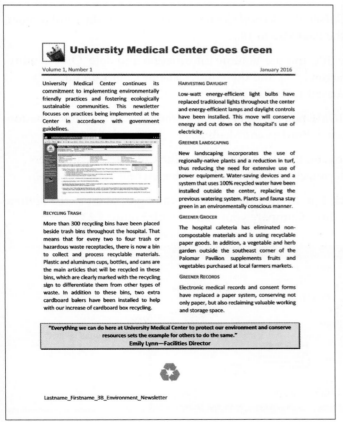

FIGURE 3.22 Project 3B Newsletter with Mailing Labels

Video W3-5

A *newsletter* is a periodical that communicates news and information to a specific group. Newsletters, as well as all newspapers and most magazines, use multiple columns for articles because text in narrower columns is easier to read than text that stretches across a page. You can create a newsletter in Word by changing a single column of text into two or more columns. If a column does not end where you want it to, you can end the column at a location of your choice by inserting a *manual column break*—an artificial end to a column to balance columns or to provide space for the insertion of other objects.

Activity 3.15 │ Changing One Column of Text to Two Columns

Newsletters are usually two or three columns wide. When using 8.5 × 11-inch paper in portrait orientation, avoid creating four or more columns because they are so narrow that word spacing looks awkward, often resulting in one long word on a line by itself.

1 Start Word. On Word's opening screen, in the lower left, click **Open Other Documents**. Navigate to your student files, and then locate and open the document **w03B_Environment_Newsletter**. If necessary, display the formatting marks and rulers. **Save** the file in your **Word Chapter 3** folder as **Lastname_Firstname_3B_Environment_Newsletter** and then add the file name to the footer.

2 Select the first paragraph of text—*University Medical Center Goes Green*. On the mini toolbar, change the **Font** to **Arial Black** and the **Font Size** to **18**.

3 Select the first two paragraphs—the title and the Volume information and date. On the mini toolbar, click the **Font Color button arrow** ，and then under **Theme Colors**, in the fifth column, click the last color—**Blue, Accent 1, Darker 50%**.

4 With the text still selected, on the **HOME tab**, in the **Paragraph group**, click the **Borders button arrow** ，and then at the bottom, click **Borders and Shading**.

5 In the **Borders and Shading** dialog box, on the **Borders tab**, click the **Color arrow**, and then under **Theme Colors**, in the fifth column, click the last color—**Blue, Accent 1, Darker 50%**.

6 Click the **Width arrow**, and then click **3 pt**. In the **Preview** box at the right, point to the *bottom* border of the preview and click one time. Compare your screen with Figure 3.23.

FIGURE 3.23

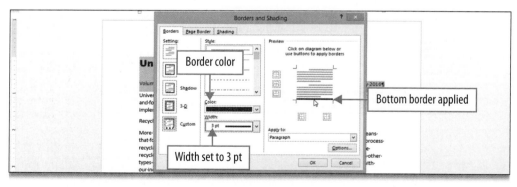

 ANOTHER WAY   In the Preview area, click the Bottom Border button .

7 In the **Borders and Shading** dialog box, click **OK**.

The line visually defines the newsletter's *nameplate*—the banner on the front page of a newsletter that identifies the publication.

8 Below the Volume information, click at the beginning of the paragraph that begins *University Medical Center continues.* By using the vertical scroll box, scroll to view the lower portion of the document, hold down Shift, and then click after the paragraph mark at the end of the paragraph that begins *Electronic medical records* to select all of the text between the insertion point and the sentence ending with the word *space.* Be sure that the paragraph mark is included in the selection. Compare your screen with Figure 3.24.

Use Shift to define a selection that may be difficult to select by dragging.

FIGURE 3.24

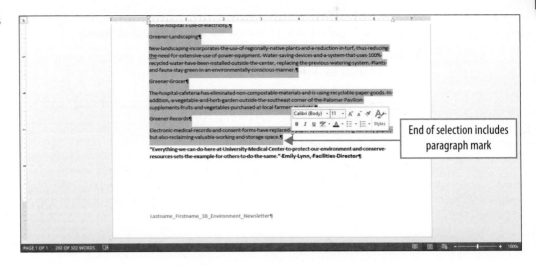

9 On the **PAGE LAYOUT tab**, in the **Page Setup group**, click **Columns**, and then click **Two**. Compare your screen with Figure 3.25, and then **Save** 💾 your newsletter.

Word divides the text into two columns and inserts a ***section break*** at the end of the selection, dividing the one-column section of the document from the two-column section of the document. A ***section*** is a portion of a document that can be formatted differently from the rest of the document. A section break marks the end of one section and the beginning of another section.

FIGURE 3.25

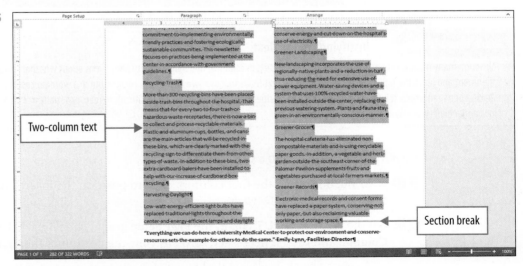

Activity 3.16 | Formatting Multiple Columns

The uneven right margin of a single page-width column is easy to read. When you create narrow columns, justified text is sometimes preferable. Depending on the design and layout of your newsletter, you might decide to reduce extra space between paragraphs and between columns to improve the readability of the document.

1 With the two columns of text still selected, on the **PAGE LAYOUT tab**, in the **Paragraph group**, click the **Spacing After down spin arrow** one time to change the spacing after to **6 pt**.

2 On the **HOME tab**, in the **Paragraph group**, click **Justify** ▤.

3 Click anywhere in the document to deselect the text, compare your screen with Figure 3.26, and then **Save** ▤.

FIGURE 3.26

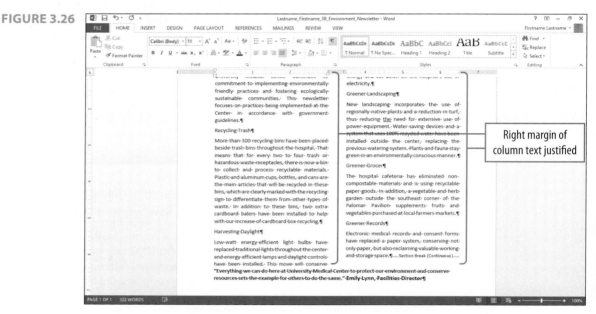

Right margin of column text justified

More Knowledge | **Justifying Column Text**

Although many magazines and newspapers still justify text in columns, there are a variety of opinions about whether to justify the columns, or to use left alignment and leave the right edge uneven. Justified text tends to look more formal and cleaner, but in a word processing document, it also results in uneven spacing between words. It is the opinion of some authorities that justified text is more difficult to read, especially in a page-width document. Let the overall look and feel of your newsletter be your guide.

Activity 3.17 | Inserting a Column Break

1 Near the bottom of the first column, click to position the insertion point at the beginning of the line *Harvesting Daylight*.

2 On the **PAGE LAYOUT tab**, in the **Page Setup group**, click **Breaks**. Under **Page Breaks**, click **Column**, and then if necessary, scroll to view the bottom of the first column.

> A column break displays at the bottom of the first column; text to the right of the column break moves to the top of the next column.

3 Compare your screen with Figure 3.27, and then **Save** ▤.

> A *column break indicator*—a dotted line containing the words *Column Break*—displays at the bottom of the column.

FIGURE 3.27

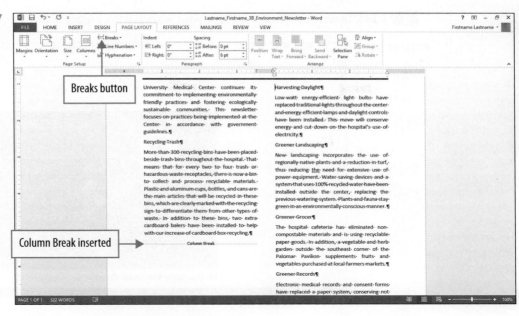

Activity 3.18 | Inserting an Online Picture

You can search for and insert online pictures in your document without saving the images to your computer. Pictures can make your document visually appealing and more interesting.

1 ▶ Press Ctrl + Home. On the **INSERT tab**, in the **Illustrations group**, click **Online Pictures**.

2 ▶ In the **Office.com Clip Art** search box, type **recycling bottles** so that Word can search for images that contain the keywords *recycling* and *bottles*. Press Enter.

3 ▶ Click the image of the recycle bin on a black background. If the image does not display, select a similar picture. Compare your screen with Figure 3.28.

FIGURE 3.28

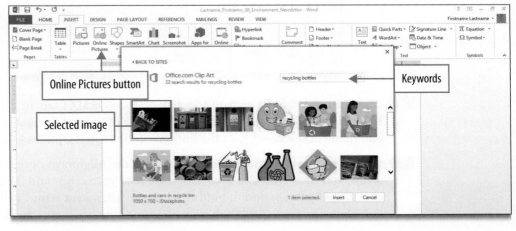

4 Click **Insert**, and then compare your screen with Figure 3.29.

FIGURE 3.29

Inserted image

5 Press `Ctrl` + `End` to move to the end of the document. On the **INSERT tab**, in the **Illustrations group**, click **Online Pictures**. In the **Office.com Clip Art** search box, type **green recycling symbol** and then press `Enter`.

6 Click the first recycling symbol and then compare your screen with Figure 3.30. If the picture is not available, choose a similar picture.

FIGURE 3.30

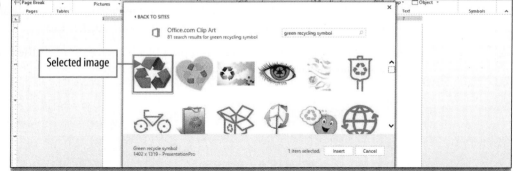

Selected image

7 Click **Insert**. With the picture selected, on the **FORMAT tab**, in the **Size group**, click in the **Height** box. Type **0.5** and then press `Enter`. To the right of the picture, click **Layout Options** 🖼, and then click **Square** 🖼. At the bottom of the **Layout Options gallery**, click **See more**.

8 On the **Position tab**, under **Horizontal**, click the **Alignment** option button. Click the **Alignment arrow**, and then click **Centered**. Click the **relative to arrow** and then click **Page**. Under **Vertical**, click the **Alignment** option button. Click the **Alignment arrow**, and then click **Bottom**. Click the **relative to arrow**, and then click **Margin**. Compare your screen with Figure 3.31.

FIGURE 3.31

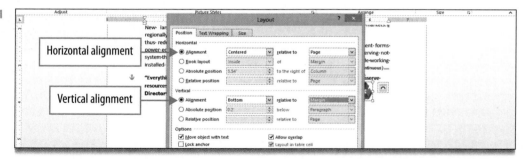

Horizontal alignment

Vertical alignment

9 Click **OK**, scroll to the bottom of the page, and then notice that the recycle image displays at the bottom of the second page. **Save** the document.

🔄 **ANOTHER WAY**   Drag the image to visually position the image.

Activity 3.19 | Cropping a Picture and Resizing a Picture by Scaling

In this activity, you will edit the recycle bin image by cropping and scaling the picture. When you *crop* a picture, you remove unwanted or unnecessary areas of the picture. When you *scale* a picture, you resize it to a percentage of its size.

1 Press Ctrl + Home to move to the top of the document, and then click the recycle bin picture to select it. On the **FORMAT tab**, in the **Size group**, click the upper portion of the **Crop** button to display crop handles around the picture. Compare your screen with Figure 3.32.

Crop handles are used like sizing handles to define unwanted areas of the picture.

FIGURE 3.32

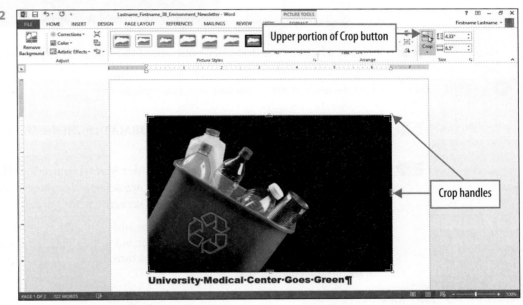

2 Point to the center right crop handle to display the ⊢ pointer. Compare your screen with Figure 3.33.

Use the *crop pointer* to crop areas of a picture.

FIGURE 3.33

3 With the crop pointer displayed, hold down the left mouse button and drag to the left to approximately **5 inches on the horizontal ruler**, and then release the mouse button. Compare your screen with Figure 3.34.

> The portion of the image to be removed displays in gray.

FIGURE 3.34

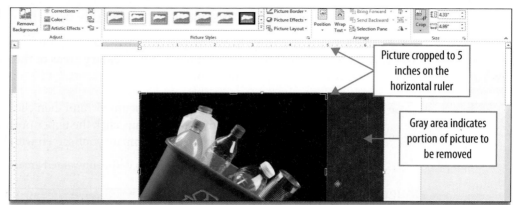

Picture cropped to 5 inches on the horizontal ruler

Gray area indicates portion of picture to be removed

4 Click anywhere in the document outside of the image to apply the crop.

ANOTHER WAY Click the upper portion of the Crop button to apply the crop.

5 Click to select the picture again. On the **FORMAT tab**, in the **Size group**, click the **Dialog Box Launcher** button.

6 In the **Layout dialog box**, on the **Size tab**, under **Scale**, be sure that the **Lock aspect ratio** and **Relative to original picture size** check boxes are selected. Select the number in the **Height box**, type **10** and then press Tab. Compare your screen with Figure 3.35.

> When *Lock aspect ratio* is selected, the height and width of the picture are sized proportionately and only one scale value is necessary. The second value—in this instance Width—adjusts proportionately. When *Relative to original picture size* is selected, the scale is applied as a percentage of the original picture size.

FIGURE 3.35

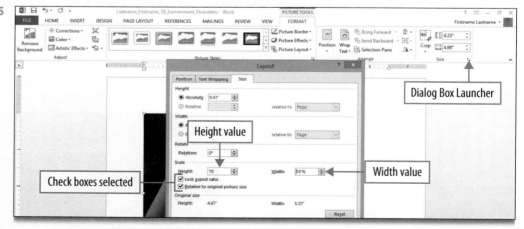

Dialog Box Launcher

Height value

Width value

Check boxes selected

7 In the **Layout** dialog box, click the **Text Wrapping tab**. Under **Wrapping style**, click **Square**.

8 Click the **Position tab**, and then under **Horizontal**, click the **Alignment** option button. Be sure that the **Alignment** indicates **Left** and **relative to Column**. Under **Vertical**, click the **Alignment** option button, and then change the alignment to **Top relative to Margin**. Click **OK**, and then compare your screen with Figure 3.36.

FIGURE 3.36

Picture cropped, scaled, and positioned → ...niversity·Medical·Center·Goes·Green¶

Activity 3.20 | Setting Transparent Color and Recoloring a Picture

You can make one color in a picture transparent using the Set Transparent Color command. When you *recolor* a picture, you change all the colors in the picture to shades of a single color.

1 On the **VIEW tab**, in the **Zoom group**, click **Zoom**, and then click **200%**. Click **OK**. Drag the scroll bars as necessary so that you can view the recycle bin picture at the top of the document.

2 If necessary, select the recycle bin picture. On the **FORMAT tab**, in the **Adjust group**, click **Color**, and then below the gallery, click **Set Transparent Color**. Move the pointer into the document to display the ✎ pointer.

3 Point anywhere in the black background of the recycle bin picture, and then click to apply the transparent color to the background. Compare your screen with Figure 3.37.

FIGURE 3.37

Transparent color applied to black background → **University·Medical·Center·Goes·Gr**

Volume·1,·Number·1

4 Press Ctrl + End to move to the end of your document, and then select the picture of the recycle symbol. On the **FORMAT tab**, in the **Adjust group**, click **Color** to display a gallery of recoloring options. Under **Recolor**, in the last row, click the fourth option— **Olive Green, Accent color 3 Light**. Compare your screen with Figure 3.38, and then **Save** 🖫 the document.

FIGURE 3.38

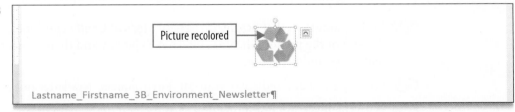

Picture recolored →

Lastname_Firstname_3B_Environment_Newsletter¶

Activity 3.21 | Adjusting the Brightness and Contrast of a Picture

Brightness is the relative lightness of a picture. *Contrast* is the difference between the darkest and lightest area of a picture.

1 If necessary, select the recycle symbol. On the **FORMAT tab**, in the **Adjust group**, click **Corrections**. Under **Brightness/Contrast**, point to several of the options to view the effect that the settings have on the picture.

Under **Brightness/Contrast**, in the last row, click the first setting—**Brightness: −40% Contrast: +40%**. Compare your screen with Figure 3.39.

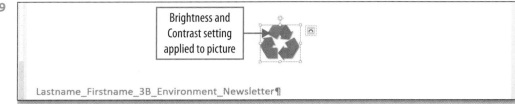

Brightness and Contrast setting applied to picture

Lastname_Firstname_3B_Environment_Newsletter¶

 On the **VIEW tab**, in the **Zoom group**, click **100%**, and then **Save** the document.

Activity 3.22 | Applying a Border to a Picture and Flipping a Picture

The *flip* commands create a reverse image of a picture or object.

1 Press Ctrl + Home to move to the top of the document, and then select the picture of the recycle bin. On the **FORMAT tab**, in the **Picture Styles group**, click the **Picture Border button arrow**. Under **Theme Colors**, in the fourth column, click the first color—**Dark Blue, Text 2**.

2 Click the **Picture Border arrow** again, and then point to **Weight**. Click **1 1/2 pt** to change the thickness of the border.

3 On the **FORMAT tab**, in the **Arrange group**, click **Rotate Objects**, and then click **Flip Horizontal**. Click anywhere in the document to deselect the picture. **Save**, and then compare your screen with Figure 3.40.

FIGURE 3.40

Picture bordered and flipped

University·Medical·Center·Goes·Green¶

Volume·1,·Number·1   →   January·2016¶

Activity 3.23 | Inserting a Screenshot

A *screenshot* is an image of an active window on your computer that you can paste into a document. Screenshots are especially useful when you want to insert an image of a website into your Word document. You can insert a screenshot of any open window on your computer.

1 In the paragraph that begins *University Medical Center continues*, click after the period at the end of the paragraph. Start Internet Explorer, and then navigate to **www.epa.gov/osw /conserve** and press Enter.

2 From the taskbar, redisplay your **3B_Environment_Newletter** document.

3 With the insertion point positioned at the end of the paragraph, on the **INSERT tab**, in the **Illustrations group**, click **Screenshot**.

All of your open windows display in the Available Windows gallery and are available to paste into the document.

4 In the **Screenshot** gallery, click the browser window that contains the EPA site to insert the screenshot at the insertion point. If a message box displays asking if you want to hyperlink the screenshot, click No, and then notice that the image is inserted and is sized to fit between the margins of the first column. Compare your screen with Figure 3.41.

By selecting No in the message box, you are inserting a screenshot without links to the actual website. Choose Yes, if you want to link the image to the website.

FIGURE 3.41

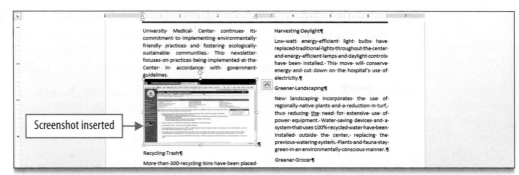

University Medical Center continues its commitment to implementing environmentally-friendly practices and fostering ecologically-sustainable communities. This newsletter focuses on practices being implemented at the Center in accordance with government guidelines.

Harvesting Daylight¶

Low-watt energy-efficient light bulbs have replaced traditional lights throughout the center and energy-efficient lamps and daylight controls have been installed. This move will conserve energy and cut down on the hospital's use of electricity.¶

Greener Landscaping¶

New landscaping incorporates the use of regionally-native plants and a reduction in turf, thus reducing the need for extensive use of power equipment. Water-saving devices and a system that uses 100% recycled water have been installed outside the center, replacing the previous watering system. Plants and fauna stay green in an environmentally-conscious manner.¶

Greener Grocer¶

Screenshot inserted

Recycling Trash¶
More than 300 recycling bins have been placed

5 With the inserted screenshot selected, on the **FORMAT tab**, in the **Picture Styles group**, click the **Picture Border button arrow**, and then under **Theme Colors**, in the second column, click the first color—**Black, Text 1**.

6 Save ⊟ the document.

Objective 6 | Use Special Character and Paragraph Formatting

Video W3-6

Special text and paragraph formatting is useful to emphasize text, and it makes your newsletter look more professional. For example, you can place a border around one or more paragraphs or add shading to a paragraph. When adding shading, use light colors; dark shading can make the text difficult to read.

Activity 3.24 | Applying the Small Caps Font Effect

For headlines and titles, *small caps* is an attractive font effect. The effect changes lowercase letters to uppercase letters, but with the height of lowercase letters.

1 Under the screenshot, select the paragraph *Recycling Trash* including the paragraph mark.

2 Right-click the selected text, and then on the shortcut menu, click **Font** to display the **Font** dialog box. Click the **Font color arrow**, and then change the color to **Blue, Accent 1, Darker 50%**—in the fifth column, the last color.

3 Under **Font style**, click **Bold**. Under **Effects**, select the **Small caps** check box. Compare your screen with Figure 3.42.

The Font dialog box provides more options than are available on the ribbon and enables you to make several changes at the same time. In the Preview box, the text displays with the selected formatting options applied.

FIGURE 3.42

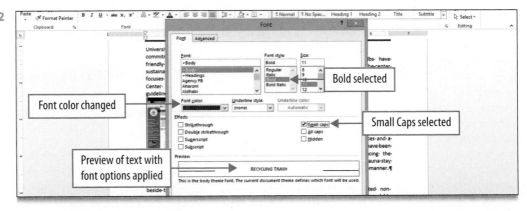

Font color changed

Bold selected

Small Caps selected

Preview of text with font options applied

4 ▶ Click **OK**. With the text still selected, right-click, and then on the mini toolbar, double-click **Format Painter** 🖌. Then, in the second column, with the 🔺I pointer, select each of the heading paragraphs—*Harvesting Daylight*, *Greener Landscaping*, *Greener Grocer*, and *Greener Records*—to apply the same formats. Press Esc to turn off **Format Painter**.

5 ▶ In the first column below the screenshot, notice that the space between the *Recycling Trash* subheading and the screenshot is fairly small. Click anywhere in the *Recycling Trash* subheading, and then on the **PAGE LAYOUT tab**, in the **Paragraph group**, click the **Before up spin arrow** two times to set the spacing to **12 pt**.

6 ▶ Compare your screen with Figure 3.43, and then **Save** 💾 your document.

FIGURE 3.43

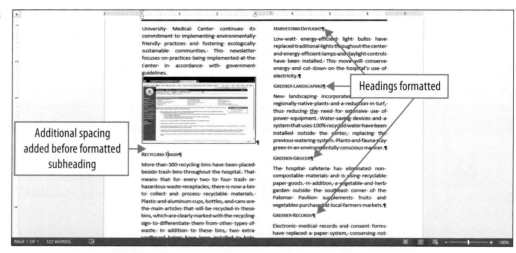

Activity 3.25 | Inserting Symbols and Special Characters

You can insert symbols and special characters in a Word document, including copyright symbols, trademark symbols, and em dashes. An ***em dash*** is a punctuation symbol used to indicate an explanation or emphasis.

1 ▶ Press Ctrl + End to move to the end of the document, and then after the name *Emily Lynn* delete the comma and the space that separates her name from her job title—*Facilities Director*.

2 ▶ With the insertion point positioned before the *F* in *Facilities*, on the **INSERT tab**, in the **Symbols group**, click **Symbol**. Below the gallery, click **More Symbols** to display the **Symbol** dialog box.

Here you can choose the symbol that you want to insert in your document.

3 ▶ In the **Symbol** dialog box, click the **Special Characters tab**. Scroll the list to view the types of special characters that you can insert; notice that some of the characters can be inserted using a Shortcut key.

4 ▶ Click **Em Dash**, and then in the lower right portion of the dialog box, click **Insert**. Compare your screen with Figure 3.44.

An em dash displays between the name *Lynn* and the word *Facilities*.

FIGURE 3.44

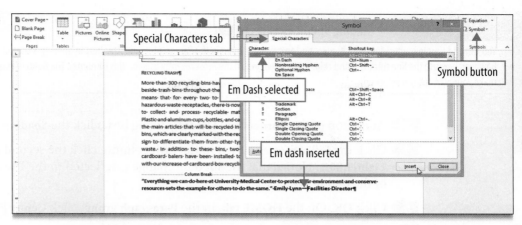

5 In the **Symbol** dialog box, click **Close**, and then **Save** 💾 your document.

Activity 3.26 | Adding Borders and Shading to a Paragraph and Inserting a Manual Line Break

Paragraph borders provide strong visual cues to the reader. You can use paragraph shading with or without borders; however, combined with a border, light shading can be very effective in drawing the reader's eye to the text.

1 At the end of the document, select the two lines of bold text that begin *"Everything we can do*.

The recycle picture may also be selected because it is anchored to the paragraph.

2 On the **HOME tab**, in the **Paragraph group**, click the **Borders button arrow** ⊞ ▾, and then click **Borders and Shading**.

3 In the **Borders and Shading** dialog box, be sure the **Borders tab** is selected. Under **Setting**, click **Shadow**. Click the **Color arrow**, and then in the fifth column, click the last color—**Blue, Accent 1, Darker 50%**. Click the **Width arrow**, and then click **1 pt**. Compare your screen with Figure 3.45.

In the lower right portion of the Borders and Shading dialog box, the *Apply to* box indicates *Paragraph*. The *Apply to* box directs where the border will be applied—in this instance, the border will be applied only to the selected paragraph.

FIGURE 3.45

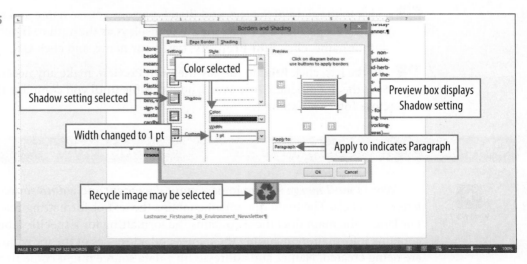

4   At the top of the **Borders and Shading** dialog box, click the **Shading tab**.

5   Click the **Fill arrow**, and then in the fifth column, click the second color—**Blue, Accent 1, Lighter 80%**. Notice that the shading change is reflected in the **Preview area** on the right side of the dialog box.

6   Click **OK**. On the **HOME tab**, in the **Paragraph group**, click **Center** ☰.

7   Click anywhere in the document to deselect, and then compare your screen with Figure 3.46.

FIGURE 3.46

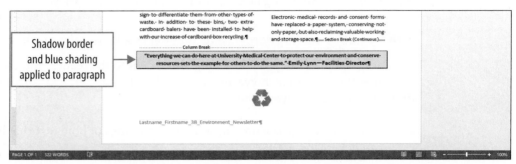

8   In the shaded paragraph, in the second line, click in front of the *E* in the name *Emily*. Hold down Shift and then press Enter.

> Holding down Shift while pressing Enter inserts a ***manual line break***, which moves the text to the right of the insertion point to a new line while keeping the text in the same paragraph. A ***line break indicator***, in the shape of a bent arrow, indicates a manual line break.

9   Press Ctrl + Home to move the insertion point to the top of the document. Click the **FILE tab** to display **Backstage** view. On the right, at the bottom of the **Properties** list, click **Show All Properties**.

10   On the list of **Properties**, click to the right of **Tags**, and then type **newsletter, January**

11   Click to the right of **Subject**, and then type your course name and section number. Under **Related People**, be sure that your name displays as the author. If necessary, right-click the author name, click **Edit Property**, type your name, and click **OK**.

12   On the left, click **Print** to display the **Print Preview**, make any necessary corrections, and then **Save** the document. **Close** Word; hold this file until you complete this project. If necessary, close Internet Explorer.

Objective 7   Create Mailing Labels Using Mail Merge

Video W3-7

Word's ***mail merge*** feature joins a ***main document*** and a ***data source*** to create customized letters or labels. The main document contains the text or formatting that remains constant. For labels, the main document contains the formatting for a specific label size. The data source contains information including the names and addresses of the individuals for whom the labels are being created. Names and addresses in a data source might come from a Word table, an Excel worksheet, or an Access database.

The easiest way to perform a mail merge is to use the Mail Merge Wizard, which asks you questions and, based on your answers, walks you step by step through the mail merge process.

Activity 3.27 | Starting the Mail Merge Wizard Template

In this activity, you will open the data source for the mail merge, which is a Word table containing names and addresses.

1 Start Word and display a new blank document. Display formatting marks and rulers. **Save** the document in your **Word Chapter 3** folder as **Lastname_Firstname_3B_Mailing_Labels**

2 With your new document open on the screen, from your student files, **Open** the file **w03B_Addresses**. **Save** the address file in your **Word Chapter 3** folder as **Lastname_Firstname_3B_Addresses** and then add the file name to the footer.

> This document contains a table of addresses. The first row contains the column names. The remaining rows contain the names and addresses.

3 Click to position the insertion point in the last cell in the table, and then press Tab to create a new row. Enter the following information, and then compare your table with Figure 3.47.

FIRST NAME	LAST NAME	ADDRESS 1	UNIT	CITY	STATE	ZIP CODE
Monica	Warren	5626 Summer Road	#234	Lakeland	TN	38002

FIGURE 3.47

4 Save, and then **Close** the table of addresses. Be sure that your blank **Lastname_Firstname_3B_Mailing_Labels** document displays.

5 Click the **MAILINGS tab**. In the **Start Mail Merge group**, click **Start Mail Merge**, and then click **Step-by-Step Mail Merge Wizard** to display the **Mail Merge** pane on the right.

6 In the **Mail Merge** pane, under **Select document type**, click **Labels**. At the bottom of the **Mail Merge** pane, click **Next: Starting document** to display Step 2 of 6.

7 Under **Select starting document**, be sure **Change document layout** is selected, and then under **Change document layout**, click **Label options**.

8 In the **Label Options** dialog box, under **Printer information**, click the **Tray arrow**, and then if necessary, click **Default tray** (Automatically Select)—the exact wording may vary depending on your printer, but select the *Default* or *Automatic* option so that you can print the labels on regular paper rather than manually inserting labels in the printer.

9 Under **Label information**, click the **Label vendors arrow**, and then click **Avery US Letter**. Under **Product number**, scroll about halfway down the list, and then click **5160 Easy Peel Address Labels**. Compare your screen with Figure 3.48.

> The Avery 5160 address label is a commonly used label. The precut sheets contain three columns of 10 labels each—for a total of 30 labels per sheet.

FIGURE 3.48

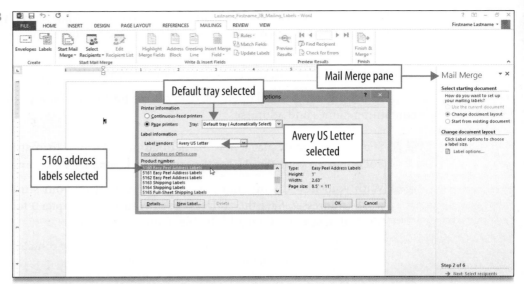

10 ▸ At the bottom of the **Label Options** dialog box, click **OK**. If a message box displays, click **OK** to set up the labels. If the gridlines do not display, on the **Layout tab**, in the **Table** group, click **View Gridlines**. At the bottom of the **Mail Merge** pane, click **Next: Select recipients**.

The label page is set up with three columns and ten rows. Here, in Step 3 of the Mail Merge Wizard, you must identify the recipients—the data source. For your recipient data source, you can choose to use an existing list—for example, a list of names and addresses that you have in an Access database, an Excel worksheet, a Word table, or your Outlook contacts list. If you do not have an existing data source, you can type a new list at this point in the wizard.

11 ▸ In the **Mail Merge** pane, under **Select recipients**, be sure the **Use an existing list** option button is selected. Under **Use an existing list**, click **Browse**.

12 ▸ Navigate to your **Word Chapter 3** folder, select your **Lastname_Firstname_3B_Addresses** file, and then click **Open** to display the **Mail Merge Recipients** dialog box. Compare your screen with Figure 3.49.

In the Mail Merge Recipients dialog box, the column headings are formed from the text in the first row of your Word table of addresses. Each row of information that contains data for one person is referred to as a *record*. The column headings—for example, *Last_Name* and *First_Name*—are referred to as *fields*. An underscore replaces the spaces between words in the field name headings.

FIGURE 3.49

13 In the lower left portion of the **Mail Merge Recipients** dialog box, in the **Data Source** box, click the path that contains your file name. Then, at the bottom of the **Mail Merge Recipients** dialog box, click **Edit**.

14 In the upper right corner of the **Data Form** dialog box, click **Add New**. In the blank record, type the following, pressing Tab to move from field to field, and then compare your **Data Form** dialog box with Figure 3.50.

FIRST_NAME	LAST_NAME	ADDRESS_1	UNIT	CITY	STATE	ZIP CODE
Sharon	Williams	1251 Parker Road	#843	Memphis	TN	38123

FIGURE 3.50

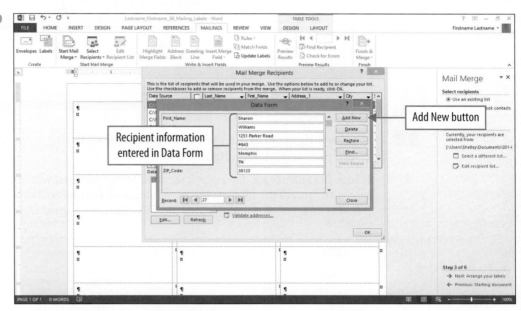

15 In the lower right corner of the **Data Form** dialog box, click **Close**. Scroll to the end of the recipient list to confirm that the record for *Sharon Williams* that you just added is in the list. At the bottom of the **Mail Merge Recipients** dialog box, click **OK**.

Activity 3.28 | Completing the Mail Merge Wizard

You can add or edit names and addresses while completing the Mail Merge. You can also match your column names with preset names used in Mail Merge.

1 At the bottom of the **Mail Merge** pane, click **Next: Arrange your labels**.

2 Under **Arrange your labels**, click **Address block**. In the **Insert Address Block** dialog box, under **Specify address elements**, examine the various formats for names. If necessary, under *Insert recipient's name in this format*, select the *Joshua Randall Jr.* format. Compare your dialog box with Figure 3.51.

FIGURE 3.51

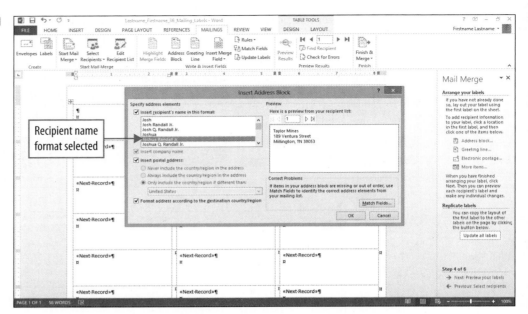

Recipient name format selected

3 In the lower right corner of the **Insert Address Block** dialog box, click **Match Fields**, and then compare your screen with Figure 3.52.

If your field names are descriptive, the Mail Merge program will identify them correctly, as is the case with most of the information in the *Required for Address Block* section. However, the Address 2 field is unmatched—in the source file, this column is named *Unit*.

FIGURE 3.52

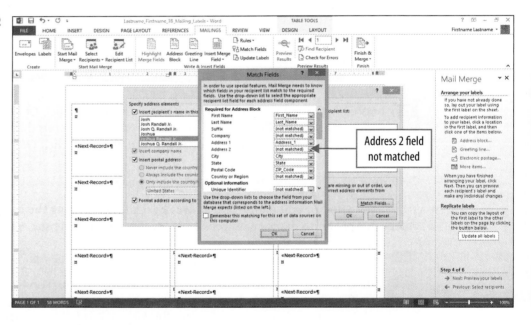

Address 2 field not matched

4 Click the **Address 2 arrow**, and then from the list of available fields, click **Unit** to match the Mail Merge field with the field in your data source.

5 At the bottom of the **Match Fields** dialog box, click **OK**. At the bottom of the **Insert Address Block** dialog box, click **OK**.

Word inserts the Address block in the first label space surrounded by double angle brackets. The *AddressBlock* field name displays, which represents the address block you saw in the Preview area of the Insert Address Block dialog box.

6 In the **Mail Merge** pane, under **Replicate labels**, click **Update all labels** to insert an address block in each label space for each subsequent record.

7 At the bottom of the **Mail Merge** pane, click **Next: Preview your labels**. Notice that for addresses with four lines, the last line of the address is cut off.

8 Press Ctrl + A to select all of the label text, click the **PAGE LAYOUT tab**, and then in the **Paragraph group**, click in the **Spacing Before** box. Type **3** and press Enter.

9 Click in any label to deselect, and notice that 4-line addresses are no longer cut off. Compare your screen with Figure 3.53.

FIGURE 3.53

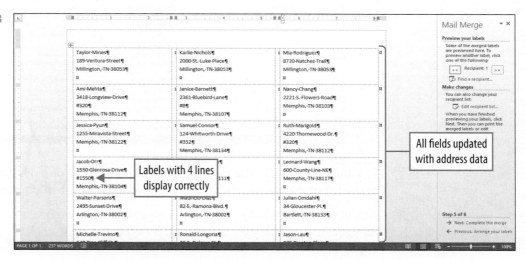

10 At the bottom of the **Mail Merge** pane, click **Next: Complete the merge**.

Step 6 of the Mail Merge displays. At this point you can print or edit your labels, although this is done more easily in the document window.

11 Save 🖫 your labels, and then on the right, **Close** ☒ the **Mail Merge** pane.

Activity 3.29 | Sorting Mail Merge Results

If you discover that you need to make further changes to your labels, you can still make them even though the Mail Merge task pane is closed.

1 Add the file name to the footer, close the footer area, and then move to the top of Page 2. Click anywhere in the empty table row, and then click the **LAYOUT tab**. In the **Rows & Columns group**, click **Delete**, and then click **Delete Rows**.

Adding footer text to a label sheet replaces the last row of labels on a page with the footer text, and moves the last row of labels to the top of the next page. In this instance, a blank second page is created, which you can delete by deleting the blank row.

2 Notice that the labels do not display in alphabetical order. Click the **MAILINGS tab**, and then in the **Start Mail Merge group**, click **Edit Recipient List** to display the list of names and addresses.

3 In the **Mail Merge Recipients** dialog box, click the **Last_Name** field heading, and notice that the names are sorted alphabetically by the recipient's last name.

Mailing labels are often sorted by either last name or by ZIP Code.

4 Click the **Last_Name** field heading again, and notice that the last names are sorted in descending order. Click the **Last_Name** field one more time to return to ascending order, and then click **OK**. Press Ctrl + Home, and then compare your screen with Figure 3.54.

FIGURE 3.54

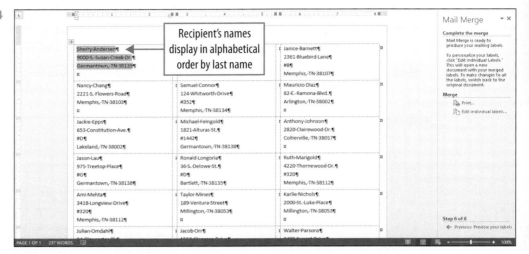

5 Click the **FILE tab**. On the right, at the bottom of the **Properties** list, click **Show All Properties**. On the list of **Properties**, click to the right of **Tags**, and then type **labels**

6 Click to the right of **Subject**, and then type your course name and section number. Be sure that your name displays as the author. If necessary, right-click the author name, click **Edit Property**, type your name, and click **OK**. Save ▭ the file. **Close** the document, and click **Yes** to save the data source.

7 As directed by your instructor, print or submit electronically.

If you print, the labels will print on whatever paper is in the printer; unless you have preformatted labels available, the labels will print on a sheet of paper. Printing the labels on plain paper enables you to proofread the labels before you print them on more expensive label sheets.

8 In addition to your labels and address document, print or submit your **Lastname_Firstname_3B_Environment_Newsletter** document as directed. **Close** Word.

END | You have completed Project 3B

GO! with Office Web Apps

Objective | **Format** a Single-Column Newsletter in Word Web App

You can use the Word Web App to insert clip art and to format text. You can change fonts and font color, and modify paragraph spacing.

A L E R T !   **Working with Web-Based Applications and Services**

Computer programs and services on the web receive continuous updates and improvements, so the steps to complete this web-based activity may differ from the ones shown. You can often look at the screens and the information presented to determine how to complete the activity.

Activity | Formatting a Single-Column Newsletter

In this activity, you will use the Word Web App to edit a single-column newsletter similar to the one you edited in Project 3B.

1 From the desktop, start Internet Explorer. Navigate to **http://skydrive.com**, and then sign in to your Microsoft account. Open your **GO! Web Projects** folder; or create this folder if necessary.

2 In the SkyDrive menu bar, click **Upload**. Navigate to your student data files, click **w03_3B_Web**, and then click **Open**.

3 Point to the uploaded file **w03_3B_Web**, and then right-click. On the shortcut menu, scroll as necessary, and then click **Rename**. Using your own last name and first name, type **Lastname_Firstname_WD_3B_Web** and then press Enter to rename the file.

4 Double-click the file that you just renamed, and then click **EDIT DOCUMENT**. On the list, click **Edit in Word Web App**.

5 Drag to select the newsletter title—*University Medical Center Goes Green*. On the **HOME tab**, in the

Font group, locate and click the **Grow Font button** two times to change the font size to **18**. With the newsletter title still selected, on the **HOME tab**, in the **Font group**, click **Font Color**, and then in the fifth column, click the last color—**Blue Gray, Accent 1, Darker 50%**. Apply the same **Font Color** to the five subheadings—*Recycling Trash, Harvesting Daylight, Greener Landscaping, Greener Grocer*, and *Greener Records*.

6 Drag to select the first subheading—*Recycling Trash*. On the **PAGE LAYOUT tab**, in the **Paragraph group**, click in the **After box**. Type **12** and then press Enter—or click the arrow as necessary. Apply the same **Spacing After** to the remaining four subheadings—*Harvesting Daylight, Greener Landscaping, Greener Grocer*, and *Greener Records*. Click anywhere in the document, and then press Ctrl + Home to move to the top of the document. Compare your screen with Figure A.

FIGURE A

(GO! with Office Web Apps continues on the next page)

7 Be sure the insertion point is positioned at the top of the document. On the **PAGE LAYOUT tab**, in the **Page Setup group**, click **Margins**, and then click **Custom Margins**. Click in the **Top** box and type **0.5** and then click in the **Bottom** box. Type **0.5** and then click **OK**.

8 On the **INSERT tab**, in the **Pictures group**, click **Clip Art**. In the **Search** box, type **recycling bottles** and then press Enter. Click the image of the recycle bin filled with plastic bottles on a black background. If the image is not available, choose a similar picture. Click **Insert**.

9 On the **FORMAT tab**, in the **Image Size group**, click in the **Scale** box. Type **10** to replace the existing number, and then press Enter. On the **FORMAT tab**, in the **Picture Styles group**, use the ScreenTips to locate and then click **Reflected Rounded Rectangle**.

10 Press Ctrl + End to move to the end of the document, and then press Enter. On the **INSERT tab**, in the **Pictures group**, click **Clip Art**. In the **Search** box, type

green recycle symbol and then press Enter. Click the image of the green recycle symbol that you used in Project 3B. If the image is not available, choose a similar picture. Click **Insert**.

11 On the **FORMAT tab**, in the **Image Size group**, click in the **Scale** box. Type **5** to replace the existing number, and then press Enter. On the **HOME tab**, in the **Paragraph group**, click **Center**.

12 In the last paragraph of the newsletter, click to position the insertion point between the second quotation mark and the letter *E* in *Emily*. Hold down Shift and then press Enter to insert a manual line break. On the **HOME tab**, in the **Paragraph group**, click **Center** to center the three lines of text in the last paragraph. Compare your screen with Figure B.

13 **Save** your file and submit as directed by your instructor. Then, on the ribbon, click the **FILE tab**, and then click **Exit**. Sign out of your SkyDrive.

FIGURE B

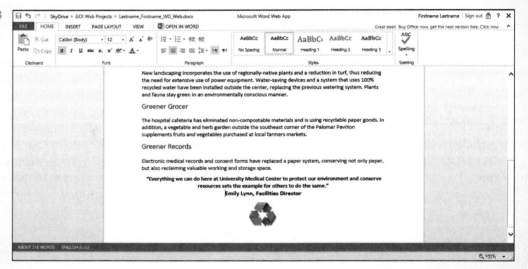

Andrew Rodriguez / Fotolia; FotolEdhar/ Fotolia; apops/ Fotolia; Yuri Arcurs/ Fotolia

The advantage of using Office 365 is that your organization does not have to purchase and install server hardware and software for sophisticated business applications and does not need a full-time IT person or staff just to manage the technology your teams need.

By using Office 365, you are able to have business-class services for your employees without investing in expensive hardware, software, and personnel. However, at least one person in an organization must be designated as the *Office 365 Administrator*—the person who creates and manages the account, adds new users, sets up the services your organization wants to use, sets permission levels, and manages the SharePoint team sites. You can have more than one Administrator if you want to share these tasks with others.

Microsoft provides easy-to-use instructions and videos to get you started, and you might also have contact with a Microsoft representative. You will probably find, however, that subscribing to and setting up the account, adding users, and activating services is a straightforward process that requires little or no assistance.

After purchasing the required number of licenses, you will add each team member as a user that includes his or her email address.

The Admin Overview page, as shown in the Figure below, assists the Office 365 Administrator. On the left, there are links to manage the users and domains in your Office 365 account. This is where you can add new users, delete users, set permission levels, enter and change passwords, and update the user properties and the licenses.

In the center, you can see the various services available to you in Office 365. In the site shown in Figure A, Outlook, Lync, SharePoint (team sites), and a public-facing website are all part of the services.

Activity | Using a Team Site to Collaborate

This group project relates to the **Bell Orchid Hotels**. If your instructor assigns this project to your class, you can expect to use a SharePoint team site in **Office 365** to collaborate on the following tasks for this chapter:

- If you are in the **Accounting Group**, you and your teammates will finalize the report to shareholders, merge the letter with the labels, and post the final report on the SharePoint team site.

- If you are in the **Engineering Group**, you and your teammates will finalize the report to the three insurance companies, merge the letter with the labels, and post the final report on the SharePoint team site.

- If you are in the **Food and Beverage Group**, you and your teammates will finalize the letter to customers planning a banquet, merge the letter with the labels, and post the final letter on the SharePoint team site.

- If you are in the **Human Resources Group**, you and your teammates will finalize the memo to employees, merge the memo with the labels, and post the final memo on the SharePoint team site.

- If you are in the **Operations Group**, you and your teammates will finalize the letter to job applicants, merge the letter with the labels, and post the final letter on the SharePoint team site.

- If you are in the **Sales and Marketing Group**, you and your teammates will finalize the letter to the 20 professional associations, merge the letter with the labels, and post the final letter on the SharePoint team site.

FIGURE A

END OF CHAPTER

SUMMARY

Word assists you in formatting a research paper for college or business by providing built-in styles and applies the most commonly used footnote and citation styles for research papers—MLA and APA.

Word helps you create the bibliography for your research paper by recording all of your citations in the Source Manager, and then generating the bibliography—in MLA, called Works Cited—for you.

Newsletters are often used by organizations to communicate information to a specific group. A newsletter can be formatted in two columns with a nameplate at the top that identifies the publication.

The Mail Merge Wizard enables you to easily merge a main document and a data source to create customized letters or labels. The data source can be a Word table, Excel spreadsheet, or Access database.

GO! LEARN IT ONLINE

Review the concepts and key terms in this chapter by completing these online challenges, which you can find at **www.pearsonhighered.com/go**.

Matching and Multiple Choice:
Answer matching and multiple choice questions to test what you learned in this chapter. MyITLab®

Crossword Puzzle:
Spell out the words that match the numbered clues, and put them in the puzzle squares.

Flipboard:
Flip through the definitions of the key terms in this chapter and match them with the correct term.

GO! FOR JOB SUCCESS

Video: Email Etiquette

Your instructor may assign this video to your class, and then ask you to think about, or discuss with your classmates, these questions:

FotolEdhar / Fotolia

Why do you think it is important to follow specific etiquette when composing email?

Why is it important to include a greeting and sign every email that you send?

What are the differences between sending a business email and a personal email, and what are three specific things you should never do in a business email?

END OF CHAPTER

REVIEW AND ASSESSMENT GUIDE FOR WORD CHAPTER 3

Your instructor may assign one or more of these projects to help you review the chapter and assess your mastery and understanding of the chapter.

		Review and Assessment Guide for Word Chapter 3	
Project	**Apply Skills from These Chapter Objectives**	**Project Type**	**Project Location**
3C	Objectives 1-4 from Project 3A	**3C Skills Review** A guided review of the skills from Project 3A.	On the following pages
3D	Objectives 5-7 from Project 3B	**3D Skills Review** A guided review of the skills from Project 3B.	On the following pages
3E	Objectives 1-4 from Project 3A	**3E Mastery (Grader Project)** A demonstration of your mastery of the skills in Project 3A with extensive decision making.	In MyITLab and on the following pages
3F	Objectives 5-7 from Project 3B	**3F Mastery (Grader Project)** A demonstration of your mastery of the skills in Project 3B with extensive decision making.	In MyITLab and on the following pages
3G	Objectives 1-7 from Projects 3A and 3B	**3G Mastery (Grader Project)** A demonstration of your mastery of the skills in Projects 3A and 3B with extensive decision making.	In MyITLab and on the following pages
3H	Combination of Objectives from Projects 3A and 3B	**3H GO! Fix It** A demonstration of your mastery of the skills in Projects 3A and 3B by creating a correct result from a document that contains errors you must find.	Online
3I	Combination of Objectives from Projects 3A and 3B	**3I GO! Make It** A demonstration of your mastery of the skills in Projects 3A and 3B by creating a result from a supplied picture.	Online
3J	Combination of Objectives from Projects 3A and 3B	**3J GO! Solve It** A demonstration of your mastery of the skills in Projects 3A and 3B, your decision-making skills, and your critical thinking skills. A task-specific rubric helps you self-assess your result.	Online
3K	Combination of Objectives from Projects 3A and 3B	**3K GO! Solve It** A demonstration of your mastery of the skills in Projects 3A and 3B, your decision-making skills, and your critical thinking skills. A task-specific rubric helps you self-assess your result.	On the following pages
3L	Combination of Objectives from Projects 3A and 3B	**3L GO! Think** A demonstration of your understanding of the chapter concepts applied in a manner that you would outside of college. An analytic rubric helps you and your instructor grade the quality of your work by comparing it to the work an expert in the discipline would create.	On the following pages
3M	Combination of Objectives from Projects 3A and 3B	**3M GO! Think** A demonstration of your understanding of the chapter concepts applied in a manner that you would outside of college. An analytic rubric helps you and your instructor grade the quality of your work by comparing it to the work an expert in the discipline would create.	Online
3N	Combination of Objectives from Projects 3A and 3B	**3N You and GO!** A demonstration of your understanding of the chapter concepts applied in a manner that you would in a personal situation. An analytic rubric helps you and your instructor grade the quality of your work.	Online
3O	Combination of Objectives from Projects 3A and 3B	**3O Cumulative Group Project for Word Chapter 3** A demonstration of your understanding of concepts and your ability to work collaboratively in a group role-playing assessment, requiring both collaboration and self-management.	Online
Capstone Project for Word Chapters 1-3	Combination of Objectives from Projects 1A, 1B, 2A, 2B, 3A, and 3B	A demonstration of your mastery of the skills in Chapters 1-3 with extensive decision making. **(Grader Project)**	In MyITLab and online

GLOSSARY

GLOSSARY OF CHAPTER KEY TERMS

American Psychological Association (APA) One of two commonly used style guides for formatting research papers.

Bibliography A list of cited works in a report or research paper; also referred to as Works Cited, Sources, or References, depending upon the report style.

Brightness The relative lightness of a picture.

Citation A note inserted into the text of a research paper that refers the reader to a source in the bibliography.

Column break indicator A dotted line containing the words *Column Break* that displays at the bottom of the column.

Contrast The difference between the darkest and lightest area of a picture.

Crop A command that removes unwanted or unnecessary areas of a picture.

Crop handles Handles used to define unwanted areas of a picture.

Crop pointer The pointer used to crop areas of a picture.

Data source A document that contains a list of variable information, such as names and addresses, that is merged with a main document to create customized form letters or labels.

Em dash A punctuation symbol used to indicate an explanation or emphasis.

Endnote In a research paper, a note placed at the end of a document or chapter.

Fields In a mail merge, the column headings in the data source.

Flip A command that creates a reverse image of a picture or object.

Footnote In a research paper, a note placed at the bottom of the page.

Hanging indent An indent style in which the first line of a paragraph extends to the left of the remaining lines and that is commonly used for bibliographic entries.

Line break indicator A non-printing character in the shape of a bent arrow that indicates a manual line break.

Mail merge A feature that joins a main document and a data source to create customized letters or labels.

Main document In a mail merge, the document that contains the text or formatting that remains constant.

Manual column break An artificial end to a column to balance columns or to provide space for the insertion of other objects.

Manual line break A break that moves text to the right of the insertion point to a new line while keeping the text in the same paragraph.

Manual page break The action of forcing a page to end and placing subsequent text at the top of the next page.

Modern Language Association (MLA) One of two commonly used style guides for formatting research papers.

Nameplate The banner on the front page of a newsletter that identifies the publication.

Newsletter A periodical that communicates news and information to a specific group.

Note In a research paper, information that expands on the topic, but that does not fit well in the document text.

Office 365 Administrator—the person who creates and manages the account, adds new users, sets up the services your organization wants to use, sets permission levels, and manages the SharePoint team sites.

Page break indicator A dotted line with the text *Page Break* that indicates where a manual page break was inserted.

Parenthetical references References that include the last name of the author or authors, and the page number in the referenced source.

PDF Reflow The ability to import PDF files into Word so that you can transform a PDF back into a fully editable Word document.

Read Mode A view in Word that optimizes the Word screen for the times when you are reading Word documents on the screen and not creating or editing them.

Recolor A feature that enables you to change all colors in the picture to shades of a single color.

Record Each row of information that contains data for one person.

Scale A command that resizes a picture to a percentage of its size.

Screenshot An image of an active window on your computer that you can paste into a document.

Section A portion of a document that can be formatted differently from the rest of the document.

Section break A double dotted line that indicates the end of one section and the beginning of another section.

Small caps A font effect that changes lowercase letters to uppercase letters, but with the height of lowercase letters.

Style A group of formatting commands, such as font, font size, font color, paragraph alignment, and line spacing that can be applied to a paragraph with one command.

Style guide A manual that contains standards for the design and writing of documents.

Suppress A Word feature that hides header and footer information, including the page number, on the first page of a document.

Windows Reader app A Windows Store app with which you can open a PDF or XPS file, zoom, find words or phrases, take notes, save changes, and then print or share the file.

Works Cited In the MLA style, a list of cited works placed at the end of a research paper or report.

CHAPTER REVIEW

Skills Review   Project 3C Diet and Exercise Report

In the following Skills Review, you will edit and format a research paper that contains information about the effects of diet and exercise. This paper was created by Rachel Holder, a medical intern at University Medical Center, for distribution to her classmates studying physiology. Your completed document will look similar to the one shown in Figure 3.55.

PROJECT FILES

For Project 3C, you will need the following file:

w03C_Diet_Exercise

You will save your document as:

Lastname_Firstname_3C_Diet_Exercise

PROJECT RESULTS

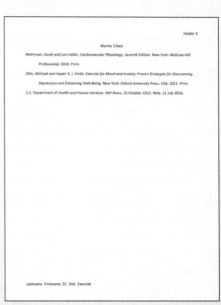

FIGURE 3.55

(Project 3C Diet and Exercise Report continues on the next page)

CHAPTER REVIEW

1 Start Word. From your student files, locate and open the document **w03C_Diet_Exercise**. Display the formatting marks and rulers. **Save** the file in your **Word Chapter 3** folder as **Lastname_Firstname_3C_Diet_Exercise**

a. Press Ctrl + A to select all the text. On the **HOME tab**, in the **Paragraph group**, click **Line and Paragraph Spacing**, and then change the line spacing to **2.0**. On the **PAGE LAYOUT tab**, change the **Spacing After** to **0 pt**.

b. Press Ctrl + Home, press Enter to create a blank line at the top of the document, and then click to position the insertion point in the new blank line. Type **Rachel Holder** and press Enter. Type **Dr. Hillary Kim** and press Enter. Type **Physiology 621** and press Enter. Type **August 31, 2016** and press Enter.

c. Type **Effects of Diet and Exercise** and then press Ctrl + E to center the title you just typed.

2 On the **INSERT tab**, in the **Header & Footer group**, click **Header**, and then at the bottom of the list, click **Edit Header**. Type **Holder** and then press Spacebar.

a. Under **HEADER & FOOTER TOOLS**, on the **DESIGN tab**, in the **Header & Footer group**, click **Page Number**, and then point to **Current Position**. Under **Simple**, click **Plain Number**.

b. On the **HOME tab**, in the **Paragraph group**, click **Align Right**. Double-click anywhere in the document to close the Header area.

c. Near the top of **Page 1**, locate the paragraph beginning *The scientific evidence*, and then click to position the insertion point at the beginning of that paragraph. Scroll to the end of the document, hold down Shift, and then click to the right of the last paragraph mark to select all of the text from the insertion point to the end of the document.

d. On the **HOME tab**, in the **Paragraph group**, click the **Dialog Box Launcher** button. In the **Paragraph** dialog box, on the **Indents and Spacing tab**, under **Indentation**, click the **Special arrow**, and then click **First line**. Click **OK**.

e. On the **INSERT tab**, in the **Header & Footer group**, click **Footer**, and then click **Edit Footer**. In the **Insert group**, click **Document Info**, and then click **File Name**. Click **Close Header and Footer**.

3 Scroll to view the top of **Page 2**, locate the paragraph that begins *Exercise also has*, and then at the end of that paragraph, click to position the insertion point to the right of the period following *Irwin*. On the **REFERENCES tab**, in the **Footnotes group**, click **Insert Footnote**.

a. As the footnote text, type **Physical activity may provide a low-risk method of preventing weight gain. Unlike diet-induced weight loss, exercise-induced weight loss increases cardiorespiratory fitness levels.**

b. In the upper portion of **Page 1**, locate the paragraph that begins *Regular cardiovascular exercise*. Click to position the insertion point at the end of the paragraph and insert a footnote.

c. As the footnote text, type **The objective of the study was to examine the effects of exercise on total and intra-abdominal body fat overall and by level of exercise. Save** your document.

4 At the bottom of **Page 1**, right-click in the footnote you just typed. On the shortcut menu, click **Style**. In the **Style** dialog box, click **Modify**. In the **Modify Style** dialog box, locate the small Formatting toolbar in the center of the dialog box, click the **Font Size button arrow**, and then click **11**.

a. In the lower left corner of the dialog box, click **Format**, and then click **Paragraph**. In the **Paragraph** dialog box, under **Indentation**, click the **Special arrow**, and then click **First line**. Under **Spacing**, click the **Line spacing button arrow**, and then click **Double**.

b. Click **OK** to close the **Paragraph** dialog box, click **OK** to close the **Modify Style** dialog box, and then click **Apply** to apply the new style. **Save** your document.

5 Scroll to view the top of **Page 1**, and then in the paragraph that begins *The scientific evidence*, click to position the insertion point to the left of the period at the end of the paragraph.

a. On the **REFERENCES tab**, in the **Citations & Bibliography group**, click the **Style button arrow**, and then click **MLA** to insert a reference using MLA style. Click **Insert Citation**, and then click **Add New Source**. Click the **Type of Source arrow**, scroll as

(Project 3C Diet and Exercise Report continues on the next page)

CHAPTER REVIEW

necessary to locate and click **Book**, and then add the following information:

Author	Otto, Michael and Jasper A. J. Smits
Title	Exercise for Mood and Anxiety: Proven Strategies for Overcoming Depression and Enhancing Well-Being
Year	2011
City	New York
Publisher	Oxford University Press, USA
Medium	Print

b. Click **OK** to insert the citation. In the paragraph, click to select the citation, click the **Citation Options arrow**, and then click **Edit Citation**. In the **Edit Citation** dialog box, under **Add**, in the **Pages** box, type **3** and then click **OK**.

c. On the upper portion of **Page 2**, in the paragraph that begins *Other positive effects*, in the third line, click to position the insertion point to the left of the period following *substantially*. In the **Citations & Bibliography group**, click **Insert Citation**, and then click **Add New Source**. Click the **Type of Source arrow**, click **Book**, and then add the following information:

Author	Lohrman, David and Lois Heller
Title	Cardiovascular Physiology, Seventh Edition
Year	2010
City	New York
Publisher	McGraw-Hill Professional
Medium	Print

d. Click **OK**. Click to select the citation in the paragraph, click the **Citation Options arrow**, and then click **Edit Citation**. In the **Edit Citation** dialog box, under **Add**, in the **Pages** box, type **195** and then click **OK**.

6 Press `Ctrl` + `End` to move to the end of the last paragraph in the document. Click to the left of the period following *loss*. In the **Citations & Bibliography group**,

click **Insert Citation**, and then click **Add New Source**. Click the **Type of Source arrow**, click **Web site**, and then select the **Corporate Author** check box. Add the following information:

Corporate Author	U.S. Department of Health and Human Services
Name of Web Page	NIH News
Year	2012
Month	October
Day	15
Year Accessed	2016
Month Accessed	July
Day Accessed	21
Medium	Web

a. Click **OK**. Press `Ctrl` + `End` to move the insertion point to the end of the document. Press `Ctrl` + `Enter` to insert a manual page break. On the **HOME tab**, in the **Paragraph group**, click the **Dialog Box Launcher** button. In the **Paragraph** dialog box, on the **Indents and Spacing tab**, under **Indentation**, click the **Special arrow**, and then click **(none)**. Click **OK**.

b. Type **Works Cited** and then press `Enter`. On the **REFERENCES tab**, in the **Citations & Bibliography group**, be sure **MLA** displays in the **Style** box. In the **Citations & Bibliography group**, click **Bibliography**, and then at the bottom, click **Insert Bibliography**.

c. Click anywhere in the *Works Cited* title, and then press `Ctrl` + `E` to center the title. **Save** your document.

7 On the **REFERENCES tab**, in the **Citations & Bibliography group**, click **Manage Sources**. On the left, on the **Master List**, click the entry for *Lohrman, David*, and then click **Edit**. In the **Edit Source** dialog box, in the **Author** box, change the *L* in *Lohrman* to **M** Click **OK**, click **Yes**, and then click **Close**.

a. On **Page 2**, in the paragraph that begins *Other positive effects*, in the third line, on the selected citation, click the **Citation Options arrow**, and then click **Update Citations and Bibliography**.

(Project 3C Diet and Exercise Report continues on the next page)

CHAPTER REVIEW

b. In the bibliography, move the pointer to the left of the first entry—beginning *Mohrman*—to display the ↗ pointer. Drag down to select all three references in the field. On the **HOME tab**, in the **Paragraph group**, set the **Line spacing** to **2.0**. On the **PAGE LAYOUT tab**, set the **Spacing After** to **0 pt**.

c. Click the **FILE tab**, and then in the lower right corner, click **Show All Properties**. Add the following information:

Title	Diet and Exercise
Tags	weight loss, exercise, diet
Comments	Draft copy of report for class
Categories	biomedical research
Company	University Medical Center
Manager	Dr. Hillary Kim

d. In the **Subject** box, type your course name and section number. Be sure that your name displays as the Author and edit if necessary. On the left, click **Save** to redisplay your document. On the **VIEW tab**, in the **Views group**, click **Read Mode**. In the upper left, click **TOOLS**, click **Find**, and then in the search box, type **Yale** and notice that the text you searched for is highlighted in the document.

e. In the upper left, click **VIEW**, and then click **Edit Document** to return to **Print Layout** view. **Close** the **navigation pane**. **Save** your document, view the **Print Preview**, and then print or submit electronically as directed by your instructor. **Close** Word.

END | You have completed Project 3C

CHAPTER REVIEW

Skills Review Project 3D Career Newsletter

In the following Skills Review, you will format a newsletter regarding professional development opportunities offered by University Medical Center, and you will create mailing labels for staff interested in these opportunities. Your completed document will look similar to Figure 3.56.

PROJECT FILES

For Project 3D, you will need the following files:

New blank Word document
w03D_Career_Newsletter
w03D_Addresses

You will save your documents as:

Lastname_Firstname_3D_Career_Newsletter
Lastname_Firstname_3D_Addresses
Lastname_Firstname_3D_Mailing_Labels

PROJECT RESULTS

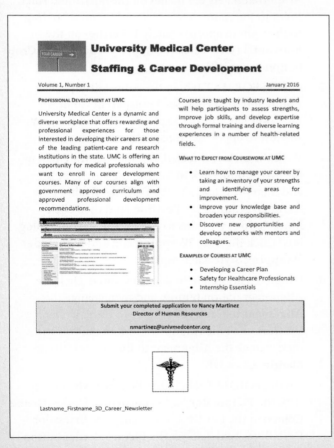

FIGURE 3.56

(Project 3D Career Newsletter continues on the next page)

CHAPTER REVIEW

1 ▶ Start Word. On Word's opening screen, in the lower left, click **Open Other Documents**. Navigate to your student files, and then locate and open **w03D_Career_Newsletter**. **Save** the file in your **Word Chapter 3** folder as **Lastname_Firstname_3D_Career_Newsletter** and then add the file name to the footer.

a. Select the first two lines of the document. On the mini toolbar, change the **Font** to **Arial Black** and the **Font Size** to **18**. Select the first three lines of the document. Click the **Font Color button arrow**, and then under **Theme Colors**, in the fifth column, click the last color—**Blue, Accent 1, Darker 50%**.

b. With the text still selected, on the **HOME tab**, in the **Paragraph group**, click the **Borders button arrow**, and then at the bottom, click **Borders and Shading**. In the **Borders and Shading** dialog box, on the **Borders tab**, click the **Color arrow**, and then under **Theme Colors**, in the fifth column, click the last color—**Blue, Accent 1, Darker 50%**.

c. Click the **Width arrow**, and then click **3 pt**. In the **Preview** box, click the bottom border. Click **OK**.

d. Click at the beginning of the paragraph that begins *Professional Development*. Scroll the document, hold down [Shift], and then click after the paragraph mark at the end of the *Internship Essentials* line. On the **PAGE LAYOUT tab**, in the **Page Setup group**, click **Columns**, and then click **Two**. With the two columns of text selected, on the **HOME tab**, in the **Paragraph group**, click **Justify**.

e. In the first column, click at the beginning of the paragraph that begins *Courses are taught*. On the **PAGE LAYOUT tab**, in the **Page Setup group**, click **Breaks**. Under **Page Breaks**, click **Column**.

2 ▶ Press [Ctrl] + [Home]. On the **INSERT tab**, in the **Illustrations group**, click **Online Pictures**. In the **Office.com Clip Art** search box, type **career** and then press [Enter]. Click the image of the sign with the text *Your Career*. If the image does not display, select a similar picture. Click **Insert**.

a. On the **FORMAT tab**, in the **Size group**, click the **Dialog Box Launcher** button. In the **Layout** dialog box, on the **Size tab**, under **Scale**, be sure the **Lock aspect ratio** and **Relative to original picture size** check boxes are selected. Select the number in the **Height** box, type **10** and then press [Tab].

b. In the **Layout** dialog box, click the **Text Wrapping tab**. Under **Wrapping style**, click **Square**.

c. Click the **Position tab**, and then under **Horizontal**, click the **Alignment** option button. Be sure that the **Alignment** indicates **Left** and **relative to Column**. Under **Vertical**, click the **Alignment** option button, and then change the alignment to **Top relative to Margin**. Click **OK**. **Save** your newsletter.

3 ▶ Press [Ctrl] + [End] to move to the end of the document. On the **INSERT tab**, in the **Illustrations group**, click **Online Pictures**. In the **Office.com Clip Art** search box, search for **caducei healthcare symbol** and then insert the picture of the gray caducei with a gray shadow. If the image does not display, select a similar picture.

a. On the **FORMAT tab**, in the **Size group**, click the upper portion of the **Crop** button. Point to the center right crop handle, and then drag to the left to approximately **5.5 inches on the horizontal ruler**. Point to the center left crop handle, and then drag to the right to approximately **1.5 inches on the horizontal ruler**. Click the upper portion of the **Crop** button to apply the crop.

b. On the **FORMAT tab**, in the **Adjust group**, click **Color**, and then click **Set Transparent Color**. In the lower left area of the picture, click in the gray shadow to apply the transparent color.

c. With the picture selected, on the **FORMAT tab**, in the **Size group**, click in the **Height** box. Type **1** and then press [Enter]. On the **FORMAT tab**, in the **Arrange group**, click **Position**, and then click **More Layout Options** to display the **Layout** dialog box. Click the **Text Wrapping tab**, and then under **Wrapping Style**, click **Square**.

d. On the **Position tab**, under **Horizontal**, click the **Alignment** option button, and then change the **Alignment** to **Centered relative to Page**. Under **Vertical**, click the **Alignment** option button, and then change the **Alignment** to **Bottom relative to Margin**. Click **OK**.

e. On the **FORMAT tab**, in the **Picture Styles group**, click the **Picture Border button arrow**. Under **Theme Colors**, in the fourth column, click the first color—**Dark Blue, Text 2**. Click the **Picture Border button arrow** again, and then point to **Weight**. Click **1 pt**.

(Project 3D Career Newsletter continues on the next page)

CHAPTER REVIEW

f. On the **FORMAT tab**, in the **Adjust group**, click **Color**. Under **Recolor**, in the first row, click the last option—**Black and White, 75%**. On the **FORMAT tab**, in the **Adjust group**, click **Corrections**. Under **Brightness/Contrast**, in the second row, click the fourth setting—**Brightness: +20% Contrast: –20%**.

4 In the paragraph that begins *University Medical Center is a dynamic*, click after the period at the end of the paragraph, and then press Enter. Start Internet Explorer, maximize the window, and then navigate to **www.ahrq.gov/clinic/**

a. Redisplay your **3D_Career_Newletter** document. With the insertion point positioned in the blank line above the column break, on the **INSERT tab**, in the **Illustrations group**, click **Screenshot**. In the **Screenshot** gallery, click the browser window that contains the website; click **No** in the message that displays.

b. Select the subheading *Professional Development at UMC* including the paragraph mark. Right-click the selected text, and then on the shortcut menu, click **Font**. In the **Font** dialog box, click the **Font color arrow**, and then in the fifth column, click the last color—**Blue, Accent 1, Darker 50%**. Under **Font style**, click **Bold**, and then under **Effects**, select **Small caps**. Click **OK**.

c. With the text still selected, right-click, and then on the mini toolbar, double-click **Format Painter**. In the second column, with the ⬛I pointer, select each of the subheadings—*What to Expect from Coursework at UMC* and *Example of Courses at UMC*. Press Esc to turn off **Format Painter**.

5 Press Ctrl + End to move to the end of the document, and then select the two lines of bold text—the graphic will also be selected. On the **HOME tab**, in the **Paragraph group**, click the **Borders button arrow**, and then click **Borders and Shading**.

a. In the **Borders and Shading** dialog box, on the **Borders tab**, under **Setting**, click **Shadow**. Click the **Color arrow**, and then in the fifth column, click the last color—**Blue, Accent 1, Darker 50%**. Click the **Width arrow**, and then click **1 pt**.

b. In the **Borders and Shading** dialog box, click the **Shading tab**. Click the **Fill arrow**, and then in the

fifth column, click the second color—**Blue, Accent 1, Lighter 80%**. Click **OK**. On the **HOME tab**, in the **Paragraph group**, click **Center**. In the shaded paragraph, click in front of the *D* in the word *Director*. Hold down Shift and then press Enter.

c. Press Ctrl + Home, and then click the **FILE tab**. At the bottom of the **Properties** list, click **Show All Properties**. Click to the right of **Tags**, and then type **newsletter, careers** Click to the right of **Subject**, and then type your course name and section number. Under **Related People**, if necessary, type your name in the Author box. Display the **Print Preview** and make any necessary corrections. **Save** the document; close Word and close Internet Explorer.

6 Start Word and display a new blank document. **Save** the document in your **Word Chapter 3** folder as **Lastname_Firstname_3D_Mailing_Labels** With your new document open on the screen, from your student files, **Open** the file **w03D_Addresses**. **Save** the address file in your **Word Chapter 3** folder as **Lastname_Firstname_3D_Addresses** and then add the file name to the footer. **Save** and then **Close** the file. Be sure that your **Lastname_Firstname_3D_Mailing_Labels** document displays.

a. Click the **MAILINGS tab**. In the **Start Mail Merge group**, click **Start Mail Merge**, and then click **Step-by-Step Mail Merge Wizard**. In the **Mail Merge** pane, under **Select document type**, click **Labels**. At the bottom of the **Mail Merge** pane, click **Next: Starting document**.

b. Under **Select starting document**, under **Change document layout**, click **Label options**. In the **Label Options** dialog box, under **Printer information**, be sure that the **Default tray** is selected.

c. Under **Label information**, click the **Label vendors arrow**, and then click **Avery US Letter**. Under **Product number**, scroll about halfway down the list, and then click **5160 Easy Peel Address Labels**. At the bottom of the **Label Options** dialog box, click **OK**. At the bottom of the **Mail Merge** pane, click **Next: Select recipients**.

d. In the **Mail Merge** pane, under **Select recipients**, under **Use an existing list**, click **Browse**. Navigate to your **Word Chapter 3** folder, select your **Lastname_Firstname_3D_Addresses** file, and then click **Open**.

(Project 3D Career Newsletter continues on the next page)

CHAPTER REVIEW

7 In the lower left portion of the **Mail Merge Recipients** dialog box, in the **Data Source** box, click the path that contains your file name. Then, at the bottom of the **Mail Merge Recipients** dialog box, click **Edit**. In the upper right corner of the **Data Form** dialog box, click **Add New**. In the blank record, type the following, pressing Tab to move from field to field:

First_Name:	Mia
Last_Name:	Orr
Address_1:	1378 Lima Ave.
Unit:	#82
City:	Memphis
State:	TN
ZIP_Code:	38123

a. In the lower right corner of the **Data Form** dialog box, click **Close**. At the bottom of the **Mail Merge Recipients** dialog box, click **OK**.

b. At the bottom of the **Mail Merge** pane, click **Next: Arrange your labels**. Under **Arrange your labels**, click **Address block**. In the lower right corner of the **Insert Address Block** dialog box, click **Match Fields**.

c. Click the **Address 2 arrow**, and then from the list of available fields, click **Unit**. Click **OK** two times.

d. In the **Mail Merge** pane, under **Replicate labels**, click **Update all labels**. At the bottom of the **Mail**

Merge pane, click **Next: Preview your labels**. Press Ctrl + A to select all of the label text, click the **PAGE LAYOUT tab**, and then in the **Paragraph group**, click in the **Spacing Before** box. Type **3** and press Enter. At the bottom of the **Mail Merge** pane, click **Next: Complete the merge**.

e. Click the **MAILINGS tab**, and then in the **Start Mail Merge group**, click **Edit Recipient List** to display the list of names and addresses. In the **Mail Merge Recipients** dialog box, click the **Last_Name** field heading to sort the names. Click **OK**. **Close** the **Mail Merge** pane.

f. Scroll the document and then click anywhere in the empty table row at the bottom. Click the **LAYOUT tab**. In the **Rows & Columns group**, click **Delete**, and then click **Delete Rows**. Add the file name to the footer, close the footer area, and then click the **FILE tab**. Click **Show All Properties**. As the **Tags**, type **labels** and as the **Subject**, type your course name and section number. Be sure your name displays as the **Author**, and then **Save** your file.

g. As directed by your instructor, print or submit electronically. **Close** the document, click **Yes** to save the data source, and then if necessary, click **Save** to save the labels. In addition to your labels and address document, submit your **3D_Career_Newsletter** document as directed. **Close** Word.

END | You have completed Project 3D

CONTENT-BASED ASSESSMENTS

Apply 3A skills from these Objectives:

1 Create a Research Paper

2 Insert Footnotes in a Research Paper

3 Create Citations and a Bibliography in a Research Paper

4 Use Read Mode and PDF Reflow

Mastering Word | Project 3E Skin Protection Report

In the following Mastering Word project, you will edit and format a research paper that contains information about skin protection and the use of sunblocks and sunscreens. This paper was created by Rachel Holder, a medical intern at University Medical Center, for distribution to her classmates studying dermatology. Your completed document will look similar to the one shown in Figure 3.57.

PROJECT FILES

For Project 3E, you will need the following file:

w03E_Skin_Protection

You will save your document as:

Lastname_Firstname_3E_Skin_Protection

PROJECT RESULTS

FIGURE 3.57

(Project 3E Skin Protection Report continues on the next page)

CONTENT-BASED ASSESSMENTS

1 Start Word. From your student files, locate and open the document **w03E_Skin_Protection**. Display formatting marks and rulers. Save the file in your **Word Chapter 3** folder as **Lastname_Firstname_3E_Skin_Protection**

2 Select all the text, change the **Line Spacing** to **2.0**, and then change the **Spacing After** to **0 pt**. At the top of the document, insert a new blank paragraph, and then in the new paragraph, type **Rachel Holder** Press Enter. Type **Dr. Hillary Kim** and press Enter. Type **Dermatology 544** and press Enter. Type **August 31, 2016** and press Enter. Type **Skin Protection** and then press Ctrl + E to center the title you just typed.

3 Insert a header, type **Holder** and then press Spacebar. Display the **Page Number gallery**, and then in the **Current Position**, add the **Plain Number** style. Apply **Align Right** formatting to the header. Insert a footer with the file name. Starting with the paragraph that begins *One way to prevent*, select all the text in the document, and then set a **First line** indent of **0.5"**.

4 On **Page 2**, at the end of the paragraph that begins *In the medical field*, insert a footnote with the following text: **The American Academy of Dermatology recommends using a broad spectrum sunscreen with an SPF of 30 or more.**

5 On **Page 2**, at the end of the paragraph that begins *Individuals should protect*, insert a footnote with the following text: **For babies, the American Academy of Dermatology recommends using a sunscreen that contains only inorganic filters, such as zinc oxide and titanium dioxide, to avoid any skin or eye irritation.**

6 Modify the **Footnote Text** style so that the **Font Size** is **11**, there is a **First line indent** of **0.5"**, and the spacing is **Double**, and then apply the style.

7 On **Page 1**, at the end of the paragraph that begins *According to an article*, click to the left of the period, and then using **MLA** format, insert a citation for a **Journal Article** with the following information:

Author	Frash, D. E., A. S. Jonason, and J. A. Simon
Title	Sunlight and Sunburn in Human Skin Cancer
Journal Name	The Journal of Investigative Dermatology

Year	1996
Pages	136-142
Medium	Print

8 In the report, select the citation you just created, display the **Citation Options**, and then edit the citation to include **Pages 136-142** At the end of the last paragraph of the report, click to the left of the period, and then insert a citation for a **Book** with the following information:

Author	Leffell, David
Title	Total Skin: The Definitive Guide to Whole Skin Care for Life
Year	2000
City	New York
Publisher	Hyperion
Medium	Print

9 In the report, select the citation you just created, display the **Citation Options**, and then edit the citation to include **Page 96** At the top of **Page 2**, at the end of the paragraph that begins *According to Dr.*, click to the left of the period, and then insert a citation for a **Web site** with the following information:

Author	Gibson, Lawrence E.
Name of Web Page	Does Sunscreen Expire?
Year	2011
Month	April
Day	01
Year Accessed	2016
Month Accessed	June
Day Accessed	30
Medium	Web

10 Move to the end of the document, and then insert a manual page break to create a new page. Display the **Paragraph** dialog box, and then change the **Indentation** under **Special** to **(none)**. Add a **Works Cited** title, press Enter, and then click **Insert Bibliography**. **Center** the *Works Cited* title.

(Project 3E Skin Protection Report continues on the next page)

CONTENT-BASED ASSESSMENTS

11 By using the **Manage Sources** command, display the **Source Manager**. On the **Master List**, select the entry for **Frash, D. E.**, and then **Edit** this source—the last name should be **Brash** instead of *Frash*. In the message that displays, update both lists. Locate the citation in the text of the report, display the **Citation Options**, and then **Update Citations and Bibliography**. On the Works Cited page, select the references, apply **Double** line spacing, and then set the **Spacing After** paragraphs to **0 pt**.

12 Update the **Document Properties** with the following information:

Title	Skin Protection
Tags	sunscreen, sun exposure
Comments	Draft copy of report for class
Categories	Dermatology
Company	University Medical Center
Manager	Dr. Hillary Kim

13 In the **Subject** box, type your course name and section number. Be sure that your name displays as the **Author** and edit if necessary. On the left, click **Print** to view the **Print Preview**, and then click **Save** to redisplay your document. Print or submit electronically as directed by your instructor. **Close** Word.

END | You have completed Project 3E

Mastering Word | Project 3F Dogs Newsletter and Mailing Labels

In the following Mastering Word project, you will format a newsletter with information about the therapy dogs handled by volunteers at the University Medical Center. You will also create mailing labels so that the newsletter can be sent to the volunteer staff. Your completed documents will look similar to Figure 3.58.

Apply 3B skills from these Objectives:

5 Format a Multiple-Column Newsletter

6 Use Special Character and Paragraph Formatting

7 Create Mailing Labels Using Mail Merge

PROJECT FILES

For Project 3F, you will need the following files:

New blank Word document
w03F_Dogs_Newsletter
w03F_Addresses

You will save your documents as:

Lastname_Firstname_3F_Dogs_Newsletter
Lastname_Firstname_3F_Addresses
Lastname_Firstname_3F_Mailing_Labels

PROJECT RESULTS

University Medical Center
Health Improvement Newsletter

Volume 3   Spring 2016

DOGS FOR HEALING

At University Medical Center, therapy dogs have been a welcomed asset to patient care and recovery since 2004. UMC works with several non-profit organizations to bring dedicated volunteers and their canine teams into the hospital to visit children, adults, and seniors. Information regarding service dog regulations, training, and laws is available on the ADA website.

BENEFITS TO PATIENTS

Medical research shows that petting a dog or other domestic animal relaxes patients and helps ease symptoms of stress from illness or from the hospital setting. Studies have shown that such therapies contribute to decreased blood pressure and heart rate, and can help with patient respiratory rate.

CUDDLES

Cuddles, a 4 year-old Labrador, is one of our most popular therapy dogs and is loved by both young and senior patients. You'll see Cuddles in the Children's wing on Mondays with his owner, Jason, who trained him since he was a tiny pup.

BRANDY

Brandy is a 6 year-old Beagle who brings smiles and giggles to everyone she meets. Over the past several years, Brandy has received accolades and awards for her service as a therapy dog. Brandy is owned by Melinda Sparks, a 17-year veteran employee of University Medical Center. Brandy and Melinda can be seen making the rounds on Wednesdays in the Children's wing and on Mondays and Fridays throughout the hospital.

To request a visit from a therapy dog, or to learn how to become involved with therapy dog training, call Carole Yates at extension 2365.

Lastname_Firstname_3F_Dogs_Newsletter

Mary Ackerman
82 E. Roxie Blvd.
Arlington, TN 38002

Anthony Borman
2820 Lincoln Ave.
Collierville, TN 38017

Jerry Camden
543 Verde Way
Memphis, TN 38120

Jacqueline Epps
653 Vista Ave.
#D
Lakeland, TN 38002

Renee Farnsworth
36 S. Levin St.
#D
Bartlett, TN 38135

Anita Figueroa
9000 S. Masters Dr.
Germantown, TN 38139

Emily Gold
888 Packard Court
Lakeland, TN 38002

Abel Heaphy
55 Amigo Lane
#4
Collierville, TN 38017

Katie Hughes
34 Sadler Pl.
Bartlett, TN 38133

Bin Lee
676 Silver St.
Memphis, TN 38120

Anh Ly
1255 Chestnut Street
Memphis, TN 38122

Priya Malik
975 Ricardo Place
#G
Germantown, TN 38138

Leland Marcus
600 Garfield Ave.
Memphis, TN 38117

Walter McKidd
2495 Holly Drive
Arlington, TN 38002

Sharon Moreno
1330 Golden Ave.
Memphis, TN 38120

Thai Nguyen
179 Sierra Court
Collierville, TN 38017

Thomas Norris
492 Mahogany Street
Bartlett, TN 38135

Daniel Scofield
1518 Price Place
Arlington, TN 38002

Erica Scott
124 Susan Drive
#352
Memphis, TN 38134

Andrew Sharma
1550 Beverly Drive
#1550
Memphis, TN 38104

Sara Thompson
4220 Glendora Dr.
#320
Memphis, TN 38112

Simone Thompson
648 Michaela St.
Bartlett, TN 38133

David Turnbull
1821 Chelsea St.
#1442
Germantown, TN 38138

Jackson Williams
15 Atlantic Rd.
Memphis, TN 38111

Miranda Yanos
1256 Loma Ave.
#34
Memphis, TN 38123

Lastname_Firstname_3F_Mailing_Labels

FIGURE 3.58

(Project 3F Dogs Newsletter and Mailing Labels continues on the next page)

CONTENT-BASED ASSESSMENTS

1 Start Word. From your student files, open **w03F_Dogs_Newsletter**. **Save** the file in your **Word Chapter 3** folder as **Lastname_Firstname_3F_Dogs_Newsletter** and then add the file name to the footer. Select the first three lines of the document, and then change the **Font Color** to **Olive Green, Accent 3, Darker 25%**—in the seventh column, the fifth color. With the text selected, display the **Borders and Shading** dialog box. Apply a **3 pt** bottom border in **Black, Text 1**.

2 Click at the beginning of the newsletter title *University Medical Center*. Insert an online picture from **Office.com Clip Art** by searching for **physician symbols** Insert the picture of the physician symbol on top of the green oval with a blue outline. Use the **Set Transparent Color** command to make the green background transparent. Change the **Brightness/Contrast** to **Brightness: 0% (Normal) Contrast: +40%**.

3 **Scale** the picture to **50%** of its **Height**, and then change the **Text Wrapping** to **Square**. Change the **Horizontal Alignment** to **Left relative** to **Margin** and the **Vertical Alignment** to **Top relative** to **Margin**.

4 Starting with the paragraph that begins *Dogs for Healing*, select all of the text from that point to the end of the document. Change the **Spacing After** to **10 pt**, format the text in two columns, and apply **Justify** alignment. Insert a **Column break** before the subheading *Cuddles*.

5 Click at the beginning of the sentence that begins with *Brandy is a 6 year-old Beagle*. Insert an online picture from **Office.com Clip Art** by searching for **beagle** Insert the picture of the beagle sitting on the grass. Rotate the picture using **Flip Horizontal**. Change the picture **Height** to **1.5** and then apply the **Square** layout option. Change the **Horizontal Alignment** to **Right relative** to **Margin** and the **Vertical Alignment** to **Top relative** to **Line**. Apply a **Black, Text 1 Picture Border** and change the **Weight** to **2 1/4 pt**.

6 Start Internet Explorer, navigate to **www.ada.gov/qasrvc.htm** and then maximize your browser window. In your **3F_Dogs_Newsletter** file, click at the end of the paragraph below the *Dogs for Healing* subheading, and then press ⏎. In the blank line, insert a **Screenshot** of the website; do not link to the URL. Apply a **Black, Text 1 Picture Border** and change the **Weight** to **1 pt**.

7 Select the subheading *Dogs for Healing* including the paragraph mark. By using the **Font** dialog box, change the **Size** to **16**, apply **Bold**, apply the **Small caps** effect, and change the **Font color** to **Olive Green, Accent 3, Darker 50%**—in the seventh column, the last color. Apply the same formatting to the subheadings *Benefits to Patients, Cuddles*, and *Brandy*.

8 Select the last paragraph in the newsletter, and then apply a **1 pt Shadow** border, in **Black, Text 1**. Shade the paragraph with a **Fill** color of **Olive Green, Accent 3, Lighter 80%**—in the seventh column, the second color. Click the **FILE tab**, and then click **Show All Properties**. As the **Tags**, type **dogs, newsletter** As the **Subject**, type your course name and section number. Under **Related People**, if necessary, type your name in the **Author box**. **Print Preview** the document and make any necessary corrections. **Save** the document and **close** Word.

9 Start Word and display a new blank document. **Save** the document in your **Word Chapter 3** folder as **Lastname_Firstname_3F_Mailing_Labels** From your student files, **Open** the file **w03F_Addresses**. **Save** the address file in your **Word Chapter 3** folder as **Lastname_Firstname_3F_Addresses** and then add the file name to the footer. **Save** and **Close** the file. Be sure that your **Lastname_Firstname_3F_Mailing_Labels** document displays.

10 Start the **Step-by-Step Mail Merge Wizard** to create **Labels**. Be sure that the **Default tray** is selected and that the label vendor is **Avery US Letter**. The **Product number** is **5160 Easy Peel Address Labels**. Select the **Use an existing list** option, and then from your **Word Chapter 3** folder, open your **Lastname_Firstname_3F_Addresses** file. Add the following record to your file:

First Name	Miranda
Last Name	Yanos
Address 1	1256 Loma Ave.
Unit	#34
City	Memphis
State	TN
ZIP Code	38123

(Project 3F Dogs Newsletter and Mailing Labels continues on the next page)

CONTENT-BASED ASSESSMENTS

11 Insert an **Address block** and match the fields. Match the **Address 2** field to the **Unit** field, and then update the labels. Preview the labels, and then select the entire document. Change the **Spacing Before** to **3** and then **Complete the merge**. Delete the last row from the bottom of the table, and then add the file name to the footer.

12 Display the document properties. As the **Tags** type **labels** and as the **Subject** type your course name and section number. Be sure your name displays in the **Author box**, and then **Save** your file. As directed by your instructor, print or submit electronically. In addition to your labels and address document, submit your **3F_Dogs_Newsletter** document as directed. **Close** Word and Internet Explorer.

END | You have completed Project 3F

CONTENT-BASED ASSESSMENTS

Mastering Word | Project 3G Research Paper, Newsletter, and Mailing Labels

Apply 3A and 3B skills from these Objectives:

1 Create a Research Paper

2 Insert Footnotes in a Research Paper

3 Create Citations and a Bibliography in a Research Paper

4 Use Read Mode and PDF Reflow

5 Format a Multiple-Column Newsletter

6 Use Special Character and Paragraph Formatting

7 Create Mailing Labels Using Mail Merge

In the following Mastering Word project, you will edit and format a research paper and a newsletter, and you will create mailing labels. Your completed documents will look similar to Figure 3.59.

PROJECT FILES

For Project 3G, you will need the following files:

New blank Word document
w03G_Electronic_Records
w03G_Newsletter
w03G_Addresses

You will save your documents as:

Lastname_Firstname_3G_Electronic_Records
Lastname_Firstname_3G_Newsletter
Lastname_Firstname_3G_Mailing_Labels
Lastname_Firstname_3G_Addresses

PROJECT RESULTS

FIGURE 3.59

(Project 3G Research Paper, Newsletter, and Mailing Labels continues on the next page)

CONTENT-BASED ASSESSMENTS

1 Start Word. From your student files, locate and open the document **w03G_Electronic_Records**, and then **Save** it in your **Word Chapter 3** folder as **Lastname_Firstname_3G_Electronic_Records** Display the header area, type **Eisler** and then press ⎵Spacebar. From the **Header & Footer group**, add a **Plain Number** page number from the **Current Position** gallery. Apply **Align Right** formatting to the header. Move to the footer area and add the file name to the footer.

Select all the text in the document, change the **Line Spacing** to **2.0**, and then change the **Spacing After** to **0 pt**. **Center** the title *Electronic Health Records*. Beginning with text below the centered title, select the text from that point to the end of the document, and then set a **First line** indent of **0.5"**.

2 At the top of **Page 1**, at the end of the paragraph that begins *There is often*, insert a footnote with the following text: **Electronic Health Records is an evolving concept that shares records in digital format across different health care settings and might include medical history, test results, and x-rays.**

At the top of **Page 2**, in the second line, at the end of the sentence that ends *if they had it*, insert a footnote with the following text: **The EMR (electronic medical record) is the patient record created in hospitals and ambulatory environments; it serves as a data source for other systems.**

3 On **Page 1**, at the end of the paragraph that begins *Those clinical practices*, click to the left of the period, and then using **MLA** format, insert a citation for a **Web site** with the following information:

Author	Sabriel, Barbara A.
Name of Web Page	Do EMRS Make You a Better Doctor?
Year	2008
Month	July
Day	15
Year Accessed	2016
Month Accessed	June
Day Accessed	30
Medium	Web

On **Page 2**, at the end of the paragraph that begins *Further research*, click to the left of the period, and then

using **MLA** format, insert a citation for a **Book** with the following information:

Author	DeVore, Amy
Title	The Electronic Health Record for the Physician's Office, 1e
Year	2010
City	Maryland Heights
Publisher	Saunders
Medium	Print

In the report, select the citation you just created, display the **Citation Options**, and then edit the citation to include **Pages 253**

4 Insert a manual page break at the end of the document. On the new **Page 3**, display the **Paragraph** dialog box, and then change the **Special** indentation to **(none)**. Type **Works Cited** and then press ⏎Enter. On the **REFERENCES tab**, click **Bibliography**, and then click **Insert Bibliography**. **Center** the *Works Cited* title.

Use the **Source Manager** to change the name of the reference *Sabriel* to **Gabriel** and update both lists. Then in the selected citation in the report, display the **Citation Options** and click **Update Citations and Bibliography**. On the Works Cited page, select the references, apply **Double** line spacing, and then set the **Spacing After** paragraphs to **0 pt**.

Update the **Document Properties** with the following information:

Title	Electronic Records
Tags	EMR, health records
Comments	Draft copy of report for class
Categories	Health Administration
Subject	(insert your course name and section number)
Company	University Medical Center
Manager	Dr. Hillary Kim

On the left, click **Print** to display the **Print Preview**, make any necessary corrections, **save** and **close** the document; leave Word open. Hold this file until you complete this project.

(Project 3G Research Paper, Newsletter, and Mailing Labels continues on the next page)

CONTENT-BASED ASSESSMENTS

Mastering Word Project 3G Research Paper, Newsletter, and Mailing Labels (continued)

5 From your student files, open **w03G_ Newsletter**. **Save** the file in your **Word Chapter 3** folder as **Lastname_ Firstname_3G_Newsletter** and then add the file name to the footer. Select the first three lines of the document and apply a **3 pt** bottom border in **Black, Text 1**.

Click at the beginning of the newsletter title *University Medical Center*. Insert an online picture from **Office.com Clip Art** by searching for **microscope** Insert a picture of a black and white microscope. **Recolor** the picture by applying **Blue, Accent color 1 Light**. Apply a **Black, Text 1 Picture Border** and change the **Weight** to **2 1/4 pt**.

Scale the picture to **10%** of its **Height**, and then change the **Text Wrapping** to **Square**. Change the **Horizontal Alignment** to **Left relative to Margin** and the **Vertical Alignment** to **Top relative to Margin**.

6 Starting with the paragraph that begins *Are You Getting a Good Night's Sleep?*, select all of the text from that point to the end of the document. Format the text in two columns, and apply **Justify** alignment. Insert a **Column break** before the subheading *Can Chemistry Help?*

Start and maximize Internet Explorer, and then navigate to **www.nhlbi.nih.gov/health** and then in the middle of the page, click **Sleep Disorders**. In your **3G_Newsletter** file, click at the end of the paragraph below the *Are You Getting a Good Night's Sleep* subheading, and then press [Enter]. In the blank line, insert a **Screenshot** of the website; do not link to the URL. Apply a **Black, Text 1 Picture Border** and change the **Weight** to **1 pt**.

Select the subheading *Are You Getting a Good Night's Sleep?* including the paragraph mark. From the **Font** dialog box, apply **Bold** and **Small Caps** and change the **Font color** to **Dark Blue, Text 2**—in the fourth column, the first color. Apply the same formatting to the subheadings *Light and Sleep*, *Can Chemistry Help?* and *Sleep Aid Apps*.

7 Select the last paragraph in the newsletter, and then apply a **1 pt Shadow** border using **Black, Text 1**. Shade the paragraph with the **Fill** color **Dark Blue, Text 2, Lighter 80%**—in the fourth column, the second color. **Center** the text.

Click the **FILE tab**, and then click **Show All Properties**. As the **Tags**, type **sleep, newsletter** As the **Subject**, type your course name and section number. Under **Related People**, if necessary, type your name in the **Author box**. On the left, click **Print** to display the

Print Preview. Make any necessary corrections. **Save** the document and **Exit** Word.

8 Start Word and display a new blank document. **Save** the document in your **Word Chapter 3** folder as **Lastname_Firstname_3G_Mailing_Labels** From your student files, **Open** the file w03G_Addresses. **Save** the address file in your **Word Chapter 3** folder as **Lastname_ Firstname_3G_Addresses** and then add the file name to the footer. **Save** and **Close** the file. Be sure that your **Lastname_Firstname_3G_Mailing_Labels** document displays.

9 Start the **Step-by-Step Mail Merge Wizard** to create **Labels**. Be sure that the **Default tray** is selected and that the label vendor is **Avery US Letter**. The **Product number** is **5160 Easy Peel Address Labels**. Select the **Use an existing list option**, and then from your **Word Chapter 3** folder, **Open** your **Lastname_Firstname_3G_Addresses** file. Add the following record to your file:

First Name	Mason
Last Name	Zepeda
Address 1	134 Atlantic Ave.
Unit	#21
City	Memphis
State	TN
ZIP Code	38123

10 Insert an **Address block** and match the fields. Match the **Address 2** field to the **Unit** field, and then update the labels. Preview the labels, and then select the entire document. Change the **Spacing Before** to **3** and then **Complete the merge**. Delete the last row from the bottom of the table, and then add the file name to the footer.

Display the document properties. As the **Tags** type **labels** and as the **Subject** type your course name and section number. Be sure your name displays in the **Author box**, and then **Save** your file. As directed by your instructor, print or submit your work electronically. In addition to your labels and address document, submit your **3G_Newsletter** and **3G_Electronic_Records** documents as directed. **Close** Word and Internet Explorer.

END | You have completed Project 3G

CONTENT-BASED ASSESSMENTS

Apply a combination of the 3A and 3B skills.

GO! Fix It   Project 3H Hospital Materials   **Online**

GO! Make It   Project 3I Health Newsletter   **Online**

Build from
Scratch

GO! Solve It   Project 3J Colds and Flu   **Online**

GO! Solve It   Project 3K Cycling Newsletter

PROJECT FILES

For Project 3K, you will need the following file:

w03K_Cycling_Newsletter

You will save your document as:

Lastname_Firstname_3K_Cycling_Newsletter

    The UMC Emergency Department publishes a newsletter focusing on safety and injury prevention. The topic for the current newsletter is bicycle safety. From your student data files, open w03K_Cycling_Newsletter, add the file name to the footer, and then save the file in your Word Chapter 3 folder as **Lastname_Firstname_3K_Cycling_Newsletter**.

    Using the techniques that you practiced in this chapter, format the document in two-column, newsletter format. Format the nameplate so that it is clearly separate from the body of the newsletter. Insert column breaks as necessary and apply appropriate formatting to subheadings. Insert and format at least one appropriate online picture and insert a screenshot of a relevant website. Apply a border and shading to the last paragraph.

    Add your name, your course name and section number, and the keywords **safety, newsletter** to the Properties area. Submit as directed.

CONTENT-BASED ASSESSMENTS

Performance Level

	Exemplary: You consistently applied the relevant skills	Proficient: You sometimes, but not always, applied the relevant skills	Developing: You rarely or never applied the relevant skills
Format nameplate	The nameplate is formatted attractively and in a manner that clearly indicates that it is the nameplate.	The nameplate includes some formatting but is not clearly separated from the body of the newsletter.	The newsletter does not include a nameplate.
Insert and format at least one online picture	An sized and positioned online picture image is included.	An online picture is inserted but is either inappropriate, or is formatted or positioned poorly.	No online picture is included.
Border and shading added to a paragraph	The last paragraph displays an attractive border with shading.	An appropriate border or shading is displayed but not both.	No border or shading is applied.
Insert a screenshot	A relevant screenshot is inserted in one of the columns.	A screenshot is inserted in the document but does not relate to the content of the article.	No screenshot is inserted.

Performance Criteria (left side label)

END | You have completed Project 3K

OUTCOMES-BASED ASSESSMENTS

RUBRIC

The following outcomes-based assessments are *open-ended assessments*. That is, there is no specific correct result; your result will depend on your approach to the information provided. Make *Professional Quality* your goal. Use the following scoring rubric to guide you in *how* to approach the problem and then to evaluate *how well* your approach solves the problem.

The *criteria*—Software Mastery, Content, Format and Layout, and Process—represent the knowledge and skills you have gained that you can apply to solving the problem. The *levels of performance*—Professional Quality, Approaching Professional Quality, or Needs Quality Improvements—help you and your instructor evaluate your result.

	Your completed project is of Professional Quality if you:	Your completed project is Approaching Professional Quality if you:	Your completed project Needs Quality Improvements if you:
1-Software Mastery	Choose and apply the most appropriate skills, tools, and features and identify efficient methods to solve the problem.	Choose and apply some appropriate skills, tools, and features, but not in the most efficient manner.	Choose inappropriate skills, tools, or features, or are inefficient in solving the problem.
2-Content	Construct a solution that is clear and well organized, contains content that is accurate, appropriate to the audience and purpose, and is complete. Provide a solution that contains no errors in spelling, grammar, or style.	Construct a solution in which some components are unclear, poorly organized, inconsistent, or incomplete. Misjudge the needs of the audience. Have some errors in spelling, grammar, or style, but the errors do not detract from comprehension.	Construct a solution that is unclear, incomplete, or poorly organized; contains some inaccurate or inappropriate content; and contains many errors in spelling, grammar, or style. Do not solve the problem.
3-Format & Layout	Format and arrange all elements to communicate information and ideas, clarify function, illustrate relationships, and indicate relative importance.	Apply appropriate format and layout features to some elements, but not others. Overuse features, causing minor distraction.	Apply format and layout that does not communicate information or ideas clearly. Do not use format and layout features to clarify function, illustrate relationships, or indicate relative importance. Use available features excessively, causing distraction.
4-Process	Use an organized approach that integrates planning, development, self-assessment, revision, and reflection.	Demonstrate an organized approach in some areas, but not others; or, use an insufficient process of organization throughout.	Do not use an organized approach to solve the problem.

OUTCOMES-BASED ASSESSMENTS

Build from Scratch

GO! Think Project 3L Influenza Report

PROJECT FILES

For Project 3L, you will need the following file:

New blank Word document

You will save your document as:

Lastname_Firstname_3L_Influenza

As part of the ongoing research conducted by University Medical Center in the area of community health and contagious diseases, Dr. Hillary Kim has asked Sarah Stanger to create a report on influenza—how it spreads, and how it can be prevented in the community.

Create a new file and save it as **Lastname_Firstname_3L_Influenza** Create the report in MLA format. The report should include at least two footnotes, at least two citations, and should include a *Works Cited* page.

The report should contain an introduction, and then information about what influenza is, how it spreads, and how it can be prevented. A good place to start is at http://health.nih.gov/topic/influenza.

Add the file name to the footer. Add appropriate information to the Document Properties and submit it as directed.

END | You have completed Project 3L

OUTCOMES-BASED ASSESSMENTS

Build from
Scratch

| **GO! Think** | Project 3M Volunteer Newsletter | **Online** |

Build from
Scratch

| **You and GO!** | Project 3N College Newsletter | **Online** |

| **GO! Cumulative Group Project** | Project 3O Bell Orchid Hotels | |
| | | **Online** |

Introduction to Microsoft Excel 2013

E
Excel 2013

Excel 2013: Introduction

Video EA

Quantitative information! Defined as a type of information that can be counted or that communicates the quantity of something, quantitative information can be either easy or hard to understand—depending on how it is presented. According to Stephen Few in his book *Show Me the Numbers*: "Quantitative information forms the core of what businesses must know to operate effectively."

Excel 2013 is a tool to communicate quantitative business information effectively. Sometimes you need to communicate quantitative relationships. For example, the number of units sold per geographic region shows a relationship of sales to geography. Sometimes you need to summarize numbers. A list of every student enrolled at your college with his or her major is not as informative as a summary of the total number of students in each major. In business, the most common quantitative information is some measure of money—costs, sales, payroll, expenses—and so on.

Rather than just a tool for making calculations, Excel is now a tool for you to communicate and collaborate with others. When you want to communicate visually with tables and graphs, Excel 2013 has many new features to help you do so. Microsoft Excel 2013 works best on a Windows 8 PC—desktop, laptop, or tablet—because if your PC is touch-enabled, you will be able to use your fingers to work with Excel.

Creating a Worksheet and Charting Data

PROJECT 1A

OUTCOMES
Create a sales report with an embedded column chart and sparklines.

PROJECT 1B

OUTCOMES
Calculate the value of an inventory.

OBJECTIVES

1. Create, Save, and Navigate an Excel Workbook
2. Enter Data in a Worksheet
3. Construct and Copy Formulas and Use the SUM Function
4. Format Cells with Merge & Center, Cell Styles, and Themes
5. Chart Data to Create a Column Chart and Insert Sparklines
6. Print a Worksheet, Display Formulas, and Close Excel

OBJECTIVES

7. Check Spelling in a Worksheet
8. Enter Data by Range
9. Construct Formulas for Mathematical Operations
10. Edit Values in a Worksheet
11. Format a Worksheet

Warren Goldswain / Fotolia

In This Chapter

In this chapter, you will use Microsoft Excel 2013 to create and analyze data organized into columns and rows. After entering data in a worksheet, you can perform complex calculations, analyze the data to make logical decisions, and create informative charts that help readers visualize your data in a way they can understand and that is meaningful. In this chapter, you will create and modify Excel workbooks. You will practice the basics of worksheet design; create a footer; enter and edit data in a worksheet; chart data; and then save, preview, and print workbooks. You will also construct formulas for mathematical operations.

The projects in this chapter relate to **Pro Fit Marietta**, a distributor of fitness equipment and apparel to private gyms, personal trainers, health clubs, corporate wellness centers, hotels, college athletic facilities, physical therapy practices, and multi-unit residential properties. The company's mission is to find, test, and distribute the highest quality fitness products in the world to its customers for the benefit of consumers. Their popular blog provides useful tips on how to use the latest workout and fitness equipment. The company is located in Marietta, Georgia, which is metropolitan Atlanta's largest suburb.

Sales Report with Embedded Column Chart and Sparklines

PROJECT ACTIVITIES

In Activities 1.01 through 1.17, you will create an Excel worksheet for Michelle Barry, the President of Pro Fit Marietta. The worksheet displays the second quarter sales of cardio equipment for the current year and includes a chart to visually represent the data. Your completed worksheet will look similar to Figure 1.1.

PROJECT FILES

For Project 1A, you will need the following file:

New blank Excel workbook

You will save your workbook as:

Lastname_Firstname_1A_Quarterly_Sales

PROJECT RESULTS

Build from Scratch

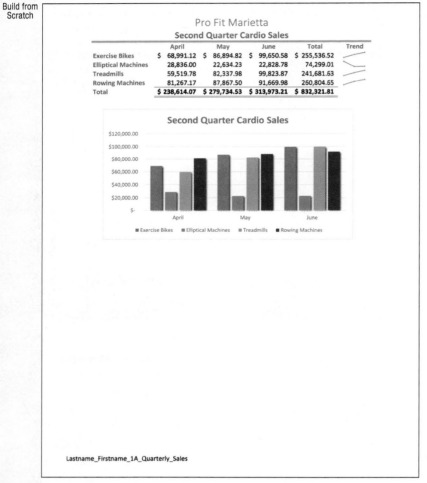

FIGURE 1.1 Project 1A Sales Report with Embedded Column Chart and Sparklines

NOTE | **If You Are Using a Touchscreen**

- Tap an item to click it.
- Press and hold for a few seconds to right-click; release when the information or commands displays.
- Touch the screen with two or more fingers and then pinch together to zoom in or stretch your fingers apart to zoom out.
- Slide your finger on the screen to scroll—slide left to scroll right and slide right to scroll left.
- Slide to rearrange—similar to dragging with a mouse.
- Swipe from edge: from right to display charms; from left to expose open apps, snap apps, or close apps; from top or bottom to show commands or close an app.
- Swipe to select—slide an item a short distance with a quick movement—to select an item and bring up commands, if any.

Objective 1 | Create, Save, and Navigate an Excel Workbook

Video E1-1

On startup, Excel displays a new blank **_workbook_**—the Excel document that stores your data—which contains one or more pages called a **_worksheet_**. A worksheet—or **_spreadsheet_**—is stored in a workbook and is formatted as a pattern of uniformly spaced horizontal rows and vertical columns. The intersection of a column and a row forms a box referred to as a **_cell_**.

Activity 1.01 | Starting Excel, Navigating Excel, and Naming and Saving a Workbook

1 ▷ Start Excel, and then on the opening screen, click **Blank workbook**. In the lower right corner of the window, on the status bar, if necessary, click the Normal button ⊞, and then to the right, locate the zoom—magnification—level.

> Your zoom level should be 100%, although some figures in this textbook may be shown at a higher zoom level. The **_Normal view_** maximizes the number of cells visible on your screen and keeps the column letters and row numbers closer.

BY TOUCH   On Excel's opening screen, tap Blank workbook.

2 ▷ Press F12 to display the **Save As** dialog box, and then navigate to the location where you will store your workbooks for this chapter.

3 ▷ In your storage location, create a new folder named **Excel Chapter 1** Open the new folder to display its folder window, and then in the **File name** box, notice that *Book1* displays as the default file name.

4 ▷ In the **File name** box, if necessary click *Book1* to select it, and then using your own name, type **Lastname_Firstname_1A_Quarterly_Sales** being sure to include the underscore (_) instead of spaces between words.

5 ▷ In the **Save As** dialog box, click **Save**. Compare your screen with Figure 1.2, and then take a moment to study the Excel window parts in the table in Figure 1.3.

***More* Knowledge** | **Creating a New Workbook by Using a Template**

On Excel's opening screen, you can select a professional-look template instead of a blank workbook. Templates have some formatting completed; you just add and modify what you want. You can select or search for a template to match your needs from Excel's opening screen; or, from the Excel window, click FILE, and then click New to search for online templates.

FIGURE 1.2

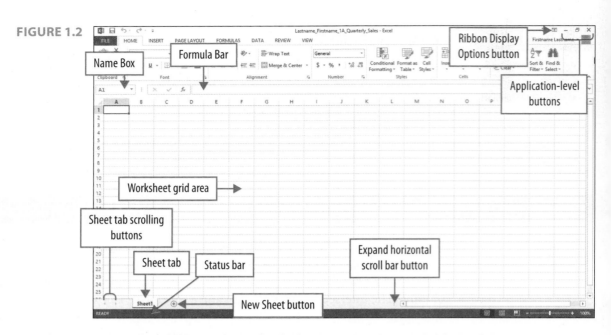

FIGURE 1.3

PARTS OF THE EXCEL WINDOW	
WINDOW PART	**DESCRIPTION**
Expand horizontal scroll bar button	Increases the width of the horizontal scroll bar.
Formula Bar	Displays the value or formula contained in the active cell; also permits entry or editing.
Sheet tab	Identifies the worksheet in the workbook.
New sheet button	Inserts an additional worksheet.
Name Box	Displays the name of the selected cell, table, chart, or object.
Sheet tab scrolling buttons	Display sheet tabs that are not in view when there are numerous sheet tabs.
Status bar	Displays the current cell mode, page number, worksheet information, view and zoom buttons, and for numerical data, common calculations such as Sum and Average.
Application-level buttons	Minimize, close, or restore the previous size of the displayed workbook.
Ribbon Display Options button	Displays various ways you can display the ribbon—the default is Show Tabs and Commands.
Worksheet grid area	Displays the columns and rows that intersect to form the worksheet's cells.

> 6 ▸ Take a moment to study Figure 1.4 and the table in Figure 1.5 to become familiar with the Excel workbook window.

FIGURE 1.4

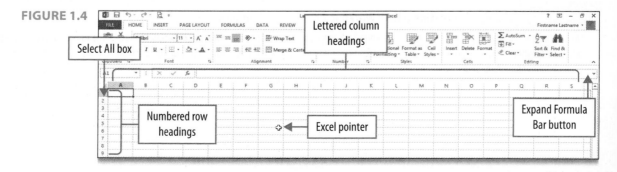

FIGURE 1.5

EXCEL WORKBOOK WINDOW ELEMENTS	
WORKBOOK WINDOW ELEMENT	**DESCRIPTION**
Excel pointer	Displays the location of the pointer.
Expand Formula Bar button	Increases the height of the Formula Bar to display lengthy cell content.
Lettered column headings	Indicate the column letter.
Numbered row headings	Indicate the row number.
Select All box	Selects all the cells in a worksheet.

7 In the lower right corner of the screen, in the horizontal scroll bar, click the **right scroll arrow** one time to shift **column A** out of view.

A *column* is a vertical group of cells in a worksheet. Beginning with the first letter of the alphabet, *A*, a unique letter identifies each column—this is called the *column heading*. Clicking one of the horizontal scroll bar arrows shifts the window either left or right one column at a time.

8 Point to the **right scroll arrow**, and then hold down the left mouse button until the columns begin to scroll rapidly to the right; release the mouse button when you begin to see pairs of letters as the column headings.

BY TOUCH   Anywhere on the worksheet, slide your finger to the left to scroll to the right.

9 Slowly drag the horizontal scroll box to the left, and notice that just above the scroll box, ScreenTips with the column letters display as you drag. Drag the horizontal scroll box left or right—or click the **left or right scroll arrow**—as necessary to position **column Z** near the center of your screen.

Column headings after column Z use two letters starting with AA, AB, and so on through ZZ. After that, columns begin with three letters beginning with AAA. This pattern provides 16,384 columns. The last column is XFD.

10 In the vertical scroll bar, click the **down scroll arrow** one time to move **Row 1** out of view.

A *row* is a horizontal group of cells. Beginning with number 1, a unique number identifies each row—this is the *row heading*, located at the left side of the worksheet. A single worksheet can handle 1 million rows of data.

11 Use the skills you just practiced to scroll horizontally to display **column A**, and if necessary, **row 1**.

12 Click **Save** 🔲.

Objective 2   Enter Data in a Worksheet

Video E1-2

Cell content, which is anything you type in a cell, can be one of two things: either a *constant value*—referred to simply as a *value*—or a *formula*. A formula is an equation that performs mathematical calculations on values in your worksheet. The most commonly used values are *text values* and *number values*, but a value can also include a date or a time of day. A text value is also referred to as a *label*.

A text value usually provides information about number values in other worksheet cells. For example, a title such as Second Quarter Cardio Sales gives the reader an indication that the data in the worksheet relates to information about sales of cardio equipment during the three-month period April through June.

1 Point to and then click the cell at the intersection of **column A** and **row 1** to make it the *active cell*—the cell is outlined in black and ready to accept data.

The intersecting column letter and row number form the *cell reference*—also called the *cell address*. When a cell is active, its column letter and row number are highlighted. The cell reference of the selected cell, *A1*, displays in the Name Box.

2 With cell **A1** as the active cell, type the worksheet title **Pro Fit Marietta** and then press Enter. Compare your screen with Figure 1.6.

Text or numbers in a cell are referred to as *data*. You must confirm the data you type in a cell by pressing Enter or by some other keyboard movement, such as pressing Tab or an arrow key. Pressing Enter moves the active cell to the cell below.

FIGURE 1.6

3 In cell **A1**, notice that the text does not fit; the text extends into cell **B1** to the right.

If text is too long for a cell and cells to the right are empty, the text will display. If the cells to the right contain other data, only the text that will fit in the cell displays.

4 In cell **A2**, type the worksheet subtitle **Second Quarter Cardio Sales** and then press Enter. Compare your screen with Figure 1.7.

FIGURE 1.7

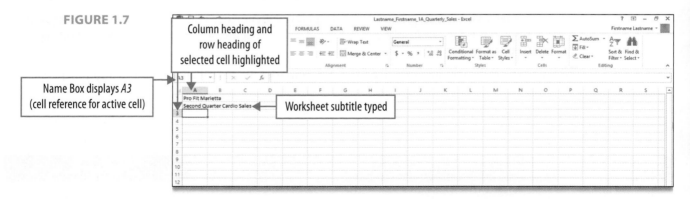

5 Above **column A**, click in the **Name Box** to select the cell reference *A3*, and then type **a4** Press Enter to make cell **A4** the active cell. In cell **A4**, type **Exercise Bikes** to form the first row title, and then press Enter.

The text characters that you typed align at the left edge of the cell—referred to as *left alignment*—and cell A5 becomes the active cell. Left alignment is the default for text values. You can type a cell address in the Name Box and press Enter to move to a specific cell quickly.

6 In cell **A5**, type **E** and notice the text from the previous cell displays.

If the first characters you type in a cell match an existing entry in the column, Excel fills in the remaining characters for you. This feature, called **AutoComplete**, assists only with alphabetic values.

7 Continue typing the remainder of the row title **lliptical Machines** and press Enter.

The AutoComplete suggestion is removed when the entry you are typing differs from the previous value.

8 In cell **A6**, type **Treadmills** and press Enter. In cell **A7**, type **Rowing Machines** and press Enter. In cell **A8**, type **Total** and press Enter. On the **Quick Access Toolbar**, click **Save** 🖫.

🔄 **ANOTHER WAY**   Use the keyboard shortcut Ctrl + S to save changes to your workbook.

Activity 1.03 | Using Auto Fill and Keyboard Shortcuts

1 Click cell **B3**. Type **A** and notice that when you begin to type in a cell, on the **Formula Bar**, the **Cancel** and **Enter** buttons become active, as shown in Figure 1.8.

FIGURE 1.8

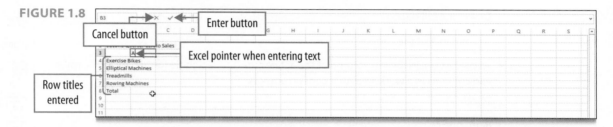

2 Continue to type **pril** On the **Formula Bar**, notice that values you type in a cell also display there. Then, on the **Formula Bar**, click **Enter** ✔ to confirm the entry and keep cell **B3** active.

3 With cell **B3** active, locate the small square in the lower right corner of the selected cell.

You can drag this *fill handle*—the small square in the lower right corner of a selected cell—to adjacent cells to fill the cells with values based on the first cell.

4 Point to the **fill handle** until the ➕ pointer displays, hold down the left mouse button, drag to the right to cell **D3**, and as you drag, notice the ScreenTips *May* and *June*. Release the mouse button.

5 Under the text that you just filled, click the **Auto Fill Options** button 🔣 that displays, and then compare your screen with Figure 1.9.

Auto Fill generates and extends a *series* of values into adjacent cells based on the value of other cells. A series is a group of things that come one after another in succession; for example, *April, May, June*.

The Auto Fill Options button displays options to fill the data; options vary depending on the content and program from which you are filling, and the format of the data you are filling.

Fill Series is selected, indicating the action that was taken. Because the options are related to the current task, the button is referred to as being *context sensitive*.

FIGURE 1.9

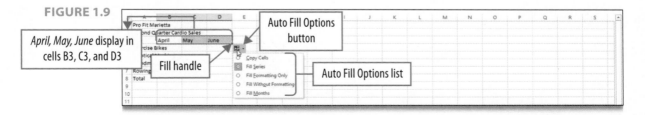

6 Click in any cell to cancel the display of the list.

The list no longer displays; the button will display until you perform some other screen action.

7 Press Ctrl + Home, which is the keyboard shortcut to make cell **A1** active.

8 On the **Quick Access Toolbar**, click **Save** 🖫 to save the changes you have made to your workbook.

9 Take a moment to study the table in Figure 1.10 to become familiar with keyboard shortcuts with which you can navigate the Excel worksheet.

FIGURE 1.10

KEYBOARD SHORTCUTS TO NAVIGATE THE EXCEL WINDOW	
TO MOVE THE LOCATION OF THE ACTIVE CELL:	**PRESS:**
Up, down, right, or left one cell	↑ , ↓ , → , ←
Down one cell	Enter
Up one cell	Shift + Enter
Up one full screen	PageUp
Down one full screen	PageDown
To column A of the current row	Home
To the last cell in the last column of the active area (the rectangle formed by all the rows and columns in a worksheet that contain entries)	Ctrl + End
To cell A1	Ctrl + Home
Right one cell	Tab
Left one cell	Shift + Tab
To the cell one worksheet window to the right	Alt + PageDown
To the cell one worksheet window to the left	Alt + PageUp
To the cell containing specific content that you enter in the Find and Replace dialog box	Shift + F5
To the cell that corresponds with the cell reference you enter in the Go To dialog box	F5

Activity 1.04 | **Aligning Text and Adjusting the Size of Columns**

1 In the **column heading area**, point to the vertical line between **column A** and **column B** to display the ✛ pointer, press and hold down the left mouse button, and then compare your screen with Figure 1.11.

A ScreenTip displays information about the width of the column. The default width of a column is 64 *pixels*. A pixel, short for *picture element*, is a point of light measured in dots per square inch. Sixty-four pixels equal 8.43 characters, which is the average number of characters that will fit in a cell using the default font. The default font in Excel is Calibri and the default font size is 11.

FIGURE 1.11

2 Drag to the right, and when the number of pixels indicated in the ScreenTip reaches **120 pixels**, release the mouse button. If you are not satisfied with your result, click Undo ⟲ on the Quick Access Toolbar and begin again.

This width accommodates the longest row title in cells A4 through A8—*Elliptical Machines*. The worksheet subtitle in cell A2 spans more than one column and still does not fit in column A.

3 Point to cell **B3** and then drag across to select cells **B3**, **C3**, and **D3**. Compare your screen with Figure 1.12; if you are not satisfied with your result, click anywhere and begin again.

The three cells, B3 through D3, are selected and form a *range*—two or more cells on a worksheet that are adjacent (next to each other) or nonadjacent (not next to each other). This range of cells is referred to as *B3:D3*. When you see a colon (:) between two cell references, the range includes all the cells between the two cell references.

A range of cells you select this way is indicated by a dark border, and Excel treats the range as a single unit so you can make the same changes to more than one cell at a time. The selected cells in the range are highlighted except for the first cell in the range, which displays in the Name Box.

When you select a range of data, the **Quick Analysis tool** displays in the lower right corner of the selected range with which you can analyze your data by using Excel tools such as charts, color-coding, and formulas.

FIGURE 1.12

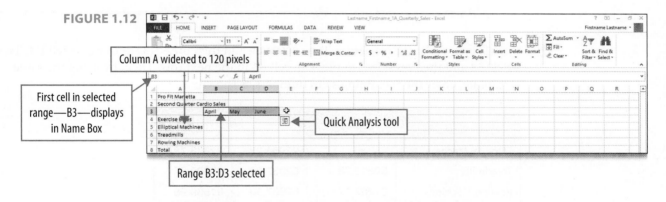

🔄 **BY TOUCH**

To select a range, tap and hold the first cell, and then when the circular gripper displays, drag it to the right, or to the right and down, to define the beginning and end of a range.

4 With the range **B3:D3** selected, point anywhere over the selected range, right-click, and then on the mini toolbar, click **Center** ⊟. On the **Quick Access Toolbar**, click **Save** 🖫.

The column titles *April, May, June* align in the center of each cell.

Activity 1.05 | Entering Numbers

To type number values, use either the number keys across the top of your keyboard or the numeric keypad if you have one—laptop computers may not have a numeric keypad.

1 ▶ Under *April*, click cell **B4**, type **68991.12** and then on the **Formula Bar**, click **Enter** ☑ to maintain cell **B4** as the active cell. Compare your screen with Figure 1.13.

By default, *number* values align at the right edge of the cell. The default *number format*—a specific way in which Excel displays numbers—is the *general format*. In the default general format, whatever you type in the cell will display, with the exception of trailing zeros to the right of a decimal point. For example, in the number 237.50 the *0* following the *5* is a trailing zero and will not display.

Data that displays in a cell is the *displayed value*. Data that displays in the Formula Bar is the *underlying value*. The number of digits or characters that display in a cell—the displayed value—depends on the width of the column. Calculations on numbers will always be based on the underlying value, not the displayed value.

FIGURE 1.13

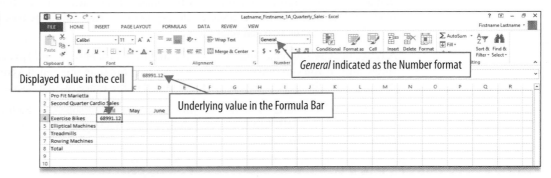

Displayed value in the cell

General indicated as the Number format

Underlying value in the Formula Bar

2 ▶ Press [Tab] to make cell **C4** active. Type **86894.82** and then press [Tab] to move to cell **D4**. Type **99650.58** and then press [Enter] to move to cell **B5** in the next row. Then, by using the same technique, enter the remaining sales numbers as shown:

	APRIL	MAY	JUNE
Elliptical Machines	28836	22634.23	22828.78
Treadmills	59519.78	82337.98	99823.87
Rowing Machines	81267.17	87867.50	91669.98

3 ▶ Compare the numbers you entered with Figure 1.14, and then **Save** 🔲 your workbook.

In the default General format, trailing zeros to the right of a decimal point will not display. For example, when you type *87867.50*, the cell displays 87867.5 instead.

FIGURE 1.14

Values entered for each category in each month

Video E1-3

A cell contains either a constant value (text or numbers) or a formula. A formula is an equation that performs mathematical calculations on values in other cells, and then places the result in the cell containing the formula. You can create formulas or use a *function*—a prewritten formula that looks at one or more values, performs an operation, and then returns a value.

Activity 1.06 | Constructing a Formula and Using the SUM Function

In this activity, you will practice three different ways to sum a group of numbers in Excel.

1 Click cell **B8** to make it the active cell and type **=**

The equal sign (=) displays in the cell with the insertion point blinking, ready to accept more data.

All formulas begin with the = sign, which signals Excel to begin a calculation. The Formula Bar displays the = sign, and the Formula Bar Cancel and Enter buttons display.

2 At the insertion point, type **b4** and then compare your screen with Figure 1.15.

A list of Excel functions that begin with the letter *B* may briefly display—as you progress in your study of Excel, you will use functions of this type. A blue border with small corner boxes surrounds cell B4, which indicates that the cell is part of an active formula. The color used in the box matches the color of the cell reference in the formula.

FIGURE 1.15

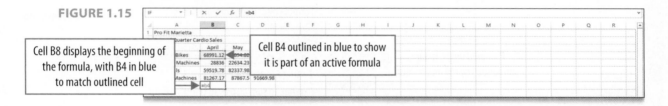

Cell B8 displays the beginning of the formula, with B4 in blue to match outlined cell

Cell B4 outlined in blue to show it is part of an active formula

3 At the insertion point, type **+** and then type **b5**

A border of another color surrounds cell B5, and the color matches the color of the cell reference in the active formula. When typing cell references, it is not necessary to use uppercase letters.

4 At the insertion point, type **+b6+b7** and then press Enter.

The result of the formula calculation—*238614.1*—displays in the cell. Recall that in the default General format, trailing zeros do not display.

5 Click cell **B8** again, look at the **Formula Bar**, and then compare your screen with Figure 1.16.

The formula adds the values in cells B4 through B7, and the result displays in cell B8. In this manner, you can construct a formula by typing. Although cell B8 displays the *result* of the formula, the formula itself displays in the Formula Bar. This is referred to as the *underlying formula*.

Always view the Formula Bar to be sure of the exact content of a cell—*a displayed number may actually be a formula.*

FIGURE 1.16

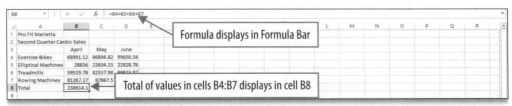

Formula displays in Formula Bar

Total of values in cells B4:B7 displays in cell B8

6 Click cell **C8** and type **=** to signal the beginning of a formula. Then, point to cell **C4** and click one time.

> The reference to the cell C4 is added to the active formula. A moving border surrounds the referenced cell, and the border color and the color of the cell reference in the formula are color coded to match.

7 At the insertion point, type **+** and then click cell **C5**. Repeat this process to complete the formula to add cells **C6** and **C7**, and then press Enter.

> The result of the formula calculation—*279734.5*—displays in the cell. This method of constructing a formula is the ***point and click method***.

8 Click cell **D8**. On the **HOME tab**, in the **Editing group**, click **AutoSum** ∑ AutoSum ▾ , and then compare your screen with Figure 1.17.

> ***SUM*** is an Excel function—a prewritten formula. A moving border surrounds the range D4:D7 and =*SUM(D4:D7)* displays in cell D8.

> The = sign signals the beginning of a formula, *SUM* indicates the type of calculation that will take place (addition), and *(D4:D7)* indicates the range of cells on which the sum calculation will be performed. A ScreenTip provides additional information about the action.

FIGURE 1.17

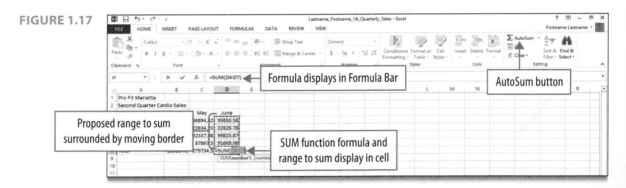

Formula displays in Formula Bar

AutoSum button

Proposed range to sum surrounded by moving border

SUM function formula and range to sum display in cell

 **ANOTHER WAY** Use the keyboard shortcut Alt + = ; or, on the Formulas tab, in the Function Library group, click the AutoSum button.

9 Look at the **Formula Bar**, and notice that the formula also displays there. Then, look again at the cells surrounded by the moving border.

> When you activate the ***Sum function***, Excel first looks *above* the active cell for a range of cells to sum. If no range is above the active cell, Excel will look to the *left* for a range of cells to sum. If the proposed range is not what you want to calculate, you can select a different group of cells.

10 Press Enter to construct a formula by using the prewritten SUM function.

> Your total is *313973.2*. Because the Sum function is frequently used, it has its own button in the Editing group on the Home tab of the ribbon. A larger version of the button also displays on the FORMULAS tab in the Function Library group. This button is also referred to as ***AutoSum***.

11 Notice that the totals in the range **B8:D8** display only one decimal place. Click **Save** 🖫.

> Number values that are too long to fit in the cell do *not* spill over into the unoccupied cell to the right in the same manner as text values. Rather, Excel rounds the number to fit the space.

> ***Rounding*** is a procedure that determines which digit at the right of the number will be the last digit displayed and then increases it by one if the next digit to its right is 5, 6, 7, 8, or 9.

Activity 1.07 | Copying a Formula by Using the Fill Handle

You have practiced three ways to create a formula—by typing, by using the point-and-click technique, and by using a Function button from the ribbon. You can also copy formulas. When you copy a formula from one cell to another, Excel adjusts the cell references to fit the new location of the formula.

1 Click cell **E3**, type **Total** and then press Enter.

The text in cell E3 is centered because the centered format continues from the adjacent cell.

2 With cell **E4** as the active cell, hold down Alt, and then press =. Compare your screen with Figure 1.18.

Alt + = is the keyboard shortcut for the Sum function. Recall that Excel first looks above the selected cell for a proposed range of cells to sum, and if no data is detected, Excel looks to the left and proposes a range of cells to sum.

FIGURE 1.18

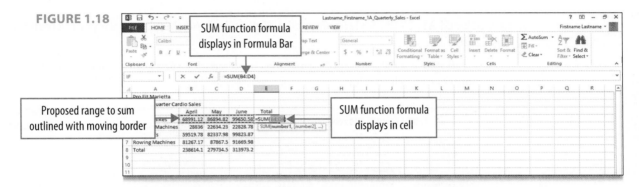

3 On the **Formula Bar**, click **Enter** ✓ to display the result and keep cell **E4** active.

The total dollar amount of *Exercise Bikes* sold in the quarter is *255536.5*. In cells E5:E8, you can see that you need a formula similar to the one in E4, but formulas that refer to the cells in row 5, row 6, and so on.

4 With cell **E4** active, point to the **fill handle** in the lower right corner of the cell until the ➕ pointer displays. Then, drag down through cell **E8**; if you are not satisfied with your result, on the Quick Access Toolbar, click Undo ↶ and begin again. Compare your screen with Figure 1.19.

FIGURE 1.19

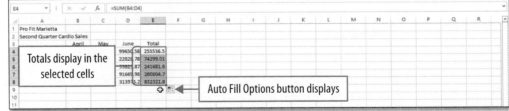

5 Click cell **E5**, look at the **Formula Bar**, and notice the formula *=SUM(B5:D5)*. Click cell **E6**, look at the **Formula Bar**, and then notice the formula *=SUM(B6:D6)*.

In each row, Excel copied the formula but adjusted the cell references *relative to* the row number. This is called a **relative cell reference**—a cell reference based on the relative position of the cell that contains the formula and the cells referred to in the formula.

The calculation is the same, but it is performed on the cells in that particular row. Use this method to insert numerous formulas into spreadsheets quickly.

6 Click cell **F3**, type **Trend** and then press Enter. **Save** 💾 your workbook.

Video E1-4

Format—change the appearance of—cells to make your worksheet attractive and easy to read.

Activity 1.08 | Using Merge & Center and Applying Cell Styles

1 Select the range **A1:F1**, and then in the **Alignment group**, click **Merge & Center**. Then, select the range **A2:F2** and click **Merge & Center**.

The *Merge & Center* command joins selected cells into one larger cell and centers the contents in the merged cell; individual cells in the range B1:F1 and B2:F2 can no longer be selected—they are merged into cell A1 and A2 respectively.

ANOTHER WAY   Select the range, right-click over the selection, and then on the mini toolbar, click the Merge & Center button.

2 Click cell **A1**. In the **Styles group**, click **Cell Styles**, and then compare your screen with Figure 1.20.

A *cell style* is a defined set of formatting characteristics, such as font, font size, font color, cell borders, and cell shading.

FIGURE 1.20

3 In the displayed gallery, under **Titles and Headings**, click **Title** and notice that the row height adjusts to accommodate the larger font size.

4 Click cell **A2**, display the **Cell Styles** gallery, and then under **Titles and Headings**, click **Heading 1**.

Use cell styles to maintain a consistent look in a worksheet and across worksheets in a workbook.

5 Select the horizontal range **B3:F3**, hold down Ctrl, and then select the vertical range **A4:A8** to select the column titles and the row titles.

Use this technique to select two or more ranges that are nonadjacent—not next to each other.

6 Display the **Cell Styles** gallery, click **Heading 4** to apply this cell style to the column titles and row titles, and then **Save** 🖫 your workbook.

Activity 1.09 | Formatting Financial Numbers

1 Select the range **B4:E4**, hold down Ctrl, and then select the range **B8:E8**.

This range is referred to as *b4:e4,b8:e8* with a comma separating the references to the two nonadjacent ranges.

🔁 **ANOTHER WAY**   In the Name Box type b4:e4,b8:e8 and then press Enter.

2 On the **HOME tab**, in the **Number group**, click **Accounting Number Format** $ ▾. Compare your screen with Figure 1.21.

The *Accounting Number Format* applies a thousand comma separator where appropriate, inserts a fixed U.S. dollar sign aligned at the left edge of the cell, applies two decimal places, and leaves a small amount of space at the right edge of the cell to accommodate a parenthesis when negative numbers are present. Excel widens the columns to accommodate the formatted numbers.

At the bottom of your screen, in the status bar, Excel displays the results for some common calculations that might be made on the range; for example, the Average of the numbers selected and the Count—the number of items selected.

FIGURE 1.21

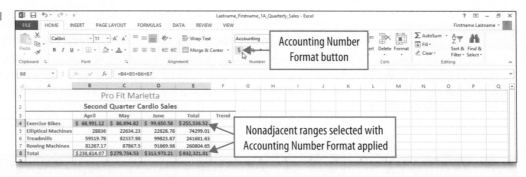

🔁 **ANOTHER WAY**   Display the Cell Styles gallery, and under Number Format, click Currency.

3 Select the range **B5:E7**, and then in the **Number group**, click **Comma Style** ▾.

The *Comma Style* inserts a thousand comma separator where appropriate and applies two decimal places. Comma Style also leaves space at the right to accommodate a parenthesis when negative numbers are present.

When preparing worksheets with financial information, the first row of dollar amounts and the total row of dollar amounts are formatted in the Accounting Number Format; that is, with thousand comma separators, dollar signs, two decimal places, and space at the right to accommodate a parenthesis for negative numbers, if any. Rows that are *not* the first row or the total row should be formatted with the Comma Style.

4 Select the range **B8:E8**. In the **Styles group**, display the **Cell Styles** gallery, and then under **Titles and Headings**, click **Total**. Click any blank cell to cancel the selection, and then compare your screen with Figure 1.22.

This is a common way to apply borders to financial information. The single border indicates that calculations were performed on the numbers above, and the double border indicates that the information is complete. Sometimes financial documents do not display values with cents; rather, the values are rounded up. You can do this by selecting the cells, and then clicking the Decrease Decimal button two times.

FIGURE 1.22

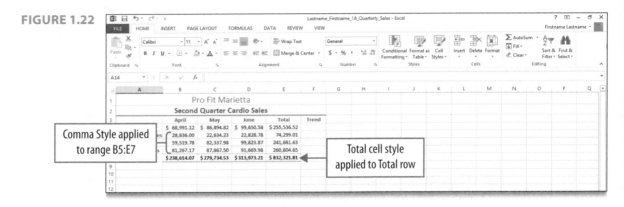

Activity 1.10 | **Changing the Workbook Theme**

A **theme** is a predefined set of colors, fonts, lines, and fill effects that coordinate for an attractive look.

> **1** Click the **PAGE LAYOUT tab**, and then in the **Themes group**, click **Themes**.

> **2** Click the **Retrospect** theme, and notice that the cell styles change to match the new theme. Click **Save** 📖.

More Knowledge | **Formatting a Cell's Font, Style, Size, or Color with Individual Commands**

Instead of using Cell Styles, you could use a combination of individual commands to format a cell. For example, on the HOME tab, in the Font group, you can change a cell's font by clicking the Font arrow and selecting a different font. You can change the font size by clicking the Font Size arrow and selecting a size. From the same group, you can apply various styles to the cell—such as Bold or Italic or Underline. To change a cell's font color, in the Font Group, click the Font Color arrow and select a different color.

Objective 5 | Chart Data to Create a Column Chart and Insert Sparklines

Video E1-5

A **chart** is a graphic representation of data in a worksheet. Data in a chart is easier to understand than a table of numbers. **Sparklines** are tiny charts embedded in a cell that give a visual trend summary alongside your data. A sparkline makes a pattern more obvious to the eye.

Activity 1.11 | **Charting Data and Using Recommended Charts to Select and Insert a Column Chart**

Recommended Charts is an Excel feature that displays a customized set of charts that, according to Excel's calculations, will best fit your data based on the range of data that you select. In this activity, you will create a **column chart** showing the monthly sales of cardio equipment by category during the second quarter. A column chart is useful for illustrating comparisons among related numbers. The chart will enable the company president, Michelle Barry, to see a pattern of overall monthly sales.

> **1** Select the range **A3:D7**.

When charting data, typically you should *not* include totals—include only the data you want to compare.

2 With the data that you want to compare selected, click the **INSERT tab**, and then in the **Charts group**, click **Recommended Charts**. Compare your screen with Figure 1.23.

> The Insert Chart dialog box displays a list of recommended charts on the left and a preview of the first chart, which is selected, on the right. The second tab of the Insert Chart dialog box includes all chart types—even those that are not recommended by Excel for this type of data.
>
> By using different *chart types*, you can display data in a way that is meaningful to the reader—common examples are column charts, pie charts, and line charts.

FIGURE 1.23

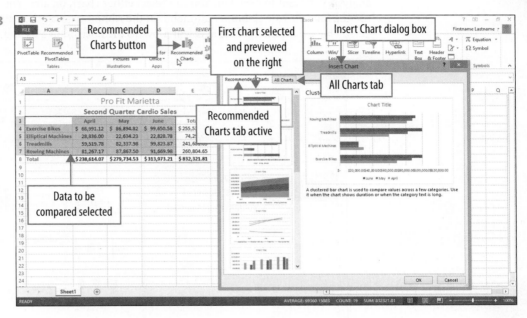

3 In the **Insert Chart** dialog box, use the scroll bar to scroll down about one-third of the way, and then click the second Clustered Column chart. Compare your screen with Figure 1.24.

> Here, *each type of cardio equipment* displays its *sales for each month*. A clustered column chart is useful to compare values across a few categories, especially if the order of categories is not important.

FIGURE 1.24

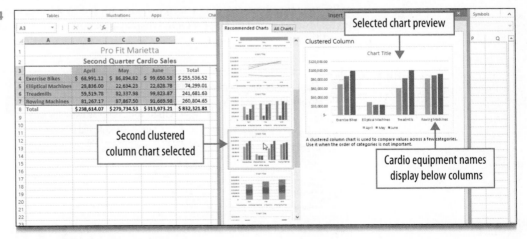

4 In the **Insert Chart** dialog box, click the chart directly above the selected chart—the first clustered column chart. Compare your screen with Figure 1.25.

In this clustered column chart, *each month* displays its *sales for each type of cardio equipment.* When constructing a chart, you can switch the row and column data in this manner to display the data in a way that is most useful to the reader. Here, the president of Pro Fit Marietta wants to compare sales of each type of equipment by month to detect patterns.

The comparison of data—either by month or by type of equipment—depends on the type of analysis you want to perform. You can select either chart, or, after your chart is complete, you can use the *Switch/Row Column* command on the ribbon to swap the data over the axis; that is, data being charted on the vertical axis will move to the horizontal axis and vice versa.

FIGURE 1.25

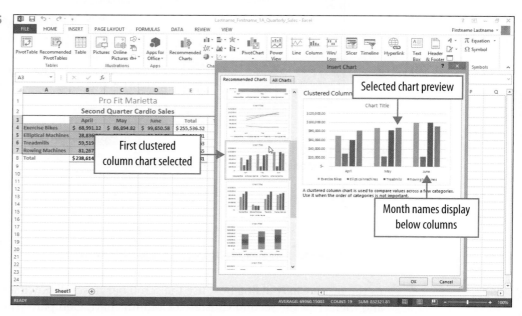

5 In the lower right corner of the **Insert Chart** dialog box, click **OK** to insert the selected chart into the worksheet. Compare your screen with Figure 1.26.

Your selected column chart displays in the worksheet, and the charted data is bordered by colored lines. Because the chart object is selected—surrounded by a border and displaying sizing handles—contextual tools named *CHART TOOLS* display and add contextual tabs next to the standard tabs on the ribbon.

FIGURE 1.26

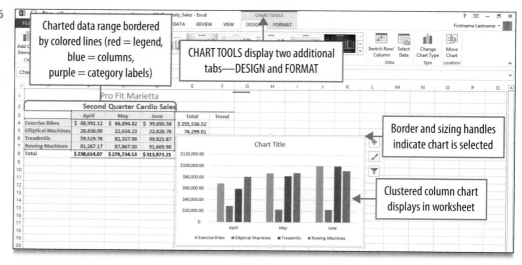

1 On the ribbon, locate the contextual tabs under **CHART TOOLS—DESIGN** and **FORMAT**.

When a chart is selected, CHART TOOLS become available and these two tabs provide commands for working with the chart.

Based on the data you selected in your worksheet and the chart you selected in the Insert Chart dialog box, Excel constructs a column chart and adds *category labels*—the labels that display along the bottom of the chart to identify the category of data. This area is referred to as the *category axis* or the *x-axis*.

Depending on which arrangement of row and column data you select in the Insert Chart dialog box, Excel arranges either the row titles or the column titles as the category names. Here, based on your selection, the column titles that form the category labels are bordered in purple, indicating the cells that contain the category names.

On the left side of the chart, Excel includes a numerical scale on which the charted data is based; this is the *value axis* or the *y-axis*. Along the lower edge of the chart, a *legend*, which is a chart element that identifies the patterns or colors that are assigned to the categories in the chart, displays. Here, the row titles are bordered in red, indicating the cells containing the legend text.

2 To the right of the chart, notice the three buttons, and then point to each button to display its ScreenTip, as shown in Figure 1.27.

The *Chart Elements button* enables you to add, remove, or change chart elements such as the title, legend, gridlines, and data labels.

The *Chart Styles button* enables you to set a style and color scheme for your chart.

The *Chart Filters button* enables you to change which data displays in the chart—for example, to see only the data for *May* and *June* or only the data for *Treadmills* and *Rowing Machines*.

FIGURE 1.27

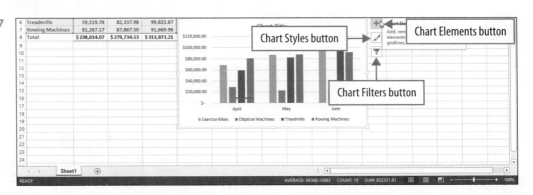

3 In the worksheet data, locate the group of cells bordered in blue.

Each of the twelve cells bordered in blue is referred to as a *data point*—a value that originates in a worksheet cell. Each data point is represented in the chart by a *data marker*—a column, bar, area, dot, pie slice, or other symbol in a chart that represents a single data point.

Related data points form a *data series*; for example, there is a data series for *April*, for *May*, and for *June*. Each data series has a unique color or pattern represented in the chart legend.

4 On the **DESIGN tab**, in the **Chart Layouts group**, click **Quick Layout**, and then compare your screen with Figure 1.28.

In the Quick Layout gallery, you can change the overall layout of the chart by selecting a predesigned *chart layout*—a combination of chart elements, which can include a title, legend, labels for the columns, and the table of charted cells.

FIGURE 1.28

5 ▸ *Point* to several different layouts to see how Live Preview displays the effect on your chart, and then click the **Quick Layout** button again *without* changing the layout.

6 ▸ In the chart, click anywhere in the text *Chart Title* to select the title box, watch the **Formula Bar** as you begin to type **Second** and notice that AutoComplete fills in the subtitle for you. Press Enter at any point to insert the subtitle as the chart title.

7 ▸ Click in a white area just slightly *inside* the chart border to deselect the chart title but keep the chart selected. To the right of the chart, click **Chart Styles** ✐, and then at the top of the **Chart Styles** gallery, be sure that **Style** is selected. Compare your screen with Figure 1.29.

> The **Chart Styles gallery** displays an array of pre-defined **chart styles**—the overall visual look of the chart in terms of its colors, backgrounds, and graphic effects such as flat or shaded columns. You can also select Chart Styles from the Chart Styles group on the ribbon, but having the gallery closer to the chart makes it easier to use a touch gesture on a touch device to format a chart.

FIGURE 1.29

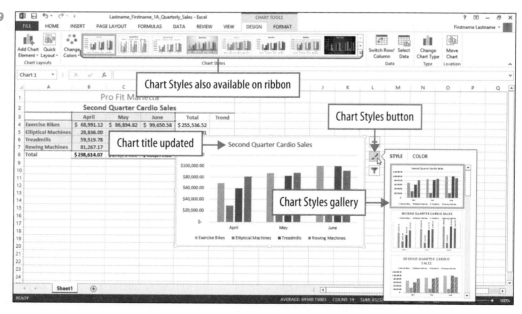

8 ▸ On the right side of the **Style** gallery, scroll down about halfway, and then by using the ScreenTips as your guide, locate and click **Style 6**.

> This style uses a white background, formats the columns with theme colors, and applies a slight shadowed effect to the columns. With this clear visual representation of the data, the president can see the sales of all product categories in each month, and can see that the sale of exercise bikes and treadmills has risen markedly during the quarter.

9 ▸ At the top of the gallery, click **COLOR**. Under **Colorful**, point to the third row of colors to display the ScreenTip *Color 3*, and then click to apply the **Color 3** variation of the theme colors.

10 Point to the top border of the chart to display the pointer, and then drag the upper left corner of the chart just inside the upper left corner of cell **A10**, approximately as shown in Figure 1.30.

FIGURE 1.30

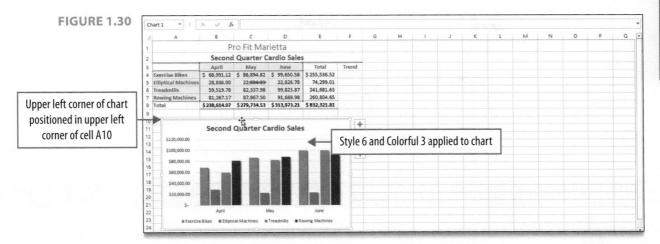

Upper left corner of chart positioned in upper left corner of cell A10

Style 6 and Colorful 3 applied to chart

11 Click any cell to deselect the chart, and notice that the chart buttons no longer display to the right of the chart and the CHART TOOLS no longer display on the ribbon. Click **Save** 🖫.

Contextual tabs display when an object is selected and then are removed from view when the object is deselected.

Activity 1.13 | Creating and Formatting Sparklines

By creating sparklines, you provide a context for your numbers. Your readers will be able to see the relationship between a sparkline and its underlying data quickly.

1 Select the range **B4:D7**, which represents the monthly sales figures for each product and for each month. Click the **INSERT tab**, and then in the **Sparklines group**, click **Line**. In the displayed **Create Sparklines** dialog box, notice that the selected range *B4:D7* displays as the Data Range.

2 With the insertion point blinking in the **Location Range** box, type **f4:f7** which is the range of cells where you want the sparklines to display. Compare your screen with Figure 1.31.

FIGURE 1.31

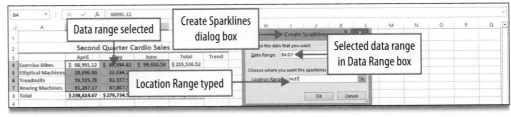

Data range selected

Create Sparklines dialog box

Selected data range in Data Range box

Location Range typed

🔄 **ANOTHER WAY**   In the worksheet, select the range F4:F7 to insert it into the Location Range box.

3 Click **OK** to insert the sparklines in the range **F4:F7**, and then on the **DESIGN tab**, in the **Show group**, click the **Markers** check box to select it.

Alongside each row of data, the sparkline provides a quick visual trend summary for sales of each cardio item over the three-month period. For example, you can see instantly that of the four items, only Elliptical Machines had declining sales for the period.

4 On the **DESIGN tab**, in the **Style group**, click **More** ⊡. In the second row, click the fourth style—**Sparkline Style Accent 4, Darker 25%**. Press Ctrl + Home to deselect the range and make cell **A1** the active cell. Click **Save** 🖫, and then compare your screen with Figure 1.32.

> Use markers, colors, and styles in this manner to further enhance your sparklines.

FIGURE 1.32

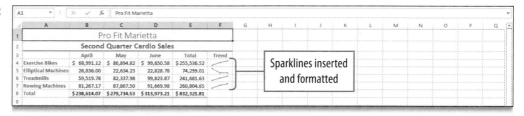

Objective 6 | Print a Worksheet, Display Formulas, and Close Excel

Video E1-6

Use the Show Formulas command to display the formula in each cell instead of the resulting value. Use the commands on the PAGE LAYOUT tab to prepare for printing.

Activity 1.14 | Creating a Footer and Centering a Worksheet

For each Excel project in this textbook, you will create a footer containing the file name, which includes your name and the project name. You will also center the data horizontally on the page to create an attractive result if your worksheet is printed.

1 If necessary, click cell **A1** to deselect the chart. Click the **PAGE LAYOUT tab**, and then in the **Page Setup group**, click **Margins**. At the bottom of the **Margins** gallery, click **Custom Margins**, to display the **Page Setup** dialog box. Compare your screen with Figure 1.33.

FIGURE 1.33

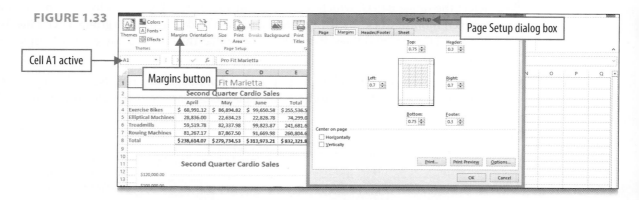

2 On the **Margins tab**, under **Center on page**, select the **Horizontally** check box.

> This action will center the data and chart horizontally on the page, as shown in the Preview area.

3 Click the **Header/Footer tab**, and then in the center of the dialog box, click **Custom Footer**. In the **Footer** dialog box, with your insertion point blinking in the **Left section**, on the row of buttons, click **Insert File Name** 🗐. Compare your screen with Figure 1.34.

> &[File] displays in the Left section. Here you can type or insert information from the row of buttons into the left, middle, or right section of the footer. The Custom Header button displays a similar screen to enter information in the header of the worksheet.

FIGURE 1.34

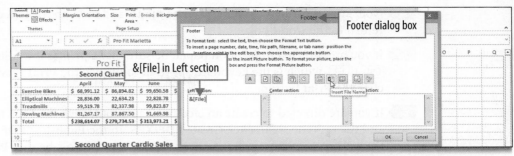

> **Footer dialog box**
> **&[File] in Left section**

4 ▶ Click **OK** two times.

The vertical dotted line between columns indicates that as currently arranged, only the columns to the left of the dotted line will print on the first page. The exact position of the vertical line may depend on your default printer setting.

🔄 **ANOTHER WAY**
Deselect the chart. On the INSERT tab, in the Text group, click Header & Footer to display Page Layout view. Click in the Left section of the displayed footer, and then in the Header & Footer Elements group, click File Name. Click any cell in the workbook to deselect the footer area, and then on the status bar, click the Normal button to return to Normal view.

Activity 1.15 | Adding Document Properties and Printing a Workbook

1 ▶ In the upper left corner of your screen, click the **FILE tab** to display **Backstage** view. In the lower right corner, click **Show All Properties**.

2 ▶ As the **Tags**, type **cardio sales** In the **Subject** box, type your course name and section number. Be sure your name displays as the author and edit if necessary.

3 ▶ On the left, click **Print** to view the **Print Preview**. Compare your screen with Figure 1.35.

FIGURE 1.35

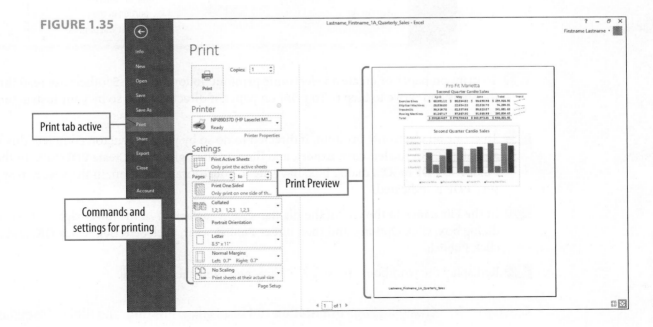

> **Print tab active**
> **Commands and settings for printing**
> **Print Preview**

4 Note any adjustments that need to be made, and then on the left, click **Save** to save and return to the workbook.

5 If you are directed to print on paper, be sure that a printer is available to your system. Press Ctrl + F2, which is the keyboard shortcut to display the **Print Preview**, and then under **Print**, click the **Print** button.

6 If you are directed to create an electronic printout, click the **FILE tab**, on the left click **Export**, and then on the right, click **Create PDF/XPS**. In the **Publish as PDF or XPS** dialog box, navigate to your storage location, in the **Save as type** box, be sure **PDF** is indicated, and then click **Publish** to create the PDF file.

Activity 1.16 | Printing a Section of the Worksheet

From Backstage view, you can print only the portion of the worksheet that you select, and there are times you might want to do this.

1 Select the range **A2:F5** to select only the subtitle and the data for *Exercise Bikes* and *Elliptical Machines* and the column titles

2 Press Ctrl + F2 to display **Print Preview**, and then under **Settings**, click the first arrow, which currently displays *Print Active Sheets*. On the list that displays, click **Print Selection**, and then compare your screen with Figure 1.36.

FIGURE 1.36

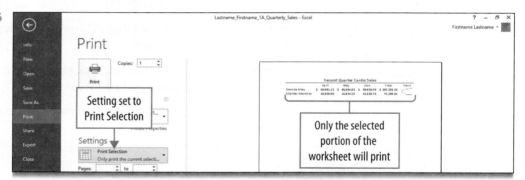

3 To print on paper or create an electronic printout, follow Steps 3-5; otherwise read through the steps and move to Step 6. To print on paper, if directed to do so by your instructor, click **Print**.

4 To create an electronic printout, if directed to do so by your instructor, complete this step and Step 5. On the left click **Export**, and then on the right, click **Create PDF/XPS**. In the **Publish as PDF or XPS** dialog box, navigate to your storage location, in the **Save as type** box, be sure **PDF** is indicated.

5 In the **File name**, to the end of the file name, add **_selection** In the lower right corner of the dialog box, click **Options**, and then under **Publish what**, click **Selection**. Click **OK**, and then click **Publish**.

6 Redisplay the workbook, press Ctrl + Home, and then click **Save** 🖫.

Activity 1.17 | Changing Page Orientation and Displaying, Printing, and Hiding Formulas

When you type a formula in a cell, the cell displays the *results* of the formula calculation. Recall that this value is called the displayed value. You can view and print the underlying formulas in the cells. When you do so, a formula often takes more horizontal space to display than the result of the calculation.

1 If necessary, redisplay your worksheet. Because you will make some temporary changes to your workbook, on the **Quick Access Toolbar**, click **Save** 🖫 to be sure your work is saved up to this point.

2 On the **FORMULAS tab**, in the **Formula Auditing group**, click **Show Formulas**.

🔄 **ANOTHER WAY**   Hold down Ctrl, and then press ~ (usually located below Esc).

3 In the **column heading area**, point to the **column A** heading to display the ⬇ pointer, hold down the left mouse button, and then drag to the right to select columns **A:F**. Compare your screen with Figure 1.37.

FIGURE 1.37

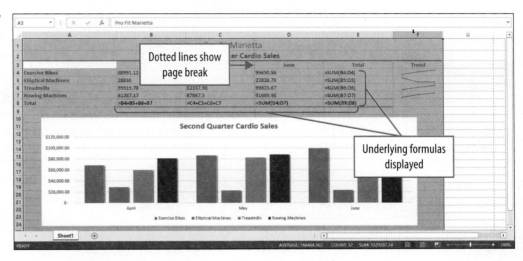

> **NOTE**   **Turning the Display of Formulas On and Off**
>
> The Show Formulas button is a toggle button. Clicking it once turns the display of formulas on—the button will be shaded. Clicking the button again turns the display of formulas off.

4 Point to the column heading boundary between any two of the selected columns to display the ➕ pointer, and then double-click to AutoFit the selected columns.

AutoFit adjusts the width of a column to fit the cell content of the *widest* cell in the column.

🔄 **ANOTHER WAY**   With the columns selected, on the HOME tab, in the Cells group, click Format, and then click AutoFit Column Width.

5 On the **PAGE LAYOUT tab**, in the **Page Setup group**, click **Orientation**, and then click **Landscape**. In the **Scale to Fit** group, click the **Width arrow**, and then click **1 page** to scale the data to fit onto one page.

Scaling shrinks the width or height of the printed worksheet to fit a maximum number of pages, and is convenient for printing formulas. Although it is not always the case, formulas frequently take up more space than the actual data.

🔄 **ANOTHER WAY**   In the Scale to Fit group, click the Dialog Box Launcher button to display the Page tab of the Page Setup dialog box. Then, under Scaling, click the Fit to option button.

6 In the **Page Setup group**, click **Margins**, click **Custom Margins**, and then on the **Margins tab**, under **Center on page**, be sure the **Horizontally** check box is selected—select it if necessary.

7 Click **OK** to close the dialog box. Check to be sure your chart is centered below the data and the left and right edges are slightly inside column A and column F—use the ⟦↖⟧ pointer to drag a chart edge and then deselect the chart if necessary.

8 Click any cell so that the chart is not selected, and then press ⟦Ctrl⟧ + ⟦F2⟧ to display the **Print Preview**. Under **Settings**, if necessary switch back to the option to **Print Active Sheets**. If directed to do so by your instructor, print on paper or click Save As and name the worksheet **Lastname_Firstname_1A_Quarterly_Sales_fomulas**

9 On the left, click **Close**, and when prompted, click **Don't Save** so that you do *not* save the changes you made—displaying formulas, changing column widths and orientation, and scaling—to print your formulas.

10 In the upper right corner of your screen, click **Close** ⟦ **✕** ⟧ to close Excel.

More **Knowledge** | **Inserting a Watermark**

Excel does not have a watermark feature like the watermark in Word, but there are two ways you can achieve the same effect. To use WordArt to mimic a watermark, on the INSERT tab, in the Text group, click Insert WordArt, and then click the style you want to use. Type the text and resize as necessary. Then, right-click the WordArt, click Format Text Effects, click Text Fill & Outline, and then drag one or both transparency sliders to the percentage you want. Or, simply create an image of a watermark and insert the image in the worksheet header or footer.

END | You have completed Project 1A

GO! with Office Web Apps

Objective | Create a Sales Report with an Embedded Column Chart Using the Excel Web App

If you are working on a computer that does not have Microsoft Office installed, you can still create new workbooks in your web browser by using the Excel Office Web App.

> **A L E R T !** **Working with Web-Based Applications and Services**
>
> Computer programs and services on the web receive continuous updates and improvements, so the steps to complete this web-based activity may differ from the ones shown. You can often look at the screens and the information presented to determine how to complete the activity.

Activity | Creating a Sales Report with Embedded Column Chart Using the Excel Web App

In this activity, you will use the Excel Web App to create a sales report and chart similar to the one you created in Project 1A.

1 Start Excel, open a new blank workbook, and then if necessary, in the upper right corner, log into Office with your Microsoft account. In cell **A1**, type **Pro Fit Marietta** press Enter, and then click the **FILE tab**. On the left, click **Save As**, and then on the right, click the name of your SkyDrive—the path to your GO! Web Projects folder on the SkyDrive may display under Recent Folders and if so, you can click there.

2 In the **Save As** dialog box for your SkyDrive, if necessary open your **GO! Web Projects** folder, and then save the file as **Lastname_Firstname_EX_1A_Web** Close Excel, launch Internet Explorer, go to http://skydrive.com, sign in, and then from your **GO! Web Projects** folder, open the file you just saved there.

3 To help you create this project quickly and to eliminate extra typing, you will import the data from a Word table. From the taskbar, open **File Explorer**, navigate to the student data files that accompany this textbook, and then open the Word document **e01_1A_Web**. Press Ctrl + A to select all of the text, right-click anywhere over the

selection, and then click **Copy**. **Close** [x] Word and **Close** [x] File Explorer.

4 Click cell **A2**, on the Excel Web App ribbon, in the **Clipboard group**, click the upper portion of the **Paste** button; if necessary click **Allow access**. Notice that number symbols display when numeric data is too wide for the cell.

5 Select column headings **A:E**, point to the border between any two selected column headings to display the [↔] pointer, and then double-click to resize all the columns to display all data.

6 Drag to select the range **A1:E1**, and then in the **Alignment group**, click **Merge & Center** [▤▾]. Merge and center the worksheet's subtitle in the same manner. Select the range **A1:A2**, and then in the **Font group**, apply **Bold** [B] and change the **Font Color** [A ▾] to **Dark Blue**.

7 Select the range **B4:E4**. In the **Number group**, click the **Number Format arrow**, and then click **Currency**. Apply the same format to the range **B8:E8**.

FIGURE A

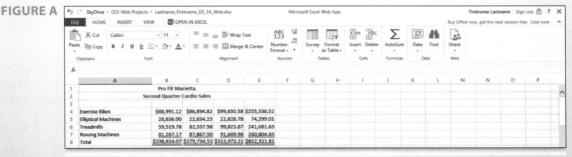

(GO! with Office Web Apps continues on the next page)

8 Select the range **B7:E7**, and then in the **Font group**, click **Underline** <u>U</u> ▾. Select the range **B8:E8**, and then in the **Font group** click **Double Underline**. Click any empty cell, and then compare your screen with Figure A.

9 Click cell **B3**, type **April** and press ⏎, and then click the cell **B3** again. Drag the fill handle to select cells **C3:D3** to complete the series. In cell **E3** type **Total** Select these four column titles and apply **Center** ▤ and **Bold** **B**.

10 Select the range **A3:D7**—the data without the totals. On the **INSERT tab**, in the **Charts group**, click **Column**, and then click the first chart type—**Clustered Column**. In the **Data group**, click **Switch Row/Column**.

11 Drag the chart so that the upper left corner of the chart is inside the upper left portion of cell **A9**. From

the **Labels group**, add a **Chart Title** in the **Above Chart** position with the text **2nd Quarter Cardio Sales**

12 Click cell **A1**, and then compare your screen with Figure B.

In the Excel Web App, you do not have the same set of features available that you have in the full version of Office; for example, you do not have Cell Styles, sparklines, and chart styles. But you can still create the data and chart in a meaningful way.

13 If you are instructed to submit your file, use one of the methods outlined in the Note box below. Then, on the ribbon, click the **FILE tab** and click **Exit**. In the Excel Web App, there is no Save button because your workbook is being saved automatically. Sign out of your SkyDrive and close Internet Explorer.

FIGURE B

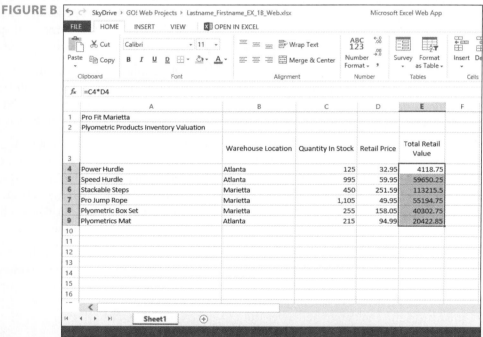

N O T E   **Printing or Creating an Electronic File from the Excel Web App**

To print on paper, click the FILE tab, click Print, click the Print button, and then click Print. In the Print Preview display, click Print. In the displayed Print dialog box, click Print to print on the printer connected to your system. To create an electronic file of your printout, from the Print dialog box, locate the printer labeled *Send to OneNote 2013*, and then click Print. When OneNote opens, click the Unfiled Notes section of the displayed notebook, and then click OK. On the ribbon, click the FILE tab, click Export, and then create a PDF of the page. A PDF created in this manner may include a blank Page 1. Close OneNote.

PROJECT

1B Inventory Valuation

MyITLab® Project 1B Training

1 EXCEL

PROJECT ACTIVITIES

In Activities 1.18 through 1.27 you will create a workbook for Josh Feingold, Operations Manager, which calculates the retail value of an inventory of plyometric training products. Your completed worksheet will look similar to Figure 1.38.

PROJECT FILES

For Project 1B, you will need the following file:	You will save your workbook as:
New blank Excel workbook	**Lastname_Firstname_1B_Plyo_Products**

PROJECT RESULTS

Pro Fit Marietta

Plyometric Products Inventory Valuation

As of September 30

	Warehouse Location	**Quantity in Stock**	**Retail Price**	**Total Retail Value**	**Percent of Total Retail Value**
Power Hurdle	Atlanta	125	$ 32.95	$ 4,118.75	1.41%
Speed Hurdle	Atlanta	995	59.95	59,650.25	20.37%
Stackable Steps	Marietta	450	251.59	113,215.50	38.65%
Pro Jump Rope	Marietta	1,105	49.95	55,194.75	18.84%
Plyometric Box Set	Marietta	255	158.05	40,302.75	13.76%
Plyometric Mat	Atlanta	215	94.99	20,422.85	6.97%
Total Retail Value for All Products				**$ 292,904.85**	

Lastname_Firstname_1B_Plyo_Products

FIGURE 1.38 Project 1B Inventory Valuation

Objective 7 | Check Spelling in a Worksheet

Video E1-7

In Excel, the spelling checker performs similarly to the other Microsoft Office programs.

Activity 1.18 | Checking Spelling in a Worksheet

1 **Start** Excel and display a new blank workbook. In cell **A1**, type **Pro Fit Marietta** and press Enter. In cell **A2**, type **Plyometric Products Inventory** and press Enter.

2 Press F12 to display the **Save As** dialog box, and then navigate to your **Excel Chapter 1** folder. As the **File name**, using your own name, type **Lastname_Firstname_1B_Plyo_Products** and then click **Save**.

3 Press Tab to move to cell **B3**, type **Quantity** and press Tab. In cell **C3**, type **Average Cost** and press Tab. In cell **D3**, type **Retail Price** and press Tab.

4 Click cell **C3**, and then look at the **Formula Bar**. Notice that in the cell, the displayed value is cut off; however, in the **Formula Bar**, the entire text value—the underlying value—displays. Compare your screen with Figure 1.39.

> Text that is too long to fit in a cell extends into cells on the right only if they are empty. If the cell to the right contains data, the text in the cell to the left is truncated—cut off. The entire value continues to exist, but is not completely visible.

FIGURE 1.39

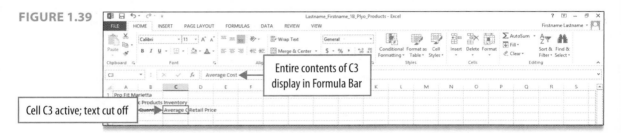

5 Click cell **E3**, type **Total Retail Value** and press Tab. In cell **F3**, type **Percent of Total Retail Value** and press Enter.

6 Click cell **A4**. *Without* correcting the spelling error, type **Powr Hurdle** and then press Enter. In the range **A5:A10**, type the remaining row titles shown below. Then compare your screen with Figure 1.40.

Speed Hurdle
Stackable Steps
Pro Jump Rope
Plyometric Box Set
Plyometric Mat
Total Retail Value for All Products

FIGURE 1.40

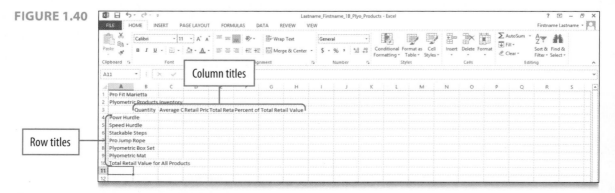

7 In the **column heading area**, point to the right boundary of **column A** to display the ⊹ pointer, and then drag to the right to widen **column A** to **215** pixels.

8 Select the range **A1:F1**, **Merge & Center** the text, and then from the **Cell Styles** gallery, apply the **Title** style.

9 Select the range **A2:F2**, **Merge & Center** the text, and then from the **Cell Styles** gallery, apply the **Heading 1** style. Press [Ctrl] + [Home] to move to the top of your worksheet.

10 With cell **A1** as the active cell, click the **REVIEW tab**, and then in the **Proofing group**, click **Spelling**. Compare your screen with Figure 1.41.

FIGURE 1.41

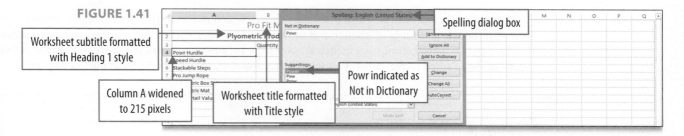

Worksheet subtitle formatted with Heading 1 style

Spelling dialog box

Powr indicated as Not in Dictionary

Column A widened to 215 pixels

Worksheet title formatted with Title style

A L E R T ! **Does a Message Display Asking if You Want to Continue Checking at the Beginning of the Sheet?**

If a message displays asking if you want to continue checking at the beginning of the sheet, click Yes. The Spelling command begins its checking process with the currently selected cell and moves to the right and down. If your active cell was a cell after A1, this message may display.

⟳ **ANOTHER WAY** Press [F7], which is the keyboard shortcut for the Spelling command.

---

11 In the **Spelling** dialog box, under **Not in Dictionary**, notice the word *Powr*.

The spelling tool does not have this word in its dictionary. Under *Suggestions*, Excel provides a list of suggested spellings.

12 Under **Suggestions**, click **Power**, and then click **Change**.

Powr, a typing error, is changed to *Power*. A message box displays *Spell check complete. You're good to go!*—unless you have additional unrecognized words. Because the spelling check begins its checking process starting with the currently selected cell, it is good practice to return to cell A1 before starting the Spelling command.

13 Correct any other errors you may have made. When the message displays, *Spell check complete. You're good to go!*, click **OK**. Save 💾 your workbook.

Objective 8 — Enter Data by Range

Video E1-8

You can enter data by first selecting a range of cells. This is a time-saving technique, especially if you use the numeric keypad to enter the numbers.

Activity 1.19 | Entering Data by Range

1 Select the range **B4:D9**, type **125** and then press [Enter].

The value displays in cell B4, and cell B5 becomes the active cell.

2 With cell **B5** active in the range, and pressing Enter after each entry, type the following, and then compare your screen with Figure 1.42:

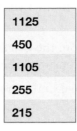

| 1125 |
| 450 |
| 1105 |
| 255 |
| 215 |

After you enter the last value and press Enter, the active cell moves to the top of the next column within the selected range. Although it is not required to enter data in this manner, you can see that selecting the range before you enter data saves time because it confines the movement of the active cell to the selected range. When you select a range of data, the Quick Analysis button displays.

FIGURE 1.42

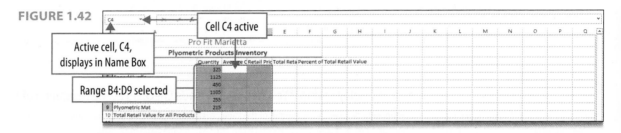

3 With the selected range still active, from the following table, beginning in cell **C4** and pressing Enter after each entry, enter the data for the **Average Cost** column and then the **Retail Price** column. If you prefer, deselect the range to enter the values—typing in a selected range is optional.

AVERAGE COST	RETAIL PRICE
15.50	32.95
29.55	59.95
125.95	251.59
18.75	49.95
85.25	159.05
49.95	94.99

Recall that the default number format for cells is the *General* number format, in which numbers display exactly as you type them and trailing zeros do not display, even if you type them.

4 Click any blank cell, and then compare your screen with Figure 1.43. Correct any errors you may have made while entering data, and then click **Save** .

FIGURE 1.43

Objective 9 Construct Formulas for Mathematical Operations

Video E1-9

Operators are symbols with which you can specify the type of calculation you want to perform in a formula.

Activity 1.20 | Using Arithmetic Operators

1 Click cell **E4**, type **=b4*d4** and notice that the two cells are outlined as part of an active formula. Then press Enter.

The *Total Retail Value* of all *Power Hurdle* items in inventory—*4118.75*—equals the *Quantity* (125) times the *Retail Price* (selling price) of 32.95. In Excel, the asterisk (*) indicates multiplication.

2 Take a moment to study the symbols you will use to perform basic mathematical operations in Excel as shown in the table in Figure 1.44, which are referred to as ***arithmetic operators***.

FIGURE 1.44

SYMBOLS USED IN EXCEL FOR ARITHMETIC OPERATORS	
OPERATOR SYMBOL	**OPERATION**
+	Addition
–	Subtraction (also negation)
*	Multiplication
/	Division
%	Percent
^	Exponentiation

3 Click cell **E4**.

You can see that in cells E5:E9, you need a formula similar to the one in E4, but one that refers to the cells in row 5, row 6, and so forth. Recall that you can copy formulas and the cell references will change *relative to* the row number.

4 With cell **E4** selected, position your pointer over the fill handle in the lower right corner of the cell until the + pointer displays. Then, drag down through cell **E9** to copy the formula.

5 Select the range **B4:B9**, and then on the **HOME tab**, in the **Number group**, click **Comma Style**. In the **Number group**, click **Decrease Decimal** two times to remove the decimal places from these values.

Comma Style formats a number with two decimal places; because these are whole numbers referring to quantities, no decimal places are necessary.

ANOTHER WAY Select the range, display the Cell Styles gallery, and then under Number Format, click Comma [0].

6 Select the range **E4:E9**, and then at the bottom of your screen, in the status bar, notice the displayed values for **Average**, **Count**, and **Sum**—*50158.89167*, *6* and *300953.35*.

When you select a range of numerical data, Excel's ***AutoCalculate*** feature displays three calculations in the status bar by default—Average, Count, and Sum. Here, Excel indicates that if you averaged the selected values, the result would be *50158.89167*, there are *6* cells in the selection that contain values, and that if you added the values the result would be *300953.35*.

You can display three additional calculations to this area by right-clicking the status bar and selecting them—Numerical Count, Minimum, and Maximum.

Activity 1.21 | Using the Quick Analysis Tool

Recall that the Quick Analysis button displays when you select a range of data. Quick Analysis is convenient because it keeps common commands close to your mouse pointer and also displays commands in a format that is easy to touch with your finger if you are using a touchscreen device.

1 In the lower right corner of the selected range, click **Quick Analysis** 📷, and then in the displayed gallery, click **TOTALS**. *Point to*, but do not click, the first **Sum** button, which shows blue cells at the bottom. Compare your screen with Figure 1.45.

Here, the shaded cells on the button indicate what will be summed and where the result will display, and a preview of the result displays in the cell bordered with a gray shadow.

FIGURE 1.45

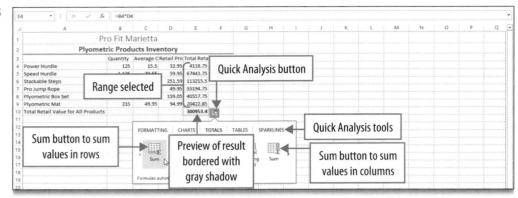

2 Click the first **Sum** button to display the column total *300953.4* formatted in Bold.

Sums calculated using the Quick Analysis tool are formatted in Bold.

3 Select the range **C5:E9** and apply the **Comma Style** ·; notice that Excel widens the columns to accommodate the data.

4 Select the range **C4:E4**, hold down Ctrl, and then click cell **E10**. Release Ctrl, and then apply the **Accounting Number Format** $ ·. Notice that Excel widens the columns as necessary.

5 Click cell **E10**, and then in the **Cell Styles** gallery, apply the **Total** style. Click any blank cell, **Save** 🖫 your workbook, and then compare your screen with Figure 1.46.

FIGURE 1.46

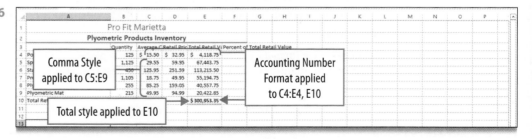

Activity 1.22 | Copying Formulas Containing Absolute Cell References

In a formula, a relative cell reference refers to a cell by its position *relative to* the cell that contains the formula. An ***absolute cell reference***, on the other hand, refers to a cell by its *fixed* position in the worksheet, for example, the total in cell E10.

A relative cell reference automatically adjusts when a formula is copied. In some calculations, you do *not* want the cell reference to adjust; rather, you want the cell reference to remain the same when the formula is copied.

1 ▶ Click cell **F4**, type **=** and then click cell **E4**. Type **/** and then click cell **E10**.

The formula =E4/E10 indicates that the value in cell E4 will be *divided* by the value in cell E10. Why? Because Mr. Feingold wants to know the percentage by which each product's Total Retail Value makes up the Total Retail Value for All Products.

Arithmetically, the percentage is computed by dividing the *Total Retail Value* for each product by the *Total Retail Value for All Products*. The result will be a percentage expressed as a decimal.

2 ▶ Press Enter. Click cell **F4** and notice that the formula displays in the **Formula Bar**. Then, point to cell **F4** and double-click.

The formula, with the two referenced cells displayed in color and bordered with the same color, displays in the cell. This feature, called the *range finder*, is useful for verifying formulas because it visually indicates which workbook cells are included in a formula calculation.

3 ▶ Press Enter to redisplay the result of the calculation in the cell, and notice that .013686, which is approximately 1% of the total retail value of the inventory, is made up of Power Hurdles.

4 ▶ Click cell **F4** again, and then drag the fill handle down through cell **F9**. Compare your screen with Figure 1.47.

Each cell displays an error message—*#DIV/0!* and a green triangle in the upper left corner of each cell indicates that Excel detects an error.

Like a grammar checker, Excel uses rules to check for formula errors and flags errors in this manner. Additionally, the Auto Fill Options button displays, from which you can select formatting options for the copied cells.

FIGURE 1.47

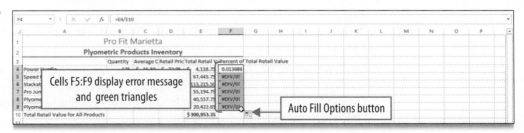

5 ▶ Click cell **F5**, and to the left of the cell, point to the **Error Checking** button ◈ ▾ to display its ScreenTip—*The formula or function used is dividing by zero or empty cells.*

In this manner, Excel suggests the cause of an error.

6 ▶ Look at the **Formula Bar** and examine the formula.

The formula is =E5/E11. The cell reference to E5 is correct, but the cell reference following the division operator (/) is *E11*, and E11 is an *empty* cell.

7 ▶ Click cell **F6**, point to the **Error Checking** button ◈ ▾, and in the **Formula Bar** examine the formula.

Because the cell references are relative, Excel builds the formulas by increasing the row number for each equation. But in this calculation, the divisor must always be the value in cell E10—the *Total Retail Value for All Products*.

8 ▶ Point to cell **F4**, and then double-click to place the insertion point within the cell.

9 ▶ Within the cell, use the arrow keys as necessary to position the insertion point to the left of *E10*, and then press F4. Compare your screen with Figure 1.48.

Dollar signs ($) display, which changes the reference to cell E10 to an absolute cell reference. The use of the dollar sign to denote an absolute reference is not related in any way to whether or not the values you are working with are currency values. It is simply the symbol that Excel uses to denote an absolute cell reference.

FIGURE 1.48

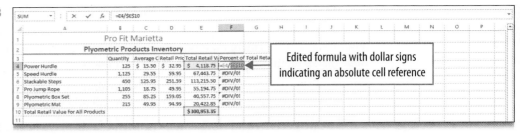

Edited formula with dollar signs indicating an absolute cell reference

 ANOTHER WAY   Edit the formula so that it indicates *=E4/$E$10.*

10 ▶ On the **Formula Bar**, click **Enter** ✓ so that **F4** remains the active cell. Then, drag the fill handle to copy the new formula down through cell **F9**. Compare your screen with Figure 1.49.

FIGURE 1.49

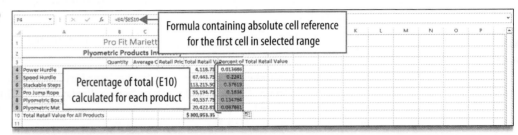

Formula containing absolute cell reference for the first cell in selected range

Percentage of total (E10) calculated for each product

11 ▶ Click cell **F5**, examine the formula in the **Formula Bar**, and then examine the formulas for cells **F6**, **F7**, **F8**, and **F9**.

For each formula, the cell reference for the *Total Retail Value* of each product changed relative to its row; however, the value used as the divisor—*Total Retail Value for All Products* in cell E10— remained absolute. You can see that by using either relative or absolute cell references, it is easy to duplicate formulas without typing them.

12 ▶ **Save** 🖫 your workbook.

More **Knowledge**   **Calculate a Percentage if You Know the Total and the Amount**

Using the equation *amount/total = percentage*, you can calculate the percentage by which a part makes up a total—with the percentage formatted as a decimal. For example, if on a test you score 42 points correctly out of 50, your percentage of correct answers is 42/50 = 0.84 or 84%.

Objective 10 | Edit Values in a Worksheet

Video E1-10

Excel performs calculations on numbers; that is why you use Excel. If you make changes to the numbers, Excel automatically *re*-calculates the results. This is one of the most powerful and valuable features of Excel.

Activity 1.23 | Editing Values in a Worksheet

You can edit text and number values directly within a cell or in the Formula Bar.

In cell **E10**, notice the column total *$300,953.35*. Then, click cell **B5**, and to change its value type **995** Watch cell **E5** and press (Enter).

> Excel formulas *re-calculate* if you change the value in a cell that is referenced in a formula. It is not necessary to delete the old value in a cell; selecting the cell and typing a new value replaces the old value with your new typing.

> The *Total Retail Value* of all *Speed Hurdle* items recalculates to *59,650.25* and the total in cell E10 recalculates to *$293,159.85*. Additionally, all of the percentages in column F recalculate.

2 Point to cell **D8**, and then double-click to place the insertion point within the cell. Use the arrow keys to move the insertion point to left or right of *9*, and use either (Del) or (Backspace) to delete *9* and then type **8** so that the new Retail Price is *158.05*.

3 Watch cell **E8** and **E10** as you press (Enter), and then notice the recalculation of the formulas in those two cells.

> Excel recalculates the value in cell E8 to *40,302.75* and the value in cell E10 to *$292,904.85*. Additionally, all of the percentages in column F recalculate because the *Total Retail Value for All Products* recalculated.

4 Point to cell **A2** so that the ⊕ pointer is positioned slightly to the right of the word *Inventory*, and then double-click to place the insertion point in the cell. Edit the text to add the word **Valuation** pressing (Spacebar) as necessary, and then press (Enter).

5 Click cell **B3**, and then in the **Formula Bar**, click to place the insertion point after the letter *y*. Press (Spacebar) one time, type **in Stock** and then on the **Formula Bar**, click **Enter** ✓. Click **Save** 🖫, and then compare your screen with Figure 1.50.

> Recall that if text is too long to fit in the cell and the cell to the right contains data, the text is truncated—cut off—but the entire value still exists as the underlying value.

FIGURE 1.50

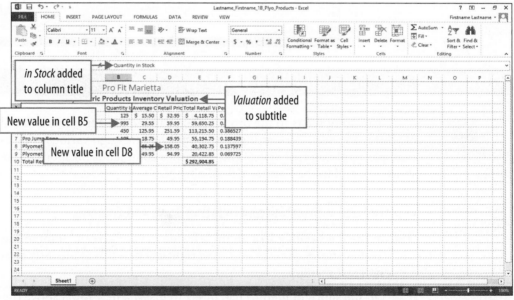

Activity 1.24 | Formatting Cells with the Percent Style

A percentage is part of a whole expressed in hundredths. For example, 75 cents is the same as 75 percent of one dollar. The Percent Style button formats the selected cell as a percentage rounded to the nearest hundredth.

1 Click cell **F4**, and then in the **Number group**, click **Percent Style** %.

Your result is 1%, which is *0.014062* rounded to the nearest hundredth and expressed as a percentage. Percent Style displays the value of a cell as a percentage.

2 Select the range **F4:F9**, right-click over the selection, and then on the mini toolbar, click **Percent Style** %, click **Increase Decimal** two times, and then click **Center** ≡.

Percent Style may not offer a percentage precise enough to analyze important financial information—adding additional decimal places to a percentage makes data more precise.

3 Click any cell to cancel the selection, **Save** your workbook, and then compare your screen with Figure 1.51.

FIGURE 1.51

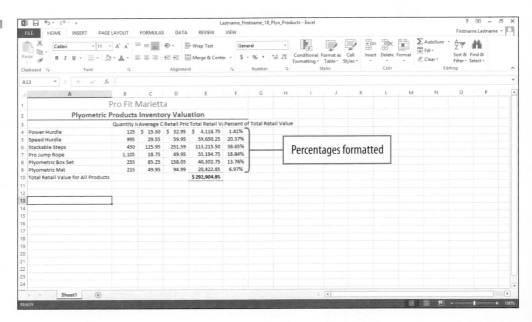

Objective 11 | Format a Worksheet

Video E1-11

Formatting refers to the process of specifying the appearance of cells and the overall layout of your worksheet. Formatting is accomplished through various commands on the ribbon, for example, applying Cell Styles, and also from commands on shortcut menus, using keyboard shortcuts, and in the Format Cells dialog box.

Activity 1.25 | Inserting and Deleting Rows and Columns

1 In the **row heading area** on the left side of your screen, point to the row heading for **row 3** to display the pointer, and then right-click to simultaneously select the row and display a shortcut menu.

2 On the shortcut menu, click **Insert** to insert a new **row 3** above the selected row.

The rows below the new row 3 move down one row, and the Insert Options button displays. By default, the new row uses the formatting of the row *above*.

 **ANOTHER WAY**   Select the row, on the Home tab, in the Cells group, click the Insert button arrow, and then click Insert Sheet Rows. Or, select the row and click the Insert button—the default setting of the button inserts a new sheet row above the selected row.

3 Click cell **E11**. On the **Formula Bar**, notice that the range changed to sum the new range **E5:E10**. Compare your screen with Figure 1.52.

If you move formulas by inserting additional rows or columns in your worksheet, Excel automatically adjusts the formulas. Excel adjusted all of the formulas in the worksheet that were affected by inserting this new row.

FIGURE 1.52

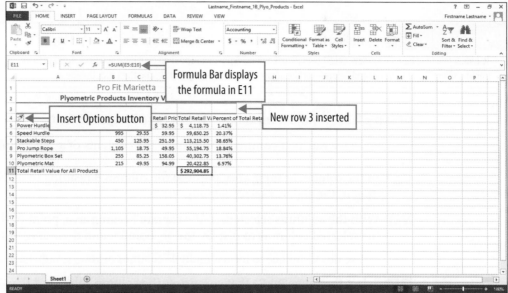

4 Click cell **A3**, type **As of September 30** and then on the **Formula Bar**, click **Enter** ☑ to maintain **A3** as the active cell. **Merge & Center** the text across the range **A3:F3**, and then apply the **Heading 2** cell style.

5 In the **column heading area**, point to **column B** to display the ⬇ pointer, right-click, and then click **Insert**.

A column is inserted to the left of column B. By default, the new column uses the formatting of the column to the *left*.

🔁 **ANOTHER WAY**   Select the column, on the Home tab, in the Cells group, click the Insert button arrow, and then click Insert Sheet Columns. Or, select the column and click the Insert button—the default setting of the button inserts a new sheet column to the right of the selected column.

6 Click cell **B4**, type **Warehouse Location** and then press Enter.

7 In cell **B5**, type **Atlanta** and then type **Atlanta** again in cells **B6** and **B10**. Use AutoComplete to speed your typing by pressing Enter as soon as the AutoComplete suggestion displays. In cells **B7**, **B8**, and **B9**, type **Marietta**

8 In the **column heading area**, point to **column D**, right-click, and then click **Delete**.

The remaining columns shift to the left, and Excel adjusts all the formulas in the worksheet accordingly. You can use a similar technique to delete a row in a worksheet.

9 Compare your screen with Figure 1.53, and then **Save** 💾 your workbook.

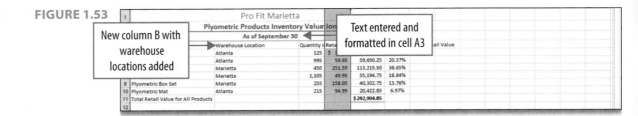

FIGURE 1.53

| New column B with warehouse locations added | | Text entered and formatted in cell A3 |

Pro Fit Marietta
Plyometric Products Inventory Valuation
As of September 30

		Warehouse Location	Quantity i Reta			ail Value
		Atlanta	125	$		
		Atlanta	995	59.95	59,650.25	20.37%
		Marietta	450	251.59	113,215.50	38.65%
		Marietta	1,105	49.95	55,194.75	18.84%
9	Plyometric Box Set	Marietta	255	158.05	40,302.75	13.76%
10	Plyometric Mat	Atlanta	215	94.99	20,422.85	6.97%
11	Total Retail Value for All Products				$ 292,904.85	
12						

More Knowledge **Hiding Rows and Columns**

To hide a row or column from view, select the row or column, right-click, and then click Hide. A border displays to indicate that data is hidden from view. To unhide, select the rows above and below—or the adjacent columns—right-click, and then click Unhide.

Activity 1.26 | Adjusting Column Widths and Wrapping Text

Use the Wrap Text command to display the contents of a cell on multiple lines.

1 In the **column heading area**, point to the **column B** heading to display the ⬇ pointer, and then drag to the right to select **columns B:F**.

2 With the columns selected, in the **column heading area**, point to the right boundary of any of the selected columns to display the ✛ pointer, and then drag to set the width to **95 pixels**.

Use this technique to format multiple columns or rows simultaneously.

3 Select the range **B4:F4** that comprises the column titles, and then on the **HOME tab**, in the **Alignment group**, click **Wrap Text**. Notice that the row height adjusts to display the titles on multiple lines.

4 With the range **B4:F4** still selected, in the **Alignment group**, click **Center** and **Middle Align**. With the range **B4:F4** still selected, apply the **Heading 4** cell style.

The Middle Align command aligns text so that it is centered between the top and bottom of the cell.

5 Select the range **B5:B10**, right-click, and then on the mini toolbar, click **Center**. Click cell **A11**, and then from the **Cell Styles** gallery, under **Themed Cell Styles**, click **40% - Accent1**. **Save** your workbook.

Activity 1.27 | Changing Theme Colors

You can change only the Theme colors of a workbook—without changing the theme fonts or effects.

1 On the **PAGE LAYOUT tab**, in the **Themes group**, click the **Colors arrow**, and then click **Green** to change the theme color. Click any blank cell, and then compare your screen with Figure 1.54.

FIGURE 1.54

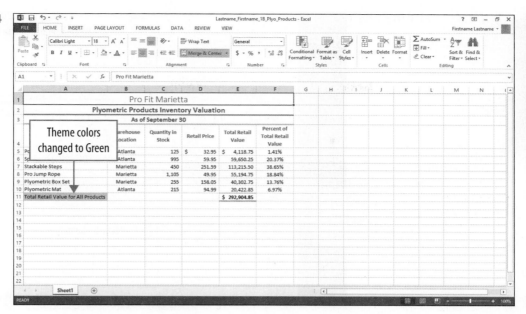

2 On the **PAGE LAYOUT tab**, in the **Page Setup group**, click **Margins**, and then click **Custom Margins**.

3 In the **Page Setup** dialog box, on the **Margins tab**, under **Center on page**, select the **Horizontally** check box.

> This action will center the data and chart horizontally on the page, as shown in the Preview area.

4 In the displayed **Page Setup** dialog box, click the **Header/Footer tab**, and then in the center of the dialog box, click **Custom Footer**. In the **Footer** dialog box, with your insertion point blinking in the **Left section**, on the row of buttons, click **Insert File Name** 🖹.

> &[File] displays in the Left section. Here you can type or insert information from the row of buttons into the left, middle, or right section of the footer. The Custom Header button displays a similar screen to enter information in the header of the worksheet.

5 Click **OK** two times.

6 Click the **FILE tab** to display **Backstage** view, and then in the lower right corner, click **Show All Properties**.

7 As the **Tags**, type **plyo products, inventory** and as the **Subject**, type your course name and section number. Be sure your name displays as the author.

8 On the left, click **Print** to view the **Print Preview**. At the bottom of the **Print Preview**, click **Next Page** ▶, and notice that as currently formatted, the worksheet occupies two pages.

9 Under **Settings**, click **Portrait Orientation**, and then click **Landscape Orientation**. Compare your screen with Figure 1.55.

> You can change the orientation on the Page Layout tab, or here, in Print Preview. Because it is in the Print Preview that you will often see adjustments that need to be made, commonly used settings display on the Print tab in Backstage view.

FIGURE 1.55

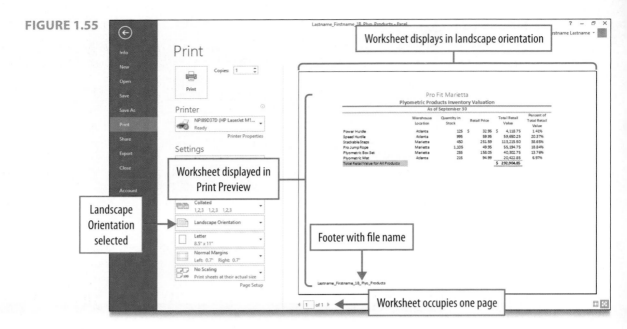

10 ▸ By using the techniques you practiced in Project 1A, print or submit electronically as directed by your instructor. If required by your instructor, print or create an electronic version of your worksheet with formulas displayed.

11 ▸ Close your workbook and Close Excel.

END | You have completed Project 1B

GO! with Office Web Apps

Objective   Calculate the Value of an Inventory in the Excel Web App

If you are working on a computer that does not have Microsoft Office installed, you can still create new workbooks in your web browser by using the Excel Office Web App.

ALERT!   **Working with Web-Based Applications and Services**

Computer programs and services on the web receive continuous updates and improvements, so the steps to complete this web-based activity may differ from the ones shown. You can often look at the screens and the information presented to determine how to complete the activity.

Activity   **Creating an Inventory Valuation Report in the Excel Web App**

In this activity, you will use the Excel Web App to create an inventory valuation similar to the one you created in Project 1B.

1 From the desktop, start Internet Explorer. Navigate to **http://skydrive.com**, and then sign in to your Microsoft account. Open your **GO! Web Projects** folder—or create and then open this folder if necessary.

2 Near the top of the screen, click **Create**, and then click **Excel workbook**. Using your own name, as the file name type **Lastname_Firstname_EX_1B_Web** and then click **Create**.

3 To help you create this project quickly and to eliminate extra typing, you will import the data from a Word table. From the taskbar, open **File Explorer**, navigate to the student data files that accompany this textbook, and then open the Word document **e01_1B_Web**. Press Ctrl + A to select all of the text, right-click anywhere over the selection, and then click **Copy**. **Close** Word and File Explorer.

4 With cell **A1** selected, on the Excel Web App ribbon, in the **Clipboard group**, click the upper portion of the **Paste** button; if necessary click **Allow access**.

5 Select column headings **A:D**, point to the border between any two selected column headings to display the ⬌ pointer, and then double-click to resize the selected columns to display all the data.

6 In cell **E3** type **Total Retail Value** and press Enter. Select the range **B3:E3**, and then in the **Alignment group**, click **Center** ▤, **Middle Align** ▤, and **Wrap Text** ▤. Widen **column E** so that *Total Retail* is on one line and *Value* is on the second line.

7 Click cell **E4** and type **=c4*d4** to create the formula and press Enter; your result is *4118.75*. Click cell **E4** again, and then drag the fill handle down through cell **E9** to calculate each row. Compare your screen with Figure A.

FIGURE A

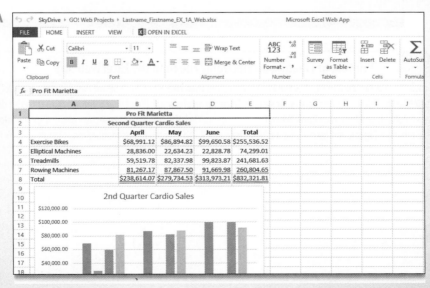

(GO! with Office Web Apps continues on the next page)

8 Click cell **E10**, and then in the **Formulas group**, click **AutoSum** and press Enter to total the column.

9 In cell **F3** type **Percent of Total Retail Value** and then apply **Center** ≣, **Middle Align** ≣, and **Wrap Text** ⊞. Widen the column to display the column title on three lines. In cell **F4** type the formula to calculate the percent of total value **=e4/e10** and press Enter, and then copy the formula down through cell **F9**. With the range **F4:F9** still selected, from the **Number Format arrow**, click **Percentage**.

10 Select the range **E4:E10** and then from the **Number Format arrow**, apply **Currency** format. Click cell **E9**, and then in the **Font group**, click **Underline**. Click cell **E10**, and then in the **Font group**, click **Double Underline**.

11 Select the range **A1:F1**, and then in the **Alignment group**, click **Merge & Center**. Merge and center the worksheet's subtitle in the same

manner. Select the range **A1:A2**, and then in the **Font group**, apply **Bold** B and change the **Font Color** A ▾ to **Orange, Darker 50%**.

12 Click cell **B3**, and then adjust the width of **column B** so that the column title displays on two lines. Click cell **C3** and adjust in the same manner.

13 In cell **A10** type **Total Retail Value for All Products** and then AutoFit **column A**.

14 Click cell **A1**, and then compare your screen with Figure B.

15 If you are instructed to submit your file, use one of the methods outlined in the Note box below. Then, on the ribbon, click the **FILE tab** and click **Exit**. Recall that in the Excel Web App, there is no Save button because your workbook is being saved automatically. Sign out of your SkyDrive and close Internet Explorer.

FIGURE B

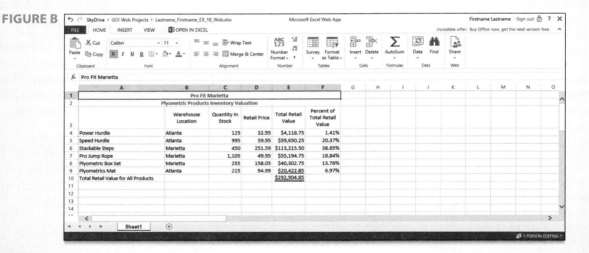

> **NOTE** **Printing or Creating an Electronic File from the Excel Web App**
>
> To print on paper, click the FILE tab, click Print, click the Print button, and then click Print. In the Print Preview display, click Print. In the displayed Print dialog box, click Print to print on the printer connected to your system. To create an electronic file of your printout, from the Print dialog box, locate the printer labeled *Send to OneNote 2013*, and then click Print. When OneNote opens, click the Unfiled Notes section of the displayed notebook, and then click OK. On the ribbon, click the FILE tab, click Export, and then create a PDF of the page. A PDF created in this manner may include a blank Page 1. Close OneNote.

GO! with Microsoft Office 365

Andrew Rodriguez / Fotolia; FotolEdhar/ Fotolia; apops/ Fotolia; Yuri Arcurs/ Fotolia

In every job, you must work and communicate with other people. A group of workers tasked with working together to solve a problem, make a decision, or create a work product is referred to as a *team*. For a team to succeed, the team members must be able to communicate with one another easily.

If all the team members work at the same location and work the same hours, communication is easy. You schedule face-to-face meetings and exchange documents and information among yourselves. But that is a rare arrangement in today's organizations. Rather, it is more likely that the members of your team work in different locations—even different countries—and work different hours or travel extensively away from the headquarters location. Also, for specific projects, teams are frequently organized across different departments of an organization or even across different organizations entirely. Then when the project is complete, the team disbands.

Collaboration is when you work together with others as a team in an intellectual endeavor to complete a shared task or achieve a shared goal; for example, when you and one or more of your classmates work together on a class project. Collaboration involves giving feedback to and receiving feedback from others on the team, and then revising the strategies to achieve the goal or produce the work product based on the feedback.

Microsoft Office 365 is a set of secure online services that enable people in an organization to communicate and collaborate by using any Internet-connected device—a computer, a tablet, or a mobile phone. Because Office 365 offers access from anywhere to email, Web conferencing, documents, and calendars, everyone on a team can work together easily. Office 365 is intended for use by multiple users in an organization and is offered on a monthly subscription basis to organizations starting as low as $6 per month per user.

Activity | Using the Exchange Online Outlook Meeting Tool to Collaborate

This team project relates to the **Bell Orchid Hotels**. If your instructor assigns this project to your class, in this chapter you can expect to use the **Outlook Meeting tool** in **Office 365 Exchange Online** to collaborate on the following tasks for this chapter:

- If you are in the **Accounting Group**, you and your teammates will meet virtually to plan a workbook to summarize hotel rooms sold over a four-week period in April.

- If you are in the **Engineering Group**, you and your teammates will meet virtually to plan a workbook summarizing Maintenance Expenses for the first quarter.

- If you are in the **Food and Beverage Group**, you and your teammates will meet virtually to plan a Menu Analysis workbook to analyze the profitability of the ten most popular entrees in the hotel's restaurant.

- If you are in the **Human Resources Group**, you and your teammates will meet virtually to plan a Salary Analysis workbook summarizing the pay of salaried employees over the first six months of operation.

- If you are in the **Operations Group**, you and your teammates will meet virtually to plan a workbook for Rooms and Housekeeping Service Analysis that will be used to determine ongoing needs for housekeeping service.

- If you are in the **Sales and Marking Group**, you and your teammates will meet virtually to plan a Rooms Sold Analysis workbook summarizing rooms sold by four salespersons during January-June that will be used to develop a marketing plan for the rest of the year.

FIGURE A

END OF CHAPTER

SUMMARY

In Excel, you work with worksheets that are contained in a workbook. A worksheet is formatted as a pattern of uniformly spaced horizontal rows and vertical columns, the intersection of which forms a cell.

A cell can contain a constant value—referred to as a value—or a formula, which is an equation that performs mathematical calculations on the values in your worksheet. Common values are text and numbers.

You can insert sparklines in an Excel worksheet, which are tiny charts embedded in a cell that give a visual trend summary alongside your data. A sparkline makes a pattern more obvious to the eye.

Charts provide a graphic representation of data in a worksheet. Use the Recommended Charts feature to display customized charts that, according to Excel's calculations, will best represent your data.

GO! LEARN IT ONLINE

Review the concepts and key terms in this chapter by completing these online challenges, which you can find at **www.pearsonhighered.com/go**.

Matching and Multiple Choice:
Answer matching and multiple choice questions to test what you learned in this chapter. MyITLab®

Crossword Puzzle:
Spell out the words that match the numbered clues, and put them in the puzzle squares.

Flipboard:
Flip through the definitions of the key terms in this chapter and match them with the correct term.

GO! FOR JOB SUCCESS

Video: Dress to Impress

Your instructor may assign this video to your class, and then ask you to think about, or discuss with your classmates, these questions:

FotolEdhar / Fotolia

If you were interviewing people for your company, what would you look for in terms of their dress and personal presentation?

What might you want to change about your personal dress for work or for an interview?

Do you feel that it's right to "judge a book by its cover"? Why or why not?

END OF CHAPTER
REVIEW AND ASSESSMENT GUIDE FOR EXCEL CHAPTER 1

Your instructor may assign one or more of these projects to help you review the chapter and assess your mastery and understanding of the chapter.

Review and Assessment Guide for Excel Chapter 1			
Project	Apply Skills from These Chapter Objectives	Project Type	Project Location
1C	Objectives 1–6 from Project 1A	**1C Skills Review** A guided review of the skills from Project 1A.	On the following pages
1D	Objectives 7–11 from Project 1B	**1D Skills Review** A guided review of the skills from Project 1B.	On the following pages
1E	Objectives 1–6 from Project 1A	**1E Mastery (Grader Project)** A demonstration of your mastery of the skills in Project 2A with extensive decision making.	In MyITLab and on the following pages
1F	Objectives 7–11 from Project 1B	**1F Mastery (Grader Project)** A demonstration of your mastery of the skills in Project 1B with extensive decision making.	In MyITLab and on the following pages
1G	Objectives 1–11 from Projects 1A and 1B	**1G Mastery (Grader Project)** A demonstration of your mastery of the skills in Projects 1A and 1B with extensive decision making.	In MyITLab and on the following pages
1H	Combination of Objectives from Projects 1A and 1B	**1H GO! Fix It** A demonstration of your mastery of the skills in Projects 1A and 1B by creating a correct result from a document that contains errors you must find.	Online
1I	Combination of Objectives from Projects 1A and 1B	**1I GO! Make It** A demonstration of your mastery of the skills in Projects 1A and 1B by creating a result from a supplied picture.	Online
1J	Combination of Objectives from Projects 1A and 1B	**1J GO! Solve It** A demonstration of your mastery of the skills in Projects 1A and 1B, your decision-making skills, and your critical thinking skills. A task-specific rubric helps you self-assess your result.	Online
1K	Combination of Objectives from Projects 1A and 1B	**1K GO! Solve It** A demonstration of your mastery of the skills in Projects 1A and 1B, your decision-making skills, and your critical thinking skills. A task-specific rubric helps you self-assess your result.	On the following pages
1L	Combination of Objectives from Projects 1A and 1B	**1L GO! Think** A demonstration of your understanding of the chapter concepts applied in a manner that you would outside of college. An analytic rubric helps you and your instructor grade the quality of your work by comparing it to the work an expert in the discipline would create.	On the following pages
1M	Combination of Objectives from Projects 1A and 1B	**1M GO! Think** A demonstration of your understanding of the chapter concepts applied in a manner that you would outside of college. An analytic rubric helps you and your instructor grade the quality of your work by comparing it to the work an expert in the discipline would create.	Online
1N	Combination of Objectives from Projects 1A and 1B	**1N You and GO!** A demonstration of your understanding of the chapter concepts applied in a manner that you would in a personal situation. An analytic rubric helps you and your instructor grade the quality of your work.	Online
1O	Combination of Objectives from Projects 1A and 1B	**1O Cumulative Group Project for Excel Chapter 1** A demonstration of your understanding of concepts and your ability to work collaboratively in a group role-playing assessment, requiring both collaboration and self-management.	Online

GLOSSARY

GLOSSARY OF CHAPTER KEY TERMS

Absolute cell reference A cell reference that refers to cells by their fixed position in a worksheet; an absolute cell reference remains the same when the formula is copied.

Accounting Number Format The Excel number format that applies a thousand comma separator where appropriate, inserts a fixed U.S. dollar sign aligned at the left edge of the cell, applies two decimal places, and leaves a small amount of space at the right edge of the cell to accommodate a parenthesis for negative numbers.

Active cell The cell, surrounded by a black border, ready to receive data or be affected by the next Excel command.

Arithmetic operators The symbols +, −, *, /, %, and ^ used to denote addition, subtraction (or negation), multiplication, division, percentage, and exponentiation in an Excel formula.

Auto Fill An Excel feature that generates and extends values into adjacent cells based on the values of selected cells.

AutoCalculate A feature that displays three calculations in the status bar by default—Average, Count, and Sum—when you select a range of numerical data.

AutoComplete A feature that speeds your typing and lessens the likelihood of errors; if the first few characters you type in a cell match an existing entry in the column, Excel fills in the remaining characters for you.

AutoFit An Excel feature that adjusts the width of a column to fit the cell content of the widest cell in the column.

AutoSum A button that provides quick access to the SUM function.

Category axis The area along the bottom of a chart that identifies the categories of data; also referred to as the x-axis.

Category labels The labels that display along the bottom of a chart to identify the categories of data; Excel uses the row titles as the category names.

Cell The intersection of a column and a row.

Cell address Another name for a cell reference.

Cell content Anything typed into a cell.

Cell reference The identification of a specific cell by its intersecting column letter and row number.

Cell style A defined set of formatting characteristics, such as font, font size, font color, cell borders, and cell shading.

Chart The graphic representation of data in a worksheet; data presented as a chart is usually easier to understand than a table of numbers.

Chart Elements button A button that enables you to add, remove, or change chart elements such as the title, legend, gridlines, and data labels.

Chart Filters button A button that enables you to change which data displays in the chart.

Chart layout The combination of chart elements that can be displayed in a chart such as a title, legend, labels for the columns, and the table of charted cells.

Chart style The overall visual look of a chart in terms of its graphic effects, colors, and backgrounds; for example, you can have flat or beveled columns, colors that are solid or transparent, and backgrounds that are dark or light.

Chart Styles button A button that enables you to set a style and color scheme for your chart.

Chart Styles gallery A group of predesigned chart styles that you can apply to an Excel chart.

Chart types Various chart formats used in a way that is meaningful to the reader; common examples are column charts, pie charts, and line charts.

Column A vertical group of cells in a worksheet.

Column chart A chart in which the data is arranged in columns and that is useful for showing how data changes over a period of time or for illustrating comparisons among items.

Column heading The letter that displays at the top of a vertical group of cells in a worksheet; beginning with the first letter of the alphabet, a unique letter or combination of letters identifies each column.

Comma Style The Excel number format that inserts thousand comma separators where appropriate and applies two decimal places; Comma Style also leaves space at the right to accommodate a parenthesis when negative numbers are present.

Constant value Numbers, text, dates, or times of day that you type into a cell.

Context sensitive A command associated with the currently selected or active object; often activated by right-clicking a screen item.

Data Text or numbers in a cell.

Data marker A column, bar, area, dot, pie slice, or other symbol in a chart that represents a single data point; related data points form a data series.

Data point A value that originates in a worksheet cell and that is represented in a chart by a data marker.

Data series Related data points represented by data markers; each data series has a unique color or pattern represented in the chart legend.

Displayed value The data that displays in a cell.

Excel pointer An Excel window element with which you can display the location of the pointer.

Expand Formula Bar button An Excel window element with which you can increase the height of the Formula Bar to display lengthy cell content.

Expand horizontal scroll bar button An Excel window element with which you can increase the width of the horizontal scroll bar.

Fill handle The small black square in the lower right corner of a selected cell.

Format Changing the appearance of cells and worksheet elements to make a worksheet attractive and easy to read.

Formula An equation that performs mathematical calculations on values in a worksheet.

Formula Bar An element in the Excel window that displays the value or formula contained in the active cell; here you can also enter or edit values or formulas.

Function A predefined formula—a formula that Excel has already built for you—that performs calculations by using specific values in a particular order.

General format The default format that Excel applies to numbers; this format has no specific characteristics—whatever you type in the cell will display, with the exception that trailing zeros to the right of a decimal point will not display.

Label Another name for a text value, and which usually provides information about number values.

Left alignment The cell format in which characters align at the left edge of the cell; this is the default for text entries and is an example of formatting information stored in a cell.

Legend A chart element that identifies the patterns or colors that are assigned to the categories in the chart.

Lettered column headings The area along the top edge of a worksheet that identifies each column with a unique letter or combination of letters.

Merge & Center A command that joins selected cells in an Excel worksheet into one larger cell and centers the contents in the merged cell.

Name Box An element of the Excel window that displays the name of the selected cell, table, chart, or object.

Normal view A screen view that maximizes the number of cells visible on your screen and keeps the column letters and row numbers close to the columns and rows.

Number format A specific way in which Excel displays numbers in a cell.

Number values Constant values consisting of only numbers.

Numbered row headings The area along the left edge of a worksheet that identifies each row with a unique number.

Operators The symbols with which you can specify the type of calculation you want to perform in an Excel formula.

Page Layout view A screen view in which you can use the rulers to measure the width and height of data, set margins for printing, hide or display the numbered row headings and the lettered column headings, and change the page orientation; this view is useful for preparing your worksheet for printing.

Picture element A point of light measured in dots per square inch on a screen; 64 pixels equals 8.43 characters, which is the average number of characters that will fit in a cell in an Excel worksheet using the default font.

Pixel The abbreviated name for a picture element.

Point and click method The technique of constructing a formula by pointing to and then clicking cells; this method

is convenient when the referenced cells are not adjacent to one another.

Quick Analysis tool A tool that displays in the lower right corner of a selected range with which you can analyze your data by using Excel tools such as charts, color-coding, and formulas.

Range Two or more selected cells on a worksheet that are adjacent or nonadjacent; because the range is treated as a single unit, you can make the same changes or combination of changes to more than one cell at a time.

Range finder An Excel feature that outlines cells in color to indicate which cells are used in a formula; useful for verifying which cells are referenced in a formula.

Recommended Charts An Excel feature that displays a customized set of charts that, according to Excel's calculations, will best fit your data based on the range of data that you select.

Relative cell reference In a formula, the address of a cell based on the relative positions of the cell that contains the formula and the cell referred to in the formula.

Rounding A procedure in which you determine which digit at the right of the number will be the last digit displayed and then increase it by one if the next digit to its right is 5, 6, 7, 8, or 9.

Row A horizontal group of cells in a worksheet.

Row heading The numbers along the left side of an Excel worksheet that designate the row numbers.

Scaling The process of shrinking the width and/or height of printed output to fit a maximum number of pages.

Select All box A box in the upper left corner of the worksheet grid that, when clicked, selects all the cells in a worksheet.

Series A group of things that come one after another in succession; for example, January, February, March, and so on.

Sheet tab scrolling buttons Buttons to the left of the sheet tabs used to display Excel sheet tabs that are not in view; used when there are more sheet tabs than will display in the space provided.

Sheet tabs The labels along the lower border of the Excel window that identify each worksheet.

Show Formulas A command that displays the formula in each cell instead of the resulting value.

Sparkline A tiny chart in the background of a cell that gives a visual trend summary alongside your data; makes a pattern more obvious.

Spreadsheet Another name for a worksheet.

Status bar The area along the lower edge of the Excel window that displays, on the left side, the current cell mode, page number, and worksheet information; on the right side, when numerical data is selected, common calculations such as Sum and Average display.

SUM function A predefined formula that adds all the numbers in a selected range of cells.

Switch Row/Column A charting command to swap the data over the axis—data being charted on the vertical axis will move to the horizontal axis and vice versa.

Text values Constant values consisting of only text, and which usually provide information about number values; also referred to as labels.

Theme A predefined set of colors, fonts, lines, and fill effects that coordinate with each other.

Underlying formula The formula entered in a cell and visible only on the Formula Bar.

Underlying value The data that displays in the Formula Bar.

Value Another name for a constant value.

Value axis A numerical scale on the left side of a chart that shows the range of numbers for the data points; also referred to as the Y-axis.

Workbook An Excel file that contains one or more worksheets.

Workbook-level buttons Buttons at the far right of the ribbon tabs that minimize or restore a displayed workbook.

Worksheet The primary document that you use in Excel to work with and store data, and which is formatted as a pattern of uniformly spaced horizontal and vertical lines.

Worksheet grid area A part of the Excel window that displays the columns and rows that intersect to form the worksheet's cells.

X-axis Another name for the horizontal (category) axis.

Y-axis Another name for the vertical (value) axis.

CHAPTER REVIEW

Apply **1A** skills from these Objectives:

1 Create, Save, and Navigate an Excel Workbook
2 Enter Data in a Worksheet
3 Construct and Copy Formulas and Use the SUM Function
4 Format Cells with Merge & Center, Cell Styles, and Themes
5 Chart Data to Create a Column Chart and Insert Sparklines
6 Print a Worksheet, Display Formulas, and Close Excel

In the following Skills Review, you will create a new Excel worksheet with a chart that summarizes the first quarter sales of fitness equipment for step training. Your completed worksheet will look similar to Figure 1.56.

PROJECT FILES

For Project 1C, you will need the following file:

New blank Excel workbook

You will save your workbook as:

Lastname_Firstname_1C_Step_Sales

PROJECT RESULTS

Lastname_Firstname_1C_Step_Sales

FIGURE 1.56

(Project 1C Step Sales continues on the next page)

Build from Scratch

CHAPTER REVIEW

1 **Start** Excel and open a new blank workbook. Click the **FILE tab** to display **Backstage** view, click **Save As**, and then navigate to your **Excel Chapter 1** folder. In the **File name** box, using your own name, type **Lastname_Firstname_1C_Step_Sales** and then press Enter.

a. With cell **A1** as the active cell, type the worksheet title **Pro Fit Marietta** and then press Enter. In cell **A2**, type the worksheet subtitle **First Quarter Step Sales** and then press Enter.

b. Leave row 3 blank, click in cell **A4**, type **Basic Step Box** and then press Enter. In cell **A5**, type **Step Storage Box** and then press Enter. In cell **A6**, type **Stackable Steps** and then press Enter. In cell **A7**, type **Step Mats** and then press Enter. In cell **A8**, type **Total** and then press Enter.

c. Click cell **B3**. Type **January** and then in the **Formula Bar**, click **Enter** to keep cell **B3** the active cell. With **B3** as the active cell, point to the **fill handle** in the lower right corner of the selected cell, drag to the right to cell **D3**, and then release the mouse button to enter the text *February* and *March*.

d. Press Ctrl + Home to make cell **A1** the active cell. In the **column heading area**, point to the vertical line between **column A** and **column B** to display the ⊞ pointer, hold down the left mouse button, and drag to the right to increase the column width to **130 pixels**.

e. Point to cell **B3**, and then drag across to select cells **B3** and **C3** and **D3**. With the range **B3:D3** selected, point anywhere over the selected range, right-click, and then on the mini toolbar, click **Center**.

f. Click cell **B4**, type **75826.99** and press Tab to make cell **C4** active. Enter the remaining values, as shown below in **Table 1**, pressing Tab to move across the rows and Enter to move down the columns.

TABLE 1

	January	February	March
Basic Step Box	75826.99	81657.32	72431.22
Step Storage Rack	85245.90	92618.95	88337.68
Stackable Steps	68751.64	71997.48	78951.23
Step Mats	63255.10	58742.67	67995.20

2 Click cell **B8** to make it the active cell and type **=**

a. At the insertion point, type **b4** and then type **+** Type **b5** and then type **+b6+b7** Press Enter. Your result is *293079.6*.

b. Click in cell **C8**. Type **=** and then click cell **C4**. Type **+** and then click cell **C5**. Repeat this process to complete the formula to add cells **C6** and **C7** to the formula, and then press Enter. Your result is *305016.4*.

c. Click cell **D8**. On the **HOME tab**, in the **Editing group**, click **AutoSum**, and then press Enter to construct a formula by using the SUM function. Your result is *307715.3*.

d. In cell **E3** type **Total** and press Enter. With cell **E4** as the active cell, hold down Alt, and then press =. On the **Formula Bar**, click **Enter** to display the result and keep cell **E4** active.

e. With cell **E4** active, point to the **fill handle** in the lower right corner of the cell. Drag down through cell **E8**, and then release the mouse button to copy the formula with relative cell references down to sum each row.

3 Click cell **F3**. Type **Trend** and then press Enter.

a. Select the range **A1:F1**, and then on the **HOME tab**, in the **Alignment group**, click **Merge & Center**. Select the range **A2:F2** and **Merge & Center** the selection.

b. Click cell **A1**. In the **Styles group**, click **Cell Styles**. Under **Titles and Headings**, click **Title**. Click cell **A2**, display the **Cell Styles** gallery, and then click **Heading 1**.

c. Select the range **B3:F3**, hold down Ctrl, and then select the range **A4:A8**. From the **Cell Styles** gallery, click **Heading 4** to apply this cell style to the column and row titles.

d. Select the range **B4:E4**, hold down Ctrl, and then select the range **B8:E8**. On the **HOME tab**, in the **Number group**, click **Accounting Number Format**. Select the range **B5:E7**, and then in the **Number group**, click **Comma Style**. Select the range **B8:E8**. From the **Styles group**, display the **Cell Styles** gallery, and then under **Titles and Headings**, click **Total**.

e. On the ribbon, click the **PAGE LAYUT tab**, and then in the **Themes group**, click **Themes** to display the **Themes** gallery. Click the **Basis** theme. (This theme widens the columns slightly). On the **Quick Access Toolbar**, click **Save**.

(Project 1C Step Sales continues on the next page)

CHAPTER REVIEW

4 Select the range **A3:D7**, which includes the row titles, the column titles and the data without the totals. Click the **INSERT tab**, and then in the **Charts group**, click **Recommended Charts**. In the **Insert Chart** dialog box, scroll down and click the fifth recommended chart—a **Clustered Column** chart in which *each month* displays its *sales for each type of step training equipment*. Click **OK**.

   a. In the chart, click anywhere in the text *Chart Title* to select the text box. Watch the **Formula Bar** as you type **First** and then let AutoComplete complete the title by pressing Enter.

   b. Click in a white area just slightly *inside* the chart border to deselect the chart title but keep the chart selected. To the right of the chart, click the second button—the **Chart Styles** button. Be sure the **STYLE** tab is selected. Use the scroll bar to scroll down, and then by using the ScreenTips, locate and click **Style 6**.

   c. At the top of the gallery, click **COLOR**. Under **Colorful**, point to the fourth row of colors to display the ScreenTip *Color 4*, and then click to apply the **Color 4** variation of the theme colors.

   d. Point to the top border of the chart to display the pointer, and then drag the upper left corner of the chart just to the center of cell **A10** to visually center it below the data.

5 Select the range **B4:D7**. Click the **INSERT tab**, and then in the **Sparklines group**, click **Line**. In the **Create Sparklines** dialog box, in the **Location Range** box, type **f4:f7** and then click **OK** to insert the sparklines.

   a. On the **DESIGN tab**, in the **Show group**, select the **Markers** check box to display markers in the sparklines.

   b. On the **DESIGN tab**, in the **Style group**, click **More** and then in the second row, click the fourth style—**Sparkline Style Accent 4, Darker 25%**.

6 Click cell **A1** to deselect the chart. Click the **PAGE LAYOUT tab**, and then in the **Page Setup group**, click **Margins**. At the bottom, click **Custom Margins** to display the **Page Setup** dialog box, and then on the **Margins tab**, under **Center on page**, select the **Horizontally** check box.

   a. In the dialog box, click the **Header/Footer tab**, and then click **Custom Footer**. With your insertion point in the **Left section**, click **Insert File Name**. Click **OK** two times.

   b. Click the **FILE tab** to display **Backstage** view. In the lower right corner, click **Show All Properties**. As the Tags, type **step sales, 1st quarter** In the **Subject** box, type your course name and section number. Be sure your name displays as the Author—edit if necessary.

   c. On the left, click **Save**.

   d. Print or submit your workbook electronically as directed by your instructor. If required by your instructor, print or create an electronic version of your worksheet with formulas displayed by using the instructions in Project 1A. **Close** Excel without saving so that you do not save the changes you made to print formulas.

END | You have completed Project 1C

CHAPTER REVIEW

Apply 1B skills from these Objectives:

7 Check Spelling in a Worksheet
8 Enter Data by Range
9 Construct Formulas for Mathematical Operations
10 Edit Values in a Worksheet
11 Format a Worksheet

Skills Review Project 1D Band and Tubing Inventory

In the following Skills Review, you will create a worksheet that summarizes the inventory of band and tubing exercise equipment. Your completed worksheet will look similar to Figure 1.57.

PROJECT FILES

For Project 1D, you will need the following file:

New blank Excel workbook

You will save your workbook as:

Lastname_Firstname_1D_Band_Inventory

Build from Scratch

PROJECT RESULTS

Pro Fit Marietta

Band and Tubing Inventory

As of June 30

	Material	Quantity in Stock	Retail Price	Total Retail Value	Percent of Total Retail Value
Super Strength Bands	Latex	225	$ 48.98	$ 11,020.50	25.16%
Medium Tubing	Rubber	198	27.95	5,534.10	12.64%
Resistance Band, Average	Latex	165	42.95	7,086.75	16.18%
Mini Bands, Medium	Latex	245	25.95	6,357.75	14.52%
Mini Bands, Heavy	Rubber	175	32.95	5,766.25	13.17%
Heavy Tubing	Latex	187	42.95	8,031.65	18.34%
Total Retail Value for All Products				$ 43,797.00	

Lastname_Firstname_1D_Band_Inventory

FIGURE 1.57

(Project 1D Band and Tubing Inventory continues on the next page)

CHAPTER REVIEW

1 **Start** Excel and display a new blank workbook. **Save** the workbook in your **Excel Chapter 1** folder as **Lastname_Firstname_1D_Band_Inventory** In cell **A1** type **Pro Fit Marietta** and in cell **A2** type **Band and Tubing Inventory**

a. Click cell **B3**, type **Quantity in Stock** and press Tab. In cell **C3** type **Average Cost** and press Tab. In cell **D3**, type **Retail Price** and press Tab. In cell **E3**, type **Total Retail Value** and press Tab. In cell **F3** type **Percent of Total Retail Value** and press Enter.

b. Click cell **A4**, type **Super Strength Bands** and press Enter. In the range **A5:A10**, type the remaining row titles as shown below, including any misspelled words.

Medium Tubing

Resistnce Band, Average

Mini Bands, Medium

Mini Bands, Heavy

Heavy Tubing

Total Retail Value for All Products

c. Press Ctrl + Home to move to the top of your worksheet. On the **REVIEW tab**, in the **Proofing group**, click **Spelling**. Correct *Resistnce* to **Resistance** and any other spelling errors you may have made, and then when the message displays, *Spell check complete. You're good to go!* click **OK**.

d. In the **column heading area**, point to the right boundary of **column A** to display the ⊕ pointer, and then drag to the right to widen **column A** to **225 pixels**.

e. In the **column heading area**, point to the **column B** heading to display the ↓ pointer, and then drag to the right to select **columns B:F**. With the columns selected, in the **column heading area**, point to the right boundary of any of the selected columns, and then drag to the right to set the width to **100 pixels**.

f. Select the range **A1:F1**. On the **HOME tab**, in the **Alignment group**, click **Merge & Center**, and then in the **Cell Styles** gallery, apply the **Title** style. Select the range **A2:F2**. **Merge & Center** the text across the selection, and then in the **Cell Styles** gallery, apply the **Heading 1** style.

2 On the **PAGE LAYOUT tab**, in the **Themes group**, change the **Colors** to **Blue Green**. Select the empty range **B4:D9**. With cell **B4** active in the range, type **225** and then press Enter.

a. With cell **B5** active in the range, and pressing Enter after each entry, type the following data in the *Quantity in Stock* column:

198

265

245

175

187

b. With the selected range still active, from the following table, beginning in cell **C4** and pressing Enter after each entry, enter the following data for the **Average Cost** column and then the **Retail Price** column. If you prefer, type without selecting the range first; recall that this is optional.

Average Cost	Retail Price
22.75	48.98
15.95	27.95
26.90	42.95
12.95	25.95
18.75	32.95
26.90	42.95

3 In cell **E4**, type **=b4*d4** and then press Enter to construct a formula that calculates the *Total Retail Value* of the *Super Strength Bands* (Quantity in Stock × Retail Price).

a. Click cell **E4**, position your pointer over the fill handle, and then drag down through cell **E9** to copy the formula with relative cell references.

b. Select the range **B4:B9**, and then on the **HOME tab**, in the **Number group**, click **Comma Style**. Then, in the **Number group**, click **Decrease Decimal** two times to remove the decimal places from these non-currency values.

c. To calculate the *Total Retail Value for All Products*, select the range **E4:E9**, and then in the lower right corner of the selected range, click the **Quick Analysis** button ▣.

(Project 1D Band and Tubing Inventory continues on the next page)

d. In the gallery, click **TOTALS**, and then click the *first* **Sum** button, which visually indicates that the column will be summed with a result at the bottom of the column.

e. Select the range **C5:E9** and apply the **Comma Style**. Select the range **C4:E4**, hold down Ctrl, and then click cell **E10**. With the nonadjacent cells selected, apply the **Accounting Number Format**. Click cell **E10**, and then from the **Cell Styles** gallery, apply the **Total** style.

f. Click cell **F4**, type = and then click cell **E4**. Type / and then click cell **E10**. Press F4 to make the reference to cell *E10* absolute, and then on the **Formula Bar**, click ✓ so that cell **F4** remains the active cell. Drag the **fill handle** to copy the formula down through cell **F9**.

g. Point to cell **B6**, and then double-click to place the insertion point within the cell. Use the arrow keys to move the insertion point to the left or right of *2*, and use either Delete or Backspace to delete *2*, and then type **1** and press Enter so that the new *Quantity in Stock* is *165*. Notice the recalculations in the worksheet.

4 Select the range **F4:F9**, right-click over the selection, and then on the mini toolbar, click **Percent Style**. Click **Increase Decimal** two times, and then **Center** the selection.

a. In the **row heading area** on the left side of your screen, point to **row 3** to display the ➡ pointer, and then right-click to simultaneously select the row and display a shortcut menu. On the shortcut menu, click **Insert** to insert a new **row 3**.

b. Click cell **A3**, type **As of June 30** and then on the **Formula Bar**, click ✓ to keep cell **A3** as the active cell. **Merge & Center** the text across the range **A3:F3**, and then apply the **Heading 2** cell style.

5 In the **column heading area**, point to **column B**. When the ⬇ pointer displays, right-click, and then click **Insert** to insert a new column.

a. Click cell **B4**, type **Material** and then press Enter. In cell **B5**, type **Latex** and then press Enter. In cell **B6**, type **Rubber** and then press Enter.

b. Using AutoComplete to speed your typing by pressing Enter as soon as the AutoComplete suggestion displays, in cells **B7**, **B8**, and **B10** type **Latex** and in cell **B9** type **Rubber**

c. In the **column heading area**, point to the right boundary of **column B**, and then drag to the left and set the width to **90 pixels**. In the **column heading area**, point to **column D**, right-click, and then click **Delete**.

d. Select the column titles in the range **B4:F4**, and then on the **HOME tab**, in the **Alignment group**, click **Wrap Text**, **Center**, and **Middle Align**. With the range still selected, apply the **Heading 4** cell style.

e. Click cell **A11**, and then in the **Cell Styles** gallery, under **Themed Cell Styles**, click **40% - Accent1**.

6 Click the **PAGE LAYOUT tab**, in the **Page Setup group**, click **Margins**, and then click **Custom Margins**. In the **Page Setup** dialog box, on the **Margins tab**, under **Center on page**, select the **Horizontally** check box.

a. Click the **Header/Footer tab**, and then click **Custom Footer**. With your insertion point in the **Left section**, click **Insert File Name**. Click **OK** two times.

b. In the **Page Setup group**, click **Orientation**, and then click **Landscape**.

c. Click the **FILE tab** to display **Backstage** view. In the lower right corner, click **Show All Properties**. As the **Tags**, type **bands, tubing, inventory** In the **Subject** box, type your course name and section number. Be sure your name displays as the author—edit if necessary.

d. On the left, click **Save** to be sure that you have saved your work up to this point.

e. Print or submit your workbook electronically as directed by your instructor. If required by your instructor, print or create an electronic version of your worksheet with formulas displayed by using the instructions in Project 1A. **Close** Excel without saving so that you do not save the changes you made to print formulas.

END | You have completed Project 1D

CONTENT-BASED ASSESSMENTS

Mastering Excel Project 1E Gym Sales

In the following Mastering Excel project, you will create a worksheet comparing the sales of different types of home gym equipment sold in the second quarter. Your completed worksheet will look similar to Figure 1.58.

Apply 1A skills from these Objectives:

1 Create, Save, and Navigate an Excel Workbook

2 Enter Data in a Worksheet

3 Construct and Copy Formulas and Use the SUM Function

4 Format Cells with Merge & Center, Cell Styles, and Themes

5 Chart Data to Create a Column Chart and Insert Sparklines

6 Print a Worksheet, Display Formulas, and Close Excel

Build from Scratch

PROJECT FILES

For Project 1E, you will need the following files:

New blank Excel workbook

You will save your workbook as:

Lastname_Firstname_1E_Gym_Sales

PROJECT RESULTS

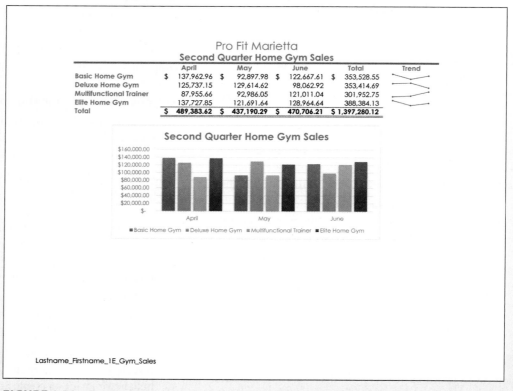

FIGURE 1.58

(Project 1E Gym Sales continues on the next page)

CONTENT-BASED ASSESSMENTS

1 Start Excel and display a new blank workbook. In cell **A1**, type **Pro Fit Marietta** and in cell **A2**, type **Second Quarter Home Gym Sales** Change the **Theme** to **Wisp**, and then **Save** the workbook in your **Excel Chapter 1** folder as **Lastname_Firstname_1E_Gym_Sales**

2 In cell **B3**, type **April** and then fill the months *May* and *June* in the range **C3:D3**. In cell **E3**, type **Total** and in cell **F3**, type **Trend**

3 Center the column titles in the range **B3:F3**. **Merge & Center** the title across the range **A1:F1**, and apply the **Title** cell style. **Merge & Center** the subtitle across the range **A2:F2**, and then apply the **Heading 1** cell style.

4 Widen **column A** to **180 pixels**, and then in the range **A4:A8**, type the following row titles:

Basic Home Gym

Deluxe Home Gym

Multifunctional Trainer

Elite Home Gym

Total

5 Widen columns **B:F** to **115 pixels**, and then in the range **B4:D7**, enter the monthly sales figures for each type of gym, as shown in the table below:

	April	May	June
Basic Home Gym	137962.96	92897.98	122667.61
Deluxe Home Gym	125737.15	129614.62	98062.92
Multifunctional Trainer	87955.66	92986.05	121011.04
Elite Home Gym	137727.85	121691.64	128964.64

6 Select the range that represents April sales, and then on the **HOME tab**, in the **Editing group**, click **AutoSum**. Copy the formula across to cells **C8:D8**. Select the range that represents the sales of the *Basic Home Gym*, and then on the **HOME tab**, in the **Editing group**, click **AutoSum**. Copy the formula down to cells **E5:E8**.

7 Apply the **Heading 4** cell style to the row titles and the column titles. Apply the **Total** cell style to the totals in the range **B8:E8**. Apply the **Accounting Number Format** to the first row of sales figures and to the total row. Apply the **Comma Style** to the remaining sales figures.

8 To compare the monthly sales of each product visually, select the range that represents the sales figures for the three months, including the month names and the product names—do not include any totals in the range. With this data selected, use **Recommended Charts** to insert a **Clustered Column** chart with the month names displayed on the category axis and the product names displayed in the legend.

9 Drag the center right sizing handle to widen the chart slightly so that all the legend items display on one line, and then position the chart so that it is visually centered below the data with its top edge aligned with the top edge of row 10 approximately as shown in Figure 1.58. Apply **Chart Style 6** and **Color 2** under **Colorful**. Change the **Chart Title** to **Second Quarter Home Gym Sales**

10 In the range **F4:F7**, insert **Line** sparklines that compare the monthly data. Do not include the totals. Show the sparkline **Markers** and apply **Sparkline Style Accent 2, Darker 50%**.

11 Center the worksheet **Horizontally** on the page, and then insert a **Footer** with the **File Name** in the **Left section**. Change the **Orientation** to **Landscape**. Display the document properties, and then as the **Tags** type **home gym, sales** As the **Subject**, type your course name and section number. Be sure your name displays as the author. Check your worksheet by previewing it in **Print Preview**, and then make any necessary corrections.

12 Save your workbook, and then print or submit electronically as directed. If required by your instructor, print or create an electronic version of your worksheet with formulas displayed by using the instructions in Project 1A. **Close** Excel without saving so that you do not save the changes you made to print formulas.

END | You have completed Project 1E

CONTENT-BASED ASSESSMENTS

Mastering Excel Project 1F Balance Sales

In the following Mastering Excel project, you will create a worksheet that summarizes the sales of balance and stabilization equipment that Pro Fit Marietta is marketing. Your completed worksheet will look similar to Figure 1.59.

Apply 1B skills from these Objectives:

7 Check Spelling in a Worksheet

8 Enter Data by Range

9 Construct Formulas for Mathematical Operations

10 Edit Values in a Worksheet

11 Format a Worksheet

PROJECT FILES

For Project 1F, you will need the following file:

New blank Excel workbook

You will save your workbook as:

Lastname_Firstname_1F_Balance_Sales

Build from Scratch

PROJECT RESULTS

Pro Fit Marietta
Balance and Stabilization Sales
Month Ending March 31

	Quantity Sold	Retail Price	Total Sales	Percent of Total Sales
Balance Pillow	275	$ 22.95	$ 6,311.25	5.43%
Slide Board	382	75.50	28,841.00	24.82%
Foam Roller	251	39.50	9,914.50	8.53%
Rebounder	162	139.95	22,671.90	19.51%
Stability Ball	380	51.50	19,570.00	16.84%
Balance Board	206	84.95	17,499.70	15.06%
Balance Pad	150	75.99	11,398.50	9.81%
Total Sales for All Products			$ 116,206.85	

Lastname_Firstname_1F_Balance_Sales

FIGURE 1.59

(Project 1F Balance Sales continues on the next page)

CONTENT-BASED ASSESSMENTS

1 Start Excel and display a new blank workbook. **Save** the workbook in your **Excel Chapter 1** folder as **Lastname_Firstname_1F_Balance_Sales** In cell **A1**, type **Pro Fit Marietta** In cell **A2**, type **Balance and Stabilization Sales** and then **Merge & Center** the title and the subtitle across **columns A:F**. Apply the **Title** and **Heading 1** cell styles respectively.

2 Beginning in cell **B3**, type the following column titles: **Product Number** and **Quantity Sold** and **Retail Price** and **Total Sales** and **Percent of Total Sales**

3 Beginning in cell **A4**, type the following row titles, including misspelled words:

Balance Pillow
Silde Board
Foam Roller
Rebounder
Stability Ball
Balance Board
Balance Pad
Total Sales for All Products

4 Make cell **A1** the active cell, and then check spelling in your worksheet. Correct *Silde* to **Slide**, and make any other necessary corrections. Widen **column A** to **180 pixels** and **columns B:F** to **95 pixels**.

5 In the range **B4:D10**, type the following data:

	Product Number	Quantity Sold	Retail Price
Balance Pillow	BP-3	275	22.95
Slide Board	SB-8	382	99.95
Foam Roller	FR-2	251	39.50
Rebounder	RB-4	162	139.95
Stability Ball	SB-5	380	51.50
Balance Board	BB-6	206	84.95
Balance Pad	BP-8	220	75.99

6 In cell **E4**, construct a formula to calculate the *Total Sales* of the *Balance Pillow* by multiplying the *Quantity Sold* times the *Retail Price*. Copy the formula down for the remaining products. Select the range **E4:E10**, and then use the **Quick Analysis tool** to **Sum** the *Total Sales for All Products*, which will be formatted in **Bold**. To the total in cell **E11**, apply the **Total** cell style.

7 Using absolute cell references as necessary so that you can copy the formula, in cell **F4**, construct a formula to calculate the *Percent of Total Sales* for the first product. Copy the formula down for the remaining products. To the computed percentages, apply **Percent Style** with two decimal places, and then **Center** the percentages.

8 Apply the **Comma Style** with no decimal places to the *Quantity Sold* figures. To cells **D4**, **E4**, and **E11** apply the **Accounting Number Format**. To the range **D5:E10**, apply the **Comma Style**.

9 Change the *Retail Price* of the *Slide Board* to **75.50** and the *Quantity Sold* of the *Balance Pad* to **150** Delete **column B**, and then **Insert** a new **row 3**. In cell **A3**, type **Month Ending March 31** and then **Merge & Center** the text across the range **A3:E3**. Apply the **Heading 2** cell style. To cell **A12**, apply the **20%-Accent1** cell style. Select the four column titles, apply **Wrap Text**, **Middle Align**, and **Center** formatting, and then apply the **Heading 3** cell style.

10 Center the worksheet **Horizontally** on the page, and then insert a **Footer** with the **File Name** in the **Left section**. Display the document properties, and then as the **Tags**, type **balance, stability, sales** In the **Subject** box, add your course name and section number. Be sure your name displays as the author.

11 **Save** your workbook, and then print or submit electronically as directed. If required by your instructor, print or create an electronic version of your worksheet with formulas displayed by using the instructions in Project 1A. **Close** Excel without saving so that you do not save the changes you made to print formulas.

END | You have completed Project 1F

CONTENT-BASED ASSESSMENTS

In the following Mastering Excel project, you will create a new worksheet that compares annual sales by region. Your completed worksheet will look similar to Figure 1.60.

Apply a combination of 1A and 1B skills:

1 Create, Save, and Navigate an Excel Workbook

2 Enter Data in a Worksheet

3 Construct and Copy Formulas and Use the SUM Function

4 Format Cells with Merge & Center, Cell Styles, and Themes

5 Chart Data to Create a Column Chart and Insert Sparklines

6 Print a Worksheet, Display Formulas, and Close Excel

7 Check Spelling in a Worksheet

8 Enter Data by Range

9 Construct Formulas for Mathematical Operations

10 Edit Values in a Worksheet

11 Format a Worksheet

PROJECT FILES

For Project 1G, you will need the following file:

New blank Excel workbook

You will save your workbook as:

Lastname_Firstname_1G_Regional_Sales

PROJECT RESULTS

Build from Scratch

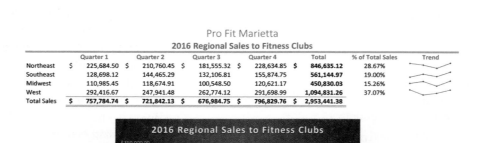

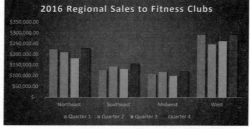

Lastname_Firstname_1G_Regional_Sales

FIGURE 1.60

(Project 1G Regional Sales continues on the next page)

1 Start Excel and display a new blank workbook. Change the **Theme** to **Retrospect**. In cell **A1**, type **Pro Fit Marietta** In cell **A2**, type **2016 Regional Sales to Fitness Clubs** and then **Save** the workbook in your **Excel Chapter 1** folder as **Lastname_Firstname_1G_Regional_Sales**

2 In cell **B3**, type **Quarter 1** and fill *Quarter 2*, *Quarter 3*, and *Quarter 4* in the range **C3:E3**. In cell **F3**, type **Total** In cell **G3**, type **% of Total Sales** and in cell **H3**, type **Trend**

3 In the range **A4:A7**, type the following row titles: **Northeast** and **Southeast** and **West** and **Total Sales**

4 Set the width of **column A** to **80 pixels** and the width of columns **B:H** to **110 pixels**. **Merge & Center** the title across the range **A1:H1**, and then apply the **Title** cell style. **Merge & Center** the subtitle across the range **A2:H2**, and then apply the **Heading 1** cell style. Select the seven column titles, apply **Center** formatting, and then apply the **Heading 4** cell style.

5 In the range **B4:E6**, enter the sales values for each Quarter as shown below.

	Quarter 1	Quarter 2	Quarter 3	Quarter 4
Northeast	225684.50	210760.45	181555.32	228634.85
Southeast	128698.12	144465.29	132106.81	155874.75
West	292416.67	247941.48	262774.12	291698.99

6 By using the **Quick Analysis tool**, **Sum** the *Quarter 1* sales, and then copy the formula across for the remaining Quarters. By using the **Quick Analysis tool**, **Sum** the sales for the *Northeast* region, and then copy the formula down through cell **F7**. Recall that the **Quick Analysis tool** formats sums in **Bold**. Apply the **Accounting Number Format** to the first row of sales figures and to the total row, and apply the **Comma Style** to the remaining sales figures. Format the totals in **row 7** with the **Total** cell style.

7 Insert a new **row 6** with the row title **Midwest** and the following sales figures for each quarter: **110985.45**

and **118674.91** and **100548.50** and **120621.17** Copy the formula in cell **F5** down to cell **F6** to sum the new row.

8 Using absolute cell references as necessary so that you can copy the formula, in cell **G4** construct a formula to calculate the *Percent of Total Sales* for the first region. Copy the formula down for the remaining regions. To the computed percentages, apply **Percent Style** with two decimal places, and then **Center** the percentages.

9 Insert **Line** sparklines in the range **H4:H7** that compare the quarterly data. Do not include the totals. Show the sparkline **Markers** and apply the second style in the second row—**Sparkline Style Accent 2, Darker 25%**.

10 **Save** your workbook. To compare the quarterly sales of each region visually, select the range that represents the sales figures for the four quarters, including the quarter names and each region—do not include any totals in the range. With this data selected, by using **Recommended Charts**, insert a **Clustered Column** with the regions as the category axis and the Quarters as the legend.

11 Apply **Chart Style 8** and **Color 3** under **Colorful**. Position the top edge of the chart in **row 10** and visually center it below the worksheet data. Change the **Chart Title** to **2016 Regional Sales to Fitness Clubs**

12 Deselect the chart. Change the page **Orientation** to **Landscape**, center the worksheet **Horizontally** on the page, and then insert a footer with the file name in the Left section.

13 Show the document properties. As the **Tags**, type **fitness clubs, sales** In the **Subject** box, type your course name and section number. Be sure your name displays as the author.

14 **Save** your workbook, and then print or submit electronically as directed. If required by your instructor, print or create an electronic version of your worksheet with formulas displayed by using the instructions in Project 1A. **Close** Excel without saving so that you do not save the changes you made to print formulas.

END | You have completed Project 1G

CONTENT-BASED ASSESSMENTS

Apply a combination of the **1A** and **1B** skills.

Build from Scratch

GO! Fix It	Project 1H New Jobs	Online

GO! Make It	Project 1I Training	Online

GO! Solve It	Project 1J Job Postings	Online

GO! Solve It	Project 1K Commission	

PROJECT FILES

For Project 1K, you will need the following file:

e01K_Commission

You will save your workbook as:

Lastname_Firstname_1K_Commission

Open the file **e01K_Commission** and save it as **Lastname_Firstname_1K_Commission** Complete the worksheet by using Auto Fill to complete the month headings, and then calculating the Total Commission for each month and for each region. Insert and format appropriate sparklines in the Trend column. Format the worksheet attractively with a title and subtitle, check spelling, adjust column width, and apply appropriate financial formatting. Insert a chart that compares the total sales commission for each region with the months displaying as the categories, and format the chart attractively. Include the file name in the footer, add appropriate properties, and submit as directed.

Performance Level

Performance Criteria		Exemplary: You consistently applied the relevant skills	Proficient: You sometimes, but not always, applied the relevant skills	Developing: You rarely or never applied the relevant skills
	Create formulas	All formulas are correct and are efficiently constructed.	Formulas are correct but not always constructed in the most efficient manner.	One or more formulas are missing or incorrect, or only numbers were entered.
	Create a chart	Chart created properly.	Chart was created but incorrect data was selected.	No chart was created.
	Insert and format sparklines	Sparklines inserted and formatted properly.	Sparklines were inserted but incorrect data was selected or sparklines were not formatted.	No sparklines were inserted.
	Format attractively and appropriately	Formatting is attractive and appropriate.	Adequately formatted but difficult to read or unattractive.	Inadequate or no formatting.

END | You have completed Project 1K

OUTCOMES-BASED ASSESSMENTS

RUBRIC

The following outcomes-based assessments are *open-ended assessments*. That is, there is no specific correct result; your result will depend on your approach to the information provided. Make *Professional Quality* your goal. Use the following scoring rubric to guide you in *how* to approach the problem and then to evaluate *how well* your approach solves the problem.

The *criteria*—Software Mastery, Content, Format and Layout, and Process—represent the knowledge and skills you have gained that you can apply to solving the problem. The *levels of performance*—Professional Quality, Approaching Professional Quality, or Needs Quality Improvements—help you and your instructor evaluate your result.

	Your completed project is of Professional Quality if you:	Your completed project is Approaching Professional Quality if you:	Your completed project Needs Quality Improvements if you:
1-Software Mastery	Choose and apply the most appropriate skills, tools, and features and identify efficient methods to solve the problem.	Choose and apply some appropriate skills, tools, and features, but not in the most efficient manner.	Choose inappropriate skills, tools, or features, or are inefficient in solving the problem.
2-Content	Construct a solution that is clear and well organized, contains content that is accurate, appropriate to the audience and purpose, and is complete. Provide a solution that contains no errors in spelling, grammar, or style.	Construct a solution in which some components are unclear, poorly organized, inconsistent, or incomplete. Misjudge the needs of the audience. Have some errors in spelling, grammar, or style, but the errors do not detract from comprehension.	Construct a solution that is unclear, incomplete, or poorly organized; contains some inaccurate or inappropriate content; and contains many errors in spelling, grammar, or style. Do not solve the problem.
3-Format & Layout	Format and arrange all elements to communicate information and ideas, clarify function, illustrate relationships, and indicate relative importance.	Apply appropriate format and layout features to some elements, but not others. Overuse features, causing minor distraction.	Apply format and layout that does not communicate information or ideas clearly. Do not use format and layout features to clarify function, illustrate relationships, or indicate relative importance. Use available features excessively, causing distraction.
4-Process	Use an organized approach that integrates planning, development, self-assessment, revision, and reflection.	Demonstrate an organized approach in some areas, but not others; or, use an insufficient process of organization throughout.	Do not use an organized approach to solve the problem.

OUTCOMES-BASED ASSESSMENTS

Apply a combination of the 1A and 1B skills.

Build from Scratch

GO! Think   Project 1L Video Sales

PROJECT FILES

For Project 1L, you will need the following file:

New blank Excel workbook

You will save your workbook as:

Lastname_Firstname_1L_Video_Sales

Michelle Barry, President of Pro Fit Marietta, needs a worksheet that summarizes the following data regarding the first quarter sales of training videos. Michelle would like the worksheet to include a calculation of the total sales for each type of video and a total of the sales of all of the videos. She would also like to know each type of video's percentage of total sales.

	Number Sold	Price
Pilates	156	29.99
Step	392	14.99
Weight Training	147	54.99
Kickboxing	282	29.99
Yoga	165	34.99

Create a worksheet that provides Michelle with the information needed. Include appropriate worksheet, column, and row titles. Using the formatting skills that you practiced in this chapter, format the worksheet in a manner that is professional and easy to read and understand. Insert a footer with the file name and add appropriate document properties. Save the file as **Lastname_Firstname_1L_Video_Sales** and print or submit as directed by your instructor.

END | You have completed Project 1L

Build from Scratch

GO! Think   Project 1M Planner   Online

You and GO!   Project 1N Personal Expenses   Online

Build from Scratch

GO! Cumulative Group Project   Project 1O Bell Orchid Hotels
Online

Using Functions, Creating Tables, and Managing Large Workbooks

GO! to Work
Video E2

PROJECT 2A

OUTCOMES
Analyze inventory by applying statistical and logical calculations to data and by sorting and filtering data.

OBJECTIVES

1. Use Flash Fill and the SUM, AVERAGE, MEDIAN, MIN, and MAX Functions
2. Move Data, Resolve Error Messages, and Rotate Text
3. Use COUNTIF and IF Functions and Apply Conditional Formatting
4. Use Date & Time Functions and Freeze Panes
5. Create, Sort, and Filter an Excel Table
6. View, Format, and Print a Large Worksheet

PROJECT 2B

OUTCOMES
Summarize the data on multiple worksheets.

OBJECTIVES

7. Navigate a Workbook and Rename Worksheets
8. Enter Dates, Clear Contents, and Clear Formats
9. Copy and Paste by Using the Paste Options Gallery
10. Edit and Format Multiple Worksheets at the Same Time
11. Create a Summary Sheet with Column Sparklines
12. Format and Print Multiple Worksheets in a Workbook

In This Chapter

In this chapter, you will use the Statistical functions to calculate the average of a group of numbers and use other Logical and Date & Time functions. Excel's statistical functions are useful for common calculations that you probably encounter frequently. You will also use Excel's new Flash Fill to automatically fill in values, use the counting functions, and apply different types of conditional formatting to make data easy to visualize. You will create a table to organize related information and analyze the table's information by sorting and filtering. You will summarize a workbook that contains multiple worksheets.

The projects in this chapter relate to **Rosedale Landscape and Garden**, which grows and sells trees and plants suitable for all areas of North America. Throughout its 75 year history, the company has introduced many new plants for the enjoyment of home gardeners. The company has nurseries and stores in the major metropolitan areas in the United States and Canada. In addition to high-quality plants and trees, Rosedale sells garden tools and outdoor furniture. Rosedale also offers professional landscape design and installation for both commercial and residential clients. The company headquarters is in Pasadena, California.

Inventory Status Report

PROJECT
2A

MyITLab®
Project 2A Training

PROJECT ACTIVITIES

In Activities 2.01 through 2.20 you will edit a worksheet for Holman Hill, President, detailing the current inventory of trees at the Pasadena nursery. Your completed worksheet will look similar to Figure 2.1.

PROJECT FILES

For Project 2A, you will need the following file:

e02A_Tree_Inventory

You will save your workbook as:

Lastname_Firstname_2A_Tree_Inventory

PROJECT RESULTS

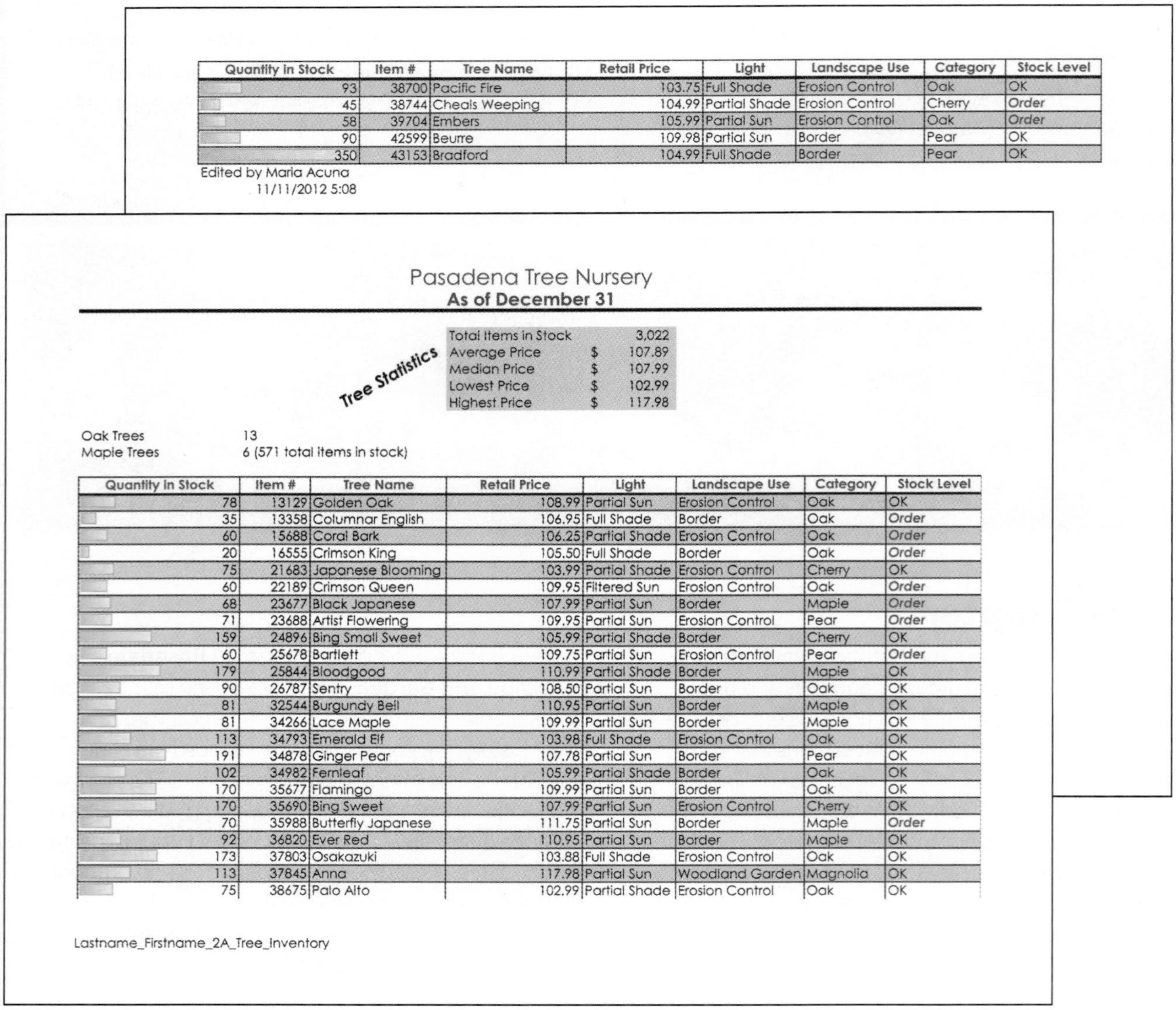

Quantity in Stock	Item #	Tree Name	Retail Price	Light	Landscape Use	Category	Stock Level
93	38700	Pacific Fire	103.75	Full Shade	Erosion Control	Oak	OK
45	38744	Cheals Weeping	104.99	Partial Shade	Erosion Control	Cherry	Order
58	39704	Embers	105.99	Partial Sun	Erosion Control	Oak	Order
90	42599	Beurre	109.98	Partial Sun	Border	Pear	OK
350	43153	Bradford	104.99	Full Shade	Border	Pear	OK

Edited by Maria Acuna
11/11/2012 5:08

Pasadena Tree Nursery
As of December 31

Tree Statistics		
Total Items in Stock		3,022
Average Price	$	107.89
Median Price	$	107.99
Lowest Price	$	102.99
Highest Price	$	117.98

Oak Trees   13
Maple Trees   6 (571 total items in stock)

Quantity in Stock	Item #	Tree Name	Retail Price	Light	Landscape Use	Category	Stock Level
78	13129	Golden Oak	108.99	Partial Sun	Erosion Control	Oak	OK
35	13358	Columnar English	106.95	Full Shade	Border	Oak	Order
60	15688	Coral Bark	106.25	Partial Shade	Erosion Control	Oak	Order
20	16555	Crimson King	105.50	Full Shade	Border	Oak	Order
75	21683	Japanese Blooming	103.99	Partial Shade	Erosion Control	Cherry	OK
60	22189	Crimson Queen	109.95	Filtered Sun	Erosion Control	Oak	Order
68	23677	Black Japanese	107.99	Partial Sun	Border	Maple	Order
71	23688	Artist Flowering	109.95	Partial Sun	Erosion Control	Pear	Order
159	24896	Bing Small Sweet	105.99	Partial Shade	Border	Cherry	OK
60	25678	Bartlett	109.75	Partial Sun	Erosion Control	Pear	Order
179	25844	Bloodgood	110.99	Partial Shade	Border	Maple	OK
90	26787	Sentry	108.50	Partial Sun	Border	Oak	OK
81	32544	Burgundy Bell	110.95	Partial Sun	Border	Maple	OK
81	34266	Lace Maple	109.99	Partial Sun	Border	Maple	OK
113	34793	Emerald Elf	103.98	Full Shade	Erosion Control	Oak	OK
191	34878	Ginger Pear	107.78	Partial Sun	Border	Pear	OK
102	34982	Fernleaf	105.99	Partial Shade	Border	Oak	OK
170	35677	Flamingo	109.99	Partial Sun	Border	Oak	OK
170	35690	Bing Sweet	107.99	Partial Sun	Erosion Control	Cherry	OK
70	35988	Butterfly Japanese	111.75	Partial Sun	Border	Maple	Order
92	36820	Ever Red	110.95	Partial Sun	Border	Maple	OK
173	37803	Osakazuki	103.88	Full Shade	Erosion Control	Oak	OK
113	37845	Anna	117.98	Partial Sun	Woodland Garden	Magnolia	OK
75	38675	Palo Alto	102.99	Partial Shade	Erosion Control	Oak	OK

Lastname_Firstname_2A_Tree_Inventory

FIGURE 2.1 Project 2A Inventory Status Report

Objective 1 | Use Flash Fill and the SUM, AVERAGE, MEDIAN, MIN, and MAX Functions

Video E2-1

Flash Fill recognizes a pattern in your data, and then automatically fills in values when you enter examples of the output that you want. Use Flash Fill to split data from two or more cells or to combine data from two cells.

A *function* is the name given to a predefined formula—a formula that Excel has already built for you—that performs calculations by using specific values that you insert in a particular order or structure. *Statistical functions*, which include the AVERAGE, MEDIAN, MIN, and MAX functions, are useful to analyze a group of measurements.

Activity 2.01 | Using Flash Fill

1 Start Excel, and then in the lower left corner of Excel's opening screen, click **Open Other Workbooks**.

🔄 **ANOTHER WAY** Press Ctrl + F12 to display the Open dialog box.

2 Navigate to the student files that accompany this textbook, and then locate and open **e02A_Tree_Inventory**. Press F12 to display the **Save As** dialog box, and then navigate to the location where you are storing your projects for this chapter.

3 Create a new folder named **Excel Chapter 2** and open the new folder. In the **File name** box, using your own name, type **Lastname_Firstname_2A_Tree_Inventory** and click **Save** or press Enter.

4 Scroll down. Notice that the worksheet contains data related to types of trees in inventory, including information about the *Quantity in Stock*, *Item #/Category*, *Tree Name*, *Retail Price*, *Light*, and *Landscape Use*.

5 In the **column heading area**, point to **column C** to display the ↓ pointer, and then drag to the right to select **columns C:D**. On the **HOME tab**, in the **Cells group**, click the **Insert button arrow**, and then click **Insert Sheet Columns**.

New columns for C and D display and the remaining columns move to the right.

🔄 **ANOTHER WAY** Select the columns, right-click anywhere over the selected columns, and then on the shortcut menu, click Insert.

6 Click cell **C11**, type **13129** and then on the **Formula Bar**, click ✓ to confirm the entry and keep **C11** as the active cell.

7 On the **HOME tab**, in the **Editing group**, click **Fill**, and then click **Flash Fill**. Compare your screen with Figure 2.2.

Use this technique to split a column of data based on what you type. Flash Fill looks to the left and sees the pattern you have established, and then fills the remaining cells in the column with only the Item #. The Flash Fill Options button displays.

FIGURE 2.2

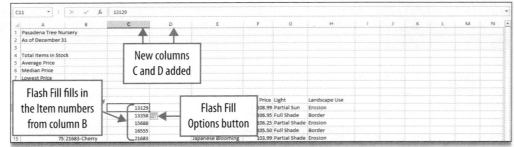

8 ▶ Near the lower right corner of cell **C11**, click the **Flash Fill Options** button, and notice that here you can *Undo Flash Fill*, *Accept suggestions*, or *Select all 28 changed cells*, for example, to apply specific formatting. Click the button again to close it.

If Excel is not sure what pattern to use, it suggests a pattern by filling with pale gray characters, and then you can use the Accept suggestions command to accept or start again.

9 ▶ Click cell **D11**, type **Oak** On the **Formula Bar**, click ✓ to confirm the entry and keep **D11** as the active cell, and then press Ctrl + E, which is the keyboard shortcut for Flash Fill.

Flash Fill extracts the text from the *Item#/Category* column and also inserts *Category* as the column name. Now that *Item #* and *Category* are in two separate columns, Mr. Hill can sort and filter by both Item # and Category.

10 ▶ Select **column B**, and then in the **Cells group**, click the **Delete button arrow**. Click **Delete Sheet Columns**. On the Quick Access Toolbar, click **Save** 💾.

ANOTHER WAY Select the column, right-click anywhere over the selected column, and then on the shortcut menu, click Delete.

Activity 2.02 | Moving a Column

1 ▶ In cell **B10** type **Item #** and press Enter. Select **column C**, and then on the **HOME tab**, in the **Clipboard group**, click **Cut** ✂. Notice that the column is surrounded by a moving border. Click cell **H1**, and then in the **Clipboard group**, click the upper portion of the **Paste** button.

ANOTHER WAY Press Ctrl + X to cut and Ctrl + V to paste.

2 ▶ Select and then delete **column C**. Select **columns A:G**. In the **Cells group**, click **Format**, and then click **AutoFit Column Width**.

ANOTHER WAY Select the columns, in the column heading area point to any of the column borders to display the ⊞ pointer, and then double-click to AutoFit the columns.

3 ▶ Press Ctrl + Home to deselect and make cell **A1** the active cell.

4 ▶ **Merge & Center** cell A1 across the range **A1:H1**, and then apply the **Title** cell style. **Merge & Center** cell A2 across the range **A2:H2**, and apply the **Heading 1** cell style. Compare your screen with Figure 2.3. **Save** 💾 your workbook.

FIGURE 2.3

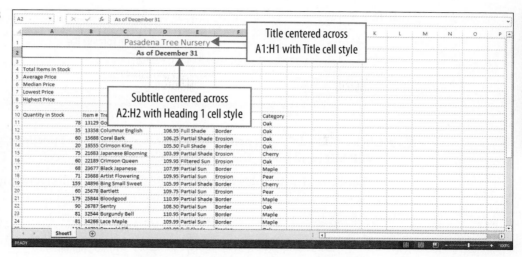

Title centered across A1:H1 with Title cell style

Subtitle centered across A2:H2 with Heading 1 cell style

Activity 2.03 | Using the SUM and AVERAGE Functions

Mr. Hill has a worksheet with information about the inventory of trees currently in stock at the Pasadena nursery. In this activity, you will use the SUM and AVERAGE functions to gather information about the product inventory.

1 Click cell **B4**. Click the **FORMULAS tab**, and then in the **Function Library group**, click the upper portion of the **AutoSum** button. Compare your screen with Figure 2.4.

The **SUM function** that you have used is a predefined formula that adds all the numbers in a selected range of cells. Because it is frequently used, there are several ways to insert the function. For example, you can insert the function from the HOME tab's Editing group, or by using the keyboard shortcut Alt + =, or from the Function Library group on the Formulas tab, or from the Math & Trig button in that group.

FIGURE 2.4

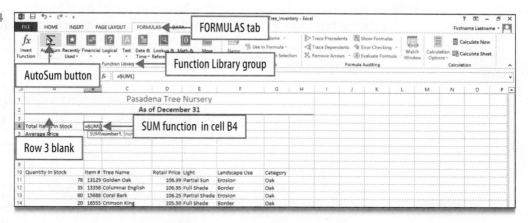

FORMULAS tab

Function Library group

AutoSum button

SUM function in cell B4

Row 3 blank

2 With the insertion point blinking in the function, type the cell range **a11:a39** to sum all the values in the **Quantity in Stock** column, and then press Enter; your result is *3022*.

3 Click cell **B4**, look at the **Formula Bar**, and then compare your screen with Figure 2.5.

SUM is the name of the function. The values in parentheses are the **arguments**—the values that an Excel function uses to perform calculations or operations. In this instance, the argument consists of the values in the range A11:A39.

FIGURE 2.5

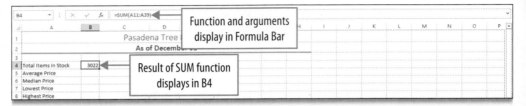

> 4 ▶ Click cell **B5**. In the **Function Library group**, click **More Functions**, point to **Statistical**, point to **AVERAGE**, and notice the ScreenTip. Compare your screen with Figure 2.6.
>
> The ScreenTip describes how the AVERAGE function will compute the calculation.

FIGURE 2.6

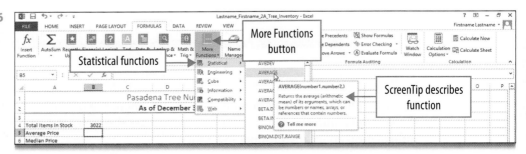

> 5 ▶ Click **AVERAGE**, and then if necessary, drag the title bar of the **Function Arguments** dialog box down and to the right so you can view the **Formula Bar** and cell **B5**.
>
> The *AVERAGE function* adds a group of values, and then divides the result by the number of values in the group. In the cell, the Formula Bar, and the dialog box, Excel proposes to average the value in cell B4. Recall that Excel functions will propose a range if there is data above or to the left of a selected cell.
>
> 6 ▶ In the **Function Arguments** dialog box, notice that *B4* is highlighted. Press Del to delete the existing text, type **d11:d39** and then compare your screen with Figure 2.7.
>
> Because you want to average the values in the range D11:D39—and not cell B4—you must edit the proposed range.

FIGURE 2.7

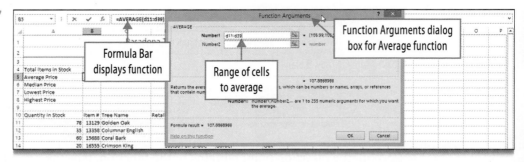

> 7 ▶ In the **Function Arguments** dialog box, click **OK**, and then click **Save** 🖫.
>
> The result indicates that the average Retail Price of all products is *107.89*.

Activity 2.04 | Using the MEDIAN Function

The *MEDIAN function* is a statistical function that describes a group of data—it is commonly used to describe the price of houses in a particular geographical area. The MEDIAN function finds the middle value that has as many values above it in the group as are below it. It differs from

AVERAGE in that the result is not affected as much by a single value that is greatly different from the others.

1 Click cell **B6**. In the **Function Library group**, click **More Functions**, display the list of **Statistical** functions, scroll down as necessary, and then click **MEDIAN**.

2 Press Del to delete the text in the **Number1** box, and then type **d11:d39** Compare your screen with Figure 2.8.

> When indicating which cells you want to use in the function's calculation—known as *defining the arguments*—you can either select the values with your mouse or type the range of values, whichever you prefer.

FIGURE 2.8

3 Click **OK** to display *107.99* in cell **B6**. Click **Save** 🖫, and then compare your screen with Figure 2.9.

> In the range of prices, 107.99 is the middle value. Half of all trees in inventory are priced *above* 107.99 and half are priced *below* 107.99.

FIGURE 2.9

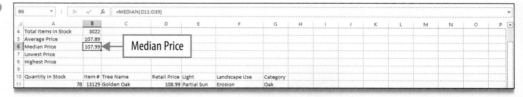

Activity 2.05 │ Using the MIN and MAX Functions

The statistical *MIN function* determines the smallest value in a selected range of values. The statistical *MAX function* determines the largest value in a selected range of values.

1 Click cell **B7**. On the **FORMULAS tab**, in the **Function Library group**, click **More Functions**, display the list of **Statistical** functions, scroll as necessary, and then click **MIN**.

2 Press Del, and then in the **Number1** box, type **d11:d39** Click **OK**.

> The lowest Retail Price is *102.99*.

3 Click cell **B8**, and then by using a similar technique, insert the **MAX** function to determine the highest **Retail Price**, then check to see that your result is *117.98*.

4 Press Ctrl + Home. Point to cell **B4**, right-click, and then on the mini toolbar, click **Comma Style** ▾ one time and **Decrease Decimal** ▵ two times.

5 Select the range **B5:B8**, apply the **Accounting Number Format** $ ▾, click **Save** 🖫, and then compare your screen with Figure 2.10.

FIGURE 2.10

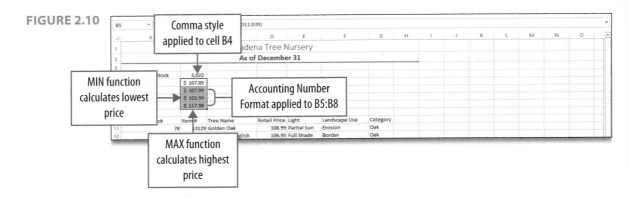

Objective 2 | Move Data, Resolve Error Messages, and Rotate Text

Video E2-2

When you move a formula, the cell references within the formula do not change, no matter what type of cell reference you use.

If you move cells into a column that is not wide enough to display number values, Excel will display a message so that you can adjust as necessary.

You can reposition data within a cell at an angle by rotating the text.

Activity 2.06 | Moving Data and Resolving a # # # # # Error Message

1 Select **column E** and set the width to **50 pixels**. Select the range **A4:B8**. Point to the right edge of the selected range to display the pointer, and then compare your screen with Figure 2.11.

FIGURE 2.11

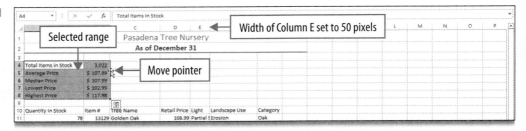

2 Drag the selected range to the right until the ScreenTip displays *D4:E8*, release the mouse button, and then notice that a series of # symbols displays in **column E**. Point to any of the cells that display # symbols, and then compare your screen with Figure 2.12.

Using this technique, cell contents can be moved from one location to another; this is referred to as *drag and drop*.

If a cell width is too narrow to display the entire number, Excel displays the ##### message, because displaying only a portion of a number would be misleading. The underlying values remain unchanged and are displayed in the Formula Bar for the selected cell. An underlying value also displays in the ScreenTip if you point to a cell containing # symbols.

FIGURE 2.12

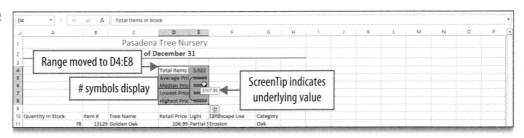

3 Select **column E** and widen it to **60** pixels, and notice that four cells are still not wide enough to display the cell contents.

4 Select **columns D:E**, and then in the **column heading area**, point to the right boundary of **column E** to display the ⊞ pointer. Double-click to AutoFit the column to accommodate the widest entry.

5 Select the range **D4:E8**. On the **HOME tab**, in the **Styles group**, display the **Cell Styles** gallery. Under **Themed Cell Styles**, click **20%-Accent1**. Click **Save** 🖫.

Activity 2.07 │ Rotating Text

1 In cell **C6**, type **Tree Statistics** Select the range **C4:C8**, right-click over the selection, and then on the shortcut menu, click **Format Cells**.

2 In the **Format Cells** dialog box, click the **Alignment tab**. Under **Text control**, select the **Merge cells** check box.

3 Under **Orientation**, click in the **Degrees** box, select the existing text, type **30** and then compare your screen with Figure 2.13.

🔁 **ANOTHER WAY**   In the upper right portion of the dialog box, under Orientation, point to the red diamond, and then drag the diamond upward until the Degrees box indicates 30.

FIGURE 2.13

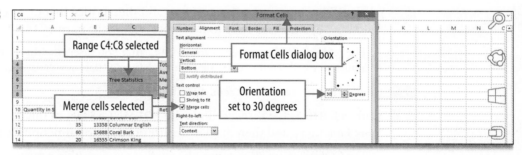

4 In the lower right corner of the **Format Cells** dialog box, click **OK**.

5 With the merged cell still selected, on the **HOME tab**, in the **Font group**, change the **Font Size** 11 ▾ to **14**, and then apply **Bold** 𝐁 and **Italic** 𝐼. Click the **Font Color arrow** 𝐀 ▾, and then in the fifth column, click the first color—**Blue, Accent 1**.

6 In the **Alignment group**, apply **Align Right** ☰. Press Ctrl + Home, **Save** 🖫 your workbook, and then compare your screen with Figure 2.14.

FIGURE 2.14

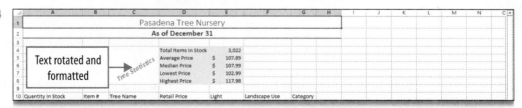

7 In the **row heading area**, point to **row 9** and right-click to select the row and display the shortcut menu. Click **Insert**, and then press F4 two times to repeat the last action and insert three blank rows.

F4 is useful to repeat commands in Microsoft Office programs. Most commands can be repeated in this manner.

8 From the **row heading area**, select **rows 9:11**. On the **HOME tab**, in the **Editing group**, click **Clear** 🖉 and then click **Clear Formats** to remove the blue accent color in columns D and E from the new rows. Click **Save** 🖫.

> When you insert rows or columns, formatting from adjacent rows or columns repeats in the new cells.

Objective 3 | Use COUNTIF and IF Functions and Apply Conditional Formatting

Video E2-3

Recall that statistical functions analyze a group of measurements. Another group of Excel functions, referred to as *logical functions*, test for specific conditions. Logical functions typically use conditional tests to determine whether specified conditions—called *criteria*—are true or false.

Activity 2.08 | Using the COUNT and COUNTIF Functions

The *Count function* counts the number of cells in a range that contain numbers. The *COUNTIF function* is a statistical function that counts the number of cells within a range that meet the given condition—the criteria that you provide. The COUNTIF function has two arguments—the range of cells to check and the criteria.

The trees of Rosedale Landscape and Garden will be featured on an upcoming segment of a TV gardening show. In this activity, you will use the COUNTIF function to determine the number of *Oak* trees currently available in inventory that can be featured in the TV show.

1 Click cell **E4**, look at the **Formula Bar**, and then notice that the arguments of the **SUM** function adjusted and refer to the appropriate cells in rows 14:42.

> The referenced range updates to *A14:A42* after you insert the three new rows. In this manner, Excel adjusts the cell references in a formula relative to their new locations.

2 Click cell **A10**, type **Oak Trees** and then press Tab.

3 With cell **B10** as the active cell, on the **FORMULAS tab**, in the **Function Library group**, click **More Functions**, and then display the list of **Statistical** functions. Click **COUNTIF**.

> The COUNTIF function counts the number of cells within a range that meet the given condition.

4 In the **Range** box, type **g14:g42** Click in the **Criteria** box, type **Oak** and then compare your screen with Figure 2.15.

FIGURE 2.15

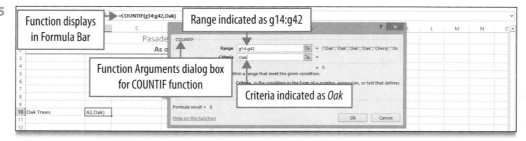

5 In the lower right corner of the **Function Arguments** dialog box, click **OK**.

> There are *13* different *Oak* trees available to feature on the TV show.

6 On the **HOME tab**, in the **Alignment group**, click **Align Left** ☰ to place the result closer to the row title. **Save** 🖫 your workbook.

Activity 2.09 | Using the IF Function

A *logical test* is any value or expression that you can evaluate as being true or false. The *IF function* uses a logical test to check whether a condition is met, and then returns one value if true, and another value if false.

For example, *C14=228* is an expression that can be evaluated as true or false. If the value in cell C14 is equal to 228, the expression is true. If the value in cell C14 is not 228, the expression is false.

In this activity, you will use the IF function to determine the inventory levels and determine if more products should be ordered.

1 Click cell **H13**, type **Stock Level** and then press Enter.

2 In cell **H14**, on the **FORMULAS tab**, in the **Function Library group**, click **Logical**, and then in the list, click **IF**. Drag the title bar of the **Function Arguments** dialog box up or down to view **row 14** on your screen.

3 With the insertion point in the **Logical_test** box, type **a14 < 75**

> This logical test will look at the value in cell A14, which is *78*, and then determine if the number is less than 75. The expression *<75* includes the < *comparison operator*, which means *less than*. Comparison operators compare values.

4 Examine the table in Figure 2.16 for a list of comparison operator symbols and their definitions.

FIGURE 2.16

COMPARISON OPERATORS	
COMPARISON OPERATORS	**SYMBOL DEFINITION**
=	Equal to
>	Greater than
<	Less than
>=	Greater than or equal to
<=	Less than or equal to
<>	Not equal to

5 Press Tab to move the insertion point to the **Value_if_true** box, and then type **Order**

> If the result of the logical test is true—the Quantity in Stock is less than 75—cell H14 will display the text *Order* indicating that additional trees must be ordered.

6 Press Tab to move to the **Value_if_false** box, type **OK** and then compare your screen with Figure 2.17.

> If the result of the logical test is false—the Quantity in Stock is *not* less than 75—then Excel will display *OK* in the cell.

FIGURE 2.17

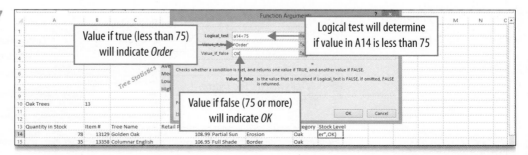

7 Click **OK** to display the result *OK* in cell **H14**.

8 Using the fill handle, copy the function in cell **H14** down through cell **H42**. Then scroll as necessary to view cell **A18**, which contains the value *75*. Look at cell **H18** and notice that the **Stock Level** is indicated as *OK*. **Save** your workbook. Compare your screen with Figure 2.18.

The comparison operator indicated <75 (less than 75) and therefore a value of *exactly* 75 is indicated as OK.

FIGURE 2.18

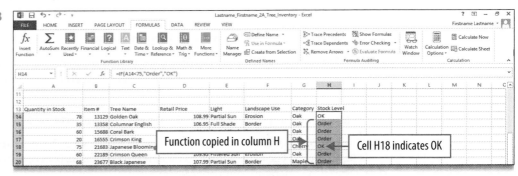

Activity 2.10 | Applying Conditional Formatting by Using Highlight Cells Rules and Data Bars

A *conditional format* changes the appearance of a cell based on a condition—a criteria. If the condition is true, the cell is formatted based on that condition; if the condition is false, the cell is *not* formatted. In this activity, you will use conditional formatting as another way to draw attention to the Stock Level of trees.

1 Be sure the range **H14:H42** is selected. On the **HOME tab**, in the **Styles group**, click **Conditional Formatting**. In the list, point to **Highlight Cells Rules**, and then click **Text that Contains**.

2 In the **Text That Contains** dialog box, with the insertion point blinking in the first box, type **Order** and notice that in the selected range, the text *Order* displays with the default format—Light Red Fill with Dark Red Text.

3 In the second box, click the **arrow**, and then in the list, click **Custom Format**.

Here, in the Format Cells dialog box, you can select any combination of formats to apply to the cell if the condition is true. The custom format you specify will be applied to any cell in the selected range if it contains the text *Order*.

4 On the **Font tab**, under **Font style**, click **Bold Italic**. Click the **Color arrow**, and then under **Theme Colors**, in the last column, click the first color—**Green, Accent 6**. Click **OK**. Compare your screen with Figure 2.19.

In the range, if the cell meets the condition of containing *Order*, the font color will change to Bold Italic, Green, Accent 6.

FIGURE 2.19

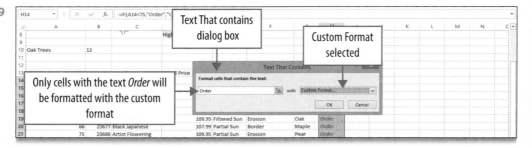

5 In the **Text That Contains** dialog box, click **OK**.

6 Select the range **A14:A42**. In the **Styles group**, click **Conditional Formatting**. Point to **Data Bars**, and then under **Gradient Fill**, click **Orange Data Bar**. Click anywhere to cancel the selection, click **Save** 🖫, and then compare your screen with Figure 2.20.

A *data bar* provides a visual cue to the reader about the value of a cell relative to other cells. The length of the data bar represents the value in the cell. A longer bar represents a higher value and a shorter bar represents a lower value. Data bars are useful for identifying higher and lower numbers quickly within a large group of data, such as very high or very low levels of inventory.

FIGURE 2.20

Activity 2.11 | Using Find and Replace

The ***Find and Replace*** feature searches the cells in a worksheet—or in a selected range—for matches, and then replaces each match with a replacement value of your choice.

Comments from customers on the company's blog indicate that using the term *Erosion Control* would be clearer than *Erosion* when describing the best landscape use for specific trees. Therefore, all products of this type will be re-labeled accordingly. In this activity, you will replace all occurrences of *Erosion* with *Erosion Control*.

1 Select the range **F14:F42**.

Restrict the find and replace operation to a specific range in this manner, especially if there is a possibility that the name occurs elsewhere.

2 On the **HOME tab**, in the **Editing group**, click **Find & Select**, and then click **Replace**.

3 Type **Erosion** to fill in the **Find what** box. In the **Replace with** box, type **Erosion Control** and then compare your screen with Figure 2.21.

FIGURE 2.21

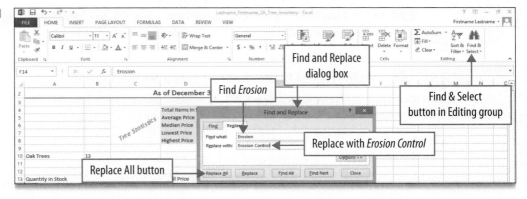

4 Click **Replace All**. In the message box, notice that 13 replacements were made, and then click **OK**. In the lower right corner of the **Find and Replace** dialog box, click **Close**. Click **Save** 🖫.

Video E2-4

Excel can obtain the date and time from your computer's calendar and clock and display this information on your worksheet.

By freezing or splitting panes, you can view two areas of a worksheet and lock rows and columns in one area. When you freeze panes, you select the specific rows or columns that you want to remain visible when scrolling in your worksheet.

Activity 2.12   Using the NOW Function to Display a System Date

The **NOW function** retrieves the date and time from your computer's calendar and clock and inserts the information into the selected cell. The result is formatted as a date and time.

1▸ To the left of the **Formula Bar**, click in the **Name Box**, type **a44** and then press Enter. Notice that cell **A44** is the active cell. In cell **A44**, type **Edited by Maria Acuna** and then press Enter.

2▸ With cell **A45** as the active cell, on the **FORMULAS tab**, in the **Function Library group**, click **Date & Time**. In the list of functions, click **NOW**. Compare your screen with Figure 2.22.

FIGURE 2.22

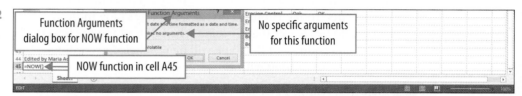

3▸ Read the description in the **Function Arguments** dialog box, and notice that this result is *Volatile*.

The Function Arguments dialog box displays a message indicating that this function does not require an argument. It also states that this function is **volatile**, meaning the date and time will not remain as entered, but rather the date and time will automatically update each time you open this workbook.

4▸ In the **Function Arguments** dialog box, click **OK** to close the dialog box and display the current date and time in cell **A45**. **Save** 🔲 your workbook.

More Knowledge   **NOW Function Recalculates Each Time a Workbook Opens**

The NOW function updates each time the workbook is opened. With the workbook open, you can force the NOW function to update by pressing F9, for example, to update the time.

Activity 2.13   Freezing and Unfreezing Panes

In a large worksheet, if you scroll down more than 25 rows or scroll beyond column O (the exact row number and column letter varies, depending on your screen resolution), you will no longer see the top rows or first column of your worksheet where identifying information about the data is usually placed. You will find it easier to work with your data if you can always view the identifying row or column titles.

The **Freeze Panes** command enables you to select one or more rows or columns and then freeze (lock) them into place. The locked rows and columns become separate panes. A **pane** is a portion of a worksheet window bounded by and separated from other portions by vertical or horizontal bars.

1 Press `Ctrl` + `Home` to make cell **A1** the active cell. Scroll down until **row 21** displays at the top of your Excel window, and notice that all of the identifying information in the column titles is out of view.

2 Press `Ctrl` + `Home` again, and then from the **row heading area**, select **row 14**. Click the **VIEW tab**, and then in the **Window group**, click **Freeze Panes**. In the list, click **Freeze Panes**. Click any cell to deselect the row, and then notice that a line displays along the upper border of **row 14**.

> By selecting row 14, the rows above—rows 1–13—are frozen in place and will not move as you scroll down.

3 Watch the row numbers below **row 13**, and then begin to scroll down to bring **row 21** into view again. Notice that rows 1:13 are frozen in place. Compare your screen with Figure 2.23.

> The remaining rows of data continue to scroll. Use this feature when you have long or wide worksheets.

FIGURE 2.23

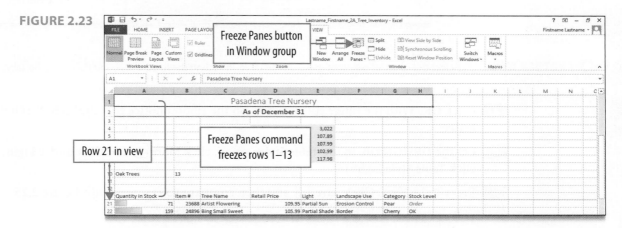

4 In the **Window group**, click **Freeze Panes**, and then click **Unfreeze Panes** to unlock all rows and columns. **Save** your workbook.

More Knowledge | **Freeze Columns or Freeze Both Rows and Columns**

You can freeze columns that you want to remain in view on the left. Select the column to the right of the column(s) that you want to remain in view while scrolling to the right, and then click the Freeze Panes command. You can also use the command to freeze both rows and columns; click a *cell* to freeze the rows *above* the cell and the columns to the *left* of the cell.

Objective 5 | Create, Sort, and Filter an Excel Table

Video E2-5

To analyze a group of related data, you can convert a range of cells to an ***Excel table***. An Excel table is a series of rows and columns that contains related data that is managed independently from the data in other rows and columns in the worksheet.

Activity 2.14 | Creating an Excel Table and Applying a Table Style

1 Be sure that you have applied the Unfreeze Panes command—no rows on your worksheet are locked.

2 ▶ Click any cell in the data below row 13. Click the **INSERT tab**. In the **Tables group**, click **Table**. In the **Create Table** dialog box, if necessary, click to select the My table has headers check box, and then compare your screen with Figure 2.24.

> The column titles in row 13 will form the table headers. By clicking in a range of contiguous data, Excel will suggest the range as the data for the table. You can adjust the range if necessary.

FIGURE 2.24

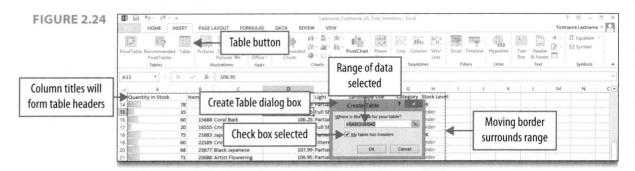

⟳ ANOTHER WAY   Select the range of cells that make up the table, including the header row, and then click the Table button.

3 ▶ Click **OK**. With the range still selected, on the ribbon notice that the **TABLE TOOLS** are active.

4 ▶ On the **DESIGN tab**, in the **Table Styles group**, click **More ▾**, and then under **Light**, locate and click **Table Style Light 16**.

5 ▶ Press [Ctrl] + [Home]. Click **Save 🖫**, and then compare your screen with Figure 2.25.

> Sorting and filtering arrows display in the table's header row.

FIGURE 2.25

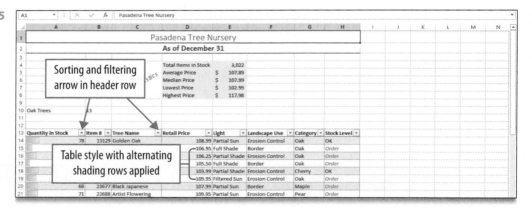

Activity 2.15 | Sorting an Excel Table

You can *sort* tables—arrange all the data in a specific order—in ascending or descending order.

1 ▶ In the header row of the table, click the **Retail Price arrow**, and then on the menu, click **Sort Smallest to Largest**. Next to the arrow, notice the small **up arrow** indicating an ascending (smallest to largest) sort.

> This action sorts the rows in the table from the lowest retail price to highest retail price.

2 In the table's header row, click the **Category arrow**. On the menu, click **Sort A to Z**. Next to the arrow, notice the small **up arrow** indicating an ascending (A to Z) sort.

> This action sorts the rows in the table alphabetically by Category, and within a Category, sorts the rows from smallest to largest by Retail Price.

3 Click the **Category arrow** again, and then sort from **Z to A**.

> This action sorts the rows in the table in reverse alphabetic order by Category name, and the small arrow points downward, indicating a descending (Z to A) sort. The Retail Price continues to be sorted from smallest to largest within each category.

Activity 2.16 | Filtering an Excel Table and Displaying a Total Row

You can *filter* tables—display only a portion of the data based on matching a specific value—to show only the data that meets the criteria that you specify.

1 Click the **Category arrow** again. On the menu, click the **(Select All)** check box to clear all the check boxes. Click to select only the **Maple** check box, and then click **OK**. Compare your screen with Figure 2.26.

> Only the rows containing *Maple* in the Category column display—the remaining rows are hidden from view. A small funnel—the filter icon—indicates that a filter is applied to the data in the table. Additionally, the row numbers display in blue to indicate that some rows are hidden from view. A filter hides entire rows in the worksheet.

FIGURE 2.26

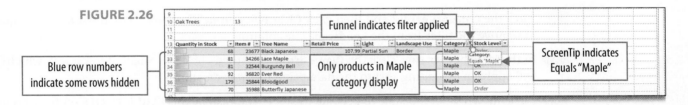

2 Point to the funnel icon to the right of *Category*, and notice that *Equals "Maple"* displays to indicate the filter criteria.

3 Click any cell in the table so that the table is selected. On the ribbon, click the **DESIGN tab**, and then in the **Table Style Options group**, select the **Total Row** check box.

> *Total* displays in cell A43. In cell H43, the number 6 indicates that six rows currently display.

4 Click cell **A43**, click the **arrow** that displays to the right of cell **A43**, and then in the list, click **Sum**.

> Excel sums only the visible rows in Column A, and indicates that 571 products in the Maple category are in stock. In this manner, you can use an Excel table to quickly find information about a group of data.

5 Click cell **A11**, type **Maple Trees** and press Tab. In cell **B11**, type **6 (571 total items in stock)** and then press Enter.

6 In the table header row, click the **Category arrow**, and then on the menu, click **Clear Filter From "Category"**.

> All the rows in the table redisplay. The Z to A sort on Category remains in effect.

More Knowledge   **Band Rows and Columns in a Table**

You can band rows to format even rows differently from odd rows making them easier to read. To band rows or columns, on the DESIGN tab, in the Table Style Options group, select the Banded Rows or Banded Columns check box.

7 Click the **Landscape Use arrow**, click the **(Select All)** check box to clear all the check boxes, and then click to select the **Erosion Control** check box. Click **OK**.

8 Click the **Category arrow**, click the **(Select All)** check box to clear all the check boxes, and then click the **Oak** check box. Click **OK**, **Save** 🔲 your workbook, and then compare your screen with Figure 2.27.

By applying multiple filters, Mr. Hill can determine quickly that eight tree names identified with a *Landscape Use* of *Erosion Control* are in the *Oak* tree category with a total of 710 such trees in stock.

FIGURE 2.27

Activity 2.17 | Clearing Filters and Converting a Table to a Range of Data

When you are finished answering questions about the data in a table by sorting, filtering, and totaling, you can convert the table into a normal range. Doing so is useful if you want to use the Table feature only to apply a Table Style to a range. For example, you can insert a table, apply a Table Style, and then convert the table to a normal range of data but keep the formatting.

1 Click the **Category arrow**, and then click **Clear Filter From "Category"**. Use the same technique to remove the filter from the **Landscape Use** column.

2 In the table header row, click the **Item # arrow**, and then click **Sort Smallest to Largest**, which will apply an ascending sort to the data using the *Item #* column.

3 Click anywhere in the table to activate the table and display the **TABLE TOOLS** on the ribbon. Click the **DESIGN tab**, and then in the **Table Style Options group**, click the **Total Row** check box to clear the check mark and remove the Total row from the table.

4 On the **DESIGN tab**, in the **Tools group**, click **Convert to Range**. In the message box, click **Yes**. Click **Save** 🔲, and then compare your screen with Figure 2.28.

FIGURE 2.28

 ANOTHER WAY   With any table cell selected, right-click, point to Table, and then click Convert to Range.

Objective 6   View, Format, and Print a Large Worksheet

Video E2-6

You can magnify or shrink the view of a worksheet on your screen to either zoom in to view specific data or zoom out to see the entire worksheet. You can also split a worksheet window into panes to view different parts of a worksheet at the same time.

A worksheet might be too wide, too long—or both—to print on a single page. Use Excel's *Print Titles* and *Scale to Fit* commands to create pages that are attractive and easy to read.

The Print Titles command enables you to specify rows and columns to repeat on each printed page. Scale to Fit commands enable you to stretch or shrink the width, height, or both, of printed output to fit a maximum number of pages.

Activity 2.18 | Modifying and Shrinking the Worksheet View

1 Press Ctrl + Home to display the top of your worksheet. On the **VIEW tab**, in the **Zoom group**, click **Zoom**.

2 In the **Zoom** dialog box, click the **75%** option button, and then click **OK**. Notice that by zooming out in this manner, you can see additional rows of your worksheet on the screen.

3 In the lower right corner of your worksheet, in the status bar, click the **Zoom In** button until the worksheet redisplays at 100%.

Activity 2.19 | Splitting a Worksheet Window into Panes

The *Split* command splits the window into multiple resizable panes that contain views of your worksheet. This is useful to view multiple distant parts of your worksheet at one time.

1 Click cell **F9**. On the **VIEW tab**, in the **Window group**, click **Split**.

Horizontal and vertical split bars display. You can drag the split bars to view any four portions of the worksheet.

2 Notice on the right that separate vertical scroll bars display for the upper and lower panes and at the bottom, separate horizontal scroll bars display for the left and right panes.

3 Drag the lower vertical scroll box down to the bottom of the scroll bar to view **line 44**. Compare your screen with Figure 2.29.

Here it could be useful to isolate the Tree Statistics at the top and then scroll to the bottom to browse the inventory items or to make a note about who edited the original worksheet.

FIGURE 2.29

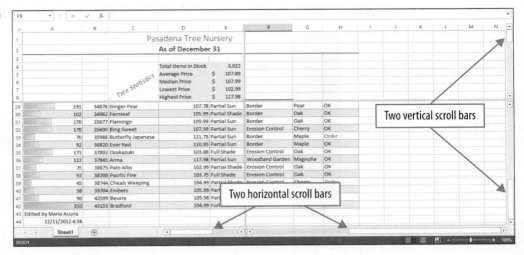

4 On the **VIEW tab**, click **Split** again to remove the split bars.

5 Press Ctrl + Home to display the top of your worksheet. On the **PAGE LAYOUT tab**, in the **Themes group**, click **Themes**, and then click **Slice**.

6 Select the range **A13:H13**. On the **HOME tab**, from the **Styles group**, apply the **Heading 4** cell style, and then apply **Center**. Click cell **A1**.

1 Click the **PAGE LAYOUT tab**, and then in the **Page Setup group**, click **Margins**. At the bottom of the gallery, click **Custom Margins** to display the **Page Setup** dialog box. Under **Center on page**, select the **Horizontally** check box.

2 Click the **Header/Footer tab**, and then in the center of the dialog box, click **Custom Footer**. In the **Footer** dialog box, with your insertion point blinking in the **Left section**, on the row of buttons, click **Insert File Name**. Click **OK** two times.

3 In the **Page Setup group**, click **Orientation**, and then click **Landscape**.

The dotted line indicates that as currently formatted, column H will not fit on one page.

4 Press Ctrl + F2 to display the **Print Preview**. At the bottom of the **Print Preview**, click **Next Page** ▶.

As currently formatted, the worksheet will print on four pages, and the columns will span multiple pages. Additionally, after Page 1, no column titles are visible to identify the data in the columns.

5 Click **Next Page** ▶ two times to display **Page 4**, and notice that one column moves to an additional page.

6 In the upper left corner of **Backstage** view, click **Back** ⊙ to return to the worksheet. In the **Page Setup group**, click **Print Titles**. Under **Print titles**, click in the **Rows to repeat at top** box, and then at the right, click **Collapse Dialog** ▦.

7 From the **row heading area**, select **row 13**, and then in the **Page Setup - Rows to repeat at top** dialog box, click **Expand Dialog** ▦. Click **OK** to print the column titles in row 13 at the top of every page.

You can collapse and then expand dialog boxes on your screen to enable a better view of your data.

8 Press Ctrl + F2 to display the **Print Preview** again. At the bottom of the **Settings group**, click the **No Scaling arrow**, and then on the displayed list, point to **Fit All Columns on One Page**. Compare your screen with Figure 2.30.

This action will shrink the width of the printed output to fit all the columns on one page. You can make adjustments like this on the Page Layout tab, or here, in the Print Preview.

FIGURE 2.30

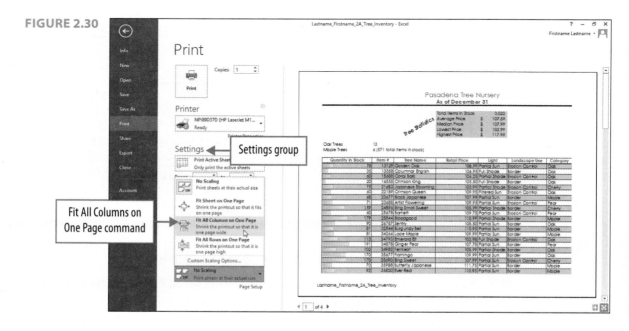

9 Click **Fit All Columns on One Page**. Notice in the **Print Preview** that all the columns display on one page.

⟳ **ANOTHER WAY**   With the worksheet displayed, on the Page Layout tab, in the Scale to Fit group, click the Width button arrow, and then click 1 page.

10 At the bottom of the **Print Preview**, click **Next Page** ▶ one time. Notice that the output will now print on two pages and that the column titles display at the top of **Page 2**. Compare your screen with Figure 2.31.

FIGURE 2.31

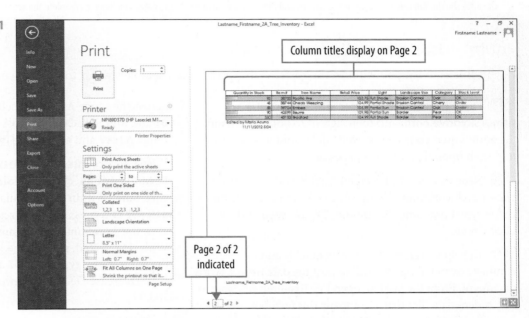

Column titles display on Page 2

Page 2 of 2 indicated

11 On the left, click **Info**, and then click **Show All Properties**. As the **Tags**, type **tree inventory, Pasadena** As the **Subject**, type your course name and section number. Be sure your name displays as the author; edit if necessary.

12 On the left, click **Save**. By using the techniques you practiced in Project 1A, print or submit electronically as directed by your instructor. If required by your instructor, print or create an electronic version of your worksheet with formulas displayed.

13 Close your workbook and close Excel.

More Knowledge   **Scaling for Data That Is Slightly Larger Than the Printed Page**

For data just a little too large to fit on a page, you can scale the worksheet to make it fit. Scaling reduces the width and height of the printed data to a percentage of its original size or by the number of pages that you specify. On the Page Layout tab, in the Scale to Fit group, click the Scale arrows to select a percentage.

END | You have completed Project 2A

GO! with Office Web Apps

Objective | Sort, Filter, and Use Functions in a Table in Excel Web App

If you are working on a computer that does not have Microsoft Office installed, you can still create new workbooks with tables in your web browser by using the Excel Office Web App.

> **ALERT!** **Working with Web-Based Applications and Services**
>
> Computer programs and services on the web receive continuous updates and improvements, so the steps to complete this web-based activity may differ from the ones shown. You can often look at the screens and the information presented to determine how to complete the activity.

Activity | Sort, Filter, and Use Functions in a Table

In this activity, you will use the Excel Web App to create a table similar to the one you created in Project 2A.

1 Launch your web browser, navigate to **http://skydrive.com**, and then sign in to your Microsoft account. Open your **GO! Web Projects** folder—or create and then open this folder if necessary.

2 Near the top of the screen, click **Create**, and then click **Excel workbook**. Using your own name, as the file name type **Lastname_Firstname_EX_2A_Web** and then click **Create**.

3 To help you create this project quickly and to eliminate extra typing, you will import the data from a Word document. From the taskbar, open **File Explorer**, navigate to the student data files that accompany this textbook, and then open the Word document **e02_2A_Web**. Press Ctrl + A to select all of the text, right-click anywhere over the selection, and then click **Copy**. **Close** ✕ Word and if necessary **Close** ⊠ the folder window.

4 With cell **A1** selected, on the Excel Web App ribbon, in the **Clipboard group**, click **Paste**; if necessary click Allow access.

5 Select column headings **A:H**, point to the border between any two selected column headings to display the ⊣⊢ pointer, and then double-click to resize all the columns to display all data.

6 Click cell **A1**, type **Pasadena Nursery: Tree Inventory** Press Enter and then **Merge & Center** the text

across the range **A1:H1**. In cell **A2**, type **As of December 31** and **Merge & Center** across the range **A2:H2**. Select the range **A1:A2** and apply **Bold** B.

7 Click cell **B4**. On the **HOME tab**, in the **Formulas group**, click the **AutoSum arrow** and then click **Sum**. Within the formula's parentheses, type **a13:a67** and press Enter for a result of *7085*. In cell **B5**, click the **AutoSum arrow** again, and then click **Average**. With *B4* selected, press Backspace one time, and then within the parentheses type **d13:d67** and press Enter. If necessary, click Decrease Decimal ⇥.0 two times for a result of *108.09*.

8 With cell **B6** selected, click the **INSERT tab**, and then click **Function**. Click the **Pick a category arrow**, click **Statistical**, and then scroll down and click **MEDIAN**. Click **OK**. Type **d13:d67)** and press Enter for a result of *106.98*.

9 In cell **B7**, click **Function**, from the **Commonly Used** group click **MIN**, click **OK**, type **d13:d67)** and press Enter for a result of *79.99*. In cell **B8**, use the same technique to compute the Highest Price for a result of *131.78*.

10 In cell **B9**, display the list of **Commonly Used** functions, scroll down, click **COUNTIF**, and then click **OK**. Type **g13:g67,"Oak")** and press Enter. Compare your screen with Figure A.

FIGURE A

1	Pasadena Nursery: Tree Inventory	
2	As of December 31	
3		
4	Total Items in Stock	7085
5	Average Price	108.09
6	Median Price	106.98
7	Lowest Price	79.99
8	Highest Price	131.78
9	Oak Trees:	20
10	Magnolia Trees:	
11		

(GO! with Office Web Apps continues on the next page)

11 Click cell **H13**. From the **Commonly Used** list of functions, insert **IF**, and then type **a13<75,"Order","OK")** and press Enter. Copy this formula down through cell **H67**, which you will have to do in sections due to the way the Excel Web App scrolls on your screen.

12 Scroll up and click cell **A12**, hold down Shift, drag the vertical scroll box down to view **row 67**, and then click cell **H67** to select the entire range of the table data. On the **INSERT tab**, click **Table**, and then click **OK**. Drag the scroll box back to the top of the vertical scroll bar.

13 Sort the **Retail Price** column in **Ascending** order. Click the **Category arrow**, click **Filter**, and then filter on **Magnolia**.

14 Scroll as necessary to view all the rows in the filtered table, click the **HOME tab**, and then in the **Tables** group, click the **Format as Table arrow**. On the list, click **Toggle Total Row**. Notice that a total row displays and indicates 8 different types of Magnolia trees. In cell **B10** type **8 types** and press Enter.

15 Click any cell in the table. Click **Format as Table** again, and then click **Toggle Total Row** to turn it off. Click the **Category arrow**, and then clear the filter. Press Ctrl + Home, and then compare your screen with Figure B.

16 If you are instructed to submit your file, use one of the methods outlined in the Note box below. Then, on the ribbon, click the **FILE tab** and click **Exit**. In the Excel Web App, there is no Save button because your workbook is being saved automatically. Sign out of your SkyDrive and close Internet Explorer.

N O T E **Printing or Creating an Electronic File from the Excel Web App**

To print on paper, click the FILE tab, click Print, click the Print button, and then click Print. In the Print preview display, click Print. In the displayed Print dialog box, click Print to print on the printer connected to your system. To create an electronic file of your printout, from the Print dialog box, locate the printer labeled *Send to OneNote 2013*, and then click Print. When OneNote opens, click the Unfiled Notes section of the displayed notebook, and then click OK. On the ribbon, click the FILE tab, click Export, and then create a PDF of the page. A PDF created in this manner may include a blank Page 1. Close OneNote.

FIGURE B

	Pasadena Nursery: Tree Inventory						
	As of December 31						
Total Items in Stock	7085						
Average Price	108.0944						
Median Price	106.98						
Lowest Price	79.99						
Highest Price	131.78						
Oak Trees:	20						
Magnolia Trees:	8 types						
Quantity in Stock	Item #	Tree Name	Retail Price	Light	Landscape Use	Category	Stock Level
20	43625	Petite Red	79.99	Partial Shade	Hedge	Oak	Order
120	55255	Canadian Boxwood	89.99	Partial Sun	Hedge	Oak	OK
190	46532	Bold Box	100.95	Partial Sun	Erosion	Maple	OK
140	78655	Honey Oak	102.78	Filtered Sun	Erosion	Oak	OK
75	38675	Palo Alto	102.99	Partial Shade	Erosion	Oak	OK
250	54635	Kagiri	102.99	Partial Shade	Border	Maple	OK

Sheet1

Weekly Sales Summary

MyITLab®
Project 2B Training

PROJECT ACTIVITIES

In Activities 2.21 through 2.35, you will edit an existing workbook for the Sales Director, Mariam Daly. The workbook summarizes the online and in-store sales of products during a one-week period in April. The worksheets of your completed workbook will look similar to Figure 2.32.

PROJECT FILES

For Project 2B, you will need the following file:

e02B_Weekly_Sales

You will save your workbook as:

Lastname_Firstname_2B_Weekly_Sales

PROJECT RESULTS

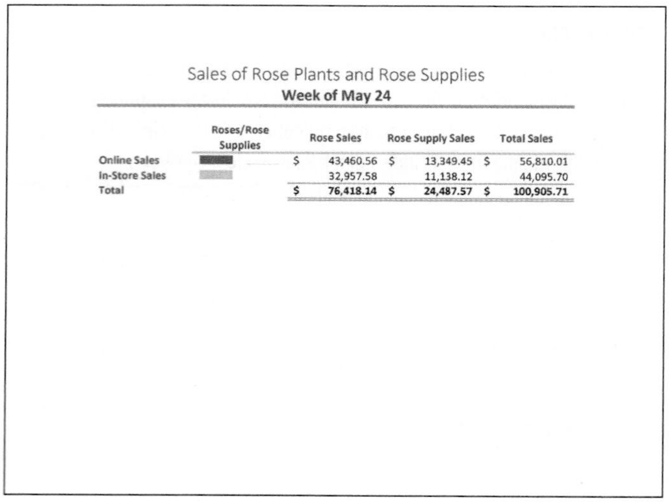

Sales of Rose Plants and Rose Supplies
Week of May 24

	Roses/Rose Supplies	Rose Sales	Rose Supply Sales	Total Sales
Online Sales		$ 43,460.56	$ 13,349.45	$ 56,810.01
In-Store Sales		32,957.58	11,138.12	44,095.70
Total		$ 76,418.14	$ 24,487.57	100,905.71

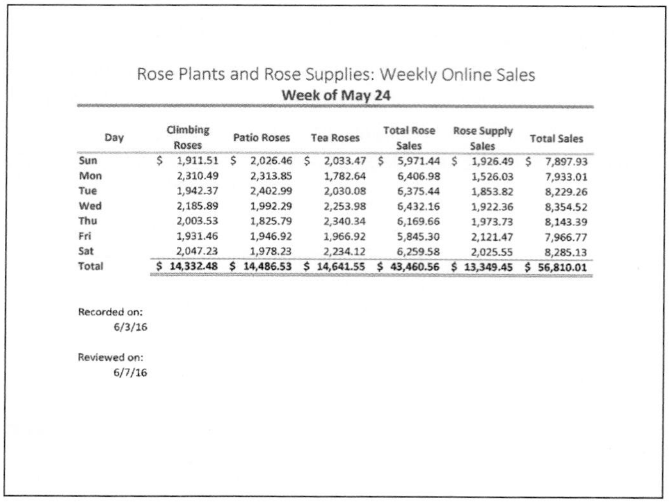

Rose Plants and Rose Supplies: Weekly Online Sales
Week of May 24

Day	Climbing Roses	Patio Roses	Tea Roses	Total Rose Sales	Rose Supply Sales	Total Sales
Sun	$ 1,911.51	$ 2,026.46	$ 2,033.47	$ 5,971.44	$ 1,926.49	$ 7,897.93
Mon	2,310.49	2,313.85	1,782.64	6,406.98	1,526.03	7,933.01
Tue	1,942.37	2,402.99	2,030.08	6,375.44	1,853.82	8,229.26
Wed	2,185.89	1,992.29	2,253.98	6,432.16	1,922.36	8,354.52
Thu	2,003.53	1,825.79	2,340.34	6,169.66	1,973.73	8,143.39
Fri	1,931.46	1,946.92	1,966.92	5,845.30	2,121.47	7,966.77
Sat	2,047.23	1,978.23	2,234.12	6,259.58	2,025.55	8,285.13
Total	$ 14,332.48	$ 14,486.53	$ 14,641.55	$ 43,460.56	$ 13,349.45	$ 56,810.01

Recorded on:
6/3/16

Reviewed on:
6/7/16

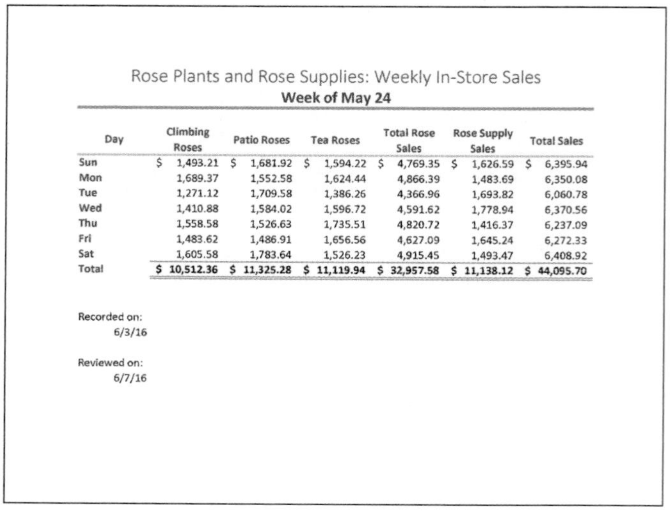

Rose Plants and Rose Supplies: Weekly In-Store Sales
Week of May 24

Day	Climbing Roses	Patio Roses	Tea Roses	Total Rose Sales	Rose Supply Sales	Total Sales
Sun	$ 1,493.21	$ 1,681.92	$ 1,594.22	$ 4,769.35	$ 1,626.59	$ 6,395.94
Mon	1,689.37	1,552.58	1,624.44	4,866.39	1,483.69	6,350.08
Tue	1,271.12	1,709.58	1,386.26	4,366.96	1,693.82	6,060.78
Wed	1,410.88	1,584.02	1,596.72	4,591.62	1,778.94	6,370.56
Thu	1,558.58	1,526.63	1,735.51	4,820.72	1,416.37	6,237.09
Fri	1,483.62	1,486.91	1,656.56	4,627.09	1,645.24	6,272.33
Sat	1,605.58	1,783.64	1,526.23	4,915.45	1,493.47	6,408.92
Total	$ 10,512.36	$ 11,325.28	$ 11,119.94	$ 32,957.58	$ 11,138.12	$ 44,095.70

Recorded on:
6/3/16

Reviewed on:
6/7/16

FIGURE 2.32 Project 2B Weekly Sales Summary

Video E2-7

Use multiple worksheets in a workbook to organize data in a logical arrangement. When you have more than one worksheet in a workbook, you can *navigate* (move) among worksheets by clicking the *sheet tabs*. Sheet tabs identify each worksheet in a workbook and display along the lower left edge of the window. When you have more worksheets than can display in the sheet tab area, use the sheet tab scrolling buttons to move sheet tabs into and out of view.

Activity 2.21 | Navigating Among Worksheets, Renaming Worksheets, and Changing the Tab Color of Worksheets

Excel names the first worksheet in a workbook *Sheet1* and each additional worksheet that you add in order—*Sheet2*, *Sheet3*, and so on. Most Excel users rename their worksheets with meaningful names. In this activity, you will navigate among worksheets, rename worksheets, and change the tab color of sheet tabs.

1 Start Excel, and then in the lower left corner of Excel's opening screen, click **Open Other Workbooks**.

> **ANOTHER WAY**   Press Ctrl + F12 to display the Open dialog box.

2 Navigate to the student files that accompany this textbook, and then locate and open **e02B_Weekly_Sales**. Press F12 to display the **Save As** dialog box, and then navigate to your **Excel Chapter 2** folder. In the **File name** box, using your own name, type **Lastname_Firstname_2B_Weekly_Sales** and click **Save** or press Enter.

> In this workbook, two worksheets display into which some data has already been entered. For example, on the first worksheet, the days of the week and sales data for the one-week period displays.

3 Along the bottom of the Excel window, point to and then click the **Sheet2 tab**.

> The second worksheet in the workbook displays and becomes the active worksheet. *Sheet2* displays in bold.

4 In cell **A1**, notice the text *In-Store*—this worksheet will contain data for in-store sales.

5 Click the **Sheet1 tab**. Then, point to the **Sheet1 tab**, and double-click to select the sheet tab name. Type **Online Sales** and press Enter.

> The first worksheet becomes the active worksheet, and the sheet tab displays *Online Sales*.

6 Point to the **Sheet2 tab**, right-click, and then from the shortcut menu, click **Rename**. Type **In-Store Sales** and press Enter. Compare your screen with Figure 2.33.

> You can use either of these methods to rename a sheet tab.

More Knowledge   **Copying a Worksheet**

To copy a worksheet to the same workbook, right-click the sheet tab, on the shortcut menu click Move or Copy, click the sheet before which you want to insert the copied sheet, select the Create a copy check box, and then click OK. To copy to a different workbook, in the Move or Copy dialog box, click the To book arrow, and then select the workbook into which you want to insert the copy.

FIGURE 2.33

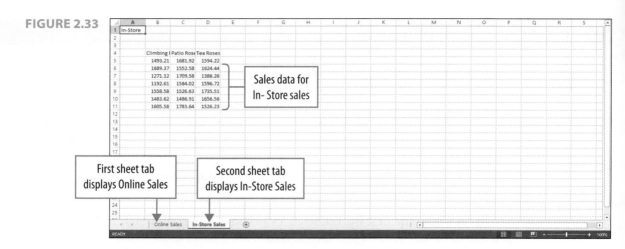

Sales data for In-Store sales

First sheet tab displays Online Sales

Second sheet tab displays In-Store Sales

7 ▶ Point to the **In-Store Sales sheet tab** and right-click. Point to **Tab Color**, and then in the last column, click the first color—**Green, Accent 6**.

 **ANOTHER WAY**   On the Home tab, in the Cells group, click the Format button, and then on the displayed list, point to Tab Color.

8 ▶ Using the technique you just practiced, change the tab color of the **Online Sales sheet tab** to **Blue, Accent 5**—in the next to last column, the first color. **Save** 💾 your workbook.

Objective 8   Enter Dates, Clear Contents, and Clear Formats

Video E2-8

Dates represent a type of value that you can enter in a cell. When you enter a date, Excel assigns a serial value—a number—to the date. This makes it possible to treat dates like other numbers. For example, if two cells contain dates, you can find the number of days between the two dates by subtracting the older date from the more recent date.

Activity 2.22   Entering and Formatting Dates

In this activity, you will examine the various ways that Excel can format dates in a cell. Date values entered in any of the following formats will be recognized by Excel as a date:

Format	Example
m/d/yy	7/4/2016
d-mmm	4-Jul
d-mmm-yy	4-Jul-16
mmm-yy	Jul-12

On your keyboard, ⊡ (the hyphen key) and ⊘ (the forward slash key) function identically in any of these formats and can be used interchangeably. You can abbreviate the month name to three characters or spell it out. You can enter the year as two digits, four digits, or even leave it off. When left off, the current year is assumed but does not display in the cell.

A two-digit year value of 30 through 99 is interpreted by the Windows operating system as the four-digit years of 1930 through 1999. All other two-digit year values are assumed to be in the 21st century. If you always type year values as four digits, even though only two digits may display in the cell, you can be sure that Excel interprets the year value as you intended. Examples are shown in Figure 2.34.

FIGURE 2.34

HOW EXCEL INTERPRETS DATES	
DATE TYPED AS:	**COMPLETED BY EXCEL AS:**
7/4/15	7/4/2015
7/4/98	7/4/1998
7/4	4-Jul (current year assumed)
7-4	4-Jul (current year assumed)
July 4	4-Jul (current year assumed)
Jul 4	4-Jul (current year assumed)
Jul/4	4-Jul (current year assumed)
Jul-4	4-Jul (current year assumed)
July 4, 1998	4-Jul-98
July 2012	Jul-12 (first day of month assumed)
July 1998	Jul-98 (first day of month assumed)

1 On the **Online Sales** sheet, click cell **A16** and notice that the cell displays *6/3*. In the **Formula Bar**, notice that the full date of June 3, 2016 displays in the format *6/3/2016*.

2 With cell **A16** selected, on the **HOME tab**, in the **Number group**, click the **Number Format arrow**. At the bottom, click **More Number Formats** to display the **Number tab** of the **Format Cells** dialog box.

Under Category, *Date* is selected, and under Type, *3/14* is selected. Cell A16 uses this format type; that is, only the month and day display in the cell.

3 In the displayed dialog box, under **Type**, click several other date types and watch the **Sample** area to see how applying the selected date format will format your cell. When you are finished, click the **3/14/12** type, and then compare your screen with Figure 2.35.

FIGURE 2.35

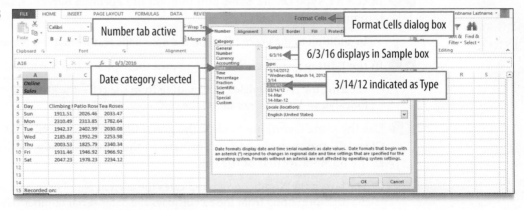

4 At the bottom of the dialog box, click **OK**. Click cell **A19**, type **6-7-16** and then press Enter.

Cell A19 has no special date formatting applied, and displays in the default date format *6/7/2016*.

A L E R T !   **The Date Does Not Display as 6/7/2016?**

Settings in your Windows operating system determine the default format for dates. If your result is different, it is likely that the formatting of the default date was adjusted on the computer at which you are working.

---

5 ▸ Click cell **A19** again. Hold down Ctrl and press ; (semicolon) on your keyboard. Press Enter to confirm the entry.

> Excel enters the current date, obtained from your computer's internal calendar, in the selected cell using the default date format. Ctrl + ; is a quick method to enter the current date.

6 ▸ Click cell **A19** again, type **6/7/16** and then press Enter.

> Because the year *16* is less than 30, Excel assumes a 21st century date and changes *16* to *2016* to complete the four-digit year. Typing *98* would result in *1998*. For two-digit years that you type that are between 30 and 99, Excel assumes a 20th century date.

7 ▸ Click cell **A16**, and then on the **HOME tab**, in the **Clipboard group**, click **Format Painter** ⊘. Click cell **A19**, and notice that the date format from cell **A16** is copied to cell **A19**. **Save** 🖫 your workbook.

Activity 2.23 | Clearing Cell Contents and Formats

A cell has *contents*—a value or a formula—and a cell may also have one or more *formats* applied, for example bold and italic font styles, fill color, font color, and so on. You can choose to clear—delete—the *contents* of a cell, the *formatting* of a cell, or both.

Clearing the contents of a cell deletes the value or formula typed there, but it does *not* clear formatting applied to a cell. In this activity, you will clear the contents of a cell and then clear the formatting of a cell that contains a date to see its underlying content.

1 ▸ In the **Online Sales** worksheet, click cell **A1**. In the **Editing group**, click **Clear** ⊘, and then click **Clear Contents**. Notice that the text is cleared, but the green formatting remains.

2 ▸ Click cell **A2**, and then press Delete.

> You can use either of these two methods to delete the *contents* of a cell. Deleting the contents does not, however, delete the formatting of the cell; you can see that the green fill color format applied to the two cells still displays.

3 ▸ In cell **A1**, type **Online Sales** and then on the **Formula Bar**, click **Enter** ✓ so that cell **A1** remains the active cell.

> In addition to the green fill color, the bold italic text formatting remains with the cell.

4 ▸ In the **Editing group**, click **Clear** ⊘, and then click **Clear Formats**.

> Clearing the formats deletes formatting from the cell—the green fill color and the bold and italic font styles—but does not delete the cell's contents.

5 ▸ Use the same technique to clear the green fill color from cell **A2**. Click cell **A16**, click **Clear** ⊘, and then click **Clear Formats**. In the **Number group**, notice that *General* displays as the number format of the cell.

> The box in the Number group indicates the current Number format of the selected cell. Clearing the date formatting from the cell displays the date's serial number. The date, June 3, 2016, is stored as a serial number that indicates the number of days since January 1, 1900. This date is the 42,524th day since the reference date of January 1, 1900.

6 ▸ On the Quick Access Toolbar, click **Undo** ↺ to restore the date format. **Save** 🖫 your workbook, and then compare your screen with Figure 2.36.

FIGURE 2.36

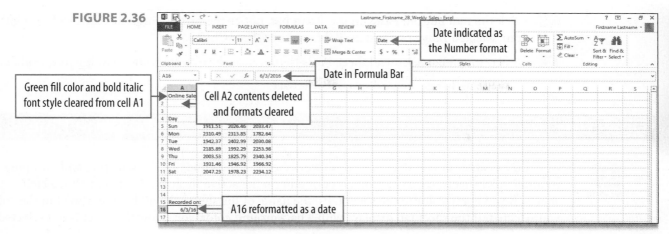

Green fill color and bold italic font style cleared from cell A1

Date indicated as the Number format

Date in Formula Bar

Cell A2 contents deleted and formats cleared

A16 reformatted as a date

More Knowledge | **Clearing an Entire Worksheet**

To clear an entire worksheet, in the upper left corner of the worksheet, click the Select All button, and then on the Home tab, in the Editing group, click Clear, and then click Clear All.

Objective 9 | Copy and Paste by Using the Paste Options Gallery

Video E2-9

Data in cells can be copied to other cells in the same worksheet, to other sheets in the same workbook, or to sheets in another workbook. The action of placing cell contents that have been copied or moved to the Clipboard into another location is called ***paste***.

Activity 2.24 | Copying and Pasting by Using the Paste Options Gallery

Recall that the Clipboard is a temporary storage area maintained by your Windows operating system. When you select one or more cells, and then perform the Copy command or the Cut command, the selected data is placed on the Clipboard. From the Clipboard storage area, the data is available for pasting into other cells, other worksheets, other workbooks, and even into other Office programs. When you paste, the ***Paste Options gallery*** displays, which includes Live Preview to preview the Paste formatting that you want.

1 With the **Online Sales** worksheet active, select the range **A4:A19**.

A range of cells identical to this one is required for the *In-Store Sales* worksheet.

2 Right-click over the selection, and then click **Copy** to place a copy of the cells on the Clipboard. Notice that the copied cells display a moving border.

3 At the bottom of the workbook window, click the **In-Store Sales sheet tab** to make it the active worksheet. Point to cell **A4**, right-click, and then on the shortcut menu, under **Paste Options**, *point* to the first button—**Paste**. Compare your screen with Figure 2.37.

Live Preview displays how the copied cells will be placed in the worksheet if you click the Paste button. In this manner, you can experiment with different paste options, and then be sure you are selecting the paste operation that you want. When pasting a range of cells, you need only point to or select the cell in the upper left corner of the ***paste area***—the target destination for data that has been cut or copied using the Clipboard.

FIGURE 2.37

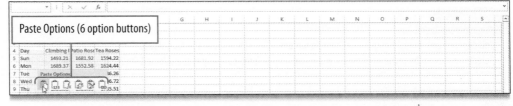

Paste Options (6 option buttons)

4 Click the first button, **Paste**. In the status bar, notice the message that displays, indicating that your selected range remains available on the Office Clipboard.

5 Display the **Online Sales** worksheet. Press (Esc) to cancel the moving border. **Save** 🔲 your workbook.

> The status bar no longer displays the message.

Objective 10   Edit and Format Multiple Worksheets at the Same Time

Video E2-10

You can enter or edit data on several worksheets at the same time by selecting and grouping multiple worksheets. Data that you enter or edit on the active sheet is reflected in all selected sheets. If you apply color to the sheet tabs, the name of the sheet tab will be underlined in the color you selected. If the sheet tab displays with a background color, you know the sheet is not selected.

Activity 2.25 │ Grouping Worksheets for Editing

1 With the **Online Sales** sheet active, press (Ctrl) + (Home) to make cell **A1** the active cell. Point to the **Online Sales sheet tab**, right-click, and then click **Select All Sheets**.

2 At the top of your screen, notice that *[Group]* displays in the title bar. Compare your screen with Figure 2.38.

> Both worksheets are selected, as indicated by *[Group]* in the title bar and the sheet tab names underlined. Data that you enter or edit on the active sheet will also be entered or edited in the same manner on all the selected sheets in the same cells.

FIGURE 2.38

3 Select **columns A:G**, and then set their width to **85 pixels**.

4 Click cell **A2**, type **Week of May 24** and then on the **Formula Bar**, click **Enter** ✔ to keep cell **A2** as the active cell. **Merge & Center** 🔲▾ the text across the range **A2:G2**, and then apply the **Heading 1** cell style.

5 Click cell **E4**, type **Total Rose Sales** and then press (Tab). In cell **F4**, type **Rose Supply Sales** and then press (Tab). In cell **G4**, type **Total Sales** and then press (Enter).

6 Select the range **A4:G4**, and then apply the **Heading 3** cell style. In the **Alignment group**, click **Center** ≡, **Middle Align** ≡, and **Wrap Text**. **Save** 🔲 your workbook.

7 Display the **In-Store Sales** worksheet to cancel the grouping, and then compare your screen with Figure 2.39.

> As soon as you select a single sheet, the grouping of the sheets is canceled and *[Group]* no longer displays in the title bar. Because the sheets were grouped, the same new text and formatting were applied to both sheets. In this manner, you can make the same changes to all the sheets in a workbook at one time.

More Knowledge   **Hide Worksheets**

You can hide any worksheet in a workbook to remove it from view using this technique:
Select the sheet tabs of the worksheets you want to hide, right-click any of the selected sheet tabs, and then click Hide.

FIGURE 2.39

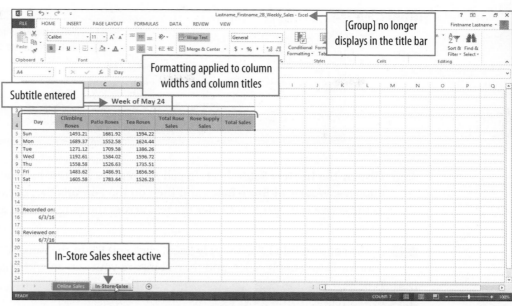

Callouts in figure:
- [Group] no longer displays in the title bar
- Formatting applied to column widths and column titles
- Subtitle entered
- In-Store Sales sheet active

ANOTHER WAY Right-click any sheet tab, and then click Ungroup Sheets.

Activity 2.26 | Formatting and Constructing Formulas on Grouped Worksheets

Recall that formulas are equations that perform calculations on values in your worksheet and that a formula starts with an equal sign (=). Operators are the symbols with which you specify the type of calculation that you want to perform on the elements of a formula. In this activity, you will enter and calculate sales for Rose Supply items from both Online and In-Store sales.

1 Display the **Online Sales** worksheet. Verify that the sheets are not grouped—*[Group]* does *not* display in the title bar.

2 Click cell **A1**, replace *Online Sales* by typing **Rose Plants and Rose Supplies: Weekly Online Sales** and then on the **Formula Bar**, click **Enter** ✓ to keep cell **A1** as the active cell. **Merge & Center** the text across the range **A1:G1**, and then apply the **Title** cell style.

3 In the column titled *Rose Supply Sales*, click cell **F5**, in the range **F5:F11**, type the following data for Rose Supply Sales, and then compare your screen with Figure 2.40.

	ROSE SUPPLY SALES
Sun	1926.49
Mon	1526.03
Tue	1853.82
Wed	1922.36
Thu	1973.73
Fri	2121.47
Sat	2025.55

FIGURE 2.40

Worksheet title entered and formatted for Online Sales sheet

Rose Supply Sales data entered

4 Display the **In-Store Sales** sheet. In cell **A1**, replace *In-Store* by typing **Rose Plants and Rose Supplies: Weekly In-Store Sales** and then on the **Formula Bar**, click **Enter** ✓ to keep cell **A1** as the active cell. **Merge & Center** the text across the range **A1:G1**, and then apply the **Title** cell style.

5 In the column titled *Rose Supply Sales*, click cell **F5**, in the range **F5:F11**, type the following data for Rose Supply Sales, and then compare your screen with Figure 2.41.

ROSE SUPPLY SALES	
Sun	**1626.59**
Mon	**1483.69**
Tue	**1693.82**
Wed	**1778.94**
Thu	**1416.37**
Fri	**1645.24**
Sat	**1493.47**

FIGURE 2.41

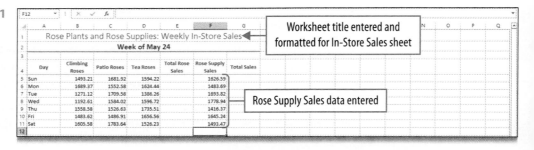

Worksheet title entered and formatted for In-Store Sales sheet

Rose Supply Sales data entered

6 Save 💾 your workbook. Right-click the **Online Sales sheet tab**, and then click **Select All Sheets**.

The first worksheet becomes the active sheet, and the worksheets are grouped. *[Group]* displays in the title bar, and the sheet tabs are underlined in the tab color to indicate they are selected as part of the group. Recall that when grouped, any action that you perform on the active worksheet is *also* performed on any other selected worksheets.

7 With the sheets *grouped* and the **Online Sales** sheet active, click cell **E5**. On the **HOME tab**, in the **Editing group**, click **AutoSum**. Compare your screen with Figure 2.42.

Recall that when you enter the SUM function, Excel looks first above and then left for a proposed range of cells to sum.

FIGURE 2.42

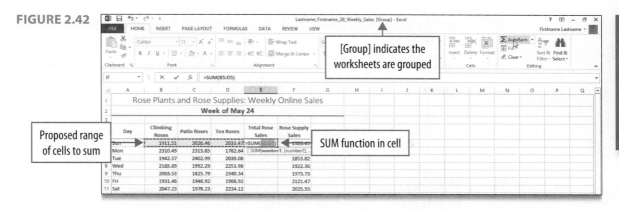

8 ▸ Press Enter to display Total Rose Sales for Sunday, which is *5971.44*.

9 ▸ Click cell **E5**, and then drag the fill handle down to copy the formula through cell **E11**.

10 ▸ Click cell **G5**, type **=** click cell **E5**, type **+** click cell **F5**, and then compare your screen with Figure 2.43.

   Using the point-and-click technique to construct this formula is only one of several techniques you can use. Alternatively, you could use any other method to enter the SUM function to add the values in these two cells.

FIGURE 2.43

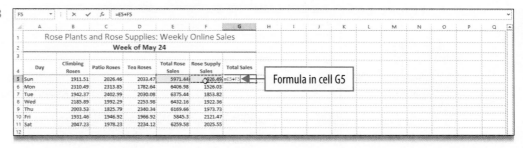

11 ▸ Press Enter to display the result *7897.93*, and then copy the formula down through cell **G11**.

Activity 2.27 | Determining Multiple Totals at the Same Time

You can select a contiguous range of cells adjacent to rows or columns of numbers and then click the Sum button—or use Alt + =—to enter the a SUM function for each row or column.

1 ▸ **Save** 🖫 your workbook. With the two worksheets still grouped, in cell **A12**, type **Total** and then select the range **B5:G12**, which is all of the sales data and the empty cells at the bottom of each column of sales data.

2 ▸ With the range **B5:G12** selected, hold down Alt and press = to enter the **SUM** function in each empty cell. Click **Save** 🖫.

   Selecting a range in this manner and then clicking the SUM button, or entering the SUM function with the keyboard shortcut Alt = =, places the Sum function in the empty cells at the bottom of each column.

Activity 2.28 | Formatting Grouped Worksheets

1 ▸ With the two worksheets still grouped, select the range **A5:A12**, and then apply the **Heading 4** cell style.

2 ▸ To apply financial formatting to the worksheets, select the range **B5:G5**, hold down Ctrl, and then select the range **B12:G12**. With the nonadjacent ranges selected, apply the **Accounting Number Format** $ ▾.

3 Select the range **B6:G11** and apply **Comma Style** [,]. Select the range **B12:G12** and apply the **Total** cell style.

4 Press Ctrl + Home to move to the top of the worksheet; compare your screen with Figure 2.44.

FIGURE 2.44

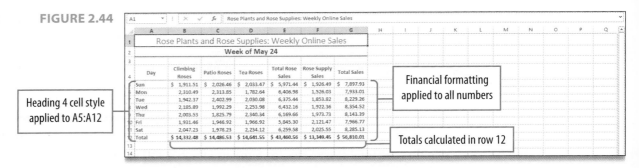

Heading 4 cell style applied to A5:A12

Financial formatting applied to all numbers

Totals calculated in row 12

Activity 2.29 | Ungrouping Worksheets

1 Click the **In-Store Sales sheet tab** to cancel the grouping and display the second worksheet. Click **Save** [💾], and then compare your screen with Figure 2.45.

With your worksheets grouped, the calculations and formatting on the first worksheet were also added on the second worksheet. As soon as you click a single sheet tab, the grouping is canceled.

FIGURE 2.45

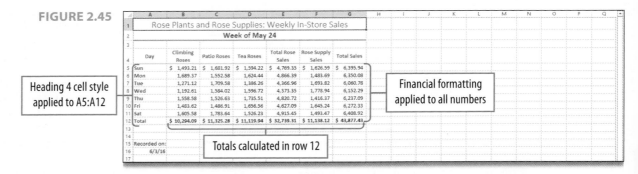

Heading 4 cell style applied to A5:A12

Financial formatting applied to all numbers

Totals calculated in row 12

Objective 11 | Create a Summary Sheet with Column Sparklines

Video E2-11

A **summary sheet** is a worksheet where totals from other worksheets are displayed and summarized. Recall that sparklines are tiny charts within a single cell that show a data trend.

Activity 2.30 | Inserting a Worksheet

1 To the right of the **In-Store Sales** sheet tab, click **New sheet** [⊕].

2 Rename the new worksheet tab **Summary** and change its **Tab Color** to **Gold, Accent 4**.

3 Widen **columns A:E** to **110** pixels. In cell **A1**, type **Sales of Rose Plants and Rose Supplies** **Merge & Center** the title across the range **A1:E1**, and then apply the **Title** cell style.

4 In cell **A2**, type **Week of May 24** and then **Merge & Center** across **A2:E2**; apply the **Heading 1** cell style.

5 Leave **row 3** blank. To form column titles, in cell **B4**, type **Roses/Rose Supplies** and press Tab. In cell **C4**, type **Rose Sales** and press Tab. In cell **D4**, type **Rose Supply Sales** and press Tab. In cell **E5**, type **Total Sales** Press Enter.

6 Select the range **B4:E4**. Apply the **Heading 3** cell style. In the **Alignment group**, click **Center** ▤, **Middle Align** ▤, and **Wrap Text**.

7 To form row titles, in cell **A5**, type **Online Sales** In cell **A6**, type **In-Store Sales** Save 🖫, and then compare your screen with Figure 2.46.

FIGURE 2.46

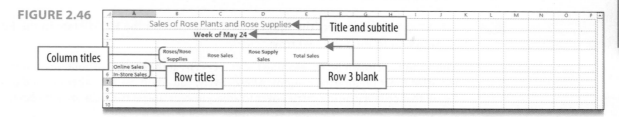

Activity 2.31 | Constructing Formulas That Refer to Cells in Another Worksheet

In this activity, you will construct formulas in the Summary worksheet to display the total sales for both online sales and in-store sales that will update the Summary worksheet whenever changes are made to the other worksheet totals.

1 Click cell **C5**. Type **=** Click the **Online Sales sheet tab**. On the **Online Sales** worksheet, click cell **E12**, and then press Enter to redisplay the **Summary** worksheet and insert the total **Rose Sales** amount of *$43,460.56*.

2 Click cell **C5** to select it again. Look at the **Formula Bar**, and notice that instead of a value, the cell contains a formula that is equal to the value in another cell in another worksheet. Compare your screen with Figure 2.47.

> The value in this cell is equal to the value in cell E12 of the *Online Sales* worksheet. The Accounting Number Format applied to the referenced cell is carried over. By using a formula of this type, changes in cell E12 on the *Online Sales* worksheet will be automatically updated in this *Summary* worksheet.

FIGURE 2.47

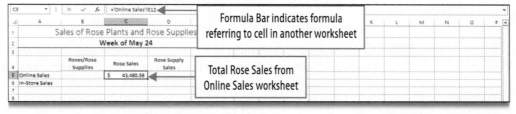

3 Click cell **D5**. Type **=** and then click the **Online Sales sheet tab**. Click cell **F12**, and then press Enter to redisplay the **Summary** worksheet and insert the total **Rose Supply Sales** amount of *$13,349.45*.

4 By using the techniques you just practiced, in cells **C6** and **D6** insert the total **Rose Sales** and **Rose Supply Sales** data from the **In-Store Sales** worksheet. Click **Save** 🖫, and then compare your screen with Figure 2.48.

FIGURE 2.48

Activity 2.32 | Changing Values in a Detail Worksheet to Update a Summary Worksheet

The formulas in cells C5:D6 display the totals from the other two worksheets. Changes made to any of the other two worksheets—sometimes referred to as **detail sheets** because the details of the information are contained there—that affect their totals will display on this Summary worksheet. In this manner, the Summary worksheet accurately displays the current totals from the other worksheets.

1 In cell **A7**, type **Total** Select the range **C5:E6**, and then on the **HOME tab**, in the **Editing group**, click **AutoSum** to total the two rows.

> This technique is similar to selecting the empty cells at the bottom of columns and then inserting the SUM function for each column. Alternatively, you could use any other method to sum the rows. Recall that cell formatting carries over to adjacent cells unless two cells are left blank.

2 Select the range **C5:E7**, and then click **AutoSum** to total the three columns. Compare your screen with Figure 2.49.

FIGURE 2.49

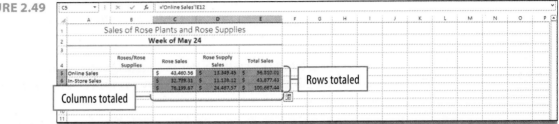

3 In cell **C6**, notice that total **Rose Sales** for **In-Store** Sales is *$32,739.31*, and in cell **C7**, notice the total of *$76,199.87*.

4 Display the **In-Store Sales** worksheet, click cell **B8**, type **1410.88** and then press Enter. Notice that the formulas in the worksheet recalculate.

5 Display the **Summary** worksheet, and notice that in the **Rose Sales** column, both the total for the *In-Store Sales* and the *Total* were recalculated.

> In this manner, a Summary sheet recalculates any changes made in the other worksheets.

6 On the **Summary** worksheet, select the range **C6:E6** and change the format to **Comma Style**. Select the range **C7:E7**, and then apply the **Total** cell style. Select the range **A5:A7** and apply the **Heading 4** cell style. **Save** 🖫 your workbook. Click cell **A1**, and then compare your screen with Figure 2.50.

FIGURE 2.50

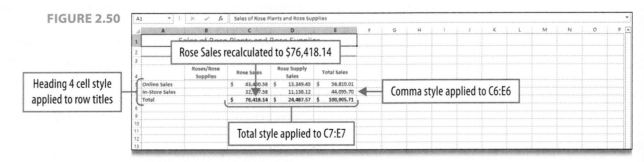

Activity 2.33 | Inserting Column Sparklines

In this activity, you will insert column sparklines to visualize the ratio of Rose sales to Rose Supply sales for both Online and In-Store.

1 On the **Summary** worksheet, click cell **B5**. On the **INSERT tab**, in the **Sparklines group**, click **Column**. In the **Create Sparklines** dialog box, with the insertion point blinking in the **Data Range** box, type **c5:d5** and then compare your screen with Figure 2.51.

FIGURE 2.51

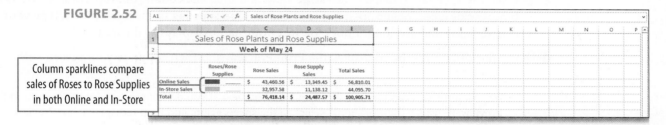

2 Click **OK**. Click cell **B6**, and then **INSERT** a **Column Sparkline** for the range **c6:d6** In the **Style group**, apply **Sparkline Style Accent 4, (no dark or light)**—in the third row, the fourth style. Press Ctrl + Home, click **Save** 🖫, and then compare your screen with Figure 2.52.

> You can see, at a glance, that for both Online and In-Store sales, Rose sales are much greater than Rose Supply sales.

FIGURE 2.52

Column sparklines compare sales of Roses to Rose Supplies in both Online and In-Store

Objective 12 Format and Print Multiple Worksheets in a Workbook

Video E2-12

Each worksheet within a workbook can have different formatting, for example different headers or footers. If all the worksheets in the workbook will have the same header or footer, you can select all the worksheets and apply formatting common to all of the worksheets; for example, you can set the same footer in all of the worksheets.

Activity 2.34 | **Moving a Worksheet, Repeating Footers, and Formatting Multiple Worksheets in a Workbook**

In this activity, you will move the Summary sheet to become the first worksheet in the workbook. Then you will format and prepare your workbook for printing. The three worksheets containing data can be formatted simultaneously.

1 Point to the **Summary sheet tab**, hold down the left mouse button to display a small black triangle—a caret—and then notice that a small paper icon attaches to the mouse pointer.

2 Drag to the left until the caret and mouse pointer are to the left of the **Online Sales sheet tab**, as shown in Figure 2.53, and then release the left mouse button.

> Use this technique to rearrange the order of worksheets within a workbook.

FIGURE 2.53

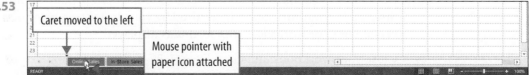

Caret moved to the left

Mouse pointer with paper icon attached

3 Be sure the **Summary** worksheet is the active sheet, point to its sheet tab, right-click, and then click **Select All Sheets** to display *[Group]* in the title bar.

4 Click the **PAGE LAYOUT tab**. In the **Page Setup group**, click **Margins**, and then at the bottom of the gallery, click **Custom Margins** to display the **Page Setup** dialog box.

5 In the **Page Setup** dialog box, on the **Margins tab**, under **Center on page**, select the **Horizontally** check box.

6 Click the **Header/Footer tab**, and then in the center of the dialog box, click **Custom Footer**. In the **Footer** dialog box, with your insertion point blinking in the **Left section**, on the row of buttons, click **Insert File Name** 📄.

7 Click **OK** two times.

The dotted line indicates the page break as currently formatted.

8 Press Ctrl + Home; verify that *[Group]* still displays in the title bar.

By selecting all sheets, you can apply the same formatting to all the worksheets at the same time, for example to repeat headers or footers.

9 Click the **FILE tab** to display **Backstage** view, and then click **Show All Properties**. As the **Tags**, type **weekly sales, online, in-store, rose plants, rose supplies** In the **Subject** box, type your course name and section number. Be sure your name displays as the author.

10 On the left, click **Print** to display the **Print Preview**, and then compare your screen with Figure 2.54.

By grouping, you can view all sheets in Print Preview. If you do not see *1 of 3* at the bottom of the Preview, redisplay the workbook, select all the sheets again, and then redisplay Print Preview.

FIGURE 2.54

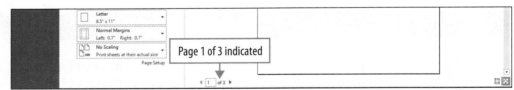

11 At the bottom of the **Print Preview**, click **Next Page** ▶ as necessary and take a moment to view each page of your workbook.

Activity 2.35 | Printing All or Individual Worksheets in a Workbook

1 In **Backstage** view, click **Save** to save your workbook before printing. In the displayed workbook, right-click the **Summary sheet tab**, and then click **Ungroup Sheets**.

2 Press Ctrl + F2 to display **Print Preview**, and then at the bottom of the window, notice that *1 of 1* is indicated.

Because the worksheets are no longer grouped, only the active sheet is available for printing.

3 On the left, under **Settings**, click **Print Active Sheets**, and then click **Print Entire Workbook**.

At the bottom of the window, *1 of 3* is indicated. By default, Excel prints only the active worksheet; however, you can use this command to print an entire workbook.

4 By using the techniques you practiced in Project 1A, print or submit electronically as directed by your instructor. If required by your instructor, print or create an electronic version of your worksheet with formulas displayed.

5 Close your workbook and close Excel.

END | You have completed Project 2B

Objective | Summarize the Data on Multiple Worksheets in Excel Web App

If you are working on a computer that does not have Microsoft Office installed, you can still create new workbooks in your web browser by using the Excel Office Web App.

> **ALERT!** **Working with Web-Based Applications and Services**
>
> Computer programs and services on the web receive continuous updates and improvements, so the steps to complete this web-based activity may differ from the ones shown. You can often look at the screens and the information presented to determine how to complete the activity.

Activity | Creating an Inventory Valuation Report in the Excel Web App

In this activity, you will use the Excel Web App to add a worksheet to a workbook created in Excel.

1 Launch your web browser, navigate to **http://skydrive.com**, and then sign in to your Microsoft account. Open your **GO! Web Projects** folder—or create and then open this folder if necessary.

2 In the SkyDrive menu bar, click **Upload**. Navigate to your student data files, click the Excel file **e02_2B_Web**, and then click **Open**.

3 Point to the uploaded file **e02_2B_Web**, and then right-click. On the shortcut menu, scroll as necessary, and then click **Rename**. Using your own name, type **Lastname_Firstname_EX_2B_Web** and then press Enter to rename the file.

4 Click the file you just renamed to open it in the Excel Web App.

5 At the bottom of the workbook, at the right end of the sheet tabs, click **New sheet** ⊕. Double-click the **Sheet4 tab**, and then name the worksheet tab **TV Sales**.

6 To help you create this project quickly and to eliminate extra typing, you will import the data from a Word table. From the taskbar, open **File Explorer**,

navigate to the student data files that accompany this textbook, and then open the Word document **e02_2B_TV_Sales**. Press Ctrl + A to select all of the text, right-click anywhere over the selection, and then click **Copy**. **Close** Word and the folder window.

7 With cell **A1** selected, on the Excel Web App ribbon, in the **Clipboard group**, click **Paste**; if necessary click Allow access. Notice that # symbols display when numeric data is too wide for the cell.

8 Select the range **A1:G1**, and then in the **Alignment group**, click **Merge & Center**. Merge and center the worksheet's subtitle in the same manner. Select the range **A1:A2**, and then in the **Font group**, apply **Bold**.

9 Select column headings **A:G**, point to the border between any two selected column headings to display the ↔ pointer, and then double-click to resize all the columns to display all data.

10 Select the range **B5:G12**, and then in the **Formulas group**, click the upper portion of the **AutoSum** button to total all the columns. Compare your screen with Figure A.

FIGURE A

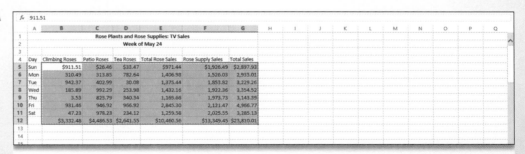

(GO! with Office Web Apps continues on the next page)

11 Display the **Summary** worksheet. Click cell **A7**, and then in the **Cells group**, click the **Insert button arrow**, and then click **Insert Rows**. In the new cell **A7**, type **TV Sales** and then press [Tab] two times to make cell **C7** active.

12 Type **='TV Sales'!E12** and press [Enter] for a result of *$10,460.56*. Notice that you cannot use the [=] plus [Enter] method in the Excel Web App, but you can simply type the command.

13 Click cell **C7** and drag the fill handle to the right to cell **E7**. Compare your screen with Figure B. Notice that Excel copies the formula and adjusts the cell references

to record the Rose Supply Sales and the Total Sales from the TV Sales worksheet. Also, the sparkline is filled in. The TV Sales had higher sales of Rose Supplies than Rose plants.

14 If you are instructed to submit your file, use one of the methods outlined in the Note box below. Then, on the ribbon, click the **FILE tab** and click **Exit**. Recall that in the Excel Web App, there is no Save button because your workbook is being saved automatically. Sign out of your SkyDrive and close Internet Explorer.

N O T E **Printing or Creating an Electronic File from the Excel Web App**

To print on paper, click the FILE tab, click Print, click the Print button, and then click Print. In the Print preview display, click Print. In the displayed Print dialog box, click Print to print on the printer connected to your system. To create an electronic file of your printout, from the Print dialog box, locate the printer labeled *Send to OneNote 2013*, and then click Print. When OneNote opens, click the Unfiled Notes section of the displayed notebook, and then click OK. On the ribbon, click the FILE tab, click Export, and then create a PDF of the page. A PDF created in this manner may include a blank Page 1. Close OneNote.

FIGURE B

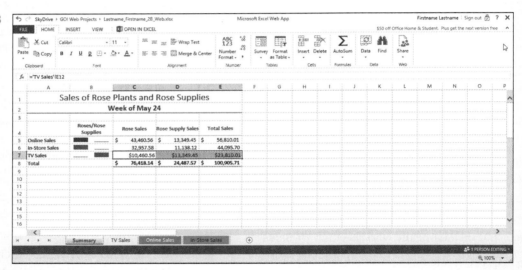

Andrew Rodriguez / Fotolia; FotolEdhar/ Fotolia; apops/ Fotolia; Yuri Arcurs/ Fotolia

Office 365 includes business-class security and is backed by Microsoft. For an organization, what does that mean?

When you and a few classmates work together on a class project, you are not concerned about the security of your data. You probably use free personal email services such as Hotmail, Gmail, or Yahoo Mail to exchange documents, or perhaps you post your documents to free services such as Google Docs.

Organizations, on the other hand—even small ones with only two or three employees—must be concerned with the privacy and security of their data. Organizations cannot entrust their data and confidential communications to free services that may change frequently or that have no legal responsibility for the security of the data.

Organizations must provide each employee with a company email address rather than having each employee use his or her own personal free email address for business communications. Organizations must provide a central storage location for its data rather than having employees store data on flash drives or local hard drives with no control or oversight.

An organization must have a *secure environment*, which is a system that uses controlled *servers*—computers that provide services on a network such as an email server or a file server—to ensure the security and privacy of email, to control the storage and use of information, and to protect against the loss of confidential data.

Most small organizations cannot afford to hire the people with the skills necessary to install and maintain servers. So to establish and maintain a secure environment, many small organizations contract with and rely on small IT—the acronym for *Information Technology*—hosting companies to host their email communications and to provide secure storage.

Activity | **Using Lync to Collaborate by Using a Video Call**

This group project relates to the **Bell Orchid Hotels**. If your instructor assigns this project to your class, you can expect to use **Lync** in **Office 365** to collaborate on the following tasks for this chapter:

- If you are in the **Accounting Group**, you and your teammates will conduct a video call to discuss and agree on a workbook to summarize hotel rooms sold over a four-week period in April.

- If you are in the **Engineering Group**, you and your teammates will conduct a video call to discuss and agree on a workbook summarizing Maintenance Expenses for the first quarter.

- If you are in the **Food and Beverage Group**, you and your teammates will conduct a video call to discuss and agree on a Menu Analysis workbook to analyze the profitability of the ten most popular entrees in the hotel's restaurant.

- If you are in the **Human Resources Group**, you and your teammates will conduct a video call to discuss and agree on a Salary Analysis workbook summarizing the pay of salaried employees over the first six months of operation.

- If you are in the **Operations Group**, you and your teammates will conduct a video call to discuss and agree on a workbook for Rooms and Housekeeping Service Analysis that will be used to determine ongoing needs for housekeeping service.

- If you are in the **Sales and Marking Group**, you and your teammates will conduct a video call to discuss and agree on a Rooms Sold Analysis workbook summarizing rooms sold by four salespersons during January-June that will be used to develop a marketing plan for the rest of the year.

FIGURE A

END OF CHAPTER

SUMMARY

Use Flash Fill to recognize a pattern in data and automatically fill in values when you enter examples of desired output. Flash Fill can split data from two or more cells or combine data from two cells.

Functions are formulas that Excel provides and that perform calculations by using specific values in a particular order or structure. Statistical functions are useful to analyze a group of measurements.

You can navigate among worksheets in a workbook by clicking the sheet tabs, which identify each worksheet in a workbook. Use multiple worksheets in a workbook to organize data in a logical arrangement.

Dates are a value you can enter in a cell to which Excel assigns a serial value—a number—so that you can treat dates like other numbers. For example, you can find the number of days between two dates.

GO! LEARN IT ONLINE

Review the concepts and key terms in this chapter by completing these online challenges, which you can find at **www.pearsonhighered.com/go**.

Matching and Multiple Choice:
Answer matching and multiple choice questions to test what you learned in this chapter. MyITLab®

Crossword Puzzle:
Spell out the words that match the numbered clues, and put them in the puzzle squares.

Flipboard:
Flip through the definitions of the key terms in this chapter and match them with the correct term.

GO! FOR JOB SUCCESS

Video: Customer Service

Your instructor may assign this video to your class, and then ask you to think about, or discuss with your classmates, these questions:

FotolEdhar / Fotolia

How could Lee have been more helpful to the customer?

What did the supervisor, Christine, do to calm the customer?

What might SunTel do on a company-wide basis to create a better customer service experience?

END OF CHAPTER

REVIEW AND ASSESSMENT GUIDE FOR EXCEL CHAPTER 2

Your instructor may assign one or more of these projects to help you review the chapter and assess your mastery and understanding of the chapter.

	Review and Assessment Guide for Excel Chapter 2		
Project	**Apply Skills from These Chapter Objectives**	**Project Type**	**Project Location**
2C	Objectives 1-6 from Project 2A	**2C Skills Review** A guided review of the skills from Project 2A.	On the following pages
2D	Objectives 7-12 from Project 2B	**2D Skills Review** A guided review of the skills from Project 2B.	On the following pages
2E	Objectives 1-6 from Project 2A	**2E Mastery (Grader Project)** A demonstration of your mastery of the skills in Project 2A with extensive decision making.	In MyITLab and on the following pages
2F	Objectives 7-12 from Project 2B	**2F Mastery (Grader Project)** A demonstration of your mastery of the skills in Project 2B with extensive decision making.	In MyITLab and on the following pages
2G	Objectives 1-12 from Projects 2A and 2B	**2G Mastery (Grader Project)** A demonstration of your mastery of the skills in Projects 2A and 2B with extensive decision making.	In MyITLab and on the following pages
2H	Combination of Objectives from Projects 2A and 2B	**2H GO! Fix It** A demonstration of your mastery of the skills in Projects 2A and 2B by creating a correct result from a document that contains errors you must find.	Online
2I	Combination of Objectives from Projects 2A and 2B	**2I GO! Make It** A demonstration of your mastery of the skills in Projects 2A and 2B by creating a result from a supplied picture.	Online
2J	Combination of Objectives from Projects 2A and 2B	**2J GO! Solve It** A demonstration of your mastery of the skills in Projects 2A and 2B, your decision-making skills, and your critical thinking skills. A task-specific rubric helps you self-assess your result.	Online
2K	Combination of Objectives from Projects 2A and 2B	**2K GO! Solve It** A demonstration of your mastery of the skills in Projects 2A and 2B, your decision-making skills, and your critical thinking skills. A task-specific rubric helps you self-assess your result.	On the following pages
2L	Combination of Objectives from Projects 2A and 2B	**2L GO! Think** A demonstration of your understanding of the Chapter concepts applied in a manner that you would outside of college. An analytic rubric helps you and your instructor grade the quality of your work by comparing it to the work an expert in the discipline would create.	On the following pages
2M	Combination of Objectives from Projects 2A and 2B	**2M GO! Think** A demonstration of your understanding of the Chapter concepts applied in a manner that you would outside of college. An analytic rubric helps you and your instructor grade the quality of your work by comparing it to the work an expert in the discipline would create.	Online
2N	Combination of Objectives from Projects 2A and 2B	**2N You and GO!** A demonstration of your understanding of the Chapter concepts applied in a manner that you would in a personal situation. An analytic rubric helps you and your instructor grade the quality of your work.	Online
2O	Combination of Objectives from Projects 2A and 2B	**2O Cumulative Group Project for Excel Chapter 2** A demonstration of your understanding of concepts and your ability to work collaboratively in a group role-playing assessment, requiring both collaboration and self-management.	Online

GLOSSARY

GLOSSARY OF CHAPTER KEY TERMS

Arguments The values that an Excel function uses to perform calculations or operations.

AVERAGE function An Excel function that adds a group of values, and then divides the result by the number of values in the group.

Comparison operators Symbols that evaluate each value to determine if it is the same (=), greater than (>), less than (<), or in between a range of values as specified by the criteria.

Conditional format A format that changes the appearance of a cell—for example, by adding cell shading or font color—based on a condition; if the condition is true, the cell is formatted based on that condition, and if the condition is false, the cell is *not* formatted.

COUNT A statistical function that counts the number of cells in a range that contain numbers.

COUNTIF function A statistical function that counts the number of cells within a range that meet the given condition and that has two arguments—the range of cells to check and the criteria.

Criteria Conditions that you specify in a logical function.

Data bar A cell format consisting of a shaded bar that provides a visual cue to the reader about the value of a cell relative to other cells; the length of the bar represents the value in the cell—a longer bar represents a higher value and a shorter bar represents s lower value.

Detail sheets The worksheets that contain the details of the information summarized on a summary sheet.

Drag and drop The action of moving a selection by dragging it to a new location.

Excel table A series of rows and columns that contains related data that is managed independently from the data in other rows and columns in the worksheet.

Filter The process of displaying only a portion of the data based on matching a specific value to show only the data that meets the criteria that you specify.

Find and replace A command that searches the cells in a worksheet—or in a selected range—for matches and then replaces each match with a replacement value of your choice.

Flash Fill Recognizes a pattern in your data, and then automatically fills in values when you enter examples of the output that you want. Use it to split data from two or more cells or to combine data from two cells.

Formula AutoComplete An Excel feature that, after typing an = (equal sign) and the beginning letter or letters of a function name, displays a list of function names that match the typed letter(s), and from which you can insert the function by pointing to its name and pressing the Tab key or double-clicking.

Freeze Panes A command that enables you to select one or more rows or columns and freeze (lock) them into place; the locked rows and columns become separate panes.

Function A predefined formula—a formula that Excel has already built for you—that performs calculations by using specific values in a particular order or structure.

IF function A function that uses a logical test to check whether a condition is met, and then returns one value if true, and another value if false.

Logical functions A group of functions that test for specific conditions and that typically use conditional tests to determine whether specified conditions are true or false.

Logical test Any value or expression that can be evaluated as being true or false.

MAX function An Excel function that determines the largest value in a selected range of values.

MEDIAN function An Excel function that finds the middle value that has as many values above it in the group as are below it; it differs from AVERAGE in that the result is not affected as much by a single value that is greatly different from the others.

MIN function An Excel function that determines the smallest value in a selected range of values.

Navigate The process of moving within a worksheet or workbook.

NOW function An Excel function that retrieves the date and time from your computer's calendar and clock and inserts the information into the selected cell.

Pane A portion of a worksheet window bounded by and separated from other portions by vertical and horizontal bars.

Paste The action of placing cell contents that have been copied or moved to the Clipboard into another location.

Paste area The target destination for data that has been cut or copied using the Office Clipboard.

Paste Options gallery A gallery of buttons that provides a Live Preview of all the Paste options available in the current context.

Print Titles An Excel command that enables you to specify rows and columns to repeat on each printed page.

Scale to Fit Excel commands that enable you to stretch or shrink the width, height, or both, of printed output to fit a maximum number of pages.

Sheet tabs The labels along the lower border of the workbook window that identify each worksheet.

Sort The process of arranging data in a specific order based on the value in each field.

Split Splits the window into multiple resizable panes that contain views of your worksheet. This is useful to view multiple distant parts of your worksheet at one time.

Statistical functions Excel functions, including the AVERAGE, MEDIAN, MIN, and MAX functions, which are useful to analyze a group of measurements.

SUM function A predefined formula that adds all the numbers in a selected range of cells.

Summary sheet A worksheet where totals from other worksheets are displayed and summarized.

Volatile A term used to describe an Excel function that is subject to change each time the workbook is reopened; for example the NOW function updates itself to the current date and time each time the workbook is opened.

CHAPTER REVIEW

2

EXCEL

Skills Review Project 2C Roses

Apply 2A skills from these Objectives:

1 Use Flash Fill and the SUM, AVERAGE, MEDIAN, MIN, and MAX Functions

2 Move Data, Resolve Error Messages, and Rotate Text

3 Use COUNTIF and IF Functions and Apply Conditional Formatting

4 Use Date & Time Functions and Freeze Panes

5 Create, Sort, and Filter an Excel Table

6 View, Format, and Print a Large Worksheet

In the following Skills Review, you will edit a worksheet detailing the current inventory of Roses at the Pasadena nursery. Your completed workbook will look similar to Figure 2.55.

PROJECT FILES

For Project 2C, you will need the following file:

e02C_Roses

You will save your workbook as:

Lastname_Firstname_2C_Roses

PROJECT RESULTS

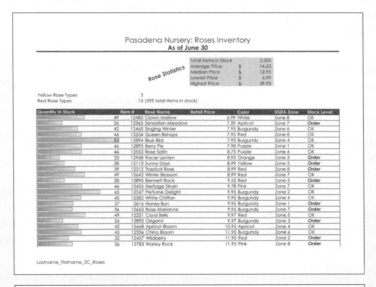

FIGURE 2.55

(Project 2C Roses continues on the next page)

CHAPTER REVIEW

1 ▶ Start Excel. From your student files, locate and open **e02C_Roses**. Save the file in your **Excel Chapter 2** folder as **Lastname_Firstname_2C_Roses**

a. In the **column heading area**, point to **column C** to display the ⬇ pointer, and then drag to the right to select **columns C:D**. On the **HOME tab**, in the **Cells group**, click the **Insert button arrow**, and then click Insert **Sheet Columns**.

b. Click cell **C14**, type **12113** and then on the **Formula Bar**, click **Enter** to confirm the entry and keep cell **C14** as the active cell. On the **HOME tab**, in the **Editing group**, click **Fill**, and then click **Flash Fill**.

c. Click cell **D14**, type **Zone 5** On the **Formula Bar**, click **Enter** to confirm the entry and keep the cell active. Press Ctrl + E, which is the keyboard shortcut for Flash Fill.

d. Select **column B**, and then in the **Cells group**, click the **Delete button arrow**. Click **Delete Sheet Columns**.

2 ▶ In cell **B13** type **Item #** and press Enter.

a. Select **column C**, and then on the **HOME tab**, in the **Clipboard group**, click **Cut**. Click cell **G1**, and then in the **Clipboard group**, click the upper portion of the **Paste** button.

b. Select and then delete **column C**. In cell **F13** type **USDA Zone** and in cell **G13** type **Stock Level**

c. Select columns **A:G**. In the **Cells group**, click **Format**, and then click **AutoFit Column Width**.

d. Press Ctrl + Home. **Merge & Center** cell **A1** across the range **A1:G1**, and then apply the **Title** cell style. **Merge & Center** cell **A2** across the range **A2:G2**, and then apply the **Heading 1** cell style. Click **Save**.

3 ▶ Click cell **B4**. On the **FORMULAS tab**, in the **Function Library group**, click **AutoSum**, and then within the parentheses, type **a14:a68** which is the range containing the quantities for each item.

a. Click cell **B5**, in the **Function Library group**, click **More Functions**. Point to **Statistical**, click **AVERAGE**, and then in the **Number1** box, type **d14:d68** which is the range containing the *Retail Price* for each item. Click **OK**.

b. Click cell **B6**. In the **Function Library group**, click **More Functions**, point to **Statistical**, and then click

MEDIAN. In the **Function Arguments** dialog box, to the right of the **Number1** box, click **Collapse Dialog** 🔳, and then select the range **D14:D68**. Click **Expand Dialog** 🔳, and then click **OK**. Recall that you can select or type a range and that you can collapse the dialog box to make it easier to view your selection.

c. Click cell **B7**, and then by typing or selecting, insert the **MIN** function to determine the lowest **Retail Price**. Click cell **B8**, and then insert the **MAX** function to determine the highest **Retail Price**.

4 ▶ Select cell **B4**. On the **HOME tab**, apply **Comma Style**, and then click **Decrease Decimal** two times. Select the range **B5:B8**, and then apply the **Accounting Number Format**.

a. Select the range **A4:B8**. Point to the right edge of the selected range to display the 🔳 pointer. Drag the selected range to the right until the ScreenTip displays *D4:E8*, and then release the mouse button. AutoFit **column D**.

b. With the range **D4:E8** selected, on the **HOME tab**, in the **Styles group**, display the **Cell Styles** gallery, and then apply **20%—Accent1**.

c. In cell **C6**, type **Rose Statistics** Select the range **C4:C8**, right-click over the selection, and then click **Format Cells**. In the **Format Cells** dialog box, click the **Alignment tab**. Under **Text control**, select the **Merge cells** check box.

d. In the upper right portion of the dialog box, under **Orientation**, point to the **red diamond**, and then drag the diamond upward until the **Degrees** box indicates *20*. Click **OK**.

e. With the merged cell still selected, change the **Font Size** to **14**, and then apply **Bold** and **Italic**. Click the **Font Color button arrow**, and then in the fifth column, click the first color—**Blue, Accent 1**. Apply **Middle Align** and **Center** to the cell.

5 ▶ Click cell **B10**. On the **FORMULAS tab**, in the **Function Library group**, click **More Functions**, and then display the list of **Statistical** functions. Click **COUNTIF**.

a. As the range, type **e14:e68** which is the range with the color of each item. Click in the **Criteria** box, type **Yellow** and then click **OK** to calculate the number of yellow rose types.

(Project 2C Roses continues on the next page)

b. Click cell **G14**. On the **FORMULAS tab**, in the **Function Library group**, click **Logical**, and then on the list, click **IF**. If necessary, drag the title bar of the **Function Arguments** dialog box up or down so that you can view **row 14** on your screen.

c. With the insertion point in the **Logical_test** box, click cell **A14**, and then type **<40** Press ⎯Tab⎯ to move the insertion point to the **Value_if_true** box, and then type **Order** Press ⎯Tab⎯ to move the insertion point to the **Value_if_false** box, type **OK** and then click **OK**. Using the fill handle, copy the function in cell **G14** down through cell **G68**.

6 ▸ With the range **G14:G68** selected, on the **HOME tab**, in the **Styles group**, click **Conditional Formatting**. In the list, point to **Highlight Cells Rules**, and then click **Text that Contains**.

a. In the **Text That Contains** dialog box, with the insertion point blinking in the first box, type **Order** and then in the second box, click the arrow. On the list, click **Custom Format**.

b. In the **Format Cells** dialog box, on the **Font tab**, under **Font style**, click **Bold Italic**. Click the **Color arrow**, and then under **Theme Colors**, in the fourth column, click the first color—**Blue-Gray, Text 2**. Click **OK** two times to apply the font color, bold, and italic to the cells that contain the word *Order*.

c. Select the range **A14:A68**. In the **Styles group**, click **Conditional Formatting**. In the list, point to **Data Bars**, and then under **Gradient Fill**, click **Red Data Bar**. Click anywhere to cancel the selection.

d. Select the range **E14:E68**. On the **HOME tab**, in the **Editing group**, click **Find & Select**, and then click **Replace**. In the **Find and Replace** dialog box, in the **Find what** box, type **Deep Burgundy** and then in the **Replace with** box type **Burgundy** Click **Replace All** and then click **OK**. In the lower right corner of the **Find and Replace** dialog box, click **Close**.

e. Scroll down as necessary, and then click cell **A70**. Type **Edited by Maria Rios** and then press ⎯Enter⎯. With cell **A71** as the active cell, on the **FORMULAS tab**, in the **Function Library group**, click **Date & Time**. In the list of functions, click **NOW**, and then click **OK** to enter the current date and time. **Save** your workbook.

7 ▸ Click any cell in the data below row 13. Click the **INSERT tab**, and then in the **Tables group**, click **Table**. In the **Create Table** dialog box, be sure the **My table has headers** check box is selected, and then click **OK**. On the **DESIGN tab**, in the **Table Styles group**, click **More** ⎯▾⎯ and then under **Light**, locate and click **Table Style Light 9**.

a. In the header row of the table, click the **Retail Price arrow**, and then from the menu, click **Sort Smallest to Largest**. Click the **Color arrow**. On the menu, click the **(Select All)** check box to clear all the check boxes. Scroll as necessary and then select only the **Red** check box. Click OK.

b. Click anywhere in the table. On the **DESIGN tab**, in the **Table Style Options group**, select the **Total Row** check box. Click cell **A69**, click the arrow that displays to the right of cell **A69**, and then click **Sum**. In cell **B11**, type the result **13** and then press ⎯Tab⎯. In cell **C11**, type **(595 total items in stock)** and then press ⎯Enter⎯.

c. In the header row of the table, click the **Color arrow** and then click **Clear Filter From "Color"** to redisplay all of the data. Click anywhere in the table. Click the **DESIGN tab**, in the **Table Style Options group**, clear the **Total Row** check box, and then in the **Tools group**, click **Convert to Range**. Click **Yes**.

8 ▸ On the **PAGE LAYOUT tab**, in the **Themes group**, click **Themes** and then click the **Ion** theme. Change the **Orientation** to **Landscape**.

a. In the **Page Setup group**, click **Margins**, and then click **Custom Margins** to display the **Page Setup** dialog box.

b. On the **Margins tab**, under **Center on page**, select the **Horizontally** check box. On the **Header/Footer tab**, display the **Custom Footer**, and then in the **Left section**, insert the file name. Click **OK** two times.

c. In the **Page Setup** group, click **Print Titles** to redisplay the **Page Setup** dialog box. Under **Print titles**, click in the **Rows to repeat at top** box, and then at the right, click **Collapse Dialog**. From the **row heading area**, select **row 13**, and then click **Expand Dialog**. Click **OK** to print the column titles in row 13 at the top of every page.

d. Press ⎯Ctrl⎯ + ⎯F2⎯ to display the **Print Preview**. At the bottom of the **Settings group**, click **No Scaling**, and

(Project 2C Roses continues on the next page)

CHAPTER REVIEW

then on the displayed list, point to **Fit All Columns on One Page**.

e. On the left, click **Info**, and then in the lower right corner, click **Show All Properties**. As the **Tags**, type **inventory, Pasadena, roses** In the **Subject** box, type your course name and section number. Be sure your name displays as the author.

END | You have completed Project 2C

9 **Save** your workbook. Print or submit electronically as directed by your instructor. If required by your instructor, print or create an electronic version of your worksheets with formulas displayed by using the instructions in Excel Project 1A, and then Close Excel without saving so that you do not save the changes you made to print formulas.

CHAPTER REVIEW

Skills Review | Project 2D Canada

In the following Skills Review, you will edit a workbook that summarizes sales in the Eastern and Western region of Canada. Your completed workbook will look similar to Figure 2.56.

PROJECT FILES

For Project 2D, you will need the following file:

e02D_Canada

You will save your workbook as:

Lastname_Firstname_2D_Canada

PROJECT RESULTS

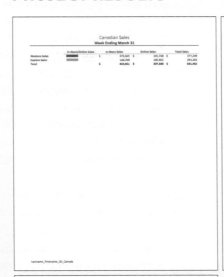

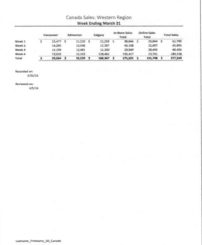

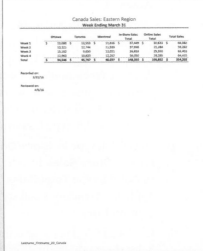

FIGURE 2.56

(Project 2D Canada continues on the next page)

CHAPTER REVIEW

1 Start Excel. From your student files, locate and open **e02D_Canada**. Save the file in your **Excel Chapter 2** folder as **Lastname_Firstname_2D_Canada**

a. Point to the **Sheet1 tab**, and then double-click to select the sheet tab name. Type **Western Sales** and then press Enter.

b. Point to the **Sheet2 tab**, right-click, and then from the shortcut menu, click **Rename**. Type **Eastern Sales** and press Enter.

c. Point to the **Western Sales sheet tab** and right-click. On the shortcut menu, point to **Tab Color**, and then in the last column, click the first color—**Green, Accent 6**. Change the **Tab Color** of the **Eastern Sales** sheet tab to **Blue, Accent 5**.

d. Click the **Western Sales sheet tab**, and then click cell **A13**. On the **HOME tab**, in the **Number group**, click the **Number Format arrow**. At the bottom of the list, click **More Number Formats** to display the **Number tab** of the **Format Cells** dialog box. Click the **3/14/12** type, and then click **OK**.

e. Click cell **A16**, type **4/5/16** and then press Enter. Click cell **A13**, and then on the **HOME tab**, in the **Clipboard group**, click **Format Painter**. Click cell **A16** to copy the date format from cell **A13** to cell **A16**.

f. Click cell **A1**. In the **Editing group**, click **Clear**, and then click **Clear Formats**.

g. Select the range **A5:A16**. On the **HOME tab**, in the **Clipboard group**, click **Copy**. At the bottom of the workbook window, click the **Eastern Sales sheet tab** to make it the active worksheet. Right-click cell **A5**, and then under **Paste Options**, click the first button—**Paste**. Display the **Western Sales** sheet. Press Esc to cancel the moving border.

2 With the **Western Sales** sheet active, make cell **A1** the active cell. Point to the sheet tab, right-click, and then on the shortcut menu, click **Select All Sheets**. Verify that *[Group]* displays in the title bar.

a. **Merge & Center** the text in cell **A1** across the range **A1:G1**, and then apply the **Title** cell style. Select **columns A:G**, and then set their widths to **100 pixels**.

b. Click cell **A2**, type **Week Ending March 31** and then on the **Formula Bar**, click the **Enter** button to keep cell **A2** as the active cell. **Merge & Center**

the text across the range **A2:G2**, and then apply the **Heading 1** cell style.

c. Select the range **B4:G4**, and then apply the **Heading 3** cell style. In the **Alignment group**, click **Center**, **Middle Align**, and **Wrap Text**.

d. With the sheets still grouped and the **Western Sales** sheet active, click cell **E5**. On the **HOME tab**, in the **Editing group**, click **AutoSum**, and then press Enter. Click cell **E5**, and then drag the fill handle down to copy the formula through cell **E8**.

e. Click cell **G5**, type **=** click cell **E5**, type **+** click cell **F5**, and then press Enter. Copy the formula down through cell **G8**. In cell **A9**, type **Total** Select the range **B5:G9**, and then hold down Alt and press = to enter the SUM function for all the columns. Select the range **A5:A9**, and then apply the **Heading 4** cell style.

f. Select the range **B5:G5**, hold down Ctrl, and then select the range **B9:G9**. Apply the **Accounting Number Format** and decrease the decimal places to zero. Select the range **B6:G8**, and then apply **Comma Style** with zero decimal places. Select the range **B9:G9**, and then apply the **Total** cell style.

3 Click the **Eastern Sales sheet tab** to cancel the grouping and display the second worksheet.

a. To the right of the **Eastern Sales sheet tab**, click the **New sheet** button. **Rename** the new worksheet tab **Summary** and then change the **Tab Color** to **Gold, Accent 4**.

b. Widen **columns A:E** to **150** pixels. In cell **A1**, type **Canadian Sales** and then **Merge & Center** the title across the range **A1:E1**. Apply the **Title** cell style. In cell **A2**, type **Week Ending March 31** and then **Merge & Center** the text across the range **A2:E2**. Apply the **Heading 1** cell style. In cell **A5**, type **Western Sales** and in cell **A6**, type **Eastern Sales**

c. In cell **B4**, type **In-Store/Online Sales** and in cell **C4**, type **In-Store Sales** In cell **D4**, type **Online Sales** and in cell **E4**, type **Total Sales** Select the range **B4:E4**, apply the **Heading 3** cell style, and then **Center** these column titles.

d. Click cell **C5**. Type **=** and then click the **Western Sales sheet tab**. In the **Western Sales** worksheet, click cell **E9**, and then press Enter. Click cell **D5**. Type **=** and

(Project 2D Canada continues on the next page)

CHAPTER REVIEW

then click the **Western Sales sheet tab**. Click cell **F9**, and then press Enter.

e. By using the same technique, in cells **C6** and **D6**, insert the total **In-Store Sales** and **Online Sales** data from the **Eastern Sales** worksheet.

f. Select the range **C5:E6**, and then click **AutoSum** to total the two rows. In cell **A7**, type **Total** Select the range **C5:E6** again. In the lower right corner of the selection, click the **Quick Analysis** button, click **Totals**, and then click the first **Sum** button. Recall there are many ways to sum a group of cells.

g. Select the nonadjacent ranges **C5:E5** and **C7:E7**, and then apply **Accounting Number Format** with zero decimal places. Select the range **C6:E6**, and then apply **Comma Style** with zero decimal places. Select the range **C7:E7**, and then apply the **Total** cell style. Select the range **A5:A7** and apply the **Heading 4** cell style.

h. Click cell **B5**. On the **INSERT tab**, in the **Sparklines group**, click **Column**. In the **Create Sparklines** dialog box, with the insertion point blinking in the **Data Range** box, select the range **C5:D5** and then click **OK**.

i. Click cell **B6**, and then insert a **Column Sparkline** for the range **C6:D6**. With the **Eastern Sales** sparkline selected, in the **Style group**, click More ▼. Apply the second style in the third row—**Sparkline Style Accent 2, (no dark or light)**.

4 ▶ Point to the **Summary sheet tab**, hold down the left mouse button to display a small black triangle, and drag

to the left until the triangle and mouse pointer are to the left of the **Western Sales sheet tab**, and then release the left mouse button to move the sheet to the first position in the workbook.

a. Be sure the **Summary** worksheet is the active sheet, and then press Ctrl + Home to move to cell **A1**. Point to the **Summary sheet tab**, right-click, and then click **Select All Sheets** to display [*Group*] in the title bar. On the **PAGE LAYOUT tab**, in the **Page Setup group**, click **Margins**, and then click **Custom Margins** to display the **Page Setup** dialog box. On the **Margins tab**, center the worksheets **Horizontally**. On the **Header/Footer tab**, insert the file name in the **left section** of the footer.

b. Display the **Print Preview** of the worksheets. Under **Settings**, click **No Scaling**, and then click **Fit All Columns on One Page**. Use the **Next** button to view all three worksheets.

c. On the left, click **Info**, and then in the lower right corner of the screen, click **Show All Properties**. As the **Tags**, type **Canada, sales** In the **Subject** box, type your course name and section number. Be sure your name displays as the author.

d. On the left, click **Save**. Print or submit electronically as directed by your instructor. If required by your instructor, print or create an electronic version of your worksheets with formulas displayed by using the instructions in Excel Project 1A, and then **Close** Excel without saving so that you do not save the changes you made to print formulas.

END | You have completed Project 2D

CONTENT-BASED ASSESSMENTS

Mastering Excel | Project 2E Plants

In the following project, you will edit a worksheet detailing the current inventory of plants at the Pasadena facility. Your completed worksheet will look similar to Figure 2.57.

Apply 2A skills from these Objectives:

1. Use Flash Fill and the SUM, AVERAGE, MEDIAN, MIN, and MAX Functions

2. Move Data, Resolve Error Messages, and Rotate Text

3. Use COUNTIF and IF Functions and Apply Conditional Formatting

4. Use Date & Time Functions and Freeze Panes

5. Create, Sort, and Filter an Excel Table

6. View, Format, and Print a Large Worksheet

PROJECT FILES

For Project 2E, you will need the following file:

e02E_Plants

You will save your workbook as:

Lastname_Firstname_2E_Plants

PROJECT RESULTS

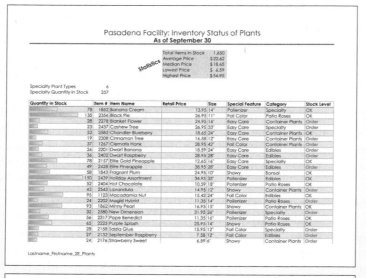

FIGURE 2.57

(Project 2E Plants continues on the next page)

CONTENT-BASED ASSESSMENTS

1 Start Excel. From your student files, locate and open **e02E_Plants**, and then **Save** the file in your **Excel Chapter 2** folder as **Lastname_Firstname_2E_Plants**

2 To the right of **column B**, insert two new columns to create **new blank columns C and D**. By using **Flash Fill** in the two new columns, split the data in **column B** into a column for *Item #* in **column C** and *Category* in **column D**. As necessary, type **Item #** as the column title in **column C** and **Category** as the column title in **column D**.

3 Delete **column B**. By using the **Cut** and **Paste** commands, cut **column C**—*Category*—and paste it to **column H**, and then delete the empty **column C**. Apply **AutoFit** to **columns A:G**.

4 In cell **B4**, insert a function to calculate the **Total Items in Stock** by summing the **Quantity in Stock** data, and then apply **Comma Style** with zero decimal places to the result. In each cell in the range **B5:B8**, insert functions to calculate the Average, Median, Lowest, and Highest retail prices, and then apply the **Accounting Number Format** to each result.

5 Move the range **A4:B8** to the range **D4:E8**, apply the **40%—Accent4** cell style to the range, and then select **columns D:E** and **AutoFit**. In cell **C6**, type **Statistics** and then select the range **C4:C8**. In the **Format Cells** dialog box, merge the selected cells, and change the text **Orientation** to **25 Degrees**. Format the cell with **Bold**, a **Font Size** of **14 pt**, and then change the **Font Color** to **Blue-Gray, Text 2**. Apply **Middle Align** and **Align Right**.

6 In the **Category** column, **Replace All** occurrences of **Vine Roses** with **Patio Roses** In cell **B10**, use the **COUNTIF** function to count the number of **Specialty** plant types in the **Category** column.

7 In cell **H13**, type **Stock Level** In cell **H14**, enter an **IF** function to determine the items that must be ordered. If the **Quantity in Stock** is less than **50** the **Value_if_true**

is **Order** Otherwise the **Value_if_false** is **OK** Fill the formula down through cell **H42**. Apply **Conditional Formatting** to the **Stock Level** column so that cells that contain the text *Order* are formatted with **Bold Italic** and with a **Color** of **Green, Accent 6**. Apply conditional formatting to the **Quantity in Stock** column by applying a **Gradient Fill Green Data Bar**.

8 Format the range **A13:H42** as a **Table** with headers, and apply the style **Table Style Light 20**. Sort the table from A to Z by **Item Name**, and then filter on the **Category** column to display the **Specialty** types. Display a **Total Row** in the table, and then in cell **A43**, **Sum** the **Quantity in Stock** for the **Specialty** items. Type the result in cell **B11**. Click in the table, and then on the **DESIGN tab**, remove the total row from the table. Clear the **Category** filter, and convert the table to a range.

9 **Merge & Center** the title and subtitle across **columns A:H**, and apply **Title** and **Heading 1** styles respectively. Change the theme to **Mesh**, and then select and **AutoFit** all the columns. Set the orientation to **Landscape**. In the **Page Setup** dialog box, center the worksheet **Horizontally**, insert a custom footer in the **left section** with the file name, and set **row 13** to repeat at the top of each page. Display the **Print Preview**. Apply the **Fit All Columns on One Page** setting.

10 As the **Tags**, type **plants inventory, Pasadena** As the **Subject**, type your course name and section number. Be sure your name displays as the **Author**. In Backstage view, on the left click **Save**, and then print or submit electronically as directed. If required by your instructor, print or create an electronic version of your worksheet with formulas displayed by using the instructions in Project 1A, and then close Excel without saving so that you do not save the changes you made to print formulas.

END | You have completed Project 2E

CONTENT-BASED ASSESSMENTS

Mastering Excel Project 2F Bonus

In the following project, you will edit a workbook that summarizes the compensation for the commercial salespersons who qualified for bonuses in the Western and Eastern Canadian regions. Your completed worksheets will look similar to Figure 2.58.

Apply 2B skills from these Objectives:

7 Navigate a Workbook and Rename Worksheets

8 Enter Dates, Clear Contents, and Clear Formats

9 Copy and Paste by Using the Paste Options Gallery

10 Edit and Format Multiple Worksheets at the Same Time

11 Create a Summary Sheet with Column Sparklines

12 Format and Print Multiple Worksheets in a Workbook

PROJECT FILES

For Project 2F, you will need the following file:

e02F_Bonus

You will save your workbook as:

Lastname_Firstname_2F_Bonus

PROJECT RESULTS

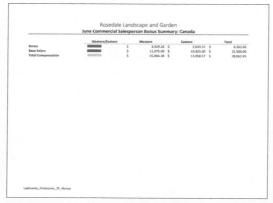

FIGURE 2.58

(Project 2F Bonus continues on the next page)

CONTENT-BASED ASSESSMENTS

1 Start Excel. From your student files, open **e02F_Bonus**, and then save the file in your **Excel Chapter 2** folder as **Lastname_Firstname_2F_Bonus**

2 Rename **Sheet1** as **Western** and change the **Tab Color** to **Brown, Accent 2**. Rename **Sheet2** as **Eastern** and change the **Tab Color** to **Orange, Accent 1**.

3 Click the **Western sheet tab** to make it the active sheet, and then group the worksheets. In cell **A1**, type **Rosedale Landscape and Garden** and then **Merge & Center** the text across the range **A1:F1**. Apply the **Title** cell style. **Merge & Center** the text in cell **A2** across the range **A2:F2**, and then apply the **Heading 3** cell style.

4 With the sheets still grouped, in cell **D5** calculate the **Bonus** for *Reid* by multiplying the **Sales Eligible for Bonus** times the **Bonus Rate**. Copy the formula down through cell **D8**. In cell **F5**, calculate **Total Compensation** by summing the **Bonus** and **Base Salary** for *Reid*. Copy the formula down through the cell **F8**.

5 In **row 9**, sum the columns for **Sales Eligible for Bonus**, **Bonus**, **Base Salary**, and **Total Compensation**. Apply the **Accounting Number Format** with two decimal places to the appropriate cells in **row 5** and **row 9** (do not include the percentages). Apply the **Comma Style** with two decimal places to the appropriate cells in **rows 6:8** (do not include the percentages). Apply the **Total** cell style to the appropriate cells in the Total row.

6 Click the **Eastern** sheet tab to ungroup the sheets, and then insert a new worksheet. Change the sheet name to **Summary** and then change the **Tab Color** to **Brown, Text 2**. Widen **column A** to 210 pixels, widen **columns B:E** to 155 pixels, and then move the **Summary** sheet so that it is the first sheet in the workbook. In cell **A1** of the **Summary** sheet, type **Rosedale Landscape and Garden** and then **Merge & Center** the title across the range **A1:E1**. Apply the **Title** cell style. In cell **A2**, type **June Commercial Salesperson Bonus Summary: Canada** and then **Merge & Center** the text across the range **A2:E2**. Apply the **Heading 1** cell style.

7 In the range **A5:A7**, type the following row titles and then apply the **Heading 4** cell style:

Bonus

Base Salary

Total Compensation

8 In the range **B4:E4**, type the following column titles, and then **Center** and apply the **Heading 3** cell style.

Western/Eastern

Western

Eastern

Total

9 In cell **C5**, enter a formula that references cell **D9** in the **Western** worksheet so that the total bonus amount for the Western region displays in **C5**. Create similar formulas to enter the total **Base Salary** for the Western region in cell **C6**. Using the same technique, enter formulas in the range **D5:D6** so that the **Eastern** totals display.

10 Sum the **Bonus** and **Base Salary** rows, and then calculate **Total Compensation** for the **Western**, **Eastern**, and **Total** columns.

11 In cell **B5**, insert a **Column Sparkline** for the range **C5:D5**. In cells **B6** and **B7**, insert **Column** sparklines for the appropriate ranges to compare Western totals with Eastern totals. To the sparkline in cell **B5**, apply the second style in the third row—**Sparkline Style Accent 2, (no dark or light)**. To the sparkline in cell **B6**, apply the first style in the fifth row—**Sparkline Style Dark #1**. To the sparkline in cell **B7**, apply the first style in the fourth row—**Sparkline Style Accent 1, Lighter 40%**.

12 Group the three worksheets, and then in the **Page Setup** dialog box, center the worksheets **Horizontally** on the page, and insert a **Custom Footer** in the **left section** with the file name. Change the **Orientation** to **Landscape**.

13 As the **Tags**, type **June, bonus, compensation** As the **Subject**, type your course name and section number. Be sure your name displays as the **Author**. Click **Save**, and then print or submit your workbook electronically as directed. If required by your instructor, print or create an electronic version of your worksheets with formulas displayed by using the instructions in Project 1A, and then close Excel without saving so that you do not save the changes you made to print formulas.

END | You have completed Project 2F

CONTENT-BASED ASSESSMENTS

Mastering Excel Project 2G Inventory

In the following project, you will edit a worksheet that summarizes the inventory of bulbs and trees at the Pasadena facility. Your completed workbook will look similar to Figure 2.59.

Apply a combination of 2A and 2B skills:

1 Use Flash Fill and the SUM, AVERAGE, MEDIAN, MIN, and MAX Functions

2 Move Data, Resolve Error Messages, and Rotate Text

3 Use COUNTIF and IF Functions and Apply Conditional Formatting

4 Use Date & Time Functions and Freeze Panes

5 Create, Sort, and Filter an Excel Table

6 View, Format and Print a Large Worksheet

7 Navigate a Workbook and Rename Worksheets

8 Enter Dates, Clear Contents, and Clear Formats

9 Copy and Paste by Using the Paste Options Gallery

10 Edit and Format Multiple Worksheets at the Same Time

11 Create a Summary Sheet with Column Sparklines

12 Format and Print Multiple Worksheets in a Workbook

PROJECT FILES

For Project 2G, you will need the following file:

e02G_Inventory

You will save your workbook as

Lastname_Firstname_2G_Inventory

PROJECT RESULTS

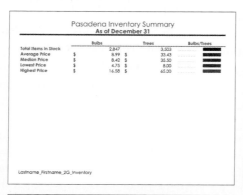

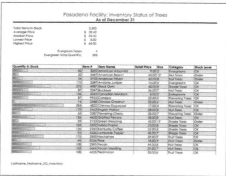

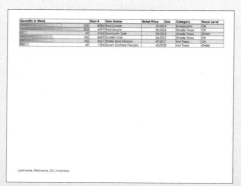

FIGURE 2.59

(Project 2G Inventory continues on the next page)

CONTENT-BASED ASSESSMENTS

1 Start Excel. From your student files, open **e02G_ Inventory**. Save the file in your **Excel Chapter 2** folder as **Lastname_Firstname_2G_Inventory.**

2 Change the **Theme** to **Slice**. Rename **Sheet1** as **Bulbs** and **Sheet2** as **Trees** Click the **Bulbs sheet tab** to make it the active sheet.

3 To the right of **column B**, insert two new columns to create **new blank columns C and D**. By using **Flash Fill** in the two new columns, split the data in **column B** into a column for *Item #* in **column C** and *Category* in **column D**. As necessary, type **Item #** as the column title in **column C** and **Category** as the column title in **column D**.

4 Delete **column B**. By using the **Cut** and **Paste** commands, cut **column C**—*Category*—and paste it to **column G**, and then delete the empty **column C**. Apply **AutoFit** to **columns A:F**.

5 Display the **Trees** worksheet, and then repeat Steps 3 and 4 on this worksheet.

6 Make the following calculations in each of the two worksheets *without* grouping the sheets:

- In cell **B4**, enter a function to sum the **Quantity in Stock** data, and then apply **Comma Style** with zero decimal places to the result.

- In cells **B5:B8**, enter formulas to calculate the Average, Median, Lowest, and Highest retail prices, and then apply the **Accounting Number Format.**

7 In each of the two worksheets, make the following calculations *without* grouping the sheets:

- In cell **B10**, enter a COUNTIF function to determine how many different types of **Tulips** are in stock on the **Bulbs** sheet and how many different types of **Evergreens** are in stock on the **Trees** worksheet.

- In cell **G14** type **Stock Level** In cell **G15**, enter an IF function to determine the items that must be ordered. If the **Quantity in Stock** is less than **75** the **Value_if_true** is **Order** Otherwise the **Value_ if_false** is **OK** Fill the formula down through all the rows.

- Apply **Conditional Formatting** to the **Stock Level** column so that cells that contain the text *Order* are formatted with **Bold Italic** with a **Font Color** of **Dark Blue, Text 2.** Apply **Gradient Fill Blue Data Bars** to the **Quantity in Stock** column.

8 In the **Bulbs** sheet, format the range **A14:G42** as a table with headers and apply **Table Style Light 20**. Insert a **Total Row**, filter by **Category** for **Tulips**, and then **Sum** the **Quantity in Stock** column. Record the result in cell **B11**.

9 Select the table, clear the filter, **Sort** the table on the **Item Name** column from **A to Z**, remove the **Total Row**, and then convert the table to a range. On the **Page Layout tab**, set **Print Titles** so that **row 14** repeats at the top of each page.

10 In the **Trees** sheet, format the range **A14:G42** as a table with headers and apply **Table Style Light 19**. Insert a **Total Row**, filter by **Category** for **Evergreens**, and then **Sum** the **Quantity in Stock** column. Record the result in cell **B11**.

11 Select the table, clear the filter, **Sort** the table on the **Item Name** column from **A to Z**, remove the **Total Row**, and then convert the table to a range.

12 On the **Page Layout tab**, set **Print Titles** so that **row 14** repeats at the top of each page, and then **Save** your workbook. **Group** the two worksheets. Center the title in cell **A1** across the range **A1:G1** and apply the **Title** cell style. Center the subtitle in cell **A2** across the range **A2:G2** and apply the **Heading 1** cell style. **Center** the worksheets **Horizontally**, change the **Orientation** to **Landscape**, display the **Print Preview**, and then change the **Settings** to **Fit All Columns on One Page.**

13 In **Backstage** view, on the left click **Save**, and then click the **Trees sheet tab** to cancel the grouping. Insert a new worksheet. Change the sheet name to **Summary** and then widen **columns A:D** to **170** pixels. Move the **Summary** sheet so that it is the first sheet in the workbook. In cell **A1**, type **Pasadena Inventory Summary** and then **Merge & Center** the title across **A1:D1**. Apply the **Title** cell style. In cell **A2**, type **As of December 31** and then **Merge & Center** the text across the range **A2:D2**. Apply the **Heading 1** cell style.

14 On the **Bulbs sheet**, **Copy** the range **A4:A8**. Display the **Summary sheet** and **Paste** the selection to cell **A5**. Apply the **Heading 4** cell style to the selection. In the **Summary sheet**, in cell **B4**, type **Bulbs** In cell **C4** type **Trees** In cell **D4** type **Bulbs/Trees** and then **Center** the column titles. Apply the **Heading 3** cell style.

(Project 2G Inventory continues on the next page)

CONTENT-BASED ASSESSMENTS

15 In cell **B5**, enter a formula that references cell **B4** in the **Bulbs sheet** so that the **Bulbs Total Items in Stock** displays in **B5**. Create similar formulas to enter the **Average Price**, **Median Price**, **Lowest Price**, and **Highest Price** from the **Bulbs sheet** into the **Summary** sheet in the range **B6:B9**. Enter formulas in the range **C5:C9** that reference the appropriate cells in the **Trees** worksheet.

16 To the range **B5:C5**, apply **Comma Style** with zero decimal places, and to the range **B6:C9**, apply **Accounting Number Format**. In cells **D5**, **D6**, **D7**, **D8**, and **D9**, insert **Column** sparklines using the values in the *Bulbs* and *Trees* columns. Format each sparkline using the first five Sparkline styles in the first row.

17 Center the **Summary** worksheet **Horizontally** and change the **Orientation** to **Landscape**. **Group** the worksheets and insert a footer in the left section with the **File Name**. As the **Tags**, type **Pasadena inventory** As the **Subject**, type your course name and section number. Be sure your name displays as the **Author**.

18 In **Backstage** view, on the left click **Save**, and then print or submit electronically as directed. If required by your instructor, print or create an electronic version of your worksheet with formulas displayed by using the instructions in Project 1A, and then close Excel without saving so that you do not save the changes you made to print formulas.

END | You have completed Project 2G

CONTENT-BASED ASSESSMENTS

Apply a combination of the 2A and 2B skills.

GO! Fix It	Project 2H Planters	Online
GO! Make It	Project 2I Salary	Online
GO! Solve It	Project 2J Sod	Online
GO! Solve It	Project 2K Products	

PROJECT FILES

For Project 2K, you will need the following file:

e02K_Products

You will save your workbook as:

Lastname_Firstname_2K_Products

From your student data files, open the file e02K_Products and save it as **Lastname_Firstname_2K_Products** This workbook contains two worksheets: one for U.S. sales data by product and one for Canadian sales data by product. Complete the two worksheets by calculating totals by product and by month. Then calculate the Percent of Total for all products by dividing the Product Total by the Monthly Total, using absolute cell references as necessary. Format the percentages with two decimal places and center in the cells. Format the worksheets attractively and apply financial formatting. Insert a new worksheet that summarizes the monthly totals for the U.S. and Canada. Enter the months as the column titles and the countries as the row titles. Include a Product Total column and a column for sparklines titled **April/May/June** Format the Summary worksheet attractively with a title and subtitle, insert column sparklines that compare the months, and apply financial formatting. Include the file name in the footer, add appropriate document properties, and submit as directed.

(Project 2K Products continues on the next page)

CONTENT-BASED ASSESSMENTS

Performance Level

	Exemplary: You consistently applied the relevant skills	Proficient: You sometimes, but not always, applied the relevant skills	Developing: You rarely or never applied the relevant skills
Create formulas	All formulas are correct and are efficiently constructed.	Formulas are correct but not always constructed in the most efficient manner.	One or more formulas are missing or incorrect; or only numbers were entered.
Create Summary worksheet	Summary worksheet created properly.	Summary worksheet was created but the data, sparklines, or formulas were incorrect.	No Summary worksheet was created.
Format attractively and appropriately	Formatting is attractive and appropriate.	Adequately formatted but difficult to read or unattractive.	Inadequate or no formatting.

Performance Criteria

END | You have completed Project 2K

OUTCOMES-BASED ASSESSMENTS

RUBRIC

The following outcomes-based assessments are open-ended assessments. That is, there is no specific correct result; your result will depend on your approach to the information provided. Make Professional Quality your goal. Use the following scoring rubric to guide you in how to approach the problem and then to evaluate how well your approach solves the problem.

The *criteria*—Software Mastery, Content, Format and Layout, and Process—represent the knowledge and skills you have gained that you can apply to solving the problem. The *levels of performance*—Professional Quality, Approaching Professional Quality, or Needs Quality Improvements—help you and your instructor evaluate your result.

	Your completed project is of Professional Quality if you:	Your completed project is Approaching Professional Quality if you:	Your completed project Needs Quality Improvements if you:
1-Software Mastery	Choose and apply the most appropriate skills, tools, and features and identify efficient methods to solve the problem.	Choose and apply some appropriate skills, tools, and features, but not in the most efficient manner.	Choose inappropriate skills, tools, or features, or are inefficient in solving the problem.
2-Content	Construct a solution that is clear and well organized, contains content that is accurate, appropriate to the audience and purpose, and is complete. Provide a solution that contains no errors in spelling, grammar, or style.	Construct a solution in which some components are unclear, poorly organized, inconsistent, or incomplete. Misjudge the needs of the audience. Have some errors in spelling, grammar, or style, but the errors do not detract from comprehension.	Construct a solution that is unclear, incomplete, or poorly organized; contains some inaccurate or inappropriate content; and contains many errors in spelling, grammar, or style. Do not solve the problem.
3-Format & Layout	Format and arrange all elements to communicate information and ideas, clarify function, illustrate relationships, and indicate relative importance.	Apply appropriate format and layout features to some elements, but not others. Overuse features, causing minor distraction.	Apply format and layout that does not communicate information or ideas clearly. Do not use format and layout features to clarify function, illustrate relationships, or indicate relative importance. Use available features excessively, causing distraction.
4-Process	Use an organized approach that integrates planning, development, self-assessment, revision, and reflection.	Demonstrate an organized approach in some areas, but not others; or, use an insufficient process of organization throughout.	Do not use an organized approach to solve the problem.

OUTCOMES-BASED ASSESSMENTS

Apply a combination of the 2A and 2B skills.

GO! Think | Project 2L Palms

PROJECT FILES

For Project 2L, you will need the following file:

e02L_Palms

You will save your workbook as:

Lastname_Firstname_2L_Palms

Melanie Castillo, Product Manager for Rosedale Landscape and Garden, has requested a worksheet that summarizes the palm tree inventory data for the month of March. Melanie would like the worksheet to include the total Quantity in Stock and Number of Items for each of the four categories of palm trees, and she would like the items to be sorted from lowest to highest retail price. She would also like a separate column for Item # and for Category.

Edit the workbook to provide Melanie with the information requested, and use the Table feature to find the data requested. Format the worksheet titles and data and include an appropriately formatted table so that the worksheet is professional and easy to read and understand. Insert a footer with the file name and add appropriate document properties. Save the file as **Lastname_Firstname_2L_Palms** and print or submit as directed by your instructor.

END | You have completed Project 2L

GO! Think | Project 2M Contracts — Online

Build from Scratch

You and GO! | Project 2N Annual Expenses — Online

GO! Cumulative Group Project | Project 2O Bell Orchid Hotels — Online

Analyzing Data with Pie Charts, Line Charts, and What-If Analysis Tools

GO! to Work
Video E3

3

PROJECT 3A

OUTCOMES
Present fund data in a pie chart.

PROJECT 3B

OUTCOMES
Make projections by using what-if analysis and present projections in a line chart.

OBJECTIVES

1. Chart Data with a Pie Chart
2. Format a Pie Chart
3. Edit a Workbook and Update a Chart
4. Use Goal Seek to Perform What-If Analysis

OBJECTIVES

5. Design a Worksheet for What-If Analysis
6. Answer What-If Questions by Changing Values in a Worksheet
7. Chart Data with a Line Chart

In This Chapter

In this chapter, you will work with two different types of commonly used charts that make it easy to visualize data. You will create a pie chart in a separate chart sheet to show how the parts of a fund contribute to a total fund. Pie charts are one type of chart you can use to show part-to-whole relationships. You will also practice by using parentheses in a formula, calculate the percentage rate of an increase, answer what-if questions, and then chart data in a line chart to show the flow of data over time and the flow of one value to the next. In this chapter, you will also practice formatting the axes in a line chart.

The projects in this chapter relate to the city of **Pacifica Bay**, a coastal city south of San Francisco. The city's access to major transportation provides both residents and businesses an opportunity to compete in the global marketplace. The city's mission is to create a more beautiful and more economically viable community for its residents. Each year the city welcomes a large number of tourists who enjoy exploring the rocky coastline and seeing the famous landmarks in San Francisco. The city encourages best environmental practices and partners with cities in other countries to promote sound government at the local level.

Enterprise Fund Pie Chart

PROJECT ACTIVITIES

In Activities 3.01 through 3.12, you will edit a worksheet for Michael Larsen, City Manager, that reports the adjusted figures for Enterprise Fund Expenditures for the next fiscal year, and then present the data in a pie chart. Your completed worksheets will look similar to Figure 3.1.

PROJECT FILES

For Project 3A, you will need the following file:

e03A_Enterprise_Fund

You will save your workbook as:

Lastname_Firstname_3A_Enterprise_Fund

PROJECT RESULTS

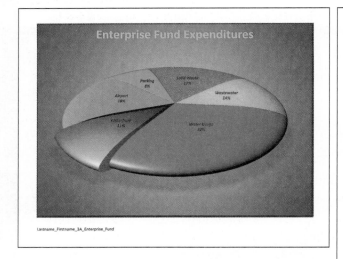

Lastname_Firstname_3A_Enterprise_Fund

Pacifica Bay
Enterprise Fund Expenditures

	Recommended Adjustments		
	Originally Proposed	Adjusted	% of Total Fund Expenditures
Airport	$ 17,610,810	$ 18,121,067	18%
Parking	6,824,865	7,897,526	8%
Solid Waste	18,695,222	17,845,287	18%
Wastewater	12,657,765	13,985,695	14%
Water Usage	30,457,903	32,356,236	32%
Waterfront	10,976,843	10,945,369	11%
Total	$ 97,223,408	$ 101,151,180	

Goal: To Reduce Waterfront Expenditures from 11% to 9% of Total Expenditures

Goal Amount:	$ 9,103,606	9%

Lastname_Firstname_3A_Enterprise_Fund

FIGURE 3.1 Project 3A Enterprise Fund Pie Chart

Video E3-1

A **pie chart** shows the relationship of each part to a whole. The size of each pie slice is equal to its value compared to the total value of all the slices. The pie chart style charts data that is arranged in a single column or single row, and shows the size of items in a single data series proportional to the sum of the items. Whereas a column or bar chart can have two or more data series in the chart, a pie chart can have only one data series.

Consider using a pie chart when you have only one data series to plot, you do not have more than seven categories, and the categories represent parts of a total value.

Activity 3.01 | Calculating Values for a Pie Chart

A **fund** is a sum of money set aside for a specific purpose. In a municipal government like the city of Pacifica Bay, the **general fund** is money set aside for the normal operating activities of the city, such as police, fire, and administering the everyday functions of the city.

Municipal governments also commonly establish an **enterprise fund** to report income and expenditures related to municipal services for which a fee is charged in exchange for goods or services. For example, Pacifica Bay receives income from airport landing fees, parking fees, water usage fees, and rental fees along public beaches, but there are costs—expenditures—related to building and maintaining these facilities and services from which income is received.

1 Start Excel. From the student files that accompany this textbook, open **e03A_Enterprise_Fund**. From **Backstage** view, display the **Save As** dialog box. Navigate to the location where you are storing your projects for this chapter.

2 Create a new folder named **Excel Chapter 3** and open the new folder. In the **File name** box, using your name, type **Lastname_Firstname_3A_Enterprise_Fund** Click **Save** or press Enter.

> The worksheet indicates the originally proposed and adjusted expenditures from the Enterprise Fund for the next fiscal year.

3 Click cell **D5**, and then type = to begin a formula.

4 Click cell **C5**, which is the first value that is part of the total Fund Expenditures, to insert it into the formula. Type **/** to indicate division, and then click cell **C11**, which is the total adjusted expenditures.

> Recall that to determine the percentage by which a value makes up a total, you must divide the value by the total. The result will be a percentage expressed as a decimal.

5 Press F4 to make the reference to the value in cell **C11** absolute, which will enable you to copy the formula. Compare your screen with Figure 3.2.

> Recall that an **absolute cell reference** refers to a cell by its fixed position in the worksheet—the cell reference will not change when you copy the formula. The reference to cell C5 is a **relative cell reference**, because when you copy the formula, you want the reference to change *relative* to its row. Recall also that dollar signs display to indicate that a cell reference is absolute.

FIGURE 3.2

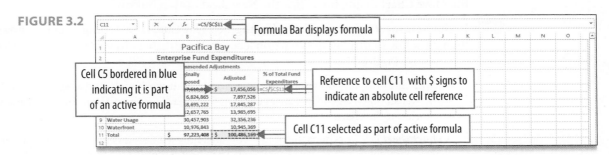

6 On the **Formula Bar**, click **Enter** ✓ to confirm the entry and to keep cell **D5** the active cell. Copy the formula down through cell **D10**, and then compare your screen with Figure 3.3.

FIGURE 3.3

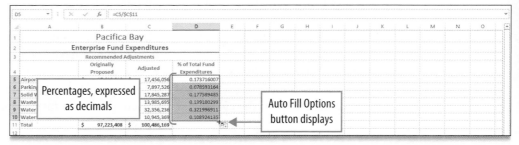

7 With the range **D5:D10** still selected, right-click over the selection, and then on the mini toolbar, click **Percent Style** % and **Center** ☰. Click cell **A1** to cancel the selection, and then **Save** 🖫 your workbook. Compare your screen with Figure 3.4.

FIGURE 3.4

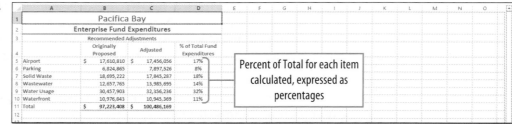

Activity 3.02 | Creating a Pie Chart in a Chart Sheet

1 Select the range **A5:A10**, hold down Ctrl, and then select the range **C5:C10** to select the nonadjacent ranges with the item names and the adjusted expenditure for each item.

> To create a pie chart, you must select two ranges. One range contains the labels for each slice of the pie chart, and the other range contains the values that add up to a total. The two ranges must have the same number of cells and the range with the values should *not* include the cell with the total.

> The item names (Airport, Parking, and so on) are the category names and will identify the slices of the pie chart. Each projected expenditure is a *data point*—a value that originates in a worksheet cell and that is represented in a chart by a *data marker*. In a pie chart, each pie slice is a data marker. Together, the data points form the *data series*—related data points represented by data markers—and determine the size of each pie slice.

2 With the nonadjacent ranges selected, click the **INSERT tab**, and then in the **Charts group**, click **Insert Pie or Doughnut Chart** 🥧 ▾. Under **3-D Pie**, click the chart **3-D Pie** to create the chart on your worksheet and to display the **CHART TOOLS** on the ribbon.

3 On the **DESIGN tab**, at the right end of the ribbon in the **Location group**, click **Move Chart**. In the **Move Chart** dialog box, click the **New sheet** option button.

4 In the **New sheet** box, replace the highlighted text *Chart1* by typing **Expenditures Chart** and then click **OK** to display the chart on a separate worksheet in your workbook. Compare your screen with Figure 3.5.

> The pie chart displays on a separate new sheet in your workbook, and a *legend* identifies the pie slices. Recall that a legend is a chart element that identifies the patterns or colors assigned to the categories in the chart.

> A *chart sheet* is a workbook sheet that contains only a chart; it is useful when you want to view a chart separately from the worksheet data. The sheet tab indicates *Expenditures Chart*.

FIGURE 3.5

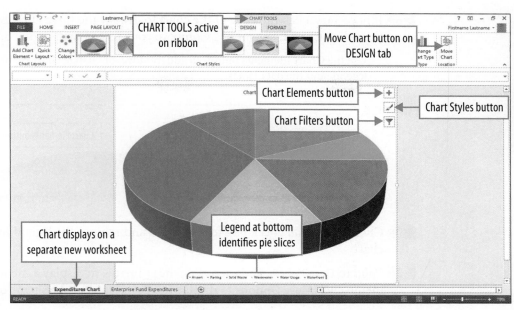

Objective 2 | Format a Pie Chart

Video E3-2

Activity 3.03 | **Formatting a Chart Title by Applying a WordArt Style and Changing Font Size**

1 Click the text *Chart Title* to surround it with selection handles, and then watch the **Formula Bar** as you type **Enterprise Fund Expenditures** Press Enter to create the new chart title in the box.

2 Click the **FORMAT tab**, and then in the **WordArt Styles group**, click **More** ⊽. In the first row, click the last style—**Fill – Gold, Accent 4, Soft Bevel**.

3 With the I pointer, drag to select the chart title text, and then on the mini toolbar, change the **Font Size** to **32**. Click the edge of the chart to deselect the title, and then compare your screen with Figure 3.6.

FIGURE 3.6

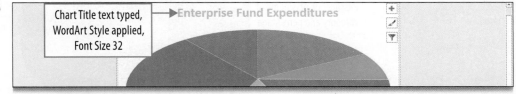

Activity 3.04 | **Formatting Chart Elements by Removing a Legend and Adding and Formatting Data Labels**

In your worksheet, for each budget item, you calculated the percent of the total in column D. These percentages can also be calculated by the Chart feature and added to the pie slices as labels.

1 If necessary, click the edge of the chart to display the three chart buttons on the right, and then click **Chart Elements** ⊞. Compare your screen with Figure 3.7.

Use the Chart Elements button to add, remove, or change chart elements such as the chart title, the legend, and the data labels.

FIGURE 3.7

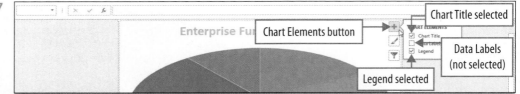

2 Click the **Legend** check box to deselect it and remove the legend from the bottom of the chart.

3 *Point* to **Data Labels**, and then click the ▶ arrow to display a menu. At the bottom of the menu, click **More Options** to display the **Format Data Labels** pane on the right.

The Format Data Labels pane displays and data labels representing the values display on each pie slice.

4 In the **Format Data Labels** pane, under **LABEL OPTIONS**, click as necessary to select the **Category Name** and **Percentage** check boxes. Click to *clear* any other check boxes in this group. Under **Label Position**, click the **Center** option button. Compare your screen with Figure 3.8.

All of the data labels are selected and display both the category name and the percentage. In the worksheet, you calculated the percent of the total in column D. Here, the percentage will be calculated by the Chart feature and added to the chart as a label.

FIGURE 3.8

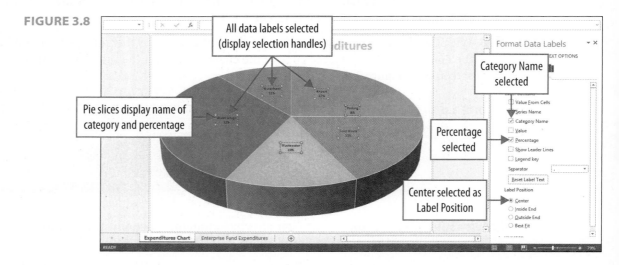

5 Point to any of the selected data labels, right-click to display a shortcut menu, and then click **Font** to display the **Font** dialog box.

6 In the **Font** dialog box, on the **Font tab**, click the **Font style arrow**, and then click **Bold Italic**. In the **Size** box, drag to select *9* and type **11** Compare your screen with Figure 3.9.

FIGURE 3.9

7 ▶ Click **OK** to close the dialog box and apply the formatting to the data labels. In the upper right corner of the **Format Data Labels** pane, click **Close** ☒.

Activity 3.05 │ Formatting a Data Series with 3-D Effects

3-D, which is short for *three-dimensional*, refers to an image that appears to have all three spatial dimensions—length, width, and depth.

1 ▶ In any pie slice, point anywhere outside of the selected label, and then double-click to display the **Format Data Series** pane on the right.

🔄 **ANOTHER WAY**   Right-click outside the label of any pie slice, and then click Format Data Series to display the Format Data Series pane. Or, on the FORMAT tab, in the Current Selection group, click the Chart Elements arrow, click Series 1, and then click Format Selection.

2 ▶ In the **Format Data Series** pane, under **SERIES OPTIONS**, click **Effects** ⬠, and then click **3-D FORMAT**. Compare your screen with Figure 3.10.

FIGURE 3.10

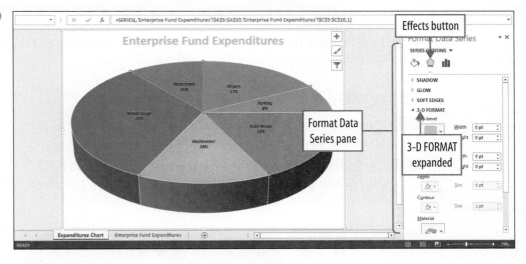

3 ▶ Click the **Top bevel arrow**, and then in the gallery, under **Bevel**, click the first bevel—**Circle**—as shown in Figure 3.11.

Bevel is a shape effect that uses shading and shadows to make the edges of a shape appear to be curved or angled.

FIGURE 3.11

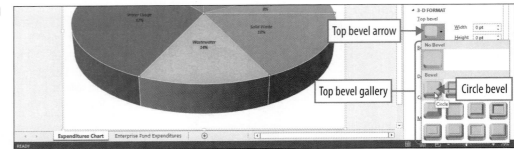

4 Under **Top bevel**, in the **Width** box, select the existing text and type **512 pt** Use the same technique to change the **Height** to **512 pt**

5 Under **Bottom bevel**, use the technique you just practiced to apply a **Circle** bevel with **Width** of **512 pt** and **Height** of **512 pt** Compare your screen with Figure 3.12.

FIGURE 3.12

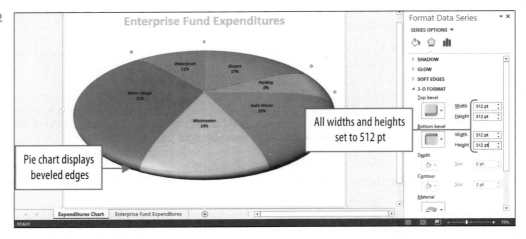

6 In the **Format Data Series** pane, scroll down as necessary, and then click the **Material arrow**. Under **Standard**, click the third material—**Plastic**.

Activity 3.06 | Formatting a Data Series with a Shadow Effect

1 If necessary, in the **Format Data Series** pane, scroll back to the top of the pane, and then click **SHADOW** to expand the options for this effect.

2 Under **SHADOW**, click the **Presets arrow**, use the scroll bar to move to the bottom of the gallery, and then under **Perspective**, in the first row, point to the third effect to display the ScreenTip *Below*. Compare your screen with Figure 3.13.

FIGURE 3.13

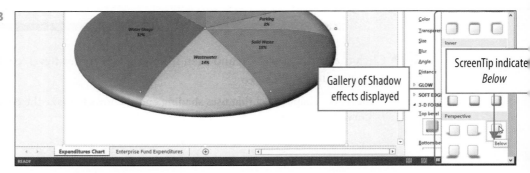

3 Click **Below** to apply the shadow to the chart.

Activity 3.07 | Rotating a Pie Chart by Changing the Angle of the First Slice

The order in which the data series in pie charts are plotted in Excel is determined by the order of the data on the worksheet. To gain a different view of the chart, you can rotate the chart within the 360 degrees of the circle of the pie shape to present a different visual perspective of the chart.

1 Notice the position of the **Water Usage** and **Waterfront** slices in the chart. Then, with the pie chart still selected—sizing handles surround the pie—in the **Format Data Series** pane, under **SERIES OPTIONS**, click **Series Options** ⚏.

2 Under **Angle of first slice**, in the box to the right, drag to select **0°**, type **250** and then press Enter to rotate the chart 250 degrees to the right.

ANOTHER WAY   Drag the slider to 250°, or click the spin box up arrow as many times as necessary.

3 Click **Save** 🖫, and then compare your screen with Figure 3.14.

Rotating the chart can provide a better perspective to the chart. Here, rotating the chart in this manner emphasizes that Water Usage is the largest enterprise fund expenditure.

FIGURE 3.14

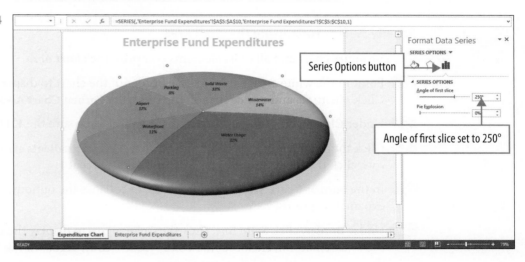

Activity 3.08 | Exploding and Coloring a Pie Slice

You can pull out—*explode*—one or more slices of a pie chart to emphasize a specific slice or slices.

1 In the **Format Data Series** pane, under **SERIES OPTIONS**, notice the slider and box for *Pie Explosion*.

When all the pie slices are selected, as they currently are, you can use this command to explode *all* of the pie pieces away from the center by varying degrees to emphasize all the individual slices of the pie chart. An exploded pie chart visualizes the contribution of each value to the total, while at the same time emphasizing individual values.

2 On the pie chart, click the green **Waterfront** slice to select only that slice, and then on the right, notice that the **Format Data Point** pane displays.

Excel adjusts the pane, depending on what you have selected, so that the commands you need are available.

3 In the **Format Data Point** pane, in the **Point Explosion** box, select the existing text, type **10%** and then press Enter.

4 With the **Waterfront** slice still selected, in the **Format Data Point** pane, under **SERIES OPTIONS**, click **Fill & Line** 🖌, and then click **FILL** to expand its options.

5 Click the **Gradient fill** option button, click the **Preset gradients arrow**, and then in the fourth row, click the last gradient—**Bottom Spotlight – Accent 6**. Click **Save** 🖫, and then compare your screen with Figure 3.15.

FIGURE 3.15

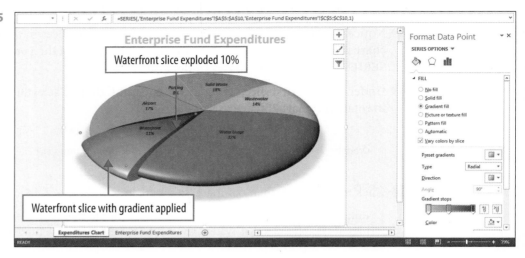

Activity 3.09 | Formatting the Chart Area

The entire chart and all of its elements comprise the *chart area*.

1 Point to the white area just inside the border of the chart to display the ScreenTip *Chart Area*. Click one time, and notice that on the right, the **Format Chart Area** pane displays.

2 Under **CHART OPTIONS**, click **Fill & Line** 🖌, and be sure the **FILL** options are still displayed.

3 Click the **Gradient fill** option button, click the **Preset gradients arrow**, and then in the fourth row, click the first gradient—**Bottom Spotlight – Accent 1**.

4 In the **Format Chart Area** pane, click **FILL** to collapse the options, and then click **BORDER** to expand its options.

5 Under **Border**, click **Solid line**, click the **Color arrow** to display the Outline colors, and then in the fourth column, click the first color—**Blue – Gray, Text 2**. In the **Width** box, drag to select the existing width, and then type **5 pt**

6 Close ☒ the **Format Chart Area** pane, and then click outside of the Chart Area to deselect the chart. Click **Save** 🖫, and then compare your screen with Figure 3.16.

FIGURE 3.16

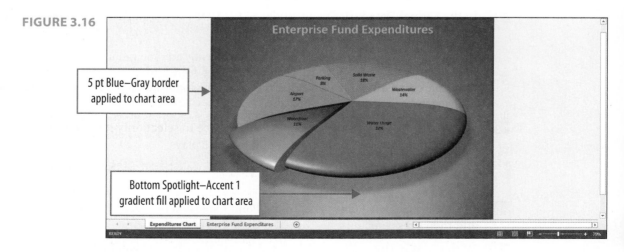

Activity 3.10 | **Editing a Workbook and Updating a Chart**

Video E3-3

If you edit the data in your worksheet, the chart data markers—in this instance the pie slices—will adjust automatically to accurately represent the new values.

1 On the pie chart, notice that *Airport* represents 17% of the total projected expenses.

2 In the sheet tab area at the bottom of the workbook, click the **Enterprise Fund Expenditures tab** to redisplay the worksheet.

3 Click cell **C5**, type **18121067** and then press Enter. Notice that the Accounting Number Format is retained in the cell.

🔄 **ANOTHER WAY**   Double-click the cell to position the insertion point in the cell and edit.

4 Notice that the total in cell **C11** is recalculated to *$101,151,180* and the percentages in **column D** are also recalculated.

5 Display the **Expenditures Chart** sheet. Notice that the pie slices adjust to show the recalculation—*Airport* is now *18%* of the adjusted expenditures. Click **Save** 🖫, and then compare your screen with Figure 3.17.

FIGURE 3.17

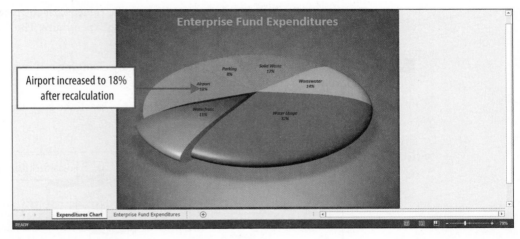

Activity 3.11 | **Using Goal Seek to Perform What-If Analysis**

Video E3-4

The process of changing the values in cells to see how those changes affect the outcome of formulas in your worksheet is referred to as *what-if analysis*. One what-if analysis tool in Excel is *Goal Seek*, which finds the input needed in one cell to arrive at the desired result in another cell.

1 Click the **Enterprise Fund Expenditures sheet tab** to redisplay the worksheet. In cell **A13**, type **Goal: To Reduce Waterfront Expenditures from 11% to 9% of Total Expenditures** **Merge & Center** the text across the range **A13:D13**, and then apply the **Heading 3** Cell Style.

2 In cell **A14**, type **Goal Amount:** and press Enter.

3 Select the range **C10:D10**, right-click over the selection, and then click **Copy**. Point to cell **B14**, right-click, and then under **Paste Options**, click **Paste** 📋.

4 Press Esc to cancel the moving border, click cell **C14**, and then compare your screen with Figure 3.18.

FIGURE 3.18

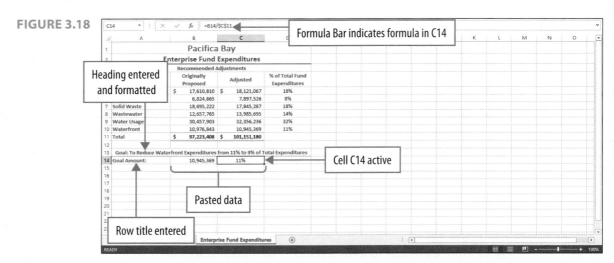

5 Be sure cell **C14** is the active cell. On the **DATA tab**, in the **Data Tools group**, click **What-If Analysis**, and then click **Goal Seek**.

6 In the **Goal Seek** dialog box, notice that the active cell, **C14**, is indicated in the **Set cell** box. Press Tab to move to the **To value** box, and then type **9%**

C14 is the cell in which you want to set a specific value; 9% is the percentage of the total expenditures that is your goal for the Waterfront Expenditure. The Set cell box contains the formula that calculates the information you seek.

7 Press Tab to move the insertion point to the **By changing cell** box, and then click cell **B14**. Compare your screen with Figure 3.19.

Cell B14 contains the value that Excel changes to reach the goal. Excel formats this cell as an absolute cell reference.

FIGURE 3.19

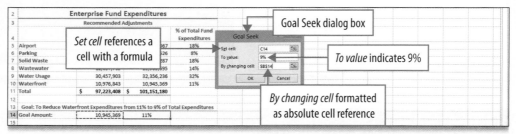

8 Click **OK**. In the displayed **Goal Seek Status** dialog box, click **OK**.

9 Select the range **A14:C14**. On the **HOME tab**, display the **Cell Styles** gallery. Under **Themed Cell Styles**, apply **20% - Accent1**.

10 Click cell **B14**, display the **Cell Styles** gallery again, and then at the bottom, under **Number Format**, click **Currency [0]**.

Use this cell style when you want to apply currency formatting with no decimal places quickly.

11 Press [Ctrl] + [Home], click **Save** 🖫, and then compare your screen with Figure 3.20.

Excel calculates that the city must budget for *$9,103,606* in Waterfront expenditures in order for this item to become 9% of the total projected budget.

FIGURE 3.20

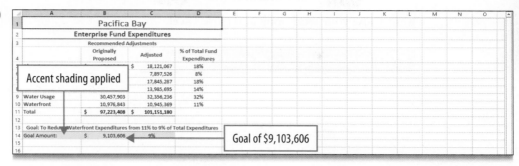

Activity 3.12 | Preparing and Printing a Workbook with a Chart Sheet

1 Click the **PAGE LAYOUT tab**. In the **Page Setup group**, click **Margins**, and then click **Custom Margins**.

2 In the **Page Setup** dialog box, on the **Margins tab**, under **Center on page**, select the **Horizontally** check box.

3 Click the **Header/Footer tab**, and then in the center of the dialog box, click **Custom Footer**. In the **Footer** dialog box, with your insertion point blinking in the **Left section**, on the row of buttons, click **Insert File Name** 📄.

4 Click **OK** two times.

The dotted line indicates the page break as currently formatted.

5 Display the **Expenditures Chart**, which must have its footer formatted separately. In the **Page Setup group**, click the **Dialog Box Launcher** 🔲.

Chart sheets are automatically centered on the page.

6 Click the **Header/Footer tab**, and then in the center of the dialog box, click **Custom Footer**. In the **Footer** dialog box, with your insertion point blinking in the **Left section**, on the row of buttons, click **Insert File Name** 📄.

7 Click **OK** two times. Click the **FILE tab**, and then click **Show All Properties**. As the **Tags**, type **enterprise fund, expenditures** As the **Subject**, type your course name and section number. Be sure your name displays as the author.

8 On the left, click **Save**. Right-click the **Expenditures Chart sheet tab**, and then click **Select All Sheets**. Verify that *[Group]* displays in the title bar.

Recall that by selecting all sheets, you can view all of the workbook pages in Print Preview.

9 Press [Ctrl] + [F2] to display the **Print Preview**. Examine the first page, and then at the bottom of the **Print Preview**, click **Next Page** ▶ to view the second page of your workbook.

N O T E	**Printing a Chart Sheet Uses More Toner**

Printing a chart that displays on a chart sheet will use more toner or ink than a small chart that is part of a worksheet. If you are printing your work, check with your instructor to verify whether or not you should print the chart sheet.

10 On the left, click **Save** to redisplay the workbook.

11 By using the techniques you practiced in Project 1A, print or submit electronically as directed by your instructor. If required by your instructor, print or create an electronic version of your worksheet with formulas displayed.

12 **Close** your workbook and close **Excel**.

END | You have completed Project 3A

GO! with Office Web Apps

Objective | Create a JPEG Photo of a Chart and Upload to a OneNote Web App Notebook

Recall that **OneNote** is a Microsoft application with which you can create a digital notebook that gives you a single location where you can gather and organize information in the form of notes. The OneNote Web App enables you to share your OneNote notebooks on the web.

> **ALERT!** **Working with Web-Based Applications and Services**
>
> Computer programs and services on the web receive continuous updates and improvements, so the steps to complete this web-based activity may differ from the ones shown. You can often look at the screens and the information presented to determine how to complete the activity.

Activity | Creating a JPEG Photo of a Chart and Uploading It to a OneNote Web App Notebook

In this activity, you will create a JPEG image of a chart, and then upload the image to a OneNote Web App notebook.

1 From File Explorer, navigate to your **Excel Chapter 3** folder, and then open your file **Lastname_Firstname_3A_ Enterprise_Fund** workbook. Display the **Expenditures Chart** worksheet.

2 Display the **Start** screen and type **snipping** Click the **Snipping Tool** program to start it.

3 In the Snipping Tool dialog box, click the **New arrow**, and then click **Rectangular Snip**. With the ⊞ pointer, point to the upper left corner of the chart, hold down the left mouse button, and then drag down to the lower right corner of the chart to create a red rectangle around the chart. Release the mouse button. Compare your screen with Figure A.

4 On the **Snipping Tool** mark-up window toolbar, click **Save Snip** 🖫. In the **Save As** dialog box, navigate to your **Excel Chapter 3** folder. Be sure the **Save as type** box displays **JPEG file**. In the **File name** box, type **Lastname_Firstname_EX_3A_Web** and then click **Save**. **Close** ⊠ the **Snipping Tool** window and **Close** ☒ Excel.

5 Launch Internet Explorer, navigate to **www.skydrive.com** and then sign in to your **Microsoft** account. Click your **GO! Web Projects** folder to open it; if necessary, create this folder.

FIGURE A

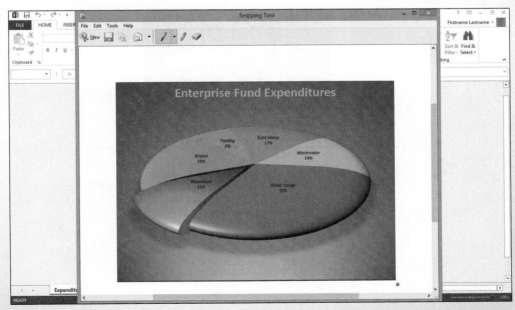

(GO! with Office Web Apps continues on the next page)

6 In the SkyDrive menu bar, click **Create**, and then click **OneNote notebook** to create a new notebook. In the **Name** box, using your own name, type **Lastname_Firstname_EX_3A_Web** and then click **Create**.

7 Point to the text *Untitled Section*, right-click, and then click **New Section**. As the **Section Name**, type **Fund Reports**, and then click **OK**.

8 With the insertion point blinking at the top of the notebook page, type **Chart of Enterprise Fund Expenditures** and press Enter. With the insertion point in the blank page, on the ribbon, click the **INSERT tab**, and then in the **Pictures group**, click **Picture**.

9 In the **Choose File to Upload** dialog box, navigate to your **Excel Chapter 3** folder, and then click the **EX_3A_Web** JPEG file that you created with the Snipping Tool. Click **Open**.

Use this technique to insert a picture to store in a OneNote notebook.

10 With the insertion point blinking below the inserted picture, click the **HOME tab**, and then in the **Tags group**,

click **Tag** to display a list of tags. Click **Important**. Below the picture, click to the right of the tag—a gold star—to position the insertion point there. Type **Attention Council Members: The expenditures from the Enterprise Fund will be discussed at the August City Council meeting.** Compare your screen with Figure B.

A note tag can help you locate specific information quickly. A note tag is both a descriptive term representing a category, such as *Important* or *To Do*, and a related icon that can be associated with a specific note. When this notebook on the SkyDrive is shared with all of the City Council members, each will be able to view the chart and see that it is important.

11 If you are instructed to submit your file, use one of the methods outlined in the Note box below. Then, on the ribbon, click the **FILE tab** and click **Exit**. In the OneNote Web App, there is no Save button because your notebook is being saved automatically.

12 Sign out of your Microsoft account, and then close all windows.

NOTE	Printing or Creating an Electronic File of a Web App OneNote Page

You can use Snipping Tool to create an electronic file or to paste the snip into a document to save and print. In the Office OneNote app, in which you can open this page, you can print pages directly to a printer.

FIGURE B

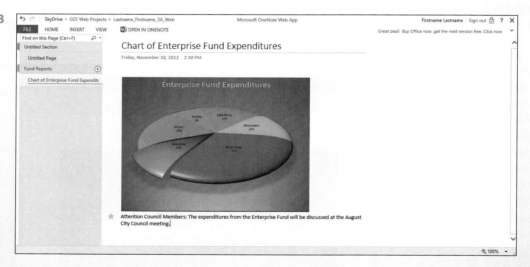

Tourism Spending Projection with Line Chart

PROJECT ACTIVITIES

In Activities 3.13 through 3.20, you will assist Michael Larsen, City Manager, in creating a worksheet to estimate future tourism spending based on two possible growth rates. You will also create a line chart to display past visitor spending. Your resulting worksheet and chart will look similar to Figure 3.21.

PROJECT FILES

For Project 3B, you will need the following files:

New blank Excel file
e03B_Surfers

You will save your workbook as:

Lastname_Firstname_3B_Tourism

PROJECT RESULTS

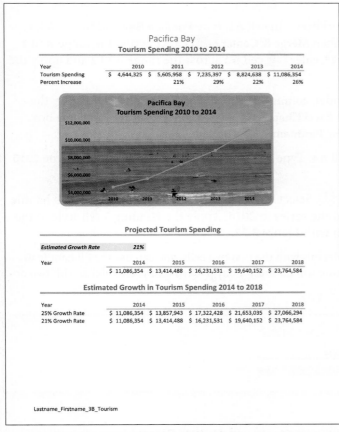

FIGURE 3.21 Project 3B Tourism Spending Projection with Line Chart

Video E3-5

If you change the value in a cell referenced in a formula, Excel automatically recalculates the result of the formula. This means that you can change cell values to see *what* would happen *if* you tried different values. Recall that this process of changing the values in cells to see how those changes affect the outcome of formulas in your worksheet is referred to as what-if analysis.

Activity 3.13 │ Using Parentheses in a Formula to Calculate a Percentage Rate of Increase

Mr. Larsen has the city's tourism spending figures for the recent 5-year period. In each year, tourism spending has increased. In this activity, you will construct a formula to calculate the *percentage rate of increase*—the percent by which one number increases over another number—for each year since 2010. From this information, future tourism spending growth can be estimated.

Excel follows a set of mathematical rules called the ***order of operations***, which has four basic parts:

- Expressions within parentheses are processed first.
- Exponentiation, if present, is performed before multiplication and division.
- Multiplication and division are performed before addition and subtraction.
- Consecutive operators with the same level of precedence are calculated from left to right.

1 ▶ Start Excel and open a new blank workbook. In cell **A1**, type **Pacifica Bay** and in cell **A2**, type **Tourism Spending 2010 to 2014** and then **Merge & Center** ⊞▾ cell **A1** across the range **A1:F1** and apply the **Title** cell style. **Merge & Center** ⊞▾ cell **A2** across the range **A2:F2** and apply the **Heading 1** cell style.

2 ▶ Widen **column A** to **150 pixels** and widen **columns B:F** to **90 pixels**. Press F12 to display the **Save As** dialog box. Navigate to your **Excel Chapter 3** folder, and then in the **File name** box, using your own name, type **Lastname_Firstname_3B_Tourism** Click **Save** or press Enter.

3 ▶ Leave **row 3** blank, and then click cell **A4**. Type **Year** and then press Tab. In cell **B4**, type **2010** and then press Tab.

4 ▶ In cell **C4**, type **2011** and then press Tab. Select the range **B4:C4**, and then drag the fill handle to the right through cell **F4** to extend the series to *2014*. Apply the **Heading 3** cell style to the selected range. Compare your screen with Figure 3.22.

> By establishing a pattern of 1-year intervals with the first two cells, you can use the fill handle to continue the series. The AutoFill feature will do this for any pattern that you establish with two or more cells.

FIGURE 3.22

AutoFill used to fill series of years

5 ▶ In cell **A5**, type **Tourism Spending** and press Enter. In cell **A6**, type **Percent Increase** and press Enter.

6 Click cell **B5**, and then beginning in cell **B5** and pressing Tab to move across the row, enter the following values for tourism spending in the years listed:

2010	2011	2012	2013	2014
4644325	5605958	7235397	8824638	11086354

7 Click cell **C6**. Being sure to include the parentheses, type **=(c5-b5)/b5** and then on the **Formula Bar**, click **Enter** ✓ to keep cell **C6** active; your result is *0.207055492*. Compare your screen with Figure 3.23.

> Recall that as you type, a list of Excel functions that begin with the letter *C* and *B* may briefly display. This is *Formula AutoComplete*, an Excel feature which, after typing an = (equal sign) and the beginning letter or letters of a function name, displays a list of function names that match the typed letter(s). In this instance, the letters represent cell references, *not* the beginning of a function name.

FIGURE 3.23

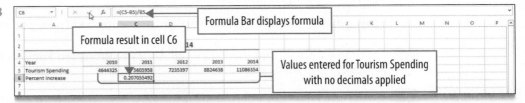

8 With cell **C6** selected, drag the fill handle to the right to copy the formula through cell **F6**.

> Because this formula uses relative cell references—that is, for each year, the formula is the same but the values used are relative to the formula's location—you can copy the formula in this manner. For example, the result for 2012 uses the 2011 value as the base, the result for 2013 uses the 2012 value as the base, and the result for 2014 uses the 2013 value as the base.

9 Select the range **B5:F5**, right-click, on the mini toolbar, click **Accounting Number Format** $ ▾, and then click **Decrease Decimal** 🔟 two times. Select the range **C6:F6**, right-click, and then apply **Percent Style** %. Click cell **C6** and look at the **Formula Bar**.

> The mathematical formula *rate = amount of increase/base* is used to calculated the percentage rate of tourism spending increase from 2010 to 2011. The formula is applied as follows:

> First, determine the *amount of increase* by subtracting the *base*—the starting point represented by the 2010 tourism spending—from the 2011 tourism spending. Therefore, the *amount of increase* = $5,605,958 – $4,644,325 or $961,633. Between 2010 and 2011 tourism spending increased by $961,633. In the formula, this calculation is represented by *C5-B5*.

> Second, calculate the *rate*—what the amount of increase ($961,633) represents as a percentage of the base (2010's tourism spending of $4,644,325). Determine this by dividing the amount of increase ($961,633) by the base ($4,644,325). Therefore $961,633 divided by $4,644,325 is equal to *0.207055492* or, when formatted as a percent and rounded up, 21%.

10 In the **Formula Bar**, locate the parentheses enclosing *C5-B5*.

> Recall that Excel follows a set of mathematical rules called the order of operations, in which expressions within parentheses are processed first, multiplication and division are performed before addition and subtraction, and consecutive operators with the same level of precedence are calculated from left to right.

11 **Save** 💾 your workbook, and then compare your screen with Figure 3.24.

FIGURE 3.24

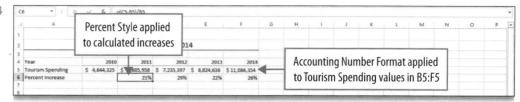

Percent Style applied
to calculated increases

Accounting Number Format applied
to Tourism Spending values in B5:F5

More Knowledge   **Use of Parentheses in a Formula**

When writing a formula in Excel, use parentheses to specify the order in which the operations should occur. For example, to average three test scores of 100, 50, and 90 that you scored on three different tests, you would add the test scores and then divide by the number of test scores in the list. If you write this formula as =100+50+90/3, the result would be 180, because Excel would first divide 90 by 3 and then add 100+50+30. Excel would do so because the order of operations states that multiplication and division are calculated *before* addition and subtraction.

The correct way to write this formula is =(100+50+90)/3. Excel will add the three values, and then divide the result by 3, or 240/3 resulting in a correct average of 80. Parentheses play an important role in ensuring that you get the correct result in your formulas.

Activity 3.14 | Using Format Painter

In this activity, you will use Format Painter to copy text (non-numeric) formats.

1 Leave **row 7** blank, and then click cell **A8**. Type **Projected Tourism Spending** and then press Enter.

2 Point to cell **A2**, right-click, on the mini toolbar, click **Format Painter** 🖌, and then click cell **A8** to copy the format.

> The format of cell **A2** is *painted*—applied to—cell **A8**, including the merging and centering of the text across the range **A8:F8**.

🔄 **BY TOUCH**   On the Home tab, in the Clipboard group, tap the Format Painter button.

3 Leave **row 9** blank, and then click cell **A10**. Type **Estimated Growth Rate** and then press Tab.

4 In cell **B10**, type **25%** and press Enter. Select the range **A10:B10**, right-click over the selection, and then from the mini toolbar, apply **Bold** **B** and **Italic** *I*.

5 Leave **row 11** blank. Click cell **A12**, type **Year** and then press Tab. In cell **B12**, type **2014** and press Tab. In cell **C12**, type **2015** and press Tab.

6 Select the range **B12:C12**, and then drag the fill handle through cell **F12** to extend the pattern of years to *2018*. Apply the **Heading 3** cell style to the selected range.

7 Point to cell **F5**, right-click, and then click **Copy**. Point to cell **B13**, right-click, and then click **Paste** 📋. Compare your screen with Figure 3.25, and then **Save** 💾 your workbook.

FIGURE 3.25

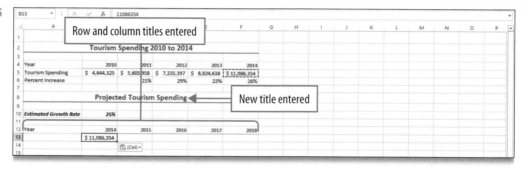

Row and column titles entered

New title entered

Activity 3.15 | Calculating a Value After an Increase

A growth in tourism spending means that the city can plan for additional revenues and also plan more hotel and conference space to accommodate the increasing number of visitors. Therefore, city planners in Pacifica Bay want to estimate how much tourism spending will increase in the future. The calculations you made in the previous activity show that tourism spending has increased at varying rates during each year from 2010 to 2014, ranging from a low of 21% to a high of 29% per year.

Economic data suggests that future growth will trend close to that of the recent past. To plan for the future, Mr. Larsen wants to prepare a forecast of tourism spending based on the percentage increase halfway between the high of 29% and the low of 21%; that is, for 25%. In this activity, you will calculate the tourism spending that would result from a 25% increase.

1 Click cell **C13**. Type **=b13*(100%+b10)** and then on the **Formula Bar**, click **Enter** ✓ to display a result of *13857942.5*. Point to cell **B13**, right-click, click **Format Painter** ✸, and then click cell **C13** to copy the format. Compare your screen with Figure 3.26.

This formula calculates what tourism spending will be in the year 2015 assuming an increase of 25% over 2014's tourism spending. Use the mathematical formula ***value after increase = base × percent for new value*** to calculate a value after an increase as follows:

First, establish the *percent for new value*. The ***percent for new value = base percent + percent of increase***. The *base percent* of 100% represents the base tourism spending and the *percent of increase*—in this instance is 25%. Therefore, the tourism spending will equal 100% of the base year plus 25% of the base year. This can be expressed as 125% or 1.25. In this formula, you will use 100% + the rate in cell **B10**, which is 25%, to equal 125%.

Second, enter a reference to the cell that contains the *base*—the tourism spending in 2014. The base value resides in cell **B13**—*$11,086,354*.

Third, calculate the *value after increase*. Because in each future year the increase will be based on 25%—an absolute value located in cell **B10**—this cell reference can be formatted as absolute by typing dollar signs.

FIGURE 3.26

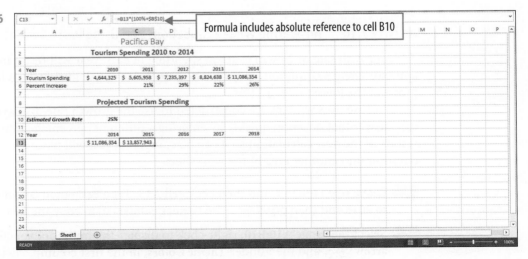

2 With cell **C13** as the active cell, drag the fill handle to copy the formula to the range **D13:F13**. Click an empty cell to cancel the selection, click **Save** 🖫 and then compare your screen with Figure 3.27.

> This formula uses a relative cell address—B13—for the *base*; the tourism spending in the year is used in each of the formulas in cells D13:F13 as the *base* value. Because the reference to the *percent of increase* in cell B10 is an absolute reference, each *value after increase* is calculated with the value from cell B10.

> The tourism spending projected for 2015—*$13,857,943*—is an increase of 25% over the spending in 2014. The projected spending in 2016—*$17,322,428*—is an increase of 25% over the spending in 2015, and so on.

FIGURE 3.27

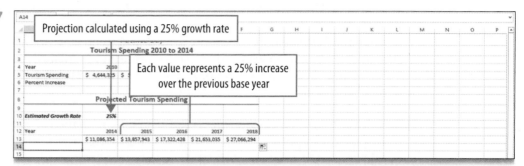

More Knowledge | **Percent Increase or Decrease**

The basic formula for calculating an increase or decrease can be done in two parts. First determine the percent by which the base value will be increased or decreased, and then add or subtract the results to the base. The formula can be simplified by using (1+amount of increase) or (1−amount of decrease), where 1, rather than 100%, represents the whole. Therefore, the formula used in Step 1 of Activity 3.15 could also be written =b13*(1+b10), or =(b13*b10)+b13.

Objective 6 Answer What-If Questions by Changing Values in a Worksheet

Video E3-6

If a formula depends on the value in a cell, you can see what effect it will have if you change the value in that cell. Then, you can copy the value computed by the formula and paste it into another part of the worksheet where you can compare it to other values.

Activity 3.16 │ Answering What-If Questions and Using Paste Special

A growth rate of 25% in tourism spending in each year will result in tourism spending of approximately $27 million by 2018. The city planners will likely ask: *What if* tourism spending grows at the lowest rate of 21%?

Because the formulas are constructed to use the growth rate displayed in cell **B10**, Mr. Larsen can answer that question quickly by entering a different percentage into that cell. To keep the results of the new calculation so it can be compared, you will paste the results of the what-if question into another area of the worksheet.

1 Leave **row 14** blank, and then click cell **A15**. Type **Estimated Growth in Tourism Spending 2014 to 2018** and then press Enter. Use **Format Painter** 🖌 to copy the format from cell **A8** to cell **A15**.

2 Select the range **A10:B10**, right-click to display the mini toolbar, click the **Fill Color button arrow** 🖍 ▾, and then under **Theme Colors**, in the first column, click the third color—**White, Background 1, Darker 15%**.

3 Leave **row 16** blank, and then in the range **A17:A19**, type the following row titles:

Year

25% Growth Rate

21% Growth Rate

4 Select the range **B12:F12**, right-click over the selection, and then on the shortcut menu, click **Copy**.

ANOTHER WAY   Press Ctrl + C; or, on the Home tab, in the Clipboard group, click the Copy button.

5 Point to cell **B17**, right-click, and then on the shortcut menu, under **Paste Options**, click **Paste**.

> Recall that when pasting a group of copied cells to a target range, you need only point to or select the first cell of the range.

6 Select and **Copy** the range **B13:F13**, and then **Paste** it beginning in cell **B18**.

7 Click cell **C18**. On the **Formula Bar**, notice that the *formula* was pasted into the cell, as shown in Figure 3.28.

> This is *not* the desired result. The actual *calculated values*—not the formulas—are needed in the range.

FIGURE 3.28

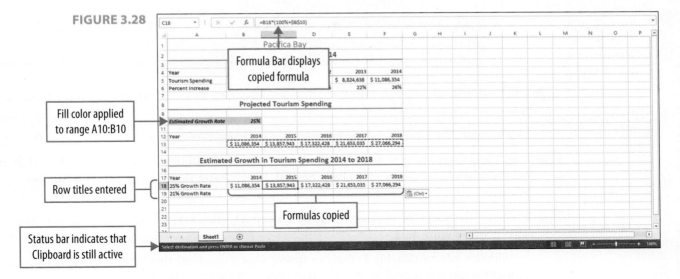

8 On the **Quick Access Toolbar**, click **Undo**. With the range **B13:F13** still copied to the Clipboard—as indicated by the message in the status bar and the moving border—point to cell **B18**, and then right-click to display the shortcut menu.

9 Under **Paste Options**, point to **Paste Special** to display another gallery, and then under **Paste Values**, point to **Values & Number Formatting** to display the ScreenTip as shown in Figure 3.29.

> The ScreenTip *Values & Number Formatting (A)* indicates that you can paste the calculated values that result from the calculation of formulas along with the formatting applied to the copied cells. *(A)* is the keyboard shortcut for this command.

FIGURE 3.29

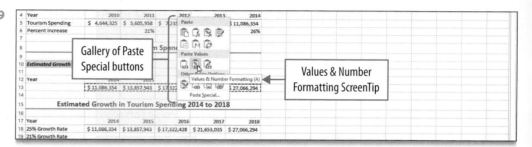

> 10 Click **Values & Number Formatting** 📋, click cell **C18** and notice on the **Formula Bar** that the cell contains a *value*, not a formula. Press [Esc] to cancel the moving border. Compare your screen with Figure 3.30.

The calculated estimates based on a 25% growth rate are pasted along with their formatting.

FIGURE 3.30

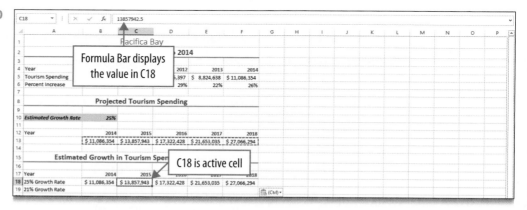

> 11 Click cell **B10**. Type **21** and then watch the values in **C13:F13** *recalculate* as, on the **Formula Bar**, you click **Enter** ✔.

The value *21%* is the lowest percent increase for the past 5-year period.

> 12 Select and **Copy** the new values in the range **B13:F13**. Point to cell **B19**, right-click, and then on the shortcut menu, point to **Paste Special**. Under **Paste Values**, click **Values & Number Formatting** 📋.

> 13 Press [Esc] to cancel the moving border, click cell **A1**, click **Save** 💾, and then compare your screen with Figure 3.31.

With this information, Mr. Larsen can answer what-if questions about the projected increase in tourism spending based on the rates of increase over the past 5 years.

FIGURE 3.31

Video E3-7

A *line chart* displays trends over time. Time is displayed along the bottom axis and the data point values connect with a line. The curve and direction of the line make trends obvious to the reader.

The columns in a column chart and the pie slices in a pie chart emphasize the distinct values of each data point. A line chart, on the other hand, emphasizes the flow from one data point value to the next.

Activity 3.17 │ Inserting Multiple Rows and Creating a Line Chart

So that City Council members can see how tourism spending has increased over the past five years, in this activity, you will chart the actual tourism spending from 2010 to 2014 in a line chart.

1 Click the **PAGE LAYOUT tab**. In the **Themes group**, click the **Colors arrow**, and then change the **Theme Colors** to **Orange**.

2 In the **row header area**, point to **row 8** to display the ➡ pointer, and then drag down to select **rows 8:24**. Right-click over the selection, and then click **Insert** to insert the same number of blank rows as you selected. Compare your screen with Figure 3.32.

> Use this technique to insert multiple rows quickly.

FIGURE 3.32

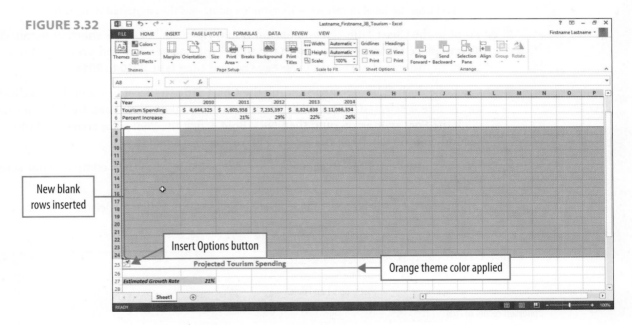

New blank rows inserted

Insert Options button

Projected Tourism Spending

Orange theme color applied

3 Near **row 25**, click **Insert Options** , and then click the **Clear Formatting** option button to clear any formatting from these rows.

> You will use this blank area to position your line chart.

4 Press Ctrl + Home to deselect the rows and move to the top of your worksheet. Select the range **A5:F5**. On the **INSERT tab**, in the **Charts group**, click **Insert Line Chart** .

5 In the gallery of line charts, in the second row, point to the first chart type to display the ScreenTip *Line with Markers*. Compare your screen with Figure 3.33.

FIGURE 3.33

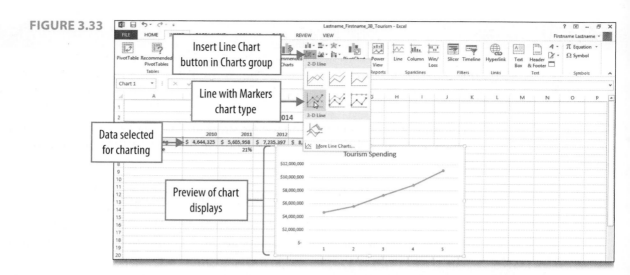

Insert Line Chart button in Charts group

Line with Markers chart type

Data selected for charting

Preview of chart displays

6 ▶ Click the **Line with Markers** chart type to create the chart as an embedded chart in the worksheet.

7 ▶ Point to the border of the chart to display the ⬚ pointer, and then drag the chart so that its upper left corner is positioned in cell **A8**, aligned approximately under the *t* in the word *Percent* above.

Excel uses the label in cell A5—*Tourism Spending*—as the suggested chart title.

8 ▶ Point to the **Chart Title** *Tourism Spending* and right-click. On the shortcut menu, click **Edit Text** to place the insertion point in the title. Type **Pacifica Bay** and press Enter. Press End to move to the end of *Spending*, press Spacebar, and then type **2010 to 2014**

9 ▶ Click the dashed border surrounding the **Chart Title** so that it is a solid line, indicating the entire title is selected. Right-click over the title, and then click **Font**. In the **Font** dialog box, click the **Font style arrow**, and then click **Bold**. Click the **Font color arrow**, and then in the second column, click the first color—**Black, Text 1**. Click **OK**.

10 ▶ On the right side of the chart, click **Chart Elements** ⊞, and then compare your screen with Figure 3.34.

Three of the available chart elements are included for this chart by default—the axes, the chart title, and the gridlines.

FIGURE 3.34

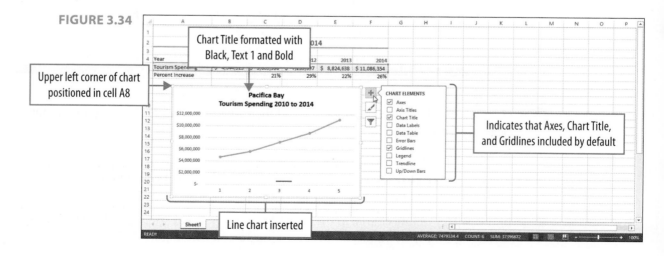

Chart Title formatted with Black, Text 1 and Bold

Upper left corner of chart positioned in cell A8

Indicates that Axes, Chart Title, and Gridlines included by default

Line chart inserted

Activity 3.18 │ Formatting Axes in a Line Chart

An **axis** is a line that serves as a frame of reference for measurement; it borders the chart **plot area**. The plot area is the area bounded by the axes, including all the data series. Recall that the area along the bottom of a chart that identifies the categories of data is referred to as the **category axis** or the **x-axis**. Recall also that the area along the left side of a chart that shows the range of numbers for the data points is referred to as the **value axis** or the **y-axis**.

In this activity, you will change the category axis to include the years 2010 to 2014 and adjust the numeric scale of the value axis.

1 Be sure the chart is still selected. At the bottom of the chart, point to any of the numbers *1* through *5* to display the ScreenTip *Horizontal (Category) Axis*, and then right-click. On the shortcut menu, click **Select Data**.

 BY TOUCH   On the ribbon, tap the DESIGN tab, and then in the Data group, tap Select Data.

2 On the right side of the **Select Data Source** dialog box, under **Horizontal (Category) Axis Labels**, locate **Edit**, as shown in Figure 3.35.

Here you can change the labels on the category axis to the years that are represented in the chart.

FIGURE 3.35

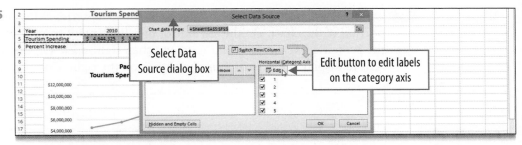

3 In the right column, click **Edit**. If necessary, drag the title bar of the **Axis Labels** dialog box to the right of the chart so that it is not blocking your view of the data, and then select the years in the range **B4:F4**. Compare your screen with Figure 3.36.

FIGURE 3.36

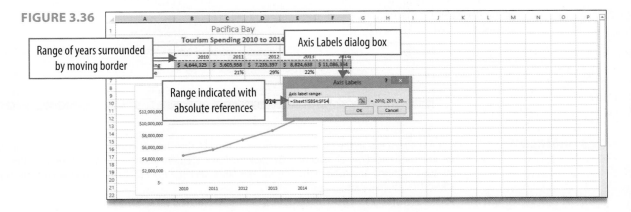

4 In the **Axis Labels** dialog box, click **OK**, and notice that in the right column of the **Select Data Source** dialog box, the years display as the category labels. Click **OK** to close the **Select Data Source** dialog box. Compare your screen with Figure 3.37.

FIGURE 3.37

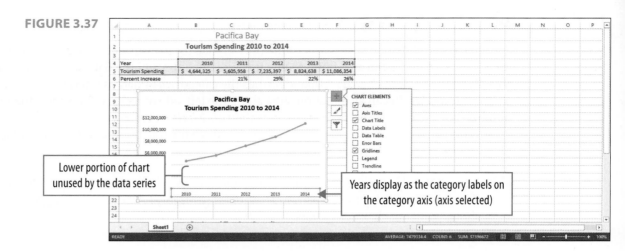

Lower portion of chart unused by the data series

Years display as the category labels on the category axis (axis selected)

5 With the **Horizontal (Category) Axis** still selected, click the **Chart Elements** button ⊞, point to **Axes**, click the ▶ arrow, and then click **More Options** to display the **Format Axis** pane.

6 Under **AXIS OPTIONS**, click **Fill & Line** 🖎, if necessary click **LINE** to expand the options, and then click the **No line** option button so that the line can become a gridline at the bottom of the chart when you format the plot area. **Close** ✕ the **Format Axis** pane.

7 On the chart, notice that the orange line—the data series—does not display in the lower portion of the chart. On the left side of the chart, point to any of the dollar values to display the ScreenTip *Vertical (Value) Axis*, and then right-click. On the shortcut menu, click **Format Axis** to display the **Format Axis** pane again on the right. Compare your screen to Figure 3.38.

FIGURE 3.38

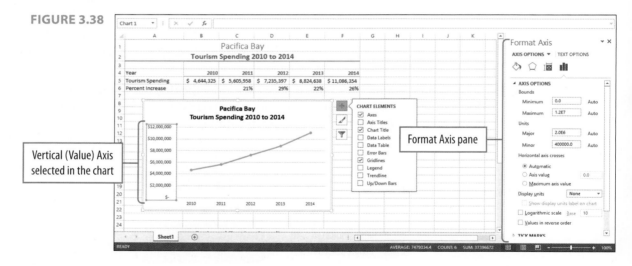

Vertical (Value) Axis selected in the chart

Format Axis pane

ANOTHER WAY On the FORMAT tab, in the Current Selection group, click the Chart Elements arrow, click Vertical (Value) Axis, and then click Format Selection. Or, click the Chart Elements button, point to Axes, click the arrow, click More Options, and then in the Format Axis pane, click the AXIS OPTIONS arrow. On the displayed list, click Vertical (Value) Axis.

8 In the **Format Axis** pane, under **Bounds**, click in the **Minimum** box, select the existing text *0.0*, and then type **4000000**

Because none of the spending figures are under $4,000,000, changing the Minimum number to $4,000,000 will enable the data series to occupy more of the plot area.

9 ▶ Under **Units**, in the **Major** box, select the text *2.0E6*, type **2000000** and press Enter. Click **Save** 🖫, and then compare your screen with Figure 3.39.

> The *Major unit* value determines the spacing between the gridlines in the plot area. By default, Excel started the values at zero and increased in increments of $2,000,000. By setting the Minimum value on the value axis to $4,000,000 and changing the Major unit to $2,000,000, the line chart shows a clearer and more pronounced trend in tourism spending.

> Numbers that display E + a number are expressed by Excel in the Scientific format, which displays a number in exponential notation.

FIGURE 3.39

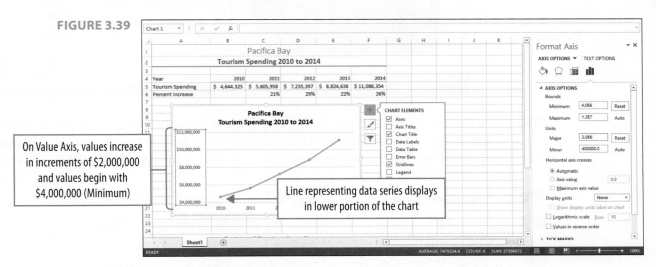

> On Value Axis, values increase in increments of $2,000,000 and values begin with $4,000,000 (Minimum)

> Line representing data series displays in lower portion of the chart

Activity 3.19 | Formatting the Chart Area in a Line Chart

An Excel chart has two background elements—the plot area and the chart area—which, by default display a single fill color. To add visual appeal to a chart, you can insert a graphic image as the background.

1 ▶ Near the top of the **Format Axis** pane, click the **AXIS OPTIONS arrow**, and then click **Chart Area** to display the **Format Chart Area** pane. Then click **Fill & Line** 🖎.

> When formatting chart elements, Excel provides multiple ways to display the panes that you need. You can right-click the area you want to format and choose a command on the shortcut menu. You can use an existing pane to move to a different pane. And you can use the FORMAT tab on the ribbon to navigate among various chart elements in the Current Selection group. Use whatever method is easiest for you.

 **ANOTHER WAY**   On the FORMAT tab, in the Current Selection group, click the Chart Elements arrow, click Chart Area, and then click Format Selection. Or, right-click slightly inside the chart to display the shortcut menu, and then click Format Chart Area.

2 ▶ In the **Format Chart Area** pane, click **FILL** to expand the options, and then click the **Picture or texture fill** option button.

> A default texture displays in the chart area.

3 ▶ In the **Format Chart Area** pane, under **Insert picture from**, click **File**. In the **Insert Picture** dialog box, navigate to the student data files that accompany this textbook, and then click **e03B_Surfers**. Click **Insert**. Compare your screen with Figure 3.40.

FIGURE 3.40

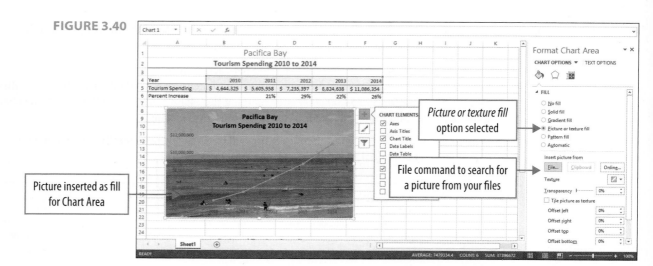

Picture inserted as fill for Chart Area

Picture or texture fill option selected

File command to search for a picture from your files

> **4** In the **Format Chart Area** pane, click **FILL** to collapse the options, and then click **BORDER** to expand the options. Click the **Solid line** option button, click the **Color arrow**, and then under **Theme Colors**, in the fifth column, notice that the first color—**Orange, Accent 1**—is already selected by default.

> **5** Click the **Color arrow** again to accept the default color and close the color palette.

> **6** Set the **Width** to **4 pt** either by selecting the existing text in the Width box and typing or by clicking the up spin box arrow as necessary.

> **7** Use the scroll bar on the right side of the **Format Chart Area** pane if necessary to scroll to the bottom of the pane, and then select the **Rounded corners** check box. On the **Quick Access Toolbar**, click **Save** 🖫, and then compare your screen with Figure 3.41.

FIGURE 3.41

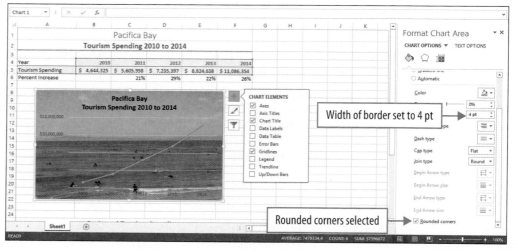

Width of border set to 4 pt

Rounded corners selected

Activity 3.20 | Formatting the Plot Area Gridlines and Axis Fonts in a Line Chart

> **1** To the right of the chart, if necessary click **Chart Elements** ➕ to display the list of elements, point to **Gridlines**, click the **arrow**, and then click **More Options** to display the **Format Major Gridlines** pane. Compare your screen with Figure 3.42.

FIGURE 3.42

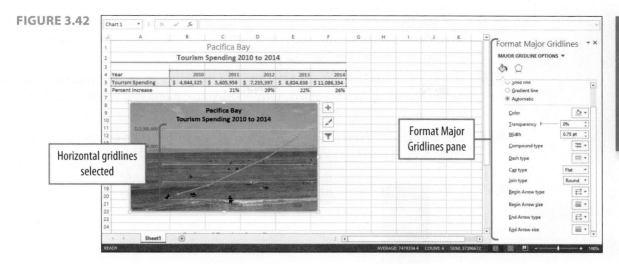

Horizontal gridlines selected

Format Major Gridlines pane

2 If necessary, in the pane, scroll to the top and click to expand **LINE**. Click the **Solid line** option button. Click the **Color arrow**, and be sure that **Orange, Accent 1**—in the fifth column, the first color—is selected.

3 Set the **Width** to **1 pt**.

4 In the chart, point to any of the dollar values on the **Vertical (Value) Axis**, right-click, and then click **Font**.

5 In the **Font** dialog box, change the **Font style** to **Bold**, and then change the **Font color** to **Black, Text 1**—in the second column, the first color. Click **OK**.

6 Use the same technique to format the font of the **Horizontal (Category) Axis** to **Bold** with **Black, Text 1**.

7 **Close** ☒ the **Format Axis** pane. Click cell **A1** to deselect the chart. Click **Save** 🖫, and then compare your screen with Figure 3.43.

FIGURE 3.43

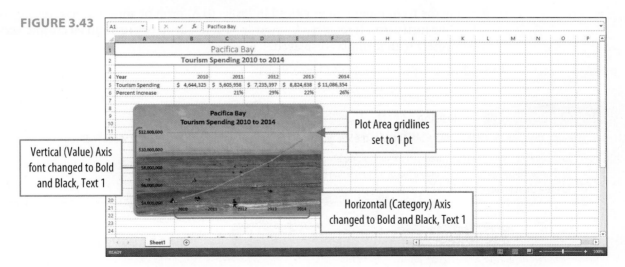

Vertical (Value) Axis font changed to Bold and Black, Text 1

Plot Area gridlines set to 1 pt

Horizontal (Category) Axis changed to Bold and Black, Text 1

8 Click the **PAGE LAYOUT tab**. In the **Page Setup group**, click **Margins**, and then click **Custom Margins**.

9 In the **Page Setup** dialog box, on the **Margins tab**, under **Center on page**, select the **Horizontally** check box.

10 ▸ Click the **Header/Footer tab**, and then in the center of the dialog box, click **Custom Footer**. In the **Footer** dialog box, with your insertion point blinking in the **Left section**, on the row of buttons, click **Insert File Name** 🗐.

11 ▸ Click **OK** two times. Click the **FILE tab**, and then click **Show All Properties**. As the **Tags**, type **tourism spending** As the **Subject**, type your course name and section number. Be sure your name displays as the author.

12 ▸ On the left, click **Print** to display the **Print Preview**, and then compare your screen with Figure 3.44. If necessary return to the worksheet and make any corrections.

FIGURE 3.44

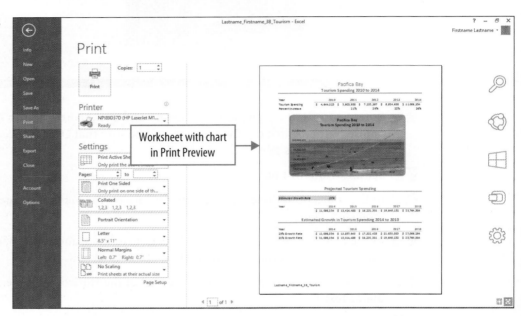

13 ▸ On the left, click **Save** to redisplay the workbook.

14 ▸ Using the techniques you practiced in Project 1A, print or submit electronically as directed by your instructor. If required by your instructor, print or create an electronic version of your worksheet with formulas displayed.

15 ▸ Close your workbook and close Excel.

More Knowledge   **Resizing a Chart**

To resize a chart, on the CHART TOOLS FORMAT tab, in the Size group, type the dimensions in the Shape Height or Shape Width box. Or:

- To change the width of a chart, drag a left or right sizing handle.
- To change the height of a chart, drag a top or bottom sizing handle.
- To size a chart proportionately, drag a corner sizing handle.

END | You have completed Project 3B

Objective   Convert an Excel Worksheet to a Google Docs Spreadsheet with a Chart

Google Docs is Google's free, web-based word processor, spreadsheet, slide show, and form service that, along with free data storage, is known as *Google Drive*. You can convert an Excel worksheet to a Google Docs spreadsheet. Google Drive and Google Docs are similar to SkyDrive and Office Web Apps—both are free, cloud-based productivity tools.

> **ALERT!** **Working with Web-Based Applications and Services**
>
> Computer programs and services on the web receive continuous updates and improvements, so the steps to complete this web-based activity may differ from the ones shown. You can often look at the screens and the information presented to determine how to complete the activity.

Activity | Converting an Excel Worksheet to a Google Docs Spreadsheet with a Chart

In this activity, you will convert an Excel worksheet to a Google Docs spreadsheet and create a column chart.

1 If you do *not* have a Google account, skip to Step 2. Start Internet Explorer, in the address bar, type **http://docs.google.com** and then press Enter. Sign in to your Google account and display the Google docs page. Now skip to Step 3.

2 From the desktop, start Internet Explorer. In the address bar, type **http://docs.google.com** and then press Enter. Locate and click the button to sign up for a new account, and then complete the information. As your email address, you can use your Microsoft account or other email address. Sign in to your new Google account.

3 Locate and click **CREATE**, and then click **Spreadsheet**. Under **Untitled spreadsheet**, click **File**, and then click **Import**. Under **Upload file**, click **Browse**, and then in the **Choose File to Upload** dialog box, navigate

to your student data files and click **e03_3B_Web**. In the lower right corner of the dialog box, click **Open**, and then click **Import**.

4 When the screen indicates that the file was imported successfully, click **Open now**. Compare your screen with Figure A.

5 Drag to select the years and values in the range **A4:F5**, and then on the menu bar, click **Insert**. On the menu, click **Chart**.

6 On the **Chart Editor** screen, under **Recommended charts**, click the second chart—the **Column chart**, and then on the left above *Recommended charts*, click to select the first check box—**Switch rows/columns**, and then the second check box **Use column A as headers**, and then the third check box, **Use row 4 as labels**.

FIGURE A

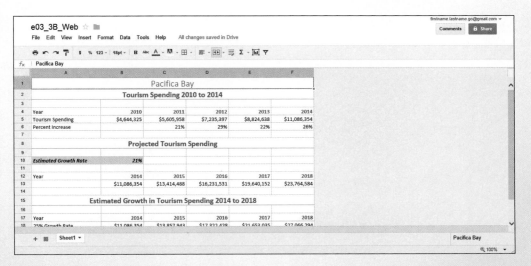

(GO! with Office Web Apps continues on the next page)

7 Click **Insert**. If necessary, click one time in the white space on the worksheet to display the chart. In the upper right corner, click the down arrow and then click **Move to own sheet**.

8 On the displayed chart, click the text *Chart title*. In the box that displays, select the existing text, and then using your own name, type **2010 – 2014 Tourism Spending Prepared by Firstname Lastname** Press Enter.

9 In the upper right corner of the chart, click the small square labeled *Tourism Spending*, and then click one time to edit the legend. In the toolbar that displays above, click **Right**, and then on the displayed list, click **None**. Compare your screen with Figure B.

10 In the upper right, click **Save image**, and then in the **Notification bar** at the bottom, click the **Save arrow**. Click

Save as, and then in the **Save As** dialog box, navigate to your **Excel Chapter 3** folder. In the **File name** box, using your own name, type **Lastname_Firstname_EX_3B_Web** and then press Enter.

11 In the upper right corner, click your Google name, and then click **Sign out**. Close Internet Explorer.

It is not necessary to save your spreadsheet, because Google Drive saves your work automatically. Your image is saved as a *.png* file, which is the file extension for an image in the *Portable Network Graphics* format. This format, like JPEG, is commonly used for graphics on the web.

12 Submit your .png image file to your instructor as directed.

FIGURE B

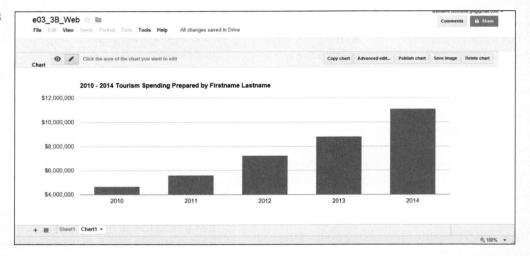

The advantage of using Office 365 is that your organization does not have to purchase and install server hardware and software for sophisticated business applications and does not need a full-time IT person or staff just to manage the technology your teams need.

By using Office 365, you are able to have business-class services for your employees without investing in expensive hardware, software, and personnel. However, at least one person in an organization must be designated as the ***Office 365 Administrator***—the person who creates and manages the account, adds new users, sets up the services your organization wants to use, sets permission levels, and manages the SharePoint team sites. You can have more than one Administrator if you want to share these tasks with others.

Microsoft provides easy-to-use instructions and videos to get you started, and you might also have contact with a Microsoft representative. You will probably find, however, that subscribing to and setting up the account, adding users, and activating services is a straightforward process that requires little or no assistance.

After purchasing the required number of licenses, you will add each team member as a user that includes his or her email address.

The Office 365 Administrator can manage the team sites, as shown in Figure A. On the left there are links to manage the site pages in the Office 365 account. Here the administrator can manage permissions, specifying which users can access and edit which team sites. The administrator can also manage and modify the look and feel of the team site.

Activity | Using a Team Site to Collaborate

This group project relates to the **Bell Orchid Hotels**. If your instructor assigns this project to your class, you can expect to use **Lync** in **Office 365** to collaborate on the following tasks for this chapter:

- If you are in the **Accounting Group**, you and your teammates will finalize the workbook to summarize hotel rooms sold over a four-week period in April and post it to your team site.

- If you are in the **Engineering Group**, you and your teammates will finalize your workbook summarizing Maintenance Expenses for the first quarter and post it to your team site.

- If you are in the **Food and Beverage Group**, you and your teammates will finalize your workbook to analyze the profitability of the ten most popular entrees in the hotel's restaurant and post it to your team site.

- If you are in the **Human Resources Group**, you and your teammates will finalize your workbook summarizing the pay of salaried employees over the first six months of operation and post it to your team site.

- If you are in the **Operations Group**, you and your teammates will finalize your workbook for Rooms and Housekeeping Service Analysis that will be used to determine ongoing needs for housekeeping service and post it to your team site.

- If you are in the **Sales and Marketing Group**, you and your teammates will finalize your Rooms Sold Analysis workbook summarizing rooms sold by four salespersons during January-June that will be used to develop a marketing plan for the rest of the year and post it to your team site.

FIGURE A

END OF CHAPTER

SUMMARY

Use pie charts when you want to show the relationship of each part to a whole. Consider using a pie chart when you have only one data series to plot and you do not have more than seven categories.

To create a pie chart, you must select two ranges. One range contains the labels for each pie slice; the other contains the values that add up to a total. Both ranges must have the same number of cells.

In formulas, Excel follows rules called the order of operations; expressions within parentheses are processed first, and multiplication and division are performed before addition and subtraction.

Use a line chart when you want to show trends over time. Time displays along the bottom axis and the data point values connect with a line. The curve and direction of the line make trends obvious.

GO! LEARN IT ONLINE

Review the concepts and key terms in this chapter by completing these online challenges, which you can find at **www.pearsonhighered.com/go**.

Matching and Multiple Choice:
Answer matching and multiple choice questions to test what you learned in this chapter. MyITLab®

Crossword Puzzle:
Spell out the words that match the numbered clues, and put them in the puzzle squares.

Flipboard:
Flip through the definitions of the key terms in this chapter and match them with the correct term.

GO! FOR JOB SUCCESS

Video: Planning and Managing Your Career
Your instructor may assign this video to your class, and then ask you to think about, or discuss with your classmates, these questions:

FotolEdhar / Fotolia

When did you start career planning and what were the main steps you took to plan your career?

What have been your best sources for networking?

What advice would you give to others about how to stay employable throughout your career?

END OF CHAPTER

REVIEW AND ASSESSMENT GUIDE FOR EXCEL CHAPTER 3

Your instructor may assign one or more of these projects to help you review the chapter and assess your mastery and understanding of the chapter.

	Review and Assessment Guide for Excel Chapter 3		
Project	**Apply Skills from These Chapter Objectives**	**Project Type**	**Project Location**
3C	Objectives 1-4 from Project 3A	**3C Skills Review** A guided review of the skills from Project 3A.	On the following pages
3D	Objectives 5-7 from Project 3B	**3D Skills Review** A guided review of the skills from Project 3B.	On the following pages
3E	Objectives 1-4 from Project 3A	**3E Mastery (Grader Project)** A demonstration of your mastery of the skills in Project 3A with extensive decision making.	In MyITLab and on the following pages
3F	Objectives 5-7 from Project 3B	**3F Mastery (Grader Project)** A demonstration of your mastery of the skills in Project 3B with extensive decision making.	In MyITLab and on the following pages
3G	Objectives 1-7 from Projects 3A and 3B	**3G Mastery (Grader Project)** A demonstration of your mastery of the skills in Projects 3A and 3B with extensive decision making.	In MyITLab and on the following pages
3H	Combination of Objectives from Projects 3A and 3B	**3H GO! Fix It** A demonstration of your mastery of the skills in Projects 3A and 3B by creating a correct result from a document that contains errors you must find.	Online
3I	Combination of Objectives from Projects 3A and 3B	**3I GO! Make It** A demonstration of your mastery of the skills in Projects 3A and 3B by creating a result from a supplied picture.	Online
3J	Combination of Objectives from Projects 3A and 3B	**3J GO! Solve It** A demonstration of your mastery of the skills in Projects 3A and 3B, your decision-making skills, and your critical thinking skills. A task-specific rubric helps you self-assess your result.	Online
3K	Combination of Objectives from Projects 3A and 3B	**3K GO! Solve It** A demonstration of your mastery of the skills in Projects 3A and 3B, your decision-making skills, and your critical thinking skills. A task-specific rubric helps you self-assess your result.	On the following pages
3L	Combination of Objectives from Projects 3A and 3B	**3L GO! Think** A demonstration of your understanding of the Chapter concepts applied in a manner that you would outside of college. An analytic rubric helps you and your instructor grade the quality of your work by comparing it to the work an expert in the discipline would create.	On the following pages
3M	Combination of Objectives from Projects 3A and 3B	**3M GO! Think** A demonstration of your understanding of the Chapter concepts applied in a manner that you would outside of college. An analytic rubric helps you and your instructor grade the quality of your work by comparing it to the work an expert in the discipline would create.	Online
3N	Combination of Objectives from Projects 3A and 3B	**3N You and GO!** A demonstration of your understanding of the Chapter concepts applied in a manner that you would in a personal situation. An analytic rubric helps you and your instructor grade the quality of your work.	Online
3O	Combination of Objectives from Projects 3A and 3B	**3O Cumulative Group Project for Excel Chapter 3** A demonstration of your understanding of concepts and your ability to work collaboratively in a group role-playing assessment, requiring both collaboration and self-management.	Online
Capstone Project for Excel Chapters 1-3	Combination of Objectives from Projects 1A, 1B, 2A, 2B, 3A, and 3B	A demonstration of your mastery of the skills in Chapters 1-3 with extensive decision making. **(Grader Project)**	In MyITLab and online

GLOSSARY

GLOSSARY OF CHAPTER KEY TERMS

3-D The shortened term for *three-dimensional*, which refers to an image that appears to have all three spatial dimensions—length, width, and depth.

Absolute cell reference A cell reference that refers to cells by their fixed position in a worksheet; an absolute cell reference remains the same when the formula is copied.

Axis A line that serves as a frame of reference for measurement and which borders the chart plot area.

Base The starting point when you divide the amount of increase by it to calculate the rate of increase.

Bevel A shape effect that uses shading and shadows to make the edges of a shape appear to be curved or angled.

Category axis The area along the bottom of a chart that identifies the categories of data; also referred to as the x-axis.

Chart area The entire chart and all of its elements.

Chart sheet A workbook sheet that contains only a chart.

Data marker A column, bar, area, dot, pie slice, or other symbol in a chart that represents a single data point; related data points form a data series.

Data point A value that originates in a worksheet cell and that is represented in a chart by a data marker.

Data series Related data points represented by data markers; each data series has a unique color or pattern represented in the chart legend.

Enterprise fund A municipal government fund that reports income and expenditures related to municipal

services for which a fee is charged in exchange for goods or services.

Explode The action of pulling out one or more pie slices from a pie chart for emphasis.

Formula AutoComplete An Excel feature which, after typing an = (equal sign) and the beginning letter or letters of a function name, displays a list of function names that match the typed letter(s).

Fund A sum of money set aside for a specific purpose.

General fund The term used to describe money set aside for the normal operating activities of a government entity such as a city.

Goal Seek A what-if analysis tool that finds the input needed in one cell to arrive at the desired result in another cell.

Google Docs Google's free, web-based word processor, spreadsheet, slide show, and form service, that along with free data storage, is known as Google Drive.

Google Drive Google's free web-based word processor, spreadsheet, slide show, and form service, that includes free data storage.

Legend A chart element that identifies the patterns or colors that are assigned to the categories in the chart.

Line chart A chart type that displays trends over time; time displays along the bottom axis and the data point values are connected with a line.

Major unit The value in a chart's value axis that determines the spacing between tick marks and between the gridlines in the plot area.

Order of operations The mathematical rules for performing multiple calculations within a formula.

Percent for new value = base percent + percent of increase The formula for calculating a percentage by which a value increases by adding the base percentage—usually 100%—to the percent increase.

Percentage rate of increase The percent by which one number increases over another number.

Pie chart A chart that shows the relationship of each part to a whole.

Plot area The area bounded by the axes of a chart, including all the data series.

Rate = amount of increase/base The mathematical formula to calculate a rate of increase.

Relative cell reference In a formula, the address of a cell based on the relative position of the cell that contains the formula and the cell referred to.

Value after increase = base x percent for new value The formula for calculating the value after an increase by multiplying the original value—the base—by the percent for new value (see the *Percent for new value* formula).

Value axis A numerical scale on the left side of a chart that shows the range of numbers for the data points; also referred to as the Y-axis.

What-if analysis The process of changing the values in cells to see how those changes affect the outcome of formulas in a worksheet.

x-axis Another name for the category axis.

y-axis Another name for the value axis.

CHAPTER REVIEW

Skills Review | Project 3C Parks

Apply 3A skills from these Objectives:

1 Chart Data with a Pie Chart
2 Format a Pie Chart
3 Edit a Workbook and Update a Chart
4 Use Goal Seek to Perform What-If Analysis

In the following Skills Review, you will edit a worksheet for Jerry Silva, City Parks Manager, which details the revenue generated from city parks and structures. Your completed worksheets will look similar to Figure 3.45.

PROJECT FILES

For Project 3C, you will need the following file:

e03C_Parks

You will save your workbook as:

Lastname_Firstname_3C_Parks

PROJECT RESULTS

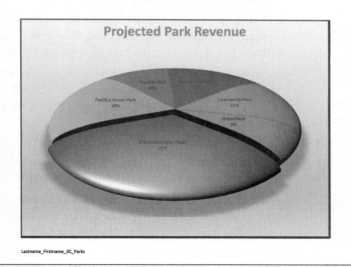

City of Pacifica Bay
Fee and Rental Revenue from City Parks
Projection for Next Fiscal Year Budget

	Current Year Revenue		Projected Revenue for Next Fiscal Year	% of Total Projected Budget
Community Park	$	2,510,980	$ 2,536,529	14%
Grand Park		1,245,730	1,395,218	8%
Diamond League Fields		3,385,050	5,896,360	33%
Pacifica Soccer Park		2,231,050	3,423,515	19%
Bayside Park		1,907,890	1,812,297	10%
Community Center		2,582,340	2,711,459	15%
Total	$	13,863,040	$ 17,775,378	

Goal: To Increase Revenue at Grand Park from 8% to 10%

Goal Amount:	$ 1,777,538	10%

Lastname_Firstname_3C_Parks

FIGURE 3.45

(Project 3C Parks continues on the next page)

CHAPTER REVIEW

1 Start Excel. From your student data files, open the file **e03C_Parks**. Save the file in your **Excel Chapter 3** folder as **Lastname_Firstname_3C_Parks**

a. Click cell **D5**, and then type **=** to begin a formula. Click cell **C5**, type **/** and then click cell **C11**. Press F4 to make the reference to the value in cell **C11** absolute. On the **Formula Bar**, click **Enter**, and then fill the formula down through cell **D10**.

b. With the range **D5:D10** selected, right-click over the selection, and then on the mini toolbar, click **Percent Style** and **Center**.

2 Select the nonadjacent ranges **A5:A10** and **C5:C10** to select the park names and the projected revenue. Click the **INSERT tab**, and then in the **Charts group**, click **Insert Pie or Doughnut Chart**. Under **3-D Pie**, click the chart type **3-D Pie**.

a. On the **DESIGN tab**, in the **Location group**, click **Move Chart**. In the **Move Chart** dialog box, click the **New sheet** option button. In the **New sheet** box, replace the highlighted text *Chart1* by typing **Projected Park Revenue Chart** and then click **OK**.

b. Click the text *Chart Title*, and then type **Projected Park Revenue** Press Enter to create the new chart title.

c. With the title selected, on the **FORMAT tab**, in the **WordArt Styles group**, click **More** to display the gallery. In the second row, select the fifth style— **Fill – Olive Green, Accent 3, Sharp Bevel**. Drag to select the chart title text, and then on the mini toolbar, change the **Font Size** to **32**.

d. Click in a white area of the chart to deselect the chart title. Click **Chart Elements**, and then click the **Legend** check box to remove the legend.

e. In the list of **CHART ELEMENTS**, point to **Data Labels**, click the **arrow** that displays, and then click **More Options**. In the **Format Data Labels** pane on the right, under **LABEL OPTIONS**, select the **Category Name** and **Percentage** check boxes, and *clear* all other check boxes. Under **Label Position**, click **Center**.

f. Point to any of the selected labels, right-click to display a shortcut menu, and then click **Font**. In the **Font** dialog box, on the **Font tab**, change the **Font style** to **Bold Italic** and change the **Size** to **11** Click **OK**.

3 In any pie slice, point anywhere outside the selected label, and then double-click to display the **Format Data Series** pane. Under **SERIES OPTIONS**, click **Effects**, and then click **3-D FORMAT**.

a. Click the **Top bevel arrow**, and then under **Bevel**, click the first button—**Circle**. Apply the **Circle** bevel to the **Bottom bevel**.

b. Set the **Width** and **Height** of both the **Top bevel** and the **Bottom bevel** to **512 pt**

c. Scroll down, click the **Material arrow**, and then under **Standard**, click the third material—**Plastic**.

d. Scroll to the top of the **Format Data Series** pane, click **SHADOW**, and then click the **Presets arrow**. Scroll down, and then under **Perspective**, in the first row, click the third effect—**Below**.

e. In the **Format Data Series** pane, under **SERIES OPTIONS**, click the third button—**Series Options**. Set the **Angle of first slice** to **50**

f. On the pie chart, click the **Diamond League Fields** slice to select only that slice, and then in the **Format Data Point** pane, set the Point Explosion to **10%**

g. With the **Diamond League Fields** slice still selected, in the **Format Data Point** pane, under **SERIES OPTIONS**, click **Fill & Line**, and then click **FILL** to expand the options.

h. Click the **Gradient fill** option button, click the **Preset gradients arrow**, and then in the fourth row, click the third gradient—**Bottom Spotlight – Accent 3**.

4 Point to the white area just inside the border of the chart to display the ScreenTip *Chart Area*, and then click one time to display the **Format Chart Area** pane.

a. Under **CHART OPTIONS**, click **Fill & Line**, and be sure the **FILL** options are still displayed.

b. Click the **Gradient fill** option button, click the **Preset gradients arrow**, and then in the first row, click the fifth gradient—**Light Gradient – Accent 5**.

c. In the **Format Chart Area** pane, click **FILL** to collapse the options, and then click **BORDER** to expand the options.

d. Click the **Solid line** option button, click the **Color arrow**, and then in the fifth column, click the last color—**Ice Blue, Accent 1, Darker 50%**. Set the **Width** of the border to **5 pt** Close the pane, and then **Save** your workbook.

(Project 3C Parks continues on the next page)

5 In the sheet tab area at the bottom of the workbook, click the **Sheet1 tab**. In cell **A13**, type **Goal: To Increase Revenue at Grand Park from 8% to 10%** and then **Merge & Center** the text across the range **A13:D13**. Apply the **Heading 3** cell style.

a. In cell **A14**, type **Goal Amount:** and press Enter. Select the range **C6:D6**, right-click over the selection, and then click **Copy**. Point to cell **B14**, right-click, and then under **Paste Options**, click **Paste**. Press Esc to cancel the moving border.

b. Click cell **C14**. On the **DATA tab**, in the **Data Tools group**, click **What-If Analysis**, and then click **Goal Seek**. In the **Goal Seek** dialog box, press Tab to move to the **To value** box, and then type **10%**

c. Press Tab to move the insertion point to the **By changing cell** box, and then click cell **B14**. Click **OK**. In the displayed **Goal Seek Status** dialog box, click **OK**.

d. Select the range **A14:C14**. From the **HOME tab**, display the **Cell Styles** gallery. Under **Themed Cell Styles**, apply **20% - Accent6**. Click cell **B14**, and then from the **Cell Styles** gallery, under **Number Format**, apply the **Currency [0]** cell style.

6 With your worksheet displayed, in the sheet tab area, double-click *Sheet1* to select the text, and then type **Projected Park Revenue Data** and press Enter.

a. Click the **PAGE LAYOUT tab**. In the **Page Setup Group**, click **Margins**, click **Custom Margins**, and then in the **Page Setup** dialog box, on the **Margins tab**, under **Center on page**, select the **Horizontally** check box.

b. Click the **Header/Footer tab**, click **Custom Footer**, and then with your insertion point in the **Left section**, on the row of buttons, click **Insert File Name**. Click **OK** two times.

c. Display the **Projected Park Revenue Chart**—recall a chart sheet must have its footer formatted separately. Display the **Page Setup** dialog box.

d. Click the **Header/Footer tab**, click **Custom Footer**, and then in the **Left section**, click the **Insert File Name** button. Click **OK** two times.

e. Click the **FILE tab**, and then click **Show All Properties**. As the **Tags**, type **park revenue** As the **Subject**, type your course name and section number. Be sure your name displays as the **Author**.

f. On the left, click **Save**. Right-click the **Projected Park Revenue Chart sheet tab**, and then click **Select All Sheets**. Print or submit electronically as directed by your instructor. If required by your instructor, print or create an electronic version with formulas displayed by using the instructions in Project 1A. Close Excel without saving so that you do not save the changes you made to print formulas.

END | You have completed Project 3C

CHAPTER REVIEW

Build from Scratch

Skills Review Project 3D Housing Permits

In the following Skills Review, you will edit a worksheet that forecasts the revenue from new housing permits that the City of Pacifica Bay expects to collect in the five-year period 2014–2018. Your completed worksheet will look similar to Figure 3.46.

PROJECT FILES

For Project 3D, you will need the following files:

New blank workbook
e03D_Housing

You will save your workbook as:

Lastname_Firstname_3D_Housing

PROJECT RESULTS

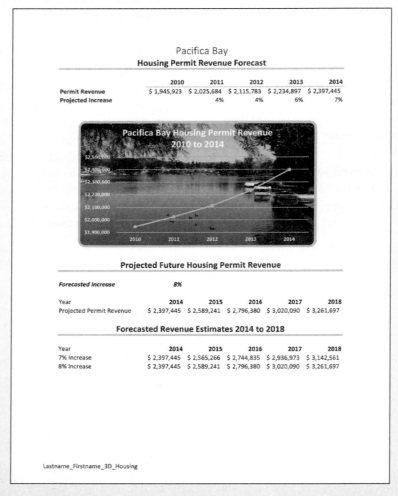

FIGURE 3.46

(Project 3D Housing Permits continues on the next page)

CHAPTER REVIEW

1 Start Excel and display a new blank workbook. By using your own name, save the file in your **Excel Chapter 3** folder as **Lastname_Firstname_3D_Housing**

a. In cell **A1**, type **Pacifica Bay** and in cell **A2** type **Housing Permit Revenue Forecast**

b. **Merge & Center** the title and subtitle across **columns A:F**. To **A1** apply the **Title** cell style and to **A2** apply the **Heading 1** cell style.

c. Widen **column A** to **175 pixels**, and widen **columns B:F to 80 pixels**.

d. In cell **A5**, type **Permit Revenue** and in cell **A6** type **Projected Increase** Apply the **Heading 4** cell style to both cells. In cell **B4**, type **2010** Press [Tab], and then in **C4**, type **2011** Use the fill handle to fill the remaining years through **column F** so that the last year that displays is 2014. Apply the **Heading 3** cell style to the years.

e. In the range **B5:F5**, type the values **1945923** and **2025684** and **2115783** and **2234897** and **2397445** Select the values you just typed, display the **Cell Styles** gallery, and then at the bottom, apply the **Currency [0]** cell style.

2 Click cell **C6**. Being sure to include the parentheses, type **=(c5-b5)/b5** and then press [Enter]. Select cell **C6**, and then apply **Percent Style**.

a. With cell **C6** selected, drag the fill handle to the right through cell **F6**.

b. In cell **A8**, type **Projected Future Housing Permit Revenue** and then press [Enter]. Point to cell **A2**, right-click, on the mini toolbar, click **Format Painter**, and then click cell **A8**. In cell **A10**, type **Forecasted Increase** leave row 11 blank, and then in cell **A12**, type **Year**

c. In cell **A13**, type **Projected Permit Revenue** and then in cell **B12**, type **2014** and press [Tab]. In cell **C12**, type **2015** and then press [Tab]. Select the range **B12:C12**, and then drag the fill handle through cell **F12** to extend the pattern of years to *2018*. Apply **Bold** to the selection.

d. Right-click cell **F5**, and then click **Copy**. Right-click over cell **B13**, and then click **Paste**.

e. In cell **B10**, type **7%** which is the percent of increase from 2013 to 2014. Select the range **A10:B10**, and then from the mini toolbar, apply **Bold** and **Italic**.

3 Click cell **C13**. Type **=b13*(100%+b10)** and then on the **Formula Bar**, click **Enter** to keep the cell active. With cell **C13** as the active cell, drag the fill handle to copy the formula to the range **D13:F13**.

a. Point to cell **B13**, right-click, click **Format Painter**, and then select the range **C13:F13**.

b. Click cell **A15**. Type **Forecasted Revenue Estimates 2014 to 2018** and then press [Enter]. Use **Format Painter** to copy the format from cell **A8** to cell **A15**.

c. In the range **A17:A19**, type the following row titles:

Year

7% Increase

8% Increase

4 Select the range **B12:F12**, right-click over the selection, and then on the shortcut menu, click **Copy**. **Paste** the selection to the range **B17:F17**.

a. Select the range **B13:F13**, right-click over the selection, and then on the shortcut menu, click **Copy**. Point to cell **B18**, right-click, and then from the shortcut menu, point to **Paste Special**. Under **Paste Values**, click the second button—**Values & Number Formatting**. Press [Esc] to cancel the moving border.

b. Click cell **B10**. Type **8** and then press [Enter]. Copy the new values in the range **B13:F13**. Point to cell **B19**, right-click, and then point to **Paste Special**. Under **Paste Values**, click **Values & Number Formatting**. **Save** your workbook.

5 In the **row header area**, point to **row 8** to display the pointer, and then drag down to select **rows 8:24**. Right-click over the selection, and then click **Insert** to insert the same number of blank rows as you selected. Under the selection area near cell **A25**, click **Insert Options**, and then click the **Clear Formatting** option button to clear any formatting from these rows.

a. On the **PAGE LAYOUT tab**, in the **Themes group**, click the **Colors arrow**, and then click **Yellow**. Select the range **A5:F5**. On the **INSERT tab**, in the **Charts group**, click **Insert Line Chart**. In the displayed gallery of line charts, in the second row, click the **Line with Markers** chart type to create the chart as an embedded chart in the worksheet.

b. Point to the border of the chart to display the [↖] pointer, and then drag the chart so that its upper left corner is positioned in cell **A9**, aligned approximately under the *c* in the word *Projected* above.

(Project 3D Housing Permits continues on the next page)

CHAPTER REVIEW

c. Point to the Chart Title *Permit Revenue* and right-click. On the shortcut menu, click **Edit Text** so that the insertion point is positioned before the word *Permit*. Type **Pacifica Bay Housing** and then press Spacebar. Press End and then press Enter to create a second line. Type **2010 to 2014**

6   At the bottom of the chart, point to any of the numbers *1* through *5*, and then right-click. On the shortcut menu, click **Select Data**. On the right side of the **Select Data Source** dialog box, click **Edit**. In the worksheet, select the years in the range **B4:F4**, and then click **OK** two times to enter the years as the category labels.

a. With the **Horizontal (Category) Axis** still selected, click **Chart Elements** ➕, point to **Axes**, click the ▶ **arrow**, and then click **More Options**. In the **Format Axis** pane, under **AXIS OPTIONS**, click **Fill & Line** ⬧, if necessary click **LINE** to expand the options, and then click the **No line** option button. **Close** the **Format Axis** pane.

b. On the left side of the chart, point to any of the dollar values, right-click, and then click **Format Axis**. In the **Format Axis** pane, under **Bounds**, select the text in the **Minimum** box, and then type **1900000**

c. Under **Units**, in the **Major** box, select the existing text, and then type **100000**

d. Near the top of the **Format Axis** pane, click the **AXIS OPTIONS arrow**, and then click **Chart Area** to display the **Format Chart Area** pane. Then, click **Fill & Line** ⬧.

e. In the **Format Chart Area** pane, click **FILL** to expand the options, and then click the **Picture or texture fill** option button. Under **Insert picture from**, click **File**. In the **Insert Picture** dialog box, navigate to your student data files, and then click **e03D_Housing**. Click **Insert**.

f. In the **Format Chart Area** pane, click **FILL** to collapse the options, and then click **Border** to expand the options. Click the **Solid line** option button, click the **Color arrow**, and then under **Theme Colors**, in the fifth column, click the first color—**Gold Accent 1**. Set the **Width** to **4 pt** Scroll to the bottom of the pane, and then select the **Rounded corners** check box

g. Right-click the chart title, and then on the shortcut menu, click **Font**. In the **Font** dialog box, change the **Font style** to **Bold**, change the **Size** to **16**, and change the **Font color** to **White, Background 1**—in the first column, the first color. Click **OK**.

7   To the right of the chart, click **Chart Elements** ➕, point to **Gridlines**, click the **arrow**, and then click **More Options** to display the **Format Major Gridlines** pane.

a. Under **LINE**, click the **Solid line** option button. Click the **Color arrow**, and be sure that **Gold, Accent 1** is the selected color. Set the **Width** to **1 pt**

b. In the chart, point to any of the dollar values on the **Vertical (Value) Axis**, right-click, and then click **Font**. In the **Font** dialog box, change the **Font style** to **Bold**, and then change the **Font color** to **White, Background 1**—in the first column, the first color. Click **OK**.

c. By using the same technique, format the **Font** of the **Horizontal (Category) Axis** to **Bold** with **White, Background 1** as the font color.

d. **Close** the **Format Axis** pane, and then click cell **A1** to deselect the chart. Click the **PAGE LAYOUT tab**. In the **Page Setup group**, click **Margins**, and then click **Custom Margins**. In the **Page Setup** dialog box, on the **Margins tab**, select the **Horizontally** check box. Click the **Header/Footer tab**, click **Custom Footer**, and then in the **Left section**, insert the file name. Click **OK** two times.

e. Click the **FILE tab**, and then click **Show All Properties**. As the **Tags**, type **housing permit revenue, forecast** In the **Subject** box, type your course name and section number. Be sure your name displays as the **Author**.

f. View the **Print Preview**, and then **Save** your workbook. Print or submit electronically as directed by your instructor. If required by your instructor, print or create an electronic version of your worksheet with formulas displayed by using the instructions in Project 1A, and then **Close** Excel without saving so that you do not save the changes you made to print formulas.

END | You have completed Project 3D

CONTENT-BASED ASSESSMENTS

Mastering Excel   Project 3E Revenue

In the following project, you will edit a worksheet that summarizes the revenue budget for the City of Pacifica Bay. Your completed worksheets will look similar to Figure 3.47.

Apply 3A skills from these Objectives:

1 Chart Data with a Pie Chart

2 Format a Pie Chart

3 Edit a Workbook and Update a Chart

4 Use Goal Seek to Perform What-If Analysis

PROJECT FILES

For Project 3E, you will need the following file:

e03E_Revenue

You will save your workbook as:

Lastname_Firstname_3E_Revenue

PROJECT RESULTS

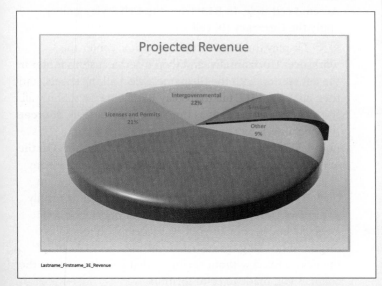

City of Pacifica Bay
Revenue Sources

Projection for Next Fiscal Year Budget

	Current Year Revenue	Projected Revenue for Next Fiscal Year	% of Total Projected Revenue
Taxes	$ 54,152,873	$ 55,956,359	37%
Licenses and Permits	28,120,500	30,854,962	21%
Intergovernmental	31,786,400	33,712,614	22%
Services	14,007,745	15,743,040	10%
Other	8,694,563	13,987,550	9%
Total	$ 136,762,081	$ 150,254,525	

Goal: Increase Intergovernmental Revenue

Goal Amount	$ 37,421,002	25%

Lastname_Firstname_3E_Revenue

FIGURE 3.47

(Project 3E Revenue continues on the next page)

CONTENT-BASED ASSESSMENTS

1 Start Excel. From your student data files, locate and open **e03E_Revenue**. **Save** the file in your **Excel Chapter 3** folder as **Lastname_Firstname_3E_Revenue**

2 In cells **B10** and **C10**, enter formulas to calculate totals for each column. In cell **D5**, construct a formula to calculate the **% of Total Projected Revenue** from **Taxes** by dividing the **Projected Revenue for Next Fiscal Year** for **Taxes** by the **Total Projected Revenue for Next Fiscal Year**. Use absolute cell references as necessary, format the result in **Percent Style**, and **Center** the percentage. Fill the formula down through cell **D9**.

3 Select the nonadjacent ranges **A5:A9** and **C5:C9** as the data for a pie chart, and then insert a **3-D Pie** chart. Move the chart to a **New sheet** named **Projected Revenue Chart** As the text for the **Chart Title** element, type **Projected Revenue** Format the **Chart Title** by using the **WordArt Style Fill – Aqua, Accent 1, Shadow**—in the first row, the second style and a **Font Size** of **32**.

4 Remove the **Legend** chart element, and then add the **Data Labels** chart element formatted so that only the **Category Name** and **Percentage** display positioned in the **Center**. Format the data labels with a **Font style** of **Bold** and a **Font Size** of **14**.

5 Format the **Data Series** by using a **3-D Format** effect. Change the **Top bevel** and **Bottom bevel** to **Art Deco**. Set the **Top bevel Width** and **Height** to **350 pt** and then set the **Bottom bevel Width** and **Height** to **0 pt** Change the **Material** to the second **Special Effect—Soft Edge**.

6 Display the **Series Options**, and then set the **Angle of first slice** to **115** so that the **Taxes** slice is in the front of the pie. Select the **Services** slice, and then explode the slice **10%**. Change the **Fill Color** of the **Services** slice to a **Solid fill** by using **Gray-50%, Accent 4**—in the eighth column, the first color.

7 Format the **Chart Area** by applying a **Gradient fill** by using the **Preset gradients Light Gradient – Accent 4**.

Format the **Border** of the **Chart Area** by applying a **Solid line** border by using **Gray-50%, Accent 4** and a **5 pt Width**. Close any panes that are open on the right.

8 Display the **Page Setup** dialog box, and then for this chart sheet, insert a **Custom Footer** in the **left section** with the file name.

9 Display **Sheet1** and rename the sheet as **Revenue Sources** Click in any blank cell to cancel any selections. In cell **A12**, type **Goal: Increase Intergovernmental Revenue** and then **Merge & Center** the text across the range **A12:D12**. Apply the **Heading 3** cell style. In cell **A13**, type **Goal Amount**

10 Copy the range **C7:D7** to the range **B13:C13**. Click cell **C13**, and then use **Goal Seek** to determine the projected amount of Intergovernmental Revenue in cell **B13** if the value in **C13** is **25%**

11 Select the range **A13:C13**, and then apply the **20% - Accent4** cell style. In **B13**, from the **Cell Styles** gallery, apply the **Currency [0]** cell style.

12 Display the **Page Setup** dialog box, center the worksheet **Horizontally**, and then insert a custom footer in the **left section** with the file name. Select all the sheets, and then click the **FILE tab** to display **Backstage** view. Show all the properties, and then as the **Tags**, type **revenue sources** As the **Subject**, type your course name and section number. Be sure your name displays as the **Author**. On the left, click **Print** to display the **Print Preview**, and note any necessary changes or corrections. In **Backstage** view, on the left click **Save**, and then print or submit electronically as directed. If required by your instructor, print or create an electronic version of your worksheet with formulas displayed by using the instructions in Project 1A, and then close Excel without saving so that you do not save the changes you made to print formulas.

END | You have completed Project 3E

CONTENT-BASED ASSESSMENTS

Mastering Excel | Project 3F Streets

Apply 3B skills from these Objectives:

5 Design a Worksheet for What-If Analysis

6 Answer What-If Questions by Changing Values in a Worksheet

7 Chart Data with a Line Chart

Build from Scratch

In the following project, you will create a worksheet that the City of Pacifica Bay Facilities Director will use to prepare a five-year forecast of the costs associated with street maintenance. Your completed worksheet will look similar to Figure 3.48.

PROJECT FILES

For Project 3F, you will need the following file:

New blank Excel workbook

You will save your workbook as:

Lastname_Firstname_3F_Streets

PROJECT RESULTS

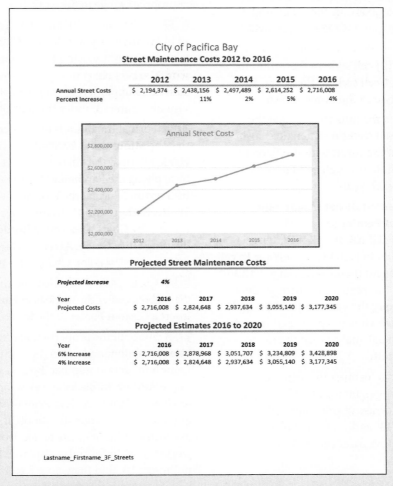

FIGURE 3.48

(Project 3F Streets continues on the next page)

CONTENT-BASED ASSESSMENTS

1 Start Excel and display a new Blank workbook. Change the **Theme Colors** to **Paper**, and then **Save** the file in your **Excel Chapter 3** folder as Lastname_Firstname_3F_Streets

2 In cell **A1**, type the title **City of Pacifica Bay** and then in cell **A2** type the subtitle **Street Maintenance Costs 2012 to 2016 Merge & Center** both the title and the subtitle across **columns A:F**, and then apply the **Title** and **Heading 1** cell styles respectively.

3 In the range **B4:F4**, fill the year range with the values 2012 through 2016. In cell **A5** type **Annual Street Costs** and in cell **A6** type **Percent Increase** Change the width of **column A** to **150 pixels**, and then change the width of **columns B:F** to **85 pixels**. In the range **B5:F5** type **2194374** and **2438156** and **2497489** and **2614252** and **2716008**

4 Apply the **Currency [0]** cell style to the values in **B5:F5**. Apply the **Heading 1** cell style to the years, and apply the **Heading 4** cell style to the range **A5:A6**.

5 In cell **C6**, construct a formula to calculate the percent of increase in annual street maintenance costs from 2012 to 2013. Format the result with the **Percent Style** and then fill the formula through cell **F6** to calculate the percent of increase in each year.

6 In cell **A8**, type **Projected Street Maintenance Costs** and then use **Format Painter** to copy the formatting from cell **A2** to cell **A8**. In cell **A10**, type **Projected Increase** and then in cell **A12**, type **Year** In cell **A13**, type **Projected Costs** and then in the range **B12:F12**, use the fill handle to enter the years 2016 through 2020. Apply **Bold** to the years. **Copy** the value in cell **F5** to cell **B13**. In cell **B10**, type **6%** which is the projected increase estimated by the City financial analysts. To the range **A10:B10**, apply **Bold** and **Italic**.

7 In cell **C13**, construct a formula to calculate the annual projected street maintenance costs for the year 2017 after the projected increase of 6% is applied. Fill the formula through cell **F13**, and then use **Format Painter** to copy the formatting from cell **B13** to the range **C13:F13**.

8 In cell **A15**, type **Projected Estimates 2016 to 2020** and then use **Format Painter** to copy the format from cell **A8** to cell **A15**. In cells **A17:A19**, type the following row titles:

> **Year**
>
> **6% Increase**
>
> **4% Increase**

9 **Copy** the range **B12:F12**, and then **Paste** the selection to **B17:F17**. Copy the range **B13:F13** and then paste the **Values & Number Formatting** to the range **B18:F18**. Complete the Projected Estimates section of the worksheet by changing the *Projected Increase* in **B10** to **4%** and then copying and pasting the **Values & Number Formatting** to the appropriate range in the worksheet. **Save** your workbook.

10 Select **rows 8:24**, and then **Insert** the same number of blank rows as you selected. **Clear Formatting** from the inserted rows. By using the data in **A4:F5**, insert a **Line with Markers** chart in the worksheet. Move the chart so that its upper left corner is positioned in cell **A9** and visually centered under the data above.

11 Format the **Bounds** of the **Vertical (Value) Axis** so that the **Minimum** is **2000000** and the **Major unit** is at **200000** Format the **Fill** of the **Chart Area** with a **Texture fill** by applying the **Parchment** texture—in the third row, the fifth texture. Format the **Plot Area** with a **Solid fill** by using **White, Background 1**—in the first column, the first color. Format the **Chart Area** with a **Border** by applying a **Solid line** by using **Olive Green, Accent 1, Darker 50%**—in the fifth column, the last color. Change the **Width** of the border to **2**

12 Click cell **A1** to deselect the chart. From the **Page Setup** dialog box, center the worksheet **Horizontally**, and then insert a **Custom Footer** in the **left section** with the file name.

13 Show all the properties, and then as the **Tags**, type **street maintenance costs** As the **Subject**, type your course name and section number. Be sure your name displays as the **Author**. In **Backstage** view, on the left, click **Print** to view the Print Preview. Print or submit electronically as directed. **Save** your workbook. If required by your instructor, print or create an electronic version of your worksheet with formulas displayed by using the instructions in Project 1A, and then close Excel without saving so that you do not save the changes you made to print formulas.

END | You have completed Project 3F

CONTENT-BASED ASSESSMENTS

Mastering Excel   Project 3G Operations

In the following project, you will edit a workbook for Jennifer Carson, City Finance Manager, that summarizes the operations costs for the Public Works Department. Your completed worksheets will look similar to Figure 3.49.

PROJECT FILES

For Project 3G, you will need the following file:

e03G_Expenses

You will save your workbook as

Lastname_Firstname_3G_Expenses

PROJECT RESULTS

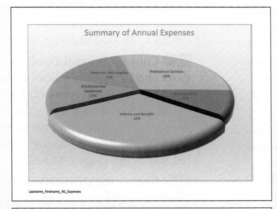

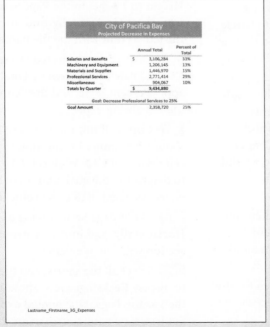

FIGURE 3.49

(Project 3G Operations continues on the next page)

CONTENT-BASED ASSESSMENTS

1 Start Excel. From your student data files, open **e03G_Expenses**. **Save** the file in your **Excel Chapter 3** folder as **Lastname_Firstname_3G_Expenses**

2 In the **Expenses** worksheet, calculate row totals for each expense item in the range **F5:F9**. Format the range **F6:F9** by applying the cell style **Comma [0]**. Calculate column totals for each quarter and for the Annual Total in the range **B10:F10**. In cell **G5**, construct a formula to calculate the **Percent of Total** by dividing the **Annual Total** for **Salaries and Benefits** by the **Annual Total** for all quarters. Use absolute cell references as necessary, format the result in **Percent Style**, and then **Center**. Fill the formula down through cell **G9**.

3 Use a **3-D Pie** chart to chart the **Annual Total** for each item. Move the chart to a **New sheet**; name the sheet **Annual Expenses Chart** As the text for the **Chart Title** element, type **Summary of Annual Expenses** Format the **Chart Title** by using **WordArt Style Fill - Blue, Accent 1, Shadow**—in the first row, the second style and a **Font Size** of **28**.

4 Remove the **Legend** from the chart, and then add **Data Labels** formatted so that only the **Category Name** and **Percentage** display positioned in the **Center**. Format the data labels with **Bold** and **Italic** and a **Font Size** of **12**.

5 Format the **Data Series** by using a **3-D Format** effect. Change the **Top bevel** and **Bottom bevel** to **Circle**. Set the **Top bevel Width** and **Height** to **50 pt** and then set the **Bottom bevel Width** and **Height** to **256 pt** Change the **Material** to the fourth **Standard Effect—Metal**.

6 Display the **Series Options**, and then set the **Angle of first slice** to **125** so that the **Salaries and Benefits** slice is in the front of the pie. Select the **Salaries and Benefits** slice, and then explode the slice **10%**. Change the **Fill Color** of the **Salaries and Benefits** slice to a **Solid fill** by using **Green, Accent 6, Lighter 40%**—in the last column, the fourth color.

7 Format the **Chart Area** by applying a **Gradient fill** using the **Preset gradients Light Gradient – Accent 4**. Format the **Border** of the **Chart Area** by adding a **Solid line** border using **Gold, Accent 4** and a **5 pt Width**.

8 Display the **Page Setup** dialog box, and then for this chart sheet, insert a **Custom Footer** in the **left section** with the file name. **Save** your workbook.

9 Display the **Expenses** worksheet, and then by using the Quarter names and the Totals by Quarter, insert a **Line with Markers** chart in the worksheet. Move the chart so that its upper left corner is positioned slightly inside the upper left corner of cell **A12**, and then drag the right sizing handle so that the chart extends slightly inside the right border of **column G**. As the **Chart Title** type **City of Pacifica Bay Annual Expense Summary**

10 Format the **Bounds** of the **Vertical (Value) Axis** so that the **Minimum** is **2100000** and the **Major unit** is at **50000** Format the **Fill** of the **Chart Area** with a **Gradient fill** by applying the preset **Light Gradient - Accent 3**—in the first row, the third gradient. Format the **Plot Area** with a **Solid fill** by using **White, Background 1**—in the first column, the first color. Close any panes on the right, click cell **A1** to deselect the chart, and then **Save** your workbook.

11 Copy the **Annual Total** in cell **F10** and then use **Paste Special** to paste **Values & Number Formatting** in cell **B35**. In cell **C35**, construct a formula to calculate the **Projected Expenses** after the forecasted increase of **3.5%** in cell **B31** is applied. Fill the formula through cell **F35**, and then use **Format Painter** to copy the formatting from cell **B35** to the range **C35:F35**.

12 Change the **Orientation** of this worksheet to **Landscape**, and then use the **Scale to Fit** options to fit the **Height** to **1 page**. In the **Page Setup** dialog box, center this worksheet **Horizontally**, and insert a **Custom Footer** in the **left section** with the file name. **Save** your workbook.

13 Display the **Projected Decrease** worksheet. In cell **C5**, calculate the **Percent of Total** for the first expense, apply **Percent Style**, and then copy the formula down for the remaining expenses.

14 Copy cell **B8**, and then use **Paste Special** to paste the **Values & Number Formatting** to cell **B13**. **Copy** and **Paste** cell **C8** to cell **C13**. With cell **C13** selected, use **Goal Seek** to determine the goal amount of Professional Services expenses in cell **B13** if the value in **C13** is set to **25%**

15 In the **Page Setup** dialog box, center this worksheet **Horizontally**, and insert a **Custom Footer** in the **left section** with the file name.

16 Select all the sheets, and then click the **FILE tab** to display **Backstage** view. Show all the properties, and then as the **Tags**, type **annual expense summary** As the **Subject**, type your course name and section number. Be sure your name displays as the **Author**. On the left, click

(Project 3G Operations continues on the next page)

CONTENT-BASED ASSESSMENTS

Print to display the **Print Preview**, and view all three worksheets. Note any necessary changes or corrections. In **Backstage** view, on the left click **Save**, and then print or submit electronically as directed. If required by your instructor, print or create an electronic version of your worksheet with formulas displayed by using the instructions in Project 1A, and then close Excel without saving so that you do not save the changes you made to print formulas.

END | You have completed Project 3G

CONTENT-BASED ASSESSMENTS

Build from
Scratch

GO! Fix It	Project 3H Schools	Online
GO! Make It	Project 3I Tax	Online
GO! Solve It	Project 3J Staffing	Online
GO! Solve It	Project 3K Water Usage	

Build from
Scratch

PROJECT FILES

For Project 3K, you will need the following files:

New blank Excel workbook
e03K_Beach

You will save your workbook as:

Lastname_Firstname_3K_Water_Usage

Pacifica Bay is a growing community and the City Council has requested an analysis of future resource needs. In this project, you will create a worksheet for the Department of Water and Power that illustrates residential water usage over a five-year period. Create a worksheet with the following data:

	2014	2015	2016	2017	2018
Water Use in Acre Feet	62518	65922	71864	76055	82542

Calculate the percent increase for the years 2015 to 2018. Below the Percent Increase, insert a line chart that illustrates the city's water usage from 2014 to 2018. Format the chart and worksheet attractively with a title and subtitle, and apply appropriate formatting. If you choose to format the chart area with a picture, you can use e03K_Beach located with your student files. Include the file name in the footer and enter appropriate document properties. Save the workbook as **Lastname_Firstname_3K_Water_Usage** and submit as directed.

Performance Level

Performance Criteria	Exemplary: You consistently applied the relevant skills	Proficient: You sometimes, but not always, applied the relevant skills	Developing: You rarely or never applied the relevant skills
Create formulas	All formulas are correct and are efficiently constructed.	Formulas are correct but not always constructed in the most efficient manner.	One or more formulas are missing or incorrect or only numbers were entered.
Insert and format a line chart	Line chart created correctly and is attractively formatted.	Line chart was created but the data was incorrect or the chart was not appropriately formatted.	No line chart was created.
Format attractively and appropriately	Formatting is attractive and appropriate.	Adequately formatted but difficult to read or unattractive.	Inadequate or no formatting.

END | You have completed Project 3K

OUTCOMES-BASED ASSESSMENTS

RUBRIC

The following outcomes-based assessments are open-ended assessments. That is, there is no specific correct result; your result will depend on your approach to the information provided. Make Professional Quality your goal. Use the following scoring rubric to guide you in how to approach the problem and then to evaluate how well your approach solves the problem.

The *criteria*—Software Mastery, Content, Format and Layout, and Process—represent the knowledge and skills you have gained that you can apply to solving the problem. The *levels of performance*—Professional Quality, Approaching Professional Quality, or Needs Quality Improvements—help you and your instructor evaluate your result.

	Your completed project is of Professional Quality if you:	Your completed project is Approaching Professional Quality if you:	Your completed project Needs Quality Improvements if you:
1-Software Mastery	Choose and apply the most appropriate skills, tools, and features and identify efficient methods to solve the problem.	Choose and apply some appropriate skills, tools, and features, but not in the most efficient manner.	Choose inappropriate skills, tools, or features, or are inefficient in solving the problem.
2-Content	Construct a solution that is clear and well organized, contains content that is accurate, appropriate to the audience and purpose, and is complete. Provide a solution that contains no errors in spelling, grammar, or style.	Construct a solution in which some components are unclear, poorly organized, inconsistent, or incomplete. Misjudge the needs of the audience. Have some errors in spelling, grammar, or style, but the errors do not detract from comprehension.	Construct a solution that is unclear, incomplete, or poorly organized; contains some inaccurate or inappropriate content; and contains many errors in spelling, grammar, or style. Do not solve the problem.
3-Format & Layout	Format and arrange all elements to communicate information and ideas, clarify function, illustrate relationships, and indicate relative importance.	Apply appropriate format and layout features to some elements, but not others. Overuse features, causing minor distraction.	Apply format and layout that does not communicate information or ideas clearly. Do not use format and layout features to clarify function, illustrate relationships, or indicate relative importance. Use available features excessively, causing distraction.
4-Process	Use an organized approach that integrates planning, development, self-assessment, revision, and reflection.	Demonstrate an organized approach in some areas, but not others; or, use an insufficient process of organization throughout.	Do not use an organized approach to solve the problem.

OUTCOMES-BASED ASSESSMENTS

GO! Think Project 3L Employment

PROJECT FILES

For Project 3L, you will need the following file:

New blank Excel workbook

You will save your workbook as:

Lastname_Firstname_3L_Employment

Sandy Ingram, the Director of the Employment Development Department for the city of Pacifica Bay, has requested an analysis of employment sectors in the city. Employment data for the previous two years is listed below:

Job Sector	2015 Employment	2016 Employment
Government	1,795	1,524
Healthcare	2,832	2,952
Retail	2,524	2,480
Food Service	3,961	3,753
Industrial	1,477	1,595
Professional	2,515	2,802

Create a workbook to provide Sandy with the employment information for each sector and the total employment for each year. Insert a column to calculate the percent change from 2015 to 2016. Note that some of the results will be negative numbers. Format the percentages with two decimal places. Insert a pie chart in its own sheet that illustrates the 2016 employment figures, and format the chart attractively. Format the worksheet so that it is professional and easy to read and understand. Insert a footer with the file name and add appropriate document properties. Save the file as **Lastname_Firstname_3L_Employment** and print or submit as directed by your instructor.

END | You have completed Project 3L

GO! Think Project 3M Population — **Online**

Build from Scratch

You and GO! Project 3N Expense Analysis — **Online**

Build from Scratch

GO! Cumulative Group Project Project 3O Bell Orchid Hotels — **Online**

Build from Scratch

Introduction to Microsoft Access 2013

A
Access 2013

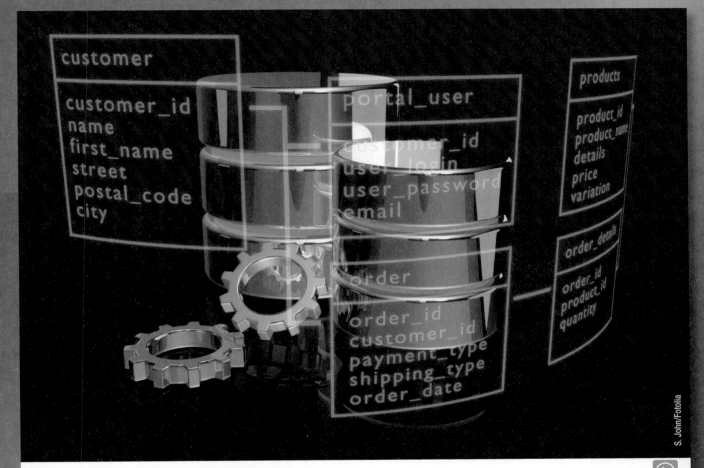

S. John/Fotolia

Access 2013: Introduction

Video AA

Microsoft Access 2013 provides a convenient way to organize data that makes it easy for you to retrieve information. Access uses tables to store data. Like Excel spreadsheets, data is stored in rows and columns in a table. So why use a database rather than an Excel spreadsheet? By using a database, you can manipulate and work with data in a more robust manner. For example, if you have thousands of records about patients in a hospital, you can easily find all of the records that pertain to the patients who received a specific type of medicine on a particular day. Information from one table can be used to retrieve information from another table. For example, by knowing a patient's ID number, you can view immunization records or view insurance information or view hospitalization records. Having information stored in an Access database enables you to make bulk changes to data at one time even when it is stored in different tables.

It's easy to get started with Access by using one of the many prebuilt database templates. For example, a nonprofit organization can track events, donors, members, and donations. A small business can use a prebuilt database to track inventory, create invoices, keep track of projects, manage pricing, track competitors, and manage quotes.

Getting Started with Microsoft Access 2013

GO! to Work
Video A1

PROJECT 1A

OUTCOMES
Create a new database.

OBJECTIVES

1. Identify Good Database Design
2. Create a Table and Define Fields in a Blank Desktop Database
3. Change the Structure of Tables and Add a Second Table
4. Create a Query, Form, and Report
5. Close a Database and Exit Access

PROJECT 1B

OUTCOMES
Create a database from a template.

OBJECTIVES

6. Use a Template to Create a Database
7. Organize Objects in the Navigation Pane
8. Create a New Table in a Database Created with a Template
9. Print a Report and a Table

Riccardo Piccinini/Fotolia

In This Chapter

In this chapter, you use Microsoft Access 2013 to organize a collection of related information. You will create new databases, create tables, and enter data into the tables. You will create a query, a form, and a report—all of which are Access objects that make a database useful for finding and analyzing information. You will also create a complete database from a template that you can use as provided, or that you can modify to suit your needs. In this chapter, you will also learn how to apply good database design principles to your Access database and to define the structure of a database.

The projects in this chapter relate to **Texas Lakes Community College**, which is located in the Austin, Texas, area. Its four campuses serve over 30,000 students and offer more than 140 certificate programs and degrees. The college has a highly acclaimed Distance Education program and an extensive Workforce Development program. The college makes positive contributions to the community through cultural and athletic programs and has significant partnerships with businesses and nonprofit organizations. Popular fields of study include nursing and health care, solar technology, computer technology, and graphic design.

Student Advising Database with Two Tables

PROJECT ACTIVITIES

In Activities 1.01 through 1.17, you will assist Dr. Daniel Martinez, vice president of Student Services at Texas Lakes Community College, in creating a new database for tracking students and their faculty advisors. Your completed database objects will look similar to Figure 1.1.

PROJECT FILES

For Project 1A, you will need the following files:

Blank desktop database
a01A_Students (Excel workbook)
a01A_Faculty_Advisors (Excel workbook)

You will save your database as:

Lastname_Firstname_1A_Advising

Build from
Scratch

PROJECT RESULTS

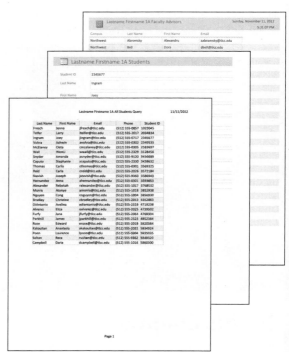

FIGURE 1.1 Project 1A Advising

Objective 1 — Identify Good Database Design

Video A1-1

A *database* is an organized collection of *data*—facts about people, events, things, or ideas—related to a specific topic or purpose. *Information* is data that is organized in a useful manner. Your contact list is a type of database because it is a collection of data about one topic—the people with whom you communicate. A simple database of this type is called a *flat database* because it is not related or linked to any other collection of data. Another example of a simple database is a list of your music collection. You do not keep information about your music collection in your contact list because the data is not related to the people in your contact list.

A more sophisticated type of database is a *relational database*, so-called because multiple collections of data in the database are related to one another; for example, data about the students, the courses, and the faculty members at a college. Microsoft Access 2013 is a relational *database management system*—also referred to as a *DBMS*—which is software that controls how related collections of data are stored, organized, retrieved, and secured.

Activity 1.01 | Using Good Design Techniques to Plan a Database

Before creating a new database, the first step is to determine the information you want to keep track of by asking yourself, *What questions should this database be able to answer?* The purpose of a database is to store the data in a manner that makes it easy to get the information you need by asking questions. For example, in a student database for Texas Lakes Community College, the questions to be answered might include:

- How many students are enrolled at the college?
- How many students have not yet been assigned a faculty advisor?
- Which students live in Austin, Texas?
- Which students owe money for tuition?
- Which students are majoring in Information Systems Technology?

Tables are the foundation of an Access database because all of the data is stored in one or more tables. A table is similar in structure to an Excel worksheet because data is organized into rows and columns. Each table row is a *record*—all of the categories of data pertaining to one person, place, event, thing, or idea. Each table column is a *field*—a single piece of information for every record. For example, in a table storing student contact information, each row forms a record for only one student. Each column forms a field for every record; for example, the student ID number or the student last name.

When organizing the fields of information in your table, break each piece of information into its smallest, most useful part. For example, create three fields for the name of a student—one field for the last name, one field for the first name, and one field for the middle name or initial.

The ***first principle of good database design*** is to organize data in the tables so that ***redundant***—duplicate—data does not occur. For example, record the student contact information in only *one* table, so that if a student's address changes, you can change the information in just one place. This conserves space, reduces the likelihood of errors when recording new data, and does not require remembering all of the different places where the student's address is stored.

The ***second principle of good database design*** is to use techniques that ensure the accuracy and consistency of data as it is entered into the table. Typically, many different people enter data into a database—think of all the people who enter data about students at your college. When entering a state in a student contacts table, one person might enter the state as *Texas*, while another might enter the state as *TX*. Use design techniques to help those who enter data into a database to enter the data more accurately and consistently.

Normalization is the process of applying design rules and principles to ensure that your database performs as expected. Taking the time to plan and create a database that is well designed will ensure that you can retrieve meaningful information from the database.

The tables of information in a relational database are linked or joined to one another by a ***common field***—a field in two or more tables that stores the same data. For example, a Students table includes the Student ID, name, and address of every student. The Student Activities table includes the club name and the Student ID of members, but not the name or address, of each student in the club. Because the two tables share a common field—Student ID—you can create a list of names and addresses of all of the students in the Photography Club. The names and addresses are stored in the Students table, and the Student IDs of the Photography Club members are stored in the Student Activities table.

Objective 2 | Create a Table and Define Fields in a Blank Desktop Database

Video A1-2

There are three methods to create a new Access database. One method is to create a new database using a ***database template***—a preformatted database designed for a specific purpose. A second method is to create a new database from a ***blank desktop database***. A blank desktop database is stored on your computer or other storage device. It has no data and has no database tools; you create the data and the tools as you need them. A third method is to create a ***custom web app*** database from scratch or by using a template that you can publish and share with others over the Internet.

Regardless of the method you use, you must name and save the database before you can create any ***objects*** in it. Objects are the basic parts of a database; you create objects to store your data, to work with your data, and to display your data. The most common database objects are tables, queries, forms, and reports. Think of an Access database as a container for the objects that you create.

Activity 1.02 | Starting with a Blank Desktop Database

1 ▶ Start Access using the same technique you used to locate and open other Office desktop apps. Take a moment to compare your screen with Figure 1.2 and study the parts of the Microsoft Access opening screen described in the table in Figure 1.3.

From this Access opening screen, you can open an existing database, create a custom web app, create a blank desktop database, or create a new web app or desktop database from a template.

FIGURE 1.2

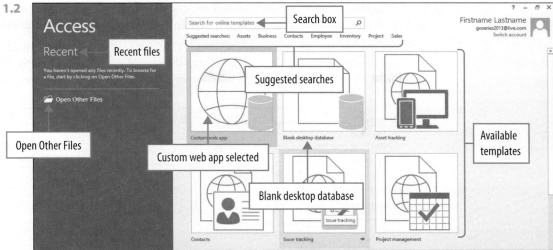

FIGURE 1.3

MICROSOFT ACCESS OPENING SCREEN ELEMENTS	
SCREEN ELEMENT	**DESCRIPTION**
Available templates	Starts a database for a specific purpose that includes built-in objects and tools ready for use.
Blank desktop database	Starts a blank database that is stored on your computer or on a storage device.
Custom web app	Starts a web app database that can be published and shared on the Internet.
Open Other Files	Enables you to open a database file from your computer, a shared location, or other location that you have designated.
Recent files	Displays a list of database files that have been recently opened.
Search box	Enables you to search the Microsoft Office website for templates.
Suggested searches	Enables you to click on a category to start an online search for a template.

> **2** In the Access opening screen, click **Blank desktop database**. In the **Blank desktop database** dialog box, to the right of the **File Name** box, click **Browse** ⬚. In the **File New Database** dialog box, navigate to the location where you are saving your databases for this chapter, create a **New folder** named **Access Chapter 1** and then press Enter. With the folder name selected, in the **File New Database** dialog box, click **Open**.

In the File name box, *Database1* displays as the default file name—the number at the end of your file name might differ if you have saved a database previously with the default name. In the Save as type box, the default database type is *Microsoft Access 2007 – 2013 Databases*, which means that you can open a database created in Access 2013 by using Access 2007, Access 2010, or Access 2013.

> **3** Click in the **File name** box. Using your own name, replace the existing text with **Lastname_Firstname_1A_Advising** and then click **OK** or press Enter. Compare your screen with Figure 1.4.

In the Blank desktop database dialog box, in the File Name box, the name of your database displays. Under the File Name box, the drive and folder where the database will be stored displays. An Access database has a file extension of *.accdb*.

FIGURE 1.4

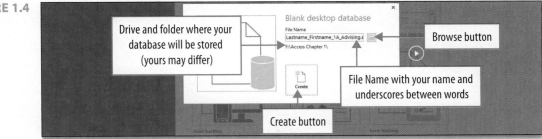

4 In the **Blank desktop database** dialog box, click **Create**. Compare your screen with Figure 1.5, and then take a moment to study the screen elements described in the table in Figure 1.6.

Access creates the new database and opens *Table1*. Recall that a table is an Access object that stores data in columns and rows, similar to the format of an Excel worksheet. Table objects are the foundation of a database because tables store the data that is used by other database objects.

FIGURE 1.5

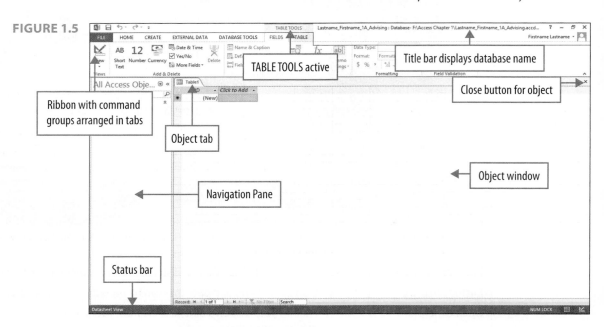

FIGURE 1.6

MICROSOFT ACCESS DATABASE WINDOW ELEMENTS	
ACCESS WINDOW ELEMENT	**DESCRIPTION**
Navigation Pane	Displays the database objects that you can open in the object window.
Object tab	Identifies and enables you to work with the open object.
Object window	Displays the active or open object (table, query, or other object).
Close button for object	Closes the active object (table, query, or other object).
Ribbon with command groups arranged in tabs	Groups the commands for performing related database tasks on tabs.
Status bar	Indicates the active view and the status of action occurring within the database on the left; provides buttons on the right to switch between Datasheet view and Design view.
Table Tools	Provides tools for working with a table object—only available when a table object is active.
Title bar	Displays the database name.

Activity 1.03 | Assigning the Data Type and Name to Fields

After you have named and saved your database, the next step is to consult your database design plan and then create the tables for your data. Limit the data in each table to *one* subject. For example, in this project, your database will have two tables—one for student information and one for faculty advisor information.

Recall that each column in a table is a field; field names display at the top of each column of the table. Recall also that each row in a table is a record—all of the data pertaining to one person, place, thing, event, or idea. Each record is broken up into its smallest usable parts—the fields. Use meaningful names for fields; for example, *Last Name*.

1 Notice the new blank table that displays in **Datasheet** view, and then take a moment to study the elements of the table's object window. Compare your screen with Figure 1.7.

> The table displays in **Datasheet view**, which displays the data in columns and rows similar to the format of an Excel worksheet. Another way to view a table is in **Design view**, which displays the underlying design—the **structure**—of the table's fields. The **object window** displays the open object—in this instance, the table object.

> In a new blank database, there is only one object—a new blank table. Because you have not yet named this table, the object tab displays a default name of *Table1*. Access creates the first field and names it *ID*. In the ID field, Access assigns a unique sequential number—each number incremented by one—to each record as it is entered into the table.

FIGURE 1.7

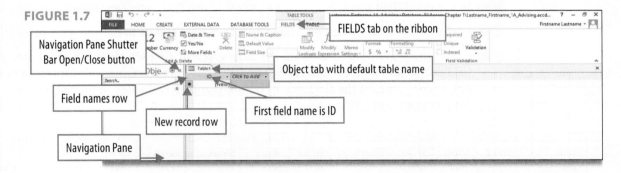

2 In the **Navigation Pane**, click **Shutter Bar Open/Close Button** « to collapse the **Navigation Pane** to a narrow bar on the left.

> The **Navigation Pane** displays and organizes the names of the objects in a database. From the Navigation Pane, you can open objects. Collapse or close the Navigation Pane to display more of the object—in this case, the table.

ANOTHER WAY Press F11 to close or open the Navigation Pane.

3 In the field names row, click anywhere in the text *Click to Add* to display a list of data types. Compare your screen with Figure 1.8.

> A **data type** defines the kind of data that you can store in a field, such as numbers, text, or dates. A field in a table can have only one data type. The data type of each field should be included in your database design. After selecting the data type, you can name the field.

ANOTHER WAY To the right of *Click to Add*, click the arrow.

FIGURE 1.8

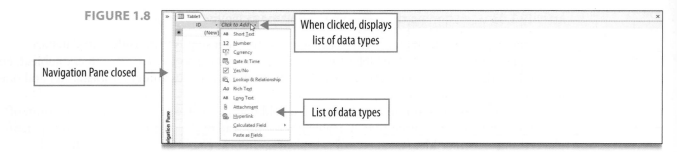

4 On the list of data types, click **Short Text**, and notice that in the second column, *Click to Add* changes to *Field1*, which is selected. Type **Last Name** and then press Enter.

> The second column displays *Last Name* as the field name, and, in the third column, the data type list displays. The ***Short Text data type*** describes text, a combination of text and numbers, or numbers that are not used in calculations, such as the Postal Code. This data type enables you to enter up to 255 characters in the field.

ANOTHER WAY With the list of data types displayed, type the character that is underscored to select the data type. For example, type *t* to select Short Text or type *u* to select Currency.

5 In the third field name box, type **t** to select *Short Text*, type **First Name** and then press Enter.

6 In the fourth field name box, click **Short Text**, type **Middle Initial** and then press Enter.

7 Create the remaining fields from the table given by first selecting the data type, typing the field name, and then pressing Enter. The field names in the table will display on one line—do not be concerned if the field names do not completely display in the column; you will adjust the column widths later.

Data Type		Short Text	Short Text	Short Text	Short Text	Short Text	Short Text	Short Text	Short Text	Short Text	Short Text	Currency
Field Name	ID	Last Name	First Name	Middle Initial	Address	City	State	Postal Code	Phone	Email	Faculty Advisor ID	Amount Owed

> The Postal Code and Phone fields are assigned a data type of Short Text because the numbers are never used in calculations. The Amount Owed field is assigned the ***Currency data type***, which describes monetary values and numeric data that can be used in calculations and that have one to four decimal places. A U.S. dollar sign ($) and two decimal places are automatically included for all of the numbers in a field with the Currency data type.

8 If necessary, scroll to bring the first column—**ID**—into view, and then compare your screen with Figure 1.9.

> Access automatically created the ID field, and you created 11 additional fields in the table.

FIGURE 1.9

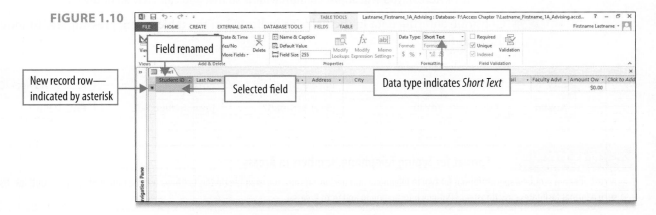

> **More Knowledge** | **Create Fields by Entering Data**
>
> You can create a new field in Datasheet view by typing the data in a new column. Access automatically assigns a data type based on the data you enter. For example, if you enter a date, Access assigns the Date/Time data type. If you enter a monetary amount, Access assigns the Currency data type. If Access cannot determine the data type based on the data entered, the Short Text data type is assigned. You can always change the data type if an incorrect data type is assigned. If you use this method to create fields, you must check the assigned data types to be sure they are correct. You must also rename the fields because Access assigns the names as *Field1*, *Field2*, and so on.

Activity 1.04 | Renaming Fields and Changing Data Types in a Table

1 In the first column, click anywhere in the text *ID*. On the ribbon, under **TABLE TOOLS**, on the **FIELDS tab**, in the **Properties group**, click **Name & Caption**. In the **Enter Field Properties** dialog box, in the **Name** box, change *ID* to **Student ID**

The field name *Student ID* is a clearer and more precise description of this field's data. In the Enter Field Properties dialog box, you have the option to change the *Caption* to display a name for a field other than the name that displays in the Name box. Many database designers do not use spaces in field names; instead, they might name a field *LastName* or *LName* and then create a caption for the field so it displays as *Last Name* in tables, forms, or reports. In the Enter Field Properties dialog box, you can also provide a description for the field.

ANOTHER WAY   Right-click the field name to display the shortcut menu, and then click Rename Field; or, double-click the field name to select the existing text, and then type the new field name.

2 Click **OK** to close the **Enter Field Properties** dialog box. On the ribbon, in the **Formatting group**, notice that the **Data Type** for the **Student ID** field is *AutoNumber*. Click the **Data Type arrow**, click **Short Text**, and then compare your screen with Figure 1.10.

In the new record row, the Student ID field is selected. By default, Access creates an ID field for all new tables and sets the data type for the field to AutoNumber. The **AutoNumber data type** describes a unique sequential or random number assigned by Access as each record is entered. Changing the data type of this field to Short Text enables you to enter a custom student ID number.

When records in a database have *no* unique value, such as a book ISBN or a license plate number, the AutoNumber data type is a useful way to automatically create a unique number. In this manner, you are sure that every record is different from the others.

FIGURE 1.10

Activity 1.05 | Adding a Record to a Table

A new contact list is not useful until you fill it with names and phone numbers. Likewise, a new database is not useful until you ***populate*** it by filling one or more tables with data. You can populate a table with records by typing data directly into the table.

1 In the new record row, click in the **Student ID** field to display the insertion point, type **1023045** and then press Enter. Compare your screen with Figure 1.11.

The pencil icon ✎ in the *record selector box* indicates that a record is being entered or edited. The record selector box is the small box at the left of a record in Datasheet view. When clicked, the entire record is selected.

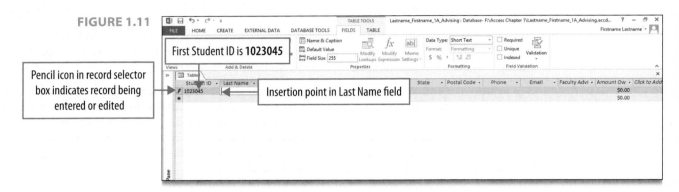

ANOTHER WAY   Press Tab to move the insertion point to the next field.

FIGURE 1.11

First Student ID is 1023045

Pencil icon in record selector box indicates record being entered or edited

Insertion point in Last Name field

2 With the insertion point positioned in the **Last Name** field, type **Fresch** and then press Enter.

NOTE   **Correcting Typing Errors**

Correct any typing errors you make by using the techniques you have practiced in other Office applications. For example, use Backspace to remove characters to the left of the insertion point. Use Del to remove characters to the right of the insertion point. Or select the text you want to replace and type the correct information. Press Esc to exit out of a record that has not been completely entered.

---

3 In the **First Name** field, type **Jenna** and then press Enter.

4 In the **Middle Initial** field, type **A** and then press Enter.

5 In the **Address** field, type **7550 Douglas Ln** and then press Enter.

Do not be concerned if the data does not completely display in the column. As you progress in your study of Access, you will adjust column widths so that you can view all of the data.

6 Continue entering data in the fields as indicated in the table given, pressing Enter to move to the next field.

City	State	Postal Code	Phone	Email	Faculty Advisor ID
Austin	**TX**	**78749**	**(512) 555-0857**	**jfresch@tlcc.edu**	**FAC-2289**

NOTE   **Format for Typing Telephone Numbers in Access**

Access does not require a specific format for typing telephone numbers in a record. The examples in this textbook use the format of Microsoft Outlook. Using such a format facilitates easy transfer of Outlook information to and from Access.

---

7 In the **Amount Owed** field, type **250** and then press Enter. Compare your screen with Figure 1.12.

Pressing Enter or Tab in the last field moves the insertion point to the next row to begin a new record. Access automatically saves the record as soon as you move to the next row; you do not have to take any specific action to save a record.

FIGURE 1.12

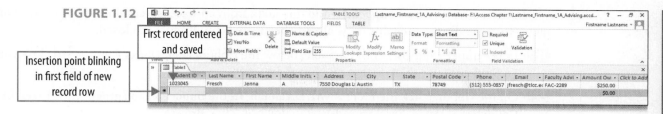

First record entered and saved

Insertion point blinking in first field of new record row

8 To give your table a meaningful name, on the **Quick Access Toolbar**, click **Save** 🔲. In the **Save As** dialog box, in the **Table Name** box, using your own name, replace the selected text by typing **Lastname Firstname 1A Students**

Save each database object with a name that identifies the data that it contains. When you save objects within a database, it is not necessary to use underscores in place of the spaces between words. Your name is included as part of the object name so that you and your instructor can identify your printouts or electronic files easily.

9 In the **Save As** dialog box, click **OK**. Notice that the object tab—located directly above the **Student ID** field name—displays the new table name that you just entered.

More Knowledge | **Renaming or Deleting a Table**

To change the name of a table, close the table, display the Navigation Pane, right-click the table name, and then click Rename. Type the new name or edit as you would any selected text. To delete a table, close the table, display the Navigation Pane, right-click the table name, and then click Delete.

Activity 1.06 | Adding Additional Records to a Table

1 In the new record row, click in the **Student ID** field, and then enter the data for two additional students as shown in the table given. Press Enter or Tab to move from field to field. The data in each field will display on one line in the table.

ent	Last Name	First Name	Middle Initial	Address	City	State	Postal Code	Phone	Email	Faculty Advisor ID	Amount Owed
677	Ingram	Joey	S	621 Hilltop Dr	Leander	TX	78646	(512) 555-0717	jingram@ tlcc.edu	FAC-2377	378.5
689	Snyder	Amanda	J	4786 Bluff St	Buda	TX	78610	(512) 555-9120	asnyder@ tlcc.edu	FAC-9005	0

2 Compare your screen with Figure 1.13.

FIGURE 1.13

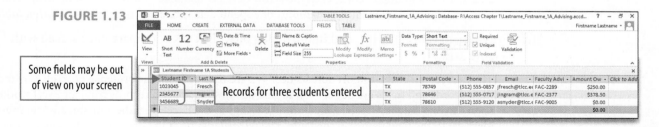

Some fields may be out of view on your screen

Records for three students entered

Activity 1.07 | Importing Data from an Excel Workbook into an Existing Access Table

You can type records directly into a table. You can also *import* data from a variety of sources. Importing is the process of copying data from one source or application to another application. For example, you can import data from a Word table or an Excel spreadsheet into an Access database because the data is arranged in columns and rows, similar to a table in Datasheet view.

In this activity, you will *append*—add on—data from an Excel spreadsheet to your *1A Students* table. To append data, the table must already be created, and it must be closed.

1 In the upper right corner of the table, below the ribbon, click **Object Close** ☒ to close your **1A Students** table. Notice that no objects are open.

2 On the ribbon, click the **EXTERNAL DATA tab**. In the **Import & Link group**, click **Excel**. In the **Get External Data – Excel Spreadsheet** dialog box, click **Browse**.

3 In the **File Open** dialog box, navigate to your student files, double-click the Excel file **a01A_Students**, and then compare your screen with Figure 1.14.

> The path to the *source file*—the file being imported—displays in the File name box. There are three options for importing data from an Excel spreadsheet: import the data into a *new* table in the current database, append a copy of the records to an existing table, or link the data from the spreadsheet to a linked table in the database. A *link* is a connection to data in another file. When linking, Access creates a table that maintains a link to the source data, so that changes to the data in one file are automatically made in the other—linked—file.

↻ ANOTHER WAY   Click the file name, and then in the File Open dialog box, click Open.

FIGURE 1.14

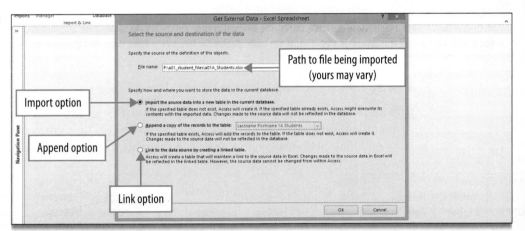

4 Click the **Append a copy of the records to the table** option button, and then, in the box to the right, click the **arrow**.

> Currently, your database has only one table, so no other tables display on the list. However, when a database has multiple tables, click the arrow to select the table to which you want to append records. The table into which you import or append data is referred to as the *destination table*.

5 Press ⌅Esc to cancel the list, and in the dialog box, click **OK**. Compare your screen with Figure 1.15.

> The first screen of the Import Spreadsheet Wizard displays, and the presence of scroll bars indicates that records and fields are out of view in this window. To append records from an Excel workbook to an existing database table, the column headings in the Excel worksheet or spreadsheet must be identical to the field names in the table. The *wizard* identifies the first row of the spreadsheet as column headings, which are equivalent to field names. A wizard is a feature in a Microsoft Office program that walks you step by step through a process.

FIGURE 1.15

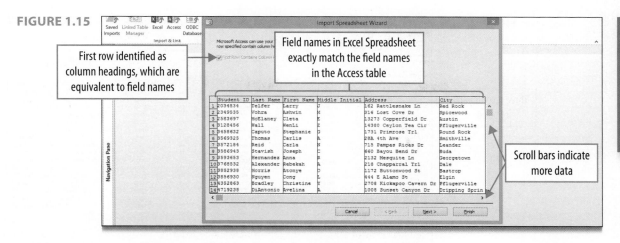

First row identified as column headings, which are equivalent to field names

Field names in Excel Spreadsheet exactly match the field names in the Access table

Scroll bars indicate more data

6 ▸ In the lower right corner of the wizard, click **Next**. Notice that the name of your table displays under **Import to Table**. In the lower right corner of the wizard, click **Finish**.

7 ▸ In the **Get External Data – Excel Spreadsheet** dialog box, click **Close**. Open ⟫ the **Navigation Pane**.

8 ▸ Point to the right edge of the **Navigation Pane** to display the ⟺ pointer. Drag to the right to increase the width of the **Navigation Pane** so that the entire table name displays, and then compare your screen with Figure 1.16.

FIGURE 1.16

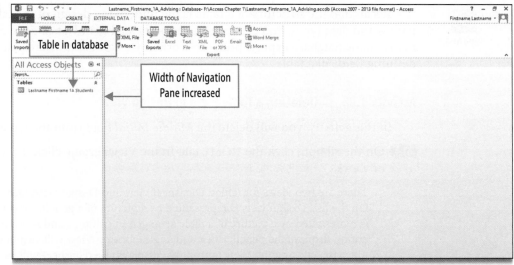

Table in database

Width of Navigation Pane increased

9 ▸ In the **Navigation Pane**, double-click your **1A Students** table to open the table in **Datasheet** view, and then **Close** ⟪ the **Navigation Pane**.

 ANOTHER WAY   To open an object from the Navigation Pane, right-click the object name, and then click Open.

10 ▸ In the lower left corner of your screen, locate the navigation area, and notice that there are a total of **25** records in the table—you entered three records and imported 22 additional records. Compare your screen with Figure 1.17.

The records that you entered and the records you imported from the Excel spreadsheet display in your table; the first record in the table is selected. The *navigation area* indicates the number of records in the table and has controls in the form of arrows that you click in order to navigate among the records.

FIGURE 1.17

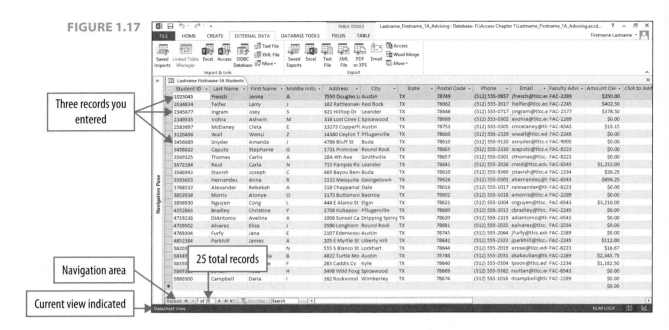

Three records you entered

Navigation area

25 total records

Current view indicated

Objective 3 | Change the Structure of Tables and Add a Second Table

Video A1-3

Recall that the structure of a table is the underlying design of the table and includes field names and data types. You can create or modify a table in Datasheet view. To define and modify fields, many database experts prefer to work in Design view, where you have more options for defining fields in a table.

Activity 1.08 | Deleting a Table Field in Design View

In this activity, you will delete the *Middle Initial* field from the table.

1 On the ribbon, click the **HOME tab**. In the **Views group**, click the **View arrow** to display a list of views.

There are two views for tables: Datasheet view and Design view. Other objects have different views. On the list, Design view is represented by a picture of a pencil, a ruler, and an angle. Datasheet view is represented by a picture of a table arranged in columns and rows. In the Views group, if the View button displays the pencil, ruler, and angle, clicking View will switch your view to Design view. Likewise, clicking the View button that displays as a datasheet will switch your view to Datasheet view.

2 On the list, click **Design View**, and then compare your screen with Figure 1.18.

Design view displays the underlying design—the structure—of the table and its fields. In Design view, the records with the data in the table do not display. You can only view the information about each field's characteristics. Each field name is listed, along with its data type. You can add more descriptive information about a field in the Description column.

You can decide how each field should look and behave in the Field Properties area. For example, you can set a specific field size in the Field Properties area. In the lower right corner, information displays about the active selection—in this case, the Field Name.

FIGURE 1.18

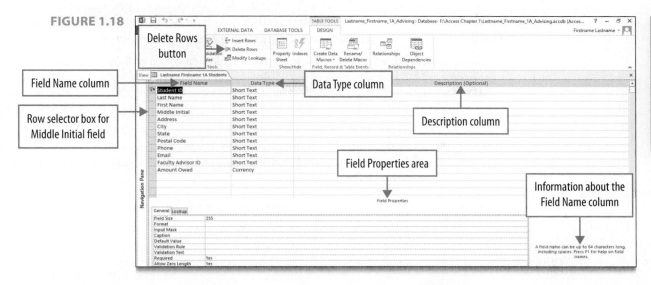

3 In the **Field Name** column, to the left of **Middle Initial**, point to the row selector box to display the ➡ pointer, and then click one time to select the entire row.

4 Under **TABLE TOOLS**, on the **DESIGN tab**, in the **Tools group**, click **Delete Rows**. Read the message in the message box, and then click **Yes**.

Deleting a field deletes both the field and its data. After you save the changes, you cannot undo this action, so Access prompts you to be sure you want to proceed. If you change your mind after deleting a field and saving the changes, you must add the field back into the table and then reenter the data for that field for every record.

⟳ ANOTHER WAY   In Design view, right-click the selected row, and then click Delete Rows; or, in Datasheet view, select the field—column—and on the HOME tab, in the Records group, click Delete.

Activity 1.09 | Changing a Field Size and Adding a Description

Typically, many different individuals in an organization have the ability to enter data into a table. For example, at your college, many registration assistants enter and modify student and course information daily. Two ways to help reduce errors are to restrict what can be typed in a field and to add descriptive information to help the individuals when entering the data.

1 With your table still displayed in **Design** view, in the **Field Name** column, click anywhere in the **Student ID** field name.

2 In the lower area of the screen, under **Field Properties**, click **Field Size** to select *255*, type **7** and then press Enter.

This action limits the size of the Student ID field to no more than seven characters. *Field properties* control how the field displays and how data can be entered into the field. You can define properties for each field in the Field Properties area by first clicking on the field name.

The default field size for a Short Text field is 255. Limiting the Field Size property to seven ensures that no more than seven characters can be entered for each Student ID. However, this does not prevent someone from entering seven characters that are incorrect or entering fewer than seven characters. Setting the proper data type for the field and limiting the field size are two ways to *help* reduce errors during data entry.

⟳ ANOTHER WAY   In Datasheet view, click in the field. On the FIELDS tab, in the Properties group, click in the Field Size box, and then type the number that represents the maximum number of characters for that field.

> **3** In the **Student ID** row, click in the **Description** box, type **Seven-digit Student ID number** and then press Enter. Compare your screen with Figure 1.19.

> Descriptions for fields in a table are optional. Include a description if the field name does not provide an obvious explanation of the type of data to be entered. If a description is provided for a field, when data is entered in that field in Datasheet view, the text in the Description displays on the left side of the status bar to provide additional information for the individuals who are entering the data.

> When you enter a description for a field, a Property Update Options button displays below the text you typed, which enables you to copy the description for the field to all other database objects that use this table as an underlying source.

FIGURE 1.19

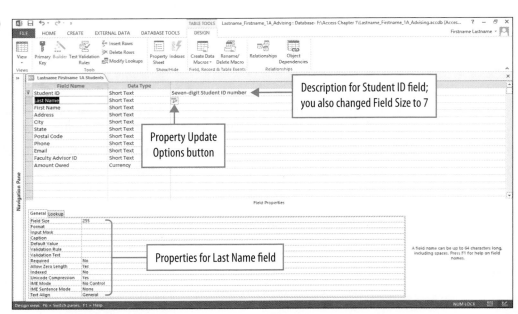

> **4** Click in the **State** field name box. In the **Field Properties** area, change the **Field Size** to **2** and in the **Description** box for this field, type **Two-character state abbreviation** and then press Enter.

> **5** Click in the **Faculty Advisor ID** field name box. In the **Field Properties** area, change the **Field Size** to **8** and in the **Description** box for this field, type **Eight-character ID of instructor assigned as advisor** and then press Enter.

> **6** On the **Quick Access Toolbar**, click **Save** 🖫 to save the design changes to your table, and then notice the message.

> The message indicates that the field size property of one or more fields has changed to a shorter size. If more characters are currently present in the Student ID, State, or Faculty Advisor ID fields than you have set as the field size, the data will be **truncated**—cut off or shortened—because the fields were not previously restricted to these specific number of characters.

> **7** In the message box, click **Yes**.

Activity 1.10 | Viewing the Primary Key in Design View

Primary key refers to the field in the table that uniquely identifies a record. For example, in a college registration database, your Student ID number uniquely identifies you—no other student at the college has your exact student number. In the 1A Students table, the Student ID uniquely identifies each student.

When you create a table using the blank desktop database template, Access designates the first field as the primary key field and names the field ID. It is good database design practice to establish a primary key for every table, because doing so ensures that you do not enter the same record more than once. You can imagine the confusion if another student at your college had the same Student ID number as your own.

1 With your table still displayed in **Design** view, in the **Field Name** column, click in the **Student ID** field name box. To the left of the box, notice the small icon of a key, as shown in Figure 1.20.

Access automatically designates the first field as the primary key field, but you can set any field as the primary key by clicking the field name, and then in the Tools group, clicking Primary Key.

FIGURE 1.20

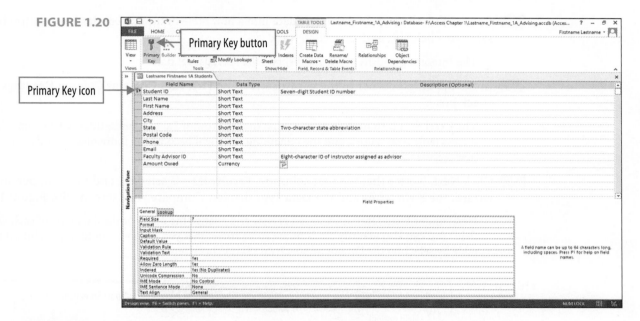

2 On the **DESIGN tab**, in the **Views group**, notice that the **View** button displays a picture of a datasheet, indicating that clicking **View** will switch the view to **Datasheet** view. Click the top of the **View** button.

If you make design changes to a table and switch views without first saving the table, Access prompts you to save the table before changing views.

Activity 1.11 | Adding a Second Table to a Database by Importing an Excel Spreadsheet

Many Microsoft Office users track data in an Excel spreadsheet. The sorting and filtering capabilities of Excel are useful for a simple database where all of the information resides in one large Excel spreadsheet. However, Excel is limited as a database management tool because it cannot *relate* the information in multiple spreadsheets in a way that you can ask a question and get a meaningful result. Because data in an Excel spreadsheet is arranged in columns and rows, the spreadsheet can easily become an Access table by importing the spreadsheet.

1 On the ribbon, click the **EXTERNAL DATA tab**, and then in the **Import & Link group**, click **Excel**. In the **Get External Data – Excel Spreadsheet** dialog box, click **Browse**.

2 In the **File Open** dialog box, navigate to the location where your student data files are stored, and then double-click **a01A_Faculty_Advisors**. Compare your screen with Figure 1.21.

FIGURE 1.21

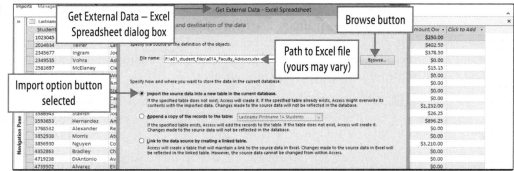

3 ▸ Be sure that the **Import the source data into a new table in the current database** option button is selected, click **OK**, and then click **Next**.

The Import Spreadsheet Wizard displays the spreadsheet data.

4 ▸ In the upper left corner of the wizard, select the **First Row Contains Column Headings** check box.

The Excel data is framed, indicating that the first row of Excel column titles will become the Access table field names, and the remaining rows will become the individual records in the new Access table.

5 ▸ Click **Next**. Notice that the first column—**Faculty ID**—is selected, and in the upper area of the wizard, the **Field Name** and the **Data Type** display. Compare your screen with Figure 1.22.

Here, under Field Options, you can review and change the name or the data type of each selected field. You can also identify fields in the spreadsheet that you do not want to import into the Access table by selecting the Do not import field (Skip) check box.

FIGURE 1.22

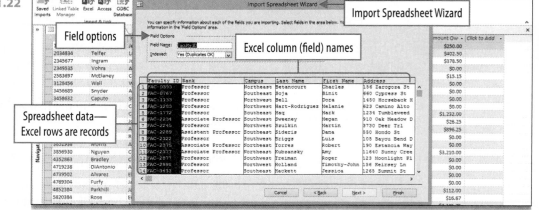

6 ▸ Click **Next**. In the upper area of the wizard, click the **Choose my own primary key** option button, and then be sure that **Faculty ID** displays in the box to the right.

In the new table, Faculty ID will be the primary key. No two faculty members have the same Faculty ID. By default, Access selects the first field as the primary key, but you can click the arrow to select a different field.

7 ▸ Click **Next**. In the **Import to Table** box, using your own name, type **Lastname Firstname 1A Faculty Advisors** and then click **Finish**.

8 ▸ In the **Get External Data – Excel Spreadsheet** dialog box, click **Close. Open** ⟩⟩ the **Navigation Pane**.

9 In the **Navigation Pane**, double-click your **1A Faculty Advisors** table to open it in **Datasheet** view, and then **Close** **«** the **Navigation Pane**.

Two tables that are identified by their object tabs are open in the object window. Your 1A Faculty Advisors table is the active table and displays the 29 records that you imported from the Excel spreadsheet.

10 In your **1A Faculty Advisors** table, click in the **Postal Code** field in the first record. On the ribbon, under **TABLE TOOLS**, click the **FIELDS tab**. In the **Formatting group**, click the **Data Type arrow**, and then click **Short Text**. Compare your screen with Figure 1.23.

When you import data from an Excel spreadsheet, check the data types of all fields to ensure they are correct. Recall that if a field, such as the Postal Code, contains numbers that are not used in calculations, the data type should be set to Short Text. To change the data type of a field, click in the field in any record.

FIGURE 1.23

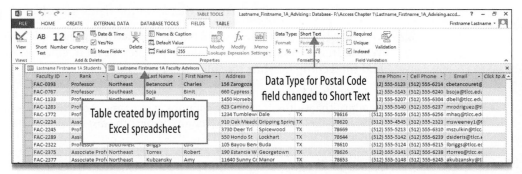

Activity 1.12 | Adjusting Column Widths

You can adjust the column widths in a table displayed in Datasheet view by using techniques similar to those you use for Excel spreadsheets.

1 In the object window, click the **object tab** for your **1A Students** table to make it the active object and to display it in the object window.

Clicking the object tabs along the top of the object window enables you to display open objects and make them active so that you can work with them. All of the columns in the datasheet are the same width, regardless of the length of the data in the field, the length of the field name, or the field size that was set. If you print the table as currently displayed, some of the data or field names will not print fully, so you will want to adjust the column widths.

2 In the field names row, point to the right edge of the **Address** field to display the ⊞ pointer, and then compare your screen with Figure 1.24.

FIGURE 1.24

3 With the ⊞ pointer positioned as shown in Figure 1.24, double-click the right edge of the **Address** field.

The column width of the Address field widens to display fully the longest entry in the field. In this manner, the width of a column can be increased or decreased to fit its contents in the same manner as a column in an Excel spreadsheet. In Access, adjusting the column width to fit the contents is referred to as *Best Fit*.

4 Point to the **City** field name to display the ⬇ pointer, right-click to select the entire column, and then click **Field Width**. In the **Column Width** dialog box, click **Best Fit**.

> This is a second way to adjust column widths.

5 If necessary, scroll to the right to view the last three fields. Point to the **Email** field name to display the ⬇ pointer, hold down the left mouse button, and then drag to the right to select this column, the **Faculty Advisor ID** column, and the **Amount Owed** column. Point to the right edge of any of the selected columns to display the ➕ pointer, and then double-click to apply **Best Fit** to all three columns.

> You can select multiple columns and adjust the widths of all of them at one time by using this technique or by right-clicking any of the selected columns, clicking Field Width, and clicking Best Fit in the Column Width dialog box.

6 If necessary, scroll to the left to view the **Student ID** field. To the left of the **Student ID** field name, click **Select All** ▢. Notice that all of the fields are selected.

7 On the ribbon, click the **HOME tab**. In the **Records group**, click **More**, and then click **Field Width**. In the **Column Width** dialog box, click **Best Fit**. Click anywhere in the **Student ID** field, and then compare your screen with Figure 1.25.

> Using the More command is a third way to adjust column widths. By using Select All, you can adjust the widths of all of the columns at one time. Adjusting the width of columns does not change the data in the table's records; it only changes the *display* of the data.

FIGURE 1.25

NOTE   **Adjusting Column Widths**

After adjusting column widths, scroll horizontally and vertically to be sure that all of the data displays in all of the fields. Access adjusts column widths to fit the screen size based on the displayed data. If data is not displayed on the screen when you adjust column widths—even if you use Select All—the column width might not be adjusted adequately to display all of the data in the field. After adjusting column widths, save the table before performing other tasks. The column width adjustments might not save with the table. When you reopen a table, be sure to readjust the column widths if you plan to print the table or work with the data in the table.

---

8 On the **Quick Access Toolbar**, click **Save** 🖫 to save the table design changes—changing the column widths.

> If you do not save the table after making design changes, Access prompts you to save when you close the table.

Activity 1.13 | Printing a Table

There are times when you will want to print a table, even though a report may look more professional. For example, you may need a quick reference, or you may want to proofread the data that has been entered. Before printing a table, be sure to apply Best Fit to all of the columns in the table.

1 On the ribbon, click the **FILE tab**, click **Print**, and then click **Print Preview**. Compare your screen with Figure 1.26.

> The table displays in Print Preview with the default zoom setting of Fit to Window, a view that enables you to see how your table will print on the page. It is a good idea to view any object in Print Preview before printing so that you can make changes to the object if needed before actually printing it. In the navigation area, the Next Page button is darker (available), an indication that more than one page will print.

FIGURE 1.26

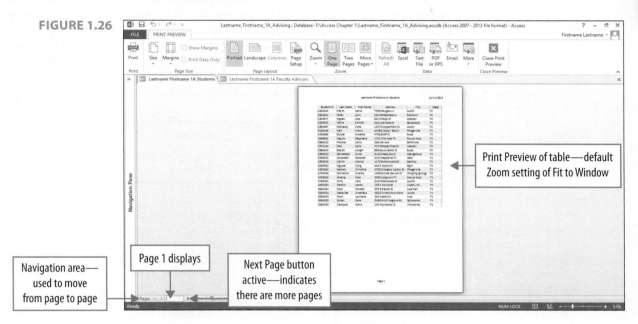

Print Preview of table—default Zoom setting of Fit to Window

Navigation area— used to move from page to page

Page 1 displays

Next Page button active—indicates there are more pages

2 In the navigation area, click **Next Page** ▶ to display Page 2. Point to the top of the page to display the 🔍 pointer, click one time to zoom in, and then compare your screen with Figure 1.27.

> The Print Preview display enlarges, and the Zoom Out pointer displays. The second page of the table displays the last five fields. The Next Page button is dimmed, indicating that the button is unavailable because there are no more pages after Page 2. The Previous Page button is available, indicating that a page exists before this page.

FIGURE 1.27

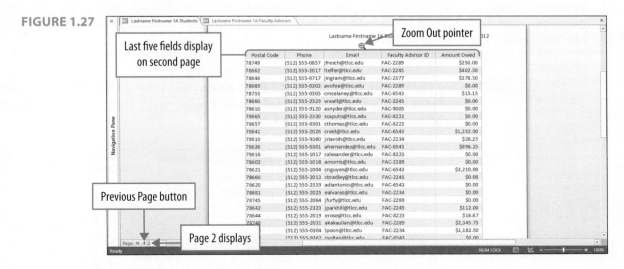

Zoom Out pointer

Last five fields display on second page

Previous Page button

Page 2 displays

3 On the ribbon, on the **PRINT PREVIEW tab**, in the **Zoom group**, click the top portion of the **Zoom** button to change the zoom setting back to the default setting of Fit to Window.

   With the 🔍 pointer displayed on the page, click to zoom back to the Fit to Window setting.

4 ▶ In the **Page Layout group**, click **Landscape**, and notice that there are only three fields on Page 2. In the navigation area, click **Previous Page** ◀ to display Page 1, and then compare your screen with Figure 1.28.

The orientation of the page to be printed changes. Included on the page are the table name and current date at the top of the page and the page number at the bottom of the page. The change in orientation from portrait to landscape is not saved with the table. Each time you print, you must check the page orientation, the margins, and any other print parameters so that the object prints as you intend. You should also be sure that Best Fit is applied to each column or to the entire table.

FIGURE 1.28

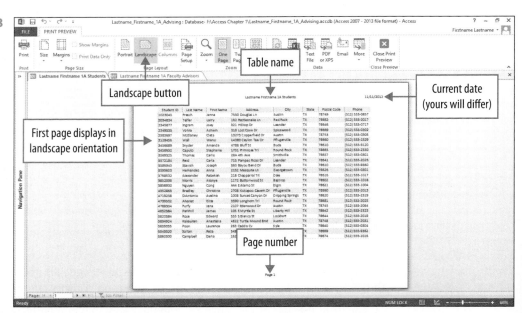

NOTE | **Headers and Footers in Access Objects**

The headers and footers in Access tables and queries are controlled by default settings; you cannot enter additional information or edit the information. The object name displays in the center of the header area, and the current date displays on the right. Adding your name to the object name is helpful in identifying your paper or electronic results. The page number displays in the center of the footer area. The headers and footers in Access forms and reports are more flexible; you can add to and edit the information.

---

5 ▶ On the **PRINT PREVIEW tab**, in the **Print group**, click **Print**. In the **Print** dialog box, under **Print Range**, verify that **All** is selected. Under **Copies**, verify that the **Number of Copies** is **1**. Compare your screen with Figure 1.29.

FIGURE 1.29

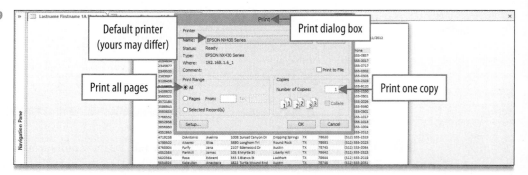

6 Determine whether your instructor wants you to submit your work for this project on paper or electronically. If submitting electronically, determine whether, in addition to submitting your Access database, your instructor wants you to create and submit electronic printouts of individual database objects.

7 To print on paper, in the **Print** dialog box, click **OK**; and then on the ribbon, in the **Close Preview group**, click **Close Print Preview**. If you are required to create and submit electronic printouts, in the **Print** dialog box, click **Cancel**, and then follow the steps in the following Note—or follow the specific directions provided by your instructor.

N O T E   **Creating a PDF Electronic Printout of an Access Object**

Display the object (table, query, form, report, and so on) in Print Preview and adjust margins and orientation as needed. On the PRINT PREVIEW tab, in the Data group, click PDF or XPS. In the Publish as PDF or XPS dialog box, navigate to your chapter folder. Use the default file name, or follow your instructor's directions to name the object. If wish to view the PDF file, in the dialog box, select the Open file after publishing check box. In the Publish as PDF or XPS dialog box, click Publish. If necessary, close the Windows 8 Reader, Adobe Reader, or Adobe Acrobat window and the Export – PDF dialog box. On the ribbon, click Close Print Preview; your electronic printout is saved.

---

8 In the upper right corner of the object window, click **Close Object** ☒ to close your **1A Students** table. Notice that the **1A Faculty Advisors** table is the active object in the object window.

🔁 **ANOTHER WAY**   In the object window, right-click your 1A Students object tab, and then click Close.

---

9 In your **1A Faculty Advisors** table, to the left of the **Faculty ID** field name, click **Select All** ☐ to select all of the columns. On the **HOME tab**, in the **Records group**, click **More**, and then click **Field Width**. In the **Column Width** dialog box, click **Best Fit** to adjust the widths of all of the columns so that all of the data display. Scroll horizontally and vertically to be sure that all of the data display in each field; if necessary, use the techniques you practiced to apply **Best Fit** to individual columns. **Save** 🖫 the changes you made to the table's column widths, and then click in any record to cancel the selection.

10 On the ribbon, click the **FILE tab**, click **Print**, and then click **Print Preview**. On the **PRINT PREVIEW tab**, in the **Page Layout group**, click **Landscape**. Notice that the table will print on more than one page. In the **Page Size group**, click **Margins**, click **Normal**, and then notice that one more column moved to the first page—your results may differ depending upon your printer's capabilities.

   In addition to changing the page orientation to Landscape, you can change the margins to Normal to see if all of the fields will print on one page. In this instance, there are still too many fields to print on one page, although the Postal Code field moved from Page 2 to Page 1.

11 If directed to do so by your instructor, create a paper or electronic printout of your **1A Faculty Advisors** table, and then click **Close Print Preview**.

12 In the object window, **Close** ☒ your **1A Faculty Advisors** table.

   All of your database objects—your *1A Students* table and your *1A Faculty Advisors* table—are closed; the object window is empty.

Video A1-4

Recall that tables are the foundation of an Access database because all of the data is stored in one or more tables. You can display the data stored in tables in other database objects such as queries, forms, and reports.

Activity 1.14 | Creating a Query by Using the Simple Query Wizard

A *query* is a database object that retrieves specific data from one or more database objects—either tables or other queries—and then, in a single datasheet, displays only the data that you specify when you design the query. Because the word *query* means *to ask a question*, think of a query as a question formed in a manner that Access can answer.

A *select query* is one type of Access query. A select query, also called a *simple select query*, retrieves (selects) data from one or more tables or queries and then displays the selected data in a datasheet. A select query creates a subset of the data to answer specific questions; for example, *Which students live in Austin, TX?*

The objects from which a query selects the data are referred to as the query's *data source*. In this activity, you will create a simple select query using a wizard that walks you step by step through the process. The process involves selecting the data source and indicating the fields that you want to include in the query results. The query—the question you want to ask—is *What is the last name, first name, email address, phone number, and Student ID of every student?*

1 On the ribbon, click the **CREATE tab**, and then in the **Queries group**, click **Query Wizard**. In the **New Query** dialog box, be sure **Simple Query Wizard** is selected, and then click **OK**. Compare your screen with Figure 1.30.

FIGURE 1.30

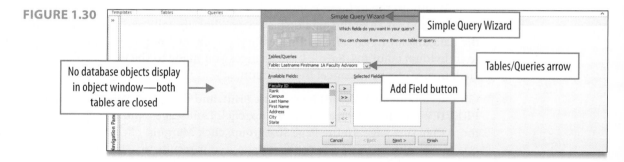

2 In the wizard, click the **Tables/Queries arrow**, and then click **Table: Lastname Firstname 1A Students**.

In the wizard, the displayed table or query name is the object that was last selected on the Navigation Pane. The last object you worked with was your 1A Faculty Advisors table, so that object name displayed in the wizard.

To create a query, first select the data source—the object from which the query is to select the data. The information you need to answer the question is stored in your 1A Students table, so this table is your data source.

3 Under **Available Fields**, click **Last Name**, and then click **Add Field** $>$ to move the field to the **Selected Fields** list on the right. Double-click the **First Name** field to add the field to the **Selected Fields** list.

Use either method to add fields to the Selected Fields list—you can add fields in any order.

4 ▸ By using **Add Field** ▸ or by double-clicking the field name, add the following fields to the **Selected Fields** list in the order specified: **Email**, **Phone**, and **Student ID**. Compare your screen with Figure 1.31.

> Selecting these five fields will answer the question, *What is the last name, first name, email address, phone number, and Student ID of every student?*

FIGURE 1.31

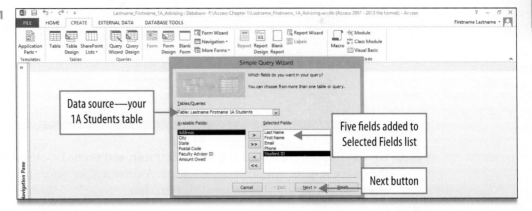

5 ▸ In the wizard, click **Next**. Click in the **What title do you want for your query?** box. Using your own name, edit as necessary so that the query name is **Lastname Firstname 1A All Students Query** and then compare your screen with Figure 1.32.

FIGURE 1.32

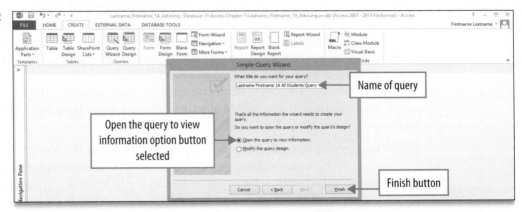

6 ▸ In the wizard, click **Finish**. Select all of the columns, apply **Best Fit**, and then **Save** 🖫 the query. In the first record, click in the **Last Name** field to cancel the selection. Compare your screen with Figure 1.33.

> Access ***runs*** the query—performs the actions indicated in your query design—by searching the records in the specified data source, and then finds the records that match specified criteria. The records that match the criteria display in a datasheet. A select query *selects*—finds and displays—*only* the information from the data source that you request, including the specified fields.

> In the object window, Access displays every student from your 1A Students table—the data source—but displays *only* the five fields that you moved to the Selected Fields list in the Simple Query Wizard.

FIGURE 1.33

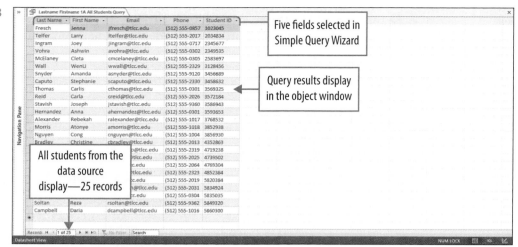

Five fields selected in Simple Query Wizard

Query results display in the object window

All students from the data source display—25 records

7 On the ribbon, click the **FILE tab**, click **Print**, and then click **Print Preview**. Notice that the query results will print on one page. As directed by your instructor, create a paper or electronic printout. Click **Close Print Preview**.

8 In the object window, **Close** ☒ the query.

Activity 1.15 | Creating and Printing a Form

A **form** is an Access object with which you can enter data, edit data, or display data from a table or query. In a form, the fields are laid out in an attractive format on the screen, which makes working with the database easier for those who must enter and look up data.

One type of form displays only one record at a time. Such a form is useful not only to the individual who performs the data entry—typing in the records—but also to anyone who has the job of viewing information in the database. For example, when you visit the Records office at your college to obtain a transcript, someone displays your record on the screen. For the viewer, it is much easier to look at one record at a time, using a form, than to look at all of the student records in the database table.

1 Open ⯮ the **Navigation Pane**. Drag the right edge of the **Navigation Pane** to the right to increase the width of the pane so that all object names display fully. Notice that a table name displays with a datasheet icon, and a query name displays an icon of two overlapping datasheets. Right-click your **1A Students** table, and then compare your screen with Figure 1.34.

FIGURE 1.34

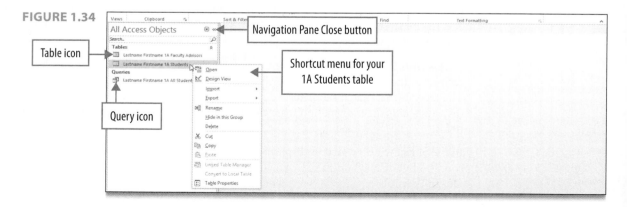

Table icon

Query icon

Navigation Pane Close button

Shortcut menu for your 1A Students table

2 On the shortcut menu, click **Open** to display the table in the object window, and then **Close** ⯭ the **Navigation Pane** to maximize your object window space.

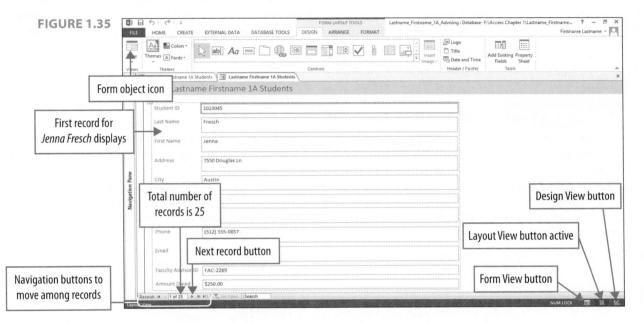

ANOTHER WAY   On the Navigation Pane, double-click the object name to open it.

3 ▶ Notice that there are 11 fields in the table. On the **CREATE tab**, in the **Forms group**, click **Form**, and then compare your screen with Figure 1.35.

The Form tool creates a form based on the active object—your 1A Students table. The form displays all of the fields from the underlying data source—one record at a time—in a simple top-to-bottom format with all 11 fields lined up in a single column. You can use this new form immediately, or you can modify it. Records that you create or edit in a form are automatically added to or updated in the underlying table or data source.

The new form displays in *Layout view*—the Access view in which you can make changes to an object while the object is open and displaying the data from the data source. Each field in the form displayed in Figure 1.35 displays the data for the first student record—*Jenna Fresch*—from your 1A Students table.

FIGURE 1.35

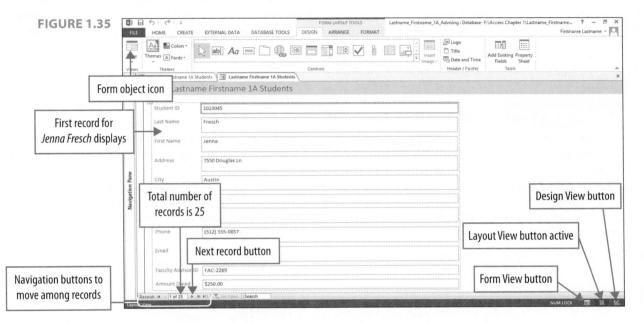

4 ▶ At the right side of the status bar, notice the three buttons. Point to each button to display its ScreenTip, and notice that **Layout View** ▤ is active, indicating that the form is displayed in Layout view.

5 ▶ In the status bar, click **Form View** ▥.

In *Form view*, you can view the records, create a new record, edit a record, and delete a record. You cannot change the layout or design of the form. Form view is useful for individuals who *access records* in your database. Layout view is useful for individuals who *design* the form.

ANOTHER WAY   On the DESIGN tab, or on the HOME tab, in the Views group, click the top portion of the View button when it displays an icon of a form.

6 ▶ In the navigation area, click **Next record** ▶ two times to display the third record—the record for *Joey Ingram*.

Use the navigation buttons to scroll among the records and to display any single record.

7 ▶ Using your own name, **Save** 🖫 the form as **Lastname Firstname 1A Student Form**

8 Be sure that Record 3 displays. On the ribbon, click the **FILE tab**, click **Print**, and then on the right, click **Print**—do *not* click **Print Preview** because you are going to print a *single* record—not all of the records.

9 In the **Print** dialog box, under **Print Range**, click the **Selected Record(s)** option button, and then click **Setup**.

10 In the **Page Setup** dialog box, click the **Columns tab**. Under **Column Size**, double-click in the **Width** box to select the existing value, type **7.5** and then click **OK**.

Forms are usually not printed, so the default width for a form created with the Form command is larger than most printers can handle to print on one page. If you do not change the width, the form will print on two pages because the last column flows over the margins allowed by the printer. If, after changing the Width to 7.5, your form still prints on two pages, try entering a different Width; for example, 7 or 6.5.

11 If instructed to print your objects, in the **Print** dialog box, click **OK** to print the record for *Joey Ingram* on one page; otherwise, click **Cancel**. If instructed to print an electronic copy, follow the steps in the following Note or the directions provided by your instructor.

After printing, along the left edge of the record, the narrow bar—the ***record selector bar***—displays in black, indicating that the record is selected.

N O T E   **Printing a Single Form in PDF**

On the FILE tab, click Print, and then on the right, click Print. In the Print dialog box, click Setup. In the Page Setup dialog box, click the Columns tab. Under Column Size, double-click in the Width box, type 7.5 and then click OK. In the Print dialog box, click Cancel. On the left edge of the form, click the record selector bar so that it is black—selected.

On the ribbon, click the EXTERNAL DATA tab. In the Export group, click PDF or XPS. In the Publish as PDF or XPS dialog box, navigate to your chapter folder, and at the lower right corner of the dialog box, click Options. In the Options dialog box, under Range, click the Selected records option button, and then click OK. In the Publish as PDF or XPS dialog box, click Publish. If necessary, close the Window 8 Reader, Adobe Reader, or Adobe Acrobat window.

---

12 **Close** ⎡×⎤ your **1A Student Form** object; leave your **1A Students** table open.

Activity 1.16 | **Creating, Modifying, and Printing a Report**

A ***report*** is a database object that displays the fields and records from a table or query in an easy-to-read format suitable for printing. Create professional-looking reports to summarize database information.

1 Open ⎡»⎤ the **Navigation Pane**, and then open your **1A Faculty Advisors** table by double-clicking the table name or by right-clicking the table name and clicking **Open**. Close ⎡«⎤ the **Navigation Pane**.

2 On the ribbon, click the **CREATE tab**. In the **Reports group**, click **Report**.

The Report tool creates a report in Layout view and includes all of the fields and all of the records in the data source—your 1A Faculty Advisors table. Dotted lines indicate how the report will break across pages if you print it now. In Layout view, you can make quick changes to the report layout while viewing the data from the table.

3 In the report, click the **Faculty ID** field name, and then on the ribbon, under **REPORT LAYOUT TOOLS**, click the **ARRANGE tab**. In the **Rows & Columns group**, click **Select Column**, and then press ⎡Del⎤. Using the same technique, delete the **Rank** field.

The Faculty ID and Rank fields, along with the data, are deleted from the report. The fields readjust by moving to the left. Deleting the fields from the report does *not* delete the fields and data from the data source—your 1A Faculty Advisors table.

ANOTHER WAY   Right-click the field name, click Select Entire Column, and then press Del.

4 ▸ Click the **Address** field name, and then by using the scroll bar at the bottom of the screen, scroll to the right to display the **Cell Phone** field; be careful not to click in the report.

5 ▸ Hold down Shift, and then click the **Cell Phone** field name to select all of the fields from *Address* through *Cell Phone*. With the six field names selected—surrounded by a colored border—in the **Rows & Columns group**, click **Select Column**, and then press Del.

Use this method to select and delete multiple columns in Layout view.

6 ▸ Scroll to the left, and notice that the four remaining fields display within the dotted lines—they are within the margins of the report. Click the **Campus** field name. Hold down Shift, and then click the **First Name** field name to select the first three fields.

7 ▸ On the ribbon, under **REPORT LAYOUT TOOLS**, click the **DESIGN tab**. In the **Tools group**, click **Property Sheet**.

The *Property Sheet* for the selected columns displays on the right side of the screen. Every object and every item in an object has an associated Property Sheet where you can make precise changes to the properties—characteristics—of selected items.

8 ▸ In the **Property Sheet**, if necessary, click the **Format tab**. Click **Width**, type **1.5** and then press Enter. Compare your screen with Figure 1.36.

The width of the three selected field names and the columns changes to 1.5", and the fields readjust by moving to the left. When you change the Width property, you do not need to select the entire column. Change the Width property if you need to move columns within the margins of a report. In this report, the fields already displayed within the margins, but some reports may need this minor adjustment to print on one page.

ANOTHER WAY   Select the column, and then drag the right edge of the column to the left to decrease the width of the field, or drag to the right to increase the width of the field.

FIGURE 1.36

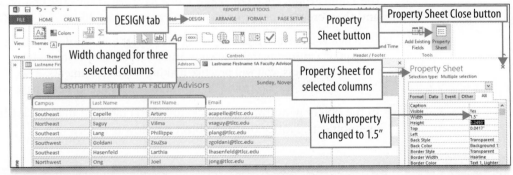

9 ▸ **Close** ☒ the **Property Sheet**. Click the **Last Name** field name. On the ribbon, click the **HOME tab**, and then in the **Sort & Filter group**, click **Ascending**.

Access sorts the report in ascending alphabetical order by the Last Name field. By default, tables are sorted in ascending order by the primary key field—in this instance, the Faculty ID field. Changing the sort order in the report does *not* change the sort order in the underlying table.

10 ▸ At the top of the report, to the right of the green report icon, click anywhere in the title of the report to select the title. On the **HOME tab**, in the **Text Formatting group**, click the **Font Size arrow**, and then click **14**. Save ☐ the report. In the **Save As** dialog box, in the **Report Name** box, add **Report** to the end of *Lastname Firstname 1A Faculty Advisors*, and then click **OK**.

11 On the **FILE tab**, click **Print**, and then click **Print Preview**. On the **PRINT PREVIEW tab**, in the **Zoom group**, click **Two Pages**, and then compare your screen with Figure 1.37.

> As currently formatted, the report will print on two pages because the page number at the bottom of the report is positioned beyond the right margin of the report.

FIGURE 1.37

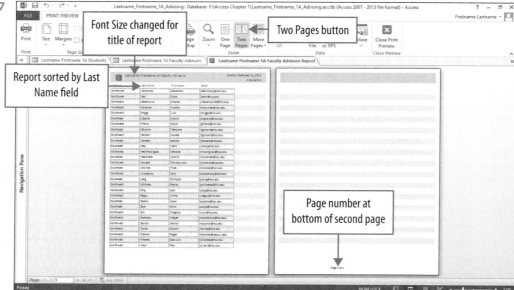

12 In the **Close Preview group**, click **Close Print Preview**. Scroll down to display the bottom of the report, and then, if necessary, scroll to the right to display the page number. Click the page number—**Page 1 of 1**—and then press ⏎Del⏎.

> Because all of the data will print on one page, the page number is not necessary for this report. If you want the page number to display, you can drag it within the margins of the report.

13 Display the report in **Print Preview**, and notice that the report will now print on one page. In the **Zoom group**, click **One Page**. Click **Save** 🖫 to save the changes to the design of the report, and then create a paper or electronic printout as directed. Click **Close Print Preview**.

> When you create a report by using the Report tool, the default margins are 0.25 inch. Some printers require a greater margin, so your printed report may result in two pages. As you progress in your study of Access, you will practice making these adjustments. Also, if a printer is not installed on your system, the electronic PDF printout may result in a two-page report.

14 In the object window, right-click any **object tab**, and then click **Close All** to close all of the open objects. Notice that the object window is empty.

Objective 5 | Close a Database and Exit Access

Video A1-5

When you close a table, any changes made to the records are saved automatically. If you make changes to the structure or adjust column widths, you are prompted to save the table when you close the table or when you switch views. Likewise, you are prompted to save queries, forms, and reports if you make changes to the layout or design. If the Navigation Pane is open when you exit Access, it will display when you reopen the database. When you are finished using your database, close the database, and then exit Access.

1 Open » the **Navigation Pane**. If necessary, increase the width of the **Navigation Pane** so that all object names display fully. Notice that your report object displays with a green report icon. Compare your screen with Figure 1.38.

FIGURE 1.38

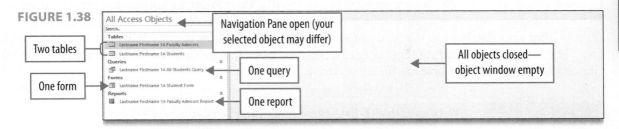

2 On the ribbon, click the **FILE tab**. Click **Close** to close the database but leave Access open. This action enables you to continue working in Access with another database if you want to do so. In the Access opening screen, in the upper right corner, click **Close** ☒ to exit Access. As directed by your instructor, submit your database and the paper or electronic printouts of the five objects—two tables, one query, one form, and one report—that are the results of this project. Specifically, in this project, using your own name, you created the following database and printouts or electronic printouts:

1. Lastname_Firstname_1A_Advising	Database file
2. Lastname Firstname 1A Students	Table (printout or electronic printout – two pages)
3. Lastname Firstname 1A Faculty Advisors	Table (printout or electronic printout – two pages)
4. Lastname Firstname 1A All Students Query	Query (printout or electronic printout)
5. Lastname Firstname 1A Student Form	Form (printout or electronic printout – Record 3)
6. Lastname Firstname 1A Faculty Advisors Report	Report (printout or electronic printout)

 **ANOTHER WAY** On the left side of the title bar, click 🗗 and then click Close, or on the right side of the title bar, click ☒ to close the database and to exit Access.

END | You have completed Project 1A

GO! with Office Web Apps

Objective	Export an Access Table to an Excel Spreadsheet, Save to SkyDrive, Edit a Record, and Save to Your Computer

Access web apps are designed to work with Microsoft's **SharePoint**, an application for setting up websites to share and manage documents. Your college may not have SharePoint installed, so you will use other tools to share objects from your database so that you can work collaboratively with others. Recall that Window's SkyDrive is a free file storage and file sharing service. For Access, you can export a database object to an Excel worksheet, a PDF file, or a text file, and then save the file to SkyDrive.

ALERT! **Working with Web-Based Applications and Services**

Computer programs and services on the web receive continuous updates and improvements. Therefore, the steps to complete this web-based activity may differ from the ones shown. You can often look at the screens and the information presented to determine how to complete the activity.

Activity | Exporting an Access Table to an Excel Spreadsheet, Saving the Spreadsheet to SkyDrive, Editing a Record in SkyDrive, and Saving to Your Computer

In this activity, you will **export**—copy data from one file into another file—your 1A Students table to an Excel spreadsheet, upload your Excel file to SkyDrive, edit a record in SkyDrive, and then download a copy of the edited spreadsheet to your computer.

1 Start Access, navigate to your **Access Chapter 1** folder, and then open your **1A_Advising** database file. If necessary, on the Message Bar, click Enable Content. In the **Navigation Pane**, click your **1A Students** table to select it—do not open it.

2 On the ribbon, click the **EXTERNAL DATA tab**, and then in the **Export group**, click Excel. In the **Export – Excel Spreadsheet** dialog box, click **Browse**, and then navigate to your **Access Chapter 1** folder. In the **File Save** dialog box, click in the **File name** box, type **Lastname_Firstname_AC_1A_Web** and then click **Save**.

3 In the **Export – Excel Spreadsheet** dialog box, under **Specify export options**, select the first two check boxes—**Export data with formatting and layout** and **Open the destination file after the export operation is complete**—and then click **OK**. In the **Microsoft Excel**

window, in the column headings row, to the left of column **A**, click **Select All**. On the **HOME tab**, in the **Cells group**, click **Format**, and then click **AutoFit Column Width**. Click in cell **A1** to cancel the selection, and then compare your screen with Figure A.

4 **Save** the spreadsheet, and then **Close** Excel. In the **Export – Excel Spreadsheet** dialog box, click **Close**, and then **Close** Access.

5 From the desktop, start Internet Explorer. Navigate to **http://skydrive.com**, and then sign in to your Microsoft account. Open your **GO! Web Projects** folder—or create and then open this folder if necessary.

6 On the menu bar, click **Upload**. In the **Choose File to Upload** dialog box, navigate to your **Access Chapter 1** folder, and then double-click your **AC_1A_Web** Excel file to upload it to SkyDrive.

FIGURE A

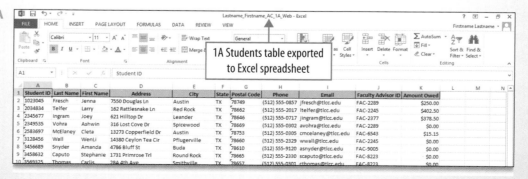

1A Students table exported to Excel spreadsheet

(GO! with Office Web Apps continues on the next page)

7 When the upload is completed, in your **GO! Web Projects** folder, click your **AC_1A_Web** file to open it in Microsoft Excel Web App.

On the ribbon, notice that you can open this worksheet in Excel instead of using the web app. If you are working on a computer that does not have Microsoft Excel installed, you can still create and modify workbooks in your web browser by using the Microsoft Excel Web app.

8 In the first record, click in the **Last Name** field. Using your own last name, type **Lastname** and then press Tab to replace *Fresch* with your last name. In the **First Name** field, using your own first name, type **Firstname** to replace *Jenna* with your own first name, and then press ↓ to save the record. Compare your screen with Figure B.

9 On the ribbon, click the **FILE tab**, click **Save As**, and then click **Download**. In the message box—usually displays at the bottom of your screen—click the **Save arrow**, and then click **Save as**. In the **Save As** dialog box, navigate to your **Access Chapter 1** folder, and then click in the **File name** box. Type **Lastname_Firstname_AC_1A_Web_Download** and then click **Save**. **Close** the message box.

10 In SkyDrive, on the title bar, click **SkyDrive** to return to your home page. At the top right corner of your screen, click your SkyDrive name, and then click **Sign out**. **Close** your browser window.

11 Start Excel. In the Excel opening screen, click **Open Other Workbooks**. Under **Open**, click **Computer**. Under **Computer**, click **Browse**. Navigate to your **Access Chapter 1** folder, and then double-click your **AC_1A_Web** Excel file. Notice that this file is the original file—the first record is not changed. If you are required to print your documents, use one of the methods in the Note box given. **Close** your Excel file, saving the changes to your worksheet, and then **Open** and print your **AC_1A_Web_Download** file by using one of the methods in the following Note. **Close** Excel, saving the changes to your worksheet. As directed by your instructor, submit your two workbooks and the two paper or electronic printouts that are the results of this project.

NOTE — **Adding the File Name to the Footer and Printing or Creating an Electronic Printout of an Excel Spreadsheet on One Page**

Click the FILE tab, click Print, and then click Page Setup. In the Page Setup dialog box, on the Page tab, under Orientation, click Landscape. Under Scaling, click the Fit to option button. In the Page Setup dialog box, click the Header/Footer tab, and then click Custom Footer. With the insertion point blinking in the Left section box, click the Insert File Name button, and then click OK. In the Page Setup dialog box, click OK.

To print on paper, click Print. To create an electronic file of your printout, on the left side of your screen, click Export. Under Export, be sure Create PDF/XPS Document is selected, and then, on the right, click Create PDF/XPS. Navigate to your Access Chapter 1 folder, and then click Publish to save the file with the default name and an extension of pdf.

FIGURE B

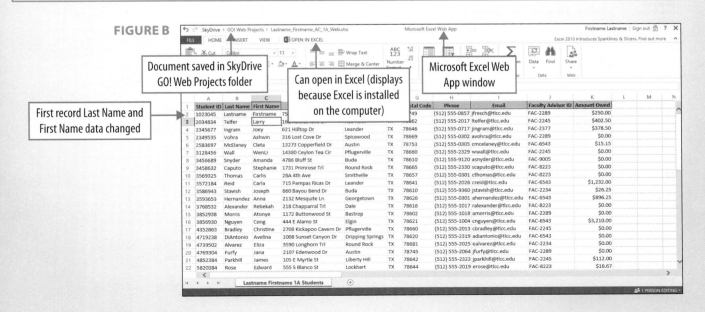

PROJECT ACTIVITIES

In Activities 1.18 through 1.25, you will assist Dr. Miriam Yong, director of student activities, in creating a database to store information about student workshops held at Texas Lakes Community College campuses. You will use a database template that tracks event information, add workshop information to the database, and then print the results. Your completed report and table will look similar to Figure 1.39.

PROJECT FILES

For Project 1B, you will need the following files:

Desktop Event Management template
a01B_Workshops (Excel workbook)

You will save your database as:

Lastname_Firstname_1B_Student_Workshops

PROJECT RESULTS

Build from
Scratch

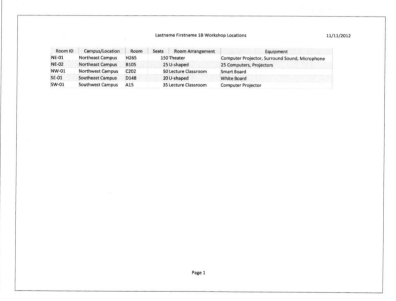

FIGURE 1.39 Project 1B Student Workshops

Objective 6   Use a Template to Create a Database

Video A1-6

A **database template** contains prebuilt tables, queries, forms, and reports that perform a specific task, such as tracking a large number of events. For example, your college may hold events such as athletic contests, plays, lectures, concerts, and club meetings. Using a predefined template, your college's activities director can quickly create a database to manage these events. The advantage of using a template to start a new database is that you do not have to create the objects—all you need to do is enter the data and modify the prebuilt objects to suit your needs.

The purpose of the database in this project is to track the student workshops that are held by Texas Lakes Community College. The questions to be answered might include:

- What workshops will be offered, and when will they be offered?
- In what rooms and on what campuses will the workshops be held?
- Which workshop locations have a computer projector for PowerPoint presentations?

Activity 1.18 │ Using a Template to Create a Database

There are two types of database templates—those that will be stored on your desktop and those that are designed to share with others over the Internet. In this activity, you will use a desktop template to create your database.

1 ▶ Start Access. In the Access opening screen, scroll down until the last templates display. Notice that there is a **Task management** template and a **Desktop task management** template. Compare your screen with Figure 1.40.

> These templates are included with the Access program. To store a database to manage tasks on your desktop, select the *Desktop task management* template. To publish a database to manage tasks and share it with others, select the *Task management* template—the one that displays a globe image. The names of templates designed to create databases stored on your computer start with the word *Desktop*.
>
> You can search the Microsoft Office website for more templates. You can also click on a category under the search box, where templates will be suggested.

FIGURE 1.40

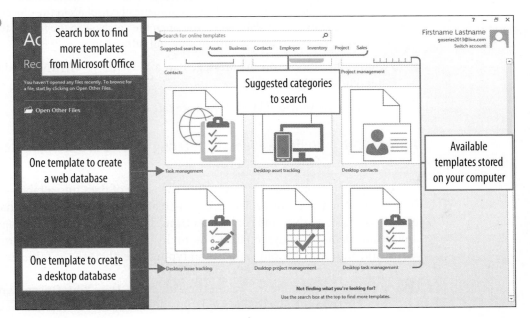

2 At the top of the window, click in the **Search for online templates** box, type **event** and then press Enter. Compare your screen with Figure 1.41.

You must have an Internet connection to search for online templates. Access displays several templates, including the Desktop Event Management template.

FIGURE 1.41

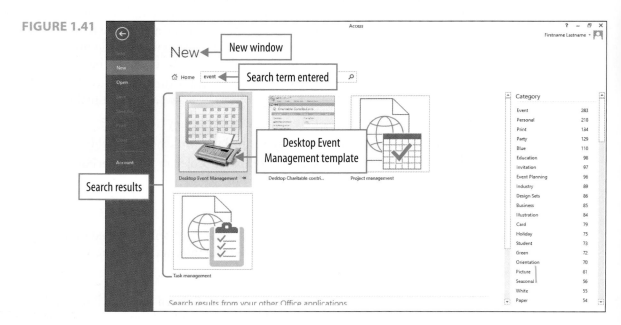

3 Click the **Desktop Event Management** template. In the dialog box, to the right of the **File Name** box, click **Browse**, and then navigate to your **Access Chapter 1** folder.

4 In the **File New Database** dialog box, click in the **File name** box to select the existing text. Using your own name, type **Lastname_Firstname_1B_Student_Workshops** and then press Enter.

5 In the **Desktop Event Management** dialog box, click **Create** to download the template and to save the database.

Access creates the *1B_Student_Workshops* database, and the database name displays in the title bar. A predesigned *form*—Event List—automatically displays in the object window. Although you can enter events for any date, when you open the database in the future, the Event List form will display only those events for the current date and future dates.

6 Under the ribbon, on the **Message Bar**, a *SECURITY WARNING* displays. On the **Message Bar**, click **Enable Content**.

Databases provided by Microsoft are safe to use on your computer.

Activity 1.19 | **Building a Table by Entering Records in a Multiple-Items Form and a Single-Record Form**

One purpose of a form is to simplify the entry of data into a table—either for you or for others who enter data. In Project 1A, you created a simple form that enabled you to display or enter records in a table, one record at a time. The Desktop Event Management template contains a *multiple-items form* that enables you to display or enter *multiple* records in a table, but with an easier and simplified layout rather than typing directly into the table itself.

1 In the new record row, click in the **Title** field. Type **Your Online Reputation** and then press Tab. In the **Start Time** field, type **3/9/18 7p** and then press Tab.

Access formats the date and time. As you enter dates and times, a small calendar displays to the right of the field. You can use the calendar to select a date instead of typing it.

> **2** In the **End Time** field, type **3/9/18 9p** and then press Tab. In the **Description** field, type **Internet Safety** and then press Tab. In the **Location** field, type **Northeast Campus** and then press Tab three times to move to the **Title** field in the new record row. Compare your screen with Figure 1.42.

> Because the workshops have no unique value, Access uses the AutoNumber data type in the ID field to assign a unique, sequential number to each record.

FIGURE 1.42

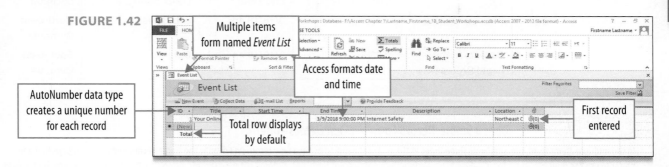

> **3** In the form, directly above the field names row, click **New Event**.

> A ***single-record form*** with the name *Event Details* displays, similar to the simple form you created in Project 1A. A single-record form enables you to display or enter one record at a time into a table.

> **4** Using Tab to move from field to field, enter the following record in the **Event Details** form—press Tab three times to move from the **End Time** field to the **Description** field. Then compare your screen with Figure 1.43.

Title	Location	Start Time	End Time	Description
Writing a Research Paper	Southwest Campus	3/10/18 4p	3/10/18 6p	Computer Skills

FIGURE 1.43

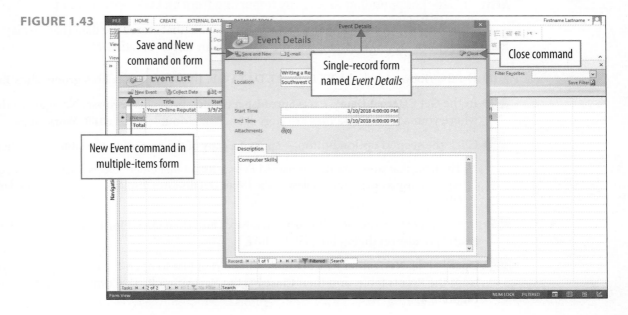

> **5** In the **Event Details** single-record form, in the upper right corner, click **Close**, and notice that the new record displays in the multiple-items form—*Event List*.

6 Enter the following records by using either the **Event List** form—the multiple-items form—or the **Event Details** form—the single-record form that is accessed by clicking the *New Event* command on the **Event List** form. The data in the table given is arranged in the same order as the **Event List** form. Be sure the multiple-items form displays, and then compare your screen with Figure 1.44.

ID	Title	Start Time	End Time	Description	Location
3	**Resume Writing**	**3/18/18 2p**	**3/18/18 4p**	**Job Skills**	**Northwest Campus**
4	**Careers in the Legal Profession**	**3/19/18 2p**	**3/19/18 4p**	**Careers**	**Southeast Campus**

ALERT! **Does a Single-Record Form—*Event Details*–Open?**

In the multiple-items form, pressing Enter three times at the end of the row to begin a new record will display the single-record form—*Event Details*. If you prefer to use the multiple-items form—Event List—close the single-record form and continue entering records, using the Tab key to move from field to field.

FIGURE 1.44

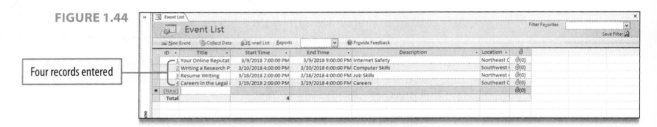

Four records entered

7 In the object window, click **Close** ✕ to close the **Event List** form.

Activity 1.20 | Appending Records by Importing from an Excel Spreadsheet

In this activity, you will append records to the table that stores the data that displays in the Events List form. You will import the records from an Excel spreadsheet.

1 On the ribbon, click the **EXTERNAL DATA tab**. In the **Import & Link group**, click **Excel**.

2 In the **Get External Data – Excel Spreadsheet** dialog box, click **Browse**. Navigate to the location where your student data files are stored, and then double-click **a01B_Workshops**.

3 Click the second option button—**Append a copy of the records to the table**—and then click **OK**.

The table that stores the data is named *Events*. Recall that other objects, such as forms, queries, and reports, display data from tables; so the Event Details form displays data that is stored in the Events table.

4 In the **Import Spreadsheet Wizard**, click **Next**, and then click **Finish**. In the **Get External Data – Excel Spreadsheet** dialog box, click **Close**.

5 **Open** » the **Navigation Pane**. Double-click **Event List** to open the form that displays data from the **Events** table, and then **Close** « the **Navigation Pane**. Compare your screen with Figure 1.45.

A total of 12 records display; you entered four records, and you appended eight records from the a01B_Workshops Excel workbook. The data is truncated in several fields because the columns are not wide enough to display all of the data.

FIGURE 1.45

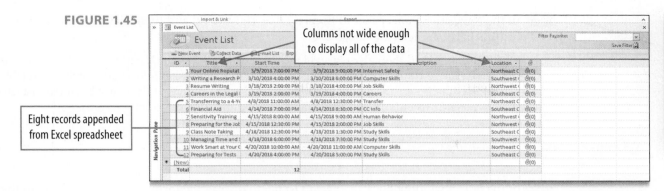

Columns not wide enough to display all of the data

Eight records appended from Excel spreadsheet

6 To the left of the **ID** field name, click **Select All** □ to select all of the columns and rows.

7 In the field names row, point to the right edge of any of the selected columns to display the ⊞ pointer, and then double-click to apply **Best Fit** to all of the columns. **Save** 🖫 the form, and then click in any field to cancel the selection.

Objective 7 Organize Objects in the Navigation Pane

Video A1-7

Use the Navigation Pane to open objects, organize database objects, and perform common tasks, such as renaming an object or deleting an object.

Activity 1.21 | Grouping Database Objects in the Navigation Pane

The Navigation Pane groups and displays your database objects and can do so in predefined arrangements. In this activity, you will group your database objects using the *Tables and Related Views* category, which groups objects by the table to which the objects are related. This grouping is useful because you can determine easily the table that is the data source of queries, forms, and reports.

1 **Open** » the **Navigation Pane**. At the top right side of the **Navigation Pane**, click ☺. On the list, under **Navigate To Category**, click **Tables and Related Views**. Compare your screen with Figure 1.46.

In the Navigation Pane, you can see the number of objects that are included in the Desktop Event Management template, including the table named *Events*. Other objects in the database that display data from the Events table include one query, two forms, and five reports. In the Navigation Pane, the Event List form is selected because it is open in the object window and is the active object. Other objects might display on the Navigation Pane; for example, Filters and Unrelated Objects. These filters are objects created for use by the Desktop Event Management template.

FIGURE 1.46

One table—data source for all other objects

Two forms

Five reports

Filters included with the template

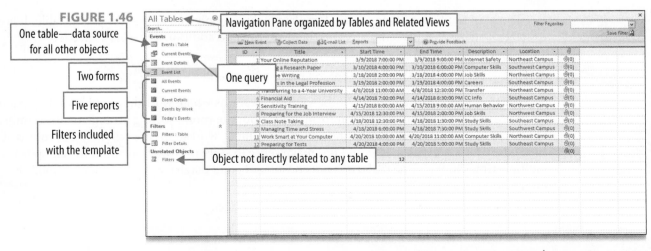

Navigation Pane organized by Tables and Related Views

One query

Object not directly related to any table

2 In the **Navigation Pane**, point to **Events: Table**, right-click, and then click **Open** to display the records in the underlying table.

The Events table is the active object in the object window. Use the Navigation Pane to open objects for use. The 12 records that display in the Event List multiple-items form are stored in this table. Recall that tables are the foundation of your database because your data must be stored in a table. You can enter records directly into a table or you can use a form to enter records.

🔁 **ANOTHER WAY**　　Double-click the table name to open it in the object window.

3 In the object window, click the **Event List tab** to display the form as the active object in the object window.

Recall that a form presents a more user-friendly screen for entering records into a table.

4 In the **Navigation Pane**, double-click the **Current Events** *report* (green icon) to open the report. Compare your screen with Figure 1.47.

An advantage of using a template to create a database is that many objects, such as reports, are already designed for you.

FIGURE 1.47

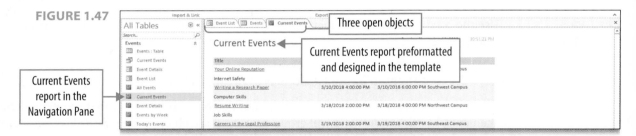

5 In the object window, **Close** ☒ the **Current Events** report.

6 By double-clicking or right-clicking, from the **Navigation Pane**, open the **Events by Week** report.

In this predesigned report, the events are displayed by week. After entering records in the form or table, the preformatted reports are updated with the records from the table.

7 In the object window, right-click any one of the **object tabs**, and then click **Close All** to close all of the objects. **Close** ☒ the **Navigation Pane**.

Objective 8　Create a New Table in a Database Created with a Template

Video A1-8

The Desktop Event Management template included only one table—the *Events* table. It is easy to start a database with a template, and then you can add additional objects as needed.

Activity 1.22 │ Using the Table Tool to Create a New Table

Dr. Yong has information about the various locations where workshops are held. For example, on the Northeast Campus, she has information about the room, seating arrangements, number of seats, and multimedia equipment. In the Events table, workshops are scheduled in rooms at each of the four campuses. It would not make sense to store information about the campus rooms multiple times in the same table. It is *not* considered good database design to have duplicate information in a table.

When data becomes redundant, it is usually an indication that you need a new table to store that information. In this activity, you will create a table to track the workshop locations, the equipment, and the seating arrangements in each location.

1 On the ribbon, click the **CREATE tab**, and then in the **Tables group**, click **Table**.

2 In the field names row, click **Click to Add**, click **Short Text**, type **Campus/Location** and then press [Enter].

3 In the third column, click **Short Text**, type **Room** and then press [Enter]. In the fourth column, click **Number**, type **Seats** and then press [Enter].

> The **Number data type** describes numbers that may be used in calculations. For the Seats field, you may need to determine the number of seats remaining after reservations are booked for a room. In the new record row, a *0* displays in the field.

4 In the fifth column, type **t** to select *Short Text*, type **Room Arrangement** and then press [Enter]. In the sixth column, type **t** and then type **Equipment** On your keyboard, press [↓].

> With the data type list displayed, you can select the data type by either clicking it or typing the letter that is underscored for the data type.

> This table has six fields. Access automatically creates the first field in the table—the ID field—to ensure that every record has a unique value. Before naming each field, you must define the data type for the field.

5 Right-click the **ID** field name, and then click **Rename Field**. Type **Room ID** and then press [Enter]. On the ribbon, under **TABLE TOOLS**, on the **FIELDS tab**, in the **Formatting group**, click the **Data Type arrow**, and then click **Short Text**. On the ribbon, in the **Field Validation group**, notice that **Unique** is selected.

> Recall that, by default, Access creates the ID field with the AutoNumber data type so that the field can be used as the primary key. Here, this field will store a unique room ID that is a combination of letters, symbols, and numbers; therefore, it is appropriate to change the data type to Short Text. In Datasheet view, the primary key field is identified by the selection of the Unique check box.

Activity 1.23 | Entering Records into a New Table

1 If necessary, in the new record row, click in the **Room ID** field. Enter the following record, pressing [Enter] or [Tab] to move from one field to the next. Do not be concerned that all of your text does not display; you will adjust the column widths later. After entering the record, compare your screen with Figure 1.48.

> Recall that Access saves a record when you move to another row within the table. You can press either [Enter] or [Tab] to move between fields in a table.

Room ID	Campus/Location	Room	Seats	Room Arrangement	Equipment
NE-01	**Northeast Campus**	**H265**	**150**	**Theater**	**Computer Projector, Surround Sound, Microphone**

FIGURE 1.48

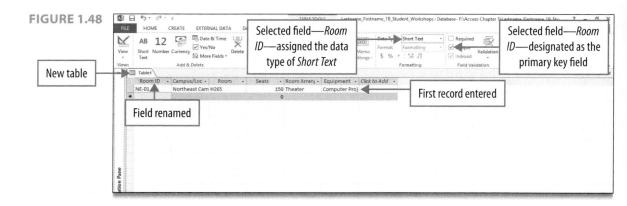

Selected field—*Room ID*—assigned the data type of *Short Text*

Selected field—*Room ID*—designated as the primary key field

New table

Field renamed

First record entered

2 In the **Views group**, click the top of the **View** button to switch to **Design** view. In the **Save As** dialog box, in the **Table Name** box, using your own name, type **Lastname Firstname 1B Workshop Locations** and then click **OK**.

Recall that when you switch views or when you close a table, Access prompts you to save the table if you have not previously saved it.

ANOTHER WAY   On the right side of the status bar, click Design View 🖾 to switch to Design view.

3 In the **Field Name** column, to the left of **Room ID**, notice the key icon.

In Design view, the key icon indicates that the field—Room ID—is the primary key field.

4 In the **Views group**, click the top of the **View** button to switch back to **Datasheet** view.

ANOTHER WAY   On the right side of the status bar, click Datasheet View 📧 to switch to Datasheet view.

5 In the new record row, click in the **Room ID** field. Enter the following records, pressing Enter or Tab to move from one field to the next.

Room ID	Campus/Location	Room	Seats	Room Arrangement	Equipment
SW-01	Southwest Campus	A15	35	Lecture Classroom	Computer Projector
NW-01	Northwest Campus	C202	50	Lecture Classroom	Smart Board
SE-01	Southeast Campus	D148	20	U-shaped	White Board
NE-02	Northeast Campus	B105	25	U-shaped	25 Computers, Projector

6 To the left of the **Room ID** field name, click **Select All** ☐ to select all of the columns and rows in the table. On the **HOME tab**, in the **Records group**, click **More**, and then click **Field Width**. In the **Column Width** dialog box, click **Best Fit** to display all of the data in each column. **Save** 🖫 the changes to the table, and then click in any field to cancel the selection. In the object window, **Close** ☒ your **1B Workshop Locations** table.

7 Open ≫ the **Navigation Pane**, and notice that your new table name displays in its own group. Point to the right edge of the **Navigation Pane** to display the ⟷ pointer. Drag to the right to increase the width of the **Navigation Pane** so that your entire table name displays. Compare your screen with Figure 1.49.

Recall that by organizing the Navigation Pane by Tables and Related Views, the Navigation Pane groups the objects by each table and displays the related objects under each table name.

FIGURE 1.49

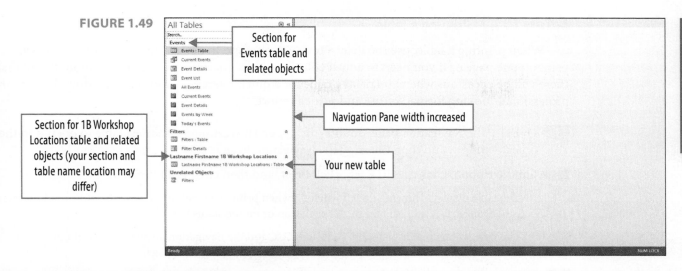

All Tables

Search...

Events

Events : Table

Current Events

Event Details

Event List

All Events

Current Events

Event Details

Events by Week

Today's Events

Filters

Filters : Table

Filter Details

Lastname Firstname 1B Workshop Locations

Lastname Firstname 1B Workshop Locations : Table

Unrelated Objects

Filters

Section for Events table and related objects

Navigation Pane width increased

Your new table

Section for 1B Workshop Locations table and related objects (your section and table name location may differ)

Ready   NUM LOCK

Objective 9 Print a Report and a Table

Video A1-9

Recall that one advantage to starting a new database with a template, instead of from a blank database, is that many report objects are already created for you.

Activity 1.24 | Viewing Reports and Printing a Report

1 In the **Navigation Pane**, double-click the report (not the form) named **Event Details** to open it in the object window.

This prebuilt Event Details report displays in an attractively arranged format.

2 Close ☒ the **Event Details** report. Open the **All Events** report, and then **Close** « the **Navigation Pane**. On the **HOME** tab, in the **Views group**, click the top of the **View** button to switch to **Layout** view.

Recall that Layout view enables you to make changes to an object while viewing the data in the fields. Each prebuilt report displays the records in the table in different useful formats.

ANOTHER WAY On the right side of the status bar, click Layout View ▤ to switch to Layout view.

3 At the top of the report, click the title—*All Events*—to display a colored border around the title. Click to the left of the letter *A* to place the insertion point there. Using your own name, type **Lastname Firstname 1B** and then press Spacebar. Press Enter, and then **Save** 🖫 the report.

Including your name in the title will help you and your instructor identify any submitted work.

4 On the right side of the status bar, click **Print Preview** 🔍. In the navigation area, notice that the navigation arrows are unavailable, an indication that this report will print on one page.

ANOTHER WAY On the HOME tab, in the Views group, click the View arrow, and then click Print Preview. Or, on the FILE tab, click Print, and then click Print Preview. Or, right-click the object tab, and then click Print Preview.

5 Create a paper or electronic printout as instructed. Click **Close Print Preview**, and then **Close** ☒ the report.

Activity 1.25 | Printing a Table

When printing a table, use the Print Preview command to determine whether the table will print on one page or if you need to adjust column widths, margins, or page orientation. Recall that there will be occasions when you print a table for a quick reference or for proofreading. For a more professional-looking format, create and print a report.

1 Open ⟩⟩ the **Navigation Pane**, double-click your **1B Workshop Locations** table to open it in the object window, and then **Close** ⟨⟨ the **Navigation Pane**.

2 On the ribbon, click the **FILE tab**, click **Print**, and then click **Print Preview**.

The table displays showing how it will look when printed. Generally, tables are not printed, so there is no Print Preview option on the View button or on the status bar.

The navigation area displays *1* in the Pages box, and the navigation arrows to the right of the box are active, an indication that the table will print on more than one page.

3 In the navigation area, click **Next Page** ▶.

The second page of the table displays the last field. Whenever possible, try to print all of the fields horizontally on one page. Of course, if there are many records, more than one page may be needed to print all of the records and all of the fields.

4 On the **PRINT PREVIEW tab**, in the **Page Layout group**, click **Landscape**, and then compare your screen with Figure 1.50. In landscape orientation, notice that the entire table will print on one page—all of the navigation buttons are unavailable.

FIGURE 1.50

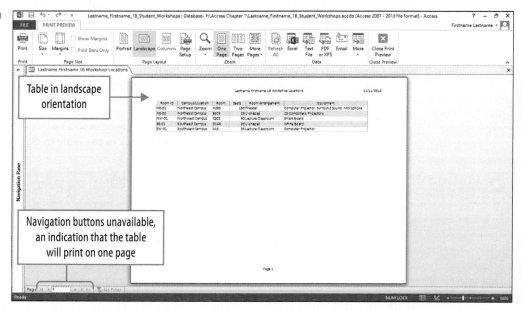

5 Create a paper or electronic printout as instructed, and then click **Close Print Preview**.

6 Close ✕ your **1B Workshop Locations** table. For the convenience of the next individual opening the database, **Open** ⟩⟩ the **Navigation Pane**.

7 On the right side of the title bar, click **Close** ☒ to close the database and to exit Access. As directed by your instructor, submit your database and the paper or electronic printouts of the two objects—one report and one table—that are the results of this project. Specifically, in this project, using your own name, you created the following database and printouts or electronic printouts:

1. Lastname_Firstname_1B_Student_Workshops	Database file
2. All Events	Report (printout or electronic printout)
3. Lastname Firstname 1B Workshop Locations	Table (printout or electronic printout)

END | You have completed Project 1B

GO! with Office Web Apps

Objective	Export an Access Table to an Excel Spreadsheet, Save to Google Drive, Add a Record, and Save to Your Computer

Access web apps are designed to work with Microsoft's SharePoint, a service for setting up websites to share and manage documents. Your college may not have SharePoint installed, so you will use other tools to share objects from your database so that you can work collaboratively with others. Recall that Google Docs is Google's free, web-based word processor, spreadsheet, slide show, form, and data storage service. Google Drive is Google's free file storage and sharing service. For Access, you can export a database object to an Excel worksheet, a PDF file, or a text file, and then save the file to Google Drive.

> **ALERT!**   **Working with Web-Based Applications and Services**
>
> Computer programs and services on the web receive continuous updates and improvements. Therefore, the steps to complete this web-based activity may differ from the ones shown. You can often look at the screens and the information presented to determine how to complete the activity.

Activity | **Exporting an Access Table to an Excel Spreadsheet, Saving the Spreadsheet to Google Drive, Editing a Record in Google Drive, and Saving to Your Computer**

In this activity, you will export your 1B Workshop Locations table to an Excel spreadsheet, upload your Excel file to Google Drive as a Google Doc, add a record in Google Drive, and then download a copy of the edited spreadsheet to your computer.

1 Start Access, navigate to your **Access Chapter 1** folder, and then **Open** your **1B_Student_Workshops** database file. If necessary, on the Message Bar, click Enable Content, and then **Close** the **Event List** form. In the **Navigation Pane**, click your **1B Workshop Locations** table to select it—do not open it.

2 On the ribbon, click the **EXTERNAL DATA tab**, and then in the **Export group**, click **Excel**. In the **Export – Excel Spreadsheet** dialog box, click **Browse**, and then navigate to your **Access Chapter 1** folder. In the **File Save** dialog box, click in the **File name** box, type **Lastname_Firstname_AC_1B_Web** and then click **Save**.

3 In the **Export – Excel Spreadsheet** dialog box, under **Specify export options**, select the first two check boxes—**Export data with formatting and layout** and **Open the destination file after the export operation is complete**—and then click **OK**. Take a moment to examine the data in the file, and then **Close** Excel. In the **Export – Excel Spreadsheet** dialog box, click **Close**, and then **Close** Access.

4 From the desktop, start Internet Explorer, navigate to **http://drive.google.com**, and sign in to your Google account; if necessary, create a new Google account and then sign in. On the right side of the screen, click the **Settings arrow** , and then point to **Upload settings**. Be sure that **Convert uploaded files to Google Docs format** is selected.

If this setting is not selected, your document will upload as a pdf file and cannot be edited without further action.

5 Open your **GO! Web Projects** folder—or create and then open this folder by clicking **New folder** . Under **Drive**, to the right of **Create**, click **Upload** , and then click **Files**. In the **Choose File to Upload** dialog box, navigate to your **Access Chapter 1** folder, and then double-click your **AC_1B_Web** Excel file to upload it to Google Drive. When the title bar of the message box indicates *Upload complete*, **Close** the message box. Compare your screen with Figure A.

FIGURE A

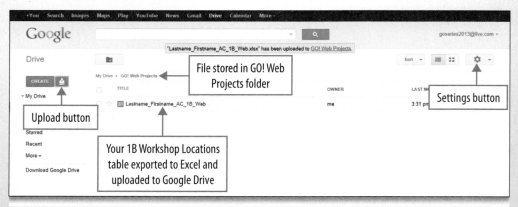

File stored in GO! Web Projects folder

Settings button

Upload button

Your 1B Workshop Locations table exported to Excel and uploaded to Google Drive

(GO! with Office Web Apps continues on the next page)

6 Click your **AC_1B_Web** file to open the file in Google Drive. If necessary, maximize the window.

The worksheet displays column letters, row numbers, and data.

7 Click in cell **A7**, type **SW-02** and then press Tab. In cell **B7**, type **Southwest Campus** and then press Tab. In cell **C7**, type **B101** and then press Tab. In cell **D7**, type **25** and then press ↓ to save the record.

The new record might display with a different font than the other records.

8 Above row **1** and to the left of column **A**, click **Select All** ⬚. On the menu bar, click **Format**, and then click **Clear formatting** so that the font is the same for all data. Click in cell **A8**, and then compare your screen with Figure B.

9 On the menu, click **File**, point to **Download as**, and then click **Microsoft Excel (.xlsx)**. In the message box—usually displays at the bottom of your screen—click the **Save arrow**, and then click **Save as**. In the **Save As** dialog box, navigate to your **Access Chapter 1** folder, click in the **File name** box, type **Lastname_Firstname_AC_1B_Web_Download** and then click **Save**. **Close** the message box.

10 In Google Drive, at the top right corner of your screen, click your user name, and then click **Sign out**. **Close** your browser window.

11 Start Excel. In the Excel opening screen, click **Open Other Workbooks**. Under **Open**, click **Computer**. On the right, under **Computer**, click **Browse**. Navigate to your **Access Chapter 1** folder, and then double-click your **AC_1B_Web** Excel file. Notice that this file is the original file—the new record is not entered. If you are required to print your documents, use one of the methods in following Note. **Close** your Excel file; and, if prompted, save the changes to your worksheet. Then **Open** and print your **AC_1B_Web_Download** Excel file using one of the methods in the following Note. **Close** Excel; and, if prompted, save the changes to your worksheet. As directed by your instructor, submit your two workbooks and the two paper or electronic printouts that are the results of this project.

> **NOTE**   **Adding the File Name to the Footer and Printing or Creating an Electronic Printout of an Excel Spreadsheet on One Page**
>
> Click the FILE tab, click Print, and then click Page Setup. In the Page Setup dialog box, on the Page tab, under Orientation, click Landscape. Under Scaling, click the Fit to option button. In the Page Setup dialog box, click the Header/Footer tab, and then click Custom Footer. With the insertion point blinking in the Left section box, click the Insert File Name button, and then click OK. In the Page Setup dialog box, click OK.
>
> To print on paper, click Print. To create an electronic file of your printout, on the left side of your screen, click Export. Under Export, be sure Create PDF/XPS Document is selected, and then, on the right, click Create PDF/XPS. Navigate to your Access Chapter 1 folder, and then click Publish to save the file with the default name and an extension of pdf.

FIGURE B

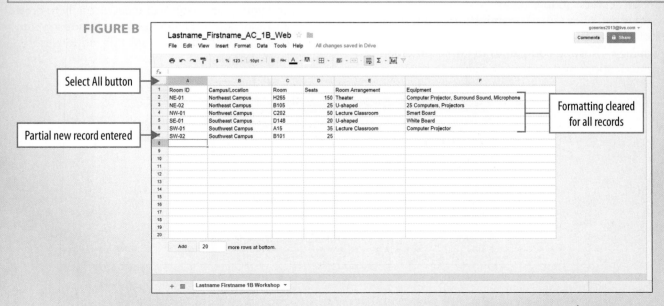

GO! with Microsoft Office 365

Office 365 includes business-class security and is backed by Microsoft. For an organization, what does that mean?

When you and a few classmates work together on a class project, you are not concerned about the security of your data. You probably use free personal email services such as Hotmail, Gmail, or Yahoo Mail to exchange documents, or perhaps you post your documents to free services such as Google Docs.

Organizations, on the other hand—even small ones with only two or three employees—must be concerned with the privacy and security of their data. Organizations cannot entrust their data and confidential communications to free services that may change frequently or that have no legal responsibility for the security of the data.

Organizations must provide each employee with a company email address rather than having each employee use his or her own personal free email address for business communications. Organizations must provide a central storage location for its data rather than having employees store data on flash drives or local hard drives with no control or oversight.

An organization must have a *secure environment*, which is a system that uses controlled *servers*—computers that provide services on a network such as an email server or a file server—to ensure the security and privacy of email, to control the storage and use of information, and to protect against the loss of confidential data.

Most small organizations cannot afford to hire the people with the skills necessary to install and maintain servers. So to establish and maintain a secure environment, many small organizations contract with and rely on small IT—the acronym for *Information Technology*—hosting companies to host their email communications and to provide secure storage.

Activity | Using the Exchange Online Outlook Meeting Tool to Collaborate

This group project relates to the **Bell Orchid Hotels**. If your instructor assigns this project to your class, you can expect to use the **Outlook Meeting tool** in **Office 365 Exchange Online** to collaborate on the following tasks for this chapter:

- If you are in the **Accounting Group**, you and your teammates will meet virtually to create a Stockholders Database to track individuals who have purchased stock in the hotel.

- If you are in the **Engineering Group**, you and your teammates will meet virtually to create a Subcontractors Database to track companies used by the Hotel for maintenance and renovation projects.

- If you are in the **Food and Beverage Group**, you and your teammates will meet virtually to create a Banquet Clients Database to track the types of functions taking place in the Hotel's banquet rooms.

- If you are in the **Human Resources Group**, you and your teammates will meet virtually to create an Employee Database for salaried employees.

- If you are in the **Operations Group**, you and your teammates will meet virtually to create a Guests Database to track guest information, as well as room rates and availability.

- If you are in the **Sales and Marketing Group**, you and your teammates will meet virtually to create an Associations Database to track industry and trade associations that book conventions for large groups.

FIGURE A

END OF CHAPTER

SUMMARY

Principles of good database design, also known as normalization, help ensure that the data in your database is accurate and organized in a way that you can retrieve information that is useful.

Databases can be created from scratch by using the blank desktop database template or a custom web app or by using a template that contains prebuilt tables, queries, forms, reports, and other objects.

Before entering records in a table, which is the foundation of a database, you must define data types and name the fields. Common data types are Short Text, Number, Currency, and Date/Time.

Forms are used to enter data into a table or view the data in a table. Queries are used to retrieve information from tables, and reports display information from tables in a professional-looking format.

GO! LEARN IT ONLINE

Review the concepts and key terms in this chapter by completing these online challenges, which you can find at **www.pearsonhighered.com/go.**

Matching and Multiple Choice: Answer matching and multiple choice questions to test what you learned in this chapter. MyITLab®

Crossword Puzzle: Spell out the words that match the numbered clues, and put them in the puzzle squares.

Flipboard: Flip through the definitions of the key terms in this chapter and match them with the correct term.

GO! FOR JOB SUCCESS

Video: Goal Setting

Your instructor may assign this video to your class, and then ask you to think about, or discuss with your classmates, these questions:

FotolEdhar / Fotolia

Is there anything you would change about Theo's behavior at his performance evaluation? Why or why not?

SMART goals are goals that are specific, measurable, achievable, realistic, and time-frame specific. Is Theo's first goal of beating his sales numbers by 10 percent next year a SMART goal?

How important do you think it is to set career development goals for yourself? Why?

END OF CHAPTER

REVIEW AND ASSESSMENT GUIDE FOR ACCESS CHAPTER 1

Your instructor may assign one or more of these projects to help you review the chapter and assess your mastery and understanding of the chapter.

Project	Apply Skills from These Chapter Objectives	Project Type	Project Location
1C	Objectives 1-5 from Project 1A	**1C Skills Review** A guided review of the skills from Project 1A.	On the following pages
1D	Objectives 6-9 from Project 1B	**1D Skills Review** A guided review of the skills from Project 1B.	On the following pages
1E	Objectives 1-5 from Project 1A	**1E Mastery (Grader Project)** A demonstration of your mastery of the skills in Project 1A with extensive decision making.	In MyITLab and on the following pages
1F	Objectives 6-9 from Project 1B	**1F Mastery (Grader Project)** A demonstration of your mastery of the skills in Project 1B with extensive decision making.	In MyITLab and on the following pages
1G	Objectives 1-9 from Projects 1A and 1B	**1G Mastery (Grader Project)** A demonstration of your mastery of the skills in Projects 1A and 1B with extensive decision making.	In MyITLab and on the following pages
1H	Combination of Objectives from Projects 1A and 1B	**1H GO! Fix It** A demonstration of your mastery of the skills in Projects 1A and 1B by creating a correct result from a document that contains errors you must find.	Online
1I	Combination of Objectives from Projects 1A and 1B	**1I GO! Make It** A demonstration of your mastery of the skills in Projects 1A and 1B by creating a result from a supplied picture.	Online
1J	Combination of Objectives from Projects 1A and 1B	**1J GO! Solve It** A demonstration of your mastery of the skills in Projects 1A and 1B, your decision-making skills, and your critical thinking skills. A task-specific rubric helps you self-assess your result.	Online
1K	Combination of Objectives from Projects 1A and 1B	**1K GO! Solve It** A demonstration of your mastery of the skills in Projects 1A and 1B, your decision-making skills, and your critical thinking skills. A task-specific rubric helps you self-assess your result.	On the following pages
1L	Combination of Objectives from Projects 1A and 1B	**1L GO! Think** A demonstration of your understanding of the chapter concepts applied in a manner that you would outside of college. An analytic rubric helps you and your instructor grade the quality of your work by comparing it to the work an expert in the discipline would create.	On the following pages
1M	Combination of Objectives from Projects 1A and 1B	**1M GO! Think** A demonstration of your understanding of the chapter concepts applied in a manner that you would outside of college. An analytic rubric helps you and your instructor grade the quality of your work by comparing it to the work an expert in the discipline would create.	Online
1N	Combination of Objectives from Projects 1A and 1B	**1N You and GO!** A demonstration of your understanding of the chapter concepts applied in a manner that you would in a personal situation. An analytic rubric helps you and your instructor grade the quality of your work.	Online
1O	Combination of Objectives from Projects 1A and 1B	**1O Cumulative Group Project for Access Chapter 1** A demonstration of your understanding of concepts and your ability to work collaboratively in a group role-playing assessment, requiring both collaboration and self-management.	Online

GLOSSARY

GLOSSARY OF CHAPTER KEY TERMS

Append To add on to the end of an object; for example, to add records to the end of an existing table.

AutoNumber data type A data type that describes a unique sequential or random number assigned by Access as each record is entered and that is useful for data that has no distinct field that can be considered unique.

Best Fit An Access command that adjusts the width of a column to accommodate the column's longest entry.

Blank desktop database A database that has no data and has no database tools—you must create the data and tools as you need them; the database is stored on your computer or other storage device.

Caption A property setting that displays a name for a field in a table, query, form, or report other than that listed as the field name.

Common field A field in two or more tables that stores the same data.

Currency data type An Access data type that describes monetary values and numeric data that can be used in mathematical calculations involving values with one to four decimal places.

Custom web app A database that you can publish and share with others over the Internet.

Data Facts about people, events, things, or ideas.

Data source The table or tables from which a query, form, or report retrieves its data.

Data type The characteristic that defines the kind of data that can be stored in a field, such as numbers, text, or dates.

Database An organized collection of facts about people, events, things, or ideas related to a specific topic or purpose.

Database management system (DBMS) Database software that controls how related collections of data are stored, organized, retrieved, and secured; also known as a DBMS.

Database template A preformatted database that contains prebuilt tables, queries, forms, and reports that perform a specific task, such as tracking events.

Datasheet view The Access view that displays data organized in columns and rows similar to an Excel worksheet.

DBMS An acronym for database management system.

Design view An Access view that displays the detailed structure of a table, query, form, or report. For forms and reports, may be the view in which some tasks must be performed, and only the controls, and not the data, display in this view.

Destination table The table to which you import or append data.

Export The process of copying data from one file into another file, such as an Access table into an Excel spreadsheet.

Field A single piece of information that is stored in every record; represented by a column in a database table.

Field properties Characteristics of a field that control how the field displays and how data can be entered in the field.

First principle of good database design A principle of good database design stating that data is organized in tables so that there is no redundant data.

Flat database A simple database file that is not related or linked to any other collection of data.

Form An Access object you can use to enter new records into a table, edit or delete existing records in a table, or display existing records.

Form view The Access view in which you can view records, but you cannot change the layout or design of the form.

Import The process of copying data from another file, such as a Word table or an Excel workbook, into a separate file, such as an Access database.

Information Data that is organized in a useful manner.

Layout view The Access view in which you can make changes to a form or report while the object is open—the data from the underlying data source displays.

Link A connection to data in another file.

Multiple-items form A form that enables you to display or enter multiple records in a table.

Navigation area An area at the bottom of the Access window that indicates the number of records in the table and contains controls in the form of arrows that you click to navigate among the records.

Navigation Pane An area of the Access window that displays and organizes the names of the objects in a database; from here, you open objects for use.

Normalization The process of applying design rules and principles to ensure that your database performs as expected.

Number data type An Access data type that describes numbers that might be used in calculations.

Object tab In the object window, a tab that identifies the object and which enables you to make the open object active.

Object window An area of the Access window that displays open objects, such as tables, queries, forms, or reports; by default, each object displays on its own tab.

Objects The basic parts of a database that you create to store your data and to work with your data; for example, tables, queries, forms, and reports.

Populate The action of filling a database table with records.

Primary key The field in a table that uniquely identifies a record; for example, a Student ID number at a college.

Property Sheet A list of characteristics—properties—for fields or controls on a form or report in which you can make precise changes to each property associated with the field or control.

Query A database object that retrieves specific data from one or more database objects—either tables or other queries—and then, in a single datasheet, displays only the data you specify.

Record All of the categories of data pertaining to one person, place, event, thing, or idea; represented by a row in a database table.

Record selector bar The bar at the left edge of a record when it is displayed in a form, and which is used to select an entire record.

Record selector box The small box at the left of a record in Datasheet view that, when clicked, selects the entire record.

Redundant In a database, information that is duplicated in a manner that indicates poor database design.

Relational database A sophisticated type of database that has multiple collections of data within the file that are related to one another.

Report A database object that summarizes the fields and records from a table or query in an easy-to-read format suitable for printing.

Run The process in which Access searches the records in the table(s) included in the query design, finds the records that match the specified criteria, and then displays the records in a datasheet; only the fields that have been included in the query design display.

Second principle of good database design A principle stating that appropriate database techniques are used to ensure the accuracy and consistency of data as it is entered into the table.

Secure environment A system that uses controlled servers to ensure the security and privacy of email, to control the storage and use of information and to protect against the loss of confidential data.

Select query A type of Access query that retrieves (selects) data from one or more tables or queries, displaying the selected data in a datasheet; also known as a simple select query.

Server A computer that provides services on a network such as an email server or a file server.

SharePoint A Microsoft application used for setting up websites to share and manage documents.

Short Text data type An Access data type that describes text, a combination of text and numbers, or numbers that are not used in calculations, such as a Postal Code.

Simple select query Another name for a select query.

Single-record form A form that enables you to display or enter one record at a time in a table.

Source file When importing a file, refers to the file being imported.

Structure In Access, the underlying design of a table, including field names, data types, descriptions, and field properties.

Table A format for information that organizes and presents text and data in columns and rows; the foundation of a database.

Tables and Related Views An arrangement in the Navigation Pane that groups objects by the table to which they are related.

Truncated Refers to data that is cut off or shortened because the field or column is not wide enough to display all of the data or the field size is too small to contain all of the data.

Wizard A feature in Microsoft Office that walks you step by step through a process.

CHAPTER REVIEW

Apply 1A skills from these Objectives:

1 Identify Good Database Design

2 Create a Table and Define Fields in a Blank Desktop Database

3 Change the Structure of Tables and Add a Second Table

4 Create a Query, Form, and Report

5 Close a Database and Exit Access

Skills Review Project 1C College Administrators

In the following Skills Review, you will create a database to store information about the administrators of Texas Lakes Community College and their departments. Your completed database objects will look similar to Figure 1.51.

PROJECT FILES

For Project 1C, you will need the following files:

Blank desktop database

a01C_Administrators (Excel workbook)

a01C_Departments (Excel workbook)

You will save your database as:

Lastname_Firstname_1C_College_Administrators

Build from Scratch

PROJECT RESULTS

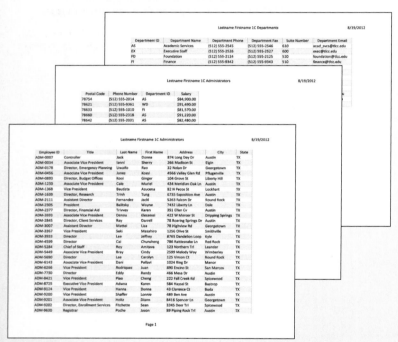

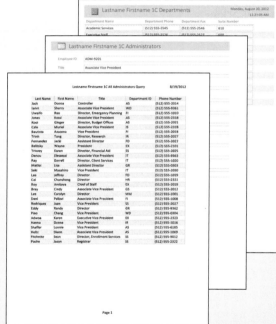

FIGURE 1.51

(Project 1C College Administrators continues on the next page)

540 Access | Chapter 1: GETTING STARTED WITH MICROSOFT ACCESS 2013

CHAPTER REVIEW

1 Start Access. In the Access opening screen, click **Blank desktop database**. In the **Blank desktop database** dialog box, to the right of the **File Name** box, click **Browse**. In the **File New Database** dialog box, navigate to your **Access Chapter 1** folder. In the **File New Database** dialog box, click in the **File name** box, type **Lastname_Firstname_1C_College_Administrators** and then press [Enter]. In the **Blank desktop database** dialog box, click **Create**.

a. **Close** the **Navigation Pane**. In the field names row, click in the text *Click to Add*, and then click **Short Text**. Type **Title** and then press [Enter].

b. In the third field name box, click **Short Text**, type **Last Name** and then press [Enter]. In the fourth field name box, click **Short Text**, type **First Name** and then press [Enter]. Create the remaining fields shown in **Table 1**, pressing [Enter] after the last field name. All of the data is typed on one line.

c. If necessary, scroll to bring the first column into view, and then click the **ID** field name. Under **TABLE TOOLS**, on the **FIELDS tab**, in the **Properties group**, click **Name & Caption**. In the **Name** box, change *ID* to **Employee ID** and then click **OK**. On the ribbon, in the **Formatting group**, click the **Data Type arrow**, and then click **Short Text**.

d. In the new record row, click in the **Employee ID** field, type, **ADM-9200** and press [Enter]. In the **Title** field, type **Vice President** and press [Enter]. Continue entering data in the fields shown in **Table 2**, pressing [Enter] or [Tab] to move to the next field and to the next row.

e. On the **Quick Access Toolbar**, click **Save**. In the **Save As** dialog box, in the **Table Name** box, using your own name, replace the selected text by typing **Lastname Firstname 1C Administrators** and then click **OK**.

f. In the new record row, enter the data for two college administrators shown in **Table 3**, pressing [Enter] or [Tab] to move from field to field and to the next row.

TABLE 1

Data Type		Short Text	Short Text	Short Text	Short Text	Short Text	Short Text	Short Text	Short Text	Short Text	Short Text	Currency
Field Name	ID	Title	Last Name	First Name	Middle Initial	Address	City	State	Postal Code	Phone Number	Department ID	Salary

Return to Step 1c

TABLE 2

Last Name	First Name	Middle Initial	Address	City	State	Postal Code	Phone Number	Department ID	Salary
Shaffer	Lonnie	J	489 Ben Ave	Austin	TX	78734	(512) 555-6185	AS	123500

Return to Step 1e

TABLE 3

Employee ID	Title	Last Name	First Name	Middle Initial	Address	City	State	Postal Code	Phone Number	Department ID	Salary
ADM-9201	Associate Vice President	Holtz	Diann	S	8416 Spencer Ln	Georgetown	TX	78627	(512) 555-1069	AS	101524
ADM-9202	Director, Enrollment Services	Fitchette	Sean	H	3245 Deer Trl	Spicewood	TX	78669	(512) 555-9012	SS	45070

Return to Step 1g

(Project 1C College Administrators continues on the next page)

g. **Close** your **1C Administrators** table. On the ribbon, click the **EXTERNAL DATA tab**, in the **Import & Link group**, click **Excel**. In the **Get External Data – Excel Spreadsheet** dialog box, click **Browse**. In the **File Open** dialog box, navigate to your student data files, and then double-click the **a01C_Administrators** Excel file.

h. Click the **Append a copy of the records to the table** option button, and then click **OK**. In the **Import Spreadsheet Wizard**, click **Next**, and then click **Finish**. In the **Get External Data – Excel Spreadsheet** dialog box, click **Close**.

i. **Open** the **Navigation Pane**. Point to the right edge of the **Navigation Pane** to display the ⟷ pointer, and then drag to the right so that the entire table name displays. In the **Navigation Pane**, double-click your **1C Administrators** table to open it, and then **Close** the **Navigation Pane**—there are 30 records in this table.

2 ▶ Click the **HOME tab**, and then in the **Views group**, click the top of the **View** button to switch to **Design** view. In the **Field Name** column, to the left of **Middle Initial**, click the row selector box to select the entire row. Under **TABLE TOOLS, o**n the **DESIGN tab**, in the **Tools group**, click **Delete Rows**. In the message box, click **Yes**.

a. Click in the **Employee ID** field name box. Under **Field Properties**, click **Field Size** to select the existing text. Type **8** and then in the **Employee ID** field row, click in the **Description** box. Type **Eight-character Employee ID** and then press Enter.

b. Click in the **State** field name box. In the **Field Properties** area, click **Field Size**, and then type **2** In the **State Description** box, type **Two-character state abbreviation** and then press Enter.

c. **Save** the design changes to your table, and in the message box, click **Yes**. On the **DESIGN tab**, in the **Views group**, click the top of the **View** button to switch to **Datasheet** view.

d. On the ribbon, click the **EXTERNAL DATA tab**, and then in the **Import & Link group**, click **Excel**. In the **Get External Data – Excel Spreadsheet** dialog box, to the right of the **File name** box, click **Browse**. In the

File Open dialog box, navigate to your student data files, and then double-click **a01C_Departments**. Be sure that the **Import the source data into a new table in the current database** option button is selected, and then click **OK**.

e. In the upper left corner of the wizard, select the **First Row Contains Column Headings** check box, and then click **Next**. Click **Next** again. Click the **Choose my own primary key** option button, be sure that **Department ID** displays, and then click **Next**. In the **Import to Table** box, type **Lastname Firstname 1C Departments** and then click **Finish**. In the **Get External Data – Excel Spreadsheet** dialog box, click **Close**.

f. **Open** the **Navigation Pane**, double-click your **1C Departments** table, and then **Close** the **Navigation Pane**. There are 12 records in your **1C Departments** table.

g. To the left of the **Department** field name, click **Select All**. On the ribbon, click the **HOME tab**. In the **Records group**, click **More**, and then click **Field Width**. In the **Column Width** dialog box, click **Best Fit**. **Save** the table, and then click in any field to cancel the selection. In the object window, click the **object tab** for your **1C Administrators** table. Using the techniques you just practiced, apply **Best Fit** to the columns, **Save** the table, and then cancel the selection.

h. With your **1C Administrators** table displayed, on the ribbon, click the **FILE tab**, click **Print**, and then click **Print Preview**. On the **PRINT PREVIEW tab**, in the **Page Layout group**, click **Landscape**. Create a paper or electronic printout as directed by your instructor—two pages result. On the ribbon, click **Close Print Preview**, and then **Close** your **1C Administrators** table.

i. With your **1C Departments** table displayed, view the table in **Print Preview**. Change the orientation to **Landscape**, and then create a paper or electronic printout as directed by your instructor—one page results. Click **Close Print Preview**, and then **Close** your **1C Departments** table.

(Project 1C College Administrators continues on the next page)

CHAPTER REVIEW

3 ▶ On the ribbon, click the **CREATE tab**, and then in the **Queries group**, click **Query Wizard**. In the **New Query** dialog box, be sure **Simple Query Wizard** is selected, and then click **OK**. In the wizard, click the **Tables/Queries arrow**, and then, if necessary, click **Table: Lastname Firstname 1C Administrators**.

a. Under **Available Fields**, click **Last Name**, and then click **Add Field** to move the field to the **Selected Fields** list on the right. Double-click the **First Name** field to move it to the **Selected Fields** list. By using **Add Field** or by double-clicking the field name, add the following fields to the **Selected Fields** list in the order specified: **Title**, **Department ID**, and **Phone Number**. This query will answer the question, *What is the last name, first name, title, Department ID, and phone number of every administrator?*

b. In the wizard, click **Next**. Click in the **What title do you want for your query?** box. Using your own name, edit as necessary so that the query name is **Lastname Firstname 1C All Administrators Query** and then click **Finish**. If necessary, apply **Best Fit** to the columns, and then **Save** the query. Display the query in **Print Preview**, and then create a paper or electronic printout as directed—one page results. Click **Close Print Preview**, and then **Close** the query.

c. **Open** the Navigation Pane, right-click your **1C Administrators** table, and then click **Open** to display the table in the object window. **Close** the **Navigation Pane**. Notice that the table has 11 fields. On the ribbon, click the **CREATE tab**, and in the **Forms group**, click **Form**. On the **Quick Access Toolbar**, click **Save**. In the **Save As** dialog box, click in the **Form Name** box, edit to name the form **Lastname Firstname 1C Administrator Form** and then click **OK**.

d. In the navigation area, click **Last record**, and then click **Previous record** two times to display the record for *Diann Holtz*. Using the instructions in Activity 1.15, print or create an electronic printout of only this record on one page. **Close** the form object, saving it if prompted. Your **1C Administrators** table object remains open.

e. **Open** the **Navigation Pane**, open your **1C Departments** table by double-clicking the table name or by right-clicking the table name and clicking **Open**. **Close** the **Navigation Pane**. On the **CREATE tab**, in the **Reports group**, click **Report**.

f. Click the **Department ID** field name, and then on the ribbon, click the **ARRANGE tab**. In the **Rows & Columns group**, click **Select Column**, and then press ⟨Del⟩. Using the same technique, delete the **Department Email** field.

g. Click the **Department Phone** field name. Hold down ⟨Shift⟩, and then click the **Suite Number** field name to select the last three field names. On the ribbon, click the **DESIGN tab**, and then in the **Tools group**, click **Property Sheet**. In the **Property Sheet**, on the **Format tab**, click **Width**, type **1.5** and then press ⟨Enter⟩. **Close** the **Property Sheet**.

h. Click the **Department Name** field name. On the ribbon, click the **HOME tab**. In the **Sort & Filter group**, click **Ascending** to sort the report in alphabetic order by *Department Name*. At the bottom of the report, on the right side, click **Page 1 of 1**, and then press ⟨Del⟩.

i. Save the report as **Lastname Firstname 1C Departments Report** and then click **OK**. Display the report in **Print Preview**, and then create a paper or electronic printout of the report as directed. Click **Close Print Preview**. In the object window, right-click any **object tab**, and then click **Close All** to close all open objects, leaving the object window empty.

(Project 1C College Administrators continues on the next page)

CHAPTER REVIEW

4 **Open** the **Navigation Pane**. If necessary, increase the width of the **Navigation Pane** so that all object names display fully. On the right side of the title bar, click **Close** to close the database and to exit Access. As directed by your instructor, submit your database and the paper or electronic printouts of the five objects—two tables, one query, one form, and one report—that are the results of this project. Specifically, in this project, using your own name, you created the following database and printouts or electronic printouts:

1. Lastname_Firstname_1C_College_Administrators	Database file
2. Lastname Firstname 1C Administrators	Table (printout or electronic printout – two pages)
3. Lastname Firstname 1C Departments	Table (printout or electronic printout)
4. Lastname Firstname 1C All Administrators Query	Query (printout or electronic printout)
5. Lastname Firstname 1C Administrator Form	Form (printout or electronic printout – Record 28)
6. Lastname Firstname 1C Departments Report	Report (printout or electronic printout)

END | You have completed Project 1C

CHAPTER REVIEW

Apply **1B** skills from these Objectives:

6 Use a Template to Create a Database

7 Organize Objects in the Navigation Pane

8 Create a New Table in a Database Created with a Template

9 Print a Report and a Table

Skills Review Project 1D Certification Events

In the following Skills Review, you will create a database to store information about certification test preparation events at Texas Lakes Community College. Your completed report and table will look similar to Figure 1.52.

PROJECT FILES

For Project 1D, you will need the following files:

Desktop Event Management template
a01D_Certification_Events (Excel workbook)

You will save your database as:

Lastname_Firstname_1D_Certification_Events

Build from Scratch

PROJECT RESULTS

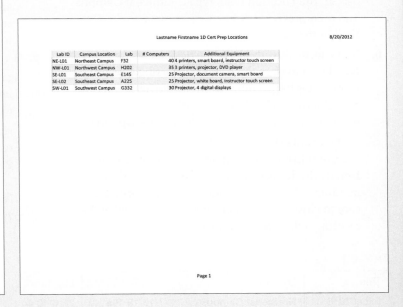

FIGURE 1.52

(Project 1D Certification Events continues on the next page)

CHAPTER REVIEW

1 Start Access. In the Access opening screen, click in the **Search** box, type **event** and then press Enter to search for a template to manage events. Click the **Desktop Event Management** template. In the **Desktop Event Management** dialog box, to the right of the **File Name** box, click **Browse**, and then navigate to your **Access Chapter 1** folder. In the **File New Database** dialog box, click in the **File name** box to select the existing text. Using your own name, type **Lastname_Firstname_1D_ Certification_Events** and then press Enter. In the **Desktop Event Management** dialog box, click **Create** to download the template and to save the database. Under the ribbon, on the **Message Bar**, click **Enable Content**.

a. In the first row, click in the **Title** field, type **Word 2013** and then press Tab. In the **Start Time** field, type **7/9/18 9a** and then press Tab. In the **End Time** field, type **7/9/18 3p** and then press Tab. In the **Description** field, type **Office 2013** and then press Tab. In the **Location** field, type **Southwest Campus** and then press Tab three times to move to the **Title** field in the new record row.

b. In the form, directly above the field names row, click **New Event** to open the **Event Details** single-record form. Using Tab to move from field to field, enter the record shown in **Table 1**. Press Tab three times to move from the **End Time** field to the **Description** field.

c. In the **Events Detail** form, click **Close**. Using either the **Event List** multiple-items form or the **Event Details** single-record form, enter the records shown in **Table 2**. If you use the **Events Detail** form, be sure to close it after entering records to display the records in the **Event List** form.

d. **Close** the **Event List** form. On the ribbon, click the **EXTERNAL DATA tab**, and in the **Import & Link group**, click **Excel**. In the **Get External Data – Excel Spreadsheet** dialog box, click **Browse**. Navigate to your student data files, and then double-click **a01D_Certification_Events**. Click the second option button—**Append a copy of the records to the table**—and then click **OK**.

e. In the **Import Spreadsheet Wizard**, click **Next**, and then click **Finish**. In the **Get External Data – Excel Spreadsheet** dialog box, click **Close**. **Open** the **Navigation Pane**, and then double-click **Event List** to open the form that displays data stored in the **Events** table—12 total records display. **Close** the **Navigation Pane**.

f. To the left of the **ID** field name, click **Select All**. In the field names row, point to the right edge of any of the selected columns to display the ⊞ pointer, and then double-click to apply **Best Fit** to all of the columns. **Save** the form, and then click in any field to cancel the selection.

2 Open the **Navigation Pane**. At the top of the **Navigation Pane**, click the arrow. On the list, under **Navigate To Category**, click **Tables and Related Views**.

a. In the **Navigation Pane**, point to **Events: Table**, right-click, and then click **Open** to display the records in the underlying table. In the **Navigation Pane**, double-click the **Current Events** report (green icon) to view this predesigned report. From the **Navigation Pane**, open the **Events by Week** report to view this predesigned report.

TABLE 1

Title	Location	Start Time	End Time	Description
Excel 2013	**Northeast Campus**	**7/16/18 10a**	**7/16/18 4p**	**Office 2013**

Return to Step 1c

TABLE 2

ID	Title	Start Time	End Time	Description	Location
3	**Access 2013**	**7/23/18 12p**	**7/23/18 6p**	**Office 2013**	**Southeast Campus**
4	**PowerPoint 2013**	**7/30/18 9a**	**7/30/18 3p**	**Office 2013**	**Northwest Campus**

Return to Step 1d

(Project 1D Certification Events continues on the next page)

CHAPTER REVIEW

b.   In the object window, right-click any of the **object tabs**, and then click **Close All**. **Close** the Navigation **Pane**.

3 On the ribbon, click the **CREATE tab**, and in the **Tables group**, click **Table**.

a.   In the field names row, click **Click to Add**, click **Short Text**, type **Campus Location** and then press Enter. In the third column, click **Short Text**, type **Lab** and then press Enter. In the fourth column, click **Number**, type **# Computers** and then press Enter. In the fifth column, click **Short Text**, type **Additional Equipment** and then press ↓.

b.   Right-click the **ID** field name, and then click **Rename Field**. Type **Lab ID** and then press Enter. On the **FIELDS tab**, in the **Formatting group**, click the **Data Type arrow**, and then click **Short Text**.

c.   In the new record row, click in the **Lab ID** field, and then enter the records shown in **Table 3**, pressing Enter or Tab to move from one field to the next.

d.   In the **Views group**, click the top of the **View** button to switch to **Design** view. In the **Save As** dialog box, in the **Table Name** box, using your own name, type **Lastname Firstname 1D Cert Prep Locations** and then click **OK**. Notice that the **Lab ID** field is the **Primary Key**. On the **DESIGN tab**, in the **Views group**, click the top of the **View** button to switch to **Datasheet** view.

e.   To the left of the **Lab ID** field name, click **Select All** to select all of the columns and rows in the table. On the **HOME tab**, in the **Records group**, click **More**, and then click **Field Width**. In the **Column Width** dialog box, click **Best Fit**. **Save** the changes to the table, and then click in any field to cancel the selection. **Close** the table, and then **Open** the Navigation Pane. Increase the width of the Navigation Pane so that your entire table name displays.

4 In the Navigation Pane, double-click the **All Events** report to open it in the object window. **Close** the Navigation Pane. On the **HOME tab**, in the **Views group**, click the top of the **View** button to switch to **Layout** view. At the top of the report, click the title—*All Events*—to display a colored border around the title. Click to the left of the letter *A* to place the insertion point there. Using your own name, type **Lastname Firstname 1D** and then press Spacebar. Press Enter, and then **Save** the report.

a.   On the right side of the status bar, click **Print Preview**, and notice that the report will print on one page. Create a paper or electronic printout as instructed. Click **Close Print Preview**, and then **Close** the report.

b.   **Open** the Navigation Pane, double-click your **1D Cert Prep Locations** table, and then **Close** the Navigation Pane. On the ribbon, click the **FILE tab**, click **Print**, and then click **Print Preview**. On the **PRINT PREVIEW tab**, in the **Page Layout group**, click **Landscape**. Create a paper or electronic printout as directed, and then click **Close Print Preview**. Close your **1D Cert Prep Locations** table.

TABLE 3

Lab ID	Campus Location	Lab	# Computers	Additional Equipment
NW-L01	Northwest Campus	H202	35	3 printers, projector, DVD player
SE-L01	Southeast Campus	E145	25	Projector, document camera, smart board
NE-L01	Northeast Campus	F32	40	4 printers, smart board, instructor touch screen
SW-L01	Southwest Campus	G332	30	Projector, 4 digital displays
SE-L02	Southeast Campus	A225	25	Projector, white board, instructor touch screen

Return to Step 3d

(Project 1D Certification Events continues on the next page)

CHAPTER REVIEW

c. **Open** the **Navigation Pane**. On the right side of the title bar, click **Close** to close the database and to exit Access. As directed by your instructor, submit your database and the paper or electronic printouts of the two objects—one report and one table—that are the results of this project. Specifically, in this project, using your own name, you created the following database and printouts or electronic printouts:

1. Lastname_Firstname_1D_Certification_Events	Database file
2. Lastname Firstname 1D Cert Prep Locations	Table (printout or electronic printout)
3. All Events	Report (printout or electronic printout)

END | You have completed Project 1D

CONTENT-BASED ASSESSMENTS

Mastering Access | Project 1E Kiosk Inventory

In the following Mastering Access project, you will create a database to track information about the inventory of items for sale in the kiosk located in the snack bar at the Southeast Campus of Texas Lakes Community College. Your completed database objects will look similar to Figure 1.53.

Apply 1A skills from these Objectives:

1 Identify Good Database Design

2 Create a Table and Define Fields in a Blank Desktop Database

3 Change the Structure of Tables and Add a Second Table

4 Create a Query, Form, and Report

5 Close a Database and Exit Access

PROJECT FILES

For Project 1E, you will need the following files:

Blank desktop database
a01E_Inventory (Excel workbook)
a01E_Inventory_Storage (Excel workbook)

You will save your database as:

Lastname_Firstname_1E_Kiosk_Inventory

PROJECT RESULTS

Build from Scratch

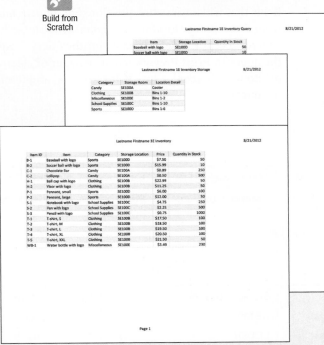

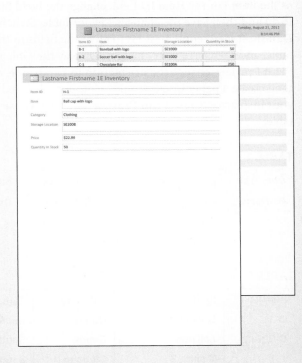

FIGURE 1.53

(Project 1E Kiosk Inventory continues on the next page)

CONTENT-BASED ASSESSMENTS

1 Start Access. Create a **Blank desktop database** in your **Access Chapter 1** folder. Name the database **Lastname_Firstname_1E_Kiosk_Inventory** and then **Close** the **Navigation Pane**. Create the fields shown in **Table 1**.

2 For the **ID** field, change the **Data Type** to **Short Text**, rename the field to **Item ID** and then enter the records shown in **Table 2**.

3 Save the table as **Lastname Firstname 1E Inventory** and then **Close** the table. From your student data files, import and then **Append** the data in the Excel file **a01E_Inventory** to your **1E Inventory** table. After importing, open your **1E Inventory** table—17 records display.

4 In **Design** view, delete the **Campus** field, which is redundant data. For the **Category** field, change the **Field Size** to **25** and enter a **Description** of **Enter the category of the item** For the **Item ID** field, change the **Field Size** to **10** and then **Save** the changes to your table. Switch to **Datasheet** view, apply **Best Fit** to all of the fields in the table, and then **Save** your changes. Display the table in **Print Preview**, change the orientation to **Landscape**, and then create a paper or electronic printout as directed by your instructor. **Close Print Preview**, and then **Close** the table.

5 From your student data files, import the **Excel** file **a01E_Inventory_Storage** into the database as a new table; designate the first row as column headings and the **Category** field as the primary key. In the wizard, name the table **Lastname Firstname 1E Inventory Storage** and then open your **1E Inventory Storage** table—five records display. In **Design** view, for the **Location Detail** field, change the **Field Size** to **30** and enter a **Description** of **Room and bin number or alternate location of inventory item Save** the design changes, switch to **Datasheet** view, apply **Best Fit** to all of the fields, and then **Save** your changes. Display the table in **Print Preview**, create a paper or electronic printout as directed, **Close Print Preview**, and then **Close** the table.

6 Use the **Query Wizard** to create a simple query based on your **1E Inventory** table. Include only the three fields that will answer the question, *For all item names, what is the storage location and quantity in stock?* In the wizard, accept the default name for the query. Display the query in **Print Preview**, create a paper or electronic printout as directed, **Close Print Preview**, and then **Close** the query.

TABLE 1

Data Type		Short Text	Short Text	Short Text	Short Text	Currency	Number
Field Name	ID	Item	Category	Campus	Storage Location	Price	Quantity in Stock

Return to Step 2

TABLE 2

Item ID	Item	Category	Campus	Storage Location	Price	Quantity in Stock
C-1	Chocolate Bar	Candy	Southeast	SE100A	.89	250
C-2	Lollipop	Candy	Southeast	SE100A	.5	500
T-1	T-shirt, S	Clothing	Southeast	SE100B	17.5	100

Return to Step 3

(Project 1E Kiosk Inventory continues on the next page)

CONTENT-BASED ASSESSMENTS

7 Open your **1E Inventory** table, and then create a **Form** for this table. **Save** the form as **Lastname Firstname 1E Inventory Form** and then display and select the fifth record. By using the instructions in Activity 1.15, create a paper or electronic printout of only this record on one page, as directed by your instructor. **Close** the form object, saving changes if prompted.

8 With your **1E Inventory** table open, create a **Report**. Delete the **Category** and **Price** fields, and then sort the **Item ID** field in **Ascending** order. Using the **Property Sheet**, for the **Item ID** field, change the **Width** to **0.75** and then for the **Storage Location** field, change the **Width** to **1.5** Scroll to display the bottom of the report, and then

delete the page number—**Page 1 of 1**. **Save** the report as **Lastname Firstname 1E Inventory Report** and then display the report in **Print Preview**. Create a paper or electronic printout as directed. Click **Close Print Preview**.

9 **Close All** open objects. **Open** the **Navigation Pane** and be sure that all object names display fully. **Close** the database, and then **Close** Access. As directed by your instructor, submit your database and the paper or electronic printouts of the five objects—two tables, one query, one form, and one report—that are the results of this project. Specifically, in this project, using your own name, you created the following database and printouts or electronic printouts:

1. Lastname_Firstname_1E_Kiosk_Inventory	Database file
2. Lastname Firstname 1E Inventory	Table (printout or electronic printout)
3. Lastname Firstname 1E Inventory Storage	Table (printout or electronic printout)
4. Lastname Firstname 1E Inventory Query	Query (printout or electronic printout)
5. Lastname Firstname 1E Inventory Form	Form (printout or electronic printout – Record 5)
6. Lastname Firstname 1E Inventory Report	Report (printout or electronic printout)

END | You have completed Project 1E

CONTENT-BASED ASSESSMENTS

Mastering Access   Project 1F Recruiting Events

Apply 1B skills from these Objectives:

6 Use a Template to Create a Database

7 Organize Objects in the Navigation Pane

8 Create a New Table in a Database Created with a Template

9 Print a Report and a Table

Build from Scratch

In the following Mastering Access project, you will create a database to store information about the recruiting events that are scheduled to attract new students to Texas Lakes Community College. Your completed report and tables will look similar to Figure 1.54.

PROJECT FILES

For Project 1F, you will need the following files:

Desktop Event Management template
a01F_Recruiting_Events (Excel workbook)

You will save your database as:

Lastname_Firstname_1F_Recruiting_Events

PROJECT RESULTS

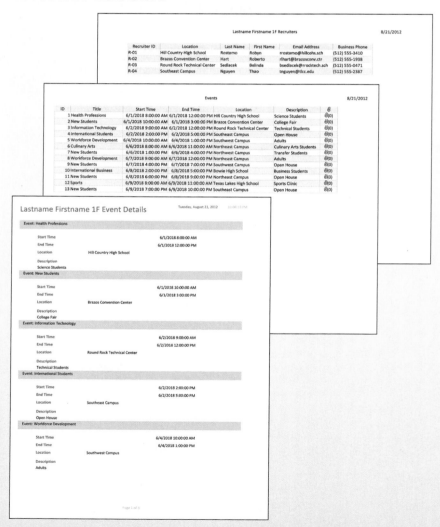

FIGURE 1.54

(Project 1F Recruiting Events continues on the next page)

CONTENT-BASED ASSESSMENTS

1 Start Access. In the Access opening screen, search for **event** and then click the **Desktop Event Management** template. Save the database in your **Access Chapter 1** folder as **Lastname_Firstname_1F_Recruiting_Events** and on the **Message Bar**, click **Enable Content**.

2 In the **Event List** multiple-items form or the **Event Details** single-record form—open by clicking **New Event** on the **Event List** form—enter the records shown in **Table 1**.

3 **Close** the **Event List** form. From your student data files, import and append the data from the **Excel** file **a01F_Recruiting_Events** to the **Events** table. **Open** the **Navigation Pane**, organize the objects by **Tables and Related Views**, and then open the **Events** table to display 13 records. **Close** the table, and then **Close** the **Navigation Pane**.

4 Create a new **Table** defining the new fields shown in **Table 2**.

5 For the **ID** field, change the **Data Type** to **Short Text**, rename the field to **Recruiter ID** and then enter the records shown in **Table 3**.

TABLE 1

ID	Title	Start Time	End Time	Description	Location
1	Health Professions	6/1/18 8a	6/1/18 12p	Science Students	Hill Country High School
2	New Students	6/1/18 10a	6/1/18 3p	College Fair	Brazos Convention Center
3	Information Technology	6/2/18 9a	6/2/18 12p	Technical Students	Round Rock Technical Center
4	International Students	6/2/18 2p	6/2/18 5p	Open House	Southeast Campus

Return to Step 3

TABLE 2

Data Type		Short Text	Short Text	Short Text	Short Text	Short Text
Field Name	ID	Location	Last Name	First Name	Email Address	Business Phone

Return to Step 5

TABLE 3

Recruiter ID	Location	Last Name	First Name	Email Address	Business Phone
R-01	Hill Country High School	Rostamo	Robyn	rrostamo@hillcohs.sch	(512) 555-3410
R-02	Brazos Convention Center	Hart	Roberto	rlhart@brazosconv.ctr	(512) 555-1938
R-03	Round Rock Technical Center	Sedlacek	Belinda	bsedlacek@rrocktech.sch	(512) 555-0471
R-04	Southeast Campus	Nguyen	Thao	tnguyen@tlcc.edu	(512) 555-2387

Return to Step 6

(Project 1F Recruiting Events continues on the next page)

CONTENT-BASED ASSESSMENTS

6 Apply **Best Fit** to all of the columns. **Save** the table as **Lastname Firstname 1F Recruiters** and then **Close** the table.

7 From the **Navigation Pane**, open the **Event Details** *report* (green icon). Switch to **Layout** view. In the report, click in the title—*Event Details*—and then click to position the insertion point to the left of the word *Event*. Using your own name, type **Lastname Firstname 1F** and then press [Spacebar] and [Enter]. If necessary, decrease the font size of the title so that the title does not overlap the date on the right side or does not extend to two lines.

Save the report, and then display it in **Print Preview**. If directed to create a paper printout, in the **Print group**, click **Print**. In the **Print** dialog box, under **Print Range**, to the right of **Pages**, click in the **From** box, type **1** and then click in the **To** box and type **1** and then click **OK** to print only the first page. If directed to create an electronic printout, in the **Publish as PDF or XPS** dialog box, click **Options**, and then under **Range**, click the **Pages** option button, and then click **OK. Close Print Preview**, and then **Close** the report.

8 From the **Navigation Pane**, open the **Events** table, select all of the columns, and then apply **Best Fit** to all of the columns by double-clicking the right edge of any one of the selected columns. **Save** the table, and then cancel the selection. Display the table in **Print Preview**, change the orientation to **Landscape**, change the **Margins** to **Normal**, and then create a paper or electronic printout as directed. **Close Print Preview**, and then **Close** the table.

9 From the **Navigation Pane**, open your **1F Recruiters** table. Display the table in **Print Preview**, change the orientation to **Landscape**, and then create a paper or electronic printout as directed. **Close Print Preview**, and then **Close** the table.

10 Open the **Navigation Pane**, and be sure that all object names display fully. **Close** Access. As directed by your instructor, submit your database and the paper or electronic printouts of the three objects—one report and two tables—that are the results of this project. Specifically, in this project, using your own name, you created the following database and printouts or electronic printouts:

1. Lastname_Firstname_1F_Recruiting_Events	Database file
2. Event Details	Report (printout or electronic printout – Page 1)
3. Events	Table (printout or electronic printout)
4. Lastname Firstname 1F Recruiters	Table (printout or electronic printout)

END | You have completed Project 1F

CONTENT-BASED ASSESSMENTS

Mastering Access Project 1G College Construction

In the following Mastering Access project, you will create one database to store information about construction projects for Texas Lakes Community College and a second database to store information about the public events related to the construction projects. Your completed database objects will look similar to Figure 1.55.

PROJECT FILES

For Project 1G, you will need the following files:

Blank desktop database
a01G_Projects (Excel workbook)
a01G_Contractors (Excel workbook)
Desktop Event Management template

You will save your databases as:

Lastname_Firstname_1G_College_Construction
Lastname_Firstname_1G_Public_Events

PROJECT RESULTS

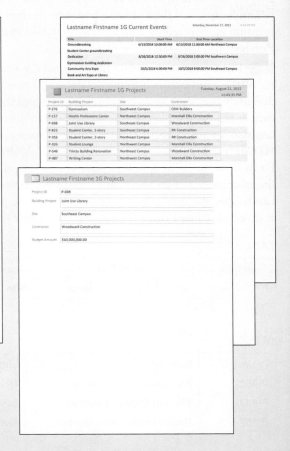

FIGURE 1.55

(Project 1G College Construction continues on the next page)

Apply 1A and 1B skills from these Objectives:

1 Identify Good Database Design
2 Create a Table and Define Fields in a Blank Desktop Database
3 Change the Structure of Tables and Add a Second Table
4 Create a Query, Form, and Report
5 Close a Database and Exit Access
6 Use a Template to Create a Database
7 Organize Objects in the Navigation Pane
8 Create a New Table in a Database Created with a Template
9 Print a Report and a Table

Build from Scratch

CONTENT-BASED ASSESSMENTS

1 Start Access. Create a **Blank desktop database** in your **Access Chapter 1** folder. Name the database **Lastname_Firstname_1G_College_Construction** and then **Close** the **Navigation Pane**. Create the fields shown in **Table 1**.

2 For the **ID** field, change the **Data Type** to **Short Text**, rename the field to **Project ID** and then enter the three records shown in **Table 2**.

3 **Save** the table as **Lastname Firstname 1G Projects** and then **Close** the table. From your student data files, import and then append the data in the **Excel** file **a01G_Projects** to your **1G Projects** table. After importing, open your **1G Projects** table—eight records display.

4 In **Design** view, for the **Project ID** field, change the **Field Size** to **5** and then enter a **Description** of **Enter the Project ID using the format P-###** Save the changes to your table. Switch to **Datasheet** view, apply **Best Fit** to all of the fields in the table, and then **Save** your changes. Display the table in **Print Preview**, change the orientation to **Landscape**, and then create a paper or electronic printout as directed by your instructor. **Close Print Preview**, and then **Close** the table.

5 From your student data files, import the **Excel** file **a01G_Contractors** into the database as a new table; designate the first row as column headings and the **ID** field as the primary key. In the wizard, name the table **Lastname Firstname 1G Contractors** and then open your **1G Contractors** table—four records display. Apply **Best Fit** to all of the fields, and then **Save** your changes. Display the table in **Print Preview**, change the orientation to **Landscape**, and then create a paper or electronic printout as directed. **Close Print Preview**, and then **Close** the table.

6 Use the **Query Wizard** to create a simple query based on your **1G Projects** table. Include only the three fields that will answer the question, *For every site, what is the building project and the budget amount?* In the wizard, accept the default name for the query. Display the query in **Print Preview**, create a paper or electronic printout as directed, **Close Print Preview**, and then **Close** the query.

7 Open your **1G Projects** table, and then create a **Form** for this table. **Save** the form as **Lastname Firstname 1G Project Form** and then display and select the seventh record. By using the instructions in Activity 1.15, create a paper or electronic printout of only this record on one page as directed by your instructor. **Close** the form object, saving changes if prompted.

8 With your **1G Projects** table open, create a **Report**. Delete the **Budget Amount** field, and then sort the **Building Project** field in **Ascending** order. For the **Building Project**, **Site**, and **Contractor** fields, using the **Property Sheet**, change the **Width** of all three fields to **2** At the bottom of the report, delete the page number—**Page 1 of 1**. Save the report as **Lastname Firstname 1G Projects Report** and then display the report in **Print Preview**. Create a paper or electronic printout as directed. **Close Print Preview**.

9 **Close All** open objects. **Open** the **Navigation Pane**, arrange the objects by **Tables and Related Views**, and be sure that all object names display fully. **Close** the database, but do *not* close Access.

TABLE 1

Data Type		Short Text	Short Text	Short Text	Currency
Field Name	ID	Building Project	Site	Contractor	Budget Amount

Return to Step 2

TABLE 2

Project ID	Building Project	Site	Contractor	Budget Amount
P-356	Student Center, 3-story	Northeast Campus	RR Construction	61450000
P-823	Student Center, 2-story	Southeast Campus	RR Construction	41960000
P-157	Health Professions Center	Northwest Campus	Marshall Ellis Construction	42630000

Return to Step 3

(Project 1G College Construction continues on the next page)

CONTENT-BASED ASSESSMENTS

10 In the Access opening screen, search for **event** and then click the **Desktop Event Management** template. Save the database in your **Access Chapter 1** folder as **Lastname_Firstname_1G_Public_Events** and on the **Message Bar**, click **Enable Content**.

11 In the **Event List** multiple-items form or the **Event Details** single-record form—open by clicking **New Event** on the **Event List** form—enter the three records shown in **Table 3**.

12 **Close** the **Event List** form. **Open** the **Navigation Pane**, organize the objects by **Tables and Related Views**, and then open the **Current Events** *report* (green icon). Switch to **Layout** view. In the report, click in the title—*Current Events*—and then click to position the insertion point to the left of the letter *C*. Using your own name, type **Lastname Firstname 1G** and then press

Spacebar and Enter. If necessary, decrease the font size of the title so that the title does not overlap the date on the right side or does not extend to two lines. **Save** the report, display it in **Print Preview**, and then create a paper or electronic printout as directed. **Close Print Preview**, and then **Close** the report.

13 Open the **Navigation Pane**, and be sure that all object names display fully. **Close** Access. As directed by your instructor, submit your database and the paper or electronic printouts of the six objects—two tables, one query, one form, and two reports—that are the results of this project. Specifically, in this project, using your own name, you created the following database and printouts or electronic printouts:

1. Lastname_Firstname_1G_College_Construction	Database file
2. Lastname_Firstname_1G_Public_Events	Database file
3. Lastname Firstname 1G Projects	Table (printout or electronic printout)
4. Lastname Firstname 1G Contractors	Table (printout or electronic printout)
5. Lastname Firstname 1G Projects Query	Query (printout or electronic printout)
6. Lastname Firstname 1G Project Form	Form (printout or electronic printout - Record 7)
7. Lastname Firstname 1G Projects Report	Report (printout or electronic printout)
8. Current Events	Report (printout or electronic printout)

TABLE 3

ID	Title	Start Time	End Time	Description	Location
1	Groundbreaking	6/13/18 10a	6/13/18 11a	Student Center groundbreaking	Northeast Campus
2	Dedication	8/26/18 12:30 p	8/26/18 2p	Gymnasium building dedication	Southwest Campus
3	Community Arts Expo	10/5/18 6p	10/5/18 9p	Book and Art Expo at Library	Southeast Campus

(Return to Step 12)

END | You have completed Project 1G

CONTENT-BASED ASSESSMENTS

Apply a combination of the 1A and 1B skills.

Build from Scratch

| GO! Fix It | Project 1H Scholarships | Online |

Build from Scratch

| GO! Make It | Project 1I Theater Events | Online |

Build from Scratch

| GO! Solve It | Project 1J Athletic Scholarships | Online |

| GO! Solve It | Project 1K Student Activities |

Build from Scratch

PROJECT FILES

For Project 1K, you will need the following files:

Desktop Event Management template
a01K_Student_Activities (Word document)

You will save your database as:

Lastname_Firstname_1K_Student_Activities

Use the Desktop Event Management template to create a database, and save it in your Access Chapter 1 folder as **Lastname_Firstname_1K_Student_Activities** From your student data files, use the information in the Word document a01K_Student_Activities to enter data into the Event List multiple-items form. Each event begins at 6 p.m. and ends at 10 p.m.

After entering the records, close the form, and arrange the Navigation Pane by Tables and Related Views. Open the Event Details *report*, and then add **Lastname Firstname 1K** to the beginning of the report title. If necessary, decrease the font size of the title so that it does not overlap the date and so that it displays on one line. Create a paper or electronic printout as directed—two pages result. As directed, submit your database and the paper or electronic printout of the report that are the results of this project. Specifically, in this project, using your own name, you created the following database and printout or electronic printout:

| 1. Lastname_Firstname_1K_Student_Activities | Database file |
| 2. Lastname Firstname 1K Event Details | Report (printout or electronic printout) |

Performance Level

Performance Criteria		Exemplary	Proficient	Developing
	Create database using Desktop Event Management template and enter data	Database created using the correct template, named correctly, and all data entered correctly.	Database created using the correct template, named correctly, but not all data entered correctly.	Database created using the correct template, but numerous errors in database name and data.
	Modify report	Event Details report title includes name and project on one line.	Event Details report title includes name and project, but not on one line.	Event Details report title does not include name and project.
	Create report printout	Event Details report printout is correct.	Event Details printout is incorrect.	Event Details report printout not created.

END | You have completed Project 1K

OUTCOMES-BASED ASSESSMENTS

RUBRIC

The following outcomes-based assessments are *open-ended assessments*. That is, there is no specific correct result; your result will depend on your approach to the information provided. Make *Professional Quality* your goal. Use the following scoring rubric to guide you in *how* to approach the problem and then to evaluate *how well* your approach solves the problem.

The *criteria*—Software Mastery, Content, Format & Layout, and Process—represent the knowledge and skills you have gained that you can apply to solving the problem. The *levels of performance*—Professional Quality, Approaching Professional Quality, or Needs Quality Improvements—help you and your instructor evaluate your result.

	Your completed project is of Professional Quality if you:	Your completed project is Approaching Professional Quality if you:	Your completed project Needs Quality Improvements if you:
1-Software Mastery	Choose and apply the most appropriate skills, tools, and features and identify efficient methods to solve the problem.	Choose and apply some appropriate skills, tools, and features, but not in the most efficient manner.	Choose inappropriate skills, tools, or features, or are inefficient in solving the problem.
2-Content	Construct a solution that is clear and well organized, contains content that is accurate, appropriate to the audience and purpose, and is complete. Provide a solution that contains no errors in spelling, grammar, or style.	Construct a solution in which some components are unclear, poorly organized, inconsistent, or incomplete. Misjudge the needs of the audience. Have some errors in spelling, grammar, or style, but the errors do not detract from comprehension.	Construct a solution that is unclear, incomplete, or poorly organized; contains some inaccurate or inappropriate content; and contains many errors in spelling, grammar, or style. Do not solve the problem.
3-Format & Layout	Format and arrange all elements to communicate information and ideas, clarify function, illustrate relationships, and indicate relative importance.	Apply appropriate format and layout features to some elements, but not others. Overuse features, causing minor distraction.	Apply format and layout that does not communicate information or ideas clearly. Do not use format and layout features to clarify function, illustrate relationships, or indicate relative importance. Use available features excessively, causing distraction.
4-Process	Use an organized approach that integrates planning, development, self-assessment, revision, and reflection.	Demonstrate an organized approach in some areas, but not others; or, use an insufficient process of organization throughout.	Do not use an organized approach to solve the problem.

OUTCOMES-BASED ASSESSMENTS

Build from Scratch

GO! Think Project 1L Student Clubs

PROJECT FILES

For Project 1L, you will need the following files:

Blank desktop database
a01L_Clubs (Word document)
a01L_Student_Clubs (Excel workbook)
a01L_Club_Presidents (Excel workbook)

You will save your database as

Lastname_Firstname_1L_Student_Clubs

Dr. Daniel Martinez, vice president of Student Services, needs a database that tracks information about student clubs. The database should contain two tables—one for club information and one for contact information for the club presidents.

Create a desktop database, and save the database in your Access Chapter 1 folder as **Lastname_Firstname_1L_Student_Clubs** From your student data files, use the information in the Word document a01L_Clubs to create the first table and to enter two records. Name the table appropriately to include your name and 1L, and then append the 23 records from the Excel workbook a01L_Student_Clubs to your table. For the Club ID and President ID fields, add a description and change the field size.

Create a second table in the database by importing 25 records from the Excel workbook a01L_Club_Presidents, and name the table appropriately to include your name and 1L. For the State and Postal Code fields, add a description and change the field size. Be sure that the field data types are correct—recall that numbers that are not used in calculations should have a data type of Short Text. Be sure all of the data and field names display in each table.

Create a simple query based on the Clubs table that answers the question, *What is the club name, meeting day, meeting time, campus, and Room ID for all of the clubs?* Create a form based on the Clubs table, saving it with an appropriate name that includes your name and 1L. Create a report based on the Presidents table, saving it with an appropriate name that includes your name and 1L, that displays the president's last name (in ascending order), the president's first name, and the phone number of every president. Change the width of the three fields so that there is less space between them, but being sure that each record prints on a single line. Delete the page number from the report.

Create paper or electronic printouts of the two tables, the query, only Record 21 of the form, and the report as directed and being sure that each object prints on one page. Organize the objects on the Navigation Pane by Tables and Related Views, and be sure that all object names display fully. As directed, submit your database and the paper or electronic printouts of the five objects—two tables, one query, one form, and one report—that are the results of this project.

END | You have completed Project 1L

Build from Scratch

GO! Think Project 1M Faculty Training ⟨Online⟩

Build from Scratch

You and GO! Project 1N Personal Contacts ⟨Online⟩

Build from Scratch

GO! Cumulative Group Project Project 1O Bell Orchid Hotels ⟨Online⟩

Sort and Query a Database

ACCESS 2013

2

GO! to Work
Video A2

Robert Kneschke/Fotolia

In This Chapter

In this chapter, you will sort Access database tables and create and modify queries. To convert data into meaningful information, you must manipulate your data in a way that you can answer questions. One question might be: *Which students have a grade point average of 3.0 or higher?* By having this list of students, you could send information about scholarships or internships to those who meet the grade point average criteria. Queries are one of the most powerful tools in an Access database—a query not only answers questions, but it also provides data for meaningful reports.

The projects in this chapter relate to **Texas Lakes Community College**, which is located in the Austin, Texas, area. Its four campuses serve more than 30,000 students and offer more than 140 certificate programs and degrees. The college has a highly acclaimed Distance Education program and an extensive Workforce Development program. The college makes positive contributions to the community through cultural and athletic programs and has significant partnerships with businesses and nonprofit organizations. Popular fields of study include nursing and health care, solar technology, computer technology, and graphic design.

Instructors and Courses Database

MyITLab®
Project 2A Training

PROJECT ACTIVITIES

In Activities 2.01 through 2.17, you will assist Dr. Carolyn Judkins, dean of the Business Division at the Northeast Campus of Texas Lakes Community College, in locating information about instructors and courses in the division. Your completed database objects will look similar to Figure 2.1.

PROJECT FILES

For Project 2A, you will need the following file:

a02A_Instructors_Courses

You will save your database as:

Lastname_Firstname_2A_Instructors_Courses

PROJECT RESULTS

FIGURE 2.1 Project 2A Instructors and Courses

Objective 1   Open and Save an Existing Database

Video A2-1

There will be instances when you need to work with a database and still keep the original, unaltered version of the database. Like the other Microsoft Office 2013 applications, you can open a database file and save it with another name.

Activity 2.01 | Opening and Saving an Existing Database

1 ▶ **Start** Access. In the Access opening screen, click **Open Other Files**. Under **Open**, click **Computer**, and then on the right, click **Browse**. In the **Open** dialog box, navigate to the location where your student data files for this chapter are stored, and then double-click **a02A_Instructors_Courses** to open the database.

2 ▶ On the ribbon, click the **FILE tab**, and then click **Save As**. Under **File Types**, be sure **Save Database As** is selected. On the right, under **Database File Types**, be sure **Access Database** is selected, and then at the bottom of the screen, click **Save As**.

> The Access Database file type saves your database in a format that enables the database to be opened with Access 2007, Access 2010, or Access 2013. If you are sharing your database with individuals who have an earlier version of Access, you can save the database in a version that is compatible with that application, although some functionality might be lost if an earlier version of Access does not have the same feature as the later version of Access.

3 ▶ In the **Save As** dialog box, navigate to the location where you are saving your databases. Create a **New folder** named **Access Chapter 2**, and then **Open** the folder. Click in the **File name** box, drag to select the existing text, and using your own name, type **Lastname_Firstname_2A_Instructors_Courses** and then click **Save** or press Enter.

> Use this technique when you need to keep a copy of the original database file.

4 ▶ On the **Message Bar**, notice the **SECURITY WARNING**. In the **Navigation Pane**, notice that this database contains two table objects. Compare your screen with Figure 2.2.

FIGURE 2.2

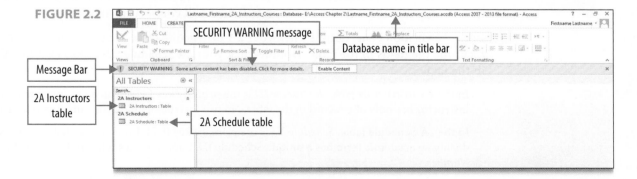

The ***Message Bar*** is the area directly below the ribbon that displays information such as security alerts when there is potentially unsafe, active content in an Office document that you open. Settings that determine the alerts that display on your Message Bar are set in the Access ***Trust Center***, an area in Access where you can view the security and privacy settings for your Access installation.

You may not be able to change the settings in the Trust Center, depending upon decisions made by your organization. To display the Trust Center, click the FILE tab, click Options, and then click Trust Center.

1 On the **Message Bar**, click **Enable Content**.

When working with the student data files that accompany this textbook, repeat this action each time you see the security warning. Databases for this textbook are safe to use on your computer.

2 In the **Navigation Pane**, right-click the **2A Instructors** table, and then click **Rename**. With the table name selected and using your own name, type **Lastname Firstname 2A Instructors** and then press Enter to rename the table. Use the same technique to **Rename** the **2A Schedule** table to **Lastname Firstname 2A Schedule**

Including your name in the table enables you and your instructor to easily identify your work, because Access includes the table name in the header of your paper or electronic printouts.

3 Point to the right edge of the **Navigation Pane** to display the ⟷ pointer. Drag to the right to increase the width of the pane until both table names display fully.

Objective 2 | Create Table Relationships

Video A2-2

Access databases are relational databases because the tables in the database can relate—actually connect—to other tables through common fields. Recall that common fields are fields in two or more tables that store the same data; for example, a Student ID number may be stored in two tables in the same database.

After you have a table for each subject in your database, you must provide a way to connect the data in the tables when you need to obtain meaningful information from the stored data. To do this, create common fields in the related tables, and then define table ***relationships***. A relationship is an association that you establish between two tables based on common fields. After the relationship is established, you can create a query, form, or report that displays information from more than one table.

Activity 2.03 | Selecting the Tables and Common Field to Establish the Table Relationship

In this activity, you will select the two tables in the database that you will use to establish the table relationship and identify the common field that will connect the tables.

1 In the **Navigation Pane**, double-click your **2A Instructors** table to open it in the object window. Examine the fields in the table. Double-click your **2A Schedule** table, and examine the fields in the table.

In the 2A Instructors table, *Instructor ID* is the primary key field, which ensures that each instructor has only one record in the table. No two instructors have the same Instructor ID.

In the 2A Schedule table, *Schedule ID* is the primary key field. Every scheduled course section during an academic term has a unique Schedule ID. Some colleges refer to this as the *Section Number*.

2 ▶ In the **2A Schedule** table, scroll to display the **Instructor ID** field—third from last column—and then compare your screen with Figure 2.3.

Both the 2A Instructors table and the 2A Schedule table include the *Instructor ID* field, which is the common field of the two tables. Because *one* instructor can teach *many* different courses, *one* Instructor ID can be present *many* times in the 2A Schedule table. When the relationship is established, it will be a ***one-to-many relationship***, which is the most common type of relationship in a relational database.

FIGURE 2.3

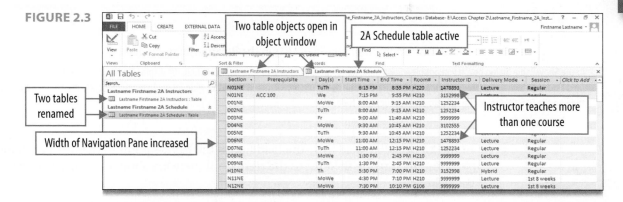

3 ▶ In the object window, right-click the **2A Schedule object tab**, and then click **Close All** to close both tables. On the ribbon, click the **DATABASE TOOLS tab**, and then in the **Relationships group**, click **Relationships**. Compare your screen with Figure 2.4.

You can close all of the open objects by right-clicking any object tab. The Show Table dialog box displays in the Relationships window. In the Show Table dialog box, the Tables tab displays the two tables that are in this database.

FIGURE 2.4

4 ▶ Point to the title bar of the **Show Table** dialog box, and then drag downward and to the right to move the dialog box away from the top of the **Relationships** window.

Moving the Show Table dialog box enables you to see the tables as they are added to the Relationships window.

5 ▶ In the **Show Table** dialog box, if necessary, click your **2A Instructors** table, and then click **Add**. In the **Show Table** dialog box, double-click your **2A Schedule** table to add it to the **Relationships** window. In the **Show Table** dialog box, click **Close**, and then compare your screen with Figure 2.5.

You can use either technique to add a table to the Relationships window. A ***field list***—a list of the field names in a table—for each of the two table objects displays, and each table's primary key is identified by the key icon. Although this database has only two tables, larger databases have many tables. Scroll bars in a field list indicate that there are fields that are not currently in view.

FIGURE 2.5

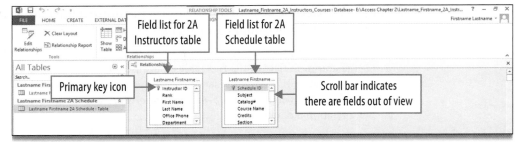

FIGURE 2.5

ALERT!   **Are There More Than Two Field Lists in the Relationships Window?**

In the Show Table dialog box, if you double-click a table name more than one time, a duplicate field list displays in the Relationships window. To remove a field list from the Relationships window, right-click the title bar of the field list, and then click Hide Table. Alternatively, click anywhere in the field list, and then on the DESIGN tab, in the Relationships group, click Hide Table.

> **6** In the **2A Schedule** field list—the field list on the right—point to the title bar to display the ⬚ pointer. Drag the field list to the right until there are about two inches of space between the field lists.

> **7** In the **2A Instructors** field list—the field list on the left—point to the lower right corner of the field list to display the ⬚ pointer, and then drag downward and to the right to increase the height and width of the field list until the entire name of the table in the title bar displays and all of the field names display.

This action enables you to see all of the available fields and removes the vertical scroll bar.

> **8** Use the same technique to resize the **2A Schedule** field list so that the table name and all of the field names display as shown in Figure 2.6.

Recall that *one* instructor can teach *many* scheduled courses. The arrangement of field lists in the Relationships window displays the *one table* on the left side and the *many table* on the right side. Recall also that the primary key in each table is the field that contains the data that uniquely identifies each record in the table. In the 2A Instructors table, each instructor is uniquely identified by the Instructor ID. In the 2A Schedule table, each scheduled course section is uniquely identified by the Schedule ID.

FIGURE 2.6

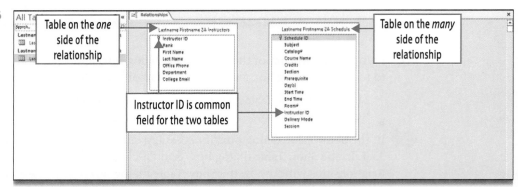

NOTE   **The Field That Is Highlighted Does Not Matter**

After you rearrange the field lists in the Relationships window, the highlighted field name indicates the active field list, which is the list that you moved or resized last. This is of no consequence for this activity.

9 ▶ In the **2A Instructors** field list, point to **Instructor ID**, and then drag the field name downward and to the right into the **2A Schedule** field list until the pointer's arrow is on top of **Instructor ID**. Release the mouse button to display the **Edit Relationships** dialog box.

> As you drag, a small graphic displays to indicate that you are dragging a field name from one field list to another. A table relationship works by matching data in two fields—the common field. In these two tables, the common field has the same name—*Instructor ID*. Common fields are not required to have the same name; however, they must have the same data type and field size.

↻ ANOTHER WAY   On the DESIGN tab, in the Tools group, click Edit Relationships. In the Edit Relationships dialog box, click Create New. In the Create New dialog box, designate the tables and fields that will create the relationship and click OK.

10 ▶ Point to the title bar of the **Edit Relationships** dialog box, and then drag the dialog box downward and to the right below the two field lists as shown in Figure 2.7.

> By dragging the common field, you create the *one-to-many* relationship. In the 2A Instructors table, Instructor ID is the primary key. In the 2A Schedule table, Instructor ID is the *foreign key* field. The foreign key is the field in the related table used to connect to the primary key in another table. The field on the *one* side of the relationship is typically the primary key.

FIGURE 2.7

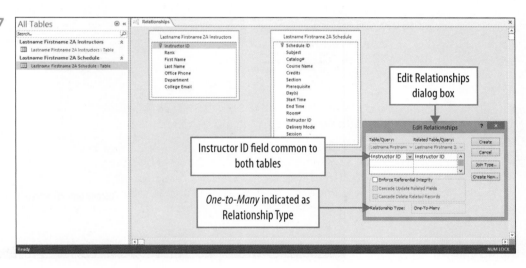

Activity 2.04 | Setting Relationship Options

In this activity, you will set relationship options that enable you to work with records in the two related tables.

1 ▶ In the **Edit Relationships** dialog box, click to select the **Enforce Referential Integrity** check box. Notice that the two options under **Enforce Referential Integrity** are now available.

> *Referential integrity* is a set of rules that Access uses to ensure that the data between related tables is valid. Enforcing referential integrity ensures that an Instructor ID cannot be added to a course in the 2A Schedule table if the Instructor ID is *not* included in the 2A Instructors table. Similarly, enforcing referential integrity without selecting a cascade option below ensures that you cannot delete an instructor from the 2A Instructors table if there is a course that has been assigned to that instructor in the 2A Schedule table.

> After selecting Enforce Referential Integrity, *cascade options*—relationship options that enable you to update records in related tables when referential integrity is enforced—become available for use.

2 In the **Edit Relationships** dialog box, click to select the **Cascade Update Related Fields** check box.

The *Cascade Update Related Fields* option enables you to change the data in the primary key field for the table on the *one* side of the relationship, and updates that change to any fields in the related table that store the same data. For example, in the 2A Instructors table, if you change the data in the Instructor ID field for one instructor, Access automatically finds every scheduled course assigned to that instructor in the 2A Schedule table and changes the data in the common field, in this case, the Instructor ID field. Without this option, if you try to change the Instructor ID number for an instructor, an error message displays if there is a related record in the related table on the *many* side of the relationship.

3 In the **Edit Relationships** dialog box, click to select the **Cascade Delete Related Records** check box, and then compare your screen with Figure 2.8.

The *Cascade Delete Related Records* option enables you to delete a record in the table on the *one* side of the relationship and also delete all of the related records in related tables. For example, if an instructor retires or leaves the college and the courses that the instructor teaches must be canceled because no other instructor can be found, you can delete the instructor's record from the 2A Instructors table, and then all of the courses that are assigned to that instructor in the 2A Schedule table are also deleted. Without this option, an error message displays if you try to delete the instructor's record from the 2A Instructors table.

FIGURE 2.8

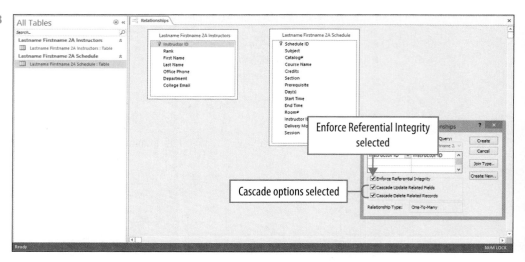

4 In the **Edit Relationships** dialog box, click **Create**, and then compare your screen with Figure 2.9.

The Edit Relationships dialog box closes and a *join line*—the line connecting or joining the two tables—displays between the two field lists. The join line connects the primary key field—Instructor ID—in the 2A Instructors field list to the common field—Instructor ID—in the 2A Schedule field list. On the join line, *1* indicates the *one* side of the relationship, and the infinity symbol (∞) indicates the *many* side of the relationship. These symbols display when referential integrity is enforced.

FIGURE 2.9

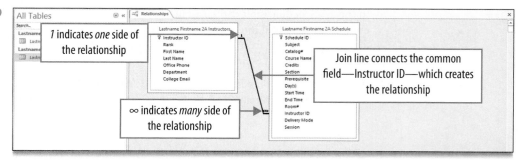

Activity 2.05 | Printing and Saving a Relationship Report

The Relationships window provides a map of how your database tables are related, and you can print and save this information as a report.

1 Under **RELATIONSHIP TOOLS**, on the **DESIGN tab**, in the **Tools group**, click **Relationship Report**.

The report is created and displays in the object window in Print Preview.

2 On the **PRINT PREVIEW tab**, in the **Page Size group**, click **Margins**, and then click **Normal** to increase the margins slightly—some printers cannot print with narrow margins. Compare your screen with Figure 2.10. Create a paper or electronic printout of the relationship report as directed.

FIGURE 2.10

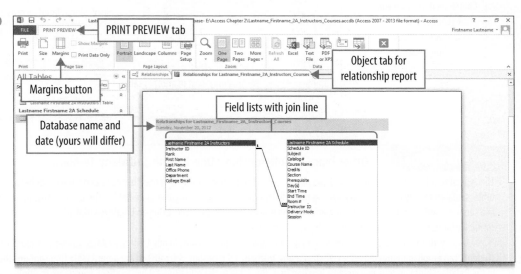

3 On the **Quick Access Toolbar**, click **Save** 🔲. In the **Save As** dialog box, click **OK** to accept the default report name.

The report name displays in the Navigation Pane under *Unrelated Objects*. Because the report is just a map of the relationship between the tables, and not a report containing records from a table, it is not associated with or related to any tables.

4 In the object window, click **Close** ✕ to close the report, and then **Close** ✕ the **Relationships** window.

NOTE	**Close Print Preview and the Relationship Report**

If you click Close Print Preview when the report is displayed in Print Preview, the Relationship Report displays in Design view in the object window. If this happens, you can Close the object while it is displayed in this view.

Activity 2.06 | Displaying Subdatasheet Records

When you open the table on the *one* side of the relationship, the related records from the table on the *many* side are available for you to view and to modify.

1 In the **Navigation Pane**, double-click your **2A Instructors** table to open it in the object window, and then **Close** « the **Navigation Pane**.

2 On the left side of the first record—*Instructor ID* of *1224567*—click ⊞, and then compare your screen with Figure 2.11.

The ⊞ symbol to the left of a record in a table indicates that *related* records may exist in another table. Click ⊞ to display the related records in a **subdatasheet**. In the first record for *Craig Fresch*, you can see that related records exist in the 2A Schedule table—he is scheduled to teach five LGL (Legal) courses. The ⊞ symbol to the left of each record displays because you created a relationship between the two tables using the Instructor ID field—the common field.

When you click ⊞ to display the subdatasheet, the symbol changes to ⊟, an indication that the subdatasheet is expanded. Click ⊟ to collapse the subdatasheet.

FIGURE 2.11

Course sections from your 2A Schedule table for *Associate Professor Craig Fresch*

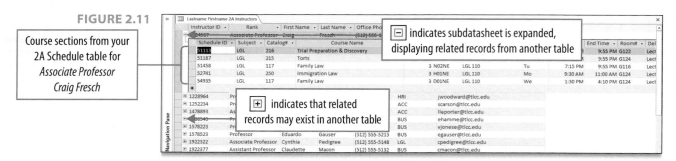

⊟ indicates subdatasheet is expanded, displaying related records from another table

⊞ indicates that related records may exist in another table

> **More Knowledge** | **Other Types of Relationships: One-to-One and Many-to-Many**
>
> The type of relationship is determined by the placement of the primary key field. A one-to-one relationship exists between two tables when a record in one table is related to only one record in a second table. In this case, both tables use the same field as the primary key. This is most often used when data is placed in a separate table because access to that information is restricted; for example, using an Employee ID field as the primary key field, there is one table for contact information and a second table with payroll information.
>
> A many-to-many relationship between tables exists when many records in one table are related to many records in another table. For example, many students can enroll in many courses. To create a many-to-many relationship, you must create a third table that contains the primary key fields from both tables. In the Relationships window, you create a join line from this table to the other two tables. In effect, you create multiple one-to-many relationships.

Activity 2.07 | **Testing Cascade Options**

Recall that cascade options enable you to make changes to records on the *one* side table of the relationship and update or delete records in the table on the *many* side of the relationship. In this activity, you will change the data in the Instructor ID field—the primary key field—for one instructor, and then delete all of the records associated with another instructor from both tables.

1 In the subdatasheet for the first record—*Instructor ID* of *1224567*—notice that the first course that this instructor is scheduled to teach has a *Schedule ID* of *51113—LGL 216*. In the **2A Instructors** table, to the left of the first record, click ⊟ to collapse the subdatasheet.

2 If necessary, in the first record, in the **Instructor ID** field, select the data—**1224567**. Type **8224567** and then press ⬇ to save the record.

Because you enabled Cascade Update Related Fields in the Edit Relationships dialog box, you can change the data in the Instructor ID field—the primary key field—and all records in the 2A Schedule table that store that Instructor ID number are automatically updated. If this option is not enabled, an error message displays.

3 Open ⟩⟩ the **Navigation Pane**. In the **Navigation Pane**, double-click your **2A Schedule** table to open it, and then **Close** ⟨⟨ the **Navigation Pane**.

 **ANOTHER WAY**   Press F11 to open or close the Navigation Pane.

4 Scroll to locate the record with a **Schedule ID** of **51113**—*LGL 216*. If necessary, scroll to the right to display the **Instructor ID** field, and notice that for this record, the **Instructor ID** is **8224567**. Compare your screen with Figure 2.12.

The Cascade Update Related Fields option enables you to change the data in the primary key field in your 2A Instructors table, and the five related records for *Craig Fresch* in the 2A Schedule table were updated to store his new Instructor ID of *8224567*.

FIGURE 2.12

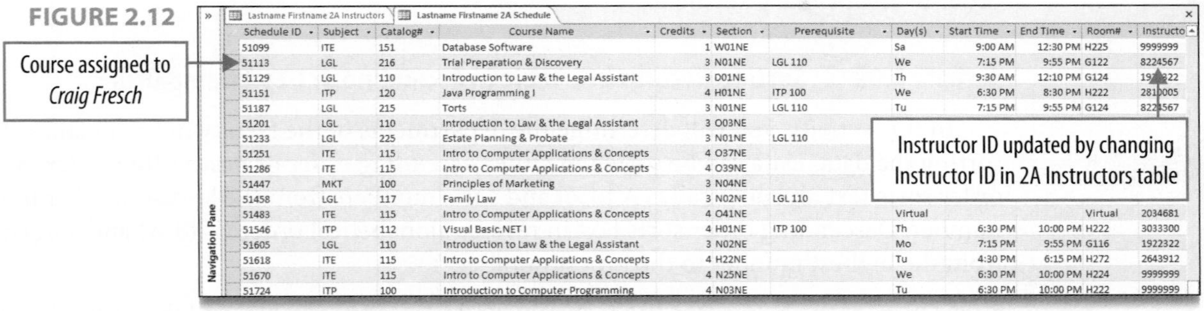

Schedule ID	Subject	Catalog#	Course Name	Credits	Section	Prerequisite	Day(s)	Start Time	End Time	Room#	Instructo
51099	ITE	151	Database Software	1	W01NE		Sa	9:00 AM	12:30 PM	H225	9999999
51113	LGL	216	Trial Preparation & Discovery	3	N01NE	LGL 110	We	7:15 PM	9:55 PM	G122	8224567
51129	LGL	110	Introduction to Law & the Legal Assistant	3	D01NE		Th	9:30 AM	12:10 PM	G124	19[illegible]22
51151	ITP	120	Java Programming I	4	H01NE	ITP 100	We	6:30 PM	8:30 PM	H222	2810005
51187	LGL	215	Torts	3	N01NE	LGL 110	Tu	7:15 PM	9:55 PM	G124	8224567
51201	LGL	110	Introduction to Law & the Legal Assistant	3	O03NE						
51233	LGL	225	Estate Planning & Probate	3	N01NE	LGL 110					
51251	ITE	115	Intro to Computer Applications & Concepts	4	O37NE						
51286	ITE	115	Intro to Computer Applications & Concepts	4	O39NE						
51447	MKT	100	Principles of Marketing	3	N04NE						
51458	LGL	117	Family Law	3	N02NE	LGL 110					
51483	ITE	115	Intro to Computer Applications & Concepts	4	O41NE		Virtual			Virtual	2034681
51546	ITP	112	Visual Basic.NET I	4	H01NE	ITP 100	Th	6:30 PM	10:00 PM	H222	3033300
51605	LGL	110	Introduction to Law & the Legal Assistant	3	N02NE		Mo	7:15 PM	9:55 PM	G116	1922322
51618	ITE	115	Intro to Computer Applications & Concepts	4	H22NE		Tu	4:30 PM	6:15 PM	H272	2643912
51670	ITE	115	Intro to Computer Applications & Concepts	4	N25NE		We	6:30 PM	10:00 PM	H224	9999999
51724	ITP	100	Introduction to Computer Programming	4	N03NE		Tu	6:30 PM	10:00 PM	H222	9999999

5 **Close** [×] your **2A Schedule** table. In your **2A Instructors** table, scroll to display the last few records. On the left side of the record for **Instructor ID** of **6145288**—*Professor Ivey Clarke*—click [+] to display the subdatasheet. Notice that this instructor is scheduled to teach two courses—*Schedule ID*s of *42837* and *42930*.

6 Click [−] to collapse the subdatasheet. For the same record—*Instructor ID* of *6145288*—point to the record selector box to display the [→] pointer, and then click to select the record. On the **HOME tab**, in the **Records group**, click **Delete**.

A message displays warning you that this record and related records in related tables will be deleted. The record you selected does not display in the table, and the next record is selected. Because you enabled Cascade Delete Related Records, you are able to delete the record for Professor Ivey Clarke and delete the two courses she is scheduled to teach from the 2A Schedule table—with no error message.

ANOTHER WAY With the record selected, press [Del]; or with the record selected, right-click within the record, and then click Delete Record.

7 In the message box, click **Yes**.

The record for *Instructor ID* of *6145288* is deleted, and the two courses she was scheduled to teach are deleted from the 2A Schedule table. On the Quick Access Toolbar, Undo is unavailable—if you mistakenly delete a record and its related records, you must enter them again in both tables.

8 **Open** [»] the **Navigation Pane**, open your **2A Schedule** table, and then **Close** [«] the **Navigation Pane**. Scroll through the records and notice that the records for a **Schedule ID** of **42837** and **42930** have been deleted from the table.

The Cascade Delete Related Records option in the Edit Relationships dialog box enables you to delete a record in the table on the *one* side of the relationship—2A Instructors—and simultaneously delete the records in the table on the *many* side of the relationship—2A Schedule—that are related to the deleted record.

9 In the object window, right-click either **object tab**, and then click **Close All** to close both tables.

Video A2-3

Sorting is the process of arranging data in a specific order based on the value in a field. For example, you can sort the names in your contact list alphabetically by each person's last name, or you can sort your music collection by the artist. Initially, records in an Access table display in the order they are entered into the table. After you close the table and reopen it, the records display in order by the primary key field.

Activity 2.08 | Sorting Records in a Table in Ascending or Descending Order

In this activity, you will determine the departments of the faculty in the Business Division by sorting the data. Data can be sorted in either *ascending order* or *descending order*. Ascending order sorts text alphabetically (A to Z) and sorts numbers from the lowest number to the highest number. Descending order sorts text in reverse alphabetical order (Z to A) and sorts numbers from the highest number to the lowest number.

1 **Open** » the **Navigation Pane**, open your **2A Instructors** table, and then **Close** « the **Navigation Pane**. Notice that the records in the table are sorted in ascending order by the **Instructor ID** field, which is the primary key field.

2 In the field names row, click the **Department arrow**, click **Sort A to Z**, and then compare your screen with Figure 2.13.

To sort records in a table, click the arrow to the right of the field name in the column on which you want to sort, and then click the sort order. After a field is sorted, a small arrow in the field name box indicates the sort order. For the Department field, the small arrow points upward, indicating an ascending sort; on the ribbon, Ascending is selected.

The records display in alphabetical order by the Department field. Because the department names are now grouped together, you can quickly scroll through the table to see the instructors for each department. The first record in the table has no data in the Department field because the *Instructor ID* of *9999999* is reserved for *Staff*, a designation that is used until a scheduled course has been assigned to a specific instructor.

ANOTHER WAY   Click in the field in any record, and then on the HOME tab, in the Sort & Filter group, click Ascending; or right-click in the field in any record, and then click Sort A to Z.

FIGURE 2.13

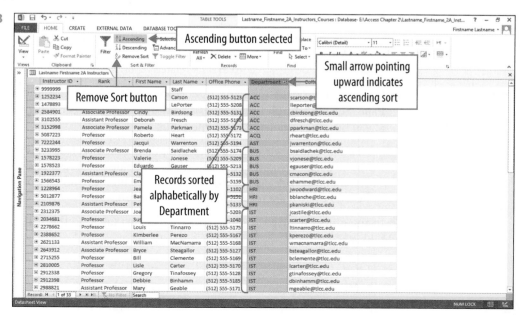

3 On the **HOME tab**, in the **Sort & Filter group**, click **Remove Sort** to clear the sort and to return the records to the default sort order, which is by the primary key field—**Instructor ID**.

4 Click the **Last Name arrow**, and then click **Sort Z to A**.

The records in the table are sorted by the Last Name field in reverse alphabetical order. The small arrow in the field name box points downward, indicating a descending sort. On the ribbon, Descending is selected.

5 In the **Sort & Filter group**, click **Remove Sort** to clear the sort.

Activity 2.09 | Sorting Records in a Table on Multiple Fields

To sort a table on two or more fields, first identify the fields that will act as the **outermost sort field** and the **innermost sort field**. The outermost sort field is the first level of sorting, and the innermost sort field is the second level of sorting. To alphabetize a table by Last Name and then First Name—also called First Name within Last Name—the Last Name field is identified as the outermost sort field. If there are duplicate last names, the records should be further sorted by the First Name field—the innermost sort field. For tables, you sort the *innermost* field *first* and then sort the outermost field.

In this activity, you will sort the records by Last Name—innermost sort field—within the Department—outermost sort field.

1 In the **Last Name** field, click in any record. On the ribbon, on the **HOME tab**, in the **Sort & Filter group**, click **Ascending**.

The records are sorted in ascending order by Last Name—the innermost sort field.

2 In any record, point in the **Department** field, right-click, and then click **Sort Z to A**. Compare your screen with Figure 2.14.

The records are sorted in descending order first by Department—the outermost sort field. Within each Department grouping, the records are sorted in ascending order by Last Name—the innermost sort field. Records can be sorted on multiple fields using both ascending and descending order.

FIGURE 2.14

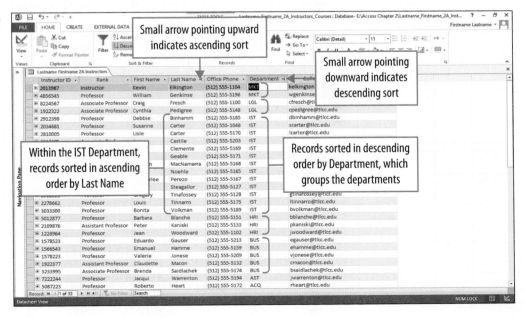

3 On the ribbon, click the **FILE tab**, click **Print**, and then click **Print Preview**. On the **PRINT PREVIEW tab**, in the **Page Layout group**, click **Landscape**. In the **Zoom group**, click **Two Pages**, and notice that the table will print on two pages.

4 In the **Print group**, click **Print**. In the **Print** dialog box, under **Print Range**, click in the **From** box, type **1** and then click in the **To** box. Type **1** to print only the first page. If directed to submit a paper printout, click **OK**. If directed to create an electronic printout, in the **Print** dialog box, click **Cancel**. On the **PRINT PREVIEW tab**, in the **Data group**, click **PDF or XPS**, click **Options**, and then under **Range**, click the **Pages** option button, click **OK**, and then click **Publish**.

5 In the object window, **Close** ⌧ the table. In the message box, click **Yes** to save the changes to the sort order.

6 Open ⟩⟩ the **Navigation Pane**, double-click your **2A Instructors** table to open it, and then **Close** ⟨⟨ the **Navigation Pane**. Notice that the table displays the sort order you specified.

7 On the **HOME tab**, in the **Sort & Filter group**, click **Remove Sort**. **Close** ⌧ the table, and in the message box, click **Yes** to save the table with the sort removed.

> Generally, tables are not stored with the data sorted. Instead, queries are created that sort the data, and then reports are created to display the sorted data.

Objective 4　Create a Query in Design View

Video A2-4

Recall that a select query is a database object that retrieves (selects) specific data from one or more tables and then displays the specified data in a table in Datasheet view. A query answers a question, such as *Which instructors teach courses in the IST department?* Unless a query has already been designed to ask this question, you must create a new query.

Database users rarely need to see all of the records in all of the tables. That is why a query is so useful; it creates a ***subset*** of records—a portion of the total records—according to your specifications and then displays only those records.

Activity 2.10　Creating a New Select Query in Design View

Previously, you created a query using the Query Wizard. To create more complex queries, use Query Design view. The table (or tables) from which a query selects its data is referred to as the ***data source***.

1 On the ribbon, click the **CREATE tab**, and then in the **Queries group**, click **Query Design**. Compare your screen with Figure 2.15.

> A new query opens in Design view, and the Show Table dialog box displays, which lists both tables in the database.

FIGURE 2.15

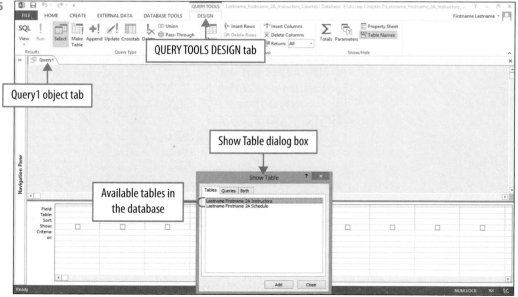

2 ▶ In the **Show Table** dialog box, double-click **2A Instructors**, and then, in the dialog box, click **Close**.

> A field list for your 2A Instructors table displays in the upper area of the query window. Instructor ID is the primary key field in this table.
>
> The query window has two parts: the upper area called the **table area** that displays the field lists for tables that are used in the query, and the lower area called the **design grid** that displays the design of the query.

A L E R T !   **Is There More Than One Field List in the Table Area?**

If you double-click a table more than one time, a duplicate field list displays in the table area of the query window. To remove a field list from the query window, right-click the title bar of the field list, and then click Remove Table.

3 ▶ Point to the lower right corner of the field list to display the ⬚ pointer, and then drag downward and to the right to resize the field list, displaying all of the field names and the entire table name. In the **2A Instructors** field list, double-click **Rank**, and then look at the design grid.

> The Rank field name displays in the design grid in the Field row. You limit the fields that display in the query results by placing only the desired field names in the design grid.

4 ▶ In the **2A Instructors** field list, point to **First Name**, drag the field name down into the design grid until the ⬚ pointer displays in the **Field** row in the second column, and then release the mouse button. Compare your screen with Figure 2.16.

> This is a second way to add field names to the design grid. As you drag the field, a small rectangular shape attaches to the mouse pointer. When you release the mouse button, the field name displays in the Field row.

FIGURE 2.16

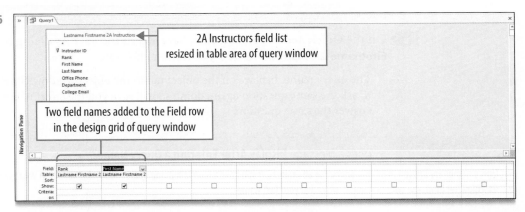

5 ▶ In the design grid, in the **Field** row, click in the third column, and then click the **arrow** that displays. From the list, click **Last Name** to add the field to the design grid.

> This is a third way to add field names to the design grid.

6 ▶ Using one of the three techniques you just practiced, add the **Office Phone** field to the fourth column and the **Department** field to the fifth column in the design grid.

A L E R T !   **Is There a Duplicate Field Name or an Incorrect Field Name in the Design Grid?**

If you double-click a field name more than one time, a duplicate field name displays in the design grid. To remove a duplicate field name, in the design grid, in the Field row, right-click the duplicate field name, and then click Cut. Use this same method to delete a field name that you placed in the design grid by mistake. As you progress in your study of query design, you will learn alternate ways to delete field names from the design grid.

After you design a query, you *run* the query to display the results. When you run a query, Access looks at the records in the table (or tables) you have included in the query, finds the records that match the specified conditions (if any), and displays only those records in a datasheet. Only the fields that you have added to the design grid display in the query results. The query always runs using the current table or tables, presenting the most up-to-date information.

1 Under **QUERY TOOLS**, on the **DESIGN tab**, in the **Results group**, click **Run**, and then compare your screen with Figure 2.17.

This query answers the question, *What is the rank, first name, last name, office phone number, and department of all of the instructors in the 2A Instructors table?* A query is a subset of the records in the table, arranged in Datasheet view, using the fields and conditions that you specify in the design grid. The five fields you specified in the design grid display in columns, and the records from the 2A Instructors table display in rows.

ANOTHER WAY On the DESIGN tab, in the Results group, click the top portion of the View button, which runs the query by switching to Datasheet view.

FIGURE 2.17

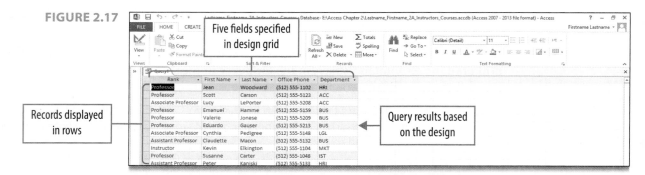

2 On the **Quick Access Toolbar**, click **Save**. In the **Save As** dialog box, type **Lastname Firstname 2A Instructors Query** and then click **OK**.

The query name displays on the object tab in the object window. Save your queries if you are likely to ask the same question again; doing so will save you the effort of creating the query again to answer the same question.

ALERT! **Does a Message Display After Entering a Query Name?**

Query names are limited to 64 characters. For all projects, if you have a long last name or first name that results in your query name exceeding the 64-character limit, use your first initial instead of your first name.

3 On the ribbon, click the **FILE tab**, click **Print**, and then click **Print Preview**. Create a paper or electronic printout as directed, and then click **Close Print Preview**.

Queries answer questions and gather information from the data in tables. Typically, queries are created as a basis for a report, but query results can be printed just like any table of data.

4 Close the query. Open the **Navigation Pane**, and then notice that your **2A Instructors Query** object displays under your **2A Instructors** table object.

The new query name displays in the Navigation Pane under the table with which it is related—the 2A Instructors table, which is the data source. Only the design of the query is saved; the records reside in the table object. Each time you open a query, Access runs it again and displays the results based on the data stored in the data source. Thus, the results of the query always reflect the most up-to-date information.

Video A2-5

You can create a new query from scratch, or you can copy an existing query and modify the design to answer another question. Using an existing query saves you time if your new query uses all or some of the same fields and conditions in an existing query.

Activity 2.12 | Copying an Existing Query

1 In the **Navigation Pane**, right-click your **2A Instructors Query**, and then click **Copy**.

ANOTHER WAY   To create a copy of the query, in the Navigation Pane, click the query name to select it. On the HOME tab, in the Clipboard group, click Copy.

2 In the **Navigation Pane**, point to a blank area, right-click, and then click **Paste**.

The Paste As dialog box displays, which enables you to name the copied query.

ANOTHER WAY   On the HOME tab, in the Clipboard group, click Paste.

3 In the **Paste As** dialog box, type **Lastname Firstname 2A Instructor IDs Query** and then click **OK**.

A new query, based on a copy of your 2A Instructors Query is created and displays in the Navigation Pane under its data source—your 2A Instructors table object.

4 In the **Navigation Pane**, double-click your **2A Instructor IDs Query** to run the query and open the query results in **Datasheet** view. **Close** `«` the **Navigation Pane**.

Activity 2.13 | Modifying the Design of a Query

1 On the **HOME tab**, in the **Views group**, click the top portion of the **View** button to switch to **Design** view.

ANOTHER WAY   On the HOME tab, in the Views group, click the View arrow, and then click Design View; or on the right side of the status bar, click Design View. If the query is not open, in the Navigation Pane, right-click the query name, and then click Design View.

2 In the design grid, point to the thin gray selection bar above the **Office Phone** field name to display the ↓ pointer, and then compare your screen with Figure 2.18.

FIGURE 2.18

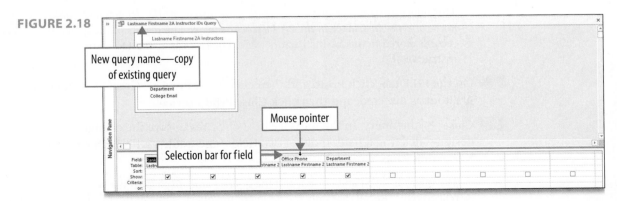

3 With the ⬇ pointer displayed in the selection bar above the **Office Phone** field name, click to select the column, and then press Del.

> This action deletes the field from the query design only—it has no effect on the field in the data source—2A Instructors table. The Department field moves to the left. Similarly, by using the selection bar, you can drag to select multiple fields and delete them at one time.

🔄 ANOTHER WAY   In the design grid, click in the field name. On the DESIGN tab, in the Query Setup group, click Delete Columns; or right-click the field name, and then click Cut; or select the column, and on the HOME tab, in the Records group, click Delete.

4 Point to the selection bar above the **First Name** column, and then click to select the column. In the selected column, point to the selection bar, hold down the left mouse button to display the 🔝 pointer, and then drag to the right until a dark vertical line displays on the right side of the **Last Name** column. Release the mouse button to position the **First Name** field in the third column.

> To rearrange fields in a query, first select the field to move, and then drag it to a new position in the design grid.

5 Using the technique you just practiced, move the **Department** field to the left of the **Rank** field.

6 From the field list, drag the **Instructor ID** field down to the first column in the design grid until the 🔝 pointer displays, and then release the mouse button. Compare your screen with Figure 2.19.

> The Instructor ID field displays in the first column, and the remaining four fields move to the right. Use this method to insert a field to the left of a field already displayed in the design grid.

FIGURE 2.19

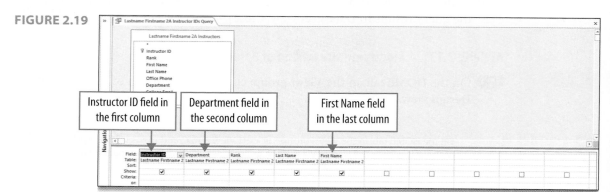

7 On the **DESIGN tab**, in the **Results group**, click **Run**.

> This query answers the question, *What is the instructor ID, department, rank, last name, and first name of every instructor in the 2A Instructors table?* The results of the query are a subset of the records stored in the 2A Instructors table. The records are sorted by the table's primary key field—Instructor ID.

8 On the **FILE tab**, click **Print**, and then click **Print Preview**. Create a paper or electronic printout as directed, and then click **Close Print Preview**.

9 **Close** ✕ the query. In the message box, click **Yes** to save the changes to the query design—deleting a field, moving two fields, and adding a field. **Open** » the **Navigation Pane**.

> The query is saved and closed, and the query name displays in the Navigation Pane under the related table. Recall that only the *design* of the query is saved; the records reside in the related table.

Video A2-6

You can sort the results of a query in ascending or descending order in either Datasheet view or Design view. Use Design view if your query results should always display in a specified sort order or if you intend to use the sorted results in a report.

Activity 2.14 | Sorting Query Results

In this activity, you will copy an existing query and then sort the query results by using the Sort row in Design view.

1 In the **Navigation Pane**, right-click your **2A Instructor IDs Query**, and then click **Copy**. In the **Navigation Pane**, point to a blank area, right-click, and then click **Paste**.

2 In the **Paste As** dialog box, type **Lastname Firstname 2A Department Sort Query** and then click **OK**. Increase the width of the **Navigation Pane** so that the names of all of the objects display fully.

> A new query is created based on a copy of your 2A Instructor IDs Query; that is, the new query includes the same fields in the same order as the query that you copied.

3 In the **Navigation Pane**, right-click your **2A Department Sort Query**, and then click **Design View**. **Close** |«| the **Navigation Pane**.

> Use this technique to display the query in Design view if you are redesigning the query. Recall that if you double-click a query name in the Navigation Pane, Access runs the query and displays the query results.

4 In the design grid, in the **Sort** row, under **Last Name**, click to display the insertion point and an arrow. Click the **arrow**, click **Ascending**, and then compare your screen with Figure 2.20.

FIGURE 2.20

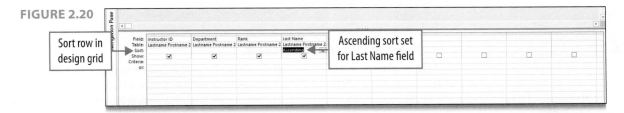

5 On the **DESIGN tab**, in the **Results group**, click **Run**.

> In the query results, the records are sorted in ascending order by the Last Name field, and two instructors have the same last name of *Carter*—*Susanne* and *Lisle*.

6 On the **HOME tab**, in the **Views group**, click the top of the **View** button to switch to **Design** view.

7 In the design grid, click in the **Sort** row under **First Name**, click the **arrow**, and then click **Ascending**. **Run** the query.

> In the query results, the records are sorted first by the Last Name field. If two instructors have the same last name, then those records are sorted by the First Name field. The two instructors with the same last name of *Carter* are sorted by their first names, and the two records with the same last name of *Fresch* are sorted by their first names.

8 ▶ Switch to **Design** view. In the design grid, click in the **Sort** row under **Department**, click the **arrow**, and then click **Descending**. **Run** the query, and then compare your screen with Figure 2.21.

In Design view, fields with a Sort setting are sorted from left to right. That is, the sorted field on the left becomes the outermost sort field, and the sorted field on the right becomes the innermost sort field. Thus, the records in this query are sorted first in descending order by the Department field—the leftmost sort field. Then, within each department, the records are sorted in ascending order by the Last Name field. And, finally, within each duplicate last name, the records are sorted in ascending order by the First Name field.

If you run a query and the sorted results are not what you intended, be sure the fields are displayed from left to right according to the groupings that you desire.

FIGURE 2.21

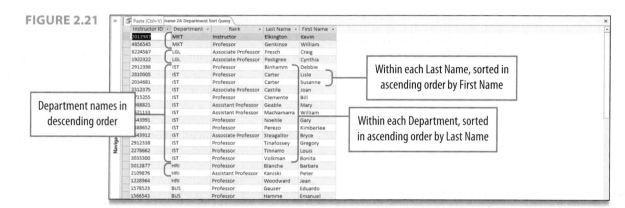

Department names in descending order

Within each Last Name, sorted in ascending order by First Name

Within each Department, sorted in ascending order by Last Name

9 ▶ Display the query results in **Print Preview**. Create a paper or electronic printout as directed, and then click **Close Print Preview**. **Close** ☒ the query. In the message box, click **Yes** to save the changes to the query design.

> **More Knowledge** | **Sorting in Design View or Datasheet View**
>
> If you add a sort order to the *design* of a query, it remains as a permanent part of the query design. If you use the sort buttons in Datasheet view, the sort order will override the sort order of the query design and can be saved as part of the query. A sort order designated in Datasheet view does not display in the Sort row of the query design grid. As with sorting tables, in Datasheet view, a small arrow displays to the right of the field name to indicate the sort order of the field.

Objective 7   Specify Criteria in a Query

Video A2-7

Queries locate information in a table based on *criteria* that you specify as part of the query design. Criteria are conditions that identify the specific records that you are looking for. Criteria enable you to ask a more specific question; therefore, you will get a more specific result. For example, to find out how many instructors are in the IST department, limit the results to display only that specific department by entering criteria in the design grid.

Activity 2.15 | Specifying Text Criteria in a Query

In this activity, you will assist Dean Judkins by creating a query to answer the question, *How many instructors are in the IST Department?*

1 ▶ On the ribbon, click the **CREATE tab**, and then in the **Queries group**, click **Query Design**.

2 ▶ In the **Show Table** dialog box, double-click your **2A Instructors** table to add it to the table area, and then **Close** the **Show Table** dialog box.

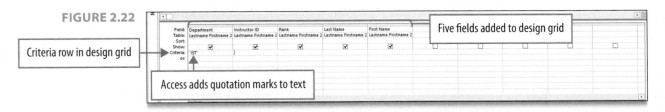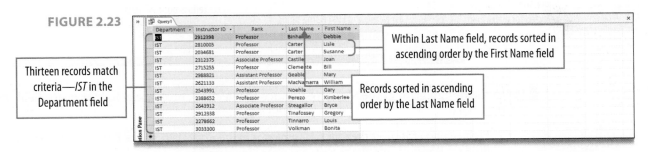**3** > By dragging the lower right corner downward and to the right, resize the field list to display all of the field names and the table name. Add the following fields to the design grid in the order given: **Department**, **Instructor ID**, **Rank**, **Last Name**, and **First Name**.

4 > In the design grid, click in the **Criteria** row under **Department**, type **IST** and then press Enter. Compare your screen with Figure 2.22.

Access places quotation marks around the criteria to indicate that this is a ***text string***—a sequence of characters. Use the Criteria row to specify the criteria that will limit the results of the query to your exact specifications. The criteria is not case sensitive; you can type *ist* instead of *IST*.

FIGURE 2.22

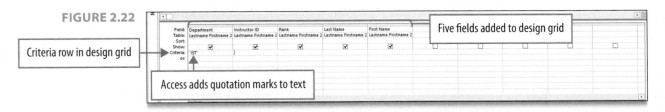

Criteria row in design grid

Access adds quotation marks to text

Five fields added to design grid

NOTE   **Pressing Enter After Adding Criteria**

After adding criteria, when you press Enter or click in another column or row in the query design grid, you can see how Access alters the criteria so it can interpret what you have typed. Sometimes there is no change, such as when you add criteria to a field that stores a numeric or currency value. Other times, Access capitalizes a letter or adds quotation marks, words, or other symbols to clarify the criteria. Pressing Enter after adding criteria has no effect on the query results; it is used here to help you see how the program behaves.

---

5 > In the design grid, click in the **Sort** row under **Last Name**, click the **arrow**, and then click **Ascending**. Click in the **Sort** row under **First Name**, click the **arrow**, and then click **Ascending**.

6 > **Run** the query, and then compare your screen with Figure 2.23.

Thirteen records display. There are 13 instructors in the IST Department; or, more specifically, there are 13 records that have *IST* in the Department field. The records are sorted in ascending order, first by the Last Name field and then by the First Name field.

FIGURE 2.23

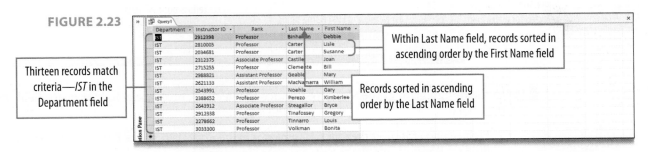

Thirteen records match criteria—*IST* in the Department field

Within Last Name field, records sorted in ascending order by the First Name field

Records sorted in ascending order by the Last Name field

ALERT!   **Do Your Query Results Differ?**

If you mistype the criteria, or enter it under the wrong field, or make some other error, the query results will display no records. This indicates that there are no records in the table that match the criteria as you entered it. If this occurs, return to Design view and examine the query design. Verify that the criteria is entered in the Criteria row, under the correct field, and without typing errors. Then, run the query again.

---

7 > **Save** the query as **Lastname Firstname 2A IST Query** and then display the query results in **Print Preview**. Create a paper or electronic printout as directed, and then click **Close Print Preview**.

8 ▸ **Close** ☒ the query, **Open** » the **Navigation Pane**, and then notice that your **2A IST Query** object name displays under your **2A Instructors** table—its data source.

Recall that in the Navigation Pane, queries display an icon of two overlapping datasheets.

Activity 2.16 | Specifying Criteria and Hiding the Field in the Query Results

So far, all of the fields that you included in the query design have also been included in the query results. There are times when you need to use the field in the query design, but you do not need to display that field in the results, usually, when the data in the field is the same for all of the records. In this activity, you will create a query to answer the question, *Which instructors have a rank of professor?*

1 ▸ **Close** « the **Navigation Pane**. On the ribbon, click the **CREATE tab**, and then in the **Queries group**, click **Query Design**.

2 ▸ In the **Show Table** dialog box, double-click your **2A Instructors** table to add it to the table area, and then **Close** the **Show Table** dialog box.

3 ▸ Resize the field list, and then add the following fields to the design grid in the order given: **Instructor ID**, **Last Name**, **First Name**, and **Rank**.

4 ▸ Click in the **Sort** row under **Last Name**, click the **arrow**, and then click **Ascending**. Click in the **Sort** row under **First Name**, click the **arrow**, and then click **Ascending**.

5 ▸ Click in the **Criteria** row under **Rank**, type **professor** and then press Enter. Compare your screen with Figure 2.24.

Recall that criteria is not case sensitive. As you start typing *professor*, a list of functions displays, from which you can select if a function is included in your criteria. After pressing Enter, the insertion point moves to the next criteria box, and quotation marks are added around the text string that you entered.

FIGURE 2.24

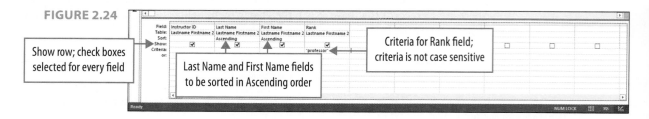

6 ▸ In the design grid, in the **Show** row, notice that a check box is selected for every field. **Run** the query.

Eighteen records meet the criteria—*professor* in the *Rank* field. In the Rank column, every record displays *Professor*, and the records are sorted in ascending order by the First Name field within the Last Name field.

7 ▸ Switch to **Design** view. In the design grid, in the **Show** row under **Rank**, click to clear the check box.

Because it is repetitive and not particularly useful to display *Professor* for every record in the query results, clear the Show check box so that the field is hidden and does not display. It is good practice, however, to run the query first before clearing the Show check box to be sure that the correct records display.

8 > **Run** the query, and then notice that the *Rank* field does not display even though it is used to specify criteria in the query.

> The same 18 records display, but the *Rank* field is hidden from the query results. Although the Rank field is included in the query design so that you can specify the criteria of *professor*, it is not necessary to display the field in the results. When appropriate, clear the Show check box to avoid cluttering the query results with data that is not useful.

9 > **Save** 🖫 the query as **Lastname Firstname 2A Professor Query** and then display the query results in **Print Preview**. Create a paper or electronic printout as directed, and then click **Close Print Preview. Close** ☒ the query.

Activity 2.17 | Using *Is Null* Criteria to Find Empty Fields

Sometimes you must locate records where data is missing. You can locate such records by using **Is Null** as the criteria in a field. *Is Null* is used to find empty fields. Additionally, you can display only the records where data has been entered in the field by using the criteria of **Is Not Null**, which excludes records where the specified field is empty. In this activity, you will design a query to answer the question, *Which scheduled courses have no credits listed?*

1 > On the ribbon, click the **CREATE tab**, and then in the **Queries group**, click **Query Design**. In the **Show Table** dialog box, double-click your **2A Schedule** table to add it to the table area, and then **Close** the **Show Table** dialog box.

2 > Resize the field list, and then add the following fields to the design grid in the order given: **Subject, Catalog#, Section, Course Name,** and **Credits**.

3 > Click in the **Criteria** row under **Credits**, type **is null** and then press Enter.

> Access capitalizes *is null*. The criteria *Is Null* examines the Credits field and locates records that do *not* have any data entered in the field.

4 > Click in the **Sort** row under **Subject**, click the **arrow**, and then click **Ascending. Sort** the **Catalog#** field in **Ascending** order, and then **Sort** the **Section** field in **Ascending** order. Compare your screen with Figure 2.25.

FIGURE 2.25

Three fields sorted in Ascending order

Is Null criteria for Credits field

5 > **Run** the query, and then compare your screen with Figure 2.26.

> Four scheduled courses do not have credits listed—the Credits field is empty. The records are sorted in ascending order first by the Subject field. Within the Subject field, the records are sorted in ascending order by the Catalog# field. Within the Catalog# field, the records are sorted in ascending order by the Section field. Using the information displayed in the query results, a course scheduler can more easily locate the records in the table and enter the credits for these courses.

FIGURE 2.26

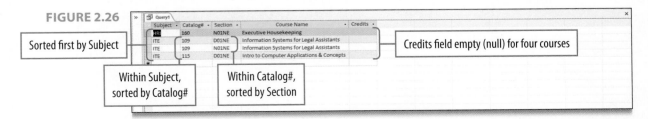

Sorted first by Subject

Within Subject, sorted by Catalog#

Within Catalog#, sorted by Section

Credits field empty (null) for four courses

6 Save 🖫 the query as **Lastname Firstname 2A No Credits Query**, and then display the query results in **Print Preview**. Create a paper or electronic printout as instructed, click **Close Print Preview**, and then **Close** ☒ the query.

7 **Open** ⟫ the **Navigation Pane**, and then notice that your **2A No Credits Query** object displays under your **2A Schedule** table object, its data source.

8 On the right side of the title bar, click **Close** ☒ to close the database and to exit Access. As directed by your instructor, submit your database and the paper or electronic printouts of the eight objects—relationship report, sorted table, and six queries—that are the results of this project. Specifically, in this project, using your own name, you created the following database and printouts or electronic printouts:

1. Lastname_Firstname_2A_Instructors_Courses	Database file
2. Relationships for Lastname_Firstname_2A_Instructors_Courses	Relationships Report (printout or electronic printout)
3. Lastname Firstname 2A Instructors table sorted (not saved)	Table sorted (printout or electronic printout - Page 1)
4. Lastname Firstname 2A Instructors Query	Query (printout or electronic printout)
5. Lastname Firstname 2A Instructor IDs Query	Query (printout or electronic printout)
6. Lastname Firstname 2A Department Sort Query	Query (printout or electronic printout)
7. Lastname Firstname 2A IST Query	Query (printout or electronic printout)
8. Lastname Firstname 2A Professor Query	Query (printout or electronic printout)
9. Lastname Firstname 2A No Credits Query	Query (printout or electronic printout)

END | You have completed Project 2A

GO! with Office Web Apps

Objective | Export an Access Query to a PDF File, Save to SkyDrive, and Add a Description to the PDF File

Access web apps are designed to work with Microsoft's SharePoint, an application for setting up websites to share and manage documents. Your college may not have SharePoint installed, so you will use other tools to share objects from your database so that you can work collaboratively with others. When you have information that you want to share with others, you can upload files to SkyDrive. Some files can be opened in SkyDrive; some can only be downloaded. Because database files are typically large in size, and free storage space on SkyDrive is limited, you can export database objects to different formats and then upload those files to SkyDrive.

> **ALERT!** | **Working with Web-Based Applications and Services**
>
> Computer programs and services on the web receive continuous updates and improvements. Thus, the steps to complete this web-based activity may differ from the ones shown. You can often look at the screens and the information presented to determine how to complete the activity.

Activity | Exporting an Access Query to a PDF File, Uploading a PDF File to SkyDrive, and Adding a Description to a PDF File

In this activity, you will export your 2A No Credits Query object to a PDF file, upload your PDF file to SkyDrive, and then add a description to the PDF File. Recall that PDF stands for Portable Document Format—a file format that creates an image that preserves the look of your file, but that cannot be easily changed. The results of the query will be available for individuals with whom you have shared your SkyDrive files or folders.

1 **Start** Access, navigate to your **Access Chapter 2** folder, and then **Open** your **2A_Instructors_Courses** database file. If necessary, on the Message Bar, click Enable Content. In the **Navigation Pane**, click your **2A No Credits Query** object to select it—do not open it.

2 On the ribbon, click the **EXTERNAL DATA tab**, and then in the **Export group**, click **PDF or XPS**. In the **Publish as PDF or XPS** dialog box, navigate to your **Access Chapter 2** folder. Click in the **File name** box, type **Lastname_Firstname_AC_2A_Web** and then be sure the **Open file after publishing** check box is selected, and the **Minimum size (publishing online)** option button is

selected. Click **Publish**, and then compare your screen with Figure A.

The PDF file is created and opens in the Windows 8 Reader, Adobe Reader, or Adobe Acrobat, depending on the software that is installed on your computer.

3 **Close** your **AC_2A_Web** file. In the **Export – PDF** dialog box, click **Close**, and then **Close** Access.

4 From the desktop, start Internet Explorer, navigate to **http://skydrive.com**, and then sign in to your Microsoft account. Open your **GO! Web Projects** folder—or create and then open this folder if necessary.

FIGURE A

Your 2A No Credits Query exported as a PDF file and opened in Adobe Reader (yours may open in Windows 8 Reader or Adobe Acrobat)

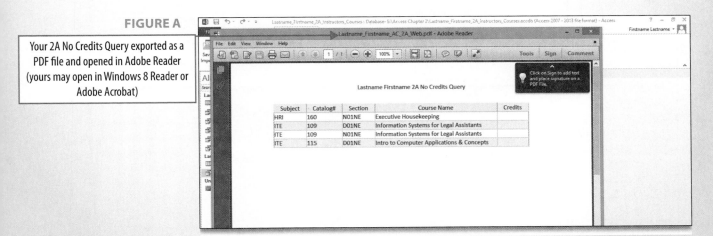

(GO! with Office Web Apps continues on the next page)

5 On the menu bar, click **Upload**. In the **Choose File to Upload** dialog box, navigate to your **Access Chapter 2** folder, and then double-click your **AC_2A_Web** file to upload it to SkyDrive.

6 In your **GO! Web Projects** folder, right-click your **AC_2A_Web** file, and then click **Properties**.

A properties panel displays on the right side of the window.

7 In the properties panel, click **Add a description**. In the box, type **This query displays courses in the schedule that do not have credits assigned to them.** and then press Enter. Compare your screen with Figure B.

8 On your keyboard, press the key, type **snip**, and then click **Snipping Tool**. In the **Snipping Tool** dialog box, click the **New arrow**, and then click **Full-screen snip**.

9 On the **Snipping Tool** toolbar, click **Save Snip** . In the **Save As** dialog box, navigate to your **Access Chapter 2** folder. Click in the **File name** box, type **Lastname_Firstname_AC_2A_Web_Snip** and then click the **Save as type arrow**. Click **JPEG file**, and then click **Save**. **Close** the **Snipping Tool** window.

10 In SkyDrive, on the title bar, click **SkyDrive** to return to your home page. At the top right corner of your screen, click your SkyDrive name, and then click **Sign out**. **Close** your browser window.

11 If directed to submit a paper printout of your pdf and snip file, follow the directions given in the Note. As directed by your instructor, submit your pdf file and your snip file that are the results of this project.

FIGURE B

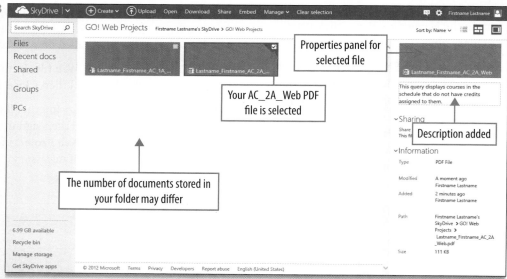

Athletic Scholarships Database

PROJECT 2B

PROJECT ACTIVITIES

In Activities 2.18 through 2.33, you will assist Roberto Garza, athletic director for Texas Lakes Community College, in creating queries to locate information about athletic scholarships that are awarded to students. Your completed database objects will look similar to Figure 2.27.

PROJECT FILES

For Project 2B, you will need the following files:

a02B_Athletes_Scholarships
a02B_Athletes (Excel workbook)

You will save your database as:

Lastname_Firstname_2B_Athletes_Scholarships

PROJECT RESULTS

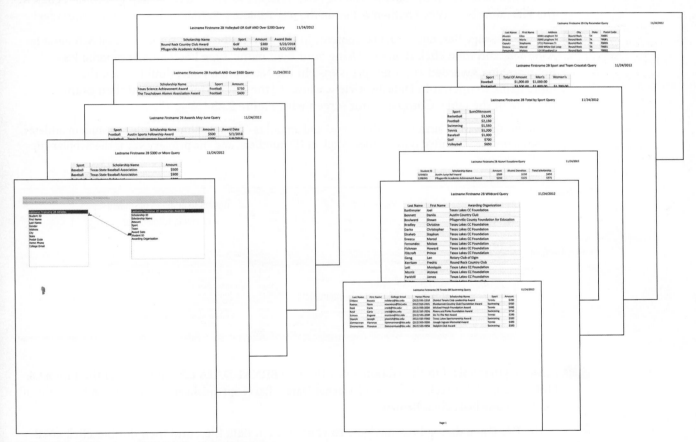

FIGURE 2.27 Project 2B Athletic Scholarships

Video A2-8

Criteria can be set for fields containing numeric data. When you design your table, set the appropriate data type for fields that will contain numbers, currency, or dates so that mathematical calculations can be performed.

Activity 2.18 | **Opening, Renaming, and Saving an Existing Database and Importing a Spreadsheet as a New Table**

In this activity, you will open, rename, and save an existing database, and then import an Excel spreadsheet as a new table in the database.

1 ▶ **Start** Access. In the Access opening screen, click **Open Other Files**. Under **Open**, click **Computer**. Under **Recent Folders**, if displayed, click the location where your student data files are stored; otherwise, click **Browse** and then navigate to the location where your student data files are stored. Double-click **a02B_Athletes_Scholarships** to open the database.

2 ▶ Click the **FILE tab**, click **Save As**, and then under **File Types**, be sure **Save Database As** is selected. On the right, under **Database File Types**, be sure **Access Database** is selected, and then click **Save As**. In the **Save As** dialog box, navigate to your **Access Chapter 2** folder, click in the **File name** box, type **Lastname_Firstname_2B_Athletes_Scholarships** and then press Enter.

3 ▶ On the **Message Bar**, click **Enable Content**. In the **Navigation Pane**, right-click **2B Scholarships Awarded**, and then click **Rename**. Using your own name, type **Lastname Firstname 2B Scholarships Awarded** and then press Enter. In the **Navigation Pane**, double-click the table name to open it in **Datasheet** view. **Close** « the **Navigation Pane**, and then examine the data in the table. Compare your screen with Figure 2.28.

In this table, Mr. Garza tracks the names and amounts of scholarships awarded to student athletes. Students are identified only by their Student ID numbers, and the primary key is the Scholarship ID field.

FIGURE 2.28

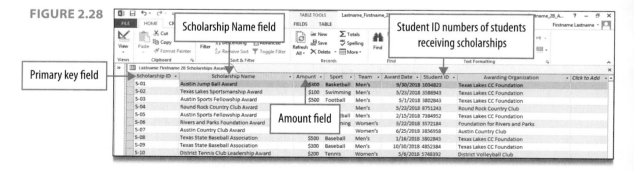

4 ▶ **Close** ✕ the table. On the ribbon, click the **EXTERNAL DATA tab**, and then in the **Import & Link group**, click **Excel**. In the **Get External Data – Excel Spreadsheet** dialog box, to the right of the **File name** box, click **Browse**.

5 ▶ In the **File Open** dialog box, navigate to your student data files, and then double-click **a02B_Athletes**. Be sure that the **Import the source data into a new table in the current database** option button is selected, and then click **OK**.

The Import Spreadsheet Wizard opens and displays the spreadsheet data.

6 ▶ In the wizard, click **Next**. In the upper left area of the wizard, select the **First Row Contains Column Headings** check box, click **Next**, and then click **Next** again.

7 In the wizard, click the **Choose my own primary key** option button, and then be sure that **Student ID** displays in the box.

In the new table, Student ID will be designated as the primary key. No two students have the same Student ID.

8 Click **Next**. With the text selected in the **Import to Table** box, type **Lastname Firstname 2B Athletes** and then click **Finish**. In the **Get External Data – Excel Spreadsheet** dialog box, click **Close**.

9 **Open** [»] the **Navigation Pane**, and increase the width of the pane so that the two table names display fully. In the **Navigation Pane**, right-click your **2B Athletes** table, and then click **Design View**. **Close** [«] the **Navigation Pane**.

10 To the right of **Student ID**, click in the **Data Type** box, click the **arrow**, and then click **Short Text**. For the **Postal Code** field, change the **Data Type** to **Short Text**, and in the **Field Properties** area, click **Field Size**, type **5** and then press Enter. In the **Field Name** column, click **State**, set the **Field Size** to **2** and then press Enter. Compare your screen with Figure 2.29.

Recall that numeric data that is not used in a calculation, such as the Student ID and Postal Code, should be assigned a data type of Short Text.

FIGURE 2.29

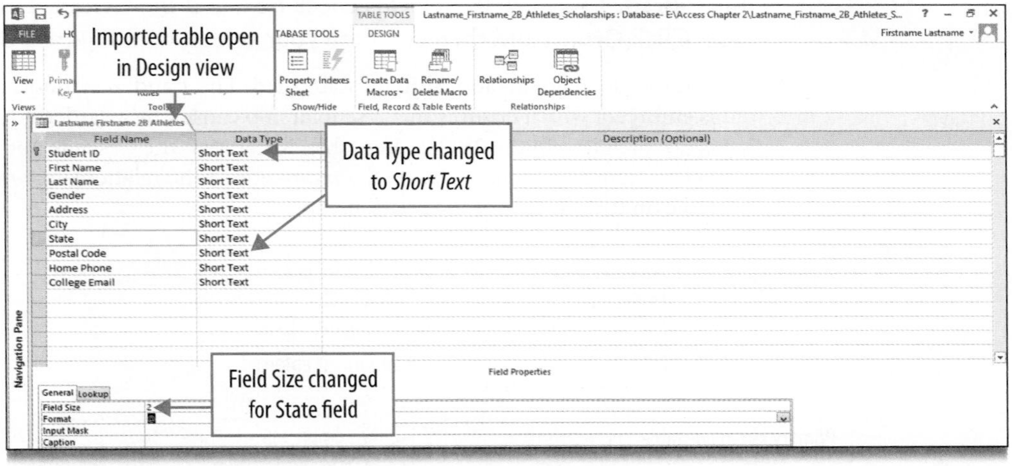

11 On the **DESIGN tab**, in the **Views group**, click the top of the **View** button to switch to **Datasheet** view. In the message box, click **Yes** to save the table. In the second message box, click **Yes**—no data will be lost. Take a moment to examine the data in the imported table.

12 In the datasheet, to the left of the **Student ID** field name, click **Select All** [ ]. On the **HOME tab**, in the **Records group**, click **More**, and then click **Field Width**. In the **Column Width** dialog box, click **Best Fit**. **Save** [ ] the table, click in any record to cancel the selection, and then **Close** [×] the table.

Activity 2.19 | Creating a One-to-Many Table Relationship

In this activity, you will create a one-to-many relationship between your 2B Athletes table and your 2B Scholarships Awarded table by using the common field—*Student ID*.

1 On the ribbon, click the **DATABASE TOOLS tab**, and then in the **Relationships group**, click **Relationships**.

2 In the **Show Table** dialog box, double-click your **2B Athletes** table, and then double-click your **2B Scholarships Awarded** table to add both tables to the **Relationships** window. **Close** the **Show Table** dialog box.

3 Point to the title bar of the field list on the right, and drag the field list to the right until there are approximately three inches of space between the field lists. By dragging the lower right corner of the field list downward and to the right, resize each field list to display all of the field names and the entire table name.

Repositioning and resizing the field lists are not required, but doing so makes it easier for you to view the field names and the join line when creating relationships.

4 In the **2B Athletes** field list, point to **Student ID**, and then drag the field name into the **2B Scholarships Awarded** field list on top of **Student ID**. Release the mouse button to display the **Edit Relationships** dialog box.

5 Point to the title bar of the **Edit Relationships** dialog box, and then drag it downward below the two field lists. In the **Edit Relationships** dialog box, be sure that **Student ID** displays as the common field for both tables.

Repositioning the Edit Relationships dialog is not required, but doing so enables you to see the field lists. The Relationship Type is *One-To-Many*—*one* athlete can have *many* scholarships. The common field in both tables is the *Student ID* field. In the 2B Athletes table, Student ID is the primary key. In the 2B Scholarships Awarded table, Student ID is the foreign key.

6 In the **Edit Relationships** dialog box, click to select the **Enforce Referential Integrity** check box, the **Cascade Update Related Fields** check box, and the **Cascade Delete Related Records** check box. Click **Create**, and then compare your screen with Figure 2.30.

The one-to-many relationship is established. The *1* and ∞ symbols indicate that referential integrity is enforced, which ensures that a scholarship cannot be awarded to a student whose Student ID is not included in the 2B Athletes table. Recall that the Cascade options enable you to update and delete records automatically on the *many* side of the relationship when changes are made in the table on the *one* side of the relationship.

FIGURE 2.30

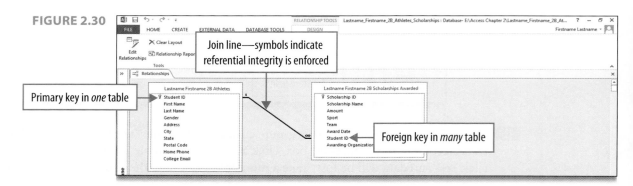

7 Under **RELATIONSHIP TOOLS**, on the **DESIGN tab**, in the **Tools group**, click **Relationship Report**. On the **PRINT PREVIEW tab**, in the **Page Size group**, click **Margins**, and then click **Normal**. **Save** 🖫 the report as **Lastname Firstname 2B Relationships** and then create a paper or electronic printout as directed.

8 In the object window, right-click either **object tab**, and then click **Close All** to close the **Relationship Report** and the **Relationships** window.

9 **Open** ⟩⟩ the **Navigation Pane**, double-click your **2B Athletes** table to open it, and then **Close** ⟨⟨ the **Navigation Pane**. On the left side of the first record, click ⊞ to display the subdatasheet for the record.

In the first record, for *Joel Barthmaier*, one related record exists in the 2B Scholarships Awarded table. Joel has been awarded the *Austin Jump Ball Award* in the amount of *$300*. The subdatasheet displays because you created a relationship between the two tables using Student ID as the common field.

10 ▶ **Close** ☒ the **2B Athletes** table.

When you close the table, the subdatasheet collapses—you do not need to click ⊟ before closing a table.

Activity 2.20 | Specifying Numeric Criteria in a Query

In this activity, you will create a query to answer the question, *Which scholarships are in the amount of $300, and for which sports?*

1 ▶ On the ribbon, click the **CREATE tab**. In the **Queries group**, click **Query Design**.

2 ▶ In the **Show Table** dialog box, double-click your **2B Scholarships Awarded** table to add it to the table area, and then **Close** the **Show Table** dialog box. Resize the field list to display all of the fields and the entire table name.

3 ▶ Add the following fields to the design grid in the order given: **Sport**, **Scholarship Name**, and **Amount**.

4 ▶ Click in the **Sort** row under **Sport**, click the **arrow**, and then click **Ascending**. Click in the **Sort** row under **Scholarship Name**, click the **arrow**, and then click **Ascending**.

The records will be sorted in ascending order by the Scholarship Name field within the Sport field.

5 ▶ Click in the **Criteria** row under **Amount**, type **300** and then press Enter. Compare your screen with Figure 2.31.

When you enter currency values as criteria, do not type the dollar sign. Include a decimal point only if you are looking for a specific amount that includes cents; for example, 300.49. Access does not insert quotation marks around the criteria because the data type of the field is Currency, which is a numeric format.

FIGURE 2.31

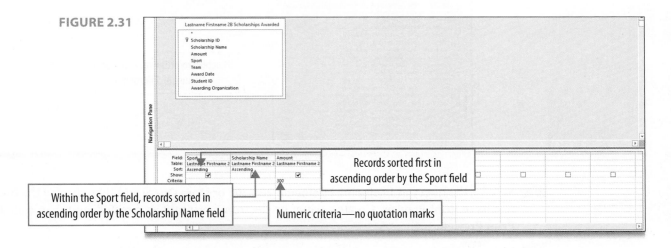

6 ▶ Under **QUERY TOOLS**, on the **DESIGN tab**, in the **Results group**, click **Run** to display the query results.

Five scholarships in the exact amount of $300 were awarded to student athletes. In the navigation area, *1 of 5* displays—1 represents the first record that is selected, and 5 represents the total number of records that meet the criteria.

7 ▶ On the **HOME tab**, in the **Views group**, click the top of the **View** button to switch to **Design** view.

Activity 2.21 | Using Comparison Operators in Criteria

Comparison operators are symbols you can use to evaluate data in the field to determine if it is the same (=), greater than (>), less than (<), or in between a range of values as specified by the criteria. If no comparison operator is specified, equal (=) is assumed. For example, in the previous activity, you created a query to display only those records where the *Amount* is *300*. The comparison operator of = was assumed, and the query results displayed only those records that had values in the Amount field equal to 300.

1 In the design grid, in the **Criteria** row under **Amount**, select the existing criteria of *300*. Type **>300** and then press ⏎. **Run** the query.

Fourteen records display, and each has a value *greater than* $300 in the Amount field; there are no records for which the Amount is *equal to* $300.

2 Switch to **Design** view. In the **Criteria** row under **Amount**, select the existing criteria of *>300*. Type **<300** and then press ⏎. **Run** the query.

Eleven records display, and each has a value *less than* $300 in the Amount field; there are no records for which the Amount is *equal to* $300.

3 Switch to **Design** view. In the **Criteria** row under **Amount**, select the existing criteria of *<300*. Type **>=300** and then press ⏎. **Run** the query, and then compare your screen with Figure 2.32.

Nineteen records display, including the records for scholarships in the exact amount of $300. The records include scholarships *greater than* or *equal to* $300. In this manner, comparison operators can be combined. This query answers the question, *Which scholarships have been awarded in the amount of $300 or more, and for which sports, arranged alphabetically by sport?*

FIGURE 2.32

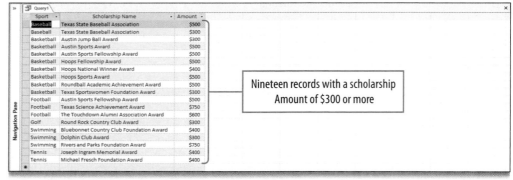

Nineteen records with a scholarship Amount of $300 or more

4 Save 💾 the query as **Lastname Firstname 2B $300 or More Query** and then display the query results in **Print Preview**. Create a paper or electronic printout as directed, and then click **Close Print Preview**.

5 Close ✕ the query. Open » the **Navigation Pane**, and notice that this new query displays under *2B Scholarships Awarded*, its data source.

Activity 2.22 | Using the Between ... And Comparison Operator

The *Between ... And operator* is a comparison operator that looks for values within a range. It is useful when you need to locate records that are within a range of dates; for example, scholarships awarded between May 1 and June 30.

In this activity, you will create a new query from an existing query, and then add criteria to look for values within a range of dates. The query will answer the question, *Which scholarships were awarded between May 1 and June 30?*

1 In the **Navigation Pane**, right-click your **2B $300 or More Query** object, and then click **Copy**. In the **Navigation Pane**, point to a blank area, right-click, and then click **Paste**.

2 In the **Paste As** dialog box, type **Lastname Firstname 2B Awards May-June Query** and then click **OK**.

> A new query, based on a copy of your 2B $300 or More Query is created and displays in the Navigation Pane under its data source—your 2B Scholarships Awarded table.

3 In the **Navigation Pane**, right-click your **2B Awards May-June Query** object, click **Design View**, and then **Close** « the **Navigation Pane**.

4 In the **2B Scholarships Awarded** field list, double-click **Award Date** to add it as the fourth column in the design grid.

5 In the **Criteria** row under **Amount**, select the existing criteria of *>=300*, and then press [Del] so that the query is not restricted by a monetary value.

6 Click in the **Criteria** row under **Award Date**, type **between 5/1/18 and 6/30/18** and then press [Enter].

7 Click in the **Sort** row under **Sport**, click the **arrow**, and then click (**not sorted**) to remove the sort from this field. Click in the **Sort** row under **Scholarship Name**, click the **arrow**, and then click (**not sorted**) to remove the sort from this field. Click in the **Sort** row under **Award Date**, click the **arrow**, and then click **Ascending**.

8 In the selection bar of the design grid, point to the right edge of the **Award Date** column to display the ⊞ pointer, and then double-click to apply Best Fit to this column. Compare your screen with Figure 2.33.

> The width of the Award Date column is increased to fit the longest entry in the column, which enables you to see all of the criteria. Access places pound signs (#) around the dates and capitalizes *between* and *and*. This criteria instructs Access to look for values in the Award Date field that begin with 5/1/18 and end with 6/30/18. Both the beginning and ending dates will be included in the query results.

FIGURE 2.33

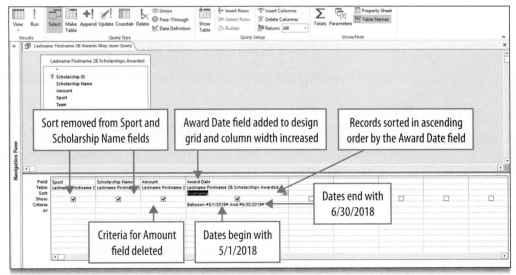

9 **Run** the query, and notice that eight scholarships were awarded between 5/1/2018 and 6/30/2018.

10 Display the query results in **Print Preview**, create a paper or electronic printout as directed, and then click **Close Print Preview**. **Close** ✕ the query, and in the message box, click **Yes** to save the changes to the query design.

Video A2-9

You can specify more than one condition—criteria—in a query; this is called **compound criteria**. Compound criteria use **logical operators** such as AND and OR. Logical operators evaluate data to determine if a condition is met (true) or not met (false). The AND and OR logical operators enable you to enter multiple criteria for the same field or for different fields.

Activity 2.23 | Using AND Criteria in a Query

The **AND condition** is an example of a compound criteria you can use to display records that match all parts of the specified criteria. In this activity, you will design a query to answer the question, *Which scholarships over $500 were awarded for football?*

1 On the ribbon, click the **CREATE tab**, and in the **Queries group**, click **Query Design**. In the **Show Table** dialog box, double-click your **2B Scholarships Awarded** table to add it to the table area, and then **Close** the **Show Table** dialog box. Resize the field list to display all of the fields and the entire table name.

2 Add the following fields to the design grid in the order given: **Scholarship Name**, **Sport**, and **Amount**.

3 Click in the **Criteria** row under **Sport**, type **football** and then press Enter.

4 In the **Criteria** row under **Amount**, type **>500** and then press Enter. Compare your screen with Figure 2.34.

> You create the AND condition by placing the criteria for both fields on the same line in the Criteria row. The criteria indicates that records should be located that contain *Football* in the Sport field AND a value greater than *500* in the Amount field. Both conditions must exist or be true for the records to display in the query results.

FIGURE 2.34

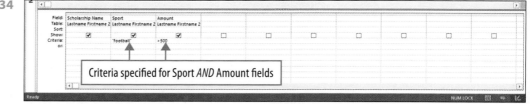

Criteria specified for Sport *AND* Amount fields

5 **Run** the query, and notice that two records display that match both conditions—*Football* in the **Sport** field AND a value greater than *$500* in the **Amount** field.

6 **Save** 🖫 the query as **Lastname Firstname 2B Football AND Over $500 Query** and then **Close** ✕ the query.

7 **Open** » the **Navigation Pane**, and then click to select your **2B Football AND Over $500 Query** object. On the ribbon, click the **FILE tab**, click **Print**, and then click **Print Preview**.

> You can view an object in Print Preview or print any selected object in the Navigation Pane—the object does not need to be open in the object window to print it.

8 Create a paper or electronic printout as directed, and then click **Close Print Preview**. **Close** « the **Navigation Pane**.

Activity 2.24 | Using OR Criteria in a Query

The **OR condition** is an example of a compound criteria you can use to display records that meet one or more parts of the specified criteria. The OR condition can specify criteria in a single field or in different fields. In this activity, you will help Mr. Garza answer the question, *Which scholarships over $200 were awarded for volleyball or golf, and what is the award date of each?*

1 On the ribbon, click the **CREATE tab**. In the **Queries group**, click **Query Design**.

2 In the **Show Table** dialog box, double-click your **2B Scholarships Awarded** table to add it to the table area, and then **Close** the **Show Table** dialog box. Resize the field list, and then add the following fields to the design grid in the order given: **Scholarship Name**, **Sport**, **Amount**, and **Award Date**.

3 In the design grid, click in the **Criteria** row under **Sport**, type **volleyball** and then press ⬇.

The insertion point is blinking in the *or* row under Sport.

4 In the **or** row under **Sport**, type **golf** and then press Enter. **Run** the query.

Six records were located in the 2B Scholarships Awarded table that have either *volleyball* OR *golf* stored in the Sport field. This is an example of using the OR condition to locate records that meet one or more parts of the specified criteria in a single field—*Sport*.

5 Switch to **Design** view. In the **or** row under **Sport**, select *"golf"* and then press Del. In the **Criteria** row under **Sport**, select and delete *"volleyball"*. Type **volleyball or golf** and then press Enter.

6 In the **Criteria** row under **Amount**, type **>200** and then press Enter. Compare your screen with Figure 2.35.

This is an alternative way to enter the OR condition in the Sport field and is a good method to use when you add an AND condition to the criteria. Access will locate records where the Sport field contains *volleyball* OR *golf* AND where the Amount field contains a value greater than *200*.

If you enter *volleyball* in the Criteria row, and *golf* in the or row for the Sport field, then you must enter *>200* in both the Criteria row and the or row for the Amount field so that the correct records are located when you run the query.

FIGURE 2.35

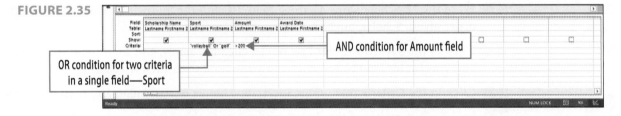

OR condition for two criteria in a single field—Sport

AND condition for Amount field

7 **Run** the query.

Two records were located in the 2B Scholarships Awarded table that have either *Volleyball* OR *Golf* stored in the Sport field AND a value greater than $200 stored in the Amount field. This is an example of using the OR condition in combination with an AND condition.

8 Save 🖫 the query as **Lastname Firstname 2B Volleyball OR Golf AND Over $200 Query** and then display the query results in **Print Preview**. Create a paper or electronic printout as directed, click **Close Print Preview**, and then **Close** ☒ the query.

Video A2-10

In a relational database, you can retrieve information from more than one table. Recall that a table in a relational database contains all of the records about a single topic. Tables are joined to one another by relating the primary key in one table to the foreign key in another table. This common field is used to create the relationship and is used to find records from multiple tables when the query is created and run.

For example, the Athletes table stores all of the data about the student athletes—name, address, and so on. The Scholarships Awarded table stores data about the scholarship name, the amount, and so on. When an athlete receives a scholarship, only the Student ID of the athlete is used to identify the athlete in the Scholarships Awarded table. It is not necessary to include any other data about the athlete in the Scholarships Awarded table; doing so would result in redundant data.

Activity 2.25 | Creating a Query Based on More Than One Table

In this activity, you will create a query that selects records from two tables. This is possible because you created a relationship between the two tables in the database. The query will answer the questions, *What is the name, email address, and phone number of athletes who have received a scholarship for tennis or swimming, and what is the name and amount of the scholarship?*

1 On the ribbon, click the **CREATE tab**, and then in the **Queries group**, click **Query Design**. In the **Show Table** dialog box, double-click your **2B Athletes** table, and then double-click your **2B Scholarships Awarded** table to add both tables to the table area. In the **Show Table** dialog box, click **Close**. Drag the **2B Scholarships Awarded** field list—the field list on the right—to the right so that there are approximately three inches of space between the two field lists, and then resize each field list to display all of the field names and the table names.

> The join line displays because you created a one-to-many relationship between the two tables using the common field of Student ID; *one* athlete can receive *many* scholarships.

2 From the **2B Athletes** field list, add the following fields to the design grid in the order given: **Last Name, First Name, College Email**, and **Home Phone**.

3 From the **2B Scholarships Awarded** field list, add the following fields to the design grid in the order given: **Scholarship Name, Sport**, and **Amount**.

4 Click in the **Sort** row under **Last Name**, click the **arrow**, and then click **Ascending**. Click in the **Sort** row under **First Name**, click the **arrow**, and then click **Ascending**.

5 Click in the **Criteria** row under **Sport**, type **tennis or swimming** and then press Enter.

6 In the selection bar of the design grid, point to the right edge of the **Home Phone** column to display the ⊞ pointer, and then double-click to increase the width of the column and to display the entire table name on the **Table** row. Using the same technique, increase the width of the **Scholarship Name** column. If necessary, scroll to the right to display both of these columns in the design grid, and then compare your screen with Figure 2.36.

> When locating data from multiple tables, the information in the Table row is helpful, especially when different tables include the same field name, such as Address. Although the field name is the same, the data may be different; for example, you might have an athlete's address or a coach's address from two different related tables.

FIGURE 2.36

Table row indicates data source

Sorted in ascending order by Last Name and First Name fields

Criteria entered for Sport field

7 ▶ **Run** the query, and then compare your screen with Figure 2.37.

Eight records display for athletes who received either a Tennis *or* Swimming scholarship, and the records are sorted in ascending order by the Last Name field, and then the First Name field. Because the common field of Student ID is included in both tables, Access can locate the specified fields in both tables by using one query. Two students—*Carla Reid* and *Florence Zimmerman*—received two scholarships, one for tennis and one for swimming. Recall that *one* student athlete can receive *many* scholarships.

FIGURE 2.37

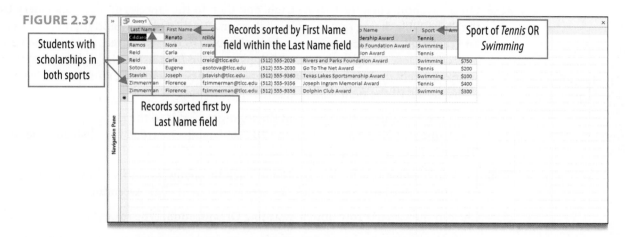

Students with scholarships in both sports

Records sorted by First Name field within the Last Name field

Sport of *Tennis* OR *Swimming*

Records sorted first by Last Name field

8 ▶ **Save** 🖫 the query as **Lastname Firstname 2B Tennis OR Swimming Query** and then display the query results in **Print Preview**. Change the orientation to **Landscape**, and the **Margins** to **Normal**. Create a paper or electronic printout as directed, and then click **Close Print Preview**.

9 ▶ **Close** ✕ the query, **Open** ≫ the **Navigation Pane**, increase the width of the **Navigation Pane** to display all object names fully, and then compare your screen with Figure 2.38.

Your *2B Tennis OR Swimming Query* object name displays under both tables from which it selected records.

FIGURE 2.38

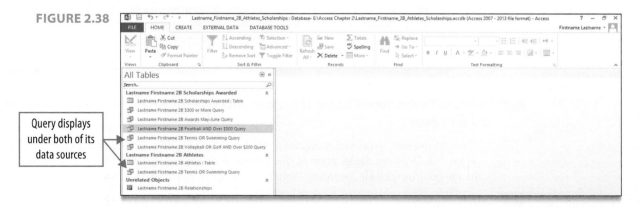

Query displays under both of its data sources

10 ▶ **Close** ≪ the **Navigation Pane**.

Video A2-11

Wildcard characters serve as a placeholder for one or more unknown characters in criteria. When you are unsure of the specific character or set of characters to include in the criteria, use a wildcard character in place of the character.

Activity 2.26 | Using a Wildcard in a Query

Use the asterisk (*) wildcard character to represent one or more unknown characters. For example, entering Fo* as the criteria in a last name field will result in displaying records containing last names of Foster, Forrester, Fossil, or any other last name that begins with *Fo*. In this activity, you will use the asterisk (*) wildcard character in criteria to answer the question, *Which athletes received scholarships from local rotary clubs, country clubs, or foundations?*

1 On the ribbon, click the **CREATE tab**, and then in the **Queries group**, click **Query Design**. In the **Show Table** dialog box, double-click your **2B Athletes** table, and then double-click your **2B Scholarships Awarded** table to add both tables to the table area. In the **Show Table** dialog box, click **Close**. Drag the **2B Scholarships Awarded** field list to the right so that there are approximately three inches of space between the two field lists, and then resize each field list to display all of the field names and the table names.

2 From the **2B Athletes** field list, add the following fields to the design grid in the order given: **Last Name** and **First Name**. From the **2B Scholarships Awarded** field list, add the **Awarding Organization** field to the design grid.

3 Click in the **Sort** row under **Last Name**, click the **arrow**, and then click **Ascending**. Click in the **Sort** row under **First Name**, click the **arrow**, and then click **Ascending**.

4 Click in the **Criteria** row under **Awarding Organization**, type **rotary*** and then press Enter.

The * wildcard character is a placeholder you can use to match one or more unknown characters. After pressing Enter, Access adds *Like* to the beginning of the criteria and places quotation marks around *rotary*.

5 **Run** the query, and then compare your screen with Figure 2.39.

Three athletes received scholarships from a rotary club from different cities. The results are sorted alphabetically by the Last Name field. If there were two athletes with the same Last Name, the records would be sorted by the First Name field.

FIGURE 2.39

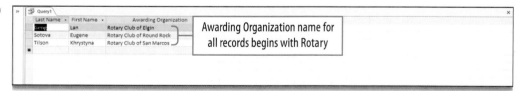

6 Switch to **Design** view. Click in the **or** row under **Awarding Organization**, type ***country club** and then press Enter.

You can use the * wildcard character at the beginning, middle, or end of the criteria. The position of the * determines the location of the unknown characters. By entering *country club*, Access will locate records with an Awarding Organization name that ends in *Country Club*.

7 **Run** the query.

Six records display for students receiving scholarships; three from organizations with a name that begins with *Rotary*, and three from organizations with a name that ends with *Country Club*.

8 ▶ Switch to **Design** view. In the design grid under **Awarding Organization** and under **Like "*country club"**, type ***foundation*** and then press Enter. Compare your screen with Figure 2.40.

This query will also display records where the Awarding Organization has *Foundation* anywhere in its name—at the beginning, in the middle, or at the end of the organization name. Three *OR* criteria have been entered for the Awarding Organization field. When run, this query will locate records where the Awarding Organization has a name that begins with *Rotary*, OR ends with *Country Club*, OR has *Foundation* anywhere in its name.

FIGURE 2.40

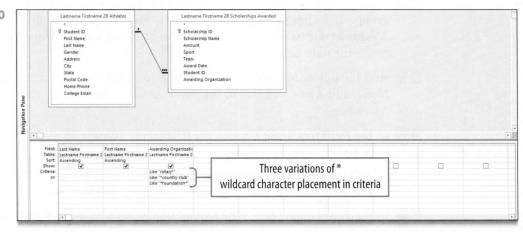

Three variations of *
wildcard character placement in criteria

9 ▶ **Run** the query.

Twenty-eight scholarships were awarded from organizations where the name of the organization begins with *Rotary*, ends with *Country Club*, or has *Foundation* anywhere in its name. The records are sorted alphabetically by the Last Name field and then by the First Name field.

10 ▶ **Save** 🖫 the query as **Lastname Firstname 2B Wildcard Query** and then display the query results in **Print Preview**. Create a paper or electronic printout as directed, and then click **Close Print Preview**.

11 ▶ **Close** ✕ the query, and then **Open** » the **Navigation Pane**. Notice that your **2B Wildcard Query** displays under both tables because the query selected data from both tables—the data sources.

More Knowledge	**Using the ? Wildcard Character to Search for a Single Unknown Character**

You can use the question mark (?) wildcard character to search for a single unknown character. For each question mark included in the criteria, the query results can display any character. For example, entering *b?d* as the criteria will result in the display of words such as *bed*, *bid*, or *bud*, or any three-character word that begins with *b* and ends with *d*. Entering *b??d* as the criteria will result in the display of words such as *bard*, *bend*, or *bind*, or any four-character word that begins with *b* and ends with *d*.

Objective 12 | Create Calculated Fields in a Query

Video A2-12

Queries can create calculated values that are stored in a ***calculated field***. A calculated field stores the value of a mathematical operation. For example, you can multiply the value stored in a field named Total Hours Worked by the value stored in a field named Hourly Pay to display the Gross Pay value for each work study student.

There are two steps to create a calculated field in a query. First, name the field that will store the results of the calculation. Second, enter the ***expression***—the formula—that will perform the calculation. When entering the information for the calculated field in the query, the new field name must be followed by a colon (:), and each field name used in the expression must be enclosed within its own pair of brackets.

Activity 2.27 | Creating a Calculated Field in a Query

For each scholarship received by student athletes, the Texas Lakes Community College Alumni Association will donate an amount equal to 50 percent of each scholarship amount. In this activity, you will create a calculated field to determine the amount that the Alumni Association will donate for each scholarship. The query will answer the question, *How much money will the Alumni Association donate for each student athlete who is awarded a scholarship?*

1 **Close** [«] the **Navigation Pane**. On the ribbon, click the **CREATE tab**, and then in the **Queries group**, click **Query Design**. In the **Show Table** dialog box, double-click your **2B Scholarships Awarded** table to add the table to the table area, **Close** the **Show Table** dialog box, and then resize the field list.

2 Add the following fields to the design grid in the order given: **Student ID**, **Scholarship Name**, and **Amount**. Click in the **Sort** row under **Student ID**, click the **arrow**, and then click **Ascending**.

3 In the **Field** row, right-click in the first empty column to display a shortcut menu, and then click **Zoom**.

Although the calculation can be typed directly in the empty Field box, the Zoom dialog box gives you more working space and enables you to see the entire calculation as you enter it.

4 In the **Zoom** dialog box, type **Alumni Donation:[Amount]*0.5** and then compare your screen with Figure 2.41.

The first element, *Alumni Donation*, is the new field name that will display the result of the calculation when the query is run. The new field name is followed by a colon (:), which separates the new field name from the expression. *Amount* is enclosed in brackets because it is an existing field name in your 2B Scholarships Awarded table; it contains the numeric data on which the calculation is performed. Following the right square bracket is the asterisk (*), the mathematical operator for multiplication. Finally, the percentage expressed as a decimal—*0.5*—displays.

FIGURE 2.41

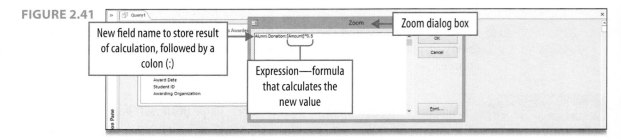

5 In the **Zoom** dialog box, click **OK**, **Run** the query, and then compare your screen with Figure 2.42.

The query results display three fields from your 2B Scholarships Awarded table and a fourth field—*Alumni Donation*—that displays a calculated value. Each calculated value equals the value in the Amount field multiplied by 0.5 or 50%.

FIGURE 2.42

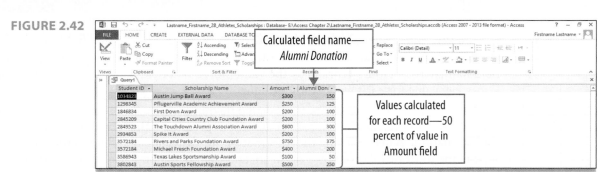

6 ▸ Notice the formatting of the values in the **Alumni Donation** field—there are no dollar signs to match the formatting in the **Amount** field; you will adjust the formatting of this field later.

> When using a number, such as 0.5, in an expression, the values that display in the calculated field might not be formatted the same as the existing field that was part of the calculation.

Activity 2.28 | Creating a Second Calculated Field in a Query

In this activity, you will create a calculated field to determine the total value of each scholarship after the Alumni Association donates an additional 50% based on the amount awarded by various organizations. The query will answer the question, *What is the total value of each scholarship after the Alumni Association donates an additional 50%?*

1 ▸ Switch to **Design** view. In the **Field** row, right-click in the first empty column to display a shortcut menu, and then click **Zoom**.

2 ▸ In the **Zoom** dialog box, type **Total Scholarship:[Amount]+[Alumni Donation]** and then compare your screen with Figure 2.43.

> Each existing field name—*Amount* and *Alumni Donation*—must be enclosed in separate pairs of brackets.

FIGURE 2.43

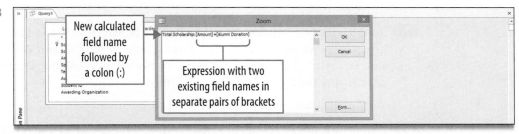

3 ▸ In the **Zoom** dialog box, click **OK**, and then **Run** the query.

> The value in the *Total Scholarship* field is calculated by adding together the values in the Amount field and the Alumni Donation field. The values in the Total Scholarship field are formatted with dollar signs, commas, and decimal points, which is carried over from the Currency format in the Amount field.

Activity 2.29 | Formatting Calculated Fields

In this activity, you will format the calculated fields so that the values display in a consistent manner.

1 ▸ Switch to **Design** view. In the **Field** row, click in the **Alumni Donation** field name box.

2 ▸ Under **QUERY TOOLS**, on the **DESIGN tab**, in the **Show/Hide group**, click **Property Sheet**.

> The Property Sheet displays on the right. Recall that a Property Sheet enables you to make precise changes to the properties—characteristics—of selected items, in this case, a field.

 **ANOTHER WAY**   In the design grid, on the Field row, right-click in the Alumni Donation field name box, and then click Properties.

3 In the **Property Sheet**, on the **General tab**, click **Format**. In the property setting box, click the **arrow**, and then compare your screen with Figure 2.44.

A list of available formats for the Alumni Donation field displays.

FIGURE 2.44

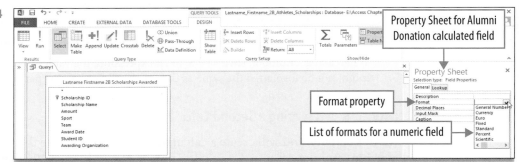

4 On the list, click **Currency**. In the **Property Sheet**, click **Decimal Places**. In the property setting box, click the **arrow**, and then click **0**.

5 In the design grid, in the **Field** row, click in the **Total Scholarship** field name. In the **Property Sheet**, set the **Decimal Places** property setting to **0**.

You do not need to set the Format setting to Currency as the field already displays with the currency symbol.

6 **Close** ☒ the **Property Sheet**, and then **Run** the query.

The Alumni Donation and Total Scholarship fields are formatted as Currency with 0 decimal places.

7 To the left of the **Student ID** field name, click **Select All** ⬚. On the **HOME tab**, in the **Records group**, click **More**, and then click **Field Width**. In the **Column Width** dialog box, click **Best Fit**. **Save** 🖫 the query as **Lastname Firstname 2B Alumni Donations Query** and then click in any field to cancel the selection.

The field widths adjust to display fully the calculated field names.

8 Display the query results in **Print Preview**. On the **PRINT PREVIEW tab**, in the **Page Layout group**, click **Landscape**. Create a paper or electronic printout as directed, and then click **Close Print Preview**. **Close** ☒ the query.

Objective 13   Calculate Statistics and Group Data in a Query

Video A2-13

You can use queries to perform statistical calculations known as *aggregate functions* on a group of records. For example, you can find the total or average amount for a group of records, or you can find the lowest or highest number in a group of records.

Activity 2.30 │ Using the Min, Max, Avg, and Sum Functions in a Query

In this activity, you will use aggregate functions to find the lowest and highest scholarship amounts and the average and total scholarship amounts. The last query in this activity will answer the question, *What is the total dollar amount of all scholarships awarded?*

1 On the ribbon, click the **CREATE tab**, and then in the **Queries group**, click **Query Design**. In the **Show Table** dialog box, double-click your **2B Scholarships Awarded** table to add the table to the table area, **Close** the **Show Table** dialog box, and then resize the field list.

2 Add the **Amount** field to the design grid.

> Include only the field to summarize in the design grid, so that the aggregate function is applied only to that field.

3 Under **QUERY TOOLS**, on the **DESIGN tab**, in the **Show/Hide group**, click **Totals** to add a **Total** row as the third row in the design grid. Notice that in the design grid, on the **Total** row under **Amount**, *Group By* displays.

> Use the Total row to select an aggregate function for the selected field.

4 In the **Total** row under **Amount**, click in the box that displays *Group By*, and then click the **arrow** to display a list of aggregate functions. Compare your screen with Figure 2.45, and then take a moment to review the available aggregate functions and the purpose of each function as shown in Table 2.46.

FIGURE 2.45

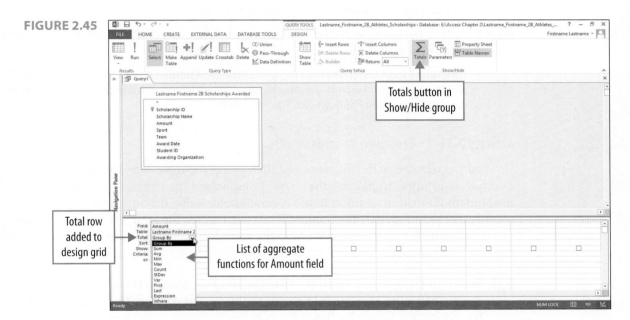

FIGURE 2.46

AGGREGATE FUNCTIONS	
FUNCTION NAME	**PURPOSE**
Group By	Groups the records alphabetically, for example, groups by Sport.
Sum	Totals the values in a field.
Avg	Averages the values in a field.
Min	Locates the smallest value in a field.
Max	Locates the largest value in a field.
Count	Displays the number of records based on a field.
StDev	Calculates the standard deviation for the values in a field.
Var	Calculates the variance for the values in a field.
First	Displays the first value in a field or column.
Last	Displays the last value in a field or column.
Expression	Creates a calculated field that includes an aggregate function.
Where	Limits the records to those that match a condition specified in the Criteria row of a field.

5 In the list of functions, click **Min**, and then **Run** the query. Point to the right edge of the first column to display the pointer, and then double-click to apply Best Fit to the field.

Access locates the minimum (smallest) value—*$100*—in the Amount field for all of the records in the 2B Scholarships Awarded table. The field name *MinOfAmount* is automatically created. This query answers the question, *What is the minimum (smallest) scholarship amount awarded to athletes?*

6 Switch to **Design** view. In the **Total** row under **Amount**, click the **arrow**, and then click **Max**. **Run** the query.

The maximum (largest) value for a scholarship award amount is *$750.00*.

7 Switch to **Design** view. In the **Total** row, under **Amount**, click the **arrow**, and then click **Avg**. **Run** the query.

The average scholarship award amount is *$358.33*.

8 Switch to **Design** view. In the **Total** row, under **Amount**, click the **arrow**, and then click **Sum**. **Run** the query.

The values in the Amount field for all records are summed displaying a result of *$10,750.00*. The field name *SumOfAmount* is automatically created. The query answers the question, *What is the total dollar amount of all scholarships awarded?*

Activity 2.31 | Grouping Records in a Query

You can use aggregate functions and then group the records by the data in a field. For example, to group (summarize) the amount of scholarships awarded to each student, you include the Student ID field in addition to the Amount field. Using the Sum aggregate function, the records will be grouped by the Student ID so you can see the total amount of scholarships awarded to each student. Similarly, you can group the records by the Sport field so you can see the total amount of scholarships awarded for each sport.

1 Switch to **Design** view. From the field list, drag the **Student ID** field to the first column of the design grid—the **Amount** field moves to the second column. In the **Total** row, under **Student ID**, notice that *Group By* displays.

This query will group—summarize—the records by Student ID and will calculate a total amount for each student.

2 **Run** the query, and then compare your screen with Figure 2.47.

The query calculates the total amount of all scholarships for each student.

FIGURE 2.47

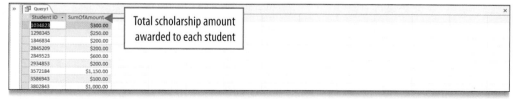

3 Switch to **Design** view. In the design grid, above **Student ID**, point to the selection bar to display the ↓ pointer. Click to select the column, and then press Del to remove the **Student ID** field from the design grid.

4 From the field list, drag the **Sport** field to the first column in the design grid—the **Amount** field moves to the second column. Click in the **Sort** row under **Amount**, click the **arrow**, and then click **Descending**.

5 On the **DESIGN tab**, in the **Show/Hide group**, click **Property Sheet**. In the **Property Sheet**, set the **Decimal Places** property to **0**, and then **Close** ☒ the **Property Sheet**.

6 **Run** the query, and then compare your screen with Figure 2.48.

Access groups—summarizes—the records by each sport and displays the groupings in descending order by the total amount of scholarships awarded for each sport. Basketball scholarships were awarded the largest total amount—*$3,500*—and Volleyball scholarships were awarded the smallest total amount—*$650*.

FIGURE 2.48

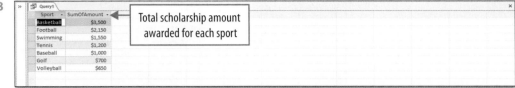

7 **Save** 🖫 the query as **Lastname Firstname 2B Total by Sport Query** and then display the query results in **Print Preview**. Create a paper or electronic printout as directed, click **Close Print Preview**, and then **Close** ☒ the query.

Objective 14 Create a Crosstab Query

Video A2-14

A ***crosstab query*** uses an aggregate function for data that can be grouped by two types of information, and then displays the data in a compact, spreadsheet-like format with column headings and row headings. A crosstab query always has at least one row heading, one column heading, and one summary field. Use a crosstab query to summarize a large amount of data in a compact space that is easy to read.

Activity 2.32 | Creating a Crosstab Query Using the Query Wizard

In this activity, you will create a crosstab query that displays the total amount of scholarships awarded for each sport and for each type of team—men's or women's.

1 On the ribbon, click the **CREATE tab**, and then in the **Queries group**, click **Query Wizard**.

2 In the **New Query** dialog box, click **Crosstab Query Wizard**, and then click **OK**.

3 In the **Crosstab Query Wizard**, click your **Table: 2B Scholarships Awarded**, and then click **Next**.

4 In the wizard under **Available Fields**, double-click **Sport** to move the field to the **Selected Fields** list and to group the scholarship amounts by the sports—the sports will display as row headings. Click **Next**, and then compare your screen with Figure 2.49.

The sport names will be grouped and displayed as row headings, and you are prompted to select column headings.

FIGURE 2.49

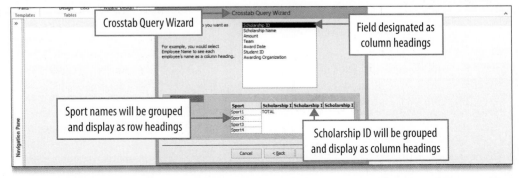

5 In the wizard, in the field list, click **Team** to select the column headings. Click **Next**, and then compare your screen with Figure 2.50.

The Team types—*Men's* and *Women's*—will display as column headings, and you are prompted to select a field to summarize.

FIGURE 2.50

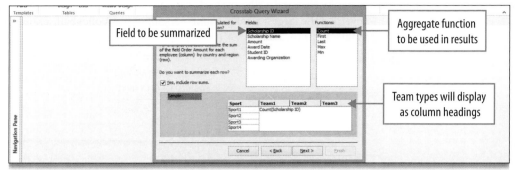

6 In the wizard under **Fields**, click **Amount**. Under **Functions**, click **Sum**.

The crosstab query will calculate the total scholarship amount for each sport and for each type of team.

7 Click **Next**. In the **What do you want to name your query?** box, select the existing text, type **Lastname Firstname 2B Sport and Team Crosstab Query** and then click **Finish**. Apply **Best Fit** to the datasheet, **Save** the query, click in any field to cancel the selection, and then compare your screen with Figure 2.51.

The field widths adjust to display fully the calculated field names.

FIGURE 2.51

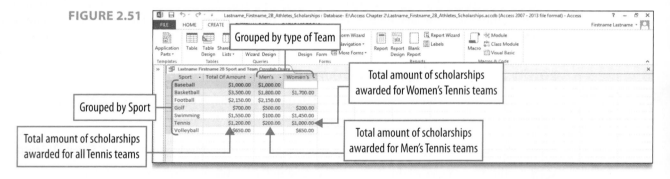

8 Display the query results in **Print Preview**. Create a paper or electronic printout as directed, click **Close Print Preview**, and then **Close** the query.

More Knowledge **Creating a Crosstab Query Using Data from Two Related Tables**

To create a crosstab query using fields from more than one table, you must first create a select query with the fields from both tables, and then use the query as the data source for the crosstab query.

Video A2-15

A ***parameter query*** prompts you for criteria before running the query. For example, you might need to display the records for students who live in different cities serviced by Texas Lakes Community College. You can create a select query and enter the criteria for a city such as Austin, but when you open the query, only the records for those students who live in Austin will display. To find the students who live in Round Rock, you must open the query in Design view, change the criteria, and then run the query again.

A parameter query eliminates the need to change the design of a select query. You create a single query that prompts you to enter the city; the results are based upon the criteria you enter when prompted.

Activity 2.33 | Creating a Parameter Query with One Criteria

In this activity, you will create a parameter query that displays student athletes from a specified city in the areas serviced by Texas Lakes Community College.

 On the **CREATE tab**, in the **Queries group**, click **Query Design**.

2 In the **Show Table** dialog box, double-click your **2B Athletes** table to add it to the table area, **Close** the **Show Table** dialog box, and then resize the field list.

3 Add the following fields to the design grid in the order given: **Last Name**, **First Name**, **Address**, **City**, **State**, and **Postal Code**.

4 Click in the **Sort** row under **Last Name**, click the **arrow**, and then click **Ascending**. Click in the **Sort** row under **First Name**, click the **arrow**, and then click **Ascending**.

5 In the **Criteria** row under **City**, type **[Enter a City]** and then press Enter. Compare your screen with Figure 2.52.

The bracketed text indicates a ***parameter***—a value that can be changed—rather than specific criteria.

FIGURE 2.52

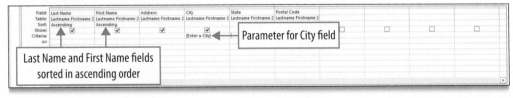

6 **Run** the query. In the **Enter Parameter Value** dialog box, type **austin** and then compare your screen with Figure 2.53.

The Enter Parameter Value dialog box prompts you to *Enter a City*, which is the text enclosed in brackets that you entered in the Criteria row under City. The city you enter will be set as the criteria for the query. Because you are prompted for the criteria, you can reuse this query without having to edit the Criteria row in Design view. The value you enter is not case sensitive—you can enter *austin*, *Austin*, or *AUSTIN*.

FIGURE 2.53

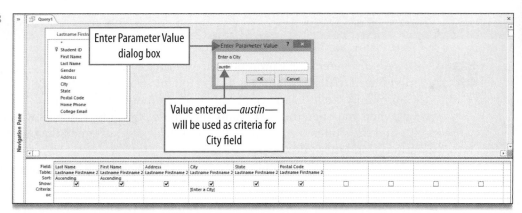

Enter Parameter Value dialog box

Value entered—*austin*—will be used as criteria for City field

---

ALERT! **Did the Enter Parameter Value Dialog Box Not Display?**

If the Enter Parameter Value dialog box does not display, you may have typed the parameter incorrectly in the design grid. Common errors include using parentheses or curly braces instead of brackets around the parameter text, which Access interprets as specific criteria, resulting in no records matching the criteria. If you type curly braces instead of brackets, the query will not run. To correct, display the query in Design view and correct the parameter entered in the Criteria row.

---

7 In the **Enter Parameter Value** dialog box, click **OK**.

Twenty-three students live in the city of Austin, and the records are sorted in alphabetical order by the Last Name field. If students have the same last name, those records will be sorted by the First Name field.

8 Save 🖫 the query as **Lastname Firstname 2B City Parameter Query** and then **Close** ☒ the query.

Recall that only the query design is saved; each time you open a query, it is run using the most up-to-date information from the data source.

9 Open ⏵⏵ the **Navigation Pane**. In the **Navigation Pane**, under your **2B Athletes** table, double-click your **2B City Parameter Query**. In the **Enter Parameter Value** dialog box, type **round rock** and then click **OK**. **Close** ⏴⏴ the **Navigation Pane**. Compare your screen with Figure 2.54.

Nine students live in the city of Round Rock. Every time you open a parameter query, you are prompted to enter criteria. You may have to apply Best Fit to the columns if all of the data in the fields does not display and you wish to print the query results—the length of the data in the fields changes as new records display depending upon the criteria entered.

FIGURE 2.54

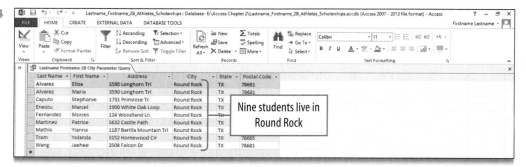

Nine students live in Round Rock

10 Display the query results in **Print Preview**, and change the orientation to **Landscape**. Create a paper or electronic printout as directed, click **Close Print Preview**, and then **Close** ☒ the query.

11 **Open** » the **Navigation Pane**, and, if necessary increase the width of the pane so that all object names display fully. On the right side of the title bar, click **Close** ✕ to close the database and to exit Access. As directed by your instructor, submit your database and the paper or electronic printouts of the 11 objects—relationship report and 10 queries—that are the results of this project. Specifically, in this project, using your own name, you created the following database and printouts or electronic printouts:

1. Lastname_Firstname_2B_Athletes_Scholarships	Database file
2. Lastname Firstname 2B Relationships	Relationships Report (printout or electronic printout)
3. Lastname Firstname 2B $300 or More Query	Query (printout or electronic printout)
4. Lastname Firstname 2B Awards May-June Query	Query (printout or electronic printout)
5. Lastname Firstname 2B Football AND Over $500 Query	Query (printout or electronic printout)
6. Lastname Firstname 2B Volleyball OR Golf AND Over $200 Query	Query (printout or electronic printout)
7. Lastname Firstname 2B Tennis OR Swimming Query	Query (printout or electronic printout)
8. Lastname Firstname 2B Wildcard Query	Query (printout or electronic printout)
9. Lastname Firstname 2B Alumni Donations Query	Query (printout or electronic printout)
10. Lastname Firstname 2B Total by Sport Query	Query (printout or electronic printout)
11. Lastname Firstname 2B Sport and Team Crosstab Query	Query (printout or electronic printout)
12. Lastname Firstname 2B City Parameter Query	Query (printout or electronic printout - Round Rock)

More **Knowledge**   **Parameter Query Prompts**

Be sure that the parameter you enter in the Criteria row as a prompt is not the same as the field name. For example, do not use *[City]* as the parameter. Access interprets this as the field name of *City*. Recall that you entered a field name in brackets when creating a calculated field in a query. If you use a field name as the parameter, the Enter Parameter Value dialog box *will not* display, and all of the records *will* display.

The parameter should inform the individual running the query of the data required to display the correct results. If you want to use the field name by itself as the prompt, type a question mark at the end of the text; for example, *[City?]*. You cannot use a period, exclamation mark (!), curly braces ({ }), another set of brackets ([ ]), or the ampersand (&) as part of the parameter.

END | You have completed Project 2B

GO! with Office Web Apps

Objective	Export an Access Query to a PDF File, Save the PDF File to Google Drive, and Share the File

Access web apps are designed to work with Microsoft's SharePoint, a service for setting up websites to share and manage documents. Your college may not have SharePoint installed, so you will use other tools to share objects from your database so that you can work collaboratively with others. Recall that Google Docs is Google's free, web-based word processor, spreadsheet, slide show, form, and data storage service. Google Drive is Google's free file storage and sharing service. For Access, you can export a database object to an Excel worksheet, a PDF file, or a text file, and then save the file to Google Drive.

ALERT! **Working with Web-Based Applications and Services**

Computer programs and services on the web receive continuous updates and improvements. Thus, the steps to complete this web-based activity may differ from the ones shown. You can often look at the screens and the information presented to determine how to complete the activity.

Activity | **Exporting an Access Query to a PDF File, Saving the PDF file to Google Drive, and Sharing the File**

In this activity, you will export your 2B Sport and Team Crosstab Query object to a PDF file, upload your PDF file to Google Drive, and then share the file.

1 **Start** Access, navigate to your **Access Chapter 2** folder, and then **Open** your **2B_Athletes_Scholarships** database file. If necessary, on the Message Bar, click **Enable Content**. In the **Navigation Pane**, click your **2B Sport and Team Crosstab Query** object to select it—do not open it.

2 On the ribbon, click the **EXTERNAL DATA tab**, and then in the **Export group**, click **PDF or XPS**. In the **Publish as PDF or XPS** dialog box, navigate to your

Access Chapter 2 folder. Click in the **File name** box. Using your own name, type **Lastname_Firstname_AC_2B_Web** and then be sure that the **Open file after publishing** check box is selected, and the **Minimum size (publishing online)** option button is selected. Click **Publish**, and then compare your screen with Figure A.

The PDF file is created and opens in Windows 8 Reader, Adobe Reader, or Adobe Acrobat, depending on the software that is installed on your computer.

FIGURE A

Your 2B Sport and Team Crosstab Query exported as a PDF file and opened in Adobe Reader (yours may open in Windows Reader 8 or Adobe Acrobat)

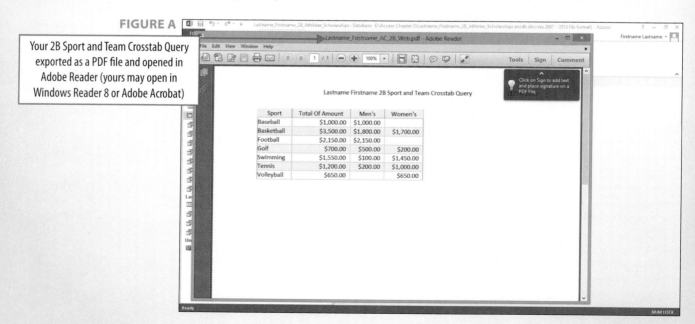

(GO! with Office Web Apps continues on the next page)

3 **Close** your **AC_2B_Web** file. In the **Export – PDF** dialog box, click **Close**, and then **Close** Access.

4 From the desktop, start Internet Explorer, navigate to **http://drive.google.com**, and sign in to your Google account, or create one.

5 Open your **GO! Web Projects** folder—or create and open this folder if necessary. Under **Drive**, to the right of **Create**, click **Upload** ⬆, and then click **Files**. In the **Choose File to Upload** dialog box, navigate to your **Access Chapter 2** folder, and then double-click your **AC_2B_Web** file to upload it to Google Drive. When the title bar of the message box indicates *Upload complete*, **Close** the message box.

6 Click your **AC_2B_Web** file to open the file in Google Drive. Notice that it displays as a PDF file on a separate tab in the browser window.

7 In the browser window, locate the tab for the PDF file, and then **Close** the tab to display your folder in Google Drive.

8 Right-click your **AC_2B_Web** file, point to **Share**, and then click **Share**.

9 In the **Sharing settings** dialog box, click in the **Add people** box, and then type your own email address that you use at your college. Click the **Can edit arrow**, and click **Can comment**. Click **Add message**, type **Please share your comments about the results of this**

crosstab query. and then compare your screen with Figure B.

10 On your keyboard, press the ⊞ key, type **snip** and then click **Snipping Tool**. In the **Snipping Tool** dialog box, click the **New arrow**, and then click **Full-screen snip**.

11 On the **Snipping Tool** toolbar, click **Save Snip** 💾. In the **Save As** dialog box, navigate to your **Access Chapter 2** folder. Click in the **File name** box, type **Lastname_Firstname_AC_2B_Web_Snip** and then be sure that the **Save as type** box displays **JPEG file**. Click **Save**, and then **Close** ✖ the **Snipping Tool** window.

12 In the **Sharing settings** dialog box, click **Share & save**. In the **Sharing settings** dialog box, click **Done**.

> You can change who has access to the file in the Sharing settings dialog box. By default, the file is private and is shared only with specific people you have designated. You can grant access to anyone on the web or to anyone who has the link to this file.

13 In Google Drive, click your Google Drive name, and then click **Sign out**. **Close** your browser window.

14 If directed to submit a paper printout of your pdf and snip file, follow the directions given in the Note. As directed by your instructor, submit your pdf file and your snip file that are the results of this project. Your instructor may also request that you submit a copy of the email that was sent to you notifying you of the shared file.

N O T E   **Printing Your PDF and Snip .jpeg File**

Use File Explorer to navigate to your Access Chapter 2 folder. Locate and double-click your AC_2B_Web file. On the toolbar, click the Print file button. Then Close the Windows 8 Reader, Adobe Reader, or Adobe Acrobat window. In your Access Chapter 2 folder, locate and double-click your AC_2B_Web_Snip file. If this is the first time you have tried to open a .jpeg file, you will be asked to identify a program. If you are not sure which program to use, select Windows Photo Viewer. From the ribbon, menu bar, or toolbar, click the Print command, and then Close the program window.

FIGURE B

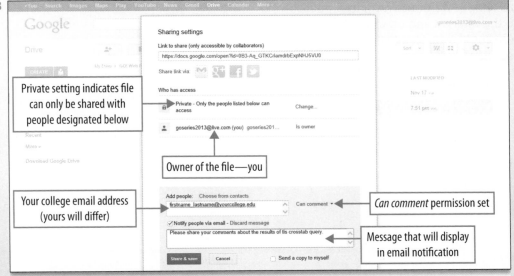

GO! with Microsoft Office 365

Andrew Rodriguez / Fotolia; FotolEdhar/ Fotolia; apops/ Fotolia; Yuri Arcurs/ Fotolia

Sharing Your Calendar in Office 365: With Office 365, you set up your Calendar in Outlook—either in Outlook Web App or on the desktop app—and then you can share your calendar, add appointments and meetings, and see your calendar from anywhere that you have Internet access. Recall that Outlook Web App and the Outlook desktop app work seamlessly together. When you use the desktop app, you have some additional features that are not available in Outlook Web App, but any information you add is available in either app. You will be able to view your calendar—and use email—from your smartphone or from anywhere you have an Internet connection.

In an Office 365 environment, the most important thing to do with your calendar is to share it with others. Recall that Office 365 is specifically designed to help teams work together, and the first step to working together successfully is to share as much information as possible to facilitate good communication.

When you create an appointment in your calendar, Outlook displays one of four indicators associated with your availability for that date and time: Busy, Free, Tentative, or Out of Office. This is referred to as your *free/busy information*. Outlook's default setting for all appointments is Busy. The free/busy indicators also display when others view your calendar on the Office 365 shared Exchange server. Recall that Exchange Server is Microsoft's system for sharing Outlook information among members on a network. Your free/busy schedule is shared automatically with all other users.

In an Exchange Online environment, you can share your calendar with other Exchange Online users in your organization. Additionally, you can publish your calendar to the Internet and other people so they can access it. You could even share your calendar with a customer or client.

Activity | Sharing Calendars

This group project relates to the **Bell Orchid Hotels**. If your instructor assigns this project to your class, you can expect to use your **Outlook Calendar** in **Office 365 Exchange Online** to set meeting times for the following tasks for this chapter:

- If you are in the **Accounting Group**, you and your teammates will set meeting times to sort, filter, and create queries for the Stockholders database you created in Chapter 1.

- If you are in the **Engineering Group**, you and your teammates will set meeting times to sort, filter, and create queries for the Subcontractors database you created in Chapter 1.

- If you are in the **Food and Beverage Group**, you and your teammates will set meeting times to sort, filter, and create queries for the Banquet Clients database you created in Chapter 1.

- If you are in the **Human Resources Group**, you and your teammates will set meeting times to sort, filter, and create queries for the Employee database you created in Chapter 1.

- If you are in the **Operations Group**, you and your teammates will set meeting times to sort, filter, and create queries for the Guests database you created in Chapter 1.

- If you are in the **Sales and Marketing Group**, you and your teammates will set meeting times to sort, filter, and create queries for the Associations database you created in Chapter 1.

FIGURE A

END OF CHAPTER

SUMMARY

Table relationships are created by joining the common fields in tables and provide a means for you to extract information from multiple tables when you create queries, forms, and reports.

Queries are created to answer questions and to extract information from your database tables; saving a query with your database saves you time when you need to answer the question many times.

Queries range from simple queries where you ask a single question to complex queries where you use compound criteria, wildcard characters, logical operators, and create calculated fields.

A crosstab query displays information grouped by two fields that is an easy way to display complex data, and a parameter query prompts you to enter the criteria when you open or run the query.

GO! LEARN IT ONLINE

Review the concepts and key terms in this chapter by completing these online challenges, which you can find at **www.pearsonhighered.com/go**.

Matching and Multiple Choice:
Answer matching and multiple choice questions to test what you learned in this chapter. MyITLab®

Crossword Puzzle:
Spell out the words that match the numbered clues, and put them in the puzzle squares.

Flipboard:
Flip through the definitions of the key terms in this chapter and match them with the correct term.

GO! FOR JOB SUCCESS

Video: Making Ethical Choices

Your instructor may assign this video to your class, and then ask you to think about, or discuss with your classmates, these questions:

FotolEdhar / Fotolia

Which behaviors in this video do you think were unethical?

Is it unethical to "borrow" things from your employer? Why? What would you do if you saw this behavior going on?

What do you think an employer could do to prevent unethical behavior?

END OF CHAPTER

REVIEW AND ASSESSMENT GUIDE FOR ACCESS CHAPTER 2

Your instructor may assign one or more of these projects to help you review the chapter and assess your mastery and understanding of the chapter.

	Review and Assessment Guide for Access Chapter 2		
Project	**Apply Skills from These Chapter Objectives**	**Project Type**	**Project Location**
2C	Objectives 1-7 from Project 2A	**2C Skills Review** A guided review of the skills from Project 2A.	On the following pages
2D	Objectives 8-15 from Project 2B	**2D Skills Review** A guided review of the skills from Project 2B.	On the following pages
2E	Objectives 1-7 from Project 2A	**2E Mastery (Grader Project)** A demonstration of your mastery of the skills in Project 2A with extensive decision making.	In MyITLab and on the following pages
2F	Objectives 8-15 from Project 2B	**2F Mastery (Grader Project)** A demonstration of your mastery of the skills in Project 2B with extensive decision making.	In MyITLab and on the following pages
2G	Objectives 1-15 from Projects 2A and 2B	**2G Mastery (Grader Project)** A demonstration of your mastery of the skills in Projects 2A and 2B with extensive decision making.	In MyITLab and on the following pages
2H	Combination of Objectives from Projects 2A and 2B	**2H GO! Fix It** A demonstration of your mastery of the skills in Projects 2A and 2B by creating a correct result from a document that contains errors you must find.	Online
2I	Combination of Objectives from Projects 2A and 2B	**2I GO! Make It** A demonstration of your mastery of the skills in Projects 2A and 2B by creating a result from a supplied picture.	Online
2J	Combination of Objectives from Projects 2A and 2B	**2J GO! Solve It** A demonstration of your mastery of the skills in Projects 2A and 2B, your decision-making skills, and your critical thinking skills. A task-specific rubric helps you self-assess your result.	Online
2K	Combination of Objectives from Projects 2A and 2B	**2K GO! Solve It** A demonstration of your mastery of the skills in Projects 2A and 2B, your decision-making skills, and your critical thinking skills. A task-specific rubric helps you self-assess your result.	On the following pages
2L	Combination of Objectives from Projects 2A and 2B	**2L GO! Think** A demonstration of your understanding of the chapter concepts applied in a manner that you would outside of college. An analytic rubric helps you and your instructor grade the quality of your work by comparing it to the work an expert in the discipline would create.	On the following pages
2M	Combination of Objectives from Projects 2A and 2B	**2M GO! Think** A demonstration of your understanding of the chapter concepts applied in a manner that you would outside of college. An analytic rubric helps you and your instructor grade the quality of your work by comparing it to the work an expert in the discipline would create.	Online
2N	Combination of Objectives from Projects 2A and 2B	**2N You and GO!** A demonstration of your understanding of the chapter concepts applied in a manner that you would in a personal situation. An analytic rubric helps you and your instructor grade the quality of your work.	Online
2O	Combination of Objectives from Projects 2A and 2B	**2O Cumulative Group Project for Access Chapter 2** A demonstration of your understanding of concepts and your ability to work collaboratively in a group role-playing assessment, requiring both collaboration and self-management.	Online

GLOSSARY

GLOSSARY OF CHAPTER KEY TERMS

Aggregate functions Calculations such as Min, Max, Avg, and Sum that are performed on a group of records.

AND condition A compound criteria used to display records that match all parts of the specified criteria.

Ascending order A sorting order that arranges text alphabetically (A to Z) and numbers from the lowest number to the highest number.

Between … And operator A comparison operator that looks for values within a range.

Calculated field A field that stores the value of a mathematical operation.

Cascade Delete Related Records A cascade option that enables you to delete a record in a table on the *one* side of the relationship and also delete all of the related records in related tables.

Cascade options Relationship options that enable you to update records in related tables when referential integrity is enforced.

Cascade Update Related Fields A cascade option that enables you to change the data in the primary key field in the table on the *one* side of the relationship and update that change to any fields storing that same data in related tables.

Comparison operators Symbols that are used to evaluate data in the field to determine if it is the same (=), greater than (>), less than (<), or in between a range of values as specified by the criteria.

Compound criteria Multiple conditions in a query or filter.

Criteria Conditions in a query that identify the specific records you are looking for.

Crosstab query A query that uses an aggregate function for data that can be grouped by two types of information and displays the data in a compact, spreadsheet-like format with column headings and row headings.

Data source The table or tables from which a form, query, or report retrieves its data.

Descending order A sorting order that arranges text in reverse alphabetical order (Z to A) and numbers from the highest number to the lowest number.

Design grid The lower area of the query window that displays the design of the query.

Expression A formula.

Field list A list of field names in a table.

Foreign key The field that is included in the related table so the field can be joined with the primary key in another table for the purpose of creating a relationship.

Free/Busy information In the Outlook calendar, one of four indicators—Busy, Free, Tentative, or Out of Office— associated with your availability for a specific date and time.

Innermost sort field When sorting on multiple fields in Datasheet view, the field that is used for the second level of sorting.

Is Not Null A criteria that searches for fields that are not empty.

Is Null A criteria that searches for fields that are empty.

Join line In the Relationships window, the line joining two tables that visually indicates the common fields and the type of relationship.

Logical operators Operators that are used to evaluate data to determine if a condition is met (true) or not met (false). With two criteria, AND requires that both conditions be met and OR requires that either condition be met for a record to display in the query results.

Message Bar The area directly below the ribbon that displays information such as security alerts when there is potentially unsafe, active content in an Office document that you open.

One-to-many relationship A relationship between two tables where one record in the first table corresponds to many records in the second table—the most common type of relationship in Access.

OR condition A compound criteria used to display records that match at least one of the specified criteria.

Outermost sort field When sorting on multiple fields in Datasheet view, the field that is used for the first level of sorting.

Parameter A value that can be changed.

Parameter query A query that prompts you for criteria before running the query.

Referential integrity A set of rules that Access uses to ensure that the data between related tables is valid.

Relationship An association that you establish between two tables based on common fields.

Run The process in which Access looks at the records in the table(s) included in the query design, finds the records that match the specified criteria, and then displays the records in a datasheet; only the fields included in the query design display.

Sorting The process of arranging data in a specific order based on the value in a field.

Subdatasheet A format for displaying related records when you click ⊞ next to a record in a table on the *one* side of the relationship.

Subset A portion of the total records available.

Table area The upper area of the query window that displays field lists for the tables that are used in a query.

Text string A sequence of characters.

Trust Center An area of Access where you can view the security and privacy settings for your Access installation.

Wildcard character In a query, a character that serves as a placeholder for one or more unknown characters in criteria; an asterisk (*) represents one or more unknown characters, and a question mark (?) represents a single unknown character.

Skills Review Project 2C Freshman Orientation

In the following Skills Review, you will assist Dr. Wendy Bowie, the director of counseling at the Southwest Campus, in using her database to answer several questions about the freshman orientation sessions that will be held prior to class registration. Your completed database objects will look similar to Figure 2.55.

PROJECT FILES

For Project 2C, you will need the following file:

a02C_Freshman_Orientation

You will save your database as:

Lastname_Firstname_2C_Freshman_Orientation

PROJECT RESULTS

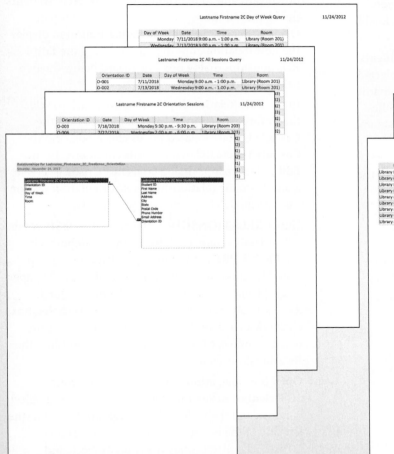
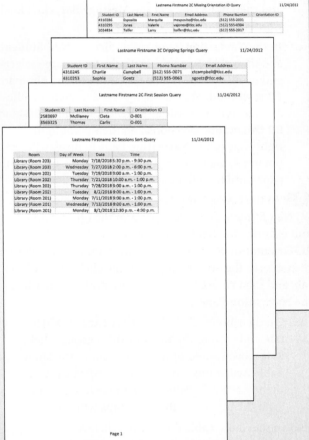

FIGURE 2.55

(Project 2C Freshman Orientation continues on the next page)

CHAPTER REVIEW

1 **Start** Access. In the Access opening screen, click **Open Other Files**. Under **Open**, click **Computer**. Under **Recent Folders**, if displayed, click the location where your student data files are stored; otherwise, click **Browse** and then navigate to the location where your student data files are stored. Double-click **a02C_Freshman_Orientation** to open the database.

   a. On the ribbon, click the **FILE tab**, and then click **Save As**. Under **File Types**, be sure **Save Database As** is selected. On the right, under **Database File Types**, be sure **Access Database** is selected, and then click **Save As**.

   b. In the **Save As** dialog box, navigate to your **Access Chapter 2** folder. Click in the **File name** box, type **Lastname_Firstname_2C_Freshman_Orientation** and then press Enter. On the **Message Bar**, click **Enable Content**.

   c. In the **Navigation Pane**, right-click **2C New Students**, and then click **Rename**. With the table name selected and using your own name, type **Lastname Firstname 2C New Students** and then press Enter. **Rename** the **2C Orientation Sessions** table to **Lastname Firstname 2C Orientation Sessions** and then point to the right edge of the **Navigation Pane** to display the pointer. Drag to the right to increase the width of the pane until both tables names display fully.

2 In the **Navigation Pane**, double-click your **2C New Students** table to open it in the object window, and examine the fields in the table. Double-click your **2C Orientation Sessions** table, and examine the fields in the table. In the object window, right-click either **object tab**, and then click **Close All** to close both tables. **Close** the **Navigation Pane**.

   a. On the ribbon, click the **DATABASE TOOLS tab**, and then in the **Relationships group**, click **Relationships**. Point to the title bar of the **Show Table** dialog box, and then drag downward and slightly to the right to move the dialog box away from the top of the **Relationships** window.

   b. In the **Show Table** dialog box, click your **2C Orientation Sessions** table, and then click **Add**. In the **Show Table** dialog box, double-click your **2C New Students** table to add it to the **Relationships** window. In the **Show Table** dialog box, click **Close**.

   c. In the **2C New Students** field list—the field list on the right—point to the title bar to display the pointer, and then drag the field list to the right until there are approximately three inches of space between the field lists. In the **2C New Students** field list, point to the lower right corner of the field list to display the pointer, and then drag downward and to the right to resize the field list and display all of the field names and the entire table name. Use the same technique to resize the **2C Orientation Sessions** field list—the field list on the left—so that the table name displays fully.

   d. In the **2C Orientation Sessions** field list, point to **Orientation ID**, and then drag the field name downward and to the right into the **2C New Students** field list until the pointer's arrow is on top of **Orientation ID**. Release the mouse button to display the **Edit Relationships** dialog box. Drag the **Edit Relationships** dialog box downward below the two field lists.

   e. In the **Edit Relationships** dialog box, click to select the **Enforce Referential Integrity** check box, the **Cascade Update Related Fields** check box, and the **Cascade Delete Related Records** check box. In the **Edit Relationships** dialog box, click **Create** to create a one-to-many relationship—*one* orientation session can be scheduled for *many* new students.

   f. Under **RELATIONSHIP TOOLS**, on the **DESIGN tab**, in the **Tools group**, click **Relationship Report**. On the **PRINT PREVIEW tab**, in the **Page Size group**, click **Margins**, and then click **Normal**. Create a paper or electronic printout as directed. On the **Quick Access Toolbar**, click **Save**. In the **Save As** dialog box, click **OK** to accept the default report name. In the object window, **Close** the report, and then **Close** the **Relationships** window.

   g. **Open** the Navigation Pane, double-click your **2C Orientation Sessions** table to open it in the object window, and then **Close** the **Navigation Pane**. On the left side of the last record—*Orientation ID* of *O-1*—click to display the subdatasheet, and notice that 13 new students are scheduled to attend this orientation session. Click to collapse the subdatasheet.

(Project 2C Freshman Orientation continues on the next page)

h. In the last record, in the **Orientation ID** field, select the existing data—*O-1*—and then type **O-001**—the first character is the letter *O* followed by a hyphen, two zeros, and the number *1*— to make the data consistent with the Orientation IDs of the other sessions. The 13 related records in your 2C New Students table are updated with the new Orientation ID because you selected **Cascade Update Related Fields** in the **Edit Relationships** dialog box.

i. Display the subdatasheet for the record with an **Orientation ID** of **O-010**, and notice that one student—*Student ID* of *8273485*—is scheduled for this orientation session. Collapse the subdatasheet. To the left of the record, point to the record selector box to display the → pointer, and then click to select the record. On the **HOME tab**, in the **Records group**, click **Delete**. In the message box, click **Yes** to delete this record and the related student record in the **2C New Students** table.

3 In the **Date** field, click in any record. On the **HOME tab**, in the **Sort & Filter group**, click **Ascending** to sort the records by the date. In the field names row, click the **Room arrow**, and then click **Sort Z to A** to sort the rooms from Room 203 to Room 201. The records are sorted first by the **Room** field and then by the **Date** field. On the **FILE tab**, click **Print**, and then click **Print Preview**. Create a paper or electronic printout as directed, and then click **Close Print Preview**. On the **HOME tab**, in the **Sort & Filter group**, click **Remove Sort**. **Close** the table, and in the message box, click **No**; you do not need to save any design changes to the table.

4 On the ribbon, click the **CREATE tab**, and then in the **Queries group**, click **Query Design**. In the **Show Table** dialog box, double-click your **2C Orientation Sessions** table, and then **Close** the **Show Table** dialog box. Point to the lower right corner of the field list to display the pointer, and then drag downward and to the right to resize the field list, displaying all of the field names and the entire table name.

a. In the field list, double-click **Orientation ID** to add the field to the first column in the design grid. In the field list, point to **Date**, and then drag the field name down into the design grid until the pointer displays in the **Field** row in the second

column, and then release the mouse button. In the design grid, in the **Field** row, click in the third column, click the **arrow**, and then click **Day of Week** to add the field to the design grid. Using one of the three techniques you just practiced, add the **Time** field to the fourth column and the **Room** field to the fifth column in the design grid.

b. Under **QUERY TOOLS**, on the **DESIGN tab**, in the **Results group**, click **Run**. This query answers the question, *What is the Orientation ID, date, day of week, time, and room for all of the orientation sessions in the 2C Orientation Sessions table?*

c. On the **Quick Access Toolbar**, click **Save**. In the **Save As** dialog box, type **Lastname Firstname 2C All Sessions Query** and then click **OK**. On the ribbon, click the **FILE tab**, click **Print**, and then click **Print Preview**. Create a paper or electronic printout as directed, and then click **Close Print Preview**. **Close** your **2C All Sessions Query**, and then **Open** the **Navigation Pane**.

5 In the **Navigation Pane**, right-click your **2C All Sessions Query** object, and then click **Copy**. In the **Navigation Pane**, point to a blank area, right-click, and then click **Paste**. In the **Paste As** dialog box, type **Lastname Firstname 2C Day of Week Query** and then click **OK** to create a new query based on an existing query.

a. In the **Navigation Pane**, right click your **2C Day of Week Query** object, and then click **Design View**. **Close** the **Navigation Pane**. In the design grid, point to the thin gray selection bar above the **Orientation ID** field name to display the ↓ pointer, click to select the column, and then press Del.

b. Point to the selection bar above the **Day of Week** field name to display the pointer, and then drag to the left until a dark vertical line displays on the left side of the **Date** column. Release the mouse button to position the **Day of Week** field in the first column.

c. **Run** the query. The query results display four fields. This query answers the question, *What is the day of week, date, time, and room for every orientation session in the 2C Orientation Sessions table?*

(Project 2C Freshman Orientation continues on the next page)

CHAPTER REVIEW

d. On the **FILE tab**, click **Print**, and then click **Print Preview**. Create a paper or electronic printout as directed, and then click **Close Print Preview**. **Close** the query, and in the message box, click **Yes** to save the changes to the design—you deleted one field and moved another field. **Open** the **Navigation Pane**.

6 In the **Navigation Pane**, right-click your **2C Day of Week Query** object, and then click **Copy**. In the **Navigation Pane**, point to a blank area, right-click, and then click **Paste**. In the **Paste As** dialog box, type **Lastname Firstname 2C Sessions Sort Query** and then click **OK** to create a new query based on an existing query. Increase the width of the **Navigation Pane** so that the names of all of the objects display fully.

a. In the **Navigation Pane**, right-click your **2C Sessions Sort Query** click **Design View**, and then **Close** the **Navigation Pane**. In the design grid, drag the **Room** field to the left of the **Day of Week** field to position it in the first column. In the design grid, click in the **Sort** row under **Room**, click the **arrow**, and then click **Descending**. Click in the **Sort** row under **Date**, click the **arrow**, and then click **Ascending**.

b. **Run** the query. This query answers the question, *For every session, within each room (with the Room field sorted in descending order), what is the day of week, date (with the Date field sorted in ascending order), and time?*

c. Display the query results in **Print Preview**, create a paper or electronic printout as directed, and then click **Close Print Preview**. **Close** the query, and in the message box, click **Yes** to save the changes to the query design.

7 On the ribbon, click the **CREATE tab**, and then in the **Queries group**, click **Query Design**. In the **Show Table** dialog box, double-click your **2C New Students** table to add it to the table area, and then **Close** the **Show Table** dialog box. Resize the field list to display all of the field names and the entire table name. Add the following fields to the design grid in the order given: **Student ID**, **Last Name**, **First Name**, and **Orientation ID**.

a. In the design grid, click in the **Criteria** row under **Orientation ID**, type **O-001**—the first character is the letter *O* followed by a hyphen, two zeros, and the number *1*—and then press Enter.

b. **Run** the query to display 13 records that meet the specified criteria—records that have *O-001* in the *Orientation ID* field. **Save** the query as **Lastname Firstname 2C First Session Query** and then display the query results in **Print Preview**. Create a paper or electronic printout as directed, click **Close Print Preview**, and then **Close** the query.

c. On the ribbon, click the **CREATE tab**, and then in the **Queries group**, click **Query Design**. In the **Show Table** dialog box, double-click your **2C New Students** table to add it to the table area, and then **Close** the **Show Table** dialog box. Resize the field list, and then add the following fields to the design grid in the order given: **Student ID**, **First Name**, **Last Name**, **Phone Number**, **Email Address**, and **City**. Click in the **Criteria** row under **City**, type **dripping springs** and then press Enter.

d. **Run** the query to display the five new students who live in *Dripping Springs*. Switch to **Design** view. In the design grid, in the **Show** row under **City**, click to clear the check box. Recall that if all of the results use the same criteria, such as *dripping springs*, it is not necessary to display that field in the query results. **Run** the query again. **Save** the query as **Lastname Firstname 2C Dripping Springs Query** and then display the query results in **Print Preview**. Create a paper or electronic printout as directed, click **Close Print Preview**, and then **Close** the query.

e. On the ribbon, click the **CREATE tab**, and then in the **Queries group**, click **Query Design**. In the **Show Table** dialog box, double-click your **2C New Students** table to add it to the table area, and then **Close** the **Show Table** dialog box. Resize the field list, and then add the following fields to the design grid in the order given: **Student ID**, **Last Name**, **First Name**, **Email Address**, **Phone Number**, and **Orientation ID**. Click in the **Sort** row under **Last Name**, click the **arrow**, and then click **Ascending**. Click in the **Sort** row under **First Name**, click the **arrow**, and then click **Ascending**. Click in the **Criteria** row under **Orientation ID**, type **is null** and then press Enter.

(Project 2C Freshman Orientation continues on the next page)

CHAPTER REVIEW

f. **Run** the query to display the three new students who have not signed up for an orientation session. **Save** the query as **Lastname Firstname 2C Missing Orientation ID Query** and then display the query results in **Print Preview**. On the **PRINT PREVIEW** tab, in the **Page Size group**, click **Margins**, and then click **Normal**. Create a paper or electronic printout as directed, click **Close Print Preview**, and then **Close** the query.

g. **Open** the **Navigation Pane**. If necessary, increase the width of the pane so that all object names display fully. On the right side of the title bar, click **Close** to close the database and to exit Access. As directed by your instructor, submit your database and the paper or electronic printouts of the eight objects—relationship report, sorted table, and six queries—that are the results of this project. Specifically, in this project, using your own name, you created the following database and printouts or electronic printouts:

1. Lastname_Firstname_2C_Freshman_Orientation	Database file
2. Relationships for Lastname_Firstname_2C_Freshman_Orientation	Relationships Report (printout or electronic printout)
3. Lastname Firstname 2C Orientation Sessions table sorted (not saved)	Table sorted (printout or electronic printout)
4. Lastname Firstname 2C All Sessions Query	Query (printout or electronic printout)
5. Lastname Firstname 2C Day of Week Query	Query (printout or electronic printout)
6. Lastname Firstname 2C Sessions Sort Query	Query (printout or electronic printout)
7. Lastname Firstname 2C First Session Query	Query (printout or electronic printout)
8. Lastname Firstname 2C Dripping Springs Query	Query (printout or electronic printout)
9. Lastname Firstname 2C Missing Orientation ID Query	Query (printout or electronic printout)

END | You have completed Project 2C

CHAPTER REVIEW

Apply 2B skills from these Objectives:

8 Specify Numeric Criteria in a Query

9 Use Compound Criteria in a Query

10 Create a Query Based on More Than One Table

11 Use Wildcards in a Query

12 Create Calculated Fields in a Query

13 Calculate Statistics and Group Data in a Query

14 Create a Crosstab Query

15 Create a Parameter Query

Skills Review | Project 2D Club Fundraisers

In the following Skills Review, you will assist Dr. Michael Bransford, the student activities director for Texas Lakes Community College, in answering his questions about fundraisers, clubs, donations, dates of fundraiser events, and fundraiser locations. Your completed database objects will look similar to Figure 2.56.

PROJECT FILES

For Project 2D, you will need the following files:

a02D_Club_Fundraisers

a02D_Clubs (Excel workbook)

You will save your database as:

Lastname_Firstname_2D_Club_Fundraisers

PROJECT RESULTS

FIGURE 2.56

(Project 2D Club Fundraisers continues on the next page)

CHAPTER REVIEW

1 ▶ **Start** Access. In the Access opening screen, click **Open Other Files**. Under **Open**, click **Computer**. Under **Recent Folders**, if displayed, click the location where your student data files are stored; otherwise, click **Browse** and then navigate to the location where your student data files are stored. Double-click **a02D_Club_Fundraisers** to open the database.

a. On the ribbon, click the **FILE tab**, and then click **Save As**. Under **File Types**, be sure **Save Database As** is selected. On the right, under **Database File Types**, be sure **Access Database** is selected, and then at the bottom of the screen, click **Save As**. In the **Save As** dialog box, navigate to your **Access Chapter 2** folder. Click in the **File name** box, type **Lastname_Firstname_2D_Club_Fundraisers** and then press [Enter]. On the **Message Bar**, click **Enable Content**.

b. In the **Navigation Pane**, right-click **2D Fundraisers**, click **Rename**, type **Lastname Firstname 2D Fundraisers** and then press [Enter]. Increase the width of the **Navigation Pane** to display the entire table name. Double-click the table name to open it, examine the fields in the table, and then **Close** the table.

c. On the ribbon, click the **EXTERNAL DATA tab**, and then in the **Import & Link group**, click **Excel**. In the **Get External Data – Excel Spreadsheet** dialog box, to the right of the **File name** box, click **Browse**. In the **File Open** dialog box, navigate to your student data files, and then double-click **a02D_Clubs**. Be sure that the **Import the source data into a new table in the current database** option button is selected, and then click **OK**.

d. In the upper left area of the wizard, select the **First Row Contains Column Headings** check box, click **Next**, and then click **Next** again. In the wizard, click the **Choose my own primary key** option button, be sure that **Club ID** displays, and click **Next**. With the text selected in the **Import to Table** box and using your own name, type **Lastname Firstname 2D Clubs**, and then click **Finish**. In the **Get External Data – Excel Spreadsheet** dialog box, click **Close**.

e. In the **Navigation Pane**, right-click your **2D Clubs** table, and then click **Design View**. **Close** the **Navigation Pane**. In the **Field Name** column, click

Club ID. In the **Field Properties** area, click **Field Size**, type **8** and then press [Enter]. Under **TABLE TOOLS**, on the **DESIGN tab**, in the **Views group**, click the upper portion of the **View** button to switch to **Datasheet** view. In the message box, click **Yes** to save the design changes. In the second message box, click **Yes**—no data will be lost. Examine the fields and data in the table. To the left of the **Club ID** field name, click **Select All**. On the **HOME tab**, in the **Records group**, click **More**, and then click **Field Width**. In the **Column Width** dialog box, click **Best Fit**. **Save** the table, click in any record to cancel the selection, and then **Close** the table.

f. On the ribbon, click the **DATABASE TOOLS tab**, and then in the **Relationships group**, click **Relationships**. In the **Show Table** dialog box, double-click your **2D Clubs** table, and then double-click your **2D Fundraisers** table to add both tables to the **Relationships** window. **Close** the **Show Table** dialog box. Point to the title bar of the field list on the right, and drag the field list to the right until there are approximately two inches of space between the field lists. By dragging the lower right corner of the field list, resize each field list to display all of the field names and the entire table name.

g. In the **2D Clubs** field list, point to **Club ID**, drag the field name into the **2D Fundraisers** table on top of **Club ID**, and then release the mouse button. Point to the title bar of the **Edit Relationships** dialog box, and then drag it downward below the two field lists. In the **Edit Relationships** dialog box, select the **Enforce Referential Integrity** check box, the **Cascade Update Related Fields** check box, the **Cascade Delete Related Records** check box, and then click **Create**. A *one-to-many* relationship is established; *one* student club can raise money for *many* fundraising events.

h. Under **RELATIONSHIP TOOLS**, on the **DESIGN tab**, in the **Tools group**, click **Relationship Report**. On the **PRINT PREVIEW tab**, in the **Page Size group**, click **Margins**, and then click **Normal**. **Save** the report as **Lastname Firstname 2D Relationships** and then create a paper or electronic printout as directed. In the object window, right-click either **object tab**, and then click **Close All**.

(Project 2D Club Fundraisers continues on the next page)

CHAPTER REVIEW

2 On the ribbon, click the **CREATE tab**. In the **Queries group**, click **Query Design**. In the **Show Table** dialog box, double-click your **2D Fundraisers** table to add it to the table area, and then **Close** the **Show Table** dialog box. Resize the field list. Add the following fields to the design grid in the order given: **Fundraiser Name**, **Donation**, and **Fundraiser Location**.

a. Click in the **Sort** row under **Fundraiser Name**, click the **arrow**, and then click **Ascending**. Click in the **Criteria** row under **Donation**, type **>=1000** and then press Enter. **Run** the query, and notice that seven records match the criteria. This query answers the question, *Where was each fundraiser held (in alphabetical order by the Fundraiser Name field) for fundraisers with a donation greater than or equal to $1,000?*

b. **Save** the query as **Lastname Firstname 2D $1000 or More Donation Query** and then display the query results in **Print Preview**. Create a paper or electronic printout as directed, click **Close Print preview**, and then **Close** your query object. **Open** the **Navigation Pane**.

c. In the **Navigation Pane**, right-click your **2D $1000 or More Donation Query** object, and then click **Copy**. In the **Navigation Pane**, point to a blank area, right-click, and then click **Paste**. In the **Paste As** dialog box, type **Lastname Firstname 2D Fundraisers June-July Query** and then click **OK**. In the **Navigation Pane**, right-click your **2D Fundraisers June-July Query** object, and then click **Design View**. **Close** the **Navigation Pane**.

d. In the **2D Fundraisers** field list, double-click **Date** to add it to the fourth column in the design grid. Click in the **Sort** row under **Fundraiser Name**, click the **arrow**, and then click (**not sorted**). Click in the **Sort** row under **Date**, click the **arrow**, and then click **Ascending**.

e. In the **Criteria** row under **Donation**, select the existing criteria of *>=1000*, and then press Del so that the query results are not restricted by a monetary value. Click in the **Criteria** row under **Date**, type **between 6/1/18 and 7/31/18** and then press Enter. **Run** the query, and notice that four records match the criteria. This query answers the question, *What is the fundraiser name, donation, fundraiser location, and date (in chronological order) for events held between June 1, 2018 and July 31, 2018?*

f. Display the query results in **Print Preview**, create a paper or electronic printout as directed, and then click **Close Print Preview**. **Close** the query, and in the message box, click **Yes** to save the changes to the query design.

3 On the ribbon, click the **CREATE tab**, and in the **Queries group**, click **Query Design**. In the **Show Table** dialog box, double-click your **2D Fundraisers** table to add it to the table area, and then **Close** the **Show Table** dialog box. Resize the field list. Add the following fields to the design grid in the order given: **Fundraiser Name**, **Fundraiser Location**, **Donation**, and **Club ID**.

a. Click in the **Sort** row under **Fundraiser Name**, click the **arrow**, and then click **Ascending**. Click in the **Criteria** row under **Club ID**, type **club-109** and then press Enter. Click in the **Criteria** row under **Donation**, type **<=1000** and then press Enter. **Run** the query, and notice that two records match the criteria. Switch back to **Design** view, and in the **Show** row under **Club ID**, clear the check box. **Run** the query again. This query answers the question, *Which fundraiser events with their locations listed had donations raised by CLUB-109 of $1,000 or less?*

b. **Save** the query as **Lastname Firstname 2D CLUB-109 Low Donations Query** and then display the query results in **Print Preview**. Create a paper or electronic printout as directed, click **Close Print Preview**, and then **Close** the query.

c. On the ribbon, click the **CREATE tab**, and then in the **Queries group**, click **Query Design**. In the **Show Table** dialog box, double-click your **2D Fundraisers** table to add it to the table area, and then **Close** the **Show Table** dialog box. Resize the field list. Add the following fields to the design grid in the order given: **Club ID**, **Fundraiser Name**, **Date**, and **Donation**.

d. Click in the **Sort** row under **Date**, click the **arrow**, and then click **Ascending**. Click in the **Criteria** row under **Club ID**, type **club-107 or club-115** and then press Enter. Click in the **Criteria** row under **Donation**, type **>1000** and then press Enter. **Run** the query, and notice that two records match the criteria. This query answers the questions, *Which fundraiser events received donations over $1,000 from either CLUB-107 or CLUB-115, and on what dates (in chronological order) were the fundraiser events held?*

(Project 2D Club Fundraisers continues on the next page)

CHAPTER REVIEW

e. **Save** the query as **Lastname Firstname 2D CLUB 107 OR 115 Over $1000 Query** and then display the query results in **Print Preview**. Create a paper or electronic printout as directed, click **Close Print Preview**, and then **Close** the query.

4 ▶ On the ribbon, click the **CREATE tab**, and then in the **Queries group**, click **Query Design**. In the **Show Table** dialog box, double-click your **2D Clubs** table, and then double-click your **2D Fundraisers** table to add both tables to the table area. **Close** the **Show Table** dialog box. Drag the field list on the right side to the right until there are approximately two inches of space between the field lists, and then resize each field list.

a. From the **2D Clubs** field list, add the following fields to the design grid in the order given: **Club Name**, **Campus**, and **Club Email**. From the **2D Fundraisers** field list, add the following fields to the design grid in the order given: **Fundraiser Name**, **Date**, and **Donation**. In the design grid, drag the **Donation** field to the left to position it as the first column.

b. Click in the **Sort** row under **Donation**, click the **arrow**, and then click **Descending**. Click in the **Criteria** row under **Campus**, type **southeast** and then press Enter. Click in the **or** row under **Campus**, type **northeast** and then press Enter. **Run** the query, and notice that 10 records match the criteria. This query answers the question, *For the Southeast and Northeast campuses, what is the donation (in descending order), club name, campus name, club email address, fundraiser name, and date of all fundraising events?*

c. **Save** the query as **Lastname Firstname 2D SE OR NE Donations Query** and then display the query results in **Print Preview**. On the **PRINT PREVIEW tab**, in the **Page Layout group**, click **Landscape**. In the **Page Size group**, click **Margins**, and then click **Normal**. Create a paper or electronic printout as directed, click **Close Print Preview**, and then **Close** the query.

5 ▶ On the ribbon, click the **CREATE tab**, and then in the **Queries group**, click **Query Design**. In the **Show Table** dialog box, double-click your **2D Clubs** table, and then double-click your **2D Fundraisers** table to add both tables to the table area. **Close** the **Show Table** dialog box. Drag the field list on the right side to the right until there are approximately two inches of space between the field lists, and then resize each field list. From the **2D Clubs** field

list, add the **Club Name** field to the design grid. From the **2D Fundraisers** field list, add the **Fundraiser Name** field to the design grid.

a. Click in the **Sort** row under **Club Name**, click the **arrow**, and then click **Ascending**. Click in the **Criteria** row under **Club Name**, type **phi*** and then press Enter. In the **Criteria** row under **Fundraiser Name**, type ***walk*** and then press Enter. **Run** the query, and notice that two records match the criteria—Club Name begins with *Phi* and Fundraiser Name has *Walk* anywhere in its name. This query answers the question, *Which clubs (in alphabetical order) that have names starting with Phi have raised money for fundraisers that involve walking?*

b. **Save** the query as **Lastname Firstname 2D Phi Walk Query** and then display the query results in **Print Preview**. Create a paper or electronic printout as directed, click **Close Print Preview**, and then **Close** the query.

6 ▶ On the ribbon, click the **CREATE tab**, and then in the **Queries group**, click **Query Design**. In the **Show Table** dialog box, double-click your **2D Clubs** table, and then double-click your **2D Fundraisers** table to add both tables to the table area. **Close** the **Show Table** dialog box. Drag the field list on the right side to the right until there are approximately two inches of space between the field lists, and then resize each field list. From the field lists, add the following fields to the design grid in the order given: **Fundraiser ID**, **Club Name**, and **Donation**.

a. Click in the **Sort** row under **Fundraiser ID**, click the **arrow**, and then click **Ascending**. Alumni will donate an additional 25 percent based on the value in the **Donation** field. In the **Field** row, right-click in the fourth column, and then click **Zoom**. In the **Zoom** dialog box, type **Alumni Donation:[Donation]*0.25** and then click **OK**. **Run** the query to be sure the new field—*Alumni Donation*—displays. In the first record, the *Alumni Donation* displays as *156.25*.

b. Switch to **Design** view. In the **Field** row, right-click in the first empty column, and then click **Zoom**. In the **Zoom** dialog box, type **Total Donation:[Donation]+[Alumni Donation]** and then click **OK**. **Run** the query to be sure that the new field—*Total Donation*—displays. In the first record, the *Total Donation* displays as *$781.25*.

(Project 2D Club Fundraisers continues on the next page)

CHAPTER REVIEW

c. Switch to **Design** view. In the **Field** row, click in the **Alumni Donation** field name box. Under **QUERY TOOLS**, on the **DESIGN tab**, in the **Show/Hide group**, click **Property Sheet**. In the **Property Sheet**, click **Format**. In the property setting box, click the **arrow**, and then click **Currency**. In the **Property Sheet**, click **Decimal Places**. In the property setting box, click the **arrow**, and then click **2**. **Close** the **Property Sheet**, and then **Run** the query. This query answers the question, *In ascending order by Fundraiser ID, what is the club name, donation, alumni donation, and total donation for each fundraising event if the alumni donate an additional 25 percent based on the value in the Donation field?*

d. To the left of the **Fundraiser ID** field name, click **Select All**. On the **HOME tab**, in the **Records group**, click **More**, and then click **Field Width**. In the **Column Width** dialog box, click **Best Fit**. **Save** the query as **Lastname Firstname 2D Alumni Donation Query** and then click in any field to cancel the selection. Display the query results in **Print Preview**. On the **PRINT PREVIEW tab**, in the **Page Layout group**, click **Landscape**. Create a paper or electronic printout as directed, click **Close Print Preview**, and then **Close** the query.

7 On the ribbon, click the **CREATE tab**, and then in the **Queries group**, click **Query Design**. In the **Show Table** dialog box, double-click your **2D Fundraisers** table to add the table to the table area. **Close** the **Show Table** dialog box. Resize the field list, and then add the **Donation** field to the design grid.

a. Under **QUERY TOOLS**, on the **DESIGN tab**, in the **Show/Hide group**, click **Totals** to add a **Total** row as the third row in the design grid. In the **Total** row under **Donation**, click in the box that displays *Group By*, click the **arrow**, and then click **Sum**. In the **Show/Hide group**, click **Property Sheet**. In the **Property Sheet**, set **Decimal Places** to **0**, and then **Close** the **Property Sheet**. **Run** the query. Point to the right edge of the first column to display the ⊕ pointer, and then double-click to apply Best Fit to the field. The sum of the Donation fields is *$20,259.*

b. Switch to **Design** view. From the field list, drag the **Club ID** field to the first column in the design grid—the **Donation** field moves to the second column. **Run** the query. This query answers the question, *For each club ID, what are the total donations?*

c. **Save** the query as **Lastname Firstname 2D Total Donations by Club Query** and then display the query results in **Print Preview**. Create a paper or electronic printout as directed, click **Close Print Preview**, and then **Close** the query.

8 On the ribbon, click the **CREATE tab**, and then in the **Queries group**, click **Query Wizard**. In the **New Query** dialog box, click **Crosstab Query Wizard**, and then click **OK**. In the **Crosstab Query Wizard**, click your **Table: 2D Fundraisers**, and then click **Next**. In the wizard under **Available Fields**, double-click **Fundraiser ID** to group the records by this field and display the Fundraiser IDs as row headings. Click **Next**.

a. In the wizard, in the field list, click **Club ID** to select the column headings, and then click **Next**. Under **Fields**, click **Donation**. Under **Functions**, click **Sum**, and then click **Next**. In the **What do you want to name your query?** box, select the existing text, type **Lastname Firstname 2D Fundraisers and Clubs Crosstab Query** and then click **Finish**.

b. On the ribbon, click the **HOME** tab, and then switch to **Design** view. In the design grid, click in the [**Donation**] column. Under **QUERY TOOLS**, on the **DESIGN tab**, in the **Show/Hide group**, click **Property Sheet**. In the **Property Sheet**, click **Decimal Places**. In the property settings box, click the **arrow**, and then click **0**. In the design grid, click in the **Total Of Donation** column, set the **Decimal Places** to **0**, and then **Close** the **Property Sheet**. **Run** the query. Select all of the columns, apply **Best Fit**, and then **Save** the query. This query answers the question, *Grouped by Fundraiser ID and Club ID, what are the total donations?*

c. Display the query results in **Print Preview**. On the **PRINT PREVIEW tab**, in the **Page Layout group**, click **Landscape**. Create a paper or electronic printout as directed—two pages result. Click **Close Print Preview**, and then **Close** the query.

9 On the ribbon, click the **CREATE tab**, and then in the **Queries group**, click **Query Design**. In the **Show Table** dialog box, double-click your **2D Fundraisers** table to add the table to the table area. **Close** the **Show Table** dialog box, and then resize the field list. Add the following fields to the design grid in the order given: **Club ID**, **Fundraiser Location**, and **Date**.

(Project 2D Club Fundraisers continues on the next page)

CHAPTER REVIEW

a. Click in the **Sort** row under **Date**, click the **arrow**, and then click **Ascending**. In the **Criteria** row under **Club ID**, right-click, and then click **Zoom**. In the **Zoom** dialog box, type **[Enter a Club ID in the format club-###]** and then click **OK**. **Run** the query. In the **Enter Parameter Value** dialog box, type **club-109** and then click **OK**. Three records match the criteria.

b. **Save** the query as **Lastname Firstname 2D Club ID Parameter Query** and then display the query results in **Print Preview**. Create a paper or electronic printout as directed, click **Close Print Preview**, and then **Close** the query.

c. **Open** the **Navigation Pane**, and increase the width of the pane so that all object names display fully. On the right side of the title bar, click **Close** to close the database and to exit Access. As directed by your instructor, submit your database and the paper or electronic printouts of the 11 objects—relationship report and 10 queries, one of which printed on two pages—that are the results of this project. Specifically, in this project, using your own name, you created the following database and printouts or electronic printouts:

1. Lastname_Firstname_2D_Clubs_Fundraisers	Database file
2. Lastname Firstname 2D Relationships	Relationships Report (printout or electronic printout)
3. Lastname Firstname 2D $1000 or More Donation Query	Query (printout or electronic printout)
4. Lastname Firstname 2D Fundraisers June-July Query	Query (printout or electronic printout)
5. Lastname Firstname 2D CLUB-109 Low Donations Query	Query (printout or electronic printout)
6. Lastname Firstname 2D CLUB-107 OR 115 Over $1000 Query	Query (printout or electronic printout)
7. Lastname Firstname 2D SE OR NE Donations Query	Query (printout or electronic printout)
8. Lastname Firstname 2D Phi Walk Query	Query (printout or electronic printout)
9. Lastname Firstname 2D Alumni Donation Query	Query (printout or electronic printout)
10. Lastname Firstname 2D Total Donations by Club Query	Query (printout or electronic printout)
11. Lastname Firstname 2D Fundraisers and Clubs Crosstab Query	Query (printout or electronic printout - two pages)
12. Lastname Firstname 2D Club ID Parameter Query	Query (printout or electronic printout - CLUB-109)

END | You have completed Project 2D

CONTENT-BASED ASSESSMENTS

Mastering Access | Project 2E Biology Supplies

In the following Mastering Access project, you will assist Greg Franklin, chair of the Biology Department at the Southwest Campus, in using his database to answer questions about biology laboratory supplies. Your completed database objects will look similar to Figure 2.57.

Apply 2A skills from these Objectives:

1 Open and Save an Existing Database

2 Create Table Relationships

3 Sort Records in a Table

4 Create a Query in Design View

5 Create a New Query from an Existing Query

6 Sort Query Results

7 Specify Criteria in a Query

PROJECT FILES

For Project 2E, you will need the following file:

a02E_Biology_Supplies

You will save your database as:

Lastname_Firstname_2E_Biology_Supplies

PROJECT RESULTS

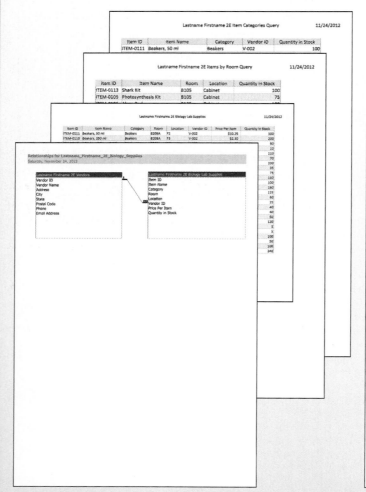
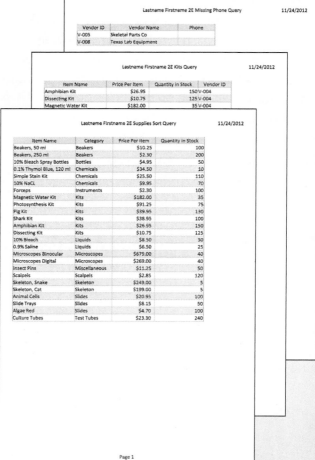

FIGURE 2.57

(Project 2E Biology Supplies continues on the next page)

CONTENT-BASED ASSESSMENTS

1 **Start** Access. From your student data files, open **a02E_Biology_Supplies**. Save the database in your **Access Chapter 2** folder as **Lastname_Firstname_2E_Biology_Supplies** and then enable the content. In the **Navigation Pane**, **Rename** each table by adding **Lastname Firstname** to the beginning of the table name. Increase the width of the **Navigation Pane** so that all object names display fully.

2 Open both tables to examine the fields and data, and then **Close** both tables. Create a *one-to-many* relationship between your **2E Vendors** table and your **2E Biology Lab Supplies** table using the common field **Vendor ID**. **Enforce Referential Integrity**, and enable both cascade options. *One* vendor can be the provider of *many* supplies. Create a **Relationship Report** with **Normal Margins**, saving it with the default name. Create a paper or electronic printout as directed, and then **Close All** open objects. Open your **2E Vendors** table. In the last record, in the **Vendor ID** field, select **V-100**, type **V-001** and then press ⬇ to save the record. **Close** the table.

3 Open your **2E Biology Lab Supplies** table. Sort the records first in **Descending** order by **Price Per Item** and then in **Ascending** order by **Category**. Using **Landscape** orientation, create a paper or electronic printout as directed. **Close** the table, and do *not* save changes to the table.

4 Create a query in **Query Design** view using your **2E Biology Lab Supplies** table to answer the question, *What is the item ID, item name, room, location, and quantity in stock for all of the items, sorted in ascending order by the Room field and the Location field?* Display the fields in the order listed in the question. **Save** the query as **Lastname Firstname 2E Items by Room Query** and then create a paper or electronic printout as directed. **Close** the query.

5 From the **Navigation Pane**, copy your **2E Items by Room Query** object to create a new query object named **Lastname Firstname 2E Item Categories Query** and then redesign the query to answer the question, *What is the item ID, item name, category, vendor ID, and quantity in stock for all items, sorted in ascending order by the Category field and in ascending order by the Vendor ID field?* Display only the fields necessary to answer the question and in the order listed in the question. Create a paper or electronic printout as directed. **Close** the query, saving the design changes.

6 From the **Navigation Pane**, copy your **2E Items by Room Query** object to create a new query object named **Lastname Firstname 2E Supplies Sort Query** and then redesign the query to answer the question, *What is the item name, category, price per item, and quantity in stock for all supplies, sorted in ascending order by the Category field and then in descending order by the Price Per Item field?* Display only the fields necessary to answer the question and in the order listed in the question. Create a paper or electronic printout as directed. **Close** the query, saving the design changes.

7 From the **Navigation Pane**, copy your **2E Supplies Sort Query** object to create a new query object named **Lastname Firstname 2E Kits Query** and then redesign the query to answer the question, *What is the item name, category, price per item, quantity in stock, and vendor ID for all items that have a category of kits, sorted in ascending order only by the Item Name field?* Do not display the **Category** field in the query results, and display the rest of the fields in the order listed in the question. Six records match the criteria. Create a paper or electronic printout as directed. **Close** the query, saving the design changes.

8 Create a query in **Query Design** view using your **2E Vendors** table to answer the question, *What is the vendor ID and vendor name where the phone number is missing from the table, sorted in ascending order by the Vendor Name field?* Display the fields in the order listed in the question. Two records match the criteria. **Save** the query as **Lastname Firstname 2E Missing Phone Query** and then create a paper or electronic printout as directed. **Close** the query.

(Project 2E Biology Supplies continues on the next page)

CONTENT-BASED ASSESSMENTS

Mastering Access Project 2E Biology Supplies (continued)

9 Be sure all objects are closed. **Open** the **Navigation Pane**, be sure that all object names display fully, and then **Close** Access. As directed by your instructor, submit your database and the paper or electronic printouts of the seven objects—relationship report, sorted table, and five queries—that are the results of this project. Specifically, in this project, using your own name, you created the following database and printouts or electronic printouts:

1. Lastname_Firstname_2E_Biology_Supplies	Database file
2. Relationships for Lastname_Firstname_2E_Biology_Supplies	Relationships Report (printout or electronic printout)
3. Lastname Firstname 2E Biology Lab Supplies table sorted (not saved)	Table sorted (printout or electronic printout - one page)
4. Lastname Firstname 2E Items by Room Query	Query (printout or electronic printout)
5. Lastname Firstname 2E Item Categories Query	Query (printout or electronic printout)
6. Lastname Firstname 2E Supplies Sort Query	Query (printout or electronic printout)
7. Lastname Firstname 2E Kits Query	Query (printout or electronic printout)
8. Lastname Firstname 2E Missing Phone Query	Query (printout or electronic printout)

END | You have completed Project 2E

CONTENT-BASED ASSESSMENTS

In the following Mastering Access project, you will assist Siobhan Reiss, the English Writing Lab coordinator, in using her database to answer questions about student publications. Your completed database objects will look similar to Figure 2.58.

PROJECT FILES

For Project 2F, you will need the following files:

a02F_Student_Publications
a02F_Student_Papers (Excel workbook)

You will save your database as:

Lastname_Firstname_2F_Student_Publications

PROJECT RESULTS

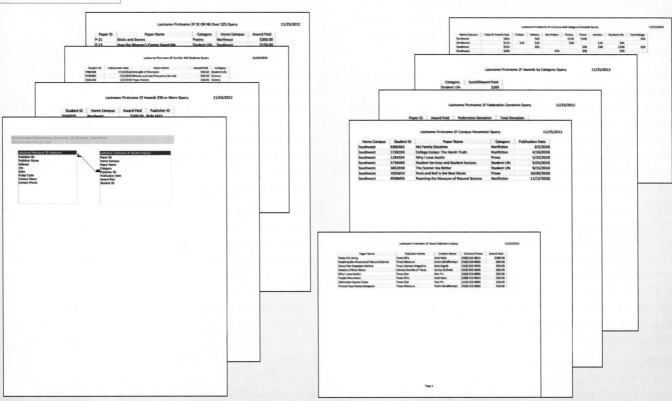

FIGURE 2.58

(Project 2F Student Publications continues on the next page)

CONTENT-BASED ASSESSMENTS

1   **Start** Access. From your student data files, open **a02F_Student_Publications**. Save the database in your **Access Chapter 2** folder as **Lastname_Firstname_2F_ Student_Publications** and then enable the content. In the **Navigation Pane**, **Rename** the **2F Publishers** table by adding **Lastname Firstname** to the beginning of the table name. From your student data files, import the **a02F_Student_Papers** Excel file as a new table in the database. Designate the first row of the spreadsheet as column headings, and designate **Paper ID** as the primary key. Name the new table **Lastname Firstname 2F Student Papers** and then increase the width of the **Navigation Pane** so that all object names display fully.

Open your **2F Student Papers** table in **Design** view. For the **Student ID** field, change the **Data Type** to **Short Text**. Switch to **Datasheet** view, saving the change, apply **Best Fit** to all of the columns, and then **Save** the table. Examine the fields and data in this table. Open your **2F Publishers** table, examine the fields and data, and then **Close All** open objects.

Create a *one-to-many* relationship between your **2F Publishers** table and your **2F Student Papers** table using the common field **Publisher ID**. **Enforce Referential Integrity**, and enable both cascade options. *One* publisher can publish *many* student papers. Create a **Relationship Report** with **Normal Margins**, saving it as **Lastname Firstname 2F Relationships** and then create a paper or electronic printout as directed. **Close All** open objects.

2   Create a query in **Query Design** view using your **2F Student Papers** table to answer the question, *What is the student ID, home campus, award paid, and publisher ID for awards greater than or equal to $50, sorted in ascending order by the Student ID field?* Display the fields in the order listed in the question. Five records match the criteria. **Save** the query as **Lastname Firstname 2F Awards $50 or More Query** and then create a paper or electronic printout as directed. **Close** the query.

3   From the **Navigation Pane**, copy your **2F Awards $50 or More Query** object to create a new query object named **Lastname Firstname 2F 2nd Qtr NW Students Query** and then redesign the query to answer the questions, *Which students (Student ID) from the Northwest campus had papers published between 4/1/18 and 6/30/18, and what was the paper name, the award paid, and the category, sorted in ascending order only by the Publication Date field?* Do not restrict the results by **Award Paid**. Do not display the **Home Campus** field in the query results, and display the rest of the fields in the order listed in the question. Three records match the criteria. Using **Landscape** orientation, create a paper or electronic printout as directed. **Close** the query, saving the design changes.

4   Create a query in **Query Design** view using your **2F Student Papers** table to answer the question, *Which paper IDs, paper names, and category for students from the Southeast or Northeast campuses were published that had an award paid greater than $25, sorted in descending order by the Award Paid field?* Display the fields in the order listed in the question. Six records match the criteria. **Save** the query as **Lastname Firstname 2F SE OR NE Over $25 Query** and then using **Normal Margins**, create a paper or electronic printout as directed. **Close** the query.

5   Create a query in **Query Design** view using both tables to answer the questions, *Which paper names were published with a publisher name that has Texas as part of its name, what is the contact name and contact phone number, and what was the award paid, sorted in descending order by the Award Paid field?* (Hint: Use a wildcard character in the **Criteria** row.) Display the fields in the order listed in the question. Eight records match the criteria. **Save** the query as **Lastname Firstname 2F Texas Publishers Query** and then using **Landscape** orientation, create a paper or electronic printout as directed. **Close** the query.

6   The college's Federation of English Faculty will donate money to the English Writing Lab based on 50 percent of the awards paid to the students. Create a query in **Query Design** view using your **2F Student Papers** table to answer the question, *In ascending order by the Paper ID field, what will be the total of each donation to the Writing Lab if the Federation donates an additional 50 percent of each award paid to students?* (Hint: First calculate the amount of the donation, naming the new field **Federation Donation**, and then run the query to be sure the correct results display. Then calculate the total donation, naming the new field **Total Donation**.) Change the property settings of the **Federation Donation** field to display with a **Format** of **Currency** and with **Decimal Places** set to **2**. For the **Publisher ID** of **P-20**, the *Federation Donation* is *$22.50*, and the *Total Donation* is *$67.50*. Apply **Best Fit** to all of the columns, **Save** the query as **Lastname Firstname 2F Federation Donation Query** and then create a paper or electronic printout as directed. **Close** the query.

(Project 2F Student Publications continues on the next page)

7 Create a query in **Query Design** view using your **2F Student Papers** table and the **Sum** aggregate function to answer the question, *What are the total awards paid for each category, sorted in descending order by the Award Paid field?* Display the fields in the order listed in the question. Change the property settings of the **Award Paid** field to display with **Decimal Places** set to **0**. For the **Category** of **Student Life**, total awards paid are *$265*. Apply **Best Fit** to the **SumOfAward Paid** column. **Save** the query as **Lastname Firstname 2F Awards by Category Query** and then create a paper or electronic printout as directed. **Close** the query.

8 Use the **Query Wizard** to create a crosstab query based on your **2F Student Papers** table. Select **Home Campus** as the row headings and **Category** as the column headings. **Sum** the **Award Paid** field. Name the query **Lastname Firstname 2F Campus and Category Crosstab Query** In **Design** view, change the property settings of the last two fields to display with **Decimal Places** set to **0**. This query answers the question, *What are the total awards paid for student publications by each home campus and by each category?* Apply **Best Fit** to all of the columns, and then **Save** the query. Using **Landscape** orientation and **Normal Margins**, create a paper or electronic printout as directed. **Close** the query.

9 Create a query in **Query Design** view using your **2F Student Papers** table that prompts you to enter the **Home Campus**, and then answers the question, *What is the home campus, student ID, paper name, category, and publication date for student publications, sorted in ascending order by the Publication Date field?* Display the fields in the order listed in the question. **Run** the query, entering **southwest** when prompted for criteria. Seven records match the criteria. **Save** the query as **Lastname Firstname 2F Campus Parameter Query** and then using **Normal Margins**, create a paper or electronic printout as directed. **Close** the query.

10 Open the **Navigation Pane**, and be sure that all object names display fully. **Close** Access. As directed by your instructor, submit your database and the paper or electronic printouts of the nine objects—relationship report and eight queries—that are the results of this project. Specifically, in this project, using your own name, you created the following database and printouts or electronic printouts:

1. Lastname_Firstname_2F_Student_Publications	Database file
2. Lastname Firstname 2F Relationships	Relationships Report (printout or electronic printout)
3. Lastname Firstname 2F Awards $50 or More Query	Query (printout or electronic printout)
4. Lastname Firstname 2F 2nd Qtr NW Students Query	Query (printout or electronic printout)
5. Lastname Firstname 2F SE OR NE Over $25 Query	Query (printout or electronic printout)
6. Lastname Firstname 2F Texas Publishers Query	Query (printout or electronic printout)
7. Lastname Firstname 2F Federation Donation Query	Query (printout or electronic printout)
8. Lastname Firstname 2F Awards by Category Query	Query (printout or electronic printout)
9. Lastname Firstname 2F Campus and Category Crosstab Query	Query (printout or electronic printout)
10. Lastname Firstname 2F Campus Parameter Query	Query (printout or electronic printout - Southwest)

END | You have completed Project 2F

CONTENT-BASED ASSESSMENTS

| **Mastering Access** | Project 2G Student Scholarships |

In the following Mastering Access project, you will assist Kim Ngo, director of Academic Scholarships, in using her database to answer questions about scholarships awarded to students. Your completed database objects will look similar to Figure 2.59.

Apply 2A and 2B skills from these Objectives:

1 Open and Save an Existing Database
2 Create Table Relationships
3 Sort Records in a Table
4 Create a Query in Design View
5 Create a New Query from an Existing Query
6 Sort Query Results
7 Specify Criteria in a Query
8 Specify Numeric Criteria in a Query
9 Use Compound Criteria in a Query
10 Create a Query Based on More Than One Table
11 Use Wildcards in a Query
12 Create Calculated Fields in a Query
13 Calculate Statistics and Group Data in a Query
14 Create a Crosstab Query
15 Create a Parameter Query

PROJECT FILES

For Project 2G, you will need the following file:

a02G_Student_Scholarships

You will save your database as:

Lastname_Firstname_2G_Student_Scholarships

PROJECT RESULTS

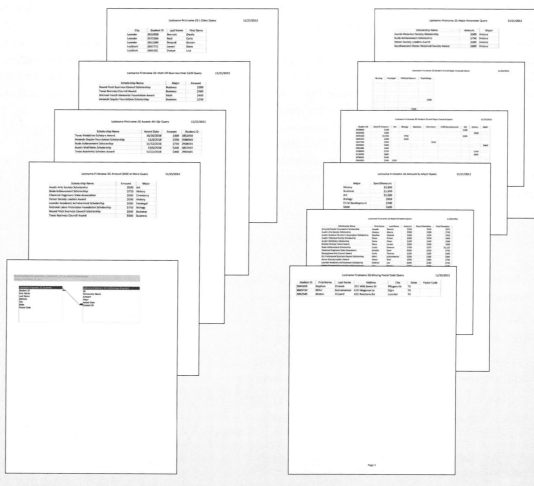

FIGURE 2.59

(Project 2G Student Scholarships continues on the next page)

CONTENT-BASED ASSESSMENTS

1 ▶ **Start** Access. From your student data files, open **a02G_Student_Scholarships**. Save the database in your **Access Chapter 2** folder as **Lastname_Firstname_2G_Student_Scholarships** and then enable the content. In the **Navigation Pane**, **Rename** each table by adding **Lastname Firstname** to the beginning of the table name. Increase the width of the **Navigation Pane** so that all object names display fully.

2 ▶ Open both tables to examine the fields and data, and then **Close** both tables. Create a *one-to-many* relationship between your **2G Students** table and your **2G Scholarships Awarded** table using the common field **Student ID**. **Enforce Referential Integrity**, and enable both cascade options. *One* student can have *many* scholarships. Create a **Relationship Report** with **Normal Margins**, saving it with the default name. Create a paper or electronic printout as directed, and then **Close All** open objects. Open your **2G Students** table. In the last record, in the **Student ID** field, select **9999999**, type **2839403** and then press ↓ to save the record. **Close** the table.

3 ▶ Create a query in **Query Design** view using your **2G Scholarships Awarded** table to answer the question, *What is the scholarship name, amount, and major for scholarships greater than or equal to $500, sorted in ascending order by the Scholarship Name field?* Display the fields in the order listed in the question. Eight records match the criteria. **Save** the query as **Lastname Firstname 2G Amount $500 or More Query** and then create a paper or electronic printout as directed. **Close** the query.

4 ▶ From the **Navigation Pane**, copy your **2G Amount $500 or More Query** object to create a new query object named **Lastname Firstname 2G Awards 4th Qtr Query** and then redesign the query to answer the question, *Which scholarships (Scholarship Name) were awarded between 10/1/18 and 12/31/18, for what amount, and for which student (Student ID), sorted in ascending order only by the Award Date field?* Display only the fields necessary to answer the question and in the order listed in the question. Do not restrict the results by amount. Five records match the criteria. Create a paper or electronic printout as directed. **Close** the query, saving the design changes.

5 ▶ Create a query in **Query Design** view using your **2G Scholarships Awarded** table to answer the question, *Which scholarships (Scholarship Name) were awarded for either Math or Business majors for amounts of more than $200, sorted in descending order by the Amount field?*

Display the fields in the order listed in the question. Four records match the criteria. (Hint: If six records display, switch to **Design** view and combine the majors on one criteria line using OR.) **Save** the query as **Lastname Firstname 2G Math OR Business Over $200 Query** and then create a paper or electronic printout as directed. **Close** the query.

6 ▶ Create a query in **Query Design** view using your **2G Students** table and a wildcard character to answer the question, *What is the city, student ID, last name, and first name of students from cities that begin with the letter L, sorted in ascending order by the City field, in ascending order by the Last Name field, and ascending order by the First Name field?* Display the fields in the order listed in the question. Five records match the criteria. **Save** the query as **Lastname Firstname 2G L Cities Query** and then create a paper or electronic printout as directed. **Close** the query.

7 ▶ Create a query in **Query Design** view using your **2G Students** table and all of the fields in the same order that they display in the field list to answer the question, *For which students is the Postal Code missing?* Three records match the criteria. **Save** the query as **Lastname Firstname 2G Missing Postal Code Query** and then using **Normal Margins**, create a paper or electronic printout as directed. **Close** the query.

8 ▶ The Board of Trustees for the college will donate an amount equal to 50 percent of each scholarship amount. Create a query in **Query Design** view using both tables to answer the question, *In ascending order by the Scholarship Name field, and including the first name and last name of the scholarship recipient, what will be the total value of each scholarship if the Board of Trustees donates an additional 50 percent of each award paid to students?* (Hint: First calculate the amount of the donation, naming the new field **Board Donation**, and then run the query to be sure the correct results display. Then calculate the total donation, naming the new field **Total Donation**.) Change the property settings of the appropriate fields to display with a **Format** of **Currency** and with **Decimal Places** set to **0**. For the **Scholarship Name** of **Amanda Snyder Foundation Scholarship**, the *Board Donation* is *$125*, and the *Total Donation* is *$375*. Apply **Best Fit** to all of the columns, **Save** the query as **Lastname Firstname 2G Board Donation Query** and then using **Landscape** orientation, create a paper or electronic printout as directed. **Close** the query.

(Project 2G Student Scholarships continues on the next page)

CONTENT-BASED ASSESSMENTS

9 Create a query in **Query Design** view using your **2G Scholarships Awarded** table and the **Sum** aggregate function to answer the question, *For each major, what is the total scholarship amount, sorted in descending order by the Amount field?* Display the fields in the order listed in the question. Change the property settings of the **Amount** field to display with **Decimal Places** set to **0**. For the **Major** of **History**, the total scholarship amount is *$1,850.* Apply **Best Fit** to all of the columns. **Save** the query as **Lastname Firstname 2G Amount by Major Query** and then create a paper or electronic printout as directed. **Close** the query.

10 Use the **Query Wizard** to create a crosstab query based on your **2G Scholarships Awarded** table. Select **Student ID** as the row headings and **Major** as the column headings. **Sum** the **Amount** field. Name the query **Lastname Firstname 2G Student ID and Major Crosstab Query** In **Design** view, change the property settings of the last two fields to display with **Decimal Places** set to **0**. This query answers the question, *What are the total scholarship amounts paid by each student ID and by each major?* Apply **Best Fit** to all of the columns, and then **Save** the query. Using **Landscape** orientation, create a paper or electronic printout as directed—two pages result. **Close** the query.

11 Create a query in **Query Design** view using your **2G Scholarships Awarded** table that prompts you to enter the **Major**, and then answers the question, *What is the scholarship name and amount for a major, sorted in ascending order by the Scholarship Name field?* Display the fields in the order listed in the question. **Run** the query, entering **history** when prompted for criteria. Four records match the criteria. **Save** the query as **Lastname Firstname 2G Major Parameter Query** and then create a paper or electronic printout as directed. **Close** the query.

12 Open the **Navigation Pane**, and be sure that all object names display fully. **Close** Access. As directed by your instructor, submit your database and the paper or electronic printouts of the 10 objects—relationship report and nine queries, one of which prints on two pages—that are the results of this project. Specifically, in this project, using your own name, you created the following database and printouts or electronic printouts:

1. Lastname_Firstname_2G_Student_Scholarships	Database file
2. Relationships for Lastname_Firstname_2G_Student_Scholarships	Relationships Report (printout or electronic printout)
3. Lastname Firstname 2G Amount $500 or More Query	Query (printout or electronic printout)
4. Lastname Firstname 2G Awards 4th Qtr Query	Query (printout or electronic printout)
5. Lastname Firstname 2G Math OR Business Over $200 Query	Query (printout or electronic printout)
6. Lastname Firstname 2G L Cities Query	Query (printout or electronic printout)
7. Lastname Firstname 2G Missing Postal Code Query	Query (printout or electronic printout)
8. Lastname Firstname 2G Board Donation Query	Query (printout or electronic printout)
9. Lastname Firstname 2G Amount by Major Query	Query (printout or electronic printout)
10. Lastname Firstname 2G Student ID and Major Crosstab Query	Query (printout or electronic printout - two pages)
11. Lastname Firstname 2G Major Parameter Query (using History)	Query (printout or electronic printout)

END | You have completed Project 2G

CONTENT-BASED ASSESSMENTS

Apply a combination of the 2A and 2B skills.

GO! Fix It	Project 2H Social Sciences	Online
GO! Make It	Project 2I Faculty Awards	Online
GO! Solve It	Project 2J Student Refunds	Online
GO! Solve It	Project 2K Leave	

PROJECT FILES

For Project 2K, you will need the following file:

a02K_Leave

You will save your database as:

Lastname_Firstname_2K_Leave

Start Access, navigate to your student data files, open a02K_Leave, and then save the database in your Access Chapter 2 folder as **Lastname_Firstname_2K_Leave** Add **Lastname Firstname** to the beginning of both table names, create a one-to-many relationship with cascade options between the two tables—*one* employee can have *many* leave transactions— and then create a relationship report saving it as **Lastname Firstname 2K Relationships** Create and save four queries to answer the following questions:

- What is the last name and first name of employees who have used personal leave, sorted in ascending order by the Last Name and First Name fields? Do not display the Leave field in the query results.
- What is the last name, first name, and email address of employees who have no phone number listed, sorted in ascending order by the Last Name and First Name fields?
- Grouped by the Leave Classification field, what is the total of each type of leave used? (Hint: Use the aggregate function Count.)
- What is the total number of leave transactions grouped in rows by the Employee# field and grouped in columns by the Leave Classification field?

As directed, create paper or electronic printouts of the relationship report and the four queries. Be sure that each object prints on one page, and that the object names display fully in the Navigation Pane. As directed, submit your database and the paper or electronic printouts of the five objects that are the results of this project.

(Project 2K Leave continues on the next page)

CONTENT-BASED ASSESSMENTS

Performance Level

Performance Criteria		Exemplary	Proficient	Developing
	Create relationship and relationship report	Relationship and relationship report created correctly.	Relationship and relationship report created with one error.	Relationship and relationship report created with two or more errors, or missing entirely.
	Create Personal Leave query	Query created with correct name, fields, sorting, and criteria.	Query created with one element incorrect.	Query created with two or more elements incorrect, or missing entirely.
	Create Missing Phone query	Query created with correct name, fields, sorting, and criteria.	Query created with one element incorrect.	Query created with two or more elements incorrect, or missing entirely.
	Create Type of Leave query	Query created with correct name, fields, and aggregate function.	Query created with one element incorrect.	Query created with two or more elements incorrect, or missing entirely.
	Create Crosstab query	Query created with correct name, row headings, column headings, and aggregate function.	Query created with one element incorrect.	Query created with two or more elements incorrect, or missing entirely.

END | You have completed Project 2K

OUTCOMES-BASED ASSESSMENTS

RUBRIC

The following outcomes-based assessments are *open-ended assessments*. That is, there is no specific correct result; your result will depend on your approach to the information provided. Make *Professional Quality* your goal. Use the following scoring rubric to guide you in *how* to approach the problem and then to evaluate *how well* your approach solves the problem.

The *criteria*—Software Mastery, Content, Format & Layout, and Process—represent the knowledge and skills you have gained that you can apply to solving the problem. The *levels of performance*—Professional Quality, Approaching Professional Quality, or Needs Quality Improvements—help you and your instructor evaluate your result.

	Your completed project is of Professional Quality if you:	Your completed project is Approaching Professional Quality if you:	Your completed project Needs Quality Improvements if you:
1-Software Mastery	Choose and apply the most appropriate skills, tools, and features and identify efficient methods to solve the problem.	Choose and apply some appropriate skills, tools, and features, but not in the most efficient manner.	Choose inappropriate skills, tools, or features, or are inefficient in solving the problem.
2-Content	Construct a solution that is clear and well organized, contains content that is accurate, appropriate to the audience and purpose, and is complete. Provide a solution that contains no errors in spelling, grammar, or style.	Construct a solution in which some components are unclear, poorly organized, inconsistent, or incomplete. Misjudge the needs of the audience. Have some errors in spelling, grammar, or style, but the errors do not detract from comprehension.	Construct a solution that is unclear, incomplete, or poorly organized; contains some inaccurate or inappropriate content; and contains many errors in spelling, grammar, or style. Do not solve the problem.
3-Format & Layout	Format and arrange all elements to communicate information and ideas, clarify function, illustrate relationships, and indicate relative importance.	Apply appropriate format and layout features to some elements, but not others. Overuse features, causing minor distraction.	Apply format and layout that does not communicate information or ideas clearly. Do not use format and layout features to clarify function, illustrate relationships, or indicate relative importance. Use available features excessively, causing distraction.
4-Process	Use an organized approach that integrates planning, development, self-assessment, revision, and reflection.	Demonstrate an organized approach in some areas, but not others; or, use an insufficient process of organization throughout.	Do not use an organized approach to solve the problem.

OUTCOMES-BASED ASSESSMENTS

Apply a combination of the 2A and 2B skills.

GO! Think | Project 2L Coaches

PROJECT FILES

For Project 2L, you will need the following file:

a02L_Coaches

You will save your database as

Lastname_Firstname_2L_Coaches

Start Access, navigate to your student data files, open a02L_Coaches, and then save the database in your Access Chapter 2 folder as **Lastname_Firstname_2L_Coaches** Add **Lastname Firstname** to the beginning of both table names, create a one-to-many relationship with cascade options between the two tables—*one* coach can participate in *many* activities—and then create a relationship report saving it as **Lastname Firstname 2L Relationships**

Create queries to assist Randy Garza, the athletic director, in answering the following questions about the coaches at Texas Lakes Community College:

- What is the last name and first name of every coach involved in *Dive* activities, sorted in ascending order by the Last Name field and First Name fields?
- What is the last name and first name of every coach involved in basketball or football activities, sorted in ascending order first by the Activity Name field and then by the Last Name and First Name fields?
- Grouped by division, what is the total number of activity names, sorted in descending order by the total number? (Hint: Use the Count aggregate function.)
- What is the skill specialty, last name, first name, and phone number for coaches in a specified position that is entered when prompted for the Position, sorted in ascending order first by the Skill Specialty field and then by the Last Name and First Name fields? (When prompted, enter the position of *director* for your paper or electronic printout.)

As directed, create paper or electronic printouts of the relationship report and the four queries. Be sure that each object prints on one page, and that the object names display fully in the Navigation Pane. As directed, submit your database and the paper or electronic printouts of the five objects that are the results of this project.

END | You have completed Project 2L

GO! Think | Project 2M Club Donations | Online

Build from Scratch

You and GO! | Project 2N Personal Inventory | Online

Build from Scratch

GO! Cumulative Group Project | Project 2O Bell Orchid Hotels | Online

Forms, Filters, and Reports

GO! to Work
Video A3

3

PROJECT 3A

OUTCOMES
Create forms to enter and delete records and to display data in a database.

PROJECT 3B

OUTCOMES
Create reports to display database information.

OBJECTIVES

1. Create and Use a Form to Add and Delete Records
2. Filter Records
3. Create a Form by Using the Form Wizard
4. Modify a Form in Layout View and in Design View

OBJECTIVES

5. Create a Report by Using the Report Tool and Modify the Report in Layout View
6. Create a Report by Using the Report Wizard
7. Modify the Design of a Report
8. Keep Grouped Data Together in a Printed Report

Ricardo Piccinini/Fotolia

In This Chapter

In this chapter, you will create forms to enter and delete data and to view data in database tables. Forms can display one record at a time with fields placed in the same order to match a paper source document. Records in a form or table can be filtered to display a subset of the records based on matching specific values. You will modify forms by adding fields, changing field widths, and adding labels to the forms. You will create professional-looking reports that summarize the data stored in a query or table. You will modify the reports by changing the fields in the report, by changing the layout of the report, by grouping data, and by making sure that groupings of data stay together on the printed page.

The projects in this chapter relate to **Texas Lakes Community College**, which is located in the Austin, Texas, area. Its four campuses serve over 30,000 students and offer more than 140 certificate programs and degrees. The college has a highly acclaimed Distance Education program and an extensive Workforce Development program. The college makes positive contributions to the community through cultural and athletic programs and has significant partnerships with businesses and nonprofit organizations. Popular fields of study include nursing and health care, solar technology, computer technology, and graphic design.

PROJECT 3A

Students and Majors Database

MyITLab®
Project 3A Training

PROJECT ACTIVITIES

In Activities 3.01 through 3.15, you will assist Sean Fitchette, director of Enrollment Services at Texas Lakes Community College, in using his Access database to track new students and their major fields of study. Your completed forms will look similar to Figure 3.1.

PROJECT FILES

For Project 3A, you will need the following file:
a03A_Students_Majors

You will save your database as:
Lastname_Firstname_3A_Students_Majors

PROJECT RESULTS

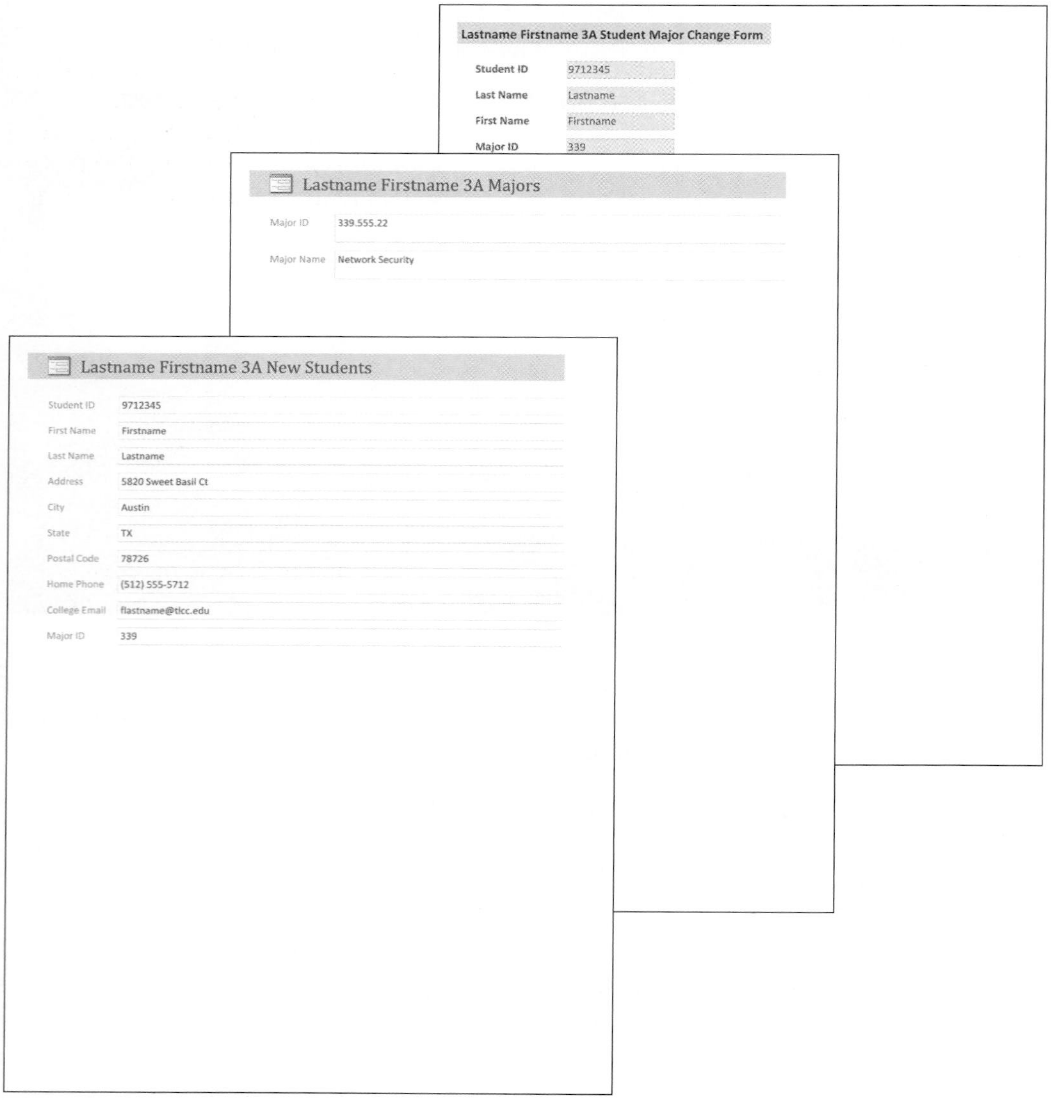

Lastname Firstname 3A Student Major Change Form
Student ID 9712345
Last Name Lastname
First Name Firstname
Major ID 339
Lastname Firstname 3A Majors
Major ID 339.555.22
Major Name Network Security
Lastname Firstname 3A New Students
Student ID 9712345
First Name Firstname
Last Name Lastname
Address 5820 Sweet Basil Ct
City Austin
State TX
Postal Code 78726
Home Phone (512) 555-5712
College Email flastname@tlcc.edu
Major ID 339

FIGURE 3.1 Project 3A Students and Majors

Objective 1 | Create and Use a Form to Add and Delete Records

Video A3-1

A *form* is a database object that you can use to enter new records into a table, or to edit, delete, or display existing records in a table. A form is useful to control access to the data. For example, you can design a form for college registration assistants so that they can see and enter the courses scheduled and fees paid by an individual student. However, they cannot see or enter grades for a student.

Some forms display only one record at a time; other forms display multiple records at the same time. A form that displays only one record at a time is useful not only to the individual who performs the *data entry*—entering the actual records—but also to anyone who has the job of viewing information in a database. For example, when you request a transcript from your college, someone displays your record on the screen. For the individual viewing your transcript, it is much easier to look at one record at a time, using a form, than to look at all of the student transcripts in the database.

Activity 3.01 | Opening and Saving an Existing Database, Renaming Tables, and Viewing a Table Relationship

1 Start Access. In the Access opening screen, click **Open Other Files**. Under **Open**, click **Computer**, and then on the right, click **Browse**. In the **Open** dialog box, navigate to the location where your student data files for this chapter are stored, and then double-click **a03A_Students_Majors** to open the database.

2 On the ribbon, click the **FILE tab**, and then click **Save As**. Under **File Types**, be sure **Save Database As** is selected. On the right, under **Database File Types**, be sure **Access Database** is selected, and then at the bottom of the screen, click **Save As**.

3 In the **Save As** dialog box, navigate to the location where you are saving your databases. Create a **New folder** named **Access Chapter 3**, and then **Open** the folder. In the **File name** box and using your own name, replace the existing text with **Lastname_Firstname_3A_Students_Majors** and then click **Save** or press [Enter].

4 On the **Message Bar**, click **Enable Content**. In the **Navigation Pane**, right-click the **3A Majors** table, and then click **Rename**. With the table name selected and using your own name, type **Lastname Firstname 3A Majors** and then press [Enter] to rename the table. Use the same technique to **Rename** the **3A New Students** table to **Lastname Firstname 3A New Students**

5 Point to the right edge of the **Navigation Pane** to display the ⟺ pointer. Drag to the right to increase the width of the pane until both table names display fully.

6 On the ribbon, click the **DATABASE TOOLS tab**. In the **Relationships group**, click **Relationships**. On the **DESIGN tab**, in the **Relationships group**, click **All Relationships**. If necessary, resize and move the field lists so that the entire table name and fields display for each field list.

> Because you renamed the tables, the field lists do not automatically display in the Relationships window.

7 In the **Relationships** window, click the **join line** between the two field lists. In the **Tools group**, click **Edit Relationships**. Point to the title bar of the **Edit Relationships** dialog box, and drag the dialog box downward below the two field lists. Compare your screen with Figure 3.2.

> *One* major is associated with *many* students. A one-to-many relationship is established between your 3A Majors table and your 3A New Students table using the Major ID field as the common field. Recall that Cascade Update Related Fields enables you to change the primary key in the 3A Majors table, and then the data in the foreign key field in the 3A New Students field is automatically updated. Recall that Cascade Delete Related Records enables you to delete a record in the 3A Majors table, and then all related records in the 3A New Students table are automatically deleted.

↻ ANOTHER WAY   In the Relationships window, double-click the join line to display the Edit Relationships dialog box.

FIGURE 3.2

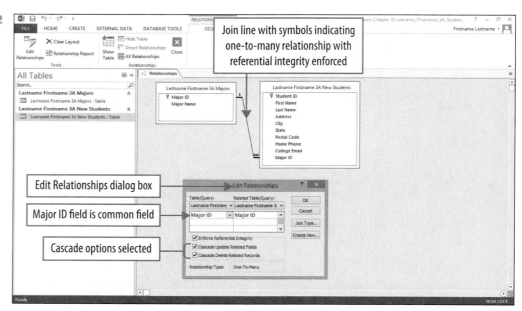

ALERT!   **Is Your Edit Relationships Dialog Box Empty?**

The Edit Relationships dialog box does not display any information if you do not first click the join line. If this happens, close the Edit Relationships dialog box, and then be sure that you click the join line—when selected, the join line is darker.

8 Close ⊠ the **Edit Relationships** dialog box, and then **Close** ⊠ the **Relationships** window. In the message box, click **Yes** to save changes to the layout of the relationships.

Activity 3.02 | Creating a Form and Viewing Records

There are several ways to create a form in Access, but the fastest and easiest way is to use the *Form tool*. With a single mouse click, all fields from the data source are placed on the form. You can use the new form immediately, or you can modify the form in Layout view or in Design view.

The Form tool uses all of the field names and all of the records from an existing table or query. Records that you create or edit using a form are automatically updated in the underlying table or tables. In this activity, you will create a form and then view records from the underlying table—the data source.

1 In the **Navigation Pane**, double-click your **3A New Students** table to open it. Scroll as needed to view all 10 fields—*Student ID, First Name, Last Name, Address, City, State, Postal Code, Home Phone, College Email,* and *Major ID.* **Close** ☒ the table.

2 In the **Navigation Pane**, be sure your **3A New Students** table is selected. On the ribbon, click the **CREATE tab**, and then in the **Forms group**, click **Form. Close** « the **Navigation Pane**, and then compare your screen with Figure 3.3.

> The form is created based on the currently selected object—your 3A New Students table—and displays in *Layout view*. In Layout view, you can modify the form with the data displayed in the fields. For example, you can adjust the size of the text boxes to fit the data.

> The form is created in a simple top-to-bottom layout, with all 10 fields from your 3A New Students table lined up in a single column. The data for the first record in the data source displays.

FIGURE 3.3

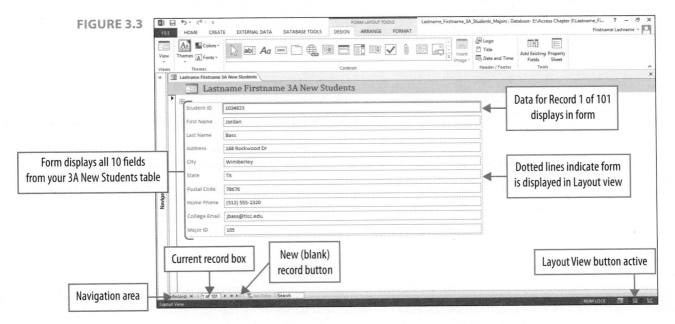

3 In the navigation area, click **Next record** ▶ four times to display the fifth record—*Student ID 1298345.* In the navigation area, select the text in the Current record box, type **62** and then press Enter to display the record for *Student ID 5720358.* In the navigation area, click **Last record** ▶▌ to display the record for *Student ID 9583924,* and then click **First record** ▍◀ to display the record for *Student ID 1034823.*

> Use the navigation buttons to scroll among the records or the Current record box to display any single record.

4 **Save** 🖫 the form as **Lastname Firstname 3A New Student Form** and then **Close** ☒ the form object.

5 **Open** » the **Navigation Pane**. Notice that your new form displays under the table with which it is related—your **3A New Students** table.

Activity 3.03 | Creating a Second Form

In this activity, you will use the Form tool to create a form for your 3A Majors table.

1 In the **Navigation Pane**, click your **3A Majors** table to select it. On the ribbon, click the **CREATE tab**, and then in the **Forms group**, click **Form**. **Close** « the **Navigation Pane**, and then compare your screen with Figure 3.4.

Because a one-to-many relationship is established, the form displays related records in the 3A New Students table for each record in the 3A Majors table. Five new students have selected a major of *Diagnostic Medical Sonography—Major ID 105.*

FIGURE 3.4

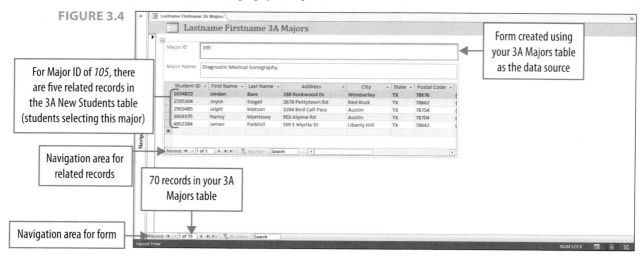

Form created using your 3A Majors table as the data source

For Major ID of *105*, there are five related records in the 3A New Students table (students selecting this major)

Navigation area for related records

70 records in your 3A Majors table

Navigation area for form

2 **Close** × your **3A Majors** form. In the message box, click **Yes**. In the **Save As** dialog box, in the **Form Name** box, type **Lastname Firstname 3A Major Form** and then click **OK**.

Recall that if you do not save an object, you are prompted to do so when you close the object.

3 **Open** » the **Navigation Pane**. Notice that your new form displays under the table with which it is related—your **3A Majors** table.

Activity 3.04 | Adding Records to a Table by Using a Form

By using a single-record form to add, modify, and delete records, you can reduce the number of data entry errors, because the individual performing the data entry is looking at only one record at a time. Recall that your database is useful only if the information is accurate—just like your contact list is useful only if it contains accurate phone numbers and email addresses.

Forms are based on—also referred to as *bound* to—the table where the records are stored. When a record is entered in a form, the new record is added to the underlying table. The reverse is also true—when a record is added to the table, the new record can be viewed in the related form.

In this activity, you will add a new record to both tables by using the forms that you just created.

1 In the **Navigation Pane**, double-click your **3A New Student Form** object to open it, and then **Close** « the **Navigation Pane**. In the navigation area, click **New (blank) record** ▶* to display a new blank form.

When you open a form, the first record in the underlying table displays in *Form view*, which is used to view, add, modify, and delete records stored in the table.

2 In the **Student ID** field, type **9712345** and then press Tab.

Use the Tab key to move from field to field in a form. *Tab order* is the order in which the insertion point moves from one field to the next when you press the Tab key. As you start typing, the pencil icon displays in the *record selector bar* at the left—the bar used to select an entire record. The pencil icon displays when a record is being created or edited.

 **ANOTHER WAY**   Press the Enter key, provided there are no special links on the form, such as a link to create a new form or a link to print the form.

3 Using your own first name and last name and using the first initial of your first name and your last name for the *College Email* field, continue entering the data shown in the following table, and then compare your screen with Figure 3.5.

Student ID	First Name	Last Name	Address	City	State	Postal Code	Home Phone	College Email	Major ID
9712345	First Name	Last Name	5820 Sweet Basil Ct	Austin	TX	78726	(512) 555-5712	flastname@ tlcc.edu	339

FIGURE 3.5

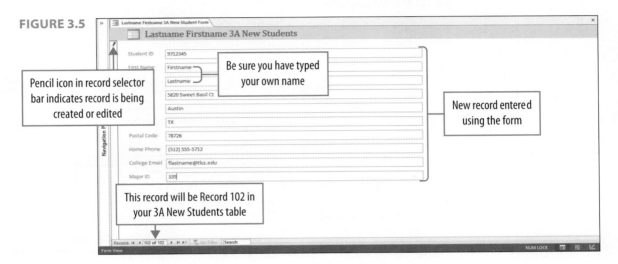

4 With the insertion point positioned in the last field, press Tab to save the record and display a new blank record. **Close** ☒ your **3A New Student Form** object.

5 **Open** ☒ the **Navigation Pane**, and then double-click your **3A New Students** table to open it. In the navigation area, click **Last record** ☒ to verify that the record you entered in the form is stored in the underlying table. **Close** ☒ your **3A New Students** table.

6 In the **Navigation Pane**, double-click your **3A Major Form** object to open it. At the bottom of the screen, in the navigation area for the form—*not* the navigation area for the subdatasheet—click **New (blank) record** ☒. In the blank form enter the data shown in the following table:

Major ID	Major Name
339.555.22	Network Security

7 **Close** ☒ your **3A Major Form** object. In the **Navigation Pane**, double-click your **3A Majors** table, and then scroll to verify that the record for *Major ID 339.555.22 Network Security* displays in the table—records are sorted by the *Major ID* field. **Close** ☒ the table.

Activity 3.05 | Deleting Records from a Table by Using a Form

You can delete records from a database table by using a form. In this activity, you will delete the record for *Major ID 800.03* because the program has been discontinued.

1 In the **Navigation Pane**, double-click your **3A Major Form** object to open it, and then **Close** « the **Navigation Pane**. On the **HOME tab**, in the **Find group**, click **Find** to open the **Find and Replace** dialog box.

↻ **ANOTHER WAY**   Press Ctrl + F to open the Find and Replace dialog box.

2 In the **Look In** box, notice that *Current field* displays. In the **Find What** box, type **800.03** and then click **Find Next**. Compare your screen with Figure 3.6, and verify that the record for *Major ID 800.03* displays.

Because the insertion point was positioned in the *Major ID* field before opening the dialog box, Access will search for data in this field—the *Current field*.

FIGURE 3.6

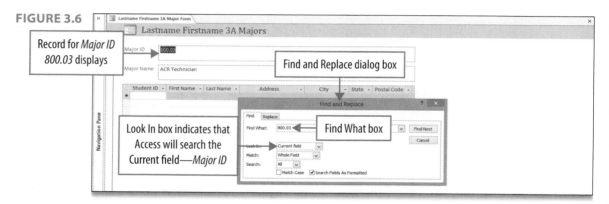

3 **Close** ☒ the **Find and Replace** dialog box. On the **HOME tab**, in the **Records group**, click the **Delete arrow**, and then click **Delete Record**.

The record is removed from the screen, and a message displays alerting you that you are about to delete *1 record(s)*. Once you click *Yes*, you cannot click Undo to reverse this action. If you delete a record by mistake, you must re-create the record by reentering the data. Because no students are associated with this major and the program is being discontinued, you can delete it from the table.

4 In the message box, click **Yes** to delete the record. In the navigation area for the form, notice that the total number of records in the table is *70*. **Close** ☒ your **3A Major Form** object.

5 **Open** » the **Navigation Pane**, and then double-click your **3A Majors** table to open it. Examine the table to verify that the *Major ID 800.03* record has been deleted from the table, and then **Close** ☒ the table.

Adding and deleting records in a form updates the records stored in the underlying table.

Activity 3.06 | Printing a Form

When a form is displayed, clicking Print causes *all* of the records to print in the form layout. In this activity, you will print only *one* record.

1 In the **Navigation Pane**, double-click your **3A New Student Form** object to open it, and then **Close** « the **Navigation Pane**. Press Ctrl + F to open the **Find and Replace** dialog box. In the **Find What** box, type **9712345** and then click **Find Next** to display the record with your name. **Close** ☒ the **Find and Replace** dialog box.

2 On the ribbon, click the **FILE tab**, click **Print**, and then on the right, click **Print**. In the **Print** dialog box, under **Print Range**, click the **Selected Record(s)** option button. In the lower left corner of the dialog box, click **Setup**.

3 In the **Page Setup** dialog box, click the **Columns tab**. Under **Column Size**, double-click in the **Width** box to select the existing value, type **7.5** and then compare your screen with Figure 3.7.

Change the width of the column in this manner so that the form prints on one page. Forms are not typically printed, so the width of the column in a form might be greater than the width of the paper on which you are printing. The maximum column width that you can enter is dependent upon the printer that is installed on your system. This setting is saved when you save or close the form.

FIGURE 3.7

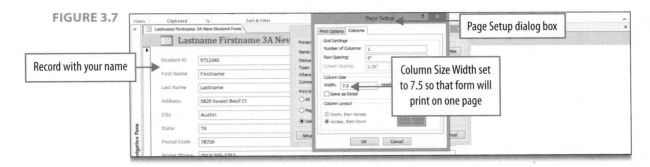

4 In the **Page Setup** dialog box, click **OK**. To create a paper printout, in the **Print** dialog box click **OK**. To create an electronic printout of this single form, click **Cancel** and then follow the instructions in the Note below.

> **NOTE** **Printing a Single Form in PDF**
>
> To create an electronic printout of a single form in PDF, change the column width to 7.5 as described in Step 3 above, and then in the Print dialog box, click Cancel. On the left side of the form, click the Record Selector bar so that it is black—selected. On the ribbon, click the EXTERNAL DATA tab. In the Export group, click PDF or XPS.
>
> In the Publish as PDF or XPS dialog box, navigate to your chapter folder. In the File name box, the form has the same name as the form. Be sure that the Open file after publishing check box is selected, and that the Minimum size (publishing online) option button is selected. In the Publish as PDF or XPS dialog box, Click Options. In the Options dialog box, under Range, click the Selected records option button, click OK, and then click Publish. Close the Windows 8 Reader, Adobe Reader or Adobe Acrobat window, and then submit the file as directed by your instructor.

5 **Close** [×] your **3A New Student Form** object, **Open** [»] the **Navigation Pane**, and then double-click your **3A Major Form** object to open it. **Close** [«] the **Navigation Pane**.

6 Use the techniques you just practiced to **Find** the record for the **Major ID** of **339.555.22**, and then create a paper or electronic printout as directed by your instructor of that record only on one page. After printing, **Close** [×] your **3A Major Form** object.

If there are no related records in the subdatasheet, the empty subdatasheet does not display in the printed form.

Objective 2 Filter Records

Video A3-2

Filtering records in a form displays only a portion of the total records—a *subset*—based on matching specific values. Filters are commonly used to provide a quick answer, and the result is not generally saved for future use. For example, by filtering records in a form, you can quickly display a subset of records for students majoring in Information Systems Technology, which is identified by the Major ID of 339.

A form provides an interface for the database. For example, because of security reasons, the registration assistants at your college may not have access to the entire student database. Rather, by using a form, they can access and edit only some information—the information necessary for them to do their jobs. Filtering records within a form provides individuals who do not have access to the entire database a way to ask questions of the database without constructing a query. You can save the filter with the form if you are going to use the filter frequently.

Activity 3.07 | Filtering Data by Selection of One Field

In this activity, you will assist a counselor at the college who wants to see records for students majoring in Information Systems Technology. In a form, you can use the *Filter By Selection* command to display only the records that contain the value in the selected field and to hide the records that do *not* contain the value in the selected field.

1 ▸ **Open** » the **Navigation Pane**, double-click your **3A New Student Form** object to open it in **Form** view, and then **Close** « the **Navigation Pane**.

2 ▸ In the first record, click the **Major ID** field name—or you can click in the field box. Press Ctrl + F to display the **Find and Replace** dialog box. In the **Find What** box, type **339** If necessary, in the Match box, click the arrow, and then click Whole Field. Click **Find Next**, and then compare your screen with Figure 3.8.

This action finds and displays a record with a *Major ID* of *339*—the major of *Information Systems Technology*. You will use this action to filter the records using the value of *339*.

FIGURE 3.8

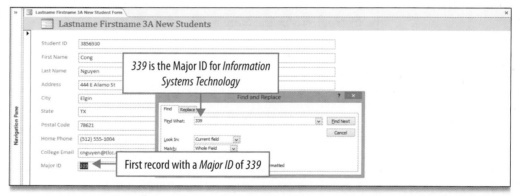

3 ▸ **Close** ☒ the **Find and Replace** dialog box. On the **HOME tab**, in the **Sort & Filter group**, click **Selection**, and then click **Equals "339"**. Compare your screen with Figure 3.9.

Seven records match the contents of the selected Major ID field—*339*—the Major ID for the Information Systems Technology major. In the navigation area, *Filtered* with a funnel icon displays next to the number of records. *Filtered* also displays on the right side of the status bar to indicate that a filter is applied. On the HOME tab, in the Sort & Filter group, Toggle Filter is active.

🔁 ANOTHER WAY   With the data selected in the field, right-click the selection, and then click Equals "339".

FIGURE 3.9

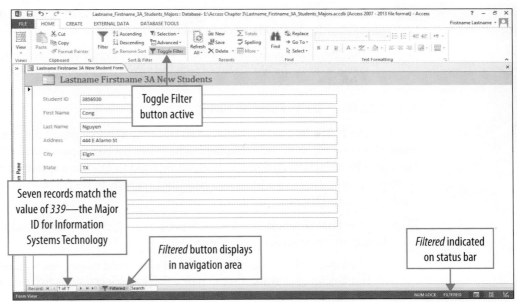

4 On the **HOME tab**, in the **Sort & Filter group**, click **Toggle Filter** to remove the filter and display all 102 records. Notice *Unfiltered* in the navigation area, which indicates a filter is created but is not active.

ANOTHER WAY Click Filtered in the navigation area to remove the filter.

NOTE **The Toggle Filter Button**

On the HOME tab, in the Sort & Filter group, the Toggle Filter button is used to apply or remove a filter. If no filter is created, the button is not available. After a filter is created, the button becomes available. Because it is a toggle button used to apply or remove a filter, the ScreenTip that displays for this button alternates between Apply Filter—when a filter is created but is not currently applied—and Remove Filter—when a filter is applied.

5 Be sure that the first record—for *Jordan Bass*—displays. On the **HOME tab**, in the **Sort & Filter group**, click **Toggle Filter** to reapply the filter. In the navigation area, click **Last record** ▶|
to display the last of the seven records that match a Major ID of *339*.

The record for *Student ID 9712345* displays—the record with your name. Use Toggle Filter to apply or remove filters as needed.

6 In the navigation area, click **Filtered** to remove the filter and display all of the records.

In the navigation area, *Filtered* changes to *Unfiltered*.

7 In the first record for *Jordan Bass*, in the **Last Name** field, select the first letter—**B**—in *Bass*. In the **Sort & Filter group**, click **Selection**, and then click **Begins with "B"**.

A new filter is applied that displays eight records in which the *Last Name* begins with the letter *B*.

ANOTHER WAY With the letter *B* selected, right-click the selection, and then click Begins with "B".

8 Use either **Toggle Filter** in the **Sort & Filter group** or **Filtered** in the navigation area to remove the filter and display all of the records.

9 In the **Sort & Filter group**, click **Advanced**, and then click **Clear All Filters**. Notice, that in the navigation area, *Unfiltered* changed to *No Filter*.

> The filter is removed from the form and must be recreated to apply it. If you toggle the filter off and save the form, the filter is saved with the form even though the filter is not currently applied.

Activity 3.08 | Using Filter By Form

Use the *Filter By Form* command to filter the records based on one or more fields, or based on more than one value in the same field. The Filter By Form command offers greater flexibility than the Filter By Selection command and can be used to answer a question that requires matching multiple values. In this activity, you will filter records to help Mr. Fitchette determine how many students live in Dripping Springs or Austin.

1 On the **HOME tab**, in the **Sort & Filter group**, click **Advanced**, and then click **Filter By Form**. Compare your screen with Figure 3.10.

> The Filter by Form window displays all of the field names, but without any data. In the empty text box for each field, you can type a value or select a value from a list. The *Look for* and *Or* tabs display at the bottom.

FIGURE 3.10

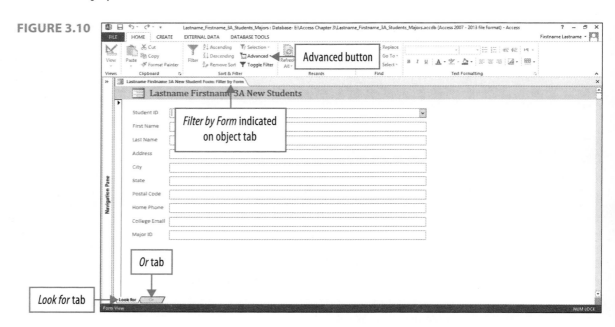

2 In the form, click the **City** field name to position the insertion point in the **City** field box. At the right edge of the **City** field box, click the **arrow**, and then click **Dripping Springs**. In the **Sort & Filter group**, click **Toggle Filter**.

> As displayed in the navigation area, four student records have *Dripping Springs* stored in the City field.

3 In the **Sort & Filter group**, click **Advanced**, and then click **Filter By Form**. In the lower left corner of the form, click the **Or tab**. Click the **City** field box **arrow**, and then click **Austin**. In the **Sort & Filter group**, click **Toggle Filter**, and then compare your screen with Figure 3.11.

> As displayed in the navigation area, 28 student records have either *Dripping Springs* OR *Austin* stored in the City field. You have created an *OR condition*; that is, records display where, in this instance, either of two values—Dripping Springs *or* Austin—is present in the selected field.

 **ANOTHER WAY** Click in the field box, and type the criteria separated by the word *or*. For example, in the City field box, type *Dripping Springs or Austin*.

FIGURE 3.11

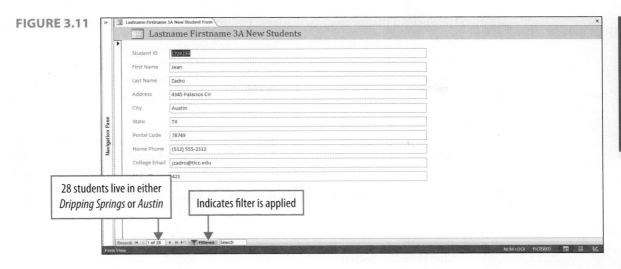

28 students live in either *Dripping Springs* or *Austin*

Indicates filter is applied

4 In the **Sort & Filter group**, click **Advanced**, and then click **Clear All Filters** to display all 102 records.

Activity 3.09 | Using Advanced Filter/Sort

In this activity, you will use the Advanced Filter/Sort command to filter records to locate students who live in Austin with a Major ID of *339*—Information Systems Technology.

1 In the **Sort & Filter group**, click **Advanced**, and then click **Advanced Filter/Sort**.

The Advanced Filter design grid displays, which is similar to the query design grid. A field list for the underlying table of the form displays.

2 In the table area, resize the field list so that the entire table name and all of the field names display.

3 In the **3A New Students** field list, double-click **City**, and then double-click **Major ID** to add both fields to the design grid. In the **Criteria** row under **City**, type **Austin** and then press [Enter]. In the **Criteria** row under **Major ID**, type **339** and then press [Enter]. Compare your screen with Figure 3.12.

FIGURE 3.12

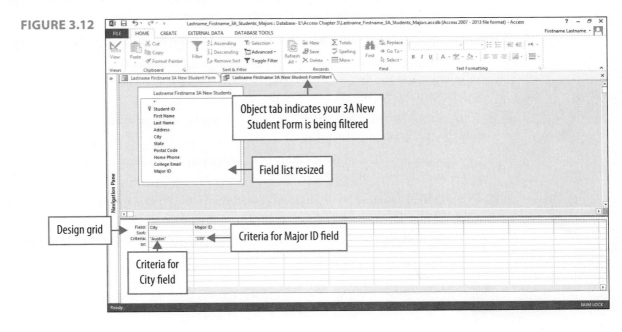

Object tab indicates your 3A New Student Form is being filtered

Field list resized

Design grid

Criteria for Major ID field

Criteria for City field

4 In the **Sort & Filter group**, click **Toggle Filter** to display the filtered records.

Three records match the criteria. You have created an ***AND condition***; that is, only records where both values—Austin *and* 339—are present in the selected fields display. There are three students who live in Austin who have declared a major of Information Systems Technology.

5 In the **Sort & Filter group**, click **Toggle Filter** to remove the filter and to display all of the records.

In the navigation area, *Unfiltered* displays, which indicates that a filter has been created for this form. Unless you click Clear All Filters, the filter is saved with the form when the form is closed. When you reopen the form, you can click Toggle Filter or Unfiltered to reapply the filter.

6 **Close** ⊠ your **3A New Student Form** object, and notice that the Advanced Filter grid also closes.

> **More Knowledge** | **Using the Filter Button**
>
> You can filter a form in a manner similar to the way you filter records in a table. Click in the field you wish to use for the filter. On the HOME tab, in the Sort & Filter group, click Filter to display a shortcut menu. Select the (Select All) check box to clear the option, and then select the data by which you want to filter your records by clicking the check boxes preceding the data. To remove the filter, redisplay the menu, and then select the (Select All) check box.

Objective 3 | Create a Form by Using the Form Wizard

Video A3-3

The ***Form Wizard*** walks you step by step through the creation of a form and gives you more flexibility in the design, layout, and number of fields in a form than the Form tool. Design a form for the individuals who use the form—either for entering new records or viewing records. For example, when your college counselor displays student information, it may be easier for the counselor to view the information if the fields are arranged in a layout that more closely matches a paper form.

Activity 3.10 | Creating a Form by Using the Form Wizard

In this activity, you will create a form to match the layout of a paper form that a student at Texas Lakes Community College completes when that student changes his or her major. This will make it easier for the individual who changes the data in the database.

1 On the ribbon, click the **CREATE tab**, and then in the **Forms group**, click **Form Wizard**.

The Form Wizard walks you step by step through the process of creating a form by asking questions. In the first wizard screen, you select the fields to include on the form. The fields can come from more than one table or query.

2 In the **Tables/Queries** box, click the **arrow** to display a list of available tables and queries from which you can create the form.

There are two tables in the database from which you can create a new form. The selected table is the one that you last worked with.

3 Click **Table: Lastname Firstname 3A New Students**, and then compare your screen with Figure 3.13.

In the Available Fields list, the field names from your 3A New Students table display.

FIGURE 3.13

Form Wizard button

Your 3A New Students table selected

Available Fields list displays field names in your 3A New Students table

Selected Fields list box

4 ▶ In the **Available Fields** list, double-click the following field names in the order given to move them to the **Selected Fields** list: **First Name**, **Last Name**, and **Major ID**. Compare your screen with Figure 3.14.

Three field names from your 3A New Students table display in the Selected Fields list.

ANOTHER WAY   Click the field name, and then click One Field > to move a field from the Available Fields list to the Selected Fields list.

FIGURE 3.14

Three fields that will display in the form

5 ▶ Click **Next**. In the wizard, be sure **Columnar** is selected as the layout, and then click **Next**. In the **What title do you want for your form?** box, select the existing text, type **Lastname Firstname 3A Student Major Change Form** and then click **Finish** to close the wizard and create the form.

The three fields and the data from the first record in your 3A New Students table display in Form view.

6 ▶ **Open** ⟫ the **Navigation Pane**. If necessary, increase the width of the Navigation Pane so that all object names display fully. Compare your screen with Figure 3.15.

In the Navigation Pane, the form displays under its data source—your 3A New Students table.

FIGURE 3.15

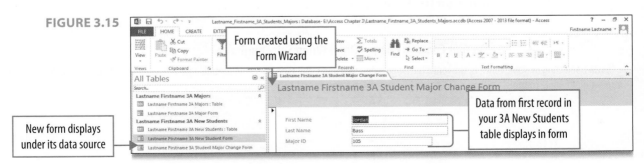

Form created using the Form Wizard

Data from first record in your 3A New Students table displays in form

New form displays under its data source

Video A3-4

After you create a form, you can make changes to it. For example, you can group the fields, resize the fields, add more fields to the form, and change the style of the form. Layout view enables you to see the data in the form as you modify the form. Most changes to a form can be made in Layout view.

Activity 3.11 | Grouping Controls in Layout View

In this activity, you will group **controls** in the form so that you can work with them as one unit. Controls are objects on a form that display data or text, perform actions, and let you view and work with information.

1 **Close** [«] the **Navigation Pane**, and be sure that your **3A Student Major Change Form** object displays in the object window. On the **HOME tab**, in the **Views group**, click the top portion of the **View** button to switch to **Layout** view. If the Field List pane displays on the right side of your screen, click Close [×] to close the pane. Compare your screen with Figure 3.16.

The field names and data for the first record in your 3A New Students record display in controls. The data for the first record displays in **text box controls**. The most commonly used control is the text box control, which typically displays data from a field in the underlying table. A text box control is a **bound control**—its data comes from a field in a table or query.

The field names—*First Name*, *Last Name*, and *Major ID*—display in **label controls**. A label control displays to the left of a text box control and contains descriptive information that displays on the form, usually the field name. A control that does not have a data source is an **unbound control**. Another example of an unbound control is a label control that displays the title of a form.

ANOTHER WAY On the right side of the status bar, click Layout View [▦] to switch from Form view to Layout view.

FIGURE 3.16

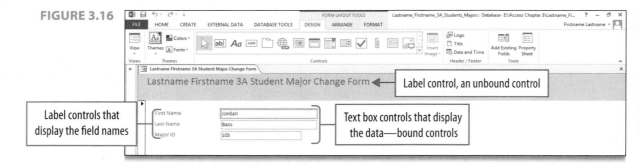

2 Click the **First Name label control**. Hold down [Shift], and then click the **Last Name label control**, the **Major ID label control**, and the three **text box controls** to select all of the label and text box controls on the form.

ALERT! **Do Your Controls Change Order When Selecting?**

If, when selecting multiple controls, the controls change order, click Undo, and then select the controls again. Be careful not to drag the mouse when you are selecting multiple controls.

3 With all six controls selected—surrounded by a colored border—on the ribbon, under **FORM LAYOUT TOOLS**, click the **ARRANGE tab**. In the **Table group**, click **Stacked**. Click the **First Name label control** to cancel the selection of all of the controls and to surround the **First Name label control** with a colored border. Compare your screen with Figure 3.17.

This action groups the controls together in the **Stacked layout** format—a layout similar to a paper form, with labels to the left of each field. Because the controls are grouped, you can move and edit the controls more easily as you redesign your form.

A dotted line forms a border around the controls, which indicates that the controls are grouped together. Above and to the left of the first label control that displays *First Name*, the **layout selector** displays. The layout selector is used to select and move or format the entire group of controls.

FIGURE 3.17

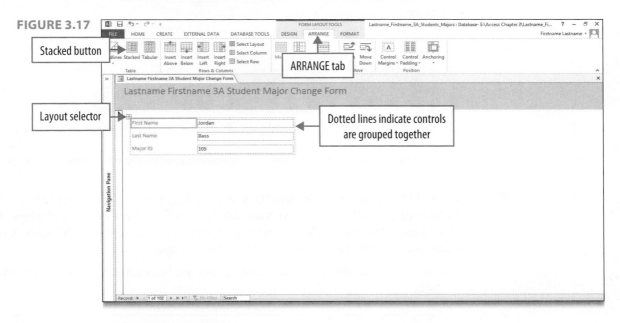

Activity 3.12 | Applying a Theme and Formatting a Form in Layout View

In this activity, you will apply a **theme** to the form in Layout view. A theme is a predesigned set of colors, fonts, lines, and fill effects that look good together and that can be applied to all of the objects in the database or to individual objects in the database.

1 On the ribbon, under **FORM LAYOUT TOOLS**, click the **DESIGN tab**. In the **Themes group**, click **Themes**. In the **Themes** gallery, using the ScreenTips, point to the **Retrospect** theme, right-click, and then click **Apply Theme to This Object Only**.

Right-click a theme so that you can apply the theme to an individual object within the database. Apply a theme before formatting any other controls in your form.

N O T E **Applying a Theme to an Object and Determining the Applied Theme**

If you click a theme rather than right-clicking it and selecting an option, the theme is applied to all objects in the database. You cannot click Undo to cancel the application of the theme to all objects. To determine the applied theme, in the Themes group, point to Themes. The ScreenTip displays the name of the current theme.

---

2 Click anywhere in the title of the form—*Lastname Firstname 3A Student Major Change Form*—to select the title. On the ribbon, under **FORM LAYOUT TOOLS**, click the **FORMAT tab**. In the **Font group**, click the **Font Size arrow**, and then click **14**. In the **Font group**, click **Bold** **B**. Click the **Font Color arrow**, and then under **Theme Colors**, in the fourth column, click the last color—**Olive Green, Text 2, Darker 50%**.

Activity 3.13 | Adding, Resizing, and Moving Controls in Layout View

In Layout view, you can change the form's **control layout**—the grouped arrangement of controls.

1 Be sure that your **3A Student Major Change Form** object displays in **Layout** view. On the ribbon, click the **DESIGN tab**, and in the **Tools group**, click **Add Existing Fields**. Compare your screen with Figure 3.18.

The Field List pane displays, which lists the fields in the underlying table—your 3A New Students table.

FIGURE 3.18

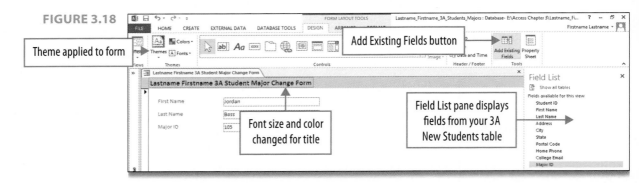

2 In the **Field List** pane, click **Student ID**, and then drag the field name to the left until the pointer displays above the **First Name label control** and a colored line displays above the control. Release the mouse button, and then compare your screen with Figure 3.19. If you are not satisfied with the result, click Undo, and begin again.

This action adds the Student ID label control and text box control to the form above the First Name controls.

FIGURE 3.19

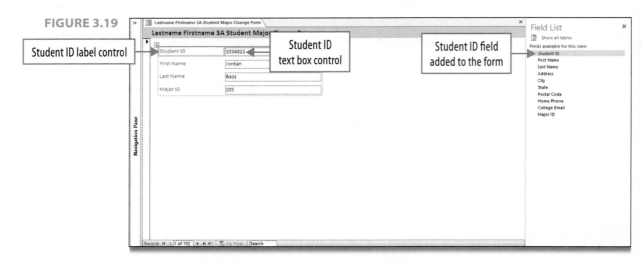

3 **Close** ☒ the **Field List** pane. Click the **Student ID text box control**, which displays *1034823*, to surround it with a border and to remove the border from the label control.

4 On the **DESIGN tab**, in the **Tools group**, click **Property Sheet**.

The Property Sheet for the Student ID text box control displays. Recall that each control has an associated Property Sheet where precise changes to the properties—characteristics—of selected controls can be made. At the top of the Property Sheet, to the right of *Selection type:*, *Text Box* displays because you selected the Student ID text box control.

5 In the **Property Sheet**, click the **Format tab**. Click **Width** to select the property setting, type **1.5** and then press Enter to decrease the width of the text box controls. Compare your screen with Figure 3.20.

All four text box controls are resized simultaneously. Because the controls are grouped together in a stacked layout, you can adjust the width of all of the text box controls at one time without having to select all of the controls. By decreasing the width of the text box controls, you have more space in which to rearrange the form controls. Because you can see the data in Layout view, you can determine visually that the space you have allotted is adequate to display all of the data in every field for every record.

ANOTHER WAY With the text box control selected, point to the right edge of the text box control until the ↔ pointer displays, and then drag left to the desired location.

FIGURE 3.20

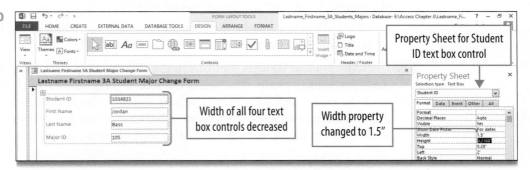

6 **Close** ✕ the **Property Sheet**. Click the **Last Name text box control**, which displays *Bass*. On the ribbon, under **FORM LAYOUT TOOLS**, click the **ARRANGE tab**. In the **Rows & Columns group**, click **Select Row** to select the text box control and its associated label control.

7 In the **Move group**, click **Move Up** to move both controls above the **First Name** controls, and then compare your screen with Figure 3.21.

ANOTHER WAY Drag the selected controls to the desired location and then release the mouse button.

FIGURE 3.21

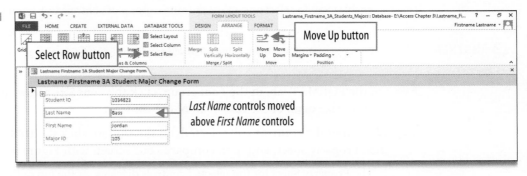

ALERT! **Did the Last Name Label Control Not Move with the Last Name Text Box Control?**

Be sure to select both the text box control and the label control before moving the controls; otherwise, only one of the controls will move. If this happens, click Undo, select both controls, and try again. Controls are stacked from top to bottom, not right to left.

8 **Save** 🖫 the changes you have made to the design of your form.

Activity 3.14 | Formatting Controls in Layout View

In this activity, you will format and change the property settings for multiple controls.

1 ▶ With the form displayed in **Layout** view, click the **Student ID text box control**, which displays *1034823*. On the **ARRANGE tab**, in the **Rows & Columns group**, click **Select Column** to select all four text box controls.

ANOTHER WAY   Click the first text box control, hold down Shift, and then click the last text box control to select all four text box controls.

2 ▶ With all four text box controls selected, on the ribbon, click the **FORMAT tab**. In the **Font group**, click the **Background Color arrow** . Under **Theme Colors**, in the last column, click the second color—**Green, Accent 6, Lighter 80%.**

All of the text box controls display a background color of light green. This formatting is not applied to the label controls on the left.

3 ▶ Click the **Student ID label control**. On the ribbon, click the **ARRANGE tab**, and then in the **Rows & Columns group**, click **Select Column**. On the ribbon, click the **FORMAT tab**, and then click the **Font Color arrow**—*not* the **Background Color arrow**. Under **Theme Colors**, in the fourth column, click the first color—**Olive Green, Text 2**. Click **Bold** **B**. Click in a blank area of the form to cancel the selection, and then compare your screen with Figure 3.22.

FIGURE 3.22

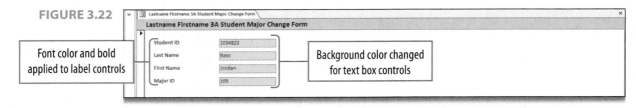

4 ▶ Click any **label control** to display the **layout selector** ⊞, and then click the **layout selector** ⊞ to select all of the grouped controls.

Recall that the layout selector, which displays to the left and above the Student ID label control, enables you to select and move the entire group of controls in Layout view.

ANOTHER WAY   Click any control, and then on the ARRANGE tab, in the Rows & Columns group, click Select Layout.

5 ▶ On the **FORMAT tab**, in the **Font group**, click the **Font Size arrow**, and then click **12** to change the font size of all of the text in all of the controls.

6 ▶ With all of the controls still selected, on the ribbon, click the **DESIGN tab**. In the **Tools group**, click **Property Sheet**, and then compare your screen with Figure 3.23.

The Property Sheet for the selected controls displays. At the top of the Property Sheet, to the right of *Selection type:*, *Multiple selection* displays because you have more than one control selected.

FIGURE 3.23

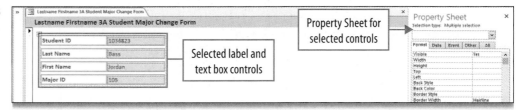

7 In the **Property Sheet**, click **Height**, type **0.25** and then press [Enter] to change the height of each selected control.

8 Click the **Student ID label control** to cancel the selection of all of the controls and to select only this label control. In the **Property Sheet**, click **Width**, type **1.25** and then press [Enter].

The width of every label control changed to 1.25 inches. Recall that because the label controls are arranged in a stacked layout, you can change the width of all controls by selecting only one control. This is one of the few properties that can be changed without first selecting the column.

9 Close [X] the **Property Sheet**, and then Save [🖫] the design changes to your form.

Activity 3.15 | Modifying a Form in Design View

Design view presents a detailed view of the structure of your form. Because the form is not actually running when displayed in Design view, the data does not display in the text box controls. However, some tasks, such as resizing sections, must be completed in Design view.

1 On the status bar, click **Design View** [🖍], and then compare your screen with Figure 3.24.

The form in Design view displays three sections, each designated by a *section bar* at the top of each section. The *Form Header* contains information, such as the form title, that displays at the top of the screen in Form view or Layout view and is printed at the top of the first page when records are printed as forms. The *Detail section* displays the records from the underlying table, and the *Form Footer* displays at the bottom of the screen in Form view or Layout view and is printed after the last detail section on the last page of a printout.

ANOTHER WAY   On the HOME tab, in the Views group, click the View arrow, and then click Design view; or right-click the object tab, and then click Design View.

FIGURE 3.24

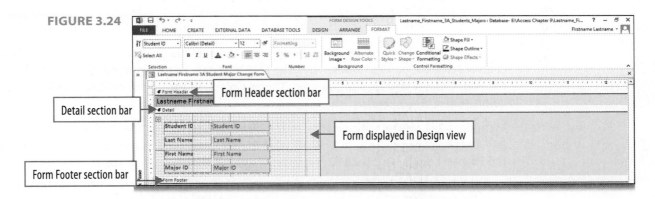

2 At the bottom of the form, click the **Form Footer section bar** to select it. On the ribbon, click the **DESIGN tab**, and in the **Tools group**, click **Property Sheet**. In the **Property Sheet**, on the **Format tab**, click **Height**, type **0.5** and then press [Enter]. Compare your screen with Figure 3.25.

In addition to properties for controls, you can make precise changes to sections of the form. Because you selected the Form Footer section bar, the Property Sheet displays a *Selection type* of *Section*, and the section is identified as *Form Footer*.

ANOTHER WAY   At the bottom of the form, point to the lower edge of the Form Footer section bar to display the [⊞] pointer, and then drag downward approximately 0.5 inch to increase the height of the section.

FIGURE 3.25

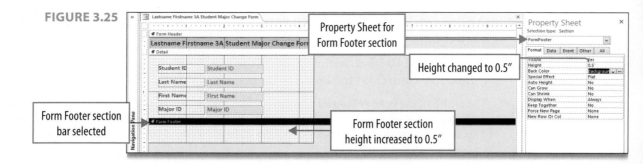

3 On the **DESIGN tab**, in the **Controls group**, click **Label** [Aa]. Move the [ᵗA] pointer into the **Form Footer** section and then position the plus sign of the [ᵗA] pointer at approximately **0.25 inch on the horizontal ruler** and even with the lower edge of the **Form Footer section bar**—the position does not need to be precise. Compare your screen with Figure 3.26.

FIGURE 3.26

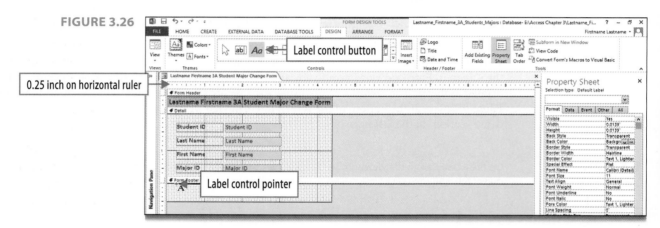

4 Click one time. Type **Texas Lakes Community College** and then press Enter. With the **label control** selected, on the ribbon, click the **FORMAT tab**. In the **Font group**, click **Bold** [B]. Click the **Font Color arrow**, and then under **Theme Colors**, in the fourth column, click the first color—**Olive Green, Text 2**.

5 With the **label control** still selected, in the **Property Sheet**, click **Top**, type **0.1** and then press Enter. In the **Property Sheet**, in the **Left** property setting, type **0.6** and then press Enter. **Close** [X] the **Property Sheet**, and then **Save** [H] the design changes to your form.

The top edge of the label control in the Form Footer section displays 0.1 inch from the lower edge of the Form Footer Section bar. The left edge of the label control aligns at 0.6 inch from the left margin of the form. In this manner, you can place a control in a specific location on the form.

6 On the right side of the status bar, click **Form View** [▦], and then compare your screen with Figure 3.27.

Form Footer text displays on the screen at the bottom of the form and prints only on the last page if all of the forms are printed. Recall, that in Form view, you can add, modify, or delete records stored in the underlying table.

↻ ANOTHER WAY   On the HOME tab, in the Views group, click the View arrow, and then click Form View; or right-click the object tab, and then click Form View.

FIGURE 3.27

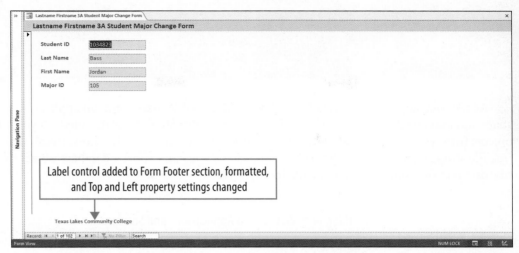

Label control added to Form Footer section, formatted, and Top and Left property settings changed

Texas Lakes Community College

7 In the navigation area, click **Last record** to display the record containing your name.

8 On the ribbon, click the **FILE tab**, click **Print**, and then on the right, click **Print**. In the **Print** dialog box, under **Print Range**, click the **Selected Records(s)** option button. Create a paper or electronic printout as directed by your instructor. To create an electronic printout, follow the directions given in the Note in Activity 3.06.

Because you decreased the width of the text box controls, you do *not* have to adjust the Column size Width in the Page Setup dialog box as you did with the form you created by using the Form tool.

9 **Close** all open objects, and then **Open** the **Navigation Pane**. On the right side of the title bar, click **Close** to close the database and to exit Access. As directed by your instructor, submit your database and the paper or electronic printouts of the three forms that are the results of this project. Specifically, in this project, using your own name, you created the following database and printouts or electronic printouts:

1. Lastname_Firstname_3A_Students_Majors	Database file
2. Lastname Firstname 3A New Student Form	Form (printout or electronic printout - Record 102)
3. Lastname Firstname 3A Major Form	Form (printout or electronic printout - Record 33)
4. Lastname Firstname 3A Student Major Change Form	Form (printout or electronic printout - Record 102)

END | You have completed Project 3A

GO! with Office Web Apps

Objective	**Export** an Access Form to an Excel Spreadsheet, Save to SkyDrive, Edit a Record, and Save to Your Computer

Access web apps are designed to work with Microsoft's SharePoint, an application for setting up websites to share and manage documents. Your college may not have SharePoint installed, so you will use other tools to share objects from your database so that you can work collaboratively with others. Recall that Window's SkyDrive is a free file storage and file sharing service. For Access, you can export a database object to an Excel worksheet, a PDF file, or a text file, and then save the file to SkyDrive.

> **A L E R T !** **Working with Web-Based Applications and Services**
>
> Computer programs and services on the web receive continuous updates and improvements. Thus, the steps to complete this web-based activity may differ from the ones shown. You can often look at the screens and the information presented to determine how to complete the activity.

Activity | Exporting an Access Form to an Excel Spreadsheet, Saving the Spreadsheet to SkyDrive, Editing a Record in SkyDrive, and Saving to Your Computer

In this activity, you will export your 3A Student Major Change Form object to an Excel spreadsheet, upload your Excel file to SkyDrive, edit a record in SkyDrive, and then download a copy of the edited spreadsheet to your computer.

1 Start Access, navigate to your **Access Chapter 3** folder, and then **Open** your **3A_Students_Majors** database file. If necessary, on the Message Bar, click Enable Content. In the **Navigation Pane**, click your **3A Student Major Change Form** object to select it.

2 On the ribbon, click the **EXTERNAL DATA tab**, and in the **Export group**, click **Excel**. In the **Export – Excel Spreadsheet** dialog box, click **Browse**, and then navigate to your **Access Chapter 3** folder. In the **File Save** dialog box, click in the **File name** box, type **Lastname_Firstname_AC_3A_Web** and then click **Save**.

3 In the **Export – Excel Spreadsheet** dialog box, under **Specify export options**, select the second check box—**Open the destination file after the export operation is complete**—and then click **OK**.

The records from the underlying table of the form display in Excel. When you export a form to Excel, the formatting and layout are automatically saved. For example, notice the olive green background color of the cells, which was the color that was applied to the text box controls in the form.

4 In the **Microsoft Excel** window, in the column headings row, to the left of column **A**, click **Select All**. On the **HOME tab**, in the **Cells group**, click **Format**, and then click **AutoFit Column Width**. Click in cell **A1** to cancel the selection, and then compare your screen with Figure A.

FIGURE A

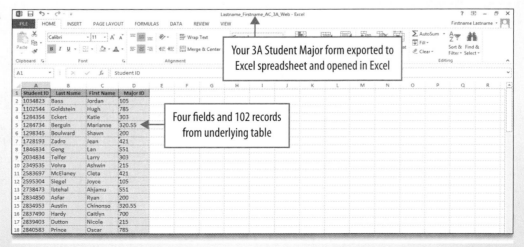

Your 3A Student Major form exported to Excel spreadsheet and opened in Excel

Four fields and 102 records from underlying table

(GO! with Office Web Apps continues on the next page)

5 Save the spreadsheet, and then **Close** Excel. In the **Export – Excel Spreadsheet** dialog box, click **Close**, and then **Close** Access.

6 From the desktop, start Internet Explorer, navigate to **http://skydrive.com**, and then sign in to your Microsoft account. Open your **GO! Web Projects** folder—or create and then open this folder if necessary.

7 On the menu bar, click **Upload**. In the **Choose File to Upload** dialog box, navigate to your **Access Chapter 3** folder, and then double-click your **AC_3A_Web** file to upload it to SkyDrive.

8 In your **GO! Web Projects** folder, click your **AC_3A_Web** file to open it in Microsoft Excel Web App.

On the ribbon, notice that you can open this worksheet in Excel instead of using the web app. If you are working on a computer that does not have Microsoft Excel installed, you can still create and modify workbooks in your web browser by using the Microsoft Excel Web App.

9 In the second record, click in the **Last Name** field, using your own last name, type **Lastname** and then press Tab. In the **First Name** field, using your own first name, type **Firstname** and then press ↓ to save the record. Compare your screen with Figure B.

10 On the ribbon, click the **FILE tab**, click **Save As**, and then click **Download**. In the message box—which usually displays at the bottom of your screen—click the **Save arrow**, and then click **Save as**. In the **Save As** dialog box, navigate to your **Access Chapter 3** folder, click in the **File name** box, and then type **Lastname_Firstname_A3A_Web_Download** and then click **Save**. **Close** the message box.

11 In SkyDrive, on the title bar, click **SkyDrive** to return to your home page. At the top right corner of your screen, click your SkyDrive name, and then click **Sign out**. **Close** your browser window.

12 Start Excel. In the Excel opening screen, click **Open Other Workbooks**. Under **Open**, click **Computer**, and then on the right, click **Browse**. Navigate to your **Access Chapter 3** folder, and then double-click your **A3A_Web** file. Notice that this file is the original file—the second record is not changed. If you are required to print your documents, use one of the methods in the Note box below. **Close** your Excel file, saving the changes to your worksheet, and then **Open** and print your **A3A_Web_Download** file following one of the methods in the Note box below. **Close** Excel, saving the changes to your worksheet. As directed by your instructor, submit your two workbooks and the two paper or electronic printouts that are the results of this project.

NOTE | **Adding the File Name to the Footer and Printing or Creating an Electronic Printout of an Excel Spreadsheet of Only One Page**

Click the FILE tab, click Print, and then click Page Setup. In the Page Setup dialog box, click the Header/Footer tab, and then click Custom Footer. With the insertion point blinking in the Left section box, click the Insert File Name button, and then click OK. In the Page Setup dialog box, click OK. Under Settings, click the *Pages* spin box up arrow to display *1* in the box. Click the *to* spin box up arrow to display *1* in the box.

To print on paper, click Print. To create an electronic file of your printout, on the left side of your screen, click Export. Under Export, be sure Create PDF/XPS Document is selected, and then click Create PDF/XPS. In the Publish as PDF or XPS dialog box, click Options. In the Options dialog box, under Page range, click Pages, and be sure the From box displays *1* and the To box displays *1*; then click OK. Navigate to your Access Chapter 3 folder, and then click Publish to save the file with the default name and an extension of pdf.

FIGURE B

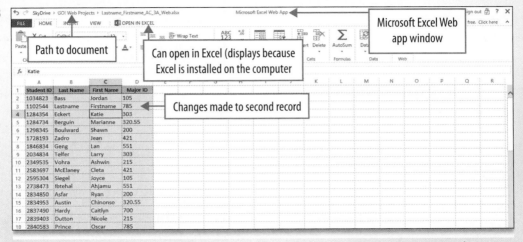

Job Openings Database

PROJECT ACTIVITIES

In Activities 3.16 through 3.24, you will assist Jack Woods, director of the Career Center for Texas Lakes Community College, in using his Access database to track the employees and job openings advertised for the annual job fair. Your completed reports will look similar to Figure 3.28.

PROJECT FILES

For Project 3B, you will need the following file:

a03B_Job_Openings

You will save your database as:

Lastname_Firstname_3B_Job_Openings

PROJECT RESULTS

FIGURE 3.28 Project 3B Job Openings

Objective 5 Create a Report by Using the Report Tool and Modify the Report in Layout View

Video A3-5

A *report* is a database object that summarizes the fields and records from a query or from a table in an easy-to-read format suitable for printing. A report consists of information extracted from queries or tables and report design controls, such as labels, headings, and graphics. The queries or tables that provide the underlying data for a report are referred to as the report's *record source*.

Activity 3.16 | Opening and Saving an Existing Database, Renaming Objects, and Viewing a Table Relationship

1 Start Access. In the Access opening screen, click **Open Other Files**. Under **Open**, click **Computer**. Under **Recent Folders**, if displayed, click the location where your student data files are stored; otherwise, click **Browse** and then navigate to the location where your student data files are stored. Double-click **a03B_Job_Openings** to open the database.

2 On the **FILE tab**, click **Save As**. Under **File Types**, be sure **Save Database As** is selected. On the right, under **Database File Types**, be sure **Access Database** is selected, and then click **Save As**. In the **Save As** dialog box, navigate to your **Access Chapter 3** folder. In the **File name** box, replace the existing text with **Lastname_Firstname_3B_Job_Openings** and then press [Enter].

3 On the **Message Bar**, click **Enable Content**. In the **Navigation Pane**, right-click the **3B Employers** table, and then click **Rename**. With the table name selected and using your own name, type **Lastname Firstname 3B Employers** and then press [Enter] to rename the table. Use the same technique to **Rename** the **3B Job Openings** table to **Lastname Firstname 3B Job Openings** and then **Rename** the first **3B Salary $40,000 or More Query** object to **Lastname Firstname 3B Salary $40,000 or More Query**

> Recall that a query that selects data from more than one table displays under both table names in the Navigation Pane. When you rename one of the query objects, the name of the second occurrence automatically changes.

4 Point to the right edge of the **Navigation Pane** to display the ⟷ pointer. Drag to the right to increase the width of the pane until all object names display fully.

5 On the ribbon, click the **DATABASE TOOLS tab**. In the **Relationships group**, click **Relationships**. Under **RELATIONSHIP TOOLS**, on the **DESIGN tab**, in the **Relationships group**, click **All Relationships**. Resize and move the field lists so that the entire table name and fields display for each field list.

> Because you renamed the tables, the field lists do not automatically display in the Relationships window.

6 In the **Relationships** window, click the **join line** between the two field lists. In the **Tools group**, click **Edit Relationships**. Point to the title bar of the **Edit Relationships** dialog box, and drag the dialog box downward below the **3B Job Openings** field list. Compare your screen with Figure 3.29.

> *One* employer is associated with *many* job openings. Thus, a one-to-many relationship is established between the 3B Employers table and the 3B Job Openings table by using Employee ID as the common field. Referential integrity is enforced, and cascade options are selected.

FIGURE 3.29

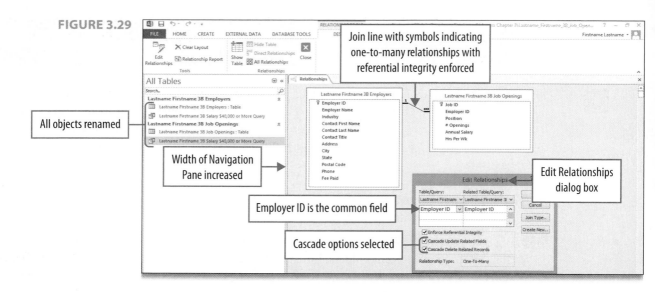

Join line with symbols indicating one-to-many relationships with referential integrity enforced

All objects renamed

Width of Navigation Pane increased

Employer ID is the common field

Cascade options selected

Edit Relationships dialog box

---

7 ▶ Close ☒ the **Edit Relationships** dialog box, and then **Close** ✕ the **Relationships** window. In the message box, click **Yes** to save changes to the layout of the relationships.

8 ▶ In the **Navigation Pane**, double-click each table, and then examine the fields and data in each table. Double-click the query object to run the query and examine the query results, apply **Best Fit** to the query results, and then **Save** the query. Switch to **Design** view to examine the design grid.

> Because you renamed the tables that are the underlying source of data for the query, you have to reapply Best Fit to the query results. The query answers the question, *What is the Job ID, position, employer name, number of job openings, and annual salary for job openings that have an annual salary of $40,000 or more, in ascending order by the Employer Name field within the Position field?*

9 ▶ In the object window, right-click any **object tab**, and then click **Close All**.

Activity 3.17 | Creating a Report by Using the Report Tool and Applying a Theme to the Report

The **Report tool** is the fastest way to create a report. This tool displays all of the fields and records from the record source that you select. You can use the Report tool to look at the underlying data quickly in an easy-to-read format, after which you can save the report and modify it in Layout view or in Design view.

In this activity, you will use the Report tool to create a report from a query that lists all of the job openings with an annual salary of at least $40,000 and apply a theme to the report.

1 ▶ In the **Navigation Pane**, if necessary, click to select your **3B Salary $40,000 or More Query** object. On the ribbon, click the **CREATE tab**, and in the **Reports group**, click **Report**. **Close** ≪ the **Navigation Pane**, and then compare your screen with Figure 3.30.

> The report is created using the query as the record source and displays in Layout view. The report includes all of the fields and all of the records from the query and the title of the query. In Layout view, the broken lines indicate the page margins in the report.

FIGURE 3.30

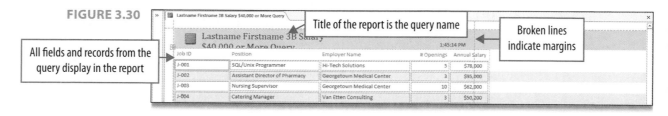

Title of the report is the query name

Broken lines indicate margins

All fields and records from the query display in the report

2 Under **REPORT LAYOUT TOOLS**, on the **DESIGN tab**, in the **Themes group**, click **Themes**. In the **Themes** gallery, use the ScreenTips to locate the **Integral** theme, right-click the **Integral** theme, and then click **Apply Theme to This Object Only**.

Recall that right-clicking a theme enables you to apply a predefined format to the active object only, which is a quick way to apply a professional look to a report. Apply a theme before formatting any other controls on the report.

Activity 3.18 | Modifying a Report in Layout View

After you create a report, you can make changes to it. For example, you can add or delete fields, resize the fields, and change the style of the report. Layout view enables you to see the data in the report as you modify the report. Most changes to a report can be made in Layout view.

1 Click the **Job ID** field name. On the ribbon, under **REPORT LAYOUT TOOLS**, click the **ARRANGE tab**. In the **Rows & Columns group**, click **Select Column** to select the field name and all of the data for each record in the field. Press Del to remove the field from the report.

The Job ID field is deleted, and the remaining fields move to the left. No fields extend beyond the right margin of the report.

 **ANOTHER WAY**   With the column selected, on the HOME tab, in the Records group, click Delete; or right-click the selected column, and then click Delete or Delete Column.

2 Scroll down, and notice that for the position of *Estimating Manager*, there is an extra blank line in the fields for this record. In the **Employer Name** field, click in the **text box control** that displays *Monroe Heating & Air Conditioning* to select all of the text box controls in this field.

3 On the ribbon, under **REPORT LAYOUT TOOLS**, click the **DESIGN tab**. In the **Tools group**, click **Property Sheet**. In the **Property Sheet**, on the **Format tab**, click **Width**, type **2.5** and then press Enter. Compare your screen with Figure 3.31.

Recall that you can use the Property Sheet to make precise changes to control properties.

ANOTHER WAY   Point to the right edge of the text box control to display the ↔ pointer. Drag to the right slightly until the data in the text box control displays on one line.

FIGURE 3.31

4 Close ☒ the **Property Sheet**. Click the **Position** field name, and then on the ribbon, click the **HOME tab**. In the **Sort & Filter group**, click **Ascending** to sort the records in ascending order by the Position field.

🔄 **ANOTHER WAY**   Right-click the selected field name and then click Sort A to Z.

5 Scroll to the bottom of the report, and then click the **calculated control** that displays *$2,157,625*, which is truncated at the bottom. Press [Del] to remove this control.

In a report created by using the Report tool, a **calculated control** is automatically created to sum any field that is formatted as currency. A calculated control contains an expression, often a formula or a function. Here, the total is not a useful number and thus can be deleted.

6 Scroll to the bottom of the report again, and then under the last column, click the horizontal line that is the border between the last record and the calculated control that you deleted. Press [Del] to remove this line, and then scroll to the bottom of the report to verify that the line has been deleted.

7 Scroll to the top of the report, and then click the **# Openings** field name. On the ribbon, click the **DESIGN tab**. In the **Grouping & Totals group**, click **Totals**, and then click **Sum**.

8 Scroll to the bottom of the report, and then click the **calculated control** that displays *100*. On the **DESIGN tab**, in the **Tools group**, click **Property Sheet**. In the **Property Sheet**, on the **Format tab**, click **Height**, type **0.25** and then press [Enter]. Compare your screen with Figure 3.32.

The total number of job openings for positions with a salary of $40,000 or more is 100.

🔄 **ANOTHER WAY**   Point to the lower edge of the text box control to display the ↕ pointer, and then double-click to resize the control, or drag downward to increase the height of the control.

FIGURE 3.32

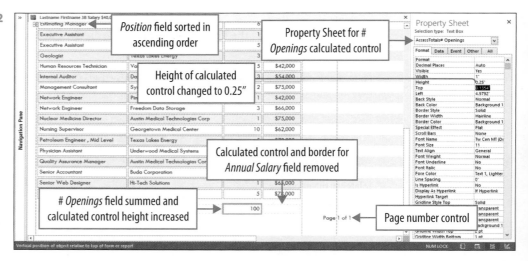

9 At the bottom of the report to the right of the calculated control, notice that the control that displays the page number does not fit entirely within the margins of the report. Click the **control** that displays *Page 1 of 1*. In the **Property Sheet**, click **Left**, type **2.5** and then press [Enter].

The control moves within the margins of the report with the left edge of the control 2.5 inches in from the left margin of the report. When you click on different controls in a report or form, the Property Sheet changes to match the selected control. Before printing, always scroll through the report to be sure that all of the controls display on one page and not outside of the margins.

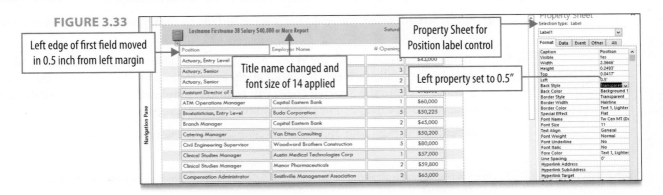

ANOTHER WAY   Click the control, point to the selected control to display the 🔈 pointer, and then drag the control to the left within the margins of the report.

10 ▶ Scroll to the top of the report, and then click the **label control** that displays the title of the report—*Lastname Firstname 3B Salary $40,000 or More Query*. On the ribbon, under **REPORT LAYOUT TOOLS**, click the **FORMAT tab**. In the **Font group**, click the **Font Size arrow**, and then click **14**.

11 ▶ With the **label control** for the title still selected, double-click **Query** to select the word, type **Report** and then press Enter to change the name of the report to *Lastname Firstname 3B Salary $40,000 or More Report*.

12 ▶ Click the **Position** field name. In the **Property Sheet**, click **Left**, type **0.5** and then press Enter to move this field 0.5 inch in from the left margin of the report. Compare your screen with Figure 3.33.

> The other fields adjust by moving to the right. The fields are centered approximately within the margins of the report.

ANOTHER WAY   Click the layout selector ⊞ to select all of the controls, and then drag it slightly downward and to the right until the columns are visually centered between the margins of the report. If your columns rearrange, click Undo and begin again.

FIGURE 3.33

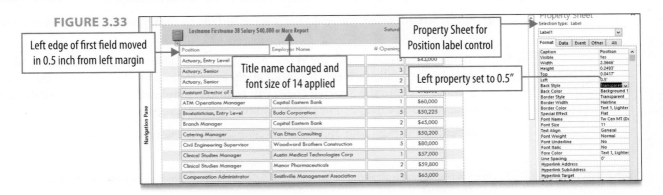

13 ▶ **Close** ✕ the **Property Sheet**, and then **Save** 🖫 the report as **Lastname Firstname 3B Salary $40,000 or More Report**

Activity 3.19 │ Printing a Report

In this activity, you will view your report in Print Preview and display the two pages of the report.

1 ▶ On the right side of the status bar, click **Print Preview** 🔍.

ANOTHER WAY   On the DESIGN tab or the HOME tab, in the Views group, click the View arrow, and then click Print Preview; or, in the object window, right-click the object tab, and then click Print Preview.

2 ▶ On the **PRINT PREVIEW tab**, in the **Zoom group**, click **Two Pages** to view the two pages of your report. Notice that the page number displays at the bottom of each page.

3 Create a paper or electronic printout as directed—two pages result, and then click **Close Print Preview**. **Close** $\boxed{\times}$ the report, and then **Open** $\boxed{\gg}$ the **Navigation Pane**.

The report displays under both tables from which the query was created. The report object name displays with a small green notebook icon.

4 **Close** $\boxed{\ll}$ the **Navigation Pane**.

Objective 6 Create a Report by Using the Report Wizard

Video A3-6

Use the ***Report Wizard*** when you need more flexibility in the design of your report. You can group and sort data by using the wizard and use fields from more than one table or query if you have created the relationships between tables. The Report Wizard is similar to the Form Wizard; the wizard walks you step by step through the process of creating the report by asking you questions and then designs the report based on your answers.

Activity 3.20 | Creating a Report by Using the Report Wizard

In this activity, you will prepare a report for Mr. Woods that displays the employers, grouped by industry, and the total fees paid by employers for renting a booth at the Job Fair.

1 On the ribbon, click the **CREATE tab**, and then in the **Reports group**, click **Report Wizard**.

In the first wizard screen, you select the fields to include on the report. The fields can come from more than one table or query.

2 In the **Tables/Queries** box, click the **arrow**, and then click **Table: Lastname Firstname 3B Employers**. In the **Available Fields** list, double-click the following field names in the order given to move them to the **Selected Fields** list: **Industry**, **Employer Name**, and **Fee Paid** (scroll as necessary to locate the *Fee Paid* field). Compare your screen with Figure 3.34.

Three field names from your 3B Employers table display in the Selected Fields list.

 ANOTHER WAY   Click the field name, and then click One Field $\boxed{>}$ to move a field from the Available Fields list to the Selected Fields list.

FIGURE 3.34

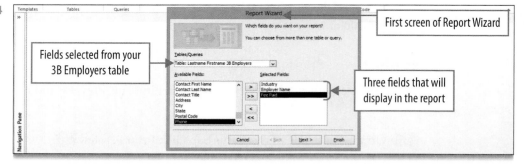

3 Click **Next**. In the wizard, notice that you can add grouping levels and that a preview of the grouping level displays on the right.

Grouping data helps to organize and summarize the data in your report.

4 On the left, double-click **Industry**, and then compare your screen with Figure 3.35.

The preview displays how the data will be grouped in the report. Grouping data in a report places all of the records that have the same data in a field together as a group—in this instance, the records will be grouped by *Industry*. Within each Industry name, the Employer Name and Fee Paid will display.

FIGURE 3.35

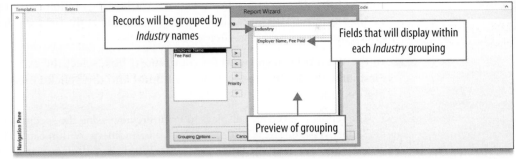

5 Click **Next**. Click the **1** box **arrow**, click **Employer Name**, and then compare your screen with Figure 3.36.

In this step of the wizard, you indicate how you want to sort the records and summarize the information. You can sort up to four fields. The Summary Options button displays because the data is grouped, and at least one of the fields—*Fee Paid*—contains numerical or currency data. Within each Industry grouping, the records will be sorted alphabetically by the Employer Name. Sorting records in a report presents a more organized view of the records.

FIGURE 3.36

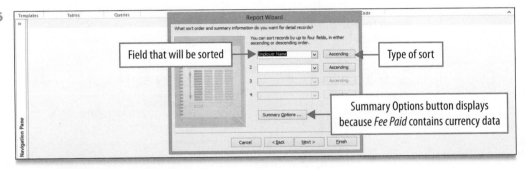

6 In the wizard, click **Summary Options**, and then compare your screen with Figure 3.37.

The Summary Options dialog box displays. The *Fee Paid* field can be summarized by selecting one of the four check boxes for Sum, Avg, Min, or Max. You can also display only summary information or display both the details—each record—and the summary information. The default setting is to display *Detail and Summary*.

FIGURE 3.37

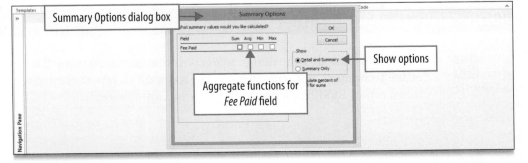

7 In the **Summary Options** dialog box, click to select the **Sum** check box. Under **Show**, be sure that **Detail and Summary** is selected, and then click **OK**. In the wizard, click **Next**.

In this step of the wizard, you select the layout and page orientation. A preview of the layout displays on the left.

8 Click each **Layout** option button, noticing the changes in the preview, and then click **Stepped** to select it as the layout for your report. Under **Orientation**, be sure that **Portrait** is selected. At the bottom of the wizard, be sure that the **Adjust the field width so all fields fit on a page** check box is selected, and then click **Next**.

9 In the **What title do you want for your report?** box, select the existing text, type **Lastname Firstname 3B Booth Fees by Industry Report** and then click **Finish**. Compare your screen with Figure 3.38.

The report is saved and displays in Print Preview using the specifications you defined in the Report Wizard. The records are grouped by Industry. Within each Industry, the records display in ascending order by the Employer Name. Within each Industry grouping, the Fee paid is summed or totaled—the word *Sum* displays at the end of each grouping.

FIGURE 3.38

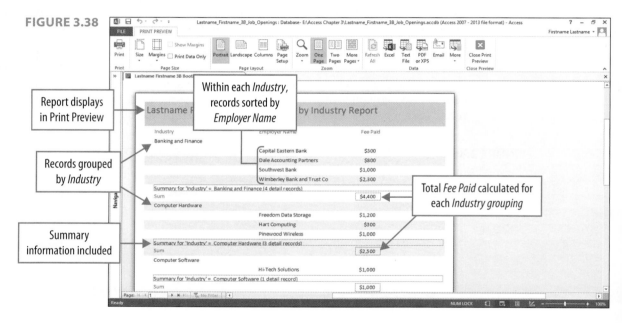

10 In the object window, right-click the **object tab** for the report, and then click **Layout View**.

 **ANOTHER WAY**   On the status bar, click Layout View ▣ ; or click Close Print Preview, and then on the HOME tab or the DESIGN tab, click the View arrow, and then click Layout View.

Objective 7   Modify the Design of a Report

Video A3-7

You can modify the design of a report that is created using the Report Wizard by using the same techniques and tools that you use to modify a report created with the Report tool. Recall that most report modifications can be made in Layout view.

Activity 3.21 | Formatting and Deleting Controls in Layout View

In this activity, you will apply a theme to the report, format the title of the report, and delete the summary information controls.

1 Be sure that your **3B Booth Fees by Industry Report** object is displayed in **Layout** view. Under **REPORT LAYOUT TOOLS**, on the **DESIGN tab**, in the **Themes group**, click **Themes**. In the **Themes** gallery, use the ScreenTips to locate the **Ion Boardroom** theme, right-click the **Ion Boardroom** theme, and then click **Apply Theme to This Object Only**.

Recall that you should apply a theme before applying any other formatting changes. Also, recall that if you click a theme—instead of right-clicking—the theme is applied to all of the objects in the database.

2 At the top of the report, click the title—*Lastname Firstname 3B Booth Fees by Industry*—to display a border around the label control. On the ribbon, under **REPORT LAYOUT TOOLS**, click the **FORMAT tab**. In the **Font group**, click the **Font Size arrow**, and then click **14**. In the **Font group**, click **Bold** B.

By changing the font size, the report name is no longer truncated and includes the word *Report*.

3 Within each *Industry* grouping, notice the **Summary for 'Industry'** information.

Because you selected Summary Options, a summary line is included at the end of each grouping that details what is being summarized—in this case, summed—and the number of records that are included in the summary total. Now that Mr. Woods has viewed the report, he has decided that this information is not necessary and can be removed.

4 Click any one of the controls that begins with **Summary for 'Industry'**.

The control that you clicked is surrounded by a border, and all of the other summary information controls are surrounded by paler borders to indicate that all controls are selected.

5 Press Del to remove the controls from the report, and then compare your screen with Figure 3.39.

ANOTHER WAY   Right-click any of the selected controls, and then click Delete to remove the controls from the report.

FIGURE 3.39

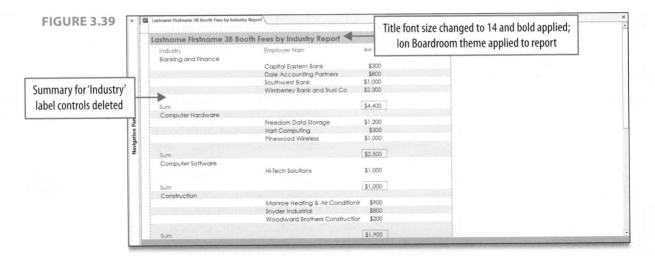

Title font size changed to 14 and bold applied; Ion Boardroom theme applied to report

Summary for 'Industry' label controls deleted

6 Save 🖫 the changes you have made to the design of the report.

Activity 3.22 | Modifying Controls in Layout View

In this activity, you will modify the text in controls, move controls, resize controls, and add a control to the report in Layout view.

1 On the left side of the report, click a **Sum label control**, which selects all of the related controls. Double-click the control to select the text—*Sum*. Type **Total Booth Fees by Industry** and then press Enter. Compare your screen with Figure 3.40.

This text states more clearly what is being summed.

FIGURE 3.40

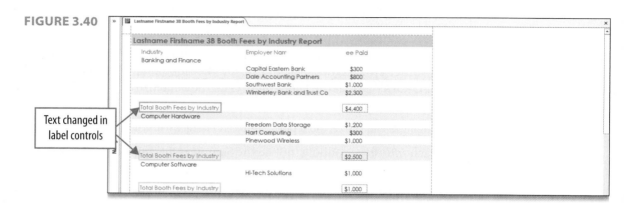

2 At the top of the report, click the **Industry label control** to select it. Hold down Shift, click the **Employer Name label control**, and then click the **Fee Paid label control** to select all three field names. On the **FORMAT tab**, in the **Font group**, click **Bold** B.

Clicking Bold also increases the size of the controls so that the text is no longer truncated.

3 At the top of the report, under the **Fee Paid label control**, click the **text box control** that displays *$300* to select the text box controls for all of the records for this field. On the ribbon, click the **DESIGN tab**. In the **Tools group**, click **Property Sheet**. In the **Property Sheet**, on the **Format tab**, click **Left**, type **7** and then press Enter. Compare your screen with Figure 3.41.

All of the Fee Paid text box controls move to the right—7" in from the left margin. Do not be concerned that the summary total and the field name are not aligned with the data; you will correct this in the next activity. The field is moved to the right so that you can increase the width of the Employer Name text box controls so that all of the data for every record displays.

FIGURE 3.41

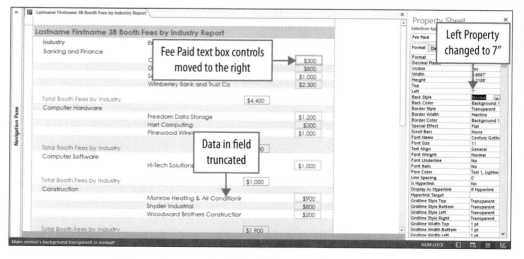

4 Scroll to view the bottom of the report. Click to select the **calculated control** for the **Grand Total,** which displays *20,400* and part of the dollar symbol. In the **Property Sheet**, click **Width**, type **0.8** and then press Enter.

> The width of the calculated control increases to display the dollar symbol. Do not be concerned that the right edge of the control no longer aligns with the control above it; you will correct this in the next activity. Recall that a calculated control contains an expression—a formula or function—that displays the result of the expression when the report is displayed in Report view, Print Preview, or Layout view.

ANOTHER WAY   Point to the left edge of the control to display the ↔ pointer. Drag to the left slightly to increase the width of the calculated control.

5 At the bottom of the report, on the left side, click the **Grand Total label control**. In the **Property Sheet**, click **Width**, type **1** and then press Enter. Compare your screen with Figure 3.42.

> The width of the label control is increased so that all of the text displays.

ANOTHER WAY   Point to the right edge of the control to display the ↔ pointer, and then double-click to resize the control.

FIGURE 3.42

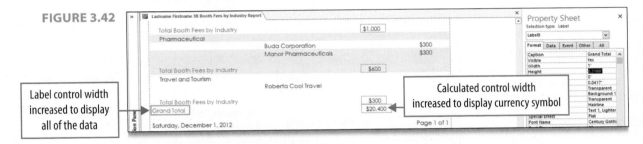

Label control width increased to display all of the data

Calculated control width increased to display currency symbol

6 Scroll to the top to display the Industry grouping of **Construction**, and notice that the first and third records have truncated data in the **Employer Name** field. In the **Construction** grouping, click, the **Employer Name text box control** that starts with *Monroe Heating* to select all of the text box controls for this field.

7 In the **Property Sheet**, click **Width**, type **3** and then press Enter. **Save** 🖫 the design changes to your report, and then compare your screen with Figure 3.43.

> The width of the Employer Name text box controls is increased so that all of the data in this field for every record displays. Recall that you moved the Fee Paid text box controls to the right to make room for the increased width of these controls.

FIGURE 3.43

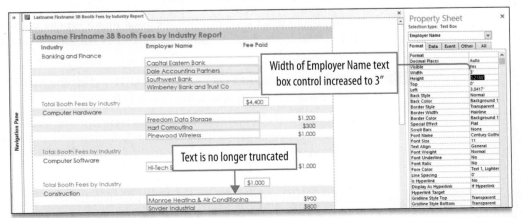

Width of Employer Name text box control increased to 3"

Text is no longer truncated

Activity 3.23 | Aligning Controls in Design View

Design view gives you a more detailed view of the structure of your report. You can see the header and footer sections for the report, for the page, and for groups. In Design view, your report is not running, so you cannot see the data from the table in the controls. In the same manner as forms, you can add labels to the Page Footer section or increase the height of sections. Some tasks, such as aligning controls, must be completed in Design view.

1 **Close** ☒ the **Property Sheet**. On the status bar, click **Design View** 📐, and then compare your screen with Figure 3.44.

Design view for a report is similar to Design view for a form. You can modify the layout of the report in this view, and use the dotted grid pattern to align controls. This report has several sections. The **Report Header** displays information at the top of the *first page* of a report. The **Page Header** displays information at the top of *every page* of a report. The **Group Header** displays the name of data in the field by which the records are grouped; in this case, the *Industry* name. The **Detail** section displays the data for each record. The **Group Footer** displays the summary information for each grouping; in this case, the Industry name. The **Page Footer** displays information at the bottom of *every page* of the report. The **Report Footer** displays information at the bottom of the *last page* of the report.

If you do not group data in a report, the Group Header section and Group Footer section will not display. If you do not summarize the data, the Group Footer section will not display.

FIGURE 3.44

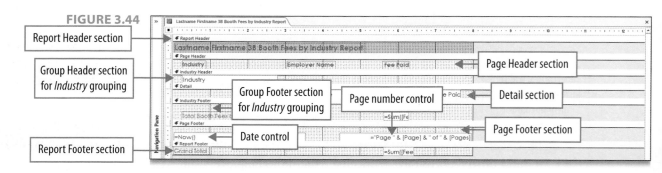

2 In the **Page Footer** section of the report, examine the two controls in this section. Recall that information in the Page Footer section displays at the bottom of every page in the report.

On the left side, the **date control** displays =*Now( )*, which inserts the current date each time the report is opened. On the right side, the **page number control** displays =*"Page " & [Page] & " of " & [Pages]*, which inserts the page number, for example *Page 1 of 2*, when the report is displayed in Print Preview or when printed. Both of these controls contain examples of functions that are used by Access to create controls in a report.

3 In the **Industry Footer** section, click the **Total Booth Fees by Industry label control**. Hold down Shift, and in the **Report Footer** section, click the **Grand Total label control** to select both label controls.

4 On the ribbon, under **REPORT DESIGN TOOLS**, click the **ARRANGE tab**. In the **Sizing & Ordering group**, click **Align**, and then click **Left**.

The left edge of the *Grand Total label control* is aligned with the left edge of the *Total Booth Fees by Industry label control*. When using the Align Left command, the left edges of the selected controls are aligned with the control that is the farthest to the left in the report.

5 In the **Page Header** section, click the **Fee Paid label control**. Hold down [Shift] while you click the following: in the **Detail** section, click the **Fee Paid text box control**; in the **Industry Footer** section, click the **calculated control** that begins with =*Sum*; and in the **Report Footer** section, click the **calculated control** that begins with =*Sum*.

> Four controls are selected.

6 On the **ARRANGE tab**, in the **Sizing & Ordering group**, click **Align**, and then click **Right**. Save [icon] the design changes to your report, and then compare your screen with Figure 3.45.

> The right edges of the four selected controls are aligned with the right edge of the *Fee Paid text box control*. When using the Align Right command, the right edges of the selected controls are aligned with the control that is the farthest to the right in the report.

FIGURE 3.45

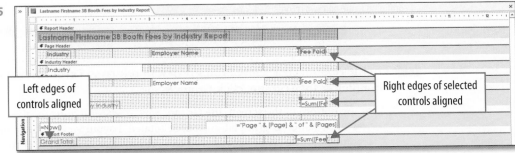

7 On the status bar, click **Layout View** [icon] to display the underlying data in the controls. Scroll to view the bottom of the report. On the left side, notice that the **Total Booth Fees by Industry label control** and the **Grand Total label control** are left aligned. Also, notice the right alignment of the controls in the **Fee Paid** column.

Objective 8 Keep Grouped Data Together in a Printed Report

Video A3-8

Before you print a report, examine the report in Print Preview to be sure that all of the labels and data display fully and to be sure that all of the data is properly grouped. Sometimes a page break occurs in the middle of a group of data, leaving the labels on one page and the data or summary information on another page.

Activity 3.24 | Keeping Grouped Data Together in a Printed Report

In this activity, you will preview the document and then will keep the data in each group together so a grouping is not split between two pages of the report. This is possible if the data in a grouping does not exceed the length of a page.

1 On the status bar, click **Print Preview** [icon]. On the **PRINT PREVIEW tab**, in the **Zoom group**, click **Two Pages**, and then compare your screen with Figure 3.46.

> The report will print on two pages. For the Industry grouping of *Hotel and Food Service*, one record and the summary data display at the top of Page 2 and is separated from the rest of the grouping that displays at the bottom of page 1. Your display may differ depending upon your printer configuration.

> In Print Preview, the One Page or Two Pages Zoom view causes the records to be compressed slightly and might display with the bottoms of records truncated. The records, however, will print correctly.

FIGURE 3.46

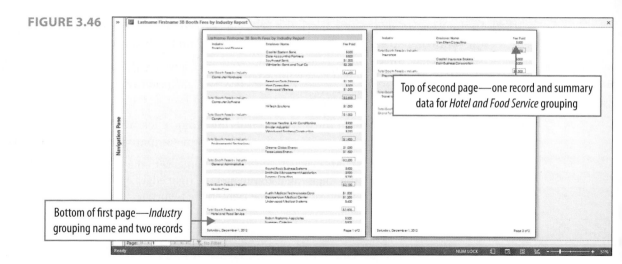

Top of second page—one record and summary data for *Hotel and Food Service* grouping

Bottom of first page—*Industry* grouping name and two records

2 On the ribbon, click **Close Print Preview** to return to **Layout** view. On the **DESIGN tab**, in the **Grouping & Totals group**, click **Group & Sort**.

At the bottom of the screen, the ***Group, Sort, and Total pane*** displays. This pane is used to control how information is grouped, sorted, or totaled. Layout view is the preferred view in which to accomplish these tasks because you can see how the changes affect the display of the data in the report.

3 In the **Group, Sort, and Total** pane, on the **Group on Industry** bar, click **More**. To the right of **do not keep group together on one page**, click the **arrow**, and then compare your screen with Figure 3.47.

The *keep whole group together on one page* command keeps each industry group together, from the name in the Group Header section through the summary information in the Group Footer section. The default setting is *do not keep group together on one page*. Next to *Group on Industry*, with *A on top* indicates that the industry names are sorted in ascending order.

FIGURE 3.47

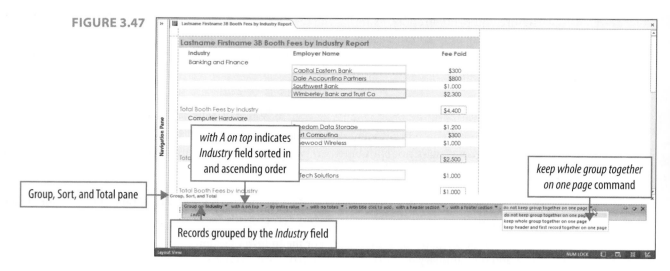

with *A on top* indicates *Industry* field sorted in and ascending order

keep whole group together on one page command

Group, Sort, and Total pane

Records grouped by the *Industry* field

4 Click **keep whole group together on one page**. On the **DESIGN tab**, in the **Grouping & Totals group**, click **Group & Sort** to close the **Group, Sort, and Total** pane.

5 On the status bar, click **Print Preview** 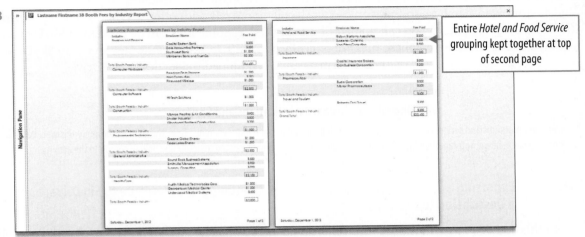. If necessary, in the Zoom group, click Two Pages. Compare your screen with Figure 3.48.

The entire grouping for the Industry of *Hotel and Food Service* displays at the top of page 2. The grouping no longer breaks between page 1 and page 2. Recall that even though the bottoms of records display truncated because of the compressed Print Preview setting of Two Pages, the records will print correctly.

FIGURE 3.48

Entire *Hotel and Food Service* grouping kept together at top of second page

6 Save the design changes to your report, and then create a paper or electronic printout of the report as directed—two pages result.

7 Close the report, and then **Open** the **Navigation Pane**. If necessary, increase the width of the Navigation Pane so that all object names display fully.

8 On the right side of the title bar, click **Close** to close the database and to exit Access. As directed by your instructor, submit your database and the paper or electronic printouts of the two reports—each report is two pages—that are the results of this project. Specifically, in this project, using your own name you created the following database and printouts or electronic printouts:

1. Lastname_Firstname_3B_Job_Openings	Database file
2. Lastname Firstname 3B Salary $40,000 or More Report	Report (printout or electronic printout - two pages)
3. Lastname Firstname 3B Booth Fees by Industry Report	Report (printout or electronic printout - two pages)

END | You have completed Project 3B

GO! with Office Web Apps

Objective | Export an Access Report to a Word File, Save to SkyDrive, and Add a Description to the Word File

Access web apps are designed to work with Microsoft's SharePoint, an application for setting up websites to share and manage documents. Your college may not have SharePoint installed, so you will use other tools to share objects from your database so that you can work collaboratively with others. When you have information that you want to share with others, you can upload files to SkyDrive. Some files can be opened in SkyDrive; some can only be downloaded. Because database files are typically large in size, and free storage space on SkyDrive is limited, you can export database objects to different formats and then upload those files to SkyDrive.

ALERT! | **Working with Web-Based Applications and Services**

Computer programs and services on the web receive continuous updates and improvements. Thus, the steps to complete this web-based activity may differ from the ones shown. You can often look at the screens and the information presented to determine how to complete the activity.

Activity | Exporting an Access Report to a Word File, Uploading the Word File to SkyDrive, and Adding a Description to the Word File

In this activity, you will export your 3B Salary $40,000 or More Report object to a Word file, upload your Word file to SkyDrive, and then add a description to the Word file. The report will be available for individuals with whom you have shared your SkyDrive files or folders.

1 Start Access, navigate to your **Access Chapter 3** folder, and then **Open** your **3B_Job_Openings** database file. If necessary, on the Message Bar, click Enable Content. In the **Navigation Pane**, click your **3B Salary $40,000 or More Report** object to select it.

2 On the ribbon, click the **EXTERNAL DATA tab**, and in the **Export group**, click **More**, and then click **Word**.

The report will be exported as a **Rich Text Format (RTF)**—a standard file format that contains text and some formatting such as underline, bold, italic, font sizes, and colors. RTF documents can be opened in many word processing programs and text editors.

3 In the **Export – RTF File** dialog box, navigate to your **Access Chapter 3** folder. In the **File Save** dialog box, click in the **File name** box to select the existing text. Type **Lastname_Firstname_AC_3B_Web** and then click **Save**. In the **Export – RTF File** dialog box, select the **Open the destination file after the export operation is complete** check box, and then click **OK**. Compare your screen with Figure A.

The RTF file is created and opens in Word.

4 Close ☒ Word. In the **Export – RTF File** dialog box, click **Close**, and then **Close** ☒ Access.

FIGURE A

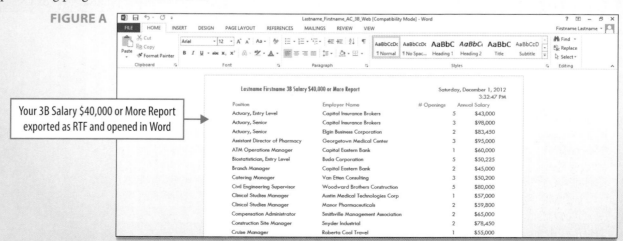

Your 3B Salary $40,000 or More Report exported as RTF and opened in Word

(GO! with Office Web Apps continues on the next page)

5 From the desktop, start Internet Explorer, navigate to **http://skydrive.com**, and then sign in to your Microsoft account. Open your **GO! Web Projects** folder—or create and then open this folder if necessary.

6 On the menu bar, click **Upload**. In the **Choose File to Upload** dialog box, navigate to your **Access Chapter 3** folder, and then double-click your **AC_3B_Web** file to upload it to SkyDrive.

7 After the file is uploaded, in your **GO! Web Projects** folder, right-click your **AC_3B_Web** file, and then click **Properties**.

A Properties panel displays on the right side of your screen.

8 In the **Properties** panel, click **Add a description**. In the box, type **This report displays job openings in our area that have a salary of $40,000 or more for which our students can apply.** Press Enter, and then compare your screen with Figure B.

9 On your keyboard, press the [⊞] key, type **snip**, and then click **Snipping Tool**. In the **Snipping Tool** dialog box, click the **New arrow**, and then click **Full-screen Snip**.

10 On the **Snipping Tool** toolbar, click **Save Snip** [💾]. In the **Save As** dialog box, navigate to your **Access Chapter 3** folder. Click in the **File name** box to select the existing text. Type **Lastname_Firstname_AC_3B_Web_Snip** and then, if necessary, click the **Save as type arrow**, and click **JPEG file**. In the **Save As** dialog box, click **Save**, and then **Close** [❎] the **Snipping Tool** window.

11 In SkyDrive, on the title bar, click **SkyDrive** to return to your home page. At the top right corner of your screen, click your SkyDrive name, and then click **Sign out**. **Close** your browser window.

12 If directed to submit a paper printout of your RTF document and snip file, follow the directions given in the Note below. As directed by your instructor, submit your RTF document, which is two pages, and your snip file that are the results of this project.

> **N O T E** **Printing your RTF Document and Your Snip .JPEG File**
>
> Using Windows Explorer, navigate to your Access Chapter 3 folder. Locate and double-click your AC_3B_Web file—it will open in Word. On the ribbon, click the FILE tab, and then click Print. To print on paper, on the right, click Print. To create an electronic file of your printout, on the left side of your screen, click Export. Under Export, be sure Create PDF/XPS Document is selected, and then click Create PDF/XPS. Navigate to your Access Chapter 3 folder, and then click Publish to save the file with the default name and an extension of pdf.
>
> In your Access Chapter 3 folder, locate and double-click your AC_3B_Web_Snip file. If this is the first time you have tried to open a .jpeg file, you will be asked to identify a program. If you are not sure which program to use, select Windows Photo Viewer. From the ribbon, menu bar, or toolbar, click the Print command, and then Close the program window.

FIGURE B

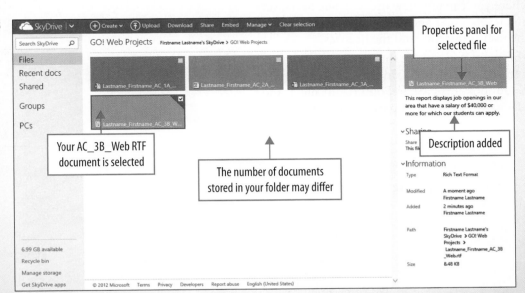

Andrew Rodriguez / Fotolia; FotolEdhar/ Fotolia; apops/ Fotolia; Yuri Arcurs/ Fotolia

The advantage of using Office 365 is that your organization does not have to purchase and install server hardware and software for sophisticated business applications and does not need a full-time IT person or staff just to manage the technology your teams need.

By using Office 365, you are able to have business-class services for your employees without investing in expensive hardware, software, and personnel. However, at least one person in an organization must be designated as the *Office 365 Administrator*—the person who creates and manages the account, adds new users, sets up the services your organization wants to use, sets permission levels, and manages the SharePoint team sites. You can have more than one administrator if you want to share these tasks with others.

Microsoft provides easy-to-use instructions and videos to get you started, and you might also have contact with a Microsoft representative. You will probably find, however, that subscribing to and setting up the account, adding users, and activating services is a straightforward process that requires little or no assistance.

After purchasing the required number of licenses, you will add each team member as a user that includes his or her email address. The Admin Overview page, as shown in Figure A, assists the Office 365 Administrator. On the left, there are links to manage the users and domains in your Office 365 account. This is where you can add new users, delete users, set permission levels, enter and change passwords, and update the user properties and the licenses.

On this page, you can see the various services available to you in Office 365. In the site shown in Figure A, Outlook, Lync, SharePoint (team sites), and a public-facing website are all part of the services.

Activity | Using a Team Site to Collaborate

This group project relates to the **Bell Orchid Hotels**. If your instructor assigns this project to your class, you will use a SharePoint team site in **Office 365** to collaborate on the following tasks for this chapter:

- If you are in the **Accounting Group**, you and your teammates will finalize the Stockholders database and post it on the SharePoint team site.

- If you are in the **Engineering Group**, you and your teammates will finalize the Subcontractors database and post it on the SharePoint team site.

- If you are in the **Food and Beverage Group**, you and your teammates will finalize Banquet Clients database and post it on the SharePoint team site.

- If you are in the **Human Resources Group**, you and your teammates will finalize the Employees database and post it on the SharePoint team site.

- If you are in the **Operations Group**, you and your teammates will finalize the Guests Database and post it on the SharePoint team site.

- If you are in the **Sales and Marketing Group**, you and your teammates will finalize the Associations database and post it on the SharePoint team site.

FIGURE A

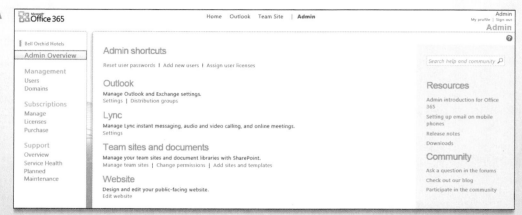

END OF CHAPTER

SUMMARY

A form is a database object that you can use to enter new records into a table, or to edit, delete, or display existing records in a table and can be used to control access to the data in a database.

Filter records in a form to display only a subset of the total records based on matching specific values to provide a quick answer to a question. Filters are generally not saved with a form.

A report is a database object that summarizes the fields and records from a query or from a table, in an easy-to-read format suitable for printing. You can group records and summarize the data in a report.

Most changes to forms and reports can be done in Layout view where the underlying data displays in the controls; however, some modifications, such as aligning controls, must be done in Design view.

GO! LEARN IT ONLINE

Review the concepts and key terms in this chapter by completing these online challenges, which you can find at **www.pearsonhighered.com/go**.

Matching and Multiple Choice:
Answer matching and multiple choice questions to test what you learned in this chapter. MyITLab®

Crossword Puzzle:
Spell out the words that match the numbered clues, and put them in the puzzle squares.

Flipboard:
Flip through the definitions of the key terms in this chapter and match them with the correct term.

GO! FOR JOB SUCCESS

Video: Performance Evaluations

Your instructor may assign this video to your class, and then ask you to think about, or discuss with your classmates, these questions:

FotolEdhar / Fotolia

What kind of message is Sara sending by forgetting to do the self-assessment review she was assigned for her evaluation? Why is it important to do a self-assessment for a review?

How should Sara react to her supervisor's criticisms in her review?

How important is it to follow a company's dress code policy? Do you think Sara's response to not following the dress code is appropriate? Why or why not?

END OF CHAPTER
REVIEW AND ASSESSMENT GUIDE FOR ACCESS CHAPTER 3

Your instructor may assign one or more of these projects to help you review the chapter and assess your mastery and understanding of the chapter.

		Review and Assessment Guide for Access Chapter 3	
Project	**Apply Skills from These Chapter Objectives**	**Project Type**	**Project Location**
3C	Objectives 1-4 from Project 3A	**3C Skills Review** A guided review of the skills from Project 3A.	On the following pages
3D	Objectives 5-8 from Project 3B	**3D Skills Review** A guided review of the skills from Project 3B.	On the following pages
3E	Objectives 1-4 from Project 3A	**3E Mastery (Grader Project)** A demonstration of your mastery of the skills in Project 3A with extensive decision making.	In MyITLab and on the following pages
3F	Objectives 5-8 from Project 3B	**3F Mastery (Grader Project)** A demonstration of your mastery of the skills in Project 3B with extensive decision making.	In MyITLab and on the following pages
3G	Objectives 1-8 from Projects 3A and 3B	**3G Mastery (Grader Project)** A demonstration of your mastery of the skills in Projects 3A and 3B with extensive decision making.	In MyITLab and on the following pages
3H	Combination of Objectives from Projects 3A and 3B	**3H GO! Fix It** A demonstration of your mastery of the skills in Projects 3A and 3B by creating a correct result from a document that contains errors you must find.	Online
3I	Combination of Objectives from Projects 3A and 3B	**3I GO! Make It** A demonstration of your mastery of the skills in Projects 3A and 3B by creating a result from a supplied picture.	Online
3J	Combination of Objectives from Projects 3A and 3B	**3J GO! Solve It** A demonstration of your mastery of the skills in Projects 3A and 3B, your decision-making skills, and your critical thinking skills. A task-specific rubric helps you self-assess your result.	Online
3K	Combination of Objectives from Projects 3A and 3B	**3K GO! Solve It** A demonstration of your mastery of the skills in Projects 3A and 3B, your decision-making skills, and your critical thinking skills. A task-specific rubric helps you self-assess your result.	On the following pages
3L	Combination of Objectives from Projects 3A and 3B	**3L GO! Think** A demonstration of your understanding of the chapter concepts applied in a manner that you would outside of college. An analytic rubric helps you and your instructor grade the quality of your work by comparing it to the work an expert in the discipline would create.	On the following pages
3M	Combination of Objectives from Projects 3A and 3B	**3M GO! Think** A demonstration of your understanding of the chapter concepts applied in a manner that you would outside of college. An analytic rubric helps you and your instructor grade the quality of your work by comparing it to the work an expert in the discipline would create.	Online
3N	Combination of Objectives from Projects 3A and 3B	**3N You and GO!** A demonstration of your understanding of the chapter concepts applied in a manner that you would in a personal situation. An analytic rubric helps you and your instructor grade the quality of your work.	Online
3O	Combination of Objectives from Projects 3A and 3B	**3O Cumulative Group Project for Access Chapter 3** A demonstration of your understanding of concepts and your ability to work collaboratively in a group role-playing assessment, requiring both collaboration and self-management.	Online
Capstone Project for Access Chapters 1-3	Combination of Objectives from Projects 1A, 1B, 2A, 2B, 3A, and 3B	A demonstration of your mastery of the skills in Chapters 1-3 with extensive decision making. **(Grader Project)**	In MyITLab and online

GLOSSARY

GLOSSARY OF CHAPTER KEY TERMS

AND condition A condition in which records display only when all of the values are present in the selected fields.

Bound A term used to describe objects and controls that are based on data that is stored in tables.

Bound control A control that retrieves its data from an underlying table or query; a text box control is an example of a bound control.

Calculated control A control that contains an expression, often a formula or function, that most often summarizes a field that contains numerical data.

Control An object on a form or report that displays data or text, performs actions, and lets you view and work with information.

Control layout The grouped arrangement of controls on a form or report; for example, the Stacked layout.

Data entry The action of entering the data into a record in a database table or form.

Date control A control on a form or report that inserts the current date each time the form or report is opened.

Design view The Access view that displays the detailed structure of a query, form, or report; for forms and reports, may be the view in which some tasks must be performed, and only the controls, and not the data, display.

Detail section The section of a form or report that displays the records from the underlying table or query.

Filter by Form An Access command that filters the records in a form based on one or more fields, or based on more than one value in the field.

Filter by Selection An Access command that displays only the records that contain the value in the selected field and hides the records that do not contain the value.

Filtering The process of displaying only a portion of the total records (a subset) based on matching specific values to provide a quick answer to a question.

Form A database object that you can use to enter new records into a table, or to edit, delete, and display existing records in a table.

Form Footer Information at the bottom of the screen in Form view or Layout view that is printed after the last detail section on the last page of a printout.

Form Header Information such as a form's title that displays at the top of the screen in Form view or Layout view and is printed at the top of the first page when records are printed as forms.

Form tool An Access tool that creates a form with a single mouse click, which includes all of the fields from the underlying data source (table or query).

Form view The Access view in which you can view, modify, delete, or add records in a table; but you cannot change the layout or design of the form.

Form Wizard An Access tool that walks you step by step through the creation of a form and that gives you more flexibility in the design, layout, and number of fields in a form.

Group Footer Information printed at the end of each group of records; used to display summary information for the group.

Group Header Information printed at the beginning of each new group of records; for example, the group name.

Group, Sort, and Total pane A pane that displays at the bottom of the screen in which you can control how information is sorted and grouped in a report; provides the most flexibility for adding or modifying groups, sort orders, or totals options on a report.

Label control A control on a form or report that contains descriptive information, usually a field name or title.

Layout selector A small symbol that displays in the upper left corner of a selected control layout in a form or report that is displayed in Layout view or Design view; used to move or format an entire group of controls.

Layout view The Access view in which you can make changes to a form or report while the object is running—the data from the underlying data source displays.

Office 365 Administrator In Office 365, the person who creates and manages the account, adds new users, sets up the services your organization wants to use, sets permission levels, and manages the SharePoint team sites.

OR condition A condition in which records display that match at least one of the specified values.

Page Footer Information printed at the bottom of every page in a report; most often includes the page number.

Page Header Information printed at the top of every page in a report.

Page number control A control on a form or report that inserts the page numbers when displayed in Print Preview or when printed.

Record selector bar The vertical bar at the left edge of a record when it is displayed in a form that is used to select an entire record.

Record source The tables or queries that provide the underlying data for a form or report.

Report A database object that summarizes the fields and records from a query or table in an easy-to-read format suitable for printing.

Report Footer Information printed at the bottom of the last page of a report.

Report Header Information printed on the first page of a report; used for logos, titles, and dates.

Report tool An Access tool that creates a report with one mouse click and displays all of the fields and records from the record source that you select.

Report Wizard An Access tool that walks you step by step through the creation of a report and that gives you more flexibility in the design, layout, and number of fields in a report.

Rich Text Format (RTF) A standard file format that contains text and some formatting such as underline, bold, italic, font sizes, and colors; RTF documents can be opened in many word processing programs and text editors.

Section bar In Design view, a gray bar in a form or report that identifies and separates one section from another; used to select the section and to change the size of the section.

Stacked layout A control layout format that is similar to a paper form, with label controls placed to the left of each text box control; the controls are grouped together for easy editing.

Subset A portion of the total records available.

Tab order The order in which the insertion point moves from one field to another in a form when you press the Tab key.

Text box control A bound control on a form or report that displays the data from the underlying table or query.

Theme A predesigned set of colors, fonts, lines, and fill effects that look good together and that can be applied to all of the objects in the database or to individual objects in the database.

Unbound control A control that does not have a source of data, such as the title in a form or report.

ACCESS

3

CHAPTER REVIEW

Apply 3A skills from these Objectives:

1. Create and Use a Form to Add and Delete Records
2. Filter Records
3. Create a Form by Using the Form Wizard
4. Modify a Form in Layout View and in Design View

Skills Review Project 3C Student Internships

In the following Skills Review, you will assist Erinique Jerlin, the dean of Business at the Northwest Campus, in using her database to track business students and their internship placements for the current semester. Your completed forms will look similar to Figure 3.49.

PROJECT FILES

For Project 3C, you will need the following file:

a03C_Student_Internships

You will save your database as:

Lastname_Firstname_3C_Student_Internships

PROJECT RESULTS

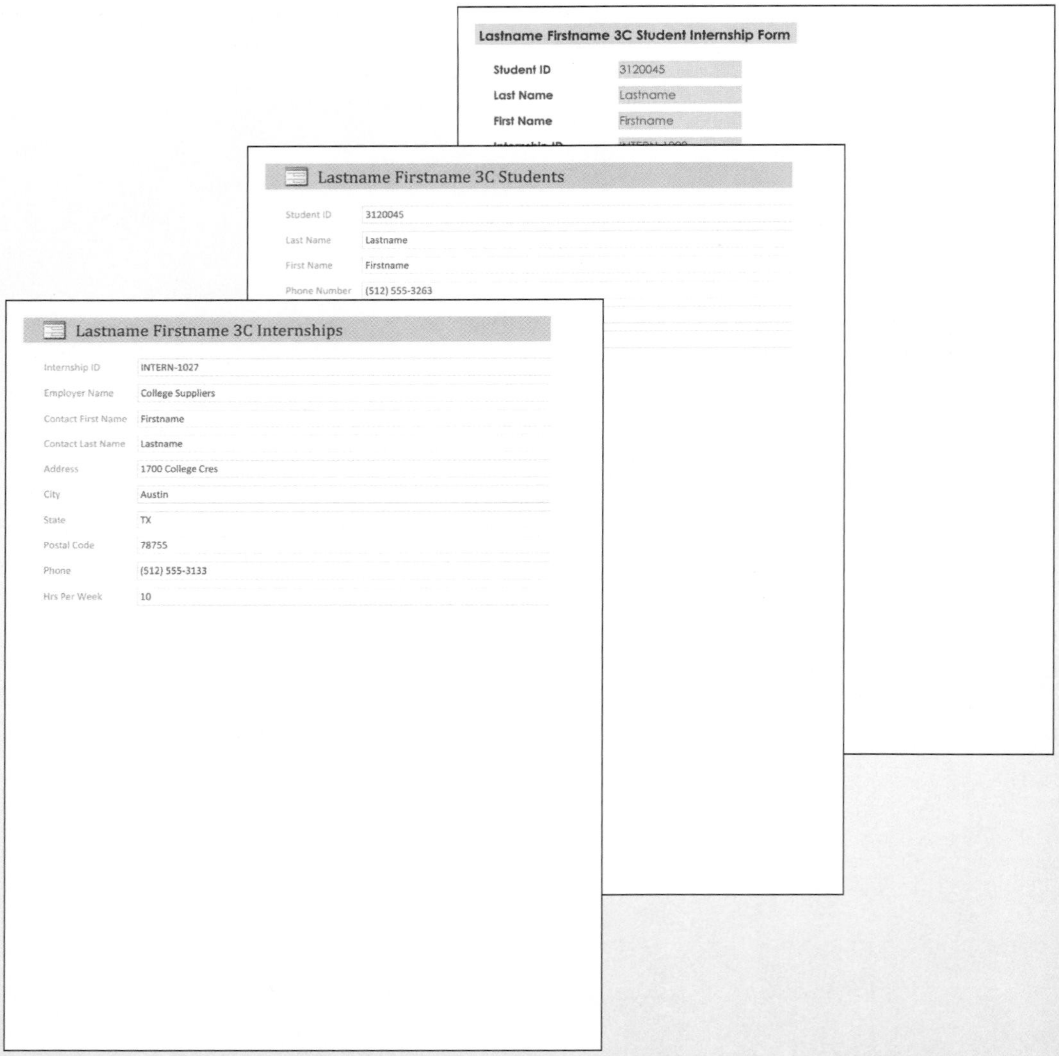

FIGURE 3.49

(Project 3C Student Internships continues on the next page)

CHAPTER REVIEW

1 Start Access. In the Access opening screen, click **Open Other Files**. Under **Open**, click **Computer**. Under **Recent Folders**, if displayed, click the location where your student data files are stored; otherwise, click **Browse** and then navigate to the location where your student data files are stored. Double-click **a03C_Student_Internships** to open the database.

a. On the ribbon, click the **FILE tab**, and then click **Save As**. Under **File Types**, be sure **Save Database As** is selected. On the right, under **Database File Types**, be sure **Access Database** is selected, and then click **Save As**.

b. In the **Save As** dialog box, navigate to your **Access Chapter 3** folder. In the **File name** box, replace the existing text with **Lastname_Firstname_3C_Student_Internships** and then press Enter. On the **Message Bar**, click **Enable Content**.

c. In the **Navigation Pane**, right-click **3C Students**, and then click **Rename**. With the table name selected and using your own name, type **Lastname Firstname 3C Students** and then press Enter. **Rename** the 3C Internships table to **Lastname Firstname 3C Internships** and then point to the right edge of the **Navigation Pane** to display the ↔ pointer. Drag to the right to increase the width of the pane until both tables names display fully.

d. On the ribbon, click the **DATABASE TOOLS tab**, and then in the **Relationships group**, click **Relationships**. Under **RELATIONSHIP TOOLS**, on the **DESIGN tab**, in the **Relationships group**, click **All Relationships**. Resize and move the field lists so that the entire table name and fields display for each field list. In the **Relationships** window, click the **join line** between the two field lists. In the **Tools group**, click **Edit Relationships**. Point to the title bar of the **Edit Relationships** dialog box, and drag the dialog box downward below the two field lists. Notice that a *one-to-many* relationship is established between

the two tables by using *Internship ID* as the common field. **Close** the **Edit Relationships** dialog box, and then **Close** the **Relationships** window. In the message box, click **Yes** to save changes to the layout of the relationships.

e. In the **Navigation Pane**, click your **3C Students** table to select it. On the ribbon, click the **CREATE tab**, and then in the **Forms group**, click **Form**. **Save** the form as **Lastname Firstname 3C Student Form** and then **Close** the form object.

f. In the **Navigation Pane**, click your **3C Internships** table to select it. On the ribbon, click the **CREATE tab**, and then in the **Forms group**, click **Form**. Notice that for the first record—*Internship ID INTERN-1000* for *Lakes Realty Inc*—there are two student records in the subdatasheet—two students have been assigned internships for this employer. **Close** the form, and in the message box, click **Yes** to save the form. In the **Save As** dialog box, type **Lastname Firstname 3C Internship Company Form** and then press Enter. If necessary, increase the width of the Navigation Pane so that all object names display fully.

g. In the **Navigation Pane**, double-click your **3C Student Form** object to open it, and then **Close** the **Navigation Pane**. In the navigation area, click **New (blank) record** to display a new blank form. In the **Student ID** field, type **3120045** and then press Tab. Using your own last name and first name, continue entering the data as shown in **Table 1**.

h. With the insertion point positioned in the last field, press Tab to save the record and display a new blank record. **Close** your **3C Student Form** object, and then **Open** the **Navigation Pane**. Double-click your **3C Internship Company Form** object to open it, and then **Close** the **Navigation Pane**. Notice that for the first record, in the subdatasheet, the record you just entered displays. Scroll to view the bottom of

TABLE 1

Student ID	Last Name	First Name	Phone Number	Email	Internship ID
3120045	**Lastname**	**Firstname**	**(512) 555-3263**	**ns3120@tlcc.edu**	**INTERN-1000**

Return to Step 1-h

(Project 3C Student Internships continues on the next page)

the form. In the navigation area for the form—*not the navigation area for the subdatasheet*—click **New (blank) record**. In the blank form, using your own first name and last name, enter the data as shown in **Table 2**.

i. In the navigation area for the form, click **First record**. Click in the **Employer Name** field, and then on the **HOME tab**, in the **Find group**, click **Find**. In the **Find and Replace** dialog box, in the **Find What** box, type **Jones Consulting** and then click **Find Next**. **Close** the **Find and Replace** dialog box. On the **HOME tab**, in the **Records group**, click the **Delete arrow**, and then click **Delete Record**. In the message box, click **Yes** to delete the record. In the navigation area for the form, notice that the total number of records is *27*.

j. Use the technique you just practiced to **Find** the form for the **Internship ID** of INTERN-1027, and then **Close** the **Find and Replace** dialog box. On the ribbon, click the **FILE tab**, click **Print**, and then on the right, click **Print**. In the **Print** dialog box, under **Print Range**, click the **Selected Record(s)** option button. In the lower left corner of the dialog box, click **Setup**. In the **Page Setup** dialog box, click the **Columns tab**. Under **Column Size**, double-click in the **Width** box to select the existing value, type **7.5** and then click **OK**. If directed to print the form, in the **Print** dialog box, click **OK**. If directed to submit an electronic printout of the form, click **Cancel**, and then follow the directions given in the Note in Activity 3.06.

k. **Close** your **3C Internship Company Form** object, and then **Open** the **Navigation Pane**. In the **Navigation Pane**, double-click your **3C Student Form** object to open it, and then **Close** the **Navigation Pane**. Use the **Find** command to display the record where the **Last Name** field contains your last name, and then create a paper or electronic printout of only

that record, being sure to change the **Column Size Width** to **7.5**

2 With your **3C Student Form** object displayed in **Form** view, in the navigation area, click **First record**, and then click the **Internship ID** field name to select the text in the field box. Press Ctrl + F to display the **Find and Replace** dialog box. In the **Find What** box, type **INTERN-1009** and then click **Find Next** to find and display the record for *Michael Fresch*. **Close** the **Find and Replace** dialog box. On the **HOME tab**, in the **Sort & Filter group**, click **Selection**, and then click **Equals "INTERN-1009"**. In the navigation area, notice that two students are assigned internships with the company identified as INTERN-1009.

a. In the **Sort & Filter group**, click **Toggle Filter** to remove the filter and display all 52 records. **Close** the form. If prompted, click **Yes** to save the form.

b. **Open** the **Navigation Pane**, double-click your **3C Internship Company Form** object to open it, and then **Close** the **Navigation Pane**. On the **HOME tab**, in the **Sort & Filter group**, click **Advanced**, and then click **Filter By Form**. In the form, click the **City** field name to position the insertion point in the **City** field box, click the **arrow**, and then click **Georgetown**. In the **Sort & Filter group**, click **Toggle Filter** to display the filtered records. In the navigation area for the form, notice that three internships are located in the *City* of *Georgetown*.

c. In the **Sort & Filter group**, click **Advanced**, and then click **Filter By Form**. In the lower left corner of the form, click the **Or tab**. Click the **City** field box **arrow**, and then click **Elgin**. In the **Sort & Filter group**, click **Toggle Filter**. In the navigation area for the form, notice that five internships are located in either *Georgetown* or *Elgin*. In the **Sort & Filter group**, click **Advanced**, and then click **Clear All Filters** to display all 27 records.

TABLE 2

Internship ID	Employer Name	Contact First Name	Contact Last Name	Address	City	State	Postal Code	Phone	Hrs Per Week
INTERN-1027	**College Suppliers**	**Firstname**	**Lastname**	**1700 College Cres**	**Austin**	**TX**	**78755**	**(512) 555-3133**	**10**

Return to Step 1-i

(Project 3C Student Internships continues on the next page)

d. In the **Sort & Filter group**, click **Advanced**, and then click **Advanced Filter/Sort**. Resize the field list. In the **3C Internships** field list, double-click **City**, and then double-click **Hrs Per Week** to add both fields to the design grid. Click in the **Criteria** row under **City**, type **Austin** and then press [Enter]. In the **Criteria** row under **Hrs Per Week**, type **>10** and then press [Enter]. In the **Sort & Filter group**, click **Toggle Filter** to display the filtered records, and notice that that there are five internships in the *City* of *Austin* offering *more than 10* hours per week of work. In the **Sort & Filter group**, click **Toggle Filter** to remove the filter and display all 27 records. **Save** and then **Close** your **3C Internship Company Form** object, which also closes the Advanced Filter grid.

3 On the ribbon, click the **CREATE tab**, and then in the **Forms group**, click **Form Wizard**. In the **Tables/Queries** box, click the **arrow**, and then click **Table: Lastname Firstname 3C Students**. In the **Available Fields** list, double-click the following field names in the order given to move them to the **Selected Fields** list: **First Name**, **Last Name**, and **Internship ID**. Click **Next**. In the wizard, be sure **Columnar** is selected as the layout, and then click **Next**. In the **What title do you want for your form?** box, select the existing text, type **Lastname Firstname 3C Student Internship Form** and then click **Finish** to close the wizard and create the form.

4 On the **HOME tab**, in the **Views group**, click the top portion of the **View** button to switch to **Layout** view. If the **Field List** pane displays on the right side of your screen, close the pane. Click the **First Name label control**. Hold down [Shift], and then click the **Last Name label control**, the **Internship ID label control**, and the three **text box controls** to select all of the controls. On the ribbon, under **FORM LAYOUT TOOLS**, click the **ARRANGE tab**. In the **Table group**, click **Stacked** to group all of the controls. Click the **First Name label control** to cancel the selection of all of the controls.

a. On the ribbon, under **FORM LAYOUT TOOLS**, click the **DESIGN tab**. In the **Themes group** click **Themes**. In the **Themes** gallery, using the ScreenTips, point to the **Wisp** theme, right-click, and then click **Apply Theme to This Object Only**. Click anywhere in the title—*Lastname Firstname 3C Student Internship Form*—to select the title. On the ribbon, under **FORM LAYOUT TOOLS**, click the **FORMAT tab**. In the **Font group**, click the **Font Size arrow**, and then click **14**. In the **Font group**, click **Bold**. Click the **Font Color arrow**, and then under **Theme Colors**, in the sixth column, click the last color—**Orange, Accent 2, Darker 50%**.

b. On the ribbon, click the **DESIGN tab**. In the **Tools group**, click **Add Existing Fields**. In the **Field List** pane, click **Student ID**, and then drag the field name to the left until the 📋 pointer displays above the **First Name label control** and a colored line displays above the control. Release the mouse button to add the *Student ID* controls to the form, and then **Close** the **Field List** pane.

c. Click the **First Name text box control**, which displays *Jordan*, to select it. On the **DESIGN tab**, in the **Tools group**, click **Property Sheet**. In the **Property Sheet**, on the **Format tab**, click **Width**, type **1.75** and then press [Enter] to decrease the width of the text box controls. **Close** the **Property Sheet**. Be sure that the **First Name text box control** is still selected. On the ribbon, click the **ARRANGE tab**, and in the **Rows & Columns group**, click **Select Row**. In the **Move group**, click **Move Down** to move both controls below the **Last Name** controls. **Save** the changes you have made to the design of your form.

d. Click the **Student ID text box control**, which displays *1010101*. On the **ARRANGE tab**, in the **Rows & Columns group**, click **Select Column** to select all four text box controls. On the ribbon, click the **FORMAT tab**, and in the **Font group**, click the **Background Color arrow**. Under **Theme Colors**, in the fourth column, click the second color—**Brown, Text 2, Lighter 80%**.

e. Click the **Student ID label control**, and then on the ribbon, click the **ARRANGE tab**. In the **Rows & Columns group**, click **Select Column** to select all four label controls. On the ribbon, click the **FORMAT tab**, and then click the **Font Color arrow**—*not* the **Background Color arrow**. Under **Theme Colors**, in the fourth column, click the first color—**Brown, Text 2**. In the **Font group**, click **Bold**.

(Project 3C Student Internships continues on the next page)

CHAPTER REVIEW

f. Click the **layout selector** ⊞ to select all of the controls. In the **Font group**, click the **Font Size arrow**, and then click **12**. With all of the controls still selected, on the ribbon, click the **DESIGN tab**, and in the **Tools group**, click **Property Sheet**. In the **Property Sheet**, on the **Format tab**, click **Height**, type **0.25** and then press ⏎ to change the height of each selected control.

g. Click the **Student ID label control** to select only that control. In the **Property Sheet**, click **Width**, type **1.75** and then press ⏎ to change the width of all of the label controls. **Save** the design changes to your form.

h. On the status bar, click **Design View**. At the bottom of the form, click the **Form Footer section bar** to select it. In the **Property Sheet**, click **Height**, type **0.5** and then press ⏎ to increase the height of the **Form Footer** section.

i. On the ribbon, under **FORM DESIGN TOOLS**, click the **DESIGN tab**. In the **Controls group**, click **Label**. Move the pointer into the **Form Footer** section and then position the plus sign of the pointer at approximately **0.25 inch on the horizontal ruler** and even with the lower edge of the **Form Footer section bar**—the placement does not need to be precise. Click one time, type **Texas Lakes Community College** and then press ⏎.

j. With the **label control** selected, on the ribbon, click the **FORMAT tab**. In the **Font group**, click **Bold**. Click the **Font Color arrow**, and then under **Theme Colors**, in the fourth column, click the first

color—**Brown, Text 2**. If necessary, double-click the right edge of the label control to resize the control so that all of the data displays.

k. With the **label control** still selected, in the **Property Sheet**, click **Top**, type **0.1** and then press ⏎. In the **Property Sheet**, in the **Left** property setting box, type **0.9** and then press ⏎. **Close** the **Property Sheet**, and then **Save** the design changes to your form.

l. On the right side of the status bar, click **Form View**. In the navigation area, click **Last record** to display the record containing your name. On the ribbon, click the **FILE tab**, and then click **Print**. In the **Print** dialog box, under **Print Range**, click the **Selected Records(s)** option button. Because you changed the field widths, you do not need to change the Column Size Width in the **Print** dialog box. Create a paper or electronic printout as directed by your instructor. To create an electronic printout, follow the directions given in the Note in Activity 3.06.

m. **Close** all open objects, and then **Open** the **Navigation Pane**. If necessary, increase the width of the pane so that all object names display fully. On the right side of the title bar, click **Close** to close the database and to exit Access. As directed by your instructor, submit your database and the paper or electronic printouts of the three forms that are the results of this project. Specifically, in this project, using your own name, you created the following database and printouts or electronic printouts:

1. Lastname_Firstname_3C_Student_Internships	Database file
2. Lastname Firstname 3C Student Form	Form (printout or electronic printout - Record 52)
3. Lastname Firstname 3C Internship Company Form	Form (printout or electronic printout - Record 27)
4. Lastname Firstname 3C Student Internship Form	Form (printout or electronic printout - Record 52)

END | You have completed Project 3C

CHAPTER REVIEW

ACCESS

3

Apply 3B skills from these objectives:

5 Create a Report by Using the Report Tool and Modify the Report in Layout View

6 Create a Report by Using the Report Wizard

7 Modify the Design of a Report

8 Keep Grouped Data Together in a Printed Report

Skills Review Project 3D Student Parking

In the following Skills Review, you will assist Carlos Medina, the chief of security, in using his Access database to track the details about students who have paid for parking in designated lots at the Southeast Campus of Texas Lakes Community College. Your completed reports will look similar to Figure 3.50.

PROJECT FILES

For Project 3D, you will need the following file:

a03D_Student_Parking

You will save your database as:

Lastname_Firstname_3D_Student_Parking

PROJECT RESULTS

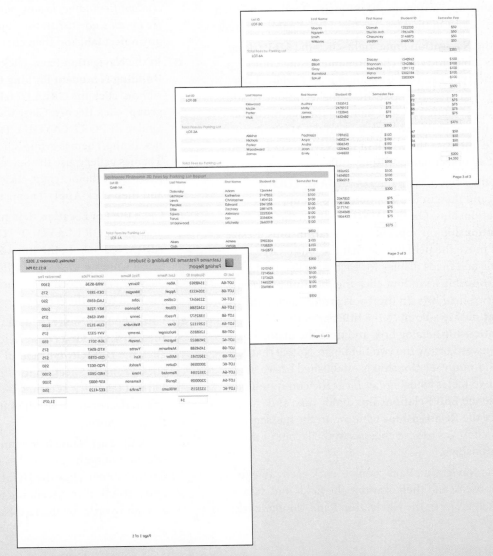

FIGURE 3.50

(Project 3D Student Parking continues on the next page)

CHAPTER REVIEW

1 Start Access. In the Access opening screen, click **Open Other Files**. Under **Open**, click **Computer**. Under **Recent Folders**, if displayed, click the location where your student data files are stored; otherwise, click **Browse** and then navigate to the location where your student data files are stored. Double-click **a03D_Student_Parking** to open the database.

a. On the ribbon, click the **FILE tab**, and then click **Save As**. Under **File Types**, be sure **Save Database As** is selected. On the right, under **Database File Types**, be sure **Access Database** is selected, and then at the bottom of the screen, click **Save As**. In the **Save As** dialog box, navigate to your **Access Chapter 3** folder. In the **File name** box, replace the existing text with **Lastname_Firstname_3D_Student_Parking** and then press [Enter]. On the **Message Bar**, click **Enable Content**.

b. In the **Navigation Pane**, right-click the **3D Parking Lots** table, and then click **Rename**. Using your own name, type **Lastname Firstname 3D Parking Lots** and then press [Enter]. Use this same technique to add your last name and first name to the beginning of the names of the two queries and the **3D Students** table. Increase the width of the **Navigation Pane** so that all object names display fully.

c. On the ribbon, click the **DATABASE TOOLS tab**, and then in the **Relationships group**, click **Relationships**. On the **DESIGN tab**, in the **Relationships group**, click **All Relationships**. Resize and move the field lists so that the entire table name and fields display for each field list. In the **Relationships** window, click the **join line** between the two field lists. In the **Tools group**, click **Edit Relationships**. Point to the title bar of the **Edit Relationships** dialog box, and drag the dialog box downward below the two field lists. Notice that a *one-to-many* relationship is established between the two tables by using *Lot ID* as the common field. **Close** the **Edit Relationships** dialog box, and then **Close** the **Relationships** window. In the message box, click **Yes** to save changes to the layout of the relationships.

d. In the **Navigation Pane**, double-click each table to open them, and then examine the fields and data in each table. In the **Navigation Pane**, double-click

your **3D Building G Student Parking Query** object to run the query and view the results. Apply **Best Fit** to the query results, and then **Save** the query. Switch to **Design** view to examine the design grid. This query answers the question, *What is the lot ID, lot location, student ID, student last name, student first name, license plate, and semester fee for students who have paid for parking in front of Building G, in ascending order by the Last Name field?* In the **Navigation Pane**, double-click your **3D Student Parking by Lots Query** object, apply **Best Fit** to the query results, **Save** the query, and then switch to **Design** view to examine the design grid. This query answers the question, *What is the lot ID, student ID, student last name, student first name, license plate, state, and semester fee for all students?* In the object window, right-click any **object tab**, and then click **Close All**.

e. In the **Navigation Pane**, click to select your **3D Building G Student Parking Query** object. On the ribbon, click the **CREATE tab**, and in the **Reports group**, click **Report**. **Close** the **Navigation Pane**. Under **REPORT LAYOUT TOOLS**, on the **DESIGN tab**, in the **Themes group**, click **Themes**. In the **Themes** gallery, use the ScreenTips to locate the **Retrospect** theme, right-click the **Retrospect** theme, and then click **Apply Theme to This Object Only**.

f. Click the **Lot Location** field name. On the ribbon, under **REPORT LAYOUT TOOLS**, click the **ARRANGE tab**. In the **Rows & Columns group**, click **Select Column** to select the field name and all of the data for each record in the field. Press [Del] to remove the field from the report.

g. Click the **Last Name** field name, hold down [Shift], and then click the **First Name** field name. On the ribbon, click the **DESIGN tab**, and in the **Tools group**, click **Property Sheet**. In the **Property Sheet**, on the **Format tab**, click **Width**, type **1.25** and then press [Enter] to decrease the width of the two fields. **Close** the **Property Sheet**.

h. Click the **Last Name** field name to cancel the selection of both fields and to select only this field. On the ribbon, click the **HOME tab**, and in the **Sort & Filter group**, click **Ascending** to sort the records in ascending order by the Last Name field.

(Project 3D Student Parking continues on the next page)

i. If necessary, scroll to the bottom of the report, and notice that the *Semester Fee* column is automatically totaled. At the top of the report, click the **Student ID** field name. On the ribbon, click the **DESIGN tab**. In the **Grouping & Totals group**, click **Totals**, and then click **Count Records**. If necessary, scroll to the bottom of the report, and notice that *14* students have paid for parking in front of Building G.

j. At the bottom of the report, under **Student ID**, click the **calculated control** that displays *14*. Hold down Ctrl, and then under **Semester Fee**, click the **calculated control** that displays *$1,075*—the two calculated controls are selected. On the **DESIGN tab**, in the **Tools group**, click **Property Sheet**. In the **Property Sheet**, click **Height**, type **0.25** and then press Enter to increase the height of both controls. At the bottom of the report, to the right of the **calculated control** that displays *$1,075*, click the **control** that displays *Page 1 of 1*. In the **Property Sheet**, click **Left**, type **2.5** and then press Enter to move the page number within the margins of the report.

k. At the top of the report, click the **label control** that displays the title of the report—*Lastname Firstname 3D Building G Student Parking Query*. On the ribbon, under **REPORT LAYOUT TOOLS**, click the **FORMAT tab**. In the **Font group**, click the **Font Size arrow**, and then click **14**. With the **label control** still selected, double-click **Query** to select the word, type **Report** and then press Enter to change the title of the report to *Lastname Firstname 3D Building G Student Parking Report*.

l. Click the **Lot ID** field name. In the **Property Sheet**, click **Left**, type **0.25** and then press Enter to move all of the fields slightly to the right from the left margin. **Close** the **Property Sheet**, and then **Save** the report as **Lastname Firstname 3D Building G Student Parking Report**

m. On the right side of the status bar, click **Print Preview**. On the **PRINT PREVIEW tab**, in the **Zoom group**, click **Two Pages**, and notice that the report will print on one page. Create a paper or electronic printout as directed, click **Close Print Preview**, and then **Close** the report.

2 On the ribbon, click the **CREATE tab**, and then in the **Reports group**, click **Report Wizard**. In the **Tables/Queries box**, click the **arrow**, and then click

Query: Lastname Firstname 3D Student Parking by Lots Query. In the **Available Fields** list, double-click the following field names in the order given to move them to the **Selected Fields** list: **Lot ID, Last Name, First Name, Student ID,** and **Semester Fee.**

a. Click **Next**. In the **How do you want to view your data?** box, click **by Lastname Firstname 3D Students**, and then click **Next**. In the list on the left, double-click **Lot ID** to group the records by this field, and then click **Next**. Click the **1 box arrow**, and then click **Last Name** to sort the records by the student's last name within each Lot ID.

b. In the wizard, click **Summary Options**. In the **Summary Options** dialog box, to the right of **Semester Fee**, click to select the **Sum** check box. Under **Show**, be sure that **Detail and Summary** is selected, and then click **OK**. In the wizard, click **Next**.

c. In the wizard, under **Layout**, be sure that **Stepped** is selected. Under **Orientation**, click **Landscape**. At the bottom of the wizard, be sure that the **Adjust the field width so all fields fit on a page** check box is selected, and then click **Next**. In the **What title do you want for your report?** box, select the existing text, type **Lastname Firstname 3D Fees by Parking Lot Report** and then click **Finish**. In the object window, right-click the **object tab** for the report, and then click **Layout View**.

3 Under **REPORT LAYOUT TOOLS**, on the **DESIGN tab**, in the **Themes group**, click **Themes**. In the **Themes** gallery, use the ScreenTips to locate the **Ion Boardroom** theme, right-click the **Ion Boardroom** theme, and then click **Apply Theme to This Object Only**. In the report, click the title—*Lastname Firstname 3D Fees by Parking Lot*—to display a border around the label control. On the ribbon, under **REPORT LAYOUT TOOLS**, click the **FORMAT tab**. In the **Font group**, click the **Font Size arrow**, and then click **14**. In the **Font group**, click **Bold**. In the body of the report, click any one of the controls that begins with **Summary for 'Lot ID'**, and then press Del. **Save** the design changes to your report.

a. On the left side of the report, click a **Sum label control**, which will select all of the related controls. Double-click the control to select the text—*Sum*. Type **Total Fees by Parking Lot** and then press Enter.

(Project 3D Student Parking continues on the next page)

CHAPTER REVIEW

b. At the top of the report, click the **Lot ID label control** to select it. Hold down Shift, and then click each one of the four other label controls that display the field names to select all five label controls. On the **FORMAT tab**, in the **Font group**, click **Bold**.

c. In the report, under **Last Name**, click the **text box control** that displays *Dolensky*. Hold down Shift, and then under **First Name**, click the **text box control** that displays *Adam*. On the ribbon, click the **DESIGN tab**. In the **Tools group**, click **Property Sheet**. In the **Property Sheet**, click **Width**, type **1.5** and then press Enter.

d. In the report, click the **Student ID label control**. In the **Property Sheet**, click **Left**, type **7.25** and then press Enter. Do not be concerned that the data in the field is not aligned with the field name; you will adjust this later in this project. Scroll to the bottom of the report, and then click the **Grand Total label control**. In the **Property Sheet**, click **Width**, type **1** and then press Enter. **Close** the **Property Sheet**, and then **Save** the design changes to your report.

e. On the status bar, click **Design View**. In the **Lot ID Footer** section, click the **Total Fees by Parking Lot label control**. Hold down Shift, and in the **Report Footer** section, click the **Grand Total label control** to select both controls. On the ribbon, under **REPORT DESIGN TOOLS**, click the **ARRANGE tab**. In the **Sizing & Ordering group**, click **Align**, and then click **Left**.

f. In the report, in the **Page Header** section, click the **Student ID label control**. Hold down Shift, and in the **Detail** section, click the **Student ID text box control**. On the **ARRANGE tab**, in the **Sizing & Ordering group**, click **Align**, and then click **Left**. On the status bar, click **Layout View** and notice the left alignment of the two sets of controls.

4 On the status bar, click **Print Preview**. On the **PRINT PREVIEW tab**, in the **Zoom group**, click **More Pages**, and then click **Four Pages** to view how your report is currently laid out. In the **Zoom group**, click the **Zoom arrow**, and then click **50%**. Notice at the bottom of Page 1 and the top of Page 2, that the grouping for **LOT-2B** breaks across these two pages. Notice at the bottom of Page 2 and the top of Page 3, that the grouping for **LOT-6A** breaks across these two pages. Your pages may display differently depending upon the printer that is installed on your system.

a. On the ribbon, click **Close Print Preview** to return to **Layout** view. On the **DESIGN tab**, in the **Grouping & Totals group**, click **Group & Sort**. In the **Group, Sort, and Total** pane, on the **Group on Lot ID** bar, click **More**. Click the **do not keep group together on one page arrow**, and then click **keep whole group together on one page**. On the **DESIGN tab**, in the **Grouping & Totals group**, click **Group & Sort** to close the **Group, Sort, and Total** pane. **Save** the design changes to your report.

b. On the status bar, click **Print Preview**. Notice that the entire grouping for **LOT-2B** displays at the top of Page 2. Keeping this group together forced the groupings for **LOT-5C** and **LOT-6A** to move to the top of Page 3—your groupings may display differently depending upon the printer that is installed on your system. Create a paper or electronic printout as directed—three pages result.

c. **Close** the report, and then **Open** the **Navigation Pane**. If necessary, increase the width of the pane so that all object names display fully. On the right side of the title bar, click **Close** to close the database and to exit Access. As directed by your instructor, submit your database and the paper or electronic printouts of the two reports—one report is three pages—that are the results of this project. Specifically, in this project, using your own name, you created the following database and printouts or electronic printouts:

1. Lastname_Firstname_3D_Student_Parking	Database file
2. Lastname Firstname 3D Building G Student Parking Report	Report (printout or electronic printout)
3. Lastname Firstname 3D Fees by Parking Lot Report	Report (printout or electronic printout - three pages)

END | You have completed Project 3D

CONTENT-BASED ASSESSMENTS

Mastering Access Project 3E Textbook Publishers

Apply 3A skills from these objectives:

1 Create and Use a Form to Add and Delete Records

2 Filter Records

3 Create a Form by Using the Form Wizard

4 Modify a Form in Layout View and in Design View

In the following Mastering Access project, you will assist Donna Rider, manager of the bookstore, in using her database to track textbooks and publishers for courses being offered by the Science Department at the Northeast Campus of Texas Lakes Community College. Your completed forms will look similar to Figure 3.51.

PROJECT FILES

For Project 3E, you will need the following file:

a03E_Textbook_Publishers

You will save your database as:

Lastname_Firstname_3E_Textbook_Publishers

PROJECT RESULTS

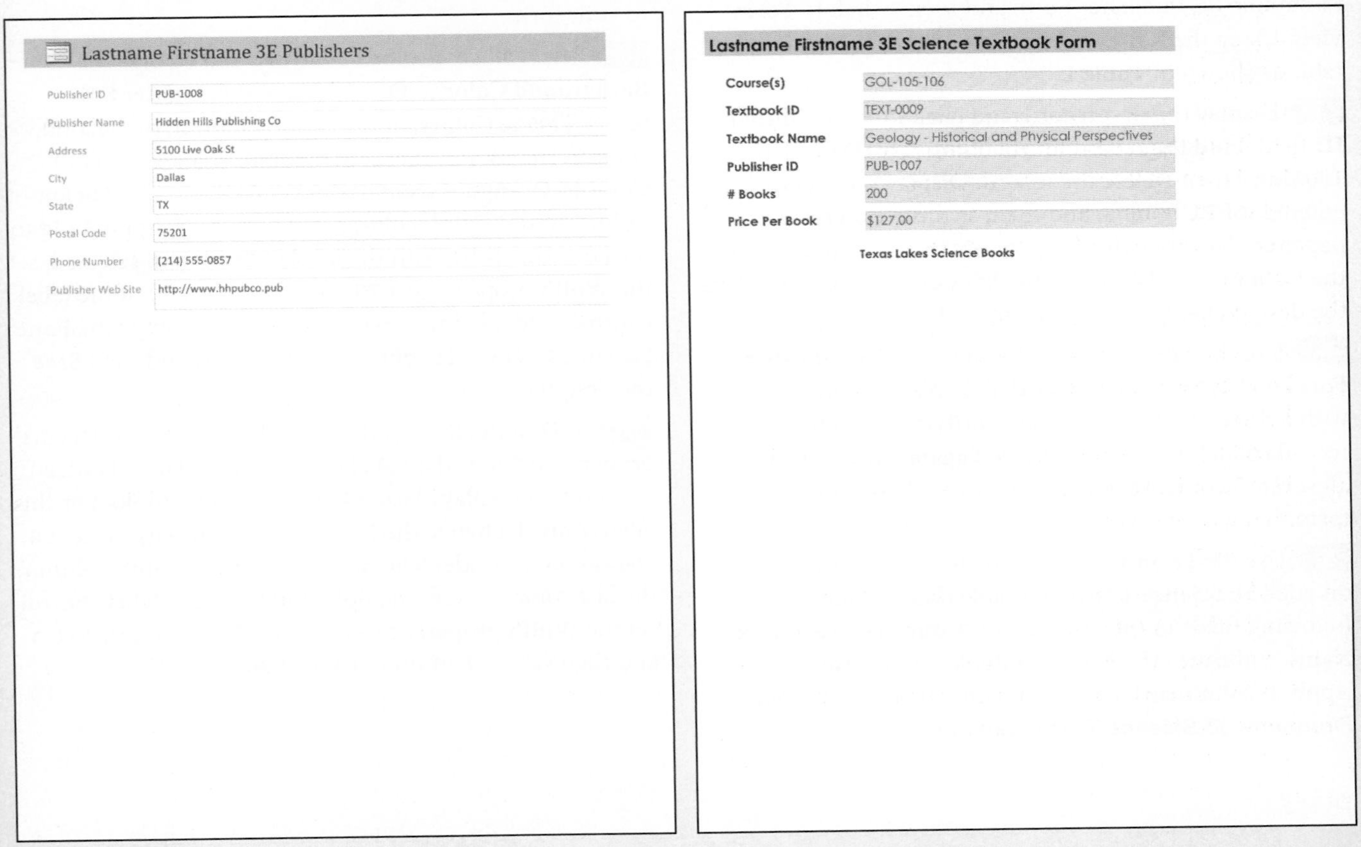

Lastname Firstname 3E Publishers	
Publisher ID	PUB-1008
Publisher Name	Hidden Hills Publishing Co
Address	5100 Live Oak St
City	Dallas
State	TX
Postal Code	75201
Phone Number	(214) 555-0857
Publisher Web Site	http://www.hhpubco.pub

Lastname Firstname 3E Science Textbook Form	
Course(s)	GOL-105-106
Textbook ID	TEXT-0009
Textbook Name	Geology - Historical and Physical Perspectives
Publisher ID	PUB-1007
# Books	200
Price Per Book	$127.00

Texas Lakes Science Books

FIGURE 3.51

(Project 3E Textbook Publishers continues on the next page)

CONTENT-BASED ASSESSMENTS

1 Start Access. From your student data files, open **a03E_Textbook_Publishers**. Save the database in your **Access Chapter 3** folder as **Lastname_Firstname_3E_ Textbook_Publishers** and then enable the content. In the **Navigation Pane**, **Rename** each table by adding **Lastname Firstname** to the beginning of the table name. Increase the width of the **Navigation Pane** so that all object names display fully. View the relationship between the *3E Publishers* table and the *3E Science Textbooks* table; *one* publisher can provide *many* textbooks for the science courses. Save the changes to the layout of the relationships.

2 Based on your **3E Publishers** table, use the **Form** tool to create a form. **Save** the form as **Lastname Firstname 3E Publisher Form** and then switch to **Form** view. Using the form, add a new record to the underlying table as shown in **Table 1**.

3 Display the first record, and click in the **Publisher ID** field. **Find** the record for the **Publisher ID** of **PUB-1006**, and then **Delete** the record. Display the record you entered for **PUB-1008**, and then, as directed, create a paper or electronic printout of only that record, changing the **Column Size Width** in the **Print** dialog box to **7.5 Save** the design changes to your form.

4 Use the **Filter By Form** tool in your **3E Publisher Form** object to create a filter that displays records with a **State** of **CA** or **TX**. After verifying that three records match this criteria, click **Toggle Filter** to display all seven records. **Save** your form, and then **Close** your form.

5 Use the **Form Wizard** to create a form based on your **3E Science Textbooks** table that includes the following fields in the order given: **Course(s)**, **Textbook Name**, **Publisher ID**, **Price Per Book**, and **# Books**. Apply a **Columnar** layout, and name the form **Lastname Firstname 3E Science Textbook Form.**

6 In **Layout** view, apply the **Stacked** layout to all of the controls, and then apply the **Ion Boardroom** theme to this form only. For the title of the form, change the **Font Size** to **16**, apply **Bold**, and then change the **Font Color** to **Dark Purple, Text 2**—under **Theme Colors**, in the fourth column, the first color. **Save** the design changes to the form.

7 From the **Field List** pane, add the **Textbook ID** field to the form directly above the **Textbook Name** field. Move the **# Books** controls directly above the **Price Per Book** controls. **Close** the **Field List** pane. Display Record 9—this record's textbook name is the longest entry of all records. Click the **Textbook Name text box control**, set the **Width** property to **4** and then **Save** the design changes to your form.

8 Select all six **text box controls**, and change the **Background Color** to **Orange, Accent 4, Lighter 80%**—under **Theme Colors**, in the eighth column, the second color. Select all six **label controls**, and change the **Font Color** to **Orange, Accent 4, Darker 50%**—under **Theme Colors**, in the eighth column, the last color. Apply **Bold** to the **label controls**. With the **label controls** still selected, set the **Width** property to **1.75** and then select all of the **label controls** and all of the **text box controls**. Change the **Font Size** to **12**, set the **Height** property to **0.25** and then **Save** the design changes to your form.

9 In **Design** view, set the **Form Footer** section **Height** property to **0.5** Add a **Label control** to the **Form Footer** section that displays **Texas Lakes Science Books** For this **label control**, change the **Font Color** to **Orange, Accent 4, Darker 50%**—under **Theme Colors**, in the eighth column, the last color—and then apply **Bold**. For this **label control**, set the **Width** property to **2.2** Set the **Top** property to **0.1** and then set the **Left** property to **1.95**

TABLE 1

Publisher ID	Publisher Name	Address	City	State	Postal Code	Phone Number	Publisher Web Site
PUB-1008	Hidden Hills Publishing Co	5100 Live Oak St	Dallas	TX	75201	(214) 555-0857	http://www. hhpubco.pub

Return to Step 3

(Project 3E Textbook Publishers continues on the next page)

CONTENT-BASED ASSESSMENTS

10 **Close** the **Property Sheet**, **Save** your form, and then switch to **Form** view. **Find** the record for the **Textbook ID** of **TEXT-0009**, and then, as directed, create a paper or electronic printout of only this record. Because you changed the field widths, you do not need to change the Column Size Width in the **Print** dialog box.

11 **Close** all open objects, and then **Open** the **Navigation Pane**. If necessary, increase the width of the pane so that all object names display fully. **Close** Access. As directed by your instructor, submit your database and the paper or electronic printouts of the two forms that are the results of this project. Specifically, in this project, using your own name, you created the following database and printouts or electronic printouts:

1. Lastname_Firstname_3E_Textbook_Publishers	Database file
2. Lastname Firstname 3E Publisher Form	Form (printout or electronic printout - Record 7)
3. Lastname Firstname 3E Science Textbook Form	Form (printout or electronic printout - Record 9)

END | You have completed Project 3E

CONTENT-BASED ASSESSMENTS

Mastering Access Project 3F Degrees and Students

In the following Mastering Access project, you will assist Tom Catogrides, the registrar, in using his database to track degrees and grade point averages for honor students in the health professions program in preparation for graduation. Your completed database objects will look similar to Figure 3.52.

Apply 3B skills from these Objectives:

5 Create a Report by Using the Report Tool and Modify the Report in Layout View

6 Create a Report by Using the Report Wizard

7 Modify the Design of a Report

8 Keep Grouped Data Together in a Printed Report

PROJECT FILES

For Project 3F, you will need the following file:

a03F_Degrees_Students

You will save your database as:

Lastname_Firstname_3F_Degrees_Students

PROJECT RESULTS

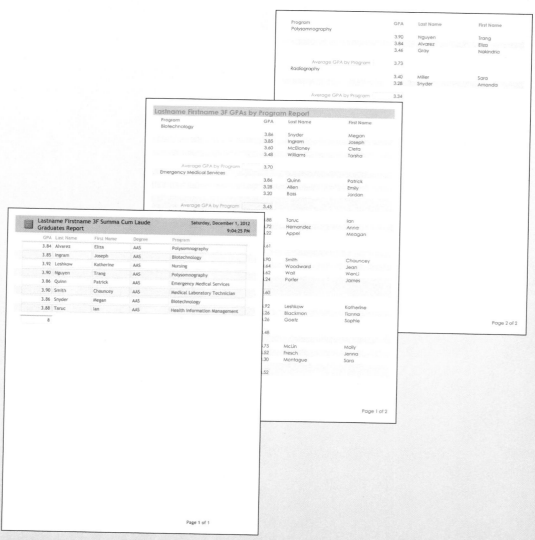

FIGURE 3.52

(Project 3F Degrees and Students continues on the next page)

1 Start Access. From your student data files, open **a03F_Degrees_Students**. **Save** the database in your **Access Chapter 3** folder as **Lastname_Firstname_3F_Degrees_ Students** and then enable the content. In the **Navigation Pane**, **Rename** the two tables and two queries by adding **Lastname Firstname** to the beginning of each object name, and then increase the width of the **Navigation Pane** so that all object names display fully. View the relationship that is established between the *3F Degrees* tables and the *3F Students* table—*one* type of degree can be awarded to *many* students. Save the changes to the layout of the relationships. **Run** each query to display the query results, apply **Best Fit**, and then **Save** each query.

Open each query in **Design** view to examine the design grid. The *3F Summa Cum Laude Graduates Query* answers the question, *What is the GPA, student ID, last name, first name, degree, and program for students graduating with a grade point average of 3.8 or higher, in descending order by GPA?* The *3F GPAs by Degree Program Query* answers the question, *What is the program, last name, first name, and GPA for all students, in ascending order by the Last Name field within the Program field?* **Close All** objects.

Based on your **3F Summa Cum Laude Graduates Query** object, use the **Report** tool to create a report. Apply the **Facet** theme to only this report. Delete the **Student ID** field from the report. For the **Last Name**, **First Name**, and **Degree text box controls**, set the **Width** property to **1.25** and then **Sort** the **Last Name** field in **Ascending** order. For the **Program text box controls**, set the **Width** property to **2.5**

At the bottom of the report, for the **calculated control**, which displays *8*, set the **Height** to **0.25** and then for the **page number control**, set the **Left** property to **5** For the title of the report, set the **Font Size** to **14** and change the word *Query* to **Report** For the **GPA** field, set the **Left** property to **0.25** to approximately center the fields within the margins of the report. **Save** the report as **Lastname Firstname 3F Summa Cum Laude Graduates Report** and then create a paper or electronic printout as directed. **Close Print Preview**, **Close** the **Property Sheet**, and then **Close** the report.

2 Use the **Report Wizard** to create a report based on your **3F GPAs by Degree Program Query** object that includes the following fields in the order given: **Program**, **GPA**, **Last Name**, and **First Name**. View your data **by 3F Degrees** and do not add any other grouping to the report. Sort first in **Descending** order by **GPA**, and second in **Ascending** order by **Last Name**. Summarize the report by averaging the **GPA** field. Be sure the layout is **Stepped** and the orientation is **Portrait**. For the report title, type **Lastname Firstname 3F GPAs by Program Report** and then switch to **Layout** view.

3 Apply the **Wisp** theme to only this report. For the report title, change the **Font Size** to **16**, and then apply **Bold**. Delete the controls that begin with **Summary for 'Program'**. Under **Program**, for the **text box controls**, set the **Width** property to **2.75** Change the text in the **Avg label control** to **Average GPA by Program** At the top of the report, select the four **label controls** that display the field names, and then apply **Bold**. Select the **GPA label control**, the **GPA text box controls**, and the **calculated controls** for the average GPA, and then set the **Width** property to **1** and the **Left** property to **3 Close** the **Property Sheet**. Display the report in **Design** view. Under **Program Header**, click the **Program text box control**, hold down ⇧Shift, and under **Program Footer**, click the **Average GPA by Program label control**. **Align** the controls on the **Right**, and then **Save** the design changes to your report.

4 Switch to **Print Preview**, **Zoom** to display **Two Pages** of the report, and examine how the groupings break across the pages. Switch to **Layout** view, display the **Group, Sort, and Total** pane, select **keep whole group together on one page**, and then close the **Group, Sort, and Total** pane. Switch to **Print Preview**, and notice that the groupings are not split between pages. **Save** the report, and then create a paper or electronic printout as directed—two pages result.

(Project 3F Degrees and Students continues on the next page)

CONTENT-BASED ASSESSMENTS

5 **Close Print Preview**, and then **Close** the report. **Open** the **Navigation Pane**, and, if necessary, increase the width of the pane so that all object names display fully. On the right side of the title bar, click **Close** to close the database and to exit Access. As directed by your instructor, submit your database and the paper or electronic printouts of the two reports—one report is two pages—that are the results of this project. Specifically, in this project, using your own name, you created the following database and printouts or electronic printouts:

1. Lastname_Firstname_3F_Degrees_Students	Database file
2. Lastname Firstname 3F Summa Cum Laude Graduates Report	Report (printout or electronic printout)
3. Lastname Firstname 3F GPAs by Program Report	Report (printout or electronic printout - two pages)

END | You have completed Project 3F

CONTENT-BASED ASSESSMENTS

Mastering Access Project 3G Career Books

In the following Mastering Access project, you will assist Rebecca Hennelly, head librarian at the Southwest Campus of Texas Lakes Community College, in using her database to track publishers and book titles that assist students in finding employment. Your completed forms and report will look similar to Figure 3.53.

PROJECT FILES

For Project 3G, you will need the following file:

a03G_Career_Books

You will save your database as:

Lastname_Firstname_3G_Career_Books

PROJECT RESULTS

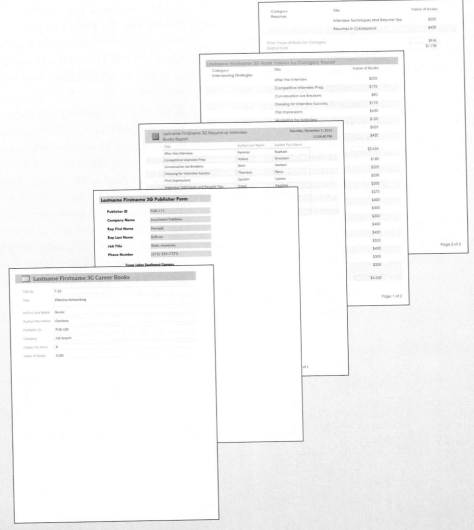

FIGURE 3.53

(Project 3G Career Books continues on the next page)

CONTENT-BASED ASSESSMENTS

1 Start Access. From your student data files, open **a03G_Career_Books**. Save the database in your **Access Chapter 3** folder as **Lastname_Firstname_3G_Career_ Books** and then enable the content. In the **Navigation Pane, Rename** the two tables and one query by adding **Lastname Firstname** to the beginning of each object name. Increase the width of the **Navigation Pane** so that all object names display fully. View the relationship that is established between the *3G Publishers* tables and the *3G Career Books* table—*one* publisher can publish *many* career books. Save the changes to the layout of the relationships.

Open the **3G Resume or Interview Books Query**, apply **Best Fit**, and then **Save** the query. Switch the query to **Design** view, examine the design of the query, and then **Close** the query object.

2 Based on your **3G Career Books** table, use the **Form** tool to create a form. **Save** the form as **Lastname Firstname 3G Career Book Form** and then switch to **Form** view. Using the form, add a new record to the underlying table as shown in **Table 1**.

3 Display the first record, and click in the **Title ID** field. **Find** the record for the **Title ID** of **T-19**, and then **Delete** the record. Display the record you entered for **T-25**, and then, as directed, create a paper or electronic printout of only that record, changing the **Column Size Width** in the **Print** dialog box to **7.5** Save the design changes to your form.

4 Use the **Filter By Form** tool in your **3G Career Book Form** object to create a filter that displays records with a **Category** of **Interviewing Strategies** or **Resumes**. After verifying that 10 records match this criteria, click **Toggle Filter** to display all 24 records. **Save** the form, and then **Close** the form.

5 Use the **Form Wizard** to create a form based on your **3G Publishers** table that includes the following fields in the order given: **Company Name, Rep Last Name, Rep First Name, Job Title,** and **Phone Number.** Apply a **Columnar** layout, and name the form **Lastname Firstname 3G Publisher Form**

6 In **Layout** view, apply the **Stacked** layout to all of the controls, and then apply the **Integral** theme to this form only. For the title of the form, change the **Font Size** to **16,** apply **Bold,** and then change the **Font Color** to **Dark Teal, Text 2, Darker 50%**—under **Theme Colors,** in the fourth column, the last color. **Save** the design changes to the form.

7 From the **Field List** pane, add the **Publisher ID** field to the form directly above the **Company Name** field. **Close** the **Field List** pane. Move the **Rep First Name** controls directly above the **Rep Last Name** controls. Click the **Job Title text box control,** set the **Width** property to **2.5** and then **Save** the design changes to your form.

8 Select all six **text box controls,** and change the **Background Color** to **Turquoise, Accent 1, Lighter 80%**—under **Theme Colors,** in the fifth column, the second color. Select all six **label controls,** and change the **Font Color** to **Dark Teal, Text 2, Darker 50%**—under **Theme Colors,** in the fourth column, the last color. Apply **Bold** to the **label controls.** With the **label controls** still selected, set the **Width** property to **1.75** and then select all of the **label controls** and all of the **text box controls.** Change the **Font Size** to **12,** set the **Height** property to **0.25** and then **Save** the design changes to your form.

TABLE 1

Title ID	Title	Author Last Name	Author First Name	Publisher ID	Category	Copies On Hand	Value of Books
T-25	Effective Networking	Nunez	Charlene	PUB-109	Job Search	6	180

(Return to Step 3)

(Project 3G Career Books continues on the next page)

CONTENT-BASED ASSESSMENTS

9 In **Design** view, set the **Form Footer** section **Height** property to **0.5** Add a **Label** control to the **Form Footer** section that displays **Texas Lakes Southwest Campus** For this **label control**, change the **Font Color** to **Dark Teal, Text 2, Darker 50%**—under **Theme Colors**, in the fourth column, the last color —and then apply **Bold**. For this **label control**, set the **Width** property to **2.2** Set the **Top** property to **0.1** and then set the **Left** property to **1** **Close** the **Property Sheet**, **Save** your form, and then switch to **Form** view. Using the form, add a new record to the underlying table as shown in **Table 2**.

10 Display the record that you just created, and then, as directed, create a paper or electronic printout of only this record. Because you changed the field widths, you do not need to change the Column Size Width in the **Print** dialog box. **Close** the form.

11 Based on your **3G Resume or Interview Books Query** object, use the **Report** tool to create a report. Apply the **Retrospect** theme to only this report. Delete the following fields from the report: **Publisher ID**, **Category**, and **Company Name**. For the **Title text box controls**, set the **Width** property to **3** and then **Sort** the **Title** field in **Ascending** order. For the **Author Last Name text box controls** and the **Author First Name text box controls**, set the **Width** property to **1.5**

12 Click the **Title** field name, and then add a calculated control that counts the number of records. At the bottom of the report, for the **calculated control**, which displays *10*, set the **Height** to **0.25** and then for the **page number control**, set the **Left** property to **5** For the title of the report, set the **Font Size** to **14** and change the word *Query* to **Report** Click the **Title** field name, and then set the **Left** property to **0.75** to move all of the controls to the right. **Save** the report as **Lastname Firstname 3G Resume or Interview Books Report** and then create a paper or electronic printout as directed. **Close Print Preview**, **Close** the **Property Sheet**, and then **Close** the report.

13 Use the **Report Wizard** to create a report based on your **3G Career Books** table that includes the following fields in the order given: **Category**, **Title**, and **Value of Books**. Group your data by **Category**, sort in **Ascending** order by **Title**, and then summarize the report by summing the **Value of Books** field. Be sure the layout is **Stepped** and the orientation is **Portrait**. For the report title, type **Lastname Firstname 3G Book Values by Category Report** and then switch to **Layout** view.

14 Apply the **Ion Boardroom** theme to only this report. For the report title, change the **Font Size** to **14**, and then apply **Bold**. Delete the controls that begin with **Summary for 'Category'**. Select the **Category, Title**, and **Value of Books label controls**, and then apply **Bold**. Under **Title**, for the **text box controls**, set the **Width** property to **3.5** For the **Value of Books label control**, set the **Left** property to **6** and then **Save** the design changes to your report.

15 At the bottom of the report in the last column, select the following three controls: **text box control** that displays *$420*, **calculated control** that displays *$945*, and the **calculated control** that displays *7,730*. Set the **Width** property to **1.25** and the **Left** property to **6** For the **Grand Total label control**, set the **Width** property to **1** and then change the text in the **Sum label control** to **Total Value of Books by Category** Click any **Title text box control**, set the **Height** property to **0.35** and then **Save** your report.

16 **Close** the **Property Sheet**, and then display your report in **Design** view. Under **Category Footer**, click the **label control** that displays *Total Value of Books by Category*, hold down Shift, and then under **Report Footer**, click the **Grand Total label control**. **Align** the controls on the **Left**, and then **Save** the design changes to your report.

TABLE 2

Publisher ID	Company Name	Rep First Name	Rep Last Name	Job Title	Phone Number
PUB-111	Associated Publishers	Marquis	Sullivan	Sales Associate	(512) 555-7373

(Return to Step 10)

(Project 3G Career Books continues on the next page)

CONTENT-BASED ASSESSMENTS

17 Switch to **Print Preview**, **Zoom** to display **Two Pages** of the report, and examine how the groupings break across the pages. Switch to **Layout** view, display the **Group, Sort, and Total** pane, select **keep whole group together on one page**, and then close the **Group, Sort, and Total** pane. Switch to **Print Preview**, and notice that the groupings are no longer split between pages. **Save** the report, and then create a paper or electronic printout as directed—two pages result.

18 **Close Print Preview**, and then **Close** the report. **Open** the **Navigation Pane**, and, if necessary, increase the width of the pane so that all object names display fully. On the right side of the title bar, click **Close** to close the database and to exit Access. As directed by your instructor, submit your database and the paper or electronic printouts of the two forms and two reports—one report is two pages—that are the results of this project. Specifically, in this project, using your own name, you created the following database and printouts or electronic printouts:

1. Lastname_Firstname_3G_Career_Books	Database file
2. Lastname Firstname 3G Career Book Form	Form (printout or electronic printout - Record 24)
3. Lastname Firstname 3G Publisher Form	Form (printout or electronic printout - Record 12)
4. Lastname Firstname 3G Resume or Interview Books Report	Report (printout or electronic printout)
5. Lastname Firstname 3G Book Values by Category Report	Report (printout or electronic printout - two pages)

END | You have completed Project 3G

CONTENT-BASED ASSESSMENTS

pply a combination of the
A and 3B skills.

GO! Fix It	Project 3H Resume Workshops	Online
GO! Make It	Project 3I Study Abroad	Online
GO! Solve It	Project 3J Job Offers	Online
GO! Solve It	Project 3K Financial Aid	

PROJECT FILES

For Project 3K, you will need the following file:

a03K_Financial_Aid

You will save your database as:

Lastname_Firstname_3K_Financial_Aid

Start Access, navigate to your student data files, open a03K_Financial_Aid, and then save the database in your **Access Chapter 3** folder as **Lastname_Firstname_3K_Financial_Aid** Using your own name, add **Lastname Firstname** to the beginning of both table names and the query name. Sivia Long, the financial aid director, would like you to create an attractive form and a report for this database, using the following guidelines:

- The form will be used to update student records in the 3K FA Students table. Be sure that the Last Name field displays above the First Name field. After the form is created, enter a new record using your own information with a Student ID of **9091246** and Financial Aid ID of **FA-07** and a Home Phone of **(512) 555-9876** and a College Email of **ns246@tlcc.edu** Create a filter that when toggled on displays the records for those students whose last names begin with the letter *S*. Add a footer to the form that displays **Texas Lakes Community College Financial Aid** Save the form as **Lastname Firstname 3K FA Student Update Form** and then create a paper or electronic printout of your record only.

- The report should use the query and list the Award Name, the Student ID, and the Award Amount for financial aid offered to students, grouped by the Award Name field, and sorted in ascending order by the Student ID field. Include a total for the Award Amount field, save the report as **Lastname Firstname 3K FA Amount by Award Report** and be sure the groupings do not break across pages when the report is printed. Create a paper or electronic printout as directed—multiple pages result.

Open the Navigation Pane, be sure that all object names display fully, and then close Access. As directed, submit your database and the paper or electronic printout of the form and report—the report is multiple pages—that are the results of this project. Specifically, in this project, using your own name, you created the following database and printouts or electronic printouts:

1. Lastname_Firstname_3K_Financial_Aid	Database file
2. Lastname Firstname 3K FA Student Update Form	Form (printout or electronic printout - Record 35)
3. Lastname Firstname 3K FA Amount by Award Report	Report (printout or electronic printout - multiple pages)

(Project 3K Financial Aid continues on the next page)

CONTENT-BASED ASSESSMENTS

Performance Level

	Exemplary	Proficient	Developing
Create 3K FA Student Update Form	Form created with correct fields, new record, footer, and filter in an attractive format.	Form created with no more than two missing elements.	Form created with more than two missing elements.
Create 3K FA Amount by Award Report	Report created with correct fields, grouped, sorted, and summarized correctly, with groupings kept together in an attractive format.	Report created with no more than two missing elements.	Report created with more than two missing elements.

Performance Criteria

END | You have completed Project 3K

OUTCOMES-BASED ASSESSMENTS

RUBRIC

The following outcomes-based assessments are *open-ended assessments*. That is, there is no specific correct result; your result will depend on your approach to the information provided. Make *Professional Quality* your goal. Use the following scoring rubric to guide you in *how* to approach the problem and then to evaluate *how well* your approach solves the problem.

The *criteria*—Software Mastery, Content, Format & Layout, and Process—represent the knowledge and skills you have gained that you can apply to solving the problem. The *levels of performance*—Professional Quality, Approaching Professional Quality, or Needs Quality Improvements—help you and your instructor evaluate your result.

	Your completed project is of Professional Quality if you:	Your completed project is Approaching Professional Quality if you:	Your completed project Needs Quality Improvements if you:
1-Software Mastery	Choose and apply the most appropriate skills, tools, and features and identify efficient methods to solve the problem.	Choose and apply some appropriate skills, tools, and features, but not in the most efficient manner.	Choose inappropriate skills, tools, or features, or are inefficient in solving the problem.
2-Content	Construct a solution that is clear and well organized, contains content that is accurate, appropriate to the audience and purpose, and is complete. Provide a solution that contains no errors in spelling, grammar, or style.	Construct a solution in which some components are unclear, poorly organized, inconsistent, or incomplete. Misjudge the needs of the audience. Have some errors in spelling, grammar, or style, but the errors do not detract from comprehension.	Construct a solution that is unclear, incomplete, or poorly organized; contains some inaccurate or inappropriate content; and contains many errors in spelling, grammar, or style. Do not solve the problem.
3-Format & Layout	Format and arrange all elements to communicate information and ideas, clarify function, illustrate relationships, and indicate relative importance.	Apply appropriate format and layout features to some elements, but not others. Overuse features, causing minor distraction.	Apply format and layout that does not communicate information or ideas clearly. Do not use format and layout features to clarify function, illustrate relationships, or indicate relative importance. Use available features excessively, causing distraction.
4-Process	Use an organized approach that integrates planning, development, self-assessment, revision, and reflection.	Demonstrate an organized approach in some areas, but not others; or, use an insufficient process of organization throughout.	Do not use an organized approach to solve the problem.

OUTCOMES-BASED ASSESSMENTS

Apply a combination of the 3A and 3B skills.

GO! Think   Project 3L Food Services

PROJECT FILES

For Project 3L, you will need the following file:

a03L_Food_Services

You will save your database as:

Lastname_Firstname_3L_Food_Services

Start Access, navigate to your student data files, open a03L_Food_Services, save the database in your **Access Chapter 3** folder as **Lastname_Firstname_3L_Food_Services** and then enable the content. Using your own name, add **Lastname Firstname** to the beginning of both table names. Luciano Gonzalez, the hospitality director, would like you to create to create an attractive form and a report to assist him with the staff scheduling of food services for a two-day student orientation workshop using the following guidelines:

- The form will be used to update records in the 3L Staff table. Be sure that the Last Name field displays above the First Name field. After the form is created, enter a new record using your own last name and first name with a Staff ID of **STAFF-1119** and a Phone Number of **(512) 555-0845** and a Title of **Server** Create a filter that when toggled on displays the records for staff with a Title of *Server*. Add a footer to the form that displays **Texas Lakes Community College Hospitality Services** Save the form as **Lastname Firstname 3L Staff Update Form** and then create a paper or electronic printout of your record only.

- The report will be used by Mr. Gonzalez to call staff members when the schedule changes. Add a report footer that displays **Texas Lakes Community College Hospitality Services** and then save the report as **Lastname Firstname 3L Staff Phone List** Create a paper or electronic printout as directed.

Open the Navigation Pane, be sure that all object names display fully, and then close Access. As directed, submit your database and the paper or electronic printout of the form and report that are the results of this project. Specifically, in this project, using your own name, you created the following database and printouts or electronic printouts:

1. Lastname_Firstname_3L_Food_Services	Database file
2. Lastname Firstname 3L Staff Update Form	Form (printout or electronic printout - Record 19)
3. Lastname Firstname 3L Staff Phone List	Report (printout or electronic printout)

END | You have completed Project 3L

GO! Think   Project 3M Donor Gifts   Online

You and GO!   Project 3N Personal Inventory   Online

Build from Scratch

GO! Cumulative Group Project   Project 3O Bell Orchid Hotels   Online

Integrating Word, Excel, Access, and PowerPoint

PROJECT 1A

OUTCOMES
Create an Excel workbook that includes data exported from Access and data copied from Word and PowerPoint.

OBJECTIVES

1. Export Access Data to Excel
2. Create an Excel Worksheet from a Word Table
3. Copy and Paste an Excel Chart into Other Programs
4. Copy and Paste an Object from PowerPoint into Excel

PROJECT 1B

OUTCOMES
Link Excel data to a Word document and complete a mail merge in Word using Access data.

OBJECTIVES

5. Link Excel Data to a Word Document
6. Modify Linked Data and Update Links
7. Create a Tabvle in Word from Access Data
8. Use Access Data to Complete a Mail Merge in Word

EpicStockMedia / Fotolia

In This Chapter

All applications in a software suite, for example Microsoft Office, are designed to work well with one another. You can input data or create objects, such as a chart or table, in one application and then export the data to another application without retyping the data or recreating the object. It is important to identify the appropriate software within the suite to produce solutions that best utilize the functions of the various applications. In this chapter, you will copy and paste data and objects between applications. You will link, modify, and update data and use mail merge to create individualized documents.

The projects in this chapter relate to **Ultimate Action Sports Gear**, one of the country's leading retailers of sports equipment and outdoor recreational merchandise. The company has a growing online business in addition to large retail stores in Colorado, New Mexico, Oregon, and Washington. Major merchandise categories include fishing, camping, golf, rock climbing, winter sports, action sports, aquatic sports, team sports, racquet sports, fitness and athletic apparel, and footwear. The company's inventory is constantly updated to provide customers with the newest products in the action sports industry.

State Sales

PROJECT ACTIVITIES

In Activities 1.01 through 1.12, you will export Access data into an Excel workbook, and then you will copy and paste Word data into the Excel workbook. In Excel, you will create a chart based on the data, and then copy the chart into a PowerPoint presentation. Your completed documents will look similar to Figure 1.1.

PROJECT FILES

For Project 1A, you will need the following files:

New blank Excel workbook
i01A_Store_Locations
i01A_State_Sales
i01A_Sales_Presentation

You will save your files as:

Lastname_Firstname_1A_Sales_Chart
Lastname_Firstname_1A_Store_Locations
Lastname_Firstname_1A_State_Sales
Lastname_Firstname_1A_Sales_Presentation

PROJECT RESULTS

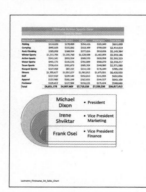

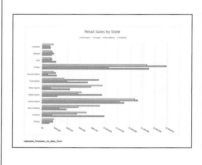
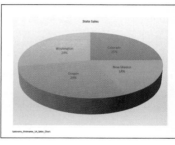

FIGURE 1.1 Project 1A State Sales

- Tap an item to click it.
- Press and hold for a few seconds to right-click; release when the information or command displays.
- Touch the screen with two or more fingers and then pinch together to zoom in or stretch your fingers apart to zoom out.
- Slide your finger on the screen to scroll—slide left to scroll right and slide right to scroll left.
- Slide to rearrange—similar to dragging with a mouse.
- Swipe from edge: from right to display charms; from left to expose open apps, snap apps, or close apps; from top or bottom to show commands or close an app.
- Swipe to select—slide an item a short distance with a quick movement to select an item and bring up commands, if any.

Objective 1   Export Access Data to Excel

Access includes a tool to export data from an Access database into an Excel workbook. When you export Access data, you create a copy of the data in Excel.

Activity 1.01 | Exporting Access Data to Excel

In the following activity, you will export Access data into an Excel workbook.

1 **Start** Access. Near the bottom left of the screen, click **Open Other Files**, and then under **Places**, double-click **Computer**. In the **Open** dialog box, navigate to your student data files, and then open the Access database **i01A_Store_Locations**. Click the **FILE tab**, and then click **Save As**. On the **Save As** screen, with **Save Database As** selected, click **Save As**.

2 In the **Save As** dialog box, navigate to the location where you are saving your files. Click **New folder**, type **Integrated Projects** and then press Enter. In the **File name** box, type **Lastname_Firstname_1A_Store_Locations** and then press Enter. On the **Message Bar** that displays a SECURITY WARNING, click **Enable Content**.

3 In the **navigation pane**, double-click the **Managers** table. At the bottom of the table, select *Firstname*, and then type your own firstname. Press Tab to select *Lastname*, type your own lastname, and then press Enter.

4 In the **navigation pane**, double-click the query **Store Locations by Manager**, and then be sure that your name displays. Compare your screen with Figure 1.2.

FIGURE 1.2

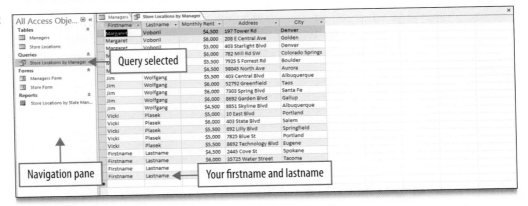

5 On the **EXTERNAL DATA tab**, in the **Export group**, click **Excel**. In the **Export - Excel Spreadsheet** dialog box, click **Browse**. Navigate to your **Integrated Projects** folder, type the file name **Lastname_Firstname_1A_Sales_Chart** and then click **Save**.

6 In the **Export - Excel Spreadsheet** dialog box, be sure that the **File format** is **Excel Workbook** (***.xlsx**). Select the **Export data with formatting and layout** check box, and then compare your screen with Figure 1.3.

FIGURE 1.3

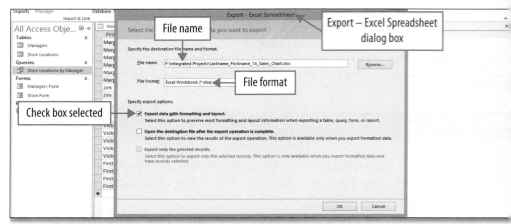

7 In the **Export – Excel Spreadsheet** dialog box, click **OK**. In the dialog box, be sure that the **Save export steps** check box is not selected, and then click **Close**.

8 **Close** ☒ Access.

9 **Start** Excel. Near the bottom left of the screen, click **Open Other Workbooks**, and then under **Places**, double-click **Computer**. In the **Open** dialog box, navigate to your **Integrated Projects** folder, and then open the Excel workbook **Lastname_Firstname_1A_Sales_Chart**.

Notice that the Excel worksheet name is changed to the exported Access query name—*Store Locations by Manager*.

Activity 1.02 | Creating and Sorting an Excel Table

To easily manage and analyze a group of related data, you can convert a range of cells to an Excel table. An Excel table typically contains data in a series of rows and columns; the Excel table can be managed independently from the data in other rows and columns in the worksheet. In the following activity, you will change a range of data into an Excel table, and then sort the data.

1 Click cell **A1**. On the **INSERT tab**, in the **Tables group**, click **Table**. In the **Create Table** dialog box, under **Where is the data for your table?**, be sure that the range is =$A$1:$E$21 and that the **My table has headers** check box is selected. Compare your screen with Figure 1.4.

FIGURE 1.4

2 In the **Create Table** dialog box, click **OK**.

3 Click in cell **E1**, click the **City arrow**, and then click **Sort A to Z** to sort the entire table. Compare your screen with Figure 1.5.

The rows display in a different order based on column E—the City column—so that city names display in ascending order.

After a column is sorted in ascending or descending order, a small arrow displays to the right of *City* to indicate the sort order.

FIGURE 1.5

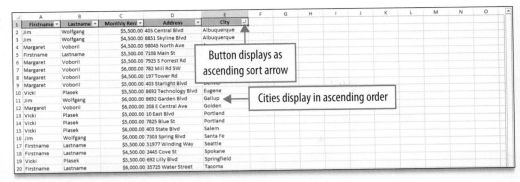

4 ▸ **Save** 🖫 your Excel workbook.

Activity 1.03 | Inserting a Total Row in an Excel Table

To quickly total the data in the columns of an Excel table, display a total row at the end of the table, and then use the functions that are provided for each cell in the total row.

1 ▸ With cell *E1* selected, on the **DESIGN tab**, in the **Table Style Options group**, select the **Total Row** check box. Click cell **E22**, and then compare your screen with Figure 1.6.

Cell E22 displays the number 20. The Total Row counts the number of cells containing text in column E. The header row is not included in the Total Row calculations.

FIGURE 1.6

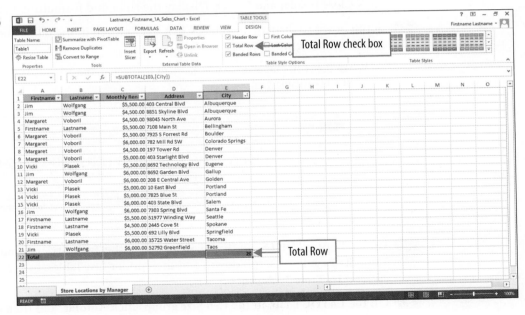

2 ▸ To the right of cell *E22*, click the **arrow**, and then click **None**.

Because the cells in column E contain text, a calculation is not required.

3 ▸ Click cell **C22**. To the right of cell *C22*, click the **arrow**, and then click **Sum**. Compare your screen with Figure 1.7.

The Total Monthly Rent for all locations displays in cell C22.

FIGURE 1.7

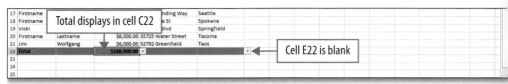

> **4** Save 🖫 your Excel workbook.

Objective 2 Create an Excel Worksheet from a Word Table

There are times when you might want to use data stored in one file in a different file without having to reenter the data.

Activity 1.04 | Formatting a Word Table

> **1** **Start** Word. Navigate to your student data files, and then open the document **i01A_State_Sales**. Press F12 to display the **Save As** dialog box. Navigate to your **Integrated Projects** folder, and then **Save** the document as **Lastname_Firstname_1A_State_Sales**

> **2** On the **INSERT tab**, in the **Header & Footer group**, click **Footer**. At the bottom of the **Footer** gallery, click **Edit Footer**. On the ribbon, under **HEADER & FOOTER TOOLS**, on the **DESIGN tab**, in the **Insert group**, click **Document Info**, and then click **File Name**. In the **Close group**, click **Close Header and Footer**. Display the ruler and formatting marks, if necessary.

> **3** Scroll down to display the table. Click the first cell in the table, and then compare your screen with Figure 1.8.

> When the entire table or a table element is selected, the TABLE TOOLS tabs—DESIGN and LAYOUT—display.

FIGURE 1.8

> **4** Under **TABLE TOOLS**, on the **DESIGN tab**, in the **Table Styles group**, click **More** ⩒. In the **Table Styles** gallery, scroll down, and then under **List Tables**, in the third row, click the last style—**List Table 3 - Accent 6**.

> **5** On the **LAYOUT tab**, in the **Cell Size group**, click **AutoFit**, and then click **AutoFit Contents**. In the **Table group**, click **Properties**. In the **Table Properties** dialog box, on the **Table tab**, under **Alignment**, click **Center**. Compare your screen with Figure 1.9.

FIGURE 1.9

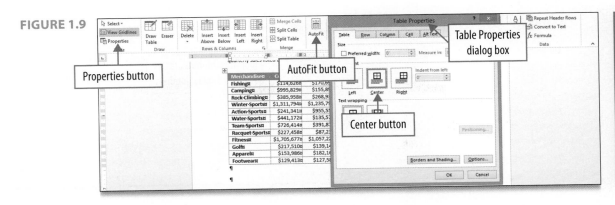

6 ▶ In the **Table Properties** dialog box, click **OK** to center the table horizontally on the page.

7 ▶ **Save** 🖫 your Word document.

Activity 1.05 | Copying and Pasting a Word Table into an Excel Workbook

After entering data in a Word document, you may realize that you can manipulate the data better in another program, such as Excel. Instead of starting over and retyping the data, you can copy the data from the Word document, and then paste the data into an Excel workbook.

NOTE	Working with Multiple Open Windows

In this chapter, you will work with a number of different files and will have a number of different windows open. When you have completed the work in one file, save the file, and then minimize the window. When you need to use the file again, click the appropriate program icon on the taskbar to maximize that window.

1 ▶ Be sure that Word is the active window. On the **LAYOUT tab**, in the **Table group**, click **Select**, and then click **Select Table**. On the **HOME tab** in the **Clipboard group**, click **Copy** 🖹.

The entire table is selected and copied.

2 ▶ On the taskbar, click the **Excel icon** 🗷 to make the Excel window active.

3 ▶ At the bottom of the worksheet, click **New sheet** ⊕ to insert a new blank worksheet. Right-click the **Sheet1** worksheet tab, and then click **Rename**. Type **Sales** and then press Enter. Compare your screen with Figure 1.10.

FIGURE 1.10

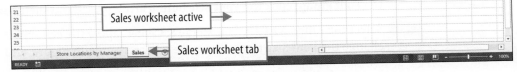

4 ▶ On the **PAGE LAYOUT tab**, in the **Themes group**, click **Themes**, and then under **Office**, click **Office**.

5 ▶ Click cell **A4** to make it the active cell. On the **HOME tab**, in the **Clipboard group**, click **Paste**. Compare your screen with Figure 1.11.

The Word data is pasted into the Excel worksheet, starting in cell A4—the active cell.

The pound sign (#) will display if a column is not wide enough to display an entire number.

FIGURE 1.11

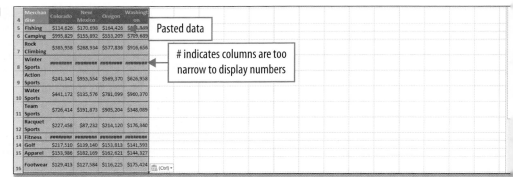

Pasted data

# indicates columns are too narrow to display numbers

6 ▶ Click cell **A4**. On the **HOME tab**, in the **Cells group**, click **Format**, and then click **Column Width**. In the **Column Width** dialog box, type **16** and then click **OK**.

7 ▶ Select the range **B4:E4**. In the **Cells group**, click **Format**, and then click **Column Width**. In the **Column Width** dialog box, type **12** and then click **OK**.

Due to the increased column widths, all data displays in the worksheet.

8 ▶ Select the range **A4:A16**. In the **Cells group**, click **Format**, and then click **Row Height**. In the **Row Height** dialog box, type **17** and then click **OK**. Click in an empty cell, and then compare your screen with Figure 1.12.

FIGURE 1.12

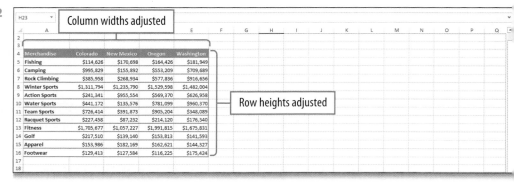

Column widths adjusted

Row heights adjusted

9 ▶ In cell **A1**, type **Ultimate Action Sports Gear** and then press Enter. In cell **A2**, type **Sales by State** and then press Enter. Select the range **A1:F1**, and then on the **HOME tab**, in the **Alignment group**, click **Merge & Center**. In the **Styles group**, click **Cell Styles**, and then click **Accent6**. In the **Font group**, click the **Font Size button arrow** ⌷11 ⌄⌷, and then click **16**.

10 ▶ Select the range **A2:F2**. Click **Merge & Center**, apply the cell style **60% - Accent6**, and then change the **Font Size** to **14**. Compare your screen with Figure 1.13.

FIGURE 1.13

Formatted cells in rows 1 and 2

11 ▶ **Save** 🖫 your Excel workbook.

Activity 1.06 | Using the SUM Function and Fill Handle in Excel

One of Excel's most powerful features is the capability to perform mathematical calculations. In the following activity, you will use the SUM function to add numbers.

1 Click cell **F4**, type **Total Sales** and then press Enter.

2 Be sure that **F5** is the active cell. On the **HOME tab**, in the **Editing group**, click **AutoSum**, and then on the **Formula Bar**, click **Enter** ✓ to confirm the entry and keep cell **F5** as the active cell. Using the technique you previously practiced, change the width of column **F** to **13**

ALERT! **The Formula Bar May Not Display**

If the Formula Bar does not display, on the VIEW tab, in the Show group, select the Formula Bar check box.

---

3 In cell **F5**, point to the fill handle until the ⊞ pointer displays, hold down the left mouse button, and then drag down to cell **F16**. Release the mouse button. In the **Font group**, click **Increase Font Size** 𝐀, and then compare your screen with Figure 1.14.

FIGURE 1.14

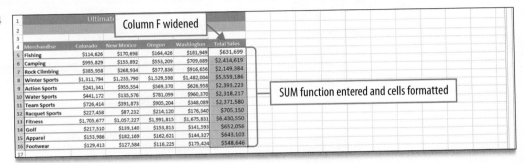

4 Click cell **A17**, type **Total** and then press Tab.

5 With cell **B17** selected, in the **Editing group**, click **AutoSum**, and then on the **Formula Bar**, click **Enter** ✓. Using the technique you just practiced, use the fill handle to copy the formula to cells **C17:F17**.

6 Select the range **A5:E16**. In the **Font group**, click the **Border button arrow** ⊞ ▾, and then click **No Border**. Select the range **B17:F17**. In the **Styles group**, click **Cell Styles**, and then under **Titles and Headings**, click **Total**. In the **Font group**, click **Increase Font Size** 𝐀. Click in an empty cell, and then compare your screen with Figure 1.15.

FIGURE 1.15

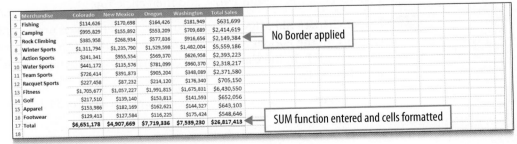

7 **Save** 🖫 your Excel workbook.

A chart displays numerical data in a visual format. You can copy an Excel chart, and then paste it in files created with other applications.

Activity 1.07 | Creating and Formatting a Bar Chart in Excel

In the following activity, you will create and format a bar chart showing a comparison of merchandise sales by state.

1 ▶ Select the range **A4:E16**. On the **INSERT tab**, in the **Charts group**, click **Insert Bar Chart arrow** ▤▾, and then under **3-D Bar**, click the first chart—**3-D Clustered Bar**. Under **CHART TOOLS**, on the **DESIGN tab**, in the **Location group**, click **Move Chart**. In the **Move Chart** dialog box, click the **New sheet** option button, type **Merchandise Chart** and then click **OK**. Compare your screen with Figure 1.16.

A 3-D bar chart is created and moved to a new chart sheet named Merchandise Chart.

FIGURE 1.16

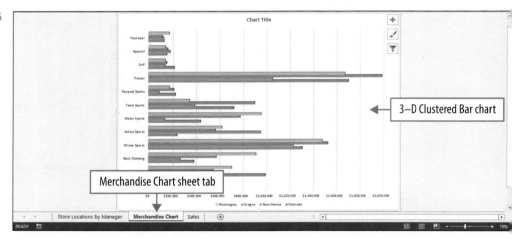

2 ▶ In the chart, select the text *Chart Title*, and then type **Retail Sales by State** Click in a blank area of the chart to deselect the chart title.

3 ▶ To the right of the chart, click **Chart Styles** ✏. In the **STYLE** gallery, scroll down, and then click **Style 10**.

4 ▶ To the right of the chart, click **Chart Elements** ⊞. Under **CHART ELEMENTS**, point to **Legend**, click the **Legend arrow**, and then click **Top**.

5 ▶ Under **CHART ELEMENTS**, point to **Axes**, click the **Axes arrow**, and then click **More Options**. In the **Format Axis** pane, under **AXIS OPTIONS**, click **Size & Properties** ▥. Under **ALIGNMENT**, in the **Custom angle** box, type **30** and then press ⏎. Compare your screen with Figure 1.17.

The numbers on the horizontal axis display at an angle of 30 degrees.

FIGURE 1.17

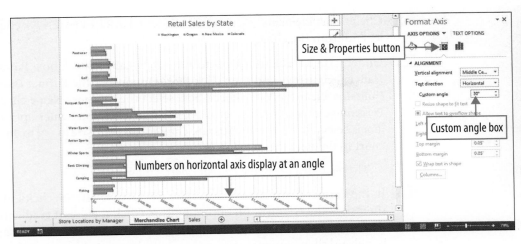

6 ▸ **Close** ☒ the **Format Axis** pane.

7 ▸ **Save** 🖫 your Excel workbook.

Activity 1.08 | Creating and Formatting a Pie Chart in Excel

In the following activity, you will create a pie chart to show each state's percentage of total sales.

1 ▸ Click the **Sales** worksheet tab. Select the range **B4:E4**, press and hold Ctrl, and then select the range **B17:E17**.

The range B4:E4 and the range B17:E17 are selected. Recall that holding down Ctrl enables you to select nonadjacent cells.

2 ▸ On the **INSERT tab**, in the **Charts group**, click **Insert Pie or Doughnut Chart arrow** 🥧▾, and then under **3-D Pie**, click **3-D Pie**. On the ribbon, under **CHART TOOLS**, on the **DESIGN tab**, in the **Location group**, click **Move Chart**. In the **Move Chart** dialog box, click the **New sheet** option button, type **State Sales Chart** and then click **OK**.

3 ▸ To the right of the chart, click **Chart Styles** 🖌. In the **STYLE** gallery, scroll down, and then click **Style 5**. Press Esc to close the gallery. Compare your screen with Figure 1.18.

FIGURE 1.18

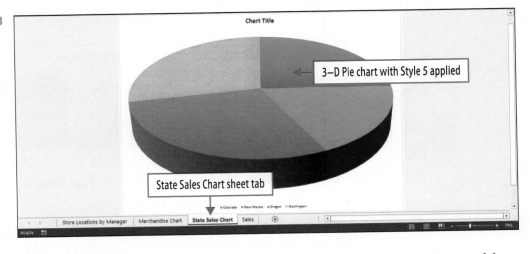

4 ▸ In the chart, select the text *Chart Title*, type **State Sales** and then click in a blank area of the chart.

5 ▶ Click **Chart Elements** ⊞, and then under **CHART ELEMENTS**, click **Legend** to remove the legend from the chart.

6 ▶ Under **CHART ELEMENTS**, select the **Data Labels** check box. Point to **Data Labels**, click the **Data Labels arrow**, and then click **More Options**. In the **Format Data Labels** pane, under **Label Contains**, clear the **Value** check box, select the **Category Name** check box, and then select the **Percentage** check box. Under **Label Position**, click the **Center** option button. With the data labels selected, on the **HOME tab**, change the **Font Size** [11 ▾] to **16**. Click in a blank area of the chart to deselect the data labels.

The pane changes to the *Format Chart Area* pane.

7 ▶ In the **Format Chart Area** pane, under **CHART OPTIONS**, click **Fill & Line** 🖎. Click **FILL**, and then click the **Gradient fill** option button. Click the **Preset gradients arrow**, and then in the first row, click the third gradient—**Light Gradient – Accent 3**. **Close** ✖ the **Format Chart Area** pane, and then compare your screen with Figure 1.19.

FIGURE 1.19

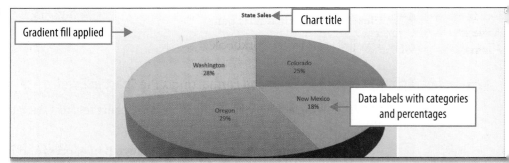

8 ▶ Press and hold Ctrl, and then click the **Merchandise Chart** sheet tab.

Both chart sheets are selected.

9 ▶ On the **PAGE LAYOUT tab**, in the **Page Setup group**, click the **Dialog Box Launcher** 🖬. In the **Page Setup** dialog box, click the **Header/Footer tab**, and then click **Custom Footer**. In the **Footer** dialog box, be sure that the insertion point is in the *Left section*, and then click **Insert File Name** 🗐. Compare your screen with Figure 1.20.

In the Left section box, the file name is inserted—*& [File]* displays.

FIGURE 1.20

10 ▶ In the **Footer** dialog box, click **OK**, and then in the **Page Setup** dialog box, click **OK**.

The file name is inserted in the footer of both chart sheets.

11 ▶ Click the **Sales** worksheet tab to make it the active worksheet and to deselect the chart sheets. Press and hold Ctrl, and then click the **Store Locations by Manager** worksheet tab.

12 On the **PAGE LAYOUT tab**, in the **Page Setup group**, click the **Dialog Box Launcher** 🔲. In the **Page Setup** dialog box, click the **Header/Footer tab**, and then click **Custom Footer**. In the **Footer** dialog box, with the insertion point in the *Left section*, click **Insert File Name** 🔲. Click **OK** two times to close the dialog boxes.

You must insert footers in worksheets separately from inserting them in chart sheets. In this case, the file name is inserted in the footer of both worksheets.

13 Press Ctrl + Home to display the top of the worksheet. Right-click the **Sales** sheet tab, and then click **Ungroup Sheets**.

14 **Save** 🔲 your Excel workbook.

Activity 1.09 | Copying and Pasting an Excel Chart into Word

1 On the **HOME tab**, in the **Clipboard group**, click the **Dialog Box Launcher** 🔲 to display the Clipboard pane. In the **Clipboard** pane, click **Clear All**. Click the **State Sales Chart** sheet tab, and then click the border of the pie chart to select the chart. On the **HOME tab** in the **Clipboard group**, click **Copy** 🔲. Compare your screen with Figure 1.21.

FIGURE 1.21

2 Click the **Merchandise Chart** sheet tab, and then if necessary, click the border of the bar chart to select the chart. In the **Clipboard group**, click **Copy** 🔲.

3 At the bottom of the screen, on the taskbar, click the **Word icon** 🔲. Press Ctrl + End to move the insertion point to the end of the document.

4 Press Ctrl + Enter.

A new blank Page 2 is inserted.

5 With the insertion point at the top of **Page 2**, type **In the chart below, our state sales managers can view their sales results.** Press Enter.

6 On the **HOME tab**, in the **Clipboard group**, click the **Dialog Box Launcher** 🔲 to display the Clipboard pane, as shown in Figure 1.22.

FIGURE 1.22

7 In the **Clipboard** pane, click the **bar chart**.

The bar chart is pasted into the Word document.

8 **Close** ☒ the **Clipboard** pane, and then press Ctrl + Home.

9 ▸ Click the **FILE tab**, and then in the lower right portion of the screen, at the bottom of the **Properties** list, click **Show All Properties**. In the **Tags** box, type **memo, state sales chart** and in the **Subject** box, type your course name and section number. Be sure your name displays as the author; edit if necessary.

10 ▸ **Save** 🔲 your Word document, and then **Close** ❌ Word.

Activity 1.10 | Pasting an Excel Chart in PowerPoint

1 ▸ Start PowerPoint. Navigate to the student data files, and then open the presentation **i01A_Sales_Presentation**. Press **F12** to display the **Save As** dialog box. Navigate to your **Integrated Projects** folder, and then **Save** the presentation as **Lastname_Firstname_1A_Sales_Presentation**

2 ▸ On the **INSERT tab**, in the **Text group**, click **Header & Footer**. In the **Header and Footer** dialog box, click the **Notes and Handouts tab**. Select the **Footer** check box, click in the **Footer** box, and then type **Lastname_Firstname_1A_Sales_Presentation** and then compare your screen with Figure 1.23.

FIGURE 1.23

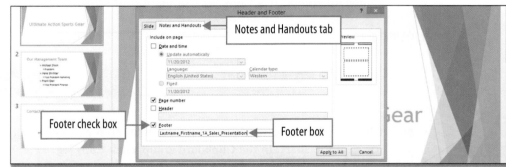

3 ▸ Click **Apply to All**.

4 ▸ In the **Slides** pane, click **Slide 2**. On the **HOME tab**, in the **Slides group**, click the **New Slide button arrow**, and then from the **Slides** gallery, click **Blank**. On the **DESIGN tab**, in the **Customize group**, click **Format Background**. In the **Format Background** pane, under **FILL**, select the **Hide background graphics** check box. Compare your screen with Figure 1.24.

A new blank Slide 3 is inserted into the presentation, and the background graphics do not display.

FIGURE 1.24

5 ▸ **Close** ❌ the **Format Background** pane. On the **HOME tab**, in the **Clipboard group**, click the **Dialog Box Launcher** ❌. In the **Clipboard** pane, click the bar chart.

The bar chart is pasted into Slide 3 of the presentation.

6 ▸ On the **HOME tab**, in the **Slides group**, click the **New Slide button arrow**, and then from the **Slides** gallery, click **Blank**. Using the technique you practiced, select the **Hide background graphics** check box. In the **Clipboard** pane, click the pie chart. Compare your screen with Figure 1.25.

FIGURE 1.25

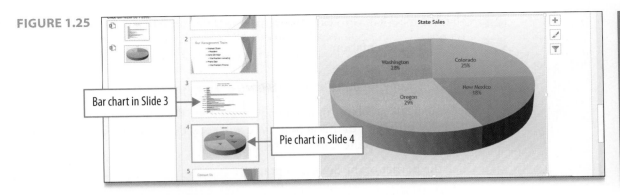

Bar chart in Slide 3

Pie chart in Slide 4

7 ▶ Close ☒ the **Clipboard** pane, and then **Save** 🖫 the presentation.

Objective 4 | Copy and Paste an Object from PowerPoint into Excel

In PowerPoint, bullet points can be converted into a SmartArt graphic to illustrate your message visually. After you create a SmartArt graphic in PowerPoint, you can copy the graphic and paste it into a file created with another program. This can save you time because there is no need to recreate the graphic.

Activity 1.11 | Inserting a SmartArt Graphic

1 ▶ Click **Slide 2** to make it the active slide. Click in the placeholder containing the names of the managers. On the **HOME tab**, in the **Paragraph group**, click **Convert to SmartArt**. In the **SmartArt** gallery, in the first row, click the fourth layout—**Target List**. If the Text Pane displays to the left of the SmartArt placeholder, click Close ☒.

2 ▶ On the ribbon, under **SMARTART TOOLS**, on the **DESIGN tab**, in the **SmartArt Styles group**, click **More** 🔽. In the **SmartArt Styles** gallery, under **3-D**, in the first row, click the third style—**Cartoon**.

3 ▶ With the **SmartArt** graphic selected, on the **ANIMATIONS tab**, in the **Animation group**, click **More** 🔽. In the **Animation** gallery, under **Entrance**, click **Wheel**. Click in a blank area of the slide to deselect the SmartArt graphic, and then compare your screen with Figure 1.26.

The number 1 displays to the left of the SmartArt graphic, which indicates that an animation effect is applied to the object.

FIGURE 1.26

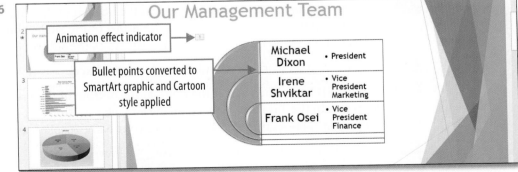

Animation effect indicator

Bullet points converted to SmartArt graphic and Cartoon style applied

Our Management Team

Michael Dixon	• President
Irene Shviktar	• Vice President Marketing
Frank Osei	• Vice President Finance

4 ▶ On the **SLIDE SHOW tab**, in the **Start Slide Show group**, click **From Beginning** to view the presentation. Press Enter to view the second slide.

5 Continue to press Enter to view the remaining slides, and then press Enter to return to **Normal** view.

6 Save 🖫 the presentation.

Activity 1.12 | Copying and Pasting a SmartArt Graphic

After you create an object in one file, you can copy the object and paste it in a file created with a different program. In this activity, you will copy the SmartArt graphic in the PowerPoint presentation, and then paste it in an Excel workbook.

1 Click the border of the SmartArt graphic.

By clicking the border of an object, you select the entire object, not just a part of the object.

2 On the **HOME tab**, in the **Clipboard group**, click **Copy** 🖹.

3 On the taskbar, click the **Excel** icon 🖾.

4 In **Excel**, click the **Sales** worksheet tab, and then click cell **A20**. On the **HOME tab**, in the **Clipboard group**, click **Paste**.

The SmartArt graphic is pasted into the Sales worksheet. The top left corner of the graphic is in cell A20.

5 Scroll down to view the entire graphic. On the ribbon, under **SMARTART TOOLS**, on the **FORMAT tab**, click **Size**, if necessary. Click in the **Shape Height** box, and then type **3.5** Click in the **Shape Width** box, type **5.5** and then press Enter.

6 Right-click the border of the SmartArt graphic, and then above the shortcut menu, click **Color**. In the **Color** gallery, under **Colorful**, click the fourth color—**Colorful Range – Accent Colors 4 to 5**. Compare your screen with Figure 1.27.

FIGURE 1.27

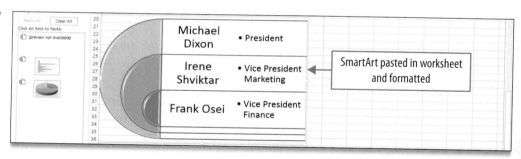

7 In the **Clipboard** pane, click **Clear All**, and then **Close** ☒ the **Clipboard** pane.

8 Click the **FILE tab**, and then at the right, at the bottom of the **Properties** list, click **Show All Properties**. In the **Tags** box, type **charts, SmartArt** In the **Subject** box, type your course name and section number. Be sure your name displays as the author; edit if necessary.

9 Save 🖫 the Excel workbook, and then **Close** ☒ Excel.

10 Click the **FILE tab**, and then at the right, at the bottom of the **Properties** list, click **Show All Properties**. In the **Tags** box, type **company info, charts, SmartArt** In the **Subject** box, type your course name and section number. Be sure your name displays as the author; edit if necessary.

11 Save 🖫 the presentation, and then **Close** ☒ PowerPoint.

12 Submit your printed or electronic files as directed by your instructor.

END | You have completed Project 1A

Taos Welcome

PROJECT ACTIVITIES

In Activities 1.13 through 1.19, you will link and update Excel data in a Word document. Because Microsoft Office programs work together, you can quickly create individualized documents in Word using data stored in a different application. You will use Word's mail merge feature and data stored in an Access database to create individualized memos. Your completed files will look similar to Figure 1.28.

PROJECT FILES

For Project 1B, you will need the following files:

i01B_Welcome_Memo
i01B_Taos_Inventory
i01B_All_Associates

You will save your files as:

Lastname_Firstname_1B_Welcome_Memo
Lastname_Firstname_1B_Taos_Memo
Lastname_Firstname_1B_Taos_Inventory
Lastname_Firstname_1B_All_Associates
Lastname_Firstname_1B_Store_Location

PROJECT RESULTS

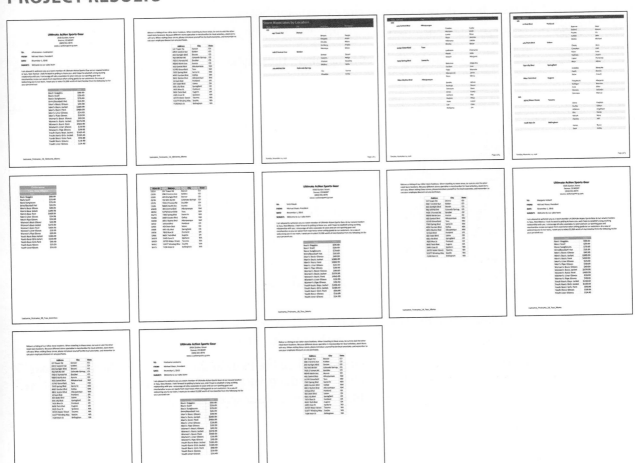

FIGURE 1.28 Project 1B Taos Welcome

Use the linking tools in Office to connect the data in an Excel worksheet to a Word document. When you link an Excel workbook to a Word document, changes you make to data in the Excel workbook will be updated in the linked Word document. Information about the link is saved with the Word document. By default, when you open the Word document, Word checks all linked files and prompts you to apply any changes.

Activity 1.13 | Using Paste Special to Link Files

In this activity, you will insert Excel data into a Word document. By selecting options in the Paste Special dialog box, you can link your Word document to the data in the Excel workbook.

1 Start Word. Navigate to the student data files and then open the document **i01B_Welcome_Memo**. Press F12, and then **Save** the document in your **Integrated Projects** folder as **Lastname_Firstname_1B_Welcome_Memo** If necessary, display the ruler and formatting marks.

2 **Start** Excel. Navigate to the student data files, and then open the Excel workbook **i01B_Taos_Inventory**. Press F12, and then **Save** the workbook in your **Integrated Projects** folder as **Lastname_Firstname_1B_Taos_Inventory**

3 On the **PAGE LAYOUT tab**, in the **Page Setup group**, click the **Dialog Box Launcher** . In the **Page Setup** dialog box, click the **Header/Footer tab**, and then click **Custom Footer**. In the **Footer** dialog box, with the insertion point in the *Left section*, click **Insert File Name** —& [File] displays. Click **OK** two times to close the dialog boxes.

4 Press Ctrl + Home to display the top of the worksheet, and then **Save** the Excel workbook.

5 Select the range **A3:B22**. On the **Home tab**, in the **Clipboard group**, click **Copy** . Compare your screen with Figure 1.29.

FIGURE 1.29

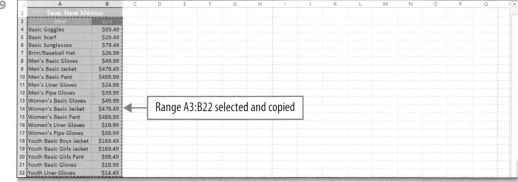

Range A3:B22 selected and copied

6 On the taskbar, click the **Word** icon . In the Word document, below the paragraph that begins *I am pleased to welcome you*, click in the blank paragraph.

7 On the **HOME tab**, in the **Clipboard group**, click the **Paste button arrow**, and then click **Paste Special**. In the **Paste Special** dialog box, click the **Paste link** option button, and then under **As**, click **Microsoft Excel Worksheet Object**. Compare your screen to Figure 1.30.

FIGURE 1.30

8 In the **Paste Special** dialog box, click **OK**.

The linked data from Excel is pasted into the Word document.

9 With the pasted object selected, on the **HOME tab**, in the **Paragraph group**, click **Center** .

10 **Save** 🖫 your Word document.

11 Click the **FILE tab**, and then click **Close** to close the document but leave Word open.

NOTE **Updating Links**

From this point forward, when you reopen a Word document that has a link to an external file, a Security Notice will automatically display. The notice will inform you that the file contains links and you have the option of updating the links or not updating them. If you trust the source of the file, you can update links. If you do not know where a file originated, you should cancel the update and investigate where the file came from before continuing.

---

12 In Word, navigate to your **Integrated Projects** folder, and then open the file **Lastname_Firstname_1B_Welcome_Memo**. A message box displays, as shown in Figure 1.31.

The message box informs you that the Word document is linked to another file, and it asks whether you want to update the data in the document.

FIGURE 1.31

13 In the message box, click **Yes**.

The linked information is updated.

Objective 6 Modify Linked Data and Update Links

It is common to make changes to your data in saved files. You can modify the data in the source file and all linked data to that source file is updated to reflect the changes.

Activity 1.14 Updating Linked Data

In the following activity, you will edit data in the linked Excel workbook, and then be sure that the updated data displays in the Word document.

1 Double-click the pasted data in the Word document to display the source file—the linked Excel workbook.

Excel becomes the active window.

If necessary, maximize the Excel worksheet, and then press [Esc] to cancel the copy. Click cell **B9**, type **389.99** and then press [Enter]. Click cell **B14**, type **379.99** and then press [Enter]. Compare your screen with Figure 1.32.

FIGURE 1.32

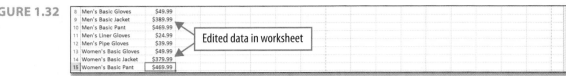

Edited data in worksheet

 Save 🖫 the Excel workbook.

4 On the taskbar, click the **Word** icon 🗏. Compare your screen to Figure 1.33.

The changes made in the Excel workbook are reflected in the linked Word document.

ALERT!   **What If the Data Is Not Updated?**

If you do not see the new numbers in the Word document, click one time in the data to select it, and then press [F9] to update the Excel data.

FIGURE 1.33

Updated data in Word document

5 **Save** 🖫 the Word document.

6 On the taskbar, click the **Excel** icon 🗏 to display the workbook.

7 Click the **FILE tab**, and then at the right, at the bottom of the **Properties** list, click **Show All Properties**. In the **Tags** box, type **edited data, linked** In the **Subject** box, type your course name and section number. Be sure your name displays as the author; edit if necessary.

8 **Save** 🖫 your changes, and then **Close** ❌ Excel.

Objective 7   Create a Table in Word from Access Data

You can export data from an Access file to another file—for example, an Excel worksheet, a Word document, or another database. Exporting is similar to copying and pasting. In Access, you can export large amounts of data by selecting the name of the object that contains the data you want to export. Exporting data eliminates the need to retype information; and, as a result, the possibility of data entry errors is reduced.

Activity 1.15 | Exporting an Access Table to an RTF File

1 **Start** Access. Navigate to the student data files and then open the Access database **i01B_All_Associates**. Click the **FILE tab**, click **Save As**, and then with **Save Database As** selected, click **Save As**.

2 In the **Save As** dialog box, navigate to your **Integrated Projects** folder, and then **Save** the database as **Lastname_Firstname_1B_All_Associates** On the **Message Bar** that displays a Security Warning, click **Enable Content**.

3 In the **navigation pane**, click the **Store Location** table to select it. On the **EXTERNAL DATA tab**, in the **Export group**, click **More**, and then click **Word**.

The Export – RTF File dialog box displays.

4 In the **Export – RTF File** dialog box, click **Browse**, and then navigate to your **Integrated Projects** folder. In the **File name** box, type **Lastname_Firstname_1B_Store_Location** and then click **Save**. Compare your screen with Figure 1.34.

The Access table is saved as a rich text format file. Rich text format is a universal file format, using the .rtf file extension, which can be read by many word processing programs.

FIGURE 1.34

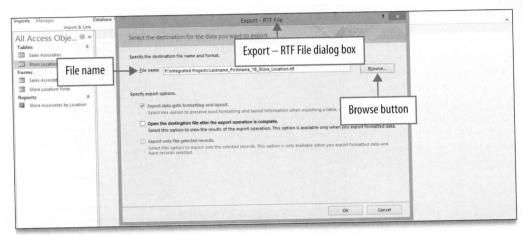

5 In the **Export – RTF File** dialog box, click **OK**. In the dialog box asking if you want to save these export steps, be sure the **Save export steps** check box is not selected. Click **Close**.

Activity 1.16 | Inserting Access Data into a Word Document

1 On the taskbar, click the **Word** icon. Press Ctrl + End to move to the end of the document.

2 On the **INSERT tab**, in the **Text group**, click the **Object button arrow**, and then click **Text from File**. In the **Insert File** dialog box, navigate to your **Integrated Projects** folder, click the file name **Lastname_Firstname_1B_Store_Location**, and then click **Insert**. Compare your screen with Figure 1.35.

FIGURE 1.35

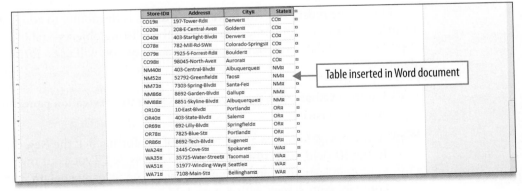

3 In the inserted table, click in the first cell, **Store ID**, to make the cell the active cell. On the ribbon, under **TABLE TOOLS**, on the **DESIGN tab**, in the **Table Styles group**, click **More**. In the **Table Styles** gallery, scroll down, and then under **List Tables**, in the third row, click the third style—click **List Table 3 - Accent 2**.

4 In the cell **Store ID**, right-click, on the mini toolbar, click **Delete**, and then click **Delete Columns** to delete the Store ID column.

5 On the **LAYOUT tab**, in the **Cell Size group**, click **AutoFit**, and then click **AutoFit Contents**.

The columns are automatically resized to fit the contents of the cells.

6 In the **Table group**, click **Properties**, and then on the **Table tab**, under **Alignment**, click **Center**. Click **OK**, and then compare your screen with Figure 1.36.

The table is centered horizontally on the page.

FIGURE 1.36

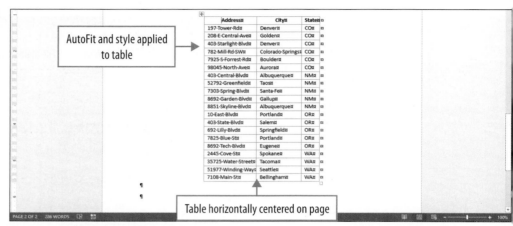

7 Save 🖫 the Word document.

Objective 8 Use Access Data to Complete a Mail Merge in Word

If you already have information in an existing data source—for example, an Access database—you do not need to enter the data again during the mail merge process. You can filter data to quickly find a portion of the total records available. Filtered data displays only the records that meet the conditions you specify and hides the records that do not meet the conditions.

Activity 1.17 │ Adding Records to an Access Table

One of the most powerful features of Access is the ability to add, edit, or delete existing records without changing the structure of the existing objects—tables, queries, forms, and reports—in the database. In the following activity, you will use a form to add a record to a database.

1 On the taskbar, click the **Access** icon 🄰. In the **navigation pane**, double-click the **Sales Associates Form**.

2 In the navigation area at the bottom of the form, click the **New (blank) record** button ▶*. In the **ID** field, type **10-60531** and then press Tab. Type your own firstname, press Tab, type your own lastname, and then press Tab. Type **Sales Associate** press Tab, type **NM52** and then compare your screen with Figure 1.37.

FIGURE 1.37

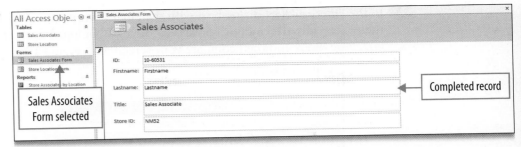

Sales Associates Form selected

Completed record

3 Press Tab to accept your record.

4 In the **navigation pane**, double-click the report **Store Associates by Location**. Scroll through the report and be sure that your name displays under **NM** for the **Taos** location.

5 Close ☒ Access.

Access automatically saves records that have been added to a database; there is no need to save the file before closing Access.

Activity 1.18 | Starting Mail Merge in Word

Mail Merge can be used to add placeholders for inserting a data field into a document to make each document unique. In the following activity, you will start the mail merge process in Word and filter the Access records.

1 On the taskbar, click the Word icon 🔳 to make the Word document active.

2 Press Ctrl + Home. On the **MAILINGS tab,** in the **Start Mail Merge group**, click the **Select Recipients** button, and then click **Use an Existing List**.

3 In the **Select Data Source** dialog box, navigate to your **Integrated Projects** folder, select the **Lastname_Firstname_1B_All_Associates** database, and then click **Open** to display the **Select Table** dialog box. Compare your screen with Figure 1.38.

The Access database contains more than one table. You need to select which table will be used for the mail merge.

FIGURE 1.38

Select Table dialog box

List of Access tables

4 In the **Select Table** dialog box, be sure that **Sales Associates** is selected, and then click **OK**.

5 In the **Start Mail Merge group**, click **Edit Recipient List**.

You can add or edit fields in the Mail Merge Recipients dialog box.

6 In the **Mail Merge Recipients** dialog box, under **Refine recipient list**, click **Filter**.

7 In the **Filter and Sort** dialog box, with the **Filter Records tab** selected, click the **Field arrow**, and then click **Store ID**. Under **Comparison**, be sure that **Equal to** is selected. In the **Compare to** box, type **NM52** and then compare your screen with Figure 1.39.

You can filter on any of the fields.

FIGURE 1.39

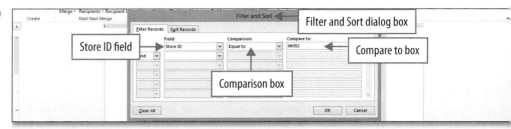

8 At the bottom of the **Filter and Sort** dialog box, click **OK**.

The three Taos records—including your record—display.

9 In the **Mail Merge Recipients** dialog box, click **OK**.

Activity 1.19 | Inserting Merge Fields

You can add merge fields as placeholders in the Word document for the information that will be inserted from the Access database. In the mail merge process, you combine a data source and a main document to create a new Word document—for example, a document that contains individualized memos, letter, or mailing labels.

1 Near the top of the document, in the heading *TO*, click to position the insertion point to the left of the paragraph mark.

2 On the **MAILINGS tab**, in the **Write & Insert Fields group**, click the **Insert Merge Field button arrow**, and then click **Firstname**. Compare your screen with Figure 1.40.

The Firstname field is inserted in the memo.

A merge field is surrounded by double angle brackets (<< >>). These formatting marks help distinguish the merge fields in the main document and do not display in the final document—after the merge process is completed.

FIGURE 1.40

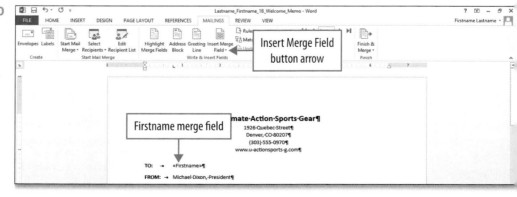

3 Press Spacebar. Click the **Insert Merge Field button arrow**, and then click **Lastname**.

This is the location in the memo where the sales associate names will be inserted.

4 In the **Preview Results group**, click **Preview Results**. In the **Preview Results group**, click **Next Record** ▶ two times to preview the three memos.

> The memo—the main document—displays with changes based on each record in the filtered data source—in this case, the sales associate's name.

5 In the **Preview Results** group, click **Preview Results**, to turn off the feature. Notice the merge fields display in the document.

6 In the **Finish group**, click **Finish & Merge**, and then click **Edit Individual Documents**. In the **Merge to New Document** dialog box, be sure that the **All** option button is selected, and then click **OK**. Compare your screen with Figure 1.41.

> A new Word document—Letters1—displays. The six-page document contains three individualized memos and is no longer connected to the Access database. The firstname and lastname in the first record displays on Page 1.

FIGURE 1.41

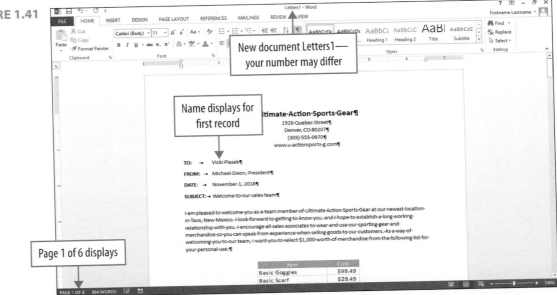

7 Press F12. **Save** the new merged document in your **Integrated Projects** folder with the file name **Lastname_Firstname_1B_Taos_Memo**

8 Right-click in the footer area, and then click **Edit Footer**. Under **HEADER & FOOTER TOOLS**, on the **DESIGN tab**, in the **Insert group**, click **Document Info**, and then click **File Name**. In the **Close group**, click **Close Header and Footer**.

9 Click the **FILE tab**, and then at the right, at the bottom of the **Properties** list, click **Show All Properties**. In the **Tags** box, type **linked table, merged** In the **Subject** box, type your course name and section number. Be sure your name displays as the author; edit if necessary.

10 **Save** 🖫 your changes, and then **Close** ✗ the **Lastname_Firstname_1B_Taos_Memo**.

11 In the **Lastname_Firstname_1B_Welcome_Memo**, right-click in the footer area, and then click **Edit Footer**. Under **HEADER & FOOTER TOOLS**, on the **DESIGN tab**, in the **Insert group**, click **Document Info**, and then click **File Name**. In the **Close group**, click **Close Header and Footer**.

12 Click the **FILE tab**, and then at the right, at the bottom of the **Properties** list, click **Show All Properties**. In the **Tags** box, type **linked table, merge fields** In the **Subject** box, type your course name and section number. Be sure your name displays as the author; edit if necessary.

13 **Save** 🖫 your changes, and then **Close** ⊠ Word.

14 Submit your printed or electronic files as directed by your instructor.

END | You have completed Project 1B

Glossary

.jpg An image file format, commonly pronounced *JPEG*, that stands for Joint Photographic Experts Group; this is a common file type used by digital cameras and computers to store digital pictures; JPEG is popular because it can store a high-quality picture in a relatively small file.

.png An image file format, commonly pronounced *PING*, that stands for Portable Network Graphic; this is an image file type that can be transferred over the Internet.

3-D The shortened term for *three-dimensional*, which refers to an image that appears to have all three spatial dimensions—length, width, and depth.

Absolute cell reference A cell reference that refers to cells by their fixed position in a worksheet; an absolute cell reference remains the same when the formula is copied.

Accounting Number Format The Excel number format that applies a thousand comma separator where appropriate, inserts a fixed U.S. dollar sign aligned at the left edge of the cell, applies two decimal places, and leaves a small amount of space at the right edge of the cell to accommodate a parenthesis for negative numbers.

Action Center Located in the notification area, a central place to view alerts and take actions related to things that need your attention.

Active cell The cell, surrounded by a black border, ready to receive data or be affected by the next Excel command.

Address bar (Internet Explorer) The area at the top of the Internet Explorer window that displays, and where you can type, a URL—Uniform Resource Locator—which is an address that uniquely identifies a location on the Internet.

Address bar (Windows File Explorer) The bar at the top of a folder window with which you can navigate to a different folder or library, or go back to a previous one; displays your current location in the folder structure as a series of links separated by arrows.

Administrator account A user account that lets you make changes that will affect other users of the computer; the most powerful of the three types of accounts because it permits the most control over the computer.

After Previous An animation option that begins the animation sequence for the selected slide element immediately after the completion of the previous animation or slide transition.

Aggregate functions Calculations such as Min, Max, Avg, and Sum that are performed on a group of records.

Alignment The placement of text or objects relative to the left and right margins.

Alignment guides Green vertical or horizontal lines that display when you are moving or sizing an object to assist you with object placement.

American Psychological Association (APA) One of two commonly used style guides for formatting research papers.

AND condition A compound criteria used to display records that match all parts of the specified criteria.

AND condition A condition in which records display only where all of the values are present in the selected fields.

Animation A visual or sound effect added to an object or text on a slide.

Animation Painter A feature that copies animation settings from one object to another.

App The term that commonly refers to computer programs that run from the device software on a smartphone or a tablet computer—for example, iOS, Android, or Windows Phone—or computer programs that run from the browser software on a desktop PC or laptop PC—for example Internet Explorer, Safari, Firefox, or Chrome. App is the shortened version of the word *application*.

App bar An area at the bottom of every Windows Store app containing various controls pertaining to the app.

App for Office A webpage that works within one of the Office applications, such as Excel, and that you download from the Office Store.

App switcher The thumbnail view of open apps that displays when you move your mouse down from the Back tip in the upper left corner; to switch to an app that is still open, you can click any of the thumbnails.

Append To add on to the end of an object; for example, to add records to the end of an existing table.

Application A set of instructions that a computer uses to accomplish a task; also called a program.

Apps for Office 2013 and SharePoint 2013 A collection of downloadable apps that enable you to create and view information within your familiar Office programs.

Arguments The values that an Excel function uses to perform calculations or operations.

Arithmetic operators The symbols +, −, *, /, %, and ^ used to denote addition, subtraction (or negation), multiplication, division, percentage, and exponentiation in an Excel formula.

Artistic effects Formats applied to images that make pictures resemble sketches or paintings.

Ascending order A sorting order that arranges text alphabetically (A to Z) and numbers from the lowest number to the highest number.

Aspect ratio The ratio of the width of a display to the height of the display.

Auto Fill An Excel feature that generates and extends values into adjacent cells based on the values of selected cells.

AutoCalculate A feature that displays three calculations in the status bar by default—Average, Count, and Sum—when you select a range of numerical data.

AutoComplete A feature that speeds your typing and lessens the likelihood of errors; if the first few characters you type in a cell match an existing entry in the column, Excel fills in the remaining characters for you.

AutoCorrect A feature that corrects common typing and spelling errors as you type, for example changing *teh* to *the*.

AutoFit An Excel feature that adjusts the width of a column to fit the cell content of the widest cell in the column.

AutoNumber data type A data type that describes a unique sequential or random number assigned by Access as each record is entered and that is useful for data that has no distinct field that can be considered unique.

AutoSum A button that provided quick access to the SUM function.

AVERAGE function An Excel function that adds a group of values, and then divides the result by the number of values in the group.

Axis A line that serves as a frame of reference for measurement and which borders the chart plot area.

Back tip The upper left corner of the screen that when pointed to displays a thumbnail image of the last screen you were on; you can use it to *go back* to your previous screen.

Background Removal A feature that removes unwanted portions of a picture so that the picture does not appear as a self-contained rectangle.

Background style A predefined slide background fill variation that combines theme colors in different intensities or patterns.

Backstage tabs The area along the left side of Backstage view with tabs to display screens with related groups of commands.

Backstage view A centralized space for file management tasks; for example, opening, saving, printing, publishing, or sharing a file. A navigation pane displays along the left side with tabs that group file-related tasks together.

Badge An icon that displays on the Lock screen, below the time, day, and date, that represents the status of your Internet connection, your battery if you are using a tablet or laptop, or any other Lock screen apps you might have selected.

Base The starting point when you divide the amount of increase by it to calculate the rate of increase.

Best Fit An Access command that adjusts the width of a column to accommodate the column's longest entry.

Between … And operator A comparison operator that looks for values within a range.

Bevel A shape effect that uses shading and shadows to make the edges of a shape appear to be curved or angled.

Bibliography A list of cited works in a report or research paper; also referred to as Works Cited, Sources, or References, depending upon the report style.

Black slide A slide that displays after the last slide in a presentation indicating that the presentation is over.

Blank desktop database A database that has no data and has no database tools—you must create the data and tools as you need them; the database is stored on your computer or other storage device.

Body The text of a letter.

Body font A font that is applied to all slide text except slide titles.

Booting the computer The process of turning on a computer when the computer has been completely shut down.

Bound control A control that retrieves its data from an underlying table or query; a text box control is an example of a bound control.

Bound A term used to describe objects and controls that are based on data that is stored in tables.

Brightness The relative lightness of a picture.

Bulleted list A list of items with each item introduced by a symbol such as a small circle or check mark, and which is useful when the items in the list can be displayed in any order.

Bullets Text symbols such as small circles or check marks that precede each item in a bulleted list.

Calculated control A control that contains an expression, often a formula or function, that most often summarizes a field that contains numerical data.

Calculated field A field that stores the value of a mathematical operation.

Caption A property setting that displays a name for a field in a table, query, form, or report other than that listed as the field name.

Cascade Delete Related Records A cascade option that enables you to delete a record in a table on the *one* side of the relationship and also delete all of the related records in related tables.

Cascade options Relationship options that enable you to update records in related tables when referential integrity is enforced.

Cascade Update Related Fields A cascade option that enables you to change the data in the primary key field in the table on the *one* side of the relationship and update that change to any fields storing that same data in related tables.

Category axis The area along the bottom of a chart that identifies the categories of data; also referred to as the x-axis.

Category labels The labels that display along the bottom of a chart to identify the categories of data; Excel uses the row titles as the category names.

Cell The intersection of a column and a row.

Cell address Another name for a cell reference.

Cell content Anything typed into a cell.

Cell reference The identification of a specific cell by its intersecting column letter and row number.

Cell style A defined set of formatting characteristics, such as font, font size, font color, cell borders, and cell shading.

Center alignment The alignment of text or objects that is centered horizontally between the left and right margins.

Charms A set of buttons that display when you point or swipe in from the right side of the screen that you can use in every app—whether a Windows Store app or a desktop app—and that enable you to search, share, access devices, or adjust your PC settings.

Chart The graphic representation of data in a worksheet; data presented as a chart is usually easier to understand than a table of numbers.

Chart area The entire chart and all of its elements.

Chart elements The various components of a chart, including the chart title, axis titles, data series, legend, chart area, and plot area.

Chart Elements button A button that enables you to add, remove, or change chart elements such as the title, legend, gridlines, and data labels.

Chart Filters button A button that displays options for changing the data displayed in a chart.

Chart layout The combination of chart elements that can be displayed in a chart such as a title, legend, labels for the columns, and the table of charted cells.

Chart sheet A workbook sheet that contains only a chart.

Chart style The overall visual look of a chart in terms of its graphic effects, colors, and backgrounds; for example, you can have flat or beveled columns, colors that are solid or transparent, and backgrounds that are dark or light.

Chart Styles button A button that displays options for setting the style and color scheme for a chart.

Chart Styles gallery A group of predesigned chart styles that you can apply to an Excel chart.

Chart types Various chart formats used in a way that is meaningful to the reader; common examples are column charts, pie charts, and line charts.

Citation A note inserted into the text of a research paper that refers the reader to a source in the bibliography.

Click The action of pressing and releasing the left button on a mouse pointing device one time.

Clip A single media file such as art, sound, animation, or a movie.

Clip art Downloadable predefined graphics available online from Office.com and other sites.

Clipboard A temporary storage area that holds text or graphics that you select and then cut or copy.

Clipboard A temporary storage area for information that you have copied or moved from one place and plan to use somewhere else.

Cloud computing Refers to applications and services that are accessed over the Internet, rather than to applications that are installed on your local computer.

Cloud storage Online storage of data so that you can access your data from different places and devices.

Collaborate To work with others as a team in an intellectual endeavor to complete a shared task or to achieve a shared goal.

Collaboration The action of working together with others as a team in an intellectual endeavor to complete a shared task or achieve a shared goal.

Column A vertical group of cells in a worksheet.

Column break indicator A dotted line containing the words *Column Break* that displays at the bottom of the column.

Column chart A chart in which the data is arranged in columns and which is useful for showing data changes over a period of time or for illustrating comparisons among items.

Column heading The letter that displays at the top of a vertical group of cells in a worksheet; beginning with the first letter of the alphabet, a unique letter or combination of letters identifies each column.

Comma Style The Excel number format that inserts thousand comma separators where appropriate and applies two decimal places; Comma Style also leaves space at the right to accommodate a parenthesis when negative numbers are present.

Commands An instruction to a computer program that causes an action to be carried out.

Common dialog boxes The set of dialog boxes that includes Open, Save, and Save As, which are provided by the Windows programming interface, and which display and operate in all of the Office programs in the same manner.

Common field A field in two or more tables that stores the same data.

Comparison operators Symbols that are used to evaluate data in the field to determine whether it is the same (=), greater than (>), less than (<), or in between a range of values as specified by the criteria.

Complimentary closing A parting farewell in a business letter.

Compound criteria Multiple conditions in a query or filter.

Compressed file A file that has been reduced in size and that takes up less storage space and can be transferred to other computers faster than uncompressed files.

Compressed folder A folder that has been reduced in size and thus takes up less storage space and can be transferred to other computers quickly; also called a *zipped* folder.

Conditional format A format that changes the appearance of a cell—for example, by adding cell shading or font color—based on a condition; if the condition is true, the cell is formatted based on that condition, and if the condition is false, the cell is *not* formatted.

Constant value Numbers, text, dates, or times of day that you type into a cell.

Content control In a template, an area indicated by placeholder text that can be used to add text, pictures, dates, or lists.

Context menus Menus that display commands and options relevant to the selected text or object; also called *shortcut menus*.

Context sensitive A command associated with the currently selected or active object; often activated by right-clicking a screen item.

Context-sensitive commands Commands that display on a shortcut menu that relate to the object or text that you right-clicked.

Contextual tabs Tabs that are added to the ribbon automatically when a specific object, such as a picture, is selected, and that contain commands relevant to the selected object.

Contiguous slides Slides that are adjacent to each other in a presentation.

Contrast The difference between the darkest and lightest area of a picture.

Control An object on a form or report that displays data or text, performs actions, and lets you view and work with information.

Control layout The grouped arrangement of controls on a form or report; for example, the Stacked layout.

Copy A command that duplicates a selection and places it on the Clipboard.

COUNTIF function A statistical function that counts the number of cells within a range that meet the given condition and that has two arguments—the range of cells to check and the criteria.

Cover letter A document that you send with your resume to provide additional information about your skills and experience.

Criteria (Access) Conditions in a query that identify the specific records you are looking for.

Criteria (Excel) Conditions that you specify in a logical function.

Crop A command that removes unwanted or unnecessary areas of a picture.

Crop handles Handles used to remove unwanted areas of a picture.

Crop pointer The pointer used to crop areas of a picture.

Crosshair pointer The pointer used to draw a shape.

Crosstab query A query that uses an aggregate function for data that can be grouped by two types of information and displays the data in a compact, spreadsheet-like format with column headings and row headings.

Currency data type An Access data type that describes monetary values and numeric data that can be used in mathematical calculations involving values with one to four decimal places.

Custom web app A database that you can publish and share with others over the Internet.

Cut A command that removes a selection and places it on the Clipboard.

Dashboard A descriptive term for the Windows 8 Start screen that provides a one-screen view of links to information and programs that matter most to the signed-in user.

Data Facts about people, events, things, or ideas.

Data bar A cell format consisting of a shaded bar that provides a visual cue to the reader about the value of a cell relative to other cells; the length of the bar represents the value in the cell—a longer bar represents a higher value and a shorter bar represents s lower value.

Data entry The action of entering the data into a record in a database table or form.

Data management The process of managing your files and folders in an organized manner so that you can find information when you need it.

Data marker A column, bar, area, dot, pie slice, or other symbol in a chart that represents a single data point; related data points form a data series.

Data point A value that originates in a worksheet cell and that is represented in a chart by a data marker.

Data series Related data points represented by data markers; each data series has a unique color or pattern represented in the chart legend.

Data source (Access) The table or tables from which a form, query, or report retrieves its data.

Data source (Word) A document that contains a list of variable information, such as names and addresses, that is merged with a main document to create customized form letters or labels.

Data type The characteristic that defines the kind of data that can be stored in a field, such as numbers, text, or dates.

Data (Excel) Text or numbers in a cell.

Data (Windows) All the files—documents, workbooks, pictures, songs, and so on—that you create and store during the day-to-day use of your computer.

Database An organized collection of facts about people, events, things, or ideas related to a specific topic or purpose.

Database management system (DBMS) Database software that controls how related collections of data are stored, organized, retrieved, and secured; also known as a DBMS.

Database template A preformatted database that contains prebuilt tables, queries, forms, and reports that perform a specific task, such as tracking events.

Datasheet view The Access view that displays data organized in columns and rows similar to an Excel worksheet.

Date & Time A command with which you can automatically insert the current date and time into a document in a variety of formats.

Date control A control on a form or report that inserts the current date each time the form or report is opened.

Dateline The first line in a business letter that contains the current date and which is positioned just below the letterhead if a letterhead is used.

DBMS An acronym for database management system.

Default The term that refers to the current selection or setting that is automatically used by a computer program unless you specify otherwise.

Descending order A sorting order that arranges text in reverse alphabetical order (Z to A) and numbers from the highest number to the lowest number.

Deselect The action of canceling the selection of an object or block of text by clicking outside of the selection.

Design grid The lower area of the query window that displays the design of the query.

Design view An Access view that displays the detailed structure of a table, query, form, or report. For forms and reports, may be the view in which some tasks must be performed, and only the controls, and not the data, display in this view.

Desktop The area in Windows 8 where you use desktop apps and that serves as a surface for your work, like the top of an actual desk.

Desktop app The term that commonly refers to a computer program that is installed on your computer and requires a computer operating system like Microsoft Windows or Apple OS to run.

Desktop background Displays the colors and graphics of your desktop; you can change the desktop background to look the way you want it.

Desktop shortcuts Desktop icons that link to any item accessible on your computer or on a network, such as a program, file, folder, disk drive, printer, or another computer.

Destination table The table to which you import or append data.

Detail section The section of a form or report that displays the records from the underlying table or query.

Detail sheets The worksheets that contain the details of the information summarized on a summary sheet.

Details pane Displays the most common properties associated with the selected file.

Details view The file list view in File Explorer that displays a list of files or folders and their most common properties.

Dialog box A small window that displays options for completing a task.

Dialog Box Launcher A small icon that displays to the right of some group names on the ribbon, and which opens a related dialog box or pane providing additional options and commands related to that group.

Displayed value The data that displays in a cell.

Document properties Details about a file that describe or identify it, including the title, author name, subject, and keywords that identify the document's topic or contents; also known as *metadata*.

Dot leader A series of dots preceding a tab that guides the eye across the line.

Double-click The action of pressing the left mouse button twice in rapid succession while holding the mouse still.

Drag The action of moving something from one location on the screen to another while holding down the left mouse button; the action of dragging includes releasing the mouse button at the desired time or location.

Drag and drop The action of moving a selection by dragging it to a new location.

Drawing objects Graphic objects, such as shapes, diagrams, lines, or circles.

Drive An area of storage that is formatted with a file system compatible with your operating system and is identified by a drive letter.

Edit The process of making changes to text or graphics in an Office file.

Editing (PowerPoint) The process of modifying a presentation by adding and deleting slides or by changing the contents of individual slides.

Ellipsis A set of three dots indicating incompleteness; an ellipsis following a command name indicates that a dialog box will display if you click the command.

Em dash A punctuation symbol used to indicate an explanation or emphasis.

Embed code A code that creates a link to a video, picture, or other type of rich media content.

Emphasis effect Animation that emphasizes an object or text that is already displayed.

Enclosures Additional documents included with a business letter.

Endnote In a research paper, a note placed at the end of a document or chapter.

Enhanced ScreenTip A ScreenTip that displays more descriptive text than a normal ScreenTip.

Enterprise fund A municipal government fund that reports income and expenditures related to municipal services for which a fee is charged in exchange for goods or services.

Entrance effect Animation that brings a slide element onto the screen.

Excel pointer An Excel window element with which you can display the location of the pointer.

Excel table A series of rows and columns that contains related data that is managed independently from the data in other rows and columns in the worksheet.

Exit effect Animation that moves an object or text off the screen.

Expand Formula Bar button An Excel window element with which you can Increase the height of the Formula Bar to display lengthy cell content.

Expand horizontal scroll bar button An Excel window element with which you can increase the width of the horizontal scroll bar.

Explode The action of pulling out one or more pie slices from a pie chart for emphasis.

Export The process of copying data from one file into another file, such as an Access table into an Excel spreadsheet.

Expression A formula.

Extract The action of decompressing—pulling out—files from a compressed form.

Eyedropper A tool that captures the exact color from an object on your screen and then applies it to any shape, picture, or text.

Field (Access) A single piece of information that is stored in every record; represented by a column in a database table.

Field list A list of field names in a table.

Field properties Characteristics of a field that control how the field displays and how data can be entered in the field.

Fields (Word) In a mail merge, the column headings in the data source.

File A collection of information that is stored on a computer under a single name, for example a text document, a picture, or a program.

File Explorer The program within Windows 8 that displays the contents of libraries, folders, and files on your computer, and which also enables you to perform tasks related to your files and folders such as copying, moving, and renaming. File Explorer is at work anytime you are viewing the contents of a library, a folder, or a file.

File list Displays the contents of the current folder or library; if you type text into the Search box, only the folders and files that match your search will display here—including files in subfolders.

File properties Information about a file such as its author, the date the file was last changed, and any descriptive tags.

Fill color The inside color of text or of an object.

Fill handle The small black square in the lower right corner of a selected cell.

Fill The inside color of an object.

Filter The process of displaying only a portion of the data based on matching a specific value to show only the data that meets the criteria that you specify.

Filter by Form An Access command that filters the records in a form based on one or more fields, or based on more than one value in the field.

Filter by Selection An Access command that displays only the records that contain the value in the selected field and hides the records that do not contain the value.

Filtering The process of displaying only a portion of the total records (a subset) based on matching specific values to provide a quick answer to a question.

Find and replace A command that searches the cells in a worksheet—or in a selected range—for matches and then replaces each match with a replacement value of your choice.

First principle of good database design A principle of good database design stating that data is organized in tables so that there is no redundant data.

Flash Fill Recognizes a pattern in your data, and then automatically fills in values when you enter examples of the output that you want. Use it to split data from two or more cells or to combine data from two cells.

Flat database A simple database file that is not related or linked to any other collection of data.

Flip A command that creates a reverse image of a picture or object.

Floating object A graphic that can be moved independently of the surrounding text characters.

Folder A container in which you store files.

Folder structure The hierarchy of folders in Windows 8.

Folder window In Windows, a window that displays the contents of the current folder, library, or device, and contains helpful parts so that you can navigate the Windows file structure.

Font A set of characters with the same design and shape.

Font styles Formatting emphasis such as bold, italic, and underline.

Footer Text that displays at the bottom of every slide or that prints at the bottom of a sheet of slide handouts or notes pages.

Footnote In a research paper, a note placed at the bottom of the page.

Foreign key The field that is included in the related table so the field can be joined with the primary key in another table for the purpose of creating a relationship.

Form An Access object you can use to enter new records into a table, edit or delete existing records in a table, or display existing records.

Form Footer Information at the bottom of the screen in Form view or Layout view that is printed after the last detail section on the last page of a printout.

Form Header Information such as a form's title that displays at the top of the screen in Form view or Layout view and is printed at the top of the first page when records are printed as forms.

Form tool An Access tool that creates a form with a single mouse click, which includes all of the fields from the underlying data source (table or query).

Form view The Access view in which you can view, modify, delete, or add to the records in a table; but you cannot change the layout or design of the form.

Form Wizard An Access tool that walks you step by step through the creation of a form and that gives you more flexibility in the design, layout, and number of fields in a form.

Format Changing the appearance of cells and worksheet elements to make a worksheet attractive and easy to read.

Formatting The process of establishing the overall appearance of text, graphics, and pages in an Office file—for example, in a Word document.

Formatting marks Characters that display on the screen, but do not print, indicating where the Enter key, the Spacebar, and the Tab key were pressed; also called *nonprinting characters*.

Formula An equation that performs mathematical calculations on values in a worksheet.

Formula AutoComplete An Excel feature that, after typing an = (equal sign) and the beginning letter or letters of a function name, displays a list of function names that match the typed letter(s), and from which you can insert the function by pointing to its name and pressing the Tab key or double-clicking.

Formula Bar An element in the Excel window that displays the value or formula contained in the active cell; here you can also enter or edit values or formulas.

Free/Busy information In the Outlook calendar, one of four indicators—Busy, Free, Tentative, or Out of Office—associated with your availability for a specific date and time.

Free-form snip When using Snipping Tool, the type of snip that lets you draw an irregular line, such as a circle, around an area of the screen.

Freeze Panes A command that enables you to select one or more rows or columns and freeze (lock) them into place; the locked rows and columns become separate panes.

Full-screen snip When using Snipping Tool, the type of snip that captures the entire screen.

Function A predefined formula—a formula that Excel has already built for you—that performs calculations by using specific values in a particular order or structure.

Fund A sum of money set aside for a specific purpose.

Gallery An Office feature that displays a list of potential results instead of just the command name.

General format The default format that Excel applies to numbers; this format has no specific characteristics—whatever you type in the cell will display, with the exception that trailing zeros to the right of a decimal point will not display.

General fund The term used to describe money set aside for the normal operating activities of a government entity such as a city.

Goal Seek A what-if analysis tool that finds the input needed in one cell to arrive at the desired result in another cell.

Gradient fill A fill effect in which one color fades into another.

Graphical user interface The system by which you interact with your computer and which uses graphics such as an image of a file folder or wastebasket that you click to activate the item represented.

Graphics Pictures, charts, or drawing objects.

Group Footer Information printed at the end of each group of records; used to display summary information for the group.

Group Header Information printed at the beginning of each new group of records; for example, the group name.

Group, Sort, and Total pane A pane that displays at the bottom of the screen in which you can control how information is sorted and grouped in a report; provides the most flexibility for adding or modifying groups, sort orders, or totals options on a report.

Groups On the Office ribbon, the sets of related commands that you might need for a specific type of task.

GUI The acronym for a graphical user interface, pronounced *GOO-ee*.

Hanging indent An indent style in which the first line of a paragraph extends to the left of the remaining lines and that is commonly used for bibliographic entries.

Hard disk drive The primary storage device located inside your computer and where most of your files and programs are typically stored; usually labeled as drive C.

Header Text that prints at the top of each sheet of slide handouts or notes pages.

Headings font A font that is applied to all slide title text.

Hierarchy An arrangement where items are ranked and where each level is lower in rank than the item above it.

Icons Small images that represent commands, files, applications, or other windows.

IF function A function that uses a logical test to check whether a condition is met, and then returns one value if true, and another value if false.

Immersive The term that describes the Windows 8 style screens, meaning they have no borders, no menus, and they behave differently from traditional Windows desktop programs because there is no taskbar, an app cannot be minimized like a desktop program, nor can an app be dragged around as a smaller window; the idea is that you are immersed in the app with no screen distractions.

Import The process of copying data from another file, such as a Word table or an Excel workbook, into a separate file, such as an Access database.

Info tab The tab in Backstage view that displays information about the current file.

Information Data that is organized in a useful manner.

Inline Object An object or graphic inserted in a document that acts like a character in a sentence.

Innermost sort field When sorting on multiple fields in Datasheet view, the field that will be used for the second level of sorting.

Insertion point A blinking vertical line that indicates where text or graphics will be inserted.

Inside address The name and address of the person receiving the letter and positioned below the date line.

Interactive media Computer interaction that responds to your actions; for example by presenting text, graphics, animation, video, audio, or games. Also referred to as rich media.

Internet Explorer The web browser program developed by Microsoft that is included with Windows 8.

Is Not Null A criteria that searches for fields that are not empty.

Is Null A criteria that searches for fields that are empty.

Join line In the Relationships window, the line joining two tables that visually indicates the common fields and the type of relationship.

JPEG An acronym for Joint Photographic Experts Group, and which is a common file type used by digital cameras and computers to store digital pictures; JPEG is popular because it can store a high-quality picture in a relatively small file. A JPEG file has a .jpg file extension.

Jump List A list that displays when you right-click a button on the taskbar, and which displays locations (in the upper portion) and tasks (in the lower portion) from a program's taskbar button.

Justified alignment An arrangement of text in which the text aligns evenly on both the left and right margins.

Keyboard shortcut A combination of two or more keyboard keys, used to perform a task that would otherwise require a mouse.

KeyTip The letter that displays on a command in the ribbon and that indicates the key you can press to activate the command when keyboard control of the ribbon is activated.

Keywords Custom file properties in the form of words that you associate with a document to give an indication of the document's content; used to help find and organize files. Also called *tags*.

Label Another name for a text value, and which usually provides information about number values.

Label control A control on a form or report that contains descriptive information, usually a field name or title.

Landscape orientation A page orientation in which the paper is wider than it is tall.

Layout The arrangement of elements, such as title and subtitle text, lists, pictures, tables, charts, shapes, and movies, on a slide.

Layout Options Picture formatting options that control the manner in which text wraps around a picture or other object.

Layout Options button A button that displays when an object is selected and that has commands to choose how the object interacts with surrounding text.

Layout selector A small symbol that displays in the upper left corner of a selected control layout in a form or report that is displayed in Layout view or Design view; used to move or format an entire group of controls.

Layout view The Access view in which you can make changes to a form or report while the object is running—the data from the underlying data source displays.

Leader character Characters that form a solid, dotted, or dashed line that fills the space preceding a tab stop.

Left alignment The cell format in which characters align at the left edge of the cell; this is the default for text entries and is an example of formatting information stored in a cell.

Legend A chart element that identifies the patterns or colors that are assigned to the categories in the chart.

Lettered column headings The area along the top edge of a worksheet that identifies each column with a unique letter or combination of letters.

Letterhead The personal or company information that displays at the top of a letter.

Library A collection of items, such as files and folders, assembled from various locations.

line break indicator A non-printing character in the shape of a bent arrow that indicates a manual line break.

line chart A chart type that displays trends over time; time displays along the bottom axis and the data point values are connected with a line.

line spacing The distance between lines of text in a paragraph.

link A connection to data in another file.

list level An outline level in a presentation represented by a bullet symbol and identified in a slide by the indentation and the size of the text.

Live Layout A feature that reflows text as you move or size an object so that you can view the placement of surrounding text.

Live Preview A technology that shows the result of applying an editing or formatting change as you point to possible results—*before* you actually apply it.

Live tiles Tiles on the Windows 8 Start screen that are constantly updated with fresh information relevant to the signed-in user; for example, the number of new email messages, new sports scores of interest, or new updates to social networks such as Facebook or Twitter.

Local account A user account in which the information associated with each user is local to a single Windows 8 computer.

Location Any disk drive, folder, or other place in which you can store files and folders.

Lock screen The first screen that displays after turning on a Windows 8 device, which displays the time, day, and date, and one or more icons representing the status of the device's Internet connection, battery status on a tablet or laptop, and any Lock screen apps that are installed such as email notifications.

Lock screen apps Apps that display on a Windows 8 Lock screen and that show quick status and notifications, even if the screen is locked, and include Calendar, Mail, Messaging, and Weather.

Logical functions A group of functions that test for specific conditions and that typically use conditional tests to determine whether specified conditions are true or false.

Logical operators Operators that are used to evaluate data to determine if a condition is met (true) or not met (false). With two criteria, AND requires that both conditions be met and OR requires that either condition be met for a record to display in the query results.

Logical test Any value or expression that can be evaluated as being true or false.

Mail merge A feature that joins a main document and a data source to create customized letters or labels.

Main document In a mail merge, the document that contains the text or formatting that remains constant.

Major unit The value in a chart's value axis that determines the spacing between tick marks and between the gridlines in the plot area.

Manual column break An artificial end to a column to balance columns or to provide space for the insertion of other objects.

Manual line break A break that moves text to the right of the insertion point to a new line while keeping the text in the same paragraph.

Manual page break The action of forcing a page to end and placing subsequent text at the top of the next page.

Margins The space between the text and the top, bottom, left, and right edges of the paper.

MAX function An Excel function that determines the largest value in a selected range of values.

MEDIAN function An Excel function that finds the middle value that has as many values above it in the group as are below it; it differs from AVERAGE in that the result is not affected as much by a single value that is greatly different from the others.

Menu bar A group of menus.

Menu A list of commands within a category.

Merge & Center A command that joins selected cells in an Excel worksheet into one larger cell and centers the contents in the merged cell.

Message Bar The area directly below the ribbon that displays information such as security alerts when there is potentially unsafe, active content in an Office document that you open.

Metadata Details about a file that describe or identify it, including the title, author name, subject, and keywords that identify the document's topic or contents; also known as *document properties*.

Microsoft account A user account that allows you to set up one Windows 8 computer and then synchronize all the same settings from that computer to any other device you have that uses Windows 8.

Microsoft Design Language The design principles in Windows 8 that include tiles with white text on deeply colored backgrounds, consistent fonts, simpler navigation, and the use of the entire screen; the idea is that you are immersed in the app with no screen distractions.

Microsoft Office 365 A set of secure online services that enable people in an organization to communicate and collaborate by using any Internet-connected device—a computer, a tablet, or a mobile phone.

MIN function An Excel function that determines the smallest value in a selected range of values.

Mini toolbar A small toolbar containing frequently used formatting commands that displays as a result of selecting text or objects.

Modern Language Association (MLA) One of two commonly used style guides for formatting research papers.

Mouse pointer Any symbol that displays on your screen in response to moving your mouse.

MRU Acronym for *most recently used*, which refers to the state of some commands that retain the characteristic most recently applied; for example, the Font Color button retains the most recently used color until a new color is chosen.

Multiple-items form A form that enables you to display or enter multiple records in a table.

Name Box An element of the Excel window that displays the name of the selected cell, table, chart, or object.

Nameplate The banner on the front page of a newsletter that identifies the publication.

Navigate The process of exploring within the organizing structure of Windows.

Navigate (File Explorer): Explore within the file organizing structure of Windows 8.

Navigation area An area at the bottom of the Access window that indicates the number of records in the table and contains controls in the form of arrows that you click to navigate among the records.

Navigation pane In a folder window, the area on the left in which you can navigate to, open, and display favorites, libraries, folders, saved searches, and an expandable list of drives.

Newsletter A periodical that communicates news and information to a specific group.

No Paragraph Style The built-in paragraph style—available from the Paragraph Spacing command—that inserts *no* extra space before or after a paragraph and uses line spacing of 1.

Noncontiguous slides Slides that are not adjacent to each other in a presentation.

Nonprinting characters Characters that display on the screen, but do not print, indicating where the Enter key, the Spacebar, and the Tab key were pressed; also called *formatting marks*.

Normal template The template that serves as a basis for all Word documents.

Normal view A screen view that maximizes the number of cells visible on your screen and keeps the column letters and row numbers close to the columns and rows.

Normalization The process of applying design rules and principles to ensure that your database performs as expected.

Note In a research paper, information that expands on the topic, but that does not fit well in the document text.

Notes page A printout that contains the slide image on the top half of the page and notes that you have created on the Notes pane in the lower half of the page.

Notes pane An area of the Normal view window that displays below the Slide pane with space to type notes regarding the active slide.

Notification area Displays notification icons and the system clock; sometimes referred to as the *system tray*.

Notification bar In Internet Explorer 10, a bar at the bottom of your screen that displays information about pending downloads, security issues, add-ons, and other issues related to the operation of your computer.

NOW function An Excel function that retrieves the date and time from your computer's calendar and clock and inserts the information into the selected cell.

Number data type An Access data type that describes numbers that might be used in calculations.

Number format A specific way in which Excel displays numbers in a cell.

Number values Constant values consisting of only numbers.

Numbered list A list that uses consecutive numbers or letters to introduce each item in a list.

Numbered row headings The area along the left edge of a worksheet that identifies each row with a unique number.

Object A text box, picture, table, or shape that you can select and then move and resize.

Object anchor The symbol that indicates to which paragraph an object is attached.

Object tab In the object window, a tab that identifies the object and which enables you to make the open object active.

Object window An area of the Access window that displays open objects, such as tables, queries, forms, or reports; by default, each object displays on its own tab.

Objects (Access) The basic parts of a database that you create to store your data and to work with your data; for example, tables, queries, forms, and reports.

Office 365 Administrator In Office 365, the person who creates and manages the account, adds new users, sets up the services your organization wants to use, sets permission levels, and manages SharePoint team sites.

Office Presentation Service A Word feature to present your Word document to others who can watch in a web browser.

Office Web Apps The free online companions to Microsoft Word, Excel, PowerPoint, Access, and OneNote.

On Click An animation option that begins the animation sequence for the selected slide element when the mouse button is clicked or the Spacebar is pressed.

One-click Row/Column Insertion A Word table feature with which you can insert a new row or column by pointing to the desired location and then clicking.

One-to-many relationship A relationship between two tables where one record in the first table corresponds to many records in the second table—the most common type of relationship in Access.

Open dialog box A dialog box from which you can navigate to, and then open on your screen, an existing file that was created in that same program.

Operating system A specific type of computer program that manages the other programs on a computer—including computer devices such as desktop computers, laptop computers, smartphones, tablet computers, and game consoles.

Operators The symbols with which you can specify the type of calculation you want to perform in an Excel formula.

Option button In a dialog box, a round button that enables you to make one choice among two or more options.

Options dialog box A dialog box within each Office application where you can select program settings and other options and preferences.

OR condition A compound criteria used to display records that match at least one of the specified criteria.

Order of operations The mathematical rules for performing multiple calculations within a formula.

Outermost sort field When sorting on multiple fields in Datasheet view, the field that will be used for the first level of sorting.

Outline View A PowerPoint view that displays the presentation outline to the left of the Slide pane.

Page break indicator A dotted line with the text *Page Break* that indicates where a manual page break was inserted.

Page Footer Information printed at the bottom of every page in a report; most often includes the page number.

Page Header Information printed at the top of every page in a report.

Page Layout view A screen view in which you can use the rulers to measure the width and height of data, set margins for printing, hide or display the numbered row headings and the lettered column headings, and change the page orientation; this view is useful for preparing your worksheet for printing.

Page number control A control on a form or report that inserts the page numbers when displayed in Print Preview or when printed.

Paint A program that comes with Windows 8 with which you can create and edit drawings and display and edit stored photos.

Pane (Excel) A portion of a worksheet window bounded by and separated from other portions by vertical and horizontal bars.

Pane A separate area of a window.

Paragraph symbol The symbol ¶ that represents the end of a paragraph.

Parameter A value that can be changed.

Parameter query A query that prompts you for criteria before running the query.

Parent folder In the file organizing structure of File Explorer, the location where the folder you are viewing is saved—one level up in the hierarchy.

Parenthetical references References that include the last name of the author or authors, and the page number in the referenced source.

Paste area The target destination for data that has been cut or copied using the Office Clipboard.

Paste Options gallery A gallery of buttons that provides a Live Preview of all the Paste options available in the current context.

Paste The action of placing cell contents that have been copied or moved to the Clipboard into another location.

Path A sequence of folders (directories) that leads to a specific file or folder.

PC settings The area from which you can control almost everything about how Windows 8 looks and works; you can change colors and backgrounds, the picture on your Lock screen, or your account picture, manage other users (if you are the administrator), connect devices like printers, or set up a network.

PDF The acronym for Portable Document Format, which is a file format that creates an image that preserves the look of your file; this is a popular format for sending documents electronically because the document will display on most computers.

PDF Reflow The ability to import PDF files into Word so that you can transform a PDF back into a fully editable Word document.

Percent for new value = base percent + percent of increase The formula for calculating a percentage by which a value increases by adding the base percentage—usually 100%—to the percent increase.

Percentage rate of increase The percent by which one number increases over another number.

Personal folder A folder created for each user account on a Windows 8 computer, labeled with the account holder's name, and which contains the subfolders *Documents*, *Pictures*, *Music*, and *Videos*.

Picture element A point of light measured in dots per square inch on a screen; 64 pixels equals 8.43 characters, which is the average number of characters that will fit in a cell in an Excel worksheet using the default font.

Picture styles Frames, shapes, shadows, borders, and other special effects that can be added to an image to create an overall visual style for the image.

Pie chart A chart that shows the relationship of each part to a whole.

PING An acronym for Portable Network Graphic, and which is a common file type that can be transferred over the Internet. A PING file has a .png file extension.

Pixel The abbreviated name for a picture element.

Placeholder A box on a slide with dotted or dashed borders that holds title and body text or other content such as charts, tables, and pictures.

Placeholder text The text in a content control that indicates the type of information to be entered in a specific location.

Plot area The area bounded by the axes of a chart, including all the data series.

Point The action of moving your mouse pointer over something on your screen.

Point and click method The technique of constructing a formula by pointing to and then clicking cells; this method is convenient when the referenced cells are not adjacent to one another.

Point to The action of moving the mouse pointer over a specific area.

Pointer Any symbol that displays on your screen in response to moving your mouse and with which you can select objects and commands.

Pointing device A mouse, touchpad, or other device that controls the pointer position on the screen.

Points A measurement of the size of a font; there are 72 points in an inch.

Populate The action of filling a database table with records.

Portable Document Format A file format that creates an image that preserves the look of your file, but that cannot be easily changed; a popular format for sending documents electronically, because the document will display on most computers.

Portrait orientation A page orientation in which the paper is taller than it is wide.

Primary key The field in a table that uniquely identifies a record; for example, a Student ID number at a college.

Print Preview A view of a document as it will appear when you print it.

Print Titles An Excel command that enables you to specify rows and columns to repeat on each printed page.

Program A set of instructions that a computer uses to accomplish a task; also called an application.

Progress bar In a dialog box or taskbar button, a bar that indicates visually the progress of a task such as a download or file transfer.

Property Sheet A list of characteristics—properties—for fields or controls on a form or report in which you can make precise changes to each property associated with the field or control.

Protected View A security feature in Office 2013 that protects your computer from malicious files by opening them in a restricted environment until you enable them; you might encounter this feature if you open a file from an email or download files from the Internet.

pt The abbreviation for *point*; for example, when referring to a font size.

Query A database object that retrieves specific data from one or more database objects—either tables or other queries—and then, in a single datasheet, displays only the data you specify.

Quick Access Toolbar In an Office program window, the small row of buttons in the upper left corner of the screen from which you can perform frequently used commands.

Quick Analysis Tool A tool that displays in the lower right corner of a selected range with which you can analyze your data by using Excel tools such as charts, color-coding, and formulas.

Range Two or more selected cells on a worksheet that are adjacent or nonadjacent; because the range is treated as a single unit, you can make the same changes or combination of changes to more than one cell at a time.

Range finder An Excel feature that outlines cells in color to indicate which cells are used in a formula; useful for verifying which cells are referenced in a formula.

Rate = amount of increase/base The mathematical formula to calculate a rate of increase.

Read Mode A view in Word that optimizes the Word screen for the times when you are reading Word documents on the screen and not creating or editing them.

Read-Only A property assigned to a file that prevents the file from being modified or deleted; it indicates that you cannot save any changes to the displayed document unless you first save it with a new name.

Reading view A view in PowerPoint that displays a presentation in a manner similar to a slide show but in which the taskbar, title bar, and status bar remain available in the presentation window.

Recolor A feature that enables you to change all colors in the picture to shades of a single color.

Recommended Charts An Excel feature that displays a customized set of charts that, according to Excel's calculations, will best fit your data based on the range of data that you select.

Record All of the categories of data pertaining to one person, place, event, thing, or idea; represented by a row in a database table.

Record selector bar The vertical bar at the left edge of a record when it is displayed in a form that is used to select an entire record.

Record selector box The small box at the left of a record in Datasheet view that, when clicked, selects the entire record.

Record source The tables or queries that provide the underlying data for a form or report.

Rectangular snip When using Snipping Tool, the type of snip that lets you draw a precise box by dragging the mouse pointer around an area of the screen to form a rectangle.

Recycle Bin A folder that stores anything that you delete from your computer, and from which anything stored can be retrieved until the contents are permanently deleted by activating the Empty Recycle Bin command.

Redundant In a database, information that is duplicated in a manner that indicates poor database design.

Referential integrity A set of rules that Access uses to ensure that the data between related tables is valid.

Relational database A sophisticated type of database that has multiple collections of data within the file that are related to one another.

Relationship An association that you establish between two tables based on common fields.

Relative cell reference In a formula, the address of a cell based on the relative positions of the cell that contains the formula and the cell referred to in the formula.

Removable storage device A portable device on which you can store files, such as a USB flash drive, a flash memory card, or an external hard drive, commonly used to transfer information from one computer to another.

Report A database object that summarizes the fields and records from a query or table in an easy-to-read format suitable for printing.

Report Footer Information printed at the bottom of the last page of a report.

Report Header Information printed on the first page of a report; used for logos, titles, and dates.

Report tool An Access tool that creates a report with one mouse click and displays all of the fields and records from the record source that you select.

Report Wizard An Access tool that walks you step by step through the creation of a report and that gives you more flexibility in the design, layout, and number of fields in a report.

Resources A term used to refer collectively to the parts of your computer such as the central processing unit (CPU), memory, and any attached devices such as a printer.

RGB A color model in which the colors red, green, and blue are added together to form another color.

Ribbon The area at the top of a folder window in File Explorer that groups common tasks such as copying and moving, creating new folders, emailing and zipping items, and changing views on related tabs.

Rich media Computer interaction that responds to your actions; for example by presenting text, graphics, animation, video, audio, or games. Also referred to as interactive media.

Rich Text Format (RTF) A standard file format that contains text and some formatting such as underline, bold, italic, font sizes, and colors; RTF documents can be opened in many word processing programs and text editors.

Right alignment An arrangement of text in which the text aligns at the right margin, leaving the left margin uneven.

Right-click The action of clicking the right mouse button one time.

Roam The ability to set up one computer, for example a desktop computer, and then synchronize—roam—all the same settings to a laptop, to a tablet PC, to a Windows phone, or to any other device to which one signs in with the same Microsoft account.

Rotation handle A symbol with which you can rotate a graphic to any angle; displays above the top center sizing handle.

Rounding A procedure in which you determine which digit at the right of the number will be the last digit displayed and then increase it by one if the next digit to its right is 5, 6, 7, 8, or 9.

Row A horizontal group of cells in a worksheet.

Row heading The numbers along the left side of an Excel worksheet that designate the row numbers.

Ruler guides Dotted red vertical and horizontal lines that display in the rulers indicating the pointer's position.

Run The process in which Access looks at the records in the table(s) included in the query design, finds the records that match the specified criteria, and then displays the records in a datasheet; only the fields included in the query design display.

Salutation The greeting line of a business letter.

Sans serif font A font design with no lines or extensions on the ends of characters.

Scale A command that resizes a picture to a percentage of its size.

Scale to Fit Excel commands that enable you to stretch or shrink the width, height, or both, of printed output to fit a maximum number of pages.

Scaling The process of shrinking the width and/or height of printed output to fit a maximum number of pages.

Screen capture An image file that contains the contents of a computer screen.

Screenshot An image of an active window on your computer that you can paste into a document.

ScreenTip A small box that that displays useful information when you perform various mouse actions such as pointing to screen elements or dragging.

Scroll arrow An arrow at the top and bottom, or left and right, of a scroll bar that when clicked, moves the window in small increments.

Scroll bar A bar that displays on the bottom or right side of a window when the contents of a window are not completely visible; used to move the window up, down, left, or right to bring the contents into view.

Scroll box The box in the vertical and horizontal scroll bars that can be dragged to reposition the contents of a window or pane on the screen.

Second principle of good database design A principle stating that appropriate database techniques are used to ensure the accuracy and consistency of data as it is entered into the table.

Section A portion of a document that can be formatted differently from the rest of the document.

Section bar In Design view, a gray bar in a form or report that identifies and separates one section from another; used to select the section and to change the size of the section.

Section break A double dotted line that indicates the end of one section and the beginning of another section.

Section header A type of slide layout that changes the look and flow of a presentation by providing text placeholders that do not contain bullet points.

Secure environment A system that uses controlled servers to ensure the security and privacy of email, to control the storage and use of information and to protect against the loss of confidential data.

Select To specify, by highlighting, a block of data or text on the screen with the intent of performing some action on the selection.

Select All box A box in the upper left corner of the worksheet grid that, when clicked, selects all the cells in a worksheet.

Select query A type of Access query that retrieves (selects) data from one or more tables or queries, displaying the selected data in a datasheet; also known as a simple select query.

Selecting Highlighting, by dragging with your mouse, areas of text or data or graphics, so that the selection can be edited, formatted, copied, or moved.

Series A group of things that come one after another in succession; for example, January, February, March, and so on.

Serif font A font design that includes small line extensions on the ends of the letters to guide the eye in reading from left to right.

Server A computer that provides services on a network such as an email server or a file server.

Shape A slide object such as a line, arrow, box, callout, or banner.

Shapes Lines, arrows, stars, banners, ovals, rectangles, and other basic shapes with which you can illustrate an idea, a process, or a workflow.

SharePoint Collaboration software with which people in an organization can set up team sites to share information, manage documents, and publish reports for others to see.

Sheet tab scrolling buttons Buttons to the left of the sheet tabs used to display Excel sheet tabs that are not in view; used when there are more sheet tabs than will display in the space provided.

Sheet tabs The labels along the lower border of the Excel window that identify each worksheet.

Short Text data type An Access data type that describes text, a combination of text and numbers, or numbers that are not used in calculations, such as a Postal Code.

Shortcut menu A menu that displays commands and options relevant to the selected text or object; also called a *context menu*.

Show Formulas A command that displays the formula in each cell instead of the resulting value.

Shut down Turning off your computer in a manner that closes all open programs and files, closes your network connections, stops the hard disk, and discontinues the use of electrical power.

Simple select query Another name for a select query.

Single spacing The common name for line spacing in which there is *no* extra space before or after a paragraph and that uses line spacing of 1.

Single-record form A form that enables you to display or enter one record at a time in a table.

Sizing handles Small squares surrounding a picture that indicate that the picture is selected.

Sizing handles Small squares that indicate a picture or object is selected.

SkyDrive A free file storage and file sharing service provided by Microsoft when you sign up for a Microsoft account.

Skype A Microsoft product with which you can make voice calls, make video calls, transfer files, or send messages—including instant message and text messages—over the Internet.

Sleep Turning off your computer in a manner that automatically saves your work, stops the fan, and uses a small amount of electrical power to maintain your work in memory.

Slide A presentation page that can contain text, pictures, tables, charts, and other multimedia or graphic objects.

Slide handout Printed images of slides on a sheet of paper.

Slide pane A PowerPoint screen element that displays a large image of the active slide.

Slide Sorter view A presentation view that displays thumbnails of all of the slides in a presentation.

Slide transitions Motion effects that occur in Slide Show view when you move from one slide to the next during a presentation.

Small caps A font effect that changes lowercase letters to uppercase letters, but with the height of lowercase letters.

Smart guides Dashed lines that display on your slide when you are moving an object to assist you with alignment.

SmartArt A designer-quality visual representation of your information that you can create by choosing from among many different layouts to effectively communicate your message or ideas.

SmartArt graphic A visual representation of information that you create by choosing from among various layouts to communicate your message or ideas effectively.

SmartArt Styles Combinations of formatting effects that you can apply to SmartArt graphics.

Snap (desktop apps): A Windows 8 desktop feature that automatically resizes windows when you move—*snap*—them to the edge of the screen.

Snip The image captured using Snipping Tool.

Snipping Tool A program included with Windows 8 with which you can capture an image of all or part of a computer screen, and then annotate, save, copy, or share the image via email.

Sort The process of arranging data in a specific order based on the value in each field.

Sorting The process of arranging data in a specific order based on the value in a field.

Source file When importing a file, refers to the file being imported.

Sparkline A tiny chart in the background of a cell that gives a visual trend summary alongside your data; makes a pattern more obvious.

Speakers icon Displays the status of the computer's speakers (if any).

Spin box A small box with an upward- and downward-pointing arrow that lets you move rapidly through a set of values by clicking.

Split Splits the window into multiple resizable panes that contain views of your worksheet. This is useful to view multiple distant parts of your worksheet at one time.

Split button A button divided into two parts and in which clicking the main part of the button performs a command and clicking the arrow opens a menu with choices.

Spreadsheet Another name for a worksheet.

Stacked layout A control layout format that is similar to a paper form, with label controls placed to the left of each text box control; the controls are grouped together for easy editing.

Start screen The first screen that displays after signing in to a Windows 8 device, which displays square and rectangular boxes—referred to as tiles—from which one can access apps, websites, programs, and tools for using the computer by clicking or tapping them.

Start search The search feature in Windows 8 in which, from the Start screen, you can begin to type and by default, Windows 8 searches for apps; you can adjust the search to search for files or settings.

Start tip The thumbnail that displays when you point to the lower left corner of your screen.

Statistical functions Excel functions, including the AVERAGE, MEDIAN, MIN, and MAX functions, which are useful to analyze a group of measurements.

Status bar The area along the lower edge of the Excel window that displays, on the left side, the current cell mode, page number, and worksheet information; on the right side, when numerical data is selected, common calculations such as Sum and Average display.

Structure In Access, the underlying design of a table, including field names, data types, descriptions, and field properties.

Style (PowerPoint) A collection of formatting options that you can apply to a picture, text, or an object.

Style (Word) A group of formatting commands, such as font, font size, font color, paragraph alignment, and line spacing that can be applied to a paragraph with one command.

Style guide A manual that contains standards for the design and writing of documents.

Subdatasheet A format for displaying related records when you click the plus sign (+) next to a record in a table on the *one* side of the relationship.

Subfolder A folder within a folder.

Subject line The optional line following the inside address in a business letter that states the purpose of the letter.

Subset A portion of the total records available.

SUM function A predefined formula that adds all the numbers in a selected range of cells.

Summary sheet A worksheet where totals from other worksheets are displayed and summarized.

Suppress A Word feature that hides header and footer information, including the page number, on the first page of a document.

Switch Row/Column A charting command to swap the data over the axis—data being charted on the vertical axis will move to the horizontal axis and vice versa

Switcher Another name for *app switcher*.

Synchronization The process of updating computer files that are in two or more locations according to specific rules—also called *syncing*.

Syncing The process of updating computer files that are in two or more locations according to specific rules—also called *synchronization*.

Synonyms Words with the same or similar meaning.

System tray Another name for the notification area on the taskbar.

Tab order The order in which the insertion point moves from one field to another in a form when you press the Tab key.

Tab stop A specific location on a line of text, marked on the Word ruler, to which you can move the insertion point by pressing the Tab key, and which is used to align and indent text.

Table A format for information that organizes and presents text and data in columns and rows.

Table area The upper area of the query window that displays field lists for the tables that are used in a query.

Table style A format applied to a table that is consistent with the presentation theme.

Tables and Related Views An arrangement in the Navigation Pane that groups objects by the table to which they are related.

Tabs (ribbon) On the Office ribbon, the name of each activity area.

Tags Custom file properties in the form of words that you associate with a document to give an indication of the document's content; used to help find and organize files. Also called *keywords*.

Taskbar The area of the desktop that contains program buttons, and buttons for all open programs; by default, it is located at the bottom of the desktop, but you can move it.

Team A group of workers tasked with working together to solve a problem, make a decision, or create a work product.

Template An existing document that you use as a starting point for a new document; it opens a copy of itself, unnamed, and then you use the structure—and possibly some content, such as headings—as the starting point for new a document.

Text alignment The horizontal placement of text within a placeholder.

Text box An object with which you can position text anywhere on a slide.

Text box control A bound control on a form or report that displays the data from the underlying table or query.

Text control A content control that accepts only a text entry.

Text effects Decorative formats, such as shadowed or mirrored text, text glow, 3-D effects, and colors that make text stand out.

Text string A sequence of characters.

Text values Constant values consisting of only text, and which usually provides information about number values; also referred to as labels.

Text wrapping The manner in which text displays around an object.

Theme A predesigned set of colors, fonts, lines, and fill effects that look good together and that can be applied to all of the objects in the database or to individual objects in the database.

Theme colors A set of coordinating colors that are applied to the backgrounds, objects, and text in a presentation.

Theme fonts The fonts to apply to two types of slide text—headings and body.

Thesaurus A research tool that provides a list of synonyms.

Thumbnail A reduced image of a graphic.

Tiles Square and rectangular boxes on the Windows 8 Start screen from which one can access apps, websites, programs, and tools for using the computer by simply clicking or tapping them.

Timing options Animation options that control when animated items display in the animation sequence.

Title bar The bar at the top edge of the program window that indicates the name of the current file and the program name.

Title slide A slide layout—most commonly the first slide in a presentation—that provides an introduction to the presentation topic.

Toggle button A button that can be turned on by clicking it once, and then turned off by clicking it again.

Toolbar In a folder window, a row of buttons with which you can perform common tasks, such as changing the view of your files and folders or burning files to a CD.

Trim A command that deletes parts of a video to make it shorter.

Triple-click The action of clicking the left mouse button three times in rapid succession.

Truncated Refers to data that is cut off or shortened because the field or column is not wide enough to display all of the data or the field size is too small to contain all of the data.

Trust Center An area of Access where you can view the security and privacy settings for your Access installation.

Trusted Documents A security feature in Office that remembers which files you have already enabled; you might encounter this feature if you open a file from an email or download files from the Internet.

Unbound control A control that does not have a source of data, such as the title in a form or report.

Underlying formula The formula entered in a cell and visible only on the Formula Bar.

Underlying value The data that displays in the Formula Bar.

Uniform Resource Locator An address that uniquely identifies a location on the Internet.

URL The acronym for Uniform Resource Locator, which is an address that uniquely identifies a location on the Internet.

USB flash drive A small data storage device that plugs into a computer USB port.

User account A collection of information that tells Windows 8 what files and folders the account holder can access, what changes the account holder can make to the computer system, and what the account holder's personal preferences are.

Value Another name for a constant value.

Value after increase = base x percent for new value The formula for calculating the value after an increase by multiplying the original value—the base—by the percent for new value (see the *Percent for new value* formula).

Value axis A numerical scale on the left side of a chart that shows the range of numbers for the data points; also referred to as the Y-axis.

Variant A variation on the presentation theme style and color.

Volatile A term used to describe an Excel function that is subject to change each time the workbook is reopened; for example the NOW function updates itself to the current date and time each time the workbook is opened.

Wallpaper Another term for the desktop background.

Web browser Software with which you display webpages and navigate the Internet.

What-if analysis The process of changing the values in cells to see how those changes affect the outcome of formulas in a worksheet.

Wildcard character In a query, a character that serves as a placeholder for one or more unknown characters in criteria; an asterisk (*) represents one or more unknown characters, and a question mark (?) represents a single unknown character.

Window A rectangular area on a computer screen in which programs and content appear, and which can be moved, resized, minimized, or closed.

Window snip When using Snipping Tool, the type of snip that captures the entire displayed window.

Windows 8 An operating system developed by Microsoft Corporation designed to work with mobile computing devices of all types and also with traditional PCs.

Windows Reader app A Windows Store app with which you can open a PDF or XPS file, zoom, find words or phrases, take notes, save changes, and then print or share the file.

Windows Store apps Apps built for specific purposes; for example, to view photos, read sports information, organize a list of contacts, or read updates to social networks like Facebook and Twitter.

With Previous An animation option that begins the animation sequence at the same time as the previous animation or slide transition

Wizard A feature in Microsoft Office that walks you step by step through a process.

WordArt A gallery of text styles with which you can create decorative effects, such as shadowed or mirrored text

Wordwrap The feature that moves text from the right edge of a paragraph to the beginning of the next line as necessary to fit within the margins.

Workbook An Excel file that contains one or more worksheets.

Workbook-level buttons Buttons at the far right of the Ribbon tabs that minimize or restore a displayed workbook.

Works Cited In the MLA style, a list of cited works placed at the end of a research paper or report.

Worksheet The primary document that you use in Excel to work with and store data, and which is formatted as a pattern of uniformly spaced horizontal and vertical lines.

Worksheet grid area A part of the Excel window that displays the columns and rows that intersect to form the worksheet's cells.

Writer's identification The name and title of the author of a letter, placed near the bottom of the letter under the complimentary closing—also referred to as the *writer's signature block*.

Writer's signature block The name and title of the author of a letter, placed near the bottom of the letter, under the complimentary closing—also referred to as the *writer's identification*.

X-axis Another name for the horizontal (category) axis.

XML Paper Specification A Microsoft file format that creates an image of your document and that opens in the XPS viewer.

XPS The acronym for XML Paper Specification—a Microsoft file format that creates an image of your document and that opens in the XPS viewer.

Y-axis Another name for the vertical (value) axis.

Zipped folder A folder that has been reduced in size and thus takes up less storage space and can be transferred to other computers quickly; also called a *compressed* folder.

Zoom The action of increasing or decreasing the size of the viewing area on the screen.

Index